A History of
ASIA

Second Edition

A HISTORY OF
ASIA

Volume II
*Old Empires, Western Penetration,
and the Rise of New Nations Since 1600*

Woodbridge Bingham
University of California, Berkeley

Hilary Conroy
University of Pennsylvania

Frank W. Iklé
University of New Mexico

Allyn and Bacon, Inc. **Boston**

TO URSULA, CHARLOTTE, AND MAURINE

© Copyright 1974 By Allyn and Bacon, Inc.,
470 Atlantic Avenue, Boston.
© Copyright 1964 By Allyn and Bacon, Inc.,
470 Atlantic Avenue, Boston.

All Rights Reserved.

No part of the material
protected by this copyright notice
may be reproduced or utilized in any form
or by any means, electronic or mechanical,
including photocopying, recording, or by any
informational storage and retrieval system,
without written permission
from the copyright owner.

Library of Congress Catalog Card Number: 73-77190

Printed in the United States of America

Acknowledgments

Frontispiece: Standing figure of a woman, print by Torii Kiyomasu (eighteenth century). Courtesy of The Art Institute of Chicago.

Chapter 1. 1.1. Turkish Information Office. 1.2. Topkapi Palace Museum, Istanbul. 1.3. University of Minnesota Library. 1.4. Punch Magazine, London.

Chapter 2. 2.1. British Museum. 2.2. Dr. L. Lockhart and Luzac and Company. 2.3. Cincinnati Art Museum. 2.4. Victoria and Albert Museum. 2.5. The Metropolitan Museum of Art.

Chapter 3. 3.1, 3.2. The Metropolitan Museum of Art, Ex. Coll. Kevorkian. Purchase, Funds donated by Kevorkian Foundation and Rogers Fund, 1955. 3.3. Victoria and Albert Museum. 3.4, 3.5. Press Information Bureau, Government of India.

Chapter 4. 4.1, 4.2. The Metropolitan Museum of Art, Rogers Fund, 1942. 4.3. The Metropolitan Museum of Art, gift of Robert E. Tod, 1937. 4.4. The Metropolitan Museum of Art, gift of Mrs. Henry J. Bernheim, 1945.

Chapter 5. 5.1. From Du Halde's *Description Geographique de la Chine*. 5.2. Peabody Museum, Salem, Mass. 5.3. From G. L. Staunton's *Authentic Account of an Embassy from the King of Great Britain to the Emperor of China*. 5.4. Culver Pictures, Inc.

Chapter 6. 6.1, 6.3, 6.4. The Art Institute of Chicago. 6.2. Brooklyn Museum. 6.5. New York Public Library.

Chapter 7. 7.1, 7.3. Rijksmuseum, Amsterdam. 7.2. Westfries Museum, Hoorn. 7.4. National Portrait Gallery, London.

Chapter 8. 8.1, 8.2. The Metropolitan Museum of Art. 8.3, 8.4. Courtesy of Prince Chula and Alvin Redman, Ltd. From the book *Lords of Life* by Prince Chula.

Chapter 9. 9.1. From B. H. Sumner, *Survey of Russian History*. Courtesy of Gerald Duckworth and Co., London. 9.2, 9.3, 9.4. From R. Kerner, *The Urge to the Sea*. Courtesy of the University of California Press.

Chapter 10. 10.1, 10.2. Government of India Tourist Office. 10.3. National Portrait Gallery, London.

ACKNOWLEDGMENTS

Chapter 11. 11.1, 11.2, 11.3, 11.4. Widener Library, Harvard University. 11.5, 11.6. From Selma Ekrem, *Unveiled*. By permission of the author.

Chapter 12. 12.1. From W. L. Bales, *Tso Tsung-t'ang* (1937). Courtesy of Kelly and Walsh, Hong Kong. 12.2, 12.3, 12.4. From S. F. Wright, *Hart and the Chinese Customs* (1950). Courtesy Wm. Mullan and Son, Belfast.

Chapter 13. 13.1. From Liberal News Agency, *The Late Emperor of Japan as a World Monarch* (Tokyo, 1913). 13.2, 13.3. From Itagaki Taisuke, compiler, *History of the Liberal Party*, Vol. I, Tokyo, 1910. 13.4. Okuma 85th Birthday Anniversary Society, compiler, Tokyo, 1926. 13.5. From J. Morris, *Makers of Japan* (1960). Courtesy of Methuen and Company, London.

Chapter 14. 14.1. Courtesy of Mr. Yoshiyuki Sakurai, from his collection. 14.2. The Bettmann Archive. 14.3. Brooklyn Museum.

Chapter 15. 15.1. National Archives. 15.2. From Arthur H. Smith, *China in Convulsion*. New York, 1901. 15.3. From S. F. Wright, *Hart and the Chinese Customs*. Courtesy of Wm. Mullan & Son, Ltd., Belfast, Ireland. 15.4. From E. T. Williams, *Short History of China* (1928). Courtesy of Harper and Bros., New York. 15.5. Courtesy of H. McAleavy.

Chapter 16. 16.1, 16.2. From J. Morris, *Makers of Japan* (1906). Courtesy of Methuen and Company, London. 16.3. Miami University Library.

Chapter 17. 17.1. Courtesy of Dr. Pardo de Tavera. 17.2. Embassy of the Philippines. 17.3. Brooklyn Museum. 17.4. Library of Congress.

Chapter 18. 18.1. Turkish Information Office, New York. 18.2. Iranian Embassy, Washington. 18.3. From M. Asad, *The Road to Mecca* (1954). Courtesy of Simon and Schuster, New York. 18.4. Arabian American Oil Company.

Chapter 19. 19.1. Press Information Bureau, Government of India. 19.2. Woodbridge Bingham. 19.3, 19.4. Press Information Bureau, Government of India. 19.5. Embassy of Pakistan.

Chapter 20. 20.1, 20.2. United Nations. 20.3. Embassy of Indonesia.

Chapter 21. 21.1. Nippon Yusen Kaisha. 21.2. From P. T. Etherton, *China, the Facts*. Courtesy of E. Benn, Ltd., London. 21.3. From W. H. Chamberlin, *Japan Over Asia*. Courtesy of Gerald Duckworth and Co., London.

Chapter 22. 22.1, 22.2. From W. H. Chamberlin, *Japan Over Asia*. Courtesy of Gerald Duckworth and Co., London. 22.3, 22.4. United States Information Agency. 22.5. Press Association, Inc. 22.6. Official U. S. Navy photograph. 22.7. U. S. Army photograph. 22.8. Defense Department photo (Marine Corps).

Chapter 23. 23.1. Iranian Oil Operating Companies. 23.2. Turkish Information Office. 23.3. Embassy of Israel. 23.4. Iraq Petroleum Company. 23.5. Arabian American Oil Company.

ACKNOWLEDGMENTS

Chapter 24. 24.1, 24.2, 24.3, 24.6. United Nations. 24.4. William B. Hubbell, Jr. 24.5, 24.7. Embassy of India. 24.8. Embassy of Pakistan.

Chapter 25. 25.1. From Prince Chula, *Lords of Life*. Courtesy of Prince Chula and Alvin Redman, Ltd. 25.2, 25.3. Embassy of Indonesia. 25.4. Federation of Malaya Embassy. 25.5. Embassy of Vietnam. 25.6. From Jean Lacouture, *Ho Chi Minh*. Editions du Seuil, Paris. 25.7. From M. Ribaud, *Face of North Vietnam*. Courtesy of Magnum Photos, New York.

Chapter 26. 26.1, 26.2. U. S. Army. 26.3, 26.4, 26.7. Wide World Photos. 26.5. Defense Department photo (Marine Corps). 26.6. Embassy of the Republic of China.

Chapter 27. 27.1. Embassy of Japan. 27.2. The White House.

Chapter 28. 28.1. Tom Fox, Dispatch News Service International.

Contents

OLD EMPIRES OF ASIA

1. **The Ottoman Empire, 1566–1856**   1

   Extent and Nature of the Ottoman Empire   1
   Beginning of Decline   7
   Period of Steady Loss of Territory   10
   Early Attempts at Reform   12
   Turkey as a Pawn of the Great Powers   16
   Later Steps Toward Reform and Westernization   19

2. **The Persian Autocratic State, 1600–1857**   25

   The Safavid Dynasty   25
   Afghan Conquest   32
   Nadir Shah   33
   Start of Active European Influences   37
   Religious Developments   42
   Afghanistan   44

3. **India from Mogul Power to British Supremacy**   50

   The Moguls After Akbar   50
   Succession Struggles of the Sons of Shah Jahan   55
   Mogul Culture   59
   Hindu Renascence   62
   European Colonial Expansion and the Rise of British Power   66
   Rule of the East India Company   73
   Cultural Trends   78

4. **Ch'ing Empire, I: Reigns, Culture, and Frontiers, 1600–1844**   83

   The Establishment of Manchu Power   83
   K'ang-Hsi Period   91

Yung-Cheng, Ch'ien-Lung, and Decline   94
Culture Under the Ch'ing   99

5. Ch'ing Empire, II: Relations with the West, 1600–1844   105

    The West in Chinese History   105
    The Portuguese in China   106
    The Jesuits in China   108
    The Coming of the Dutch   111
    The Coming of the English   113
    The Canton System   116
    Anglo-Chinese Conflict and the First Anglo-Chinese War   123

6. Tokugawa Japan   132

    Establishment of the Tokugawa Regime   132
    Tokugawa Economy and Society   139
    Tokugawa Culture and Thought   143
    The Opening of Japan   151
    End of the Shogunate   153

WESTERN PENETRATION

7. Dutch Empire in the Far East to 1850   161

    Establishment of a Dutch Commercial Empire in the Indies   161
    The Eighteenth Century: Transition from Commercial to Territorial Empire   172
    Reforms, 1800–1824   176
    Restoration of Dutch Rule   179

8. Colonial Empires of Southeast Asia to 1914   182

    Netherlands Indies   182
    The British Colonial Empire: Burma, Malaya, Borneo   187
    French Colonial Expansion   192
    Siam   196

9. Russia in Asia, 1600–1895   203

    Geography   203
    Russian Expansion Across Asia   204
    Siberian Administration   214
    Early Relations with the Manchu Empire   215
    Siberian Colonization and Far Eastern Expansion, After Nerchinsk   219
    Russian Expansion into Central and Western Asia   223

10. India: Empire and Nationalism, 1858–1914   229

Imperial Organization and Expansion   229
British Foreign Policy   232
Impact of British Ideas   236
Indian Intellectual and Religious Currents   239
Nationalism in Politics   243

11. The Challenge of Western Ideas in Southwest Asia, 1857–1914   253

Anglo-Russian Rivalry in Persia   254
Persian Constitutional Movement   258
The Ottoman Empire and Increased Western Pressure   263
Non-Turkish Peoples of the Empire   271

12. Decline of the Ch'ing, 1844–1894   278

Loss of Independence   278
Weakness and Rebellion   283
The T'ung-chih Restoration   287
Semicolonial Status and Foreign Pressure   290

13. Japan: Meiji Restoration and Modernization to 1895   298

Destruction of Feudalism   300
Westernization and Centralization   303
Creation of a National Government   307
Beginnings of Expansion   313

14. Korea: From Seclusion to International Conflict, 1600–1895   317

Seclusion Under the Yi   318
Opening of Korea   324
International Rivalry   328
The Sino-Japanese War   331

15. China: The First Revolution, 1895–1914   338

Internal Efforts and External Pressures, 1895–1899   338
The "Open Door" and the Boxer Movement, 1899–1901   344
The Manchus Attempt Reform   349
Revolution and Republic   352

16. Japan and Northeast Asia, 1895–1914   363

Internal Effect of Sino-Japanese War   363
Japan Under the Elder Statesmen   364

Industrialization of Japan   367
Rivalry in Northeastern Asia   371
The Russo-Japanese War   377
End of Korean Independence   380
American-Japanese Relations   381

17. The Philippines, 1600–1913, and American Expansion to the Far East   386

   The Discovery of the Philippines   386
   Period of Spanish Rule   388
   Open Trade and Revolution in the Philippines   394
   Americans Cross the Pacific   398

REVOLUTION AND NEW NATIONS

18. Nationalism in Southwest Asia, 1914–1939   409

   Turkey   410
   Persia   420
   Afghanistan   427
   The Arab States and League Mandates   429

19. India, 1914–1947   442

   Military Effort and Disillusionment   442
   Mohandas Gandhi Leads Nationalists   445
   Moslem-Hindu Divergence   449
   The British Seek Stability   450
   Modernization   456
   India and World War II   457

20. Southeast Asia: Colonies and New Nations, 1914–1946   467

   Common Characteristics of Modern Southeast Asia   467
   Thailand (Siam)   470
   The Philippine Islands   473
   Indonesia   476
   Indochina   479
   British Colonial Empire   484

21. Chinese "Republic" and Japan, 1914–1928   489

   Peking "Republic" and the Warlords   489
   Japan in World War I   490
   Siberian Intervention   494
   Versailles and Washington Treaties   496
   Growth of the Chinese Nationalist Movement   500

The Kuomintang Revitalized and Victorious   503
Japan's Liberal Era   507
Weakness of Japanese Liberalism   509
Rise of Ultranationalism in Japan   511
Intervention in China   513

22. **Japan's Road to War: In China and the Pacific, 1928–1945**   517

    Japanese Pressure on China   521
    Kuomintang Leadership, 1928–1937   525
    Japan Seizes Key Areas of China   529
    Japanese Relations with Europe   533
    Relations with the United States   536
    The Pacific War   540
    China and the Pacific War   549

23. **Southwest Asia: Since World War II**   556

    Iran   558
    Government of and by the Shah   566
    Development, Land Reform, and Politics   567
    Power and Stability in Southwest Asia   569
    Turkey   570
    The Arab League and Israel   573
    Afghanistan   590

24. **India and Pakistan, Since 1947**   594

    Independence and Its Problems   594
    World Relations   604

25. **New Nations of Southeast Asia, Since 1946**   613

    General   613
    Thailand   614
    Philippines   616
    Indonesia   618
    Burma   621
    Malaysia   623
    Indochina   624

26. **Divergence and Division in East Asia: Japan, China, and Korea, 1945–1960**   637

    The Occupation of Japan   637
    Organizational Structure and Policy Objectives   640
    The Stage of Democratization, 1945–1948   643
    The Stage of Recovery, 1948–1952   **648**
    Renewal of Chinese Civil War   649
    The People's Republic Established   653

Nationalists on Formosa 655
The Question of Recognition 657
The Division of Korea 659
War and Truce in Korea 662
East Asia in the Later 1950's 665

27. New Giants of Asia: Japan's Capitalist Democracy and China's People's Republic, Since 1960 678

Japan 679
China 686

28. The United States and Asia 696

Russia and the Far East to 1945, and Russian-American Relations 696
Cold War 700
American Attitudes and Policies Toward Asians 704

Index 715

Maps

Southwest Asia about 1650   8
Ch'ing Empire about 1750   90
Tokugawa Japan   134
Southeast Asia about 1750   173
Russia in Asia, 1600–1895   222
Indian Empire   230
Southwest Asia about 1914   272
China in 1900   340
Japanese Expansion, 1875–1912   379
Southwest Asia about 1937   411
Far East, 1922   499
Japanese Conquests, 1941–1943   546
The Arab World and Israel in 1970   577
Eastern Asia in 1960   674
Asia in 1971   709

Preface to Volume II

The reader is referred to the preface and the introduction to Volume I for an explanation of the scope and organization of this history of Asia, remarks on the spelling and pronunciation of Asian names, the use of the reading lists, and acknowledgments to the many persons who assisted the authors in various ways. For Volume II we are additionally indebted to Professors Holden Furber and Michael Pearson of the University of Pennsylvania for assistance with outlines and criticism of the chapters on modern India respectively, to Professor Alexander V. Riasanovsky of the University of Pennsylvania for criticism of the chapter on Russian expansion in Asia, to Professor Thomas Naff of the University of Pennsylvania for criticism of the chapter on Southwest Asia, 1857–1914, to Mr. Toru Takemoto of the University of Pennsylvania and Mrs. Sharlie C. Ushioda of the University of California (Irvine) for criticism of the chapters on Japan, and to Mr. Wayne K. Patterson of the University of Pennsylvania for assistance with sections of the chapters on Korea and the People's Republic of China.

Mrs. Evelyn B. Prosser prepared all the maps for this revised edition.

Once again, however, all responsibility in the matter of facts and interpretation is our own.

W. B., H. C., F. W. I.

Chapter 1

The Ottoman Empire, 1566-1856

This period of Ottoman history reveals the steady decline of an "Asiatic empire." But the process of decline is not limited to Turkey alone; it occurs during the same period in the Persian, Mogul, and Ch'ing empires to the east. How then, and for what reasons, does this decline among once powerful empires take place? In this chapter an analysis will be made of the factors contributing to the decline of the Turkish empire. Internal weakness and forces from the outside will be stressed and one should bear in mind that similar strains and stresses affected the other great empires of Asia.

To understand Ottoman history from 1566 to 1856, four approaches may be considered: first, to analyze the internal structure of the state; second, to illustrate the weakness of this structure and the seeds of internal decay; next, to discuss the problem of Western influence and Western-style reforms; and, finally, to look at Turkey during the period when she was the pawn of the great powers.

EXTENT AND NATURE OF THE OTTOMAN EMPIRE

By the middle of the sixteenth century the Ottoman empire reached Vienna in the north, Arabia and the Sudan to the south, Persia and the Caspian Sea in the east, and Oran in the west. The government of Suleiman the Magnificent controlled thirty million people of twenty nationalities, brought terror to Europe, and acted as the chief threat to Charles V. The power of this state was based upon an excellent and unique system of imperial administration that held together a vast conglomeration of 24 provinces.[1]

[1] All but four of them were in Asia and Africa. The empire also included self-governing principalities under the suzerainty of the sultan: the kingdoms of Hungary

FIGURE 1.1. *Mosque of Selim at Edirne, one of the most magnificent works of Ottoman architecture.*

In the internal structure of the Ottoman empire the historical roots are always apparent. The state, a military despotism, was based on a mixture of the organizations and aims of the civilizations of the nomad and those of Islam. The Ottoman empire in this sense was an "Asiatic empire." Although ruled from a capital in Europe it was distinct from and foreign in thought and values to the new national states of post-Renaissance Europe. The problem of the Ottoman Turks was that of a very small minority group ruling a large population of intelligent and civilized subject peoples. This problem was solved by means of a unique system carefully thought out and executed whose ultimate aim was the preservation of the leadership of the Ottoman Turk.

The Ruler

The Ottoman governmental organization can be broken down into three basic elements: the ruler, the officials, and the ruled. The ruler was

and Transylvania, the principalities of Moldavia and Wallachia, the khanate of the Crimea, the sherifate of Hejaz and the Barbary states of Tripoli, Algiers, and Tunis.

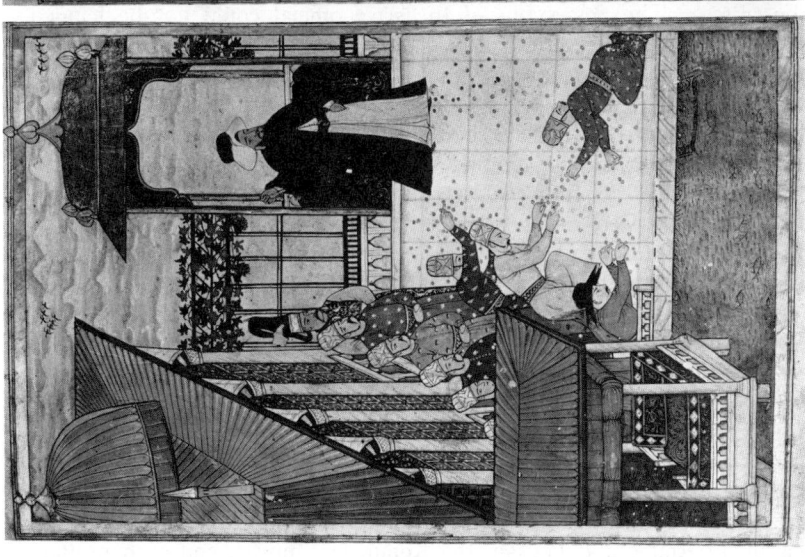

FIGURE 1.2. The sultan, Ahmed III (early eighteenth-century) scattering alms. A contemporary print.

the sultan, an autocratic monarch, a descendant of the family of Osman, but in practice frequently a descendant of a slave, since his mother was usually a slave in the imperial harem. To prevent succession rivalry within the dynasty the fundamental law promulgated by Muhammad II established the right to exterminate one's rivals: "those of my illustrious children who ascend the throne may execute their brothers, in order to assure the peace of the world." Thus the rule of the sultan, the autocratic despot, was preserved, reflecting the unlimited power of the nomad chieftain, garbed in the religious authority of the descendant of Muhammad.

The Officials

It was, however, the system of officials that was the most interesting, and the most striking part of Ottoman government. With few exceptions all officials were slaves. Known as the Ottoman "slave household," this arrangement represented the outgrowth of nomadic forms of political ideals: the Turk conquered, the conquered served the conqueror in those capacities in which he excelled. The creation of the empire and its increasing expansion gave rise to greater need for officials, with the result that the system soon became highly developed and applied on a very large scale. The natural desire of the Ottoman ruler to place dependable and personally devoted adherents in key positions was accomplished by making all officials slaves of the autocratic sultan. From the Grand Vizir, who had wide powers in all fields of administration, and who frequently was the supreme commander of the army, to the ministers of state who aided in the government, to the secretaries, down to the lowest possible official—all were slaves at the mercy of the sultan. The possessions of the slave official could not be handed down to his son; they reverted upon death of the official to his master, the sultan. Hereditary office, under this system, did not exist. The effective power of the state rested in the hands of a non-hereditary officialdom.

The members of the slave household were recruited from the non-Moslem population of the empire, either through periodic roundups of children (blood tax), or from children bought from professional slave traders. The slave children were carefully selected, their functions were differentiated from the earliest moment, and they remained under perpetual and close supervision. Constantly graded and judged, ruthlessly disciplined, they were also stimulated to keenest competition by the use of differential pay scales. The highest goal, open to all, was the position of the Grand Vizir. Conversion to Islam came voluntarily, as a by-product of this education. Forcible conversion was hardly needed when the unconscious acceptance of the Islamic religious milieu served so well instead.

The brightest, most intelligent boys were selected to serve as pages in anticipation of an administrative career. They were trained in colleges in Constantinople and Adrianople, in a curriculum which consisted of a literary education in Arabic and Persian, the Koran, law, music, and such military skills as archery, musketry, horsemanship, javelin throwing, and tactics. After the completion of this training they entered the household service of the sultan, performing minor duties, and at the age of twenty-five they were

FIGURE 1.3. *A seventeenth-century German print of Spahis (cavalry) and Janissaries.*

given appointments as administrative officials. If successful in their careers, the ablest would eventually rise to the positions of governor-generals of provinces, commanders of armies, ministers of state, and even to the pinnacle of Grand Vizir.

Those boys who seemed intelligent and also possessed a strong physical constitution were selected for the army. They were sent into the interior of Anatolia to learn Turkish and to be toughened by hard labor on the land. The fittest of them were selected for service in the famous Ottoman guard corps, the Janissaries. This privileged corps of trained infantry came to number about twelve to fourteen thousand. They wore as their special insignia a white felt cap and a spoon (to indicate that they were "eating the Sultan's soup"), they could be punished only by their own officers, and even the Grand Vizir had only limited powers over them. They formed a compact, small, zealous, and at their height, formidable, element of Ottoman military strength. Finally, the least promising of the slave boys, and those who failed in their training, were assigned as servants, laborers, or were given minor tasks.

This system of the slave household had as its key strong point the concept that only those able and conditioned by hard training were fitted for the highest positions. Thus it made advancement subject to merit, ensured a dependable, loyal, and efficient body of officials, both military and civil, and carefully eliminated the evils of a hereditary officialdom. Since the free-born Moslem could not enter this public service, and since the son of the slave-official became a free Moslem, the system worked well. It seemed to constitute an excellent solution to the problem of a small ruling group administering a vast empire.

The only exception to slave-officials was in the realm of religion and law, which were closely intertwined and where the influence of Islam was dominant. In these fields it was the free Moslem who served as religious official (*ulama*), or as interpreter (*mufti*) and administrator (*kadi*) of the law. Headed by the Grand Mufti, this officialdom played but a minor role in the great administrative structure of the Ottoman state.

The Subjects

The third element in this structure was the subject people, who were organized into a number of religio-political divisions. Technically known as a *millet*, each of these groups was headed by a religious official and was organized along religious lines, but each one also possessed political functions such as the raising of taxes and the maintenance of its own law courts. This system of millets, extending throughout the empire, again reflects the hierarchial structure of nomad society with the inherent purpose of greater ease of ruling, and served as another excellent device for the maintenance of Ottoman supremacy over a vast multitude of subject people.

Highest in this hierarchy were the Ottoman Turks. They were free Moslems and possessed the greatest privileges. Some were great landholders of vast estates. But, as has been pointed out, they were deprived of access to political and military service which was the prerogative of slaves. Then came the rest of the non-Ottoman free Moslems, including the Arabs, consisting of both privileged landholders and Moslem peasants. Although the technical term millet was not applied to this group, nevertheless that is what the Islamic community essentially was, since it was headed by a religious leader, the Grand Mufti of Constantinople, who possessed both religious and political functions. Although the Moslem millet was dominant, it frequently was victimized by an inefficient and corrupt government, and the poorer Turks were often worse off than their Christian neighbors.

Below the Moslems were the other subjects of the sultan, organized in millets: Orthodox Christians, Latins, Armenians, Jews, and even Protestants. All of these were identically organized. At the head of each group stood a religious figure, be it the Grand Rabbi of the Jews or the Ecumenical Patriarch of the Orthodox Church at Constantinople, and all combined purely religious functions with those of a political nature, such as tax collection and the administration of law.

This system of millets came to be applied even to the foreigner residing within the Ottoman state. Whether he was French, English, Venetian, or Dutch, he found himself grouped together with his fellow countrymen into a millet which was headed by his ambassador or consul. These millets of foreigners, for the most part traders, were given certain rights of self-government and privileges which were embodied in charters called capitularies or capitulations, granted by the sultan and revocable at his will. These millets were another fine instrument of control, yet this system had its dangers which became only too clear in the nineteenth century when the Western powers found in the capitularies useful wedges against the integrity of the Turkish state.

As a whole, Ottoman rule of the non-Moslem population was a severe one. There existed a Turkish proverb to the effect that "the bended head is not to be stricken off," yet Turkish rule was designed to keep the head of the subject well bowed. A series of discriminatory decrees maintained a clear distinction between ruler and subject. The latter could not bear arms, was forbidden to ride a horse, and was forced to wear identifying costume. In the realm of taxation the hand of the master seemed particularly oppressive. Taxes were numerous and heavy. In addition to the dreaded "blood tax" (the periodic round-up of children for the slave household), there were taxes on land, on sheep, on pasture, on commerce, on mills, a poll tax, tithes, a tax on celibates, and, in order to produce equal justice, a tax on those who married.

A summary of the internal structure of the Ottoman Empire shows these essential features: the sultan as the absolute ruler, relying in turn on a body of dependent slaves for his officials, and the rule of his subjects by means of closely supervised and controlled millets. Embodying both the nomad heritage and Islamic political thought, this ingenious and efficient system created a strong Ottoman state which found its most powerful expression in the sixteenth century. Yet after 1566 the Ottoman empire declined and became gradually weaker.

BEGINNING OF DECLINE

When studying Ottoman decline, it becomes obvious that there existed definite and dangerous signs of weakness within the internal structure of the Turkish state, which, however, do not alone explain the decline of the empire. It was the combination of internal weakness with the impact of a new and greatly changed outside world which accounts for it.

If the analysis of the internal structure of the Ottoman empire has shown its three keys to be the ruler, officialdom, and ruled, one may also expect that internal decay manifested itself among all three. As for the ruler in his capacity as absolute monarch, personal ability was extremely important, and the fact that Suleiman the Magnificent was succeeded by Selim the Sot may tell a considerable part of the story. In fact, the sultans frequently proved to be weak and the period after 1566 was characterized by harem politics: "The sultan governs no longer, the Grand Vizir is hindered in governing, the power is actually in the hands of Negro eunuchs and purchased slave girls." Weak rulers, isolated in the palace, such as Muhammad III, who was controlled by his mother, or Ahmed I, slave to his wife, were common from the 17th century on.

In addition there were the signs of decay and weakness apparent among the officials in the slave household. The system showed alarming

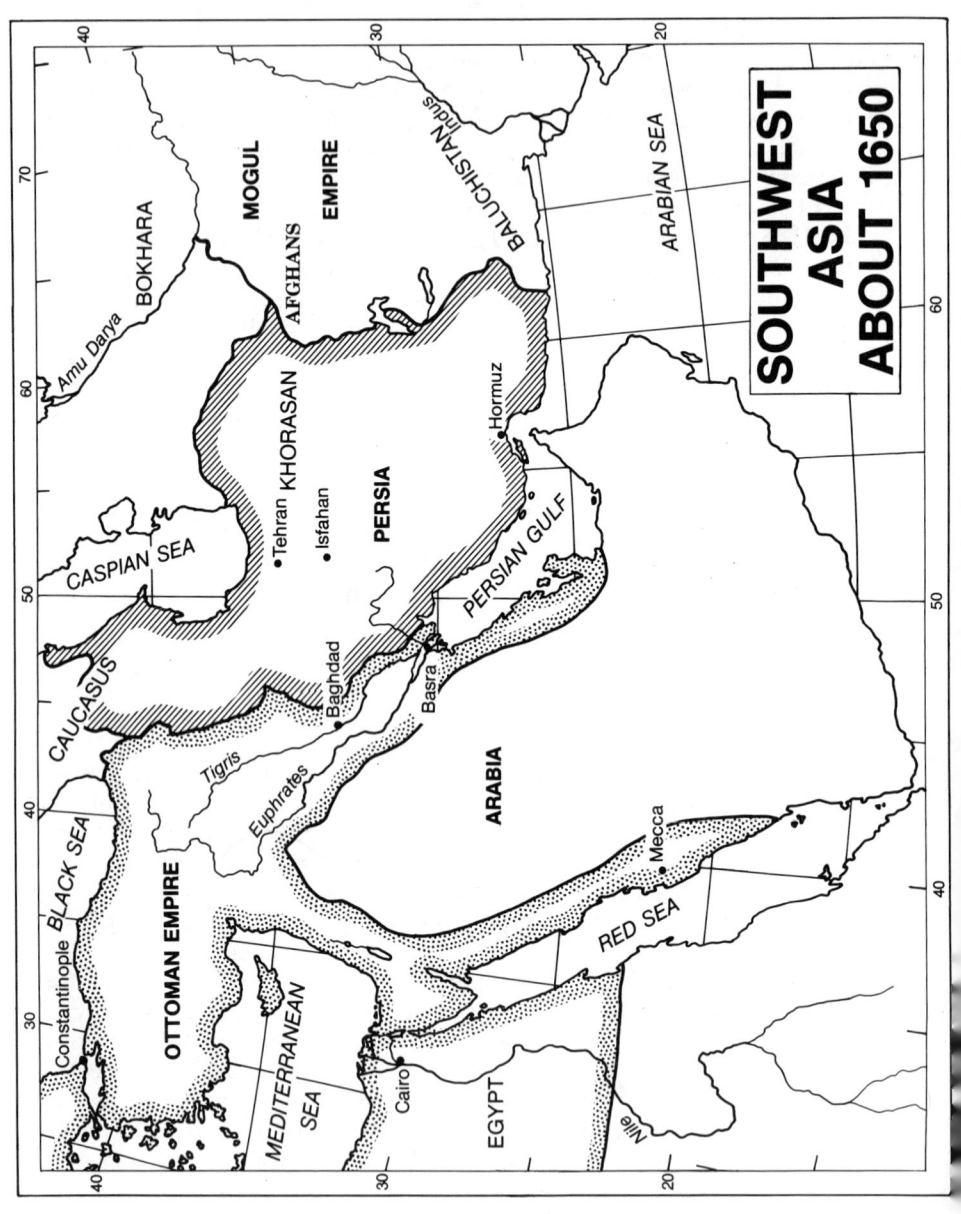

symptoms after 1600, primarily because of the desire of the slave-official to create a hereditary position. Successful in compelling the sultan to permit enrollment of their sons in the slave household, they transformed their positions into a hereditary officialdom and a hereditary Janissaries corps. Constantly gaining power and influence, these hereditary bodies undermined the system. This happened especially among the Janissaries, whose devotion and discipline seemed to vanish and whose constant demands for ever greater privileges were manifested in frequent mutinies. But it was also the free Moslem who contributed to an increase in corruption and the widespread purchase of offices. Hitherto denied service, he now clamored for entrance to public office. As a result of the hereditary system Ottoman officialdom declined; graft, bribery, and corruption flourished; and rule became more arbitrary, exacting, and severe.

As for the subject peoples, a number of developments presaged the breakdown of the structure. With weakening government at the center, some of the great feudal lords among the Ottomans began to set themselves up as "Lords of the Valley" (Derebeys). These semi-independent lords, mostly in Anatolia, gradually became a danger to the ruling dynasty. With increased taxation and corruption, general dissatisfaction grew among the subject population. Decline was manifested in intellectual life as well; little interest was paid to literature and the fine arts.

Still more threatening was an actual rebellion of a subject people, particularly when it was coupled with religious fanaticism. Such a direct challenge to the rule of the Ottoman Turks was a religious movement which arose in central Arabia in the mid-eighteenth century, the movement of the Wahhabi.

Arabia had been conquered by the Ottomans under Suleiman the Magnificent in the sixteenth century, but Turkish rule had always sat lightly upon the peninsula. The Arab chieftains, called Sherifs and possessing both religious and political functions, soon opposed the Turkish caliphate, and from the seventeenth century onward relations had been increasingly strained. After 1642 Arabia for all practical purposes had become autonomous, and Turkish tax gatherers and soldiers were conspicuous by their absence.

The founder of the movement, Muhammad Abd-al-Wahhab, a soldier-preacher of scholarly background, held to a strict monotheism and repudiated all authority except that of the Koran. His ascetic puritanism rejected the cult of the prophet and the worldliness of the caliphate and insisted on rigid adherence to the religious orders of the Koran. The purification of Islam and the expulsion of the Turk thus became the twofold aim of his movement.

In 1742 Abd-al-Wahhab converted to his cause a local emir of the Nejd district, Ibn Sa'ud. Arabia soon became united under the religious leadership of Abd-al-Wahhab and the political power of Ibn Sa'ud. Proclaiming the return of all Arabs to the true faith, the Wahhabi movement combined religious revival with a declaration of holy war (*jihad*) against Ottoman rule. In the early nineteenth century the Wahhabis captured Mecca and Medina where they stripped the tombs of the saints and the prophet of all decorations and treasures. Bold raids led by Ibn Sa'ud's grandson brought the Wahhabis almost to the gates of Damascus.

The Turkish sultan became increasingly concerned at the threat of a new and formidable Arab invasion and, as caliph, was harassed by appeals from the faithful to free the holy cities and the pilgrim roads. The sultan, Mahmud II, hopelessly involved in European complications, turned for aid to Mehemet Ali, the Pasha of Egypt. After a series of protracted campaigns, Egyptian forces captured and destroyed the Wahhabi stronghold of Daraiya in 1818. The last Wahhabi prince was executed in Constantinople and the movement was brought under control. A result of these campaigns was renewed attention to Arabia on the part of the European powers. Great Britain feared French influence in Arabia and in 1839 obtained from Mehemet Ali the excellent harbor of Aden at the entrance of the Red Sea.

PERIOD OF STEADY LOSS OF TERRITORY

In view of these danger signals, Ottoman military weakness was most serious. It was demonstrated in a series of failures and defeats. A gradual, but steady, shrinkage of empire was the chief development of seventeenth- and eighteenth-century Ottoman history. Continuous wars against Venice, Austria, Russia, and Persia ended in defeat and loss of territory. This military misfortune was especially striking since the Turkish government was making serious and partially successful attempts at internal reform during the same period. Despite some able sultans, several outstanding administrators, and the start of military and naval reforms, reverses on the battlefield did not abate. Internal decay might perhaps be brought under some control, but outward pressure from the West was relentless in the direction of the spoliation of the Ottoman state.

The sixteenth century ended with the serious defeat of the Ottoman navy at the hands of the Venetians and Spanish in 1571 at the Battle of Lepanto. The seventeenth century began with foreign wars against Austria and Persia, the reigns of weak sultans, frequent mutinies and revolts, and general dissatisfaction, but it also saw determined efforts to maintain the power of the sultanate. Murad IV, who ruled from 1623 to 1640, successfully reasserted his autocratic control and ruthlessly suppressed a mutiny of the Janissaries. Strong-willed and determined, he restored order and enforced laws. There is a story to the effect that he would wander disguised through the streets of Constantinople, where smoking tobacco had been forbidden, and if he discovered in some inn or other an unfortunate who smoked, the sultan with his own hands executed the culprit on the spot. Murad IV, leading the Turkish troops in person, managed to retake Baghdad from the Persians in 1638.

The Koprulus and Attempts at Reform

Soon after the rule of Murad IV there rose to power as successive Grand Vizirs four members of a remarkable Albanian family, the Koprulus. This period, also known as the "rule of the vizirs," was a period of steady reform and improved administration, yet it too was accompanied by military failure and loss of territory. In 1656 Muhammad Koprulu, grandson of a Moslem

Albanian, who had begun service as a kitchen boy, became Grand Vizir at the age of 70. He demanded and received unlimited powers, and these he exercised ruthlessly for the benefit of the state. All his measures were to be ratified without discussion; he was to have unquestioned power to appoint, to reward, and to punish; no great man or favorite was to be allowed any influence against him; and all accusations against him were to be instantly rejected.

As an unchecked dictator he opposed bribery and corruption with severe measures. He ordered the execution of 36,000 persons, regardless of position. The chief executioner strangled with his own hands 4,000 culprits in five years, an average of three a day. These efforts produced results. Muhammad Koprulu restored financial order by borrowing when necessary from the sultan's private funds, curtailing incomes of the clergy, and confiscating money from religious institutions and he managed to put a temporary stop to corruption in the imperial administration. In 1661, when dying, he succeeded in having his son, Ahmed Koprulu, appointed as next Grand Vizir. His son turned out to be a statesman of the first rank; able, humane, and pious, he held power from 1661 to 1676. He insisted on equal justice for all, saw to it that the public service remained efficient and tolerably free from corruption, and put through a series of successful reforms of the army and navy. Nevertheless, the military decline of the Ottoman empire continued.

A series of wars against Christian Europe brought defeat after defeat. Against Austria, Turkish arms lost two spectacular battles: in 1664 the Battle of St. Gotthard, where superior Western military weapons, such as artillery, and the infantry wrought great havoc, and again in 1683 when the Grand Vizir and son-in-law of Ahmed Koprulu, Kara Mustafa, was defeated before the walls of Vienna. Turkish losses were very great, and the execution of Kara Mustafa and the presentation of his head to the sultan on a silver platter did nothing to improve Turkish military morale. A similar fate overtook Turkish military power in the wars against Venice, Poland, and Russia. Ottoman possessions in Europe were reduced by half. The rule of Mustafa Koprulu (1689), brother of Ahmed, again brought into power an able administrator, but it witnessed further military defeats.

Defeat by Persia

The eighteenth century, like the preceding one, produced a series of crushing military disasters. These were not all administered merely by the European powers, but also by neighboring Asian states. Time and time again Turkish armies were defeated in warfare against the Persians. Under the ex-brigand chief and usurper, Nadir Shah, Persian cavalry defeated Turkish infantry at the battle of Kirkuk in 1733. Two years later Nadir Shah inflicted heavy losses at the battle of Baghavand. This forced the Ottoman sultan to make peace, to surrender Tiflis, Erivan, and nearby territory to Persia, and to abandon claims to Persian lands which had been alloted to Turkey a bit prematurely under a joint Turkish-Russian plan for the dismemberment of northwestern Persia. The first war against Nadir Shah of Persia was followed by a second in 1743. The result was another decisive Persian victory, near

Kars, in 1745. Here, the Turks were utterly routed with heavy losses and a force of 100,000 cavalry and 40,000 infantry was put to flight in hopeless disorder.

Defeat by Russia

There followed a short interlude of peace and even some cultural progress under Raghib Pasha, who was Grand Vizir between 1757 and 1763. But this was soon followed by further serious military reverses. These were the defeats in the Turkish wars against Austria and Russia which occupied the last half of the century. The Ottoman empire faced in Catherine the Great an able, unscrupulous, and relentless adversary, bent on the eventual dismemberment of the Ottoman territory and the restoration of a Greek state ruled by her son Constantin.

In the first Russo-Turkish war of 1768–74, the Turks lost the Danube delta after heavy fighting in the Dniester and Danube mouths; a Russian fleet from the Baltic operating in the Aegean inflicted heavy losses on the Ottoman navy in the Battle of Chesme, off the island of Chios; and the Greeks were incited successfully to revolt against their masters. The war was ended by the Treaty of Kuchuk Kainarji, a small village in Bulgaria. In effect this treaty made Turkey a kind of Russian province. Not only did it entail the loss of the Crimea, which was to be an independent state, but a clause was inserted in the treaty which heralded Russian interference in the affairs of the subjects of the sultan. Russia reserved for herself the right to intervene on behalf of all the Christian subject people within the Ottoman state. But these gains were not sufficient for the empress.

Catherine was determined to acquire the Crimea for Russia, and she was successful in this attempt in 1783. She had drawn up a joint scheme with Joseph II of Austria which envisaged the disruption of the Ottoman empire and a division of the Balkans between Russia and Austria. Consequently, when the second Russo-Turkish War broke out in 1787 the Russians were joined by the Austrian armies. The latter took Belgrade, and the Russians advanced to the Danube. The alliance lasted only until 1791 and Russia concluded the Peace of Jassy the next year. This treaty was as disastrous to Turkish prestige and power as had been the Treaty of Kuchuk Kainarji. The impotence of Ottoman rule had been made clear to the world, so much so that it aroused British and French fears of a Russian seizure of the Bosphorus.

EARLY ATTEMPTS AT REFORM

Steady military decline was a symptom not merely of the internal decay of the state, but also of the fact that Turkey had not progressed in comparison with the rest of the world. The West had undergone profound changes, changes which immeasurably strengthened the European powers in all aspects, not merely the military. For Turkey it was no longer a question of a reform of military nature, but it had become one of a basic readjustment in order to survive. Government, justice, and education, and many other aspects of Ottoman life required drastic changes. A government in which the provinces were ruled by pashas who had obtained their position by bribery, and whose sole interest in ruling was to recover their expenditures as quickly as possible through extortion, corruption, and the wholesale exploitation of their powerless subjects, could not continue.

The sultan, the "Lord of the Age and the Shadow of the Universe," exercised little control over his officials; in addition, he was not obeyed at all in those regions where the Derebeys (the great landholders and local magnates) chose to resist all government orders even to the extent of refusing military service when it was demanded.

In a state where the ruler was Moslem caliph as well as sultan, Christians were carefully excluded from both army and civil service, and from all imperial offices, with the sole exception of the post of the Grand Dragoman, the interpreter responsible for dealing with the Western ambassadors. Christian subjects were relegated to agriculture and trade, but even here suffered discrimination. Moslems engaged in commerce paid only half of the customs duties exacted from Christian merchants. Although some of the Christian subjects, notably the Greeks, were well enough off, and even had become indispensable as superior merchants and skilled sailors, the lot of the South Slav, Bulgarian, Albanian, and Armenian peasant was extremely hard. Oppressive government, confiscatory taxation, and Turkish religious fanaticism made his life one of desolation and misery. This was particularly true as far as justice and the law was concerned. In court an incontrovertible Christian claim stood no chance against the simple allegation of a Moslem, unsubstantiated, and not even backed by oath. The verdict almost invariably was in favor of the Moslem, in part because he could afford to pay more in bribes than could the impoverished Christian.

There were no educational facilities but those for the training of the slave household and those conducted for Moslems by teachers attached to mosques. These ulamas were paid by the government to teach religion to the faithful, and education was limited to a knowledge of the Koran, some law, and some elementary rules of behavior. In Constantinople and in some of the more important provincial cities there existed mosque schools which provided free religious instruction and which opened a career of teaching for the Moslem subject, but Christians were deprived of education in the old Ottoman state. Thus reform required more basic reconstruction than simply the reform of the military. An acute French observer, Baron de Tott, who helped in the reorganization of the Turkish artillery, could write, in 1760, of the state of the Ottoman empire as follows:

> The Turk's weapons are the same as those used in the days of Sennacherib. As for their ships, they are utterly worthless. The men know absolutely nothing and their superstition baffles belief. They are very brave and very religious, but otherwise quite useless. The Janissaries are the terror of the country and will submit to no sort of discipline. They refuse to live in their barracks, which are filthy, and their insolence to foreigners is beyond endurance. As for the Courts of Law, nothing can exceed the disorder which reigns in them. If the Empire is to be saved, everything is to be reorganized on a new basis.

None of the old Ottoman techniques and methods proved valid against the impact of the new power—the new world of nineteenth-century Europe, the world of the West.

The impact of Western ideas was at the core of Turkish history during the nineteenth century. The effect of Western influence was twofold. On the one hand, the lessons learned at the cost of the humiliating treaties which Turkey had been forced to conclude with Russia made it clear to the government that reform of at least the military forces was an absolute necessity if the state were to survive. On the other hand, Western ideas and ideals reached the subject peoples of the sultan and were destined to cause far-reaching repercussions. As pointed out, the subject people had been carefully left out of the administration of the state. They had been granted a measure of limited autonomy, but had no active part in the government. Left alone, they were free to turn to the West. It was among the Greeks in particular, who as merchants and traders traveled about, that a certain familiarity with Western languages, science, arts, and political institutions manifested itself. Visitors to the West brought back Western ideals, not the least of which was nationalism with its demands for independence and complete severance from the Ottoman empire. Thus, Western thought produced an ever-growing gap between the ruler and the ruled.

Military Reform

More direct, more pressing, and far more immediate, at least to some Ottoman rulers, was the problem of reform of the armed forces. Military reform was to be adopted as a state policy. The reasons for this appeared obvious: if it were due to superior military strength that Turkish armies had been defeated, then Turkey must take over those features of the West which made for this superiority. It was not really understood by the Ottoman government that the military strength of the West represented merely an element of Western superiority but did not in itself contain the key to this superiority. This military power was based on the tremendous intellectual, political, and economic changes which Europe had undergone. The Ottoman government's aim was a narrow one: to create a new, really efficient body of troops and to do away with the Janissaries. Reform of the Turkish army was to be the sole concession to Western thought and power, and it was attempted rather late in a period of crisis. As might be expected reform threatened vested interests, and it at once encountered internal opposition from the slave household, certain sections of the Islamic community at large, and, above all, from the intended victims of reform, the Janissaries.

Selim III

Selim III, who ruled from 1789 to 1807, was an able and intelligent sultan. Eager for victory and reform, he met failure in both endeavors. Turkey against her will became embroiled in the Napoleonic wars upon the landing of Napoleon in Egypt in 1798. Napoleon's plan was to make Egypt, then a Turkish province, a French military base. The Turks, entering the war on the side of England, were severely defeated by the French at the Battle of Aboukir in 1799.

Selim was also determined to create a new, small, but modern military force and to eliminate the power of the Janissaries once and for all. The attempt ended in complete disaster; it cost him his throne and his life. The Janissaries had become increasingly dangerous and turbulent. In 1807 their particularly oppressive rule of Serbia resulted in a general massacre of the Serbs, and the Serbs revolted in a spontaneous uprising against the Janissaries. Selim was actually sympathetic to Serb resistance to the Janissaries but a virtually independent Serbia was the result of this revolt. A war against Russia and Britain in 1807 complicated matters. Russia demanded the right of intervention on behalf of the Christian subjects of the Turks, invoking the famous clause of the Treaty of Kuchuk Kainarji. The British fleet threatened Constantinople, at which point Selim attempted to reorganize the army and to do away with the power of the Janissaries. The sultan hoped to enroll the youngest and best of the Janissaries in a new corps, clothed, drilled, and paid along the lines of the most modern European model, which at that moment meant the French army. (Selim had come under the influence of Sebastiani, Napoleon's able ambassador who was a monk turned diplomat.)

When this edict was issued, the Janissaries mutinied in 1807. They inquired from the Grand Mufti what punishment was deserved by one who had established the new military force and the answer was unequivocal: "Death, and that according to the Koran since the Diwan[2] has introduced among Moslems the manners of infidels and manifested an intention to suppress the Janissaries, who are the true defenders of the law and the prophets." The mutiny was successful. Selim III was forced to abdicate and was hastily executed in 1808 when it appeared that he might be restored. Reform, even along purely military lines, did not have a promising beginning.

Mahmud II

Selim's successor was his nephew Mahmud II. A mere child in 1808, the puppet of the mutineers, his life was spared only because he was the last surviving member of the Ottoman dynasty. He was forced to repeal all reform measures, was greatly humiliated, and for all practical purposes the Janissaries became virtual rulers of the Ottoman empire. Under the circumstances Mahmud II could do nothing but bide his time. A very able, resolute, strong-willed, and patient man, he was convinced that military reform was a matter of survival for the empire. Although peace had been restored for the moment with the Treaty of Bucharest of 1812 which terminated the war with Russia, it seemed likely that Turkey might fall a victim to either Napoleon or Tsar Alexander, depending on the success of the French invasion of Russia. Internally, chaos reigned in almost every part of the state. In the rural areas of Anatolia, the Derebeys acted as virtually independent rulers, thus challenging the rule of the Sultan. The distant

---

[2] The high council of the empire, composed of the Grand Vizir, vizir, and secretaries.

provinces were governed by rebellious pashas, Egypt and Albania were practically independent, the army was most ineffective, and the terror of the Janissaries was ever present.

Mahmud II decided finally to eliminate the Janissaries. Patiently he organized a small force of artillery personally loyal to him. The decisive clash came on June 15, 1826. When the Janissaries refused to obey an edict of reorganization and mutinied, storming the streets toward the palace, Mahmud used his artillery against them. Four thousand Janissaries were killed in the capital itself and many others in the provinces. The Janissaries were completely wiped out. "Such of the corpses as were not burned in the fires which blazed in all directions were cast into the sea, and for many months fish in Constantinople were not eatable." This time the Mufti pronounced a malediction against them. Their banner and their special badge, the white cap, were dragged through the mud, and the mosques and cafes which they had habitually frequented were destroyed. The very name of the Janissaries was erased from official records.

Mahmud II was now free to reorganize the army. He himself read French books on tactics, drilled his own troops, and created a new model army in which at first French and later Prussian influence predominated. Mahmud II also founded a number of military and naval schools and the reform of the military was completed when conscription was introduced in 1843. Mahmud II had accomplished the military reform of the Ottoman empire, yet it was insufficient to save the state. The history of the nineteenth century showed only too clearly the fatal tardiness of the Turks to come to grips with the world around them, a world in which the military reform, the change from Janissaries to a modern army, amounted to very little when measured against the more profound changes of the Industrial Revolution, the rise of great new powers, and the all-pervasive ideals of nationalism.

It was the new Western idea, nationalism, which seemed to spell the doom of the disintegrating empire. After maturing for a long period among the subject peoples of the Turks, it broke out in a series of revolutions which shook the Turkish state to its core. It seemed as if this disintegrating state would fall easy prey to one of the great new powers of Europe, Russia. The tsar, it appeared, would be heir to the defenseless Turkish state and would gain access to Constantinople and the Straits. But precisely this possibility was to ensure the continued though feeble existence of the Ottoman empire. England, the rival of Russia, would not tolerate Russian control in this area. As early as 1792 the younger Pitt had declared that "the true doctrine of the balance of power requires that the Russian empire should not, if possible, be allowed to increase, nor that of Turkey to diminish."

TURKEY AS A PAWN OF THE GREAT POWERS

Western influence, in the form of nationalism, which demanded that each nationality or group of people with common language, culture, and tradition should constitute a united, independent sovereign state, lay behind the second rising of the Serbs, 1815–1817, and the more spectacular insurrection of the Greeks in 1821. These nationalist revolts, these "wars of independence," illustrated the crumbling internal structure of the Ottoman empire. But what they demonstrated even more was that European powers had begun to take an active interest in the problem of Turkey, an interest which was soon to appear on the stage of European diplomacy as the great, haunting "Eastern question"—the problem of the fate of the Turkish state.

Greek Insurrection

The Greeks rebelled in 1821, killing the Turkish garrisons wherever they could, and the Turks replied in kind. The sultan hanged the Greek patriarch in his pontifical robes at Constantinople, and there were frightful scenes of destruction and barbarism, of which the famous massacre of Chios, where the Turks killed or sold in slavery all of the unfortunate inhabitants of that island, was but the most celebrated one. Mahmud II called on his subordinate, the pasha of Egypt, Mehemet Ali for aid in the suppression of the Greeks. In 1825 a large part of the modernized Egyptian army was transported across the Mediterranean, and under the leadership of Ibrahim, the son of Mehemet Ali, large areas of the ravaged country were reconquered and the Greek insurgents, who were split into factions, were gradually crushed. But stubborn refusal on the sultan's part to accept the terms proposed by the British foreign secretary, George Canning, and the eagerness on the side of the Western powers to help the sons of ancient Greece in their struggle against oriental barbarism (Byron's poetry made it appear as if the days of Marathon and Salamis were back again), resulted in a resounding Turkish naval defeat at the Battle of Navarino in 1827. A British admiral who had orders to stop the warfare of the Turks against the Greeks, but not to engage in hostilities, found a solution to this impossible command when Egyptian ships opened fire on the British fleet which was ranged along the joint Egyptian-Turkish navy. The Ottoman fleet was almost completely destroyed in the ensuing battle and the Egyptian troops were expelled from Greece.

In 1828 Tsar Nicholas I declared war on Turkey to bring an end to the situation. A daring march across the Balkan mountains by the Russian general, Diebitch, with only 15,000 troops and the capture of Adrianople forced Mahmud II to conclude the humiliating Treaty of Adrianople in 1829. In this treaty the sultan was forced to concede independence to Greece, autonomy to Serbia, and the principalities of Wallachia and Moldavia came under strong Russian influence. As a consequence Mahmud II shut himself up in his palace for weeks in deepest gloom.

Revolt of Mehemet Ali and European Intervention

After internal revolt and defeat, disintegration next threatened in the direct challenge to the rule of the Ottoman sultan from Mehemet Ali, the pasha of Egypt. Born in 1769, son of an Albanian fisherman, he was a penniless orphan who never learned how to read or write, but gained a fortune by speculations in tobacco. Making a name for himself in the campaigns against Napoleon in Egypt in 1798 and against the English in 1808, he won constant promotion and was named pasha of Egypt. In Egypt, he created an excellent modern army and a strong navy with the use of French advisors and military instructors left from the Napoleonic Wars. In 1811 he succeeded in grasping absolute power in Egypt by treacherously murdering the remaining Mamluks at a banquet in the citadel of Cairo, at the conclusion of which 300 of them were shot down in its narrow alleyways. An excellent ruler and statesman of real genius, he built up a conscript army of over 100,000 men, strengthened by a powerful fleet. As he grew stronger, the relationship between Mehemet Ali and Mahmud II, his suzerain, soon became merely a matter of formality. Mehemet Ali broke the Wahhabi revolt in Arabia, and aided the sultan in the suppression of the Greeks, but his own final break with Constantinople and the proclamation of his independent, hereditary position was merely a matter of time.

In 1832 Mehemet Ali defeated the Turkish forces and captured Syria, and the Egyptian troops under the able leadership of his son, Ibrahim Pasha, advanced into Asia Minor. No obstacles lay between the victorious Egyptian army and Constantinople, but it was precisely the alarming possibility of the collapse of Ottoman rule which turned out to be the salvation of the Turkish state. Mahmud II appealed for aid to the European powers. Refused help at first by Britain, he next turned to Russia, as a drowning man clings to a serpent, and Russian aid was forthcoming. A Russian fleet entered the Bosphorus and 15,000 Russian troops were landed. This Russian intervention by Nicholas I, who feared an active, reorganized Turkey under the reformer Mehemet Ali, at once caused the very greatest alarm in the West. Britain above all, but also France, now agreed to the cardinal principle which was to govern their relationship with the Turks for a long time to follow: Turkey was to be preserved as an empire, dependent on Britain, as a bulwark against Russia.

The result of this policy was Western pressure against Mehemet Ali. The Egyptians held Syria and Adana but withdrew from most of Asia Minor. Mahmud II was guaranteed his position and the Russians withdrew from the Straits. First, however, they concluded the Treaty of Unkiar Skelessi (1833) with the Ottoman ruler. This represented the highest point of Russian influence and brought Turkey virtually under the tutelage of the tsar. In time of need, according to a secret article, the Turks promised to keep the Straits closed to all foreign warships. The establishment of Russia's protectorate and the real danger of Russian control of the Ottoman state acted to preserve Turkey. More than ever Britain was convinced that her diplomacy must maintain an independent Turkey as a bastion against Russian expansion and its threat to the British empire's lifeline to India.

The interest of the powers in the fate and the survival of the Ottoman state soon was shown again when the struggle between the sultan and the Egyptian pasha was renewed. Mahmud II was determined to crush his refractory subordinate, while Mehemet Ali thought that through a renewed war he might establish hereditary rule for himself and his son in Egypt and

Syria. In the war of 1839 the Turkish model army suffered a complete defeat by the Egyptians (Battle of Nesib). Meanwhile, the Turkish fleet sailed straight into the harbor of Alexandria, not to fight, but to surrender. Mercifully Mahmud II was spared the news of these disasters; he died before the dispatches arrived.

Mahmud was succeeded by his timorous son, Abdul Mejid. The Ottoman empire again seemed likely to be dissolved, parts falling into the eager hands of Mehemet Ali, while Russia waited to share in the spoils in the north. England had no desire to see either of these results. Palmerston, supported by Austria, delivered an ultimatum to Mehemet Ali who, relying upon French support, decided to ignore it. For a moment, this seemed to strain Anglo-French relations to the possibility of war. Soon thereafter Mehemet Ali lost the French support of Louis Philippe and when he continued to prove stubborn toward the demands of Britain, the latter acted at once. A joint Austrian-British fleet bombarded Egyptian forces in Syria and then proceeded to sail to Alexandria, whereupon Mehemet Ali was forced to agree to negotiations. Mehemet Ali obtained hereditary possession of Egypt, but not of Syria.

England obtained Aden, the strategic port which controls the Red Sea exit to the Indian Ocean, on the basis of a lease "in perpetuity," while her position in Mesopotamia, astride the most direct route to India, was also strengthened. As early as 1835 an English colonel had transported a dismantled steamer overland from Syria to the Euphrates, then reassembled it and sailed down the river. At this time an English resident was stationed in Baghdad, with his own guard of Indian troops and a gunboat on the river. The English organized a special camel post system from Mesopotamia to the Mediterranean, while an English company obtained special privileges on the two great Mesopotamian rivers, the Tigris and the Euphrates.

The Ottoman sultan once again was preserved in his role as a bulwark against the danger from the north. In 1841 a convention was signed whereby the Straits were to be closed to all warships in times of peace.

LATER STEPS TOWARD REFORM AND WESTERNIZATION

The preservation of the Ottoman empire as a bulwark against Russia introduced to Britain the difficult question of Turkish internal reform. Military support of a weak Turkey was one thing; political reformation whereby the state became internally strong and reinvigorated was quite another. To accomplish both objectives, opposing Russia at every turn and urging complete reform upon the Turkish state, Stratford Canning was sent as ambassador to Constantinople. A charming, truthful, and persuasive man, he managed to obtain enormous influence with the sultan Abdul Mejid, and proved most successful as far as opposition to Russia was concerned; however, he could not surmount the problem of reform.

Changes in the direction of westernization were begun. Some students were sent to the West, in particular to France, and the first printing press, newspapers, Western drama, and French poetry made their appearance at

Constantinople. In addition some public schools were opened. Nevertheless, the attempt to change the Ottoman empire proved to be a failure.

Hatt-i-sherif of Gulhané

Reform was attempted in a decree of the Grand Vizir, Rezhid Pasha, the Hatt-i-sherif of Gulhané. Rezhid Pasha was the former Turkish ambassador to London and there had become a fervent believer in constitutional and parliamentary forms of government. With the backing of Canning he promulgated the Reform Decree of 1839. This document was solemnly proclaimed to the accompaniment of a salute of 101 guns before an assembly of foreign diplomats and Turkish, Greek, Catholic, and Jewish subjects of the sultan. It promised equal security of life, honor, and property to all. Calling for equitable apportioning of taxes, it also established a five-year military service for the Moslems, and exempted the Christians from their service upon payment of a special tax. Provincial councils were to be set up, tax farming was abolished, state banks and secondary education were to be instituted, and judicial reform was promised. A comment on the state of justice in the old Ottoman empire is one of the provisions of this document which stated that no one henceforth was to be killed by poison before judgment was rendered.

This reform document was received with bitter opposition by the old order. Provincial councils when called obstructed all innovations, tax farming was soon back again, inequality of taxation continued, and in 1843 the death penalty was decreed for apostasy from Islam. Rezhid Pasha himself had little illusion regarding the reform attempts, since he agreed that "our government is bad, but we prevent it from becoming worse." The court faction opposed to him caused his fall, despite Canning's wishes, and very little progress was made toward reform before the Crimean War.

The Crimean War

While the domestic reformation of the Ottoman state seemed difficult, the attempts at saving Turkey from dismemberment were more successful. In a famous conversation in early 1853 between Tsar Nicholas I and Hamilton Seymour, the British ambassador in St. Petersburg, the tsar prophesied the doom of Turkey and the need for a mutual agreement regarding its partition: "We have on our hands a sick man—a very sick man. It will, I tell you frankly, be a great misfortune if one of these days he should slip away from us before all necessary arrangements were made." Her Majesty's government was less inclined to subscribe to the prophecy of a speedy death, if it could be prevented by English support. Again, British fears of a Russian advance to the Straits resulted in the propping up of the Ottoman empire. Canning was sent out once more, to serve his second tour of duty as ambassador in Constantinople where he labored strenuously to check Russian influence.

In 1852, a quarrel broke out between France and Russia, a dispute over a mere trifle—whether the Latin or the Greek monks in Jerusalem were to

CONSULTATION ABOUT THE STATE OF TURKEY.

FIGURE 1.4. Cartoon from Punch *showing a worried France and Britain in discussion about the seemingly inevitable decease of moribund Turkey.*

have certain prerogatives in the holy places. France, as protector of the Catholic church in Ottoman dominions, posed the question whether or not the Latins could be asked to celebrate mass at the church of the Virgin upon a schismatic slab of marble, and before a crucifix which had its feet separated. The Turkish government rendered a decision favorable to the French, and Nicholas I was annoyed. The tsar then sent Prince Menchikov, a rude, tactless, and arrogant soldier, to Constantinople to intimidate the Turks and to demand that all Orthodox clergy within the Turkish empire be put under Russian supervision. Outmaneuvered by Canning, Menchikov left after the Turks had refused to accept his ultimatum, and Russian troops began to occupy the Rumanian principalities of Wallachia and Moldavia.

The Turks protested and were only restrained by the powers from declaring war against Russia. Negotiations continued at Vienna, but in October 1853, a joint British-French fleet entered the Dardanelles. Louis Napoleon was eager for a victorious war to secure glory to France and to strengthen his own position, and in England a bellicose Palmerston had taken over from a peace-minded Aberdeen. When a Russian fleet destroyed a Turkish squadron at Sinope in March 1854, the Crimean War began.

This, the most unnecessary of all modern wars in the opinion of some historians, was fought by the Turks in the Danubian provinces, where they forced the Russians back, and by the Allies in the Crimea. Ignorant of the country, of the strength of the enemy, or of his fortifications, British and French troops fought heroically against stubbornly resisting Russians, who put up a gallant fight to save Sebastopol. The Treaty of Paris of 1856 ended the war after Russia's defeat and the death of Nicholas, and guaranteed Turkish integrity and independence, and the closure of the Bosphorus and the Dardanelles to warships of all nations during peace. The chief policy of the Western Allies remained that of preserving Turkey against Russia. Further, in order to deprive Russia of future pretexts at intervention, the Western powers now insisted on Turkish internal reform.

Hatt-i-Humayun

The result was the edict of Hatt-i-Humayun of 1856, the most important Turkish reform edict of the nineteenth century. In this decree the stipulations of the reform edict of Gulhané of 1839 were once more affirmed. In addition, Christian subjects of the Ottoman ruler were given the right to enter every civil office, all ranks of the military service and to be represented on the provincial councils. The reform edict provided also for an annual budget, the creation of a regular foreign service instead of irregular missions, and the establishment of state schools. Torture was to be abolished and prisons reformed. All legal proceedings were to be held in public, and evidence of witnesses was to be accepted without distinction of race and creed, as taxes were to be levied without religious or racial discrimination. In order to end the frequent scandals of the disposition of the patriarchs of the Christian churches they were to be appointed for life, and obtained fixed salaries from the government. In addition, some measures were instituted against tax farming, bribery, and corruption.

As a whole, the reform decree remained a dead letter. Christians continued preferring to pay the poll tax to military service, Moslems refused to obey Christian officials, and equal justice was denied to Christian subjects in Turkish courts. Reform made very slow, almost painful, progress. Education proved perhaps the most encouraging field of endeavor for the labor of the reformers. Here the Ottoman government established new public grade schools and high schools in the capital cities of the provinces, and a more modern curriculum of reading, writing, and arithmetic supplemented the learning by memory of passages from the Koran. Professional schools for law, medicine, the civil service, engineering, the army, and the navy were also established. Apart from the efforts of the government to improve education, the Greeks and Armenians of the empire made a particular point to establish better private schools which used materials printed in their national languages. Thus these two subject races of the sultan became soon the intellectual elite of the empire.

Western missionary activity became a new influence. Jesuit, Greek Orthodox, and Protestant missionaries all established private schools. In 1863 an American philanthropist, Charles Robert, established a college named after him on the Bosphorus, with an American faculty offering American education. Robert College and a similar American college for girls across the Straits at Scutari were to be extremely influential in the introduction of Western thought to Turkey.

Nevertheless, the major problem, that of a complete renovation of the Ottoman empire, remained. Turkey, the "sick man," pretended to be well. Kept alive by outside powers, the state still faced the task of adjustment to the new forces of the West which made themselves felt everywhere in the world. This simply had not been accomplished by 1860.

BASIC DATES

1623–1640	Murad IV
1656–1678	Koprulus serve as Grand Vizirs
1730–1735, 1743–1746	Turks defeated by Nadir Shah
1757–1763	Raghib Pasha
1768–1774, 1787–1792	Turks defeated in Russia
1789–1807	Selim III
1803	Wahhabis capture Mecca
1808–1839	Mahmud II
1815–1817	Revolt of Serbia
1821–1830	Revolt of Greece
1832, 1839	Mehemet Ali of Egypt defeats Turks
1854–1856	Crimean War
1856	Hatt-i-Humayun

SUPPLEMENTARY READING

Brockelmann, C. *History of the Islamic Peoples.* New York, 1947. Authoritative, but somewhat difficult reading. Capricorn reprint, N.Y., 1960.
Eversley, G. and V. Chirol. *The Turkish Empire from 1288 to 1924.* London, 1924. Dated but solid account.
Fisher, S. *The Middle East.* New York, 1959. A more recent text.
Hitti, P. *The Near East in History.* Princeton, N.J., 1961. Another text.
Itzkowitz, N. *The Ottoman Empire and Islamic Tradition.* New York, 1972.
Jackh, E. *Background of the Middle East.* Ithaca, N.Y., 1952. Includes a brief, but good chapter on Turkey.
Lewis, Raphaela. *Everyday Life in Ottoman Turkey.* London, 1971.
Toynbee, A. and K. Kirkwood. *Turkey.* New York, 1927.
Vucinich, W. *The Ottoman Empire: Its Record and Legacy.* Princeton, N. J., 1965.

ADVANCED READING

Alderson, A. *The Structure of the Ottoman Dynasty.* Oxford, 1956.
Anderson, M. S. *The Eastern Question, 1774–1923.* London, 1966.

Berkes, N. *The Development of Secularism in Turkey.* McGill University, 1964.
Coles, P. *The Ottoman Impact on Europe.* New York, 1968.
Creasy, E. *History of the Ottoman Turks.* New York, 1878.
Hogarth, D. *Arabia.* Oxford, 1922.
Hurewitz, J. C. *Diplomacy in the Near and Middle East: A Documentary Record, 1535–1914.* Princeton, N.J., 1956.
Lewis, B. *The Emergence of Modern Turkey.* New York, 1961.
Miller, B. *Beyond the Sublime Porte.* London, 1931. A study of the Ottoman imperial palace.
Saunders, J. *The Muslim World on the Eve of Europe's Expansion.* Englewood Cliffs, N.J., 1966.
Wittek, P. *The Rise of the Ottoman Empire.* London, 1938.

Chapter 2

The Persian Autocratic State, 1600-1857

THE SAFAVID DYNASTY

In a survey of the history of Persia and Afghanistan of this period a comparison with the Ottoman empire is exceedingly valuable. Persia, like Turkey, was governed by an autocracy, and the key position of the ruler remained a basic factor in the strength of the government. Yet, the Persian monarch in contrast to the sultan-caliph at Constantinople had a much more religious character. At the root of the Persian state was the Shi'ite Moslem sect which contributed to a unique Persian national feeling, which was limited to Iran. Furthermore, Persia as a whole was much less complex than the Ottoman empire with its "slave household" and great numbers of subject people of varying races and religions occupying a vast geographical area. Despite this contrast, both Persia and Turkey, and for that matter even Afghanistan, came to share the same fate in the nineteenth century. They became victims of the great power rivalry between Great Britain and Russia, and served as pawns in this struggle. The powerful impact of the West did not overthrow a strong and vigorous Persia, just as it did not cause the decline of the great Ottoman empire; both of these oriental states were already victims of their own internal decay when the outside force appeared.

Shah Abbas I

Abbas I and Persia faced a difficult position when he came to power in 1587. In the west the Ottomans had taken Georgia, Armenia, Azerbaijan, and Baghdad, and in the east the Uzbek ruler of Bukhara had taken the region of Khorasan including the centers of Herat and Meshed. Abbas decided to attack the weaker power of the Uzbeks first. In order to do this in

FIGURE 2.1. Portrait of Sir Robert Sherley.

1590 he concluded a humiliating peace with Turkey in which he conceded most of the disputed possessions to the Ottomans. Shah Abbas was successful in his campaigns against Bukhara. By 1597 its power had been broken, and Abbas was now ready to turn against the Turks. But before embarking upon this venture he made excellent use of the services of two English adventurers, the Sherley brothers, who were of great aid to him in his plan to reorganize the Persian army.

Anthony and Robert Sherley, with 24 retainers, arrived in Persia in 1598, and offered their services to the shah. Their plan was to render their services to the Persian shah in order to strike a blow at the Ottoman empire. They flattered Shah Abbas, who began to realize the value of these Elizabethans in his attempt to reorganize the Persian army.

His Army. A completely new Persian army was organized. Originally this army had consisted entirely of Qizilbash horsemen who obeyed only their tribal chiefs, and who possessed no tactics other than their cavalry charge, in contrast to the Turkish army which had excellent infantry and good artillery. The Sherley brothers reduced the tribal contingents to 30,000 men and built up a force of 10,000 cavalry and 12,000 infantry paid and officered directly by the crown. In addition, the army was supplied with 500 guns made by a cannon founder in the service of the English brothers. Further, the army was reorganized so as to break the power of the tribes and to get away from the turbulent and often domineering Qizilbash, by the creation of a completely new tribe, the Shah Savan, or "Friends of the Shah." Open to all friends of the shah, this force supposedly possessed the virtue of direct loyalty to the shah himself, and it at once attracted a number of the shah's followers who came from a variety of tribes.

An attack on Turkey was postponed until the new army had been created. The war, which lasted from 1602 until 1627, was completely successful. Abbas took Tabriz, captured all of northwest Persia, took Erivan, and won a decisive victory against the Turks at a battle near Lake Urmia. The conquest of Azerbaijan and Kurdistan was followed in 1624 by the seizure of Baghdad. Persian prestige as a great military power was completely restored.

His Administration. Shah Abbas also excelled as an administrator. During his reign each provincial governor and local magistrate was made responsible for the security of the roads within his area. Falsehood within the bureaucracy was so frequently and severely punished that the belief sprang up that spirits informed the shah whenever anyone lied to him. He was particularly concerned with furthering trade and commerce. For this purpose Shah Abbas built roads and bridges and established and maintained caravansaries and bazaars.

Interest in stimulating trade led to a joint Anglo-Persian expedition against the Portuguese at Hormuz in 1622, and with the capture of this strategic island the English East India Company was given special commercial privileges. On the mainland opposite Hormuz a new port, Bander Abbas, was constructed to serve as chief export center for the silk trade. To promote commerce and in accordance with an enlightened policy of religious toleration Shah Abbas gave the Armenians a privileged position in business, and he used the Christian Georgians in the Persian army. In his reign even Catholic Carmelites were permitted to reside at the capital. Yet Abbas never for a moment forgot the Shi'a basis of his rulership and the theocracy over which he presided. A religious aura clothed his reign and was publicly demonstrated in the many long pilgrimages which the shah personally undertook. He once walked 800 miles to Meshed, a specially venerated Shi'a shrine.

His Diplomacy. Another feature of Abbas' reign which illustrates the renewed power of Persia in the seventeenth century was the attempt to establish diplomatic relations with European powers in order to work out plans for a concerted attack against the Ottoman empire, the enemy of both Christian Europe and Persia. In 1599 Shah Abbas sent Anthony Sherley to Europe to obtain cooperation for this scheme from the Emperor Rudolph II and the King of Spain.

Although Sherley's mission was a failure, it caused a new interest in Persia on the part of the European powers. Europe became conscious of the aid which Persia might furnish against the Ottoman empire, and as a result a number of diplomatic missions were sent. There were embassies from the Pope, Paul V (1608), from Spain (1602, 1618), from England

FIGURE 2.2. General view of the Masjid-i Shah from the Ali Kapu, the large pavilion leading to the royal gardens.

(1618, 1627), and Holland (1623, 1629). Despite Sherley's failure, Shah Abbas made a second attempt to obtain a power coalition against the Turks, and in 1602 he dispatched Robert Sherley on an identical mission abroad. Traveling via Poland he reached Prague and then Rome in 1609 and finally visited Spain, but the great scheme of concerted action of a league against the Ottomans did not materialize. Attacks on Turkey from both west and east remained uncoordinated.

Isfahan. In 1598 Shah Abbas made the city of Isfahan his new capital, and constructed new buildings so that it became, and remains until today, one of the great artistic centers of Persia. Shah Abbas ushered in the last splendid age of Persian art. The city of Isfahan possessed a good central location, and soon attracted a large population of about half a million. It was laid out on the basis of a completely new plan, and its splendor gave rise to the Persian saying that "half the world is Isfahan."

At the center of Isfahan is a large, open space, 560 yards long, the "Maidan" used for the playing of polo and for horseracing. Overlooking it still stands the "Sublime Porte," the "Ali Kapu," a large pavilion which leads to the royal gardens, and from which the shah watched the events which unfolded on the Maidan. Across the square stands the small, but exquisite mosque of Shah Abbas' father-in-law, the mosque of Sheik Lutfullah. This is a masterpiece of Safavid architecture in which the color of the beautiful tile work is particularly admirable. One of the most impressive buildings of Isfahan is the royal mosque, the Masjid-i Shah. Illustrating strong Sassanian influence, it shows great mastery of the arch and vault construction. Its gigantic porch, open across the entire width of the building, and reaching to its full height, is a good example of the excellence of engineering achieved by Safavid architects. The practice of adorning buildings with colored tiles reached its peak under the Safavid rulers. Every color was used in decorating tiles, and in particular all the various shades of blue, which, when seen against the background of the Persian sky produce an effect of striking brilliance. Another part of the city was built along an avenue of monumental proportions, which was lined with palaces and graced with pools of water and playing fountains. Everywhere there is an emphasis on garden settings, which is explained by the geographical location of Isfahan on a dry, dusty plateau. This added great beauty and charm to the overall effect of architectural splendor. It was estimated that Isfahan contained 162 mosques, and 273 public baths. The total effect of the great buildings, bridges, and gardens utterly charmed the European envoys at the court of the shah.

Safavid Culture

In the seventeenth century the Safavid period produced a fine school of painting. This continued the tradition of the blending of Chinese influence, particularly Ming, in drawing, composition, and in color, with the purely native Persian feeling apparent in treatment of space and form. Essentially an aristocratic art, Safavid painting depicted scenes from court life, hunting expeditions, and flowers and animals. The portraits of courtiers show slender graceful figures of beautiful youths and lovely ladies, all possessed of a delicate elegance and a somewhat languid grace. Aristocratic elegance and lightness coupled with expert drawing characterize these studies, as well as those of animals and even flowers. The school of painting which flourished here at Isfahan had many masters and, under Shah Abbas, Agha Riza was perhaps the greatest. A rather special art was displayed in the great fresco paintings of the great palace, the Chehil Sutun. Here large mural compositions, one of which depicted Shah Abbas himself, showed distinct Italian influence in the splendor of their gold tones and in the richness of the fabrics.

If Safavid Persia produced beautiful buildings and exquisite paintings, it nevertheless obtained its highest achievement in the decorative arts, above all in the carpet. The Persian carpet is the image of a garden: flower beds, floral borders, tiled walks, gleaming pools are all woven into textiles. An attempt is made to reproduce the flowering gardens of Persia, a lifelike glow is given it by the skillful use of colors, and the patterns are taken from the floral world, such as palmettes, blossoms, spiral vines, and flowerettes. Usually at the center of the carpet are rich palmettes which are contrasted with the lively rhythms of the swirling tendrils at the border. This contrast makes for energy and strength and gives a good Persian carpet great elegance and dignity. Hunting scenes or combats between animals are also

FIGURE 2.3. *The prayer cloth of Shah Abbas. An excellent example of floral patterns.*

used as decorative schemes, but in all of the great masterpieces it is the floral and geometrical decoration which is magnificent. Some of the carpets, known technically as "Polonaise," were woven with silver and with gilded silver threads. As Migeon says: "Nothing could be more remarkable than a fine carpet of this school. The composition displays a lavish imagination which is quite fairylike. Yet crowded and intricate though the motives are, they are nonetheless subject to a rigorously logical law of symmetry. No painter's work could achieve such supreme harmonies and rare touches of subtlety than that which the great weavers of Isfahan displayed in these enchanting works."[1]

Persian literature of the Safavid period, both in prose and poetry, is chiefly remarkable for the interest taken in the form of expression; it delights in figures of speech and in ornate and elaborate designs given to the language. This surely is a counterpart to the interest taken in the decorative arts illustrated in the weaving of the carpets.

[1] René Grousset, *The Civilizations of the East*, Vol. I (Paris, 1931), p. 384.

Persia and Europe

Consequently it is not surprising that the impression which the Persia of Shah Abbas made upon Europe was that of a rich and civilized country. The Frenchman, Chardin, reported, after leaving Persia for the last time in 1677:

> The Persians are the most civilized people of the East, and the greatest complimenters in the world. The polite men amongst them are upon a level with the politest men in Europe. Their air, their countenance, is very well composed, lovely, grave, majestical, and as fond as may be, they never fail complimenting one another about the precedence, either going out or coming into a house or when they meet.

Mention has already been made of the diplomatic interest taken by the European powers in Persia as counterweight against Turkey, and this interest continued all through the seventeenth century. Frequent embassies arrived at the court of Isfahan from England, Holland, and from Peter the Great of Russia, and some from German duchies (1637), Sweden (1683), and even a somewhat irregular embassy headed by a woman from the court of France in 1706. But it was more than merely the interest in Persia in terms of a balance of power against the Ottoman empire which fascinated Europe. Soon Persia was looked upon as an important gateway to the riches of India; the commerce in silk and Indian textiles which centered primarily on Hormuz made a deep impression on the imagination of great European poets, such as Milton. The interest in exotic things for a while stimulated Charles II of England to consider the adoption of Persian dress as obligatory court costume, while later on this interest was made the effective vehicle for the thinkers of the Enlightenment, as in the *Lettres Persanes* of Montesquieu. At its height the Persia of the Safavids began to exercise a cultural influence on the West, but it was brief and proved superficial. Instead, Persia was soon destined to be overwhelmed by Western ideas.

Successors of Shah Abbas

In discussing the history of the later Safavids, the successors of Shah Abbas, it may be helpful to refer to a parable in the Koran. Solomon was depicted as dead and standing up supported by the staff on which he leaned until the woodworm ate through that staff and his body fell to the ground.

The Safavid dynasty stood up after the reign of Abbas the Great by following a policy which he began. Sons of his successors were brought up among the women and the eunuchs, and received a poor education. They proved, almost without exception, quite incapable. Being incapable they also feared that they might be done away with by the more enterprising members of the family, and as a consequence the period is one in which wholesale executions, massacres, and harem rule abound. The rapid decline began at once with Shah Safi, who ruled from 1629 to 1642. He put to death all the princes and the princesses of the royal blood, and then he murdered his generals and councillors.

Taking advantage of such conditions the Turks, led by the very able Sultan Murad IV, were able to reconquer large parts of Persian territory. Azerbaijan, including Tabriz, was lost in 1635; Baghdad was retaken by Murad in 1638. However, it was not Turkey which was to end the declining Safavid rule in Persia, but Afghanistan. Native control in Persia was to be replaced for a brief period by the rule of foreign Afghan tribesmen.

AFGHAN CONQUEST

From the sixteenth until the eighteenth century Afghanistan was governed in part by the Persians, by the Moguls, and by the Uzbek khans of Bukhara. In the early eighteenth century some of the Afghan tribes rebelled successfully against Persia. The leader of the Afghans at Kandahar, Mir Vais, perceived the weakness of the Persian state, and led the early movement for independence. His son eventually conquered Persia. Mir Vais had been a hostage at the court of Isfahan, and there had clearly seen the weakness of the Persian monarchy. A successful intriguer, he dissimulated his true intentions and won the trust of the Persian shah. He also armed himself with a religious weapon. While on a pilgrimage to Mecca, Mir Vais, a Sunni, had obtained from the religious doctors a document in which his mission to exterminate the followers of Shi'a as heretics was approved. In consequence the Afghan movement soon achieved the propaganda value of a holy war.

In 1721 Mir Vais' son, Mir Mahmud, invaded Persia with 20,000 Afghan soldiers. The Persian court, already thoroughly demoralized, was panic-stricken. There had been portents in the sky and an earthquake at Tabriz that very same year. The monarch, Shah Husain, was an incompetent ruler. Above all, the low morale of the Persian state facilitated the Afghan conquest. One contemporary observer reported on the state of Persia under the last Safavids as follows: "Merit became an empty sound; all offices and dignities were given to those who paid the highest price; money decided everything, and the immense riches which were accumulated by this means seemed rather to whet than to glut the appetite of those base ministers. Every part of the state felt the effect of this disorder. The troops, discouraged by ill discipline and worse pay, served with reluctance. Robbers infested the highways and interrupted commerce . . . justice was sold in the very capital of the Emperor." Despite the fact that the Persian army had a numerical and material superiority, when the two forces met at the Battle of Gulnabad, the Persians fled. Isfahan was besieged and the shah decided to surrender. He rode out in person to the Afghan camp and surrendered his kingdom to Mir Mahmud.

While the Afghans captured the capital city and Mir Mahmud became shah in 1722, Persia's neighbors made good use of the opportunities presented to them. Both Russia and Turkey seized Persian territory. In 1722 Peter the Great, always eager for Russian expansion, occupied Baku and Derbent. In the next year the Turks took Tiflis in Transcaucasia. In 1724, Turkey and Russia arrived at an agreement for the dismemberment of Persia, in which the Turks were to obtain Hamadan, Tabriz, and Kermanshah, while the Russians assigned to themselves the Persian provinces on the Caspian.

The reign of Shah Mir Mahmud at first seemed stable. He permitted Persian officials to remain at their posts, and he appeared to be just and tolerant. Yet, because most Afghans drifted back to their native country, and since Mir Mahmud received few recruits from home, he felt that his position was becoming more and more insecure as time went on, and he began to institute a reign of terror against the Persians. He gave a banquet and used this occasion to assassinate many Persian officials. Persian forces which he had collected were massacred, and Mir Mahmud, who perhaps was somewhat insane, then proceeded to kill all Persian nobles, large numbers of soldiers, and even Persian civilians. He himself was murdered by his own Afghan troops when only twenty-seven years old. After his murder the Afghan army soldiery selected Ashraf as their ruler.

Ashraf was a moderate and released many prisoners. At the same time he was singularly effective in diplomacy against the Turks. He dispatched four Sunni religious leaders to the Turkish army where they successfully made the point that orthodox Turks should not fight against orthodox Afghans who were engaged in overthrowing the Persian heretics. This propaganda made an impression and some Turkish troops deserted while on a campaign against the Afghans. As a consequence a peace was concluded in 1727 between Turkey and Ashraf in which the Afghans were permitted to remain in Isfahan, while the Turks kept the conquered provinces of the west.

NADIR SHAH

The Afghans in Iran generally showed more skill as soldiers than as administrators. Their rule was brought to a rapid end by the rise of a truly remarkable Persian leader, Nadir Shah. He was born in Khorasan, a Turk of the Afshar tribe, and a Sunni Moslem. He entered the service of the governor of the province of Khorasan and rose rapidly because of his ability and his marriage to the governor's daughter. Nadir distinguished himself particularly in attacks against the Uzbeks and in these campaigns he gained excellent military experience. A rash claim to the deputy governorship of Khorasan changed his fortunes, and he was dismissed. As a consequence of this fall Nadir became a robber and a brigand chief.

Very successful in his new occupation, Nadir offered his services to the last remaining Safavid, the fugitive Shah Tahmasp II, to fight against the Afghan invaders of Persia. He set in motion a national reaction against foreign rule and expelled Ashraf and his Afghans from Isfahan in 1728. The final defeat of the Afghans took place in 1730 and the unlucky Ashraf was killed while fleeing to Afghanistan. Afghan forces everywhere were routed and few escaped.

Nadir was given the title sultan by the grateful Safavid Shah. Nadir's successes against the Afghans were at once followed by attacks against the Turks. These campaigns against the Ottomans lasted from 1730–32 and again from 1733–35. Nadir at first was successful; he defeated a Turkish army near Hamadan and the province of Azerbaijan became once more Persian. A revolt at Herat in the east drew Nadir off and in his absence Shah Tahmasp decided to finish off the Turks. In this campaign the shah lost everything which Nadir had won; Shah Tahmasp was forced to return Tabriz, Hamadan, and Kermanshah to the Ottomans. Infuriated at this turn of events, Nadir decided to make good use of this defeat and of the humiliating terms as an excuse to grasp power for himself. In 1732 Nadir arrested Shah Tahmasp, deposed him, and in turn proclaimed an infant son of the shah as Persian ruler. In reality all power after 1732 was held by Nadir himself, who had fortified his position by marrying Shah Tahmasp's sister. After a series of setbacks in battle with the Turks, Nadir replaced his losses and renewed his attacks.

The Persian army under his leadership managed to inflict a decisive defeat upon the Ottomans in 1735, at the Battle of Baghavand. As a consequence the Turks returned the cities of Tiflis and Erivan to Persia.

Successful first against the Afghans, then against the Turks, Nadir now decided to regain the Persian territories lost to Russia, which Peter the Great had seized in 1722. The tsarist government by now was suitably impressed with the renewed vigor and the leadership displayed by Nadir, and Baku and Derbent on the Caspian were voluntarily restored to Persian rule in 1735.

Nadir's victories and the successful expulsion of the Afghans, the Turks, and the Russians from Persian territory won him enormous acclaim. Since the last Safavid ruler, an infant, had died in 1736 there was no legal obstacle to block his desire to ascend the empty throne, and in 1738 Nadir called a large assembly of all the Persian chiefs in order to consider the election of a shah. The meeting was a farce, everyone knew that Nadir was determined to become shah himself, and the opposition was discouraged by the fate of the chief mullah, who declared that everyone really preferred the Safavid dynasty over Nadir and was strangled the next day. Nadir treated the whole assembly to lavish banquets where wine was liberally dispensed, in order, as some skeptics declared, for Nadir to see who among the assembled betrayed his true sentiments while intoxicated. At first Nadir repeatedly refused the throne when it was offered to him, but he finally yielded, outwardly at least with reluctance. He declared he would accept only under the condition that Persia would renounce Shi'a and adopt Sunni Islam. Coming from a man who was not deeply religious himself, this clause probably served the mundane interest of facilitating a temporary settlement with the Turks. In any case, this was distasteful to the Persians, since Shi'a was too deeply embedded in Iran for a successful promotion of the Sunni orthodoxy.

Nadir Shah's Conquests

After becoming shah, Nadir began a career of conquest. In 1739 he attacked Afghanistan. He captured Kandahar and Kabul, and by the end of the year controlled all of Afghanistan and Bactria. The great lure was then

Mogul India, and like many others before him, Nadir also decided to invade the subcontinent. Crossing the Khyber Pass, he attacked the Mogul empire on the pretext of Mogul refusal to reply to a demand by Nadir that Afghan refugees be surrendered.

By 1739 the Mogul empire was but a shadow of its former self. The emperor, Muhammad Shah, who was "never without a mistress in his arms and a glass in his hands," was an utter weakling. After crossing the Indus river, Nadir Shah attacked the Mogul army about 60 miles from Delhi, at Karnal. The result was a complete defeat for the Mogul forces. Nadir Shah entered the Mogul capital in triumph, with the trembling Mogul emperor at his side. At first the visit of the conqueror seemed to be little else than a visit of courtesy, but when a number of Persian military police were killed by mob action in the narrow streets of Delhi, Nadir gave the order to massacre the population of that unfortunate city. This sack of Delhi of 1739 lasted for five hours, and approximately 20,000 people were put to the sword. According to an Indian historian the gutters ran with blood. "The streets were strewn with corpses like a garden with dead leaves. The city was reduced to ashes and looked like a burnt plain." Nadir Shah impassively observed the general massacre; his remarkable control over his soldiers was shown by the fact that when he ordered an end to the slaughter they stopped at once.

After the sack of Delhi, Nadir withdrew from India, carrying with him enormous booty. Included was the fabulous Peacock Throne of the Mogul emperor Jahangir, encrusted with jewels, the famous Koh-i-Noor, or "mountain of light" diamond, and the Mogul imperial goldplate, together with innumerable jewels, elephants, and horses. The total loot permitted Nadir to proclaim an amnesty from taxation for Persia for three years. In addition, the area west of the Indus river was ceded to the Persian Shah and one of his sons married the daughter of the Mogul emperor.

Still the conquests of Nadir Shah continued. In 1740 he began campaigns against the Uzbek khanates of Bukhara and Khiva, whose frequent raids into Persian territory had always been troublesome. Bukhara submitted that very same year, and the Amu Darya River was made the boundary between the two states, and the resistance of the Khan of Khiva was crushed by military force shortly thereafter. Nadir Shah was also interested in establishing Persia as a naval power on the Persian Gulf. For this purpose he had seized the island of Bahrein in 1738. In 1743 followed a successful Persian attack on Basra, and further to the west, on Mosul. The restlessness of ambition drove Nadir to continue military exertions in attacks against the Georgians in the Caucasus and also in campaigns against the hill tribe of the Lesghians in Daghestan. In these Nadir Shah suffered defeats which infuriated him and which indicated that at last the furthest extent of the military ambitions of this soldier had been reached.

The Fall of Nadir Shah

After his return, booty-laden, from India, Nadir Shah changed in character. His ability as a statesman, never a strong point to begin with, declined con-

FIGURE 2.4. A contemporary Mogul portrait of Nadir Shah.

siderably. Nadir Shah after 1740 turned more and more into a cruel, suspicious, bloodthirsty miser and tyrant. Fearful that his son plotted an attempt on his life, Nadir had him blinded. With despotic rule and complete arbitrariness, he killed hundreds of his subjects at his slightest whim and erected great pyramids out of the skulls of these unfortunates. Ever in need of sums to finance his unending campaigns, he increased taxes by the year and forced enormous exactions from the people. In the final analysis this change to a bloodthirsty tyrant seems to have resulted from the fact that Nadir Shah became insane with power and fearful that this power might be wrested from him.

A natural result was increased discontent among his subjects. Nevertheless, Nadir's military successes continued despite the hatred which the people began to bear him. In his second war against the Turks, between 1743 and 1745, he won what was perhaps his greatest military victory. In a battle which was fought in 1745 near Kars, Nadir utterly routed an Ottoman army of 100,000 cavalry and 40,000 infantry.

But Nadir's tyrannical rule, increasingly heavy and ruthless, became unbearable. Finally in 1747 he was murdered in his tent by fellow tribesmen of his bodyguard. Surprised in his sleep, he was still able to kill two of his assailants before he was finally cut down.

The rise and fall of Nadir Shah illustrates clearly the central position of the ruler in the Persia of the seventeenth and eighteenth centuries. As an autocrat it was very largely his personal character which determined the fate of the state. Nadir was a great soldier, but he was not a statesman or administrator. The Persia of both the Safavids and Nadir Shah depended for its strength on the personal character of the shah. What Nadir lacked in administrative ability and statesmanship he made up by his undeniably great military skill. He has sometimes been compared to Napoleon, but the resemblance of Nadir to Timur is perhaps closer. In both cases, the empires they created remained ephemeral. Tactical skill and strategic excellence alone were not enough, and whereas Napoleon may be remembered also for his code, his educational and administrative reforms, both Timur and Nadir Shah impress themselves upon posterity by reason of their ruthlessness and cruelty. In the history of Persia Nadir's reign is of short duration, but is indicative of the importance of the character of the ruler in this type of autocracy.

When Nadir Shah was assassinated in 1747 a dispute over the throne ensued, and for three years Persia suffered from political division and civil war. With the breakup of the army, which had been forged into such an excellent instrument by Nadir, the Afghan components went their own way. In Afghanistan a former general of Nadir's proclaimed himself an independent ruler and established the Durani dynasty. In Persia itself there were many rival claimants to the vacant throne and civil war lasted until 1750. In that year Karim Khan of Zand won and established the Zand dynasty at Shiraz which lasted until 1794. Karim Khan was an exceptionally just and benevolent ruler who gave Persia an admirable government and peace, and who did not neglect to further artistic endeavors at Shiraz. However, he did not rule the entire country. Since Afghanistan had been lost and the province of Khorasan in the east remained also under independent leadership, the Zand dynasty ruled only the southern section of Persia. Karim Khan evinced eagerness for trade and invited the English East India Company to Bushire, where a factory was established in 1763, and to Basra, where a factory was founded three years later. This short but peaceful and happy interlude was brought to an end in 1794 with the overthrow of the Zand dynasty by Aga Muhammad Khan, founder of the Kajar dynasty.

START OF ACTIVE EUROPEAN INFLUENCES

The rise of the Kajar dynasty, which ruled Persia from 1794 to 1925, saw the beginning of active European influence, during which Persia was reduced, as had been Ottoman Turkey, to a pawn in the diplomatic game played between Great Britain and Russia.

The Kajar Dynasty

The Kajars were a Turkish tribe from Merv, northeast of Khorasan, and the founder of the dynasty was Aga Muhammad. He was a eunuch, and an exceptionally cruel, avaricious, and bloodthirsty tyrant who was eventually murdered by two of his own servants. Yet he was a very shrewd judge of character and could win devoted adherents. After successfully overthrowing the last ruler of the Zand dynasty, Aga Muhammad selected Tehran for his capital and from there began a series of campaigns which won back parts of former Persian territory. First Tiflis was recaptured and later Khorasan was brought back under Persian rule, although in the northwest Derbent and Baku were temporarily lost to Catherine the Great. Aga Muhammad was able to reunify Persia and to establish the long-lasting Kajar dynasty. This dynasty ruled Persia in the accustomed fashion of an autocratic monarchy, but the forces at work which molded the history of the country were gradually more and more those of the West.

Fath Ali Shah

Fath Ali Shah, the nephew and successor of Aga Muhammad, ruled from 1797 to 1835. In contrast to his uncle, he was weak and without military ability. He was famous for only three things: his enormous beard, his incredibly large family and, not the least, his ardent love for money and jewels, and of wealth and splendor in general.

Some authorities reported that Fath Ali Shah had a total of 57 sons and 46 daughters, and that 158 wives bore him his offspring. He gave the inspiration to the Persian proverb that "camels, lice, and princes are to be found everywhere." The economic consequences of this rule may well be imagined; Fath Ali Shah drained Persia. The harem, which on the average contained about forty women, dominated the court. The finances of the court were managed by some of the slave women attached to the harem. One of these, the serving woman of the royal coffee table, had the special privilege of bringing a flea caught in the royal blouse to one of the princes, who in turn had the honor of purchasing the insect which had afflicted the sanctified body of the ruler and killing it for a large sum of money which the shah himself had specified in advance. Despite the personal miserliness of Fath Ali, the court managed to spend a vast fortune for kitchen spices alone every year.

British Interest in Persia

During Fath Ali Shah's reign Persia became involved in European politics and experienced the rapid infiltration of European influence. By 1800 Persia was drawn into the Napoleonic upheaval and from then until the present the history of Persia can only be understood in terms of the great power struggles between European nations. In the reign of Fath Ali Shah, Persia became involved in the diplomatic contest between Russia and Britain. To the north there was a steady and successful Russian advance into Transcaucasia and Central Asia, and Russian influence made itself felt strongly in Persia; while to the south there was constant British concern with this Russian pressure threatening India, the jewel of her empire.

The key event in the impact of Western diplomacy on Persia was Napoleon's invasion of Egypt in 1798 which opened the area to Western influence and Western ideas. This direct threat to India caused Britain to make every effort to stem and counterbalance the French influence in the Near East. The British had previously made overtures to Persia when they had supported Aga Muhammad against Afghanistan in order to curb Afghan raids. With the possibility that Napoleon now would make a reality of his plan to attack India, Britain took definite measures to secure Persia. Britain was more concerned since Tsar Paul, upon the death of his overbearing mother, Catherine the Great, had reversed the traditional Russian policy of support of England and now joined Napoleon in a scheme of an overland attack on India.

In 1800 Great Britain sent John Malcolm, a servant of the East India Company, to Persia to thwart the French designs. A British-Persian treaty was concluded in that year and the East India Company promised aid against the French, an annual subsidy to the shah, and in addition lavished many presents on him. Another clause of the treaty provided for Persian cooperation against the Afghans; until the ruler of that country renounced his designs on Indian territory the Persians were to make no peace with him. From the commercial point of view the treaty called for free importation of British goods into Persia and the unrestricted right of English and Indian traders to settle and trade within that country. This at first seemed a successful attempt to bring Iran under British influence. The British, however, gave very little aid to the Persians.

In 1800 the Russians were active in the Caucasus and annexed Georgia, thus becoming the immediate neighbor of Persia and a competitor for territory in the same area. The shah's government was in need of support against Russia and, when French-Russian hostilities broke out in 1805, Persia tended to favor France.

In 1806 Napoleon's envoy, Jaubert, arrived in Tehran and made a generous offer to Fath Ali Shah. Napoleon proposed to restore Georgia to Persia and to subsidize the Persian army if in return that army would launch an attack on India. Since no immediate British counterproposal was forthcoming, Fath Ali Shah agreed and a French military mission consisting of 70 officers and noncommissioned officers headed by General Gardanne arrived at the Persian capital from Warsaw to undertake the training of the Persian army in preparation for the attack. Thus, the French were able to take advantage of British lack of interest and in 1807 a treaty of alliance, the Treaty of Finkenstein, was signed between Fath Ali Shah and Napoleon. Later the rapid change in European politics caused a different power alignment. After the meeting at Tilsit between Napoleon and Tsar Alexander, Persia was abandoned by the French and left to face the Russian danger by herself. Then, a little late, in 1808, the British again arrived on the scene; but by this time the French danger had passed.

John Malcolm, representing the East India Company, landed at Bushire to obtain a reversal of Persian policy. This achievement, however, was reserved for Sir Hartford Jones who acted directly for the British government, and who declared, somewhat pompously perhaps, that he had come to Tehran to "throw the aegis of the British Crown over the imperilled destinies of India." Jones promised Fath Ali Shah aid against the French, an annual subsidy of £120,000, and endeared himself particularly to the shah when he presented to him a large diamond, the gift of George III. In consequence of these various exertions the English were given a magnificent reception, and the French general, Gardanne, and his military entourage were dismissed.

The British obtained the primary position in the Persian army and a number of British officers served as advisors, some of them with great distinction. One of these, Henry Lindsay, an artillery officer, later became commander-in-chief of the Persian army. By 1810 British influence had been firmly established in Persia. The definitive treaty of 1814 between Persia and Great Britain outlined the mutual obligations of the two states. Persia was not to make any treaties with nations hostile to England while Britain committed herself to the very large annual subsidy of £150,000, and, in case of need, military aid to Persia. In this situation it was no longer the power of France which posed the main threat to Persia. Rather, it was Russian advances and pressure against Persia which brought British fears of an attack on India to a new height and resulted in Britain's determination to block the Russian advance in Persia, just as Russian advances were to be blocked in Turkey as well.

Russian Advance

The Russian annexation of Georgia resulted in the Persian-Russian war of 1804–1812. In 1813 the Peace of Gulistan was concluded between the two foes. The peace was certainly most timely, for not only had the Persians been defeated in battle, but at the same time the shah faced a revolt in Khorasan and in Khiva. Under the terms of the Treaty of Gulistan most of Transcaucasia was ceded to Russia as well as the cities of Derbent and Baku, and the Russians obtained the exclusive right to maintain a navy on the Caspian Sea from which all Persian warships were to be excluded. Peace was kept between the two nations until 1825 when the Russian occupation of the Gokcha district in Transcaucasia (not previously assigned to either side), precipitated war once more.

This second war (1825–1827) of Fath Ali Shah against Russia had a promising beginning, inasmuch as the Persians scored initial successes. However, when the Persian advance was routed by the Russians, the heir apparent lost his head and fled, and the Persian army followed in a state of chaos. Poor leadership, together with the fact that the army was inadequately supplied and not properly paid, made continued Persian retreat inevitable. In November 1827, the Russians sacked Ardebil, the revered birthplace of the Safavid dynasty, and in the same year the able Russian general, Paskievich, captured Erivan and later Tabriz. The result of this war was the Treaty of Turkomanchai of 1828, a landmark in the history of Russian Asiatic expansion. Under the terms of this treaty the boundaries between Persia and Russia were fixed along the present boundary lines of Iran and the U.S.S.R. The Persians ceded the districts of Erivan and Nakhichevan, and the exclusive rights of a Russian navy on the Caspian were reaffirmed. In addition, attached to this treaty were a number of clauses regarding trade and commercial privileges and in these clauses Russia successfully asserted her rights to extraterritoriality in Persia, giving Russian consuls sole authority over Russian subjects on Persian territory.

It was stipulated in this treaty that other powers might obtain the same commercial privileges and the powers were not slow to follow. By a series of capitularies based on the clauses of the Treaty of Turkomanchai, other nations gained similar rights of extraterritoriality. In short, the treaty signaled the end of complete Persian independence. But it also signaled increased British anxiety lest Persia become dominated by Russia, thus becoming a danger to India. Consequently, it ushered in a period in which the British exerted diplomatic and, when necessary, military efforts to redress the balance, and to obtain for England a predominant influence in Persia. The other war which Persia fought during the first part of the nineteenth century, a short war against Turkey between 1821 and 1823, had no serious consequences. It was terminated by the Peace of Erzerum, which caused little change in previous conditions.

Muhammad Shah

Since it evidently had become impossible for Persia to fight Russia, Persian policy turned to the east, against the Afghans. Western losses were to be made good by the recovery of eastern provinces and from 1832 to 1857 Persia made strenuous efforts to recover Herat from the Afghans. This attempt created great British apprehensions. While the British for the time being felt that little could be done to counteract Russian influences at the Persian court, where Russian and British diplomats engaged in rivalry to obtain the ear of Fath Ali Shah, a procedure which was facilitated by the shah's avarice, the British definitely did not want any further extension of Persian or Russian power in Herat and Afghanistan. Fath Ali Shah could be swayed by presents, but when he died in 1834 he was succeeded by Muhammad Shah (1835–1848) who took a definitely pro-Russian stand. Muhammad Shah began a series of Russian-supported attacks against the Afghans in Herat in 1837 to 1838. A British mission to the court at Tehran was given a very hostile reception.

The British then decided to support the Afghan cause against Persia. British intervention saved Herat and the shah was forced to retire from the siege. In an attempt to put pressure on the Persian flanks, the British also occupied the island of Kharg in the Persian Gulf and maintained a garrison on that island until 1842. But Russian influence was firmly established at the Persian court and the Russian envoy, Simonich, had the ear of Muhammad Shah. In 1838, the Russians landed on the island of Astrabad in the Caspian and proceeded to establish a naval base there.

As far as internal conditions were concerned, Muhammad Shah's reign was one in which abuses flourished. He himself made it a practice to sell offices to the highest bidder and thus extorted exorbitant purchase prices. At the death of Muhammad Shah in 1848 Persia was a thoroughly exhausted country. Money had been spent in vain on the Afghan campaigns and everywhere there was corruption.

Nasir-ud-din

Muhammad Shah was succeeded by Nasir-ud-din, who reigned from 1848 to 1896 and who was the ablest ruler of the Kajar dynasty. Only sixteen at the time of his accession, he relied, with excellent results, upon the services of Mirza Taki Khan, his chief minister. Mirza Taki Khan was capable, hardworking, and above all honest, a rare quality in nineteenth-century Persia. Up to 1852 a number of financial and military reforms were effected, although they proved to be merely temporary. The sale of offices was stopped, soldiers received regular pay, and the worst abuses of the administration were eliminated. But reforms made some very powerful enemies for the vigorous minister. One of these was the queen mother, and because of her pressure the shah was forced to sacrifice Mirza Taki Khan, who was executed in 1852. Attempts at internal reform were abandoned.

Persia then turned again to external aggression and tried to recover Afghan territories in the east. In 1856 Nasir-ud-din was able to capture Herat, whereupon the British declared war on Persia. British troops were landed once again on the island of Kharg and then on the mainland at Bushire in southern Persia. They advanced a short distance inland and after a brief fight a new Persian peace treaty was concluded. In the Treaty of Paris of 1857 the shah agreed to evacuate Herat, to renounce all claims to Afghan territories, and to recognize the nominal independence of Afghanistan. He was let off rather easily since he did not have to pay any indemnities.

After 1857 the court of Nasir-ud-din relapsed again into the pattern of a despotic regime, with a shah who had absolute command over the life and property of every one of his subjects, but had no responsibilities beyond those which fear of foreign opinion might instill in him. The omnipotence of the shah, "the shadow of God on earth," continued to be accepted without much challenge. He visited Europe three times but paid relatively little attention to foreign ideas. Nevertheless, foreign ideas penetrated Persia and were first felt in Bahaism, the offshoot of a new religion called Babism.

RELIGIOUS DEVELOPMENTS

Babism

In 1820 there was born in Bushire the son of a merchant, soon orphaned, later known by the name of Sayid Ali Muhammad. In 1844, at the age of twenty-four, this man proclaimed himself to be the Bab, or the "gate." To understand the meaning of this term and to understand the new religion, Babism, preached by Sayid Ali Muhammad, one must first briefly review the religion of Shi'a. Most believers of the Shi'i community declared that Muhammad had appointed Ali, his son-in-law, as his spiritual successor and that this spiritual succession was continued through twelve religious leaders known as the twelve imams. This divine right of the imams to temporal supremacy and to spiritual guidance of the faithful had also been strengthened by the tradition that Ali's son had married a Sassanian princess. Thus,

Shi'a acquired a connection with the Persian past and Persian national feeling was expressed in this distinctly Persian sect of Islam.

The twelfth imam in the succession had mysteriously disappeared, but not without leaving behind him the belief that he would reappear once more in the role of a messiah. It was this role of the resurrected twelfth imam which Sayid Ali Muhammad assumed in the year 1844. This year supposedly coincided with the 1,000th year after disappearance. Sayid Ali Muhammad declared himself to be the Bab of the twelfth imam, the gate by which mankind could be united with the imam, the executor of the divine will, and finally he chose to consider himself to be the actual incarnation of the divine revelation.

Babism was a new religion, both mystical and obscure: "God is eternal and unapproachable; all things come from Him and exist by Him." God was one, and the Bab was the mirror in which He was reflected. This new religion soon developed its own doctrine and dogmas in which ancient Persian national ideas played some part. Zoroastrian influences were discernible in the greeting to the sun on Friday morning and in the burial habit of putting the corpses in stone coffins in order to avoid defilement of the earth. The Bab chose 19 as a sacred number and the year was divided into 19 months, each consisting of 19 days. In addition to being a religion of ardent mysticism, Babism also carried a social message and that was a message of reform. The Bab came out directly against the worldliness and immorality of the mullas, the Moslem clergy, and against the rapacity and injustice of the Persian civil authorities. Babism also espoused the right of women to emancipate themselves; it opposed polygamy and the wearing of the veil for women. Politically, its claims were vast. Nothing less than the dominion of the world by Persia was asked since infidels could not be tolerated as rulers. The Bab went on a pilgrimage to Mecca and upon his return his teachings gained many adherents. The government arrested him at Shiraz and he was declared at first a heretic and then a madman. In 1846 the Bab temporarily resided at Isfahan where he enjoyed the favor of the local governor, but he was then imprisoned in a frontier fortress under considerable hardship. His followers caused a disturbance in Meshed in 1848 and a revolt of the Babis against the government broke out in the next year. The Babis stood off the royal armies for months. At last the Babis surrendered upon the promise of their life, but were massacred instead.

The crushing of this revolt did not cause an abatement of the movement. The number of followers of the Bab increased steadily and the government became more and more alarmed. As a result it was decided to execute the Bab himself. In 1850 he was brought before a firing squad at Tabriz. The soldiers aimed and fired and when the smoke of the volley had cleared away, the Bab had disappeared. The miracle, if miracle it was, would have assuredly served to strengthen the infant religion immeasurably but it did not end that way. The shots had cut the ropes by which the Bab had been tied to a stake. He escaped, but committed the tactical error of escaping in the wrong direction and was recaptured. The Bab was taken out again and killed.

A martyr's death, as is known, only arouses increased resistance and this was also the case among the Babis. Opposition against the government continued and there was even an attempt in 1852 against the life of the shah himself. As a consequence of the plot to assassinate the shah, the Babis were cruelly persecuted and since persecution bred further resistance, the cycle continued in ever more brutal fashion. A formal inquisition was established by the government to hunt out, persecute, and torture the adherents of the Bab, but his followers still were able to make successful efforts at proselytizing.

Bahaism

The leaders of Babism finally decided to leave Persian territory and the center of the sect was transferred to Turkish soil in Baghdad. The Persian government's fear of the Babis caused remonstrances with the Turks and the leaders had to migrate once more, this time to Adrianople in the European part of Turkey. In Adrianople the followers of Babism split in 1863. The schism divided Babism into two branches, one of which retained a mystical Iranian character and was truer to the original teachings of the Bab, while the other and far more important branch, was the one founded by Baha Allah, the "splendor of God," and known consequently as Bahaism.

In Bahaism, Western ideas are much more pronounced. With its center at Acre, Bahaism formulated a syncretistic faith, deeply influenced by the extreme liberal ideas of contemporary Europe. It proclaimed a universal cosmopolitan religion without either special rites or a priestly hierarchy and thus abandoned the stricter Islamic tradition.

AFGHANISTAN

Closely connected with the history of Persia is that of Afghanistan. As noted above that country prior to the eighteenth century had been ruled in part by Persia, in part by the Mogul empire of Delhi, and in part by the Uzbek khan of Bukhara. Early in the eighteenth century the Afghans had gained freedom from Persian rule. In 1706 Kandahar became independent and Herat soon followed. In 1722 the Afghan conquest terminated the rule of the Safavids in Persia. Afghan rule of Persia in turn had given way after a few years to a renewed Persian conquest of Afghanistan in 1737 by Nadir Shah, the great soldier, but at his death in 1747 Afghanistan permanently achieved the status of an independent country.

The Durani Dynasty

One of the generals of Nadir Shah, Ahmad Shah of the Abdali tribe in 1747 established the Durani dynasty. A successful general with sufficient means at hand, since he had captured the treasure of Nadir after his assassination, he ruled Afghanistan, Baluchistan, Kashmir, and the Punjab from 1747 to 1773. During this period he made a series of nine devastating raids into India for plunder and food. The unfortunate Mogul capital of Delhi was

FIGURE 2.5. Kabul, Afghanistan.

sacked again in 1755 and Sind was added to the Afghan territories. Ahmad Shah was careful to see to it that the freedom-loving Afghan tribes were left under the rule of their own chiefs and little was asked from them beyond occasional levies of troops and some payments. Indeed the success of Ahmad Shah was due to his great liberality in sharing the spoils and the plunder of India with these chiefs. Thus he reigned by popular acclaim and by not interfering in tribal affairs, but this practice of course, was not in the interest of a strong central government. He ruled by soliciting the advice of a council of nine major chiefs, whose offices continued to be hereditary.

In 1761, the Afghans inflicted a very important defeat upon the forces of the Marathas at the Battle of Panipat (see Chapter 3). The Marathas of India were the most powerful opponents of the British in India and this defeat facilitated the British task of the conquest of India. In 1762, the Afghans scored again, this time against the Sikhs. Afghan cavalry accompanied by rapid-fire swivel guns mounted on camels mowed down the Indian troops.

Ahmad Shah died in 1774 and all central authority disintegrated at once. His son Timur, who had succeeded him at Kabul, lost the border provinces, notably Sind, and faced a series of internal revolts. He died in 1793 and until 1835 the history of Afghanistan was one of repetitious tribal wars and indecisive dynastic conflicts. The first ruler during this period was Zaman Shah whose career was mostly occupied in putting down the rebellions of his brothers and defending himself in 1799 against a Persian attack of Fath Ali Shah who was supported in this venture by the British. Next in line was Mahmud Shah, a weak ruler, under whom the tribes revolted at frequent intervals and who lost Khorasan to Persia. Finally in 1803 came Shuja Shah, who after bludgeoning his able minister, faced yet another rebellion and fled the country seeking refuge among the British in India. So ended the Durani dynasty.

The Barakzai Dynasty

The Durani were replaced in Afghanistan by the Barakzai, whose founder Dost Muhammad triumphed over Shuja Shah in 1835. He became emir of Afghanistan at Kabul in 1835 and ruled until 1863. European interest in Afghanistan began during his reign.

Dost Muhammad at first was in sympathy with the British and had wanted a British alliance against the Sikhs in the Punjab, but the British government had given him little encouragement. However, when a Russian agent, Captain Vikovich, arrived on the scene, the great fear of Russian expansion toward India once more took possession of the British official mind. A possible alignment of Persia and Afghanistan, with Russia playing the predominant part in both countries, seemed the blackest of combinations to the English. In order to split the Persians from the Afghans, the British promised the shah the town of Herat, which his forces had besieged unsuccessfully for two years, together with financial aid. The British decided to depose Dost Muhammad by force and to restore Shuja Shah who was conveniently in British hands. British policy was formulated in this statement:

The welfare of our possession in the East requires that we should have on our Western frontier an ally who is interested in resisting aggression and establishing tranquility, in the place of chiefs ranging themselves in subservience to a hostile power and seeking to promote schemes of conquest and aggrandizement.[2]

Palmerston was responsible for the decision for armed intervention. In 1839 the British invaded Afghanistan from India and the first Afghan War began. Twenty-one thousand men easily took Kandahar, then Ghazni, and finally Kabul, while Dost Muhammad fled and the British installed Shuja Shah. Initial military conquest was one thing, but permanent British influence in Afghanistan quite another. The British resident in Kabul aroused the greatest possible antagonism since he constantly interfered in local administration and the independent Afghans developed a great hatred for the British. Discontent was soon rife. In 1840, Dost Muhammad attempted a return to power, but was captured and exiled by the English. Foolishly enough the British local administration reduced the subsidies to the hill tribes and the line of communication with India consequently became increasingly tenuous.

The revolt which soon afterwards broke out was spectacular. Five thousand British troops were killed and one lone survivor returned to tell the tale. It was a great blow to British prestige. In order to save appearances the British reoccupied Kabul in 1842 but this was done merely as a gesture. They evacuated Afghanistan soon after. Shuja Shah was murdered in the disturbances which had followed the revolt and Dost Muhammad returned once more.

The British tried to save what they could and now aligned themselves with Dost Muhammad. A British-Afghan alliance was signed, and arms and munitions were furnished him from India. In 1856 the Persians finally wrested Herat from Afghan rule, and as a consequence Britain declared war on Persia. The war was ended by the Treaty of Paris of 1857, which brought Afghanistan under British control. Herat was ceded by Persia to Afghanistan, the Afghan ruler received a British subsidy, and a British resident was installed at Kabul.

Relations between British and Afghans remained cordial until the death of Dost Muhammad in 1863. Afghanistan had become entirely dependent on Britain and British influence seemed solidly established in these critical border areas. As a result of British determination to block the expansion of Russia from the north, Afghanistan also shared the fate of Turkey and of Persia and became a pawn of the great powers.

BASIC DATES

1587–1629   Shah Abbas I
1622   British East India Company at Hormuz

[2] Quoted in Sir Alfred Lyall, *The Rise and Expansion of the British Dominion in India* (London: John Murray, 1905), p. 308.

1635	Turks invade Azerbaijan
1638	Turks seize Baghdad
1709	Afghans independent at Kandahar
1722	Mir Mahmud takes Isfahan
1736–1747	Nadir Shah
1737–1738	Conquest of Bactria and Afghanistan
1738–1739	Invasion of India
1743–1747	Successful wars against Turks
1747	Assassination of Nadir Shah
1747–1773	Ahmad Shah in Afghanistan
1750–1779	Karim Khan in South Persia
1755	Afghan plunder of Delhi
1761	Afghan victory over Marathas
1762	Afghan victory over Sikhs
1794–1797	Aga Muhammad of Kajar dynasty
1797–1835	Fath Ali Shah
1835–1839	Dost Muhammad founds Barakzai dynasty in Afghanistan
1835–1848	Muhammad Shah
1839–1842	First British-Afghan war
1848–1896	Nasir-ud-din

SUPPLEMENTARY READING

Arberry, A. *The Legacy of Persia.* Oxford, 1953. Topical essays.
Avery, P. *Modern Iran.* New York, 1965.
Fletcher, A. *Afghanistan, Highway of Conquest.* Ithaca, N.Y., 1965.
Frye, R. *Persia.* London, 1968.
Grousset, R. *The Civilizations of the East, Vol. 1: The Near and Middle East.* New York, 1934. Stresses artistic developments.
Hitti, P. *The Near East in History.* Princeton, N.J., 1961.
Sykes, P. *Persia.* Oxford, 1922. An abbreviated version of the author's major work, listed below.
Wilber, D. *Iran, Past and Present.* Princeton, N. J., 1948.

ADVANCED READING

Algar, H. *Religion and State in Iran, 1785–1906.* Berkeley, 1970.
Browne, E. G. *A History of Persian Literature in Modern Times.* Cambridge, 1924.
Fisher, W. B., ed. *Cambridge History of Iran.* Vol. I. Cambridge, England, 1968.
Hurewitz, J. C. *Diplomacy in the Near and Middle East: A Documentary Record, 1535–1914.* Princeton, N.J., 1956.
Kelly, J. B. *Britain and the Persian Gulf, 1795–1880.* Oxford, 1968.
King, P. *Afghanistan: Cockpit in High Asia.* London, 1966.
Lockhart, L. *Nadir Shah.* London, 1938.
———— *The Fall of the Safavi Dynasty and the Afghan Occupation of Persia.* Cambridge, England, 1958.

Nimat, R. *History of the Afghans.* Pasadena, 1965.
Norris, J. *The First Afghan War.* London, 1967.
Pope, A. *A Survey of Persian Art.* London, 1938. A major work in its field.
Ramazani, R. *The Foreign Policy of Iran, 1500–1914.* Charlottesville, 1966.
Ross, E. D. *Sir Anthony Sherley.* London, 1933.
Sykes, P. *History of Persia.* Oxford, 1922. Still a valuable account.
Upton, J. *History of Modern Iran.* Harvard, 1960.

Chapter 3

India from Mogul Power to British Supremacy

THE MOGULS AFTER AKBAR

By 1605 the Mogul Empire in India, which had been founded by Babur, included the valleys of the Indus and the Ganges and all Indian territory north of the Vindhya mountains, as well as part of the Deccan and Afghanistan, Baluchistan, and Kashmir. There remained only a few independent Moslem states in the south—Ahmadnagar, Bijapur, and Golconda—and Hindu rule of a sort remained in the Tamil country at the southern tip of the subcontinent. The Mogul empire had reached its apex under Akbar who died in 1605. A man of exceptional ability, Akbar had a great vision of a truly united India. His governmental machinery had been efficient and during his reign India was the most prosperous and one of the largest empires in the world. However, none of his successors was as able as he had been and after his death came the gradual decline of Mogul power, eventual political anarchy, and the establishment of British supremacy. Unlike the Ottoman and Persian empires, discussed in the two previous chapters, the Mogul empire disintegrated internally before the arrival of a great European power, and for this reason the process of decline and decay was of a somewhat different nature.

Jahangir

Akbar's successor in 1605 was Prince Salim, who ascended the Mogul throne as Jahangir, or "world grasper," and reigned until 1627. The beginning of his reign was promising enough, since his first act in the capital at Agra was to proclaim a series of reforms. He promised protection to Islam, a general amnesty, the end of punishments such as mutilation, the suppression of rob-

FIGURE 3.1. Jahangir and his father, Akbar. Mogul painting.

bery, the prohibition of liquor, and he confirmed his nobles in their possessions. In order to secure the loyalty of the Rajputs and to keep his Hindu subjects content, he agreed that he would follow his father's policy of toleration.

Interested in religion and religious discussion, Jahangir also showed a renewed interest in the Portuguese Jesuits. They received imperial favors and were permitted to display religious pictures and to conduct religious processions at Agra, which scandalized devout Moslems. Jahangir also showed an interest in the rising power of the English, since to his discerning eye Portuguese strength seemed to be on the wane. Some Portuguese ships had committed the blunder of attacking some Mogul ships transporting pilgrims to Mecca, and this had irritated the emperor. Then some English vessels beat off a Portuguese attack in full sight of the native population, and Portuguese influence declined rapidly.

In 1609 there appeared at Jahangir's court a rather remarkable Englishman, William Hawkins, who had travelled widely in the Levant. He was sent by the East India Company to open the port of Surat to English trade. Hawkins at first was liked by Jahangir, since he proved an amiable companion during the emperor's drinking bouts. Hawkins was given an Armenian girl from Jahangir's harem, but he later fell into disfavor, and died in 1612 on the trip back to England.

In 1615 the English sent an embassy from James I led by Sir Thomas Roe. His objectives were the same as Hawkins'—to get the necessary trading concessions for the East India Company. Sir Thomas was a man of cultured intelligence and shrewd common sense. His diplomacy was successful, and in 1619 the English received further permission to establish posts on Indian soil.

In 1611 Jahangir married a famous beauty, Nur Jahan. She had been the wife of the governor of Bengal, whose loyalty Jahangir suspected and whom he had killed. Nur Jahan was not only a woman of outstanding beauty; she also had great intelligence and fearless courage, which she demonstrated by killing four tigers on one occasion. Jahangir fell completely under the influence of his wife, who was exceedingly capable and used her power well. The Mogul empire profited by her rule. Her name, which appeared on the coinage and the imperial decrees, added strength to that of Jahangir. She was always open to audience, and everyone had free access to her to air their grievances and to obtain redress from injustice.

However, the reign of Jahangir did not increase the military glory of the Moguls. There was constant, but indecisive, fighting in the Deccan, and in 1622 Shah Abbas of Persia seized Kandahar from the Moguls. Military power seemed somewhat weaker than it had been under Akbar, and there were also perhaps the first signs of administrative decline.

Jahangir was in some respects very much like his famous father. He too had a passing interest in religion including Christianity and the beliefs of Hindu ascetics. He believed in God, but not in any special creed. He was accomplished in writing and poetry, and wrote elegant memoirs; he was a distinguished connoisseur of painting, he liked music, and loved the beauties of nature. But Jahangir was given to greater extremes. Although often gentle, he could be barbarously cruel. His opponents he had torn to bits by elephants, and he once killed a clumsy huntsman who had spoiled his shot at a wild bull. Unfortunately, he was indolent and weak, and very much under the influence of drink and opium. Jahangir's last years were spoiled by the rebellion of his son, Khurram, but Jahangir managed to defeat his future successor on the Mogul throne and continued to rule until 1627, when he died, the victim of addiction to drugs and alcohol.

Shah Jahan

At the death of Jahangir a succession dispute between his sons broke out, but the rebellious Prince Khurram won out against his rivals, and he ascended the Mogul throne at Agra as Shah Jahan, or "king of the world." He had all his male relatives killed, and banished his mother, Nur Jahan. In 1628 Shah Jahan married Mumtaz Mahal, whose death in childbirth after she had been the mother of fourteen of his sixteen children plunged the emperor into abysmal grief, and whose memory he honored by building the Taj Mahal.

Shah Jahan was a capable administrator for most of the years of his reign (1628–1658). But unlike his great predecessors, Shah Jahan was a devout, orthodox, and intolerant Moslem, and he began to abandon the policy of religious toleration with which Akbar had so successfully united the various Indian subjects of his empire. In 1632 Shah Jahan ordered the destruction of all new Hindu temples and the demolition of all Christian churches, although not all of these decrees were enforced. He also attacked the declining power of the Portuguese by sending in 1632 a large army against their settlement of Hooghly in Bengal. Although the pretext for this campaign was found in a charge of kidnapping, the real intention of Shah Jahan was to oust the Portuguese and monopolize the trade of Bengal.

Shah Jahan's greatest military campaigns were waged in the Deccan, against the Shi'a Moslem kingdoms which still maintained their independence from Mogul rule. In 1632 Ahmadnagar was annexed to the Mogul dominions, and then Golconda submitted and recognized Mogul suzerainty. In 1635 the most important of them all, Bijapur, after being ravaged by the Moguls, also succumbed finally and was temporarily made into a subject state. Not until fifty years later were Golconda and Bijapur finally destroyed.

FIGURE 3.2. Shah Jahan on horseback; miniature from an album compiled for Shah Jahan.

But Shah Jahan had less success in warfare against the Persians. In 1645 his troops captured Balkh, but that they could not hold it is an indication of the beginning of Mogul military decline.

After the annexation of the Moslem kingdoms in the Deccan, Shah Jahan appointed his son Aurangzeb viceroy for that region. Aurangzeb, who hated the unorthodox Shi'a, had distinguished himself in the campaigns in the Deccan, where he employed European-serviced artillery; he also proved himself a capable ruler over the lands entrusted to him. He reorganized their finances, made a better land survey, and encouraged agriculture and the building of irrigation works. Shah Jahan treated his other three sons, all equally brave, in similar fashion, establishing each as a virtually independent ruler in the provinces which were assigned to them. In 1657, when the emperor's health began to fail, a contest for power among the sons broke out in violent fashion. It was won by Aurangzeb against his father's favorite, Dara Shukoh, who had been kept at the court and had been showered with titles, honors, and wealth by Shah Jahan. In this civil war Aurangzeb gained Agra by force and he kept his father captive in the fort of the capital for eight years until Shah Jahan's death in 1666.

In some respects the reign of Shah Jahan was the golden age of the Mogul empire. It was characterized by unexcelled magnificence and the construction of splendid buildings, such as the world-famous Taj Mahal at Agra. Shah Jahan was a munificent patron of the arts, who spent immense sums on architecture which made lavish use of marble and precious stones, and on fabulous display, such as the famed Peacock Throne which was built in seven years at the estimated cost of five million dollars in present values. Yet at the same time the economic system of India was nearing collapse, indicated by increasing oppression and poverty. Shah Jahan's building expenditures created a crushing burden, and tax assessments were raised by 50 per cent with the inevitable consequence that agriculture became neglected and fields were abandoned. Terrible and frequent famines also contributed to a decline in production and a weakened economic structure of the state. Officials were more cruel and oppressive than they had been before, and the life of the Indian peasant degenerated into one of abysmal misery. Bernier, a French doctor who travelled in India during this period, gloomily describes the condition of the country:

> The despotic tyranny of local governors was often so excessive as to deprive the peasant and artisan of the necessaries of life, and leave them to die of misery and exhaustion—a tyranny owing to which these wretched people either have no children at all or have them only to endure the agonies of starvation, and to die at a tender age—a tyranny in fine, that drives the cultivator of the soil from his wretched home to some neighboring state, in hopes of finding milder treatment, or to the army, where he becomes the servant of some trooper. The country is ruined by the necessity of defraying the enormous charges required to maintain the splendour of a numerous court, and to pay a large army maintained for the purpose of keeping the people in subjection. No adequate idea can be conveyed of the sufferings of that people. The cudgel and the whip compel them to incessant labor for the benefit of others; and driven to

despair by every kind of cruel treatment their revolt or their flight is only prevented by the presence of a military force. Thus do ruin and desolation overspread their land.[1]

SUCCESSION STRUGGLES OF THE SONS OF SHAH JAHAN

In the struggle for power the contest was primarily between the third son of Shah Jahan, Aurangzeb, and his favorite and oldest, Dara Shukoh. The great contrast between the two men lent a most dramatic touch to their rivalry. Dara was enlightened, amiable, popular, and of a liberal trend of mind. Influenced by the Sufis, he had shown a marked interest in the religious aspects of Hinduism, and he was somewhat hostile to orthodox Islam. What Dara lacked in military experience, he made up by popular support. Aurangzeb, on the other hand, was cruel, cold, and crafty, a Sunni Moslem who detested his brother with all the hate of a religious bigot. Aurangzeb made use of his other two brothers in the struggle against Dara, and then treacherously betrayed them, executing one and forcing the other to flee. Dara too was betrayed, captured, and then executed in 1658 by Aurangzeb, who was fearful of the support of the masses in favor of his older brother. Dara's eldest son managed to flee to the Rajputs, but he too eventually was captured and sent to the state prison of Gwalior where he was slowly poisoned to death, by being forced to drink a concoction of opium.

Aurangzeb

Aurangzeb became Mogul emperor formally in 1659 in a great ceremony conducted at Delhi. The forty-year-old son of Shah Jahan was very able and an administrator of wide experience, having served his father as viceroy in the Deccan for many years. Aurangzeb possessed a cool and clear head, he was courageous, energetic, and a scholar in his own right. His personal life was above reproach. He knew the Koran by heart, read it every evening, and spent many nights in the mosque in the company of devout men. He abstained from the slightest overindulgence in food, drink, or dress. Every action of his life was governed by rigid austerity.

Aurangzeb's rule began with great promise. He decreed a series of useful edicts against rapacity and dishonesty in government and took great interest in the encouragement of agriculture. Military campaigns into Assam and the Arakan coast and in the northwest indicated the vigor of his armies. Delhi during the first twenty years of Aurangzeb's reign was the political center of the Moslem world, and attracted embassies from Mecca, Persia, and other Moslem countries as well as from infidel countries such as Abyssinia and Holland.

But there was one trait of Aurangzeb's personality—his religious attitudes—which undid all his energy, ability, and devotion to government, and which was in a real sense responsible for the rapid collapse of the Mogul

[1] Bernier, *Travels* (London: Constable, 1891), p. 230.

empire. He was truly pious, but a fanatic, motivated by grim religious zeal. Precisely because he was not hypocritical, his decision to purify the land of all idolatry and return to the strictest orthodox Islam was a disastrous one. He began his policy of a return to purest Islam by sweeping reforms designed to curtail court pleasure and suppress all vices. Drinking, gambling, and music were outlawed and the great artists of the Mogul court were summarily dismissed. As time went on he also became increasingly distrustful of everyone in his administration. He in turn won universal distrust. Since the emperor attempted to do everything in person and delegated no authority, the administrative system began to break down.

The really fateful step taken by Aurangzeb was the adoption of a policy of religious intolerance. In 1669 he ordered Hindu temples and schools to be desecrated and destroyed, and this order was partially carried out. Apostates from Islam were executed, while converts to Islam were honored and rewarded. Laws discriminated against Hindus in every aspect of their lives. In 1671 Aurangzeb dismissed all Hindu clerks from his government, a measure which could not be carried out. One-half of them were finally retained in the administration of the state, but not many Hindus could expect to occupy high office. The final blow came in 1679 when Aurangzeb reinstated the hated poll tax. This impolitic and very unpopular measure produced the greatest consternation among the Hindus, but to no avail.

These actions of a religious bigot produced disastrous results. In vain did Aurangzeb receive a famous anonymous protest, in which it was pointed out to him that under Akbar Moslems, Christians, Jews, Hindus, Jains, sky-worshippers, and atheists all had lived in harmony. It prophesied the alienation of Aurangzeb's subjects, loss of territory, and a future of devastation and depopulation for the whole of India.

Since the religious fanaticism of Aurangzeb could not be swayed by argument, revolts broke out. There was a peasant rebellion in the Punjab, followed by a revolt of the Rajputs. Aurangzeb, who looked upon the toleration of the Rajputs as an offense against Islam, then made his greatest mistake and alienated his most powerful supporters. Even his own son rebelled when Aurangzeb attempted to annex the Rajput states by force. He sided with the Rajputs, but promptly became a victim to the cunning of his father. Aurangzeb forged a letter in which he made it appear as if his son had joined the Rajputs only to betray them, and he saw to it that this letter fell into Rajput hands. His son had to flee, first into the Deccan, and then to Persia where he died.

Aurangzeb moved inconclusively against the Rajputs in 1679. He then turned to warfare in the Deccan where he intended finally to annex to his dominions the remaining heretical Moslem states, Bijapur and Golconda. Bijapur, sorely beset by a food shortage, surrendered to the huge Mogul forces in 1686, and the last of the independent states, Golconda, was taken by treachery the following year. By 1690 Aurangzeb had conquered the whole of southern India. The Mogul flag was planted everywhere from Kabul to Cape Comorin; but the victories of Aurangzeb were illusive and hollow for the Mogul empire was on the verge of collapse.

Everywhere in the newly conquered Deccan Aurangzeb's armies en-

FIGURE 3.3. Portrait of Aurangzeb as an old man.

countered fierce guerrilla warfare by the Marathas. The Marathas had been organized by a Hindu leader, Shivaji, who had broken off from the state of Bijapur and had founded an independent Hindu state, as part of a general movement of Hindu resistance against the Moguls (see pp. 62–63). His forces, speedy and lightly armed, successfully ambushed the Mogul lines of communications and inflicted defeat after defeat upon the unwieldy Mogul armies. Despite the fact that some Maratha leaders, including Shivaji's son, were captured and executed after the most refined tortures, Maratha resistance did not lessen. Large areas of India were devastated, Aurangzeb's campaigns were a terrible drain upon his treasury, and the emperor himself, absent twenty years from his capital, lost all control over the Mogul government which became rapidly even more inefficient and oppressive. With his wealth and control gone, his troops unpaid, and an ineffective but interminable war continuing against the Marathas and the rebels in the Punjab, the emperor in 1704 appeared a pathetic and even tragic figure to the Italian traveler, Manucci, who was struck by his personality and the stateliness of his appearance, tall, with a flowing white beard, the very figure of a patriarch:

> Most of the time he sits doubled up, his head drooping. When his officers submit a petition, or make report to him of any occurrence, he raises his head and straightens his back. He gives them such an answer as leaves no opening for reply, and still looks after his army in the minutest particulars. But those who are at a distance pay very little attention to his orders. They make excuses, they raise difficulties; and under cover of these pretexts, and by giving large sums to the officials at court, they do just what they like. If only he would abandon his mock

sainthood and behead a few of those in his Empire, there would not be so much disorder, and he would be better obeyed.[2]

But Aurangzeb was no mock saint. He was sincere and with his sincerity he ruined the Mogul empire. In 1705, still fighting an endless war in the Deccan, he was attacked by fever. He finally made his retreat to the north, but he died in 1707 at the age of eighty-nine. As he had requested, his body was shrouded in coarse cloth and buried in a humble tomb. Aurangzeb was simple, austere, religious. He had wanted to purify India, but he ended by ruining it.

End of the Mogul Empire

After the death of Aurangzeb the Mogul empire almost at once broke up into separate parts, each ruled by officials who now became hereditary princes in the provinces which they had formerly governed for the Moguls. Oudh was established as a kingdom, the rich province of Bengal became virtually independent, and in the south, Mysore and Hyderabad also became independent principalities, paying only the most shadowy allegiance to the nominal Mogul ruler of Delhi. Aurangzeb's death caused a scramble for power among his sons, from which Bahadur Shah emerged victor, but he was weak and died in 1712. Bloodshed and disorder at the capital followed and a series of puppet emperors occupied ruined halls and governed beneath tattered canopies. Some of these phantom emperors were maltreated, blinded, or murdered by their subordinates. In 1739 Delhi underwent the ordeal of the foreign invasion of Nadir Shah of Persia, who gave his troops a free hand to massacre and plunder. When he left the stricken city he carried with him the fabled Peacock Throne, the symbol of former Mogul greatness.

Nevertheless all the powers which struggled for supremacy in India, even the Hindu Marathas, invoked the imperial Mogul name and titles and acted under nominal Mogul authority. The series of nominal emperors lasted until the great Indian Mutiny of 1857, when the British deposed the last of these descendents of Babur, Akbar, and Aurangzeb.

The causes for the downfall of the Mogul empire are many and complex. Although the Moguls were foreigners to India, alien both by race and religion, there was at least the possibility that Akbar's enlightened policy and his great vision of a united India might have created a more substantial and durable Mogul dominion. There is certainly no question that Aurangzeb's religious policy had a direct bearing upon the collapse of Mogul power. He alienated the Hindus, ended the Rajput support essential to his government, and caused a Hindu revival, while his long absence proved fatal to effective government. Yet, important as Aurangzeb's reign is, and important as personality was in Indian statecraft, other factors also contributed to the decline of the Moguls.

Among these the Maratha revolt was certainly a primary cause for the

[2] Manucci, in H. G. Rawlinson, *India: A Short Cultural History*. (London: Cresset Press, 1937), p. 350.

Mogul decline, since it was not only a religious rebellion but also a very successful political movement, using guerrilla style warfare.

The Mogul nobility suffered from the losses attendant upon frequent succession struggles to the throne, and was not reinvigorated by new blood. The aristocracy was perhaps more degenerate in the eighteenth century than it had been in the sixteenth. The Mogul armies, too, showed increasing signs of weakness, which was illustrated in their fiasco against the Persians (see Chapter 2). By the eighteenth century Mogul armies were merely armed rabble and Mogul artillery was of the crudest sort. Another important factor in the decline was the economic degeneration of the empire. The revenue system began to break down after the death of Akbar, and formerly equitable taxes became mere extortion to support the increasing extravagance of the court. At the same time government became more unstable and oppressive.

One factor which did not contribute to the fall of the Mogul Empire was outside force. When the empire crashed it did so for internal reasons, much more so than empires of the Ottomans and of the Persians. The Mogul decline preceded the coming of the British; when England appeared, the Indian scene was one of political anarchy in which many powers struggled for political supremacy on equal terms.

MOGUL CULTURE

The Mogul era was one of the very great periods in Indian art. Works of supreme beauty in architecture and in painting were produced. This was primarily an aristocratic art, and the overtaxed and frequently starving peasantry did not share in it.

Architecture

In architecture a distinct Indo-Persian style was developed. The Persian contribution and trademark was the bulbous dome, while Hindu masons and stonecutters were responsible for the lavish ornament of the buildings. Mogul architecture was executed in hard white marble, a much more lasting material than the rapidly crumbling Persian faience. The white marble was inlaid by the technique known as *pietra dura*, in which agate, carnelian, jasper, and turquoise were used to furnish elaborate and splendid decorative patterns.

The Taj Mahal, built during the reign of Shah Jahan, represents the apex of Mogul architecture. The central marble mausoleum with its lofty vaulted gateway stands amidst formal gardens and fountains, and is surrounded by four lofty, slender minarets. Its superb beauty and the simple grandeur of its design mark it as the masterpiece and triumph of Indo-Persian architecture.

The Taj Mahal was begun in 1632 and was not completed until 1647. Its chief architect was probably a Turk, Usted Isa, who possibly was influenced by Italian architectural developments.

FIGURE 3.4. Pearl Mosque, Agra.

Other great buildings of Mogul architecture include the tomb of Jahangir, the Pearl Mosque, and the palace at Delhi. With their glittering white marble, their beautifully inlaid stonework and their exquisite openwork tracery, they stand in striking contrast to the earlier simplicity of Akbar's red sandstone buildings at Fathpur Sikri.

Painting

Mogul painting also represents a fusion of Persian and Hindu elements. Persia contributed the forceful line and design, and India its naturalism and realism. In addition European, especially Italian, influence was seen in the use of perspective, shading and a sense of atmosphere. This influence was introduced by copies of Italian works brought to the Mogul court by the Jesuits, just as was architecture. Mogul painting, with its excellent calligraphic lines and fine designs, also exerted influence on such great masters as Rembrandt and Reynolds in the West. Mogul painting was an art of the court. The subject matter was primarily the pomp and splendor of an aristocratic society, but it also came to include animated hunting scenes and charming studies of flowers, animals, and birds. Above all, Mogul painting excelled in portraiture. The portraits of the Mogul rulers, such as those of Akbar and Shah Jahan, are masterpieces of intense psychological analysis and they convey the personality of these masters of India with a finesse and delicacy similar to that of the great portraits done by Dürer, Holbein, and Clouet. There are also striking portraits of saints, fakirs, and holy men, in which their mystic ardor and religious fanaticism are captured to perfection. In landscapes a love of nature pervades and a wealth of detail is witness to close observation of wildlife and floral beauty.

Akbar was a great patron of painting and employed many artists, both Persian and Hindu, in his royal studios, which he visited regularly. Mogul painting reached its zenith in Jahangir's reign. He himself was proud to be known as a connoisseur of painting, and in a composite picture, done by several different masters, he could detect which artists had painted the eyes or which had done the eyebrows of a face.

A special, and quite separate, school of painting existing during Mogul times is known as Rajput painting. This was a strictly Hindu art practiced in Rajputana and the upper Punjab. It was a popular art primarily concerned with religious scenes which were rendered with great tenderness and love. It was influenced by Mogul painting, but much of it was derived from the purely Hindu tradition which took its inspiration from the art of Ajanta. There were also some outstanding accomplishments in the minor arts such as jewelry, textiles, and numismatics.

Literature

The Mogul rulers themselves were skillful writers, as the memoirs of Babur and Jahangir testify, and they patronized many poets and historians, among whom the greatest was Abul Fazl, the author of the *Life of Akbar* and the *Institutes of Akbar*. There was also interest in Hindu works of literature and philosophy, and many of these, such as the *Bhagavad Gita*, were translated into Persian from their native Sanskrit. Outside the Mogul court a vernacular literature sprang up, particularly in Bengal, where Tulsi Das was responsible for a version of the *Ramayana* written in Hindi, a work of considerable religious impact.

The Mogul rulers did not neglect education for their subjects. Each Moslem mosque had a school attached to it, and there the fundamentals of knowledge, reading, writing, and arithmetic, were taught together with the Koran. Higher learning included theology, mathematics, and physics.

Mogul culture took a sharp and decisive turn for the worse when Aurangzeb became emperor. He dismissed all artists from the court, and forbade new buildings. Although he himself was a poet, he discouraged poetry since it interfered with religious contemplation. He ordered all paintings destroyed since they were idolatrous, and he considered history tainted. Small wonder that after Aurangzeb Mogul culture ceased to exist at the capital, although Mogul Persian and Urdu culture continued to flourish into the 18th century, especially in the fields of poetry and scholarship.

HINDU RENASCENCE

The Marathas

Despite India's conquest by the Moslems, Hinduism retained great vitality, most of which was centered in the devotional movement known as *bhakti* or love. This popular cult, a sort of religious patriotism, had survived all persecutions, but when Moslem persecution under Aurangzeb became fierce the bhakti movement became a political one. The movement was anti-Brahmanical and was most successful among the frugal and hardy peasant stock of the Marathas and the Sikhs, who rose to power in the seventeenth century.

The Maratha power was derived from the energetic and self-reliant peasants of the Western Ghats, the mountain area parallel to the west coast of the Deccan. Here the bhakti movement had great strength with the pious and courageous farmers who made a scant living from poor soil, but whose devotion, frugality, and endurance made them excellent soldiers. Among the Maratha people a kind of national tradition was kept alive by many venerated poets and saints, and only a strong military leader was needed to make them a cohesive and formidable force.

Shivaji. This leader was Shivaji, who was born in 1627. His father, Shahji, a soldier of the Moslem state of Bijapur, was possessed with love for his country and the Hindu religion. He educated his son on the great Indian epics and inculcated in him a hatred for the alien rulers. Shivaji eventually gained control of some hill fortresses around Poona, and successfully defeated the armies of the ruler of Bijapur which had been sent to bring him to subjection. Shivaji then proceeded to create a completely Hindu state based on impregnable fortresses. Shivaji at first had seemed to be hardly more than a robber baron, but he soon proved his military and administrative ability and won reluctant admiration even from his enemies, the Moguls, who attempted to crush him after Bijapur had failed.

Aurangzeb, who systematically planned the whole conquest of the Deccan, tried negotiations with Shivaji at first. Shivaji, after what he considered an insult by Aurangzeb, and fearing for his life, made a clever escape from the Mogul court, by hiding himself in a basket of food. Once back in the fastnesses of the Western Ghats, he began a series of daring exploits against the Moguls. He and a small group of his followers disguised themselves as a wedding party and entered Poona where, at night, they attacked the Mogul commander and captured the strategic city. Shivaji, an excellent soldier, conducted also a series of successful raids which reaped much plunder. In 1664 the wealthy port of Surat was his target, and later, in 1676, he extended his power into the region of the Carnatic in the south, the first effective Hindu power there since the collapse of Vijayanagar.

In 1674 Shivaji was proclaimed king of the Marathas. His administration was thoughtful and efficient, and the Deccan was better governed during his time than was the Mogul empire. He reigned through a council of eight and broke the power of the hereditary nobles. Agriculture was encouraged by loans and by careful tax assessments which did not deprive the cultivator of the incentive to produce more. Shivaji was a gifted leader, and consequently he was able to enforce strict discipline among his troops; they did not molest women nor did they desecrate mosques, but on the contrary treated copies of the Koran with great respect.

The Peshwas of Poona. Shivaji, the founder of Maratha greatness, died in 1680 and was succeeded by his son Sambhaji, an inept and dissolute fellow, who did not oppose the conquest of the sultanates of Bijapur and Golconda by Mogul forces. In due time Sambhaji was captured by Aurangzeb, tortured, and then executed, but this did not stop the Marathas from continuing the war against the Moguls. At first it was the second son of Shivaji, and then his widow, who continued to lead the Marathas in successful guerrilla warfare against the unwieldy and undisciplined Mogul troops. Eventually Maratha leadership fell into the hands of the prime minister of the state, the *peshwa*, and it was he and his sons who as hereditary prime ministers of the Marathas can be considered the second founders of Maratha power.

The peshwa ruled from Poona, and expanded Maratha power into all directions. In continuous warfare against the Moguls, in which the Marathas fought not only for their freedom but soon also for plunder, and in which the earlier discipline of Shivaji gave way to arson, murder and mutilation of innocent civilians, Maratha forces carved out for themselves new states in central India, such as Gwalior, Baroda, and Indore. These all became part of the Maratha confederacy, ruled by the peshwa at Poona who was able to keep central power in his hands. The hereditary prime minister, a Brahman, gave his dominions good administration which was entrusted to other Brahmans, who possessed the necessary education and learning.

By the middle of the eighteenth century Maratha power reached its zenith. It now extended into Hyderabad in the south and into the Punjab in the north. In 1758, after having previously interfered in affairs in Delhi, the Marathas made a supreme effort to establish their supremacy over all India, and to oust the Moguls completely. They occupied Lahore and then moved north against the Afghans, and it seemed that despite the unpopularity due to their destructiveness, tyranny, and oppression of peasants, a chance had come again to restore a Hindu empire in India. But in 1761 the Maratha forces were severely defeated by the Afghans under Shah Durani at the Battle of Panipat. Panipat was such a great blow that the Maratha confederacy never recovered from it. Since the Afghans did not stay in India, and the Marathas had been seriously weakened by their clash with them, the Battle of Panipat, the last one fought with an invader from Central Asia, paved the way for the English conquest of India.

The final downfall of the Marathas in India was due largely to the astute diplomacy of Hastings and Wellesley, who succeeded in exploiting and interfering in the intrigues and succession disputes which took place at Poona. In 1802 the peshwa asked for British protection, which was given to him, but when he tried to shake it off the next year he found that to be another matter. In 1803 the British defeated the Maratha confederacy decisively at the Battle of Assaye, which put an end to their power and which foreshadowed the annexation of their territory by the English. The Marathas had had a genuine chance to establish a Hindu empire in India upon the ruins of Mogul greatness, but they failed and Britain was to occupy their place.

The Sikhs

The other great movement of the Hindu renascence of the seventeenth century was that of the Sikhs. Like the Maratha movement, it also had its origin in the devotional bhakti doctrine and attracted adherents from the peasantry and the lower classes. The founder of Sikhism was Guru Nanak, born in 1469, who had been greatly influenced by the teachings of Kabir before him (see page 224, Volume I). Nanak rejected the authority of the Brahmans, the Vedas, and the caste system, although he retained the concepts of karma and transmigration. He argued that neither race, nor nationality, nor caste mattered, since God could be found everywhere: "there is no Hindu and no Moslem." It was Nanak's vision to find a common bond between Hindus and Moslems, and the religion of Sikhism was based upon a synthesis of both.

Nanak preached both in Hindu temples and Moslem mosques in the Punjab, and before his death he appointed his spiritual successor, the *guru* or teacher. Of these there were ten in succession, who led the movement which at first was peaceful enough. The Sikhs were granted land at Amritsar by Akbar, but they got into difficulties with Jahangir. Their guru Arjuna had aided Jahangir's son, Khusru, in the revolt against his father, and in 1606 he was executed. With the policy of religious intolerance adopted by Aurangzeb, the Sikhs turned into active enemies of the Moguls, and, after 1675, they revolted. In the war which followed Sikhism, which had begun as a peaceful peasant religious movement, became a military fighting order, similar perhaps to the Templars of Europe, and their creed and institutions were formalized. The Sikhs adopted as their chief authority the *Adi Granth*, or "book," which contains hymns, prayers, and the writings of their teachers from Kabir on. After 1708 there were no more gurus, and all authority was henceforth vested in this holy book. All Sikhs take the name Singh, or lion, and they undergo an initiation ceremony in which they forswear tobacco, wine, and the caste system. As symbols the Sikhs adopt the wearing of long hair, short drawers, and the possession of a special comb, dagger, and iron discus.

Ranjit Singh. During the second half of the eighteenth century, the Sikhs suffered severely at the hands of the Afghans who destroyed their temple at Amritsar, and their fortunes reached low ebb, but this decline was remedied by Ranjit Singh, the greatest leader of the Sikhs, who made out of what had become little more than a band of robbers a strong, theocratic military confederacy. Ranjit Singh, a man of exceptional courage, perseverance and endurance, was thoroughly successful in his aim to make the

INDIA FROM MOGUL POWER TO BRITISH SUPREMACY

FIGURE 3.5. Golden Temple, Amritsar.

Sikhs a separate nation. Ranjit Singh, although a small man with but one eye, possessed an awe-inspiring personality. He was a fine fighter, an excellent horseman, and soon recovered Amritsar for the Sikhs, where he built their famed Golden Temple. He employed French and Italian generals who trained his infantry, and he soon gained control over Multan, Peshawar, the whole of the Punjab, and Kashmir.

British Conquest of the Punjab. The Sikh state, a formidable military power under Ranjit Singh, concluded a treaty with Britain in 1809, wherein the Sutlej river was established as the boundary between the Sikh dominions and those of Britain to the east. In 1841 Britain entered the First Afghan War to counter Russian influence in that country, but she met with disaster when her expeditionary forces were wiped out. This greatly reduced British prestige in India, and it gave added impetus to Sikh desires to encroach upon English territory in the Ganges valley. Ranjit Singh, a steadying influence, died in 1839, and successive troubles, strife, mutiny, and assassination made the Sikhs more turbulent than ever. They threw caution to the wind and attacked the British in 1845 when they crossed the Sutlej. A band of 50,000 Sikhs attempted to plunder Delhi, but after bloody and obstinate fighting were driven back. As a result of this war the British obtained Kashmir, and they installed a British resident, Sir Henry Lawrence, in Lahore. He and his brother, John Lawrence, were brilliant men of exceptional ability who took over the administration of the Sikh territories with the sole instructions: "to settle the country, make the people happy, and take care there are no rows." They reduced the taxes of the peasants, assisted agriculture and irrigation, built village schools where there had been none before, and made the Punjab into a prosperous and peaceful country.

But the proud Sikh aristocracy did not accept British control, and in 1848 the Sikhs revolted. The British accepted the challenge with considerable heat, Dalhousie, the Governor-General, exclaiming that: "The Sikh nation has called for war, and upon my word, Sirs, they shall have it with a vengeance." In the ensuing fierce campaign the Sikhs were defeated at the Battle of Gujarat, in 1849, and with that battle the Sikh nation ceased to exist. The Punjab now became a part of the British possessions in India.

Both the Maratha and the Sikh movements were attempts to restore Hindu power in India, and one of them, the Maratha, came close to success during the middle of the eighteenth century when India was torn by political and economic chaos. The situation in India around 1750 was that of a political vacuum in which any one power, whether Mysore, Hyderabad, the Marathas, or one from the outside might rise to supremacy; what all India desired was peace, security, and stability.

The power which filled this political vacuum and which restored orderly government in the subcontinent was Great Britain.

EUROPEAN COLONIAL EXPANSION AND THE RISE OF BRITISH POWER

Among the Europeans, the sixteenth century had been the century of the Portuguese, whose twofold interest in trade and religion had led to the establishment under the leadership of Albuquerque of a maritime empire based on seapower and a few fortified strategic bases (see Volume I). The Portuguese were replaced during the seventeenth century by the Dutch, who successfully challenged the Portuguese monopoly of the trade in spices from the Spice Islands by creating a monopoly of their own. The Dutch East India Company, chartered in 1602, was an institution of wide powers and representing nation-wide interests. But the Dutch made relatively little impact upon India, even less than their Portuguese predecessors. Except for the purchase of Indian textiles, Dutch interests centered entirely on the riches of the Southeast Asian archipelago, and little need be said about them in the context of Indian history. The eighteenth century was the age of the British and the French. Their impact on India was to be profound and revolutionary.

The Coming of the British

The interest of Britain in Eastern waters began in the Elizabethan age, when many minds were fascinated by the idea of trade with India, China, and the East Indies. There were the fabulous stories of Marco Polo and other travellers; there were the concrete facts of an increased demand for spices; and there was the no less concrete example of the prosperity which the Portuguese and then the Dutch derived from trade with the East. Between 1558 and 1603 a number of chartered companies were founded in England to engage in monopoly trade, such as the Baltic, Venetian, Turkish, and Muscovite companies, while a number of attempts were also made to reach the East either by land or sea. Efforts to penetrate Turkistan and Persia via Russia and Turkey were on the whole unsuccessful, and the search for a Northwest Passage by sea was even more so. Davis got as far as Baffin Land in 1586, but then was blocked by impenetrable ice. In the meantime Drake, the privateer, had sailed around the world in the years 1577–1580, and after looking in vain for the western end of the Northwest Passage had sailed south into the Moluccas, where he traded with an anti-Portuguese sultan.

The destruction of the Spanish Armada in 1588 gave a great boost to British voyages, and in 1591–95 the first English vessel sailed on the first direct voyage to India around the Cape of Good Hope, to be followed by many ships which were now no longer checked by Portuguese naval supremacy. Disasters and privations, losses by sea and scurvy, did not check the rapidly increasing number of trading voyages to Eastern markets, and by 1600 the East India Company, the greatest trading and empire-building corporation in English history, received its charter.

The first English voyages early in the seventeenth century usually went to Red Sea ports, such as Aden, and ports in the Persian Gulf, Hormuz, which was captured by the English from the Portuguese in 1622, in particular; but soon afterwards India became the chief attraction. We have already seen how William Hawkins, the boon companion of Jahangir, attempted to obtain a trading concession at Surat for the East India Company. He had been thwarted in this aim in 1608 by the Portuguese Jesuits. In 1612 two British ships fought vigorously and victoriously against thirty Portuguese vessels off Surat, and the Moguls had witnessed this event with much interest. Shortly afterwards the Portuguese seized a Mogul ship carrying pilgrims to the Moslem holy places, and as a result of this incident the Mogul government permitted the English to establish themselves in Surat. Further established trading rights were secured for Britain by her ambassador, Sir Thomas Roe, who was at the Mogul court from 1615 to 1619. From Surat British ships traded as far as Bantam on Java, and with the Spice Islands further east, and they easily outstripped the Portuguese wherever they encountered them. Nevertheless, the English East India Company was still much inferior to the Dutch in those waters, since the Dutch East India Company had at least four times as many ships as the English company.

The English East India Company

The term *factory* which was applied to the first English settlement in Surat, and then subsequently to other British establishments in India, denoted merely a group of residences, offices, and warehouses under the protection of the local government, where goods were stored pending the arrival and departure of ships to the home country. The factories were governed by a president, aided by members of the staff, all living under strictest discipline and engaged in purely commercial activities. The sole aim of the East India Company in India was trade, and since no political issues were involved, early relations with the Mogul government were usually friendly. Since the Moguls possessed no seapower of their own they welcomed the English as counterpoise against the Portuguese. Later, in 1640, the English established another factory at Fort St. George, Madras. In 1661 Bombay, a Portuguese island, was added to these English outposts in India as part of the dowry of Catherine of Braganza who had married Charles II, and it was leased to the Company from the Crown in 1669. In Bengal the Portuguese were driven out in 1632 by Shah Jahan, ostensibly because they engaged in slave trading and piracy, but really because the Moguls wanted the profitable trade in the Bay of Bengal for themselves. This action opened the Hooghly estuary to the Dutch and the English, and in 1690 the village of Calcutta was rented by the British East India Company.

From Surat, which was the chief establishment of the company in India, and from Madras, Bombay, and Calcutta the East India Company created an effective commercial organization whose prime purpose was profitable trade. Since the company in London was governed by cautious merchants, averse above all to expense and unnecessary risk, neither interference in local politics, missionary activities, nor the thought of conquest were tolerated. England, so it was argued by the Board of Directors, had America for colonization and the East for trade.

In the 17th century the English had great difficulty finding anything to sell in India except bullion, and a few fabrics such as broadcloths, velvet, and brocades, but the export of precious metal, silver in particular, aroused the ire of the mercantilists. In addition the English Civil War and the Puritan Revolution also brought little but grief to the East India Company. This situation gradually began to improve when the Company involved itself in the "country-trade," exporting Indian goods to China, and made use of the profits to be had in this in the purchase of Asian goods destined for Europe, such as cottons, silk, indigo, pepper, other spices, sugar, and opium. The Stuart Restoration also aided the fortunes of British trade, since Charles II was interested in and supported the company. By 1700 trade had assumed large and important proportions, with great profits being realized.

Development of Territorial Settlements

The second stage in the rise of colonial powers in India was the transition by which the factory became a fort. Due to the insecurity of the conditions which prevailed in India after the death of Aurangzeb, and even earlier when the Marathas were attacking Mogul supremacy, the need was felt to protect the factory, a pure trading establishment, with a small garrison and some fortifications. For instance, the English built a fort on the island of Bombay after Shivaji had raided Surat and made trade there temporarily impossible. Due to raids, local disturbances, or activities of pirates, the company erected small forts wherever necessary to safeguard its trading interests, and in turn these places of security attracted the people of the surrounding countryside. These forts, whether they were at Madras, Bombay, or Calcutta, were the germs of future territorial dominion. They possessed self-government and independent jurisdiction, they collected local customs duties, and coined money, and employed a native militia for their protection.

The final step in the process of dominion took place when the fort expanded into a territorial settlement. This change occurred when Europeans began to think how they might decrease the costs of maintaining an expensive garrison and then solved the problem by obtaining self-supporting settlements, which met all expenses and were not a drain upon the profits of the company. It must be stressed that in this process the trading companies relied on their own wealth and energy, the English government being merely a kind of silent partner who bore no risks and slight responsibility, and who only acted when it seemed likely that the general political interests of England were compromised by the activities of the trading companies in India. It was the weakness of the Mogul empire and the absence of any effective central authority which furnished both the motive and the opportunity for change. The view that Britain might well establish political power in India was first stated by Sir Josiah Child, a company director in 1690, but it will be noted that when he outlined his views he argued for the establishment of a British dominion *in* India and not over the whole of it. The company was:

> to establish such a politic of civil and military power, and create and secure such a large revenue, as may be the foundation of a large, well-grounded, sure English dominion in India for all time to come.[3]

The development from factory to fort and then to territorial settlement was not restricted to the British East India Company. It had its first really fully conscious political expression among the French, the great rivals of the English. Colbert, the great mercantilist finance minister of Louis XIV, had founded the *Compagnie des Indes Orientales* in 1664 and this French monopoly trading company obtained sites on the east coast of India when they acquired Pondicherry in 1674, and Chandernagore on the Hooghly delta in 1690. The worldwide Anglo-French rivalry thus also included India where the two companies faced each other on the Coromandel coast, the English at Madras, and the French at Pondicherry. Both trading companies desired peaceful trade, but both companies appeared in an era of

---
[3] A. C. Lyall, *The Rise and Expansion of the British Dominion in India* (London: John Murray, 1905), p. 49.

increasing political anarchy and growing turbulence in India, and they engaged from the beginning in economic rivalry against each other, which soon led to private and then national war. In the ensuing wars the English company won since it was backed by the largest seafaring population and the most opulent city of the world, and because it enjoyed the favor of its government to a degree which the French company never did. But the successful establishment of Western power securely on Indian soil was done by a Frenchman of great vigor and ability, Joseph Dupleix, who was the first European to think of India not merely in economic, but also in political and territorial terms.

Dupleix

Dupleix, who became governor-general at Pondicherry in 1742, realized that the French East India Company must acquire territory in India in order to become economically self-sufficient, so as to permit greater profits from trade and the end of silver imports from France. He also understood the problem of political power in India in its most general terms. Seeing the utter weakness of the Mogul empire and the political instability of the times, he concluded that it was certain that eventually a European power would rule India, and this to Dupleix meant, of course, France.

Dupleix began his political activities by becoming involved in the rivalries of the native Indian powers, in order to obtain Indian allies and puppets which would be useful in the elimination of his own rivals, particularly the English. The scene of his activity was the region known as the Carnatic.[4] After increasing the military strength of the French East India Company by enlisting, training, and equipping native soldiers, known as sepoys, who served as musketeers with field artillery (a measure which the English promptly copied from the French), Dupleix plunged into war against the English in India when the outbreak of the War of the Austrian Succession provided a pretext. In 1746 Dupleix captured Madras, and the French at once gained superior prestige in Indian affairs. The English invoked the aid of the nawab of Arcot, but his cavalry was useless against French muskets and guns. France gained undisputed control on land, but the French fleet was shattered by a hurricane in the Bay of Bengal and had to return home. Lack of seapower eventually proved to be the decisive factor in the decline of French fortunes. For the time being, however, the French seemed in no way inferior to the English in means and resources.

When the news of peace between France and England arrived from Paris, Dupleix was able to employ his large military forces at once to intervene in the affairs of Hyderabad. It was Dupleix's policy to make the French supreme in India by installing rulers friendly to them in Indian provinces, and he seemed well on the way to success. Between 1750 and 1755 French influence was becoming firmly rooted at the court of the

---

[4] The area lying between the Eastern Ghats and the Bay of Bengal, which belonged to the *nizam* of Hyderabad who ruled this territory through his provincial governor, the *nawab* at Arcot.

Nizam of Hyderabad through Dupleix's very able representative, Charles de Bussy. A strip of territory on the coast, known as the Northern Circars, was assigned to the French to furnish the expenses of their troops which they maintained in Hyderabad. The English, on the other hand, supported the nawab of the Carnatic. War broke out soon again between the French-supported Nizam and the English-backed nawab, but this time it was the English who gained success, prestige, and power in the struggle over the Carnatic.

Clive

The English victories were due mostly to Robert Clive, a man in whom Dupleix found his master. Clive, who had come out to India in the service of the company as a poor clerk, was, in Macaulay's words, a man of "great faults, but truly great in arms and councils." The turning point in the struggle between Indian and Indian, each supported by a rival European power, came in 1751 when Clive with a display of great bravery captured Arcot. As a result of this disaster, Dupleix was recalled to France, and died in poverty there, neglected and discredited. The execution of the idea of founding a vast European empire in India belongs to Dupleix, and it is a fact that Clive adopted his methods in order to establish British dominion in the subcontinent. India had attracted schemes for conquest before: Bernier, the traveller at Aurangzeb's court, had maintained that the "great" Condé of European fame might take all of it with 20,000 men; and in 1746 a Colonel James Mill had submitted a similar scheme to the Austrian emperor, but it was Dupleix, and then Clive, who put these plans into practice. After the capture of Arcot Clive began to train sepoys in imitation of the French, and he was consequently in a strong position in 1756 when the Seven Years War in Europe again made France and Britain enemies on Indian soil. This time Clive was determined to eliminate the French for all time, and he was successful. In the new war between the French and British in India the French had a "fine" commander named Lally, but he was hotheaded and a stiff-necked martinet and was detested by his own officers who often thwarted him. Lally also quarreled with Bussy in Hyderabad and got no help from that quarter, and he was unable to take Madras and drive the English out. By 1759 British seapower played its decisive role, and blocked all reinforcements to the French. Seapower, as Mahan later pointed out, was the deciding factor in the Anglo-French rivalry, and in 1761 the English captured Pondicherry, thereby putting an end to French aspirations in India forever.

The Founding of British Rule in India

Clive did more than expel the French from a position of power in India; he also extended British control to the north into Bengal, the most valuable of the provinces of India and one of easy access for the British navy. There the young and impetuous Mogul viceroy or nawab Siraj-ud-daula, who ruled practically as an independent potentate, began to realize the dangers of European aggression. He had seen what Dupleix had achieved in the south, and he did not trust Clive's policy. Consequently in 1756, when the English had their hands full in the Carnatic, Siraj-ud-daula attacked their settlement at Calcutta on the Hooghly. All those who could, including the governor, fled aboard ship, the fort surrendered, and the remnant of the English garrison that held out to the last was put into a small cell where many of them suffocated. This story of the "Black Hole of Calcutta" gave Clive ample excuse to attack Siraj-ud-daula. The English retook Calcutta, and then in 1757 they captured the French fort of Chandernagore. In the meanwhile the position of Siraj-ud-daula had deteriorated rapidly among his own subjects, for he was cruel and cowardly and had alienated wealthy Hindus by extortion. His nobles intrigued against him and supported Mir Jafar, his erstwhile general, whom Clive quickly recognized as new nawab. After some rather unethical behavior, involving misrepresentation and forgery, Clive managed to obtain sufficient native support to march against Siraj-ud-daula. In 1757 Clive with 3,000 men met 50,000 Indian troops at Plassey, and with the total cost of only 22 killed and 49 wounded he won a decisive victory against the nawab of Bengal. After the skirmish of Plassey (it was hardly a battle; since Clive, by bribery, had won it beforehand) Clive held the predominant position in Bengal. His control was further strengthened two years later when he beat off a small Dutch expedition sent from Batavia.

In 1760 Clive returned to England, with Calcutta safe in English hands, but with the relations between the company and Mir Jafar, the new nawab, still unsettled. At home Clive was bitterly assailed for his acceptance of bribes from Mir Jafar at the time of Plassey, and for his use of a fictitious document. The attack on Clive in England was the result of popular opposition against the so-called *nabobs*, Englishmen who had gone out to India as company servants and had made quick and vast fortunes by private trade, bribes, extortion, and corruption.

While Clive was absent in England a new clash between the English and Mir Jafar's successor took place over a question of trade. The company had been exempt from transit dues on their goods, but many of the company servants extended this claim also to cover their private trade, the surest road to personal enrichment. After an incident at Patna a short war broke out in which the new nawab was also defeated. In order to settle this quarrel and to reform the abuses by company servants, in 1765 Clive again was sent as governor. Clive made a settlement with the Mogul emperor, the nominal ruler of India. The emperor was given Allahabad, the province of Oudh became a buffer state between him and the company, and, by far the most important point, the East India Company was appointed by the emperor as the *diwan*, or revenue administrator, for the provinces of Bengal and Bihar. It was this step, the appointment of the English East India Company as revenue collector, which marked the actual beginning of the British empire in India, since the company now became in fact a territorial ruler, rather than a mere trading organization. It controlled the revenue of the two richest provinces in India, estimated at three times the revenue of any other province, and its law was supreme in Bengal.

Clive left India in 1767 to return for a few unhappy years to Britain, where he continued to be the target of those who saw in him the worst of the Indian nabobs. Depressed by a parliamentary inquiry into his conduct in India, he committed suicide in 1774.

Most of India in the eighteenth century just prior to the establishment of British power was a country of widespread disorder and misery, torn by political instability, and weakened by an economy which had declined steadily since the death of Akbar. In this land in which peace was continually disturbed by the predatory activities of Mysore, the Marathas, and other provincial rulers, in which agricultural production declined, in which trade had waned, and in which culture had sunk to a low state, the rule of the East India Company initiated the first phase of British dominion.

RULE OF THE EAST INDIA COMPANY

The British Parliament had been sufficiently aroused by the corruption, bribery, and private trade during Clive's regime to demand reform in stormy sessions. Not only did the House of Commons believe that England was involuntarily responsible for a country plunged into violent disorder, but there was the added argument that bad government made for bad profits. Finally, there was the feeling that the East India Company was an anomalous institution, an *imperio in imperium*, which could not be tolerated without prejudice to the rights of the Crown, as Burke eloquently pointed out. For these reasons a number of measures were passed by Parliament beginning with the Regulating Act of 1773, which separated the company's governing and trading functions. A governor-general was appointed with authority over all the territory controlled by the company; he was to be assisted by a council and a supreme court in Calcutta. Some questions of jurisdiction had been left unanswered which resulted in frequent collisions between the council and the court. In 1784, therefore, Parliament passed Pitt's India Act, under which the company was brought under the direct rule of Parliament, the president of the Board of Control of the company became a member of the British ministry, and the governor-general was chosen from outside the ranks of the company. These were the first English attempts to give a definite and recognizable form to the vague and arbitrary rule which the company had exercised in India since the days of Clive.

Warren Hastings

The work of Warren Hastings, under whom these changes were enacted, can be separated into two main areas: successful internal reform and shrewd diplomacy in dealing with the rival Indian powers. Hastings came to India in 1772 as governor of Bengal. As the result of the Regulating Act of 1773 his authority was extended over Madras and Bombay as well. His main task in the company territory was to create an effective administrative system, and to transform a trading company into a government. He faced many difficult problems, for his staff was unfamiliar with life in India, they were paid ridiculously low salaries, and the reason for which almost all of them came to India was to engage in private trade, precisely the abuse that Hastings wanted to abolish. Hastings made some headway in this task, and from his time dates the beginning of the gradual evolution of the Indian civil service. He facilitated internal trade by abolishing tolls, and established local courts of justice, in which civil and criminal cases were clearly differentiated and which were under the supervision of the chief civil and criminal courts at Calcutta. Hastings' measures were not successful in establishing a workable system of administration of land revenue, and it was left to his successor to settle that complicated and vexing problem.

The English faced a formidable threat to their power in India when a coalition of the Marathas, Hyderabad, and Mysore was formed in 1779. It certainly had the potential of ejecting all British forces from the country. The leaders of this coalition were the rulers of Mysore, father and son, Haidar Ali and Tipu, who were hostile to the English-supported nawab of Arcot in the Carnatic. These two implacable enemies of Great Britain made use of the French to stir up trouble for the English in India. In 1780 Haidar Ali overran the Carnatic, and in the next year his son Tipu, now supported by the French, became a real menace to the survival of British power. However, Hastings' able diplomacy ended this threat. He negotiated a separate peace with the Marathas in 1781, resulting shortly after in the collapse of the anti-British alliance. The British, having neutralized the Marathas, were now at leisure to settle their score with Tipu of Mysore, and they defeated him in battle in 1783.

Cornwallis

Hastings' successor was Lord Cornwallis, the general defeated by the Americans at Yorktown, who served as governor-general in India between 1786 and 1793. He continued the struggle against Tipu with energy. Cornwallis was also an excellent organizer, and extended vastly the work of setting up a civil administration which Hastings had begun. Cornwallis insisted on and obtained high ethical standards and strict discipline from his officials. More Englishmen than Hindus were now employed in the higher positions in the Indian civil service, and a modern police force was organized. The most important of Cornwallis's measures was the reform of land revenue administration embodied in the so-called Permanent Settlement of Bengal of 1793. This measure provided for a fixed amount of revenue, similar to the English quitrent, to be paid by the cultivator to the government by way of the *zamindars*, or hereditary rent collectors. This measure gave the peasants little security, since no safeguards were provided against speculation or famine. To follow closely an English model proved to be a distinct mistake under Indian conditions.

Wellesley

The final steps of establishing English supremacy in India were taken by Wellesley. The successor of Cornwallis, Marquess Wellesley, was ambitious, energetic, hard-working and imperious. He had a clear and comprehensive vision wherein he would eliminate all rival powers in India and insure British sovereignty. His military and diplomatic skills were first employed against the veteran foe of Britain, Tipu of Mysore. Napoleon's campaign in Egypt had caused the greatest anxiety among the British in India, which only increased when the French concluded an alliance with Tipu in 1799, under which "Citoyen Tipu" was furnished with French soldiers. After neutralizing Hyderabad, Wellesley successfully attacked the fortress of Seringapatam in Mysore. Tipu was killed in its defense, and finally Mysore came under English control.

Wellesley was a firm believer in what might be called the "forward policy," which was based on the faith that the extension of British rule was an unquestionable benefit to Indians. Finally, Wellesley pursued a policy of subsidiary treaties such as the one concluded with Hyderabad in order to establish the ascendancy of English power over all the states in India so as "to deprive them of the means of prosecuting any measure or of forming any confederacy hazardous to the security of the British empire, and to enable us to preserve the tranquility of India by exercising a general control over the restless spirit of ambition and violence which is characteristic of every Asiatic government."

After disposing of Mysore, and forcing a subsidiary alliance upon Hyderabad and Oudh under which the Indian princes were left only nominal control of their domain, Wellesley completed his work by destroying the power of the Marathas. The peshwa of Poona, due to internal intrigues, had sought British protection, which offended the Marathas as a whole, and the war between them and the English which soon followed was the final struggle before the unquestioned military and political superiority of England in India was established. After fierce fighting the Marathas were crushed in 1803 at the Battle of Assaye, when Colonel Arthur Wellesley (the brother of the governor-general and the future Duke of Wellington) with 5,000 men defeated a foe ten times as numerous. The British victory extended the boundaries of Bengal into the Punjab, and made the shadowy Mogul emperor a state pensioner of the British. Battles that Britain fought in India for the next half-century against Nepal, Burma, Afghanistan, and the Sikhs were concerned only with the aims of securing borders and eliminating foreign dangers; after the victory of Assaye the last chance of a restoration of a native Indian power had passed away.

Frontier Problems

Great Britain's troubles with the warlike Gurkhas of Nepal was due to their frequent border raids into the Ganges plains, and after desperate fighting in 1814–1816 the Gurkhas were defeated and their borders defined. During the first sixty years of the century there were also successful wars fought against Burma, which are described in greater detail in Chapter 8.

The most important war fought during this period in defense of British possessions in India was the First Afghan War (1839–1844). It resulted in a first-class disaster and then in the voluntary withdrawal of England from Afghanistan (see Chapter 2).

As a consequence of the defeat and loss of prestige which Britain suffered in the First Afghan War, and also because of the English annexation of Sind on a flimsy pretext in 1843, the Sikhs began hostilities against Britain, only to be fully defeated by 1849. Their territory, the Punjab, was annexed to the rest of the vast British possessions in India.

Reform

Reform was the chief problem that Britain faced during the period of her rule from the Battle of Assaye until 1857. In an age of liberal thinking characterized by the Reform Act of 1832 and of British utilitarianism and evangelism much interest was current in Britain concerning her responsibilities toward her subjects in India. Much of the westernization and modernization of India had its beginning at this time.

By rule of Parliament the charter of the East India Company came up for renewal at 20-year intervals, to be preceded by a long and careful inquiry into its administration. The charter of 1813 ended the trade monopoly of the company in India, except for trade with China, and that act also contained numerous reform provisions. The next renewal in 1833 ended all trading activities of the company, which became merely a government agency, and its administration was also improved by the special college training now given its recruits in England.

Among the governor-generals who were distinguished reformers, Bentinck and Dalhousie deserve special mention. Bentinck, who ruled from 1828 to 1835, was genuinely interested in his subjects' welfare, and it was his avowed policy to "establish British greatness upon Indian happiness." He opposed with success the practices of slavery, infanticide, and *suttee*, the last of which, he pointed out, had never been practiced in ancient Hinduism and was "a foul stain upon British rule." Another practice which was curbed was *thuggee*, an organized secret system of religious murder. The Thugs worked in unarmed gangs, disguised as pilgrims or merchants on trade routes, who strangled their victims as sacrifices to the goddess Kali. One gang alone killed some 719 human beings, but Bentinck effectively crushed their organization, thereby restoring safety to internal travel. He also employed more Indians in the civil service, although most of them in low-level positions. The most important innovation was the result of the recommendation of Macaulay, the great English historian, that in the organization of higher education in India, English should be the language of instruction. This was a fundamental decision with profound consequences, since it enabled India in the nineteenth century to adjust herself more easily to the impact of Western power and ideas, in striking contrast to the agonies of China which clung to ancient traditions. It is not too much to say that Macaulay's advice paved the way toward the gradual and peaceful evolution of Indian independence. But it also left India with no national language.

Dalhousie was convinced that the masses of India were better off under British rule than under the abuses of their native rulers, and he developed the doctrines of lapse and of paramountcy as instruments of further annexation. Under the doctrine of lapse the government of an independent Indian state ceased and the state lapsed to Britain when there was a failure in the direct line of its rulers. According to the doctrine of paramountcy Britain reserved to herself the right to interfere in any native state when that state was misgoverned. The first principle was successfully applied against three Maratha states which were brought under company rule, the second temporarily against Mysore in 1831, and against Oudh in 1856, where misgovernment by "an administration of fiddlers and eunuchs" was notorious. Dalhousie, who was a student of Adam Smith, also took a great interest in Indian economics and finance. He developed irrigation, canals, and forest conservation. Communications in India were improved by the establishment of a mail system and the first telegraph, and it was under Dalhousie also that India's rail system was mapped out and the great trunk road from Calcutta to Delhi was constructed.

Dalhousie also took an interest in art, and he set up an administration for ancient monuments whose first important task was the restoration of the Kutb Minar at Delhi. Increased attention was paid to the system of education, both on the primary and secondary level. Elementary education was promoted in the vernacular, and higher education was provided in English as Macaulay had proposed. But the most important of Dalhousie's measures was the introduction of the English legal code in India, and with it the rule of law. Internal peace and order prevailed in India for the first time since Aurangzeb, and disputes were decided before courts rather than with arms. The rule of law, which became a reality with the administration of Dalhousie, is perhaps Great Britain's best claim toward greatness as a colonial power.

But many of these reforms and innovations added fuel to the flames of discontent against British rule in India. The doctrine of lapse deprived the Maratha rulers of power and of income, and it also meant the end of the pension paid to the peshwa. Many Moslems were disturbed by the English system of education in which Indian vernacular languages replaced Persian, and state and church became separated. The annexation of Oudh to the company's domains in 1856 especially caused unrest because many of the landholders in that province were dispossessed. This unrest became dangerous since Oudh was the recruiting ground for most of the troops of Bengal. Above all these specific instances there was general resentment against British innovations, such as railways and the telegraph, the abolition of native customs such as suttee, and the substitution of the hated English legal code for ancient Indian customs. Missionary activities also contributed to discontent by teaching against the established system of caste, and by raising the spectre of mass conversions to Christianity.

The Indian Mutiny

This general discontent broke out into open rebellion in May, 1857. The Indian Mutiny of 1857 was neither a war of independence nor a national movement; rather it was a sudden outburst of violence produced by British incompetence in the face of long-smouldering unrest and dissatisfaction with some aspects of British rule. The actual incident which provoked the Mutiny was an episode dealing with the issue of new Enfield rifles with greased cartridges to Indian troops. When loading, the end of the cartridge had to be bitten off. Since the fat was that of either cows or pigs this meant utter sacrilege and unspeakable pollution to both Hindus and Moslems. Faced with what they construed to be an attack upon their caste and religion, the sepoys of a regiment of the Bengal army mutinied at Meerut. British government in India was taken completely by surprise, and the Mutiny spread rapidly among the Indian troops of Bengal. The great arsenals of Delhi and Allahabad fell into the hands of the mutineers, and at Delhi sepoys proclaimed the last Mogul emperor as their leader. The English were numerically weak in India, British troops being engaged in Persia and in China, and the situation seemed very desperate for a moment. But the very facts that outside the Gangetic plain the Mutiny did not develop into a popular uprising against English rule and that the Indian princes remained loyal to England soon made the Mutiny a hopeless cause. The Indian princes, the Sikhs, and Nepal sent troops to aid the English, while Afghanistan remained neutral. Since the leaders of the Mutiny lacked a common aim the movement was soon crushed, however, not before both sides committed atrocities on a wide scale. It was only the quick suppression of the Mutiny which caused the legacy of blind hate on both sides to be less than it might have been had the Mutiny been prolonged. With the fall of Delhi in June, 1858 the back of the Mutiny was broken. The unfortunate last Mogul emperor was deposed and banished to Rangoon, and in 1858, as a result of the Mutiny, company rule in India was ended.

The Sepoy Mutiny caused tremendous excitement in England. It had become clear that the outdated administration of the company would have to yield to direct government of India by the Crown. This was done by the Proclamation of Queen Victoria in 1858 in which she appointed Lord Canning as her first viceroy of India. In her proclamation she announced a general amnesty, the promise of complete religious freedom, and the guarantee to the Indian princes that there would be no further British encroachment upon their territories.

The successful establishment by 1858 of British rule in India was due to a combination of direct effort and favorable circumstances, in which Britain's mastery of the sea played a decisive role, but it was not an inevitable development, foreplanned and executed. Lyall, the distinguished historian of British rule in India, wrote: "It was a unique instance of the dominion over an immense alien people in a distant country acquired entirely by gradual expansion from a base of the sea."[5]

CULTURAL TRENDS

Indian Influence on the West

The effect of European contacts with India in the cultural sphere caused both a revived interest in things Indian in the West, as well as major

[5] Lyall, op. cit., p. 4.

changes within the framework of Hindu civilization.

In the eighteenth and early nineteenth century the Europeans in India lived very much according to the customs and the habits of the country in which they found themselves, and there was some social intercourse with Indian Moslems and Hindus, as well as interest in their culture. For instance, one of the British residents at Hyderabad married a Moslem woman, spoke fluent Persian, and wore Moslem dress. Warren Hastings, in order to establish sound government in Bengal, strongly encouraged the study of ancient Hindu literature, language, and legal codes. The study of Sanskrit literature in particular, which was inaugurated by the fine work of Sir William Jones, was to have a tremendous influence in the West, similar perhaps to the impact of Greek in Renaissance Italy. Translations from the great Indian classics, such as the *Bhagavad Gita*, the *Upanishads*, *Sakuntala* and others, which were prepared under the guidance of Jones and the newly founded Asiatic Society of Bengal, reached Europe and America where they shaped the thinking of such men as Goethe and Schopenhauer, and where they were highly influential in the philosophy of English and American transcendentalists such as Coleridge, Carlyle, and Emerson.

In return India benefited from the European literary and historical interest in her past. Pre-Islamic history was studied systematically, and with the decipherment of the Brahmi and Karoshti alphabets in 1834, the history of periods such as the reign of Asoka was rediscovered for modern times. Western scholars also took great interest in the doctrines of the Buddha, while Western artists and art historians were attracted by and began collecting Indian art.

Western Influence on India

If Indian civilization made an impression upon the West, the impact of Western thought upon India was far more pervasive. The English in the eighteenth century were not particularly interested in anything but indigenous education, and they had no use for Western missionary activities, Protestant missionaries being kept out of India except for a few Baptists in the Danish settlement of Serampore near Calcutta. A few Jesuits followed an approach in India of identifying themselves with the predominant culture of the country in which they worked. In southern India, for instance, de Nobili followed the Brahman model and permitted the institution of caste among his converts. But with the advent of reforming governor-generals, such as Bentinck, a great change took place. To many of these Western liberals before the Mutiny it seemed as if India could be modernized only by the spread of European knowledge and ideas. Indeed, to Macaulay, the formulator of the famous Minute on Education of 1835, all Hinduism was nothing more than "false history, false astronomy, false metaphysics, and false religion." He urged the use of the English language in Indian education, in order "to civilize India." Consequently, European education was now greatly encouraged by Western liberals. Missionaries actively took the lead in the spread of Western thought by setting up the first printing press, by establishing Bengali newspapers, and by translating the Bible into the Indian vernacular. A Hindu college was founded as early as 1816, and

Western education made rapid headway in India, especially after 1835 when Macaulay's recommendation was given official sanction.

Ram Mohun Roy

One of the most important Indian reformers during this period was Ram Mohun Roy. He was born in 1772 of a Brahman family in Bengal, served the East India Company for ten years, and then made Calcutta his home. As a youth he had learned English, Greek, and Hebrew, after having been thoroughly trained in Persian, Sanskrit, and Arabic. Influenced by Western learning, Ram Mohun Roy concluded that Hinduism needed to be purified. He opposed the worship of idols, and found truth only in the Vedas and the *Upanishads*. From a study of the ancient Hindu literature Ram Mohun Roy then turned to a study of the Bible, and in 1820 he published what was perhaps his most influential book, the *Precepts of Jesus*, in which he denied miracles and the divinity of Jesus Christ, but argued rather for the acceptance of the moral principles of the gospel as the guiding principles for all mankind. With his belief in pure theism and the recognition that inspiration could be found in the scriptures of all creeds, Ram Mohun Roy thus anticipated the theosophical movement.

As a social reformer Ram Mohun Roy popularized Western education, opposed such social evils as child marriage, infanticide, suttee, and the thugs, and promoted writing in the vernacular. In 1828 he founded a small élite society, the Brahmo Samaj, which he conceived of as a kind of church open to all men "for the worship and adoration of the Eternal, Unsearchable, and Immortal Being Who is the Author and Preserver of the Universe." Since to Ram Mohun Roy Western knowledge was a useful thing, and reform in India highly desirable, he decided to make the journey to England in 1830. His visit was a great social success, and he was listened to with attention by the debaters of the pending great reform bill. He was also instrumental in securing passage of the Charter Act of 1833, which ended the commercial character of the Company in India. Ram Mohun Roy died in England before he could return to his native country, the first of a line of Indian thinkers who accepted Western thought and the need of social reform in India as necessary prerequisites for the modernization of their country.

BASIC DATES

1600	British East India Company founded
1605–1627	Reign of Jahangir
1615–1619	Embassy of Sir Thomas Roe
1628–1658	Reign of Shah Jahan
1639	British acquisition of Madras
1658–1707	Reign of Aurangzeb
1661	British acquisition of Bombay
1674	French company establishes Pondicherry
1680	Shivaji dies

1690	Calcutta founded
1725–1774	Robert Clive
1746–1754, 1757–1760	Anglo-French rivalry in India
1757	Battle of Plassey
1761	Battle of Panipat
1765	British East India Company becomes diwan for Bengal and Bihar
1772–1785	Warren Hastings governor and governor-general
1784	Pitt's India Act
1786–1793	Cornwallis governor-general
1803	Battle of Assaye
1814–1816	War against Nepal
1824–1826	First Anglo-Burmese War
1828	Brahmo Samaj founded
1828–1835	Bentinck governor-general
1839	Ranjit Singh dies
1839–1844	First Afghan War
1845–1849	Sikh Wars
1848–1856	Dalhousie governor-general
1849	Battle of Gujarat
1852	Second Anglo-Burmese War
1857–1858	Sepoy Mutiny

SUPPLEMENTARY READING

Brown, W. N. *The United States and India and Pakistan.* Cambridge, Mass., revised, 1963.
Ikram, S. M. *Muslim Civilization in India.* New York, 1964.
Moreland, W. H. and A. A. Chatterjee. *A Short History of India.* 3rd ed., London, 1953.
Rawlinson, H. G. *India: A Short Cultural History.* London, 1937.
Smith, V. A. *The Oxford History of India,* 3rd ed. Oxford, 1958. A detailed standard reference.
Spear, P. *India: A Modern History.* Ann Arbor, Michigan, 1972.
Wolpert, S. *India.* Englewood Cliffs, N.J., 1965.

ADVANCED READING

Collier, R. *The Great Indian Mutiny.* New York, 1964.
De Bary, W. T., ed. *Sources of Indian Tradition.* New York, 1958. A useful collection of writings.
Dodwell, H. *The Cambridge History of India,* Vol. IV. Cambridge, 1932.
———— *Dupleix and Clive.* London, 1920.
Furber, H. *John Company at Work.* Cambridge, Mass., 1948. An account of the East India Company.
Graham, G. S. *Great Britain in the Indian Ocean: A Study of Maritime Enterprise, 1810–1850.* Oxford, 1967.

Griffiths, P. *The British Impact on India.* London, 1952.
Hutchinson, L. *European Freebooters in Moghul India.* London, 1965.
Kopf, D. *British Orientalism and the Bengal Renaissance.* Berkeley, 1969.
Langdon-Davies, J. *The Indian Mutiny, a Collection of Contemporary Documents.* London, 1966.
Marshall, P. J. *Problems of Empire: Britain and India, 1757–1813.* New York, 1968.
Philips, C. *India.* London, 1949.
Rawlinson, H. G. *The British Achievement in India.* London, 1948.
Sarkar, J. *Mughal Administration,* rev. and enlarged ed. Calcutta, 1952.
───── *Short History of Aurangzeb.* Calcutta, 1962.
Sen, S. P. *The French in India.* Calcutta, 1958.
Woodruff, P. *The Men Who Ruled India: The Founders.* London, 1953.

Chapter 4

Ch'ing Empire, I: Reigns, Culture, and Frontiers, 1600-1844

THE ESTABLISHMENT OF MANCHU POWER

The Late Ming

In 1600 China had been governed for over two hundred years by the Ming dynasty, which had come to power in 1368 when it expelled the Mongols. By 1600 the Ming was an old dynasty, and its traditional and conservative tendencies, which had begun almost with its inception, had been greatly strengthened and fortified. The Ming had represented a Chinese revival after the many dynasties of conquest that for centuries had subjected the country to foreigners, and, rather like the Safavids in contemporary Persia, the Ming was interested in restoring a purely Chinese society, and in looking back to past glories. At the same time, in the early years of the Ming dynasty a vigorous foreign policy had been pursued. In the fifteenth century there had been active expansion into Chinese Central Asia at the expense of the Mongols, and a number of Chinese voyages into the *nan-yang* (the "Southern Ocean area") and beyond into the Indian Ocean carried the Chinese flag to such far distant parts as Colombo in Ceylon and Mogadiscio in East Africa. By the sixteenth century this early vigor had been succeeded by contraction, increasing isolation, and growing weakness. Instead of carrying war into Central Asia and Mongolia, the Ming became satisfied to remain behind the shelter of the Great Wall. Instead of active maritime expansion, China itself was ravaged so seriously by Japanese pirates that the later Ming rulers bribed the Ashikaga shogun of Japan to suppress piratical depredations, while they actually moved the Chinese coastal population out of the threatened areas. Imperial weakness was further marked by the fact that even small countries, such as Vietnam, ceased to pay tribute to the Ming. Finally, in 1592 the Japanese invaded Korea, a prelude to Hideyoshi's vast project of the conquest of all China, clearly indicative of the weakened state of affairs within China. Indeed, by the end of the sixteenth century, not only was foreign policy far less effective, but rather the very basis of Ming rule showed dangerous signs of decay and collapse.

The critical years of the Wan-li reign (1573–1620) showed this decline very clearly. The Wan-li emperor had begun his career with considerable promise, but after 1582 the vigor of his early reign was succeeded by utter irresponsibility and neglect on his part. He paid no further attention to his ministers, avoided any semblance of governing, and squandered large sums of money. The court, rapidly coming under the baneful influence of eunuchs, began to develop rival groupings, which in turn led to factional strife, misgovernment, increasing governmental weakness, and widespread distress.

A contemporary Chinese historian pointed out that the abuse of power by the eunuchs had never been as great in the past as it was during the late Ming dynasty, when the eunuchs controlled all aspects of government, the writing of imperial decrees, the collection of taxes, and the dispensation of justice. The power of the eunuchs surpassed all others as an evil of the political system. When one of these eunuchs, a certain Wei Chung-hsien, usurped all imperial power, Chinese government had sunk to a deplorable state of corruption and decline. Such abuses meant, of course, oppressive taxes, agricultural distress, and popular discontent directed against the corruption and wealth of the bureaucracy and the landlords. In short, the Ming dynasty gave every indication that it might crumble from within before much time had passed.

Rise of the Manchus

It was under these circumstances that a new power that eventually conquered all of China arose to the northeast in Manchuria. Certain parts of Manchuria, the south and the area east of the Liao river, the Liaotung region, had been under Ming control. Here the Ming had developed a compromise form of political organization, suitable for rule over the Chinese settlers in south Manchuria, as well as flexible enough to cope with the problems of administration over the neighboring tribes in this frontier region. The dual nature of Ming government in Manchuria permitted these tribes, above all the strongest of them, the Manchus, to learn from the Chinese without being completely absorbed into the Chinese society. It was this very fact that the Manchus were a people of mixed culture, living on the margin of Chinese society, which partially explained the ease of their success in establishing a new dynasty in China.

The Manchus were a Tungusic people, inhabiting the great pine, fir, and larch forests of northeastern Manchuria, especially the Sungari valley. They were related to the Jurchen, the people who had carved out the Chin empire in north China in the twelfth century. The Manchus were organized on a tribal basis, consisting of a number of rival clans, but they were not pure nomads. Their economy was supported by agriculture as well as hunting and herding. Although they were horsemen, they lived in walled towns. They maintained a flourishing trade with China, had been deeply influenced by Chinese civilization, and had learned much about Chinese administration before they subjugated China itself.

Manchu Administration

In the early seventeenth century the Manchus began to abandon their earlier loose tribal system in favor of the strong personal leadership of military men. The first of these leaders was Nurhachi (1559–1626), who began the task of welding the Manchus into a powerful people. Courageous and intelligent, he rose from obscure origins and by means of alliances, marriages, and sporadic warfare was successful in uniting the four main Manchu tribes. He then created new administrative institutions, the most important of which was the banner system.

In this system, adapted from the Ming system of frontier guards, all tribesmen were enrolled under the rule of a tribal chief into banners, or military units, each with a distinctive banner or flag of yellow, white, red, or blue and of variations of these basic colors which included banners of one color with a different colored border. This system provided an efficient administrative unit, in which the population could be registered, taxed, and generally controlled. Eventually, as Manchu power increased, Mongols and Chinese were also included in these units. In addition to the creation of the banners, under Nurhachi the Manchurian language adopted the Mongol alphabetic script, thus permitting writing. In 1631 a Confucian type of government was established when the traditional six boards, rites, revenue, civil office, war, punishment, and public works, were set up. The essential fact is that the Manchus had already mastered the Confucian art of government before they ever entered China proper.

Nurhachi also began the gradual process of extending Manchu frontiers north to the Amur, east to the sea, west into western Manchuria and eastern Mongolia, and south against the Ming in southern Manchuria. Large numbers of Mongols were subdued and submitted, and from them the Manchus obtained the dynastic seal of the Great Yuan dynasty. They benefited from the military and internal weaknesses of Ming China, and from the willingness of many Chinese officials in south Manchuria to serve a Manchu regime which rewarded them generously and which was far from being a barbarian society. Nurhachi defeated a Chinese force in 1622, and by 1625 had moved his capital to Mukden in south Manchuria which he had captured from the Ming. He then gained contol over the entire Liao river basin, as well as of the Liaotung peninsula, and before his death in 1627 the Manchus had wrested all of the territory lying north of the Great Wall from the Chinese. At this point the power of the Manchus was checked until the advent of Abahai.

Abahai

Nurhachi's successor Abahai (ruled 1627–1643) in 1636 proclaimed the new Manchu dynasty, the Ta Ch'ing, or "Great Pure" dynasty, from his capital at Mukden, thereby proclaiming his intention to conquer all of the Middle Kingdom. Under the strong leadership of Abahai the Manchus in 1627 began to invade the Korean peninsula, sacking the Korean capital of Seoul and forcing the Korean king to acknowledge their supremacy. It was Abahai also who made many preparations for the final conquest of China. Between 1629 and 1638 the Manchus frequently broke through the Great Wall and raided north China, but they were not able to obtain a permanent foothold south of the Great Wall until the Ming itself was torn by internal rebellion. It was not Manchu military superiority so much as the Ming China's internal weakness which made the Manchu conquest of China possible.

The Revolt of Li Tzu-ch'eng

In China, meanwhile, conditions had deteriorated seriously. As early as 1621 discontent had produced popular outbreaks in various parts of the empire in protest against the heavy burden of taxation, aggravated by special levies for defense against the Manchus and the Japanese. These outbreaks were stimulated further by severe droughts, widespread destruction of property in the north, and general discontent caused by the oppressive government of the eunuchs. These riots and disturbances, clear symptoms of widespread suffering and of discontent with the ruling dynasty, increased and came to a head with the outbreak of a full-scale rebellion led by Li Tzu-ch'eng. Li Tzu-ch'eng, a native of Shensi province, was a cruel, superstitious, unscrupulous, but courageous peasant, who turned bandit as the result of oppressive taxation and famine. He began his operations as a leader of brigands in the northwest, from Shensi. His ability soon earned him the sobriquet of "the Dashing General," and he became the most formidable of the many opponents of the Ming dynasty. As early as 1637 he had tried to capture Szechuan, unsuccessfully, but a few years later, by 1642, he had full control over Honan and parts of Shensi province, and he assumed the imperial title for himself the following year.

In 1644 Li, with 200,000 followers, advanced on the imperial capital, Peking. The poorly led Ming armies were defeated, most of the troops surrendered, and Peking was taken by Li. The last of the Ming emperors, Ch'ung-cheng, faced with this final disaster, hanged himself. Li massacred any member of the Ming family he could find and then ascended the imperial throne. But his reign was brief. Li was essentially a bandit chief, incapable of establishing a system of administration and orderly taxation, and his persecution and execution of members of the scholar gentry alienated that important class. His inability to solve the fundamental problems of establishing a new dynasty cost him his life, and it opened the way to the Manchu conquest of China.

Manchu Conquest of Peking

While Li indulged his bloodthirstiness in the capital, a splendid opportunity to invade China presented itself to the Manchu forces. An important Ming general, Wu San-kuei, in charge of defending the northeast frontier where the Great Wall meets the sea against a Manchu breakthrough, chose to join forces with the Manchus. Freed of his former obligations because of the overthrow of the Ming, Wu preferred the Manchus to Li, the bandit, perhaps (at least there is a story to this effect) because Li had also snatched his favorite concubine. Wu's decision was certainly not unique; it was the decision of many Chinese officials, who, even before the Ch'ing conquest of Peking, supported a government based on a traditional Chinese system and traditional Chinese ideas, rather than an anarchic oppressor of the landed gentry. It was the support of individuals such as Wu San-kuei that was responsible for the rapidity and ease of the Manchu conquest.

Wu San-kuei, after joining his forces with those of the eager Manchus, in 1644 advanced upon Peking under cover of a violent dust storm, and the combined forces had no difficulty in capturing the city and driving Li Tzu-ch'eng out. Li, retreating to the west, was soon abandoned by most of his supporters, and probably was killed by peasants, although there is another tradition which ascribes to him a peaceful end as a Buddhist monk.

Conquest of China

The capture of Peking in 1644 was, of course, a great victory, but the Manchus still faced the formidable task of conquering the rest of China. Adherents of the Ming dynasty tried to rally their forces, a new Ming emperor was proclaimed at Nanking, and there were some signs of determined resistance, but again some of the basic weaknesses of the Ming, disunity and lack of coordination, undermined efforts to check the Manchus. Six Ming emperors, all weak personalities, contended against each other in rapid succession, while no joint effort to stem the advance of the Manchus materialized. By 1645 Nanking had fallen, Szechuan was conquered in 1646, and Canton was taken in 1647. Even so, Ming resistance survived, led by the longest lived of the many contenders, Prince Kuei Wang, who held out in Yunnan, and who tried a comeback in 1648. For a brief moment it looked as if he might be successful, since most of the Chinese officials south of the Yangtze supported him, but the Manchus regained what territory they had lost by 1650. Kuei Wang fled to Burma where he was strangled and this marked the end of most Ming resistance.

There remained another leader of opposition who plagued the Manchus and became a major thorn in their side. This was the famous pirate Koxinga, or Cheng Ch'eng-kung, the vain and handsome son of a Chinese Christian father and a Japanese mother. After his father and his brothers who had supported the Ming had been executed by the Manchus, he swore vengeance and for a number of years, until his premature death at the age of 39 in 1662, he made good his threats. For some sixteen years he led a relentless campaign against the Manchus, operating for his own account along the coast of China. In 1653 he gained a naval base at Amoy and soon thereafter he became a veritable terror on the South China coast, especially that of Fukien province. So destructive were his depredations and so serious his danger that the Manchu government resorted to a wholesale evacuation of the population of Fukien province. In 1661 he expelled the Dutch from Formosa.

Even after his death his son, following in the footsteps of his father, remained as a serious nuisance to Manchu power along the China coast.

Nevertheless by 1650, for all practical purposes, the Manchu conquest of China had been completed, and the reign of the Shun-chih emperor (1644–1661) witnessed the founding of the strong Ch'ing empire, the greatest in the contemporary world (in view of the decline of the Moguls). The Shun-chih emperor himself was a psychopath, a religious fanatic, and politically impotent, but it was during his reign that the basic foundations of Manchu rule in China were laid.

The Nature of Manchu Rule

In the nineteenth century a common notion was that all foreign conquerors had been inevitably absorbed by the superior civilization of China, until they became increasingly Chinese in blood and outlook. However, an analysis of Manchu culture and institutions proves this theory of absorption not applicable in this case. The Manchus were not absorbed at all. They maintained their separate identity, but ruled through Chinese institutions. The essential problem was how 10 million Manchus, or some two per cent of the total population of China, could control some 350 million Chinese, without becoming swamped by them, and still preserve their own power. The Manchu answer was to always remain a privileged group of conquerors, retaining special status and rights. At the same time their power depended upon a state modeled on Chinese lines, and on the employment of Chinese officials. The Manchus never were absorbed by the Chinese because they carefully guarded their separate culture. They attempted to preserve their native Manchu language, their clan organization, even their special diet which included the drinking of *kumiss*. The position of Manchu women was much higher than that of Chinese women, and intermarriage with the Chinese was either forbidden or severely frowned upon. Differentiation was further indicated by dress. The Manchus were forbidden to wear Chinese costume; at the same time they forced all male Chinese to adopt the queue as a special form of hairstyle indicative of their loyalty to the Ch'ing, although the Chinese were allowed burial in Ming-style clothes.

At the same time that they were concerned with preserving their own cultural and racial identity, the Manchus were adopting the Confucian political system; in fact they preserved and continued Ming administrative structure. By accepting the new principle of a Confucian monarchy, which superseded their traditional clan government, the Manchus ensured for themselves the adherence of the all important class of Chinese scholar-officials. The emperor, supreme and autocratic, albeit Manchu, was once again at the center of all government, enjoying the Mandate of Heaven, while Confucian orthodoxy was preserved in the traditional examinations based on the Confucian classics. Every effort was made to attract and conciliate the upper strata of Chinese society, the landlord gentry families, and for the most part the Manchus were successful. They reduced taxes, gave privileged treatment to scholars, and honored Confucius and his disciples by increasing the dignity of the highest Confucian academy, the Hanlin Academy, which was housed in splendid new quarters. In adopting Confucianism the Manchus also took over the external forms of Ming government with the adoption of the Grand Secretariat, the traditional Six Boards or ministries, the institution of the censors (always an important independent organ of Confucian statecraft), and the local forms of Ming provincial and district government. Even the Manchu law code was merely a reissue of an earlier Ming code. China itself was divided into eighteen provinces, and the majority of all provincial positions including those of the highest rank, as well as positions in the capital, were open to the Chinese.

At the same time, the Manchus also instituted some modifications designed to guard their supremacy. Although government posts were held by Manchus and Chinese in about an equal ratio, the Chinese predominated in the lesser posts, while some of the most influential positions went to Manchus exclusively. Manchu supremacy was especially clear in the military administration of China. Here the Manchus continued to employ the banner system in such a way that throughout China Manchu garrisons were located in strategic cities and areas. These were composed of the eight traditional Manchu banners, each under a Manchu general, and each having about 4,000 men. This arrangement assured that military control, the final criterion of power, would continue to be vested ultimately in Manchu hands. There was also, it is true, the so-called Green Standard army, recruited from the Chinese, but it was poorly armed, poorly drilled, and poorly paid, and was used only as a local defense and police force.

Another modification, undertaken somewhat later, was the creation in 1729 of the Grand Council, or *Chün Chi Ch'u*, instead of the Grand Secretariat. It brought the highest governing body, now composed mainly of Manchus, under much closer control of the Manchu emperor. Finally, the Manchus also took steps to preserve their own homeland, Manchuria, from the influx of Chinese. In 1668 north and central Manchuria was closed to Chinese immigration, and Mukden always remained as a kind of subsidiary capital in addition to Peking.

The Ch'ing dynasty, which lasted from 1644 to 1912, was not only one of the longest lived dynasties in China's history, but it also ruled the largest Chinese empire in history. Under the Manchus, China, Manchuria, Mongolia, Sinkiang, and Tibet were all integral parts of the empire, while Nepal, Burma, Laos, Siam, Annam, the Liu-ch'iu islands, and Korea became members of the Chinese tributary system and voluntarily recognized Chinese supremacy. It was an orderly, prosperous, and populous empire which, well into the eighteenth century, could be compared favorably with the British, Spanish, French, Russian, Ottoman, and Mogul empires in terms of size, population resources, and material wealth. It was, however, at the same time an empire devoted to cultural orthodoxy, necessarily so since the Manchus had no choice if they wanted to rule China than to use Confucian statecraft, and a civil service which was based on the teachings of the Confucian Classics. Hence little originality or creativity characterized the Ch'ing period. Finally, in the nineteenth century the Manchus had to

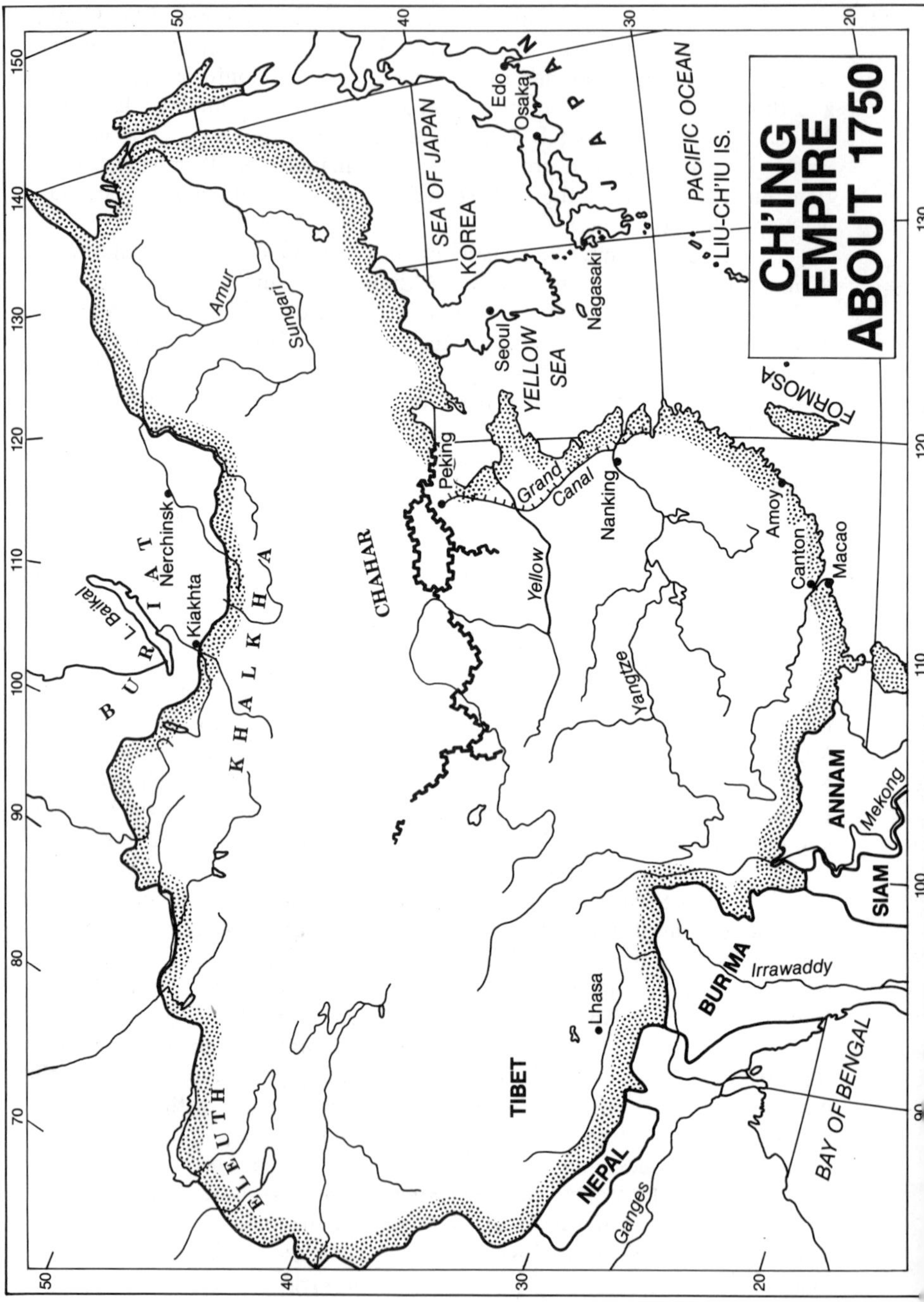
CH'ING EMPIRE ABOUT 1750
SEA OF JAPAN
KOREA
JAPAN
Edo
Osaka
PACIFIC OCEAN
LIU-CH'IU IS.
Nagasaki
Seoul
YELLOW SEA
FORMOSA
Amur
Sungari
Peking
Grand Canal
Nanking
Amoy
Canton
Macao
Yellow
Yangtze
CHAHAR
BURIAT
Nerchinsk
Kiakhta
L. Baikal
KHALKHA
ANNAM
Mekong
SIAM
BURMA
Irrawaddy
Lhasa
TIBET
NEPAL
Ganges
BAY OF BENGAL
ELEUTH

face the greatest challenge that China ever faced—the impact of the West. After 1839 Manchu power crumbled, traditional China perished, and the country was remade and emerged in a strikingly different way.

K'ANG-HSI PERIOD

Much of the success and greatness of the Manchu dynasty is due to two very important reigns, those of the K'ang-hsi and the Ch'ien-lung emperors respectively, both of whom were very able and long-lived. The K'ang-hsi (his reign name, not his personal name) emperor ruled from 1662 to 1722. His reign coincided with those of Peter the Great in Russia and Aurangzeb in India, but the K'ang-hsi emperor surpassed both of these outstanding monarchs in ability. A vigorous man who enjoyed strenuous outdoor activity (he loved hunting tigers, deer, and antelopes, as well as military exercises), he also possessed many intellectual interests, an excellent memory, and strong qualities of leadership. One of his greatest assets was his constant concern for the welfare of his subjects, and the close personal attention he paid to the problems of government. Always frugal himself in his personal life, he cut court expenses, refused to increase the land tax in 1712 when he declared that the treasury had sufficient revenue, and tried his best to curb the growth of large landed estates. Among the measures which contributed greatly to his success were the extensive travels he personally undertook throughout the width and breadth of the huge Manchu empire. On six of the great tours to the south, with only a small retinue accompanying him, and forbidding celebrations and offerings in honor to his person, he inquired into existing conditions, and kept the provincial and district officials to strict account.

On these trips the emperor managed to convey the impression of being many things: the serious-minded scholar steeped in the classics, the sensitive aesthete gazing at an exquisite plum tree in early spring bloom, and the skilled archer and horseman shooting at targets from a galloping horse. He even made a point of talking alone to the people, remarking, so it is said, that one should see everything for oneself. A patron of Confucian scholars, his administration rested squarely upon Confucian doctrines, but at the same time his intense personal interest in government gave China a most vigorous administration.

Suppression of Internal Revolt

The first and most pressing task faced by the K'ang-hsi emperor was the suppression of the dangerous opposition to Manchu rule that had developed in southwest China, in Yunnan and Szechuan provinces, led by Wu San-kuei, the famous general. Showered with honors by the Manchus after his part in the capture of Peking, he ran a splendid court and had become virtually an independent ruler in his role of viceroy of the southwest. The Manchu court became increasingly disturbed with his growing power, and soon regarded him as a serious menace. After rejecting repeated demands

FIGURE 4.1. The K'ang-hsi emperor (1662–1722).

that he appear in Peking, in 1673 Wu began a rebellion, in which he was soon joined by a number of other Chinese generals in the south, as well as by the Chahar Mongols of Inner Mongolia. This rebellion, known as the San-fan revolt or the Revolt of Three Feudatories, soon assumed menacing proportions, as more and more Chinese joined the movement against the Manchus, while the son of Koxinga, heartened by this outbreak, resumed operations along the coast. Most of south China fell into the hands of the rebels, but the K'ang-hsi emperor, in the face of crisis, acted with promptness and energy. When the old general, Wu San-kuei, died of natural causes in 1678, the fate of the rebels became increasingly hopeless. They quarreled among themselves, and by 1681 they had been completely suppressed and almost totally exterminated.

The result of the unsuccessful rebellion was to establish Manchu rule more firmly than ever. Henceforth all officials were required to report to Peking at stated intervals, while in 1683 the Manchus also conquered Formosa, putting an end to that troublesome pirate base.

Foreign Expansion

Having greatly strengthened his position at home, the K'ang-hsi emperor then turned to expansion beyond the Chinese frontiers. Here, again, the K'ang-hsi emperor adopted a bold policy to cope with a threat, this time in the form of the Mongols.

The Mongols were divided into two main branches, the Eastern Mongols and the Western Mongols. In turn, the Eastern Mongols were split into two groups, the Khalkas in the north, and the Chahar Mongols in the south of Inner Mongolia. Among the Western Mongols the Kalmuks were the leading group. One of their tribes, the Eleuths, had become dominant under the strong leadership of their chieftain, Galdan. Galdan had been educated as a lama in Lhasa, and maintained close ties with Tibet that eventually led to his intervention in that country. His capital was in Zungaria, in the Ili river valley to the north of the T'ien-shan mountains, but he also controlled the major oasis city states of Kashgar, Turfan, and Hami in Turkistan and the Tarim basin. By 1670 Galdan controlled all of Chinese Turkistan, and, strengthened by his successes, he began to dream of reestablishing a Mongol empire on the model of Chingis Khan's. Therefore, Galdan attacked the Eastern Mongols, and by 1690 he had subdued the Khalkas. The Manchus were sufficiently disturbed at Galdan's desire to intervene in Tibet (Galdan was a convert of the Yellow Caps, the leading branch of Tibetan Buddhism), but the specter of a new Mongol empire impelled the K'ang-hsi emperor to decisive action.

In 1696 the K'ang-hsi emperor personally led his troops, equipped with artillery, into Mongolia against Galdan's armies. The ambitious Eleuth leader, who had proclaimed himself the protector of the Khalka Mongols, was repeatedly defeated during that year. Late in 1696 Galdan sustained a crushing disaster; he was forced to flee and died the next year. The defeat of Galdan ended the threat of a reinvigorated Mongol empire, and Chinese troops now controlled the Eastern Mongols. However, the Eleuths continued to vex the Manchus, due to their activities in Tibet where they had become most influential as adherents and supporters of the Yellow Sect.

Before the defeat of Galdan, the K'ang-hsi emperor in 1684 had called for the cooperation of the Dalai Lama, the head of the Yellow Sect, in securing peace among the unruly Khalkas. The chief minister of the Dalai Lama did little to help the Chinese. Furthermore, he had also had dealings with Wu San-kuei, and thus had incurred the suspicion of the Manchus. After 1696, with Galdan out of the way, the K'ang-hsi emperor sent Chinese troops to the Tibetan frontier. Trouble in Tibet erupted soon enough, giving the K'ang-hsi emperor the pretext to intervene. In 1717 there was a disputed succession for the position of Dalai Lama. The candidate supported by the Eleuths won with the help of troops sent into Tibet by the nephew of Galdan, Tsewang Rabdan. His army captured the capital, Lhasa, in 1719, and put to death pro-Chinese Tibetans. This act furnished the excuse desired by the K'ang-hsi emperor, and in 1720 two Chinese armies from two directions entered Tibet. In this first Chinese military intervention into Tibetan affairs, the Manchu armies entered Lhasa, and put the Chinese protégé and candidate for the position of Dalai Lama on the throne. In addition, Chinese troops were established as garrison forces in Tibet, and two Chinese high commissioners were stationed at the court of the Dalai Lama as counsellors. Thus, by 1720, Tibet came under the political control of the Chinese.

The K'ang-hsi emperor checked a new power in another direction— Russia in the northeast. Russian expansion across Siberia in the seventeenth century had been exceedingly rapid, and by the middle of that century the Russians had reached the Amur basin (see Chapter 9). Here, however, the Russians were checked by the Manchus, and they fought a series of brief battles which culminated in the Chinese capture of the Russian fort of Albazin in 1685. Negotiations followed, which led to the Treaty of Nerchinsk of 1689. This treaty, a milestone in Sino-Russian relations, was a victory for China. The Amur basin remained in the hands of the Chinese, and the Sino-Russian border was fixed along the watershed to the north of the Amur.

Domestic Policies

The successful foreign policy of the K'ang-hsi period was paralleled by a time of domestic prosperity and order. The emperor was deeply involved in promoting the material welfare of his subjects. Reduction of taxes, an honest bureaucracy, stable currency, and the construction of great public works, especially along the Yellow river, were among his goals and projects. In addition, the K'ang-hsi emperor, a genuine scholar and intellectual, was especially concerned with the encouragement of culture. He subsidized schools, and commissioned new editions of the Classics. Many great compilations were prepared, and a famous dictionary, known by his reign title as the K'ang-hsi Dictionary, appeared. He personally studied the Confucian Classics, was an avid book collector, and was also the author of sixteen short moral maxims, which he issued in 1671 as "sacred edicts" for the guidance of his people. These maxims, such as "Explain the laws in order to warn the ignorant and obstinate," or "Esteem economy that money be not lavishly wasted," or again "Instruct the youth in order to restrain them from evil," were, of course, tinged with propaganda, indicating how the emperor himself, a widely read and learned man, used literature as a weapon with which to buttress Manchu rule. His reign is also famous for the fine porcelain produced in the imperial kilns.

YUNG-CHENG, CH'IEN-LUNG, AND DECLINE

The illustrious K'ang-hsi emperor was succeeded by the short reign of the Yung-cheng emperor (1722–1735), which was followed by the second of the two great Manchu reigns, that of the Ch'ien-lung emperor.

Yung-cheng Reign

The Yung-cheng reign is not particularly important. This emperor, a son of the K'ang-hsi emperor, was forty-six years old when he succeeded his father, and he governed an empire then at the height of its power, with no decline in sight. He was hardworking, diligent, and conscientious, although not as tolerant as his father, and his reign was somewhat marred by court intrigues and family quarrels. On the other hand, he continued the successful campaigns against the Eleuths in the West. When he died in 1735 he left the power of the Ch'ing dynasty undiminished. During the reign of his son and successor, the Ch'ien-lung emperor (reigned 1736-1796), the Manchus reached the pinnacle of their power.

Ch'ien-lung Reign

The Ch'ien-lung emperor possessed indefatigable energy, a strong sense of order and discipline, and great ability. Like the K'ang-hsi emperor, he gave his personal attention to the details of his administration and traveled widely throughout his realm, but he was also a man fond of outdoor life, a scholar, and a great patron of the arts.

Foreign Affairs. The Ch'ien-lung emperor settled finally the troublesome frontier problem posed by the Eleuths, a Kalmuk tribe, by the permanent elimination and destruction of that people. In a succession dispute among the Eleuths, the Manchus in 1755 supported successfully a pretender, Amursana. However, in that same year Amursana revolted against his protectors, and the Chinese garrison in the Ili river valley was massacred by the Eleuths. This success emboldened other frontier tribes, and the Manchus were faced again with unrest not only from among the Eleuths, but from the Khalka Mongols as well. However, in 1757 a vigorous Chinese general, Chao-hui, completely broke the power of the Eleuths for all time. Amursana himself fled to Siberia, while an estimated 600,000 of his subjects were slaughtered by the Chinese, and many others perished as the result of smallpox. This event marked the end of the Eleuths as a nation, as only a pitifully small remnant found refuge on Russian territory. After the destruction of the Eleuths, no important obstacles remained for the victorious Chinese in extending their power over the entire Tarim basin, and by 1759 the various Moslem principalities, such as Kashgar, Yarkand, and Khotan, all had fallen or had submitted to the Manchus. It was at this time that the Tarim basin became an integral part of the Chinese empire. It was named the New Dominion, or Sinkiang, and was colonized and settled by Manchus and Chinese.

This vigorous foreign policy was paralleled in other areas, of which Tibet was the most important after the Central Asian land frontier. In 1751 a series of uprisings occurred in Tibet, during which a number of Manchus and Chinese were killed. A Manchu army was sent into Tibet, and it restored Manchu rule and strengthened it beyond its previous level. The Dalai Lama was confirmed as the supreme ruler of Tibet, but from this time on two *ambans*, or Chinese representatives, were constantly at his side, supervising his political acts, and also having a predominant voice in the determination of his successor. Furthermore, as a check on the Dalai Lama, the Chinese strengthened his arch-rival, the Panchen Lama of Tashilunpo, the supposed reincarnation of the Amitabha Buddha. Chinese power was extended even beyond Tibet itself, to Nepal on the other side of the Himalayan range. When the Gurkhas, the warlike inhabitants of Nepal, encroached upon the frontiers of Tibet, a Manchu army of some 70,000 was sent into Nepal in 1792. It drove the Gurkhas back, and Nepal was forced to recognize the suzerainty of Peking, becoming enrolled as a member of the Chinese tributary system.

Manchu military forces also saw service on the southwestern borders of the Chinese empire. Here Chinese colonization resulted in serious resistance and opposition from the hill tribes in Szechuan province, and the severe fighting which broke out in this area led to friction and conflict with Burma, which claimed authority over some of these tribes. War resulted between Burma and China between 1765 and 1769. Twice the Manchus invaded Burma, but Burmese resistance, disease, and the tropical climate halted these invasions; but even so Burma also agreed to pay tribute and to recognize the supremacy of the Ch'ing. Similarly, the Manchus during the Ch'ien-lung reign also interfered successfully in Vietnam.

Learning and the Arts. The same energy and vigor displayed in foreign affairs also characterized learning and the arts during the Ch'ien-lung reign. Like his distinguished predecessor, the K'ang-hsi emperor, he too was interested in learning and in scholarship. He wrote poetry and essays, and during his reign a series of new editions of the Classics was produced, as well as encyclopedias on government, law, and administrative geography. It is true these displayed little originality, but they served to preserve Chinese literary tradition. Especially famous was the great collection of all Chinese literature ordered by the emperor, and known as the "Complete Library of the Four Treasuries." The catalogue contained a condensed description and appraisal of 10,000 books. Fifteen thousand calligraphers and 361 editors worked on the copying, selection, and rejection of titles. This compendium was too long to be printed, and only seven manuscript copies were made for the imperial libraries.

There was also an attempt to curb sedition in written work, and to suppress all anti-Manchu literature by means of strict censorship. By order of the emperor some 2,300 works were suppressed, whose contents were either "rebellious" or insulting in any way to the barbarian dynasties not only of the Manchus, but of the Khitans, the Jurchen, and the Mongols as well. All works on frontier and defense problems were also sought out and destroyed, and so thorough was this "literary inquisition" that even inscriptions on monuments which could, however vaguely, be interpreted as deleterious to Manchu rule were erased.

The Ch'ien-lung emperor was also a great patron of the arts, especially of architecture. He continued the building project of the magnificent imperial summer palaces outside Peking, and he also built in 1771 a complex of palaces, parks, and temples, including a replica of the Potala of Lhasa, in Jehol, 140 miles north of Peking.

Symptoms of Decline

As a whole, internal order, peace, prosperity, and vigorous administration are the hallmarks of the great Ch'ien-lung reign, yet certain signs of decline were also present, especially in the latter part of that long reign. There were occasional revolts against the rule of the Manchus among the Moslems in the region of Kokonor, in Formosa, and among the primitive hill tribes, such as the Miaos of Szechuan. In later years activities of anti-Manchu secret societies, especially the White Lotus Society in Honan after 1775, were also a serious danger signal.

Another grave warning that the zenith of the Ch'ing had been passed was the increase in personal favoritism at the imperial court, which, again after 1775, gave rise to a serious scandal. The Ch'ien-lung emperor became captivated by a trusted favorite, Ho-shen, who, handsome, intelligent, able, clever, and possessed of a ready wit, rose spectacularly from bodyguard of the emperor to the position of his chief minister. Ho-shen soon held great power, which he used to amass a vast fortune. He built up a clique of supporters and controlled a series of offices in his own hands. He was a master of nepotism and corruption, which were his chief weapons. At one time he occupied simultaneously twenty offices; he also levied a fixed percentage on the pay of the troops and established a regular traffic for the sale of all imperial offices. It is no wonder that Ho-shen's private residence outshone in magnificence the imperial palace and that his rooms were full of precious jewels and jade.

Another weakness which became apparent during the Ch'ien-lung reign was the increasing military ineffectiveness of the Manchu banner forces. Their idleness and inactivity, coupled with poor training and shoddy and inadequate supplies, contributed to a general demoralization of the Chinese military at the end of the eighteenth century.

But outdistancing all of these symptoms in the effect it was to have upon the history of China in the nineteenth century was the enormous population increase of the empire. Even conceding lack of reliable statistics and granting large errors, this growth was very great. In 1578 it was estimated that the population of China was 60 million; by 1710 this figure had risen to 116 million, by 1814 to 374 million, and by the middle of the nineteenth century it had grown to over 400 million. In the absence of technical advances, growth of industry, wars and natural catastrophes, and internal disturbances, this population growth was to become one of the chief problems of modern China, for the agricultural production of the country began to lag behind the needs of the large population. Increased population required increased cultivation, which in turn led to the cutting down of forest cover and to soil erosion, putting yet more pressure on arable land. Certainly part of the Chinese revolution which was to shake China from the nineteenth century on was the simple fact of population growth, which was greatly stimulated by the peace and stability of the two great Manchu

FIGURE 4.2. Ho-shen (1750–1799), the infamous favorite of the Ch'ien-lung emperor.

reigns. As in Mogul India so also in the China of the Manchus internal decay and decline preceded the revolutionary impact of the West.

Chia-ch'ing Reign

The Ch'ien-lung emperor abdicated in 1796, after a sixty-year reign, in respect for his grandfather the K'ang-hsi emperor, who had also ruled for sixty years. Even so, until his death three years later he continued to govern, although nominally the year 1796 is the beginning of the Chia-ch'ing reign, which lasted until 1820. The Chia-ch'ing emperor tried to come to grips with some of the problems that had arisen in the last years of his illustrious predecessor. He tried to practice economy, and one of his first moves was to suppress Ho-shen. He had his enormous wealth confiscated, and then graciously permitted him to commit suicide. He also tried to crush some of the revolts which troubled China, but without complete success. The White Lotus Society in particular increased their activities until they covered six provinces, and it was only after resort to drastic measures that they were subdued finally in 1800, only to be succeeded by a revolt of the Miao tribesmen in the southwest in 1801. Furthermore, the Chia-ch'ing emperor himself was given over to pleasure, and again the influence of the palace eunuchs, with attendant widespread graft and corruption, could be discerned at the court. The emperor adopted a policy of arrogance and disdain toward Westerners, but judging from the frequent outbreak of rebellions in many provinces of the empire, this position of strength was not solidly based. There were many pirates along the Fukien and Chekiang coasts, there was a mutiny in the army, and in 1813 the emperor himself was almost assassinated in a plot hatched by a society entitled "Heaven's Law."

Tao-kuang Reign

The Tao-kuang emperor (reigned 1821-1850) was talented, frugal, and courageous, yet was a relatively weak ruler. Corruption continued to flourish at the capital, and rebellions also were practically continuous, sparked largely by the rapacity of the imperial officials. There were rebellions in Kiangsi, Szechuan, Hupei, and Shansi provinces, as well as in Formosa, on Hainan, and in Sinkiang. It was still possible to suppress these outbreaks, and in 1839 the Chinese empire was still, at least outwardly, a wealthy, prosperous, and imposing empire, but this was a façade which crumbled when the great crisis of the relations between China and the West resulted in the disaster of the First Anglo-Chinese War, which will be treated in the next chapter. With the first treaty settlements which resulted from that war a new era began in Chinese history.

CULTURE UNDER THE CH'ING

The Manchus preserved the authority of the Chinese traditions of the past, with its base of the Confucian Classics which had been shaped in the Han, T'ang, Sung, and Ming periods.

Porcelain

The Ch'ing period produced little painting of high quality, but it excelled in the decorative arts where manual skills were blended with a technical proficiency to produce fine work in lacquer and wood, ivory and jade carving, and splended textiles. However, the highest achievement of Manchu art was undoubtedly in the making of porcelain. The famous kilns of Ching-te-chen in Kiangsi were reopened in 1680, and the imperial porcelain

FIGURE 4.3. White porcelain vase with four romping lions from the K'ang-hsi period.

factory, under direct control of the court, turned out new masterpieces in that medium. The Ming dynasty already had used polychrome porcelain, but the Ch'ing period is famous for the rich splendor of its color and a variety of new glazes. Especially famous among the monochromes are apple green, sang-de-boeuf or oxblood (a brilliant red), and some fine dark blue; among the polychromes, blue and white, and a lustrous and intense black are notable. The zenith of the art of porcelain was reached during the reign of the K'ang-hsi emperor. By the time of the Ch'ien-lung emperor signs of decline were already present, decorative motifs became increasingly ingenious and complicated, colors sometimes were almost cloying, and elegance turned increasingly toward the artificial.

Literature

The Ch'ing period is characterized by enormous output of literature based upon able scholarship and the official Confucian ideology. Vast collections and reference works abound including works on geography, and new editions of the classics were published, such as the complete works of Chu Hsi (see Volume I, pp. 401–402). In one field outside the orthodox literature there was true excellence, and that was in the field of the novel.

The finest novel in all Chinese literature, the *Hung Lou Meng*, or *Dream of the Red Chamber*, was written in the vernacular by Tsao Hsüeh-ch'in, who died in 1763. Its subject is the decline of a rich family in the service of the Manchu court, whose property eventually is confiscated. This was most likely the family of Ts'ao Yin, a high Ch'ing official under the K'ang-hsi emperor. It is also the story of that family's decadent son's love for a young, beautiful, and emotional woman, ending in tragedy. Al-

FIGURE 4.4. Pair of bowls (Ch'ien-lung period) with covers decorated in iron red on opaque white enamel incised with all-over floral scroll design.

though written in an easy style, and dealing often with affairs of everyday life, the novel contains overtones taken from Buddhist and Taoist philosophy, and its insight into Chinese thought and life are combined with a delicate and imaginative style.

Philosophy

In philosophy, there was considerable creativity during the Manchu period. The very fact of the conquest of China by the alien Manchus prompted Chinese thinkers to ask questions about the apparent weakness of the Chinese state. This speculation resulted in considerable reaction by a number of distinguished philosophers against the dominant Neo-Confucianism of the Ming period. They argued that it was because Chinese intellectuals and officials were absorbed in books and fruitless discussions, were sterile in their thought, and rigid in the pattern of the examination system, that the Manchus found it so easy to master China. Some critics advocated instead hard labor and the cultivation of character in order to strengthen the fiber of the Chinese. They denounced the stereotyped essay, and instead urged knowledge which would be of practical use to society.

Another aspect of Ch'ing philosophy was the attempt to return to the original Classics and unadulterated thought of the Han period. This led to the development of the so-called "Han" school of philosophy, whose chief founder was Ku Yen-wu. This critical school tried to ascertain the authenticity of the ancient Han Confucian texts by means of empirical research and the study of phonetics. Great energy was expended by scholars of the "Han" school in philology and historical criticism, involving critical analysis and thought. One of their great triumphs was to prove that the *Shu ching*, or *Classic of Documents*, was really a forgery of later times. This same critical spirit also increasingly turned against the Taoist and Buddhist accretions of Confucian philosophy.

By and large, however, despite the existence of a group of thinkers who critically questioned the past, the Ch'ing period was still one in which Sung Neo-Confucianism remained the orthodox school, strengthened and reinforced through the civil service examinations based in turn upon official Confucian ideology.

Influence on Europe

No account of Chinese culture during the Ch'ing period would be complete without a brief account of the admiration which this highly developed and sophisticated civilization aroused abroad, especially in Europe. Chinese influence was apparent both in the art and thought of eighteenth-century Europe, although for only a brief period.

Chinese influence on the fine arts, although remaining marginal, was successful in creating a new style in Europe, that of chinoiserie. Chinese silks, embroideries, porcelain, and lacquer were much admired for their delicacy, grace, and fantasy, and imitation was but a short step from admiration. What appealed especially to European taste was the exoticism, the irregularity, and asymmetry of Chinese art. Rococo wallpaper employed Chinese motives; the Chinese pagoda made its European appearance in French and English gardens; and the Chinese-style garden, with its bridges and grottoes, was developed in Western Europe as a precursor of the Romantic garden of the early nineteenth century.

Much more important than chinoiserie in Europe was Chinese influence on the thought of the European Enlightenment. China, known to Europe by means of the admirable descriptions of the Jesuits, to many intellectuals emerged as a model which Europe would do well to follow. There was a great deal of enthusiasm for the Chinese social system and Confucius was widely read; Voltaire himself, the high priest of the Enlightenment, declared that Confucianism was the "perfect moral science," that it was the "religion of philosophers" par excellence, and that Chinese society was founded on the highest moral principles. The monadism of Leibnitz in Germany also showed clearly Chinese influence. Even Chinese military weakness was declared to be a virtue, and Chinese argricultural practices and philosophy also managed to greatly impress liberal economic thinkers, the Physiocrats, in their ideas.

However, important as this influence of China on Europe was, it was short-lived. First the French Revolution, and then the Industrial Revolution, completely changed the European outlook towards the Far East. The China which had been admired by the Jesuits and the philosophers of France was given quite a different appraisal by the merchants and free traders of the nineteenth century, who saw there nothing but a decrepit and backward absolutism, fit only for being replaced by European progress and the gospel of utilitarianism.

In summary, the Ch'ing period in Chinese history seemed to be one of its most glorious epochs. In the eighteenth century Chinese power reached its zenith, in both the extent of its domain and its success in establishing domestic peace, tranquility, and order. It was a period of marked prosperity, population increase, and artistic and intellectual activity. At the same time the Manchu period also led toward the nadir of the Chinese state. Lack of creative thought, sterility, uncritical adherence to the past, and growing population pressure all contributed to an eventual collapse. This collapse affected every aspect of Chinese life and thought by the middle of the nineteenth century.

BASIC DATES

1559–1626	Nurhachi
1625	Manchus gain control of Liaotung peninsula
1627	Invasion of Korea
1627–1643	Abahai
1636	Ch'ing empire proclaimed
1644	Peking captured
1644–1661	Shun-chih emperor
1647	Canton captured
1662–1722	K'ang-hsi emperor
1681	Suppression of the San-fan Rebellion
1689	Treaty of Nerchinsk
1696	Defeat of Galdan
1722–1735	Yung-cheng emperor
1736–1796	Ch'ien-lung emperor
1751	Chinese gain control of Tibet
1757	End of Eleuth power
1765–1769	War with Burma
1792	Defeat of Gurkhas
1796–1820	Chia-ch'ing emperor
1799	Death of the Ch'ien-lung emperor
1821–1850	Tao-kuang emperor

SUPPLEMENTARY READING

Fairbank, J. K., ed. *The Chinese World Order: Traditional China's Foreign Relations.* Cambridge, Mass., 1968.

Fitzgerald, C. P. *China.* London, 1965. A good chapter on the Manchus.

Hsü, Immanuel, C. Y. *The Rise of Modern China.* New York, 1970, Chaps. 1–6.

Latourette, K. S. *The Chinese: Their History and Culture.* New York, 1964. A classic account; contains good bibliography of older studies.

Lattimore, O. *Inner Asian Frontiers of China.* New York, 1951. A classic study of China's frontier.

Lee, S. E. *A History of Far Eastern Art.* Englewood Cliffs, N.J., 1964.
Michael, F. *Origin of Manchu Rule.* Baltimore, 1942. An authoritative monograph on the rise of the Manchus to power.
Reischauer, E. O. and J. K. Fairbank. *East Asia: The Great Tradition.* Boston, 1958. Revised and abbreviated edition, 1973.

ADVANCED READING

Backhouse-Bland, J. O. *Annals and Memoirs of the Court at Peking.* London, 1914. Anecdotal, but nevertheless interesting account of Manchu rulers.
Bishop, J. L. *Comparative Studies of Governmental Institutions in Chinese History.* Cambridge, Mass., 1968.
Bodde, D. and C. Morris. *Law in Imperial China.* Cambridge, Mass., 1967.
Fairbank, J. K. and S. Y. Teng. *Ch'ing Administration: Three Studies.* Cambridge, Mass., 1960.
Goodrich, L. C. *The Literary Inquisition of Ch'ien Lung.* Baltimore, 1935.
Hedin, S. *Jehol, City of Emperors.* New York, 1932.
Hsieh, P. C. *The Government of China.* Baltimore, 1925. Old but still useful account of the governmental structure of Manchu China.
Hummel, A. *Eminent Chinese of the Ch'ing Period.* Washington, 1943, 1944.
Kahn, H. L. *Monarchy in the Emperor's Eyes: Image and Reality in the Ch'ien-lung Reign.* Cambridge, Mass., 1970.
Lee, R. H. *The Manchurian Frontier in Chinese History.* Cambridge, Mass., 1970.
Levenson, J. R., ed. *Modern China: An Interpretive Anthology.* London, 1971.
Reichwein, A. *China and Europe.* New York, 1925, reprinted 1968. Fascinating account of the impact of Chinese culture on Europe during the eighteenth century.
Spence, J. *T'sao Yin and the K'ang-hsi Emperor, Bondservant and Master.* New Haven, 1966.
Sun, E-tu zen. *Ch'ing Administrative Terms.* Cambridge, Mass., 1961.
Wang, C. C. *Dream of the Red Chamber.* New York, 1958. A famous novel.

Chapter 5

Ch'ing Empire, II: Relations with the West, 1600-1844

THE WEST IN CHINESE HISTORY

Chinese relations with the modern West introduce an entirely new and profoundly different phase in the history of the Far East. In order to comprehend completely the impact of the coming of the West, it is necessary to understand this event as it appeared in Chinese eyes. It must be remembered that the events recorded here loomed large to Western individuals and nations, but much less so to the Chinese. The importance of the coming of the West with all its manifestations—Christianity, new demands for trade, and, above all, the appearance of the new strong national state (personified by Britain)—has been stressed by Western historians. However, to the Chinese in the early period of relations with the West these contacts were, at best, of secondary importance.

One basic reason for this attitude was the fact that for the Manchu empire the greatest source of danger was the land frontier; the coast, where the West made its appearance, was never a source of great concern. It was no accident that Peking, the Ch'ing capital, was located in the north facing the long land frontiers of China.

A second reason lay in the nature of China's system of international relations—cultural imperialism based on Confucian ideology. Without an understanding of the rationale behind the conduct of China's foreign relations in this period, one must remain puzzled, uncomprehending, and eventually outraged, precisely as did the baffled Western nations. Chinese policy was based on the following principles. China was the center of the world, and its culture was the only acceptable one. Hence, all the world

105

voluntarily looked to China for enlightenment. The task of China was to teach civilization to the "barbarian." In the relationships between China and the barbarian, Confucian ritual, *li*, governed, just as it did in the family relationship between the elder and the younger brother. China was the elder brother, while the more or less barbarian "dependent" state was the younger one. The barbarian looked to China for its culture, used Chinese seals and the Chinese calendar, and his ruler was invested as a "tributary ruler" by the Son of Heaven himself. Korea is perhaps the best example of a dependent state. There was no interference in the internal affairs of such tributary states by the Chinese; except in cases of emergency, they were permitted to conduct their own affairs.

As part of this tributary system, each dependent state had the privilege (not an exaction) of sending tributary missions to China. These, in fact, were an economic incentive to the dependent nation, since they were essentially trading missions, usually profitable. Hence, trade (in theory a subordinate feature of Chinese government) played in practice an important role in relations between China and her neighbors. Trade along the southeast China coast had been carried on by Arabs and Persians among others for many centuries. It was trade which eventually became one of the opening levers used by the West to force China to abandon her position of cultural supremacy, but more important than trade were the basic concepts of international relations conducted upon principles of Confucian ethics and China's age-old assumption of cultural supremacy. In the nineteenth century it was these concepts which produced the profound clash between two world views. The West, with its own ideas of sovereignty and diplomacy and its interest in free trade, found Chinese interpretations of sovereignty incredible and incomprehensible. Consequently, the shattering impact of the West went far beyond questions of opium or trade. An ethnocentric China, secure in its belief of being the center of the world and the fountain of all civilization, was confronted with the great powers of the nineteenth century and the demands of the Industrial Revolution. The clash was to be fundamental and formidable.

THE PORTUGUESE IN CHINA

The first Western people to make their impact felt in China were the Portuguese who, motivated by the desire for commercial profits and for making conversions to Christianity, arrived first in the sixteenth century. Because of the slow pace of their early expansion and the small scale of their activities, the Portuguese were eventually surpassed in influence and power by other Western commercial powers, such as Spain, the Netherlands, Great Britain, and the United States. However, the early relations between the Chinese and Portuguese provide an understanding of Chinese attitudes and of their treatment of the Western "barbarians," and explain many of the developments of the nineteenth century.

Portuguese interest in China was a natural outgrowth of the establishment of their power in India. In 1511 they conquered the strategic seaport of Malacca, and in 1514 the first European vessel in the China Sea, a Portuguese ship, was well received at Canton. In 1517 the first official Portuguese embassy, which included Thomas Pires, the royal ambassador carrying a letter to the Chinese emperor, arrived off Canton. Pires brought as a gift a shipload of pepper and was cordially received by Chinese officials, who considered him a tributary envoy and allowed him to travel to the capital, where he hoped to obtain a treaty for trade. However, this early success was short-lived.

While Pires was traveling north, another Portuguese, Simon de Andrade, arrived on the coast and constructed a fort on St. John's Island in the West River estuary. He also constructed a gallows and executed some Chinese delinquents. Chinese officials were annoyed by this assumption of the prerogatives of sovereignty, but Andrade further aggravated the situation by refusing to pay local duties, beating a Chinese official, and behaving in a generally arrogant manner. The initial favorable impression made by the Portuguese vanished quickly. Soon stories were circulating that the Portuguese roasted Chinese children for their banquets.

Pires' arrival at Peking had been preceded by reports of these events. Additional reports about the Portuguese made to the Ming court by Arab traders did not improve the Portuguese position. Tales of Portuguese ruthlessness from the Moslem sultans of the East Indies, coupled with news of Simon de Andrade's swashbuckling behavior, blackened the Portuguese reputation and Pires was arrested and charged with spying. Why, the Ming court inquired, did the Portuguese war relentlessly against the Arabs? Had not the Chinese welcomed Arab traders? Why should trade be influenced by religion? If the Portuguese could not behave correctly, their trading activities would not be tolerated. Pires himself was condemned to death, a sentence commuted to life imprisonment, and he died in prison. Many Portuguese were driven off or massacred, but some managed to maintain an unofficial foothold near Canton.

After 1550, however, Sino-Portuguese relations showed marked improvement. The Portuguese learned that they would have to respect Chinese customs and laws if they wanted to trade; the Chinese, on the other hand, found that there were certain advantages to Portuguese trade. Henceforth, the Portuguese were tolerated on condition of good behavior, as had been earlier foreign traders such as the Jews, Arabs, and Persians in T'ang and Sung times. Mutual benefit was found in the carrying trade with Japan. The Portuguese vessels, the large carracks, were superior to the ships of the Japanese pirates (wakō) who had disrupted trade between Ming China and Ashikaga Japan. The safe Portuguese vessels allowed the Chinese to resume this profitable trade. The Portuguese also aided the Ming government in suppressing local coastal pirates and in return for this service in 1557 were allowed to establish a permanent residence on the narrow peninsula of Macao.

On Macao the Portuguese were permitted to build factories consisting of sheds and warehouses, but the settlement remained under strict Chinese supervision. A Chinese resident official governed Macao, and the Portuguese were obliged to pay rent, customs duties, and anchorage dues. To emphasize Chinese control, a wall was built across the neck of the peninsula separating it from the mainland. The Portuguese were permitted to send two ships a year to Canton but they were required to leave immediately following the trading period. Despite these restrictions, Macao soon became a flourishing entrepôt of Far Eastern trade. In addition to China, the Portuguese traded with the Spice Islands, Java, and Japan, and in the factories of Macao were stored silk, musk, pearls, gold, ivory, lacquer ware, porcelain, spices, tropical woods, dyes, perfumes and drugs. Portuguese trade was monopolistic, in accordance with the spirit of contemporary European mercantilist economic theory. Each voyage was led by the captain-major, a noble or *fidalgo*, who had exclusive trading rights and could sell shares in ventures, a very lucrative enterprise.

The Portuguese settlement at Macao, with its restrictions and financial arrangements, was essentially the kind of place Canton became in the eighteenth century. This same system was applied to the English as the Canton system. The underlying Chinese philosophy remained basically the same: trade by the barbarians would be tolerated provided they behaved properly and recognized Chinese control.

THE JESUITS IN CHINA

It must be remembered that Portuguese expansion had been motivated not only by economic incentives. The call to spread the gospel also led the Portuguese to the East. Upon his arrival in India, Vasco da Gama himself reportedly declared, "I have come to look for spices and for Christians." Christianity as well as trade accompanied the Portuguese to China.

The leaders of the missionary movement in China were the ardent and efficient Jesuits who had developed a special relationship with the Portuguese king and been granted by him spiritual hegemony in the Far East. The outstanding personality among the early Jesuit missionaries was St. Francis Xavier. He had been highly successful in introducing Christianity to Japan and wanted to work in China as well, but died near Macao before reaching the interior.

Matteo Ricci and His Successors

Xavier was now followed to China by other Jesuits. After some early failures, there appeared in 1582 a most remarkable and successful Italian Jesuit, Matteo Ricci, who developed the formula followed by later Jesuits in China. Ricci was a highly learned man, especially in mathematics and astronomy. He realized the importance of scholarship in Chinese civilization, and gained acquaintance with Chinese intellectuals by his study of their language and classics. It was Ricci's firm belief that Christianity could be introduced successfully to China only if the Chinese literati had respect for its bearers. Over a twenty-year period Ricci became a friend of Chinese scholars and earned a reputation for his wide learning. He was finally permitted to go to Peking where his personality and knowledge earned him a cordial reception. He instructed the court astronomers in the use of scientific instruments, taught how to cast cannon, prepared a new map of the world (wisely putting China in the center), and brought with him books on literature, science, geography, architecture, and mathematics. By the time of his death in 1610 Ricci had made a number of converts to Christianity from the scholar class, including an imperial prince and some members of the Hanlin Academy. The Jesuits who succeeded Ricci followed his example. Their policy was to serve the Chinese as educators, scholars, and courtiers, and this approach of working from the top of Chinese society met with considerable success both in late Ming and early Manchu days.

After their capture of Peking in 1644, the Manchus continued to make use of the services of the Jesuits and during the early reigns of that dynasty the order reached the peak of its influence and success in China. A German, Adam Schall, was given high official rank by the Shun-chih emperor and became an important technical advisor to the Manchus. He won great renown for his reform of the calendar, in which he pointed out the errors of Moslem astronomers, and his prestige won for him permission by the emperor to build a church within the palace precincts. It was Schall and his successors who brought the triumphs of European science to China, in the works of da Vinci, Copernicus, Galileo, Newton, Boyle, and Descartes. As early as 1644 more than 150 books had been translated by them into Chinese, dealing with European mathematics, natural science, physics, philology, astronomy, and geography. Schall's successor, a Belgian, Ferdinand Verbiest, was valued by the Chinese for his ability in medicine, cartography, gun casting, and diplomacy. One of his colleagues, the French Jesuit, Father Gerbillon, in 1689 was employed by the K'ang-hsi emperor in negotiating the Treaty of Nerchinsk with the Russians.

Essentially, the Jesuits won acceptance because of their scholarship and practical services. Their religious mission, the fundamental reason for their very presence, met with considerably less success. At the peak of their influence the Jesuits could claim but 200,000 converts from the vast Chinese population, and their religious impact was neither very extensive nor lasting.

That the Jesuits were valued primarily for their secular uses is clearly evident in the language of the imperial decree issued by the K'ang-hsi emperor in 1692 which generously responded to their contributions:

". . . these men, after having corrected the calculation of the calendar and having in wartime repaired the old cannons and manufactured new ones, employing their energies for the empire, and giving themselves much trouble, have recently accompanied the military expeditions against the Russians and deserve great credit for their assistance given in the final settlement of that affair."

The learning of the Jesuits made a deep impression on the Chinese, but it did not effect a change in Chinese thought. Western knowledge

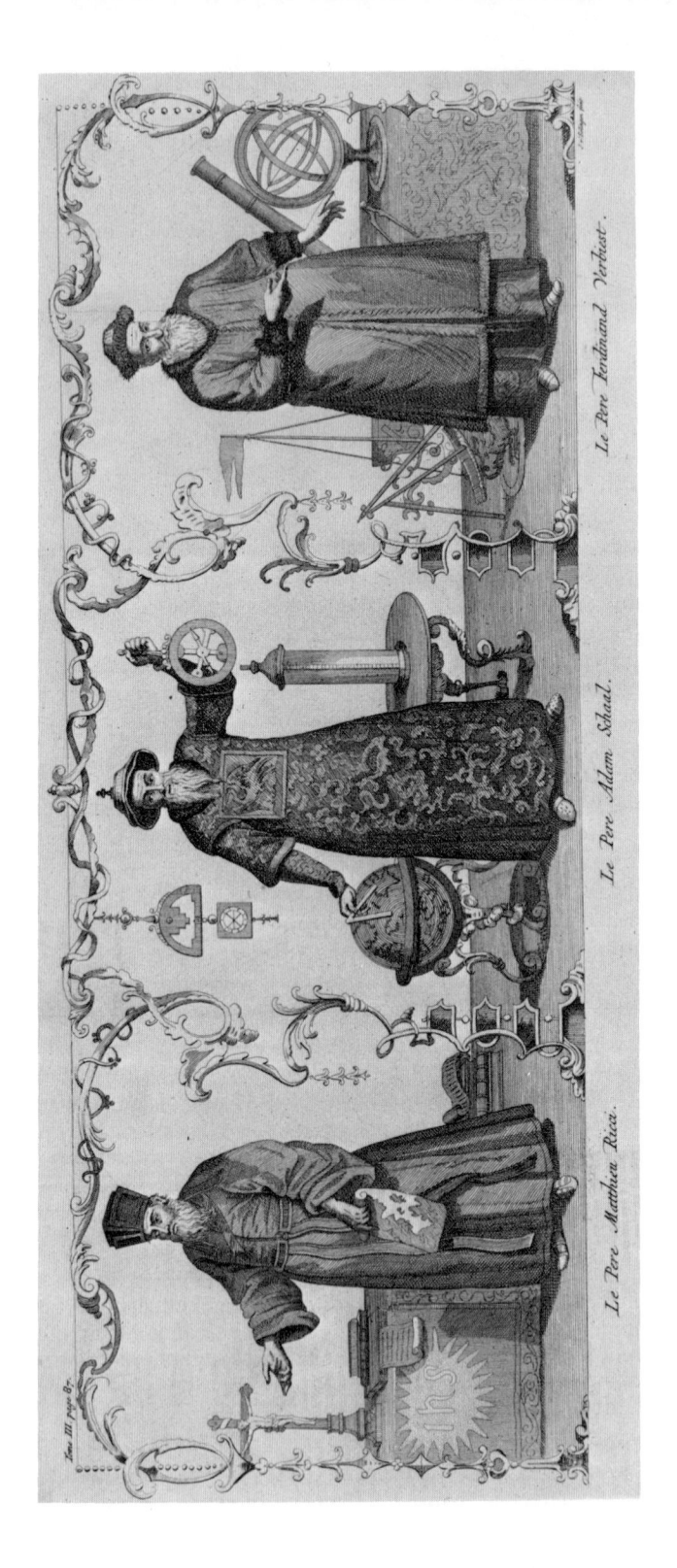

Le Père Matthieu Ricci.   *Le Père Adam Schaal.*   *Le Père Ferdinand Verbiest.*

was found amusing and often quite useful, but, in the final analysis, not very important. Chinese conservatism had no basic interest in Christianity, and the efforts at conversion made by the early Jesuits were soon nullified by the opposition to them which grew both in China and Europe.

The Rites Controversy

In Europe the Jesuits had aroused the antagonism and jealously of the mendicant orders (the Dominicans and Franciscans). These orders had been established successfully in the Philippines under Spanish auspices. They operated out of Manila and wanted their share of missionary activities in China, bitterly criticizing the Jesuit method of introducing Christianity through the top levels of Chinese society. In Rome they soon raised the question of whether or not compromises by the Jesuits with Chinese customs could be tolerated. On this point Ricci and his successors had maintained that Confucian ceremonial was only a social and political act, without religious significance. This civil interpretation of Confucian rites, favored by the Jesuits as an accommodation to Chinese customs, was severely attacked by the mendicants, as was the use of the word "t'ien" to be used as equivalent for the Christian "God." They urged the pope to condemn Jesuit methods.

The dispute grew into a great controversy. The papal legate, de Tournon, sent to China in 1704, antagonized the K'ang-hsi emperor who had been in favor of a tolerant approach to the dispute, but who became thoroughly angered at the appeal to an outside authority. He declared that no foreigner should attempt to enforce decrees counter to Chinese customs or to oppose the imperial will. The Jesuits were given the choice of abiding by his decrees or leaving the country. The Jesuits, appalled at the course of events, appealed again to Rome for a favorable decision on the Rites Controversy. However, due to their enemies, primarily the Franciscans, their appeals were rejected. Another papal legate, Mezzabarba, sent in 1719 produced the final disaster. In claiming papal supremacy he raised a political issue intolerable to any Chinese emperor. The Chinese restricted missionary activities but continued to use Jesuit services at court. In 1742 the pope decided against the Jesuits and their policies of toleration, and in 1773 their order was dissolved by the pope. Even before that date the Jesuits' influence in China had declined. They were subject to mild persecution in the form of occasional arrests, and the number of their converts dwindled. Christianity did not have an important role in China; like trading, it would be tolerated if it was not obnoxious to the Chinese.

THE COMING OF THE DUTCH

Following the Portuguese were the Dutch, a nation whose primary interests were commercial. They had amassed great amounts of capital in the

FIGURE 5.1 (opposite). Fathers Ricci, Schall, and Verbiest, the three most eminent Jesuits in China. All are dressed in Chinese robes and are shown with the symbols of their Western learning—the map, the astronomical instrument, and the cannon.

sixteenth century in the carrying trade of Europe, when they controlled the navigation of the Baltic, the North Sea, and the Channel. The Dutch had been excluded from Lisbon and the spice trade by the union of Spain and Portugal in 1580 under Philip II, but by 1600 launched their own voyages into the Far East where they challenged successfully the seapower of the Portuguese (see Chapter 7).

The first Dutch ship to touch China arrived in 1604. Its captain was refused permission to trade by the Chinese officials at Canton, at the suggestion of the Portuguese. In 1607 another attempt at opening trade also failed. Some disappointed Dutch shippers turned to plunder, and in 1619 they captured a number of Chinese junks bound for the Philippines and Java and massacred their crews, but this action at once led to sharp Chinese measures, reminiscent of the reaction to the Portuguese after Simon de Andrade's behavior, and Dutch trading was forbidden.

The Dutch blamed most of their difficulties, quite correctly, upon the Portuguese in Macao, who had persuaded the Chinese officials in Canton to prohibit trade. Consequently, at the suggestion of Jan Pieterszon Coen, the Dutch governor-general in Batavia, in 1622 the Dutch launched an attack against Macao. A Dutch fleet of fifteen ships, carrying with it 800 men, under the command of Admiral Cornelius Ryerszon, arrived off Macao in 1622. The Portuguese, however, with Chinese help and some luck, were able to drive the Dutch off. A lucky hit by the Portuguese blew up a Dutch powder barrel, and after having 300 men and the admiral himself killed in action, the Dutch drew off. The Dutch fleet then seized the Pescadores Islands off Formosa, to the great annoyance of the Chinese, who launched several attacks against them in order to force them to evacuate these islands. After some fighting and negotiations, the Dutch agreed to leave the islands, but in return established themselves upon the island of Formosa, a kind of "no man's land," where they built a fort, Fort Zeelandia, on the southwest coast, a red brick building with solid walls six to eight feet thick. Controlling Formosa, the Dutch were in an excellent position to intercept the carrying trade of the Portuguese between Macao and Japan, and thus remained a thorn in the sides of both the Portuguese and the Chinese.

Yet the persistent goal of the Dutch was permission to trade with China. The Dutch East India Company now sent a large embassy to attempt to gain direct access to the wealth of China. This was in 1655, when the mission of Peter de Goyer and Jacob de Keyzer was sent out. It was a regular, and rather large, diplomatic mission, including four merchants, six servants, a steward, a secretary, a doctor, two interpreters, a trumpeter, and a drummer. The experiences of this mission were recorded by the steward, and were published in London in 1669. In the account appear remarks about China which are no longer laudatory, which foreshadow later reports of Chinese complacency and corruption, and which indicate European contempt for the Middle Kingdom.

The mission traveled from Canton via Nanking to Peking, where it was treated as a regular tributary mission. Although the emperor was not impressed by the gifts of the Dutch (which did not include the scientific instruments highly valued by the Chinese), the Manchu emperor nevertheless graciously permitted an audience after the Dutch envoys had performed the kowtow, the ceremonial three kneelings and nine prostrations. The Dutch envoys, who represented the Dutch East India Company, not the Dutch government, were then given permission by the Board of Ceremonies to send tribute once every eight years. This tributary mission was to be limited to one hundred men, who were to arrive at the Kwangtung coast, but only twenty of them were to be permitted to travel to the capital. No Dutchman was to reside permanently at the seacoast. In short, the Dutch were to be treated just as the Portuguese, as a tributary nation allowed to trade by the Chinese government on condition of good behavior. The Chinese policy of controlling and restricting trade, permitting it as long as the Dutch remained peaceful, continued to govern the relations between China and Holland during the rest of the seventeenth and all of the eighteenth century.

In 1662 the Dutch lost Formosa to the famous half-Japanese pirate Koxinga, or Cheng Ch'eng-kung, a staunch partisan of the Ming, who had vowed eternal vengeance against the Manchus. This event caused the Dutch to aid the Manchus against Koxinga. Dutch ships cooperated with the Manchus in the capture of the port of Amoy, a stronghold of Koxinga. The Chinese government, in recognition of Dutch services, permitted the Dutch to send tributary envoys and conduct trade once every two years instead of eight. Yet these cordial relations were soon disturbed again by Dutch disregard for Chinese law and acts which brought immediate Chinese retribution. After some Dutch had descended upon the island of P'u-to Shan, one of the Chusan group of islands off the coast of Chekiang, and a famous Buddhist shrine and sanctuary, pillaged some temples, burnt a number of shrines, and maltreated some monks, the Ch'ing court in 1666 declared that all trade be prohibited, except at Canton, and that the tributary missions could again come only once every eight years.

China's policy of restricted and controlled trade with foreign nations continued to govern relations between the Dutch and Chinese until the nineteenth century. This same policy was followed with the English.

THE COMING OF THE ENGLISH

British interest in China, like that of the Dutch, was based on trade. When the English arrived at Canton on the heels of the Dutch they were looking for markets for English woolen goods, and seeking oriental products such as silk, spices, and, later, tea.

Actually, early British efforts to reach China predated the Elizabethan age. Willoughby and Frobisher were both unsuccessful in the search for a northern passage to the Far East. Yet the lure of Chinese riches remained a powerful incentive. Cavendish, who between 1586 and 1588 circumnavigated the globe, and had visited the Philippines, painted a glowing picture of China's wealth. In 1600 an expedition under Benjamin Wood departed for China with a letter from the Virgin Queen in Latin addressed to the ruler of China, seeking reciprocal trading privileges. However, the expedition never reached its destination, being waylaid by the Spanish, Wood himself being murdered.

The Stuart kings continued to show an interest in the possibilities of trade with China. The first successful English attempt to open relations with China was launched in 1636 by the Courteen Association, the rival of the East India Company, and was headed by Captain John Weddell. Weddell's four ships arrived in Macao in June 1637, but here they encountered Portuguese obstacles and hostility. Weddell reached Canton, but only after some initial hostilities did the Chinese promise liberal trade terms for the future. Weddell's attempt at forcing trade indicated an ominous beginning to Anglo-Chinese relations. However, Portuguese obstruction, rivalry with the Dutch in the East (which came to a climax with the Amboina Massacre of 1623, see Chapter 7), greater interest in the Indian market, the existence of competing rival companies and interlopers (such as the Courteen Association) which for a time even threatened the very existence of the British East India Company, and, most important, the civil war and the Puritan uprising in England all contributed to a temporary slack in English interest in overseas expansion.

It was only after two major events—the Manchu conquest and the Stuart Restoration of 1660—that the English resumed their interest in trade with China. The Manchu conquest brought to China peace, and renewed prosperity, and a favorable climate for trade. The Manchu government in 1679 invited the East India Company to send a vessel to Canton. In 1685 the K'ang-hsi emperor himself proclaimed the official opening of Chinese ports for foreign trade. During these years in England the power of the East India Company was growing rapidly. It enjoyed the strong royal favor of the last two Stuart monarchs and no longer had to fear rivalry from interlopers and competing companies. Peace had been arranged with the Dutch, and, perhaps even more important, British mercantilist theories distinctly favored company monopoly. Added to this growing power and interest in trade was the growing use of tea which became a new staple product from China. In addition to silk and chinaware, tea was a major trade item. Since tea soon became the fashionable drink of all England, it eventually became the chief import from China.

The real beginning of Great Britain's "China Trade" was in 1699, when the Manchus granted the first permanent privileges to the English at Canton, promising favorable trading conditions, civil treatment, and the right to establish a factory. This was the beginning of the Canton system, so-called since after 1757 all trade was restricted by the Manchus to the port of Canton alone (previously, trade had also been permitted at Amoy, Foochow, and Ningpo). The Canton system, which operated from 1757 to 1842, was the final solution of the Chinese problem of control of the foreign trader.

The Canton system was a remarkable institution. It embodied the general political philosophy of the Confucian world state in regard to the British, and the West in general, and toward the problem of trade specifically. It was the perfect expression of Chinese attitudes toward foreign relations. Under this system the ancient Confucian ethics were pitted against the expanding commercial empire of Britain, with revolutionary consequences for China. In Canton the impact of the West was felt and this encounter between China and the West involved not merely questions of trade or even diplomacy, but basic views of the world.

At first, there was little Chinese interest in the West and much confusion. Portugal and France were described as Buddhist kingdoms before they had become Catholic, and a Ch'ing document of 1750 recorded that the pope had come in person to Canton to pay tribute to China in 1725. Scant attention was paid to the English who were regarded as "red-haired barbarians" of inferior culture who were to be brought into the Chinese tributary system.

In 1852 a British interpreter summed up the persistent Chinese attitude:

> The Chinese do habitually call and consider Europeans barbarians, meaning by that term peoples in a rude, uncivilized state, morally and intellectually uncultivated. They are always surprised, not to say astonished, to learn that we have surnames, and understand the family distinctions of father, brother, wife, sister, etc., in short that we live otherwise than as a herd of cattle.[1]

Needless to say, the British did not share this opinion of themselves. Changing Western attitudes toward China are found in the accounts of the officers and men of the first ship of the British navy, the *Centurion* under Captain John Anson, to call at Canton (1742). Anson had just captured the Spanish treasure galleon bound from Manila to Acapulco, Mexico, with booty worth close to two million dollars. He went to Canton for supplies and repairs at first forbidden to him by the Chinese, but later granted when he threatened force. He felt that "in artifice, falsehood, and an attachment to all kinds of lucre, many of the Chinese are difficult to be paralleled by other people." One of his officers pointed out in letters to England how ingenious Cantonese tradesmen were, putting stones in chickens and ducks, and injecting water into the carcasses of pigs, in order to increase their weight. According to him, the magistrates were crafty, corrupt, and venal, the people thievish, and China was in no position to defend herself against an outside power. The *Centurion* alone could dispose of the naval power of the Chinese empire, he maintained.

Since their kingdom was the center of all civilization and since their emperor represented all mankind in his functions as moral and ceremonial intermediary between nature and human society, the Chinese expected that all foreigners would recognize their inferiority as a fact of nature and would gladly enter into the tributary system. Foreign nations were graciously permitted to trade after sending tributary envoys who were expected to perform the kowtow acknowledging Chinese overlordship, and paying meticulous attention to Chinese regulations.

To cope with the arrival of the English and the growth of maritime trade with Europe, the Manchus employed the administrative mechanism

---

[1] J. K. Fairbank, quoting Thomas Taylor Meadows in *Trade and Diplomacy on the China Coast* (Cambridge, Mass.: Harvard University Press, 1953), p. 19.

which had been developed earlier by the T'ang, Sung, and Ming for the regulation of commerce at the ports. First, the supervision and taxation of trade was conducted by officials directly responsible to the capital. Secondly, trade itself was to be confined to certain ports, chiefly Canton. Finally, the foreigners themselves were to be confined to these ports in their own quarters under the authority of their own headman. This application of the tributary system was the method of control which we know as the Canton system.

THE CANTON SYSTEM

The Hoppo

Heading the Canton system was an official known as the *hoppo*, or superintendent of maritime customs. The hoppo was an imperial agent first appointed in 1685 who served as a representative of the court when the bulk of foreign trade became concentrated at Canton. His primary job was to collect duty on foreign trade at Canton and to remit it to the Board of Revenue at the capital.

The hoppo, always a Manchu and responsible directly to the court, had no easy task. The Canton area, a river delta, afforded excellent opportunities for smuggling and evasion of customs. Also, because of provincial and local interests, the office of the hoppo underwent frequent administrative change and reorganization. One of his most difficult problems was to obtain cooperation from the provincial officials since provincial and dynastic interests frequently diverged. After 1750, in order to obtain greater cooperation, the hoppo, after collecting revenue, would make a joint report to Peking with the Kwangtung provincial governor, while later there also grew the practice of having the governor-general report secretly every month to the Board of Revenue. His reports would be compared with those of the hoppo himself. This practice resulted perhaps in greater honesty, but, more importantly, it caused both imperial and provincial officials at Canton to develop an interest in foreign trade.

The imperial government in Peking always expected to receive from customs a fixed annual sum and additional fixed surpluses. The hoppo was required to fulfill these expectations. He was appointed to his position for three years, during which, in the words of a critical Westerner: "It took the net profit of the first year of his tenure to obtain his office, of the second year to keep it, and of the third year to drop it and provide for himself."[2]

The Cohong Merchants

In order to accomplish his duties, the hoppo made use of a group of Chinese merchants to act as his agents, a traditional procedure. These

---

[2] H. B. Morse, *The International Relations of the Chinese Empire*, Vol. I (London: Longmans Green, 1910), p. 34.

merchants or middlemen were known as the *cohong* merchants. In the seventeenth century a number of individual *hong* merchants had been active, but in 1720 the government united a group of thirteen hong traders in a cohong monopolistic guild. The cohong became agents of the government and were given certain official standing. The thirteen firms of merchants who formed the cohong swore a blood oath based upon a code of thirteen articles which governed their commercial practices. This creation of a monopolistic guild enabled the cohong to put up a common front against the foreign trader and, one might add, against Chinese officialdom as well.

The cohong system was further refined when in 1745 there was established the security system under which one hong would assume the responsibility for a particular foreign ship, seeing to it that it paid its duties and that its crew conducted itself properly. By 1760 all trade with the West at Canton was handled exclusively by the cohong merchants. From 1760 to about 1834, the heyday of the Canton system, as taxation proliferated and more restrictions upon the freedom of Western merchants were promulgated, the duties of the hong merchants increased rapidly. The hong merchants had to set prices, sell goods, negotiate with and restrain the foreigners, lease factories to them, and guarantee the payment of their duties. They had to act as interpreters and manage a banking business, they were expected to control smuggling and to support all manner of military and educational institutions, and finally, they were expected to give presents and contributions to the authorities, the famous "squeeze."

The real profits from foreign trade, however, did not go to the cohong merchants, but rather to the bureaucracy. The great maritime profits flowed to the imperial coffers in both Canton and Peking, while the cohong merchants often suffered bankruptcies and failure. The government, although officially having no direct contact with trade, had a most profitable interest in it. At the same time the fiscal importance of the growing foreign trade was never acknowledged in the official ideology of the Manchu dynasty. Its formal policy remained anticommercial, based upon the traditional view that foreign trade, at best, was a boon granted to the barbarian and, at worst, was a channel through which the foreigners might spy on the weaknesses and strength of China.

Restrictions on the Foreigners

The Canton system was also designed to restrict the foreigner as much as possible. The traders were permitted in Canton only during the trading season but were not allowed to winter there. After the trading they were forced to retire to Macao, where they had left their families while they were allowed in Canton. In Canton the foreigner was forced to live in a restricted area; he was not permitted to bear arms, to buy certain Chinese books, or to learn the Chinese language. Foreigners were not permitted to use sedan chairs while in Canton, they could not row for pleasure on the river, nor walk far on shore for exercise. The actual conditions of trade were determined exclusively by the Chinese. Charges were variable and levies normally as high as traffic would bear. In addition to tonnage dues, anchorage fees, export and import duties, service charges of all kinds, never fixed and subject to constant variation, there were always the necessary but unforeseeable presents made mandatory by "squeeze." Certain products, such as saltpeter, gunpowder, and iron goods, could not be purchased at all for strategic reasons. When foreigners had grievances, they had to be expressed in "petitions," through the hong merchants, but no direct contact with the Chinese government was allowed. Then there were also legal difficulties between the foreigners and the Chinese, especially over the vexing question of criminal jurisdiction. A good example of this occurred in 1789 when the British vessel *Lady Hughes* fired a salute during which two Chinese were killed accidentally. The unfortunate gunner was turned over to Chinese authorities and executed after the Chinese threatened to stop all trade. This was a form of justice which was repellent to most British. However, it was the uncertainties, the cumbersome restrictions, and the constant fluctuations in trade, rather than the financial exactions (which were not really so large in view of the profits) which most irked the foreign trader.

Since the trade remained profitable, the Canton system with the hoppo, its cohong monopoly, and its restrictions upon the barbarian flourished for almost a century, for in order to maintain this profitable trade the foreign trader was ready to endure almost any inconvenience. Indeed, most of the time the relations of the foreign trader with the Chinese cohong merchant assigned to him were most cordial.

Foreign Quarters in Canton

By the middle of the eighteenth century the English well outstripped their competitors in the China trade. In 1715 the British East India Company established their factory at Canton where their merchants lived in the restricted Shameen district outside the Canton city walls. They employed their own English clerks, but they also made use of a Chinese clerk known as the *compradore*, who served as a buffer between the foreign firm he served and the hong merchants. In addition they employed Chinese interpreters and servants. The foreigners trading at Canton were entirely dependent on the good will of the Chinese for their food, their water, and their servants. Their supplies could be, and were occasionally, cut off, if trouble arose. The traders' recreations and their pleasure grounds were similarly restricted by Chinese officialdom.

The British East India Company

The East India Company at Canton enjoyed monopoly status since the bulk of British trade was conducted under its control. The company had the right to trade, to engage Chinese servants, to purchase provisions, to repair its ships; it was freed from having to pay duty on unsold goods and it was to be protected from insult. Other Englishmen were permitted to come to Canton and to trade only under a license issued by the East India Company and even if such a license were granted, other Englishmen had only limited access to this trade.

FIGURE 5.2. A view of the factories at Canton about 1800.

The East India Company was represented at Canton by a superintendent who, because of the predominance of the English, in large measure became the spokesman for all foreigners engaged in the China trade. He had control over his fellow countrymen, and the Chinese held him responsible for their good conduct, a responsibility reminiscent of that given to the headmen of the Arab traders in Canton during T'ang times and later. The East India Company was granted wide powers by the British government, but, unlike India where these powers were exploited by Company servants to transform the Company into a government, in China the Company never lost its purely mercantile character. It remained an organization devoted entirely to profits, which, although not exorbitant, hovered steadily around a satisfactory eight per cent.

By and large the Company did not object to having trade restricted to Canton. It felt that there was an advantage in having a well-established and dependable market in one place, and its earlier experiences of trade in Amoy and the Chusan Islands bore out this point. Furthermore, the Company, as a monopoly itself, had no particular objection to dealing with another monopoly, the Chinese merchants' cohong. Thus, despite the fact that the Company often chafed and fretted at the restrictions imposed by the Chinese, that it complained about interminable delays in business, constant uncertainties and legal conflicts, that it worried about bad debts and stoppages of trade, it remained basically satisfied with the Canton system. Its relations with the hong merchants remained cordial.

American Traders

Second only to the British in importance and volume of trade were the Americans. American traders had appeared at Canton for the first time in 1789 (see also Chapter 17), and their trading activities had grown very rapidly. They came as individual traders, not under the aegis of a company, and their trade was freer as compared with that of the British. However, their relations with the Chinese were perhaps poorer, and they had more trouble in obtaining articles of trade. These articles of the China trade were tea, silk, and porcelain, which were paid for with silver. Opium, which was imported by the British from India, became increasingly important and was destined to play a major role in future Anglo-Chinese relations.

Macartney's Mission

Yet, despite the fact that the China trade under the Canton system was satisfying to all who engaged in it, new forces, economic and political, worked for its overthrow. These forces were the demands of the Industrial Revolution and the growth of Great Britain into a world power.

The Industrial Revolution gave impetus to expanding trade and its regularization. An outlet was needed for new British manufactures, especially cotton textiles which flowed in ever-increasing quantities from the new mills in the Midlands, and guarantees for foreign trade were sought by the British government. The demands of the Industrial Revolution were felt at the end of the eighteenth century, even before Britain as the result of the Napoleonic wars became the foremost power in the world.

As early as 1787 a certain Lt. Col. Cathcart had been appointed by the British government as envoy to China, to obtain trade guarantees, but his mission was abandoned following his death en route to Canton. In 1792 the British government appointed a new embassy, despite the apprehensions and objections of the East India Company.

This mission was the famous one under the Earl of Macartney. Its aim was to remove the restraints and exactions on the Canton trade, to regularize the amounts which were payable to the Chinese and which had always been irregular and arbitrary, and to expand trade, obtaining the right to trade at ports other than Canton as well.

Macartney's embassy was large and splendid, and a good account of it was written by his secretary. The retinue, which included two Chinese interpreters from the Jesuit college at Naples, arrived in China in August 1793, carrying very valuable presents. The Chinese received Macartney as a tributary envoy, and the boats and carts assigned to his embassy while en route to Peking bore flags with the inscription "ambassador bearing tribute from the country of England." Macartney was very well received at the Manchu court and requested permission for the English to trade at the north China ports of Ningpo, Chusan Islands, and Tientsin, for printed tariff schedules, and for the rights to establish a factory at Peking and to maintain a British representative at the Manchu capital. Macartney also presented the court with many presents, including mathematical and scientific instru-

FIGURE 5.3. Ch'ing soldiers attending the passage of Ambassador Macartney. Note the Manchu flags, the firecracker, and the men towing the junk.

ments, a field gun, a carriage, and Wedgwood china (much admired by the Chinese), and, of course, as befitting a tributary envoy, the Chinese bestowed upon him in return a large quantity of gifts.

Macartney, before being dismissed from China, was given a letter from the Ch'ien-lung emperor to his royal master, King George III of England. This very famous document, couched in the traditional phraseology of the tributary system, was issued as an imperial edict and illustrates marvelously the Chinese attitude of cultural supremacy and its disdain for trade:

> You, O king, are so inclined toward our civilization that you have sent a special envoy across the seas to bring to our court your memorial of congratulations on the occasion of my birthday and to present your native products as an expression of your thoughtfulness. On perusing your memorial, so simply worded and sincerely conceived, I am impressed by your genuine respectfulness and friendliness and greatly pleased.
>
> As to the request made in your memorial, O king, to send one of your nationals to stay at the Celestial Court to take care of your country's trade with China, this is not in harmony with the state system of our dynasty and will definitely not be permitted.
>
> The Celestial Court has pacified and possessed the territory within the four seas. Its sole aim is to do its utmost to achieve good government and to manage political affairs, attaching no value to strange jewels and precious objects. The various articles presented by you, O king, this time

are accepted by my special order to the office in charge of such functions in consideration of the offerings having come from a long distance with sincere good wishes. As a matter of fact the virtue and prestige of the Celestial dynasty having spread wide and far, the kings of the myriad nations come by land and sea with all sorts of precious things. Consequently there is nothing we lack, as your principal envoy and others have themselves observed. We have never set much store on strange and ingenious objects, nor do we need any more of your country's manufacture.[3]

Macartney's mission, then, was a failure. Before the British could take further action, they were engaged full-time in the Napoleonic wars. When, as the result of Napoleon's occupation of Portugal, the British occupied Macao in the Far East, giving as their reason the need to protect the Chinese from French attack, the Chinese viceroy at Kwangtung was furious: "Knowing as you ought to know, that the Portuguese inhabit a territory belonging to the Celestial Empire, how could you suppose that the French would ever venture to molest them?" Trade with England was promptly cut off. The English, at the behest of the Company, yielded and abandoned Macao.

Lord Amherst's Embassy

It was only after Waterloo that Britain made a new attempt to regularize and expand trade with China. In 1816 Lord Amherst was appointed head of a new British embassy which was to establish a British representative in Peking, obtain information on trading conditions in north China, and put the Canton trade on a secure footing. Amherst's mission was a dismal failure, largely because of discourtesy and general inability to communicate on the part of both sides. Amherst had arrived at Peking after a hard journey, and he was fully determined to avoid making the kowtow. Travel-worn, dusty, exhausted, and in stained clothes, he was rushed by the Chinese officials on the night of his arrival to the summer palace where he was told an audience would be granted him at 5:00 A.M. Since Amherst had neither credentials nor his court uniform with him, he asked for a postponement, and when this request was denied he pleaded illness. Diplomatic indisposition was an inadequate excuse, since the emperor sent his own physician to examine the irritated Briton. The doctor needed little time to discover the sham involved, and reported it to the Dragon Throne, whereupon the Chia-ch'ing emperor was furious and issued an edict expelling the unmannerly envoy at once. The unlucky Amherst was escorted back to Canton and returned home with empty hands. Diplomacy had failed again.

The unsatisfactory situation remained. Either Britain could abandon trade with China completely, a near impossibility since tea had become the established British drink and since China loomed larger as a limitless market for British woolen goods and cotton textiles, or she could use force, compelling China to allow further trade and terminate irksome restrictions. In any event, for the next few years, Britain did neither. At the advice of the

---

[3] E. Backhouse and J. O. P. Bland, *Annals and Memoirs of the Court of Peking* (Boston: Houghton Mifflin, 1914), p. 323.

East India Company, always fearful where profits were concerned, British trade with China continued to operate under the Canton system with all its arbitrariness and irregularity. But this policy could not, and did not, last for very long.

End of the Canton System

The forces of the Industrial Revolution and those of British world power were working hand in hand to shatter ideas of Chinese cultural supremacy and to destroy the traditional Confucian system. Great Britain was the supreme power in the world, both economically and politically. Economically she was far in advance of any of her rivals, she dominated world trade and shipping, and was crucially interested in expanding her economy. Politically, no rival was left after Napoleon had been defeated. France was weak, Germany disunited, Italy lacked cohesion, the Dutch had no political ambitions, the monarchy of Austria-Hungary was fully occupied in keeping together its patchwork of nationalities, and the young American republic was pushing into its own West.

While the East India Company could accept restrictions and humiliating conditions in Canton as long as trade was profitable, Britain as a world power could not. This situation, fundamentally a political and economic issue, became critical a few years later in the early 1830's, when the Company monopoly ended and the British government took over its affairs at Canton.

ANGLO-CHINESE CONFLICT AND THE FIRST ANGLO-CHINESE WAR

The East India Company lost its trade monopoly in 1832 as the result of the new economic philosophy then prevailing. Manchester liberalism or laissez faire looked upon the idea of trade restrictions as unnatural, abhorred the notion of monopoly, could see no sense in a country's closing its portals to the free flow of trade, and firmly believed in universal free trade. At the same time the opium problem became critical. For Britain the China trade became increasingly one-sided, with silver being drained from England, and by 1750 a new product was needed to obtain a favorable balance of trade, since few British goods except woolens were sold in exchange for Chinese products. Opium filled this need.

The Opium Question

To China, the opium problem was relatively new. Chinese demand for the drug was recent, since it was not widely used before the eighteenth century when it was introduced by the Dutch on Formosa. However, once the drug had gained a foothold, there was a rapid increase in demand. Increasing consumption led to increased production of the opium poppy, especially in India, whence opium was exported to China in so-called "country ships" licensed by the East India Company. This led to the creation of vested interests in the opium trade. By 1773 the importation of opium became a Company monopoly. By that time, according to one estimate, the flourishing trade in opium had accounted already for fifty per cent of all the British exports to China.

As early as 1729 the Manchu government prohibited the importation of opium, and further orders to halt that trade followed unsuccessfully, primarily because it was too profitable a business to be stopped by official prohibitions. Official prohibition merely meant that the trade in opium became illegal, but it flourished as smuggling became widespread and chronic, and no real attempt was made to curb its importation. Illegal opium trading boomed because of the rapacity of the local officials, who took their profits from it in the time-honored practice of the squeeze. Yet, increasingly, the imperial government at Peking was disturbed about the extent of the opium trade. Not, one must hasten to add, primarily because of the deleterious effects it had upon its subjects, but rather for economic reasons. The importation of opium reversed the silver situation and resulted in an increasing drain of silver from China. It was this drain of specie which led to a series of memorials and petitions being submitted to the throne, advocating one of two choices for the solution of the problem. China should either regularize and restrict the opium trade, or should prohibit it entirely. The Manchu government decided to prohibit the importation of the drug and to enforce its prohibition.

In the 1830's these two factors—the end of Company monopoly and the sudden fortuitous boom in opium together with its imperial prohibition—coincided, and, in an already explosive situation at Canton, they precipitated the conflict between Great Britain and China.

Lord Napier

With the end of the Company monopoly in 1834, the British government decided to send to China an official representative, not merely a commercial agent, who was to insist upon equal treatment at the hands of Chinese officials as the diplomatic representative of the greatest power in the world. Lord Palmerston, the British foreign minister, selected a naval officer, Lord Napier, as his envoy. Napier was told to announce his arrival to the Chinese viceroy at Canton by letter, asserting equality of status. No show of force was to accompany him, since it was taken for granted by Palmerston that British might was sufficiently well known to make such measures unnecessary.

The arrival of Lord Napier, who was used to prompt obedience and whose naval training had accustomed him to stand for "no nonsense," created a major problem for the Chinese and produced immediate friction between them and the British. The Chinese officials knew that the Company monopoly at Canton had come to an end, and they were curious to see who would succeed the Company superintendent as headman of the British. What they wanted, as the viceroy had intimated to the hong merchants, was a commercial agent, nothing more. Lord Napier, as a diplomatic representative insisting upon equality with the viceroy, was quite another matter.

There was no place for such a person within the tributary system, unless he came as tributary envoy.

Lord Napier proceeded to Canton without permission. In Canton he insisted on communicating with the viceroy directly, refusing the customary practice of dealing with Chinese officialdom through the hong merchants. He attempted to shift relations from a commercial to a diplomatic basis. His attempt produced a series of abortive negotiations, and it culminated in the decision of the viceroy, in order to preserve the traditional principles of international relations between China and the rest of the world, to refuse to accept the letter Napier had brought with him:

> The great ministers of the Celestial Empire are not permitted to have private intercourse by letters with outside barbarians. If the said barbarian headman [Lord Napier] throws in letters, I, the viceroy, will not at all receive or look at them . . . To sum up; the nation has its laws; it is so everywhere. Even England has its laws, how much more the Celestial Empire! How flaming bright are its great laws and ordinances! More terrible than the awful thunderbolt![4]

The refusal of the viceroy to accept his letter annoyed Napier, but he was more angered when he discovered that his name was transliterated by the Chinese as "Laboriously Vile," and in his ire he referred to the Manchu officials as "presumptuous savages," who had committed an outrage upon the British Crown and should be chastised.

Since neither side was willing to yield, a deadlock ensued. The viceroy, to emphasize his view, ordered all trade with Britain to be stopped and the Chinese servants of the British in Canton to be withdrawn. Lord Napier returned to Macao, where he caught fever and died. The impasse of the Napier mission left Britain in an intolerable position. In view of her political supremacy and her economic interests, the restrictions imposed upon her and her treatment as an inferior nation were unrealistic. She could do no less than to assert equality of position with China. Furthermore, her private traders and merchants engaged in trade with China wanted an end of the cohong monopoly and the opening of additional Chinese ports to trade, and they urged the use of force on the British government. As stated in the *China Repository*:

> Nor indeed should our valuable commerce and revenue both in India and Great Britain be permitted to remain subject to a caprice, which a few gunboats laid alongside this city would overrule by the discharge of a few mortars. The results of a war with the Chinese could not be doubted.[5]

The Napier affair, in Chinese eyes, had been quite successful, and upon his departure normal relations were restored at Canton. The presumption of the barbarian had been ended, and he had been forced to retire. This strengthened Chinese confidence and confirmed their feeling that in the final analysis the barbarian was dependent on Chinese wishes. While one side

---

[4] H. B. Morse, *International Relations of the Chinese Empire*, Vol. I (London: Longmans Green, 1910–1918), p. 126.
[5] *Chinese Repository*, January, 1840, Macao.

remained supremely confident that its treatment of the foreigner was correct, the other side was contemplating the use of force, if necessary, to terminate an intolerable arrangement. In these conditions it was impossible to avoid conflict. For a few years matters continued to drift, but then in 1838 the issue flared up again over the question of control of the opium trade, and this time the crisis flared into open war.

Commissioner Lin

The illegal opium trade, now carried on by private traders from their armed ships at Lintin island in defiance of the hong merchants and the viceroy at Canton, had become very important business indeed. Its income exceeded that of official trade. The Manchus, greatly concerned with this vast illegal activity, decided to put a stop to it, and for this reason the emperor appointed a new imperial commissioner, Lin Tse-hsü. Commissioner Lin, a man of vigor and great integrity, was given unlimited power by the court to end the opium trade. Upon his arrival at Canton in 1839 Lin took decisive action by demanding the surrender of all opium chests in British hands. Captain Elliot, the British superintendent of trade, agreed to this procedure on behalf of the merchants in Canton, and Lin then burned the chests in public. For the opium merchants themselves this was not bad business, since they got rid of half a year's supply at a price guaranteed to them by the British government in the person of Captain Elliot, but they all refused to sign bonds required from them by Commissioner Lin not to engage further in the trade of the drug. After this the British retired from Canton to the rocky off-shore island of Hong Kong.

FIGURE 5.4. The Nemesis in action. She is seen here destroying Chinese war junks.

To Commissioner Lin it seemed as if the issue had been settled, once the opium chests had been destroyed upon his orders. As a matter of fact he was interested in encouraging and continuing foreign trade, and he firmly believed that the barbarians were dependent on China: "Foreign countries cannot get along without tea and rhubarb for a single day."

But the destruction of the opium chests by Lin was a *casus belli*, and within a year a British expeditionary force was fighting the Ch'ing empire. The fundamental issue was not merely opium, but equality and trading conditions, and to call the ensuing war the "Opium War" is an oversimplification. The opium problem was merely a symptom of a much graver malady. The American John Quincy Adams recognized this:

> The fundamental principle of the Chinese Empire is anti-commercial. It admits no obligation to hold commercial intercourse with others. It utterly denies the equality of other nations with itself, and even their independence. This is the truth, and, I apprehend, the only question at issue between the governments and nations of Great Britain and China. It is a general, but I believe altogether mistaken opinion that the quarrel is merely for certain chests of opium imported by the British merchants into China, and is a mere incident to the dispute; but no more the cause of war than the throwing overboard of the tea in Boston harbor was the cause of the North American revolution.[6]

The First Anglo-Chinese War, to give it its formal name, began in the summer of 1840 with the arrival of about 10,000 British troops. The British enjoyed, of course, technological superiority over their foes. This superiority of science, in 1840, was embodied in the armed steamer *Nemesis*, a 630-ton iron sidewheel vessel, with a flat bottom which gave her great maneuverability. *Nemesis* carried a crew of 90 and had only two guns, but she appeared invulnerable.

The British blockaded Canton, and then they moved northward along the coast. They carried with them a letter from Palmerston regarding all outstanding issues between the two nations, and they were instructed to deliver that letter to Peking. The British were unsuccessful in their attempt to deliver the letter, and they were persuaded by the Manchu government to return to Canton for the opening of negotiations.

These negotiations were carried on by a shrewd Manchu official, Ch'i-shan, and by Elliot for the British. The result was the Convention of Chuenpi. Under its terms the Chinese agreed to cede the island of Hong Kong and to grant equality of intercourse to the British. However, this convention pleased neither the masters of Ch'i-shan nor those of Captain Elliot. Ch'i-shan was promptly cashiered, his wealth was confiscated by imperial decree, and he himself left Canton in chains, while Elliot was disavowed by his government. Queen Victoria declared that he had "completely disobeyed his instructions and tried to get the lowest terms he could." He was recalled, but at least he was spared the chains.

The failure of these talks led to a second British campaign in August 1841. Its plan was suggested to Palmerston and Sir Henry Pottinger, who

---

[6] Lecture, Massachusetts Historical Society (December, 1841).

was to be in charge of it, by one Jardine, a leading British merchant on the China coast. In order to get the desired peace terms and the opening of a number of ports such as Amoy, Foochow, Ningpo, and Shanghai, he advised that the British military expedition should not only blockade the coast but should also sail up the Yangtze river as far as Nanking, thereby cutting China in half. His advice was followed, and the British advance up the Yangtze was a decisive action, since it was followed by the signing on August 29, 1842, of the Treaty of Nanking, which terminated the First Anglo-Chinese War.

The First Treaty Settlement

In the First Anglo-Chinese War China for the first time faced Western military superiority, and the Manchu dynasty, fearful for its very existence, chose to bow to the West rather than to continue resistance. The advocates of appeasement at court argued that if peace was not made with the barbarian the dynasty might well be undone, as they expected more than just commercial demands from the British, since to the Chinese trade served merely as a cloak for political conquest. Moreover, there was always the constant nightmare for the Manchus of the "traitorous Chinese" waiting for a chance to topple alien rule. To cope with this problem of "rebellious barbarians without and bandits within," the court decided to entrust negotiations into the hands of Ch'i-ying, the son of a rich and corrupt Manchu clansman, who had risen in service by a series of rapid promotions. He was given full powers by the court, but not much in the way of firm directions. The court itself vacillated as to the proper course of action, and it was motivated by a mixture of hopes and fears. Sometimes the court was optimistic, even thinking of recapturing Hong Kong. At other times, such as when the British naval forces captured Chinkiang on the Yangtze and cut the Grand Canal connection to the north, the court was plunged into deepest gloom and was willing to secure peace at any price.

In his negotiations with the British Ch'i-ying at first used his subordinates, who were unable to make definite commitments, but this infuriated the British, who insisted on dealing with an envoy of high rank. Unable to avoid the British demands, Ch'i-ying was finally forced to meet with them in person. His chief aim was to remove barbarians from the Yangtze valley at any cost. He did not inform the emperor of all the British demands, and the formal recognition of equality, upon which the English insisted, was not evident in the documents sent to Peking where the characters for "England" were not written large as were the characters for the "Middle Kingdom."

The Treaty of Nanking marked the beginning of a series of unequal treaties which China was forced to enter into with the West. Under its terms China ceded the island of Hong Kong to the English, and she also agreed to pay indemnities for the war and for the destruction of the opium which had preceded it. Five Chinese ports were to be opened to foreign trade: Canton, Amoy, Foochow, Ningpo, and Shanghai. At these ports foreign merchants had the right to trade, reside, and to maintain a consul to look after their interests. The monopoly of the cohong was terminated, and a uniform and moderate tariff was to be drawn up. Finally, the schedule of customs duties was to be fixed and was not to be increased except by mutual consent. This last clause was of special importance, since under it China was no longer able to raise her import and export duties as she wished. It marked the beginning of inequality, a new era in Chinese history.

In 1844 the Treaty of Wanghsia was signed with Caleb Cushing of the United States, and it included a clause concerning extraterritoriality, by which the Chinese gave up their right to try foreigners according to Chinese law. Foreign residents came under the jurisdiction of their consuls instead. With these two treaties China lost judicial as well as financial autonomy. Finally, in the Treaty of Whampoa signed with France in 1844, the Chinese agreed to tolerate the Christian faith. These three treaties, Nanking, Wanghsia, and Whampoa, collectively are referred to as the First Treaty Settlement. These and other rights granted by China in these treaties were extended to other foreign powers on the basis of the so-called "most-favored-nation" clause.

Despite the conclusion of the First Treaty Settlement, the Ch'ing continued to think in the old terms. Ch'i-ying's ideas were to use trade as bait, to mollify the British with a treaty, and to win the confidence and friendship of Sir Henry Pottinger. In his memorial to the court at Peking, Ch'i-ying stated that one must secure the foreigners' allegiance by deigning to treat them compassionately, to get them under peaceful control by bringing them within the Confucian order, and to subdue them through negotiation. His attitude was well summarized in his own writings:

> With this type of people from outside the bounds of civilization if we adhered to the proper forms of official communications and let them be weighed according to the status of superior and inferior truly it would be of no advantage in the essential business of subduing and conciliating them. To fight with them over empty names and get no substantial result would not be so good as to pass over these small matters and achieve our larger aims.[7]

However, these "small matters" were exceedingly important. Because of them, and because of the First Treaty Settlement, China found herself in an inferior position for the first time since she had been conquered by the nomads of the northern borderland.

BASIC DATES

1557	Macao founded by the Portuguese
1610	Matteo Ricci's death in Peking
1630–1662	Dutch in Formosa
1637	First English ship at Canton
After 1700	Regular trade at Canton
1704	Mission of de Tournon

[7] T. F. Wade, *Correspondence Relative to the Earl of Elgin's Special Mission to China and Japan, 1857–1859* (London, 1859), p. 175.

1719	Mission of Mezzabarba
1742	Rites Controversy decided against Jesuits
1757–1842	European trade restricted to Canton
1793	Macartney embassy
1816	Amherst embassy
1834	End of Company monopoly and mission of Lord Napier
1839	Lin Tse-hsü burns opium at Canton
1839–1842	First Anglo-Chinese War
1842–1844	First Treaty Settlement

SUPPLEMENTARY READING

Fairbank, J. K. *The United States and China,* rev. ed. Cambridge, Mass., 1972.

Hsü, Immanuel C. Y. *The Rise of Modern China.* New York, 1970, Chaps. 7–8.

Hudson, G. F. *Europe and China.* London, 1931. An excellent study of cultural interrelations.

Latourette, K. S. *The Chinese: Their History and Culture.* New York, 1964.

Morse, H. B. *International Relations of the Chinese Empire,* Vol. I. London, 1910.

Rowbotham, A. H. *Missionary and Mandarin.* Berkeley, Calif., 1942. A study of the Jesuits at the court of Peking.

Spence, J. *To Change China.* Boston, 1969.

ADVANCED READING

Chang, H. P. *Commissioner Lin and the Opium War.* Cambridge, Mass., 1964.

Chang, T. *Sino-Portuguese relations.* Leiden, 1934.

Clyde, P. H. *United States Policy Toward China: Diplomatic and Public Documents, 1839–1939.* Durham, N.C., 1940.

Dulles, F. R. *The Old China Trade.* Princeton, N.J., 1946.

Fairbank, J. K. *Trade and Diplomacy on the China Coast, 1842–1854.* Cambridge, Mass., 1953. An excellent book on the events of and subsequent to the first treaty settlement.

Fu, L. S. *A Documentary Chronicle of Sino-Western Relations (1644–1820).* Tucson, 1966.

Greenberg, M. *British Trade and the Opening of China, 1800–1842.* Cambridge, Mass., 1951. A careful study written from the point of view of the expansion of British trade.

Holt, E. *The Opium Wars in China.* London, 1964.

Hunter, W. C. *The Fan Kwae at Canton Before Treaty Days, 1825–1844.* London, 1882. A good description of the life of the foreigners at Canton.

MacNair, H. F. *Modern Chinese History: Selected Readings.* Shanghai, 1927.

Morse, H. B. *The Chronicles of the East India Company Trading to China, 1635–1834.* Oxford, 1929.

Morse, H. B. and H. F. MacNair. *Far Eastern International Relations.* Boston, 1931.

Pritchard, E. *Crucial Years of Anglo-Chinese Relations.* Urbana, Ill., 1930.

Reichwein, A. *China and Europe: Intellectual and Artistic Contacts in the Eighteenth Century.* New York, 1925. Reprinted, 1968.

Staunton, G. *An Authentic Account of an Embassy from the King of Great Britain to the Emperor of China.* Philadelphia, 1799. The contemporary account of the Macartney mission; full of interesting material.

Teng, S. and J. K. Fairbank, eds. *China's Response to the West: A Documentary Survey, 1839–1923.* Cambridge, Mass., 1954. An excellent collection.

Waley, A. *The Opium War Through Chinese Eyes.* London, 1958.

Chapter 6

Tokugawa Japan

ESTABLISHMENT OF THE TOKUGAWA REGIME

After his victory at Sekigahara in 1600 (see page 558, Volume I), Tokugawa Ieyasu moved swiftly to consolidate his power. Tokugawa relatives (*shimpan*) were given strategically located fiefs, while the already established feudal lords (*daimyō*) were divided into two groups, according to a very simple division: those who had actively supported his cause and those who had not. The latter included both the opposition camp and those who were merely lukewarm before the decisive battle. To his supporters he gave additional land and, when possible, strategically located land. From the others, in so far as he could, he took land, either adding it to the Tokugawa domain directly or putting it under the control of lords who had supported him. The loyal feudal lords were called hereditary daimyo (*fudai*); the suspect lords were called "outside" daimyo (*tozama*). Individually the holdings of the hereditary lords were not large, few of them reaching the level of 100,000 koku (a rice income measure of land value), so that even by augmenting these Ieyasu needed have no fear of allies turning into rivals. The Tokugawa holdings after the redistribution amounted to 4,200,000 koku. A number of the outside lords had held huge estates, some almost on a par with Tokugawa, and after the redistribution these remained larger than any except the Tokugawa estates themselves. However, since the largest of these, Maeda of Kaga and Shimazu of Satsuma, were of one million koku, the vast superiority of the Tokugawa position can be seen both in terms of outright territorial holdings and directly received income. Nothing short of a coalition of the outside lords could hope to challenge the Tokugawa, and, although eventually such a coalition did develop, the measures which Ieyasu and the other early Tokugawa took proved sufficient to make such a development impossible for over two hundred and fifty years.

Actually on the matter of land redistribution Ieyasu, with typical caution, did not push too far, stopping short of what might have given rise to desperate rebellion against him. And he relied on a system of checks and balances rather than on a crude centralization of power to maintain the Tokugawa position. For the time being Hideyori was left at Osaka castle, as feudal lord of some 600,000 koku, and in 1603 Ieyasu received the title *shōgun* from a compliant emperor. With typical reserve he kept the title personally only two years, then resigned to establish his son as shogun while he worked behind the scenes for eleven years more, until his death in 1616, to perfect a system which would perpetuate Tokugawa family rule, whether his shogunal descendants were able or inept.

The Tokugawa System

By 1616 "Tokugawa stability" had not been entirely established, though giant strides had been made toward its achievement, but by the mid-point of the reign of Ieyasu's grandson, Iemitsu (1622–1651), the finishing touches had been applied. Even before Ieyasu's death the last potential focal point of revolt was eliminated. This was young Hideyori, who, after Sekigahara had been left at Osaka, married a granddaughter of Ieyasu and was surrounded with Tokugawa advisors. At first Ieyasu apparently thought this sufficient to prevent the revival of a "Toyotomi faction," but in an interview in 1611 he found the young man to be intelligent and astute, and thereafter a breach developed. In 1614 on the occasion of the dedication of a great Buddhist bell in Osaka, Ieyasu discovered that his name had been "improperly placed" and he took the position that he had been insulted. The following year there were "rumors of rebellion" from Osaka and in that year the Tokugawa forces attacked Osaka castle, took it, and after Hideyori was killed in the fray, they hunted down and killed his heirs. With no further rallying point for revolt, the outside lords subsided completely to the point where in the time of Iemitsu they accepted the institution of "alternate residence" (*sankin kōtai*) at the insistence of the shogun. Each feudal lord was required to maintain an "alternate residence" in Edo, the Tokugawa capital, where he must spend part of each year and where family members, wives and sons especially, were required to live in the intervening months literally as hostages of the shogun. The "alternate residence" had the double function of putting the various feudal lords under the physical control of the shogun during part of the year and of burdening them with great expenses. Each daimyo was required to bring along a certain number of retainers, relative to the size of his fief, and had to pay the expense of the journey for these, their servants and various others who made up the feudal entourage, as well as the upkeep of a sumptuous establishment in Edo to maintain his standing and prestige.

While the road to Edo was always open for the performance of alternate residence, roads and bridges leading from one fief to another were carefully manned and watched by agents of the shogun. Barriers blocked the traveler's way at every turn. Castle building was carefully watched and duly reported. The statement "a castle with a wall more than 10 feet thick by 30 feet high is harmful to a fief; high walls and deep moats are

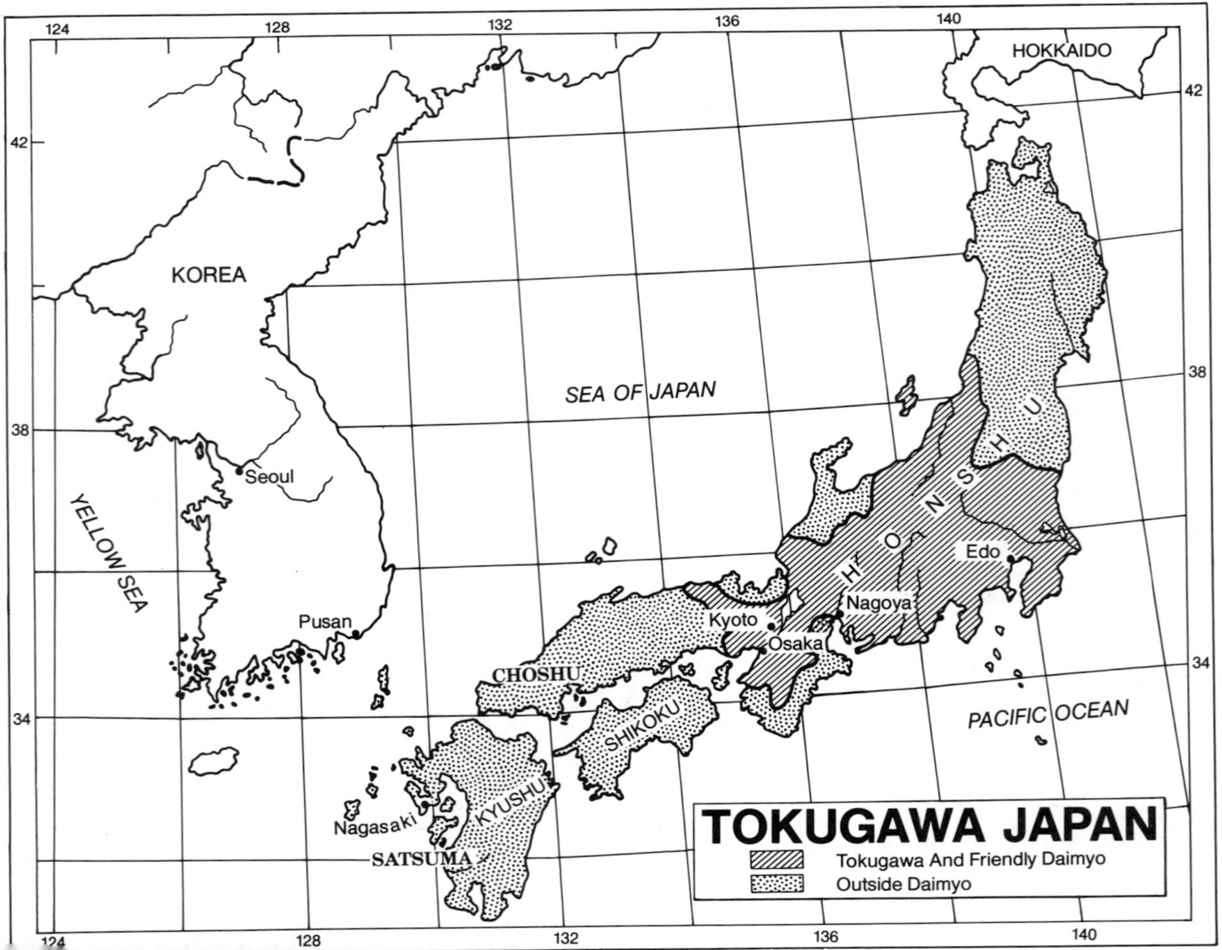
TOKUGAWA JAPAN
Tokugawa And Friendly Daimyo
Outside Daimyo
HOKKAIDO
KOREA
SEA OF JAPAN
YELLOW SEA
PACIFIC OCEAN
HONSHU
SHIKOKU
KYUSHU
CHOSHU
SATSUMA
Seoul
Pusan
Nagasaki
Kyoto
Osaka
Nagoya
Edo
124
128
132
136
140
42
38
34

the causes of upheavals," represented shogunal thinking on this matter. Also realizing that "nefarious plots" could develop out of marriage alliances among the feudal lords' families, the Tokugawa took precautions in this regard, emphasizing that "marriages must not be privately arranged." In addition the shogun maintained a widespread system of censors and spies who reported independently of the regular feudal bureaucracy.

Clearly the Tokugawa system was designed to keep rival lords in check, but it was also a system which supported the "legitimate" aspirations of the entire feudal warrior or *samurai* class of which the Tokugawa were the leading members. During the sixteenth century there had been a great deal of class mobility in Japan arising out of civil war, the development of trade and commerce, and contact with foreigners. Hideyoshi himself seems to have risen from a peasant background. But the Tokugawa wanted no more Hideyoshis, and their system was designed to block vertical movement between classes just as much as it was designed to inhibit horizontal movement between fiefs.

Thus the Tokugawa aided the feudal lords in carefully defining the position and status of the samurai class, emphasizing the latter's role as the administrators of a feudal bureaucracy and their singular right to be armed. Hence developed the concept of the two-sworded samurai, who was privileged, if offended, to cut down a commoner on the roadside without further ado. There was an elaborate code for the samurai, the *Buke Sho-Hatto*, first promulgated in 1615, which emphasized the duties of that class, but also emphasized its superiority.

The economic position of the samurai was based on rice income received from the lord's domain, collected, of course, from the labors of the farmers. This was a factor in stabilizing the samurai position of control in the early Tokugawa period but, as we shall see, later developments tended to make it less decisive.

Other classes of society were carefully separated from the samurai and strictly regulated. The court aristocracy and the emperor at Kyoto were considered "very precious and decorative, like gold and silver," but not so useful as the samurai class. Hence the court, including the emperor, was limited to cultural activities. The ways of the ancients, poetical composition, and such things as flowers, birds, snow, and wind, and the moon were recommended as fine subjects for study. The ranks of court nobles were very carefully established with the shogun as the arbiter, and shogunal authority guarded the court and its environs carefully, preventing unauthorized people from approaching. The farmers were lauded as essential to society and its chief productive element. But they were reminded that "any combination of persons for whatever purpose" was unlawful, and were urged to till their fields in the daytime, make straw mats and other useful things at night, to eat coarse grain and wear coarse clothing, and to pay attention to the distinctions between the ranks of society.

Lowest on the social scale, except for outcasts, were townspeople, including both artisans and merchants. This class was regarded as much less valuable than farmers, especially the merchants who, being completely unproductive, were the target of many special regulations to emphasize their inferiority. Amongst both farmers, who lived in village or hamlet clusters, and townspeople a system of collective responsibility laid the weight of feudal authority on every household. Each house was linked with four others in a five-house group and required to report unusual happenings in any of them to the authorities, under pain of sharing the responsibility of a "guilty" party.

Foreign Relations

One of the key problems which Ieyasu and Iemitsu faced in their effort to organize a stable and self-perpetuating Tokugawa-dominated political and social system was that of foreign relations. Ieyasu very quickly reversed Hideyoshi's expansionist projects, recalled the troops from Korea, and proceeded to make settlements both with Korea and China which permitted the resumption of friendly, though restricted, relations.

Korean relations with Japan were defined by both sides as "neighborly," which placed them immediately in marked contrast to Korean relations with China which came under the heading of "serving the great" and which emphasized Korea's status as a dependent state of the Chinese empire. Between Japan and Korea in Tokugawa times there was no hint of subordination on the part of Korea; in fact, if anything the Koreans assumed a rather superior attitude. Thus, a Japanese trading settlement at Pusan was closely circumscribed, which the Japanese accepted for the sake of trade. Occasionally envoys came from Korea, particularly to congratulate a new shogun on his accession, but these were far from humble and through most of the period they came only as far as the island of Tsushima, where Tokugawa envoys met them and seem to have paid their expenses. Actually, it was the daimyo of Tsushima who was principally interested in this Korean exchange, for his island location between Japan and Korea made it important and profitable for him to maintain good feeling between the two sides.

While the bitter hostility and arrogance toward China generated by Hideyoshi was dissipated, the Tokugawa by no means resumed the humble "King of Japan to Emperor of China" relationship of the Ashikaga shoguns. Instead the Chinese "permitted" Japan not to send tributary missions, which the Tokugawa certainly would not have done anyway, and so official relationships between the two governments were almost nonexistent. However, there was some trade between Japanese and Chinese merchants at Nagasaki and, although it was much curtailed after 1641, it persisted through the Tokugawa period. The most important relationship between Tokugawa Japan and China was cultural, and since no Japanese was allowed to go to China, at least officially, this cultural influence seems to have been the result of the importation of Chinese books in the Nagasaki trade, which will be considered subsequently in the discussion of intellectual currents in Tokugawa Japan.

The principal problem of foreign relations for the early Tokugawa concerned the Westerners, chiefly Portuguese, Spanish, and, to a lesser extent,

Dutch and English, who had found a ready welcome in the troubled Japan of the sixteenth century by bringing arms and other goods to Japanese merchants who transmitted them to eager feudal lords. Also Catholic Christianity had found many converts, whether by genuine conviction or for the tactical purpose pursued by Nobunaga of undermining the powerful Buddhist sects of sixteenth-century Japan (see Volume I, Chapter 27).

When Ieyasu came to power he did not seem to have clearly defined attitudes towards the Westerners. He was mainly concerned with enhancing the fortunes of the Tokugawa house and with stabilizing its regime in Japan, and as was characteristic of this calculating man, he seems to have considered the relations with Western countries in terms of what they contributed to or detracted from this larger purpose. Probably the key to understanding Ieyasu's attitude to Westerners lies in the question which he posed to them: would they come to Edo? He seems to have disliked from the first the fact that the Western trade, whether Portuguese, Spanish, English, or Dutch, was going mainly to the northern Kyushu and southwestern Honshu area, where some of his most potent rivals were located. But he seem to have had no original animosity for the Westerners as such. In fact, he specifically invited the Spanish, through a Spanish priest brought before him in 1598, to visit Edo, trade with Tokugawa vassals, and "teach them how to develop silver mines." The Spanish did send a number of ships from the Philippines to eastern Japan and thence on to Mexico, but they asked Ieyasu to expel the Dutch, which he refused to do. Indeed, he was befriending the Dutch too and hoping to get them also to come to Edo.

Ieyasu first came into contact with Dutch traders through the visit of the ship *de Liefde*, which arrived in 1600, and which had aboard an Englishman, Will Adams, who quickly won his favor. When the Dutch captain returned to Holland with an invitation to trade, Adams stayed with Ieyasu to give advice on shipbuilding and act as a general advisor on foreign trade matters. Adams, while getting in some good words for the English as well as the Dutch, warned Ieyasu against their Spanish rivals and may have succeeded in arousing suspicions of them in Ieyasu. But when the Dutch returned to Japan in 1609 to found a factory in line with Ieyasu's invitation, they found it more convenient to establish themselves in northern Kyushu than in the Edo area. Similarly, when the English came in 1613, they established themselves alongside the Dutch factory, rejecting a specific invitation proffered through Will Adams to come to eastern Japan.

Meanwhile Ieyasu's suspicions of Christianity grew. In the so-called Arima Incident (1612) he found a Christian dealing with other Christians in some chicanery regarding the transfer of a fief in northern Kyushu. As a result the principals were executed and, in addition, Ieyasu withheld their revenue as punishment for other Christian officers. Although this plot had little to do with Christianity, he seems to have regarded it as a Christian affair. About the same time the so-called Okubo Conspiracy involving a Christian in an embezzlement case resulted in an order for the destruction of Christian churches in Kyoto and the expulsion of foreign priests to Nagasaki. In 1613 the feudal lord of Sendai in northern Honshu, Date

Masamune, startled Ieyasu by sending an elaborate mission of some sixty people to Mexico, Spain, and then to the Vatican without first getting specific permission from the shogunate. And in 1615 there were Christian banners and Christian military leaders in the opposition to the Tokugawa at the reduction of Osaka castle.

Ieyasu died in 1616, disappointed in the failure of the Westerners to take up his invitation to come to the Edo area, and increasingly inclined to persecute Christians, although he himself never decreed a death penalty for a foreign missionary. However, in the next twenty years his successors concluded that Christianity must be exterminated and Westerners driven from Japan before the Tokugawa regime could feel secure. In 1617 four foreign priests were killed and in 1622 nine more. During the course of the 1620's a widespread and deliberate persecution of Japanese Christians developed, whereby many kinds of tortures were devised to force them to recant. In the face of this most Japanese Christians, especially those of the samurai class, gave up the faith, but some persisted. Many of those who held firmly to their Christian beliefs lived in the Nagasaki area.

The English, whose trade had never been profitable, withdrew from Japan in 1623 and the Spaniards, accused of various plots, were expelled in 1624. The Dutch and the Portuguese remained, however, the Dutch becoming more and more obsequious toward the Japanese, whose animosity they had excited by establishing control over part of Formosa and becoming involved in incidents there with Japanese traders. The Portuguese tried to do business as usual at Nagasaki but with increasing obstacles placed in their way. The climax came in 1637–1638 in the form of the Shimabara Revolt, a rising of Japanese peasants in the Nagasaki area. There the exactions of a local feudal lord touched off a revolt in which some thirty thousand people, armed with scythes, sickles, spears, and a few hundred matchlocks, challenged the feudal authority and waged a desperate struggle. They brought forth banners with crosses, which seemed to the authorities to indicate the existence of a Christian plot, and which brought down the wrath of the shogunate as a mere peasant riot might not have done. Shogunal commanders were sent to organize the forces of Kyushu in suppressing the uprising, and it is interesting that the samurai army, though vastly superior numerically, was defeated in several encounters. However, the rebels gradually ran out of supplies and were eventually forced to Hara castle and its rocky point on the Shimabara peninsula, where in the end the whole force was massacred. Immediately thereafter, in 1639, an order expelling the Portuguese was issued and shortly a definitive policy of preventing any Japanese from going abroad was instituted. The Dutch had handled themselves with the greatest circumspection in this crisis, emphasizing that they had no missionary intention and no sympathy for the rebels. One of their ships actually fired on the beleaguered castle to help the government forces quell the revolt. At any rate, when the final decision was made, the Dutch were informed that they might continue a very limited relationship with Japan. They were required to move their establishment to a tiny island, Deshima, in Nagasaki harbor, where, under very close supervision and maddening restrictions, they were allowed to continue their trade on a very small scale.

Neo-Confucianism

In addition to restraining feudal rivals, regulating feudal classes, and excluding foreigners, the early Tokugawa shoguns added an intellectual component to their search for stability. This was Neo-Confucianism, called Shushi Learning in Japan. Neo-Confucianism, it will be remembered, had been developed by the great Chinese philosopher, Chu Hsi (in Japanese Shushi), and his school during the late Sung period (see Chapter 20, Volume I) had found great favor in official circles there, especially in the Ming period. The first important advocate of this Neo-Confucianism in Japan was Fujiwara Seika (1561–1617), a Zen Buddhist priest who, becoming dissatisfied with what he considered to be a lack of interest of society in Zen, learned Neo-Confucianist doctrines from a Chinese visitor to Japan and became an advocate of that philosophy. He met Tokugawa Ieyasu about 1592, the two became good friends, and Ieyasu employed him as a teacher at Edo.

Among others, Fujiwara Seika taught Hayashi Razan (1583–1657), who took over his school at Edo in 1608. At this time Ieyasu was developing and promulgating the basic laws of the Tokugawa regime, and Hayashi seems to have worked closely with government leaders in working out philosophic precepts which reinforced the Tokugawa position. Beyond that he and his students began work on a mammoth history of Japan, called *The Comprehensive Mirror of Japan* (Honchō Tsugan), which although not completed for many years, reviewed the whole history of Japan in such a way as to justify the emergence of the Tokugawa regime and to counsel loyalty to feudal hierarchy. Feudal warriors, who had been all too warlike in the preceding era, were now urged to add Neo-Confucian learning to the military arts as necessary to the performance of their duty as samurai-administrators of feudal estates. Neo-Confucianism gradually became a basic philosophy of the ruling class in Tokugawa Japan. Neo-Confucianism purported to explain the "natural order" of the universe and by giving the Tokugawa political and social structure an important place in this natural order, the official scholars of Tokugawa Japan were able to establish a strong ideological base for the system instituted by the early Tokugawa shoguns. Only when irregularities developed was the concept of the Tokugawa regime as a part of natural order questioned in intellectual circles.

TOKUGAWA ECONOMY AND SOCIETY

While the Tokugawa have been censured in Western books for the brutality which accompanied their institution of the seclusion policy, for the time being that policy effectively turned aside the first stage of European expansion to Japan. Also there was a certain honesty which accepted the loss of such benefits of foreign contact as a potentially rich trade and opportunity for national expansion in seeking the security that isolation presumably would bring.[1]

At any rate, by the middle of the seventeenth century the Tokugawa had achieved stability based on isolation and a samurai-dominated class structure. "Pax Tokugawa," which gave Japan more than two hundred years of domestic peace and freedom from foreign strife, was a considerable achievement, for it has been rarely matched in world history. But developments within Japan itself during the period indicated that its foundations of social rigidity and isolation were shaky. Signs of ultimate breakdown were the gradual impoverishment of the samurai class, even as it maintained its monopoly of political power and social prestige; the gradual achievement of economic power by the merchant class, even though it remained politically impotent and low in the social scale; increasing restiveness on the part of the farmers; and a growing alienation of intellectuals from the Shushi Neo-Confucian norm. Since these seem in retrospect to have been rather natural developments, one could almost say that the Tokugawa regime was doomed from the beginning. We shall take up these phenomena one by one though it will be observed that they are interdependent.

Economic Changes

Economically speaking it could be said that the warrior class ruined itself. This occurred on three levels, at the very top in the Edo shogunate; among the daimyo, lords of the great feudal estates; and among the lower samurai (their feudal retainers), the administrators of those estates. The shogunate under Ieyasu began in a frugal way. Ieyasu argued that "if a stringent economy is not followed then the state will not be governed well. Whoever becomes extravagant will automatically fall into distress." He wanted a full treasury, sought to control and develop mines to obtain precious metals, and exhorted the members of the ruling class to be thrifty. However, after his death, signs of extravagance at the highest level of government were not long in appearing. Indeed, it is ironic that the first great extravagance involved the erection during the reign of Ieyasu's grandson, Iemitsu, of a huge mausoleum at Nikko to the memory of Ieyasu. Nevertheless, the finances of the central government were relatively good until the middle of the seventeenth century.

Then a great fire at Edo in 1657 required the shogunate to expend huge amounts of money in reconstruction, including some 800,000 ryō for the rebuilding of Edo castle itself. The annual income of the shogunate was about 770,000 ryō, which is indicative of the relative size of this expenditure. Repeated famines in the late 1600's demanded aid from the central government and by the end of the seventeenth century the shogun, Tsunayoshi, who was himself very extravagant, in 1703 found to his chagrin that there was not money enough in the treasury to finance a projected

---

[1] A contrast can be drawn with the later American experiment in "partial isolation," which in a sense sought the advantages but refused the disadvantages of separation from the rest of the world.

pilgrimage to Nikko. Taxes were immediately increased, but in addition a new idea was entertained, that of recasting and debasing the coinage. This seemed like a windfall for a time, but a brilliant economist and government official, Arai Hakuseki, in 1712 pointed out that such measures could lead to disaster. Arai had some success in stabilizing the coinage, and he turned a very suspicious eye on the small Dutch settlement at Deshima, thinking that perhaps precious metal in Japan was leaking out through that point. This resulted in greater restriction on the Dutch trade, but the real problem lay in the fact that the population in Japan had increased to near thirty million and internal commerce required an expanded supply of money. After Arai there were no more serious efforts to stabilize the coinage and debasement was indulged in again and again.

Among the daimyo similar financial troubles were developing. One of the largest factors in daimyo expenditures was the shogunal inspired practice of alternate residence at Edo. Over one-half the total expenditure of every daimyo went into the upkeep of his establishment in Edo and into frequent travel expenses from the capital. At first daimyo and their retinues came to Edo because they were required to do so, but they found life there so pleasant and so exciting that they were soon establishing miniature Edos all over the country. The relatively isolated, mountain-fastness type of feudal fortress of the civil war period disappeared as peace and stability prevailed. Since there was less reason to guard the frontiers of an individual fief, many fiefs were consolidated; and when a feudal lord obtained sufficient means, he would erect a grand castle and around it a "castle town," which, as the administrative center of his domain, was soon populated with samurai retainers and guards, the latter hardly necessary any longer. Samurai constituted over fifty per cent of the population of these castle towns, and though their populations were small in comparison with Edo's million, like Edo they were centers of consumption where the luxuries of life might be had. Not only the lord, but practically all his samurai sought these luxuries, and even if a samurai could not gain entry into the Edo establishment, he was a poor manipulator if he could not get to the castle town of his own domain.

However, the upkeep of the towns was expensive and to obtain the necessary capital the daimyo and their retainers pressed the farming population ever harder for taxes. Their "agrarian mentality" considered wealth in terms of land, products of the land, and people who worked the land. Hence farmers, while given great praise by their feudal superiors as the foundation of society, were squeezed unmercifully. Although basic land taxes remained at approximately fifty per cent of the yield, many extras, public labor taxes, supplementary rice levies, special taxes on villages near highways, and so-called taxes on "little things" were added, as were completely illegal exactions by individual tax collectors. Despite the fact that the amount of land under cultivation increased remarkably from about five million acres in 1600 to some eleven and a half million acres in 1868, the condition of farmers deteriorated steadily.

The extent of rural poverty may be estimated from the widespread resort to infanticide and abortion to keep down the number of mouths to feed, and from the increase in tenancy. Farmer discontent is shown graphically in the increasing number of farmers' uprisings which occurred as the Tokugawa era progressed. These were aimed at local grievances: an unusually grasping tax collector, the appointment of new officials whose stipends had to be borne by the locality, special levies and such. They did not develop into a widespread rebellion against feudal superiors, but their frequency shows that they represented a national rather than a local phenomenon. In addition, some farmers, especially those who lived near cities, began to be discontented with merely "grasping the hoe" as they were enjoined to do. They wanted better clothing and housing, so that even if they were fairly well off by minimum standards, they fell into debt for "extras."

Rise of the Merchant Class

It was the merchant class which profited from the mistakes and appetites of their betters. In a very real sense, Japan's fourth-ranking class, the merchants and their various townspeople allies, who ranked beneath aristocrats, samurai, and farmers, captured Tokugawa Japan. This they did without demanding or acquiring political power, merely by catering to the frivolous tastes of the other classes. So thorough was this capture, it is interesting to note, that the most successful merchants tended more and more to identify themselves with the feudal regime to the extent that in its last days, when they had the opportunity to strike for political power, they were not inclined to do so. Instead they seemed to hope for an indefinite prolongation of that old regime which had once heaped so many disabilities on them, and only at the last moment when its impending downfall was obvious did some of them switch sides.[2]

The secret of the success of the merchant class lay basically in the development of urban life in Japan. And since urbanization is a widespread phenomenon inseparable from the development of higher civilization itself, it seems unwise in the case of Japan to view it merely as a class struggle between merchants and samurai. Rather it might be said that those who came to live in the cities were seeking a higher standard of living, better shelter, more conveniences, and a more pleasurable and sophisticated existence than that afforded by the farming village.

To supply the needs of the towns came the merchants. Making connections with the great merchant houses of Osaka, which survived from the open trade days of the sixteenth century, they could arrange the marketing of the rice which poured into the lord's granaries. From the merchants the lord received the money which he and his retainers so sorely needed for the upkeep of their sumptuous establishments and their pilgrimages to Edo, but in the hands of merchants the stores of rice became a type of fluid wealth, which could be held for times of scarcity or transported to consum-

[2] On this point it may be that small village merchants and itinerant peddlers, who operated outside the area of direct Tokugawa control and had close contacts with the wealthy peasants, played a larger role in undoing feudalism than did the wealthy merchant houses, but this matter needs further study.

ing areas to be sold at immense profits. The case of one merchant establishment, called Yodoya, may be cited as an example of the way in which merchant prosperity developed. The foundation of the fortune of Yodoya lay in a commission given by the daimyo Maeda in the sixteenth century to market one hundred thousand koku of rice for him. By the end of the seventeenth century the master of this merchant house was in the financial service of the lords of thirty-three fiefs in western Japan, possessed forty-eight warehouses, and maintained a magnificent residence.

Merchants who began as marketing agents for individual daimyo soon became independent and were operating on a very large regional or even countrywide basis. Since the merchants had no political power, it may be asked, how could they force members of the samurai class to pay their bills? It seems they used subtle coercion of various types, mainly involving the credit of a particular lord or samurai. Sometimes they were so bold as to place "no credit" signs on the doors of the residences of samurai who did not pay their debts. If this were impossible, by banding together in official or unofficial liaison, the merchants of an area could bring a samurai to heel by refusing to cooperate in his business needs. Indeed, merchants began to develop a kind of "protestant ethic" about their business (shingaku) in which they held that making an honest profit was a reward for service not unlike the samurai's stipend.

TOKUGAWA CULTURE AND THOUGHT

Both a reflection and a cause of samurai economic discomfiture can be found in the cultural sphere amidst the emerging prosperity of a bourgeois class in Tokugawa Japan. By the Genroku era (1688–1704) the merchants and their townspeople adherents were not only enjoying literature, art, and the theater, which in earlier periods had been largely reserved to court aristocrats and samurai, but they were setting the pace and the standards, with their "betters" finding the new bourgeois culture too exciting to resist. In every town, and especially in Edo and Osaka, there emerged an amusement quarter, liberally staffed with entertainers and entertainment of many varieties. In this Ukiyo, the "Floating World," any man from any class who had money and was willing to spend it could find release from the restrictions, the duties, and the drabness of feudal society. Here geisha, who might be prostitutes but who were also accomplished actresses, musicians, and conversationalists, held court nightly, and bath houses, restaurants, sake shops, and theaters flourished.

The government saw a certain subversive tendency in these trends and tried to legislate against the gaiety. One regulation required all roles in the Kabuki popular theater to be taken by men. However, the Floating World was elusive. While Kabuki was somewhat restricted for a time by the males-only regulation, a completely uninhibited puppet theater called Bunraku arose in Osaka and began to set a pace which Kabuki later copied. Printing now received a tremendous impetus from the use of movable type, knowledge of which had been obtained from Korea in the late sixteenth

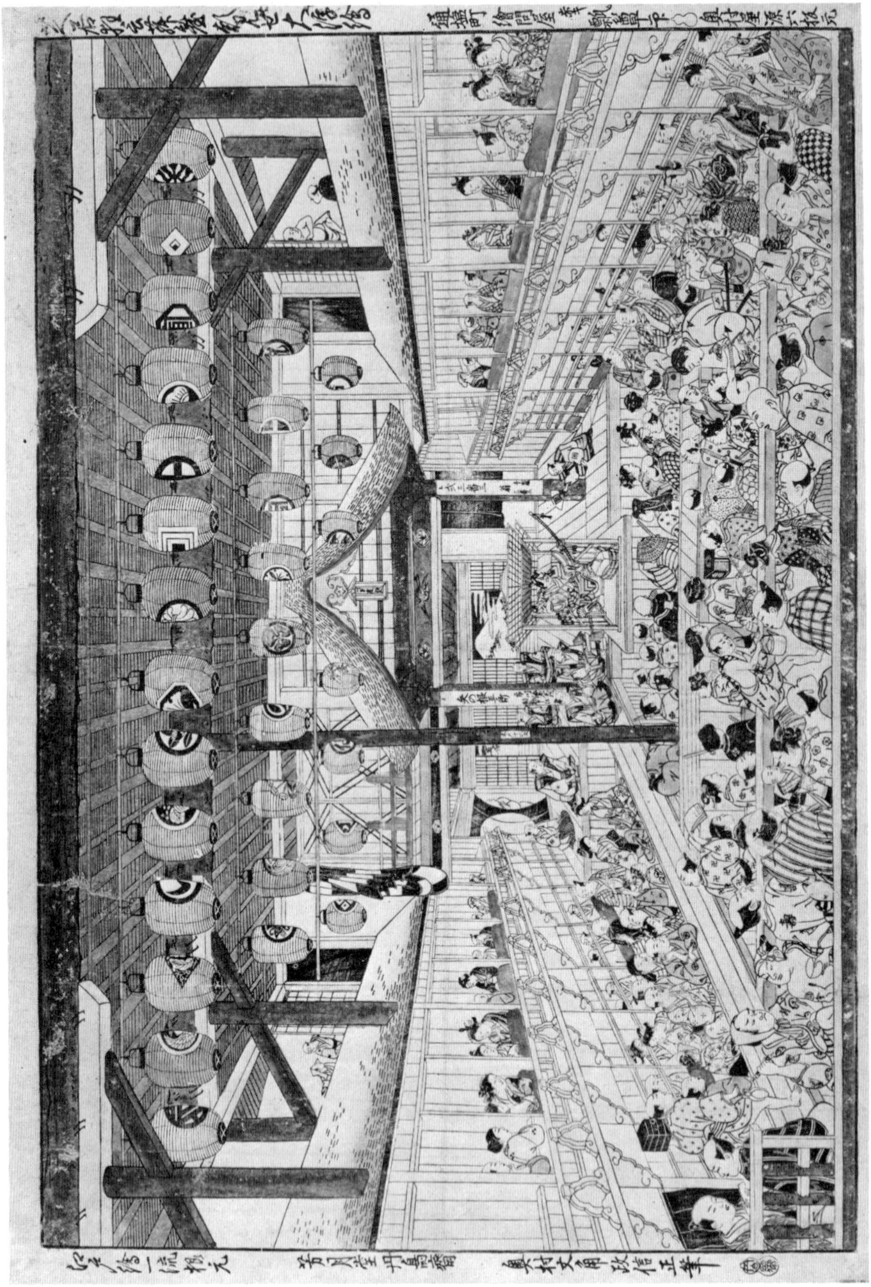

century. This made possible the cheap production and widespread distribution of novels, plays, and advertisements which edified the popular taste. Sophisticated developments in the technique of making woodcut prints made possible the distribution of popular art which also gained its inspiration from city life. The chief subjects of both art and literature were romance, adventure, and some mild social satire, the latter frequently taking the form of low class townspeople appearing to possess many of the virtues which samurai were supposed to have. There was also a great deal of unashamed ribaldry and sex in the production.

Literature

Chikamatsu Monzaemon (1653–1725) stands far above the other writers of his time. He was Japan's greatest dramatist and can be ranked with Kalidasa and Shakespeare. In the fifty-one plays he produced he utilized both poetry and prose and proved himself a master of comedy, tragedy, and the historical drama. He wrote especially for the puppet-theater, seemingly because it was a freer medium at the time, but his plays were later adapted to live Kabuki. He had a remarkable ability to keep his audience on edge, even in the loosely knit historical plays, which mixed history and fiction for this purpose. The most enduring of these, still popular in motion pictures, is *Chushingura*, the story of the Forty-seven *Rōnin* (masterless warriors) who killed a shogunal official to avenge their dead master and paid for the deed with their lives. Based on events of 1702–3, the play was laid in the fifteenth century to confuse censors, who were further confused by the idealistic handling of the loyalty theme. Another historical play is *The Battles of Koxinga* (*Kokusenya Kassen*), the story of the half-Japanese Ming partisan who held out on Formosa against the Manchus. Perhaps better known and loved by his audiences were Chikamatsu's domestic plays, which used the themes of duty and sentiment frequently in opposition to one another. In these dramas he often showed common people, caught in a net of conflicting obligations, rising to remarkable heights of courage, and on his pages many a townsman dies for love as a feudal warrior might be expected to die for his lord.

More cynical than Chikamatsu but fully as popular was Ihara Saikaku (died 1693) who also centered his activities in Osaka and wrote prolifically, both novels and sketches of contemporary city life. Since he did not have "a single Chinese character in his belly," he wrote in the language of the newly semiliterate townsman. His principal themes were sex and money, and schemers and scoundrels were his heroes. His titles such as *Five Amorous Women* and *The Man Who Spent His Life at Lovemaking* suggest why his works were in such demand.

Takizawa Bakin (1767–1848) also loved scoundrels, and he gave some of his stories adventurous twists which made them delightful, if incredible. Jippenshu Ikku (1775–1831) produced a rollicking tale of two Falstaffian

FIGURE 6.1 (opposite). A contemporary Japanese print showing the interior of the Kabuki theatre in Edo in the seventeenth century.

FIGURE 6.2. *Kiyomasu print of a Kabuki actor, Fujimura Handaya, as a courtesan. The actor, dressed for his role, is not distinguishable from women as portrayed by the same artist. The robes are exceedingly elegant.*

characters, lovable cowards, who traveled along the Tōkaidō,[3] from Edo to Kyoto, like samurai in reverse. They engaged in all sorts of adventures which show them to be superstitious, fools, and liars, yet lovable all the while.

The Woodcut Print

If the literature of the Floating World, except for Chikamatsu, was perhaps too bawdy to be great, this cannot be said of the art. In the woodcut medium popular prints were produced by the thousands, as illustrations for stories, plays, theater posters and so on, with actresses, courtesans, "frail

---

[3] The eastern sea road between Kyoto and Edo.

FIGURE 6.3. A woodblock print of three geisha by Utamaro, a master of the art of the Floating World. Utamaro is especially famous for his studies of women.

beauties," "robust beauties," and even "foreign beauties" as central figures often placed against scenic backgrounds. This was in contrast to the dominant tradition of Chinese painting and that of earlier Japanese artists, which usually subordinated human figures to the landscape. The titles of some of the prints of Utamaro (1753–1805) are instructive: *Three Women on a Journey Under a Mosquito Net*, *Women Chasing Fireflies*, and *The Ryōgoku Bridge with Nine Women on It*. Although some of these productions were ribald, in the hands of several of the masters of the late Tokugawa period they were truly great art. About 1765 Harunobu developed polychrome prints in which as many woodblocks as colors were used in the reproduction, and minute attention to details of coloration now became possible. Kiyonaga (1752–1815) was perhaps the most skillful of all the artists although Hokusai (1760–1849) and Hiroshige (1797–1858) became probably the most popular in the West. Hiroshige's series entitled *Fifty-three Way Stations of the Tokaido* is perhaps the most famous of all these Tokugawa works of popular art.

FIGURE 6.4. The Debarkation by Kiyonaga, probably the greatest artist of the Tokugawa period. The stateliness of human forms, the composition of the print and the composure of the faces lead to comparisons with the art of Periclean Greece or Renaissance Italy.

148

Intellectual Currents

As the attractions of the Floating World led many people to stray from the restrictions of the Tokugawa system, serious intellectual inquiry began to question its very foundations. We have observed that the shogunate fostered the orthodox Neo-Confucianism of Chu Hsi, which in the hands of official scholars provided a powerful rationale for the Tokugawa system. However, scholarship could not be completely controlled in Japan, and even within the framework of Confucianism there developed alternative schools of thought. Like the orthodox school these followed Chinese models, one of them, the Ōyōmei, being a Japanese manifestation of China's Wang Yang-ming School, which placed greater emphasis on introspection and intuitive perception of truth than did the rationalistic Neo-Confucians. Kumazawa Banzan (1619–1691) was perhaps the leading figure of this school and, enjoying the favor of his feudal lord, he was able to train many students in the Kyoto area especially in ideas which, if not inimical to, were at least critical of the prevailing philosophy. He emphasized that the Tokugawa had risen because "they put the country in order," and he thought the imperial court should never rule. But he said that the imperial institution had an important role in providing stability and continuity through periods of change, implying, at least, that there could be change if the Tokugawa failed to maintain order.

Similarly the Han Learning school, which criticized Neo-Confucians as being too far removed from the original Confucian texts, had its counterpart in Japan. Itō Jinsai (1627–1705), Ogyū Sorai (1666–1723), and others of this school emphasized that older texts must be studied before truth could be ascertained. Ogyū decided that the Classics did not support the idea of a natural order of society handed down from Heaven. Rather the sages themselves had invented the system of four classes to enable people to live together in harmony. Indeed, he argued, the "true" way in any society was not "true" in any absolute sense, but was the contrivance of the rulers, who, if they were to be successful, must obtain and maintain the acquiescence of the ruled. His philosophy was utilitarian and in some ways akin to the Legalism of ancient China (see Volume I, Chapter 17).

Shinto

However, the search for old books led beyond Confucianism into a phenomenon best described as the Shinto revival, whose implications for the security of Tokugawa rule were extremely serious. Shinto, although very closely identified with the oldest Japanese traditions, with the imperial court, and with nature and fertility cults that were deeply involved in peasant life, had in the centuries after the influx of Chinese learning been largely engulfed by Buddhism and had lost its separate identity. Buddhism had flourished magnificently in the Heian, Kamakura, and Ashikaga periods, but its armed monks had been defeated and its organization seriously disrupted by the wars of the sixteenth century. And while most people in

Tokugawa Japan were technically Buddhists, including the shoguns, there was little intellectual stimulation or zeal left in the religion. Yet Shinto remained subordinate to it, even to the degree that Buddhist priests managed Shinto shrines.

Ironically, since it played a considerable role in the downfall of the shogunate, the revival of Shinto received an early impetus from a member of the Tokugawa clan, Mitsukuni of the Mito district where relations with the senior Tokugawa branch were sometimes strained. In the latter half of the seventeenth century Mitsukuni made Mito a center for historical study, and scholars there began to emphasize old Japanese sources as vital for explaining the history of Japan, especially the importance of the imperial line.

In the eighteenth century this scholarship was carried much further by Motoori Norinaga (1730–1801), who, perhaps significantly, was a non-samurai who turned scholar. He denounced Chinese studies and Confucianism and devoted half a lifetime to translating the oldest "purely Japanese" book, the *Kojiki*, into contemporary language and explaining its significance—to wit, that the Japanese emperor, appointed by the gods, "is the immovable ruler who must endure to the end of time." Evil men, like the Hōjō and the Ashikaga, "influenced by Chinese learning," had risen against him to Japan's sorrow. Motoori did not specifically link the Tokugawa with these earlier "usurpers," but others might see a connection later.

These several schools of heterodox thought should probably be called potentially rather than outrightly subversive, for they were seeking possible ways to place the existing socio-political structure on firmer foundations. They were by no means spokesmen for popular discontent. Indeed, very few intellectuals had much concern on this score, though there was one whose privately circulated writings took issue not only with Confucianism but with all the "paternalistic" norms of aristocratic feudal society. This was Andō Shōeki (born c. 1700), an obscure country physician, who denounced "sages," warrior-aristocrats, priests, and merchants alike as parasites who stole rice from the common people. He wanted to return them all to working the soil but he was so far from the mainstream of intellectual activity that he was unnoticed.

Andō Shōeki's denunciation of the whole mainstream of Sino-Japanese tradition may have been in part conditioned by acquaintanceship with Dutch Learning (Rangaku), of which, as a physician, he doubtless had some knowledge.

Dutch Learning

After the Dutch factory was removed to Deshima, its trade amounted to very little, hardly worth the effort of keeping it open. But "Dutch Learning" was to have a real importance in the latter part of the Tokugawa period, although its circle of participants was small. Most Japanese thought of these strange Westerners in terms of clichés. This depth of ignorance was the result of the extreme vigilance of Tokugawa censors against any printed reference even remotely related to Christianity. After 1685 this meant the wholesale expurgation of European references even from Chinese books.

However, in 1720 the shogun, Yoshimune, impressed by the arguments of a calendar maker of the desirability of exploring Western calendar lore which he found mentioned in Chinese books, decreed a relaxation of the restrictions, and in 1741 ordered the Dutch language to be studied so that direct translations might be made. By the end of the eighteenth century "Dutch Learning" in the fields of mathematics, geography, and medicine, especially, was exciting great interest among intellectuals. Sugita Gempaku, perhaps the outstanding member of the school, in 1771 presided at the first scientific dissection of a human body, Dutch textbook in hand, on an execution field.

During the early nineteenth century some of those associated with Dutch Learning became active critics of the seclusion policy, and in the era of the opening of Japan many of them served as translators, interpreters, and teachers of Western knowledge.

THE OPENING OF JAPAN

Russian Contacts

Meanwhile, from the outside came occasional reminders that seclusion would become increasingly difficult to maintain. Russians had crossed Siberia with remarkable speed and, having established themselves in Kamchatka in the 1690's, began to make contact with Japan. Ships under the command of Bering's assistant, Spanberg, actually touched at several points along the Japanese coast in 1738–39 and their officers were entertained by local Japanese. Also a number of Japanese castaways were picked up by Russian vessels, some of whom were taken to Russia and used as teachers of the Japanese language. In 1771 one Benyovsky (alias Hangenboro), a Hungarian-born adventurer who was exiled to Kamchatka by the Russian government, escaped, together with fellow exiles, took a ship, and sailed to Japan. There he left letters expressing good will to the Japanese, but claiming that he had been ordered by Russia to reconnoiter the islands in preparation for Russian raids. This stirred great excitement and suspicion in Japan.

However, when a Russian expedition did come in 1792, under Professor Erik Laxman and his son, Lieutenant Adam Laxman, it behaved scrupulously, received warm Japanese hospitality, and engaged in rather lengthy negotiations with Japanese officials in Hokkaido at Nemuro, Hakodate, and Matsumae City. The Japanese accepted shipwrecked repatriates, but under instructions from Edo, refused to modify the exclusion laws to allow trade, even though Lieutenant Laxman was given a certificate of entry to Nagasaki harbor for a future visit there "according to regulations."

Not until 1805 did the Russians try to use this "pass." In that year Nikolai Rezanov of the Russian-American (Fur) Company of Alaska, in ill-health and bad temper, arrived, made a poor impression on the Japanese, as did they on him, and sailed away empty handed and angry. The following year two young off-duty naval lieutenants, Khvostov and Davidov, acting under instructions from Rezanov, conducted raids of reprisal in Sakhalin and the southern Kurils, destroying several villages and killing many Japanese, and they destroyed Japanese boats off Hokkaido. Though they were court-martialed for this, to the Japanese it seemed the fulfillment of Benyovsky's prophecy. When the next Russian ship ventured near Hokkaido in 1811, its commander, Golovnin, was lured ashore and sent prisoner "in a cage" to Matsumae City near Hakodate. He was kept prisoner two years, although, as his diary records, he became quite fond of his Japanese captors and they of him. Meanwhile in 1808 the British warship *Phaeton*, pursuing a Dutch vessel, invaded Nagasaki harbor, then departed, and in subsequent years several American and British trading vessels made abortive attempts to trade at points along the Japanese coast.

The United States Opens Japan

In the face of these contacts the shogunate first attempted to tighten the seclusion laws, but by the 1840's when news of events along the China coast reached them through the Dutch, their resolve began to weaken. In fact, in 1837 when an American ship, the *Morrison*, privately outfitted by merchants at Canton, came to Edo itself seeking trade, one of the shogun's counsellors advocated a friendly reception. However, despite warnings from the Dutch, including a personal plea from King William II of Holland (1844) that world events like the Anglo-Chinese War were making seclusion untenable, the rather elaborate Biddle Mission, making an official American request for a trade treaty, was turned away (1846), as were a number of trading vessels of various nationalities.

In order to insure better treatment for shipwrecked Yankee sailors from north Pacific whaling vessels, to obtain whaling stations in Japan as part of the great circle route of American steamships from San Francisco to Canton, and to gain access to Japanese trade, in July 1853 came the American Commodore Matthew Calbraith Perry, bearing a friendly letter from President Fillmore, while implying threat with his own imperious bearing and the guns on his ships. He was empowered to voice "in the most unequivocal terms" the insistence of the United States for a government-to-government agreement on matters mentioned in the letter: treatment of shipwrecked sailors in Japan, coaling stations, and general trade (see also Chapter 17). Perry simply delivered the letter, informed the Japanese that he expected a formal reply and would return for it, moved his ships up Edo Bay for a close look at the Tokugawa capital, and departed. When he returned the following February, with additional ships, the shogun's officials informed him that the shogun was willing to sign a treaty. At Kanagawa, south of Edo, they signed, agreeing to open Hakodate and Shimoda as ports of call to American ships. Although it was not realized at the time, this breach of the seclusion policy sounded the death knell of the Tokugawa regime.

FIGURE 6.5. The meeting of Commodore Perry with Japanese officials at Yokohama. From Narrative of the Expedition of an American Squadron, New York, 1856.

END OF THE SHOGUNATE

In the face of external danger and many internal problems the Tokugawa government decided to seek the backing of the country at large, including outside daimyo, on the matter of dealing with the demands of Perry. It seems to have anticipated that most of the feudal lords would favor compromise of some sort and that it could then give some ground to Perry, but at the same time maintain its dignity and position and secure for the future a solid base of support around the country. The result was civil war and overthrow of the feudal order. But it is incorrect to assume therefore that powerful forces were simply waiting to pounce on and end the old regime. In fact, the movement that brought down the Tokugawa was far from revolutionary in the beginning, and compromise seemed possible as late as 1867.

Internal Repercussions of Perry's Visit

Nevertheless, the "American question" stirred the feudal lords to serious argument, and three groups emerged. One, led by the lord of Mito, the dissident Tokugawa relative, advocated an uncompromising position including war if necessary. A second, which gathered around Ii Naosuke, the leading hereditary daimyo, advocated dealing with the Westerners temporarily while building the military forces of the country to oust them eventually. A third group, led by the powerful lord of Satsuma, advocated avoiding hostilities but at the same time refusing to deal with the Americans. The policy adopted when Perry returned for his answer in 1854 was one of conciliation of the Americans without any definite decision on what the future course would be.

Meanwhile, another factor became prominent. In addition to notifying the various feudal lords of the problem and asking their advice, the shogunate had notified the imperial court at Kyoto. This also seems to have been a part of its effort to obtain as wide as possible a basis of support for its handling of foreign policy, for the Tokugawa had almost never in 250 years of rule asked imperial advice on anything. This provided an alternative rallying point to which the various disputants might appeal if their voices were not sufficiently heard at Edo.

Abe Masahiro, who was the chief counsellor to the shogun, was the person most responsible for the effort to secure the opinions of the various feudal lords and to obtain their cooperation. In the years immediately following the Kanagawa treaty with Perry he was able to make significant strides in welding together the three groups which had emerged. The chief of the Mito faction was given a high position in the shogun's advisory counsel, a marriage alliance was arranged with Satsuma, and Hotta Masayoshi, a follower of Ii Naosuke, was invited to become the counsellor in charge of foreign affairs. However, Abe died in 1857 before he could obtain his goals. Shortly after his death certain tensions between the various lords began to come into the open and the death of the shogun himself the following year provided the opportunity for real competition. A candidate from Mito, Keiki, was supported by the Mito and Satsuma groups, with many other lords joining in that coalition. Opposed was the long-time "inside," fudai group, led by Ii Naosuke. Both groups tried to sway the court at Kyoto in their favor, but at Edo and Kyoto alike the traditional advantage of the fudai group proved decisive and Ii won a complete, although short-lived victory. His candidate Iemochi became shogun, but both the Mito and Satsuma groups were embittered and became more inclined to attack shogunal policy than to cooperate in the coalition.

Ii took drastic steps to defeat their interference, placing several daimyo under house arrest and jailing or executing many of the lower ranking samurai involved. Yoshida Shōin, who had supported a return to imperial power in Chōshū and become a hero to many young samurai there, was among those executed. This "Great Persecution of Ansei" excited bitter personal animosity against Ii. Also he had the shogun sign a treaty with the United States in 1858, after Hotta had negotiated the treaty with Townsend Harris without obtaining the emperor's signature. For such "high-handedness" Ii was assassinated by a group of masterless warriors (rōnin) from Mito in the spring of 1860. This, however, was more a rejection of Ii and the old-line shogunate policy of running important governmental affairs without consulting the court or the outside lords than an attack upon the institution of the shogunate itself. In fact, after the assassination of Ii there were indications that the compromise arrangement at the center of the government, which Ii had destroyed, might be re-established. The jails were emptied and those daimyo who had been placed under house arrest by Ii were restored to favor. In addition, the long-established system of alternate residence at Edo was modified so that feudal lords were less frequently required to come, and they were allowed to take their wives and children to their estates without special permission. The shogun invited Keiki of Mito to be his counsellor and tutor.

If their demands had remained the same these measures might have satisfied the opponents of the *fudai* faction, but by this time (1861) Kyoto had become a center for dissident groups, including not only the top leaders of several "outside" clans but many younger men whose ideas were much more radical. From various discussions and negotiations emerged a so-called *Sonnō-Jōi* group which demanded reverence for the emperor (*Sonnō*) and expulsion of foreigners from Japan (*Jōi*). Also implicit in their demands was the abolishment of the shogunate. Several court nobles, including Iwakura Tomomi and Sanjo Sanetomi who later achieved fame, were involved in the schemes of the Sonnō-Jōi group, and Choshu clansmen from southwestern Honshu were very active. The emperor Komei himself was opposed to this group and very much in favor of the sort of compromise arrangement which had been offered by the shogunate after Ii's death. In fact, the only element which remained hard and fast in opposition to compromise was Choshu. A marriage alliance between the court and shogunate was arranged to further the process of compromise, and in 1863 Keiki, representing the shogun, instituted regular meetings with leading feudal lords from most of the large fiefs, including Satsuma, but excluding Choshu. Choshu men, meanwhile, plotted to seize control of the court. Although foiled in 1863, they began to make secret alliances and arrangements with certain Satsuma samurai which anticipated that Satsuma participation in the coalition government with Tokugawa would fail.

In 1864 a quarrel took place within the council of lords on the issue of how strong a stand to take against the foreigners, and all the members resigned. This brought a temporary crisis, but Keiki was able in the late fall of 1865 to obtain the imperial sanction for the treaties, and to keep up the non-grata status of Choshu, against whom a shogunal punitive expedition had been launched. Then Keiki became shogun in 1866 and the possibility of uniting all factions seemed to be better than ever. He attempted to restore the coalition in full strength and even to conciliate Choshu and bring it back into cooperation. Perhaps the decisive event which ruined the chances for success of a Tokugawa-arranged coalition was the death of the emperor Komei in December, 1866. He seems never to have been swayed in the slightest by the radical schemes that had been proposed to him and to have consistently advocated the cooperation of all groups with the Tokugawa. But the new emperor, called Mutsuhito or by his reign title, Meiji, was a young boy of fifteen, and soon after his accession Sanjo and other anti-Tokugawa court nobles attained great influence at court. Furthermore, the lower level Satsuma-Choshu negotiations began to bear fruit in terms of bringing Satsuma into opposition to the Tokugawa. Other leading feudal lords, led by the lord of the Tosa fief on Shikoku island, still expected to arrange the political situation in Japan in terms of coalition, with the Tokugawa continuing to play the leading role.

The Politics of the Meiji Restoration

However, in a series of conferences in 1867 it became clear that Satsuma, whose policy was being formulated by two energetic young samurai, Saigo and Okubo, had moved away from its original position of supporting the Tokugawa to one of cooperation with Choshu against them. Even though Keiki was the shogun, they insisted that he be eliminated from the government and, perhaps more important for the future of the Tokugawa house, be deprived of the immense land holdings which the shogun traditionally held. Keiki, while prepared and even anxious to accept a reordering of the government in which he would have a subordinate role, was not prepared to be eliminated entirely. Anticipating a Choshu-Satsuma coup, in the fall of 1867 he announced his decision to surrender his political powers to the emperor and bring the institution of Tokugawa government to an end. This came just in time, for Choshu and Satsuma had received a secret imperial rescript authorizing them to attack the shogunate, but the attack was now postponed. During December, 1867, and January, 1868, there was sharp argument among the feudal lords in meetings at Kyoto, with the Tosa group urging that the shogun not be stripped of his lands and that he be included as a leading element in the new government. But Choshu and Satsuma leaders, along with Iwakura of the court who proved to be a very able organizer of anti-Tokugawa sentiment, remained adamant. The result was that the shogun and his immediate supporters were summarily dismissed and ordered to surrender their lands to the throne. Almost simultaneously, the Satsuma "headquarters" in Edo became a center of intrigue and violence as Saigo ordered his followers there to quarrel with the Tokugawa.

In February the shogun accepted the challenge and, after putting down the disturbances in Edo, sent an army toward Kyoto in what he called a punitive expedition against Satsuma. This was more ill fated than had been the earlier "punitive" expedition against Choshu. The shogun's troops were defeated and he himself was forced to flee. Soon thereafter, upon the advice of some of his subordinates, Keiki surrendered and accepted the inevitable—loss of his lands as well as his political position. He was required to retire to Mito and although some Tokugawa partisans tried to continue the fight from Hokkaido, the war essentially was over by May, 1868, when the so-called "imperial forces" took over the former Tokugawa stronghold of Edo and signified the beginning of a new regime by renaming it Tōkyō or Eastern Capital, and moving the emperor into the old shogunal palace. The new Meiji era of "Enlightened Government" had begun.

Causes of the Tokugawa Collapse

Before proceeding to a discussion of this new era it is necessary to say a few words concerning the problem of interpretation of the downfall of the Tokugawa regime.

Perhaps the simplest is the Sonnō Jōi (revere the emperor and expel the barbarians) interpretation, which holds that four western clans, Satsuma, Choshu, Tosa, and Hizen, long dissatisfied at their "outside" status, with collaboration of the renegade Mito branch of Tokugawa, organized a movement around this slogan and focused it against the shogunate, whose usurpation of the imperial authority and weakness before the foreigners' demands were thus brought into clear relief. Certainly, the idea of restoring the emperor provides a key ideological clue to the whole process. However, it should be observed that the Jōi part of this slogan was lost long before matters came to a climax in the civil war. It is true that the opportunity for argument against the shogunate came as a result of Perry's demands and the shogun's equivocation concerning them. Also, samurai of these anti-Edo clans in the 1850's and early 1860's were noted for their anti-foreign acts, which included the murder of one Heusken, the Dutch interpreter for the American legation in 1860, an attack on British representatives in Edo the same year by Mito samurai, and the famous Richardson affair of September, 1862, when a group of British were attacked by Satsuma men and one of the party, Richardson, was slain. And in June, 1863, Choshu ships, under orders of the daimyo of Choshu, attacked an American ship near the Straits of Shimonoseki. These and other incidents led the Western powers to take action, not against the shogunate, which it was realized had no part in or control over these unauthorized activities, but directly against Choshu and Satsuma to whose ports punitive naval expeditions were dispatched. The "punishment" by bombardment of Kagoshima in the Satsuma domain and Shimonoseki in the Choshu, may have been the beginning of a turn toward interest in, rather than absolute hostility to the Westerners by these outside clans. At any rate by the time the Meiji Restoration took place the anti-shogunate forces were wavering in their commitments to Jōi, "expel the barbarians," as a part of their ideology.

Enough has been said of the complication of relationships between the various clans and the shogunate, including the fact that all of them except perhaps Choshu spent a good deal of effort in trying to arrange a coalition with the Tokugawa, to indicate that the Sonnō Jōi explanation is overly simple. In this regard it should be noted that the final factor in the overthrow of the shogunate was the Choshu-Satsuma coalition, which may go far to explain why the other cooperating clans tended to fall out of the Restoration government after the overthrow of the shogunate was accomplished. But "revere the emperor" and the Satsuma-Choshu coalition do not tell the whole story.

The general intellectual ferment which had its beginnings in the Mito school gradually produced the idea of "learning for leadership" and, by the mid-nineteenth century, this had evolved into a demand that leadership be entrusted to men of ability, regardless of their rank or background. When the shogunate did not prove sufficiently responsive, growing numbers of angry young men developed a "culture of action" which began to disrupt the established order with violent tactics. Yoshida Shoin was only the first of these, and after his execution, many others broke from their feudal positions and began to roam the country as "unattached patriots" advocating and plotting not only social but political change.

Social and economic factors also loom large behind the Tokugawa overthrow. A political scientist will be quick to see the explosiveness inherent in a situation in which the class with political power (samurai) had fallen heavily in debt to a class ranked last in the social scale (merchants), to whom political power was effectively denied. Samurai, merchants, and farmers, too, as indicated by the growing number of peasant uprisings in the late Tokugawa period, had their grievances. But is it possible to locate more specifically those factors, or groups, which were most influential in bringing about the disintegration of the old regime? Some have argued that it was "rich merchants" combined with "lower samurai." Certainly, some rich merchants supported the Restoration movement, but when one comes to name them one finds only a few, the outstanding one being Mitsui. Similarly, one finds lower samurai playing a leading role in the movement, men like Saigo, Okubo, and their counterparts from other clans. But these "lower samurai" were certainly not low in terms of influence in their own clans, where they were literally right-hand men to their feudal lords, and it is questionable whether we can say that a lower samurai revolt against "upper samurai" provides the key to the Restoration story. Similarly, wealthy farmers and small merchants who were interconnected very likely provided a considerable amount of wealth and enthusiasm for the Restoration movement, perhaps more than the rich merchants, yet we should be wary of calling them the decisive factor. The peasants were certainly restive, and many of them joined the anti-Tokugawa movement, but since no peasant leadership emerged to play a significant role in the Restoration and peasant disillusionment with the new regime became speedily apparent, we cannot accent the peasant role too strongly. Perhaps it is best to say that the ingredients of the Restoration were a mixture of all of these plus certain momentary impulses, such as Ii Naosuke's Ansei persecutions and Iwakura's conniving, which was stimulated as much by months of languishing under house arrest as anything else. The Meiji Restoration was truly a complex phenomenon, and its complexity no doubt justifies the fact that more studies have been written about it than about any other event in Japanese history.

BASIC DATES

1600	Tokugawa Ieyasu triumphs at Sekigahara
1603	Ieyasu becomes first Tokugawa shogun; shogunate at Edo, 1603–1867
1605	Ieyasu resigns as shogun, but continues to dominate government
1615	Revolt at Osaka castle; Hideyori killed; Buke Sho-Hatto promulgated
1616	Death of Ieyasu
1622–1651	Tokugawa Iemitsu rules as third shogun
1637	Shimabara Rebellion
1639–1641	Policy of national seclusion inaugurated; Dutch allowed limited contact at Deshima; suppression of Christianity

c. 1660	Completion of orthodox "Comprehensive Mirror" (*Honchō Tsugan*) and start of unorthodox Mito school
1688–1704	Genroku era; flowering of bourgeois culture
1720	Shogun Yoshimune eases ban on Dutch books; "Dutch Learning" begins
1730–1801	Motoori Norinaga and Shinto revival
1792–1812	Russians seek trade with Japan; Japanese refuse
1837	American ship *Morrison* seeks trade at Edo, refused
1844	Dutch advise Japan to end seclusion
1846	Biddle Mission fails to open Japan
1853–1854	Perry's visits and opening of Japan
1858	Townsend Harris negotiates commercial treaty
1860	Ii Naosuke, Tokugawa counsellor and advocate of the treaties, assassinated
1862–1863	Attacks on Westerners; retaliation against Satsuma and Choshu
1860–1867	Imperial restoration movement
1867	Resignation of last Tokugawa shogun

SUPPLEMENTARY READING

Beasley, W. G. *The Modern History of Japan.* New York, 1964.
Borton, H. *Japan's Modern Century.* New York, rev. ed., 1970. The first four chapters cover the closing years of the Tokugawa era.
Brown, D. M. *Nationalism in Japan.* Berkeley, Calif., 1955. Gives evidence of national consciousness in the Tokugawa period.
De Bary, W. T., ed. *Sources of the Japanese Tradition.* New York, 1958.
Hall, J. W. *Japan: From Prehistory to Modern Times.* New York, 1970, Chaps. 10–12.
Hane, M. *Japan: A Historical Survey.* Scribner's (paperback), 1972.
Inoue, M. *Introduction to Japanese History Before the Meiji Restoration.* Tokyo, rev. ed., 1968, Chaps. 10–12.
Keene, D. *Anthology of Japanese Literature.* New York, 1955.
Kitagawa, J. *Religion in Japanese History.* New York, 1968.
Lee, Sherman E. *A History of Far Eastern Art.* Englewood Cliffs, N.J., 1964.
Munsterberg, H. *The Arts of Japan.* Tokyo, 1957.
Reischauer, E. O. *Japan: Story of a Nation.* New York, 1970.
Reischauer, E. O. and J. K. Fairbank. *East Asia: The Great Tradition.* Boston, 1960. Well-balanced account of the period. Revised and abbreviated ed., 1973.
Sansom, G. *Japan, A Short Cultural History.* New York, rev. ed., 1962.
Terry, C. *Masterworks of Japanese Art.* Rutland, Vt., 1956.

ADVANCED READING

Beasley, W. G., ed. *Select Documents on Japanese Foreign Policy, 1853–1868.* London, 1955.

Bellah, R. N. *Tokugawa Religion: The Values of Preindustrial Japan.* Glencoe, Ill., 1957.
Boxer, C. *Jan Compagnie in Japan.* The Hague, 1936. Describes the Dutch at Hirado and Deshima.
Craig, A. M. *Choshu and the Meiji Restoration.* Cambridge, Mass., 1961.
Craig, A. M. and D. H. Shively, eds. *Personality in Japanese History.* Berkeley, 1970. Pp. 29–263 deal with Tokugawa personalities.
Dore, R. P. *Education in Tokugawa Japan.* Berkeley, 1965.
Earl, D. M. *Emperor and Nation in Japan: Political Thinkers of the Tokugawa Period.* Seattle, 1964.
Goodman, Grant K. *The Dutch Impact on Japan.* Leiden, 1967.
Hall, J. W. *Tanuma Okitsugu, 1719–1788: Forerunner of Modern Japan.* Cambridge, Mass., 1955.
Hall, John W. and Marius B. Jansen, eds. *Studies in the Institutional History of Early Japan.* Princeton, N.J., 1968.
Harootunian, H. D. *Toward Restoration: The Growth of Political Consciousness in Tokugawa Japan.* Berkeley, Calif., 1970.
Henderson, D. F. *Conciliation and Japanese Law.* Seattle, 1965.
Jansen, M. *Sakamoto Ryōma and the Meiji Restoration.* Princeton, 1961.
Keene, D. *The Japanese Discovery of Europe: Honda Toshiaki and Other Discoverers, 1720–1798.* London, 1951.
Lensen, G. A. *The Russian Push Toward Japan, 1697–1875.* Princeton, 1959.
Murdoch, J. *History of Japan.* London, 1925.
Paine, R. T. and A. Soper. *The Art and Architecture of Japan.* Baltimore, 1955.
Sadler, A. L. *The Maker of Modern Japan: The Life of Tokugawa Ieyasu.* London, 1937.
Sansom, G. B. *A History of Japan, 1615–1867.* Stanford, Calif., 1963.
——— *The Western World and Japan.* New York, 1950.
Sheldon, C. D. *The Rise of the Merchant Class in Tokugawa Japan, 1600–1868.* Locust Valley, N.Y., 1958.
Smith, T. C. *The Agrarian Origins of Modern Japan.* Stanford, Calif., 1959.
Spae, J. J. *Itō Jinsai, a Philosopher, Educator, and Sinologist of the Tokugawa Period.* New York, 1967.
Totman, C. *Politics in the Tokugawa Bakufu, 1600–1843.* Cambridge, 1967.
Tsukahira, T. G. *Feudal Control in Tokugawa Japan.* Cambridge, 1966.
Webb, H. *The Japanese Imperial Institution in the Tokugawa Period.* New York, 1968.

Chapter 7

Dutch Empire in the Far East to 1850

ESTABLISHMENT OF A DUTCH COMMERCIAL EMPIRE IN THE INDIES

The Portuguese and the Spanish had led the way from Europe to the Far East, but after 1600 they met a formidable challenge to their power from the Dutch. The Dutch, in the Far East fighting primarily the seapower of Portugal, were eminently successful, and since their only possible rivals, the English, were fully preoccupied with a civil war, the seventeenth century was the century of Dutch supremacy par excellence all over the world.

European Background

In order to understand the creation of a Dutch empire in the East it is necessary to sketch briefly the background of Holland during the sixteenth century. This was a period of vast expansion of European economic activity, producing what has been called the Commercial Revolution. This term meant that because of overseas expansion European trade greatly increased in both the variety and volume of goods, which in turn led to an increase in the wealth of those nations which participated in this expansion and in the availability of great amounts of risk capital to a class of capitalist bourgeois for further investment. In this revolutionary development, the Low Countries managed to obtain a goodly share of the benefits and some of the most important early centers of this development were located there, such as Antwerp and, somewhat later, Rotterdam. To these centers came many foreign merchants, from Portugal, Spain, Italy, Germany, England, the Hansa, and Holland itself, to engage in trade. In Antwerp the first great European stock exchange, the Bourse, became established in 1531

FIGURE 7.1. Interior of the stock exchange at Amsterdam. Painting by Berckheyde.

where speculating with stocks could produce spectacular profits, and where such capitalist techniques as life and marine insurance were developed. The reason for the Low Countries' development as centers of the Commercial Revolution was simply that they were able to monopolize the carrying trade of Western Europe. Since they were part of the empire of Charles V, they benefited by this connection with Spain, as Dutch ships went to Spain and Portugal to purchase goods in Seville and Lisbon, which they then carried to the Netherlands for sale and distribution. In addition, the Netherlands benefited also from large-scale trade with England, Scandinavia, the Baltic, and Russia. This extensive trade conducted by organized commercial companies resulted in rapid prosperity and the creation of a very large commercial fleet which dominated the carrying trade of the North Sea and the Baltic, and practically monopolized the distribution of colonial goods from the Iberian peninsula. In addition to this large commercial fleet, there were many fishing vessels operating in the North Sea and the Baltic, where they provided a fine training ground for young sailors.

The Commercial Revolution had very extensive effects in the Netherlands by the middle of the sixteenth century. With the coming of the Reformation and the revolt of the Protestant Netherlanders against their sovereign, Philip II of Spain, it was the northern province of the Low Countries, or Holland proper, which gained the predominance in commercial affairs. When Antwerp fell to Spanish forces in 1584, Amsterdam in the north became the new headquarters for commercial activities.

The difficulties of the Netherlands with Spain resulted in open war after 1566 which threatened its prosperity. Many Dutch ships were detained or seized in Spain, and when the union of Spain and Portugal was consummated in 1580, Portuguese harbors, notably Lisbon, were also closed to the Dutch, or, at the most, permitted only limited access to their shipping. This threat to Dutch prosperity caused Holland to extend its commercial sphere beyond Europe, and in turn Dutch determination was greatly facilitated by the defeat of the Spanish Armada in 1588, a disaster which cost the Portuguese and Spanish their naval supremacy and ultimately the loss of control of the sea.

By the end of the sixteenth century Holland possessed many advantages over the rest of Europe. She had superiority in ships, in trained manpower, in capital, and in vigor. By this time, too, much knowledge of the East Indies had come into the possession of the Dutch. This was contributed in 1595 by Jan Linschoten, who wrote a brilliant encyclopedic account, the *Itinerario*, of the East Indies, while he served as secretary to the archbishop of Goa, the Portuguese center for activities in Eastern waters. In this work Linschoten gave an account of the trade possibilities, with special emphasis upon the spice trade, and described the strengths and weaknesses of the Portuguese. For the Dutch to gain a position in Asia meant not only a commercial and political victory against the hated Spanish, but profits which would also furnish the material resources needed by the Dutch in their long struggle against the military might of Philip II. It was for this reason then that the Dutch attacked Portuguese seapower in Asia, since, as the result of the union with Spain, Portugal also had become an enemy. This struggle which began in 1595 lasted to 1641, and the final defeat of the Portuguese resulted in Dutch supremacy which was maintained for the rest of the century. It was only after 1700 that first British seapower and later the demands of the Industrial Revolution caught up with and ended the great Dutch century.

Indonesia Before the Coming of the Dutch

Before describing the arrival of the first Dutch expedition, it might be well to discuss the conditions in Indonesia at the end of the sixteenth century, because they greatly influenced the success of the Dutch in creating an empire in the East.

Briefly stated, the most significant factor in the general political situation was the absence of a strong and unified power after the collapse of the Madjapahit empire of Java, and this significantly favored the ease of eventual European conquest. Lack of a strong political power was coupled with the spread of a new faith, that of Islam. The propagation of Moslem doctrines had followed the major trading and shipping routes in Southeast Asia, from Malacca to east Java and thence to the principal islands of the Moluccas. From these central points it spread along the coasts of many other islands, although the interior of the Indonesian archipelago was touched barely or not at all by this new religion. Islam did not involve a major break with the old traditions and beliefs of the area; rather, it was sponsored by a small group of foreign traders located in the principal ports, having at their disposal relatively large resources, and to whom the petty princes on the coast of Java and some of the other islands were only too glad to marry their sons and daughters. In more primitive parts, such as Borneo and Celebes, Moslem traders propagated the new faith in the interior by means of the sword, thereby profitably combining salvation with an expansion of their commercial activities. But a most important point was the fact that the coming of the new faith did not result in a powerful new Indonesian state. Rather, there existed by the end of the sixteenth century a multiplicity of small Moslem sultanates, fierce rivals of each other, possessing no power beyond their particular narrow confines.

On Java there were two of these. In west Java there was the Moslem sultanate of Bantam, which was important as a producer of pepper, while in central Java there was the state of Mataram, almost exclusively an agricultural state, lacking any kind of naval power, and fully occupied with vicious and frequent succession disputes. However, the really important areas, as far as European interests were concerned, were the so-called Spice Islands, or Moluccas, further east. These were the legendary sources of great wealth derived from the cultivation of nutmeg and clove.

Clove was derived from the dried flowers and buds of the clove tree, which grew originally only on the small islands of Ternate and Tidore. Its cultivation was easy enough work, since a fully grown clove tree produced for 75 years; but because of the high risk of a long sea voyage the spice fetched an enormous price in Europe, and profits could be made at the rate of 2,500 per cent. Nutmeg came from the tree of the same name, grown specifically on Amboina and some of the Banda Islands, again with little effort, since a nutmeg tree normally lasted 100 years, and again with chances of enormous profits. Small wonder that the Portuguese, once they had established themselves at the strategic port of Malacca, were hopeful of obtaining a monopoly of both spices. This they could do by eliminating the native middleman, and by restricting export by a policy of policing the sea routes between Indonesia and Arabia, a task in which they were fairly successful because of their superior ships and gunnery.

In order to maintain an effective monopoly the Portuguese also needed a permanent base and a garrison in the Spice Islands. They debated over the choice of Ternate or Tidore for this purpose. Both were petty Islamic states, both wanted a treaty with the Portuguese, and both expected great profits from such an arrangement. Eventually, the Portuguese concluded such a treaty with the sultan of Ternate, which gave them in effect absolute control over the clove trade, but it left their relations with the Banda Islands in a less satisfactory state. Here several independent republics, which monopolized nutmeg production, resisted the Portuguese so they could neither establish any fortified points, nor create an iron-clad monopoly in that commodity. The Portuguese soon ran into further trouble when their greed led them to murder treacherously the sultan of Ternate in 1570, an event which led to a general revolt against the Portuguese and their expulsion from the Spice Islands by 1574. In effect, then, Portuguese authority was not strong in Indonesia beyond Malacca at a time when foreign competition, first the Spanish, then the Dutch, already threatened them. The Spanish government, securely established in the Philippine Islands to the north, had already shown some interest in the Spice Islands, despite vigorous Portuguese protests. On occasions, the Spanish had supported the sultan of Tidore against the Portuguese at Ternate, but the real threat to Portuguese monopoly which put an end to their power came from the Dutch.

The Arrival of the Dutch

Holland had explored several possibilities for the expansion of its trade outside Europe. As early as 1561, for instance, trading stations had been established on the north Russian route to China, but here the climate was prohibitive, and the search for a Northeast Passage was abandoned in 1597. In the west, too, the Dutch encountered difficulties in meeting such notable Elizabethan freebooters as Drake and Frobisher, so that the Dutch decided to try to follow the Portuguese and sail around Africa to the east. This route had been explored partially when a Dutch squadron visited the Cape Verde Islands in 1585.

Ten years later the first successful Dutch voyage to the East Indies was made. This was the expedition of van Houtman, a rather disgruntled ruffian and boaster, who had served the Portuguese before. He left Amsterdam with four ships, 250 experienced sailors, and 60 guns. He reached the small Islamic principality of Bantam, in northwest Java, in 1596, after losing 145 men of his crew. The sultan at Bantam welcomed van Houtman cordially, seeing in him an ally against the Portuguese, and a treaty was concluded between the Dutch and Bantam. Even the Portuguese at Bantam were pleasant enough at first, but the Portuguese in Goa were much more upset at the appearance of an interloper, and they decided to punish the sultan of Bantam for making a treaty with the Dutch. After van Houtman had started his return trip a Portuguese fleet appeared off Bantam, but it was beaten off by the local ruler, an indication of the decline of Portuguese power in Indonesian waters. Van Houtman's successful return to Holland in August 1597 with a profitable cargo produced an immediate fever of speculation and the beginning of a boom. Between 1598 and 1605 some 12 separate expeditions, totalling some 65 ships in six years, were launched from Holland to garner the riches of the East, one competing against the other for profits. Most of these vessels visited Bantam on Java, but some also penetrated farther east into the Moluccas where the first Dutch ships loaded their precious cargo of nutmeg, cloves, and mace at Amboina and Banda in 1599.

The formation of many rival companies engaged in ruinous competition with each other pointed out to the shrewd Dutch the need for pooling capital in a unified effort, if the whole of the Eastern enterprise should not end in a financial fiasco. Therefore in 1602 the Dutch Estates General granted a charter establishing the famous United Dutch East India Company. It was the largest commercial company then in existence. The Estates General granted the Company a 21-year monopoly (extended later on into the 18th century) for the entire world lying between the Cape of Good Hope and the Straits of Magellan, with rights to trade, to make treaties and agreements with local rulers, to build forts and maintain troops, and to establish law courts. The East India Company was a joint stock company with a capital of 6½ million guilders, and shares were bought with immense enthusiasm. Returns were enormous, averaging some 37 per cent annually, and in some years dividends shot up to 75 per cent. So vast were the profits reaped that in 1624 one of its original stockholders left to his heirs eight tons of gold, and even a hundred years later, in 1723, Company shares were quoted at the value of 22,000 florins, representing an original investment of only 840 florins.

Following the establishment of a unified organization, the Dutch launched a systematic war of attrition against the Portuguese. In Europe in 1606 they blockaded the harbor of Lisbon, and in 1608 they defeated a Spanish fleet off Gibraltar. In the Indies they defeated a Portuguese squadron off Bantam in 1602, giving the Dutch command of the Sunda Straits and opening the road to the Moluccas, and they repeated their success in 1609 off Malacca. The main effort of the Dutch in the East was directed towards obtaining trade both at Bantam and in the Moluccas. By the use of bribery and promises of justice, here the Dutch were able to secure forts and some territorial footholds on the small islands of Amboina (1605) and on Banda (1609), where the local chiefs acknowledged Dutch suzerainty by treaty. The rulers of Tidore and Ternate more or less were also drawn into supplying and supporting the Dutch East India Company. However, the center of Portuguese activities, Malacca, with its superb control of the Straits of the same name between the Malay peninsula and the island of Sumatra, still eluded the Dutch grasp. Nevertheless, in the commercial war which the Hollanders waged against the Portuguese, the former had the advantages. Dutch ships, although small vessels of only 500–1,000 tons, were far superior to those of their opponents, and they effectively managed to capture Portuguese ships encountered on the high seas, as well as to blockade successfully Portuguese ports in Eastern waters. In order to obtain a monopoly of trade, especially the spice trade, the Dutch also turned against indigenous shipping, whether Hindu, Malay, Siamese, Annamese, Chinese, or Japanese.

In their efforts to obtain undisputed commercial control of the East, the Dutch were aided by the political situation in Indonesia itself, where no strong central power or empire existed to block them (see pp. 163–164). The Dutch position was further strengthened by the discovery of a new route to the East in 1616 when Schouten van Hoorn discovered the wind-torn cape named after him, and Dutch monopoly became an undisputed fact when the only other European rivals of the Dutch in the Spice Islands, the English, were reduced to insignificance after 1623, as the result of the Amboina massacre.

Coen and the Founding of the Dutch Empire

In theory and on paper Holland and England cooperated with each other against their common enemies, the Spanish and the Portuguese. This alliance worked in Europe, but not in the East. It is true that a treaty of cooperation between the Dutch and the English had been signed which provided for the equal sharing of the trade of the Indies and the creation of a combined Anglo-Dutch defense fleet for Eastern waters, but in practice Dutch-English relations began to cool as soon as Portuguese power had been weakened. Hostilities between the two rivals broke out in Java, where in 1619 the Dutch attacked a fleet of four English ships and sank one of them, and where, in the same year, the Dutch seized land in Java as a base and fortified it against the English. This was the founding of Batavia (today Djakarta), the city which became the center of Dutch activity in the East. Its seizure and fortification was due to a Dutch official, Jan Pieterszon Coen, the founder of the Dutch empire in the East Indies, who had just become, while only 31, the Dutch governor-general. He was very hostile to the English, and had written that friendship with them was possible only at the cost of giving them the whole earth. With the acquisition of Batavia as a fortified base, Coen laid the permanent foundations of the Dutch dominion in the East.

An English attack on Batavia was repulsed, and there were further disputes between the two Protestant powers two years later when a joint Anglo-Dutch expedition which had been sent against the Spanish in Manila broke up after squabbles between the antagonistic commanders. This friction between the Dutch and English culminated in the Amboina massacre of 1623. In Amboina the Dutch governor arrested on suspicion of a conspiracy the entire staff of the English trading post—ten Englishmen, one Portuguese, and nine Japanese. After torture and a highly irregular trial, the governor ordered the prisoners executed, an act which caused a great stir of popular opinion in England. All pretense of cooperation between the Dutch and English ended, and the English withdrew from Indonesia. Henceforth, the Dutch monopoly was unchallenged in the East either by European or Asian rivals.

Much of the success in creating a Dutch empire in the East was due to Jan Pieterszon Coen. This devout, gruff, ambitious, and strict Calvinist had the great dream of an empire, accomplished by the conquest of all Portuguese key ports, and the elimination of all rivals. At the age of 13 Coen had been sent to Rome to work as clerk in a commercial house. When he was 25 the young man was sent to the Indies in command of two ships. There he became the director of the Dutch factory at Bantam in west Java. He was then described as an "honest and devout young man, very modest in his conduct, sober and of good character, no drunkard, not arrogant, very capable in council and well-versed in bookkeeping." When, shortly thereafter, in 1618, Coen became governor-general, he was enabled to realize his ambitious visions. In addition to defeating the Portuguese and English rivals of the Dutch, and in creating in Batavia a center of Dutch power, Coen also believed in the necessity of colonization. He outlined his views in a treatise, *Discourse on the State of India*, in which he argued that commerce in the Indies was necessary for the welfare of Holland, but that settlement of the Indies was of equal importance. He argued that the Dutch had a legal right to trade and to establish a monopoly by virtue of the treaties concluded with Amboina and other native states, and they had also the duty to drive out their rivals, the English in particular, in order to prevent

FIGURE 7.2. Portrait of Jan Pieterszon Coen.

smuggling. In addition, in order to maintain Dutch power, Coen stressed the importance of drawing settlers to the East, Dutchmen preferably, but Chinese and Japanese if no Hollanders were willing. He even went so far as to advocate the kidnapping of Chinese, and also stressed the high quality of Japanese soldiers employed by the Company, who he felt would make excellent colonists. After the complete annihilation of foreign and native shipping, Coen believed that Batavia would become the hub of all of the Asian carrying trade, thus realizing great profits. The real wealth, as Coen quite rightly saw, was to be found in the Asian carrying trade, which the Dutch would monopolize, thereby gaining import and export taxes.

Coen wrote to the directors of the Company in Holland declaring that if they followed his advice, establishing a commercial monopoly and bringing out colonists to strengthen the Dutch position in the Indies, they would reap a ten-fold profit. However, the Company attitude in Holland agreed only partially with Coen's argument. A monopoly of trade was acceptable, but settlements were rejected. They would cost money, and what the Company wanted was immediate profit with minimum expenditures. Therefore, only the first part of Coen's program was accepted, and plans for colonization were shelved.

The policy of monopoly, expounded by Coen and supported by the Company at home, was implemented by some very vigorous measures carried out by Coen while governor-general. In order to obtain a complete monopoly of cloves and prevent smuggling in 1621 the Dutch launched a ruthless attack against the Banda Islands. Many of the inhabitants of these islands were either executed or sold into slavery, and their land was given to employees of the Company. Production of clove trees was carefully controlled by the Company, all excess being periodically destroyed in order to keep the market price high. Coen even went so far as to cut off the rice supply to these islands, forcing the natives to subsist on a less nutritious sago, and to encourage civil war, all measures designed to discourage the people from growing cloves and thus preventing a surplus.

Thenceforth, every year or so, the Dutch sent armed fleet raids, or as they were more euphemistically called "inspection tours," through the Spice Islands to destroy spice surpluses, and to maintain a tight monopoly. In 1622 Coen attempted to seize the Portuguese stronghold of Macao, but here the Dutch met stiff opposition, and the Portuguese, aided by the Chinese, were able to drive away the Dutch. The Dutch admiral then proceeded to seize the Pescadores Islands and Formosa, where they established a garrison at Fort Zeelandia, which became a center of distribution for Japanese silver. From Batavia, Coen also defended the Dutch position in the Indies, when in 1627 he repulsed a major attack launched against the city by the sultan of Mataram. When Coen died of cholera two years later in Batavia, his work had been accomplished and a Dutch empire in the Indies had become a reality.

The Successors of Coen

One of his successors was Anthony van Diemen, who served as governor-general between 1636 and 1645. Van Diemen was a businessman, statesman, and naval officer, and thus was well suited to consolidate the gains of his patron, Coen. As an admiral, Van Diemen began an intelligent and well-directed offensive against the remnants of Portuguese strength. By making excellent use of his superior naval power and his greater resources of economic strength, manpower, and shipping, he ended the Portuguese colonial empire, replacing it with complete Dutch dominion in the East Indies. After 1633 annual Dutch fleets cruised the Straits of Malacca, and raided and captured Portuguese ships; by 1639 nearly 150 Portuguese vessels had been destroyed. In 1636 a Dutch blockade of the port of Goa in India and the entire Malabar coast was also begun; and in the next year the Dutch began the conquest of Ceylon. While Ceylon was not finally taken until 1658, the Dutch did gain access to the cinnamon trade in this fashion.

In 1639 Spanish and Portuguese seapower suffered a further and irremediable loss when a joint fleet was defeated by the Dutch admiral Tromp in the English Channel. The fall of Malacca to the Dutch in 1641 after a short siege was an event of prime importance, since it assured the Dutch of complete monopoly over the spice trade, while it also permitted the exploitation of the tin supplies in Malaya. In 1663, when the Portuguese made a treaty of peace with Holland, the Portuguese had been reduced to insignificance in the East.

Van Diemen's work was carried on by Jan Matsuycker, who was governor-general between 1653 and 1678. During his regime the Dutch gained control over the whole of Ceylon and a monopoly over the pepper exports from Sumatra and the Malabar coast of India. In the second half of the seventeenth century the Dutch had reached the zenith of their power; they had created a far-flung empire which reached from the Cape of Good Hope (1660), to Ceylon (1638), the Indies, into the south Pacific as far as Samoa, and to the north to Japan (Hirado 1609, Nagasaki after 1641). It was a commercial empire, based upon control of the sea rather than territorial possessions, and upon the monopoly of shipping which the Dutch enjoyed over intra-Asian trade. At its height this empire was 58 times the size of the mother country, and its profits seemed to flow in a never-ending stream into the coffers of the Dutch burghers.

Batavia

Batavia, the center of the Dutch empire in the East, was founded by Coen in a swamp on a desolate coast, surrounded by wild forested hinterland. Batavia served as the great entrepôt of all the intra-Asian trade, since all goods from Persia, India, and Ceylon to the Moluccas and Japan, were cleared and transshipped here. In Batavia all records of commercial transactions were kept and were sent once a year to Holland on the so-called "tea and book ship," a vessel which had no other cargo than these two items. Batavia was a fortified city and the seat of government and administration. Its walled castle contained a garrison of some 1,200 men, and in its small space merchants and officers worked and lived together. The castle was surrounded by houses in Dutch style along canals, and by the dwellings of the many Chinese who were attracted to Batavia.

Living conditions in the city were difficult, to put it mildly. The Dutch were afraid of sea air and fresh wind, and kept their windows closed tightly both day and night. They continued to dress in heavy European fashion, worked long hours, from 6 A.M. to 6 P.M., smoked heavily, and drank gin in vast quantities. The day was begun with gin before breakfast, and gin was consumed thereafter all day long. Coen put it this way: "Our nation must drink or die." They did both, and Batavia was notorious for its heavy mortality rate. The two great dangers were fever and the flux, and a Company servant had the choice of being carried away by either. Those gentlemen who drank liquors to excess usually managed to avoid the flux, but they were carried off by fever, whereas those who abstained managed to avoid fever, but were carried off by the flux.

Company Policy

The Dutch East India Company was really a state within a state, since the Dutch Estates General exercised no control over its affairs. It was the company, or rather its committee of seventeen (*Heeren XVII*), who appointed the governor-general in Batavia, who in turn was aided by a council. Some of the Dutch residents in Batavia were appointed as governors of some

---

FIGURE 7.3 (opposite). The fleet of the Dutch East India Company on the roadstead off Batavia; painting by A. Cuyp. The cane points directly at the source of this Dutch bourgeois couple's wealth.

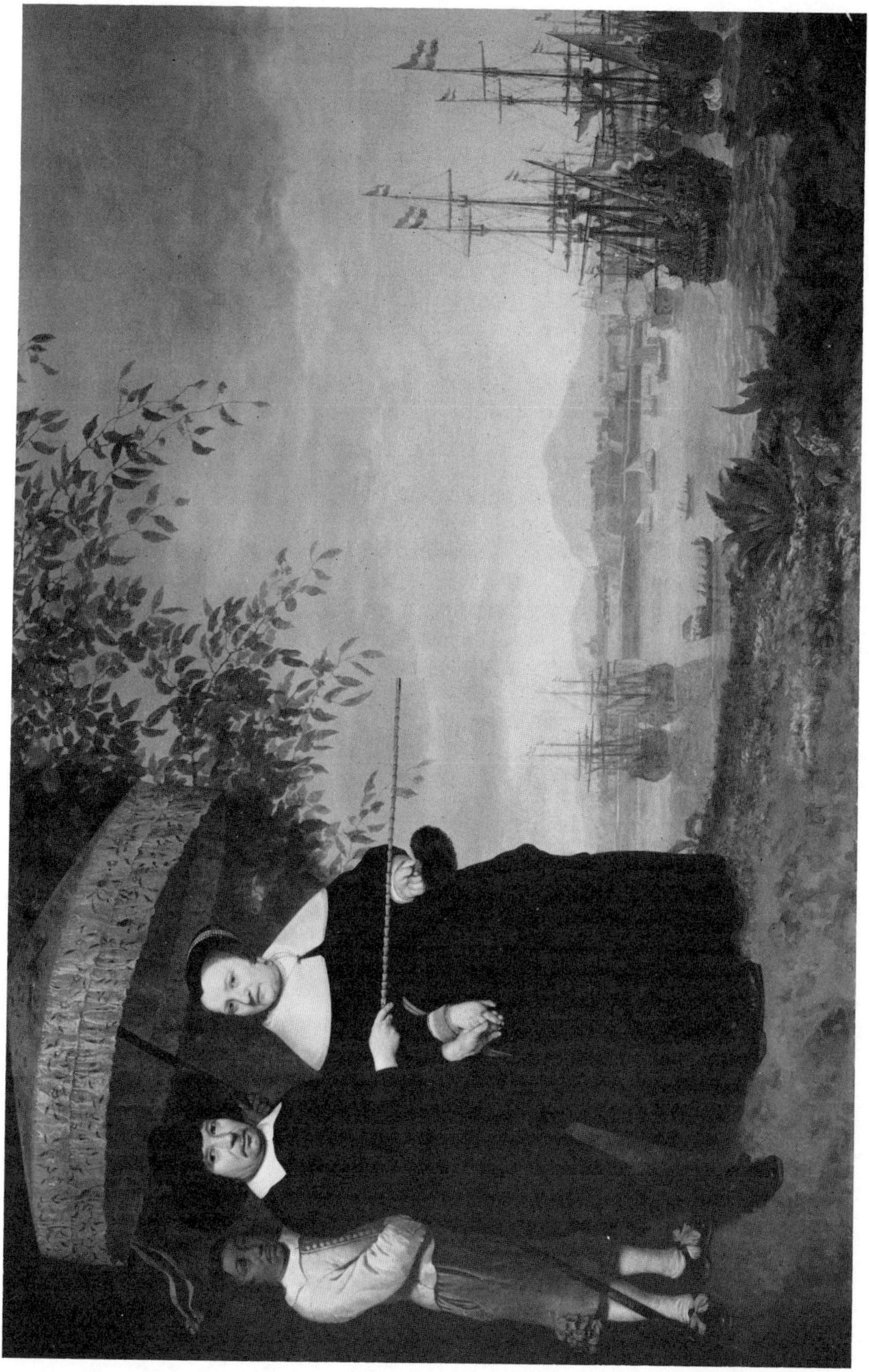

inland provinces, a development which came with the later growth of the company. Beneath these governors were native regents in charge of districts, who in turn relied upon village headmen to carry out orders and maintain law and order. But, as has been mentioned before, the basic interest of the company was purely commercial. It opposed the acquisition of territory, it had no interest whatsoever in colonization, since no direct profit could accrue from it, and it even refused to exploit discoveries made by individual Dutch navigators such as Abel Tasman who explored the South Pacific in 1642–1644.

Acquisition of territory was made only when trade made it imperative, as in the case of Batavia, Banda, or Amboina; for the rest, the company much preferred to rule through native kings by treaty arrangements. This philosophy of the company was clearly expressed in its decision when the annexation of Ceylon was once proposed: "This would be the work of a great and ambitious king, and not one of merchants who only look for profit." In Java the company was satisfied in playing off one native state against another. Bantam versus Mataram was the usual alignment, while in the Moluccas, too, the company ruled by indirect methods, as far as possible. Most local sultans, except for the one at Ternate who was reduced to complete dependency in 1683, were left as nominally sovereign rulers, but bound to the company in all economic matters. All through the seventeenth century the company tried to avoid rule over native areas, and where it could not be avoided because of involvement in political rivalry, the company always managed to rule through a native regent who could do as he pleased as long as he supplied the Dutch with the products they wanted. Profit was what the Dutch were after, and profit they obtained. As the world's sole supplier of cloves and nutmeg their profits were fabulous. About 1,400 to 1,800 tons of cloves were shipped annually to Amsterdam. Their purchase price was equivalent to about five cents a pound in the Spice Islands, and their cost about double when they reached Amsterdam, but a pound of cloves was sold there at over a dollar.

THE EIGHTEENTH CENTURY: TRANSITION FROM COMMERCIAL TO TERRITORIAL EMPIRE

At the turn of the eighteenth century, great changes were taking place in the nature of the Dutch empire in the East. Dutch seapower had begun to wane, and the Dutch had lost important outposts of their commercial empire. Formosa had been taken over by the formidable pirate Koxinga, the Dutch had suffered losses in Ceylon, India, and Persia, while trade with Japan had radically declined when that nation closed itself to the outside. The result of these changes was very profound.

The original goal of the Dutch, which was to interpose themselves as monopolist middlemen and carriers between the main sources of supply of Southeast Asia and the world markets, began to give way to a new concept, that of the intensive agricultural exploitation of one particular region, namely the island of Java. This policy hopefully would compensate the Dutch for

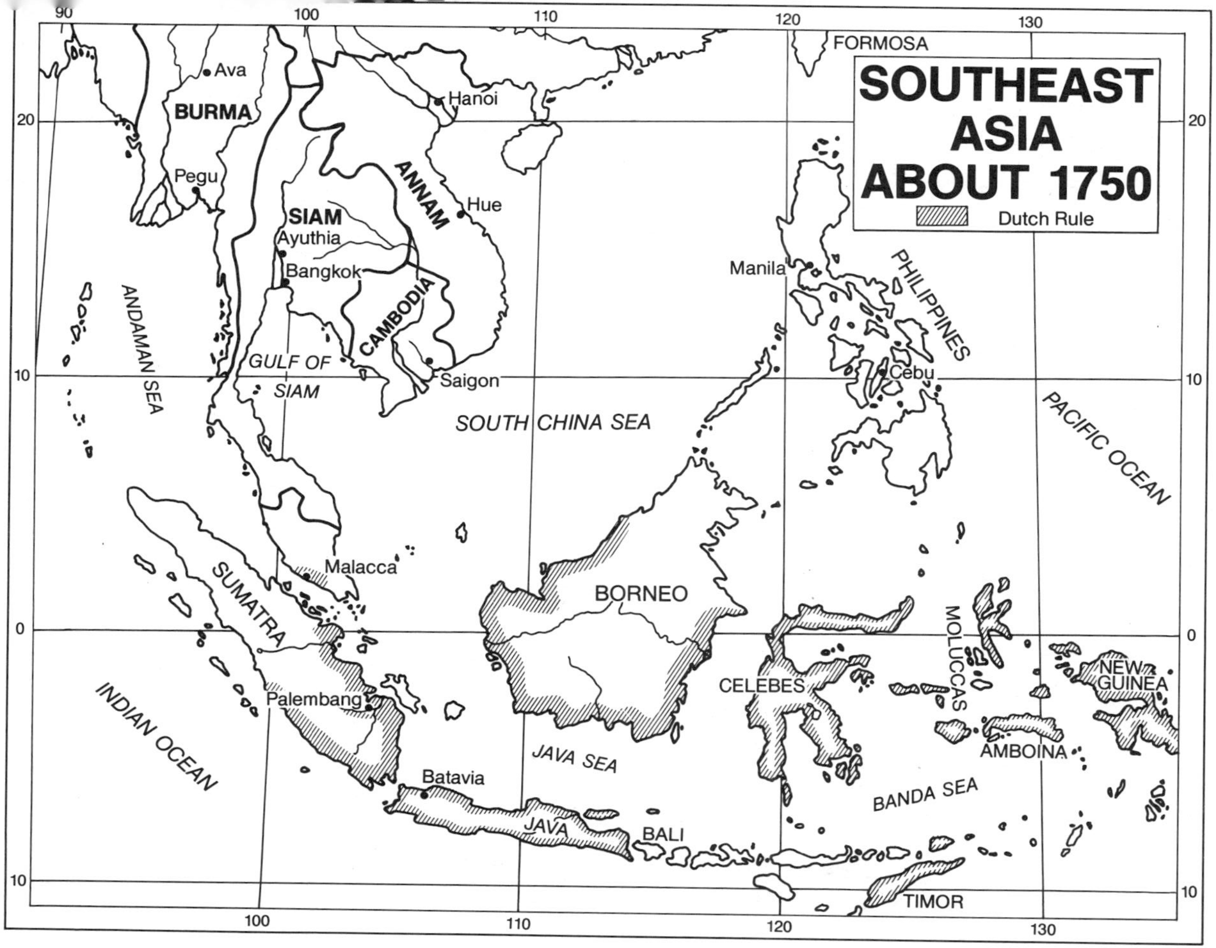
SOUTHEAST ASIA ABOUT 1750
Dutch Rule
FORMOSA
BURMA
Ava
Pegu
SIAM
Ayuthia
Bangkok
ANNAM
Hanoi
Hue
CAMBODIA
Saigon
GULF OF SIAM
ANDAMAN SEA
SOUTH CHINA SEA
PHILIPPINES
Manila
Cebu
PACIFIC OCEAN
Malacca
SUMATRA
Palembang
BORNEO
CELEBES
MOLUCCAS
NEW GUINEA
AMBOINA
BANDA SEA
JAVA SEA
JAVA
Batavia
BALI
TIMOR
INDIAN OCEAN
90
100
110
120
130
20
10
0
10

trade losses suffered. It also contained the political implication of Dutch domination over that island. The growth of Dutch political influence in Java was made easy by the absence of political unity on the island, and the existence of rival petty states, so that the Dutch found themselves in a position somewhat similar to that of the British in India.

About 1680 the Dutch interfered in a civil war that tore the sultanate of Mataram in east Java apart, and they obtained land as payment for their services. A strip of the north coast and the port of Semarang was ceded to the Dutch, and the districts of Cheribon and the Preanger were added in 1705. In 1743 the Dutch secured Madura, including the port of Surabaya. In west Java, the Dutch pursued a similar policy of interference in the kingdom of Bantam, where, because of frequent internal strife, the Dutch also obtained control of the throne. The further extension of Dutch sway over the entire island was the inevitable result of their assumption of the role of a territorial power, and it entailed extensive political supervision, so that by the early eighteenth century the company had, in fact, become the master of Java.

Beginnings of the Plantation System

Beginning in 1703, when the Dutch set up a puppet on the throne of Mataram (the "susuhunan" or supreme ruler), the Dutch set up a system of puppet governors with whom they made alliances and to whom they gave military assistance, while in return they were given extensive commercial privileges. Money was still the sole interest of the company, but money now meant the cultivation of plantation crops for export, rather than income derived from commerce. The first years of the new century saw the large-scale development of agriculture in Java, notably of such plantation crops as sugar (originally brought in from China), coffee (introduced from Arabia), indigo, tea, and cotton. As the plantation system grew and expanded, the Dutch worked out two methods of operation—the system known as forced delivery and the contingent system.

The forced delivery system was based on a quota which the regents, or native rulers, were required to deliver to the Dutch. Fixed amounts of products, such as coffee, pepper, and other tropical raw materials, at company-imposed prices, had to be provided. The contingent system, on the other hand, was merely payment of tribute in kind. Since tribute in kind was paid in the form of export crops, and since their prices depended upon the world market, the demand for these various staple products by the company was subject to arbitrary fluctuation. When prices were high in Europe, the company would suddenly demand additional tribute; when prices at the exchange in Amsterdam were low, tropical products such as coffee and spices might actually be destroyed in order to keep the price up. Under either system the Dutch found themselves involved in the general supervision of production in Java, and since profit was basically the only interest of the Dutch, the result was oppressive misgovernment for the island. Since the Dutch desired to economize as much as possible in their administration, they took no interest whatever in the misrule of the local regents, as long as the desired products arrived. Both systems resulted in a very heavy burden on the native cultivator, and due to erratic demands, the peasants were sometimes even compelled to grow crops on unsuitable soils, neglecting the growing of rice, their basic foodstuff, in order to produce the required amounts for delivery or tribute.

Furthermore, under this system, Java was not only saddled with oppressive government, but as the aims of European activity were solely commercial, Western culture had practically no impact on the island. Because education or Christianizing would cost money, the Dutch discouraged missionary efforts and showed no interest in educating the natives. Even the language used by the Dutch with the Javanese remained a sort of debased Portuguese, and no efforts were made to introduce the Dutch tongue. Consequently, during the eighteenth century the influence of the West made practically no impression on Java, and the life of the peasant villages in particular continued perfectly unchanged in its traditional patterns.

The Arrival of the Chinese

The only major social change which occurred as the result of the Company's shift towards a territorial empire was the great influx of Chinese. Many of these came from China's south coast, especially Fukien province in the aftermath of the unsuccessful San Fan Rebellion against Manchu rule, and they arrived in the Indies as artisans, traders, overseers of sugar plantations, and also as moneylenders and bankers. Their ability to extract work from the Javanese pleased the Dutch, and their own industriousness and thriftiness soon gave them an important role in the economy of the Indies. The Chinese maintained their own traditions and customs, and remained a separate middle-class community apart from the Dutch and the Javanese, forming the beginnings of the so-called "plural society" in Indonesia, where in addition to the ruling class of the whites and the bottom rung of native peasants, there was also an alien middle class. By 1720 some 100,000 Chinese had settled in Java, of whom perhaps 80 per cent lived in or near Batavia. The Dutch gave them the right of residence, but at times their numbers seemed a threat to the Dutch government, and sometimes, as in 1740, there were massacres of the Chinese at Batavia. The massacre of 1740 started as a result of the false rumor that Chinese who were being deported has been thrown from ships and left to drown, and it caused a general panic which lasted twelve days and cost the lives of 10,000 Chinese.

Decline of the Company

In the long run, however, the policy of immediate profit to the exclusion of all else proved to be a mistaken one. By the late eighteenth century the Dutch East India Company began to show very serious signs of decline and decay due to mismanagement, graft, smuggling, corruption, and private trading. The practice of false economy especially was damaging. Ships would not be repaired, and they would sink. The lowering of salaries of company officials, to a point where they were not enough to live on, attracted only individuals from a lower-class background, who in order to live had to resort to private trade. Many of them took temporary native wives, and among the soldiers, too, barrack-room mating, as it was called, became common. The resultant growth of a mixed race was not discouraged by the Dutch, and with it too came many new and formidable problems. Fortified sites in the Indies were inadequately garrisoned and supplied, for economy's sake, and the company was thus unable to prevent the appearance of British, Danish, and American merchant ships.

Nevertheless, in order to maintain appearances and confidence, the company continued to issue huge dividends, and it did not shrink from fraud and dishonesty. The economic decline of the company's fortunes late in the eighteenth century, originally the result of miserliness and poor management, culminated in disaster with the outbreak of the French Revolution and the Napoleonic Wars. After 1780 British control of the seas and the resultant blockade caused the company to go hopelessly into debt, so that by 1796 it was forced to suspend dividends, and two years later in 1798 company rule ended. A new Dutch government, that of the French-controlled Batavian republic, democratic in character and hostile to a commercial oligarchy, prepared to take over the affairs of the Dutch in the East. With the spread of the French Revolution Holland in fact became part of France, and a new era of reform dawned for the Dutch empire.

REFORMS, 1800–1824

The first years of the nineteenth century were the era of reform for the Dutch possessions in the East, the result both of the principles of the philosophy of the Enlightenment, as well as of the practical results of the French Revolution and Napoleonic rule. Reforms were carried out first by the Dutch, and later by the English when the East Indies came temporarily into their possession.

The leaders in the reform movement were men imbued with the liberal principles of the philosophers of the Enlightenment, notably those of Locke who had declared that "men are born, and always continue, free and equal in respect of their rights." John Locke's doctrine of the natural rights of men went hand in hand, on the economic side, with the theories of the Physiocrats who also believed in principles of natural law which, in agriculture, implied the abolition of all special privileges and monopolies.

Hermann Daendels

Among the liberal reformers in Southeast Asia who were influenced by these ideas, two men stand out in particular for their role in shaping developments in the Dutch East Indies. One of these was Dutch, the other British. The first of these was Hermann Daendels, who had been trained as a lawyer in Holland. He had become a great admirer of Napoleon, whom he served as a soldier with considerable distinction, becoming known as the "Thundering Marshal." In 1808 he was sent to Java by Napoleon to strengthen the defenses of the island against the British and to institute liberal administrative and judicial reforms. For the next two years Daendels worked with tremendous energy to accomplish his task. It was Daendels who laid the groundwork of reform in the Dutch possessions by replacing the system of indirect rule by a more direct rule, by bringing the native regents under close control of Dutch officials, and by centralizing the government in order to create a more efficient bureaucracy. Other measures were designed to curb administration graft and corruption, and Javanese law courts were established which dispensed native (adat) law, thereby ensuring greater justice to the Javanese peasant. Daendels was also responsible for the building of a great road which ran the length of the island from Batavia to Surabaya, and which made defense easier by permitting rapid shifting of military forces. In the economic sphere Daendels abolished forced deliveries in spices, although the system was kept for other products; at the same time he tried to increase overall production. The net effect of Daendels' administration was an improvement in government, but as one might expect, he created many enemies. Bitter complaints were made against him, and in 1810 he was recalled.

Thomas Stamford Raffles

In July of that same year Holland became an integral part of France by being annexed by Napoleon, and so Java, together with all the rest of the Dutch possessions overseas, was considered enemy territory by Great Britain. The result was a British invasion during August 1811 by some 100 ships and 12,000 men under Lord Minto, which quickly secured the surrender of all Java. The British appointed as governor-general Thomas Stamford Raffles, the second of the great liberal reformers. At that point in his career Raffles was only thirty years old, but was ambitious and brilliant.

Raffles envisioned Java as becoming a permanent British possession, and his administration (1811 to 1816) during the British occupation was based on liberal principles. He believed that it was necessary to "give justice, humanity, and moderation to the native people . . . let us do all the good we can," so that in some respects at least Raffles continued the program of Daendels, while in others he greatly differed from that program.

Essentially, what Raffles did was to promote direct rule (as had Daendels) and direct taxation (as Daendels had not). Raffles, in introducing new aims and methods of colonial administration, was more liberal than his predecessor, and his administration marked a sharper turning point, since he believed that the supreme end of government was to provide for the welfare of the people. Both men had tried to do away with the system of native regents, substituting instead a government operating through a European bureaucracy. However, whereas Daendels was no liberal in the economic sphere, increasing production and retaining the system of forced deliveries for some products, Raffles decreed the complete abolition of the forced delivery system, and followed the example of India in leasing out the land to the peasant for money rent. Raffles also introduced the liberal principle of a free market, in which the cultivator could grow and sell his

FIGURE 7.4. Portrait of Sir Thomas Stamford Raffles painted in 1817 by G. F. Joseph.

crops as he desired. Raffles argued that if you gave economic freedom to the peasant, the result would be economically advantageous to government, since the peasant could use his cash income after paying rent to purchase products of British industry and commerce, such as cotton goods. Opening Java as a market for free trade was, of course, the very opposite of Daendels' economic policy. Raffles' economic policy did produce an eightfold increase in revenues and seemed to promise a higher standard of living for the Javanese, but this policy came to an early end with the departure of the British. In another respect Raffles showed himself to be more imbued with the principles of the Enlightenment than Daendels. This was Raffles' humanitarian approach to a foreign culture. Raffles studied the language of Java, he wrote a classic *History of Java*, and ordered the first survey to be made of the magnificent Borobodur monument of medieval times.

The work of Raffles in Java did not survive, since, as the result of negotiations at the Congress of Vienna, Britain decided to return the East Indies to the Dutch. In order to restore the balance of power in Europe, Great Britain needed a strong Netherlands. For this reason the British occupation of Java came to end in 1816, and in 1824 the final treaty returning all islands in the East Indies to the Dutch was signed. Reform came to an end with the resumption of direct Dutch control.

RESTORATION OF DUTCH RULE

From 1816 to 1848 the Dutch established a system in which the governor-general and his council ruled directly for the Dutch king. In order to protect Dutch commercial interests in Java and to secure ready money, there was a rapid return to a monopolistic economic organization. This was accomplished by the Netherlands Trading Company formed in 1824 at the Hague, a company which, of course, was the very opposite in concept to free trade. The Netherlands need for money soon became very acute, following a slump in the price of coffee, a costly revolt in Belgium, and, finally, an even more costly revolt in Java itself. The latter was the work of a Javanese prince, Dipo Negara of Jogjakarta, who from 1825 to 1830 led against the Dutch a guerrilla military action, which he proclaimed to be a Moslem holy war. This bitter struggle, whose ultimate effect was to force the Dutch to conquer the interior of the island and to extend their control, ended only after Dipo Negara was captured at great cost in manpower and in money. By 1830, as the result of the war in Java, and the long drawn out Belgian insurrection, the Dutch revenues showed an annual deficit, and the cry for more money was louder than ever. To ease this financial crisis a new scheme was proposed in 1830 by Johannes Vandenbosch. A bitter critic of what he called "perverted liberalism," Vandenbosch had quarreled with Daendels and his ideas of colonial administration. Now, in 1830, he proposed a new system which was to be "the life belt on which the Netherlands would be kept afloat."

The culture system was an attempt to concentrate in the hands of the government all of the productive capacity of the Indies, and it was modeled to a large extent on the slave plantations of the United States. In a sense, this was not really a new system of production; rather, it was a reversion to the old forced delivery system, because under the culture system the government claimed either one fifth of the produce, or sixty-six working days from the native cultivator. This meant complete government control over commercial agriculture and the intensive exploitation of Java. After the introduction of the culture system, the island became virtually a vast state plantation in which export crops, notably coffee, sugar, and indigo, but also kapok, tapioca, quinine, tobacco, tea, cotton, and pepper, were produced by forced labor under state compulsion. This scheme, once instituted, almost at once resulted in expanded production and increased revenue, and during the years 1840 to 1848, the heyday of the culture system in terms of production and profits, the Netherlands enjoyed enormous cash returns. Vast sums flowed directly into the royal treasury at the Hague, and they constituted a veritable financial lifebuoy for Holland. These were in the neighborhood of 14 to 15 million guilders each year, and were used to redeem public debts, reduce taxes, finance public works, and strengthen the Dutch merchant marine. All of this was of little benefit to Java. The culture system, profitable as it was for the Dutch, in reality meant a heavy burden of compulsory labor for the Javanese peasant. It was a demoralizing method of human exploitation which at times produced famine since it seriously interfered with and curtailed the rice production necessary to sustain the Javanese.

This period of direct royal control and of financial monopoly by the Netherlands Trading Company may have been economically rewarding, but it once again induced complacency and lack of interest in the affairs of the Indies. Since responsibility of the officials was directly to the king, to most Hollanders events in their overseas possessions in the East mattered little. Holland extended her territory somewhat into Sumatra and Borneo, and in 1828 the western part of the huge island of New Guinea was brought under Dutch control, but these events were scarcely noted at home, and it was not until the revolutionary year of 1848 that exclusive royal control over the Indies came to an end. Even so, when constitutional reforms were made and some changes instituted following that year of upheaval, the colonial question remained still very much in the background. After 1848 the Dutch parliament received the right to an annual report, but that was all. It was left to the powerful and impassioned pen of Douwes Dekker, who wrote under the pseudonym Multatuli, to awaken the public opinion and conscience of the Dutch to the abuses of their government and of the culture system in the Indies. When he published his famous book *Max Havelaar* in 1860, after having returned from service in Java, the impact of that work was rather like that of *Uncle Tom's Cabin*; literature was enlisted as a potent force for change.

BASIC DATES

1595	*Itinerario* by Jan Linschoten
1595–1596	Voyage of van Houtman
1602	Foundation of Dutch East India Company
1619	J. P. Coen establishes Batavia
1622	Dutch attack on Macao
1623	Amboina massacre
1641	Dutch capture of Malacca
1703	Dutch set up puppet ruler of Mataram
c. 1750–1798	Dutch Company sovereignty
1808–1810	Hermann Daendels
1811–1816	Thomas Stamford Raffles

1830   Vandenbosch and the culture system
1848   End of direct royal control
1860   Max Havelaar

SUPPLEMENTARY READING

Bastin, J. S. and H. Benda. *A History of Modern Southeast Asia.* Englewood Cliffs, N.J., 1968.
Cady, J. *Southeast Asia: Its Historical Development.* New York, 1963.
Harrison, B. *South-East Asia: A Short History,* 2nd ed. London, 1963, Brief, well-written.
Vlekke, B. H. M. *Nusantara: A History of the East Indian Archipelago.* Cambridge, Mass., 1943.

ADVANCED READING

Fieldhouse, D. K. *The Colonial Empires: A Comparative Survey from the Eighteenth Century.* New York, 1969.
Furnivall, J. S. *Netherlands India.* New York, 1944. A careful analysis by a famous British colonial administrator of the success and failure of Dutch policy in the Indies.
Hall, D. G. E. *A History of South-East Asia.* New York, 1955.
Marselman, G. *The Cradle of Colonialism.* New Haven, 1963.
Raffles, T. S. *The History of Java.* London, 1966. Originally published 1817.
Steinberg, D. J. *In Search of Southeast Asia.* New York, 1961.

Chapter 8

Colonial Empires of Southeast Asia to 1914

NETHERLANDS INDIES

In the last chapter the creation of a Dutch empire in the East was discussed, and it seems fitting to complete the story of this process up to 1914 first, and then to turn to the history of the British and French colonial empires in Southeast Asia, concluding this survey with an account of the history of Siam, the one remaining independent country in that area prior to the outbreak of the First World War.

Beginnings of Reform

The second half of the nineteenth century in the Netherlands Indies was a period in which the liberal movement in the Netherlands was sufficiently strong to produce economic and social changes in the Dutch colonies. After 1848 the administration of the Dutch East Indies came under the direction of the Dutch parliament which now had a voice in the control of the colonies and was an institution responsive to aroused opinion, and some mention has been made of the very important role of the book *Max Havelaar* (published 1860) as an impetus to reform (see Chapter 7).

By 1854 the Dutch parliament had adopted what was called the Colonial Constitution, first milestone of the reform movement. Regulation of forced labor was instituted, a beginning was made in the gradual abolition of slavery, a civil service was established, the first step was taken for the provision of schools for the Indonesians, and decrees were issued making possible the leasing of unused lands to Europeans. A little later, in 1864, the colonial budget was put under the scrutiny of the parliament, and the first steps were taken to abolish the culture system. One product at a time was released, first tea, then indigo, tobacco, and cinnamon, so that by 1870 all crops except coffee and sugar were exempt from the culture system (although it must be realized that it was precisely these two latter commodities which were the most important ones from the point of view of cash export crops, and coffee continued to be grown under the culture system until 1917). It is true that reform had begun, but it made very slow headway as far as political and social affairs were concerned, whereas in the economic field the doctrines of liberalism were fully triumphant.

Economic Developments

Economic liberalism, with its accompanying belief in free enterprise and its principle that the desire for individual gain would also promote the general welfare without formal planning, became the accepted gospel of the day. Its advocates argued that the government should get out of business, and that instead private capital and enterprise should exploit the Dutch colonies. They also pointed out that a colony based on free labor would provide a much better market for European goods, and that an increase in private enterprise also would certainly mean increased production which would supply greater revenues to the government from increased land rents and customs payments. With the passing of the agrarian law of 1870 the way was prepared for the acceptance of these principles of economic liberalism.

Under this law private plantations could be established, while at the

FIGURE 8.1. A Javanese house in a kampong, *or village. From* Gleason's Pictorial, *June 11, 1853.*

same time the law protected the native cultivator against exploitation. It forbade the outright sale of land to non-Indonesians, permitting only leases to plantation owners. The result was a great flow of European investment capital into the Dutch East Indies. Most of the early private capital investments went into sugar, but some also into tin mining on the islands of Bangka and Billiton, and later oil when in 1888 petroleum was discovered in Sumatra and east Borneo. In 1890 the Royal Dutch Oil Company was founded to exploit these new riches, but the really great increase in capital flow to the Indies came after 1900, and it was concerned primarily with the island of Java. From this time investment capital was not only Dutch, but increasingly from British, American, French, Belgian, and German sources, and it went into new tropical products, such as palm oil and rubber which had been introduced with striking success from Brazil.

As Europe and the United States became highly industrialized, the demand for colonial products steadily increased, and the market for tropical products expanded ceaselessly. This trend was accompanied by the fall in cost of transportation, made possible in particular by the opening of the Suez Canal. The production of all tropical raw materials, especially sugar, tobacco, and tea, virtually doubled overnight, bringing ever higher returns on investment capital.

However, despite its advantages economic liberalism brought with it by 1900 state intervention once again to protect the natives who were powerless in the face of the large-scale plantation system, and after the turn of the century the Dutch government found a need for an active economic and social program designed to protect the natives against the evils of capitalism. From this period dates the so-called "ethical policy" of the Dutch in Indonesia, which stressed the welfare of the people, but at the same time did not run counter to the interests of the Dutch manufacturer or foreign investor. The moral duty of the Netherlands toward the people of the Indies was emphasized in an article, "Debt of Honor," in 1899 by C. Th[eodore] van Deventer, who maintained that it was the duty of the government to support education in partial return at least for the wealth which Indonesia had given to the Dutch. A beginning was made in the establishment of village schools, although progress was very slow, and the level of education remained low. By 1913 only 7,000 schools could be found in all Java. The increase in enrollment fell far behind the population growth, and higher education was almost completely neglected.

By 1900, also, the general development of the agricultural and mineral resources of the East Indies was no longer restricted to Java alone, and a notable feature of economic development prior to World War I was the activity in territories outside Java. In order to work plantations in Sumatra and Borneo there was an increased need for labor, and since Java had the largest population, labor was imported from there, usually under the contract system with low wages and many penal sanctions. The economy of the Dutch East Indies was also aided by the rise in prices of tropical products, so that the Dutch enjoyed a period of great prosperity. On the other hand, there was no corresponding rise in the standard of living of the Indonesians; rather, just as in India, the effect of prosperity was to increase population, a development which was soon to pose some very serious problems. During the period from 1815 to 1860 the population of Java doubled, reaching about 11 million, but by 1900 this figure had risen to a formidable 28 million.

Political Expansion

The shift of attention to areas other than Java, the original scene of development, brought with it also extension of Dutch political control. After 1824 the Dutch had been satisfied to leave the sultans of Sumatra untrammeled, but increasing economic development and the problem of piracy led to the Dutch conquest of the whole of that large island. The source of most trouble in this respect, and the home of some truly ferocious pirates, was the Moslem sultanate of Achin on the northwest tip of Sumatra. Hostilities between the Dutch and Achin finally broke out in 1873, ironically enough over the issue of abolition of debt slavery which the Dutch insisted upon. The Achin war lasted 30 years and cost one quarter of a million lives. Not until 1907 were the Dutch able to take over the whole island of Sumatra, with the consent of the British. By this time the Dutch also had extended their political control into the outer territories, which comprised everything beyond Java and adjacent Madura. The outer islands were taken over by the Dutch to prevent possible foreign intervention, and by 1900 the islands of Bali and Lombok had come under direct Dutch rule. By that date, too, the Dutch had explored the interior of Borneo, and had established their political control over a portion of that island and over western New Guinea. Extension of Dutch political control into the outer territories was accompanied by economic exploitation of their great natural riches, such as pepper, coffee, copra, rubber, sugar, tea, tobacco, tin, and petroleum.

Nature of Dutch Rule

Dutch rule in Indonesia was exercised through the governor-general in Batavia, who was assisted by an advisory council, composed of Hollanders. He also was served by a cabinet, also all-Dutch in composition, and there was, of course, no popular representation involved in Dutch rule prior to the First World War. The authoritarian and paternalistic structure of Dutch government in the Indies, ever since the inception of the "ethical policy" early in the twentieth century, was, however, concerned with measures which would protect the native peasant proprietor from the worst effects of a money economy. Some of these measures, designed to safeguard native society, included legislation which prevented the alienation of land to non-Indonesians. Land which was unsuitable for wet-rice production and which had to be cleared first, but which could be used for tea and rubber plantations, was given on long-term leases, to large-scale operators, whereas land which was suitable for the growing of rice, as well as for sugar and tobacco, could be leased only on an annual basis, thereby preventing the possibility of insufficient amounts of staple food. The government also controlled the rents involved, to protect the peasant. In order to protect the Javanese from moneylenders after 1900 the Dutch government also began to institute government pawn shops, as well as private village banks, where loans for seed and tools were possible at moderate rates. A further step was taken when the Village Act of 1906 was passed, which attempted to restore social solidarity to the native village by providing for local responsibility for local social welfare under the traditional *adat* law of Java. In general, Dutch policy in the Indies attempted to improve the lot, or at least safeguard the interests, of the natives; it was a policy of adaptation, but it was not one of assimilation whereby the Indonesians would be culturally absorbed by their masters.

Seeds of Nationalism

Although the Dutch did not attempt to bring Western ideas and methods to the Indies, nevertheless these ideas did begin to make their appearance in the first decade of the new century. An outgrowth of these ideas was the emergence of an Indonesian nationalist movement, as a reaction against Dutch colonial rule. Nationalism in Indonesia began as a cultural movement, founded by Western-trained Indonesian intellectuals, in part stimulated by Western ideas of nationalism introduced through Western education. The national movement, which moved from acquiescence to Dutch rule to the demand for total national independence, began with the foundation in 1908 of a society called Budi Utomo, or "high endeavor." This society was the work of a physician, Radin Sutomo, who greatly admired the ideas of Tagore and Gandhi in India. Its program was primarily concerned with education. The society stressed the necessity of establishing Indonesian schools which would provide improved educational standards and opportunities for Indonesia, thereby promoting social and economic progress. One marked feature of the program was that it stressed the revival of the Indonesian cultural tradition. The Budi Utomo gained the support of a number of Indonesian intellectuals, officials, and members of the native aristocracy, and it flourished for a while in Java and Madura, but it was soon eclipsed by a far more popular form of Indonesian nationalism, that which found its expression in the movement founded in 1910 known as Sarekat Islam. As its title indicates, this movement played upon the religious motive of strengthening the faith of Muhammad, and thus it had a wider appeal than a purely educational movement. Sarekat Islam also stood for the promotion of commercial enterprise among Indonesians by means of mutual economic support, and it opposed in this way the economic influence of the Chinese who played such a prominent part in Indonesian economic life. The Sarekat Islam, in its short official life before it was suppressed in 1911, even organized anti-Chinese riots. It was reorganized in 1912, declaring loyalty to the Dutch, but it soon became more outspoken, and with the outbreak of the First World War Sarekat Islam was the first Indonesian mass movement to profess radical nationalistic ideas.

THE BRITISH COLONIAL EMPIRE: BURMA, MALAYA, BORNEO

The changes which took place during the last quarter of the nineteenth century in the Dutch East Indies may be seen as the beginning of a general process by which other countries of Southeast Asia developed along parallel lines with Java. They, too, were impelled to increase their production for export; they, too, became increasingly dependent upon world markets and shared in a general transition from a subsistence to a commercial economy; and they, too, were part of a colonial world in which the sources of political power were half a world away, in London or in Paris.

British colonial possessions in this part of the world included Burma, Malaya, and Borneo.

Burma

Burma originally derived its culture from India across the Bay of Bengal. It had developed into a strong Hinayana Buddhist kingdom by the eleventh century, but had suffered greatly from the inroads of the Mongols in the thirteenth century and the subsequent migration of Shan tribes into northern Burma in the wake of the Mongol destruction. From 1280 to 1762 the native Toungoo dynasty ruled the country, but at the beginning of the seventeenth century Burma was weakened by wars and disruption. Very little control was exercised by the royal court, which after 1635 had retired inland and withdrawn to Ava. By the eighteenth century Burma was completely exhausted due to frequent civil wars and absence of strong royal control. It was divided and utterly impoverished, a victim of complete anarchy, so much so that no foreigners evinced interest in foreign trade with her. Burma was left strictly alone, leading a self-sufficient existence.

Alaungpaya and Burmese Expansion. After the middle of the eighteenth century, however, Burma was once more reunited under the very energetic leadership of a new ruler of Ava, Alaungpaya. During the years 1753 to 1760 Alaungpaya unified Burma and established a new dynasty. In this task he had the assistance of the British East India Company who furnished him weapons and munitions, since they feared the possibility of the French seizing Burma, and in return the British obtained favorable commercial terms. So successful was Alaungpaya within Burma that he soon directed his aggressiveness against his neighbor to the east, Siam. A clash on the frontier was followed by a Burmese invasion of Siam in 1759, and after Alaungpaya's death in 1760, his successors continued the war. In 1769 a new Burmese invasion was most successful, sweeping away the Siamese defenders, and the Burmese army captured, plundered, and almost destroyed the Siamese capital at Ayuthia.

In their attempt to establish their overlordship over Siam the Burmese eventually were checked by Manchu China. China had extended her control over Tibet, and she had forced Nepal to acknowledge Chinese suzerainty and enlist in the tributary system. During 1766–69 a clash took place between Chinese and Burmese troops over the issue of control over some hill tribes in Yunnan, and the great Ch'ien-lung emperor ordered a Chinese army into Burma. His forces were outmaneuvered by the Burmese, but nevertheless his power was so formidable that in 1770 the Burmese agreed to a peace treaty which relinquished Burmese control of Siam. In Siam itself a native resistance movement had begun to spring up, after 1768, and the Siamese had been able to recapture Ayuthia and to reestablish their power.

Restrained in the east, Burmese energy and vigor then searched for an outlet in the west along the coast of the Bay of Bengal. By 1784 the Burmese had conquered the Arakan coast, and they began to encroach upon territory claimed by the government of India, while by 1793 Burma also had acquired the Tenasserim coast in the south.

British Conquest. The extension of Burmese power to the north along the coast of Arakan into Assam, a region previously subject to Burma, caused friction between Burma and the British, and it precipitated the First Anglo-Burmese War. The Burmese king, Bagyidaw, was determined to reassert Burmese authority over Assam, and after some preliminary activity along the Assamese frontier, in 1822 he proceeded to invade Assam after the British in Calcutta had declared it to be a protectorate. The East India Company had decided to make Assam a buffer state, since it feared the very real danger of an invasion of Bengal should the Burmese be successful in their claims. For this reason in 1824 the first war broke out between the British and the Burmese. A British naval expedition from Bengal overran the Arakan coast, and captured Rangoon and Pegu, despite vigorous Burmese resistance. With British forces proceeding up the Irrawaddy valley, King Bagyidaw decided to bow to the inevitable, at least temporarily, and in 1826 the war ended. As spoils of victory the British obtained the whole of the Arakan and Tenasserim coasts, Burmese agreement to British control of Assam, and an indemnity. In addition, the British obtained a commercial agreement and the right to station a British resident at the Burmese court in Ava.

But the Burmese were not ready to acquiesce. They continued to be as uncooperative and obstructive as possible, they treated the British with contempt, and they opposed strenuously Britain's desire to trade. Quarrels between Burma and Britain, mostly of a commercial nature, thus led to the Second Anglo-Burmese War in 1852 when Rangoon and Pegu were both taken by British forces. The result of this debacle was that Burma was forced to surrender her entire coastline, becoming an inland country in the upper Irrawaddy valley.

A few years later, the Burmese, still in a defiant mood, tried to shake off the encroachments of the British lion by playing it off against the power of the French. This was attempted by King Thibaw, a rather apathetic and highly imprudent ruler. In 1878 he negotiated with the French for the establishment of a French-controlled royal bank and the construction of a railroad line to the Indian frontier. This was a most dangerous move by the king, since the British were alarmed at the aggressive nature of the colonial policy formulated by Jules Ferry in Paris, and there was real

FIGURE 8.2. A view of Rangoon, principal port of Burma. From Gleason's Pictorial, *August 14, 1852.*

anxiety in London that the French might possibly gain control of upper Burma. When another quarrel flared up between the English and Thibaw, this time the result of a fine which was levied by the king against a British timber company (a fine curiously enough for precisely the same amount as a loan which this company had refused to hand over to the king), the British government issued an ultimatum to Burma in which it demanded that Thibaw receive a British envoy at his court, now in Mandalay, who was to be in charge of the foreign relations of the country. Upon rejection of this ultimatum the British declared war in 1885, the third and last Anglo-Burmese War. The result was not hard to foretell. Mandalay was captured, the unlucky king sent into exile to India, upper Burma was annexed, and Burma as an independent nation ceased to exist. It took a little longer for the British to establish full control over Burma, and guerrilla warfare continued for some years, particularly in northern Burma in the Shan states, but once established, British control survived until World War II.

British Rule. Burma was administered by the British as a province of India. The British tried to apply the ideas they had learned in India to Burma. This carried with it some advantages, inasmuch as British reforms in India applied also to Burma, but it also meant some disadvantages, since social conditions were often quite different, as in the realm of landownership, and it also brought about the economic exploitation of Burma by the *chettyars*, a Hindu caste of moneylenders and bankers, who flocked to Burma from Madras and soon controlled a large segment of Burmese agriculture in the lower Irrawaddy delta. Burma thus became a plural society, as had Indonesia. Burma was of great economic value to Great Britain, with its resources of oil, teakwood, rice, rubies, and other mineral products. The British introduced modern systems of transportation and communication, they gave Western law and a centralized colonial government to the country, but Burma remained to the English a lucrative colony ruled with a minimum of administrative expense.

Malaya

The other mainland area in Southeast Asia to become part of the British colonial empire was Malaya. The peninsula had already demonstrated its great strategic importance when the Portuguese took Malacca in 1511, and the Dutch captured it from them and ended Portuguese power in the East in 1641. Apart from Dutch-controlled Malacca the peninsula was composed of many rival Malay principalities. A private trader, Francis Light, was responsible for laying the foundation of British power in Malaya by using the political rivalries of the various sultans and exploiting the disturbed conditions of the peninsula. The peninsula also suffered from the frequent inroads of the ferocious Bugis, seamen, or rather pirates, from Celebes, who invaded and plundered the region at frequent intervals. Light, by supporting the sultan of Kedah against the Bugis, obtained in return the island of Penang in 1786, and a few years later he added to Penang the territory lying opposite the island, which was then called Province Wellesley. Further to the south the British held Malacca, taken from the Dutch as the result of the Napoleonic Wars; however, together with Java, Malacca was restored to Holland in 1818.

This restoration brought about the acquisition of Singapore, a key British position in Malaya. Sir Stamford Raffles, the ex-governor of Java and no friend of the Dutch, had protested strongly but futilely the return of Java and Malacca, and in order to counterbalance this loss he now pressed upon the government in London the necessity of obtaining the uninhabited island of Singapore from the sultan of Johore. He told his government, "You may take my word for it, this is by far the most important station in the East." Sir Stamford had a keen eye and a persuasive pen, and in 1819 Britain acquired Singapore, then a swamp which had been abandoned for centuries, but soon to become the keystone of Britain's colonial empire in Southeast Asia. The Dutch protested for the next five years, and it was only in a treaty concluded between Holland and Britain in 1824 that they finally acquiesced.

Malacca, too, in 1824, once more became British, but in return the English agreed to get out of Sumatra altogether, where they had a small trading station in Bencoolen. The port of Singapore, which Raffles founded, soon became important commercially, and the British government found itself in the possession of a first-rate deep water harbor of the greatest strategic importance, since Singapore controlled all traffic through the Straits of Malacca and defended the eastern approaches to the Indian Ocean.

Raffles made Singapore a free port, thereby attracting trade, and provided law courts, a code of law, and schools for the city.

After 1830 all three bases, Penang, Malacca, and Singapore, were ruled separately from Calcutta, but in 1867 the three became the crown colony of the Straits Settlements. Their economic development was most rapid, particularly with the exploitation of their resources of tin, and then, somewhat later, with the growing of rubber trees. Growing prosperity attracted a large number of Chinese, especially after 1850, so that in Malaya, too, a plural society was being formed.

At first the British did not interfere with the local Malay states to the north, but after 1872 the British began to expand in that direction also. Based on the argument that prevailing anarchy made intervention necessary, some of the petty Malay sultanates were placed under British protection. This process began in Perak, where the chiefs had revolted in 1875 and where the sultan concluded a treaty agreeing to accept a British resident, and it continued with a similar treaty with Pahang a few years later after a revolt had been put down there in 1894. In 1895 four Malay states were joined as the Federated Malay States. These four were Perak, Selangor, Negri Sembilan, and Pahang. The Federated Malay States were administered by a British resident general with supervisory powers stationed at Kuala Lumpur, and local British residents at the courts of the four sultans.

With the Malay sultanates located further north and to the south of the Federated Malay States, treaties were also concluded which resulted in their union into the Unfederated Malay States. These were Kelantan, Kedah, Perlis, Trengganu, and Johore (in 1914), and each agreed to receive assistance from British advisors who were given the rank of "resident ministers." In an Anglo-Siamese treaty signed in 1909, Siamese suzerainty over these sultanates was clearly terminated.

The results of the establishment of British rule in Malaya were very rapid and very drastic economic changes in the peninsula. The English provided modern means of communication, telegraph, telephone, a postal service, roads, and railways, they introduced modern medicine and Western law, but above all they developed Malaya's natural wealth. The economy of the area became based on large-scale plantations and large-scale mining. The production of sugar, coffee, coconuts, and (after 1900) especially rubber, together with the mining of tin, was largely in the hands of foreigners. Plantations were held by the British, while mines were controlled by the Chinese as well. So great was this economic revolution that even the basic foodstuff of Malaya, rice, was imported from abroad. Profits were enormous. New immigrants, Chinese, and to a lesser degree Indians, came in such numbers that they outnumbered the Malays, and by 1914 the population of the city of Singapore was 80 per cent Chinese.

The British in Borneo

Beyond the mainland, and in the island world of Southeast Asia, the British established themselves on the island of Borneo in Sarawak, Labuan, and

North Borneo. The story of Sarawak is a rather romantic one. It became the possession of a private adventurer, James Brooke, who handed it down as personal property in his family. Brooke was a wealthy, retired officer of the British East India Company who in 1839 visited the sultan of Brunei on Borneo. This ruler was plagued by many pirates and the consequent absence of profitable foreign trade, but Brooke furnished him valuable military assistance against the pirates. In appreciation of these services the sultan gave him Sarawak in 1841, and from that year on Sarawak was ruled by Rajah Brooke. He was succeeded by his nephew, and he in turn by his son, who ruled until 1946. The Brooke family governed as a benevolent autocracy, enlarging the borders of Sarawak, developing public works, education, public health, forestry, and trade. The foreign relations of Sarawak were conducted by the English government, and the officials employed were all British civil servants, while from 1888 on Sarawak was declared a British protectorate, but even so there clung to this region the unique flavor of a family enterprise.

Another British possession in Borneo was the island of Labuan, off the coast of North Borneo. It was acquired by the British in 1846 from James Brooke, as a coaling station between Singapore and Hong Kong. Finally, in North Borneo itself, British rule was exercised through the British North Borneo Company, a chartered company with both British and Austrian capital, which from 1881 on ruled that part of the great island, and ruled it well. The British North Borneo Company developed rubber plantations and the area soon enjoyed great prosperity. North Borneo, like Sarawak, was made a British protectorate in 1888.

FRENCH COLONIAL EXPANSION

Vietnam and the French

The French colonial empire in Southeast Asia was built in Vietnam, known to the Chinese as Annam, and its origins go back to French missionary efforts in the seventeenth century.

The reigning family in Vietnam, since 1428, was the Le dynasty whose founder had overthrown Chinese political control without rejecting the culture of Ming China. During the sixteenth century two noble families gained power as rival rulers in Vietnam, the Trinh at Hanoi in Tonkin (or Tongking) where after 1592 the Le emperors maintained their court, and the Nguyen, since 1558, at Hué in the south. There was open warfare between the two from 1620 to 1673; the Le had become mere puppets. Nguyen princes meanwhile used some of their forces to extend Vietnamese rule to the south; they gained control of Quinhon in 1602 and Saigon in 1658. In the process the ancient principality of the Cham was eliminated and the Vietnamese moved into territory which had been dominated by the Cambodians. In extending their rule and their culture the Nguyen made use of Chinese settlers, including those who fled from China at the fall of the Ming, and who spread from Saigon to the Mekong delta. During their wars the Nguyen were also aided by Portuguese and Dutch who came to trade in the area but who found little demand for their imports.

This was a time of Buddhist revival in Vietnam, both north and south. The Thien (or Ch'an) sects came in from China during the seventeenth century. In their religion the Vietnamese developed a syncretism of faiths, but this did not include Christianity. On the contrary, there was opposition to the French Catholic missionaries (mostly Jesuits) who entered the country after 1664.

During most of the eighteenth century the Trinh maintained an effective government at Hanoi while the Nguyen in the south continued to expand at the expense of the Cambodians. Both Vietnamese regimes were disrupted by rebels from Tayson who commenced by capturing Quinhon in 1773 and who contested the rule of the Nguyen until 1801.

During the time of the Tayson rebellion, one of the contestants, Nguyen Anh, was befriended by a French bishop, Pigneau de Behaine. The latter recruited in India a French military force which came to the assistance of Nguyen Anh. He defeated the rebels in 1801 and gained control of northern Vietnam in 1802. As the Emperor Gia Long, he unified the country, gained Chinese recognition, and established a centralized administration north and south. He reigned until 1820, the first of a new dynasty.

The fact that the French had aided in establishing a new strong Nguyen dynasty in Vietnam did not result in immediate advantages to them. As long as Gia Long himself reigned, he continued to employ French advisors and officers. His successors, absolute monarchs ruling through a Confucianist bureaucracy, were all strongly anti-French in their policies and began to persecute missionaries and their native converts. In 1848, for instance, the Emperor Tu-Duc issued a decree ordering his subjects to seize missionaries and throw them into the sea with rocks around their necks. Even so, some French missionaries undauntedly continued their labors, while some were murdered by the Vietnamese authorities. The treatment of their missionaries finally furnished an excuse for the new, vigorous French imperialism of Napoleon III to establish a colonial empire in Vietnam.

French Conquest

The new French imperialism was founded upon an identity of interests between the French church, French businessmen in search of new markets, and the patriotic and selfish motives of Napoleon III, who wanted colonies for personal and national power and prestige. When in 1858 a French and a Spanish priest were killed, a joint Franco-Spanish expedition was organized. The allies bombarded and took Danang (Tourane), and in 1859 the French seized Saigon in Cochin China. They forced Vietnam to accept being "opened" to trade and to give up eastern Cochin China when they concluded the Treaty of Saigon with the Annamese emperor in 1862. Under the terms of this treaty Vietnam also paid an indemnity, tolerated Christianity, and not only opened its ports to foreign trade but also gave the French the right to navigate the Mekong river. The French thus came to rule first in the southern part of Vietnam, the region which had been

Vietnamese the shortest time and was inhabited by a very mixed population. Much of the land in the south also was owned by absentee landlords.

In 1863 France made Cambodia a protectorate. In this case the French were welcomed by the Cambodian monarch and the French advisor at Phnom-Penh received with open arms, since the Cambodians feared the Siamese more than the French. In 1867 Siam recognized the fact of a French protectorate over its neighbor. With the acquisition of Cochin China, the western part of which was ceded in 1867, and of Cambodia, the French had created a foothold of empire for themselves, after which they attempted to expand to the north and to obtain control of the rest of Annam and of Tonkin.

The north was homogeneous in population and was more conscious of the ancient Vietnamese national traditions. Thus, when in 1873 a young French naval lieutenant, Francis Garnier, was sent to Hanoi in Tonkin, with orders to explore the Red River and possibly to gain access to trade with southwest China, he was met with hostility by the local Vietnamese, who refused to let him proceed. Thereupon the impetuous young man took matters in his own hands, attacked and took Hanoi and the Red River delta. But he was subsequently killed by a band of Chinese irregular troops, the Black Flags, and his death delayed the final conquest of Tonkin by the French for some ten years. Even so, the French obtained a treaty with Vietnam in 1874 by which they obtained the right to trade and to advise the emperor.

The Franco-Prussian War, as well as the death of Garnier, delayed but did not stop French expansion, and in 1884 France declared Annam to be a protectorate, despite strong Chinese objections. The Chinese, fearing the loss of a member of the Chinese tributary system, asserted their suzerainty over Annam and sent Chinese volunteer forces into the country, and a Franco-Chinese war followed (1884–1885). Surprisingly enough, the Chinese won a minor victory in this struggle, at Langson near the Chinese border, an event which led to the overthrow of Jules Ferry, the French prime minister who had pushed French expansion, but in the long run the declining Manchu empire could not resist the French. After the French navy destroyed a Chinese fleet at Foochow, and blockaded the Yangtze River, the Chinese were forced to conclude a peace, the Treaty of Tientsin, negotiated by Li Hung-chang, in which the Chinese acknowledged a French protectorate over Annam, permitted French trade with south China, and gave the French strong preference over other powers in construction works in Yunnan province.

After the conquest of Annam and Tonkin, the French in 1893 established a protectorate over Laos, the vast region of high valleys and plateaus along the Mekong River. The territory of Laos had been claimed by the Siamese, but again the French, after some local resistance and minor warfare, had no great difficulty in conquering it and forcing Siam to recognize French suzerainty over the kingdom. In order to round out the French empire further demands were served upon Siam in 1904, after which the Siamese were forced to hand over the provinces of Battambang and Siemreap, close to the Cambodian frontier, in return for a minor modification of the Laos frontier to the advantage of Siam. In 1907 the French demanded the cession of the whole of the lower Mekong valley by Siam to France, and again the Siamese had to yield.

The Nature of French Rule

French colonial administration had the unenviable reputation of being the worst in all of Southeast Asia, and this was certainly true in the first few years when the French treated their acquisitions as conquests and left them in the hands of naval officers. This "rule of the admirals" was characterized by frequent quarrels, maladministration, graft, and excessive taxation. After 1879 civil government took over with some improvements, but even then the French government faced continuous budget losses and frequent native outbreaks and rebellions which had to be pacified by the French military. The French governor-general resided at Hanoi, but he was a political appointee for two years only, and was at the mercy of the permanent French officials, as well as of the Minister of Colonies in Paris and of secret inspection visits from France. He was at the head of a strongly centralized administrative system, comprised of the governors of Cochin China and of the protectorates. In order to improve efficiency, in 1887 Cochin China, Cambodia, Annam, and Tonkin were administratively united as "French Indochina."

The French ruled through a hierarchy of Vietnamese officials, the Mandarinate. They permitted kings of the Nguyen dynasty to continue to "reign" at Hue in Annam. But in the period from 1885 to 1916 three out of five reigning monarchs were deposed by the French and deported.

After 1896 French Indochina did benefit from reforms inaugurated by Paul Doumer, who was governor-general until 1902. He dismissed the worst officials, appointed in their stead more honest ones, and in general attempted to create better government. Doumer wanted France to become a great Asiatic power, and in his reforms he emphasized a policy of assimilation. The policy of assimilation was the very opposite of the Dutch policy of adoption; it tried to make the people of the colonial possessions as far as possible French in language and in customs. At the same time, Doumer also was interested in making the colonies economically self-sufficient. This he did by stimulating rice production, particularly in the Red river and Mekong deltas, and by developing rubber, coal, zinc, and tin, all raw materials valuable to French industry. In the economic sphere the French monopolized trade and investment; whereas the scale of living of the native population remained very low. French Indochina's economy was dominated by French banks, investment houses, insurance companies, and trading firms, while the masses generally lived in poverty subject to heavy taxation and to labor conscription. The policies of Doumer, both economic as well as his policy of assimilation, could well be criticized. Economically, they did much for France but almost nothing for the Indochinese; and politically, while only a handful of Indochinese acquired French culture, this handful soon became a leading segment of a population which was increasingly bitter and hostile toward the French. The creation of a class of Western-trained Vietnamese intellectuals, imbued with French ideas, led to the revival of Vietnamese nationalism. This nationalism became especially strong after 1904 and Japan's victory over Russia. Vietnamese students in Japan and France began to form organizations and to publish propaganda literature. A further stimulus was given to this movement by the influence of Chinese reformers such as K'ang Yu-wei and Liang Ch'i-ch'ao. After 1905 popular discontent against the French resulted in the "era of plots," all of which were suppressed by the French. Especially important were the peasant tax demonstrations of 1908 in central Vietnam. The French, in order to check this Vietnamese nationalism, conducted widespread raids and arrests, and even went so far as to close the French University of Hanoi in 1908, an institution which had been established because of widespread demand for education just a short time before.

Demands for changes in French colonial rule came also as a result of the Chinese overthrow of the Manchus in 1911. In this period the anti-colonialist leader Phan Boi Chau was organizing Vietnamese revolutionaries in China, and Nguyen Ai Quoc (later famous as Ho Chi Minh) went to Europe after spending some years at sea.

SIAM

Among the countries of Southeast Asia only one, Siam, retained its independence from the Western colonial powers. The reasons for its survival can be found both in its geographical position and in the fact that it became the pawn of two competing great powers, Britain and France.

Early French Interest

Siam was drawn into the commercial rivalries of European powers early in modern history. Already in the seventeenth century European and Japanese traders had made it a point to come to trade at Ayuthia, the capital of the Tai kingdom on the Chao Phraya, sometimes called the Menam. By 1664 the Dutch had obtained a trade monopoly with Siam. They also were favored by the fact that their Japanese rivals had vanished as the result of Japan's adoption of a closed-country policy; but the Dutch did not long enjoy their position of dominance, and before the century was over they were challenged in Siam by the French. In Siam the French used as their tool a Greek adventurer, Constantine Phaulkon, who arrived in 1659 in the East and who afterwards rose rapidly to power in the service of the Siamese government.

Phaulkon was appointed first superintendent of foreign trade by the Siamese government, and then became chief minister to the king, Phra Narai. As the holder of such high offices it was not difficult for him to invite the French into Siam, and their first trading factory was opened in Ayuthia in 1680. In France there was considerable enthusiasm in government circles about developing trade with Southeast Asia and exercising political control in Siam. This was kindled by the dispatch of a Siamese mission to the court of Louis XIV in 1684; France concluded a commercial treaty with Siam in response. The British were disturbed at this turn of events, but for the time being were powerless to prevent it. Once entry had been gained by means of trade the ambitions of the Sun King soon led to the ambitious plan of establishing a French protectorate over Siam. In 1687 the French sent to Siam French goods such as textiles, clocks, and mirrors, in the care of some 600 soldiers and 300 technicians. Upon arrival in Ayuthia, the French troops were distributed throughout Siam, garrisoning such places as Bangkok and Mergui, and the technicians furnished technical aid, designed to bring Siam under close French control. In these efforts the French were also strongly supported by the strong missionary labors of their priests, and by the unflagging encouragement of Phaulkon who won for them further trade concessions. It seemed as if Siam was not only to enter a close trade relationship with the French, but also that the country was destined to become a French colony, but a sudden reversal came in 1688.

In Siam strong French political and missionary influence resulted in a popular reaction and revolt against the French in 1688 which was completely successful. Phaulkon himself was arrested, tortured, and executed; his Japanese wife and family were sold into slavery; French missionaries were imprisoned and their native converts slain; and the French military force was expelled. The reaction against the French was so strong that even the king, Phra Narai, lost his throne and was replaced. This outbreak put an end to French ambitions in Southeast Asia for a long period, but it did not strengthen Siam. Rather, after 1688 extreme disorder, a period of civil war, and weakness culminated in the successful Burmese invasion of Siam by the heir of Alaungpaya in 1767 and the utter destruction of Ayuthia.

Chakkri Dynasty

The anarchy and disorder in Siam were ended by the end of the eighteenth century after the coming in 1782 of a new dynasty, the Chakkri which rules to the present, and the establishment of a new capital, Bangkok. The first king of the new house, Rama I who ruled from 1782 to 1809, ended the long conflict with Burma, and began a policy of steady internal reform and improvement to which Siam owed, at least partially, its survival as an independent nation. Some reform in justice was made, and more capable officials were selected, and Rama's successors concluded new treaties with the great Western powers. In 1826 Siam signed a commercial treaty with Great Britain, just after the British had finished their first war with Burma, and in 1833 Siam concluded a similar treaty with the United States. These treaties permitted the arrival of missionaries, both French Catholics and American Protestants, although they did not grant the powers the right of extraterritoriality. By 1844 Siam felt strong enough to make Cambodia a protectorate of the Siamese throne.

Westernization and Reforms

A major step forward toward modernization came with the reign of Rama IV Mongkut, who ruled Siam from 1851 to 1868. A studious and intelligent man, who as a monk had learned English, French, and Latin from missionary teachers, he realized that a policy of gradual westernization was absolutely necessary for Siam if the country were to avoid the fate of Burma and other regions of the Far East. Rama IV was willing, therefore, to adopt legal and commercial methods from the West, to establish educational institutions, and to open Siam to Western influence, if by doing so he could avoid giving a pretext for intervention to the Western powers. He concluded a new commercial treaty with Great Britain in 1855, which included the right of extraterritoriality, forbade the levying of duties on opium imports, and gave Britain further trading privileges. Similar treaties were made with France and the United States. Rama IV also hired foreign advisors and tutors, of whom Anna of *Anna and the King of Siam* fame is

FIGURE 8.3. King Rama IV Mongkut, the westernizer of Siam.

the best-known example, opened a mint and issued modern currency, built modern hospitals, and founded an academy of foreign languages.

There is no question that the wisdom of adopting a policy of westernization was partially responsible for saving Siam's independent existence, but even so, Siam in the nineteenth century was a country belonging to a colonial economy, substantially dependent upon foreign investment, mainly British and some Chinese. Furthermore, Siam also soon experienced great pressure from the rival colonial powers, France and Great Britain, both eager to extend their claims in Southeast Asia. Geographical accident, because Siam lay as a buffer zone between the British in Burma in the west and the Malay peninsula in the south, and the French in Annam and Cambodia in the east, also played a role in the survival of Siam as an independent country. The bitter colonial rivalry of France and Great Britain resulted eventually in the willingness of both to leave Siam as a neutral buffer state. This mutual agreement did not take place, however, until the

FIGURE 8.4. *King Rama V Chulalonkorn and his son.*

French had nibbled sizable slices of territory away from control of Bangkok. The French advanced into Cambodia, and in 1893 their interests in Laos led them to demand from Siam the entire left bank of the Mekong. The resultant crisis almost led to a war between France and Great Britain when the French sent a gunboat to Bangkok, which served a stiff ultimatum upon the Siamese king and blockaded the port. The crisis passed, but in 1896 the French and the British signed a treaty whereby they recognized the integrity of Siam and guaranteed the Menam basin, but even afterwards there were some minor frontier rectifications always resulting in loss to Siamese suzerainty. In 1904, and again in 1907, Siam ceded territory to France along the Cambodian frontier, and in 1907 and 1909 Siam agreed to the establishment of British protectorates in the Malay peninsula where she previously had exercised overlordship.

Still, because of geographic location and because of the wise internal policy of her capable kings, Siam remained as the one country in Southeast Asia free from foreign political domination. The policy of internal reforms, which had begun so well with Rama IV Mongkut, was continued by his successor, Rama V Chulalonkorn. This monarch, who ruled from 1868 to 1910, presents a rather striking analogy with the Meiji emperor of Japan (see page 298). Their reigns are contemporaneous, and so were their policies; both strove for governmental and social reforms within their respective countries. Rama V, often referred to as the real founder of modern Siam, was a man modern in thought who had travelled overseas in India, Europe, and the Dutch East Indies, and who had received a modern Western education by English tutors. Although he personally clung to some of the privileges of the past (he was addicted to smoking opium and maintained a huge harem), he issued a veritable flood of reform edicts to modernize the country. Slavery was abolished, a new law code and Western-type courts were established, and he built a telegraph line (1883), the first railroad (1893), and highways. He instituted a postal service, created a small but efficient army, and gave to his kingdom a central bureaucracy which put through important reforms in the fields of taxation and finance. Rama V relied heavily upon foreign advisors in his policies, using both Americans and Belgians, and he also inaugurated the policy whereby bright Siamese students were sent abroad for their studies to benefit from Western education at its source.

These policies of profound reform began to show signs of success just before the outbreak of the First World War, and Siam was able to obtain revised treaties from the great powers who relinquished their right to extraterritoriality. In 1909 Britain concluded such a treaty and the beginnings of Siam as a modern state were thus successfully recognized by the world.

BASIC DATES

1659–1688   Constantin Phaulkon in Siam
1753–1760   Alaungpaya in Burma

1769	Burmese destroy Ayuthia
1782	Chakkri dynasty at Bangkok
1786	Francis Light obtains Penang
1802–1820	Reign of Gia Long in Vietnam
1819	Raffles obtains Singapore
1824	First Anglo-Burmese War
1841	James Brooke obtains Sarawak
1846	Great Britain acquires Labuan
1851–1868	Reign of Rama IV Mongkut
1852	Second Anglo-Burmese War
1859	French seize Saigon
1860	Max Havelaar
1863	Cambodia becomes a French protectorate
1867	Straits Settlements become a crown colony
1868–1910	Reign of Rama V Chulalonkorn
1873–1907	Dutch war with Achin
1885	Annam becomes a French protectorate
1885	Third Anglo-Burmese War
1893	Laos becomes a French protectorate
1896–1902	Paul Doumer governor-general of French Indochina
c. 1900	Establishment of "Ethical Policy" in Dutch East Indies; development of outer territories
1908	Budi Utomo founded
1910	Sarekat Islam founded

SUPPLEMENTARY READING

Bastin, J. S. *The Emergence of Modern Southeast Asia, 1511-1957.* Englewood Cliffs, N.J., 1967.

Benda, H. J. and J. A. Larkin. *The World of Southeast Asia: Selected Historical Readings.* New York, 1967.

Cady, J. *Southeast Asia: Its Historical Development.* New York, 1963.

Hammer, E. *Vietnam Yesterday and Today.* New York, 1966.

Harrison, B. *South-East Asia: A Short History,* 2nd ed. London, 1963.

Vlekke, B. *Nusantara: A History of the East Indian Archipelago.* Cambridge, Mass., 1943.

ADVANCED READING

Buttinger, D. *The Smaller Dragon: A Political History of Vietnam.* New York, 1958.

Cady, J. F. *A History of Modern Burma.* Ithaca, N.Y., 1958.

────── *Roots of French Imperialism in Asia.* Ithaca, N.Y., 1954. A good study of French expansion in Indochina.

Chula, C. *Lords of Life: A History of the Kings of Thailand.* London, 1967.

Clair, C. *Sir Stamford Raffles, Founder of Singapore.* Watford, 1963.

Furnivall, J. *Netherlands India.* New York, 1944.

Hall, D. G. *A History of South-East Asia,* 3rd ed. New York, 1968.
Harvey, G. *History of Burma from the Earliest Times to 10 March 1824, the Beginning of the English Conquest.* London, 1925.
Kennedy, J. *A History of Malaya, A.D. 1400-1959.* London, 1967.
Marr, D. G. *Vietnamese Anticolonialism, 1885-1925.* Berkeley, 1971.
Mills, L. *British Malaya, 1824-1867.* New York, 1967.
Roff, W. R. *The Origins of Malay Nationalism.* New Haven, 1967.
Steinberg, D. J. *In Search of Southeast Asia.* New York, 1970.
Thompson, V. *French Indo-China.* London, 1937.
——— *Thailand.* New York, 1942.
Truong, B. L. "Intervention versus Tribute in Sino-Vietnamese Relations, 1788-1790," in J. K. Fairbank, *The Chinese World Order: Traditional China's Foreign Relations.* Cambridge, Mass., 1968, pp. 165-179.
Winstedt, R. *Malaya and Its History,* 4th ed. London, 1957.

Chapter 9

Russia in Asia, 1600-1895

GEOGRAPHY

This chapter deals with the development of Russia as a power in Asia, and thus it concerns the story of the almost continuous advance and expansion of that nation across the Eurasian continent, beginning in the sixteenth century and ending with the late nineteenth century. In those three hundred years Russia obtained common boundaries with China, Mongolia, Manchuria, Afghanistan, and Persia. As her conquests of Siberia and other parts of Asiatic Russia became consolidated, and as Asiatic Russia grew in population and economic importance, so increased the influence of Russia as a world power, until she came to play a vital part in the whole of Asian history.

To show the origins and the course of this great development a brief study of geography is necessary since physiography, hydrography, soils, and climate all played important roles in the historical development of Russia as an Asian power. First there is the immensely vast Eurasian plain, which extends from the Baltic and the Black Sea almost to the shores of the Pacific, containing perhaps some eight million square miles. The Ural mountains, the only major break in the otherwise continuous sweep, do not really constitute a significant barrier across the Eurasian realm, since they are not steep enough to prevent travel. In the north the Eurasian plain is bordered by the Arctic Ocean, to the south by the Caspian Sea, the Iranian highlands, and then the towering ranges of the snowclad Pamir and Hindu Kush mountains, while to the southeast and east a whole series of mountain ranges, beginning with the T'ien Shan mountains, and continuing with the Altai, the Sayan, the Yablonoi, and finally the Stanovoi mountains form an effective barrier. This immense plain is drained by a number of great rivers and their tributaries, all flowing northward to the Arctic Sea. These are the Ob and Irtysh in western Siberia, the Yenissei in central Siberia, and the Lena in eastern Siberia.

Climatically, the Eurasian plain is divided into a number of zones, beginning with the tundra in the north and ending in steppe and desert areas and some fertile river valleys in Central Asia and Turkistan. The tundra zone in the north is an area of permanently frozen subsoil, in which vegetation is restricted to mosses and lichens, in which there are no trees, in which agriculture is impossible, and where the native economy is based on the herding of reindeer. The next zone to the south consists of the taiga, the vast coniferous forest lands of Siberia, which have their close analogy in the great Canadian North. This is the region of the pine and fir belt, across the central part of Asiatic Russia, and it is also the home of a vast number of fur-bearing animals, which gave the economic impetus for the original Russian conquest of Siberia. Further south again comes the zone of temperate climates, but with frequent precipitation deficiencies, a region primarily of steppes and occasional true deserts with rainfall of less than ten inches per year. Where rainfall is sufficient, or where river valleys debouch from the mountains and irrigation is feasible, agriculture is possible. The bulk of the early population of Asian Russia was concentrated in the last two of these zones, the forest and the steppe lands. The mountain ranges which form the boundary of the Eurasian plain to the northeast reflect the climatic zones in their vegetative cover; on their northern slopes they are usually clad with coniferous trees, while on the southern slopes deciduous vegetation predominates.

One final significant point must be mentioned, and that is the general northeastward direction of the mountain ranges, beginning from the Altais to the Stanovoi mountains, as this physical feature also contributed to the historical development of Siberia, deflecting Russian expansion to the northeast, to the Pacific and beyond, and forming an early obstacle to Russian penetration to the southeast.

The native populations of Siberia and their mode of life reflect closely the major geographical zones. In the north there were the inhabitants of the tundra, the Giliaks, Ostiaks and other nomads whose lives depended upon the reindeer; in the forest zone were Tungus and other tribes, mainly hunters and fishers; while the steppe and desert zone supported a nomadic horse economy of such peoples as the Buriats and the Kirghiz.

It was in this geographical setting that the Russian expansion across Asia began, and it was these geographic factors which contributed to the nature of its development.

RUSSIAN EXPANSION ACROSS ASIA

The conquest of Siberia is rather similar in many ways to the conquest of the American continent, and it is remarkable for the speed of the Russian advance.

Early Siberian History

Siberian history begins only with the Mongols. In the thirteenth century, when the Mongols created the greatest empire the world had ever seen, large parts of Siberia, especially western Siberia, came under the dominion of the Mongol rulers. When that empire began to fall apart in the fourteenth and fifteenth centuries, there were established in its wake a number of local Islamic khanates, of which the most important one in Siberia was in the Ob river basin, entitled the khanate of Sibir, which was established by Kuchum, a Mongol Moslem prince who originally came from Bukhara in Turkistan. It is the name of his principality which gave the name Siberia to all of the vast expanse of land in Asiatic Russia stretching to the Pacific. To the west across the low Ural mountains from Sibir was European Russia, also for a long time subject to and part of the Mongol empire. The Golden Horde, or the Kipchak portion of the Mongol world state, had controlled the Russian princes since the thirteenth century, and it was to them that Russia had been forced to pay tribute. Just as in the case of Sibir, where a local ruler established his power in the wake of the Mongol disintegration, so here in Russia, too, as the power of the Moslem Mongols (or Tatars, as they were called by the Russians) weakened, the power of the local Russian princes began to increase. This was especially true of the Grand Dukes of Moscow, who had the advantage of a central location, and the luck of having among them some very clever politicians. One of these was Ivan Kalita, or "John Moneybag," who had collected taxes for the Mongols and had benefited from this employment by strengthening Moscow over the rest of his Russian competitors. Under his successors Moscow developed a strong frontier policy of expansion into Siberia, although Moscow had inherited already an interest in Siberia from the great merchant community of Novgorod. Western Siberia had been known to the merchants of Novgorod the Great as early as the eleventh century. The Kiev chronicle *Tale of Bygone Years*, for instance, spoke of Yugria, a fabled land on the lower Ob, where Alexander the Great was supposed to have discovered the unclean peoples, and fenced them in among mountains so that they would not corrupt the rest of the earth. We read of a treaty of 1263 which includes among the Novgorodian possessions the trans-Ural territories of Petchora and Yugria, and furthermore we read of a large expedition setting out from Novgorod in 1364, when a large army reached the Ob, sailed down to the mouth of that river to the Arctic Ocean, and returned from Yugria with enormous spoils taken from the natives. Yet the permanent Russian conquest of Siberia really began with Moscow's rise to power. Ivan III, the Great, who ruled from 1462 to 1505, felt strong enough to overthrow the Tatar yoke in 1480. He ruled as an independent sovereign, and his territory extended to the north, the Arctic, and to the northeast beyond the Urals.

Under the rule of his successor, Ivan IV, "the Terrible," who was no longer merely a grand prince, but tsar, the earlier Russian attempts from Novgorod and Moscow were pursued, and during his reign (1533–1584) Siberia was made a Russian territory. In 1552 Ivan the Terrible captured the Tatar khanate of Kazan on the Volga river, a major step in Russian expansion, since that vast river was opened for trade, and in 1566 the whole of the Volga basin was brought under Russian control following the Russian capture of Astrakhan at the river's mouth in the Caspian Sea. As early as 1554 Ivan IV, in a letter to Edward VI of England, proclaimed himself "commander of all Sibir." The realization of the increase of Russian power subsequent to the capture of Kazan was not lost on the prince of Sibir, Kuchum, who hastened to congratulate the Russian tsar upon his accomplishment, and thought seriously of curtailing some of his raids into Russian territory.

Reasons for Russian Expansion

The real importance of the capture of Kazan was that the route to the Urals along some of the major tributaries of the Volga, notably the Kama river, was now open for exploration. An easy route, coupled with the economic impetus of the search for furs, gave Russia the road and the vital force for expansion which carried the Russians across the whole of the continent in less than fifty years, and which justified the classic saying of the great Russian historian, Klyuchevsky, who stated in his *History of Russia* that "migration and colonization characterized all Russian history."

The greatest economic resource of Siberia was its wealth of fur-bearing animals, especially sable, but also beaver, ermine, fox, and squirrel. This abundance coincided with the prevailing European fashion, which had started in the sixteenth century, of wearing furs. The quickened economic development of Western Europe due to the great discoveries of the fifteenth century and the influx of gold and silver in large quantities from the New World, provided a demand for greater luxuries in dress, including fur. As Moscow gained its independence, and also established an easy route to Germany via Smolensk, and while the first English traders arrived in the north in 1553 at the northern Dvina and in 1585 at Archangelsk, the quantities of furs which came from Russia rapidly increased, resulting in the depletion of the fur-bearing animals in the forest belt of European Russia. The need to find new regions, and the ease of the Kama river route across the Urals, propelled Russia into the acquisition of Siberia.

The actual agent was, however, not the Russian government, but rather a famous Russian commercial family, the Stroganovs. The Stroganovs of Novgorod, revered in gourmet circles whenever beef à la Stroganov is served, were early Russian capitalists and members of a commercial dynasty, which is first mentioned in chronicles in 1395. This family of entrepreneurs had become wealthy from many sources—developing salt works, exploiting forest land grants, establishing early iron works for the supply of mines, developing grain, and also in the fur trade. When the fur trade declined on the European slope of the Ural mountains as depletion took its toll, the Stroganovs began to turn to the regions across the Urals. In 1574 they obtained from the tsar new concessions and land grants across the Urals, on condition that they would suppress robbery along the Tobol river and would establish an iron work. This territory was actually part of the khanate of Sibir, ruled by Kuchum, who logically and promptly repudiated the suggestion of the Stroganov family to exploit these areas, but he had underrated both the enterprise and the greed of that family. Balked by Kuchum, they now turned to the use of force, employing one Yermak, a Cossack leader from south Russia.

Yermak's Conquest of Siberia

The term "cossack" seems originally to have denoted the lowest elements of the Mongol or Tatar armies. In Russian the name appears for the first time early in the sixteenth century in a monastery charter, where it is used to describe an itinerant worker or bandit. The name "cossack" became applied to that restless group of men who, fleeing Russian taxes and serfdom, had established themselves as frontiersmen, paying no taxes, but instead rendering military service to the Russian state against the Crimean and Kipchak Tatars. These cossacks were drawn from ex-galley slaves, absconded peasants, brigands, and similar elements of Russian society, and they were by and large a rather turbulent, though freedom-loving group. They had created self-governing communities, especially in the lower Don valley, where the government had had the good sense to grant them land without taxation, in return for their frontier services, but their chief occupation when not defending the boundaries of the state seems to have consisted in rather indiscriminate plundering. One of these cossack leaders, Yermak Timofeyevitch, a man of broad shoulders and sturdy frame who had begun his career as a cook on a river boat, had made the mistake of robbing a Persian embassy en route to the tsar's court. He fled the wrath of Moscow, went to the Stroganov territory in the Urals, and seemed to them the perfect instrument

FIGURE 9.1. Yermak's conquest of Siberia. From the Rezanov Mss., c. 1700.

FIGURE 9.2. An ostrog and portage in Siberia.

for extending their power into Siberia. He and his small group of followers, some five hundred and forty cossacks and an additional three hundred volunteers, were staked to food and arms by the Stroganov family, with the object of establishing a Russian base across the Urals. When Yermak started out on his career as conquerer of Siberia he had a most important advantage over his adversaries, the Sibir Mongols, in artillery and good muskets. This military superiority greatly facilitated his conquest, rather similar to the ease of conquest by which the great *conquistadores*, Cortez and Pizarro, conquered the Aztec and Inca empires in the New World. By September 1581, Kuchum, the Khan of Sibir, was defeated in a rather hard battle, his capital captured, and he himself was in full flight.

When the news of Yermak's conquest reached Moscow, the tsar, Ivan IV, was at first furious, since he had originally opposed the use of force for fear of Mongol depredations, but the splendid furs sent him by Yermak soon mellowed him, and by 1582 the Russian government had decided to support the conquest of Siberia. In return for Yermak's appeal for aid and reinforcements to make good his losses in manpower and supplies, the government sent some five hundred men, while the tsar himself graciously extended a full pardon to Yermak.

The change in attitude of the tsar was the result of his own keen appreciation of the opportunities in the fur trade. With support from

FIGURE 9.3. Fur tribute (iasak) paid at a Siberian ostrog.

Moscow the first settlement in Siberia was established in 1587 at Tobolsk at the union of the Irtysh and Tobol rivers. After the death of Ivan IV in 1584, his successor, Boris Godunov (first regent to the infant son of Ivan, then tsar), continued to display a very lively interest in the eastward expansion of the Russian state. This interest is illustrated in the detailed instructions to establish a government in Siberia which Boris gave to the leader of a new expedition.

Nature of the Conquest of Siberia

Unfortunately, this early vigor came to a somewhat sudden stop with the death of Yermak in 1584 and, more importantly, with the "Time of Troubles," the civil disturbances which racked Russia after Boris' death (1605). Civil war and confusion had a direct effect on conditions in Siberia, the most important of which was perhaps the fact that while expansion into Siberia by the Russians continued, it continued under different circumstances. It lost its early planned character, and instead it became the work of private individuals, frontiersmen, adventurers, and pioneers. These were the private enterprisers, or *promyshlenniks*, as they were called in Russian, merchants, trappers, hunters, and frontiersmen, very much like the North American *coureurs de bois*. This wave of invaders and adventurers, attracted by the enormous wealth of furs in the frontier region of

Siberia, continued the eastward advance across the continent by horses, sleighs, carts, and above all, boats. Individuals of this type, and groups of promyshlenniks working for themselves and constantly looking for new regions of fur-bearing animals, were responsible for the conquest of most of eastern Siberia.

With the restoration of strong government in Moscow in 1615 when Michael Romanov came to the throne, these pioneers were also supported once more by the government, a government which had a strong interest in trade; but the flavor of private enterprise of the Russian advance into the rest of Siberia was to remain strong.

The methods of the Russian advance into Siberia were very simple. The great system of natural communications, furnished by the river systems of Siberia, was used, and control was maintained by the building of forts and blockhouses, the so-called *ostrogs*, on strategic points along the rivers and astride the portages connecting the various river systems. The government built these forts in the wake of the promyshlenniks for the purpose of commanding rivers and portages, and for the supervision of the collection of tribute from the natives.

Each ostrog contained various buildings, such as the residence of the *voevoda*, or governor, his office, barracks, other living quarters, store and supply houses, perhaps even a church. In addition to its strategic function, an important purpose of the ostrog was the collection of *iasak*, or tribute. This was a tax collected from the natives, chiefly in furs. Iasak varied according to local conditions, but as a whole it was not overly heavy, averaging perhaps some seven sable furs per native per year. The government also had the right to collect 10 per cent of the best furs from the private Russian trappers and traders, as well as the right to buy the best of the furs offered for sale by them in Moscow. In addition, the government also enjoyed a monopoly on sables and black foxes sold to China.

Russian government policy toward natives was designed to assure a minimum of interference. The Russians carefully avoided involvement in native tribal affairs; instead they tried to win over the most powerful natives by a paternalistic policy. The Russians demanded an oath of loyalty from these tribal leaders, and kept some as hostages, but preserved the native customs and their tribal organization. The Russian government even went so far as to discourage the Russian clergy from their missionary activities, since when baptized a native was raised to the same level as a Russian and no longer was required to pay tribute. Time and time again instructions were issued to the clergy to leave the natives strictly alone.

The nature of expansion into eastern Siberia remained somewhat different from that of western Siberia. In western Siberia it had been the state in the persons of Ivan the Terrible and Boris Godunov which had led the advance. In western Siberia, too, colonization by peasants and serfs was encouraged by the Russian government, and efforts were made to encourage local agriculture and the growing of basic foodstuffs, especially cabbage, so that a minimum of supplies would have to be imported from European Russia. Efforts were even made, although unsuccessful ones, to teach the natives agriculture. But the situation in eastern Siberia was quite different.

Instead of advance according to government plan, expansion was much more in the nature of a free, independent, orderless movement by enterprisers, the promyshlenniks, who were drawn to adventure and exploration by hopes for personal wealth.

Rapidity of Russian Expansion

The Russian advance across the Asiatic continent moved with very great speed, again somewhat reminiscent of the American frontier expansion across the Great Plains, and as early as 1638 it had reached the shores of the Pacific. The advance was hastened partially because of the rapid depletion and exhaustion of hunting grounds, partially because of the continuing heavy demand for Russian furs, but also because of the introduction of better hunting methods. The rapid exhaustion of one promising hunting ground led to the discovery of a new one, and the process continued rapidly so that all of Siberia soon was made subject to Russian rule. The major steps were as follows. In 1587 Tobolsk had been founded on the Irtysh river at its junction with the Tobol; in 1604 came Tomsk on the junction of the Ob and Tom rivers; then in 1619 the important ostrog of Yenisseisk was established on the Yenissei, at a point where that river meets one of its major tributaries, the Upper Tunguska; in 1632 came the very important (in terms of further explorations) settlement of Yakutsk on the Lena; and in 1638 the Russians reached the borders of the Pacific Ocean at Okhotsk on the shores of the gulf of that name. In less than fifty years (1587-1632), using the magnificent natural system of river passages, which led from one major Siberian river by means of short portages to the next, the entire enormous distance to the Pacific was covered. Geography had provided for this easy passage from one of the four major rivers and their tributaries to the next river basin, and this accounts for the ease and rapidity of pace. From the tributaries of the Pechora and Kama rivers in Europe, to the tributaries of the Lena river, which gave access to the Pacific shore, almost the entire

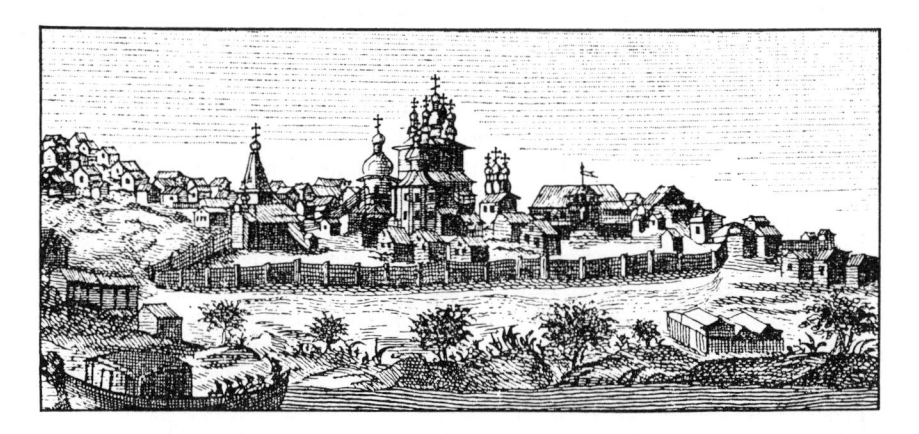

FIGURE 9.4. A view of Yakutsk in the eighteenth century.

distance could be travelled by boat, except for a five-mile portage between the Ob and Yenissei river systems, and a ten-mile portage between the Yenissei and Lena basins.

The northeasterly direction of the eastern Siberian mountain ranges also played a geographical role in the nature of expansion, as it deflected the Russian advance to the northeast, the Pacific, and thence out into the Aleutians, Alaska, California, and the Kurils. Always leading the inexorable advance was the search for furs, which propelled promyshlenniks and cossacks alike to conquer eastern Siberia regardless of obstacles. Only the rate of exhaustion of hunting grounds determined the speed of expansion of these two groups of men, who, combining all the virtues of frontiersmen, such as boldness, courage and endurance, with their vices such as greed and ruthlessness, were the agents of the conquest, a conquest in which state planning and direction played no part or very little. Everywhere the Russians went they imposed iasak, or tribute, payable in furs. The native Ostiak, Vogul, Samoyed, Tatar, and Kirkhiz tribes whom they encountered, nomadic, backward, disunited, and powerless in the face of Russian military superiority, had no alternative but to submit.

Discovery of Sakhalin, Kamchatka, and the Kurils

The ease with which wealth could be acquired, and the veritable fur fever which had taken possession of the Russian adventurers soon led to renewed advances beyond the Gulf of Okhotsk. Sakhalin was discovered in 1643, and by 1697 the Russians had begun their push into Kamchatka against the bitter resistance of the native Koriak and Itelmen tribes. The advance into that great peninsula was led by a typical Russian frontiersman, Atlasov, a poorly educated, cruel, greedy, but fearless and energetic leader, who by 1699 had completed the conquest of Kamchatka, imposed fur tribute everywhere, and secured Russian control by a series of ostrogs.

By 1711 the exploration of the Kurils, the great chain of volcanic islands extending southward from Kamchatka toward Japan, had begun, and in 1717 Peter the Great sent out two geodesists with secret instructions to chart the islands and to find out whether gold could be found on them.

Bering's Voyages

The keen interest of Peter the Great in questions of national wealth, and his desire for profitable trade, which would enable Russia to compete with the Western powers, also resulted in his sponsorship of the grandly planned and executed scientific expeditions of Vitus Bering, which were to establish proof of whether Asia and America were separated and find a sea route south from Kamchatka to tap the trade of Japan and the even more fabled treasures of the Chinese empire. Bering, a Danish sea captain in the employ of the Russian government, sailed in 1728 on his first voyage, after careful preparations, but his first voyage was inconclusive, and he turned back before he had discovered the straits which now bear his name. The unlucky

Dane was given a cool reception upon his return to court, but in 1741 he sailed again, after even more grandiose and expensive preparations. He explored the Bering Straits and reached Alaska, where he stayed but one day. On his return voyage he suffered shipwreck and died on a desolate island in the north Pacific. Actually, however, Bering's discovery of Alaska had been already antedated by the voyage of a certain Gvosdev, a promyshlennik, who had reached Alaska in 1732. Part of the great Bering expeditions was a plan to find a sea route from Kamchatka to Japan, and this now led to the first of a number of unsuccessful attempts by Russia to open relations with Japan.

Russian Interest in Japan

One of these attempts consisted of the expedition (1738–1742) of Lt. Martin Spanberg of the Russian navy, who reached Hakodate on the northernmost of the Japanese main islands, Hokkaido, and attempted to repatriate some shipwrecked Japanese, among whom was an Osaka merchant, who had become a Christian during his stay in Russia. Spanberg was given a friendly reception by the Japanese in Hakodate, and food and water were furnished him, but he attained no other goals. Another vessel of the same expedition actually managed to reach the Japanese coast as far south as Shimoda on Honshu, but again without any lasting success.

The next Russian attempt to open relations with Japan was made at the end of the eighteenth century, when Catherine the Great supported a plan to enter into treaty negotiations with Japan. In 1792 this resulted in the arrival of Adam Laxman off Hakodate port with the first official Russian expedition, but again the Japanese politely refused to enter into negotiations. The Russians, whose excuse it was to return two Japanese castaways, were pleasantly but firmly told that all questions of trade could only be decided at Nagasaki, the Japanese port open to the Chinese and the Dutch in the south of Japan.

This argument was next used as an excuse by the Russian government in 1804 when it sent out as its ambassador Rezanov, who was instructed by the imperial government to conclude a treaty with Japan. He arrived at Nagasaki in 1804 with a large retinue and splendid gifts. After some six months of fruitless discussions in Nagasaki, the Japanese broke off negotiations and forced Rezanov to abandon his mission. The advent of a new anti-foreign shogun, who refused to accept the letters and gifts from the tsar, brought with it the refusal of the Japanese authorities in Nagasaki harbor even to supply the Russians with food, so that Rezanov was forced to return to Kamchatka in 1805.

Rezanov then decided to use force against Japan. Convinced that the Japanese people themselves would welcome the opening of trade, and hoping that a show of force would cause the Japanese to have second thoughts about the possibility of losing their fishing grounds in northern waters, he rather indirectly instructed two young Russian navy lieutenants, Davidov and Khvostov, to attack the Japanese on Sakhalin and the Kurile Islands. During 1806 and 1807 they burned villages, captured Japanese, seized food supplies, and destroyed ships. Eventually, the use of force and terror was disavowed by the Russian government, but the net effect had been much what Rezanov had at least partially hoped. It instilled a great fear of Russia among the Japanese, without, however, bringing with it the desired effect of better trade relations (see Chapter 6).

SIBERIAN ADMINISTRATION

Russian official policy and administration regarding Siberia was largely determined by Siberia's position as a financial investment and as a producer of vast quantities of valuable furs.

Originally, the Russian government in Moscow controlled all affairs in Siberia by means of an office called the Siberian *prikaz*, established in 1637. The Siberian prikaz, or desk, was headed by a number of nobles, who were aided by a staff of clerks. They were in charge of all affairs pertaining to Siberia: development of government, justice, army, finances, border affairs, colonization, supervision of officials, care of furs, and the sable treasury. The original Siberian prikaz was practically an autonomous governmental institution collecting reports, directing Russian officials in Siberia, and at the same time supervising and managing the fur trade. Within Siberia the administration was permitted to develop rather freely on its own, as long as the necessary reports and petitions were sent to Moscow. To each major fort or ostrog in Siberia was appointed from Moscow a chief official, the *voevoda*, the military and administrative head. The voevodas were responsible only to Moscow, being autonomous in the administration of their respective territories. However, as a check upon their activities, an associate voevoda, or *tovarishch*, was usually also appointed from Moscow, for the same period of service, to act as a countercheck upon the activities of the voevoda. Each ostrog also had a number of clerks who carried on the chief business of each ostrog, that of collecting the fur tribute, and a number of soldiers to garrison the fort. These were either cossacks or *streltsy* ("shooters"), professional infantrymen. Cossacks were either employed on active duty as salaried garrison troops, or they served as agricultural colonists in settlements where they were exempt from the land tax, but were expected to serve as military units in times of need. Since furs were one of the best sources of revenue for the seventeenth-century Russian state and formed the largest single item in the foreign trade of Muscovy, special attention was paid to the fur trade by the Siberian prikaz as well as by the local voevodas. The government levied a ten per cent duty on all furs, had the right to confiscate choice furs, and was especially concerned to ensure that its portion was not lost through graft, corruption, or smuggling. Therefore, border customs checkpoints were maintained across the Urals, and all voevodas had to render a careful personal account upon entering and leaving their official appointments. Early Siberian administration, in the words of a distinguished historian, then was a system in which "the elements of feudal society blended with new ideas of bureaucratic centralized monarchy." It was a system which "lacked orderliness and cohesion, marred by corrupt practices and oppression, but it seemed to satisfy the needs of the Muscovite state at a particular stage of its development."[1]

Later on, under Peter the Great, in order to increase the efficiency of the Russian government, the old autonomous system of voevodas was replaced by new administrative measures, the whole of Siberia being made into one *gubernia* (or "province"), the center of which was Tobolsk. This system, however, had many weaknesses. Since the governor in Tobolsk was far from the capital, the result was an increase in graft, oppression of the people, and lack of information of events in Siberia. The governors were appointed for long terms and were not required to give an accounting of their services. Frequently they enriched themselves, and one of them was tried and hanged for graft by Peter himself.

After Peter, the failure of this system led to a reorganization of the Siberian administration under Count Michael Speransky, who served as governor-general of Siberia from 1819 to 1821. Taking a personal interest in Siberian affairs, he made governmental appointments responsible once more directly to the Russian capital, and he insisted on short tenure appointments. Speransky was motivated by the social, economic, and political ideals of the Enlightenment, and he prepared new legislation for Siberia in 1822 which resulted in the creation of an orderly, bureaucratic organization. Siberia was separated into two governor-generalships, Tobolsk in the west, and Irkutsk in the east, with their own local administrative subdivisions. This permitted a greater amount of decentralization of responsibility, and led to greater freedom of local development. Speransky also inaugurated less state control over trade and fewer restrictions, resulting in freer trade, while protective laws for the natives and measures encouraging the immigration of peasants from Russia to Siberia were also included in his reforms.

In one area of Russian expansion, however, an entirely different concept of government prevailed. In Alaska, government was put into the hands of the Russo-American Company, founded in 1799 in St. Petersburg, which under the capable leadership of Baranov exercised exclusive control of the fur business (mainly in sea otters) in the Aleutians, the Kurils, and Alaska, and which was originally given a twenty-year fur trade monopoly by the government. Government in those areas was conducted by a commercial company, exercising administrative powers within the framework of a mercantilist economic philosophy, analogous to that which lay behind the operations of the British and Dutch East India Companies.

EARLY RELATIONS WITH THE MANCHU EMPIRE

As the Russian population in Siberia and Alaska increased, the problem of obtaining the food supplies necessary for the support of that population grew in intensity, as there was little agriculture except in the Ob basin. The problem was greatest in eastern Siberia and in Alaska, and it motivated Russian expansion from both of these regions.

From Alaska this expansion took form in the mission of Rezanov to

---

[1] George Lantzeff, *Siberia in the Seventeenth Century* (Berkeley, Calif.: University of California Press, 1943), p. 205.

California. Rezanov, the unsuccessful Russian envoy to Japan in 1804, upon his return was made head of the Russo-American Company. On a voyage of inspection to Alaska, he was appalled at the state of conditions there, specifically the lack of food, and he decided in 1805 to sail south to California in order to obtain an agreement with the Spanish which would guarantee Russian access to ample food stores. Rezanov was granted the use as a Russian base of Fort Ross, on the coast north of San Francisco, but that base turned out to be utterly inadequate, and was eventually relinquished by the Russo-American Company. Thus, the attempt to use California as a supply base was a failure.

Russian Conquest of Transbaikalia

This same demand for access to a grain producing area, coupled with an interest in trade, also led to Russian expansion from eastern Siberia to the south, into Transbaikalia and the Amur river basin, resulting in contact between the Russian and the Chinese empires. Transbaikalia, the region beyond Lake Baikal, was brought under Russian control from 1630 to 1665. The Russians were attracted to that area originally by rumors of gold and silver, but they found its conquest no easy matter. Difficult topography, rivers hard to navigate, and, above all, the fierce resistance of the warlike Buriats, made the conquest of Transbaikalia a much more formidable matter than had been the original conquest of Siberia. In 1661 the Russians founded as their base in Transbaikalia Irkutsk, near the shores of Lake Baikal. Even before that, further rumors had spread about the presence of silver and of a rich grain-producing area to the south of Transbaikalia, in the land of a great river, the Amur. A number of exploratory parties were sent out, the first of which was entrusted to the command of a cossack officer, Vasily Poiarkov. In 1643 his expedition set out from Yakutsk on the Lena and reached the upper Amur river basin. He sailed down the whole length of the Amur, and made his way back by sea to Okhotsk. Poiarkov returned in 1646. He had made maps of his trip, and he wrote an account of his expedition in which he described the fertility of the Amur basin. In 1648 Poiarkov's exploits were followed by yet another exploratory party, which resulted in the Russian conquest of parts of the Amur river region.

Khabarov and the Amur

Khabarov, a wealthy and successful trader and promyshlennik, who had prospered in life as a fur trader and a patron of salt works, proposed to the local voevoda at Yakutsk an offer to establish Russian authority on the Amur river at his own expense, with his own men, at no cost to the government. His party of some 150 volunteers left Siberia in 1649. After reaching the Amur basin, Khabarov established a fort at Albazin, and then sailed down the river. In 1651 he arrived at the confluence of the Amur and Ussuri rivers, where yet another ostrog was built on a site which was given his own name, Khabarovsk. On his way to the Amur and down river, Khabarov had employed a policy of terror and destruction toward the local inhabitants.

Wherever his detachments went they plundered the villages, seized the crops, and frequently slaughtered members of the local Dauri tribes. Russian terror and cruelty led the tribes to appeal to the Manchus, who saw in the Khabarov expedition a challenge to the control of their own homeland, Manchuria, and who soon responded. On the other hand, Khabarov, much impressed by the fertility and climate of the Amur river basin, came to the conclusion that colonization of the territory was in the best interests of Russia, hence he appealed to Moscow for military aid in his attempt to establish permanently Russian control. A clash between Russia and China over control of the Amur river followed soon.

Sino-Russian Relations

Hostilities between the Russians and the Chinese began in 1652, and they lasted intermittently until 1686. At first the Chinese attempts to drive the Russians out of the Amur basin were not successful. In 1652, for instance, a Chinese attack on Khabarovsk failed largely because of Chinese orders to take the Russians alive, and not to kill them. The Russians, perceiving the lack of aggressiveness on the part of the Chinese, had no trouble in warding them off. But the attack was sufficiently impressive to cause Khabarov to evacuate Khabarovsk, and to move his forces upstream to Albazin. There Khabarov's role in the Amur came to an end, as his volunteers mutinied against his leadership, and he was forced to leave. But battles between the Chinese and the Russians continued, now over control of Albazin. These continued hostilities led the Russians to found yet another fort, Nerchinsk, further up river on the Shilka, and it also led the Russian government to decide to try a diplomatic approach to China.

Moscow's attempt to use diplomacy instead of force led to the dispatch of two missions to Peking. The first (1653–1656), under Baikov, was instructed by the Ministry of Finance to obtain, if possible, commercial relations, and to obtain as much information as possible about China and her intentions toward Russia. Baikov carried a letter from the tsar, Alexis, addressed to the Chinese emperor, and he was strictly warned against performing any kind of humiliating ceremonies before the Chinese court. But as Baikov refused to perform the kowtow, or ceremonial prostration, and insisted on delivering the tsar's letter directly to the Chinese emperor, his mission resulted in failure, and no trade privileges were granted to Russia. In 1676 a new embassy, headed this time by a Greek adventurer, Spafarii, was ordered to establish trade with China and to discover the best route between Siberia and Peking. Spafarii had little success in China, but he brought back to Russia a keen awareness of Chinese power, so that the government in Moscow came to realize the need for a settlement along the Amur frontier.

Here hostilities had continued. As the result of continued cossack depredations, the Chinese had managed in 1658 to exterminate a rather sizeable band of cossacks, led by Stepanov. By this time the Chinese had cleared the lower portion of the Amur river basin of Russians, but the Russians still controlled the upper river, with their bases at Albazin and

Nerchinsk. The Chinese then began to make serious and elaborate preparations for a major campaign to drive the Russians entirely out of the Amur river. Albazin was taken in 1685 but was reoccupied in 1686, leading to further hostilities. Finally both sides concluded that serious and unabated warfare served the interest of neither. Russia felt that she could not hope for secure possession of the Amur river basin as long as there existed a major Chinese threat, and besides, the government in Russia was far more interested in opening profitable trade relations with Peking. On the other hand, the Chinese also were increasingly interested in settling their frontier dispute with Russia, since the attention of the K'ang-hsi emperor and his advisors was directed chiefly toward the destruction of the formidable Eleuths in Central Asia.

Treaty of Nerchinsk

The result was the Treaty of Nerchinsk (1689), concluded by the governments of the K'ang-hsi emperor and Peter the Great, which remained a major landmark in Russo-Chinese relations until 1858. In the negotiations Jesuit missionaries were used as interpreters, and Latin served as the common language. The treaty was the first between China and a European power. It was signed on the basis of equality, and in effect, was a major Chinese victory.

The negotiations at Nerchinsk began with the Chinese putting forth some very large claims. China claimed all the land clear to the Lena and the Gulf of Okhotsk. The Russians replied to this by putting forth a demand for the Amur river itself as a boundary line between the Russian and Chinese empires, but in view of the Chinese pressure, and military preponderance, they had to yield so that the boundary finally settled upon was the watershed to the north of the Amur, atop the Yablonoi range separating the Lena and Amur drainage.

The Russians were pushed out of the Amur basin. However, they did obtain the right to maintain their fort at Nerchinsk, and trade with China was permitted and regularized, so that caravans operated by the Russian government on a monopoly basis were allowed to go to Peking. Russian furs were traded for traditional Chinese wares, such as tea, silk and porcelain, and this trade, although not on a large scale, became profitable for the Russians.

However, precisely because trade with China was profitable, Russian private merchants attempted to evade state control, resulting in much smuggling to the annoyance of the Chinese. The Chinese were further chagrined by frontier friction due to cossack activities along the border and by Russian actions in regard to a Chinese embassy sent to the tribe of the Torguts. These people, former inhabitants of north Mongolia, had migrated far to the west to Russia, where they settled between the Don and Volga rivers. The Manchus, in their struggle against the Eleuths, looked upon the Torguts as natural allies, and sent a mission to persuade them to join in the attack, but the Russian government prevented this. For these reasons, the Chinese decided to stop all trade with Russia.

In order to adjust these disputes the Russian government sent out in

1719 a captain of the Lifeguards, Ismailov. He arrived laden with valuable gifts which included furs, a microscope, barometers, watches, clocks, and spyglasses, some of them made by Peter himself, and with an ample supply of money with which to bribe the Chinese officials. Ismailov, at first, refused to perform the kowtow, but the K'ang-hsi emperor, who received him graciously and spoke to him in person, eventually persuaded him to go through the ceremony, urging that it did not imply the acknowledgment of Russian inferiority. The result of this mission was the resumption of the caravan trade, while the Russian government also obtained the right to station a consul in Peking and to establish there an ecclesiastical mission to minister to the Russian prisoners of war who had been captured by the Chinese at the siege of Albazin.

Treaty of Kiakhta

In 1727, another treaty signed at Kiakhta, a town southeast of Irkutsk on the Chinese frontier, resulted in further Russian commercial and some minor diplomatic gains. Under its terms Russia recognized Chinese suzerainty over Outer Mongolia and agreed to a final settlement of some outstanding minor points of frontier demarcation, and in return Russia received the right to trade at Kiakhta and the right to send every three years a caravan of 200 men to Peking to trade directly at the capital. Russian interest in trade with China became the guide of Russian policy. Kiakhta soon became the center of a very flourishing Russo-Chinese trade, although, in all probability, it was the Chinese merchants who were able to drive better bargains.

The major Russian exports were, of course, furs, but textiles, glass, leather, hides, cattle, horses, and camels were also sold by the Russians, in return for Chinese silk, cotton cloth, tea, porcelain, sugar, ginger, lacquered goods, and rhubarb. The yearly volume of trade reached the proportions of four million rubles, of which a half million rubles was clear profit to the Russian government.

SIBERIAN COLONIZATION AND FAR EASTERN EXPANSION, AFTER NERCHINSK

The Treaty of Nerchinsk (1689) remained a landmark until the middle of the nineteenth century, when Russian expansion again produced major changes in her Asian possessions. The basic motivation for the renewal of expansion again is to be found in the problem of food supply, which became increasingly acute with the increase of the permanent population in Siberia. The problem of food supply was especially urgent in eastern Siberia, Kamchatka, and Alaska, since by 1700 western Siberia produced enough grain to support most of its population. Eastern Siberia continued to experience an inflow of cossacks, peasants, and, from the time of Catherine the Great, criminals and political exiles who were used especially to develop silver and copper mines in the vicinity of Nerchinsk, but whose life was not overly unpleasant as they were permitted to take their families along with them.

But the greatest single factor in the growth of the Russian population in Siberia was Russian peasant immigration. Peasants flowed in ever larger numbers to Siberia where there was no serfdom, and where free land was available. By 1800 the population of Siberia was estimated to be about a million, but at the end of the century it had increased at least to ten times that number. Russian administrators, faced with the problem of how to feed a rapidly growing population, had, of course, never forgotten the very real attractions of the Amur basin, with its fertility, its hospitable climate, and its excellent resources.

Muraviev and the Acquisition of the Amur Basin

The lure of the Amur lay behind the resumption of Russian expansion. In 1842 China's weakness had been shown to the whole world by her defeat in the First Anglo-Chinese War and the subsequent humiliating First Treaty Settlement. As early as 1843 the Russian government sponsored an explorer, Middendorf, who was sent to see whether the Amur delta was navigable for vessels entering the river from the sea. His report was negative, but this did not deter the energetic Russian governor-general, Count Nicholas Muraviev, who was the real driving force behind renewed Russian expansion in the Far East in the nineteenth century. Nicholas Muraviev, only thirty-eight years old in 1847 when he became governor-general, was an exceedingly aggressive, unscrupulous, but also a very capable individual. His idea was to promote once more Russian interests in the Amur by sending out new expeditions which were to explore the region, and then to create permanent Russian settlements, while he also proposed to build a Russian naval base at Petropavlovsk on Kamchatka which would strengthen Russia's hold on her eastern provinces. The renewed interest of Muraviev stemmed from the fact that he felt it necessary for Russian interests, in addition to solving the food supply problem, to counterbalance the increasing British trade in south China and the growing strength of the British navy in the Pacific with Russian control of the Amur basin and the establishment of Russian seaports on the Pacific. This would protect her trade interests, her settlements in Kamchatka, the growing activities of the Russo-American Company in Alaska, and her whaling industry in the Bering Sea. It was Muraviev who decided upon the launching of a new expedition which was to find out, specifically, whether or not the Amur had a navigable mouth, and whether or not Sakhalin was an island. For this reason Nevelskoi, a young Russian navy lieutenant, prompt and decisive in his actions, was selected by Muraviev, who impressed upon him the need for Russia's special interest in the Amur region and for definitive information. Nevelskoi was sent out from St. Petersburg in command of a navy transport vessel with instructions to settle once and for all the question of the Amur estuary and its navigability and the question of Sakhalin.

The impetuous Nevelskoi, after establishing a number of small Russian posts on Sakhalin island, against Japanese protests, sailed up the Amur river and at a point upstream, subsequently the city of Nikolaevsk, he raised the Russian flag and took possession of the Amur basin for his country. Nevelskoi's act infuriated the Russian foreign minister Nesselrode, who insisted upon a court-martial and degradation for Nevelskoi, but the lieutenant was supported by the tsar, Nicholas I, who came forth with the grandiloquent declaration that "where the Russian flag is once raised, it can not be lowered." Thus did the Amur basin become Russian territory. Nevelskoi continued his explorations, next in the Ussuri river area, but the series of Russian posts which he had established on Sakhalin island were withdrawn by Russia in 1853 because of Japanese protests and the Crimean War. It only remained for Russia to legalize the *fait accompli* of her seizure of the Amur basin, and this came when the weak Manchu government signed the Treaty of Aigun (1858) with Russia, negotiated by Muraviev. The territory on the left bank of the Amur became Russian, while the land between the Ussuri river and the Pacific was to be held jointly by Russia and China. Shortly thereafter Nicholas I declared the Amur to be indispensable to Russia.

Treaty of Peking

In 1860 the Russians once more took advantage of the weakness of China to gain further prominence in the Far East. During that year the Allies began their advance upon Peking, in the Second Anglo-Chinese War. The Russian envoy to the Manchu court, General Ignatiev, at that time posed as the friend of China and as indispensable negotiator who could intervene and prevent Allied aggression, while simultaneously he urged the Western Allies to take a firm line with the Chinese. He would save Peking from destruction, he told the Chinese court, while in return he merely wanted an insignificant frontier rectification, nothing more than the cession to Russia of the trans-Ussuri region, a region, in his words: "sterile, inhabited by robbers and infested by tigers, where no mandarin could make a living, fit only for a penal settlement, with a rugged seacoast where no Chinese sail was ever seen." Prince Kung thereupon signed the Treaty of Peking with Russia, by which all territory east of the Ussuri river, some 350,000 square miles, the so-called Primorsk or Maritime Province of the Russian empire, was handed over to Russia, cutting off Manchuria from the sea.

With the signing of the Treaties of Aigun (1858) and Peking (1860), the Amur question had been settled to the satisfaction of Russia. All that was left to be done was to energetically develop the new possessions. In 1860 the city of Vladivostok, "ruler of the East," was founded, giving the Maritime Province and Siberia a well-situated outlet to the sea. After the abolition of serfdom in 1861 large numbers of colonists began to move into Siberia and the newly acquired Maritime Province. Paralleling these great advances was a general reorientation of Russian policy after the Crimean War. The Russian government concluded that in view of its weakness vis-à-vis British seapower it might do well to get rid of its overseas possessions, especially Alaska, which was sold to the United States in 1867, and instead to emphasize the development of Russian Siberia. This view was further strengthened after 1888 when Russia turned away from the Balkans, so that the government was free to turn its full attention to the Far East.

RUSSIA IN ASIA 1600–1895

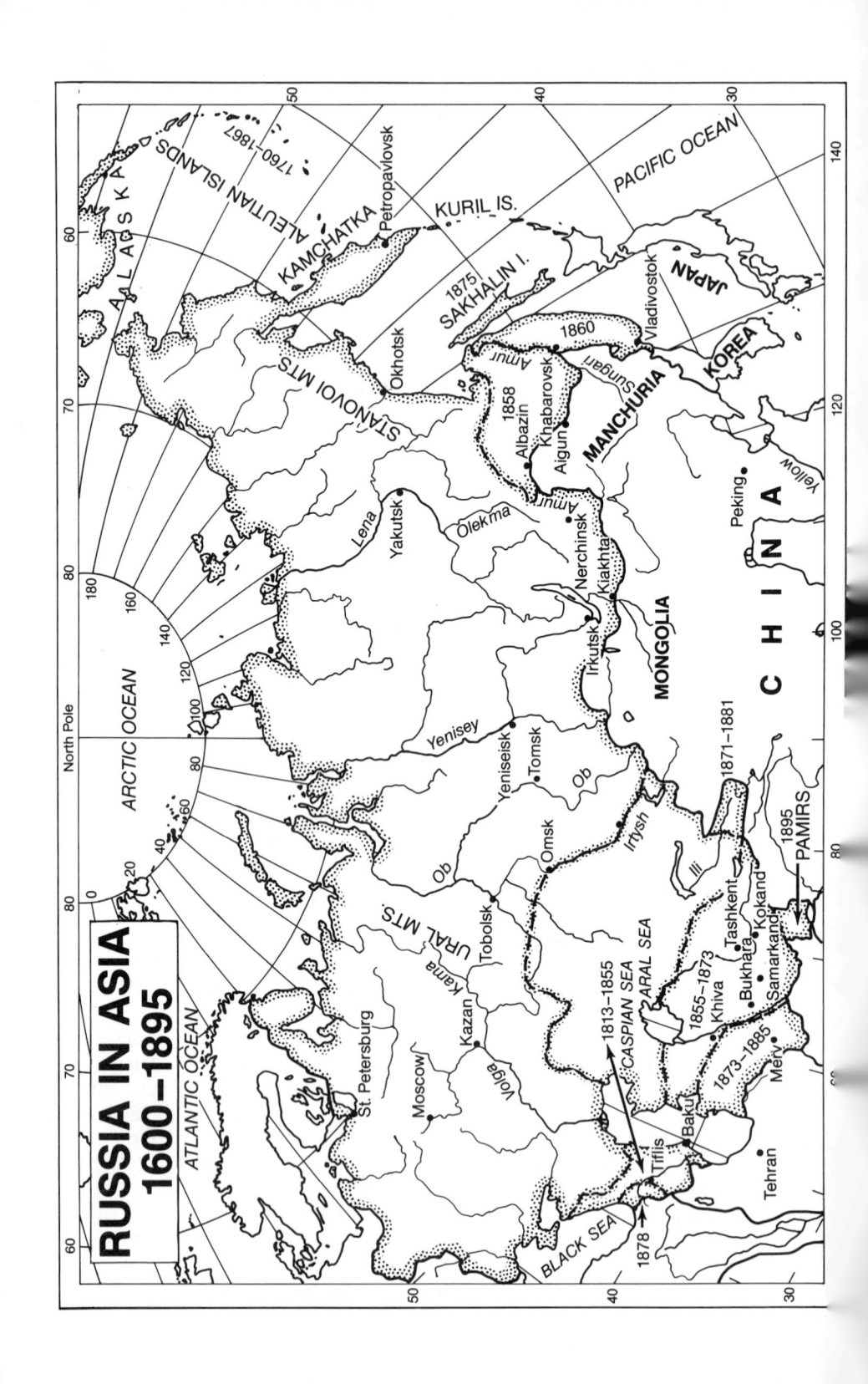

The Building of the Trans-Siberian Railroad

The development of Siberia required transportation facilities. The idea of building a railroad line to Siberia from Russia had first been conceived in 1858, and Muraviev himself had shown an interest in such a project in conversations during the early 1880's, but this project of enormous scope and cost really came under serious consideration only with the completion of the Trans-Ural Railroad in 1884. The building of a Trans-Siberian Railroad, which was to carry on the line from the Urals across all of Asiatic Russia, was the work of the Russian finance minister, the very able Count Witte, who urged its construction both for economic as well as for strategic considerations. The building of the Trans-Siberian Railroad was begun in 1891 in seven sections, and was completed in 1903.

The significance of the Trans-Siberian Railroad in channeling a vast stream of immigration from Russia and in promoting trade became clear at once. Whereas in 1861 the population of Eastern Siberia totaled 630,000 people, by 1939 it had risen to four and one-half million, of whom two and one-half million were located in the Amur basin. It was the Trans-Siberian Railroad which really made Eastern Siberia, the Amur river region, and the Maritime Province into a Russian area.

The Russian empire also made gains during the last part of the nineteenth century in yet another direction—the waters dividing its possessions from those of Japan. The Russo-Japanese Treaty of 1855, which Admiral Putiatin had negotiated, in addition to permitting trade, also provided for the joint possession by both nations of the island of Sakhalin, and for the division of the Kurils. Russia was much interested in obtaining sole ownership of Sakhalin, and in a treaty with Japan in 1875 she obtained that objective at the cost of turning all of the islands of the Kuril chain over to the Japanese.

RUSSIAN EXPANSION INTO CENTRAL AND WESTERN ASIA

It was not only in the Far East that Russia made vast gains during the nineteenth century. In the same period Russia also made great advances into Central Asia, present Russian Turkistan in particular, while all along her West Asian boundaries, toward Persia and Afghanistan, Russia also became a formidable power exercising vast influence.

Early Advances

Russian expansion into Central Asia began with Peter the Great. Peter's interest in a land route to China and India led to the first of many Russian expeditions into the Kirghiz steppe and into Turkistan. Peter's appetite was also whetted by the rumor of gold in Central Asia. For these reasons a certain guard officer, Prince Bekovich Cherkassky, was sent on a series of exploratory expeditions on the Caspian Sea during 1715 and 1716. He sailed along the coasts of that great body of water, leaving behind sizable garrisons wherever he went, but since he may have been demented he chose as sites places where no water, nor any kind of vegetation, could possibly be found, so that ninety per cent of his soldiers perished. In 1717 Bekovich Cherkassky marched against the Moslem principality of Khiva, on the Amu Darya river. However, only three men of his expedition eventually returned to Russia; the rest of his army and he himself were massacred by the inhabitants of Khiva.

This early attack against a Central Asian state was a failure. However, in their drive into the Kirghiz steppe the Russians were far more successful. Operating from fortified bases such as Omsk (1716) and Semipalatinsk (1718), they constructed a series of fortified lines which enabled the Russians to gain control of the interfluvial regions, thereby cutting off the grazing grounds and preventing free movement of the nomads. In short, control of the steppe area was won, as had been Siberia, by a line of military blockhouses, or ostrogs. Once Kazakhstan had been encircled by a series of these ostrogs and the power of the fierce and turbulent Kazakhs broken, Russians began to settle in the upper Irtysh valley. By the first decades of the nineteenth century Russian military power had been extended south, to the Syr-darya valley and the region of Lake Balkash. From here, the lure of a trade route to India via Bukhara led the Russian government once again to undertake another attempt to conquer Khiva, but with the same dismal failure as a result.

Conquest of Turkistan

Fifteen years later, however, after the Crimean War had given Russia the impetus to expand into the cotton growing territories of Russian Turkistan, the advance up the Syr-darya valley was taken up with vigor and new methods. Forts were built on Lake Balkash and Lake Aral, and river steamboats were built to facilitate the advance on the Central Asian khanates. The successful conquest of the Syr-darya valley began when Kokand was captured in 1865. Next, Russian military superiority in terms of modern firearms against the lances and flintlocks of the oasis city states of Tashkent and Bukhara sealed their respective doom in 1867 and 1868. They were captured by the Russians under the ambitious General Chernaiev, and the fabled city of Samarkand fell to the forces of General Kauffman in 1868. Russian domination of these Moslem states seemed necessary in order to forestall a possible English advance into Turkistan, and eventually all of these either became vassals of the Russian tsar, as did the emir of Bukhara, or they came under direct Russian control as did Kokand after a brief unsuccessful revolt in 1875. In 1867 a governor-generalship of Turkistan was created, with General Kauffman being appointed as the first governor-general at Tashkent. This left only Khiva, and an old score was settled when it was finally conquered in 1873.

Russia in Zungaria

General Kauffman, an energetic and far-seeing soldier, acted on his own initiative in 1871 when he sent Russian troops eastward into the Ili river valley, the most fertile and most populated part of Chinese Turkistan. He occupied that area as the result of the Moslem revolt in Chinese Turkistan. The Russian troops, originally sent "to preserve peace," stayed on for seven years of occupation. The Chinese government tried to end this situation through diplomacy in the form of two treaties. The terms of the first treaty (1879) were most disadvantageous to China. The Chinese envoy agreed that Russia could keep most of the Ili river valley, and that China would pay indemnities to Russia for the costs of her occupation. For agreeing to these terms the envoy was sentenced to be beheaded upon his return to China, and a new treaty was subsequently concluded in 1881. The Russians returned to Chinese control most of the Ili valley, in return for which Russia gained the right to trade, reduced customs duties, and the right to establish consulates in Turkistan and Mongolia. This change in Russian attitude was due, however, not so much to Chinese diplomatic skill, as to the arrival of the well-trained Chinese forces under Tso Tsung-t'ang in Chinese Turkistan, which had crushed the Moslem revolt, and which seemed to promise difficulties for too intransigent a Russian stand.

Pressure on Persia and Afghanistan

Mention must also be made, however briefly, of Russian expansion to the south, in the direction of Persia and Afghanistan. From their position in Transcaucasia the Russians had waged war against Persia in 1804, in 1812, and again from 1825 to 1828, with the result that Russian influence in north Persia had come to be an accepted fact after the Treaty of Turkomanchai (1828). This situation contributed greatly to the rivalry between the British and the Russians. After the conquest of Russian Turkistan in the 1860's, Russian pressure could now also be exercised upon yet another segment of the Persian border, and Russia lost no time in moving against the Turkmen tribes who lived in that area. At first this attempt ended in disaster, when a Russian force was ambushed and suffered severe losses in 1879, but by 1884 the Turkmen stronghold of Geok Tepe was captured and Russian troops occupied the city of Merv, close to the Persian border (again causing great anxiety among the British who feared a Russian threat to India). The Russians used their advantage in obtaining a trade route from Persia and defining their mutual border, and then they continued to exert pressure, this time against Afghanistan. Fear of Russian penetration into that kingdom had already produced the First and Second Afghan Wars, and it produced promptly yet another major crisis, the result of the Panjdeh Incident in 1885. There Russian troops had fired upon some Afghan cavalry along the Amu-darya river, almost causing war between Great Britain and Russia. After this tense situation had been settled, a new crisis between Britain and Russia arose over boundary conflicts in the Pamir mountains. This conflict was adjusted by mutual agreement in 1895, but it again illustrated the dominant fact of the great Anglo-Russian rivalry, pitting seapower against land power, all across Asia from the Straits in Constantinople, where Turkey was propped up by British power and was saved by that country in the Crimean War, through Persia, Afghanistan, and Tibet to the Far East.

Russian Rule in Turkistan

The Pamir frontier rectification in 1895 ended further acquisitions by Russia in Central Asia. Russia had conquered and annexed vast areas in Central Asia, comparable in size to Western Europe, in less than fifty years at a total cost of some four hundred soldiers. Russian Central Asia, or Russian Turkistan, including the present Kazakh, Kirghiz, Uzbek, Turkmen, and Tadzhik Soviet Socialist Republics, is one great basin, half the size of the United States. It is primarily a steppe and desert area, but with valuable irrigated agricultural land along the Amu and Syr-darya rivers. Before the advent of Russian power in the mid-nineteenth century it was a region isolated from the rest of the world, depressed economically, ruled tyrannically and oppressively by Moslem principalities, of whom the three most important had been Khiva, Kokand, and Bukhara. These were slave states, despotic and lawless, with widespread illiteracy and superstition, and indulging in frequent internecine warfare among themselves. The Russians did establish a more efficient, although still ruthless government, and they did improve the economic condition of Russian Turkistan. General Kauffman, who was governor-general (1868–1882), contributed greatly to the rapid economic development of the area. The government encouraged colonization, and many settlers from European Russia responded, usually appropriating the best irrigated lands. The development of cotton was of special interest to the Russian government, which had suffered from a shortage of cotton due to the Crimean War and the American Civil War. A new American strain from Texas was introduced, and new, improved methods of cotton cultivation and processing were being employed, while other irrigation projects allowed flourishing fruit orchards. The growing of cotton was further stimulated by low freight rates and tax privileges, and above all by the construction of new railroad lines. The Trans-Caspian Railroad had been completed in 1881, and by 1906 a direct line had been completed from Tashkent to Orenburg, with easy access from Orenburg to European Russia. Russian domination of Russian Turkistan meant economic improvement for that whole vast area, and it also implied a gain for the natives, although compared with the rest of Russia, Russian Turkistan in 1914 was still a backward area.

BASIC DATES

1552	Ivan IV captures Kazan
1581	Yermak overthrows khanate of Sibir
1587	Tobolsk founded
1604	Tomsk founded
1619	Yenisseisk founded
1630–1665	Russians gain control of Transbaikalia
1632	Yakutsk founded
1638	Russians reach Pacific at Okhotsk
1649–1651	Khabarov in Amur basin

1654	Nerchinsk founded
1661	Irkutsk founded
1689	Treaty of Nerchinsk
1697–1699	Conquest of Kamchatka
1711	Exploration of the Kurils
1732	Exploration of North America
1739	Exploration of Japan
1792	Laxman
1804	Rezanov
1806–1807	Davidov and Khvostov
1828	Treaty of Turkomanchai
1847	Muraviev appointed governor-general of Siberia
1850	Nevelskoi at Nikolaevsk
1858	Treaty of Aigun
1860	Treaty of Peking; founding of Vladivostok
1865	Kokand captured
1867	Alaska sold to the United States; Bukhara captured
1868–1882	Kauffman governor-general of Turkistan
1871–1881	Ili valley occupied by Russia
1873	Khiva captured
1875	Sakhalin obtained by Japan
1881	Trans-Caspian Railroad completed
1884	Trans-Ural Railroad completed
1885	Panjdeh Incident
1891–1903	Trans-Siberian Railroad built
1895	Pamir boundary settlement
1906	Tashkent-Orenburg Railroad built

SUPPLEMENTARY READING

Fisher, H. *The Russian Fur Trade.* Berkeley, Calif., 1943.
Harrison, J. A. *The Founding of the Russian Empire in Asia and America.* Coral Gables, Fla., 1971.
Lantzeff, G. *Siberia in the Seventeenth Century.* Berkeley, Calif., 1943.
Treadgold, D. G. *The Great Siberian Migration.* Princeton, N.J., 1957.

ADVANCED READING

Allworth, E. *Central Asia: A Century of Russian Rule.* New York, 1967.
Becker, S. *Russia's Protectorates in Central Asia: Bukhara and Khiva, 1865-1924.* Cambridge, Mass., 1968.
Chen, V. *Sino-Soviet Relations in the Seventeenth Century.* The Hague, 1966.
Fisher, R. H. *Records of the Russian-American Company, 1802, 1817-1867.* Washington, D.C., 1971.
Khalfin, N. A. *Russia's Policy in Central Asia, 1857-1868.* London, 1964.
Lensen, G. A. *The Russian Push Toward Japan, 1697-1875.* Princeton, N.J., 1959.

Pierce, R. *Russia in Central Asia, 1867-1917: A Study in Colonial Rule.* Berkeley, Calif., 1960. Stresses primarily Russian administration and economic development, with little material on Russian expansion itself.

Vladimir (pseudonym of Z. Volpicelli). *Russia on the Pacific and the Siberian Railway.* London, 1899.

Weigh, K. *Russo-Chinese Diplomacy, 1689-1924.* Bangor, Maine, 1967.

Chapter 10

India: Empire and Nationalism, 1858-1914

IMPERIAL ORGANIZATION AND EXPANSION

The great Indian Mutiny of 1857 had been a tremendous shock to British public opinion, perhaps more so than its extent warranted since it was not a national movement. After all, it had been restricted to the Indian troops in Bengal, and there had been no trouble whatever in either Madras or Bombay. Further, the princely states too had not participated in the futile attempt to shake off the British yoke, and indeed some of them from the Punjab and from Nepal had even sent military forces of their own to aid the English in the suppression of the Mutiny. Nevertheless, the impact of the year 1857 in London was so great that there was a demand for a general reorganization of British rule in India. In British governing circles it seemed that nothing short of a fundamental change would do. Fundamental change was duly provided with the passing by royal proclamation of the "Act for the Better Government of India of 1858." The essential element in this change was the establishment of the complete and direct supremacy of Parliament over India, with the consequent location of responsibility for all Indian affairs in London. The act provided then for the transfer of authority from the Board of Control of the directors of the East India Company to a secretary of state for India, who was to be a member of the British cabinet and was to be responsible to Parliament. He was to be aided at the India Office in London by the Council of India, composed of expert officials.

The Administrative System

In turn, the secretary of state in London was represented in India by the governor-general, who now was called viceroy (Lord Canning being the first), and who ruled from the capital of Calcutta over the governors of the

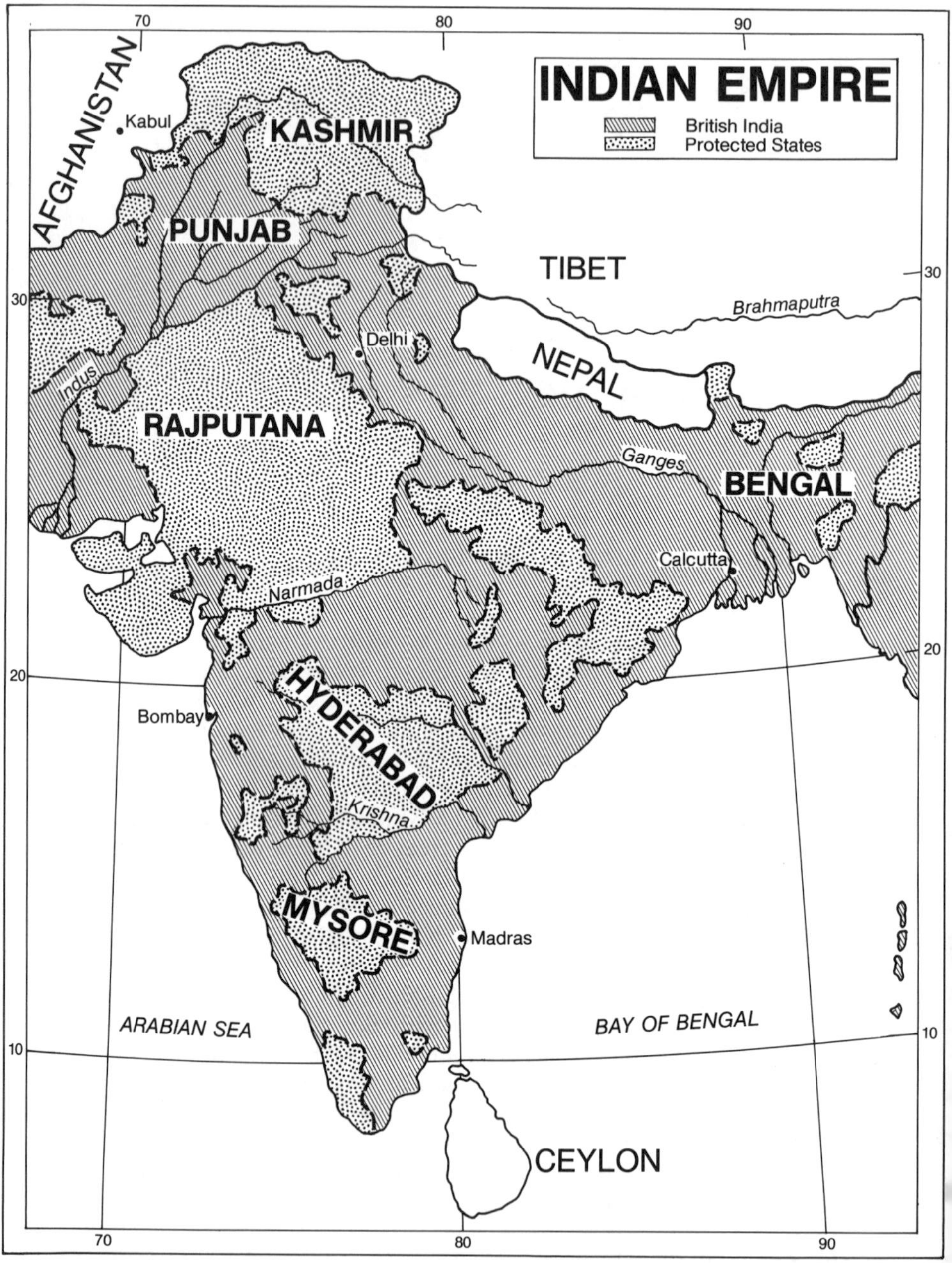
INDIAN EMPIRE
British India
Protected States
AFGHANISTAN
Kabul
KASHMIR
PUNJAB
TIBET
Brahmaputra
Delhi
NEPAL
Indus
RAJPUTANA
Ganges
BENGAL
Calcutta
Narmada
HYDERABAD
Bombay
Krishna
MYSORE
Madras
ARABIAN SEA
BAY OF BENGAL
CEYLON
70
80
90
30
20
10

provinces. British India was organized into two main divisions: that part of the country subject to direct British rule, and the so-called "protected states" which were bound to Britain by treaties of friendship and commerce. To the former belonged the provinces of Bombay, Madras, the Ganges provinces, Punjab and Burma; to the latter belonged the "protected states" of Hyderabad, Mysore, Kashmir, a series of Rajput principalities, and some others, in which control was exercised by the British government through a British resident at the court of each prince. In order to assure British supremacy in the native states, all foreign relations and relations with other states on the part of the protected states were to be handled only by the British viceroy; at the same time, in order to gain the loyalty of the princes to British rule, the hated doctrine of lapse was ended by the British government in 1859, thus permitting an adopted son to be recognized as the legal heir of the native state. Coupled with this announcement came the reassurance that the British government henceforth had no desire to extend its territories. The right to intervene in the affairs of the native states in case of maladministration was, however, still reserved to the viceroy.

The viceroy after 1861 was assisted by an executive council of five European members, each of whom was given a special portfolio, such as the Army, etc. There was no Indian on this council until 1909, and the decisions of the members, who were appointed by the Crown, were subject to the viceroy's veto. A similar autocratic relationship existed between the viceroy and his legislative council, dating also from 1861. This council was composed of the executive council and such additional members as were appointed by the viceroy, but its functions were limited to a mere discussion of bills proposed, and even these could be overruled by either the viceroy or the secretary of state for India. The judicial branch of the British government in India was equally closely controlled by the viceroy since the members of the high courts of the various provinces were appointed by him.

In the provinces each governor had the assistance of a provincial council, but here, too, except for the fact that these councils were enlarged in 1892 and the seed of the elective principle was introduced at that time, full power to overrule them was held by the governor. At the bottom of the structure of British government in India was perhaps the most important British official, the district officer, on whom the whole administrative system depended.

All of these British officials belonged to an able and dedicated bureaucratic elite organization, the Indian Civil Service. The I.C.S., as it was abbreviated, established high standards of admission based on competitive examinations and offered life careers with excellent salaries and generous pension allowances to its members. While these men governed India well, they were slow to recognize and to respond to Indian demands. Less than 4,000 members of this service, of whom the vast majority were British, ruled an Indian population of hundreds of millions.

Military Reorganization

In addition to administrative changes, the Mutiny also resulted in drastic changes in the military. No longer were special troops to be recruited in

Britain for service in India; after 1858 the army which garrisoned India was composed of regular units of the British army and of Indian troops officered by Englishmen. Especially important was the fact that all artillery was solely in the hands of British army units, and that Indians were denied commissions. Furthermore, in order to make the defense of India more efficient and reliable, the British army in India relied for recruitment of its Indian troops upon the so-called "martial races" of the Punjab, the northwest, and of Nepal, areas which remained unaffected by the disloyalty evinced among the ranks of the mutineers from Bengal. Additional support to the British military system came from limited native contingents maintained by some princes, but trained by British officers.

Nature of British Rule

As a whole one can say that these changes, both political and military, resulted in some improvements, but there were also distinct disadvantages. For one thing, after the Act for the Better Government of India of 1858, Parliament ceased to take much interest in Indian affairs. English party politics no longer were made turbulent by Indian issues, and the debate on the Indian budget came to mean lengthy hours of unmitigated boredom. The India Office itself was now merely one of several ministries, and the secretary of state for India showed little interest in reforms in India. Thus Parliament no longer dispatched independent parliamentary inquiries, such as those which had resulted in the Pitt Act. In India, as the British historian Philips puts it, power confined the English rather than corrupted them. On the other hand, the viceroy himself tended to have less and less contact with India. He spent half the year in the cool hills of Simla and the rest in Calcutta where he dealt primarily with English professional civil servants, merchants, and industrialists. The very closeness of London to Calcutta, which came with the establishment of the first overland telegraph line in 1865, soon to be followed by the opening of the Suez Canal in 1869 and the first submarine cable the year after, worked against close personal relations between British officials and Indian reality. With this coincided also the development of the less optimistic view among British officialdom that Western ideas would not be able to transform Indian customs and traditions. In short, British policy after 1858 tended to be much more conservative in spirit, more cautious about reforms, and more concerned in maintaining the status quo, rather than being occupied in what seemed increasingly a vain attempt of improving and transforming.

BRITISH FOREIGN POLICY

The maintenance of the status quo, which was now the chief aim of British policy was also, as one might expect, reflected in the conduct of British foreign policy regarding India. During the years which followed 1858 this policy was one of the gradual extension and consolidation of British authority over the entire peninsula, and in certain strategically important regions on the Indian frontier.

INDIA: EMPIRE AND NATIONALISM, 1858–1914

FIGURE 10.1. The Victoria Memorial, Calcutta. This "British Taj Mahal" illustrates well the solidity and impressive qualities of permanence which Englishmen at the end of the nineteenth century thought reflected their rule in India.

The second half of the nineteenth century was the very apogee of Britain's greatness as an imperial power, and for India this was symbolized by Disraeli's proclamation on January 1, 1877, declaring Queen Victoria Empress of India. This act not merely symbolized the rising tide of imperialism, but it also made the independent princely rulers of India the Empress' vassals. The Indian princes and rulers of the various protected states, such as Hyderabad, Mysore, Kashmir, and the Rajput principalities, to name only the most important ones, continued to be treated as independent sovereigns, but the government of India became increasingly interested in their internal affairs and sometimes did not hesitate to interfere in them when conditions became exceptionally arbitrary and tyrannical. Under the doctrine of paramountcy, the British resident at each princely court had the duty to protect both British and native interests if he decided that the administration of these states had fallen below certain standards.

Beyond the confines of the Indian peninsula this period also saw the gradual extension of British authority in those regions which seemed vital to the British rule of India. To the north relations with Nepal continued to be friendly, as they had been since 1816. However, the British did not hesitate to take action against the smaller Himalayan principality of Bhutan, located on the northern frontier of Bengal, which was punished in 1865 for raids into the Ganges valley and was forced to cede some 4,000 square miles of territory. In the east, the final annexation of what was left of Burma occurred in 1885. Burma became a province of the British empire in India. Finally, to the west, the British government added Baluchistan to its possessions, in order to obtain a broader frontier in the strategic area around Afghanistan.

The Problem of Afghanistan and Russian Power

If there was one single overriding consideration in all of British foreign policy during this period it was the fear for the security of India, especially as it was threatened by the worldwide Anglo-Russian rivalry of the nineteenth century. This fear had already inspired the British to engage in the disastrous First Afghan War, and it was now to cause the second. The amir of Afghanistan, Dost Muhammad, who had been friendly to the English, died in 1863. After his death the country was plunged into a seven-year civil war in which twelve brothers contended for the throne. During this period the British had pursued a policy of "masterly inactivity," criticized by its opponents as cheap, cold-blooded, and overly cautious. It was only after one brother, Sher Ali, had won in 1870 that the British government in India recognized and supported him, but his attitude toward the English remained cool. While civil war had raged in Afghanistan the Russians had most successfully advanced into Central Asia, and by 1867 had reached the borders of Afghanistan (see Chapter 9). The creation of a Russian Turkistan, under a Russian military government, was motivated strongly by the implied threat of weakening British support to the Turks at Constantinople by stabbing at India, the "crown jewel" of the empire. Sher Ali himself had become disturbed at these developments, and in 1873 he asked for definite British support, only to be refused by Gladstone. Sher Ali then turned to the Russians instead, and began to accept Russian support. With the outbreak of the Russo-Turkish War in 1877 Anglo-Russian rivalry became critical once more, leading to the annexation of Baluchistan by British military forces. This move was designed to check Afghan power since the Afghan flank was now turned, and since Quetta, the Baluchi capital, was located in a most strategic spot on the road to Afghan Kandahar. This move greatly annoyed Sher Ali, but by this time, Disraeli, supported by his viceroy in India, Lord Lytton, had discarded the policy of "masterly inactivity." Aroused by what seemed to be the newest evidence of the Russian menace, he substituted a new "forward policy," designed, if necessary, to go to war with the Afghans in order to keep Russian influence out of that country. Matters came to a head when Sher Ali received a Russian envoy, General Stolietov, in July 1878 while refusing at the same time to receive a British envoy at his court. Disraeli, who had heretofore vainly attempted to persuade the Russians to change their policy and to discontinue their friendly relations with the amir, now issued an ultimatum to Sher Ali, demanding a full apology and the acceptance of a British resident at the court in Kabul. Sher Ali rejected it promptly, and in November, 1878, the British launched the Second Anglo-Afghan War, for which there was little enough reason and which was the result of previous English ineptness. Afghanistan was invaded by a punitive expedition which had no difficulty in driving Sher Ali into exile in Russia where he soon died. His son, Yakub Khan, agreed in 1879 to sign the Treaty of Gandamak with the British, in which Yakub agreed to accept a British representative in Kabul and to hand over to the English control of Afghan foreign relations. In addition, he agreed to cede the strategic Khyber Pass and some additional territory, including the valley of Kurram, to the British government. British victories and the peace of Gandamak remained, however, hollow successes, since the resentful Afghans promptly revolted against the British army in September of 1879. The British resident in Kabul, Cavagnari, was murdered, and heavy losses convinced the British of the impossible expense of permanent military control of the kingdom. In the aftermath of this affair, Yakub Khan abdicated, and was succeeded by his nephew, Abdurraman, who was amir from 1880 until 1910. In his reign a new British "good-will" policy approach to the Afghan problem was adopted, and was greatly strengthened after Lord Dufferin became viceroy in 1884, who, in order to keep the Afghan frontier safe, cultivated the good will of Abdurraman without interfering in Afghan internal affairs.

This policy was most successful. In 1885 there occurred a clash between a Russian military patrol and some Afghan forces at Panjdeh on the Amu-darya river, and Britain appeared in the role of the defender of Afghanistan. The Panjdeh Incident was a most serious one, and war between the two great European powers, Britain and Russia, seemed imminent. A British army corps was mobilized in India, but this display of readiness had the desired result of Russia's backing down. After 1885 Britain gave Afghanistan a guarantee as to its independence, and an annual generous subsidy. Consequently, without having to station British troops in Afghanistan, the country had become an effective buffer state against Russian expansionist tendencies.

Russian activities in the high Pamirs in 1891 led to further British countermeasures to guard India. The British occupied the principalities of Hunza and Nagar in the Gilgit valley in 1892 to strengthen the defenses against invasion across the icy passes of the Hindu Kush, and in 1895 British control was extended to the petty state of Chitral, west of Gilgit. The Pamir frontier dispute with Russia was settled also in 1895, and contributed to an easing of tension.

Fear of Russian expansion had also led the English to take a most active interest in Chinese Turkistan. There the Moslems had revolted against their Chinese overlords in 1874, and for some three years the province of Sinkiang had become de facto an independent state. The British government in India was very concerned about Sinkiang becoming pro-Russian, but their fears were allayed when the Chinese suppressed the Moslem revolt (see Chapter 12).

The Tibetan Problem

British anxiety about possible Russian maneuvers in Tibet to the north led also to British interference. Tibet had interested the English in India as far back as the days of Warren Hastings, who had sent Bogle in 1774 and Samuel Turner in 1783 to establish diplomatic relations, but the Tibetans remained isolated behind their mountain barrier as a dependent state of the Manchu empire. But here, too, fear of Russia eventually led to renewed British action. In 1901, Dorjeff, an envoy from the Dalai Lama of Tibet to the tsar at St. Petersburg, had been most cordially received by the Russians, while at the same time a letter from Lord Curzon, the British viceroy in India, had been returned unopened. Fearing the worst, and imagining the Russian menace settling down on the high Tibetan plateau to haunt India, the British ordered Colonel Younghusband in 1903 at the head of a military expedition to penetrate into the fastnesses of Tibet. The Tibetans resisted, but Younghusband received reinforcements and entered Lhasa in August, 1904. He obtained a treaty from Tibet which provided that a British representative was to be established in the Tibetan capital, and that the Tibetans would pay a small indemnity. However, in the treaty Chinese suzerainty over Tibet was once more reaffirmed.

The great Anglo-Russian rivalry, which had occupied the minds of most European diplomats throughout the nineteenth century, ended in 1907 with the conclusion of the Triple Entente between Britain, Russia, and France. In its wake came a settlement of all outstanding issues between Russia and Britain, including Tibet. A convention was signed between the two great powers settling conflicting claims.

The Northwest Frontier

However, with the termination of this great diplomatic struggle Britain's troubles had not quite ended, since there remained the vexatious question of the warlike, unruly frontier tribes on the northwest frontier between India and Afghanistan. These Pathan tribes, who were excellent soldiers, had made it a permanent habit to raid India and then to retire with booty, and a series of policy solutions was attempted by the British to curb them. Punitive expeditions and attempts to isolate the tribes were unsuccessful, since the basic problem was an economic one. It was only with the adoption of the policy of economic aid, which provided better living and agricultural conditions in the tribes' impoverished country, that some pacification resulted. By the promotion of agriculture, the creation of local militias paid by the British, the establishment of a separate Northwest Frontier Province in 1901, and the building of roads, the worst of the frontier troubles was over by the end of the century, although the fighting qualities of the tribes themselves did not appreciably diminish.

IMPACT OF BRITISH IDEAS

The years after 1858 were one of the most formative periods in all Indian history. The most impressive feature in that time span was the introduction and impact of many British ideas, resulting in profound changes in the economy of India and preparing for a vast cultural transformation.

Economic Activities

The British approach in economics, based upon the principles of free enterprise and free trade, achieved great progress in the unification of Indian markets, the development of communications, the foundation of an industrial base, and the development of Indian agriculture and a greatly increased foreign trade. Since the nineteenth-century Englishman fervently believed in free economic play, no fixed ideas or planning was discernable in the creation of modern trade and industry in India.

The unification of Indian markets was the result of closer relations with England and the European continent, which permitted large-scale trade and resulted in stable prices for Indian products. Communication between Europe and India was facilitated by the establishment of the first telegraph line from London to India via Baghdad and Basra in 1865, the opening of the Suez Canal in 1869 (an event of crucial importance to India's economy), and the laying of reliable submarine cable connections in 1870, connecting Bombay with London via Aden, the Red Sea, and the Mediterranean. India became a unified economic region, and because of improved communications with Europe the exploitation of India's economic resources by the British was stimulated. Consequently there followed the creation of a modern internal system of communications, which in turn was a powerful factor in unifying the subcontinent. The construction of railroads (some 24,000 miles by 1890), the extension of an efficient post, telegraph, and mail system, and the beginnings of a modern road system all contributed to the growth of industry and foreign trade.

The seeds of India's industrialization were found in Bengal. Here the first of many jute mills was established in Calcutta in 1854. Jute processing, which was practically a monopoly held by Scots from Dundee, was soon followed by the establishment in rapidly increasing numbers of factories producing cotton, leather, paper, and woolen goods. Textile production tended to center in Bombay. There were ten cotton mills there in 1861, a number which rose to over fifty in less than twenty years. The boom in cotton as the result of the American Civil War also led to the gradual rise of an Indian industrial class, led by the Parsees[1] from Bombay. After 1900 large-scale factories financed and run by Indians were no longer a rarity, and the European monopoly of industrial management disappeared. The first native large-scale industrial planning came with the creation of the Chota Nagpur steel mills at Jamshedpur, where ore, coal, and limestone all were easily available. This new industry was in the hands of the Tata family, Parsees from Bombay. The growth of industry was closely followed by the exploitation of India's mineral resources, such as coal, and the establishment of modern banks and banking procedures. Increase of industrial production did deal a heavy blow to the native handicrafts industry, and it also raised many new social problems, such as working conditions, child labor, etc.

Perhaps more important than industrial raw materials in the way of

---

[1] The Parsees were a religious sect who sought refuge from persecution of their Zoroastrian religion in their native Persia.

export goods were Indian agricultural products. By 1860 crops grown on plantations for export, such as tea, coffee, cotton, and indigo, became the chief items of foreign trade. Here, however, European capital and European management predominated. Coffee and tea production was exclusively reserved to the Englishmen who began to come to India in the 1860's in a veritable flood tide of managerial and supervisory talent.

Toward the end of the century the British government began to take an increasing interest in the agricultural development of India and the lot of the peasant. Great irrigation works were built, particularly in the Punjab and in Sind, which brought extensive new lands under cultivation, and direct government aid to agriculture and legislation protecting the peasant were provided. Cooperative societies were introduced for loan purposes, moneylenders were somewhat curbed by frequent legislation, agricultural research institutes were established, and there is considerable truth in the statement of Lord Curzon that "the peasant has been in the background of every policy for which I have been responsible." By 1900 the Indian currency was also stabilized, and a definite ratio between the pound sterling and the rupee had been established, doing away with some of the earlier financial stress which had had its origin in the devaluation of the rupee. However, another major economic question concerned the special countervailing excise taxes on Indian cotton cloth, the result of pressure by Lancashire textile interests who were fearful of Indian competition. This tax was especially resented by Indian industrialists since it was an obvious breach of the gospel of British free trade.

Public Health

Certainly two of the greatest reforms for which British rule was responsible were in the areas of public health and the prevention of famine. These reforms resulted in an outstanding phenomenon of the history of India in the nineteenth century, the rapid rise of its population. British successes in removing the positive checks upon population growth—war, famine, pestilence—led to India's population explosion. Such major diseases as malaria, cholera, and smallpox were endemic in India, while bubonic plague was an import from abroad. Even though today there are still ten million annual admissions to Indian hospitals for the treatment of malaria, and even though in 1960 infant mortality was still around 50 per cent (a staggering figure to an American), some of the British public health measures which were introduced in the last decades of the nineteenth century stemmed other killers such as the worst of the great cholera and plague epidemics, and began to work against the prevailing unhygienic habits and apathy, which in turn had been based upon poverty and perhaps also upon Indian religious convictions of the unalterability of fate. Mortality rates began to decline slowly and gradually, and they were further reduced by British attempts to tackle the old, and horrible, problem of famine. A famine in Orissa in 1865 had resulted in more than a million deaths of starvation, but when crop failure struck in Bengal in 1874 countermeasures for the first time in Indian history prevented famine. Famines were again very widespread and acute in 1896, 1897, 1900, and 1908, but by this time previous experience had resulted in the adoption of a famine code which could be invoked to avoid disaster. By timely forecasts of probable famine conditions, by bringing in supplies from other parts of India and from overseas, by organizing in advance plans for large-scale public works and the remission of land revenue from affected areas, and by borrowing from a special central famine fund, most of the earlier horrors of famine conditions in India were overcome successfully. The greatest single factor in combating famine was perhaps the railroad, which made possible rapid and large-scale transportation of foodstuffs from one end of India to the other.

Growth of Population

The direct result of both public health advances and famine prevention was the unceasing increase of population pressure in India. For example, between 1881 and 1891, despite, or rather precisely because of, the great death toll from the bubonic plague, India's population increased an enormous ten per cent, due to the impetus given to public health by the epidemic itself. In the face of such tremendous increases, Indian emigration abroad provided merely the smallest and most insufficient of safety valves. Indians did go overseas as contract laborers to Mauritius, Natal, British Guiana, Trinidad, and Burma; but except for the last area the conditions they encountered abroad amounted to virtual slavery. Bound to their indenture contracts, frequently abused and discriminated against, especially in South Africa where even free Indians were relegated to a definitely inferior position, their status as overseas unskilled labor was anything but enviable. The crucial point, however, is that they emigrated in insufficient numbers. Thus population increase in India resulted soon in constantly increasing pressure upon the available land. Despite rising prices, which might make for temporary prosperity, pressure on land inevitably caused both the progressive subdivision of holdings, to the point where land was no longer sufficient to feed a family, and an increase of debt. With industrialization just barely beginning and offering only the meagerest of outlets to population pressure, and with emigration amounting to a mere trickle, the dark shadow of insufficient land and the tight bonds of the moneylender weighed increasingly upon the Indian farmer.

INDIAN INTELLECTUAL AND RELIGIOUS CURRENTS

The most important effect of British thought in nineteenth-century India was the transformation of India's culture, which was manifested in the rise of a new middle class, educated along Western lines, and imbued with a feeling of a common destiny.

The New Middle-Class Intelligentsia

The rise of a new bourgeois middle class in India was the result of the increasing necessity for educated young men to find employment, which was made possible by the increasingly mercantile character of India's nineteenth-century economy. The old leisure class of educated landholders, or *zamindars*, who made their living from the collection of land rents, became faced with the problems of growing family size and rising cost of living. A young man from this class, faced with the problem of making a living, had few careers open to him. To go abroad to England for training was almost impossible due to the high expense involved and the loss of caste incurred when crossing the ocean. To enter the Indian Civil Service was almost equally impossible, since the British government looked upon the I.C.S. as a service for Europeans and had made it increasingly more difficult to enter, for instance, by reducing in 1877 the age at which examinations had to be taken to nineteen. The independent professions of law, journalism, and teaching remained. The best brains became lawyers, and there was a real need for them with the rapid proliferation of courts and the many lawsuits accompanying a commercial economy. Others became independent journalists or teachers in schools. These lawyers, journalists, and teachers were able people and masters of the spoken and written word, filled with independent spirit, and eventually formed that class which produced future Indian political figures.

This new ambitious and dynamic middle class was also well acquainted with the principles of Western education. All higher education was in the English language, the result of Macaulay's celebrated memorandum of 1835, and it brought with it exposure to English history with its emphasis on national unity and upon the growth of democratic and liberal ideas. The widespread use of English by this class led to a feeling of growing unity and to a sound knowledge of nineteenth-century liberal political philosophy, both of which were to be most powerful forces in molding the growth of an Indian national spirit. As higher education spread with the establishment of universities at Calcutta, Madras, Bombay and elsewhere, so these Western values spread, to which were also added later a growing interest in Western science and technology. At the same time Indians took renewed pride in their own traditions exemplified by the growth of vernacular literature in drama, poetry, and prose (the result of the teaching of vernacular languages in village schools), and by the rediscovery of much of India's own great past due to archaeological and historical discoveries.

A new middle class, intellectually trained in Western principles and bound by common interests, in turn gave rise to a growing consciousness of unity throughout India. The feeling of a common destiny and unity was greatly strengthened not only by the extension of a modern system of communications, railways, telegraph, and a postal service, but also by the uniform British system of administration throughout the country, and by the rule of one law for all of India. Above all it was now the English language, the language of the courts, of the press and of the universities, which greatly cemented the concept of all-Indian unity.

Yet at the same time, while there was in India a growing sense of unity, pride in tradition and group assertiveness also produced an increasing consciousness of separateness between the Hindus and the Moslems. Nationalism in India was not entirely a secular movement, but took on religious overtones, intensifying the racial, sectional, and religious antagonisms between Hindus and Moslems. In a sense this was due to the heritage of the Moslem past, as both the Delhi sultanate and the Mogul empire (Akbar always excepted) had carefully maintained their identity as Moslem conquerors over Hindu subjects. This consciousness of separateness was greatly strengthened as the result of the impact of modern political ideas, and it led to new movements both in Islam and in Hinduism.

The Moslems and Reforms

Among the Moslems the man most responsible for the introduction of modern influences, and the undisputed leader of nineteenth-century Islam, was Sayyid Ahmed Khan. He was born in Delhi of an old Moslem family, became a judge, and was a man of keen intelligence and of a persuasive personality. Possessing a liberal outlook on religious and social questions, he urged his coreligionists to regenerate themselves by accepting Western education and by prompting social reform, and he did succeed (as one authority puts it) "in arresting the degeneration of a whole people." In order to introduce modern knowledge he published books, a monthly journal, and pioneered in making modern Urdu the most important language of India's Moslems. In 1877 he founded the Moslem university of Aligarh, his most important accomplishment since Aligarh gave to Moslem nationalism its intellectual center and leadership.

Sayyid Ahmed Khan visited England himself where he had been most impressed with Victorian splendor, and he remained perfectly loyal to British rule, but he gave to the Moslems in India a new spirit of self-assertiveness and he restored to them the confidence lost after the decline of Mogul greatness. This spirit and this confidence came to be directed more and more against the Hindus, not against the English, as the Moslems feared permanent domination, educationally, economically, and politically, by the numerically superior Hindus. In 1906 the Moslems organized a political organization, the Moslem League, to get their share of government posts. The activities of the Moslem League, headed by the Aga Khan, were soon welcomed by the British as a counterweight against the Indian National Congress. The Moslem League, however, was not a British creation; rather it came into being as the result of Hindu militant nationalism. The League further alienated the Indian Moslems from a unified national movement, and the seeds for India's partition in the twentieth century were thus laid by the religious expression of Indian nationalism.

The Hindu Renaissance

Among the Hindus a number of reform movements appeared which were influenced by Western ideals and which also proclaimed pride in their own past and traditions. There was the already existing Hindu society of the Brahmo Samaj, founded by Ram Mohun Roy in the first half of the nineteenth century, which was primarily concerned with the growth of social reform and social responsibility, and which continued to attract a few adherents of rather high quality who believed in the theistic personal religion of its founder. There now appeared a number of new Hindu movements suffused with religion and possessed of great fervor and emotional strength.

The leader of one of these purely Hindu groups was Ramakrishna. He was born a Brahman in 1834, but forsook the world and for a time worked as a scavenger in a temple. There he had visions of Krishna and Jesus and concluded that all creeds were merely facets of the same truth: "Every man should follow his own religion. A Christian should follow Christianity, a Mohammedan should follow Mohammedanism. For Hindus the ancient path is the best." Thus Ramakrishna believed in the restoration of ancient Hinduism, with all of its traditional sacrifices, ceremonies, and images, and he led the way toward a cultural renaissance of Hinduism in India. Since Ramakrishna himself had led a saintly life, and since his teachings were easily understood, he soon attracted a large following. His teachings were handed down very successfully by his most important pupil, Swami (or "ascetic") Vivekenanda. To him everything in Hinduism was right, everything in Western thought was wrong. He painted a bleak picture of Western materialism and degradation and became well known for his attempt to graft Hindu beliefs on modern thought. Because of his dynamic personality, he soon became a world figure, making even a number of American converts.

Another Hindu group, more eclectic and selective than the group founded by Ramakrishna, was the Arya Samaj founded in 1875 by the Swami Dayanand. Dayanand rejected the traditional deities of Hinduism and instead proclaimed that true religion as well as all knowledge was solely contained in the Vedas. Dayanand argued that these sacred writings contained everything worth knowing, even the seeds of modern science with its railways and steamships. Dayanand also rejected caste and the authority of the Brahmans, and at the same time urged the need for social and moral reform, for better education, and for an improvement in the status of women. In his teachings, which were especially well received in the Punjab, there is a strong note of truculency, and the nationalism which he instilled in his followers was both ardent and militant. The militant Hinduism of the Arya Samaj condemned everything foreign as evil, and also denounced in violent language the teachings, not only of the Christians, but also of the Moslems. Vigorously condemning cow killing, and attacking Islam in strong polemical language, this Hindu movement soon turned into one of the major divisive factors in Indian national life.

For a time at least, however, Indian national feeling could still be united, and both Hindus and Moslems could focus on issues dear to both of them, such as the so-called Service question. This dealt with the vexations aroused by the fact that the British reserved all higher positions in the Indian Civil Service to Britishers (although that had not been so in the days of Cornwallis). Legally, entrance to the coveted service was open to all, but after 1853 the competitive examinations and the training courses which prepared an individual for such examinations were given exclusively in England, with the result that it had become virtually impossible for an Indian to be employed in the Civil Service. In 1878 there were exactly nine Indians in the I.C.S. Eventually though, Indian national feeling went

FIGURE 10.2. Great Hindu Temple at Madura, built in the seventeenth century.

its separate ways along religious lines, and instead of one, there were to be two national movements in India, a Hindu one and a Moslem one.

NATIONALISM IN POLITICS

The Indian National Congress

From nationalist movements in religion to nationalist movements in politics was but a short step, quickly taken. In the rise of Indian nationalist politics no date is of greater significance than December, 1885, when the Indian National Congress met for the first time in Bombay. Lest the term lead to false conclusions, the Indian National Congress was neither connected with the government nor was it national in composition. The Indian National Congress was a self-constituted body, composed of the urban intelligentsia, meeting for purposes of political discussion and social reforms. The composition of its members (originally seventy) was predominantly drawn from Hindu lawyers, teachers, editors, and journalists, and it had no connection with either the peasants, the laborers, or the landholders. Since the Moslems abstained from participation in it (there were only two Moslem members at first, though there were more later on), its aim could not properly be called national, but rather Hindu. The Indian National Congress was sponsored by a retired British official, Allen O. Hume, who felt that such a body, modeled on British practice and subject to English advice, would serve as a safety valve for moderate, secular, middle-class nationalist aspirations, and such it proved to be in the beginning. Its demands for reform were moderate, "constructive criticism" was its slogan, and it praised and admired all that was British. But in the long run the Congress provided the most powerful force in Indian politics and the germs for the movement toward independence.

Aided by English supporters, and utilizing English procedures, Congress's earliest demands were indeed moderate. Led by such apostles of moderation as Gopal Krishna Gokhale, a law professor, it demanded increased use of Indians trained by Western education in the I.C.S., to be made possible by holding entrance examinations in India as well as in England. Other demands included reductions in the salt tax, the appointment of Indian commissioned officers in the Indian armed forces, and Indian representation in the legislative council of the viceroy. Although the British government as a whole refused to take the activities of the Congress seriously, and dismissed it as a "microscopic minority," it did feel the wisdom of granting certain minor reforms. For instance, provincial legislative councils were enlarged in 1892 and the principle of election was introduced in them in such a way that members of these councils were to be nominated by various bodies such as associations of landholders, chambers of commerce, universities, and rural boards. Control of the press was also relaxed by the government after it repealed in 1882 the Vernacular Press Act which had required the editor of a publication in an oriental language to post bond not to publish articles objectionable to the government.

Success, however minor, greatly increased the prestige of the Congress. That body tended to become increasingly revolutionary, and at the same time more truly a representative body of Indian public opinion. By the 1890's the Indian National Congress had undergone remarkable growth; it ceased to be satisfied with a moderate and constitutional program, but rather attacked further British reforms and agitated for direct action and terrorism as a means of fulfilling its ever more radical goals. This was particularly true after 1904 when the moderates in the Congress lost control, and a left-wing majority advocated revolutionary changes by means of boycotts and violence. At the same time Congress also began to take an interest in economic problems and questions of social responsibility, since the subject of economics had attained new importance in the universities, and since universal primary education had drawn the attention of the newly educated Indian classes to the many social evils existing in India. The defeat of Russia by Japan in 1904 provided another great stimulus to nationalism in Asia, coming as it did after the British difficulties suffered during the Boer War (1899–1902). The growing Indian spirit of self-assertion came to a head when the Indian National Congress demanded self-rule, or *swaraj*, as its objective in 1906. The agitation within the ranks of Congress regarding the wisdom of such radical aims resulted in a split in 1907, when the extremists left that body under the leadership of Bal Gangadhar Tilak. Tilak, a man of tremendous industry, strong will, and great courage, was born a Brahman in Poona. He had received an excellent Western education, together with a good grounding in the Sanskrit and Marathi classics. However, he began to feel, despite the fact that he was in modern journalism, that all of India's evils could be attributed to the English and conversely, that everything indigenous was sacred. Tilak came soon to be the "father of Indian unrest," as one British historian has christened him. He used the Age of Consent Bill, which attempted to eliminate child marriage by raising the age of marriage for Hindu girls to twelve, as an excuse to attack the British ("religion in danger"), and he utilized even more so the great plague of 1907, which killed some two million people, as a convenient excuse to agitate against British sanitary measures. When British officers attempted to enforce these measures in Poona they were attacked and plague riots broke out in the Maratha region. These riots were led by Tilak, who had revived the cult of the Marathas and made Shivaji, their great seventeenth-century leader, into a semidivine being. His journalistic agitation was, however, not only confined to urging revolutionary crimes against the English; he reviled the Moslems as well, and contributed to the growing gap between the two religions. Tilak was imprisoned, but his radical views continued to influence the Indian National Congress and the Indian press, and they contributed greatly to the growing sense of hostility against the British which became noticeable by the end of the 19th century.

Anglo-Hindu Tension

This feeling of mutual hostility between Hindus and English was further embittered with a growing sense of racial antagonism, which was clearly demonstrated in the bitter debate which centered around the so-called Ilbert Bill of 1883, which provided that Englishmen, as well as Indians, should be tried by Indian district magistrates. The indigo planters in the remote districts began a vicious press attack on the bill, with racial slurs and overtones, which forced the British government to rescind the bill, and promise the whites the right to trial by a jury of their own peers.

British interference with Hindu religion as in the Age of Consent Bill of 1891, and the very bad press stemming from the Ilbert bill discussions increased hostility toward the British, which came to a head during Lord Curzon's viceroyalty of India from 1899 to 1905. The irony of this was that perhaps no man since Dalhousie worked harder or did more for the material benefit of India than Curzon.

Lord Curzon

Lord Curzon was ambitious, energetic, and most courageous. He had traveled widely in Persia, Central Asia, the Far East, and he had published several scholarly books. His term as viceroy marked the climax of British rule in India. Curzon improved the land revenue system, organized rural banks and cooperative credit institutions, and devoted his talents to improving the lot of the peasant. Furthermore he was responsible for preserving India's ancient monuments. He appointed as Director General of the Archaeological Service John Marshall, who restored the Taj Mahal, the Buddhist monuments of Sanchi and of Taxila in the Punjab, and discovered the Indus river valley civilization of Mohenjo-Daro and Harappa. Yet Curzon, excellent administrator and statesman that he was, managed to draw upon himself an unparalleled storm of protest from India's new national leaders. The reason for this seeming contradiction was largely due to Curzon's character, which was brusque, haughty, and aloof. While he dominated the government he brooked no criticism, and he was exceedingly tactless and scornful in his attitude toward Indian aspirations. His actions, lacking sympathy and antagonizing even the moderate elements in the Congress, culminated in his attempt to put into force two very unpopular measures, the partition of Bengal and government control over universities.

In 1905 Curzon decided to partition the province of Bengal for purely administrative reasons, only to reap a whirlwind of opposition from its Hindu inhabitants who displayed their regional patriotism by uttering the cry that "the motherland was to be torn into two" and who expressed their feelings by a successful boycott of English goods. The reality and extent of this national feeling came as a genuine surprise to Curzon, and it resulted in very heavy pressure against him, which was compounded by Curzon's passing of the Universities Act. This act was designed to eliminate the manifold abuses current at institutions of higher learning in India, and to give more power to the universities in raising the standards of education and in supervising teaching, but it was interpreted by Indian nationalists as an attempt to fetter academic independence. In overriding brusquely feelings of fear of government control of the universities, Curzon again displayed his lack of understanding of Indian aspirations. So great was the furor aroused by these measures that Lord Curzon, who also had lost a power struggle with Lord Kitchener, the British army commander-in-chief in India, resigned as viceroy in 1905.

In the decade just before World War I hostility increased against the British in India. Anti-British agitation was carried on by men with genuine grievances, students who had failed their exams in England, journalists desirous of increasing the circulation of their papers, honest fanatics, and outright criminals, but it began to take on an overtone of a new and most disturbing kind, that of racial antagonism. Now Indians came to look upon

FIGURE 10.3. Portrait of Lord Curzon after J. S. Sargent.

white men as brutal, bullying, raucous, and arrogant, while some British went out of their way to foster racial antagonism. A great deal of bad feeling was created by the racial issue which was intensified and exploited by the press on both sides. The arrival of a large number of low-class Englishmen in India in the 1860's had done a good deal of damage. They brought with them a strong belief in their racial superiority, and ignorantly and contemptuously despised the Indians. They regarded themselves as a favored breed of men whose task it was to keep the Indians in their proper place. Hence the increase in individual incidents, such as the exclusion of Indians from English clubs, or the ousting of Indians from railway compartments when Englishmen boarded a train. This was not a universal trend; some Englishmen still maintained friendships with Indians and remained popular among them. But it was a very dangerous trend. Unscrupulous accusations and violent agitation by anti-Indian business groups, such as the indigo planters who were completely hostile to Indian social and political aspirations, taught the Indians to use the same methods against the British. Worse yet, the racial issue contributed not only to an increase in Indian resentment against the British, but also to increased Hindu-Moslem antagonism.

Hindu-Moslem Antagonism

In the past, Hindus and Moslems by and large had managed to live side by side peacefully, but when the shrill voice of intensive and strident nationalism was raised it found targets not only in the ruling classes, but also among those who differed in religious thought and practices. Hindu-Moslem differences, or communal differences as they came to be called, soon became violent and deeply antagonistic in their outbursts against the outward forms of each faith. Hindu processions and the Hindu reverence for the cow came under attack by the Moslems who ate beef and ridiculed Hindu ritual; Hindus reciprocated by insulting Moslem beliefs and rites. It was precisely the Hindu militant nationalist movements, such as the Arya Samaj of Dayanand, which led the way in communal violence and bitter religious strife. By conducting inflammatory propaganda and aggressively promoting "cow protection," the activities of the Arya Samaj led to deepening tension and an increase of mutual suspicion between Hindus and Moslems.

By 1890 relations between Hindus and Moslems had degenerated into frequent, and often great, violence, instigated by unscrupulous agitators, and wildly exaggerated by the press of both sides. A natural reaction to this situation was increased Moslem self-assertiveness, marked by pride in the Islamic past, and deep interest in the ideas of Panislamism. Among Hindus this growing spirit even percolated down to the lowest strata of Indian society, the untouchables. Aided by American Protestant missionaries, members of this group began to question their outcaste status. Even on the highest intellectual level national self-assertiveness characterized the period. For example, the great poet Rabindranath Tagore (1861–1941), who had won international reputation and gained a Nobel prize for his literary works, was an ardent lover of Indian culture and a critic of the West. He established traditional Indian schools, and he vigorously opposed the West's "driving the tentacles of its machinery deep down into the Indian soil."

However, except for a minority in the Indian National Congress, Hindu popular feeling as a whole was as yet not directed toward the termination of British rule in India. Prior to the outbreak of World War I it lacked effective political aims. A good example of the general satisfaction that Indians felt with the status quo was the great enthusiasm shown during the state visit to India in 1911 of King George V and Queen Mary, the first reigning British sovereigns to set foot upon Indian soil. Their welcome at the great *durbar* at Delhi, India's new capital, was overwhelming, and demonstrated the devotion of the Indian masses to the British *raj*, a devotion which was carefully fostered by the announcement that the hated partition of Bengal had been rescinded. The scene was one of great splendor, and it gave to Englishmen renewed assurance that their empire in India was destined for long life.

Morley-Minto Reform

Nevertheless, following the success of Japan in war with Russia and the surprising Indian protests against the measures of Lord Curzon, the British government began to consider the wisdom of instituting new reforms. The result was the Morley-Minto governmental reform of 1909 (Lord Minto was viceroy in India, Morley was secretary of state for India). These reforms enlarged the existing legislative councils in India and somewhat extended their powers; but at the same time they avoided responsible government. Morley, speaking privately, made this perfectly clear when he said that it was "neither desirable nor possible or even conceivable to adopt English political institutions to the nations who inhabit India." The British government, when granting these reforms, had no intention of giving India responsible parliamentary institutions which would ultimately eliminate English rule. The legislative council of the viceroy was increased to sixty members, of whom twenty-seven were elected, while the provincial legislative councils were enlarged to fifty members, of whom the majority was elective. In order to guarantee representation to the minorities, such as the Moslems, a number of seats in the legislative councils were set aside for them under the principle of communal representation. Of course, it will be remembered that these legislative councils were merely advisory bodies without real power. In addition, as a further gesture representing British concessions, the viceroy appointed an Indian lawyer to his executive council, while Indians were also made eligible to serve as members on the council of the secretary of state for India in London and on the provincial executive councils of Bengal, Madras, and Bombay.

The Morley-Minto reform, while not really instituting responsible government for all, did instill greater confidence in Indian public opinion. Indians, while still a minority in the legislative council of the viceroy, could get at least a hearing for their views, while on the provincial level Indians had a majority and could at least disapprove those British measures which they disliked.

Terrorism

This limited measure of reform was denounced by those left-wing revolutionaries who preferred direct action or terrorism. Political unrest in its most violent form of terror, bombings, and assassination increased sharply in the last decade before the First World War. Behind most of these activities stood Tilak, who had formed a number of so-called "gymnasiums" where he trained students for political warfare. Here, too, the impetus of Japan's victory over Russia stimulated fervor, while discrimination against Indians in the Dominions, notably South Africa, fanned the flames of resentment against British rule in India. Violence at first was rather ineffective, beginning with some crude attempts to bomb railroad trains, but after some students were sent to Paris to study the fine art of dynamiting and a special bomb factory was established in Calcutta, bombings and political murders sharply increased in their effectiveness. There were gang robberies of banks to secure funds; there were assassination attempts on the viceroy in 1909 and again in 1921 (a rather spectacular one in which Lord Hardinge barely escaped), and there were murders even in the staid clubs of London's West End. Although Tilak was promptly imprisoned, terroristic activities continued, especially in Bengal and the Punjab, and funds for such purposes were collected not only throughout India, but even in the United States by Indian societies for that purpose. In 1914 when a shipload of Sikhs and Moslems of the Punjab were denied admission by Canada and were returned to Indian soil, there were great riots. Political discontent was clearly visible to all, and was barely suppressed by the Press Act of 1908, which was designed to control such activities.

Without question, nationalism was the most powerful force in India, shaping her future destiny in the last decades of the nineteenth and the first decade of the twentieth century. Unfortunately, this nationalism was not to be unified, but became a Hindu and a Moslem nationalism, sharply split against each other.

During this period, too, the British missed a chance of introducing an English-type parliamentary system in India at a time when conditions were still favorable for such an attempt, since the Indian National Congress at first had been eager enough to cooperate with their British rulers. But by and large the English had lacked clarity of mind and directness of approach, and this resulted in an attitude of coolness and concealed inflexibility toward Indian national aspirations. Uncertain English policy in turn provided for merely temporary stop-gap measures such as the Morley-Minto reforms, granted too late to satisfy the wishes of the bulk of India's educated public opinion.

It is true, of course, that British rule in India in the critical years between 1858 and 1914 provided universal peace and justice in the form of rule of law, ensured by an organized police system and an elaborate court system, while the peasant was assured protection under the existing land tenure structures. These conditions would have served well enough in a stationary society, but this was precisely what India was not. Western liberal ideas and nationalist thought, demanding constitutional and parliamentary reforms as a minimum, had profoundly changed India from the days of Maurya and Mogul autocracy, when nothing stood between the will of the ruler and the silent masses. The masses were to be silent no longer.

BASIC DATES

1865	England-India telegraph line begins operation
1869	Suez Canal opened
1875	Arya Samaj founded
1877	Aligarh Moslem University founded
1877	Victoria proclaimed empress of India
1878–1879	Second Anglo-Afghan War

1879	Treaty of Gandamak
1880–1901	Reign of Abdurraman in Afghanistan
1885	Indian National Congress founded
1885	Panjdeh Incident
1885	Conquest of Upper Burma
1887	Conquest of Shan states
1891–1905	Agitation against British reforms
1899–1905	Curzon viceroy
1901–1904	Anglo-Russian rivalry in Tibet
1905	Boycott and violence
1906	Swaraj (self-rule) demanded
1907	Tilak and extremists leave Congress
1909	Morley-Minto reform
1911	Durbar at Delhi

SUPPLEMENTARY READING

Metcalf, T. R., ed. *Modern India: An Interpretive Anthology.* London, 1971.
Moreland, W. H. and A. C. Chatterjee. *A Short History of India.* London, 1945.
Rawlinson, H. G. *The British Achievement in India.* London, 1948.
Smith, V. A. *The Oxford History of India,* 3rd ed. Oxford, 1958.
Spear, P. *India: A Modern History.* Ann Arbor, Michigan, 1972.
Wallbank, T. W. *India in the New Era.* Chicago, 1951.
Wolpert, S. *India.* Englewood Cliffs, N.J., 1965.

ADVANCED READING

Alder, G. *British India's Northern Frontier, 1865-1895.* London, 1963.
Argov, D. *Moderates and Extremists in the Indian Movement, 1883-1920.* New York, 1967.
Bose, N. *The Indian Awakening and Bengal.* Calcutta, 1960.
De Bary, W. T., ed. *Sources of Indian Tradition.* New York, 1958.
Desai, A. *Social Background of Indian Nationalism.* Bombay, 1941.
Dodwell, H. *Cambridge History of India.* Vol. VI. Cambridge, 1932.
Edwardes, M. *High Noon of Empire: India under Curzon.* London, 1965.
Griffiths, P. *The British Impact on India.* London, 1952.
Heimrath, C. *Indian Nationalism and Hindu Social Reform.* Princeton, N.J., 1964.
Kumar, R. *India and the Persian Gulf Region, 1858-1907: A Study in British Imperial Policy.* New York, 1965.
Marriott, J. A. R. *The English in India.* Oxford. 1932.
Mehrotra, S. *India and the Commonwealth.* New York, 1965.
Metcalf, T. *The Aftermath of Revolt: India, 1857-1870.* Princeton, N.J., 1964.
Panikkar, K. M. *Asia and Western Dominance.* London, 1953.
Singh, Khushwant. *A History of the Sikhs: Vol. 2, 1839-1964.* Princeton, N.J., 1967.

Singh, V. B. *Economic History of India, 1857-1956.* New York, 1965.
Smith, W. R. *Nationalism and Reform in India.* New Haven, 1938.
Thompson, E. and G. Garratt. *The Rise and Fulfillment of British Rule in India.* London, 1934.
Wolpert, S. *Tilak and Gokhale: Revolution and Reform in the Making of Modern India.* Berkeley, 1962.
Woodruff, P. *The Men Who Ruled India: The Guardians.* London, 1953.

Chapter 11

The Challenge of Western Ideas in Southwest Asia, 1857-1914

The history of Southwest Asia from the latter half of the nineteenth century until World War I is primarily the story of the decline and collapse of two formerly great Asiatic empires, the Persian and the Ottoman. This decline was in part due to the fact that these empires became the principal victims of a gigantic diplomatic, and sometimes military, struggle between Great Britain and Russia. The rivalry of these imperial protagonists manifested itself across the whole breadth of Asia, from the Dardanelles to the Sea of Japan. Caught between the European giants, Persia and Turkey suffered constant loss of territory and ever increasing interference in their governments until they retained little sovereignty.

But Anglo-Russian rivalry was not the sole cause of the collapse of these Asiatic empires. Western ideas were beginning to challenge time-honored practices which had been considered proper and sufficient answers to problems of government and society. To keen-minded Persians and Turks who visited Europe or became acquainted with Westerners it was soon apparent that social and technological change were essential if the empires were to survive at all, and prodigious efforts were made to save them by westernizing them—in vain. The last years prior to World War I witnessed a new force in Southwest Asia, a popular nationalism which was stimulated by the West and directed against the old corrupt regimes of shah in Persia and sultan in the Ottoman empire. Although insufficient in itself to produce thoroughgoing reform, this new force resulted in partial acceptance of the idea of parliamentary controls on hitherto absolute rulers. It led to the dethronement of a shah in 1908 and a sultan in 1909. By 1914, even though the earlier expectations of the reform movement had turned to disillusionment, strong currents were running in the direction of change.

ANGLO-RUSSIAN RIVALRY IN PERSIA

Competition between the British and the Russian empires was brought to a focus in Persia. This is shown by the fact that later when the two powers reached agreement on Persia (1907), the way became clear for diplomatic rapprochement throughout Europe and Asia and resulted in the formation (with France) of the Triple Entente. The reason for the intensity of the struggle in Persia was not only its relation to European politics, but also because the British regarded Persia as a strategic area involving their vital interests in India, a matter about which they were extremely sensitive. Because of British concern about the empire, and because the Persians throughout most of this period were more responsive to the Russians than to the British, British representatives in Persia were often inclined to exasperation with Persia and the Persians, and spoke disparagingly of them. In 1856 Britain made war on Persia, as a pawn of Russian influence, to end Persian designs on Afghanistan. The peace treaty (1857) put Afghanistan effectively under British influence, and forced the Persians to withdraw from Herat. For a time the Afghan border seemed secure.

British Anxiety

The matter of Russian aims in Central and Southwest Asia, however, was far from settled. During the 1860's Russian expansion in Central Asia reached out in several directions, toward Kokand, Khiva, and Bukhara. "Turkistan" became a Russian province in 1867; the city of Samarkand was taken in 1868. This had been anticipated in a memorandum on Central Asian policy drawn up by the Russian imperial chancellor, Prince Gortchakoff, in 1864 and circulated to the various European governments. The explanation for the advance and consolidation anticipated therein emphasized peaceful intents, the necessity of quelling tribal disorders in these regions and extending Russian rule to a point at which it would "no longer encounter such unstable entities as nomad tribes, but more regularly organized states," for civilization's sake as well as Russia's. Presumably such "regularly organized states" would include Persia and Afghanistan, but the British were not sure that Russia would stop at their frontiers, especially since these borders themselves were in dispute. For example, the Persians claimed the town of Merv but they rarely controlled it. In fact Merv was in the hands of just such "unstable entities" whose presence might invite Russian interference.

The British on their part were cautious in their policies in Persia. They feared war with Russia on very disadvantageous ground. John Lawrence, who had gone through the Indian Mutiny as chief commissioner in the Punjab and who was governor-general of India in 1864–1869, was wary of even pushing British involvement in Afghanistan too far, and the British Foreign Office studiously avoided any promise of support for Persia in the event of Russian encroachment on Persian borders. The British waited to see how far Russian expansion would go and to see whether a modus vivendi might be reached whereby the Russians would refrain from encroachment on Afghanistan, with the hope that that country would thus be left as a buffer between a Russian-controlled Central Asia and British India.

The British after 1874 successfully gained complete control of Afghanistan even at the cost of a second Afghan war. But in Persia they faced a different problem. Russia enjoyed an immense advantage from proximity alone in any diplomatic or military duel there, and it was obvious that the most strenuous efforts would be required if Britain were to dislodge her. In this situation the essential question for British policy makers was: How far might Persia be related to the defense of India? There was no matter of oil yet to be considered, and trade with Persia was small. Except for possible involvement with the defense of India, nineteenth-century British interest in Persia was only one aspect of a widespread international rivalry between Britain and Russia. From the British point of view there was considerable room for give and take. Their policy might even permit Russian superiority in Persia, but they would be firm in defending their position in India.

The alarmist view was expressed by Sir Henry Rawlinson. He held posts at Tehran on several occasions, including service as British minister there. As director of the East India Company and a member of the Indian Council he also saw clearly the connection between India and Persia. Sir Henry argued in a "Memorandum on the Central Asian Question" drawn up in 1868 that Persia was a vital link in the defense of India. His reasoning was that Russia would be likely to threaten India not through central Afghanistan and the mountain passes of the Hindu Kush range, but by an easier route, farther west, along the eastern frontier of Persia to Herat and on into the lower Indus valley. Therefore, Persia was important, indeed vital, to the defense of India, and British diplomacy in Persia should be directed towards bringing Persia into the British orbit.

Subsequent events led British policymakers to try desperately to throw stumbling blocks in the way of Russian intrusions into Persian affairs, but at the same time their concern over the possible consequences prevented their making any commitments to support Persia against Russia, even when the Persian government on a number of occasions sought such assurances. In the final settlement (1907) they were highly relieved that they could secure the corner of Persia adjacent to India in return for relinquishing most of Persia as a Russian sphere of influence. This was British government policy but many British officials in the field chafed at their being outdone by Russians and were bitterly frustrated by the "weakness" of Britain's Persia policy.

Russian Successes

The buildup of Russian influence in Persia proceeded gradually at first, with many protestations of pacific intentions. On the northeast frontier activity was most pronounced. Having established an anchor point at the southeastern tip of the Caspian Sea in the 1860's the tsarist government moved farther east to secure Russian Turkistan as has been mentioned above. They turned farther west again to take Khiva in 1873 and then proceeded across the Amu Darya toward Persia. Persia obtained temporary respite while Russian agents again became active in Afghanistan and while Russia fought a war against the Ottoman empire in Europe, but in 1881 the Persian government found it discreet to sign a convention with Russia in which various of the northeast boundary questions were settled in Russia's favor. Persia thereby gave up all claim to Turkoman-controlled areas west of the Amu-darya. Russia then also disclaimed any interest in Merv. As a possible starting point on the road into India, Merv was a place about which the British, and particularly Rawlinson, were extremely sensitive. In spite of this fact, two years later the Turkomans asked to be incorporated; Russia could scarcely refuse, and Merv was annexed.

In relations with Persia Russia gained a definite superiority over Britain all along the line. The tradition of British advisors in military affairs, which extended back to the Sherley brothers of the early seventeenth century, was upset by the arrival in 1878 of Russian officers to organize Persian forces. Here lay the ultimate basis of Russian power inside Persia. Colonel Liakhoff in 1908 bombarded and closed the Majlis (parliament) and Liakhoff was for a time clearly the dictator of Tehran.

In matters of commerce and finance, where one would expect the British to be more adroit, the Russians also gained the advantage, despite a head start by the British. The latter built up a telegraph system in the 1860's which was connected with London in 1870, and two years later, Julius de Reuter, an English financier, obtained from a foolish and greedy grand vizir a whole network of concessions, including railways, mines, and an imperial bank. The bank was established in 1889 as a convenient vehicle for Shah Nasir-ud-din's borrowings, but the other concessions were cancelled. The Russians opposed these and the British government did not see fit to push their development. This fact became clear to the shah after he made visits to London and St. Petersburg in 1873. He was entertained in London by Her Majesty Queen Victoria and received the Order of the Garter from her, but no promise of support against Russia was forthcoming, and after this he moved very carefully in all relations with the tsar. On his European tour in 1878 the shah visited St. Petersburg but omitted London. It was on his return from this journey that the shah was accompanied by his new Russian military advisors.

Beginning in 1889 and continuing through the 1890's Russia received most of the concessions which had been tentatively given to de Reuter in 1872. In addition the shah agreed to consult with Russian representatives before granting further concessions to other foreigners. This went far beyond the "most-favored-nation" treaty stipulation and further than any of the Ottoman capitulations. By 1900 the ruler of Persia, Shah Muzaffar-ud-din, was so deeply in debt to Russia that the Persian customs, nominally under the direction of a Belgian, had to be turned over to Russian control. The British did what they could to counter these moves. They tried to match the Russians loan for loan, and the spendthrift shah took advantage of this to make use of all the funds he could get. The British also prevented the extension of Russian railroad building into south Persia and the concession to Russia of a port on the Persian Gulf. But in their competition with the Russians the British diplomats doubtless welcomed the change that came with the Russo-Japanese war in 1904.

Anglo-Russian Settlement

After the war with Japan, Russia found it necessary to abandon the most advanced positions gained in the late nineteenth century, and the way was cleared for an agreement concerning Persia. The British were more than willing, especially because of the development of Germany as a rival in Europe. To forestall an agreement between Germany and Russia following the conversations of Kaiser Wilhelm II with Tsar Nicholas II in 1905, the British felt that they must seek a settlement of their long-standing rivalry with Russia.

The prospects of agreement were much enhanced by the appointment of Alexander Isvolsky as Russian minister of foreign affairs. He favored an agreement, as did the French, who were anxious to complete their alliance system against Germany by bringing their separate allies together. Negotiations were carried on from London by Foreign Secretary Sir Edward Grey, and an Anglo-Russian Convention was signed on August 31, 1907. It settled outstanding questions of Afghanistan and Tibet; Afghanistan was excluded from the Russian sphere of influence. But the heart of the agreement concerned Persia. Persian "independence" was to be "respected," but to facilitate this the country was to be divided into three zones. The northern half of the country, which contained almost all the major cities including the capital, was designated a Russian sphere of influence, and in the southeast a section bordering India and Afghanistan equivalent in area to about one fifth the total area of Persia was designated a British sphere of influence. Between the two an area which included the entire Persian Gulf coast on the west and narrowed to a corridor as it ran northeast toward the Afghan border was designated a neutral zone. Some years later in his memoirs Sir Edward Grey described the agreement in this way:

> What did Russia get in return? On paper it was an equal bargain. The part of Persia by which India could be approached was made secure from Russian penetration. The part of Persia by which Russia could be approached was made secure from British penetration. The gain was equal—on paper. In practice we gave up nothing. We did not wish to pursue a forward policy in Persia; nor could a British advance in Persia have been the same menace to Russia that a Russian advance in Persia might be to India.

Thus tension was eased, India was secure, and perhaps a European war between Britain and Russia was avoided. But what were the effects on Persia? To discover them it is necessary to consider the internal politics of that country.

PERSIAN CONSTITUTIONAL MOVEMENT

Persian Absolutism under Nasir-ud-din and Muzaffar-ud-din

During the period discussed Persia had two shahs, Nasir-ud-din, who ruled from 1848 until his assassination in 1896, and his son Muzaffar-ud-din, who ruled from 1896–1907. These two rulers of the Kajar line were the last two absolute monarchs to occupy the throne of the Iranian King of Kings. Nasir-ud-din and Muzaffar-ud-din followed a tradition of absolute rule that went back more than two thousand years to Darius. All ministers and government officials were expendable. However influential they might be at one moment, at a word from the shah, they could be cut down at the next. The taxes collected by the government belonged to the shah; he could do as he pleased with the resources of the country; he could seize the lands of anyone great or small; he could squander as he pleased. But heretofore these matters had been a question of the shah and his subjects and traditional right was on the side of the shah.

However, with increasing clarity a new element was interjected into the reigns of Nasir and Muzaffar, that of the foreigners, principally the Russians and the British. When the shah took from his subjects, that was tradition; but when it went to benefit the foreigners and to fasten their influence on the country, that was something to be talked about in the bazaars.

Despite the despotic tradition of the King of Kings there were two persistent undercurrents in Persia which, given proper conditions, might rise to dispute it. The first was a sort of national consciousness (not so highly developed as nationalism, but akin to it) which had through the centuries helped preserve Persia and Persian ways from being trampled underfoot by foreign intruders. It had resisted the Hellenization of the Parthian period, had Persianized invading Arabs (considerably) and Turks (thoroughly), and had even survived the depredations of the Mongols. It served to support the royal institution so long as the shahs represented and espoused Persianism. But if they failed and instead became puppets of foreigners, then the force of national consciousness might work towards their overthrow.

The second force was an undercurrent of independence, or perhaps merely unruliness among the more mobile elements in Persian society. This is characteristic of all nomadic peoples because their mobility is a safeguard against the measures a despotic ruler can impose upon a sedentary population. Persian society was by no means or even principally nomadic in the nineteenth century, yet among two groups, the "tribes," particularly of the south, and the merchants, whose fortunes were intimately connected with displaying their wares in the right place at the right time, a considerable mobility was characteristic.

The tribes had never been fully integrated into the political system of the country. Living far from the centers of government they maintained a group solidarity whose loyalty was first to the tribal chiefs and then to the shah. The shah's government therefore dealt with the chiefs and left them to deal with the tribesmen. But the situation was always unstable. Even when the tribesmen were incorporated into the shah's armies they were an unruly element, fighting fiercely for the shah if it pleased them but ready to desert his cause to settle tribal enmities at any time.

The status of the bazaar (merchant community) was more complicated. There a man might rise from poverty to opulence overnight if by skill or luck he could calculate the direction and velocity of the winds of trade. Thus the bazaar was attuned to catch intelligence of all sorts, from the slightest whim of the shah to crucial international political currents, and in the absence of widespread newspaper circulation or other communications media, the bazaar was news (and rumor) dispenser to the nation. But it did more than carry the news, often with the speed of wireless telegraphy. In addition it commented on the news, editorialized, magnified, distorted, and above all approved the news until out of the process might emerge something akin to public opinion of a limited variety. This could influence the course of events, and make the bazaar so important a pressure group in political affairs that the court could not control it.

These undercurrents were not sufficient in themselves to start a constitutional movement in Persia, but once begun they could speed it along and sustain it in adversity. In addition a deep tradition in Persia became important in protecting the lives of individual leaders of the constitutional movement. This was the inviolability of holy buildings in which a fugitive could find sanctuary.

The constitutional movement may be said to have begun with Jamal-ud-din al-afghani, to whom Shah Nasir-ud-din was temporarily attracted, perhaps out of nostalgia for the reforms he had once begun but abandoned early in his reign. Jamal-ud-din had traveled widely in Europe, and was frequently a guest at the shah's court in the 1880's and early 1890's. While he merely talked reform to the shah all was well, but when a reform party commenced to gather around him, the shah expelled him from the country. However, he carried on the reform campaign from Europe. In 1896 one of his disciples in Persia, Mirza Muhammad Riza, assassinated the shah, giving as his reason that the shah was selling out the country to foreigners.

Other than the assassination the most spectacular evidence of growing popular antagonism to the shah's actions was vigorous opposition to a tobacco concession granted to a British speculator in 1890. By this concession one Major G. F. Talbot obtained the monopoly right to buy and sell tobacco in Persia, one quarter of the profits going to the shah and the other three quarters to his corporation. There was a widespread popular reaction, and religious leaders advocated a boycott against the use of tobacco. The response was overwhelming and the boycott swept the country. The shah finally rescinded the concession.

During the succeeding reign of Muzaffar-ud-din Anglo-Russian rivalry reached its peak. The shah squandered even more than his father, and as the concessions to foreigners grew in number, a nationalist party was formed, chiefly by European-educated members of the upper class, and more forthright demands for reform were heard. Affairs reached a climax in July, 1906, with a bloodless revolution. Large numbers of people in Tehran sought sanctuary in various places, including the compound which housed the British legation. They were peaceful but their spokesmen were insistent,

FIGURE 11.1. Nasir-ud-din Shah.

first that the extremely reactionary minister, Ayn-ud-dola, should be dismissed, and secondly that a constitution should be granted. The shah, perhaps mindful of his father's assassination, conceded these demands and agreed also to the convening of an elected Majlis to draw up the constitution. This was accomplished during the autumn and the shah signed the new constitution just before he died, of natural causes, in December, 1906.

Muhammad Ali

Matters might have gone reasonably well, or at least not so badly, with the constitutional regime if the old shah had lived longer. He was succeeded by his son, Muhammad Ali, formerly governor of Azerbaijan, where he had shown a distinct cordiality to the Russians. Muhammad Ali was described by an indignant American as "the most perverted, cowardly, and vice-sodden monster that had disgraced the throne of Persia in many generations."[1] He first pledged himself to observe the constitution and respect the Majlis (now

[1] W. Morgan Shuster, *The Strangling of Persia* (New York: The Century Company, 1912), p. xxi.

FIGURE 11.2. Muhammad Ali Shah.

seated as a parliament), but he quickly came into conflict with it. He was forced to dismiss the Belgian customs director, who in addition to collecting for Russia apparently pocketed large sums himself. But the shah, with Russian aid, contrived to bring back to Persia as prime minister Atbak-i-azam, who had been sent into exile in 1903 after his corrupt sponsorship of

FIGURE 11.3. Revolutionaries of 1909.

Russian loans. However, Atbak-i-azam was assassinated by a nationalist fanatic on August 31, 1907, the same day on which the Anglo-Russian convention was signed, and most of Persia handed over to unimpeded Russian influence. Up to this point the British, through their legation, had given some encouragement to the parliamentary forces; their mediation at the time of the bloodless revolution played a part in evoking the promise of a constitution from the shah. After the signing of the Anglo-Russian convention the British were most reluctant to interfere, and the Majlis was left to fend for itself against the shah, his Russian-officered Cossack brigade, and the Russian embassy.

The Majlis fought to maintain its position, and considering the very recent break with despotism, elicited amazing support from various segments of Persian society. The shah moved to crush the Majlis for good in June, 1908, turning his Cossack brigade against it and bombarding the building in which it met. Volunteer defenders held out for a few hours, but shortly thereafter the capital city was in the hands of the brigade and the shah. However, as the news of the counterrevolution reached the provinces, violent reactions set in, especially in Tabriz where the deposition of the shah was proclaimed. There was civil war for some months, in which important tribal groups supported the nationalists. As a result, and despite intervention of some Russian troops to "guarantee the protection of foreign consulates," the nationalists finally retook Tehran in July, 1909. Thereupon Muhammad Ali abdicated and soon departed for Russian exile.

Ahmad Shah

Muhammad Ali's successor was his twelve-year-old son Sultan Ahmad Shah, for whom an elder member of the ruling Kajar family was declared regent. Muhammad Ali Shah made an attempt to regain his throne the following year but this was abortive. At the end of 1910 the Majlis undertook a bold and dramatic plan in an attempt to inaugurate a new era in Persia. Certain progressive elements in the Majlis took the lead and after obtaining a recommendation from the State Department of the United States, sent an invitation to W. Morgan Shuster, an American financial expert, to come to Persia to assume unusual powers as treasurer-general and to put the finances of the country in order.

Shuster plunged into the unfamiliar job with energy and determination. He found the Belgian-run, but Russian-dominated, customs service ready with a plan which would have subordinated him to the director of that service, but he went immediately and directly to the Majlis, demanded and got control of such funds as the government had, thus bypassing the customs.

Shuster soon decided that to accomplish the sort of sweeping reforms he felt necessary to put the finances of the country on a sound basis, he needed a force of treasury agents, a "Treasury Gendarmerie" as he called it, to obtain an honest and thorough collection of the taxes. He got the Majlis' approval of his gendarmerie, but when he tried to install Major C. B. Stokes, a Britisher completing a term as military attaché at the British legation, as its chief he ran up against the Anglo-Russian convention of 1907.

Shuster preferred to read the convention only as far as the pronouncement of mutual respect by the British and Russians for the integrity and independence of Persia. Stokes was willing to be appointed but the British government informed the Persian Foreign Office that, if the Persian government persisted in the appointment, it would recognize Russia's right to take such steps as she thought necessary to safeguard her interests in northern Persia.

Meanwhile Russian "steps" were in the making. The ex-shah, Muhammad Ali, emerged from his exile in Odessa and his partisans succeeded in taking Tabriz, with Russian troops helping to "keep order" there. The Majlis responded by declaring a state of siege, putting a price on the head of the ex-shah, and attempting to put military forces into the field against him. They had practically no army, but popular feeling ran high and tribesmen began to arrive from the south. Disorganized as it was, the constitutional army routed the ex-shah. When the latter escaped the Majlis promptly ordered the confiscation of estates belonging to participants in the plot. But when Shuster's gendarmes went to take over the estates they were met by Cossack guards sent out by the Russian consul-general to seize the property on the grounds that the former owners owed money to the Russian bank (a "fictitious obligation," according to Shuster). There was an incident in which no one was killed, but Russian officials were "insulted," and the Russian government shortly issued an ultimatum demanding the surrender of the estates to the Russian consulate and an apology. The Majlis was in a defiant mood, but the Persian cabinet, especially after receiving British advice to comply and hearing that Russian troops were en route, agreed. Shuster turned over the estates, getting "receipts in full."

On November 29 Russia presented a second ultimatum, demanding that Shuster be replaced. The cabinet again decided to yield, but when the approval of the Majlis was sought, with excitement running high in the streets outside, and amidst the tears and applause of the spectators, the Majlis voted to retain Shuster and to oust the cabinet. Despite the vote there was much wavering in the days thereafter as frantic meetings were held to plan ways to stave off the coming Russian invasion. Turmoil and indecision mounted and on December 24 the deposed cabinet with Russian backing expelled deputies from the Majlis grounds, barred the gates, and pronounced the Majlis abolished.

Constitutional government was dead for the time being. Russian troops stayed in the country, while Shuster left Persia in January, 1912. In spite of this Shuster's name remained a symbol of the promise of freedom in Persia.

THE OTTOMAN EMPIRE AND INCREASED WESTERN PRESSURE

By the Treaty of Paris (1856), which ended the Crimean War, the Ottoman empire was formally inducted into the European state system, the first non-Western state to be so "honored." And the European powers all signed a statement that "none of them, either collectively or individually, has the right to interfere in the relations of H.M. the Sultan with his subjects or in the internal administration of his empire."

Not even in the interests of that sovereign's much abused Christian subjects would they interfere. They were clear on this point, for it was remembered that Russia's mission of "protecting" the Orthodox Christians in the Ottoman Danubian provinces had led to the Crimean War. Neither the Russians nor the English had profited from that bloody and inconclusive conflict, and the French, with their finances strained and their army ravaged by disease, were especially anxious to call a halt. It was agreed that the powers would not fight among themselves for the privilege of doctoring the Ottoman "sick man"; they would return to him his territories, remind him of his duty to carry on reforms in line with Hatt-i-Humayun precepts, and allow him to do his own doctoring. Ironically, this "hands off" treaty of 1856 may be said to have inaugurated an era of dislocation, frustration, and turmoil in Southwest Asia such as had not been known for centuries.

For three immediate and obvious reasons the Ottoman empire could not reconstitute and transform itself: (1) the court was unwilling to make the necessary readjustments and sacrifices; a few enlightened ministers were willing, but sultans, harems, court cliques, and other vested interests were not; (2) even if the court had made its best efforts toward reform, it might not have been enough; subject peoples, imperfectly assimilated non-Turkish groups within the empire, were becoming emboldened to defy their Ottoman masters; (3) the powers, for all their promises, not only continued to interfere in Ottoman affairs but began to nibble at the fringes of the Ottoman domain. Each of these points deserves some elaboration.

The Problem of Reform and Midhat Pasha

The best hope for a court-directed reform program lay in the efforts and the personality of Midhat Pasha, who, after a distinguished career as a reform governor of a Danubian province and then of Mesopotamia, in 1876 was able amidst bizarre circumstances to assume the direction of affairs at Constantinople and to attempt drastic reform measures. The background of events leading up to his opportunity and his great effort was indicative of the magnitude of the difficulties which faced any reformist group at court.

After the Treaty of Paris, reform was neglected, and old abuses multiplied. A new sultan, Abdul Aziz, came to the throne in 1861. He began his career with a pronouncement of good intentions, particularly with regard to economies at court, but he soon gave way to enormous spending for the upkeep of his palace and harem, and he and his associates set a record for borrowing money.

By 1875 the Ottoman government could not even pay the interest on its debts, and it began to issue worthless bonds to give creditors in lieu of interest payments. Money which reached Constantinople was generally marked for military refurbishment or other "reform" endeavors, but most of this was siphoned off by the court and officials. The approaching financial debacle was accompanied by frantic efforts on the part of Ottoman authorities to collect more taxes from the already overburdened population; this created an immediate prospect of revolt in the provinces, regardless of what the powers might do. The powers meanwhile prepared to assume control of the finances of the empire by means of an international commission.

This was the uninviting situation into which Midhat Pasha stepped. However, his career in the provinces indicated that he had an unusual grasp of the main problems of the empire. He had served in areas in which there were mixed populations and he had made a good record at the provincial level in gaining the cooperation of the leaders of non-Turkish subjects. He had stressed educational programs which were designed to serve the whole community and he had experimented in administrative reforms, inviting the advice of councils. He was in Mesopotamia for only three years (1869–1872), but from his administration there developed such important reforms as the land registry which undertook to encourage and regularize land settlement, irrigation works, the introduction of a middle class urbanite officialdom, and many schools. In addition, as his seizure of power at Constantinople revealed, he was an experienced politician.

Midhat Pasha skillfully planned his coup d'état. He sent an anonymous notification of his intentions to the British, French, and German governments which stated that Islamic law required the chief of state to be sane, and that since Abdul Aziz did not meet this qualification it had become necessary to depose him. Late in May, 1876 the plotters, armed with a testament from the Grand Mufti that the Sultan was not sane and must therefore be deposed, invaded the palace, arrested Abdul Aziz, and proclaimed his nephew, Abdul Mejid, to be the new sultan, Murad V. Less than a week later Abdul Aziz died under mysterious circumstances, the cause being certified as suicide.

The elevation of Murad V to replace his "mentally incompetent"

FIGURE 11.4. Midhat Pasha.

uncle had a certain irony about it, since Murad was really insane. Intelligent and liberal as a young man, he had excited the suspicions of conservatives who forced him into a life under house arrest, wherein he had become both neurotic and alcoholic. Then the sudden and completely unexpected turn of events which placed him on the throne, the grisly demise of his predecessor, and the glare of the spotlight now focused upon him seem to have deprived Murad of what little sanity his previous indulgences had left him. At the end of August another proclamation by the Mufti, prepared, of course, in collaboration with Midhat Pasha and the other ministers, announced what was really true this time, that Murad was mentally unfit to continue as sultan, and was therefore deposed. Next day Murad's brother, who agreed to uphold the constitution, ascended the throne as Abdul Hamid II.

With a new and presumably dependable monarch at last, Midhat Pasha accepted the post of grand vizir and moved to initiate a reform program. It would be difficult to envision an Ottoman official in a stronger position. He had deposed two sultans, and his intentions must be adjudged to have been earnest. He had a clear idea of the empire's needs, and his vision included not only the obviously necessary financial reforms, but broad political changes which included the adoption of constitutional government.

His hand was further strengthened and a sense of the absolute urgency of his reform created by the imminence of a conference of the powers on the future of Turkey, growing out of the general financial crisis, but more immediately of the "black outrages" which occurred during the late spring and summer of 1876 in Bulgaria. There the Christian peasant population had become extremely disaffected by the extortions of Moslem landlords, aggravated by an intensified tax collecting campaign on orders from Constantinople. Even as the successive coups d'état which brought Midhat Pasha to power were being planned and executed, revolt broke out in Bulgaria. This was speedily put down by Turkish troops and the affair might have ended there had not the Turkish commander in the field allowed his troops, including utterly undisciplined irregulars, to be turned loose on the Christian population of the rebellious district, to plunder and ravage as they pleased. Thousands were killed and whole villages despoiled. An English newspaperman kept the British public fully informed as the story of atrocity after atrocity unfolded. At first the tale of horror was discounted by political leaders in England, including Disraeli, who felt that British interests were best served by the continuance of the Ottoman empire, however wicked and effete, as a bulwark against Russia.

Moralistic elements in Great Britain insisted that the Turks be called to account. Gladstone published a furious pamphlet entitled "The Bulgarian Horrors and the Question of the East" in which he demanded a complete reversal of British policy and the application of all Britain's "vigour to obtain the extinction of the Turkish executive power in Bulgaria." He called the Turkish deeds in Bulgaria the "basest and blackest outrages" on record in the nineteenth century.

Disraeli tried to calm the growing popular rage against the Turks by inciting some bitterness against Russia, who he rightly presumed would soon be seeking a renewed opportunity to come to the aid of the Christian provinces of the Ottoman empire, and thus to bring them under Russian protection. But he could not dissipate the demand that Turkey be disciplined. With Turks committing atrocities as well as declaring moratoriums on their interest payments, with anti-Turkish feeling developing in England, and with the tsar talking of protecting Christians in Ottoman provinces by Russian power alone, if necessary, it was time for another conference. This was called for Constantinople in late December, 1876.

Midhat Pasha was quite aware that this conference would make heavy demands on the Ottoman government, especially if there was no prior evidence that a reform program was underway in earnest. In this state of real emergency Sultan Abdul Hamid and Ottoman leaders who might otherwise have opposed such sweeping changes accepted the grand vizir's blueprint for reform. After feverish work the new era was proclaimed on the day before the opening of the powers' Constantinople Conference with the announcement of what amounted to a constitution for the Ottoman empire. Based on the Belgian constitution, it was a liberal document, establishing equality before the law for all subjects of the empire, Turk and non-Turk, Moslem and non-Moslem alike; all were to be called "Ottoman" thereafter. Representative government was established with a bicameral elected legislative parliament and a new court system to interpret laws. The lower house was to set the state budget. The provinces were to enjoy a much larger voice in their local government than before, and universal education for all was to become a reality.

Bringing the Ottoman government to such a position was a magnificent achievement for Midhat Pasha, and the powers would have been wise to have aided him and his reform group at this point, but they did not. The Conference took the view that these pronouncements were paper measures only and that on the key issues, that of the "Christian provinces," there was no satisfactory proposal offered. The Turks had already proved by their atrocious behavior that they could not be trusted in dealing with Christian populations, and the powers demanded that the governments of these "Christian provinces" be rendered autonomous and that the appointment of governors for them be made only on approval of the powers. Such an arrangement, of course, constituted a clear infringement on Ottoman sovereignty, the very sort of thing which Midhat Pasha, by his reform program, was seeking to forestall.

Abdul Hamid II

Deadlock ensued, and the parties involved in the dispute now reverted to form. The sultan, whose personal strength Midhat Pasha had probably underestimated, shortly accused his grand vizir of complicity in the murder of the former Sultan Abdul Aziz and produced two witnesses who "admitted" that they had murdered that ruler on orders from Midhat Pasha. Midhat Pasha was convicted of high treason and banished to Arabia, where, presumably on orders of the sultan, he was later killed.

Abdul Hamid II was not again to allow his authority to be challenged by a mere minister. He ruled more than thirty years, until he was ousted by revolution in 1909, and during that time he completely dominated the Ottoman government. He made the constitution a dead letter, his ministers mere puppets of his will; he reasserted the dominant position of Islam as the state religion and of himself as the caliph; and though he promoted military and technological reforms thereafter, they were mainly with a view to keeping subject peoples within the empire and holding off the foreigners from its borders. His conception of the empire was a traditional one: a multinational state dominated and run by an Ottoman minority, which he presumed would be supported by the religious cohesion of the Islamic community. But in spite of his strenuous efforts the forces of disruption were too strong. The pressure of the powers now took its toll in territory; and the variegated populations within the empire, including even the Turks themselves, proved more susceptible to the new current of nationalism than Abdul Hamid, with his pan-Islamic outlook, dreamed possible.

Renewed European Intervention

Indications that the powers were not going to watch idly while Abdul Hamid reverted to despotism were not too long in coming. From a conference in London came one more demand for reform, which was promptly rejected by the sultan (April, 1877), and then the Russian government, claiming to act on behalf of all the powers, declared war on the Ottoman empire.

High councils in Britain were divided in regard to Turkey. While it was realized that Russia might make immense territorial gains, yet in line with Gladstonian principles there was a strong feeling that the Turks had become too vicious. The British declared for neutrality, which meant for

FIGURE 11.5. Sultan Abdul Hamid II.

the time being that as far as they were concerned the Ottomans would be left to their "just deserts," namely the mercies of the Russian army.

The Russians invaded the Ottoman empire on both its European and Asiatic fronts, and except for a few difficulties encountered in the early days of the European campaign, less from Turks than from terrain, they were everywhere successful. While their Asiatic forces moved through Armenia taking fortress after fortress from Turkish garrisons, the European contingents closed in on Constantinople. They took Adrianople in January, 1878, and would certainly have been before Constantinople shortly thereafter had not the British, now thoroughly alarmed at the impending upset in the Near Eastern power balance, moved part of their fleet into the Dardanelles and given notice that they would not see Constantinople fall to the Russians. At first the Russians responded belligerently by moving units to within sight of the city, but in reality the Russian government was no more anxious for hostilities with the British than was the British government anxious for war with the Russians. The long and increasingly bitter rivalry between these powers, which, as noted earlier in this chapter, was of supreme importance in Persian affairs and a very vital factor across the whole breadth of Asia in the latter years of the nineteenth century, was still in the sparring stage. As long as one of them did not try to push its opportunities too far, there was always the possibility of diplomatic settlement. Such was the case in 1878.

The Russians started negotiations with the Turks which they intended would lead to the breaking up of the European part of the Ottoman empire. At the same time talks were initiated with the British with a view to ascertaining how far such a break-up might proceed and still be acceptable to London. The results were the Treaty of San Stefano between Russia and Turkey (March 1878) and the Congress of Berlin (June–July 1878), at which all the major powers were represented. The details of these agreements are of more concern to the student of European than of Asian history, and therefore need not be related here. It is sufficient to say that the Turks were deprived of most of their European holdings, which became either autonomous or independent states. Careful adjustments were made, however, to satisfy the British that the result of this would not be complete Russian ascendancy in the Balkans. In addition the Turks yielded part of Armenia to Russia and the island of Cyprus to Britain, the better, presumably, for these two powers to guarantee that the Turks carried out their promises of good government for the Christians remaining in the empire, as well as to keep watch on each other.

The British seizure of Cyprus at the end of the long course of San Stefano-Berlin negotiations is of particular interest for its implications for the future. It indicated clearly and precisely, though in a small and tentative way, that Britain was done with supporting the Ottoman "sick man" in his efforts to hold on to his territory. Hereafter the British would keep pace with the Russians or other powers in nibbling at the fringes of the empire. For example, British units began to consolidate a sphere of influence along the Persian Gulf coast of Arabia by taking under their protection Bahrain Island (1880), Oman (1891), and Kuwait (1899).

Entry of Germany into Great Power Rivalry

The European power rivalry in Turkey was further complicated in the 1890's by the intrusion of Germany into the politics of the region. This was facilitated by the growing Turkish realization that Britain could no longer be counted on to befriend the empire or even to restrain herself from seizing Ottoman territory. Hence, when Kaiser Wilhelm II began to make overtures of friendship toward Turkey, a period of German-Ottoman friendship was inaugurated. Kaiser Wilhelm came to the rescue of a languishing railway enterprise begun in the 1870's by Abdul Hamid with the cooperation of German financiers, and which by 1890 had at last connected Belgrade and Constantinople and had made a beginning on Asiatic soil. With money supplied by the Deutsche Bank, which established a Constantinople branch after Wilhelm visited that city in 1889, the railroad was pushed through to Ankara, and, with loud fanfare from Wilhelm, aimed for Baghdad. Britain and Russia rallied their diplomacy to stop it. But the Kaiser worked hard to cement German-Ottoman friendship. He sent German military experts to advise and train the sultan's army, and after another "friendship" visit to Constantinople in 1898 obtained the right to build modern port facilities at Haydar Pasha, opposite Constantinople on the Asia Minor coast, which was to serve as the connecting link between the European railroad system leading to Constantinople and the Asiatic system running on to Baghdad.

While the work on the Baghdad line was proceeding, the sultan used some of the money at his disposal to push ahead with a project dear to his heart, a railroad line linking the Ottoman heartland of Asia Minor with the important cities of the Moslem world, Beirut, Damascus, and the Arabian holy cities of pilgrimage, Mecca and Medina. This might have had the effect of strengthening the sultan's hold on such remote places as Arabia, had not other conditions adverse to this goal prevailed.

The principal effect of the German "menace" in Turkey was to facilitate Anglo-Russian cooperation. In the long run this contributed to the Anglo-Russian settlement of 1907 and the formation of the Triple Entente.

The Young Turks

Another effect of German friendship, certainly not anticipated by the sultan, was the growing disaffection of some members of his army. This was noticeable particularly among the group which came to be called the "Young Turks," a group which found its principal leadership among youthful officers stationed in Macedonia where their main duty was to keep the Christian population under control. The Turkish army was singularly inept at this task, and frequent riots with their resulting atrocities brought a series of diplomatic interventions by European powers, some of which by 1908 were demanding that the Turkish forces be put under the command of European officers.

The Young Turks had been learning military tactics from German advisors, but they were fiercely resentful of the idea of foreign commands for the army and of foreign pressure generally. They regarded the Sultan Abdul Hamid as being spineless and they plotted revolution against him.

The leader of the conspirators was a young officer named Enver Bey, who had formerly been a military attaché in Berlin. A lesser figure in the organization, who became supremely important after World War I, was Mustafa Kemal. The conspirators had their organization working not only on the European side of the Straits, with their headquarters at Salonica, but also in places like Beirut, Jerusalem, and Damascus, among members of the army garrisons stationed there. Connections among the various groups were not always well maintained, but all had the same spirit.

The Young Turk movement must be defined as principally a *nationalist* movement. While calling "union and progress" their long range objective, they made Midhat Pasha's almost forgotten constitution of 1876 their rallying point and its reactivation their immediate goal. In this the Young Turks had the support of the more truly liberal groups such as the one headed by the former grand vizir Kâmil Pasha, an advocate of a British-type parliamentary system.

Although these groups did not plot revolution, Enver Bey and his radical and nationalist Committee of Union and Progress thought that armed revolt was the best road to reformed government. With support from a considerable section of the army, now infected with the new nationalist sentiment, they staged a coup d'état in July 1908 and offered Sultan Abdul Hamid his choice between abdication and the acceptance of the constitution of 1876. He accepted the constitution, invited Kâmil Pasha to be his prime minister, and under the watchful eyes of Enver Bey and the "Committee," he seemingly moved ahead toward a liberal constitutional regime.

The nationalistic Young Turks soon found themselves in difficulties with the subject nationalities and with conservative groups. In the struggle with the latter, parts of the army aligned themselves with both sides. Following the outbreak of fighting in which the sultan opposed the Young Turks (1909), they were able to force his abdication. Enver Bey led a second coup and Abdul Hamid was deposed. Although they elevated another of his family to the office of sultan, the Young Turks actually took over the government.

Enver Bey now became a virtual military dictator, and the liberal aspect of the regime speedily disappeared. He proclaimed a program of extreme Turkish nationalism, by which the non-Turkish groups within the empire were to be integrated into the Turkish state. They were no longer to be allowed to go their own subordinate but relatively undirected ways, as had been the custom in the past; rather they were to use the Turkish language, serve in the Turkish army, and to abandon aspects of their own culture, in favor of Turkish mores. This policy, naturally enough, alienated most of the non-Turkish peoples of the empire, and it may be well at this point to review briefly their condition in the first decade of the twentieth century.

NON-TURKISH PEOPLES OF THE EMPIRE

Christian subjects of the Ottoman empire were generally restive. Among those living in Asia an important group were the Armenians, whose land

SOUTHWEST ASIA ABOUT 1914

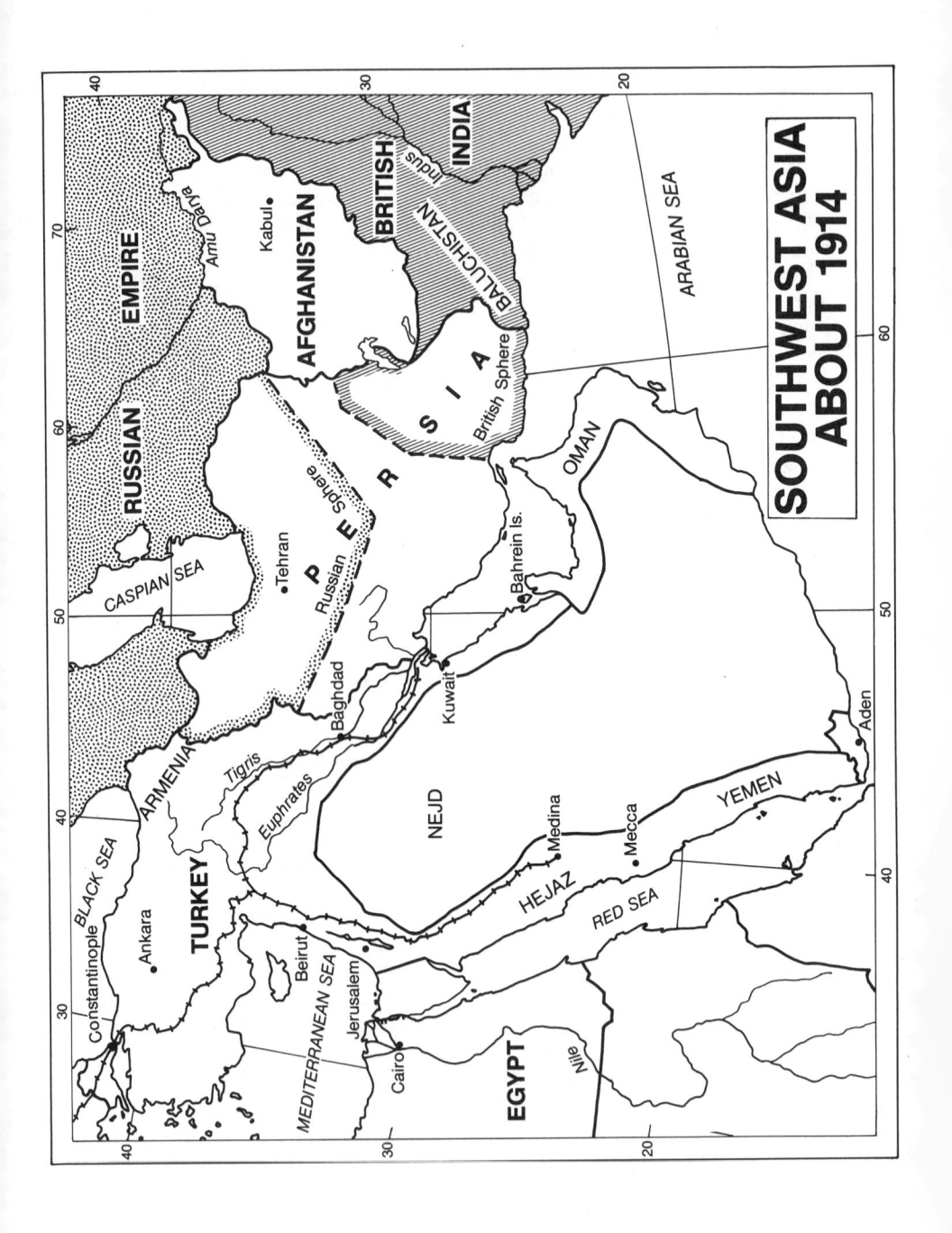

extended from inner Anatolia to the Caspian Sea. As previously noted this region had been a crossroads and a battleground of empires since Roman-Parthian times. Armenian aspiration for an independent national existence was very ancient, and though the idea of political independence had been smothered in recent centuries by Ottoman rule, the Armenians had stubbornly maintained a cultural and religious aloofness. Furthermore, by assiduous attention to economic matters they had managed to become a relatively wealthy group in spite of their inferior political position. Their troubles with "turkification" actually antedated the Young Turk government program, for in Abdul Hamid's last years as sultan there had been efforts to tie them more securely to Ottoman rule. The great railway project had a spur line for them, running from central Anatolia through their principal city, Erzerum, and on beyond toward the Caspian. While this railway link to Constantinople promised obvious economic advantages to the Armenians, it also promised to make their cultural and religious independence more difficult to maintain. There were large-scale massacres of Armenians in 1905, which if not specifically ordered by the sultan, were certainly abetted by his disinclination to stop them. The Young Turks' emphasis on nationalism and their dictatorial approach to affairs of state clearly envisaged no relief for the Armenians and in fact promised an acceleration of persecution. Hence Armenian restiveness was on the increase.

South of Armenia, and like Armenia a borderland of the empire, lay three Ottoman provinces which now constitute the state of Iraq. The ancient cultural unity of Mesopotamia had in large measure been lost in the centuries just preceding the Ottoman assumption of control and there had been no recovery during the succeeding centuries of Ottoman rule.

Iraq in the early twentieth century was united in the negative aspect of being non-Turkish, but otherwise sharply divided. The population in the north was largely composed of Kurds, fiercely proud and often rebellious herdsmen who considered themselves superior even to the Turks. The latter handled the Kurds with great circumspection and used up their energies in various military tasks. The population of the Baghdad and Basra provinces was largely Arabic speaking, but they were rather clearly divided on the question of religion, since the northern area, including both Mosul and Baghdad, was largely of the Sunni branch of Islam, while the southern (Basra) area was almost exclusively Shi'a. Between the two was always latent and often active hostility. In addition, scattered through the whole area were groups of Persians, Jews, and Christians of various types. Each of these groups formed a minority element. All were under Turkish rule which enforced the use of the Turkish language in official business and in such educational institutions as existed.

For the inhabitants of Iraq, making a living from the narrow river valley was hard and from the nearby desert impossible. Despite some lovely date gardens, the general aspect of life was squalid and unpleasant, especially in the crowded, ill-drained, disease-ridden cities. The land had lost the excellent flood control and irrigation systems of ancient times. By this period, however, some new activities were commencing. Westerners were becoming aware of the resources of the area, particularly oil, and there was some inclination for Europeans to enter into shipping on the Tigris-Euphrates and into Iraqi trade generally. The foreign contacts, though they promised little in the way of economic advantage to the Iraqi under conditions where the Ottoman government was quick to absorb any profits, nevertheless made the region aware of the course of events in Europe and the western part of the Ottoman domain. While the Ottoman spy system had long made political organization outside governing circles unthinkable, the nascent bitterness of subjects toward their masters was reflected in the great interest with which the Iraqis watched the Ottoman government flounder in its efforts to "stabilize" rebellious subject populations, particularly those in eastern Europe, who, with the aid of outside powers, were winning their way to freedom from Ottoman rule.

The Young Turks' seizure of power in 1908 tended to crystallize and clarify the relationship between Iraq, or rather the various sections of Iraq, and the Ottoman government. Immediately after the promise of constitutional government was issued, leaders of various groups in Iraq, both Turkish officials and non-Turk leaders of the various religious and population groups, sought to enter the political arena.

With the establishment of the dictatorship of Enver Bey it soon became clear not only that non-Turks might not expect to participate in the new regime, but that the turkification program would soon be disrupting even their customary non-Turkish mode of existence. Out of resistance to this an Iraqi-Arab nationalism was born. It was most pronounced in Basra, where a young Arab leader who had first tried to cooperate with the Young Turks broke with them and began to lead a movement for independence. The independence movement itself did not prosper, but strong sentiment for some sort of autonomous regime developed in Baghdad. By 1914 there was strong resistance among the Iraqis against conscription into the Ottoman armies, Turkish officials were murdered, and pent-up grievances were aired in numerous recently established newspapers. This was the situation in the Iraqi borderland of the Ottoman empire in 1914.

In Arabia Ottoman authority in the decade before World War I was mainly nominal. While the old Wahhabi separatism of the early nineteenth century had died down, the interior of the peninsula was the scene of struggles for power between rival Arab tribal leaders. The Ottoman government repeatedly sent contingents of troops into the area, but they neither settled the strife nor proved to be a decisive influence in favor of one group or another. Gradually the house of Sa'ud forged ahead in the competition, and beginning about 1910, Ibn Sa'ud, an able and energetic scion of that house, began to rekindle the fires of Wahhabiism and to begin a drive for power, which after World War I was to bring about the birth of a new nation, Saudi Arabia.

Ottoman influence was most pronounced along the western coast of Arabia. An Arab leader, Husain, who lived long in Constantinople, was installed as Emir at Mecca by Enver Bey's government in 1908. At first he aided in promoting Turkish interests, but by 1913 he already showed evidence of his future anti-Turkish leadership in opposing the building of the Hejaz railway.

FIGURE 11.6. The governor of Jerusalem receiving the friendship oath of an Arab chief shortly before World War I. The photograph illustrates the contrasts found within the Ottoman empire: here the Turkish official in modern Western uniform beside the Arab sheik in his traditional robes.

While specific mention has been made only of the frontier areas, Armenia, Iraq, and Arabia, all of the non-Turkish provinces of the Ottoman empire may be said to have been sullen, restive, or both during the decade preceding the first World War. It later took a minimum of disruption to bring about their separation from the Ottoman domain. World War I, together with the various intrigues that accompanied it, provided the disruptive factor. Indeed, the empire felt the maximum impact of the war because, in the frantic alignment of combatants in 1914, the Young Turk government allowed itself to be persuaded to join Germany and the Central Powers. This was natural perhaps, in view of the Young Turk officers' early training and association with German teachers and the great interest and "friendship" the Kaiser had so often expressed in describing his feeling toward the Ottoman empire. But it proved to be a fatal decision, and the break-up of the empire was its end result.

This chapter has treated the history of the Persian and Ottoman empires in considerable detail through what was for the peoples of those empires an extremely critical period, 1857–1914. Both empires, though very different in their internal problems and organizations, nevertheless were alike in responding to the impact of the West with a rebellious nationalism, which expressed itself in a determination to reform the old regime or to be rid of it.

BASIC DATES

1848–1896	Nasir-ud-din
1861–1876	Abdul Aziz sultan
1864–1907	Intense Anglo-Russian rivalry in Persia
1866–1868	Nationalist uprisings in Crete
1869	Suez Canal opened
1870–1876	Nationalist uprisings in Balkans
1874	Financial collapse of Ottoman empire
1876	Midhat Pasha and parliamentary constitution
1876–1909	Abdul Hamid II sultan
1877	Absolutism reestablished in Turkey
1878	Congress of Berlin
1878–1903	Insurrections in Crete, Balkans, Armenia
1880	British in Bahrain
1882	Ottoman revenues placed under foreign control
1891	British in Oman
1896–1908	Young Turk movement
1899	British in Kuwait
1899	Germans secure Baghdad railway concession
1900–1908	Hejaz railway constructed
1906	Calling of Majlis; constitution granted in Persia
1907	Anglo-Russian agreement
1907–1909	Muhammad Ali Shah reigns in Persia
1908–1909	Nationalist revolution in Turkey
1909	Anglo-Persian Oil Company founded
1909–1915	Muhammad V sultan
1909–1925	Ahmad Shah reigns in Persia
1911	Turkish war with Italy
1912	First Balkan War
1913–1918	Rule of Young Turks under Enver Bey
1914	Turkey enters First World War

SUPPLEMENTARY READING

Anderson, Matthew S. *The Eastern Question, 1744-1923.* London, 1966.
Avery, Peter W. *Modern Iran.* London, 1965.
Brockelmann, C. *History of the Islamic Peoples.* New York, 1960.
Davison, R. H. *Turkey.* Englewood Cliffs, N.J., 1968. A Spectrum paperback.

Fisher, S. N. *The Middle East.* New York, 1959.
Hitti, P. *The Near East in History.* Princeton, N.J., 1961.
Leiden, Carl, ed. *The Conflict of Traditionalism and Modernism in the Muslim Middle East.* Austin, Texas, 1968.
Lewis, B. *The Emergence of Modern Turkey.* London, 1961.
─────── *The Middle East and the West.* London, 1964.
Toynbee, A. and K. Kirkwood, *Turkey.* New York, 1927.
Upton, J. *The History of Modern Iran: An Interpretation.* Cambridge, Mass., 1960.

ADVANCED READING

Ahmad, Feroz. *The Young Turks.* London, 1969.
Banani, Amin. *The Modernization of Iran, 1921-1941.* Stanford, Calif., 1961.
Berkes, Niyazi. *The Development of Secularism in Turkey.* Montreal, 1964.
Busch, B. C. *Britain and the Persian Gulf, 1894-1914.* Berkeley, Calif., 1967.
Chambers, Richard L. and W. R. Polk. *The Beginnings of Modernization in the Middle East: The Nineteenth Century.* Chicago 1968.
Cottam, R. W. *Nationalism in Iran.* Pittsburgh, Pa., 1964.
Davison, R. H. *Reform in the Ottoman Empire, 1856-1876.* Princeton, N.J., 1963.
Devereux, Robert. *The First Ottoman Constitutional Period: A Study of the Midhat Constitution and Parliament.* Baltimore, 1963.
Entner, Marvin L. *Russian-Persian Commercial Relations, 1828-1914.* Gainesville, Fla., 1965.
Haas, W. S. *Iran.* New York, 1946. Reprinted 1966.
Hogarth, D. *Arabia.* Oxford, 1922.
Hurewitz, J. C., ed. *Diplomacy in the Near and Middle East: A Documentary Record, 1535–1914.* Princeton, N.J., 1956. A useful source.
Kazemzadeh, Firuz. *Russia and Britain in Persia, 1864–1914: A Study in Imperialism.* New Haven, 1968.
Keddie, Nikki R. *An Islamic Response to Imperialism.* Berkeley, 1968.
─────── *Religion and Rebellion in Iran: The Tobacco Protest of 1891–1892.* London, 1966.
Mardin, Serif. *The Genesis of Young Ottoman Thought.* Princeton, N.J., 1962.
Midhat, Ali Haider. *The Life of Midhat Pasha.* London, 1903. Biography of the constitutionalist by his son.
Ramsaur, E. *The Young Turks.* Princeton, N.J., 1957.
Shuster, W. M. *The Strangling of Persia.* New York, 1912. An interesting account of the Anglo-Russian rivalry by an active eyewitness.

Chapter 12

Decline of the Ch'ing, 1844-1894

LOSS OF INDEPENDENCE

Although the Ch'ing had surpassed all previous dynasties of China and indeed most of the world in extent of territory controlled, number of people governed, degree of sophistication in political, economic, and social structures, and, since the establishment of peace in the realm in 1683, had developed remarkably in the arts as well, it was barely to survive the nineteenth century.

The years 1839–1844 had seen many reverses. The efforts of Commissioner Lin to root out the opium traffic in Canton had failed, Chinese forces had been completely defeated in war with Great Britain, and the Nanking and other treaty settlements were completely one-sided in favor of the foreigners (see Chapter 5). Yet the Ch'ing government and most of its leading officials seemed almost to congratulate themselves on winning the victory. The foreigners had won trade concessions, a money indemnity, an unused and presumably not very important island (Hong Kong) which the Emperor "graciously granted" to England, and the right to consular jurisdiction. But to the Chinese these were much less important considerations than the things that had been avoided: recognition of the foreigners as equals and the stationing of foreign representatives at Peking. The indemnity was heavy, but the money came from the local Canton area with the hong merchants bearing a large part of the burden. The wealthy hong merchant Wu Ch'ung-yueh (Howqua) is said to have paid one million dollars himself. Consular jurisdiction, or extraterritoriality, was eventually to compromise seriously Chinese independence, but at the time it seemed to the Chinese to be merely a way of avoiding unnecessary contacts with foreigners.

At any rate, the outcome from the Chinese point of view did not seem to be as bad as it might have been. The Confucian system was undisturbed. The "barbarians" seemed to be satisfied with the sort of sugar plums of trade with which China had bought off other barbarians in earlier times, and there was as yet little inclination to regard the Westerners as barbarians of a different and more dangerous breed than those which Chinese civilization had absorbed in the past. Ch'i-ying, who negotiated and signed the treaty, replaced Commissioner Lin as the imperial representative to deal with the foreigners at Canton. Grand Counsellor Mu-chang-a backed Ch'i-ying in his efforts to pursue a conciliatory policy and the emperor, Tao-kuang, was content to have it that way, temporarily at least. Assuming that the demands of the foreigners could be kept within reasonable bounds by diplomatic means, he had those high officials at Peking who had backed the vigorous policies of Commissioner Lin demoted.

However, several factors augured ill for the continuance of peaceful relations. At bottom, the problem was that while the Chinese were expecting to minimize the effects of the treaties, the Westerners, particularly the British, expected to carry them out to their fullest extent. The first specific problem regarded the question of the foreigners' right to enter the city of Canton itself. Canton was a walled city, where, during the war, a great deal of anti-British propaganda had been promoted, with incentive rewards offered for every dead Englishman. It was difficult to change this sentiment overnight, even though the Treaty af Nanking clearly marked Canton as one of the port cities to be opened to British trade and residence. Ch'i-ying urged the British to be patient, and promised to arrange for their entrance inside the walls as soon as possible. The British did not immediately try to force entrance into Canton, but there were various incidents with walking parties and individuals entering the city, while British negotiators kept demanding that the Chinese set a date when they could legally establish themselves inside the walls. In 1847 there was a very serious incident in which six Englishmen walking near the city were attacked and killed. Ch'i-ying rounded up the Chinese perpetrators of the killings and had four of them executed. However, the incident had repercussions in Peking where there was much criticism of Ch'i-ying for taking the side of the foreigners.

Another matter that caused difficulty was the continued and accelerated importation of opium. Nothing had been said about opium in the treaty settlement, except that the Chinese were required to pay six million dollars for the destruction of "property" and, of course, a considerable amount of the "property" was opium. But the question of the continued illegality of the importation of opium was not settled. After the Treaty of Nanking the importation of opium was simply winked at by Chinese officials and more and more was imported. The British several times indicated their willingness and desire to have the importation legalized and the opium taxed, hence presumably made subject to control, but the Chinese, with their anti-opium laws still on the books, refused to consider this.

Another explosive possibility developed out of smuggling and piracy along the southeast China coast and their relationship to foreign shipping. Chinese law and order was in a state of disarray, and in order to cope with piracy the foreigners, particularly the Portuguese from Macao and the British from Hong Kong, began to organize a sort of convoy system. At first a foreign gunboat would escort legitimate Chinese trading vessels to insure their protection; later an arrangement was worked out whereby the Chinese trading boats might register at Hong Kong and, for a fee, become entitled to the "protection" of British registry expressed symbolically in the right to fly the British flag. Presumably no pirate would dare to attack such a vessel. This practice lay in the background of the famous Lorcha Arrow Incident of October, 1856, which will be discussed shortly.

One more factor in the increasing tension at Canton was the removal from office there of the conciliatory Ch'i-ying. This occurred early in 1848, and it meant that advocates of a stronger policy in dealing with the foreigners were becoming more influential at the capital. The new appointee was Yeh Ming-ch'en, a man who was noted for his ability to suppress bandits and handle financial problems. However, he was also something of a believer in divination, or at least he professed to believe that important affairs could be conducted only on "auspicious days," and there proved to be very few "auspicious days" for the conduct of negotiations with foreigners. He was regarded by the foreigners as arrogant and obstructionist, and they soon found that the long-standing demand for entrance into the walled city of Canton would not be considered during his regime.

Arrow Incident and War

According to the American treaty, the terms might be renegotiated after twelve years, and this being applicable by the most-favored-nation clause to all the treaties, the British took the lead in demanding treaty revision to clarify and make more definite their rights. Since there was no inclination on the part of the Chinese to move in this direction, negotiations were deadlocked when, in 1856, the Lorcha Arrow case occurred. The term "Lorcha" means a boat that is in its design half-Chinese and half-Western, and the Arrow was one of those Chinese-owned trading boats which was sailing under British registry at Hong Kong, under the command of an English captain with a Chinese crew. It flew the British flag. On October 8, 1856, while the Arrow lay anchored at Canton, Chinese authorities came aboard and arrested several members of the crew as former pirates. Sir Harry Parkes, the British consul for the Canton area, who prided himself on his ability to handle "Orientals," demanded the return of the men and an apology for the insult to the British flag. (Later it developed that the British registry at Hong Kong had expired eleven days before the incident, but Parkes did not feel that that altered the fact that the British flag had been insulted.) The Chinese authorities returned the men but refused to apologize, and the argument became intensified.

Other events in 1856 and 1857 which added to the tension included the murder of a French Catholic missionary, August Chapdelaine, who was proselytizing in the interior in Kwangsi province. According to the French treaty, Christianity was to be tolerated in the empire, but Father Chapdelaine, like other foreigners, actually had no right to go beyond the treaty port area, though he had been in the interior since 1853. After his arrest in 1856 he was subjected to terrible tortures, decapitated, and his body thrown to dogs, all with the approval or at least the non-interference of the local magistrate. Another incident involved the killing of a British sailor near Canton in early December, after which British troops attacked and set fire to houses in the village where the event occurred. In retaliation a Chinese mob attacked and set fire to foreign factories along the Pearl river. Then a Chinese baker named Ah-Lum poisoned the bread in Hong Kong with arsenic, which endangered the lives of many Englishmen, although none actually died from the effects. Incidents continued through 1857, and British and French negotiators empowered to serve an ultimatum arrived from Europe. When it went unanswered British and French forces bombarded Canton on December 28, 1857 and entered the city on the following day. On January 5, 1858 Governor Yeh was captured and taken prisoner to Hong Kong. Later, in February, he was shipped to India where he was placed under house arrest in Calcutta. There he remained until his death by natural causes a year later.

These, of course, were acts of war, but Chinese governmental controls were by this time in such a precarious state that it was not declared as such and in fact trade with Westerners went on as before at other ports, particularly at Shanghai.

However, the British and French governments were determined not to leave matters unsettled, despite the fact that Canton was now under the control of the British consul, Sir Harry Parkes. It was decided that there should be a combined action, including a military expedition to Peking if necessary, to obtain revision of the Treaties, and the British and French representatives, Lord Elgin (James Bruce) and Baron Jean Louis Gros, consulted with Russian and American representatives, who had arrived upon the scene, as to the best way to bring the Chinese to accept the treaty revisions they all desired. The American envoy was William D. Reed; the Russian was Count Putiatin. Unlike Elgin and Gros they did not have authority to employ force, but they helped draw up a note for presentation at Peking. The four envoys waited at the mouth of the Peiho river near Tientsin for a reply. This river leading to Peking was guarded by the Taku forts. When the Chinese refused all of their demands, the French and British commissioners opened hostilities and took the forts. After that the Chinese agreed to negotiate and actually signed separate treaties at Tientsin with all four powers, the so-called Treaties of Tientsin of 1858.

In the negotiations the British interpreter, H. N. Lay, played a leading role. He was domineering and truculent, emphasizing repeatedly to the Chinese that there would be war if they did not give in completely to the British demands. Ch'i-ying, old and out of favor, was sent from Peking in a last attempt at conciliating the barbarians, but the British this time rudely disregarded him and produced documents captured at Canton to show his ambivalence. Dispirited, he returned to Peking without being specifically recalled. For this he was denounced for appeasement and cowardice by court enemies, who demanded his execution. The emperor showed "compassion" by merely requiring him to commit suicide.

The Tientsin settlement guaranteed Western diplomats the right to reside at Peking and deal directly with important ministers of state. Missionaries and other foreigners with passports could travel in the interior, erect churches, and own property. Indemnities demanded by the British and the French were accepted by the Chinese, the tariff was revised downward, and the importation of opium was legalized and made subject to import duties. The Americans accepted in their treaty, somewhat shamefacedly perhaps, a provision that "if any other nation should act unjustly or oppressively, the United States will exert their good offices on being informed of the case, to bring about an amicable arrangement of the question, thus showing their friendly feeling." The Russians also gave the impression of playing a role of friendship to the Chinese to mitigate the Franco-British demands, but all were tied together by most-favored-nation clauses. The Tientsin treaties called for ratifications to be exchanged at Peking a year later, but in June, 1859, when the envoys returned, they found the Chinese unwilling to ratify. Furthermore, the way to Peking up the Peiho river was barred with a chain across the river and shore batteries were ready to contest the entrance of the envoys. The British and French ministers again ordered attack and a fierce fight ensued, with the European forces being at first badly beaten. The American ship at hand, under Commodore Tatnall, USN, though under orders to observe strict neutrality, actually aided the British at a crucial point in the battle by helping to bring up British reserves. At this time Tatnall is said to have explained his action with the expression, "Blood is thicker than water." This attempt to force the river failed, and the envoys and their supporting military units withdrew to Shanghai. However, Elgin and Gros returned with reinforcements in June of 1860, broke the chain, silenced the shore batteries, and fought their way to Peking. While the Chinese court fled to Jehol, Franco-British forces took control of the capital and burned various buildings. These included the famous Summer Palace, Yuan-ming Yuan, where European prisoners, taken under a flag of truce, had been held.

Peking Convention

Prince Kung, the half-brother of the emperor, finally returned, partly by reason of the mediation of the new Russian envoy, General Ignatiev, who received for Russia the cession of the Maritime Province for his "honest brokerage" (see Chapter 9). Prince Kung, with imperial authority, negotiated with the Europeans the so-called Peking Convention of 1860. Its principal provisions included an increase in indemnities, the opening of Tientsin as a port for foreign residence and trade, the addition of nine other cities to the treaty port list (with the right of foreign warships to visit them), the cession of Kowloon, a mainland area opposite Hong Kong, to the British, an agreement on the part of the Chinese to establish a Western-style foreign office, and an apology from the emperor for the attack upon the British and French parties which had come for the ratification in 1859. In addition the provisions of the Treaties of Tientsin were endorsed.

With the signing of the Peking Convention and the acceptance of the

Treaties of Tientsin the power of the Ch'ing government to control its affairs, at least in the area of foreign relations, was ended. The Middle Kingdom, which for centuries had acted the role of universal state in the Far East, treating other nations and peoples with condescension and paternalistic benevolence, was now reduced to a condition in which she was clearly not able to preserve her sovereignty before the Western powers she had scorned. Whether the dynasty would be able to survive this crisis of prestige was much in doubt in 1860, because throughout China the long series of defeats in foreign relations that had begun with the first outbreak of war with the British in 1839 was reverberating in domestic affairs, and internal rebellion was shaking the very foundations of the Peking government.

WEAKNESS AND REBELLION

Perhaps the key assumption of the Confucian state was that it was governed by "superior men," who had passed through an elaborate examination system to qualify for office and who were presumed to be relatively incorruptible in their service to the state and the emperor. Of course, the system never worked perfectly, and controls such as the periodic transfer of officials and the institution of a censorate to denounce wrongdoing in official posts had been traditional safeguards in the system. In the Ch'ing period these worked tolerably well until about the 1790's when, with the rise of the imperial guardsman Ho-shen, there began an era of corruption in the bureaucracy on a grand scale extending through the first half of the nineteenth century. This involved admission to the bureaucracy by purchase, extensive development of landlordism, use of office to obtain private fortunes by which officials supported hordes of relatives, general evasion of difficult problems by the emperors and their court favorites. The result of these abuses was a widespread loss of confidence in and support for the dynasty expressed in a half dozen major rebellions which almost succeeded in destroying the Ch'ing government in the mid-nineteenth century.

The practice of admission to the bureaucracy by purchase was actually an old one in China, which was often utilized in times of stress to finance special needs of the government. In some ways it was not as disastrous a practice as the term "sale of office," which is sometimes used to describe it, may imply. Offices themselves were not actually offered for sale, rather rank or eligibility for office could be purchased by a "public donation." Not many of the purchasers of rank actually obtained an office, at least not a high office, in the bureaucracy, until after 1800, when the need for special funds to meet various crises became perennial, and the practice was resorted to more and more frequently. The development of landlordism and local sinecures accompanied the breakdown of the practice of transferring officials every three years, which had been customary, along with the growth of the practice of "squeeze," or extra collections by officials which were used for their personal benefit. The circumstances surrounding foreign trade at Canton provided excellent opportunities for "squeeze." Strangely, nepotism, if it is considered narrowly as the practice of an official's promoting the advancement in the hierarchy of his relatives without regard to merit, did not become a serious problem; rather, the use of "squeeze" to enhance family incomes was the pattern.

Another indication of bureaucratic breakdown was the increasing use of Manchu clansmen in office, in favor of often better qualified Chinese candidates, though this practice was reversed after the climactic Second Anglo-Chinese War (1858–1860). The evasion of responsibility by the highest authority at court is illustrated by the banishment of Commissioner Lin and the sentencing to suicide of Ch'i-ying for their failures to solve the "barbarian" problem, which in the terms of reference of the imperial court was insoluble. Great men and great ideas were conspicuous by their absence in China during the entire Tao-kuang (1821–1850) and Hsien-feng (1851–1861) reign periods. During that time of crucial relations with the West the pattern of government in China was for lower officials to use their offices at least in part for private gain and for high officials to evade responsibility by blaming those unfortunate enough to be placed in the position of having to negotiate with the supposedly inferior barbarians when in reality it was the central government's failure to recognize the problems of China and to plan a program for dealing with them that was at fault. In the absence of competence at Peking it is not surprising that the leadership of the country almost slipped into other hands.

T'ai-p'ing Rebellion

The greatest rebellion of the period and one of the most remarkable the world has ever seen was the T'ai-p'ing, which swept through south and central China from 1850 to 1864 and which during a large part of that period maintained Nanking as the capital of an empire within an empire. Although the social forces which generated the T'ai-p'ing rebellion may be found in widespread peasant discontent at the iniquity and incompetence of Manchu rule, the inception of the rebellion rests with one man, Hung Hsiu-ch'üan, whose career and ideas were most remarkable. Hung was a member of the very low, almost outcast, Hakka element of south China, being born in Kwangtung province. However, he was a very bright boy whose education his family and friends decided to support, and he studied hard with the goal of passing the provincial examinations. Although he passed the district examination and stood for the provincial examinations several times, he failed to pass them, and after his failure in 1837 he seems to have suffered a nervous collapse lasting some weeks. During his illness Hung seems to have had visions or hallucinations wherein a mysterious old man appeared to him urging him to go forth and repel demons, change perverse hearts, and rejuvenate the depraved people and conditions around him. Also, he thought he talked to a middle-aged man whom he called his elder brother.

At the time of his illness, Hung had in his possession several Christian tracts which he had been given by a foreign missionary on the occasion of one of his visits to Canton. He had not read them, however, and in fact he did not connect them with his vision or illness for another six years, when quite by accident a cousin of his, who happened to read them, urged Hung to study them because of their very interesting ideas. Reading these tracts in 1843 was like another revelation to Hung, and he began to see in them the meaning of his vision; the old man was God, the Christian Jehovah, and his middle-aged elder brother was Jesus. False teachings and idol worship were the demons he was to slay, and the ordinary people were his brothers and sisters to be saved. He then became officially a Christian, but, as many missionaries were to attest later, his version of Christianity was to be quite unsatisfactory to them. The very idea of a Chinese prophet was not congenial to Christian beliefs in the nineteenth century, and Hung was soon alienated from the missionaries. Nevertheless, his movement gained great momentum, spread into the Yangtze valley, and soon attracted thousands of followers. In July, 1850, government troops were sent against the converts, but Hung and his followers defeated them, and the rebels began to set up a government structure of their own. This they called the "Heavenly Kingdom of Peace" or T'ai-p'ing T'ien-kuo. Hung was declared the "celestial king" and the year 1851 was designated the year one of the new era of "great peace." During the next several years the T'ai-p'ings took control of several cities in the Yangtze river valley and persistently moved eastward. During the late 1850's, as the Peking government came into conflict with England and France, the T'ai-p'ings established their capital at Nanking (March, 1853) and exerted their influence over an enormous area in central and southern China.

Although the T'ai-p'ings gained tremendous popular support in their

FIGURE 12.1. Tso Tsung-t'ang.

rise to power, Hung and his associates proved to be very inept at government. Rivalries and strife within their own ranks, the political irresponsibility of Hung himself, and an increasing arrogance in their leadership lost for the T'ai-p'ing movement the possibility of organizing a new state in China. Also Westerners, who at first were inclined to favor the movement as semi-Christian, became alienated at its violence and radicalism, and came to the conclusion that they could do business better with the regular government at Peking. The Peking Convention of 1860 had the effect of placing the Westerners definitely on the side of the Manchu dynasty, and several Western soldiers of fortune including an American, Frederick Townsend Ward, and an Englishman, George "Chinese" Gordon, were employed by the business community of Shanghai to lead irregular troops against the T'ai-p'ings in 1861–1862. Endorsed by the Imperial government as the "Ever Victorious Army," they relieved rebel pressure on Shanghai and surrounding Kiangsu province. However, it was mainly the efforts of three Chinese officials, Tseng Kuo-fan, Li Hung-chang, and Tso Tsung-t'ang, which defeated the T'ai-p'ings and saved the Manchu dynasty. Realizing the inadequacy of bannermen and other imperial forces, they raised regional armies in Hunan, Anhwei (Huai River area), and Chekiang respectively, imbued them with devotion to Confucian ideology and, beginning in 1862, rapidly reversed the T'ai-p'ing fortunes. "Heavenly King" Hung gave up the direction of political affairs and, as government forces closed in on Nanking, committed suicide on June 1, 1864. Tseng Kuo-fan captured Nanking on July 19, and the great rebellion was over.

It had wrought tremendous and terrible effects. Probably twenty million people were killed or died of starvation during the fourteen years of struggle. In the last stages there were ferocious reprisals against the T'ai-p'ings, the rebel soldiers being slain almost to a man. Although at the time the T'ai-p'ing Rebellion was regarded largely as a religious or ideological movement, more recent evaluations of it have tended to emphasize the importance of social and economic components. Such things as the T'ai-p'ing system of communal landownership, their emphasis on equality of the sexes, and the general air of social revolution in the movement has led the Chinese Communists to consider the T'ai-p'ing a precursor to their own revolution.

Other Rebellions

The T'ai-p'ing, though the greatest, was not the only rebellion in China during the mid-nineteenth century. We cannot go into the others in such detail, but they deserve mention. One was the Triad Rebellion. The Triads (Heaven and Earth Society) were at first associated with the T'ai-p'ings in the Yangtze valley, but they broke off from that movement and took an independent course. They captured Shanghai in 1853, causing the flight of the imperial magistrate to the American consulate and the flight of thousands of Chinese to the foreign-controlled international settlement just outside the city.

A group called the Nien-fei ravaged Shantung during the 1850's and

1860's, being suppressed completely only in 1868 by the armies of Tso Tsung-t'ang and Li Hung-chang. Muslims revolted in Yunnan province and also in the far northwest, with riots continuing for 20 years. Also, unintegrated Miao tribesmen ran out of control in Kweichow province.

The effect of these rebellions was so devastating that it is a wonder that China even partially recovered as a political entity. It should be noted that the saving of the dynasty was accomplished only at the cost of the creation of a new kind of regionalism, whereby the saviors, like Tseng and Li, combined civil and military leadership functions in their provinces, becoming governors as well as army commanders and establishing fiscal systems to pay their troops. Also dissident elements, former rebels and secret societies, remained, especially in south China. Nevertheless, considerable recovery was made during the 1860's and early 1870's.

THE T'UNG-CHIH RESTORATION

The name T'ung-chih is given by the Chinese to the period 1862–1874. It is an era name or reign title, the characters for which are taken from a sentence in the *Book of Documents* (*Shu-ching*); see Volume I, Chapter 17. Its meaning, impossible to translate exactly, in the minds of those who chose the name was something like "Union for Order." At the beginning of this period in 1862 China was bordering on chaos. With the T'ai-p'ing and other rebellions still unsuppressed, with Westerners exercising a large degree of control in most of China's port cities, and with Western diplomats in a commanding position at Peking, the dynasty had to make a supreme effort to restore order and strengthen itself if it were to endure as the government of China. Although at the time of the death of the Hsien-feng emperor in 1861 and the succession of his son, a child, to the throne, such reestablishment of order and control seemed nearly impossible, it was the remarkable achievement of the T'ung-chih era that the dynasty was strengthened almost to the point of regaining its equilibrium. Within the Confucian frame of reference it accomplished, perhaps, all that could be done. The so-called "self-strengthening movement" reduced corruption and incompetence in government, refurbished the loyalty of the Chinese officialdom to the throne, and rebuilt the confidence of the Chinese people in their government, at least to the extent that they desisted from rebellion. So impressive were these achievements that Western governments, including Britain, decided temporarily to reverse their policies of encroachment. On this issue British merchants were often in vigorous disagreement with British official policy, for they wanted ever widening privileges in China but the British Foreign Office for a decade was adamant that China should be treated with more consideration.

Credit for the achievements of the T'ung-chih Restoration belongs largely to Prince Kung, who had negotiated the Peking Convention of 1860, and to the aforementioned Chinese Confucian officials, Tseng Kuo-fan, Tso Tsung-t'ang, and Li Hung-chang. It should be noted also that the mother of the new emperor, the empress dowager Tz'u-hsi, was a part of the new leadership. However, she was still a young woman and during the era of the T'ung-chih Restoration she did not exercise the decisive influence which she was to have later, a fact that allowed more flexibility and more intelligent handling of problems, for her great gift was in the area of court intrigue rather than in the area of national leadership. The role of Prince Kung was most important in the early stages, for it was only he at first who had the confidence and trust of the foreign envoys which allowed him and his Chinese supporters to reorganize the government and reestablish its authority throughout the country. To 1861 the British had been inclined to give de facto recognition to the T'ai-p'ings in Central China and deal with them, but then Prince Kung convinced them that he and his supporters could take the situation in hand. Seeing that he could, they acted through the balance of the 1860's with considerable restraint.

On the Prince's recommendation a special office, the Tsungli Yamen, was created in 1861. This became in effect a foreign office for Western-style diplomatic dealings and also an agency for promoting modernization. Naturally this pleased the Westerners, as did Prince Kung's somewhat accidental conversion to Western-style international law when he discovered, in 1864, that it could be invoked against misbehavior in Chinese territorial waters. Furthermore, a "cooperative policy" was worked out by the Western diplomats whereby all the Western powers restrained themselves to give the Ch'ing government a chance to restore order. Relations between the Western diplomats and Chinese officials became much more cordial than they had ever been before.

The general program of the T'ung-chih Restoration is revealed in cer-

FIGURE 12.2. Prince Kung, first president of Tsungli Yamen.

tain slogans of that era. The term "self-strengthening" seems to have been invented by a scholar named Feng Kuei-fen, whose writings also provided the inspiration for "Chinese learning as the basis, Western learning for practical use." The Wuhan governor, Chang Chih-tung, was to popularize this later as a catch-all guideline for China's future development. Tseng Kuo-fan even spoke of "the people's welfare," by which he meant a renewed attention to the welfare of the peasant masses of China in contrast with the merchant group which had been enriching themselves at the latter's expense. Also the Restoration leadership abandoned the practice of seeking scapegoats for every unpleasant situation, and worked on problems of government with considerable vigor. The former practice of giving Manchus long-term and superior positions over the Chinese, which had become endemic since 1840, was ended, and the Chinese bureaucrats, who were generally more able than their Manchu counterparts, gave a fuller measure of devotion to the cause of the dynasty. The Confucian basis of society and government was never questioned, but the Restoration leadership tried hard to purify it of evils that had crept in. They greatly curtailed the "purchase of rank" by "public donation," placed greater reliance on the examination system and broadened it, cut down on practices of "squeeze," emphasized the moral standards that Confucianism demanded of the official class, and called attention to the tremendous responsibility imposed by the times on ranks of government officials.

In addition, although the various rebellions were put down brutally, once rebellion had ceased, programs of economic improvement and social welfare were undertaken. Free food distribution centers were set up in areas of great need and supplies of grain from more stable areas were transported to famine-threatened areas. Public health programs were instituted, and programs of public works were established both to give employment and to improve transport and flood control in China. In short, there was a good deal more attention given to economic matters than the noneconomically minded Confucian bureaucracy usually gave.

Nevertheless, in some ways the economic rehabilitation program was shortsighted. It was typically Confucian in that it had no sufficient appreciation of the possibilities of commerce, either in the areas of foreign trade or domestic exchange. Agriculture was considered to be the key to economic rehabilitation in an era when commercial development might have greatly increased the wealth of China. Though a "China Merchants' Steamship Company" was established, the revenues derived from foreign trade and from domestic commerce were generally regarded as for emergency use rather than a major element in the country's financial structure, although the foreign management of the Chinese customs service provided China with more money than they had expected to obtain from this un-Chinese activity.

Industrial development hinged upon the location of and development of new ores and raw materials. This was not pursued sufficiently, although there were some experiments undertaken. But nothing like the program of government stimulation of industries such as was shortly to occur in Japan developed in China. Only an imperfect appreciation of technology developed. Some arsenals and foundries were constructed with foreign aid, and some students were sent abroad to study, but these efforts were essentially dependent on local officials who were too often hidebound, fearful, or both.

Surprisingly, considering the age-old traditions that had to be combated, in the area of diplomacy the Chinese began to utilize Western methods with some success. Li Hung-chang became the expert in this, and considering the lack of military strength behind him, he and the Tsungli Yamen did surprisingly well. They modernized and reorganized China's approach to foreign relations until by the late 1860's they were on the verge of obtaining equal treaties with Western countries. Unfortunately the Restoration leadership was not quite able to accomplish treaty revision, although both the British minister at Peking, Rutherford B. Alcock, and the American minister, Anson Burlingame, were convinced by 1868 that treaty revision in China's favor was desirable.

The factors which blocked such treaty revision and rendered the remarkable effort of the T'ung-chih Restoration abortive were the demands of British merchants for more extensive privileges, particularly in the internal trade of China, where they bitterly resented the Chinese practice of imposing internal transit dues, and secondly the friction between foreign missionaries and Chinese Christians on the one hand, and anti-foreign Chinese groups on the other.

The anti-Christian feeling had a spectacular outbreak in the "Tientsin Massacre" of 1870 when a Chinese mob destroyed a Roman Catholic orphanage and church and killed nearly fifty people, including priests, nuns, and a French official. This event so enraged foreign feeling against the Chinese that the British merchant groups, which had been opposing the treaty revision recommended by Minister Alcock, were able to obtain powerful support for their position both in China and in London. As a result Alcock's convention was not ratified. Although the T'ung-chih period continued for another four years, it began to lose momentum after the difficulties of 1870, and gradually the many programs of "rehabilitation and self-strengthening" which had been inaugurated were discarded. Tseng Kuo-fan, whose leadership had been indispensable to the "self-strengthening" program, died in 1872. After him the others seemed to lack the incentive to carry on with the same enthusiasm, and at court the influence of Prince Kung came more and more to be replaced by that of the empress dowager, Tz'u-hsi, who proved to be an extremely strong person, but one whose attitudes and methods were unsuitable to the progress of reform, even of the limited Confucian variety that had characterized the T'ung-chih era.

SEMICOLONIAL STATUS AND FOREIGN PRESSURE

H. B. Morse, the author of the classic three-volume *International Relations of the Chinese Empire*, describes the period from 1861 to 1893 as the "period of submission." Certainly by the latter date the Chinese had lost

FIGURE 12.3. Robert Hart, 1866.

control of several aspects of government which commonly are associated with sovereignty. We have already mentioned the fact that tariffs after 1842 were set by treaty and these "convention tariffs," as they were called, could not be changed unilaterally by the Chinese. Indeed, by a curious set of coincidences, Westerners came also to be in charge of the very customs service which collected the import and export duties. This state of affairs arose from developments at Shanghai during the period of Triad rebel control of that city (see p. 286 also), and the general breakdown of imperial authority through central China caused by the T'ai-p'ing Rebellion.

The Westerners were bound by their own treaties with China to pay certain tariffs, but there were no imperial officials on hand to collect them. Furthermore, during the period 1856–1860, the English and French were at war with Peking and so could hardly pay the duties there directly. Nevertheless, it was deemed desirable to maintain the treaty commitments on the Western side, for the whole idea of the argument was to emphasize to the Chinese the legality and even sanctity of the treaties. Hence the Westerners collected taxes on their goods themselves, kept the money in a fund, and later turned it over to the imperial authorities at Peking. They did such a scrupulous job of this that the Chinese, who were accustomed by this time to operations of "squeeze" and private graft by their own officials, were much impressed, and after the 1860 settlements the imperial government invited a British subject, Robert Hart, to organize and take charge of the Customs Service. Hart brought in other foreigners to assist him, together with Chinese, and from 1863 to 1911, under his direction, the collection of tariffs in China was a joint Sino-Western operation. The obvious impairment of Chinese sovereignty which such an arrangement entailed was perhaps compensated for by the fact that the Customs Service under Hart was efficiently managed and produced more dependable revenues to the Peking government than Chinese management could probably have done. Yet the need for foreign direction of such an important area of government was indicative of the sorry state of Chinese government.

Another similar indication, which again had both positive and negative aspects, was the Peking government's appointment of an American, Anson Burlingame, to represent it abroad in 1868. Burlingame had been American minister to China since 1861. A sensitive and understanding man, he was sympathetic to the plight of China, and this was appreciated by the Chinese. Feeling that he might present China's case abroad better than any Chinese could, the imperial government offered to make him *its* representative. He accepted and toured the world (1868–1870), trying to present China's case and to enlist cooperation with China in securing a favorable revision of her treaties with Western countries. But he died of pneumonia in Russia before much could be accomplished. Perhaps he did harm, by overemphasizing China's readiness to partake of new ways, especially Christianity, but his intentions were good. The treaty of 1868 with the United States, which Burlingame drew up and which bears his name, was a considerable step forward toward reciprocity emphasizing mutual good will and the rights of Chinese and Americans respectively to travel, trade, and live in each others' countries. However, even this turned out badly, for within a decade anti-Chinese sentiment rose to such a degree in the American West Coast area, to which many coolies had come to work on railroad construction, that the Congress repudiated the Burlingame Treaty and suspended Chinese immigration.

China, during the "period of submission," also saw large areas of her territory and large numbers of Chinese removed from her control. The extraterritoriality arrangements contained in the early treaties were constantly enlarged and many new areas were declared to be foreign enclaves, where Chinese authority might not intrude. Such events as the Tientsin Massacre of 1870 and the murder of an Englishman named Margary in Yunnan province in 1875 resulted in increased foreign interference. The Chefoo Convention of 1876, which finally settled the Margary affair, opened four interior "ports" on the Yangtze River to foreign residence and authority and explicitly recognized a "British Supreme Court for China." Thus foreigners in China were not subject to Chinese law and authority; but beyond that many Chinese Christian converts began to use their semi-Western status to advantage by getting missionaries and other foreigners to intercede for them when they had brushes with Chinese laws and officials. Also many non-Christian Chinese preferred life in foreign settlements under foreign jurisdiction and contrived to enter them. As Professor Fairbank has said, "Further analysis of the Western century in China should make it plain that the treaty system gradually became a basic component of the power structure of the Chinese state."[1]

---

[1] John K. Fairbank, *Trade and Diplomacy on the China Coast*, Vol. I (Cambridge: Harvard University Press, 1953), p. 476.

FIGURE 12.4. Shanghai bund (landing stage) in the early 1850s.

Borderland Pressures

While Westerners were becoming intricately involved in the governing process in China, they were also exerting strong pressure on border areas around China, and they detached certain dependent states or "hedge countries," as the Chinese often called bordering territories. These pressures were produced by the Russians in the northwest, the British in the southwest from Burma and India, and the French in the south from Indochina. The Russians were the least successful between 1861 and 1893, though they had gained the Maritime Province and the Amur River boundary in the negotiations culminating in 1860. Their next opportunity for expansion at China's expense came as a result of the Moslem rebellion in Chinese Turkistan, or, more broadly, the "new dominion," Sinkiang. There a young Moslem from Tashkent, Yakub Beg, succeeded in ousting Chinese authority and setting up an independent Moslem state, taking the title of emir in 1873. The Russians entered into the far northwestern area of Sinkiang, called Ili, ostensibly to prevent its falling into Yakub Beg's hands (see Chapter 9). They promised to restore it to China whenever she could restore order in Turkistan, which Westerners did not expect to happen. However, they were to be surprised.

Peking sent General Tso Tsung-t'ang, victor over the T'ai-p'ings and other rebels in China proper, to Turkistan and, though it required more than three years, he restored the imperial authority everywhere save Ili. That required another three years of difficult negotiations with the Russians during which one Chinese negotiator, Ch'ung Hou, a neophyte at Western-style diplomacy, almost gave away the whole area and an indemnity besides! Peking denounced the agreement and sentenced Ch'ung to death, but British intervention saved him and brought about a reopening of negotiations. In 1881 the matter was finally settled, and Russia returned sovereignty over the Ili valley to China, in return receiving extensive trading privileges in Chinese Central Asia in a treaty signed at St. Petersburg.

On the southern borderlands China was not so lucky (see also Chapter 8). The British gradually took over the rest of her former dependent state of Burma, the southern part of which had been annexed in 1852. The climax came after Britain's third Burmese war in 1885, which placed the British in control of the entire country. China helplessly recognized British suzerainty in 1886 with the proviso that Burmese decennial missions still be permitted to come to Peking. One more, the last, came in 1895. In addition, Chinese suzerainty over the Himalayan border kingdoms of Sikkim and Bhutan was surrendered in 1886. Tibet was also on the British agenda, but they left it in abeyance for the time being.

Meanwhile the French had penetrated Indochina. They occupied the southern part during the 1860's, and in the 1870's French military forces and explorers penetrated northern Vietnam, seizing Hanoi. The Vietnamese emperor, who as "King of Annam" was a tributary of China, appealed to Peking, and Chinese troops were sent in. In 1884 the French forced the Annamese king to sign a treaty of protection at Hue and then pressed negotiations at Peking for the withdrawal of Chinese troops. Li Hung-chang signed the Li-Fournier Convention, agreeing to withdraw Chinese troops, but, under pressure from pro-war critics at Peking (the *ch'ing-i* "purists"), he could not set a precise date. When the Chinese did not withdraw after a short interlude, the French attacked not only in Vietnam, but with warships along the China coast. The Chinese, now thoroughly alarmed, gave in and signed the Treaty of Tientsin with France in June, 1885, by which China recognized French suzerainty over Vietnam (Annam) unconditionally.

Trouble with Japan

During the 1870's China also began to feel the pressure of her newly modernizing neighbor, Japan. The Japanese, shortly after establishing their new Foreign Office, entered into negotiations with China and established Western-style diplomatic relations with a treaty signed at Tientsin in 1871. The Japanese, new at the game of diplomacy, did not demand a most-favored-nation clause. Hence in this case, in contrast to her treaties with Western nations, China had an equal treaty. However, Japan and China were soon embroiled in argument over the Liu-ch'iu Islands, which China had long considered as one of her dependent kingdoms, but to which Japan also had certain long standing claims, and more importantly over Korea, China's favorite dependent state, for which the Japanese supported independent status. These controversies were to reveal the weakness and ineptness of China even more glaringly than the border controversies with Western countries. With Korea, especially, the Chinese made a desperate effort to maintain their ancient ties, yet failed. However, since these relationships with Japan form the background of the Sino-Japanese War, which marked the final denouement of the Chinese imperial system, they are better left for discussion in subsequent chapters.

Population

Behind all the other problems was one which was only dimly seen, that of population increase. Though Chinese census figures were certainly inaccurate, the population increase from the early Ch'ing period to the mid-nineteenth century was stupendous, rising from about 150 million in 1740 to over 400 million by 1850. After that, with the many rebellions, there seemed to be a decrease—to about 380 million in 1882. However, it should be noted that the machinery of collecting census data had also broken down during the rebellions so that great areas of population went unreported. We cannot be sure of the figures, but the Chinese population by the 1890's had certainly become so large that only a miracle of industrialization and/or some unprecedented program of national coordination for agricultural production could hope to support it above the most marginal level of existence.

By 1894, although the Ch'ing dynasty had been almost miraculously preserved amidst the seemingly overwhelming domestic and foreign pressures that beset it in the middle years of the century, it still had found no solutions to the basic problems of China. There had been a temporary resuscitation during the T'ung-chih Restoration (1862–1874), but the depth of the challenges the modern age presented went completely unmeasured. Nothing but stopgap measures had been taken, and they were about to give way.

BASIC DATES

1821–1850	Reign of Tao-kuang emperor
1844	Final phase of first treaty settlements: American (Wanghsia) and French (Whampoa) Treaties
1850–1864	T'ai-p'ing Rebellion
1851–1861	Reign of Hsien-feng emperor
1853	Nanking falls to T'ai-p'ings; Triad Rebellion
1853–1868	Nien-fei Rebellion
1854	British demand new treaty negotiations
1855–1873	Moslem rebellion in Yunnan
1855–1881	Miao rebellion
1856	Arrow Incident and war
1858	Treaties of Tientsin
1859–1860	Renewal of war; Anglo-French attack in north China
1861–1908	Empress Dowager Tz'u-hsi holds power
1862–1874	T'ung-chih Restoration
1862–1877	Moslem rebellion in Turkistan
1863	Robert Hart becomes superintendent of Chinese customs
1868	Burlingame Treaty with the United States
1868–1870	Burlingame mission
1870	Tientsin Massacre
1875	Margary murder
1876	Chefoo Convention (third treaty settlement)
1881	Ili area regained from Russia
1882	United States closed to Chinese immigration
1884–1885	Sino-French War; French take Annam
1885	British take Burma
1880's–1894	Sino-Japanese rivalry over Korea

SUPPLEMENTARY READING

Fairbank, J. K., E. O. Reischauer, and A. M. Craig. *East Asia: The Modern Transformation.* Boston, 1965. Revised and abbreviated edition, 1973.

Hsü, I. C. Y. *The Rise of Modern China.* New York, 1970. Chaps. 9–14.

Latourette, K. S. *The Chinese: Their History and Culture.* New York, 1948.

Li, C .N. *The Political History of China, 1840–1928.* Princeton, N.J., 1956.

Li, Dun J. *The Ageless Chinese, A History.* New York, 1965.

Teng, S. Y. and J. K. Fairbank. *China's Response to the West: A Documentary Survey 1839–1923.* Cambridge. Mass., 1961.

ADVANCED READING

Banno, M. *China and the West, 1858–1861: The Origins of the Tsungli Yamen.* Cambridge, Mass., 1964.

Boardman, E. P. *Christian Influences upon the Ideology of the Taiping Rebellion, 1851–1864.* Madison, Wis., 1952.

Ch'en, G. *Tseng Kuo-fan, Pioneer Promoter of the Steamship in China.* Peking, 1935.

―――― *Tso Tsung-tang, Pioneer Promoter of the Modern Dockyard and the Woolen Mill in China.* Peking, 1938.

Cohen, P. A. *China and Christianity: The Missionary Movement and the Growth of Antiforeignism, 1860–1870.* Cambridge, Mass., 1963.

Fairbank, J. K. *Trade and Diplomacy along the China Coast, 1842–1854.* Cambridge, Mass., 1953.

Fairbank, J. K., ed. *The Chinese World Order: Traditional China's Foreign Relations.* Cambridge, Mass.. 1968.

Feuerwerker, Albert. *China's Early Industrialization: Sheng Hsuan-huai (1844–1916) and Mandarin Enterprise.* Cambridge, Mass., 1958.

Haldane, Charlotte. *The Last Great Empress of China.* London, 1965.

Hsü, I. C. Y. *China's Entrance into the Family of Nations: The Diplomatic Phase, 1858–1880.* Cambridge, Mass., 1968.

―――― *The Ili Crisis: A Study of Sino-Russian Diplomacy, 1871–1881.* Oxford, 1965.

Hsü, I. C. Y., ed. *Readings in Modern Chinese History.* New York, 1971.

Hummel, A. W., ed. *Eminent Chinese of the Ch'ing Period.* Washington, D.C., 1944.

King, Frank H. H. *Money and Monetary Policy in China, 1845–1895.* Cambridge, Mass., 1965.

Latourette, K. S. *History of Christian Missions in China.* London, 1929; Taipei, 1966.

Levenson, J. R. *Confucian China and Its Modern Fate.* Berkeley, Calif., 1964–1965. Vols. 2 and 3 are pertinent.

―――― *Modern China and Its Confucian Past.* Garden City, N.Y., Doubleday Anchor Book, 1964.

Levenson, J. R., ed. *Modern China: An Interpretive Anthology*. London, 1971.
Liu, K. C. *Anglo-American Steamship Rivalry in China, 1862–1874*. Cambridge, Mass., 1962.
MacNair, H. F., ed. *Modern Chinese History: Selected Readings*. Shanghai, 1927. Translations of original sources.
Meadows, T. T. *The Chinese and Their Rebellions*. London, 1856. Old, but excellent.
Michael, Franz and Chung-Li Chang. *The Taiping Rebellion: History and Documents*. Seattle, 1966.
Morse, H. B. *The International Relations of the Chinese Empire*. London, 1910-1918. A three-volume work; Vols. I and II provide a wealth of detail for this period. Morse worked in the Chinese Customs under Robert Hart.
Pelcovits, N. *Old China Hands and the Foreign Office*. New York, 1948. A sophisticated study of British policy arguments.
Rawlinson, J. L. *China's Struggle for Naval Development*. Cambridge, Mass., 1967.
Schurmann, Franz and O. Schell, eds. *Imperial China*. New York: Vintage Book, 1967.
Selby, John. *The Paper Dragon: An Account of the China Wars, 1840–1900*. London, 1968.
Shih, Vincent Y. C. *The Taiping Ideology: Its Sources, Interpretation and Influences*. Seattle, 1967.
Spector, Stanley. *Li Hung-chang and the Huai Army: A Study in Nineteenth Century Chinese Regionalism*. Seattle, 1964.
Spence, Jonathan. *To Change China: Western Advisers in China, 1620–1960*. Boston, 1969. Chaps. 2–5.
Swisher, E. *China's Management of the American Barbarians: A Study of Sino-American Relations, 1841–1961, With Documents*. New Haven, 1953.
Teng, S. Y. *The Taiping Rebellion and the Western Powers*. New York, 1971.
Wakeman, F. E. *Strangers at the Gate: Social Disorder in South China, 1839–1861*. Berkeley, 1966.
Williams, S. W. *The Middle Kingdom*. New York, 1883. The work of a contemporary observer.
Wright, M. C. *The Last Stand of Chinese Conservatism: The T'ung-chih Restoration*. Stanford, Calif., 1957.

Chapter 13

Japan: Meiji Restoration and Modernization to 1895

The years 1868 to 1895 were years of tempestuous change for Japan, matched in intensity in only two preceding eras of Japanese history, the Taika Reform era of the seventh century, which produced the first coherent governmental structure in Japan, and the sixteenth century era of national unification (see Vol. 1, pp. 486 and 555). This first and most vital part of the Meiji era, which began with the restoration of Japan's imperial house to a position of prestige and authority it had not enjoyed since Heian times and ended with Japan's first foreign war in almost three centuries, the Sino-Japanese War of 1894–95, saw the destruction of a now archaic and outmoded feudal system, a remarkable degree of modernization in all areas of Japanese life, the establishment of a national political structure, and the beginnings of Japanese territorial expansion.

Although the main emphasis in these early Meiji years was on progress and activity, there was also a strong emphasis on caution and control; caution against involvement in projects that would upset the financial equilibrium of the nation, and control by government leaders of unauthorized behavior and even of thought. Descriptions of the Meiji era almost always begin with reference to the Charter Oath, a declaration issued in the name of the Meiji emperor in April, 1868. It is an extremely progressive document, whose five main points, when taken together, clearly sounded the death knell of feudalism and pointed in the direction of uninhibited change. In this document the emperor proclaimed that: (1) deliberative assemblies shall be widely established and all matters settled by public discussion; (2) all classes, high and low, shall unite in vigorously carrying out the administration of affairs of state; (3) the common people, no less than civil and military officials, shall each be allowed to pursue his own calling so that there may be no discontent; (4) evil customs of the past shall be broken off

FIGURE 13.1. The Meiji emperor.

and everything based upon the just laws of Nature; (5) knowledge shall be sought throughout the world so as to strengthen the imperial rule.[1]

However, lest the caution and control aspect of the Meiji era be forgotten, three other documents, each in its own way, contain ideas as important for understanding the Meiji psychology as the Charter Oath itself. These are the Imperial Rescript on Education, the "Reasons for Opposing the Korean Expedition" by Okubo Toshimichi, and the Commentaries on the Constitution by Ito Hirobumi. The Imperial Rescript on Education was not issued until 1890, but it reflected the thinking of Meiji government leaders as to the limits which should be put on westernization in general and Western-style education in particular. In it the Emperor speaks the language of the Confucian tradition:

> Know Ye our subjects: Our Imperial ancestors have founded Our empire on a basis broad and everlasting, and have deeply and firmly implanted virtue; Our subjects ever united in loyalty and filial piety have from generation to generation illustrated the beauty thereof. This is the glory of the fundamental character of Our Empire, and herein also lies the source of Our education. Ye, Our subjects be filial to your parents, affectionate to your brothers and sisters; as husbands and wives be harmonious, as friends true . . . and thus guard and maintain the prosperity of Our Imperial throne coeval with heaven and earth. So shall ye not

---

[1] William T. De Bary, ed. *Sources of the Japanese Tradition* (New York: Columbia University Press, 1958), p. 644.

only be Our good and faithful subjects, but render illustrious the best traditions of your forefathers . . .[2]

Okubo's "Reasons for Opposing the Korean Expedition" is a rather long document presented to the Council of State in the fall of 1873 in answer to advocates of a strong foreign policy and of overseas expansion. Expansion, like westernization, was pursued, but it is important to realize the cautious limits which the Meiji government set on expansion and these are nowhere better expressed than in Okubo's arguments. Okubo declared that the Meiji reign must consolidate its strength in Japan itself. He warned that the tremendous expenditures necessary for foreign wars would drain Japan and undermine the government's domestic projects. He also saw clearly the danger of accumulating a large debt in war which would open the way for European intervention. Okubo further wrote that the goal of the government should be elimination of unequal treaties and the restoration of complete Japanese independence rather than overseas adventures such as a war with Korea.

In the domestic policies in early Meiji Japan there was a strong drive for parliamentary and constitutional government, but here again the elements of caution and control were powerfully exercised by government leaders. Ito Hirobumi, the principal author of the Meiji Constitution, which was promulgated in 1889, has left many commentaries on his handiwork. But the following excerpt from an address to the heads of prefectural assemblies is a succinct statement of his main idea:

> The Constitution recently promulgated is, needless to say, a constitution by imperial grant. As you well know, the term "imperial grant" means that it was initiated by the sovereign himself and that it was sanctioned and granted to his subjects by the sovereign. It is my hope that you will always remember this fact—and inscribe it in your hearts—that this Constitution is the gift of a benevolent and charitable emperor to the people of his country.[3]

In the following pages as we discuss the destruction of feudalism, the process of modernization, the various political developments that led to the establishment of a new governmental structure, and the beginnings of expansion in these early Meiji years, we should bear in mind not only the promise of progress contained in the Charter Oath, but also the elements of caution and control exemplified in the Imperial Rescript on Education, Okubo's "Reasons," and Ito's commentary.

DESTRUCTION OF FEUDALISM

The coalition of four western clans, consisting of Satsuma, Choshu, Tosa, and Hizen (Sat-Cho Do-Hi), by May 1968 had defeated the Tokugawa

[2] Ibid., pp. 646–647.
[3] Ibid., p. 666.

and overthrown the shogunate (see Chapter 6). This did not necessarily mean that the victorious party would now do away with feudalism and the various institutions through which the Tokugawa had governed the country. As has been shown, up to the very outbreak of the civil war there had been various negotiations looking toward a settlement with the Tokugawa regime, and even after its demise, some elements in the coalition no doubt expected a four-clan dominated feudal regime to replace the old one. The new leadership was quite confused in its ideology, having abandoned the Jōi (expel the barbarian) part of its slogan, and even the Sonnō (revere the emperor) part might not have been taken too seriously, since the Meiji emperor was still a young boy. It was by no means a foregone conclusion that the change of government leadership would mean the destruction of the feudal order, for the great fiefs of Japan, with the exception of the Tokugawa, were still intact. However, two factors presaged changes of a more drastic nature than a mere feudal reordering: (1) the pressure of relations with the outside world, which made it desirable or even necessary for Japan to act as a unit if it were to escape from the inequalities of the treaty network which had already been forged, and (2) the fact that the real leadership of the new government lay not in the feudal lords themselves, but in a group of young, lower ranking samurai who could more easily than their masters conclude that the feudal system was inadequate, because they had less stake in it. Practical considerations were paramount with them. They were to become, as one scholar has called them, "ministers of modernization."

These new leaders included Okubo Toshimichi and Saigo Takamori of Satsuma, Kido Koin, Yamagata Aritomo, Ito Hirobumi, and Inoue Kaoru of Choshu, Goto Shojiro, Fukuoka Kotei, and Itagaki Taisuke of Tosa, Okuma Shigenobu and Eto Shimpei of Hizen, and Iwakura Tomomi of the imperial court. Though Kido was perhaps the most brilliant and sensitive and Saigo the most potent in samurai virtues, it was the austere Okubo "like an iceberg in the Arctic Ocean" who dominated the government until his death in 1878. After that, Ito in civilian affairs and Yamagata in military were the key men.

Anticipating the reemergence of clan rivalries after the defeat of the Tokugawa, they immediately undertook to persuade the leaders of their clans to relinquish their feudal land titles to the throne. The Tokugawa in defeat had, of course, surrendered most of their vast land holdings, but as yet it had not been decided whether these would remain in imperial hands or be redistributed among other feudal lords. The crux was whether or not the four cooperating clans could be persuaded to turn over their land titles, and the leaders of the new government exerted all their energies to convince the daimyo of their own clans that this policy would be in their own interest as well as that of the nation. They played upon various themes, such as the necessity of presenting a united front to foreign countries, the assurance that daimyo would play a leading role in the new governmental structure, and the promise of a very generous financial settlement. The surrender of the fiefs was accomplished by stages, the first being the acceptance in principle of the idea by the daimyo of the great Sat-Cho Do-Hi clans in early 1869, after which they were quickly appointed to governorships of their former lands and granted an income equal to one-half their previous revenue. The central government assumed payment of the stipends of the samurai who served the daimyo.

This settlement was much too generous as it proved, for it could not be reconciled with the financial problems and needs of the government, and it did not remain the permanent settlement. The land titles remained in the hands of the central government, but the pensions and stipends of the daimyo and their samurai were curtailed considerably before the feudal settlement was completed. By 1873 the government had drawn up a plan whereby the pensions and stipends were to be converted voluntarily into government bonds, bearing interest and with periods of maturity ranging up to fifteen years. This was made compulsory in 1876, and had the effect of relieving the government of the necessity of making huge cash outlays each year to daimyo and samurai and gave it a chance to establish a minimum of financial equilibrium. This final settlement, though far less attractive than the original one, was by no means ungenerous, particularly to the daimyo and wealthier samurai. These, if they lived on their interest (which ranged from five to ten per cent) and later invested their principal wisely, could achieve financial leadership in the new Japan. Numbers of them accomplished this, and lower samurai, whose interest receipts were not nearly enough to support livelihood in the manner to which they were accustomed, were literally forced into business. Of course, many could not make the transition and became embittered, but the samurai spirit unleashed into business "for the good of the nation" became a major input in developing aggressive entrepreneurship.

Another aspect of the liquidation of feudalism was a new land tax, collected in money. Though there has been much argument concerning the extent to which landholders succeeded in undervaluing their land and its rice yield to minimize their taxes, there is no doubt that the new government realized a great deal of revenue from the reorganization. To obtain additional funds the government took forced loans from various wealthy merchants, and received a particularly large credit from the house of Mitsui, which was given thereby a privileged position in managing government finance, and whose credit made possible the floating of a seven per cent loan in London.

While the financial settlements were being made, the feudal structure was further undermined by the abolition of the very classes and class distinctions which had comprised it. This does not mean that the new regime was egalitarian, but new types of class distinction were substituted for old, and highest honors went to a new nobility which had performed some service for the state or were somehow associated with its leadership, the *kazoku*; the samurai, now relieved of their swords, became *shizoku* (gentry), which while an honored ranking, carried none of the privileges over life and property of the common people which the samurai had formerly had; all others became *heimin* (commoners), with presumably equal rights, although the former *eta* class (butchers, scavengers, etc.) continued to suffer social discrimination.

WESTERNIZATION AND CENTRALIZATION

While Okubo, Iwakura, and the others of the inner circle of Meiji leadership were destroying the forms of feudalism, they were also establishing the foundations of a highly centralized political, social, and economic structure that was to endure until the mid-twentieth century. This began in the spring of 1868 with the transfer of the imperial residence from Kyoto to Edo, now renamed Tokyo or Eastern Capital. The move to Tokyo had removed the court and the government from the immediate supervision of those clans which had backed the Restoration, and it gave young samurai leaders of the government such as Okubo a freedom of action they might not otherwise have had. To carry out the "imperial wishes" a Council of State (*Dajokan*) was organized as the supreme lawmaking and enforcing body. This contained six executive departments—civil affairs, imperial household, finance, justice, foreign affairs and war—in which princes of the blood held titular control, while the real leaders at first were merely "advisors" to these august personages. Later the actual leaders assumed some of the high offices themselves. The inner organization of the government underwent a number of changes in the early years of Meiji, but these did not seriously affect the operation of the government, which remained centralized in the hands of the dozen or so leaders who had directed the Restoration. In fact it narrowed somewhat after 1873 following a split in the Council over the question of war with Korea. This matter will be discussed subsequently in connection with other expansionist activities, but its political effect was to eliminate from the government most of the Hizen and Tosa elements and Okubo's Satsuma rival, Saigo Takamori, leaving ultimate authority in the hands of Okubo, Iwakura, and Kido, with Okubo assuming the leading position until his death in 1878.

Religion

One of the most interesting changes in these early years involved the Department of Religion, which for a time occupied a preeminent position in the governmental structure, since it was placed outside and "above" the other departments. The Tokugawa system of tacitly approving Buddhist supervision of all religious bodies, and the management of Shinto shrines by Buddhist priests, was replaced in the Shintoist fervor of the Restoration by a new bureau which was anti-Buddhist, actually being a "Department of Shinto" given "supreme control over matters regarding the worships of the Gods and the different orders of the Priesthood." Various laws were promulgated which required that Shinto shrines which had been utilizing Buddhist statuary and had been under the management of Buddhist priests must "correct themselves." The new situation provoked a reaction from the Buddhists, who set up such an outcry that the "Department of Shinto" was abolished in April, 1872, and replaced by a more neutrally oriented Department of Religion, which would have supervision over all religious bodies and which made an obvious effort at rapprochement with the Buddhists. Nevertheless, there was a great deal of tension between Buddhists and Shintoists during the next several years, and in 1877 the Department of Religion was reorganized and demoted, this time becoming a Bureau of Temples and Shrines and being placed under the direction of the Home Ministry Department. Shinto and Buddhism were to have official equal but separate status.

The Tokugawa ban of Christianity, which had been ritualized into cross-trampling ceremonies, was still in effect as the Meiji government took hold; indeed, there was intensified persecution of Japanese Christians amid the Shintoist temper of the early years of the new regime. However, as Westerners appeared in increasing numbers in Japan it became apparent that there would be serious international repercussions if this continued. Hence government leaders reviewed the religious situation, desiring at once to be able to present to the world a policy of religious toleration, but at the same time wishing to utilize the Shinto creed as an ideological buttress for the restored emperor and the new government. Their final resolution of this problem was to make a division in Shinto, which, however artificial and illogical, was extremely useful. In earlier chapters traditional Shinto has been described as a combination of nature worship, fertility cults, myths about the gods and the creation of Japan, and the divine origin and nature of the emperor. The new division of Shinto separated the imperial tradition from the rest of the cult and made loyalty to and worship of the emperor the function of Shinto *shrines*, which were differentiated from Shinto *churches*. The latter could carry on whatever peculiar forms of nature or other worship they might have developed. Japanese subjects were free to practice these, or Buddhist, Christian, or other religious observances as they pleased—hence there was religious freedom. But every Japanese, as a condition of his nationality, must be connected with a Shinto shrine, which was designated a nonreligious institution, but wherein worship of the Emperor and his god ancestors would be required. This division of Shinto into shrines and churches was first made in 1882 and after that the development of state Shinto as the "national faith" of Japan proceeded steadily.

Education

Another area in which centralization was accomplished was education. Education was related to the religious system described above since state Shinto observances became prominent features of public school programs, and on many special occasions required formal obeisance to the emperor and the gods. Indeed, it might be said that the "national faith" became the ultimate frame of reference of the entire educational system. However, the goal of the Meiji leaders was not only "national faith," but also national ability, and they realized that the old-fashioned feudal idea of tutoring limited to a few would not equip Japan for competition in the modern world.

In 1871 a Ministry of Education was established whose primary objective was the elimination of illiteracy. The Council of State proclaimed that in the future there should be "no community with an illiterate family and no family with an illiterate person," and in 1872 a compulsory primary school education law was put into effect. French models were employed in the educational administrative system at first. The country was divided into eight university districts, and these were subdivided into middle and primary school districts. However, there was much experimentation in the 1870's, emphasizing practical subjects and the stimulation of the individual. This was partly the result of American influence, for beginning with Professor David Murray of Rutgers in 1873 numerous American advisors worked on Japanese educational problems, and partly the result of the efforts of Western-inspired Japanese liberals. In the latter category Fukuzawa Yukichi's brilliant *Encouragement of Learning*, which sold over three million installments between 1872 and 1876, was perhaps the most significant. Fukuzawa, denouncing Confucian scholars as "rice-consuming dictionaries," advocated "learning that is close to the needs of everyday life," and built on principles of independence and self-respect for the individual.

By the end of the 1870's old line Confucianist opposition was almost routed, and in 1879 a brief attempt at educational decentralization was made in which local school boards were formed. The country proved unready for this step. Local communities would not support the schools, and the following year there was a reversion to centralized control. Then, during the 1880's, the concept of education for individual improvement lost ground to that of state service. For some years this trend remained quite Western, especially German, in orientation. Mori Arinori, who was much influenced by Bismarckian concepts, as minister of education from 1885 to 1889 gave a strong impetus to making education state centered while retaining "foreign" subjects as the core of the curriculum. This was, as we shall see later, quite in line with what Ito Hirobumi, the author of the Meiji Constitution, was attempting to do in the political world. Indeed, it was Ito who appointed Mori as minister.

Private schools, like Fukuzawa's Keio University and a few others, resisted this trend, but the Ministry of Education did not allow their certificates equal accreditation with the national schools and they lost ground. In addition, in the climate of state centered education, truly reactionary tendencies began to appear. Confucian-Shinto advocates, while applauding the idea that state ends must be served by education, sought to define those state ends by stressing traditional patterns of morality and loyalty. The emperor's Confucian tutor, Motoda Eifu, setting forth his ideas under the banner of "imperial wishes," stressed that however practical Western learning might seem, it was inferior to oriental ideas on morals and ethics. As early as 1884 in daily audiences with the emperor, Motoda was stressing the need for settling upon a "national doctrine" which would give voice to "the teachings of our ancestors" and make "rebellion out of the question." The Western-oriented leaders of the Meiji government did not like Motoda (Ito once threatened to resign if Motoda's imperial audiences were not confined to morning hours only), but they did not want rebellion either, and Motoda was plucking at chords of loyalty that were deeply imbedded in Japanese society. In 1889 the assassination of Mori by a "patriot" who considered that the minister had not showed sufficient veneration for the imperial ancestors at Ise Shrine brought educational issues to something of a climax. The warnings of Motoda were heeded, and in November 1890, the emperor issued the famous Imperial Rescript on Education, which, in words cited at the beginning of this chapter, proclaimed filial piety and loyalty to emperor and state as the basis of the Japanese educational system, presumably for all time.

Industrialization

Government sponsored industrialization was yet another factor in the trend toward centralization of power in the early Meiji period. No private group had the courage, money, or vision to undertake the steps to begin catching up with Western countries economically, but the Sat-Cho Do-Hi oligarchs had the courage, and (excepting Saigo, who balked at building railroads) the vision. Money was secured from the new tax structure and certain carefully placed loans. With an English loan they began railroad building in 1871, and though it took a full decade to complete the first hundred miles of track, the line was planned carefuly so that by 1880 the main eastern (Kanto) cities were linked, as were the main Kansai (Kobe-Osaka-Kyoto area) cities, and the joining of the two districts was not far in the future. The Tokyo-Yokohama line reduced the cost of overland transport between those cities by 98 per cent and carried 2,000,000 passengers in 1880. Furthermore the government's success in railroad construction and operation stimulated private capital to enter the field as well, and private lines were soon blossoming.

Other industries followed a similar pattern. The government entered mining and shipbuilding especially, employing foreign technicians and modern equipment, and established models for private venture later to follow. It also went into cement, glass and brick production, silk reeling, and textile manufacture. Government enterprise in these many fields did not hamper private development; on the contrary, the government also endeavored to attract private investment, worked out many production difficulties to the later benefit of private industry, and sold many of its plants to private interests after they were operating soundly. Indeed, only in the field of telegraph construction did the government maintain an absolute monopoly, and it is clear that the government's active entry into industrial development was largely responsible for Japan's building up a modern industrial plant in the almost incredibly short period of two decades after the Restoration.

However, it is also true that government industrial enterprise was a major contributor to centralization of power. It controlled the direction of industrial development, significantly placing emphasis on strategic industry, and in its gradual disposition of government properties it made sure that they went to insiders or to those groups whom it would be profitable to bind closely to the governing oligarchy. The ease with which government officials shuttled between the financial and industrial world illustrates this policy, and it is clear that the foundations of what was later to be known and condemned as the *zaibatsu* (financial clique) system, which intertwined money power and political power, were laid in the early Meiji period.

The Army

Another instrument favorable to centralization which the oligarchy held was the army, or more precisely, the power of conscription. Conscription, which was instituted in 1870, following French and (after the Franco-Prussian War) German models, contributed to the breakup of the feudal class structure. Older samurai resented the arming of peasants and for a time, the peasants may have liked the idea of receiving arms. But conscription was by no means a liberalizing measure. Peasants soon feared and evaded it, and the term blood tax (*ketsu eki*), by which the system was known, did not add to its popularity.

The conscript army of the early Meiji period was ragged and unwilling, barely able to put down the two diehard samurai revolts which challenged the new government in the 1870's (1874 in Hizen; 1877 in Satsuma). However, Minister of War Yamagata Aritomo, the chief organizer of the conscript system, worked hard on morale and indoctrination, issuing admonishments against "idle chatter about people's rights." An Imperial Rescript to Soldiers and Sailors in 1882 reminded the conscripts:

> We [the emperor] are your supreme Commander-in-Chief. Our relations with you will be most intimate when we rely upon you as Our limbs and you look up to Us as your head. . . . The soldier and sailor should consider loyalty their essential duty . . . neither be led astray by current opinions nor meddle in politics, but with single heart fulfill your essential duty of loyalty, and bear in mind that duty is weightier than a mountain, while death is lighter than a feather.

Certainly by 1894, when the first test of foreign war since Hideyoshi's invasion of Korea came, Japanese conscripts and their officer corps were particularly responsive to centralized direction in pursuit of whatever national goals the oligarchs, through the emperor, might prescribe.

CREATION OF A NATIONAL GOVERNMENT

The politics of the Meiji era to 1895 were turbulent and exciting. Both a constitution and a national Diet became part of the governmental apparatus before the smoke cleared away. Nevertheless, a long range assessment shows that the main theme of the politics was not to be the victory of parliamentary forces, but rather the triumph of the conservative oligarchy which had engineered the Restoration and undertaken to build Japan into a strong, Western-style, but authoritarian, state.

Despite the concentration of power which the overthrow of the feudal system and centralization in the several areas already discussed brought to the oligarchy, the ultimate political composition of the new Japan was determined only after the oligarchy had met and mastered severe tests in the political arena. These were of two types, which, however, were not mutually exclusive. The first challenge was from the side of reaction. This may be dismissed quickly, as its overt influence in the Meiji era was dissipated soon after major flareups in the 1870's, although the sentiments it engendered were to remain as a sullen ideological undercurrent through decades of westernization and were to flare into prominence again in the 1930's as a principal ingredient of the ultranationalism of that era.

This reactionary opposition centered around the defection of Saigo Takamori, Eto Shimpei, and others from the Restoration coalition in 1873. The immediate issue was whether the government would launch a "samurai" expedition against Korea to avenge alleged insults from that kingdom, an idea which, taken in the domestic Japanese political scene, embodied a last effort of disgruntled samurai to regain their place in the sun as heroes and leaders of Japan. The more Western-minded and experienced oligarchs, rallying around Okubo and Iwakura, vetoed the plan, ousted the war advocates, and repressed the subsequent samurai revolts with their new conscript army. Saigo himself, his forces defeated and scattered, committed suicide in approved samurai fashion in 1878. Rebellion did not recur; however, adherents and admirers of Saigo organized a secret society, the Genyosha or Black Ocean Society, in 1881 to keep alive his memory, samurai ideals, and reactionary-ultranationalist attitudes. It remained a pressure group through the middle Meiji years and became a sort of parent society to

FIGURE 13.2. Saigo Takamori.

many similar groups which were organized after the turn of the twentieth century.

More important and more troublesome to the government oligarchs than the reactionary opposition was the opposition of those groups which entered the political lists to demand a parliament and a constitution. These we may call the liberals, although their liberalism was often imperfect and confused. In their formative stage they had much in common with the reactionaries, and their leadership was also composed of disaffected samurai. Indeed, Itagaki Taisuke, the first great liberal leader and the founder of the Liberal party (*Jiyūtō*), left the government with Saigo in 1873. Okuma Shigenobu, who ranked second only to Itagaki in the movement, was ousted from the oligarchy for exposing a Hokkaido development scandal. These men, significantly, were from Tosa and Hizen respectively, elements which had been gradually dropped from the Restoration coalition. Hence their disaffection may in the first instance have been due largely to sectional rather than ideological differences. However, both the weapons with which they chose to fight the oligarchy and the goals they set were important. Rejecting rebellion and reaction, they chose the newly learned Western-style course of political action, declaring as their goals "people's rights" and an elective national parliament. In support of these goals Itagaki's Liberal party, formally organized in 1881 after several years of preliminary activities, especially attracted rural elements of all classes. Okuma's party, organized

FIGURE 13.3.   Itagaki Taisuke.

FIGURE 13.4. Okuma Shigenobu.

in 1882 after his ouster from the government and known as the Progressive party (Kaishintō), particularly attracted bourgeois elements.

Just before the formation of these parties the pressure of "people's rights" advocates against the government had reached a peak of intensity. Okubo, the strongest of the oligarchs, had been assassinated in 1878, Iwakura (d. 1883) was nearing the end of his powers, and their younger protégé, Ito, was not yet in command of the situation. The government tried to counter the rising tide with a law against public meetings in 1880, but Okuma, who, though still a member of the oligarchy, had become more and more estranged from the others and more and more sympathetic to the popular movement, submitted a petition directly to the emperor early in 1881 urging the election of representatives to a national assembly the following year. This antagonized his colleagues further, but, though they isolated him, he found his chance to strike back hard that summer by denouncing the Hokkaido affair. This was the final straw and Okuma was forced to resign. But something had to be done to stem the popular fury. On October 12, 1881, the day after Okuma left the government, the emperor announced that a national assembly would be convened, although not until 1890, and that meanwhile careful study of plans for a constitution would be undertaken. After this government pressure against the formation of parties and the holding of meetings was temporarily relaxed, with the result that the formation of the two major popular parties occurred. Of course, they expected to influence the form and content of the new constitution.

Such was not the case. To oppose the popular parties the government sponsored a party of its own, the Constitutional Imperial party (*Rikken Teiseitō*), but beyond that, during the ensuing decade, it did its best to undermine the popular movement. This included attempts to "buy off" its leaders. Itagaki was enticed into accepting a government invitation to go abroad in 1883 at a very crucial time for his party. Later Goto Shojiro, his chief party lieutenant, was brought into the government as communications minister, and Okuma himself was enticed back into the government as foreign minister early in 1888. In addition, the parties did much to hurt each other and themselves. They obtained the financial backing of rival interests, Mitsubishi (Progressives) and Mitsui (Liberals) respectively, and much of the pressure they could exert was channeled into business rivalries, rather than focused on securing real parliamentary government. Furthermore, the parties split into factions, with the left wing of the Liberal party, especially, becoming extremely chauvinistic and violent. This element was led by Oi Kentaro, who was an advocate of French revolutionary ideas, but who sometimes cooperated with reactionary-ultranationalist members of the Genyosha in "direct action" plots to embarrass the government. With economic depression and much unrest in the mid-eighties, the government used the excuse of such plots to muzzle the press and harass public meetings.

As for the planning of constitutional government, not only were political party leaders and their advocates not consulted, they were not even allowed to know what was going on. Ito Hirobumi, now chief of the oligarchs, was the key figure in the planning. As chairman of the Commission on the Constitution he visited Europe to obtain ideas; then, with his assistants, he drafted the document in secret. He had visited Prussia in 1872 and his chief assistant, Inoue Kowashi, had translated the Prussian constitution. Ito again visited Europe in 1882 to gather further ideas, and although there was strong support for a British style parliamentary system from Okuma's Progressive party, he found the advice of experts on the Bismarckian system, Rudolph von Gneist, Lorenz von Stein, and Hermann Roesler, more to his liking. Amply warned by them against allowing a popularly elected legislature to interfere in matters pertaining to military and foreign affairs and the imperial household, he took pains that this should not happen.

When the new constitution was unveiled by imperial proclamation in 1889, it was as a gift of the emperor to his subjects, and a new peerage, a Privy Council and a Cabinet, had already been established. The peerage, made up of loyal supporters of the oligarch regime, would provide members for an upper, stabilizing "House of Peers" in the new constitutional structure; the privy council, a group of imperial advisors especially appointed to review and approve the new constitution before its promulgation (with Ito as chairman), was given constitutional status as the principal advisory body to the emperor; the cabinet, whose several ministers were in charge of the executive departments of the government, was after the constitution as before to be appointed by the emperor and to be responsible to him.

FIGURE 13.5. Ito Hirobumi, the architect of the Meiji Constitution.

Imperial household and military budgets remained the same with or without Diet approval (the Diet could increase, but not decrease them).

Despite the restricted nature of the Japanese parliamentary system as established under the Constitution of 1889, when the first elected Diet met in 1890 it became clear immediately that the oligarchs were not going to be able to hold their power without a struggle. Although the qualified voter ranks were limited to 450,000 (men over 25 who paid 15 yen or more national tax), the lower house of the first Diet was largely made up of political party men who were vehement critics of the oligarchy. Their power was largely negative, based on the Constitution's Article XXXVII, which specified that every law required the consent (or according to Ito, the "approval") of the imperial Diet. It could not force a cabinet out of office by a vote of no confidence, nor could it withhold funds from the administration (for the previous year's budget would continue until a new one had been voted), nor could it pass legislation over the veto of the cabinet. But it could refuse its consent to any law submitted by the administration. This it did again and again in the first four years of its existence, bringing about such a deadlock that the cabinet was shuffled three times in order to allay opposition. First Yamagata was premier, while Ito held the chairmanship of the Privy Council; then the oligarchy's financial wizard, Matsukata, took the premiership; and in 1892, Ito, himself, but at no time did the cabinet admit responsibility to the Diet. By 1894 the Diet had been dissolved four times, with new elections held in the hope of obtaining a more passive lower house, but, despite the fact that repressive police measures were employed by the Home Ministry to influence the elections, the Lower House remained obdurate.

Although the political struggle involved various matters, the real issue was that of cabinet responsibility to the Diet. This became very clear in Ito's premiership, when the lower house twice voted no confidence, the last time after new elections in the spring of 1894 by a huge majority, 253 to 17. Yet Ito did not resign. However, he and his government and perhaps the whole system of oligarchic control was saved by the outbreak of the Sino-Japanese War in July of that year. The following autumn a contrite and patriotic Diet reconvened to vote for the entire government program, including huge war budgets. Ito remained premier until September, 1896. The failure of the parliamentary parties to establish the principle of Cabinet responsibility to the Diet at this point was crucial, for they were not to have such an opportunity until after World War II. This failure was in part the result of oligarchic manipulation, but it was in no small measure the fault of the party politicians themselves, especially their irresponsibility on matters of foreign policy. For it is a fact that they contributed a great deal, perhaps even more than the oligarchs, to the coming of that very Sino-Japanese War which spoiled the first and best chance for parliamentary government in Japan. In their efforts to discredit the oligarchs wherever possible, they frequently employed the device of calling them weak-kneed, afraid to be "strong" in foreign affairs, to the point that when the oligarchs went to war, they had no choice but to support them. In favor of the oligarchs it should be said that the election of 1890, which seems to have been quite fairly conducted, was a landmark, the first popular election in Asia. And, although others of his oligarchic colleagues remained obdurate, Ito himself during the 1890's came to feel that cabinets of the future could not rule without popular party support.

BEGINNINGS OF EXPANSION

The Sino-Japanese War will be discussed more fully in the next chapter, but the background of Japanese expansion deserves mention here. The foreign policy of the Meiji government, at least until 1894, was much less expansionist than one might expect looking back over the aggressive expansionism of the World War II era. The government oligarchy under Okubo, as we have seen, purged itself of the advocates of expansionist adventures in Korea in 1873 at the cost of creating very serious internal tension in Japan. The remaining oligarchs, smarting under accusations of cowardice from dissident samurai, sought to retrieve their reputations by maneuvering China into helping Japan obtain a treaty with Korea in 1876 and by capitalizing on China's diplomatic blunders to make effective shadowy earlier Japanese claims to the Liu-ch'iu Islands. The Liu-ch'iu affair included a Japanese expedition to Formosa in 1874 to obtain redress for the killing of a party of Liu-ch'iu islanders by Formosan savage tribes. This helped to quiet samurai criticism of the oligarchs' "weakness" over Korea by giving them some relatively safe military employment, and it worried the Chinese so much about the possibility of their being made to pay damages for the Formosan cruelties that they forgot to contest the Liu-ch'iu ownership question seriously.

Otherwise Japan's early Meiji diplomacy was decidedly mild. There was the possibility of a clash with Russia over boundary questions. Nationals of both countries were colonizing Sakhalin and the Kuril Islands. Sakhalin was felt by both parties to be the more valuable, but the Japanese accepted the lesser end of the bargain for the sake of amity, giving up their claims to Sakhalin in return for Russian recognition of Japan's suzerainty over the Kurils. A treaty to this effect was signed at St. Petersburg in 1875. Another example of Japan's avoidance of adventurism in foreign affairs in this period is to be seen in her relations with Hawaii. She had many opportunities for political meddling there between 1880 and 1898, but her governing oligarchy scrupulously avoided this, even when the temptations were greatest, as in 1881 when the Hawaiian king invited the Japanese emperor to arrange a marriage alliance between the respective royal families, or in 1887 and 1893 when the American element in the islands took steps to secure control of the government, or at the time of annexation by the United States in 1898.

With regard to Korea, after the treaty of 1876, the Japanese government tried to strengthen commercial and political ties in a cautious way, but specifically rejected the attempt of overzealous Korean and Japanese "progressives" to establish a "reform" administration in Korea by coup d'état in 1884 and then stood by while Chinese control of the Korean government was gradually tightened between 1885 and 1894. There is no doubt that this Chinese ascendancy was galling to the Japanese, but until 1894 when several simultaneous crises culminated in war, the Japanese oligarchs avoided entanglement on the Korean question to the point of increasing their unpopularity with their own countrymen.

Actually the major foreign policy goal in the early Meiji period was revision of the unequal treaties, by securing Western recognition of the principle of Japan's equality in their treaty relationships with the West. The oligarchs worked incessantly for this, from the time of Iwakura's world mission in 1872. Yet here too they were patient and cautious, though the populace and the party politicians became inflamed as the powers delayed on various grounds, claiming that this institution or that in Japan was not sufficiently modern and civilized to permit the end of extraterritoriality. In 1888 popular criticism was so vehement that the oligarchs took their archrenegade and chief critic, Okuma, back into the government as foreign minister. Okuma found, as the others had, that it was not easy to convince the powers, his attempt ended in failure, and he was the victim of an assassination attempt by a "patriot" who considered that he had betrayed Japan's honor by his "weak-kneed" negotiating. The patience and caution paid off in 1894 when the powers at last recognized the principle of full treaty equality for Japan. Doubtless the feeling that the powers, particularly Britain, were favorably inclined, taken together with their desire to control the domestic political scene more effectively, helped to convince the oligarchs that to challenge China on the Korean question would help rather than hinder their larger project of building Japan into a strong centralized modern state. Thus they opted for war in 1894.

The record of Japan's transformation in the Meiji era may perhaps properly be evaluated as both an inspiration and a warning to other areas undertaking modernization in Asia and elsewhere. Undeniably there was tremendous achievement and the oligarchs who led the way must be credited with remarkable sagacity, practicality, and skill. But some things were missing for an ultimately successful system. There was too much concern with state organization, power, and methods of control, and too little with the development of individual initiative and political responsibility.

BASIC DATES

1868	Emperor "restored" and moved to Tokyo; Charter Oath
1869–1871	Liquidation of feudalism
1871–1873	Iwakura Mission
1873	Government splits on Korean issue
1874	Formosan expedition
1875	Treaty with Russia
1876	Treaty of Kanghwa (with Korea)
1877	Satsuma Rebellion
1879	Incorporation of Liu-ch'iu Islands as Okinawa prefecture
1881	Okuma ousted from government, promise of Constitution and formation of political parties
1885	Li-Ito Convention with China settles Korean issue temporarily
1889	Promulgation of Constitution
1890–1894	Diet versus Cabinet "oligarchs"
1894	Revision of treaties; outbreak of Sino-Japanese War
1895	Treaty of Shimonoseki; acquisition of Formosa

SUPPLEMENTARY READING

Borton, H. *Japan's Modern Century,* rev. ed. New York, 1970.
Brown, D. M. *Nationalism in Japan.* Berkeley, Calif., 1955. See Chaps. 5–7.
De Bary, W. T., ed. *Sources of the Japanese Tradition.* New York, 1958; paper ed., 1964.
Hall, J. W. *Japan: From Prehistory to Modern Times.* New York, 1970. Chaps. 13–16.
Hane, M. *Japan: A Historical Survey.* New York, 1972.
Ishida, T. *Japanese Society.* New York, 1971.
Jansen, M. B., ed. *Changing Japanese Attitudes Toward Modernization.* Princeton, N.J., 1965.
Reischauer, E. O. *Japan: The Story of a Nation.* New York, 1970.

Scalapino, R. A. *Democracy and the Party Movement in Prewar Japan.* Berkeley, Calif. 1953.
Shively, D. H., ed. *Tradition and Modernization in Japanese Culture.* Princeton, N.J., 1971.
Yanaga, C. *Japan Since Perry.* New York, 1949; reprinted, 1966.

ADVANCED READING

Akita, G. *Foundations of Constitutional Government in Modern Japan, 1868–1900.* Cambridge, Mass., 1967.
Allen, G. C. *A Short Economic History of Japan,* 2nd rev. ed. London, 1963.
Blacker, C. *The Japanese Enlightenment: A Study of the Writings of Fukuzawa Yukichi.* Cambridge Univ., 1969.
Conroy, H. *The Japanese Seizure of Korea, 1868–1910.* Philadelphia, 1960.
────── *The Japanese Frontier in Hawaii, 1968–1898.* Berkeley, Calif., 1953.
Craig, A. M. and D. H. Shively. *Personality in Japanese History.* Berkeley, Calif., 1970. Pp. 264–334.
Hackett, R. *Yamagata Aritomo and the Rise of Modern Japan.* Cambridge, Mass., 1971.
Harrison, J. A. *Japan's Northern Frontier,* Gainesville, 1953.
Hirschmeier, J. *The Origins of Entrepreneurship in Meiji Japan.* Cambridge, Mass., 1964.
Holtom, D. C. *The National Faith of Japan, Shinto.* London, 1938.
Ike, N. *The Beginnings of Political Democracy in Japan.* Baltimore, 1950.
Lockwood, W. W. *The Economic Development of Japan,* rev. ed. Princeton, N.J., 1968.
Mason, R. H. P. *Japan's First General Election.* Cambridge, England, 1969.
Nakamura, J. I. *Agricultural Production and the Economic Development of Japan.* Princeton, N.J., 1966.
Norman, E. H. *Japan's Emergence as a Modern State.* New York, 1946. A classic study.
Pittau, J. *Political Thought in Early Meiji Japan.* Cambridge, Mass., 1967.
Presseisen, E. L. *Before Aggression: Europeans Prepare the Japanese Army.* Tucson, 1965.
Pyle, K. B. *The New Generation in Meiji Japan.* Stanford, 1969.
Rosovsky, H. *Capital Formation in Japan, 1868–1940.* New York, 1961.
Sansom, G. B. *The Western World and Japan.* New York, 1949. See Chaps. 13–16.
Schwantes, R. S. *Japanese and Americans: A Century of Cultural Relationships.* New York, 1955.
Silberman, B. S. *Ministers of Modernization: Elite Mobility in the Meiji Restoration, 1868–1873.* Tucson, 1964.
Smith, T. C. *Political Change and Industrial Development in Japan, 1868–1880.* Stanford, Calif., 1955.
Smith, W. *Confucianism in Modern Japan.* Tokyo, 1959.
Treat, P. J. *Diplomatic Relations Between the United States and Japan, 1853–1895.* Stanford, 1932.

Chapter 14

Korea: From Seclusion to International Conflict, 1600-1895

The fact that no previous chapter has exclusively discussed Korea does not mean that early Korean history is unimportant, or that information on it is lacking. Rather, requirements of space, coupled with realization that pre-1600 Korean history was much involved with China and Japan, led the authors to include prior Korean developments in chapters primarily devoted to those countries in Volume I. Only after 1600 did Korea develop the characteristics associated with the term "hermit nation" (a name given by W. E. Griffis, the first serious American historian of Korea, in his classic *Corea: The Hermit Nation*, first published in 1882). Although "hermit" attitudes and characteristics came to dominate Korea, leaving her ill prepared for participation in the modern world she was forced to enter in the late nineteenth century, it is well to recall that Korea was an international highway in early times, a cultural bridge across which Chinese characters, Buddhism, and Confucianism were transmitted to Japan, that Korean artisans helped to build Nara and Kyoto, and that Korean ships and mariners were probably the best in the early Far East.

During the Three Kingdoms (Koguryo, Paekche, Silla) period Korea was in close touch with both China and Japan, yet held off aggressive inroads from either side. After the unification of Korea by Silla with Chinese aid in T'ang times, Korea's relations with her more powerful neighbors became more stable, being friendly and equal with Japan, and "respectful" with China; that is, Korea came to accept China's Confucian theory of international relations which held that smaller countries should accept subordinate status to China, whereby China was honored and paid tribute as the superior country, and she in turn rewarded this "filial" loyalty with special privileges, gifts, protection if needed, and noninterference in the lesser state's internal affairs. This does not mean that Korea became a completely Confucian monarchy. Indeed, until Mongol times Buddhism was probably the strongest of the many elements of Chinese culture that had flowed into the peninsula, and the concept of a Confucian bureaucracy had to compete with an earlier tribal "bone rank" (*kolp'um*) system. But as far as relationships with China were concerned, after ousting her erstwhile T'ang allies in the 670's, Korea continued them on the basis described above, not only through the rest of the T'ang era, but also through the Five Dynasties and Sung periods. This was despite a change of dynasty and the name of the state from Silla to Koryo (the basis of the name Korea) and serious problems with the Manchurian Khitan and Jurchen tribes in the north. At any rate, until the thirteenth century Korea's international relations, though not without vicissitudes and problems, had perhaps been more enriching than troublesome. Certainly they had not been such as to cause the nation to seek isolation.

Beginning with the Mongol conquest of China, however, Korea began to be buffeted by alien winds so strong that her people were to develop almost a psychosis of withdrawal. The Mongols invaded, ravaged, and ruled Korea through a puppet administration, then forced Korean participation in their ill-starred attempts to invade Japan (1274, 1281) (see Volume I). After that, though the Mongols were overthrown (1368), the Japanese had been aroused, and the fourteenth and fifteenth centuries saw a rising tide of Japanese piratical maraudings of the Korean coast, climaxed in the 1590's by Hideyoshi's brutal invasions. Although the Chinese came to Korea's aid against Hideyoshi, the rise of the Manchus was causing new alarms even as the Japanese withdrew. It is little wonder that Korean efforts were directed toward keeping contacts with foreigners at a minimum after 1600.

SECLUSION UNDER THE YI

The seclusion policy which Korea developed under its last royal house, the Yi (1392–1910), was in part the result of understandable fears generated by these catastrophic foreign entanglements and the possibility of others, and in part the result of increasing political and cultural rigidity, which by the mid-nineteenth century had become almost a paralysis. But this policy developed only gradually, and with the establishment of a new capital at Seoul by the dynasty's vigorous founder, Yi T'aejo, and the invention of movable type in 1403 (nearly fifty years before Gutenberg's press in Europe), a veritable renaissance began. King Sejong (1419–1450) promoted all the arts, including medicine, music, astronomical science, agricultural manuals, the invention of a pluviometer (long before Europe), and an ingenious new alphabet, *Han-gul*, achievements which easily rank him with Frederick II of Prussia. In addition a new philosophic framework for political institutions was discovered and utilized.

Neo-Confucianism

Neo-Confucianism, that remarkable, sophisticated redefinition of Confucian principles prepared by Chu Hsi and his school in late Sung China (see

Volume I, Chapter 20), was first introduced to Korea, it is said, by one An Hyang, who visited the Peking of Kublai Khan in the retinue of his king. There he studied with Chinese scholars and returned to Korea with prized new books and new knowledge to found a school which became, after the establishment of the Yi dynasty, the intellectual center of the kingdom. The fact that Ming China adopted Neo-Confucianism also, no doubt, solidified its position in Korea, but Korean intellectual interest in this school even before that time was also a factor in its subsequent strength.

During the early years of the Yi dynasty Neo-Confucianism helped in establishing the regime at Seoul and in supporting excellent relations with China. As in China it brought a presumably ancient (pre-Mongol and pre-Buddhist) authority to bear on problems of the day and at first, while its philosophic subtleties (and deficiencies) remained obscure, it had great practical value. It brought fervor, reform, and organization to the construction of the new government. It began in a pragmatic mood, avoiding excessive philosophic disputations. The early Yi leaders might even be called Confucian-Legalists, combining a Confucian regard for moral principles with a Legalist urge to get things done. Laws and precepts for the people were written down and rules of conduct, ritual for officials, a canon of legitimacy for the royal house, and a clarification of the role of local government were established. The last step was very important, for previously there had been no clear definition of the functions or the extent of the authority of local officials, with the result that almost all matters had to wait on the decision of the capital. Now local scholar-officials, called *yangban*, were given authority to operate in accordance with relatively standardized village codes and instructional examples of wrong adjudication which were circulated. These officials were also given lands in relatively permanent tenure, which, though later detrimental by creating a landlord class, for the time gave them an added attachment to and interest in their local duties.

Relations with China and Japan

Relations with China, where a "legitimate" (the Ming) dynasty now ruled, were fostered by frank admiration and imitation. Yi T'aejo had in fact disobeyed orders to march against the Ming in the Yalu river region previous to seizing the Korean throne. Later he asked for and received a Ming seal investing him with the right to rule. The Ming code of punishment was adopted, Confucian examinations for public officials decreed, and Ming models generally followed in the governmental reorganization. Official relations were regularized by carefully patterned exchanges of missions, in which the Koreans at designated intervals brought tribute in the form of "products of the country" (sea eagles were once refused as not being "products of the country") and on special occasions offered congratulations or condolences. The Chinese in turn sent missions bearing "gifts" to Korea and statements expressing the pleasure of the Ming emperor at the various evidences of Confucian rectitude to be found in Korea. In these exchanges Korea was defined as a *shu-kuo*, "dependent" or "belonging" country of China, a designation the Chinese also used for such places as Vietnam, Liu-ch'iu, Burma, Siam, and other small states. But it should be emphasized that in Confucian terminology this was a respected, even honored status, given only to civilized countries who knew proprieties and practiced right conduct, and was sharply differentiated from "barbarian" states which did not. Furthermore, Korea was the most respected of the shu-kuo, the favorite son in Ming China's Confucian international family.

The strength of the bond between Korea and Ming China was demonstrated in the 1590's in Korea's refusal to join Hideyoshi in his plan to invade China or to allow his troops to pass through Korean territory (see Volume I, Chapter 27), and in China's dispatch of military forces (albeit too few) to rescue the peninsula from Japanese invasion.

Although Ming China, Korea, and the model Confucian relationship between them survived Hideyoshi's Japanese invasion of the continent, it was not to last long thereafter. By 1600 the Japanese threat had ended, when the disillusioned Japanese made an armistice and began withdrawing shortly after Hideyoshi's death. The Tokugawa, after taking control of the Japanese government in 1600, made it clear that they had no intention of renewing the war, and a formal peace settlement was negotiated on Tsushima Island in 1609.

By that time a new threat was forming north of the Yalu river, the Manchus. As they took over the Chinese-controlled commanderies in southern Manchuria, they began to jeopardize Korea's comfortable relations with the Ming, finally demanding that Korea recognize and pay tribute to their leader as the rightful claimant to the Dragon Throne.

Korea stoutly resisted the Manchu pressure for many years, sent 20,000 men to assist the Ming armies in 1619, but suffered defeat and finally, in 1627, invasion by the Manchus. The king fled from Seoul to Kanghwa Island and it seemed for a time as if there would be another Mongol-type occupation of the country. But the Manchus proved to be much more sophisticated and sinified than the Mongols. Indeed, they had shown a certain appreciation of the Confucian father-son relation at the time of the fighting involving Korea in 1619, when after defeating and capturing many Koreans, they sent the prisoners home with a statement that they understood the obligations Korea owed the Ming, but admonished their king not to persist in his anti-Manchu attitude. In 1627 they invited the king to negotiate according to terms which were remarkably subtle. Korea would accept the Manchus as "elder brother" and exchange missions with them in the vein of "elder brother-younger brother." The Koreans accepted this, but did not in fact carry out the incumbent obligations. In 1632 the Manchus complained: "Your country looks upon the Ming as a father, and many times you have sent them tribute rice. Now we are your elder brother, can you not give it us once?"

Receiving no satisfaction, in 1637 the Manchus invaded Korea again, capturing the whole royal family and leading ministers. This time they forced the king to give up the Ming seal, accept the Manchu calendar, promise yearly tribute, and give two royal sons as hostages. However, they still preferred persuasion to force, and in 1644, having seized Peking and proclaimed the Ch'ing dynasty, the new Manchu emperor returned the Korean hostages, remitted Korean tribute for two years, and otherwise salved Korean wounds to the point that at the official level, at least, Korea accepted Ch'ing suzerainty in accordance with Confucian norms.

Despite the fact that relations with Japan and the new power in China had been settled, it soon became clear that Korea was not enthusiastic about contact with either side. The new treaty with Japan called for the exchange of envoys and "neighborly relations," but it is evident that Korea thought of this in minimal terms. Japanese envoys were not allowed to go beyond Pusan, where Korean officials went to meet them, often keeping them waiting, and the Japanese colony that had inhabited Pusan from early times was sharply circumscribed. Tsushima Island, whose feudal lord owed allegiance to the Tokugawa and served as the shogunate's intermediary in negotiations preceding the treaty of 1609, had close connections and a brisk trade with the Pusan Japanese. This was allowed to continue, but was more closely regulated, the lord of Tsushima being required to accept a semitributary position and a Korean seal of office to keep it going.

Korean missions to Japan were to be sent to Edo to offer congratulations on events of "great national importance" (usually the accession of a new shogun), their expenses from Tsushima to Edo to be paid by the Japanese. Eleven were sent up to 1763, after which there was a long delay and an altercation over protocol and expense. One more mission went in 1811, but only as far as Tsushima. The Japanese had tried to cut expenses, which were considerable since a typical embassy numbered 500 people, and Korea took the opportunity of the argument to end the relationship. Although four new shoguns came to power after 1811, Korea sent no "congratulations."

In relations with Manchu China, her "elder brother" turned "father" after 1644, Korea was scrupulously correct in her performance of *sadae* (serving the great), as the relationship was called. But a certain suspicion had replaced the frank admiration of Ming times. This was not so much suspicion that the Manchus would again violate Korean territory, for the Manchus themselves were very circumspect on that score, demarking a "no man's land" at the Yalu river through which no unauthorized person might pass, and forbidding Chinese activity, even fishing, along the Korean coast. They obligingly and even affectionately adhered to the precise ceremonial the Koreans prescribed for missions coming from Peking to Seoul, whereby most of the retinue would be left at the Yalu frontier and the chief envoy kept in seclusion at Seoul, and even "corrected" their records of Korean relations in accordance with what the Koreans thought "proper." Rather it was laxness on the part of Peking that worried Korea. Members of Korean missions to Peking circulated quite freely after their official duties had been performed and they sometimes came back with noxious ideas, about which Seoul complained. Korea did not want mingling of peoples, even with China.

The Introduction of New Ideas

The fear of new ideas was an expression of the rigidity which Neo-Confucianism, a healthy political philosophy in early Yi times, had assumed. Its life as the official creed of government had not been complicated by a dynastic turnover, as had occurred in China, and as a result it had become more and more firmly entrenched but increasingly divorced from real problems. The so-called School of Rites (ceremonies), which had been only one part of the Neo-Confucian complex, tended to become all-embracing and suffocating, in political and even social affairs. Correct ritual was everything, from court circles down to ordinary family circles. Bitter feuds were fought over ritual, over such questions, for example, as that which occupied the country in the 1670's: should the period of mourning for a dead queen extend beyond one year?

For a time in the eighteenth century there were signs of intellectual stimulation rather similar to the Han Learning movement in China, which, it will be remembered, found the seeds of the Ming dynasty's ruin in the undue reverence it had paid to Chu Hsi and Neo-Confucianism (see Chapter 4). This Korean school, called the *Sirhak*, also criticized Neo-Confucianism and preferred an inductive method of research to deductions from Chu Hsi's philosophy. There was a healthy creativity about this school and it began to be politically significant as a rallying ground for critics of the status quo, especially a so-called "Southerners" group of political outcasts. These included concubine sons of scholar-officials who, their rank being determined by their mothers' status, were doomed to perpetual inferiority in the hierarchy. The movement found a leader in the brilliant Chong Ta-san (1762–1836), who almost attained sufficient political power to effect changes. But the traditionalists had broken him by 1800, and while he spent the last half of his life in enforced retirement, Korea fortified her orthodoxy. Ta-san had advocated land reform, tax equalization, and improved administration, in addition to seeking a more scientific approach to knowledge, but he was felled as a potential subversive.

It is interesting and significant that a part of the case against Ta-san was the argument that he might have been touched by an even more frightening alien influence than his errant Confucianism suggested, namely, Christianity. This was another subversive doctrine learned at Peking by inquisitive members of Korean tribute missions. While there was no doubt some knowledge of it before, it is clear that a member of the mission of 1784, who was a distant relative of Ta-san, studied with Jesuits at Peking and returned home with a Bible in Chinese and other Western books. This began a new heresy, which was promoted by several French and Chinese priests who stole into Korea, and led to increasingly severe persecution of all unorthodox behavior.

By the middle of the nineteenth century, though there may have been 10,000 to 20,000 Christian converts in Korea and many disaffected Confucianists, no group could advocate a foreign policy other than seclusion. The Confucian educational establishment, from the great Academy at Seoul and its provincial colleges to the local academies built around Confucian shrines, were dedicated to tradition and were concerned mainly with details of form and administration. And the heterodox elements stemming from the revolt of Ta-san, ironically enough, found that they could most successfully challenge the regime by backing the ultra-seclusionist Taewongun (regent) who came to power in 1863.

With the rise of the Taewongun the final decay of Yi seclusion policies set in. The Taewongun was born in 1811, the fourth son of a prince of the royal clan. His own son became king of Korea in 1863, and he became the power behind the throne. The Taewongun sought to centralize authority further, and in so doing he stressed foreign dangers as the compelling issue. Indeed, the opening of Peking to Western diplomats in 1860 created a sort of panic in Seoul and in their desperation Korean leaders decided they must increase security regulations regarding missions to and from Peking lest pernicious doctrines creep in. The Taewongun then began increasing controls. He stressed military preparations to ward off foreign danger and as a corollary decreed the closing of many Confucian schools, which might have challenged his control as well as his greater stress on physical fitness than on books. He did not succeed in creating adequate defenses, but he did succeed in creating factional strife between himself, supported by the "Southerners" political faction which had once espoused Ta-san, and the old cliques which solidified around the queen's Min clan. Unfortunately the issue was no longer new ideas versus traditional ones, but rather who could suppress foreign influences and maintain seclusion the most thoroughly. While old line missions to China urged officials there not to allow any disturbance of Korea's hermit calm on the grounds that her people were poor, her resources meager, and her territory too small to be valuable, the Taewongun was carrying out a massacre of Christians, including a number of foreign priests, and attacking any foreign vessels which ventured to land.

Western Pressure

These actions excited foreign retaliation, specifically from France and America. France was angered by the killing of several French missionaries who had entered Korea clandestinely. Having informed the Chinese government of outrages committed by its "former vassal," the French chargé at Peking, in cooperation with the commander of France's Far East squadron, organized and dispatched a punitive expedition of six hundred men to Korea in 1866. It was beaten off, however, soon after landing on Kanghwa Island, and later the French government disavowed the action. American intervention was brought on by the case of the United States schooner *General Sherman*, which ran aground off Pyongyang in 1866. Koreans attacked and burned her and killed her crew, which consisted mainly of Southeast Asians and Chinese but included three Americans and two Europeans.

The United States first brought the affair to the attention of China's new-style Foreign Office, the Tsungli Yamen, in Peking, which immediately disavowed any responsibility by explaining that the only connection between Korea and China was a "ceremonial" one; this was true, of course, but it failed to communicate to non-Confucian minds the depth and importance of "ceremonial" ties in this case. The United States then decided to deal directly with Korea on the matter, and, in the hope of obtaining a treaty which would guarantee safety for shipwrecks and open regularized relations, sent the American minister to Peking, Mr. Frederick P. Low, with a squadron of five warships to Korea. They reached the mouth of the Han river, which led to Seoul, in late May, 1871. Korean officials met them, but refused to discuss a treaty and refused permission for the Americans to take surveys in the river, which they started to do anyway. Thereupon a Korean coastal fort opened fire. The survey boats retreated, but ten days later 650 Americans charged and reduced the fort, 350 Koreans and three Americans being killed in bitter fighting. Later two other forts were taken easily, but since there was no prospect of a treaty and no desire or real possibility to attack Seoul, the entire expedition withdrew.

These "defeats" of the Western "barbarians" made the Taewongun the more intransigent in his seclusion policy. When Japan sent a message via Tsushima informing Korea of the establishment of the new Meiji government and asking for a renewal of diplomatic relations, the Korean reply was arrogant and insulting, accusing Japan of abandoning civilized (Confucian) ways and refusing to accept the idea of her having an "emperor." This gave rise to samurai war fever in Japan, and almost served as sufficient excuse for the launching of a Korean war, as proposed by Saigo Takamori and other Japanese leaders in 1873. The warhawks were defeated in Tokyo, however, and Japan continued peaceful efforts to negotiate at Pusan, while laying plans for a direct approach to Seoul, which will be discussed shortly.

Before concluding this discussion of Korean seclusion it should perhaps be said that the extreme malevolence which it developed in the 1860's, when as many as 10,000 people were put to death, often after torture, was not so much the expression of those Confucian doctrines which set the intellectual framework of seclusion, as of a fearful sense of emergency. Indeed, as late as 1855 four Americans who had deserted ship and a harsh captain off the Korean coast and become the first Americans to set foot in Korea were treated kindly. They spent a month in a Korean village, were given food and clothing, and then sent on horseback with an escort to the Yalu frontier where they were turned over to Chinese authorities who in turn brought them to the American consul at Shanghai, the nearest United States representative. Even in the 1860's there were cases of kindness amidst the cruelties. But the suspicion, for example, that a shipwrecked crew could have some ulterior intention would set off persecution, as may have been the case with the *General Sherman*. Some visitors unquestionably did have base motives, for example the grave-robbing expedition headed by a shady merchant, Oppert, which included an American, Jenkins, and a French priest, Feron, which sailed from Shanghai to rob a royal Korean graveyard in 1867. Such private depredations plus the official pressures Western powers were applying in the Far East at the time were enough to justify Korea's fears, if not her persecutions.

OPENING OF KOREA

Western states in their early attempts to negotiate with Korea were troubled by their lack of understanding of the Confucian relationship between Korea and China. Whereas Korea's presentation of tribute at Peking was mainly ceremonial and Korea, as the Chinese were wont to say, "managed its own affairs," the Western nations concluded inaccurately that Korea, though perhaps "formerly" a vassal of China, was in all essential matters an independent state. The Confucian dependent state relationship, while unobtrusive and subtle, was nonetheless strong, especially in the case of Korea. This would not be obvious in normal circumstances when indeed Korea was self-governing, but in a crisis the same attitudes which governed a Confucian social situation would prevail. The father's authority was supreme, to be enforced gently if possible, but with an iron hand if necessary.

While other elements of the Chinese government, notably the Board of Rites which received the Korean and other tributary missions, remained relatively hidebound, the Foreign Office (Tsungli Yamen), which was actively in touch with Western diplomats, began to have misgivings about Korea's absolutist seclusion position in the mid-1860's. After the Christian persecutions of 1866 and the French expedition it recommended that the Board of Rites inform Korea that it might be possible to negotiate with France. The Board of Rites refused and the Foreign Office could only register its contention that Korea might find it necessary to enter into international relations in the future, while forwarding various informational materials on international affairs to the Koreans.

Later, as problems multiplied, the Board of Rites became more responsive to the advice of the Foreign Office and particularly to that of Li Hung-chang, who was becoming known as the most skilled Chinese negotiator on "barbarian affairs." In Korea the seclusionist attitude became slightly less adamant in 1873 with the withdrawal (temporarily) of the Taewongun from the active direction of affairs upon the king's reaching his majority. And in Japan the "peace faction," now in control of the central government, decided in 1875 to take up the Korean problem again, which would help satisfy smouldering samurai resentment, but in a manner calculated to improve rather than injure Japan's international position. The emphasis was to be on peace, not war, and on opening Korea to the currents of progress, not revenge.

Japan "Opens" Korea

The occasion for action was a fracas involving a Japanese shore party seeking water near Kanghwa for a Japanese survey ship, the *Unyo*. Korean shore batteries then fired on the *Unyo*, which in turn reduced the batteries. Amidst rising war fever in Japan, the Japanese government decided to use the incident to obtain a treaty with Korea. American representatives in Tokyo and the records of Perry's expedition were consulted, while a threatening Perry-like squadron was readied to carry two negotiators, Kuroda and Inoue, to Kanghwa. Their instructions, however, called for peace, not hostilities, and they were armed with plenipotentiary powers to make a treaty. In addition, to seek the cooperation of China, another emissary, Mori Arinori, was dispatched to Peking. Mori discussed matters with the Tsungli Yamen, and though they would make no promises as a body, they referred him to Li Hung-chang. Li explained at length Korea's status as a depen-

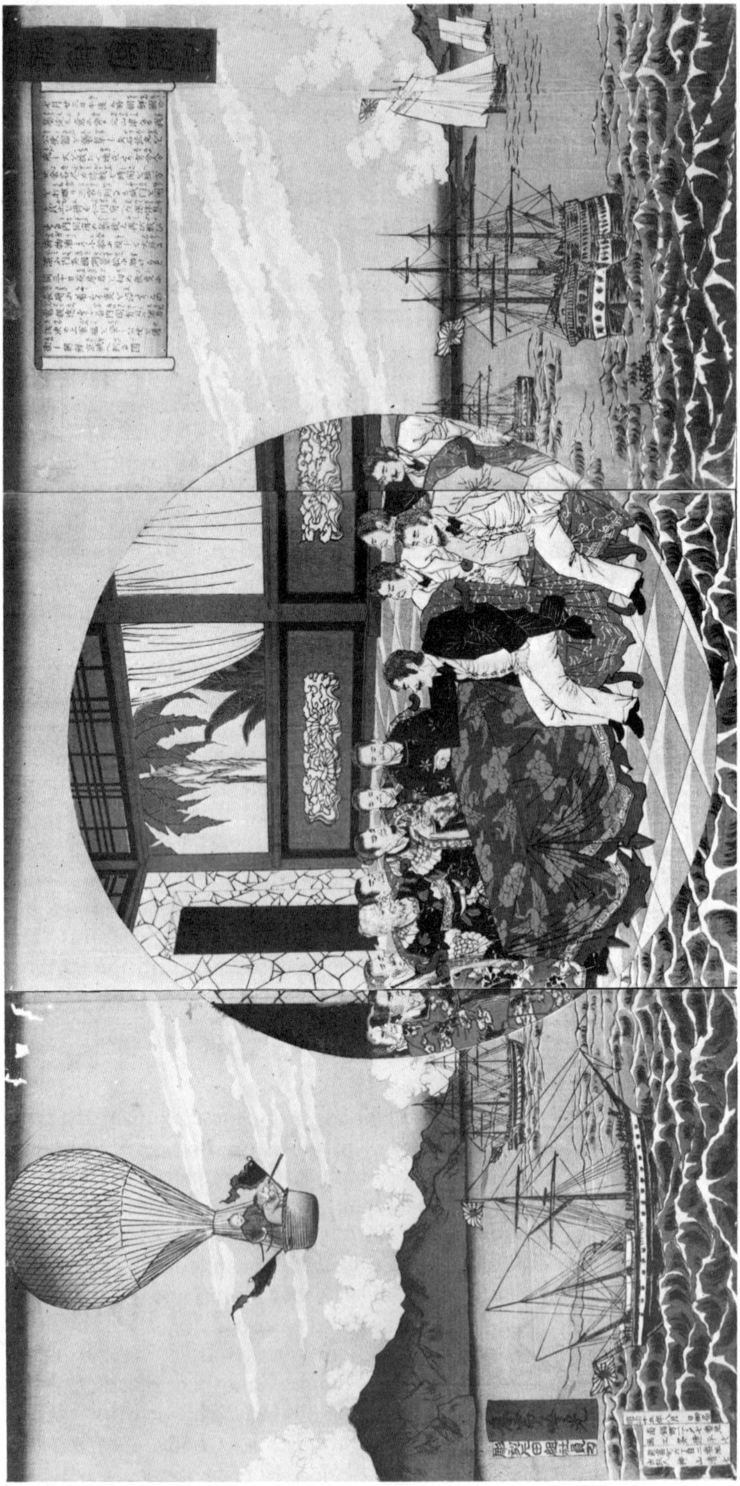

dent state of China, but he accepted Mori's argument that the time had come for Korea to make a treaty with Japan and agreed to use his influence to obtain a courteous reception for the Japanese negotiators. Thereafter the channels of Confucian advice worked as if by magic, and Kuroda and Inoue, who arrived in Korea on February 6, 1876, had their treaty by February 26. The treaty promised the opening of three ports to trade, the establishment of diplomatic relations, the allowance of coastal surveys, and perhaps most important of all, referred to Korea as an "independent," or "self-governing," country. The Japanese and Westerners were to prefer the former reading, China the latter.

The Japanese did not push for their new treaty rights too rapidly, leaving time for the seclusionist climate to change, which it did to some extent. After prolonged negotiation Japan was allowed to establish a legation at Seoul and trade began to develop in the opened ports of Pusan, Inchon, and Wonsan. In addition, from among Koreans who visited Japan and a few others, a "progressive" party began to form. Growing Japanese influence aroused alarm on two sides. In Korea the Taewongun was angered, especially since his political rivals, the Min (Queen's) clan and its adherents who had gained in power after 1873, had allowed the Japanese treaty to be made. Also China began to worry about Japanese influence, especially after certain arguments revealed quite clearly diverging interpretations of "independent" and "self-governing." Japan's takeover of the Liu-ch'iu Islands, also by Chinese definition a "dependent state," caused a number of her officials to worry lest the same fate befall Korea.

Treaties with Other Powers

In the circumstances the Chinese, acting on the advice of Li Hung-chang, decided to urge Korea to open her doors further, making treaties with various Western nations, which would at least give Japan some competition as the apostle of progress. The United States, which had failed to obtain a treaty in 1871, was in fact making another try in 1878, when one Commodore Shufeldt of the American navy tried to approach the Koreans via Japanese introductions to explain the 1871 affair and obtain a treaty. He had almost given up when he was invited to discuss the matter with Li Hung-chang in China. After that, as with the Japanese treaty, matters went smoothly. Shufeldt obtained full treatymaking powers and returned to Inchon in 1882 to sign the treaty with Korea's representatives in a ceremony supervised by two Chinese officials. The only troublesome "detail" was Li's insistence that a statement of Korea's dependent status to China be included in the treaty. Shufeldt refused on the grounds that such a thing would invalidate the whole treaty, for a treaty presumed sovereign powers on either side. (He did not seem to see any incongruity in the fact that he was arguing treaty terms with Li, not the Koreans.) A compromise

FIGURE 14.1. *Japanese Minister Hanabusa negotiating with the Korean king after the 1882 Seoul incident, while, according to the Japanese, Chinese spies watch from a balloon.*

was finally reached, whereby Li agreed to omit the clause about dependent status from the treaty itself on the understanding that Shufeldt would forward to the president of the United States a separate letter from the king of Korea covering this point.

Translations of the king's letter differ, but the main points may be summarized as follows: Korea is a dependent country to China, but the management of her governmental affairs, both domestic and foreign, has always been vested in her king; treaty relations with the United States shall be carried out in good faith in accord with "universal rules" (international law?); as regards Korea's duties as a dependent of China the United States shall have no concern whatever with them. In ratifying the treaty the United States Senate had the king's letter before it, but gave it no special notice. The treaty provided for friendship, commerce, and extraterritorial rights for Americans until Korea's legal structure should be modernized. Similar treaties with Britain, Germany, Italy, Russia, and France were signed shortly thereafter, to whom the king's letter was also duly sent. China was helping to lead Korea into modern international intercourse, while reminding the world that China's special dependent state overlordship still prevailed.

In Korea, although the king and the Min clan were agreeable to following Li Hung-chang's advice in these matters, the Taewongun was not. In the midst of the treaty negotiations of 1882, he advocated seclusion as the best policy dramatically and violently. In late July he attempted a coup d'état, during which antiforeign sentiments were unleashed, several Min ministers killed (the queen narrowly escaping assassination), the Japanese legation burned, and the government temporarily brought under his control again. While Japan dispatched an expedition to demand apologies and restitution, the Chinese took the situation in hand. Chinese warships were sent, and the Taewongun was firmly "invited" to come aboard one of them, which speedily removed him to Tientsin, where he remained for the next three years. While he was away various legations were established in Seoul, traders and missionaries came, Koreans traveled abroad. A sense of excitement and adventure began to stir the opened "hermit nation."

INTERNATIONAL RIVALRY

Attendance at the schools of "progress" was popular and respectable in the early 1880's as bright young Korean aristocrats became frequent visitors at the Japanese, American, and other foreign legations. Through them the king and court were influenced to introduce many examples of progress, from "Edison electric lights" to postage stamps. Also the idea of "independence" began to take hold, to the extent that some began to stress the "sovereign" nature of Korea to the exclusion of any mention of "dependence" on China. Two young highborn Koreans, Pak Young-hyo and Kim Ok-kiun, who studied at Fukuzawa Yukichi's school of "independence and self respect" in Tokyo were leaders of the party of progress, but many others, who had been to Japan, the United States, or Europe were among its advocates. The king wavered between the old and the new.

KOREA: FROM SECLUSION TO INTERNATIONAL CONFLICT, 1600–1895 329

FIGURE 14.2. *The Korean embassy, headed by Min Yong-ik, calls upon the American president, Chester A. Arthur, at the Fifth Avenue Hotel, New York, September 18, 1883.*

Attempt at Revolution in 1884

The progressives counted heavily on Min Yong-ik, who was leader of the influential Min party and was very close to the queen, to further their cause. He had been induced to go abroad as chief of an embassy to the United States in the winter of 1883–1884, returning to Korea in May, 1884. However, he apparently was not impressed with what he saw abroad, spent much of the home voyage reading Confucian books, and back in Korea he became estranged from the progressives. Fearing loss of influence, Pak, Kim, and other progressives, with help from some Japanese adventurers, attempted to assassinate Min and take over the government by coup d'état on the night of December 4, 1884. Min, though severely wounded, lived, but it was a night of fearful violence. The rebels tried to obtain assistance from the Japanese legation in stabilizing their new regime, and succeeded in persuading the Japanese minister, Takezoe, who was sympathetic to them but without orders from Tokyo, to send his 200 legation guards to control the palace. On the 6th an anti-Japanese reaction swept the city, the Japanese legation was attacked and burned, and Chinese forces, of which there was an encampment of 1500 (left from the 1882 affair) outside the city, moved in to take control. The Japanese legation guards left the palace and with Minister Takezoe, Japanese civilians, and other foreigners fled to Inchon. Kim and Pak and some of the other rebels also escaped to Inchon and thence abroad, although many of them were killed in Seoul in the aftermath of the incident. Battle between Chinese and Japanese troops had narrowly been averted. Japanese and other foreign ships gathered at Inchon.[1]

The Japanese government was embarrassed by Takezoe's complicity, and it was not favorably inclined toward the Korean progressives, who were too much involved with Japanese liberals and other government critics in Japan to suit its oligarchic inclinations. It wanted Korea to be open to Japanese commerce and influence, but did not want a serious international embroilment and was willing to sacrifice something of the former to avoid the latter. China also did not want a showdown, especially inasmuch as the Western powers tended to favor Japan at this point. Hence both sides wanted a settlement and Japan's leading statesman, Ito Hirobumi, went to Tientsin to meet with Li Hung-chang to settle outstanding issues. This was accomplished by the Li-Ito (Tientsin) Convention of April, 1885, which agreed that neither side would keep troops in Korea, nor send them in an emergency without notifying the other. Ito had hoped to get Li to make some statement verifying Korea's sovereignty, but he would not, and so the "dependent state" issue was left to be interpreted by the various parties interested in their own way.

Chinese Determination to Maintain Control over Korea

In accepting the commitment not to use force in Korea, Ito was probably assuming, as the representatives of the Western powers also assumed, that time was on their side and that without troops to back it up China's Confucian overlordship would eventually disappear. In this he underestimated China and the strength of ties which, the American minister once wrote, "can accomplish the purposes of marching armies." Chinese troops were withdrawn, but Chinese influence, far from abating, became stronger and stronger until it could be said that Li Hung-chang, through his representative in Korea, was directing the Korean government's every move. Distressed at the unmanageability of "progress" in Korea, Li decided to bring the time-honored Confucian relationship in all its oriental splendor to bear against it. In what the Japanese and the Westerners liked to think of as the Chinese "legation" he established his favorite protégé, Yuan Shih-k'ai, who in the fall of 1885 distributed calling cards designating himself as "His Imperial Chinese Majesty's Resident in Korea." The foreigners thought he must mean "minister resident," but it soon became clear that he was much more than that. Also the Chinese sent the Taewongun back to Seoul in the fall

---

[1] For an eyewitness account see Lucius H. Foote, United States Minister at Seoul, to Secretary of State, Dec. 17, 1884, printed in George M. McCune and John A. Harrison, eds., *Korean-American Relations* (Berkeley: University of California Press, 1951), pp. 97–113.

of 1885. He soon had an antiforeign group around him again, though the Chinese worked mainly through the Min clan to bring pressure on the king to conform to Confucian traditions. Occasionally the king was rebellious, but in general the years 1885–1894 saw Yuan Shih-k'ai pulling the wires behind the Seoul government. Foreigners were still treated cordially, but they were circumscribed in various ways, from increasing formality demanded in royal audiences (although Yuan Shih-k'ai obviously saw the king whenever he pleased) to arrangements which favored Chinese commerce over all other, especially Japanese.

The foreigners fell back on their treaty agreements and complained that the Chinese were making a mockery of most-favored-nation clauses, which guaranteed each of them that they would be treated as favorably as any other nation. But China could reply with quotations from the king's letters reminding complainants that the duties Korea owed the "father nation" were beyond their area of inquiry. Of course, foreign influence did not cease, and the powers in Korea jealously watched each other as well as the Chinese. Britain occupied Port Hamilton, an island off the south Korean coast, from 1885 to 1887 in response to rumors that a Korean Foreign Office advisor, Möllendorff, who had been appointed by Li Hung-chang, was secretly dealing with Russia. Li discharged Möllendorff and the British finally withdrew. Another altercation concerned an American legation representative in Seoul, Ensign George Foulk, who, Yuan learned, had been sympathetic to the Korean progressives at the time of the 1884 attempted coup. He demanded and obtained Foulk's ouster. Also, Yuan and the American legation were at odds over a projected Korean mission to Washington in 1887. Yuan tried to block the mission, which was a favorite project of Americans in Seoul, then insisted that it must be subordinate to the Chinese embassy in Washington while in America. Dr. H. N. Allen, the American member of the delegation, made sure that the Koreans did not subordinate themselves to the Chinese in Washington, for which Yuan had the chief delegate exiled after his return to Korea. Japan tried to get telegraph concessions and keep up its trade, but was only partially successful. Yuan Shih-k'ai was probably the most influential individual in Seoul from 1885 to 1894.

THE SINO-JAPANESE WAR

By the early 1890's the powers were much annoyed at what they considered to be China's highhandedness in Korea. The Westerners had little appreciation of Confucian relationships, and they considered China's tactics violations of Korean independence. Japan understood more Confucianism, and sometimes gained a point by routing a diplomatic demand through China, as in the case of a grain export controversy, but her government, too, was Western-style in diplomacy and resented China's position. Furthermore, Japan, emerging as a new nation, full of self-conscious nationalism, began to look on Korea as a security problem vis-à-vis other powers, especially Russia. The years since 1885 had been increasingly antiforeign and especially anti-Japan, in Korea. This was fostered by Yuan and also by the

Taewongun's party, not in an overt sense against the foreigners themselves, but in the sense that for a Korean to be a "progressive" now was tantamount to treason. The prime "traitors," Kim and Pak, remained abroad, with a price on their heads.

Yet political and social injustice was rife in Korea. Confucian virtue was talked about, but the *yangban* class, which was supposed to possess it, had become avaricious and self-indulgent to an extreme. The luxury of high officials close to the court was jealously resented by lower officials in the countryside and they fairly outdid one another in exactions from farmers, small manufacturers, and other producing members of society. A promising cotton industry was ruined by "cloth taxes"; an "ever normal granary" system which was supposed to aid farmers became a mechanism for maintaining high interest rates. Bribery, sale of offices, unjust taxation, legalized extortion, brutal punishments carried out at the whim of officials, and social discriminations were the rule. A whole class of hereditary outcastes did the most menial jobs and were considered beyond the pale of human society, and ordinary people, mostly farmers, were little more than beasts of burden for the parasitic officials. The large class of free farmers created at the beginning of the Yi era had become largely a class of debt slaves.

The Tonghak Society

Nevertheless a movement arose which aimed to rectify some of these abuses, one which proved unusually tenacious because it took on an antiforeign, traditionalist, rather than an alien-inspired reformist cast. This was the Tonghak (Eastern Learning) movement. It had not, it seems, been antiforeign in the beginning. In fact its founder, Ch'oe (Choi), may have been influenced by Christianity to undertake a serious reevaluation of life's meaning. At any rate, in 1859 he experienced what he thought to be a revelation from the "Lord of Heaven" which resulted in his founding a new religion. He rejected Christianity as false, except perhaps for the idea of a supreme deity, and he drew generously on Buddhist, Confucianist, and Taoist teachings to construct a new set of tenets which had important social and political implications. Rejecting class distinction and urging improvement in the lot of the common people, his teaching challenged the corruptness and arbitrariness of officials. Ch'oe was executed in 1864, and his Tonghak society outlawed. But as a movement it continued to grow, employing passive measures to bring pressure on government officials and making use of the right of petition to obtain redress of grievances. It became particularly strong in south Korea.

In 1893 its adherents appeared at the palace gates in Seoul, petitioning the king for removal of the bans against them and complaining that foreigners, even Christians, were now tolerated. They were driven away by palace guards. Early in 1894 the movement took a violent turn. With dissatisfaction rife in the southern provinces, the Tonghak took control of a wide belt across south Korea, and, tying their grievances to foreign influences in the capital, proclaimed their intention of ousting them. With mass support from impoverished farmers and villagers, they were joined by many disaffected Confucianists and fallen nobles, and it may be that the Taewongun aided them. In addition they seem to have had support from certain reactionary elements in Japan which, dissatisfied with the course of modernization in their own country, were seeking ways to restore "Eastern virtue" in the world, and perhaps to give vent to samurai energies.

As the Tonghak affair was coming to a climax, an unrelated but spectacular assassination incident increased the tension. Kim Ok-kiun, the famous Korean progressive who had been in exile since 1884, was killed in 1894 by a Korean agent who had trailed him to a Shanghai hotel, and his body was taken on a Chinese ship to Korea where it was dismembered. This inflamed Japanese liberals, who had befriended Kim and who had since the Tientsin convention been critical of the Japanese government's "let-alone" policy on Korean matters. Although pressed by antigovernment critics of both the reactionary and liberal variety to intervene in Korea, the Japanese government, led by the ever cautious Ito, was at first not inclined to do so. But it was buffeted by interventionist storms in Japan, and at a singularly inopportune moment China responded to a Korean government entreaty for aid and sent troops "to put down rebellion in our tributary state." This was really not necessary, for by the time the troops arrived, the Korean government had the rebellion under control.

Japan Decides on War

The Japanese government now decided to send troops "in line with the Tientsin convention" to "match the Chinese" and to effect a "joint evacuation." However, the tension mounted as Japanese troops poured in and came face to face with the Chinese. Japan had long smarted at Yuan Shih-k'ai's "arrogance" in Korea and was particularly offended at China's renewed reference to Korea as her tributary state. In addition, the political

FIGURE 14.3. A conference of Japanese naval officers aboard their ship during the Sino-Japanese War.

opposition in the Japanese Diet was threatening to overthrow the government, the Japanese military was anxious to test its mettle, and businessmen wanted to enlarge Korean trade. Finally, the realities of Far Eastern power politics, particularly the rise of Russian power, which was symbolized by the construction of the Trans-Siberian Railroad, made the oligarchs desirous, even at the risk of war, of strengthening Japan's position in Korea. Accordingly, in June, 1894, with troops already in Korea, the Japanese cabinet reconsidered the Korean situation and decided not to accept a merely "joint evacuation," but instead to demand that China accept far-reaching reforms in the Korean government as the price of withdrawal. Ito was, at first, cautious about this, lest there be international repercussions, but finding that international sentiment, particularly British, was favorable to Japan, decided on war with an attack on a Chinese troopship on July 25.

Hostilities lasted from July, 1894 to March, 1895, and the Japanese, to the surprise of many, were everywhere victorious. They ousted the Chinese from Korea, occupied Seoul and other strategic points, and invaded and occupied southern Manchuria and the Shantung peninsula, where they seized the important port of Weihaiwei. Their fleet, victorious on the sea, also controlled the Formosa Strait and forces were landed on that island. With Japan's Manchurian army poised for a march into China proper, the Chinese sued for peace. On March 20 Li Hung-chang himself arrived at Shimonoseki to meet with Ito and other Japanese negotiators. He asked for an armistice while peace terms could be negotiated. At first the Japanese refused to grant the armistice, insisting that the war would proceed while negotiations went on, which would, because of the realities of the military situation, put tremendous pressure on the Chinese. However, an unexpected incident happened. A Japanese ultranationalist fanatic attempted to assassinate Li Hung-chang, which turned world sympathy toward China, and the Japanese emperor, in partial atonement, granted the armistice immediately.

Treaty of Shimonoseki and the Triple Intervention

After Li's recovery the negotiations proceeded and the Treaty of Shimonoseki ending the war was signed on April 18, 1895. The terms called for the abandonment of all Chinese claims to Korea and her recognition of the complete independence of the peninsula. In addition, Japan obtained "compensation." China ceded the Liaotung peninsula in south Manchuria, Formosa, and the Pescadores Islands to Japan "in perpetuity," and 200 million Chinese dollars were to be paid, with Japan continuing to occupy Weihaiwei until payment was received.

Even before the treaty terms were made known there were rumors that an intervention by Western powers would take place if Japan's terms were too severe. The Japanese cabinet considered these, but decided "not to give in at all to China" in the treaty terms and later, if necessary, to make adjustments in accordance with the demands of the powers. Otherwise, Ito thought the settlement would be endlessly complicated by arguments with other powers. The intervention, when it came on April 23, was blunt and demanding. Organized by Russia, it took the form of nearly identical notes from Russia, France, and Germany demanding that Japan restore the Liaotung peninsula to China lest its possession by Japan be a "perpetual obstacle to the peace of the Far East." There was more than a hint that force would be employed if Japan did not give in. The Japanese looked not too hopefully toward London and Washington for aid, and tentatively proposed to give up most, but not all, of the Manchurian peninsula. The Triple Intervention remained firm. On May 5 Japan capitulated, and announced to the three powers and the world that she accepted their "recommendation." The three powers expressed their "congratulations."

At home the capitulation to the Triple Intervention seriously embarrassed the Japanese government. There were outcries from various quarters demanding that Japan fight the interfering powers, but the government by press censorship and an emphasis on the emperor's determination to "bear the unbearable" controlled the situation. At least Japan had Formosa, an indemnity and, presumably, a strong position in "independent" Korea.

Japanese Reforms in Korea

In Korea, since their seizure of power in late July, the Japanese had been trying to effect radical reforms. One of their ablest diplomats, Inoue Kaoru, was sent to Seoul to build a new regime, employing pro-Japanese Korean progressives who now came out of hiding and, led by Pak Young-hyo, formed a new "reform" ministry. Certainly reforms were long overdue and many of the Japanese-sponsored measures, if they had been accomplished with due regard for Korean independence, would have been most worthwhile. For example, a clearly departmentalized central government structure was inaugurated. Also decreed were the separation of the royal household from political affairs (aimed primarily at the queen's clan), abolition of many sinecures, financial reforms, and legal reforms, many of which had far reaching social implications, such as Resolution 37, which liberated the outcastes.

Inoue became so interested in the reform program that at times he was quarreling with his own government on behalf of loans for Korea. However, ultimately his and the Japanese government's concern was with Japanese and not Korean interests, realization of which stirred Korean resentment, even among pro-Japanese ministers like Pak. Inoue was spectacularly successful for a while, but by the spring of 1895 the Korean old guard was blocking his every move and about that time Pak and other reformist ministers ceased to cooperate also. Finally Inoue gave up in disgust and the Japanese government decided to abandon reform and merely maintain Japanese interests through a holding operation with a tough former general, Miura Goro, in charge of the Japanese legation at Seoul. Miura found the Min clan implacable and became involved in a plot with the Taewongun to murder Queen Min. This was accomplished on October 8, 1895, but it was a diplomatic fiasco for Japan. Although Miura, who had disobeyed his instructions, was recalled and made to stand trial, his actions had made Japan so hated and distrusted in Seoul that she could now hope to accomplish nothing there except by force. The Tokyo government, wary of world opinion and disillusioned with Korean affairs, decided against this. They made a halfhearted effort to keep control of the palace precincts through the closing months of 1895, but early in February 1896 the king and crown prince escaped to the Russian legation, where they took up residence, and from whence the king issued proclamations branding collaborators of the Japanese as traitors and rescinding the Japanese-tainted reforms.

With Confucian ties with China severed and Japanese tutelage broken, Korea thus began her career as an independent state, as it were, from the front porch of the Russian legation.

BASIC DATES

1392–1910	Yi dynasty
1598	End of Japanese (Hideyoshi's) invasions of Korea
1609	Treaty settlement with Japan
1619	Korea defeated in aiding Ming against Manchus
1627	Korea invaded by the Manchus
1637	Korea accepts Manchu suzerainty
1784	Beginnings of Christianity in Korea
1800	Fall of Chong Ta-san, orthodoxy strengthened
1811	End of missions to Japan
1864	Kojong king (to 1907); Taewongun in power as regent (to 1873)
1865–1870	Intense persecution of Christians and foreigners
1866	French expedition; *General Sherman* affair
1871	American expedition
1873	Japanese samurai unsuccessfully demand war with Korea
1876	Japan opens Korea, obtains Kanghwa Treaty with Chinese aid
1882	American treaty, followed by other Western treaties. Taewongun removed to China following antiforeign incident
1884	Korean progressives attempt unsuccessful coup d'état
1885	Li-Ito (Tientsin) Convention, followed by Chinese ascendancy (to 1894)
1894	Tonghak Rebellion; murder of Kim; outbreak of Sino-Japanese War
1895	Treaty of Shimonoseki; Triple Intervention; murder of Queen Min; followed by decline of Japanese influence

SUPPLEMENTARY READING

Choy, B. Y. *Korea: A History.* Rutland, Vt., 1971.

Hatada, T. *A History of Korea.* Trans. and ed. by W. W. Smith, Jr. and B. Hazard. Santa Barbara, Calif., 1969.

Reischauer, E. O. and J. K. Fairbank. *East Asia: The Great Tradition.* Boston, 1960. Contains an excellent chapter titled "Traditional Korea."

Sohn, P. K., C. C. Kim, and Y. S. Hong. *The History of Korea.* Seoul, 1970.

ADVANCED READING

Chien, F. F. *The Opening of Korea: A Study of Chinese Diplomacy, 1876–1885.* Hamden, Conn., 1967.
Conroy, H. *The Japanese Seizure of Korea, 1868–1910.* Philadelphia, 1960. An interpretive study of Japanese policies toward Korea.
Griffis, W. E. *Corea: The Hermit Nation.* New York, 1882. Old, but still available and useful.
Harrington, F. H. *God, Mammon and the Japanese.* Madison, Wis., 1944. Discusses Korea and the powers from the 1880's to 1905.
Hulbert, H. B. *History of Korea.* Seoul, 1905; Rev. ed. by C. N. Weems, New York, 1962.
Hulbert, H. B. *The Passing of Korea.* New York, 1909; reprinted, Seoul, 1969.
Kang, Y. *The Grass Roof.* New York, 1932. A novel on Korea in transition.
Kim, C. Y. E. and H. K. Kim. *Korea and the Politics of Imperialism.* Berkeley, Calif., 1967.
Lee, Y. B. *Diplomatic Relations Between the United States and Korea, 1886–1887.* New York, 1970.
McCune, E. B. *The Arts of Korea.* Tokyo, 1961.
McCune, S. B. *Korea's Heritage: A Regional and Social Geography.* Rutland, Vt., 1956.
Nelson, M. F. *Korea and the Old Orders in Eastern Asia.* Baton Rouge, La., 1946; reprinted, New York, 1967. Excellent work emphasizing Sino-Korean relationships.
Yang, K. P. and G. Henderson. "An Outline of Korean Confucianism," *Journal of Asian Studies,* XVIII (February 1959), pp. 81–101, 259–276. Difficult but important material.

Chapter 15

China: The First Revolution, 1895-1914

China's defeat in the Sino-Japanese war not only revealed her military weakness to outsiders, but awoke many Chinese to the fact that the rather complacently carried out "self-strengthening" program had failed. "Self-strengthening," which had been promoted by such leaders as Tseng Kuo-fan, Tso Tsung-t'ang, and Li Hung-chang, had sought to adapt Western technical skills to China to improve her military capacity without seriously altering her social, political, or ideological structure. Implicit in it was still a sense of China's age-old superiority over other nations. It was grounded in confidence rather than fear. After 1895, however, a note of fear, even desperation, came into the Chinese efforts to save the situation, whether through frantic concessions to Western nations, frantic resistance to their inroads, overnight decrees of change in ancient institutions, or, finally, revolution to wipe out the past and start anew.

INTERNAL EFFORTS AND EXTERNAL PRESSURES, 1895-1899

Chang Chih-tung, who had been one of the more active "self-strengtheners," touched one alarm bell in August, 1895, when he urged that China must have a military alliance with Russia "to save the critical situation today." Russia had "kept treaty agreements with us for more than two hundred years" and so could be trusted more than the other powers. Her navy could patrol China's seas. Others besides Chang, impressed by the way Russia had forced Japan to give up the Liaotung peninsula, backed the same idea with the result that Li Hung-chang, attending the coronation of Tsar Nicholas II in 1896, made a "mutual defense" treaty. It specified only Japan as the potential invader of Chinese or Russian territory and its *quid pro quo* was the granting to Russia of the right to build and control what was to be the Chinese Eastern railroad across Manchuria connecting the Trans-Siberian line with Vladivostok. This was the beginning of an almost disastrous round of concessions.

Scramble for Concessions

A more detailed discussion of these concessions will be made in the next chapter. Suffice it to say here that, although this Russian treaty might temporarily have restrained Japan, it opened the floodgates to demands by other European powers for territorial and economic privileges in China until by the summer of 1898 it seemed that China was being cut up "like a melon." Russia was staking out Manchuria, Mongolia, and north China as her sphere; Germany had laid claim to a privileged position in the Shantung peninsula and was looking acquisitively behind it to the whole Yellow river valley; France had staked off south China as her preserve; and Britain, while opposed to the idea of spheres because she wanted to trade in all parts of China, nonetheless pointed to the whole heart of China, the Yangtze valley, as her prerogative in case carving up was to be the order of the day. Also, Britain obtained Weihaiwei in north China and the whole of the Kowloon peninsula in south China as *"points d'appui"* in alienated areas. The number of "treaty ports" where foreigners enjoyed their own jurisdiction, which had begun with five in the Treaty of Nanking in 1842, had reached nearly a hundred by the end of the century. And, ironically, they included cities, like Chungking, which were as much as a thousand miles inland from the coastline.

In the face of these disastrous developments Tz'u-hsi, the dowager empress, who had remained the power behind the Chinese throne since 1861, temporarily lost her hold on affairs and her nephew, the Kuang-hsü emperor, a liberally inclined though not especially brilliant young man, took the reins of power at court. Beginning in June, 1898, the emperor gave over the effective leadership of the government to one of China's most brilliant scholars, perhaps the most original thinker the Confucian tradition had produced since the Han Learning criticism of orthodox Confucianism had dwindled away in the literary inquisition of Ch'ien-lung. This was K'ang Yu-wei (1858–1927), who shortly after the Sino-Japanese War had submitted a petition of "Ten Thousand Words," signed by 1300 imperial examination candidates at Peking, urging widespread reforms in many fields, from education to agriculture.

K'ang Yu-wei

Although the changes he demanded were far-reaching, K'ang was not a revolutionary. He never questioned the authority of the Manchu government and, in fact, hoped to restore it even after the Revolution of 1911. He was consistently a reformer, advocating peaceful, albeit sweeping, change, in a progressive direction. And he based his program for reform on the best possible Chinese authority, Confucius. Since Confucius, even in his own day, invoked the guidance of the past and Confucianism had remained a

CHINA IN 1900

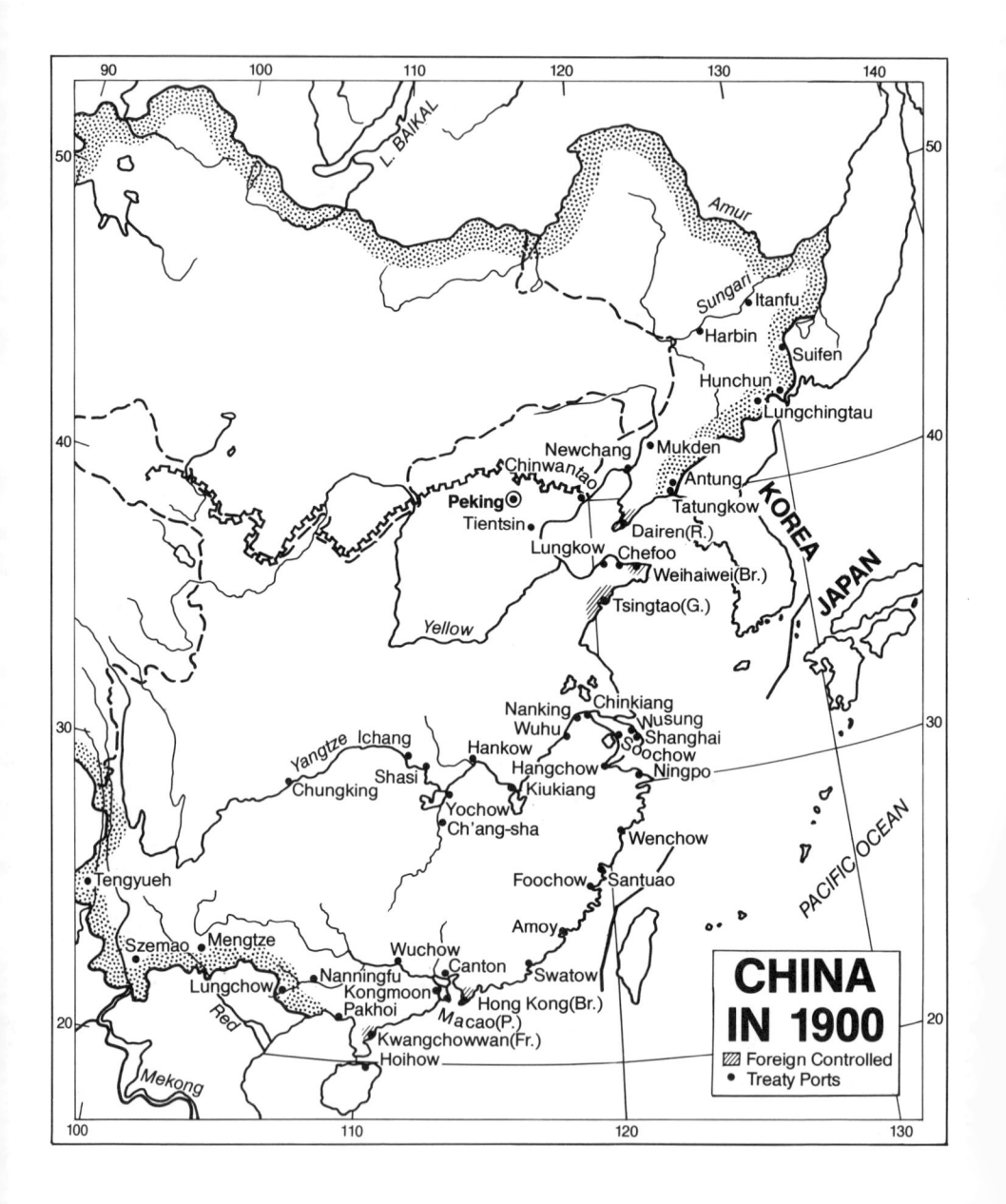

- ▨ Foreign Controlled
- • Treaty Ports

conservative philosophy through the centuries, it is necessary to explain briefly how K'ang could reconcile Confucianism with a program for progress that to be meaningful in the late nineteenth century had to include much that was new to China and Western in origin. He did this by reinterpreting the framework and meaning of Confucius' teaching.

In three remarkable works K'ang set the philosophical background for the sort of reform program he envisioned for China. In an essay on "The Forged Classics of the Wang Mang Period" (or the "False Classics of the Hsin Learning") he rejected certain standard Confucian "texts" as forgeries of a later period, thus clearing the way for his utilization of other texts, more congenial to his theory, as the basis of Confucian teaching. In a second work entitled "Confucius as a Reformer" he utilized what he considered to be more authentic texts, which to that time had been little used, to show that Confucius was a progressive, not a conservative. Confucius, he said, had deliberately constructed a fictitious utopian past in order to indicate what society's future goals should be. His appeal to past tradition was a sort of figure of speech, not a real guide. K'ang's third treatise, called "The Book of the Great Harmony," expressed his ultimate ideal of a utopian Confucian future toward which the Western world was also journeying, a future combining East and West in unselfish human understanding. To realize his thesis he played down the elements of class division in orthodox Confucianism, emphasizing egalitarianism, sharing of property, and unselfishness. There were nine barriers to be removed, he said, among them those between nation and nation, race and race, and men and women. Once these barriers were removed a world government could be constructed, elected by world citizens. All men and women would be free and equal.

As for his practical plan of reform K'ang spoke in its behalf in a historic audience with the emperor Kuang-hsü on June 16, 1898, at a moment when the magnitude of China's problems had been revealed more starkly than ever before in the "melon slicing" concession diplomacy of that spring. The audience lasted an unprecedented five hours. During it K'ang impressed upon a receptive emperor not only the need for reforms, but the necessity of his setting them forth as rapidly as possible by imperial decree. Most of the high ministers, K'ang argued, were very old and conservative, lacking understanding of foreign countries. To rely on them for reform would be like "climbing a tree to seek for fish."

The "100 Days" of Reform

The Emperor agreed. K'ang was appointed secretary of the Tsungli Yamen and given the privilege of submitting memorials directly to the throne. Arrangements were made to bypass conservative ministers, numerous young reformers, such as Liang Ch'i-ch'ao and T'an Ssu-t'ung, were given the opportunity to express their views, and from the palace came decree after decree bearing the imperial seal, instituting reform measures. In a hundred days between June and September, these decrees changed China—on paper, at least. The bureaucracy was revitalized, with many meaningless or potentially obstructive offices abolished, and the authority of the central government over the provinces reemphasized. Since behind officeholding lay the traditional examination system, built around the "eight-legged essay" with its orthodox Confucian subject matter, K'ang attacked that too, and decrees were issued to alter it drastically, introducing the arts and sciences of the West on a par with Chinese subjects and broadening the whole educational structure. Education and officeholding were no longer to be the monopoly of those trained in the narrow classical tradition. Many economic changes were likewise decreed; railroads were to be built, mining and industries to be encouraged, and scientific budgetary controls introduced. Confucius, said K'ang, would have liked this.

Whether Confucius would have liked it is difficult to say, but conservative government officials definitely did not. Fearing loss of their influence and possibly their posts, they found ways to minimize the effect of the decrees. The governor of Shantung and the governor-general of Szechuan, confident of favor in conservative circles at court, simply disobeyed; others avoided the issues. Of all the high provincial officials perhaps only one, the governor of Hunan province, earnestly tried to put the reforms into effect. In a sense, however, provincial officials may have merely been waiting for the outcome of the struggle for power which the sudden onslaught of the reformers had produced at Peking. By September it was clear that very powerful elements of the central court and government structure had been alienated: Manchu princes, palace eunuchs, army commanders, and the empress dowager herself, who, along with her favorite, General Jung-lu, became the focus of anti-reformist sentiment. K'ang had acted too rapidly and alienated too many vested interests. Perhaps he had hoped to take them by surprise and rout them before they realized what was happening, but he knew by September that he had failed, and that, unless military force could be found to back up the reformist position of the emperor, reaction would set in.

The specific problem was Jung-lu, who as governor-general of the metropolitan province of Chihli, wherein Peking was located, and commander of its military forces, was in a position to seize control of the palace whenever he wished. To forestall such an eventuality the reformers sought to enlist the support of Yuan Shih-k'ai. This was the same Yuan Shih-k'ai who had been Chinese "resident" in Korea preceding the Sino-Japanese War. In those days he had been the protégé of Li Hung-chang, but Li's prestige declined after the Sino-Japanese War and Yuan, who had played the game of politics strategically and, it seems, cynically ever since his purchase of an official title in 1880 had launched his career, attached himself to the rising star of Jung-lu after the war. He had been given an important army command and had made the most of it, developing perhaps the best military unit in China in his "Newly Created Army" and its officer corps. The fact that he had utilized Western techniques and advisors, plus the fact that he had been a member of a reform party in 1895, may have led K'ang's group to consider Yuan more progressive than he was, or they may have counted on his ambition. At any rate they attempted to separate him from Jung-lu, had the emperor promote him, and invited his support against his former patron. According to some accounts, Yuan was to seize Jung-lu and the empress dowager and execute them.

Triumph of Reaction

Meanwhile the empress dowager, who had become convinced that the reform measures would undermine the position of her family and her favorites, her main concern, was biding her time for an opportunity to reassert her former authority. In this situation of plot and counter-plot Yuan and his "modern" army were sought by both sides, and Yuan decided to "remain loyal" to his patron and former commander, Jung-lu, or to "betray" the emperor, however one defines it. On September 21, 1898, with military support from Jung-lu and Yuan Shih-k'ai, the empress dowager seized control of the government, imprisoned the emperor in the winter palace, and ordered the execution of the reform leaders. K'ang and Liang fled the country, but six of their colleagues, including T'an Ssu-t'ung, were taken and executed. The reform edicts were quickly revoked.

The wheel now turned full circle to reaction. In only one field, the military, were reforms continued where Yuan and Jung-lu directed continuing modernization. Even here, however, the old provincial decentralization was preserved so that their programs had little effect outside their immediate commands, and scant attention was given to the industrial development behind modern weaponry. Politically the focus was on preserving the

FIGURE 15.1. Empress Dowager Tz'u-hsi, in her latter years.

imperial structure intact, and ideologically there was a reaction against all forms of Western innovation, which found its most extreme expression in the so-called "Boxer" movement.

THE "OPEN DOOR" AND THE BOXER MOVEMENT, 1899–1901

The defeat of the reformers, though it comforted the empress dowager and conservative officials, only deepened the chaos in China. Undoubtedly K'ang Yu-wei had been doctrinaire and his reform group overbearing under the heady wine of imperial patronage, to the point that they had alienated cautious reformers who might have helped them. For example, Weng T'ung-ho, the imperial tutor who had recommended K'ang to the emperor, had been alienated by the boldness of his plans. But after K'ang was gone, there was for a time a complete vacuum of constructive leadership, with the result that the powers moved to tighten their holds on their respective spheres of influence in anticipation of whatever further breakdown might occur in China.

The "Open Door"

The first moves to stem disintegration came from abroad, specifically from Great Britain where, amidst indulgence in the competition of sphere grabbing, there was also uneasiness. Far better for British trade and interests would be the preservation of open rights of trade in all parts of China. Here was the germinating idea of the "Open Door" which, in fact, had been an unnamed attribute of both British and American policy in China since the first treaties in the 1840's. During 1898 the British government put out several feelers to the United States to ascertain whether the latter would support such a position, and in the winter of 1898–1899 Lord Charles Beresford, returning to London from a trip to China, traveled by way of the United States making "a continuous after-dinner speech." He had one central theme: China was being torn apart by concession diplomacy. It must stop or Russia would shut out all others from north China and Manchuria. Shortly thereafter he published his warnings in a book called *The Break-up of China*.

American opinion was cool. There was wariness of involvement in China, particularly in concert with Great Britain which to most Americans was fully as imperialist as other European powers. However, a very important American had been converted to the idea. John Hay as ambassador at London had been acquainted with the early formulation of the idea, and in August, 1898 he was recalled to Washington to become secretary of state. When another English visitor, Alfred E. Hippisley, lately of the China Customs Service, and William W. Rockhill, Secretary Hay's chief China policy advisor, began to draw up a suggested version of an "open door" policy statement, he encouraged them, while warning that "the senseless [anti-British] prejudices in certain sections of the 'Senate and people' compel us to move with great caution." By September, 1899, however, the

American climate was more favorable, and having received President McKinley's approval, Secretary Hay issued the famous "Open Door" notes to the various powers with interests in China, asking their assurances that there would be no interference with the rights of trade of other countries. The replies were rather evasive, admiring the general principle but pointing out special "problems" in each power's special area, even the British studiously avoiding mention of Hong Kong and Kowloon though they endorsed the principle elsewhere. However, Hay, in cavalier fashion, simply shut the replies up in his desk and announced to the world that the Open Door principle had been accepted by all. Of course, even if it were observed, this first formulation of the Open Door policy only aimed to keep the sphere holders from maintaining them as exclusive preserves. It did not attempt to restore them to Chinese administration.

Nevertheless Hay's dramatic appeal may have produced a momentary pause in the concessions race. Then in the following year he added a much more far reaching corollary to the Open Door doctrine. This was a unilateral pronouncement by the United States that its objective, in addition to maintaining the principle of equal and impartial trade with all parts of China, was "to preserve Chinese territorial and administrative entity." This elicited no promises or replies from other powers; it asked for none. But it set forth a goal and an ideal to which the United States would refer again and again in subsequent diplomatic arguments about China. The statement was issued at a critical time, on July 3, 1900, when north China was plunged into chaos by the antiforeign Boxer Rebellion, and an international intervention was being organized. Hay was trying to forestall the possibility of the intervention turning into a partition of China.

The Boxer Rebellion

The Boxer Rebellion, or movement, was a violent reaction against foreign influences in China which began among secret societies in Shantung and, as it spread, found support among court reactionaries to such an extent that it has been argued that the Peking government initiated it deliberately. However, it now seems clear that the movement was popularly rather than officially inspired. It was rebellious but not revolutionary, for it supported the Manchu government, while demanding the suppression of foreign influences in China. It was ignorant and blind, but like the Tonghak Rebellion in Korea and the Satsuma Rebellion in Japan contained within it real grievances, the greatest of which was the arrogance of foreign imperialism in China. Recent research indicates that unemployment along the Grand Canal, which was falling into disuse because of the development of steam navigation in coastal waters, provided a particular economic grievance.

The Boxers (I Ho Ch'üan or "Righteous Harmony Fists") drew on certain Buddhist and Taoist traditions together with tales of the supernatural in popular operas and novels of Shantung to put together a sort of religious ideology. This held that a man by practicing a special ritual of calisthenics ("boxing") could beget a supernatural spirit in him which would render him impervious to bullets, change the direction of the wind, foretell enemies'

FIGURE 15.2. First railroad train passing through the wall of Peking illustrates the impact of the West.

plans, command divine fire to burn enemy places, etc. The "Red Lanterns," a sort of women's auxiliary sect, could learn to walk on water and even to fly, it was said. The existence of an I Ho Secret Society which practiced boxing rituals goes back at least as far as 1815 and probably earlier, but in 1898, amidst general rumors and allegations concerning foreign penetration of China, it took on a distinctly antiforeign and particularly anti-Christian complexion. It began to issue propaganda against the foreigners and to urge villagers to join in attacks on Christian churches and other establishments and on Chinese Christian converts, who were especially hated because, it was claimed, they obtained special privileges through their foreign connections and enjoyed the intercession of missionaries in their behalf even in legal cases.

The first attacks against Christians occurred in the fall of 1898 by which time Boxers were operating on both sides of the boundary between Shantung and Chihli provinces. Within a few months there had been many killings and burnings of buildings in Shantung especially, as the Boxers put extreme pressure on neutral villagers to participate in the maraudings. For example, a typical call to action would warn: "After this notice is issued to instruct you villagers, no matter which village you are living in, if there are Christian converts, you ought to get rid of them quickly. The churches that belong to them should be unreservedly burned down. Everyone who intends to spare someone, or to disobey our orders by concealing Christian converts, will be punished according to the regulations when we come to his place, and he will be burned to death to prevent his impeding our program."[1]

Beginning in December, 1899, however, Boxer activity in Shantung was sharply curtailed when Yuan Shih-k'ai was sent there as acting governor. Yuan dealt very sternly with the Boxers and broke up their Shantung organization. However, they became all the more active in the neighboring province of Chihli where in the spring of 1900 they launched an all-out attack on railroads, telegraphs, and other foreign establishments as well as on native Christians in that province, cutting off communication between Peking and the coast. One reason that the Boxers could operate so freely in the Peking area was that they had begun to have many sympathizers at court. These were notably the Manchu grand councillor, Kang I, and the imperial princes, Tuan, father of the heir apparent, and Chuang. These reactionaries at court at first secretly and then openly encouraged the Boxers to the point that even Yuan Shih-k'ai, always reading the political signs, began to be less anti-Boxer in his attitude. Several provincial viceroys and several important members of the central government, especially those who had experience in dealing with foreigners, sent in strongly worded memorials warning the court that the Boxer disturbances could be ruinous and that they must be dealt with severely, but the ear of the empress dowager was being turned to favor the Boxers and these warnings were to no avail. As the Boxers approached Peking Manchu troops made a few halfhearted efforts to stop them, but with the reactionaries taking control of the court they began more and more to merge with imperial troops with the result that Peking was entered in early June, churches and foreign residences burned, and the foreign diplomatic representatives besieged in the legation quarter. Hundreds of Chinese Christians, a member of the Japanese legation, and the German ambassador were killed, but a call for help had reached British Admiral Seymour at Tientsin and he and other foreign military officers there began to organize a relief expedition. The first detachment left for Peking on June 8, but was forced back with heavy losses. Then several thousand foreign troops, English, German, Japanese, Russian, and American, were rushed to the Tientsin area, and, finding the way blocked by the Taku forts, bombarded and captured them. The imperial council, summoned in Peking, was dominated by reactionaries. It decided to induct the Boxers, "young and strong," into the imperial army, and on June 21, 1900, issued a declaration of war by China against the intervening powers.

Despite the fact that the Peking government had in effect joined the

---

[1] S. Y. Teng and J. K. Fairbank, eds., *China's Response to the West, 1839–1923* (Cambridge: Harvard University Press, 1954), p. 190.

Boxers and decided on war, eight of the southern provincial viceroys joined together to oppose the position and to urge that Li Hung-chang, then viceroy at Canton, be appointed to negotiate with the powers. Li Hung-chang, himself, disregarded orders of the court and advised Chinese ministers abroad not to break relations with foreign governments. The effect of this was to keep the southern provinces entirely out of the war. At Peking, too, there were some officials who risked, and lost, their lives by warning the court that it was making a terrible mistake to join forces with the Boxers.

As the renewed international relief expedition approached Peking, government there broke down completely and shortly after the allied force entered Peking early in the morning of August 15, the empress dowager, her emperor prisoner, the child heir apparent, and important officials fled from the city in confusion, making their way eventually to the old T'ang capital site, Sian (formerly Ch'ang-an). What Arnold Toynbee has called "zealotism," a frantic, last effort to reverse the tides of change, had failed. China's capital was in the hands of the Western "barbarians."

The Boxer Settlement

The Boxer affair had brought out the worst in both sides. The Boxers and their high-placed supporters had been ruthless and irrational in the extreme, but to its discredit the allied relief expedition had been marauding and vengeful. Chinese officials had equivocated and lied to the foreigners and to each other, while certain of the powers, as will be discussed in the next chapter, sought to use the opportunity to seize Chinese territory and they all demanded huge indemnities and more controls in China. However, there were brighter aspects to the affair. Hay's circular of July 3 had sounded a warning, and when the powers discussed what was to be done after having defeated the Chinese, they soon became aware that a world war over Chinese territory might result if they were too greedy. Southern viceroys, as already mentioned, were anxious to restore good relations with the powers and Yuan Shih-k'ai had avoided throwing his modern army into the fray, which, had he done so, would have made the war much more prolonged and bloody.

Thus, settlement short of the dismemberment of China was possible. The allies insisted on severe punishments, not only of the Boxer leaders but of the court officials who had first encouraged and then led them. This included death for Prince Chuang, who, according to their indictment, had become commander-in-chief of the Boxers, Prince Tuan, Kang I, and several other high personages. Kang I died of illness before sentence could be pronounced, and Prince Tuan's punishment was commuted to life imprisonment, but most of the others paid with their lives. China was required to outlaw "forever" antiforeign societies (membership in which was to be punished by death), and to pay an indemnity based on the whole cost of the expedition and damages of $330,000,000 in gold (the American representative refused to approve the sum, demanding it be lowered to $200,000,000, a figure based on China's ability to pay). The Chinese government accepted the former amount, however, to be paid over thirty-nine years at four per cent interest, with customs and salt tax receipts pledged as security. The United States finally accepted the settlement, but later returned large portions of its share, which the Chinese government used for the education of Chinese students in the United States. In addition, the forts at Taku were to be permanently razed and the powers were to have the right to station permanent forces at Peking to defend their legations, a privilege which the Japanese were to utilize and expand in the 1930's as they sought to control north China.

Having reached agreement on these and various lesser issues on September 7, 1901, the powers gave back the throne to the Manchu dynasty, with both sides constructing a rather elaborate pretense that the Boxer affair had been a "rebellion" against the dynasty which the intervention had helped to suppress.

THE MANCHUS ATTEMPT REFORM

Reaction having failed, the empress dowager now turned for advice and support to those viceroys and governors who had opposed the Boxer movement and the war. These included Li Hung-chang, Chang Chih-tung, Liu K'un-i (viceroy at Nanking), and Yuan Shih-k'ai. Though Li died in 1901 and Liu in 1902, these four were responsible for setting forth proposals which were implemented into what is best described as a "conservative reform" program (in contrast to K'ang Yu-wei's "radical" program of 1898 and in further contrast to the newer revolutionary ideas of Sun Yat-sen). The "conservative reform" lasted until the death, in November, 1908, of the empress dowager, who, having at last been convinced of the dire need for serious changes, supported the program in her last years but was unable to project it beyond her death.

Conservative Reform

Conservative reform focused on the educational and civil service system, the military, and finally on constitutional change. During the long negotiations for the Boxer settlement, Chang and Liu submitted a joint proposal pointing out that China had "a dearth of men of ability due to our limited knowledge and unsubstantial learning" and urging that "both ancient and modern methods" be considered in the educational process and the examination system. Students should be encouraged to study abroad and civil service examinations should include "the politics, geography, military systems, agriculture, industry, mathematics and the like, of all countries." They urged the establishment of a nationwide primary school system and commented favorably on such systems in the West. These proposals were actually almost as radical as the educational proposals of the "100 Days" in 1898, but they contained more solicitude for the well-being of scholars trained in the classical style and more concern for precedents. Also they advocated Western military training and the abolition of old military garrisons, but cited the earlier Ch'ing precedent of employing Western Jesuits such as Ferdinand Verbiest to design cannon and they urged planning for the livelihood of Manchu bannermen, who would be displaced.

In addition they proposed that industry be promoted, necessary technical schools established, fiscal policies revised so as to eliminate the pur-

FIGURE 15.3. Chang Chih-tung, a leader of conservative reform.

chase of offices and titles, and the tax structure improved. To help raise revenue they proposed the establishment of a revenue-producing postal system and government control and taxing of opium, rather than addition to traditional taxes. All of these things, they averred, were very different from K'ang Yu-wei's proposals, for he had only promoted himself and "treacherously sought to disturb the basic order of things."

The empress dowager agreed that reforms outlined by Chang and Liu should be put into practice "from time to time." This was not very specific, but it was an invitation of a sort for provincial governors to proceed, and a number of reforms were instituted, especially in the metropolitan province, Chihli, which was now under the governorship of Yuan Shih-k'ai and in the Yangtze "Hu" provinces under Chang Chih-tung. A grand reform of education was proclaimed in 1904 and the ancient examination system spectacularly abolished by decree in September, 1905.

That this could be done without widespread protest from the gentry class indicated their tacit admission at last that the old Confucian style education could no longer stand as "the ladder of success" in twentieth century China. Many gentry sons were soon scrambling for entry into "new-style" schools where Western subjects were taught or for government scholarships to study abroad. A degree of social change was implicit in this, for lower gentry and wealthy merchant families were especially quick to take advantage of the broadening educational horizon. Within a few years over a million students were attending the new schools or studying in

Japan, and not a few were pursuing their studies in the United States or in Europe.

Military Reforms

The most discernible progress was in the military. With the help of German military advisors, by 1905 Chang had trained a crack brigade, divided into infantry, artillery, cavalry, and engineer units, as the core of a modernized central China army. This strengthened his personal position in many ways, and was part of his purpose, for he no doubt took into account the probability that his reformist position might be undercut by rivals if he did not possess military strength. Yuan, being in command at the capital and having the Manchu treasury to draw on, instead of merely the resources of two provinces as did Chang, was even more successful. During these years Yuan built the *Pei-yang* (Northern) army into a formidable organization, complete with an officer clique that was personally loyal to him, and backed by military and technical schools. Taken together, Chang and Yuan had rather remarkable success in training modern armies, and, perhaps unfortunately, in making a military career an avenue to leadership in China. Chang's army did not have a lasting influence, partly because it was several times broken up by the transfer of its units to places like Canton, outside of Chang's jurisdiction. But Yuan's remained relatively intact despite the urgings of some court advisors that it be broken up. Both Chang and Yuan were "kicked upstairs" to high positions at Peking in 1907 to separate them from their commands. Chang did lose touch with his, but Yuan, by very clever manipulation, managed to maintain control through his subordinates.

The entrance of provincial governors like Chang and Yuan into the central administration at Peking was not simply an effort to deprive them of control of their armies, although this was a partial factor. It was also an expression of the imperial court's desire to achieve more centralization in government generally and to make some of its best provincial leaders a part of it. The court was gradually coming to the realization that such matters as military development, railroad construction, and fiscal reforms needed central planning. A difficult question, however, was whether the provinces would regard this merely as a sort of power grab by the faltering dynasty, an attempt to deprive the provinces of those traditional areas of autonomy which had made their submission to a "foreign" Manchu rule tolerable. The court was not unaware of this problem and, realizing that any attempt to tighten the lines of authority from Peking might lead to provincial disaffection or even revolt, it sought to give assurances of magnanimity with the promise of constitutional government.

Steps Toward Constitutionalism

Constitutionalism of a very limited, monarchical variety was envisioned, but nevertheless several serious steps were made in that direction. The empress dowager dispatched missions to Europe and America in 1905 to investigate constitutional governments, and the model provided by Japan was closely watched. Reports recommended that the monarch grant a constitution, reserving all unspecified powers to the throne and thus avoiding the problem and danger of a constitution being forced upon the monarch from below, as had happened in many European countries. It was also argued that a constitution would help to make the country strong, enlisting the support of all the people behind the dynasty. Tz'u-hsi issued various edicts in support of this principle, the most noteworthy in the summer of 1908 promising constitutional government within nine years (strikingly like the emperor Meiji's promise of 1881). Experimentation was begun with consultative provincial assemblies, which were to be a training ground for a consultative national assembly.

Meanwhile legal reforms, advocated especially by Yuan Shih-k'ai, which mitigated torture and punishment and introduced some Western and Japanese concepts, were introduced, and currency reform was talked about. However, none of the reforms, with the exception of the opium control program, which so impressed the British that they agreed to reduce the opium import coming from India to whatever extent the Chinese decreased opium production in China, was very far advanced by November, 1908, when the death of the empress dowager brought everything to a standstill again. Her death was preceded, ironically and suspiciously, by the death one day earlier of the long imprisoned Kuang-hsü emperor.

Power at court was then seized by Prince Ch'un, father of the three-year-old emperor-designate, Hsuan-t'ung (also known as P'u-yi), who became regent. Prince Ch'un was fearful of the power and influence of Yuan Shih-k'ai, and he contrived to have him retired, which Yuan accepted on the excuse of "foot trouble," perhaps to bide his time. Apparently Prince Ch'un expected to rely primarily on Chang Chih-tung for political advice, but Chang died in 1909, and one by one the reformist measures and promises, even the opium control, went into eclipse. On his own Prince Ch'un was unduly solicitous of the position of the Manchu nobility, which offended their Chinese colleagues. A relatively handpicked advisory assembly was convened at Peking in 1910. Although enjoined from discussing the constitutional problem, it did so anyway, demanding that the nine-year program be speeded up. The assembly was dismissed, but a promise was issued that a parliament would be convened in 1913.

Events did not wait upon this promise. Discontent, rife in many parts of China, was fanned further by the so-called railroad controversy in 1911, wherein the central government tried to "nationalize" existing railroads and take control of new construction. This was bitterly resented by merchant groups, especially in Szechuan, who had invested in railway enterprise to make large profits and now foresaw the government reimbursing them on a fractional basis. Beset with problems from many sides and with revolution breaking out at Wuhan, the Regent swallowed his pride and recalled Yuan Shih-k'ai on October 14, 1911. But it was too late to save the dynasty.

REVOLUTION AND REPUBLIC

Liang Ch'i-ch'ao

The Revolution of 1911, which overthrew the Manchu dynasty, was born in the minds and hearts of Chinese living in exile. The most important and by far the best known of these, of course, was Sun Yat-sen. However, there were several others who contributed almost as much as he to the new Chinese nationalist spirit which produced the Revolution, even though they may not themselves have intended to be revolutionists. The best example of this type, who deserves a brief discussion before we proceed to Sun, was Liang Ch'i-ch'ao. Liang had been one of the leading reformers of the "100 Days" period in 1898 and after the reaction set in he had fled for his life to Japan. There during the next seven years he was a leading journalist and editor whose ideas strongly influenced the many young Chinese who studied in Japan. Liang's influence declined after 1905 because he refused to take an outright revolutionary position, while his followers, becoming impatient, were increasingly attracted by Sun's outright revolutionist program. Nevertheless Liang's influence in promoting what turned out to be a climate of revolution also was considerable.

Liang was a well-trained classical scholar who was able to synthesize his classical education with a new and vigorous appeal to the intellects and emotions of sensitive and dissatisfied students, who, studying in Japan, saw only too clearly the comparative deficiencies of the China they had left behind. Liang's main theme was that a new spirit must be generated in China among the people themselves and must flow up to the government to make that government responsible, strong, active, and progressive. What he called for in simplest terminology was nationalism. He said that the European powers coming into Asia had found China

> "the largest country with the most fertile territory, the most corrupt government, and the most disorganized and weak people . . . and they mobilized their national imperialism as swarms of ants attached themselves to what is rank and foul and as a myriad of arrows concentrate on a target."[2]

Liang said that the Chinese people must rejuvenate themselves. They did not have to discard their entire heritage, but like a tree they had to grow new branches every year. Otherwise it and they would wither away. His ideas were expressed chiefly in his reformist society's newspaper, the *Ch'ing-i Pao*, which was published in Yokohama. Liang's reformist society, the "Protect the Emperor Society," which had for its official objective the restoration of the deposed Kuang-hsü emperor, was formed in collaboration with his mentor, K'ang Yu-wei, who was in Japan for a time. Liang and K'ang were very close to Okuma Shigenobu and other members of his Progressive Party and probably received financial help from them.

Actually Liang was much more active than K'ang in Japan, and also more accessible. It is not surprising, therefore, that Sun Yat-sen's revolutionaries contacted him with a view to joining forces. Liang explored their proposition, though it was opposed from the beginning by K'ang, and he even made a trip to Hawaii to meet Sun's brother and uncle and to be introduced to active Chinese leadership there. He spent the first several months of 1900 in Hawaii, where his popularity began to cause misgivings on the part of Sun, especially as he seemed more interested in enlisting a

[2] Teng and Fairbank, *op. cit.*, pp. 221–222.

Hawaiian Chinese following for his own reformist approach than in furthering Sun's cause. Sun rebuked him for this, and thereafter the two went their separate ways, with Liang's following gradually dwindling while Sun's increased. In addition to the issue of monarchical reform versus antimonarchical revolution between them, a second issue that also divided Sun and Liang was that of socialism. Sun regarded his economic program as essentially socialist, while Liang wrote scathing attacks on socialism, and although neither had a very clear idea of many important socialist doctrines, it was a point of bitter argument between them.

Despite the importance of Liang and other reformists in probing the possibilities for change, the strongest movement leading China to revolution was led by Sun Yat-sen. Sun and the group with whom he worked in establishing his first revolutionary society, the Hsing-Chung-hui (Revive China Society) were very unlike the "100 Days" reformers in background and outlook. The latter were Confucian scholars, whereas Sun and his friends could never have passed Confucian examinations. They were lower-class, Canton area people mostly, and those who, like Sun, obtained an education got it in Western or mixed Chinese-Western surroundings.

Sun Yat-sen

Sun Yat-sen was born in 1866 in the Chungshan district of Kwangtung province, of which Canton was the capital. Sun's early education was at a village school but at the age of twelve he was sent to Hawaii, to live with an elder brother who had gone there some years before and prospered as a storekeeper. Sun spent about six years in Hawaii, where he attended an English language missionary school. His brother sent him back to China partly because he was becoming too alienated from his Chinese heritage. Back in China in the mid-1880's he became a Christian and argued vehemently against local traditions of worship in his home community, from which he was finally expelled for breaking images in the ancestral temple. He then began attending school in Hong Kong, studying Chinese among other subjects, returned briefly to his home to marry a neighboring farmer's daughter, but centered his activities thereafter in Hong Kong, Macao, and Canton. He obtained a medical degree as a student of Dr. James Cantlie and he practiced for a while, but more and more he drifted into political activity, reformist at first.

In the summer of 1894, accompanied by a boyhood friend, he went north to Tientsin to seek an audience with Viceroy Li Hung-chang to present reform ideas. He received no audience, but seems to have had some encouragement from one of Li's secretaries on the matter of establishing an agricultural association. That autumn he went to Hawaii to raise funds for the "agricultural association," which, however, took on a wider dimension and was organized as the Hsing-Chung-hui in Honolulu in November. Early in 1895 he returned to Hong Kong to establish a second branch of the society there. That spring, with the defeat of China by Japan in the Sino-Japanese War, the society became frankly revolutionary and hatched a plot to seize control of Canton, which came to a climax late in October. The plot was uncovered by Canton officials, and Sun barely escaped with his life, fleeing to Japan. After that he did not return openly to China (or even Hong Kong) until the successful revolution of 1911, though he kept alive contacts with friends and secret societies in China and may have crossed the border from Indochina briefly in 1907. Occasionally he saw the coast of China from ships off Hong Kong or Shanghai.

Between 1896 and 1911 Sun Yat-sen traveled extensively, raising money and enlisting support for a revolution against the Manchus. In Hawaii, San Francisco, New York, London, and Paris he obtained contributions, sometimes their life savings, from overseas Chinese. Other agents of the Revive China Society worked in Southeast Asia, the Philippines, Hong Kong, and in China itself. Sun was not at first the undisputed leader of the revolutionary movement, since Yang Ch'ü-yün, who was several years older than Sun, was the first "elected" president of the Society and of a "provisional government" if and when the Revolution should succeed. However, Sun became world famous in 1896 as the result of being kidnapped by Manchu agents in London and held prisoner at the Chinese legation there. As he was about to be shipped to China, where certain execution awaited him, he succeeded in smuggling out word of his captivity to his friend and teacher, Dr. James Cantlie, who notified the British Foreign Office and the press. His release was demanded and secured at once, and this "shanghai-ing" in the heart of London blackened the name of the Manchu dynasty while it exalted Sun as the great Chinese revolutionary. While in the West Sun's active mind absorbed the ideas and ideals of republican government and social justice. Also he became a professional revolutionist, putting family, career, and all other considerations aside.

However, it should also be remembered that Sun's main base of operations during these years was Japan. There he lived most of the time, and he often traveled as a Japanese, having acclimatized himself to the language and customs of that country. It is interesting, and something of a contradiction to his republican ideals, that his particular friends in Japan were ultranationalist members of the reactionary Black Ocean and Black Dragon societies. They were far from republicans, but Sun found common ground with them in their opposition to Western imperialism and their cry of Asia for the Asians. That Sun wanted a China run by Chinese and they envisioned a China ruled by Japanese did not become clear at this early stage. No doubt they expected to use Sun to further Japanese domination of the continent, but for the time being he used them to obtain funds and support for his revolutionary movement. Indeed, it was at the headquarters of Uchida Ryōhei, the Black Dragon chieftain, in Tokyo in 1905 that Sun's rather diverse revolutionary connections were finally formulated into the hard core revolutionary party that was to execute the Revolution. This was the *T'ung-meng-hui* (Together Sworn Society), which was the direct antecedent of the *Kuomintang* (Nationalist Party), which name was taken by the revolutionary organization in 1912 after the Revolution had been successful. The members of the T'ung-meng-hui took an oath to overthrow the Manchu "barbarians," restore China to the Chinese, establish a republic, and distribute the land equally. Members must support the cause

FIGURE 15.4. Sun Yat-sen, leader of the Chinese Revolution of 1911.

loyally, and if one broke faith, he would be punished by the other members as they saw fit. Sun was elected "general director."

After this the revolutionary movement picked up momentum, while the Protect the Emperor Society of Liang Ch'i-ch'ao became weaker. Sun found two able publicists in his following, Wang Ching-wei and Hu Han-min, who assumed the editorship of his revolutionary news organ, the *People's Tribune*, and produced a vehement literary challenge to Liang. To the secret society and overseas former coolie element in Sun's entourage was now added a large number of Chinese intellectuals, especially those studying in Japan. Liang's arguments for constitutional monarchy soon seemed pale when compared with the exciting program of the revolutionists, and some seven abortive attempts at revolution in China between 1906 and 1908, in which most of the planning and leadership was handled by Together Sworn members, produced a number of spectacular assassinations and equally spectacular reprisals against those revolutionaries who were caught. In 1909 Wang Ching-wei went to China and attempted to assassinate the Prince Regent. He failed, was captured and condemned to death, but by that time public opinion in China was becoming so aroused that the government was afraid to carry out the sentence, imprisoning him instead.

The Revolution of 1911

During the early part of 1911 the antirailroad nationalization movement in central and south China added a new element to the general revolutionary ferment. Merchants who stood to lose by the nationalization began to pour money into revolutionary activities. The outbreak that finally brought down the Manchu government occurred at a place where it might be said that the railroad restiveness, which had its center in Szechuan, met a branch of T'ung-meng-hui plotting, whose center was Canton. This was on the middle Yangtze, at the twin cities of Hankow and Wuchang, called together Wuhan. Revolution had been attempted several times at Canton, most recently in April, 1911. There the revolutionaries were well organized, but so was the governor-general's office, which was always alert for clandestine activities and which had smashed the April affair with great severity, killing or jailing most of the revolutionary leaders in the area. The defeat at Canton shifted the revolutionary focus to Wuhan, where the T'ung-meng-hui cadre was anxious to try its luck. Sun Yat-sen, in America on another fund-raising campaign, was informed of the plan by cable, but too late for him to give any active direction.

The Wuhan uprising was originally planned for October 6, then rescheduled for October 16. But it actually occurred on the night of October 10, because an accidental explosion the day before was being investigated by the authorities, who seemed likely to discover the revolutionary plan. The revolutionists seized an ammunition dump and attacked the governor-general's headquarters, and the governor-general in a crucial moment of panic fled to a gunboat on the river. This gave the revolutionaries their great chance. Some of the imperial troops, especially the more modernly trained ones, deserted to the revolutionary side. Their commander, Colonel Li Yuan-hung, after being captured, was persuaded to stop "being a slave of the Manchus and injuring his own brothers" and to become instead commander of the revolutionary forces. He was very reluctant about this at first, but the revolutionary tide swept him on and he was soon moving on Nanking as the popular leader of the insurgents. In the end in the cities of central and south China only the old bannermen remained loyal to the Manchus and these were quickly routed. Nanking was taken on December 12 and proclaimed the new revolutionary capital. During the ensuing two weeks there was some danger that the revolutionists would split among themselves over the formation of a new government, but on December 25 Sun Yat-sen arrived in Shanghai. He had returned to China rather slowly after receiving news of the Revolution, taking the long way around through London and Paris where he had received assurances from the British and French governments that they would hold up financial outlays to the Manchus pending the outcome of the revolutionists' attempt to establish a new government. On December 29 Sun was elected provisional president by an almost unanimous vote of the revolutionary assembly. Li Yuan-hung was elected vice-president.

In the north the frightened prince regent, immediately after the successful revolt at Wuhan, had recalled Yuan Shih-k'ai to take charge of the

FIGURE 15.5. Yuan Shih-k'ai as a Manchu official in 1904.

central provinces and suppress the rebellion. Yuan, however, dallied on various excuses (recuperation from his "foot trouble," etc.) until the situation was desperate. Then Yuan demanded and received sweeping powers as prime minister as well as overall army commander of the imperial forces. At Peking he quickly consolidated his position, putting his own men in control of the court guards and reactivating those elements of the Pei-yang army which he knew were loyal to him. By December the whole Pei-yang army was responding to his leadership, and on December 6, the prince regent resigned. Hence, when Sun took over the provisional presidency of the "Republic" he faced a formidable rival in the north. However, compromise was possible. Yuan, while he at first demanded that the revolutionists accept the principle of constitutional monarchy, was far from enthusiastic about preserving the Manchu dynasty, and Sun felt that if a basis of republican government were laid, it did not matter who was president so long as China could unite behind him. A compromise was reached early in 1912. Yuan secured the abdication of the Manchu dynasty (February 12) and two days later Sun resigned as provisional president, recommending Yuan to succeed him on condition that he take an oath to uphold a provisional republican constitution, which at the same time set up a National Council consisting of representatives from all the provinces, Mongolia, and Tibet. This was to have all legislative and taxing powers for ten months, after which a new National Assembly would be elected to assume legislative power and frame a permanent constitution. Another condition which Sun was very anxious to impose was that Yuan should take office at Nanking.

Yuan Shih-k'ai

Yuan was enthusiastically elected, and he accepted the provisional constitution and agreed to execute the laws passed by the National Council. But he did not wish to come to Nanking, and when informed that he was expected there for his inauguration, he replied that unsettled conditions in the north required his continued presence at Peking. Representatives of the Nanking government were sent north to fetch him, but instead of their persuading him, he convinced them of the desirability of his continued presence in the north. Opportunely and perhaps with Yuan's connivance, several riots broke out during the crucial days while the argument was going on, producing great uncertainty and fear at the foreign legations that another Boxer affair might arise. The foreigners sided with Yuan in the argument, and Nanking's representatives were persuaded to recommend that the essential thing was for China to show unity. Sun had misgivings, but others at Nanking won him over, and Yuan was allowed to accept the presidency at Peking on March 10.

Between Peking and Nanking there was a very brief honeymoon of expressions of mutual confidence followed by developing animosity and then an all-out struggle for power. The provisional constitution had anticipated that the president would do the bidding of the legislature, but Yuan had other ideas. After he succeeded in getting the National Council to convene in Peking, he began to ignore it. Also he speedily transformed the Cabinet, which had originally been a compromise cabinet under T'ang Shao-i, Yuan's able Western-educated assistant who was popular with and sympathetic to the revolutionaries, into his own instrument. T'ang and the four T'ung-meng-hui members of the cabinet resigned when they found that Yuan was relying on his Pei-yang army clique rather than on them for advice. The Pei-yang leader, Tuan Ch'i-jui, was Minister of War, having been selected over the revolutionists' candidate, Huang Hsing, for that post, and he was especially unsubtle in his "devotion" to Yuan and his antagonism to the Nanking element. Seeing their influence weakening rapidly, the T'ung-meng-hui revolutionary brotherhood decided to transform itself into a political party and enter actively into political campaigning. It became the Kuomintang in the summer of 1912 and its members campaigned so actively and successfully that it elected a clear majority of its people to the National Assembly, which was to take over from the National Council in April, 1913. A leading candidate for Prime Minister was Sung Chiao-jen, who had worked hard to build the Kuomintang party and carried on a nationwide campaign to emphasize the idea that the premier must be a member of, and answerable to, the majority party. But Sung was assassinated just before the National Assembly met, and there was strong evidence that the murder was done at Yuan's bidding. The Assembly met in an attitude of extreme bitterness, and immediately expressed opposition to Yuan's money raising tactics, which included the obtaining of loans from foreign bankers without waiting for legislative sanctions. (It should be noted that several European governments and Japan were betting on Yuan as the man to stabilize China and were pleased to back the loans.)

During the summer of 1913 Yuan tried to replace provincial revolutionary governors with his own military followers, and this gave rise to a "second revolution" in the Yangtze valley. Sun Yat-sen and other former revolutionaries encouraged it, though the Kuomintang did not officially take a stand. After its failure Sun, his most faithful adherents, and a number of members of the National Assembly fled from China to escape accusations of treason. The Assembly under strong pressure from Yuan elected him to a regular presidential term of five years in October, with Li Yuan-hung again vice-president, but it showed a reaction to the presidential pressure in the constitution it produced, one in which the chief executive's powers were sharply curtailed. This infuriated Yuan, and he prevented ratification of the document by leveling accusations of treason against the entire Kuomintang organization and expelling its members from the Assembly. Without a quorum that body was now defunct, and Yuan decreed its dissolution. Early in 1914 he convened another constitution-drafting body, which, being made up of his supporters, produced a document much more to his liking. It lengthened the presidential term to ten years and gave the president sweeping powers. This was promulgated on May 1. Yuan Shih-k'ai had become a virtual dictator.

BASIC DATES

1895	End of Sino-Japanese War; beginnings of Chinese re- and revolutionary movements
1896	China grants Manchurian railroad rights to Russia
1898, Spring	China grants concessions to Russia, Britain, Germany, and France
1898, Summer	K'ang Yu-wei, under sponsorship of Kuang-hsü emperor, attempts "100 Days" reform
1898, September	Reform defeated; Dowager Empress Tz'u-hsi seizes power
1899	Secretary Hay enunciates Open Door Policy
1899–1901	Boxer uprising, war, and settlement
1902–1908	Tz'u-hsi and Yuan Shih-k'ai sponsor "conservative reform"
1905	Sun Yat-sen and other revolutionaries organize T'ung-meng-hui (predecessor to Kuomintang) in Japan
1908	Deaths of Kuang-hsü emperor and Dowager Empress Tz'u-hsi; retirement of Yuan Shih-k'ai
1908–1911	Regency of Prince Ch'un; parliament promised, but reform falters; railroad controversy
1911	Revolution at Wuhan; revolutionary government at Nanking; Yuan Shih-k'ai recalled to power at Peking

1912	Revolutionaries compromise with Yuan; Manchus abdicate, Yuan provisional president; Kuomintang formed, controls legislature
1913	Yuan purges Kuomintang, becomes "dictator-president"

SUPPLEMENTARY READING

Clubb, O. E. *Twentieth Century China.* New York, 1964.
Fairbank, J. K., E. O. Reischauer, and A. M. Craig. *East Asia: The Modern Transformation.* Boston, 1965. Revised and abbreviated edition, 1973.
Griswold, A. W. *The Far Eastern Policy of the United States.* New York, 1938; reprinted, 1964.
Hsü, I. C. Y. *The Rise of Modern China.* New York, 1970, Chaps. 15–20.
Li, C. *The Political History of China, 1840–1928.* Princeton, N.J., 1956.
Li, D. J. *The Ageless Chinese: A History.* New York, 1965.
Sharman, L. *Sun Yat-sen: His Life and Its Meaning.* New York, 1934.
Teng, S. Y. and J. K. Fairbank, eds. *China's Response to the West: A Documentary Survey, 1839–1923.* Cambridge, Mass., 1954.

ADVANCED READING

Cameron, M. E. *The Reform Movement in China, 1898–1912.* Stanford, Calif., 1931; reprinted, N.Y., 1963.
Ch'en, J. *Yuan Shih-k'ai (1859–1916): Brutus Assumes the Purple.* London, 1961.
Chu, S. C. *Reformer in Modern China: Chang Chien, 1853–1926.* New York, 1965.
Feuerwerker, A. *The Chinese Economy, 1870–1911.* Ann Arbor, Mich., 1969.
Fitzgerald, C. P. *Revolution in China.* New York, 1952.
Haldane, C. *The Last Great Empress of China.* London, 1965.
Ho, P. T. *The Ladder of Success in Imperial China.* New York, 1962.
Hsüeh, C. T. *Huang Hsing and the Chinese Revolution.* Stanford, Calif., 1961.
Levenson, J. R. *Confucian China and Its Modern Fate.* Berkeley, Calif., 1958.
——*Liang Ch'i-ch'ao and the Mind of Modern China.* Cambridge, Mass., 1953.
Lo, J. P., ed. and tr. *K'ang Yu-wei.* Tucson, Ariz., 1967.
Powell, R. L. *The Rise of Chinese Military Power, 1895–1912.* Princeton, N.J., 1955.
Schiffrin, H. Z. *Sun Yat-sen and the Origins of the Chinese Revolution.* Berkeley. Calif., 1968.
Schrecker, J. E. *Imperialism and Chinese Nationalism: Germany in Shantung.* Cambridge, Mass., 1971.

Schwartz, B. I. *In Search of Wealth and Power: Yen Fu and the West.* Cambridge, Mass., 1964.
Spence, J. *To Change China: Western Advisers in China, 1620–1960.* Boston, 1969.
Steiger, G. N. *China and the Occident.* New Haven, 1927.
Tan, C. C. *The Boxer Catastrophe.* New York, 1955.
Wright, M. C., ed. *China in Revolution: The First Phase, 1900–1913.* New Haven, Conn., 1968.

Chapter 16

Japan and Northeast Asia, 1895-1914

INTERNAL EFFECT OF SINO-JAPANESE WAR

The principal result of the Sino-Japanese War in Japan itself was to confirm and strengthen the political power of the oligarchy. Ito, Yamagata, Matsukata, and the other leaders of the preconstitutional regime had sought to make the inauguration of a constitution and Diet as painless to their leadership as possible. But the years 1889 to 1894 had been a sore trial. Yamagata had anticipated the difficulties and urged as early as 1889 that the cabinet must above all maintain its unity in the face of party politics. Individual cabinet ministers had a "moral responsibility" to deliberate in secret, seek unity, and never, as individuals, express views in such a way as to cause public debate (no doubt Yamagata had in mind Okuma's transgressions in 1881).

Ito also intended that the cabinet should be transcendental, beyond the control of and responsibility to the Diet, and his basic approach to the constitution and the parliamentary structure emphasized this. Nevertheless, although they tried to govern serenely above the Diet, the early oligarchic cabinets were jolted by obstreperousness in the parliamentary body, and perhaps only war and the call for national unity thereby provided could have saved the "transcendentalism" of the cabinet in 1894. In fact one scholarly appraisal considers the Japanese cabinet's anxiety to quiet domestic political turmoil as the essential cause of the war. This is probably an oversimplification, but there can be no doubt that the Sino-Japanese War fortified the oligarchy and seriously injured the cause of parliamentary government in Japan.

JAPAN UNDER THE ELDER STATESMEN

After the war the Liberal and Progressive parties found themselves so weakened that they began to seek the favors of office from the oligarchs. Ito, who was more open and optimistic than Yamagata, saw opportunity in this to build party support for the Government, an idea which repelled the stern ministers, like the army, should be "above politics." Thin-voiced and nerparties to form and debate in the Diet, but insisted that the Emperor's ministers, like the army, should be "above politics." Thin-voiced and nervous in Diet politics, he advised Ito against playing the political game. Nevertheless, Ito went ahead, and therein began an estrangement between the two samurai comrades from Choshu which resulted in some stretching of the oligarchy, although Yamagata, who outlived Ito by a dozen years, was able to counter all threats to the transcendental cabinet ideal until 1918.

Ito began by taking Itagaki into his cabinet in 1896 in return for Liberal party support. Then in 1898 he enlisted the Progressives by resigning his third premiership in favor of Okuma, the Progressive leader, with Itagaki remaining as Home Minister. Yamagata was so appalled that he threatened to wreck the Cabinet by withdrawing the Army minister, a device by which the military were to control many cabinets in the future. However, this time it proved unnecessary, for Okuma and Itagaki quarreled and began to denounce each other. To Yamagata's vast relief this first (and last,

FIGURE 16.1. *General Yamagata, creator of Japan's army.*

to 1919) experiment in party government completely failed, the cabinet resigning in hopeless disunity after four months, never having met a single session of the Diet.

Another matter that displayed the feebleness of the parties of "liberty" and "progress" when it came to defending such crucial issues as independence of thought and freedom of speech was the handling of the famous "Republican Speech" incident of August, 1898. Ozaki Yukio, minister of education and as strong an advocate of parliamentary government as Japan had or was to have before World War II, in an address to educators made some remarks on political morality which compared Japan unfavorably with the United States, a republic. This was misconstrued as advocating a republican form of government in Japan and Ozaki was attacked as subversive, not only by the antiparliamentary forces but by Itagaki and his Liberal party. It raised such a storm that Okuma, himself, who had been supported by Ozaki, also demanded the latter's resignation.

The Genro

The fiasco of 1898 ended the argument about responsible government for a long time to come, and Japan entered into a period of rule by the now aging Meiji oligarchs through their younger protégés. The Diet, of course, continued to meet, parties were formed and disbanded and re-formed under various names, and parliamentary politics were often tumultuous, but they revolved around secondary issues, often patronage. The "Elder Statesmen" (Genrō), as the oligarchs were now called, were firmly in control on major matters, peace and war, overseas policies, army-navy expansion, control of "radical" movements, and the economic structure. Regarding the last, there were signs in the late Meiji period of the emergence of a new financial aristocracy which would eventually have important political influence, but since this group had been helped to affluence by the Meiji oligarchs, they were still in a state of political sycophancy to them, a condition which persisted until about the end of World War I. Their money was always available to the oligarchs when it was needed to influence political parties or individual politicians.

Indeed, it can be said that the Genro "captured" the two main political parties. The major part of the old Jiyuto, which had almost fallen apart after Itagaki's resignation in 1898, accepted the sponsorship of Ito as the lesser of evils among the oligarchs. They reorganized under his leadership as the Seiyūkai, accepting as part of their party platform the idea they had fought so bitterly in the past, that Cabinets were above parties and in no way responsible to them, however strong their representation in the Diet. On these terms Ito and his protégé, Saionji Kimmochi, ran the Seiyukai for several years. Meanwhile Yamagata and his protégé, Katsura Taro, utilized other party remnants, not so formally, but effectively.

"Civilian" and "Military" Factions of the Oligarchy

Actually, with the parties little more than pawns, the real political division, as already suggested, had become intra-Genro rivalry between Ito and Yamagata. They would close ranks and make their party supporters do likewise at any hint of challenge from below to the principle of cabinet authority, but there was a real and often bitter struggle between Ito's "civilian" faction and Yamagata's "military" faction. When Ito quit the premiership for the last time in 1901, the circumstances were rather different from previous occasions when under a barrage of party criticism in the Diet, he had turned over the premiership to Matsukata or Yamagata or another oligarchic choice. This time the pressure to resign came from Yamagata himself, who had strong support from government bureaucrats at various levels, and who wanted a large-scale military expansion program to which Ito was adverse. This was a principal point of argument between the two factions. Another concerned foreign policy, where Yamagata favored a stronger policy and was not reluctant to resort to war, while Ito was more inclined to seek compromises, especially with Russia. On domestic issues Ito was inclined to be more liberal than Yamagata, and after 1907 the two factions clashed on Korean issues.

In 1901, when Ito resigned, Yamagata began the practice of Genro abstention from the premiership by installing his protégé, General Katsura, instead of himself as premier. From 1901 to 1913 the premiership alternated between Katsura and Ito's man, Saionji. Katsura was premier from 1901 to January, 1906, then Saionji (1906–1908), Katsura (1908–1911), Saionji (1911–1912), and Katsura for a third time (1912–1913). The three to two ratio in favor of Katsura and the lengthy terms of his first two ministries should not be taken to mean that the Ito faction was powerless most of the time. The "militarists" compromised with Ito on numerous occasions, as when he demanded a free hand as resident-general in setting up the Korean protectorate after the Russo-Japanese War, and Ito, however reluctantly, went along with the Katsura ministry on such large issues as the Anglo-Japanese Alliance, war with Russia, and eventually Korean annexation, even on occasion ordering the Seiyukai party to support Katsura if it seemed necessary "in the national interest." Certainly there was no chance for old-style "people's rights" advocates or new-style socialist radicals to exert much influence, except clandestinely. Their newspapers, such as *Heimin Shimbun* (Common People's Newspaper), were suppressed and their leaders jailed or, in the case of Kotoku Shusui, executed for treason. Most successors of the early Meiji liberals climbed on the bandwagon of imperial Japan, or, if they had misgivings, retreated into nonpolitical literary activities. Suicide became a frequent alternative for those students who reacted negatively to the strong emphasis on nationalism in education and religion.

In Katsura's last ministry the military faction overplayed its hand. Katsura, who had become increasingly overbearing, tried to use the prestige of the throne to force through large army increases, to the point that he alienated even the navy subfaction, controlled by Satsuma men. (The army was primarily identified with Choshu clansmen, of whom Yamagata and Katsura were the leaders.) Ozaki Yukio, who was emerging from his earlier misadventures to become an outstanding, though lonely, advocate of parliamentary rule, denounced Katsura's manipulation of the throne in a spectacular speech in the Diet, and public opinion as well as bureaucratic opponents castigated Katsura to the point that he resigned on February 20, 1913, after only seven weeks in office. Admiral Yamamoto Gombei, with support from the civilian faction (now under Saionji after Ito's death in 1909) and the Seiyukai party, took the premiership for a year. And Saionji, now graduated into the ranks of the Genro, experimented with what was to become a favorite political device with him: to call in an admiral when the army became too pugnacious. The Yamagata faction was by no means finished; its leader remained senior among the Genro until his death in 1922 and a number of military adventures were undertaken before that time. However, from the fall of the last Katsura cabinet until 1931 Japanese politics was mainly business oriented.

INDUSTRIALIZATION OF JAPAN

During the period 1895–1914 the government-sponsored industrialization program designed by the oligarchs in the years immediately after the Restoration bore fruit to the extent that Japan equalled at least the second rank of European industrial powers, and certainly far surpassed any other Asian, African, or South American country. And by 1914 the stage was set for further, almost unlimited, industrial expansion while Europe was preoccupied with World War I.

The abolition in 1885 of the Ministry of Industry, to which Ito, himself, had given primary attention in the early stage of his government career, was indicative of a gradual change in policy from organization and direction of industries by the government to the release of them to private ownership, while continuing government subsidies guaranteed their further growth. Major exceptions to this were railroads and steel. The government continued to build and operate the main railroads, although private ones were encouraged also. What was to be the largest iron and steel processing plant, the Yawata Iron Works, was set up by the government in 1896 after the Sino-Japanese War experience convinced government leaders that iron and steel production was not developing satisfactorily. Private enterprise was not moving ahead despite government encouragement, because of technical difficulties and uncertainty as to sources of ore. For the Yawata works the government hired foreign technical advisors, surveyed ore deposits all over Japan, and obtained the best equipment available. Whereas in 1892 only 18,000 tons of steel had been produced in Japan, by 1906 Yawata alone could produce 180,000 tons per year and this increased to 350,000 tons by 1914. With such a remarkable increase the question of source of ore supply became an expanded one, beyond the home islands, involving northeast Asia. The political aspects of this problem will be considered shortly.

The Zaibatsu

In areas other than railroads and steel the characteristic economic pattern of this period was the emergence of giant, privately owned, but government-favored business combines called *zaibatsu*. At their core these were family corporations, if the term family is regarded in the broader oriental sense, including adopted children, nephews, cousins, in-laws, and more distant relatives. The main zaibatsu houses were the Mitsui, whose roots in the Tokugawa era have been mentioned, several *nouveaux riches*, Iwasaki (controlling the Mitsubishi company), Sumitomo, and Yasuda. Each of these had at its center a bank and trust company, and although each had begun with some more or less special endeavor (e.g., Mitsubishi's early concentration was on shipping), by the first decade of the twentieth century they were branching into every conceivable phase of economic activity, until by 1919 the four companies controlled 75 per cent of the corporate wealth of Japan. Mitsui alone by that time controlled 120 corporations and subsidiaries.

Chemical, electrical, metallurgical, textile, food processing, and other modern industries, as well as the financial apparatus of the country, were all developed with zaibatsu capital. This does not mean that small private enterprises were stamped out. Indeed, in retail trade and small crafts Japan was very much a nation of small shopkeepers, and it is well to remember this so as not to overemphasize the reach of the tentacles of the zaibatsu, but it was they who possessed the capital for developing industrial and commercial enterprise, introducing advanced techniques, employing foreign technicians, and, in short, moving Japan ahead toward economic self-sufficiency.

Production Growth

In terms of absolute capital growth remarkable strides were made in the late Meiji era. For example, in 1902 there were 27 milling companies with a paid-up capital of 735,000 yen. In 1912 there were 31 companies with a paid-up capital of 5,407,000 yen. There were many similar increases when figures of 1902 are compared with 1912. In paper manufacture 40 companies with 10,275,000 yen increased to 70 companies with 22,151,000 yen; in sugar refining eight companies with 2,738,000 yen increased to 13 companies with 15,017,000 yen, this being largely a reflection of the acquisition of sugar producing Formosa; in ship building 17 companies with 10,653,000 yen increased to 25 companies with 28,033,000 yen; in electricity 62 companies with 10,347,000 yen increased to 270 companies with 159,808,000 yen.

Population Growth and Standards of Living

Such striking increases were to be found in many fields of industrial production. In addition, agricultural production increased remarkably. However, these increases were offset by two other developments, first, a rapid increase in population and second, ever accelerating outlays for armaments. As to population there was no accurate national census until 1920, although a rather crude one had been taken in 1872 and totals were adjusted periodically thereafter according to birth and death recordings in family registers.

From the base figure of the 1872 census, 33,110,796, the total population had apparently increased to 46,041,786 by 1902 and to 52,522,752 by 1912. Statistical recapitulations applied to this after the 1920 census, however, resulted in estimated totals which changed these figures somewhat, placing the 1872 figure at 37,806,000; the 1902 figure at 44,964,000; and the 1912 figure at 50,577,000. However one looks at it, the population was increasing so fast that the average person in 1912 had only slightly more rice to consume than he had had in the early Meiji period, and furthermore prices and taxes had gone up so much that all the extra money earned by the farmer in sericulture or by his sons and daughters in low-paying factory jobs barely maintained the average family's already low standard of living.

After 1895 military expenditure was consistently an item of top priority in the national budget, absorbing from 35 per cent to 50 per cent of national government expenditures. Until about 1900 the government, still imbued with Okubo's caution, tried to hold these expenditures down, preferring, for example, a diminution of Japanese influence in Korea to uncontrolled expenditures there, and exerted economy efforts sufficient to put Japan on the gold standard. But after 1900 the lure of power politics prevailed, and the cost of the Russo-Japanese War alone was enough to prevent any significant rise in Japanese living standards.

Labor

With production and prices rising, but living standards remaining at low levels, some segments of Japan's working population made sporadic, though largely fruitless, attempts to improve conditions. With the government intent on production and business leaders anxious for profits and trade, the position of laborers declined seriously. This was especially true in the mining, iron, and textile industries. A combination of entrepreneurial callousness toward industrial accidents and the importation of socialist ideas produced the beginnings of a labor movement in the 1890's. During that decade several socialist journals were published sporadically and unions of iron workers, railway engineers and firemen, and other smaller unions were formed, and nearly 100 strikes (mostly small) were called. Despite this there was little improvement in conditions until 1899, when some 200 miners were burned to death in a Kyushu mine and 31 female textile workers died in a fire in a locked company dormitory. Public opinion was aroused to the point of giving considerable support to the radical leader, Oi Kentaro, whose left wing Oriental Liberal party had sponsored a "Japan Labor Association." The government responded with the Public Peace Preservation Law, in 1900, making it virtually a crime for a worker to agitate, even gently, on wages and hours, let alone to advocate a strike, but did take some steps to improve safety conditions, which culminated in a mine safety act in 1905.

Meanwhile between 1900 and 1905 the labor movement became increasingly identified with socialism. Deprived of the weapon of the strike, labor's advocates responded to the plea of Oi and others for political or, at least, educational action. The railway workers' union passed a resolution in 1901 advocating socialism as the only way out of labor's dilemma, and a Social Democratic party, which included public ownership of both land and capital as a plank in its platform, was organized (and banned) the same year. Various publishing ventures were undertaken by the socialists thereafter, culminating in the Common People's Newspaper which, from 1903 until it was forced to close in January, 1905, defiantly campaigned against imperialism, war, and capitalist exploitation. The leaders were Abe Isoo, a persistent democratic socialist, Uchimura Kanzo, a Christian socialist and founder of the Churchless Christian movement, Katayama Sen, later a communist, and the aforementioned Kotoku Shusui, who became an anarchist.

In its revival after the Russo-Japanese War the socialist movement tended to become more violent, in words at least, as suppression by the government produced exaggerated bitterness in the socialist leadership, from which the milder members dropped out. Two riotous mine strikes in 1907 forced some concessions from mine owners, but brought the police down all the harder on the socialists who applauded these as workers' revolts and staged "red flag" parades in defiance of police regulations. There were many arrests of radicals in 1908 and 1909. These events, together with the seizure of Kotoku and most of his followers in 1910 and the execution of twelve of them on charges of plotting to harm the emperor, effectively squelched the socialist movement for the duration of the World War I era. However, the stir produced by the idea of socialism and the various labor strikes of the preceding decade had a legislative effect at last in 1911, when Japan's first factory act was passed by the Diet. It was really very little and very late, especially inasmuch as it was not enforced until 1916. Applying to all mines and factories employing over fifteen persons it limited the working day to twelve hours, including one hour of rest, for women and for children under fifteen. The minimum working age was twelve.

It is not surprising that workers and their sympathizers considered the Factory Act of 1911 inadequate. However, with socialism and radicalism under strict surveillance, the leadership of the labor movement fell to the mildest of advocates, one Suzuki Bunji, who in 1912 organized a Friendly (Labor) Society (*Yuaikai*) which stressed the idea of harmony between capital and labor and restricted its efforts on behalf of labor to remedying the most obvious abuses, such as night work and child labor. Suzuki was influenced by the American Federation of Labor and its pragmatic approach to labor's immediate problems, while keeping clear of wider political issues.

In retrospect we can see that Suzuki Bunji and his Friendly Society gave the government and the zaibatsu a second chance to come to friendly terms with labor on a basis of minimum concessions, but they were not interested, with the result that when the struggle was joined again after the temporary prosperity of World War I, workers and peasants were more willing to think in terms of the necessity of overthrowing the "capitalists' government." Of course, the greed of business and the blindness of government were not the only factors in labor's unhappy plight. Longstanding social traditions of class distinction and paternalism made "lower class" people submissive and a vast reservoir of excess farm population competed in a cheap labor market.

RIVALRY IN NORTHEASTERN ASIA

Reasons for Japan's Expansion

While government and business leaders in Japan showed little interest in the general standard of living there, they were greatly concerned about Japan's international position. The fear of colonial control, which was a very real threat in the early Meiji years, had given tremendous impetus and excellent justification to the government's program of building national strength, both militarily and industrially. However, by 1900 Japan was free of all semicolonial restrictions, after the last of the unequal treaties was abrogated in 1897 and extraterritoriality ended in 1899 (some tariff restrictions remained until 1911, but only because the Japanese government did not consider them important enough to abrogate). Secondly, the Japanese industrial machine needed more raw materials to feed it than were available in Japan. Japan had good resources for electric power in her mountain streams, but was deficient in iron ore, coal, other minerals, raw cotton, and oil.

There was enough for a good start, but as the industrial system grew larger and more complex after 1900 there were arguments that iron and coal, as well as foodstuffs, must be had from the Asian mainland. Of course, Japan might have obtained these peacefully, by trade and mutually profitable investment arrangements with China and other nations, if her diplomacy had been considerate of their interests as well as her own. Thirdly, population pressure was a self-justifying reason for expansion. It is somewhat suspect because, although the population was very large considering the size of the country, the colder parts of Japan itself, notably Hokkaido, whose climate is no worse than New England's, were not fully utilized. In addition, although the large population was a factor in depressing the general standard of living, Japan's leadership might have improved this situation by measures to raise working class purchasing power.

Japanese expansion on the northeast Asian mainland was motivated to a certain extent by the above factors, but above and beyond them the most important reason (or lack of reason) for Japan's penetration of Korea, Manchuria, and China proper in this period was the factor of power politics, the international rivalries involving Britain, Germany, France, the United States, and, especially, Russia. To the Japanese the question seemed to be one of "national security" and those in charge of foreign policy thought of themselves as preventing strong potential enemies from being able to threaten Japan through Korea or China, thereby justifying the extension of their "defense" perimeter.

Russo-Japanese Rivalry in Korea

The main Far Eastern rivalry was between Japan and Russia, but from a broader perspective this was only one aspect of a larger rivalry between Britain and Russia, a rivalry which extended all the way from the Yellow Sea, across China, Central Asia, Afghanistan, and Persia to the Ottoman empire and ended in European alignments. Japanese antagonism toward

Russia may have begun before the Sino-Japanese War. Certainly Russia's Trans-Siberian Railway construction program did not go unnoticed in Japan; General Yamagata warned as early as 1892 that the completion of the railroad would mean a vast augmentation of Russian power in the Far East, and that Japan must be ready. However, it was the Triple Intervention of 1895 which turned Japanese popular hostility and governmental suspicion against Russia. After that it seemed almost as if Russia, not Japan, had won the Sino-Japanese War.

When the Korean king sought refuge from his Japanese "advisors" by taking up residence in the Russian legation, the Russian star went into ascendancy in Korea and the Japanese one into eclipse. To maintain a modicum of influence Japan had to sign two agreements with Russia, the Weber-Komura and Lobanov-Yamagata agreements of May and June, 1896, respectively. By these Japan preserved control over the Pusan-Seoul telegraph she had built and retained the right to maintain up to 200 guards in the Japanese settlements at Seoul, Pusan, and Wonsan. However, this was far less than the influence Japan's leaders expected to exert in Korea, and it was humiliating to have to accept Russian-imposed limitations, especially inasmuch as the king's presence and favor at the Russian legation had concrete results for Russia in the form of timber and mining concessions, the use of Russian officers to train Korean soldiers, and a Russian director for the Korean customs and tax collection office. These developments occurred between 1896 and 1898, but by the spring of 1898 Russian activities in Manchuria had enjoyed such striking success that the Russian foreign minister, Muraviev, was willing, even anxious, to retreat somewhat in Korea lest Japan be antagonized too much. Also, a reaction to russification was developing among Koreans. Hence in April, 1898 the Nishi-Rosen Convention was made by which Russia and Japan agreed not to interfere in Korea's internal affairs unless it be by mutual agreement; and Russian military and financial personnel were withdrawn thereafter.

Russia in Manchuria

However, Manchuria was definitely becoming part of the Russian orbit. In 1896, as a reward for her leadership of the Triple Intervention, which had restored south Manchuria to China from Japanese hands, the Chinese government gave Russia the right to run its Trans-Siberian Railroad across Manchuria to Vladivostok, the Manchurian (Chinese Eastern) section to be controlled by a Russo-Chinese bank, which operated as a "slightly disguised branch of the Russian treasury." The railroad would be a fine distance saver for Russia, but it made Japan nervous. Then, in March, 1898, Russia and China reached another agreement whereby Russia would be given a twenty-five-year renewable lease of the south Manchurian (Liaotung, later called Kwantung) peninsula, including the ice-free port of Port Arthur, and the right to connect it by rail northward to the Chinese Eastern. To obtain these agreements the Russians put heavy pressure, including bribes, on Li Hung-chang and other Chinese officials. About the same time Germany, another erstwhile "friend" of China in the Triple Intervention, used the excuse of the murder of missionaries in Shantung to demand and obtain a leasehold at Kiaochow (March, 1898); and France, the third Intervention partner, obtained concessions in south China on Kwangchow Bay (April, 1898).

As noted above, Russia partially assuaged Japan with the Nishi-Rosen Convention, but Britain took a dim view of these entire proceedings and began actively to plan ways to thwart the Russian Bear in the Far East as she had previously done in the Near East (Crimean War; Congress of Berlin) and the Middle East (Afghan diplomacy and wars). Her first move was to seize the strategic port of Weihaiwei, on the Shantung peninsula opposite Port Arthur, and to obtain a lease of its facilities from China "for as long as the Russians shall occupy Port Arthur." Japan, some of whose troops were still in Weihaiwei awaiting final payment by China of the Sino-Japanese War indemnity, cooperated with Britain by accepting British occupation, and it seems that China did not oppose the change of tenants, which occurred in April, 1898. The scramble for concessions and "spheres of interest" which followed among the European powers left Japan as something of a breathless bystander. More adventurous elements in the Japanese government, responding to urgings from the governor-general of Formosa, wished to take advantage of the Boxer affair in north China to "assist" Sun Yat-sen's revolutionaries in south China, where there was a small incident at Amoy, but Ito Hirobumi threw his great weight against this and insisted that Japan cooperate with the Western powers in the expedition against the Boxers, urging, as did Britain and the United States, that it not be used as an excuse to violate Chinese territorial integrity further, which they suspected Russia of intending to do.

Actually the Russians entered into the Boxer relief expedition with some misgivings. They were not anxious to be identified with an international concert against China, having been quite successful as the "friend of China" in recent years; yet the anti-Western nature of the outbreaks, the nearness of Russian troops at Port Arthur, and the urge to be "in" on whatever diplomacy occurred at Peking encouraged Russian entry. Russia sent 4000 troops from Port Arthur, which constituted the decisive element in gaining the initiative for the intervening powers, but it is interesting that she did not seek the overall command, which was given to the German general, Waldersee. In the negotiations for settlement at Peking Russia played a moderating role.

However, where Russian interests were most directly affected, in Manchuria, she reacted sharply. Between 1900 and 1902 Russian troops took effective control not only of the railway zones, but of all strategic points in Manchuria, and even then, although an evacuation agreement was reached in April, 1902, they did not withdraw. The spread of the Boxer uprisings to Manchuria and attacks on Russian railway construction posts there provided the reason (or excuse) for large-scale military intervention. Thousands of Chinese had emigrated from north China to Manchuria seeking economic opportunity. Some sixty thousand of them were employed on the Russian railway projects, but others were in a rather drifting condition. Among the latter group Boxerism first made its appearance and, as outsiders to the projects, they launched several, not too serious attacks on railway properties.

Russian Finance Minister Count Witte, for whom railroads were a favorite project, took alarm immediately and obtained from the War Ministry the dispatch of some 11,000 additional railway guards. At first he hoped that the disturbances could be quelled by these alone, but, unlike China proper where most of the viceroys and provincial governors did not accept the idea that the Chinese court favored the Boxers and worked against them as rebels, in Manchuria many Chinese officials, including a lieutenant-governor who put his superior under house arrest, took the view that China was at war with the intervening powers and sent imperial troops into action against the Russians. On July 9, 1900, Russian columns invaded Manchuria from north of the Amur river and speedily "pacified" the country. An anti-Boxer revolt which divided the Chinese helped the process. On October 1 Mukden was taken and on October 6 Russian control had been reestablished over all Russian railway zones in Manchuria.

But complete pacification of Manchuria proved a very difficult matter. Bandits continued to operate in the hinterland, and the Russians were soon embarrassed by problems of administration they were not equipped to handle. It seemed to Russian advantage to terminate the affair, but the Russians also could not resist the opportunity to make some gains from the situation. Witte, thinking largely in terms of extending Russia's railroad empire, sought a special agreement with China guaranteeing Russia a monopolistic position in Manchuria, turning over control of the Imperial Northern Railway, which ran north of the Great Wall, to the Chinese Eastern Railway organization, and in addition, guaranteeing the future exclusion of non-Russian railroad enterprises throughout the entire region north of the Great Wall, including Mongolia and Chinese Central Asia. These were really maximum proposals and embodied Witte's dreams of economic empire.

When the Chinese refused, negotiations continued until April, 1902, when the evacuation agreement was signed. Its terms were much more agreeable to China, along the lines of the *status quo ante* in Manchuria. Russian troops were to be evacuated in three stages, each six months in duration. Russia's agreement was doubtless hastened by the fact that the famous Anglo-Japanese Alliance, which will be discussed shortly, had been concluded in January. Count Witte, who calculated diplomacy largely in financial terms, was willing to give ground to avoid a larger crisis which might injure his favorite projects, the railways and related economic activities in Manchuria. However, the crisis was to deepen. While Witte was willing, even anxious, to have Russian troops evacuated from Manchuria, more chauvinistic groups in St. Petersburg were not willing to do so. Several factors undermined Witte, among them the Bezobrazov faction whose leader was interested in Yalu timber concessions and anxious to pursue a stronger policy in Korea and the Russian War Ministry which controlled the troops. The first stage of the evacuation was carried out, even slightly ahead of schedule, but in the second stage troops were merely shifted around, and then all pretense of evacuation was abandoned. Witte was "kicked upstairs" from his position as minister of finance, and out of power, on August 28, 1903. Russia was drifting into the adventurous policy that would eventually spell war.

The Anglo-Japanese Alliance

Meanwhile Britain and Japan were coming together. The Anglo-Japanese Alliance (January, 1902) was the product of a community of interests between Japan and Great Britain against Russia which had been growing since the Sino-Japanese War. At the outbreak of that war Britain had nodded approvingly toward Japan; also it was noteworthy that Britain did not protest Japan's efforts to take southern Manchuria, as did the Triple Powers. Japan's acquiescence to British control over Weihaiwei in 1898 has also been noted. However, more than these accidental incidents was necessary for the formulation of a hard and fast military alliance. From the British side there had to be a determination that a Japanese alliance would truly be useful. While still thinking of Japan perhaps as a second-rate power, Britain through 1900–1901 repeatedly sounded out Germany on the possibility of a rapprochement, with particular reference to containing Russia in the Far East. But the German Foreign Office was not interested. Then the British began to consider Japan.

A memorandum of Lord Selborne, son-in-law of Prime Minister Lord Salisbury and first lord of the admiralty, dated September 4, 1901, gave the following specific military reasons for a Japan alliance. The "recognized standard" of British naval strength, necessary to the security of the empire, was to maintain equality with the next two greatest naval powers combined. It was becoming impossible to do this in both the European area and the "China Seas." Russia and France would soon have nine battleships to Britain's four in the China area and a like superiority in smaller warships. To remedy this Britain would soon have to draw vessels from her Mediterranean and/or English Channel fleets. However, Britain and Japan together could show eleven battleships in Far Eastern waters against the Russo-French coalition's nine and a preponderance of cruisers, without drawing from Britain's European fleets. The argument was militarily impeccable and although some in the British Cabinet and Parliament tried to argue for seeking agreement with Russia, the breakdown of certain Anglo-Russian negotiations over Persia shortly thereafter sealed the determination of the British Foreign Office to seek the Japanese alliance, and provided a rationale to silence criticism.

As for Japan, her leaders had regarded Russia with antagonism and suspicion ever since the Triple Intervention, while the several instances of cooperation with Britain inclined them to look to her for international bolstering. By 1900 there was a younger element in the Japanese government, led by Foreign Minister Kato Takaaki, who had been minister at London, which favored a definite orientation toward Britain and against Russia. His successor at London, Hayashi Tadasu, worked wholeheartedly in that direction from 1900 to the successful conclusion of the alliance. Military leaders in Japan were also favorable to the alliance idea. The chief obstacle was the ever cautious Ito, who realized fully that too close an alignment with Britain might close the door to negotiations with Russia and lead to war. However, Russia's failure to respond to his special efforts to find a means of reconciliation of outstanding issues weakened his argument, and in June,

FIGURE 16.2. Admiral Togo.

1901, the military-oriented Katsura ministry took office and gave Hayashi a go-ahead sign to negotiate in earnest in London. By January, 1902 the alliance was sealed, and Ito accepted it.

However, Ito was not ready to give up the idea that relations with Russia could be worked out amicably and he persuaded his colleagues to try to use the alliance as a means of pressuring Russia into an agreement, rather than merely affronting her. The basis of this was to be *Man Kan Kōkan* (exchanging Manchuria for Korea). Between 1902 and 1904 Japan, and particularly Ito, tried to persuade Russia to accept the idea that if Manchuria were considered primarily a Russian sphere of interest, with Russian economic and security interests predominant there, then Korea was an area where Japanese economic and security interests should prevail. However, Russia was moving to a more aggressive position (climaxed by the fall of Witte in August, 1903) and talked of a division of interests in Korea at the thirty-ninth parallel as her minimum consideration, with Manchuria "of no concern to Japan." Even if Ito had accepted this, his colleagues would not, and a tragic situation resulted whereby the more aggressively inclined elements in both Russia and Japan (and Britain also) prevailed. In January, 1904, negotiations broke down into ultimatums; Japan broke relations with Russia on February 6; the tsar ordered the Russian fleet to attack any Japanese ships moving north of the thirty-ninth parallel on February 8; and Japan attacked Russia's Port Arthur Squadron on the night of February 8–9. Declarations of war were issued on February 10.

THE RUSSO-JAPANESE WAR

Course of Hostilities

Japan undertook the Russo-Japanese War at considerable risk, for her military potential had never been tested against a European power. The Anglo-Japanese Alliance, though of such importance that Japan would certainly not have risked the war without it, nevertheless did not provide specific military assistance unless a third power joined on the side of Russia. Since that did not happen, Japan enjoyed only the benevolent neutrality of her ally, which included important loans in London. However, her forces were ready and concentrated, whereas Russia's were spread out over the whole Eurasian continent, with her fleet split into three: in the Baltic, at Vladivostok, and at Port Arthur. The Japanese attack at Port Arthur and on two Russian warships at Inchon gave Japan unquestioned command of the seas in the war area for several months, until the ice melted at Vladivostok and the Baltic fleet could move.

By that time Japanese troops had occupied Korea and begun to cross the Yalu river, cut off Port Arthur from the main Russian forces in Manchuria, and begun to push the latter forces back northward. Nevertheless the fighting was bitter, bloody, and costly. Japan poured half a million troops into Manchuria, but it was January, 1905, before Port Arthur was taken, and a stalemate was reached north of Mukden in March after the Japanese had taken the city at terrific cost. Meanwhile, the main Russian fleet was en route from the Baltic Sea. Its progress was slow, for it had to go around Africa to avoid possible involvement with the British at Suez, and it stopped for supplies in French Indochina, which brought rumors of world war lest the British interpret this as French intervention. The Japanese naval commander, Togo, shrewdly anticipated the route of the Russian fleet towards Vladivostok and lay in wait as the Russian ships approached the narrow Tsushima Straits, and catching the Russians in unwieldy array, destroyed almost the entire fleet in the Battle of Tsushima Straits (May 27–28, 1905). Russia now could not possibly hope to dislodge Japan from her newly won positions on the continent without undertaking a new long range program of military build-up.

Treaty of Portsmouth

It was not likely that Russia would do this, but it was possible, considering the vastness of Russian resources, and the Japanese, having already strained their own resources to the limit, decided in the hour of victory to seek a negotiated peace. For this they invited President Theodore Roosevelt, who along with most Americans had generally favored the cause of "little" Japan against "giant" Russia, to bring about negotiations through his good offices. Although Roosevelt did not wish to see Japan become too demanding, to the point perhaps of trying to take control of eastern Siberia, the only conditions he imposed on Japan in proffering his good offices were that she agree to

FIGURE 16.3. The tsar, Nicholas II, blessing a group of infantry before their departure for the Manchurian front against the Japanese.

respect the Open Door in Manchuria and restore Manchuria to Chinese sovereignty. Roosevelt asked no conditions regarding Korea. Indeed, shortly before the convening of the peace conference Secretary of War Taft, representing the President, negotiated a secret "agreed memorandum" in Tokyo with Prime Minister Katsura by which the United States approved Japan's "suzerainty over" Korea in return for a Japanese disavowal of any aggressive intentions toward the Philippines.

The peace conference opened on August 5, 1905, in Portsmouth, New Hampshire. Neither Korea nor China was represented, although both were "sovereign" states and the war's land operations had been fought entirely on their soil. Russia was represented at the peace table by Count Witte, who accepted the assignment after several members of the pro-war faction turned it down as unlikely to add to their laurels. And the Japanese negotiator, Komura, literally had to sneak back to Tokyo, so unpopular were the terms of the treaty in Japan.

By the Treaty of Portsmouth Russia acknowledged Japan's "paramount" interests in Korea (also acknowledged by Britain in the renewal of the Anglo-Japanese Alliance on August 12, while the peace conference was in session). She relinquished to Japan the Russian leasehold and railway rights in South Manchuria, ceded to Japan the southern half of Sakhalin Island, and acknowledged the right of Japanese fishing in certain Siberian waters. The

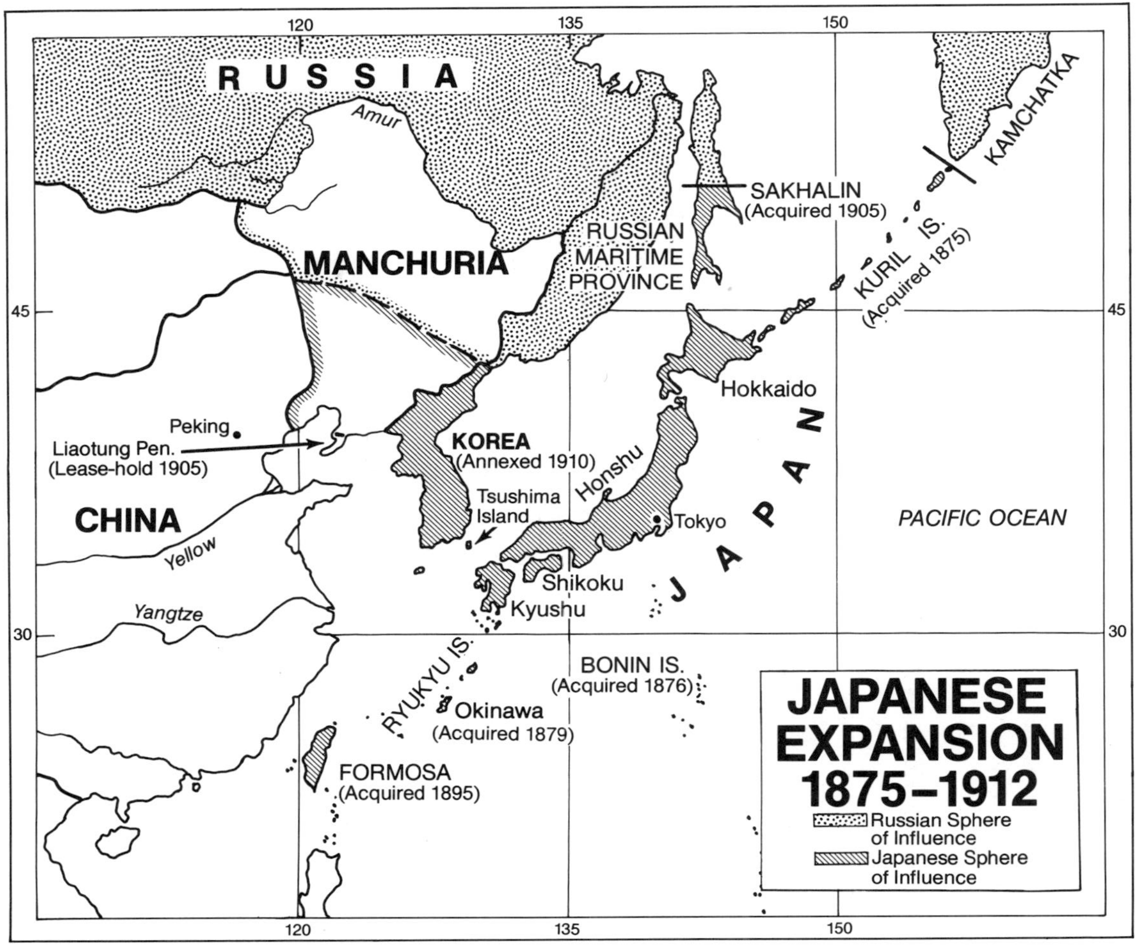

JAPANESE EXPANSION 1875–1912
Russian Sphere of Influence
Japanese Sphere of Influence
RUSSIA
Amur
MANCHURIA
RUSSIAN MARITIME PROVINCE
SAKHALIN (Acquired 1905)
KURIL IS. (Acquired 1875)
KAMCHATKA
Hokkaido
Honshu
Tokyo
Shikoku
Kyushu
JAPAN
PACIFIC OCEAN
KOREA (Annexed 1910)
Tsushima Island
Peking
Liaotung Pen. (Lease-hold 1905)
CHINA
Yellow
Yangtze
RYUKYU IS.
Okinawa (Acquired 1879)
BONIN IS. (Acquired 1876)
FORMOSA (Acquired 1895)
120
135
150
45
30

cession of southern Sakhalin was a compromise on the thorniest issue of the conference, for the Japanese had demanded a money indemnity, which the Russians refused to pay. Finally the Japanese accepted the Sakhalin cession in lieu of money, but the withdrawal of the indemnity demand and the general fact that this was a negotiated peace after a "victorious" war made the settlement unpopular in Japan, where ultranationalist groups led popular demonstrations against it. Although the sovereignty of Korea was nowhere mentioned, both Russia and Japan admitted the principle of Chinese sovereignty in Manchuria, and Japan acknowledged that the transfer of the Russian concessions to her should be approved by China.

END OF KOREAN INDEPENDENCE

From the Japanese standpoint the cause of the war had been her sense of insecurity about Korea. It was a war of "self defense" for Japan because Russia had refused to admit that unsettled conditions in Korea and "meddling" there by other powers menaced Japanese security. Japan had offered to trade "Manchuria for Korea" but Russia had refused. At the end of the war Japan's paramount interest in Korea had been fully recognized, explicitly by Russia, Britain, and the United States, and implicitly by all other Western powers when they did not object to the Portsmouth Treaty terms. China also had nothing to say, she having given up any interest in Korea ten years before at Shimonoseki. The only ones left to consider were the Koreans themselves.

During the war Japan had established effective military control over Korea. Nevertheless, Ito Hirobumi, who of all the Japanese leaders was the most sensitive to the wider currents of world opinion and the need for restraint in the pursuit of Japan's national interests, was determined that the regime to be established there should be an example of benevolent and enlightened control. He was opposed to outright annexation and he took precautions that the Japanese military should not force his hand. These included his own personal supervision at Seoul as resident-general, his insistence (over the heads of military leaders) that he be in military as well as civilian command in Korea, and his establishment of a line of direct responsibility from the resident-general to the Japanese emperor which left him relatively free of interference from the Foreign Office and even the prime minister in Tokyo. Also he could offer numerous inducements to Koreans who would cooperate with his protectorate regime.

Ito may have convinced the outside world, at least its governments, but he did not convince the Koreans, who became more and more restive under his proddings to "progress," and his regime became subject to increasing criticism in Japan, where ultranationalists took the lead in criticizing it as "weak-kneed." In 1907 the Korean king (now called "emperor") secretly dispatched an appeal against Japan to the Hague international peace conference. This was thrown out as "uninvited" by the Conference, which, according to the London *Times*, could not allow itself to be distracted from its "momentous work" for peace by giving time to "lost causes and submerged nationalities." But the aftermath in Korea and Japan was such that the office of resident-general never regained its equilibrium. For his "breach of faith" the "emperor" was required to abdicate in favor of his feeble-minded son and the Korean army was ordered disbanded. Ito hoped that these measures, which were concurred in by pro-Japanese Korean ministers of state, would remedy obstructionism and open the road to "progress" but the ministers were widely denounced as traitors and riots broke out all over Korea. Ito moved to quell these by military force, but this only further inflamed Korean hate of Japanese rule, while annexationists in Japan called for stronger action. Ito resigned in 1909, willing, apparently, to concede that annexation was necessary if Korea was not to be a thorn to Japanese security, but he was assassinated in Harbin by a Korean before any concrete step toward annexation had been taken. Then, ironically, the assassination became an added excuse for outright annexation and the Katsura government, which contained many leading advocates of annexation, sent War Minister Terauchi to Korea to end the last pretense of respect for Korean independence. In August, 1910, Korea was proclaimed annexed to Japan and a harsh colonial rule, which lasted until 1945, was inaugurated.

AMERICAN-JAPANESE RELATIONS

Manchuria and the Open Door

While Japan had a completely free hand in Korea, insofar as international rivals were concerned, she was soon in the thick of international arguments regarding Manchuria. The Portsmouth settlement gave her Russia's holdings in south Manchuria but also committed her to uphold Chinese sovereignty there. The Chinese government, weak and corrupt, was obliging enough in acknowledging the transfer and giving Japan further economic concessions by the Treaty of Peking, December, 1905, but it was not immediately clear how far Japan would push her advantageous position in Manchuria. In particular, would she violate the Open Door idea, so enthusiastically pronounced by American Secretary of State John Hay at the time of the Boxer uprising as the measure of restraint the powers must practice in China if that empire was not to be torn apart in international rivalries? With Britain allied to Japan and Russia quiescent, the United States especially watched to see whether Japan would try to shut out other countries from Manchurian enterprises.

There were momentary signs that an era of American-Japanese cooperation was dawning, as American railroad magnate E. H. Harriman proposed joint development of Manchurian railways to the Japanese. He could supply capital, which the Japanese lacked. A number of Japanese leaders were seriously interested in the idea, but in the end they decided to turn Harriman down and obtain such loans as they needed in London, while vesting control in a Japanese government-owned South Manchurian Railroad Company. This angered Harriman and a vehement supporter of his project, Willard Straight, who as American consul-general at Mukden from 1906–1908, was something of a knight errant battling against Japanese influence.

The Immigration Issue

President Roosevelt, although he liked Straight personally, had other worries. Since the annexation of Hawaii a steady stream of Japanese had been coming to California from this Pacific "vestibule" and by 1905 California was seething with anti-Japanese feeling. In that year the San Francisco school board decreed the segregation of Japanese students and an Exclusion League was launched to exclude Japanese and Koreans (as earlier the Chinese) from the United States. Roosevelt had to consider the interrelationship of various Pacific problems, as his letter to Henry Cabot Lodge, dated June 3, 1905, indicates:

> These Pacific Coast people wish grossly to insult the Japanese and to keep out the Japanese immigrants on the ground that they are an immoral, degraded, and worthless race; and at the same time that they desire to do this for the Japanese and are already doing it for the Chinese they expect to be given advantages in Oriental markets; and with besotted folly are indifferent to building up the navy while provoking this formidable new power—a power jealous, sensitive and warlike, and which if irritated could at once take both the Philippines and Hawaii from us if she obtained the upper hand on the seas. . . .[1]

During the next three years Roosevelt worked to calm the Californians, soothe the Japanese, and protect the American national interest, as he conceived it, namely her Pacific possessions. He was able to accomplish a compromise on the immigration problem, the so-called "Gentlemen's Agreement," whereby Japan promised to reduce the immigration to a point where exclusion would presumably become a dead issue. She agreed to refuse passports for America to all laborers, whether skilled or unskilled, except those who were returning to a previously established home in the United States or joining parents, wife, or children residing there, or were "settled agriculturalists" returning to their farms. This put the exclusion on an economic rather than a racial basis and eased the affront to the "gentlemen" of Japan. In return, by the Root-Takahira Agreement (1908), Japan received an implicit, but nonetheless actual, guarantee that her status quo in Manchuria would be undisturbed by the United States, and she in return would respect the American status quo in the Pacific (meaning the Philippines and Hawaii). China's "independence and integrity" were mentioned, but the word "territorial" which had been attached to Secretary Hay's definition of "integrity" was conspicuously omitted. The Root-Takahira Agreement was of the executive variety, binding only the Roosevelt administration, but in his advice to his successor, Taft, Roosevelt in 1910 emphasized that

---

[1] Quoted in A. W. Griswold, *The Far Eastern Policy of the United States* (New York: Harcourt, Brace and Co., 1938), p. 348.

"the vital interest of the Japanese . . . is in Manchuria and Korea. It is therefore peculiarly to our interest not to take any steps as regards Manchuria which will give the Japanese cause to feel, with or without reason, that we are hostile to them. . . . The "Open Door" policy, as a matter of fact, completely disappears as soon as a powerful nation determines to disregard it."[2]

Dollar Diplomacy

President Taft chose to disregard Roosevelt's advice. Responding to urgings from Willard Straight and banking interests anxious to push American investments, he had already given implicit official sanction to renewed efforts by Harriman's group to compete with Japan in Manchuria, and, after the death of Harriman in September, 1909, had caused some hesitation on the part of many investors, his secretary of state, Philander Knox, pushed "dollar diplomacy" in Manchuria with all the resources of the State Department. Knox urged Britain to join the United States in "neutralizing" the foreign-controlled railroads by loaning China sufficient money to buy back both the Japanese South Manchurian and the Russian Chinese Eastern Railroad systems. The British were not enthusiastic and in a sense answered by renewing the Anglo-Japanese Alliance in 1911, to the embitterment of American relations. Knox meanwhile tried various projects to bring in American capital, but the result was meager. Japan and Russia had responded to Willard Straight's activities at Mukden in 1907 with an agreement to maintain the status quo, which secretly delimited their respective "spheres," and now in 1910 they affirmed that they would, if necessary, take "common action" in defense of their special interests in Manchuria.

Though ejected from Manchuria, Knox did not give up. Instead, he changed his focus to China proper and succeeded in organizing a four-power consortium consisting of France, Britain, Germany, and the United States to make loans to China for railways. However, Britain balked when he tried to require that China put all these loans through the consortium, with obvious intent to keep Japan out, but it is some indication of Knox's success that Japan and Russia then demanded entrance and were received into the group. After becoming president Woodrow Wilson, however, reviewed the whole consortium operation and decided that it was itself violating principles of Chinese integrity by taking liens on Chinese tax and postal receipts as loan security, and he withdrew American participation. This, plus the outbreak of World War I in Europe which distracted the interests and the finances of the European powers, left investment financing in China wide open to the Japanese, whose now business-minded government leaders were to make the most of the opportunity.

In evaluating the history of the first stage of Japanese expansion onto the Northeast Asian mainland most American scholars have attributed it to calculated and nefarious Japanese design, with the United States a well-meaning but entirely futile proponent of Open Door ideals. Since the American people would not go to war for the Open Door, such efforts as

[2] *Ibid.*, pp. 131–132.

Philander Knox's attempt to keep the door ajar with American capital were foolish, and only Theodore Roosevelt's realism was praiseworthy. However, there are many problems. From a close-up view one finds indications that the Japanese expansionist drive was not necessarily immutable, that it was conditioned by Social Darwinism which the British alliance and general world power attitudes stimulated. Weak countries, "decadent" peoples *should* be controlled, said that attitude, and there is little doubt that Roosevelt shared these opinions. He was contemptuous of the Chinese for their lack of fighting qualities and organization, qualities which he found and frankly admired in the Japanese, and his approach to the two countries may be said implicitly, if not explicitly, to have invited the idea of a ruled China and ruling Japan.

The Straight-Taft-Knox approach may actually have been a little better, for it had the merit of trying to block the strong from preying on the weak. But its "defense" of the weak charged heavy interest, and the loan schemes offered were "business-like" enough to threaten to put a lien on several generations of Chinese. With Britain and the United States, the "good" nations, acting as they did and Russia perhaps worse, it is small wonder that Japan did not show much sensitivity to the problems of the weak and the poor in her push onto the Asian mainland.

BASIC DATES

1896	Flight of Korean king to Russian legation
1898	Attempt and failure of party government in Japan; powers take spheres of interest in China
1900	Emergence of Elder Statesmen (*Genrō*) in Japan; Boxer movement in China; Russian seizure of Manchuria
1901–1913	Katsura-Saionji alternation of premiership; emergence of zaibatsu in Japan; suppression of socialist movement
1902	Anglo-Japanese Alliance
1904–1905	Russo-Japanese War; Japanese protectorate established over Korea
1907	Korean appeal to Hague tribunal
1907–1908	"Gentlemen's Agreement" between United States and Japan
1907–1910	Russo-Japanese division of Manchuria as American intervention fails
1910	Japanese annexation of Korea
1911	Renewal of Anglo-Japanese Alliance

SUPPLEMENTARY READING

Beasley, W. G. *The Modern History of Japan.* New York, 1963.
Borton, H. *Japan's Modern Century,* rev. ed. New York, 1970.
Brown, D. M. *Nationalism in Japan.* Berkeley, Calif., 1955.
Griswold, A. W. *The Far Eastern Policy of the United States.* New York, 1938; 5th printing, 1966.

Hall, J. W. *Japan: From Prehistory to Modern Times.* New York, 1970. Chap. 16.
Hane, M. *Japan: A Historical Survey.* New York, 1972.
Iriye, Akira. *Across the Pacific: An Inner History of American-East Asian Relations.* New York, 1967; *Pacific Estrangement* (1972).
Jansen, M. B., ed. *Changing Japanese Attitudes Toward Modernization.* Princeton, N.J., 1965.
Reischauer, E. O. *The United States and Japan,* 3rd ed. Cambridge, Mass., 1965.
Scalapino, R. A. *Democracy and the Party Movement in Prewar Japan.* Berkeley, Calif., 1953.
Yanaga, C. *Japan Since Perry.* New York, 1949; reprinted, 1966.

ADVANCED READING

Allen, G. C. *A Short Economic History of Modern Japan,* 2nd rev. ed. London, 1963.
Arima, T. *The Failure of Freedom: A Portrait of Modern Japanese Intellectuals.* Cambridge, Mass., 1969.
Beale, H. K. *Theodore Roosevelt and the Rise of America to World Power.* Baltimore, 1946.
Conroy, H. *The Japanese Seizure of Korea, 1868–1910.* Philadelphia, 1960.
Esthus, R. A. *Theodore Roosevelt and Japan.* Seattle, 1966.
Kajima, M. *The Emergence of Japan as a World Power, 1895–1932.* Rutland, Vt., 1967.
Kim, C. I. E. and H. K. Kim. *Korea and the Politics of Imperialism, 1876–1910.* Berkeley, Calif., 1967.
Kublin, Hyman. *Asian Revolutionary: The Life of Sen Katayama.* Princeton, N.J., 1964.
Lockwood, W. W. *The Economic Development of Japan,* rev. ed. Princeton, N.J., 1968.
Lockwood, W. W., ed. *The State and Economic Enterprise in Japan.* Princeton, N.J., 1965.
Malozemoff, A. *Russian Far Eastern Policy, 1881–1904.* Berkeley, Calif., 1958.
Najita, Tetsuo. *Hara Kei in the Politics of Compromise, 1905–1915.* Cambridge, Mass., 1967.
Nakamura, J. I. *Agricultural Production and the Economic Development of Japan, 1873–1922.* Princeton, N.J., 1966.
Neu, C. E., Jr. *An Uncertain Friendship: Theodore Roosevelt and Japan, 1906–1909.* Cambridge, Mass., 1967.
Nish, Ian. *The Anglo-Japanese Alliance.* London, 1966.
Notelfer, F. G. *Kōtoku Shūsui: Portrait of a Japanese Radical.* New York, 1971.
Spaulding, R. M. *Imperial Japan's Higher Civil Service Examinations.* Princeton, N.J., 1967.
White, J. A. *The Diplomacy of the Russo-Japanese War.* Princeton, N.J., 1964.

Chapter 17

The Philippines, 1600-1913, and American Expansion to the Far East

This chapter will deal with two essentially different themes, first the Spanish occupation of the Philippines and the long period of Spanish control, and secondly, American expansion in the Pacific area. These two themes were united by the historical accident of the extension of the Spanish-American War to the western Pacific in 1898. Thereafter the Spanish-oriented Philippines Islands became a colony of and a problem for an American republic, which was founded on a basis of anticolonialism.

THE DISCOVERY OF THE PHILIPPINES

Pre-Spanish Philippines

Almost every schoolboy knows that Ferdinand Magellan discovered the Philippines for Spain near the end of his circumnavigation in 1521. However, he may not know that a great variety of people, including Negritoes, Indonesians, and Malaysians, had found them centuries earlier and, after them, preceding the Spanish, had come Chinese, Japanese, and Moslem traders, the latter from as far away as India and Arabia. When the Spaniards arrived, the Philippines already had a written language which may have had Sanskrit origins, an active trade, and a fairly well-developed social system. Religion was primitive, except for certain areas, especially Mindanao, where Islam was becoming strong, and the political organization was quite primitive. There was no centralized political system. The seven thousand-odd islands were divided into an even larger number of petty local political groups, headed by chiefs or, if Indian or Moslem in inspiration, by a "raja" or a "sultan." Local chiefs, called *dato*, were the spokesmen for some thirty to one hundred families, collectively called *barangay* after the Malay sailboats that brought early immigrants. Linguistically they were also divided, with nearly a hundred different languages being spoken. One called Tagalog, however, was the most prevalent, and all were related to Malay.

Magellan

In the Philippine archipelago Magellan landed on a small uninhabited island near Leyte. Natives came from nearby and welcomed the Europeans, and Magellan was then led to Cebu, the largest island in the vicinity, where he was also welcomed. There the Cebuans allowed Mass to be said and the conversion to Christianity of several hundred people followed. Magellan and the chief of Cebu entered into a blood pact, and then Magellan with his Cebuan allies invaded a neighboring island, Mactan. In the fight that followed Magellan was killed on the beach (April, 1521). After that the Cebuan chieftain also turned against the Spaniards. Many were killed, and the rest put to sea on their remaining ships, two of which were yet to be lost before the last handful of men successfully completed the circumnavigation of the globe and returned to Spain.

Later Spanish Explorers

Although Magellan's results in the Philippines were decidedly negative, other Spanish explorers went to the islands. Villalobos, sailing from Mexico in 1542, reached Leyte or its vicinity the following year and christened one of the islands he touched "Philippine" in honor of Crown Prince Philip (later Philip II), a name which was later to grace all the islands. Villalobos sailed on to the Moluccas where he was taken prisoner by the Portuguese and later died, but between 1565 and 1571 the flag of Spain was firmly planted in the Philippines. This was the work of Miguel Lopez de Legaspi. Legaspi reached the Philippines at Cebu from Mexico in mid-February, 1565. However, the Cebuans were hostile, so he withdrew to Samar and then Leyte where he was able to make compacts with the native chiefs. With their aid, he attacked Cebu and forced those islanders to accept Spanish rule. Legaspi's first intention seems to have been to organize Spanish control in the southern islands of the Philippines, but some of his men explored further north and discovered that on the main island, Luzon, was a fine port, Manila, where a flourishing trade was going on under the control of a Moslem merchant prince. The Moslem prince, Suleiman, refused to accept Spanish suzerainty, and Legaspi attacked in 1570. Suleiman was defeated in 1571, Spanish control over Manila became effective, and gradually other parts of the island of Luzon were pacified.

Legaspi carried with him a commission as first governor-general of the Philippine Islands, and before his death at Manila in August, 1572, he had established the first Spanish government there. Many years were required to complete the organization of Spanish control, but after the capture of Manila and the pacification of most of Luzon, it went on rapidly. The Augustinian friars, who accompanied Legaspi, and other orders (Franciscans after 1577, Jesuits after 1581, and Dominicans after 1587) used the persuasions of religion effectively to bring the Filipinos into the new Spanish order. The most serious resistance was on the large southern island of Mindanao, where Islam had made the strongest inroads. There the Moslem inhabitants, called Moros, adamantly refused to accept either Catholicism or Spanish rule. Some mountain tribes also remained independent and hostile, but in general from the late sixteenth century until 1898 Spanish rule prevailed over the accessible lowland areas where at least nine-tenths of the population lived.

PERIOD OF SPANISH RULE

Spain's Colonial Administration

Colonial administration in the Philippines was remotely under the control of Spain's Council of the Indies, which was the royal body in charge of all Spanish colonial affairs. In addition, more direct supervision of the Philippine administration came from the Spanish colonial government of Mexico, until 1821 when Mexico became independent of Spain. Hence the connection with Mexico, both politically and commercially, was very close. Most communications to the Philippines came via Mexico, gubernatorial appointees arrived from Mexico, often after serving there, and troops and traders were available from there.

However, the trip to Mexico was long, to Spain even longer, and once in the Philippines the governor-general, with his appointment as the king's military, civil, and even ecclesiastical representative, could rule with almost absolute power. Presumably he was checked on by a royal Audiencia, composed of Spanish nobles and justices, which provided him with advice, which acted as a supreme court in judicial cases, and which formulated many of the laws put into force. It also audited financial records and reported on these to Spain. However, the governor-general was the Audiencia's president, and it was only in rare instances that he could not control it.

A better check on the governor-generalship came from the so-called Residencia, a body set up by an incoming governor-general to compile a report on the state of affairs as the new administration found it. Since an outgoing governor's reputation could be ruined by an unfavorable report, he was presumably anxious to do a good job while in office, although in most cases he was also determined to make a fortune, and usually did.

A third element in the Spanish government of the Philippines was the Catholic Church. Roman Catholicism was the state religion of the Philippines as it was of Spain, and the Church had unusual rights of tax collection and even of local administration, for there were far too few civil officials to carry the government into local areas. The Church organization was headed by an archbishop at Manila who usually worked closely with the governor-general but who sometimes quarrelled with him.

Whereas the usual term of office of a governor-general was from two to six years, the archbishops tended to stay much longer. Frequently they would serve as acting governors-general while that office was being turned over, and many of them were not averse to interfering in secular affairs. Though the archbishop was dependent on the king of Spain for his recommendation to office, his appointment was officially made by the Pope, and this gave him a certain independence of action if he chose to use it.

The ecclesiastical authority was further complicated by the presence of members of the several orders of friars, whose primary duty was the conversion of the populace, but who also served as parish priests when the latter were lacking. As parish priests they were responsible to the archbishop and the several bishops under him, but as regular clergy they were responsible through their provincial superiors to the heads of their respective orders, who were outside of the Philippines and even outside of Spain. Since the missionary role was their primary one, they often refused to accept the authority of the archbishop, even when he was backed by the governor, and as a matter of policy they refused to allow the bishops' rights of canonical visitation (and investigation) in their parishes. On a number of occasions in which the issue of visitation was squarely joined they won the day by threatening to resign as parish priests if the archbishop enforced his authority.

The Encomienda System

For the Filipinos the result of these several layers of military, civil, and religious authority was a life of hardship and near slavery. The Filipino population was divided into so-called *encomiendas* and assigned to the over-

FIGURE 17.1. Church and bell tower built with Filipino labor during the Spanish period.

sight of individuals or institutions. In the first division after the conquest about two-thirds of the encomiendas were designated as "private" and given to Spanish conquistadors as rewards for their services, the remaining one-third being retained for the Crown. However, after three generations the private encomiendas returned to the Crown for reassignment. It should be noted that the encomienda was a division of population, not of land. Ownership of the land presumably remained with the Filipinos, who held it collectively in their barangays, although gradually in the nineteenth century private ownership began to prevail. The encomienda privilege was one of income, or "tribute." The encomienderos had the right and duty to collect tribute from every adult male, age 18 to 60, under their sway to defray the cost of the secular and religious administration provided by Spain.

The system operated as originally planned only until the mid-seventeenth century, when complaints by the clergy led to its being ended officially, although there was no real relief.

Supposedly the amount collected was under careful regulation, but actually it was not, and it usually amounted to extortion from the Filipinos of as much as they could pay, whether in goods, money, or services.

Even this was not enough to support the Spanish administration and there were frequent special emergencies, such as the Dutch Wars (1600–1648), during which Manila was attacked seven times, and the anti-Moro piracy campaigns, when special levies, particularly of forced labor and of special products, were made to develop ship construction and other public projects.

While the encomienda system was probably no more tyrannical than the plantation system in Java or the slave system in the United States, it was undoubtedly a very harsh experience for the rather carefree and easygoing Filipinos. The regimentation which it entailed certainly developed the land, but it broke the spirit of the Filipinos to the point that it required the outside influences of the nineteenth century to revive a spirit of freedom in them.

The Question of a Filipino Clergy

One of the most bitter aspects of Spanish rule over the Philippines was that the very church to which the Filipinos had been so persuasively converted, after conversion discriminated against them. This was more the doing of the regular orders and their friars than of the archbishop's organization. In fact, the archbishops of Manila were anxious to build a native clergy to oversee the various local parishes into which the islands had been divided, and between 1768 and 1776 a number of them were put into Filipino hands. However, the friars of the several monastic orders, having served in the early period as parish priests, had become reluctant to relinquish these posts and complained bitterly that the Filipinos were incompetent, and worse, that they tended to be too tolerant of pagan native traditions. Actually the Filipinos appointed in the 1770's did not do very well and the practice of appointing them as parish priests was suspended in 1776. After that, even though many qualified Filipinos were graduated from the schools established by the several orders in the Philippines, they were allowed to serve only as assistants. The parish priest was almost always a white man.

Furthermore, the regular orders remained closed to Filipinos, as illustrated in the famous case of Apolinario de la Cruz (1815–1841). Deeply religious, Apolinario studied hard, dreaming of the day when he might join one of the monastic orders, but when he went to Manila to try to do so he was informed that Filipinos were not eligible. He then returned to his home area and set about organizing a new religious order honoring St. Joseph and the Virgin. It attracted many followers, but when he sought official recognition for it he was turned down by both ecclesiastical and governmental authorities. Then he was ordered to disband his organization. When he did not, the authorities arrested many of his followers, but he escaped. In the fall of 1841, he and his remaining followers rose in revolt against the authorities, demanding religious freedom. The provincial governor led a small contingent of soldiers and friars against him, but the rebels won the first engagement and the governor was killed. Now thoroughly alarmed, the governor-general sent overwhelming forces against Apolinario, who was defeated, captured, and executed in November, 1841.

Other Riots and Uprisings

Though Apolinario's revolt was quite spectacular, it should be characterized only as one of the last of a long succession of local uprisings against Spain, sometimes for secular and sometimes for religious reasons, which preceded the emergence of a sense of Philippine nationality and a more general revolutionary spirit in the late nineteenth century. Of the earlier revolts the most serious were the following: one on the island of Samar (1649–1650) against the impressment of men to work in shipyards; one in the Lingayen area of Luzon (1660–1661) over requisitions for timber and seizures of rice; one on the island of Bohol in 1744 over the punishment of a Filipino Christian who renounced the faith. This became widespread and endemic on that island, with the rebels finally retreating into the mountains and remaining unsubdued, their descendants being resettled under Spanish authority more than half a century later. There was a series of uprisings around Manila (1745–1746) over the alleged usurpation of certain lands by the Jesuit order; and uprisings associated with the temporary seizure of Manila by the British in 1762–1764, which will be discussed shortly.

All of these and other lesser uprisings were suppressed by the Spanish authorities, but an especially persistent defiance of Spanish rule was that of the previously mentioned Moslem Moros. From the beginning they resisted the Spanish, and with the arrival of the Dutch in the East Indies area they found new support in their struggle. In 1644 the heir to the sultanate of Sulu actually visited Batavia and made an alliance with the Dutch, which complicated matters for the Spanish for a few years. After the Dutch Wars ended with the Treaty of Münster in Westphalia, the end of the Thirty Years War, in 1648, the Spanish went on the offensive and obtained control of part of Mindanao. In 1737, the Moros signed a treaty with the Manila authorities promising to set free those Christian captives they held. However, this agreement, and others, were soon broken, and in the late eighteenth and early nineteenth centuries the Moros again attacked Christians and Christian settlements all through the southern islands and even along the coast of Luzon. The raids were stopped only after 1848, when the Spanish acquired steamships at Manila which could chase down and destroy the Moro sailing ships.

The Manila Galleon

Despite the encomienda tribute system and the use of forced labor, the Philippines was not a profitable colony for Spain. Many officials who served there made private fortunes, and most of the Spaniards in the islands lived affluently, but in the mercantilist balance sheets of the Spanish empire the Philippines were a constant deficit. This was because the costs of maintaining the government, the religious establishment, and the defense establishment (against Dutch and English encroachment especially) were very high. The productivity of the islands and their people was simply not enough to pay for these, and Spain might have had to abandon the islands for financial reasons had it not been for the remarkable galleon trade that developed with Mexico and brought Mexican silver into the Philippines in exchange for oriental products, largely imports from China.

Of course, from an overall imperial view, the dispatching of Mexican treasure to the Philippines represented a loss to Spain itself, for had there been no importation of oriental goods from the Philippines, Mexico would probably have bought their equivalent from Spain. It is interesting to note that the merchants of Cadiz and Seville realized this and exercised pressure at Madrid to cut down the Mexico-Manila galleon trade, but the Spaniards in Mexico loved the oriental products and those in Manila needed the silver so badly that the result was a compromise whereby the galleon trade was limited, to one ship a year after 1734, and quite strictly regulated, but was allowed to continue. Needless to say the Manila-Acapulco organizers utilized every possible inch of cargo space and made the ships as large as possible. (With the result that an overloaded ship occasionally went to the bottom, and all were in jeopardy of fast-moving raiders manned by Dutch and English soldiers of fortune.) The goods exported from Manila included a veritable treasure of silks and other fabrics, porcelains, spices, perfumes, and jewels, which brought profits up to three hundred per cent in Mexico.

The Chinese in the Philippines

The galleon trade required much commercial activity in Manila, an area in which Chinese merchants took the lead. Many already lived in the Philippines when the Spanish arrived, but the galleon trade opened new opportunities to them as importers and transshippers of oriental goods and the recipients of Mexican silver, and they came in ever increasing numbers. The Spanish authorities, while regarding them as inveterate heathens, were in no small measure dependent on their commercial abilities. In fact, the term *Sangleys* by which the Chinese were known in the Philippines was a corruption of a south China term meaning, "We came to trade." The Chinese were not politically ambitious, but they resisted excessive exactions and discrimination, with the result that relations between them and their Spanish overlords were always tense and sometimes explosive. On several occasions (1603, 1639, 1662, 1686, 1762, and 1819) the Spanish suspected the Chinese of plotting and retaliated with terror campaigns in which thousands of Chinese were massacred. Probably the only real threat to Spanish control posed by the Chinese was in 1662 when the famous half-Chinese, half-Japanese Ming partisan, Koxinga, who controlled Formosa, threatened invasion of the Philippines if the Spanish did not meet his demands for tribute. Many Chinese in the islands might have joined him if he had come, but he died in the midst of his preparations, and the only result was a bloody suppression of Chinese "rebels" and "potential rebels" in the islands.

Foreign Trade

The dependence on the Chinese for the importation of oriental products was certainly galling to the Spanish, especially in view of their unresponsiveness to Christianity, the propagation of which the Spanish took very seriously, since it was their main justification for the maintenance of the unprofitable Philippine colony. However, the alternatives to dealing with the Chinese were even more unsatisfactory. For a few years in the early seventeenth century it seemed as though trade relations with Japan might be established, and indeed several Spanish ships visited Japan and various negotiations were undertaken with Tokugawa Ieyasu himself. Ieyasu was willing to have Spanish trade if it would come to Edo, if it would involve artisans more than priests, if it would operate alongside the Dutch and English, if, in short, it met his terms. However, Ieyasu had become increasingly suspicious of Christians during his later years, and in 1624 his son, Hidetada, had banned the Spaniards completely, fifteen years before the Portuguese exclusion.

Control of Formosa by the Dutch and then Koxinga, and the Dutch control of the South China Sea made direct approaches to the China mainland impossible, even if the Portuguese at Macao had been friendly to Spanish overtures, which they were not. Actually the best possibility for avoiding dependence on the Chinese junk traders was to develop trade with the Indian ports, especially Madras. An English East India Company merchantman came to Manila as early as 1644 to test the possibility of opening trade relations there. At that time Manila had been experiencing the effect of a Dutch blockade and was very much in need of the goods it brought, and, although the Spanish authorities refused officially, they negotiated unofficially for part of the cargo. Subsequently high-level talks between London and Madrid considered the possibility of trade and failed of agreement, but a limited trade developed in a disguised condition, nevertheless. Not the English East India Company, but "free merchants" in

Madras outfitted ships, gave them appropriate Spanish saints' names, or Indian names, listed the owners as "Armenians" or other innocent parties, and visited Manila fairly frequently, trading cloth, and Indian articles for Mexican silver.

As the result of the Seven Years War (1756–1763), when Spain and England became enemies, Manila was captured by a powerful English squadron from India in October 1762. The English controlled Manila and its environs for nearly two years, but they did not extend their authority further. Two years later, in 1764, the English withdrew and power was restored to Spain. The earlier Madras-Manila trade then was again resumed, and Indian goods continued to constitute a secondary source of supply in the foreign trade of the Philippines.

End of the Galleon Trade

The galleon trade continued almost to the time of the separation of Mexico from Spain (1821), but in the later years it languished. One reason was that in 1785 the Royal Company of the Philippines was licensed by the King of Spain and given monopoly rights to trade directly between the Philippines and Spain. With the westward route through the East Indies now relatively unimpeded by enemies and Philippine products allowed to enter Spain duty free, this became a more profitable trade than that with Mexico, where the prices offered for oriental products declined steadily. Also the growing spirit of free trade in the world was leaving the Spanish monopoly philosophy far behind the times.

The galleon trade had been a remarkable adventure, and it had supplied the Philippines with enough wealth to bring the colonial budget not into balance, but close enough to it so that the Spanish government, which regarded the Philippine enterprise as the noble and self-sacrificing one of bringing civilization and Christianity to benighted heathens, was not moved to abandon it, although there were times when this was talked about.

OPEN TRADE AND REVOLUTION IN THE PHILIPPINES

Although English ships and some American ones were calling at Manila with increasing frequency in the late eighteenth and early nineteenth centuries, it was not until 1834 that the Spanish government decided to declare Manila open to world trade. By that time the Manila-Mexico trade was long dead and the Royal Company of the Philippines, trading directly with Spain, was bankrupt. Actually during the brief period of the 1813 Cortes in Spain the Philippines had sent a delegate, a Manila merchant, who urged the end of the galleon monopoly and obtained the promise of freer trade. Subsequently the Philippines sent delegates to the Cortes of 1820–1823, but without favorable results. The Cortes of 1834–1837 was also abortive for the Philippines in the political sense, since Philippine delegates were excluded in 1837. However, the opening of Manila to world trade in 1834 was to have widespread effects, not only commercially, but intellectually and eventually politically.

Effects of the Opening of Manila

Philippine commerce increased by leaps and bounds as American and British merchants began to seek and obtain from the Philippines not merely the valuable articles from China and India that had characterized the earlier monopoly trade, but bulk products such as sugar, hemp, rice, and tobacco. Total exports which before the opening were never valued at more than five million pesos per year soared to the order of 25 million by the 1880's. The demand for Philippine agricultural products was reflected in increasing agricultural production, the prospects for which were improved by the suppression of Moro depradations at mid-century.

With the increased trade came new ideas. The English and American merchants who now operated openly in Manila began to extend their activities into agricultural and engineering projects, as well as banking. Technical experts of various kinds began to arrive, and most of the newcomers were Protestants. An educated Filipino middle class began to emerge, which found stimulation in books and pamphlets on liberal themes which began to circulate in Manila. In 1868 a revolt in Spain against the absolutism of Queen Isabella II led to the appointment of a new liberal-minded governor-general for the Philippines, Carlos de la Torre, who encouraged freedom of expression and a sense of equality among the Filipinos. It seemed like the dawn of a new era, and educated Filipinos welcomed the opportunity to explore new ideas and vistas with the friendly new governor and his entourage. Various discussion groups and cultural societies were formed, much to the consternation of the friars and parish priests, who were deeply entrenched in habits of paternalism.

Had de la Torre's policies continued a new Spanish-Filipino relationship based on equality might have gradually emerged, but the opportunity ended with the restoration of monarchy in Spain and the replacement of de la Torre in 1871 by an autocrat of the old school. The immediate result of the new governor's reestablishment of restrictions was a mutiny of Filipino troops at Cavite in 1872. It was thought to have been inspired by Filipinos who had emerged as active cultural and semi-political leaders under de la Torre, and many of these were hunted out and executed or imprisoned. Spain was trying to turn the clock back, but it was too late.

The "Propaganda" Movement and Rizal

During the later 1870's and the 1880's the Philippine intellectual movement moved forward despite vigorous attempts by the Manila authorities to thwart it. Bright young Filipinos who had imbibed liberal ideas were banished to remote places in the Philippines. But many contrived to go abroad, to Japan, to Hong Kong, and to Europe. Even in Spain they had much more freedom of expression than in the Philippines. These young people managed to keep in touch with each other and with their friends in the Philippines through letters, circulars, and pamphlets, and they gradually developed a coherent movement for reform, the "Propaganda Movement," which demanded freedom of speech and movement for Filipinos and equal right with Spaniards before the law. As for relations with Spain at this stage there was no demand for independence, but rather for representation at Madrid.

By the late 1880's the Propaganda Movement had found a leader of great stature, José Rizal, one of the most brilliant men of the nineteenth century of any country. Of mixed Filipino-Chinese ancestry, he was first taught by his mother, a cultured woman who suffered a period of imprisonment by the Spanish authorities. Nevertheless she saw to it that the boy learned Spanish and later attended Jesuit schools and Santo Tomás University in the Philippines. In 1882 he went to Spain, where he was graduated in medicine from the Central University of Madrid. Though medicine was his profession, languages and humanistic studies interested him even more. He learned to read a dozen European languages besides Spanish, and traveled and studied in various European university centers. While in Berlin in 1887 he published a novel, *Noli Me Tangere* (literally, "Touch Me Not"), which brought him immediately to the forefront of the Propaganda Movement. Though the novel circulated in Spain, it was condemned by the Permanent Censorship Commission of the Philippines as "libelous, immoral, and pernicious," indicating that it had struck home. Against a rich and real background of life in the Philippines, Rizal had his characters speak out on problems of politics and religion and through them voiced an eloquent plea for reform.

With this and another novel, *El Filibusterismo*, published in Belgium in 1891, and with various articles and essays, Rizal, like other Filipino members of the Propaganda Movement, hoped particularly to draw the attention of government and intellectual circles in Spain to conditions in the Philippines, so that the Spanish constitution might be applied there and discrimination against Filipinos ended. But some of his writing is possessed of a universality beyond his own time and place. In his pleas for racial equality and human dignity for colonial peoples and subject races he foreshadowed some of the major themes of the twentieth-century world.

After enjoying the stimulation and companionship of European intellectual circles for nearly a decade Rizal decided in 1892 to return permannently to the Philippines to practice medicine and to further the reform movement. Shortly after his arrival he founded *La Liga Filipina* to encourage Filipino participation in civic affairs and to obtain the cooperation of the Spanish authorities in bringing about reforms. He was immediately arrested and exiled to a remote village in Mindanao, where he was allowed to practice medicine but forbidden to engage in political activity.

The Katipunan Society and Revolution

With the removal of Rizal the leadership of the reform movement passed into more radical hands. One Andrés Bonifacio, who had been a member of Rizal's group, organized a secret society of patriots, the Katipunan, which

FIGURE 17.2. José Rizal.

began to plot outright revolution. Tied together with oaths, passwords, and other secret apparatus, its members began to collect weapons and to organize for revolt against Spain. They tried to contact Rizal, but he refused to endorse their violent intentions. In 1895 a young man with unusual military abilities, Emilio Aguinaldo, joined the society. Aid was sought in Hong Kong and Tokyo, with the result that helpful contacts were made with Japanese ultranationalists and Chinese revolutionists. In 1896 the call to revolution was sounded.

Meanwhile Rizal, who had been living quietly in Mindanao, had decided to volunteer his medical services for Cuba, was granted permission to leave, and was actually aboard ship for Spain when the revolution broke out. Immediately the Manila authorities sent out an order for his arrest, and he was brought back to the Philippines, given a speedy trial, and shot on December 30, 1896. With Rizal now a martyr the revolution spread. It might have succeeded in overthrowing the power of Spain within the next year except for a split between Bonifacio and Aguinaldo which developed when they tried to set up a provisional government. Open fighting broke out between the factions, and Bonifacio was killed. After that a stalemate developed between the Spanish forces and those of Aguinaldo, and finally negotiations were begun. The governor-general offered amnesty and an indemnity to the rebels and the promise of reforms, equality for Filipinos, freedom of speech and press, changes in property and tax laws, if Aguinaldo would call off the rebellion and go into voluntary exile. Aguinaldo accepted, received a large sum of money, and retired to Hong Kong to see how the new arrangement would work. It did not. Some of the rebels would not accept the terms, and on the excuse of punishing these the Spanish authorities shortly began new persecutions.

This was the situation when the Spanish-American War broke out on April 24, 1898. At that time Aguinaldo was actually in Singapore, where he had some conferences with the American consul-general. Shortly thereafter he returned to Hong Kong, to be taken on an American ship to Manila, where the destinies of Filipinos and Americans were to be joined.

AMERICANS CROSS THE PACIFIC

Although the saga of early American commercial, missionary, and diplomatic activities in the Pacific and Far Eastern area forms the background of United States involvement in the Philippines, it should perhaps be emphasized that the annexation of the islands was not necessarily a natural outgrowth of those activities. Indeed, it might be argued that the Cuban imbroglio and the war with Spain produced in 1898 a temporary state of mind which induced the American government and public to forget their customary caution and circumspection in Far Eastern affairs and plunge into actions that were quite inconsistent with past attitudes and policies. Exactly why this urge to empire took hold of the country at this time we leave for historians of the United States to discover; here we shall recount only a few of the main events linking America and the Far East before 1898.

Early Trade at Canton

American involvement in the Far East began very early in the life of the republic, in 1784, when one Samuel Shaw, acting on behalf of a group of New York merchants, brought the first American ship, the *Empress of China*, to Canton to trade. Shaw arranged with one of the cohong merchants to exchange furs, cotton, ginseng (a plant whose root was much prized in the Far East for its medicinal qualities), and a few other items for Chinese tea, silks, and porcelain. The exchange being mutually profitable, within a few years the visits of ships from east coast American cities became frequent at Canton, and a regular route and system was developed. The ships would load cotton, ginseng, blankets, trinkets, rum, and guns at Boston, Salem, New York, Baltimore, or Norfolk and proceed around South America via the Straits of Magellan and up the western American coast to the Oregon-Vancouver area. There the blankets, trinkets, "fire water," and weapons would be traded to American Indians and white trappers for furs. Then the ships would proceed to Hawaii where sandalwood, which was much in demand in China as raw material for chests, fine paneling, and incense, would be added to the cargo. And thence to Canton.

By the 1840's American commercial activity was outdistancing all rivals approaching China from the Pacific side. This was largely because of the advanced design and speed of the famous clipper ships, one of which, the *Rainbow*, set a remarkable record of 88 days for the journey from New York to Canton in 1845. Of course, the English trading volume at Canton continued to be preponderant, with the bulk of the English trade coming via the Indian Ocean and the South China Sea, but some American merchants even tried to compete there, sending ships via the Atlantic-Cape of Good Hope route, and also obtaining opium at Persian Gulf ports for sale in China.

Although the United States neither sought territorial holdings, nor participated in military ventures against China, the Americans did profit from Britain's Nanking Treaty when Caleb Cushing, the American negotiator, obtained most-favored-nation treatment in the first American treaty with China in 1844, the Treaty of Wanghsia. It has also been noted in Chapter 12 that the American Commodore Tattnall did not refrain from helping the Franco-British cause slightly in the war against China in 1859 even though it violated his instructions. And in the 1860's, as British pressure on China seemed to relax, United States policy became "cooperative" with Britain. Even so, American aloofness from the more intense pressures exerted by the British helps to explain the good will China showed America in appointing Anson Burlingame to represent her abroad in 1868.

Steamships and the Opening of Japan

The exuberant trade of the clipper ships, together with anticolonial sentiments remembered from the Revolutionary War days, rather firmly implanted the idea in the United States that American business in the Far East was commerce, not politics or territory. And the American concept of an "open door" for trade, fair, equal, and competitive, though not put into words, was already born in that early era. However, in the 1840's and early '50's dark steam-engine smoke began to cloud the carefree horizons of the clipper ship era. The development of steamships injured the American competitive position, partly because the British developed better steamships faster than did the United States and partly because the vastness of the Pacific approach to China made coal supplies on board seem always inadequate. This, together with a variety of lesser matters, quickened American interest in Japan.

Japan had become known to American traders as early as 1790 when a New England merchant named John Kendrick, having failed to get the price he wanted at Canton, tried to sell some of his cargo of furs in Japan. Japan's exclusion laws defeated him, but other Americans glimpsed Japan, sailing in the Dutch service from Batavia during the next two decades. However, when they tried later to go into Nagasaki or other Japanese ports on their own they were repulsed. Meanwhile, over the years, Japanese castaway fishermen were occasionally picked up by English or American vessels, a few even survived drifting across the Pacific to the Oregon coast, and a number of shipwrecks or deserters from American ships found their way ashore in Japan.

In 1837 an enterprising American merchant at Canton, Charles W. King, obtained custody of a group of Japanese castaways and determined to organize a rather elaborate return to Japan for them, hoping that successful trade relations might be inaugurated. He sent them, together with a cargo, directly to Edo Bay aboard the brig *Morrison*. Though the ship's officers tried to stress their friendly purpose and showed the American flag, the Japanese opened fire, and the *Morrison* returned to China without having been able to leave even the Japanese castaways.

Though the *Morrison's* was not an authorized voyage, the United States government took notice of the fact that the American flag had been fired on. When Caleb Cushing went to China to negotiate the American treaty in 1844, there was a general understanding that he might proceed thereafter to Japan to try to obtain a treaty there also, but specific instructions were not forthcoming and he did not go. However, stories of cruel treatment of American seamen by the Japanese attracted considerable attention, and in 1846 Commodore James Biddle was sent to Japan to obtain a treaty. Like the *Morrison* he avoided Nagasaki and went directly to Edo Bay. The Japanese did not fire this time, and offered water and provisions, but they were adamant about retaining their seclusion policy, and Biddle finally sailed away.

During the next several years American commercial interests became increasingly concerned with Japan. The advent of steam called attention to the need for coaling stations, and American ships bound for the China coast as well as whaling vessels, which penetrated ever further into the north and west Pacific as whaling grounds near Hawaii were exhausted, eagerly eyed Japan. Some landed there and various incidents occurred, which were

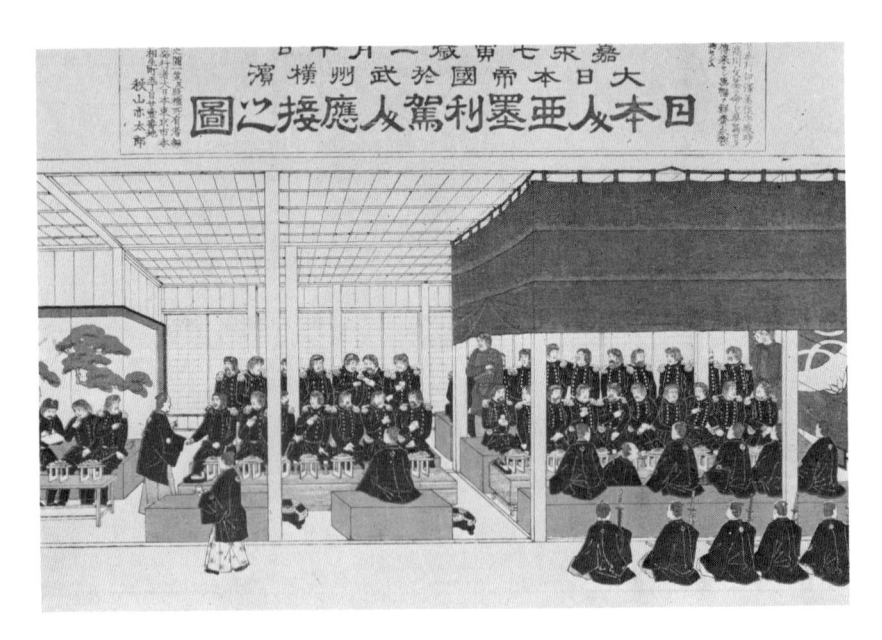

FIGURE 17.3. Reception of American naval officers of the Perry mission in Japan. Contemporary Japanese print.

colorfully described in reports to Congressmen and government officials. In 1851 Commodore James Aulick proposed to Secretary of State Daniel Webster that another group of Japanese castaways be returned to Japan as an entering wedge for another attempt to obtain a treaty. Aulick was shortly appointed commander of America's "East India Squadron" and authorized to proceed on the mission he had advocated. However, in February, 1852, Aulick was relieved of his command, and Matthew Calbraith Perry was appointed to replace him.

Perry was allowed to write his own orders; he took a large view of his mission and organized it well. He was one of a small group, consisting of American naval officers and a few missionaries who were looking forward to a vast augmentation of American power and overseas activity, and he had plans for establishing American bases in the Bonins, the Liuch'ius, and on Formosa. However, his superiors and the State Department were much more cautious, and while he was allowed a free hand in exerting a considerable amount of pressure on the Japanese, his further schemes were vetoed.

During Perry's two voyages to Japan, in July, 1853 and March, 1854, his strategy of stern invitation to open relations and later return for a reply worked well, but it should also be remembered that many previous contacts had prepared the way for him, and that the Tokugawa shogunate was well aware that further delay in making treaties with Western countries might

FIGURE 17.4. American merchant in Yokohama, c. 1860. Contemporary Japanese print.

result in the kind of military disasters which China had suffered. Therefore they accepted Perry's demands, which were not for a full commercial agreement, but for a limited arrangement, opening two undesirable ports, Hakodate and Shimoda, to American ships for refueling and supplies, promising protection to shipwrecked seamen, and admitting that consular officials might be exchanged if either country, according to the American reading, or both, according to the Japanese, desired it. This, and a most-favored-nation clause, was all Perry's treaty, the Treaty of Kanagawa of March 31, 1854, obtained.

Townsend Harris, the first American consul, who was sent, uninvited, in 1856, negotiated a full-scale commerical agreement, which was signed on June 29, 1858. Harris won the opening of six additional ports, the best in Japan, to American trade and residence, rights of extraterritoriality, religious toleration, and full diplomatic representation, a tariff agreement, and at the same time he won the confidence and friendship of the leading officers of the shogunate. There was to be a full decade of bitter argument between pro- and anti-treaty Japanese (see Chapter 6) before the "opening" of Japan was fully accepted, but when it was finally endorsed by the new Meiji government in 1868 there was not only no hint of animosity toward the United States, but an evident appreciation for the services Americans had rendered and might render in the future.

America as a Popular Neighbor, 1868–1898

If the success of foreign policy may be judged by the degree of popularity it engenders, the three decades from 1868–1898 must be considered an age of fine American relations with Far Eastern countries. Beginning with the Burlingame mission in China and the Meiji restoration in Japan, America and Americans were quite clearly regarded as friends in the Far East, with a sort of climax to this era of good feeling being reached in 1894 when both China and Japan, belligerents in the Sino-Japanese War, asked the United States to be custodian of their interests in the respective enemy country. This despite the fact that the United States had in 1882, in response to West Coast agitation, renounced the right of Chinese immigration granted in the Burlingame Treaty, and the fact that Americans in Hawaii had shown discriminatory attitudes against Orientals both in the advice they tendered the Hawaiian monarchy in setting up the Hawaiian constitution of 1887 (by which Westerners were allowed to vote, but not Orientals) and in the laws of the Hawaiian provisional government which they established in 1893. Thus where Americans met Far Easterners at close range in intergroup contact there were already signs of trouble, but these did not seriously disturb the rather smooth course of American relations with Far Easterners in their home countries during this era.

In Japan American advisors and advice were much sought after, beginning with a very active mission under Horace Capron and William Alexander which inaugurated the agricultural and industrial development of Hokkaido in the early 1870's. Teachers like William E. Griffis and Ernest Fenollosa helped in many educational and cultural projects, businessmen like Robert

W. Irwin, who organized Japanese immigration to Hawaii, and even an adventurer like Charles LeGendre, who helped to scheme the Japanese expedition to Formosa in 1874, had wide circles of friends in Japan. Also the official representatives of the United States, such as John A. Bingham, Richard B. Hubbard and Edwin Dun, who served as ministers at Tokyo, were appreciated for their sympathetic attitudes to Japan's problems. In particular they frequently expressed a favorable attitude toward the treaty revision the Japanese so ardently desired and gave freely advice on how to go about obtaining it. The fact that the United States did not offer unilaterally to revise its treaty seems not to have dampened the feeling of Japanese leaders that the United States was on the right side on the issue.

In China the suspension of immigration in 1882 caused some adverse reaction, including boycotts, but the issue was clouded by the argument that the odious coolie traffic was being quashed. Also the United States was conspicuously absent from the power rivalries and territorial demands of Britain, France, and Russia, and the plight of China was almost universally sympathized with by American missionaries and travelers there. To have no territorial ambitions and yet to be friendly and interested was a brilliant policy, though no one in Washington particularly thought it out in those terms. The State Department was mainly anxious to avoid embarrassing involvements, which resulted in the missing of certain opportunities to build foundations of equality between Asians and Westerners—as on the Japanese treaty revision issue—but at least it did not excite suspicion. However, the fact that policy was not really formulated at all may have been a factor in allowing a developing American school of imperialists, led by Alfred Mahan and Theodore Roosevelt, to bring about the annexationist fever of 1898.

Annexations and Suspicions

The United States first became involved in Far Eastern power politics as the result of the Spanish-American War in 1898. In that year American expeditionary forces, having taken Guam and Wake Island en route, arrived at Manila, where, backed by Dewey's fleet and aided by Aguinaldo's Filipino insurrectionists, they took the city on August 13. However, the Spanish forces surrendered to American General Wesley E. Merritt, and he issued orders that the Filipino insurgents not be allowed to enter the city. The same day (August 12 in Washington) a peace protocol had been signed between Spain and the United States. In the months that followed the fate of the Philippines hung in the balance, but in December, 1898, with the conclusion of the Treaty of Paris, the Philippines were awarded to the United States by purchase, for twenty million dollars. Aguinaldo protested immediately upon receiving the news, and he and his subordinates went about organizing a Filipino government. A Philippine republic, with Aguinaldo as president, was inaugurated on January 23, 1899.

When the United States refused to recognize this government, open hostilities broke out between Filipino and American forces. Aguinaldo's army soon faced defeat as an organized unit, but it disbanded and guerrilla warfare was waged in the islands for over two years. General Arthur Mac-

Arthur, father of Douglas MacArthur, finally captured Aguinaldo in March, 1901, after which the Filipino resistance gradually died out, although it did not cease entirely until the spring of 1902.

One noteworthy point is that during the Philippine war Aguinaldo's emissaries visited various countries seeking recognition. They had their greatest success in Japan, where they were allowed to purchase arms and where there was open sympathy for them, though they were denied recognition. The American annexations of both Hawaii and the Philippines in 1898 were discussed in critical terms in the high councils of the Japanese government, but it was decided that friendship with the United States should not be imperilled by opposition to these acts. Aguinaldo's cause also received sympathy and some support from Chinese elements, particularly those associated with the developing Chinese revolutionary movement of Sun Yat-sen.

It might be added than while the Philippine imbroglio was still unresolved, the United States for the first time joined imperialist powers in military intervention in China, with American troops joining the international expedition to relieve the Peking legations and suppress the Boxers in 1900. Of course, Secretary of State Hay's pronouncement of the Open Door doctrine emphasized that the American purpose was the opposite of territorial aggrandizement, but recent reevaluations of that policy have argued that it was to become, in long-range effect, a kind of nonmilitary imperialism building an "informal empire" through international business. Whatever the truth of this, it is clear that American possession of the Philippines made it seem hypocritical for the United States to interpose the Open Door policy against Japan in Manchuria.

American Rule in the Philippines to 1913

The Philippines insurrection was a bitter experience for the United States. More than 120,000 American troops and three years of fighting were required, and debates amongst Americans themselves concerning moral issues and policy issues became extremely acrimonious. President McKinley was sorely pressed by the imperialism issue and he was extremely anxious to begin the making of a benevolent record for American tutelage in the islands. Hence, while the insurrection was still raging, he sent out a Philippine commission, headed by Judge William Howard Taft of Ohio and consisting of jurists and scholars, to organize a civil government structure. Taft and General MacArthur quarrelled, for MacArthur felt that a great deal more pacification was necessary before the government could be entrusted to civilian hands, but Taft was put in charge as civil governor on July 4, 1901.

Taft felt that kindness and good government would win the support of the Filipinos, and to an extent he was right, except that an ingredient which he had not specifically anticipated had to be added, namely, the promise of future self-government. Taft avoided giving this, as did his successor, who was inaugurated as governor-general early in 1904. Taft had sponsored a "Federal" political party in 1900 for those Filipinos who would swear allegiance to the United States, and his vision was that this party would become a popular party whose members could eventually take responsible positions in the government. On the duration of American rule Taft made statements stressing such things as "increasing popular government," "quasi-independence," and the need for the people "to show themselves fit for self-government."

The machinery of government as established permanently in 1904 followed in large part Taft's recommendations and practices. It included a governor-general, with the full executive authority Taft had possessed and veto power over local legislation. It confirmed the judiciary he had set up, and gave permanence to his Philippine commission, now enlarged to include loyal Filipino members, as the appointive upper house of a bicameral legislature. The principal innovation was the establishment of a lower house, called the Assembly, to have equal legislative power with the now permanent commission. This was to be elected by a qualified electorate of Filipinos after peace had been maintained in the islands for at least two years. The Philippines were allowed special tariff advantages and some constitutional rights, but the United States Supreme Court decided in several famous "insular cases" which tested these issues that tariff and constitutional privileges would apply only insofar as the Congress of the United States deemed it proper to apply them. Two nonvoting Filipino delegates, called resident commissioners, were to be allowed to sit and to speak in the United States House of Representatives.

A census of the islands was completed in 1905 as a preliminary step to holding elections, local elections were allowed shortly thereafter, and in March, 1907 certification was issued that there had been peace and order for two years previously; hence national elections for the Assembly could be held. The chief result of the election of 1907 was the victory of a "Nationalist" (*Nacionalista*) party, which had organized in opposition to Taft's Federal party and which had in its platform a definite demand for independence, with some factions calling for *immediate* independence. The Federal party ran a poor second even though it had changed its name to the "Progressive" party and had enlarged its platform to include independence after Filipinos had proved themselves fit for self-government. Despite the emphasis on independence in party platforms, the elected Filipinos accepted the government structure, and as long as American administrators refrained from expressing themselves as opposed to eventual independence, affairs went fairly smoothly.

Remarkable progress was indeed made in education, health, railroad building, harbor development, trade, banking, and agriculture, including government purchase and redistribution of friar-owned lands, introduction of farm machinery, and restocking depleted farm animal resources. Church and state were separated, a system of free primary school education established, and religious freedom declared. Protestant missionaries, whose church officials had advocated taking the Philippines to uplift and Christianize them, were somewhat embarrassed at finding that most of the population were already Roman Catholic. While some wished to de-Catholicize the Filipinos, in general they avoided open religious rivalry. Instead they concentrated on the non-Christian population, mountain tribesmen and Moslems, for proselytism, and on the establishment of hospitals, clinics, and social welfare programs for the general population. In addition they founded several institutions of higher learning.

The Philippines were moving ahead rapidly by 1913, but the question of ultimate direction, whether toward fuller incorporation into the United States or toward independence, was unresolved. In 1909 Manuel Quezon, who had been a fiery spokesman for independence as floor leader of the Philippine Assembly, was elected by the legislature as resident commissioner in Washington. There he carried on a campaign for defining Philippine independence in specific terms as the goal of American rule in the islands, to which Congressmen, especially of the incoming Wilson administration, lent an increasingly sympathetic ear. Meanwhile, with English now the language of education, close ties to America were guaranteed, whatever the political future.

BASIC DATES

1521	Magellan reaches Guam, Leyte, Cebu
1565	Legaspi begins conquest of the Philippines
1570	Manila taken by the Spanish
1570–1750	Spread of Spanish influence and authority in Philippines; Dutch wars (to 1648); Moro resistance; Manila-Acapulco galleon trade
1762–1764	British occupation of Manila
1784	Beginning of American Canton trade
1785–1820	Decline of galleon trade with Mexico
1821	Separation of Philippines from Mexico
1834	Manila becomes an open port
1844	Treaty of Wanghsia
1853–1854	Perry mission to Japan
1868	Burlingame Treaty with China
1868–1871	Reform administration of de la Torre
1872	Cavite revolt
1887	Publication of Rizal's *Noli Me Tangere*
1891–1892	Rizal founds La Liga Filipina; Rizal exiled
1892	Katipunan revolutionary society founded
1896	Aguinaldo leads insurrection; Rizal executed
1898	Spanish-American War; Spain cedes Guam and Philippines to the United States
1899	Aguinaldo proclaims Philippine republic; war with United States (to 1902)
1900	Taft Commission establishes civil administration
1907	First Philippine assembly elected
1910–1913	Quezon works in Washington for independence

SUPPLEMENTARY READING

Agoncillo, Teodoro and O. Alfonso. *A Short History of the Filipino People.* Quezon City, Philippines, 1960.
Clyde, P. H. and B. F. Beers. *The Far East,* 5th ed. Englewood Cliffs, N.J., 1966.
Griswold, A. W. *The Far Eastern Policy of the United States.* New York, 1938; reprinted, New Haven, 1962.
Iriye, Akira. *Across the Pacific: An Inner History of American-East Asian Relations.* New York, 1967.
Lafeber, Walter. *The New Empire: An Interpretation of American Expansion, 1860–1898.* Ithaca, N.Y., 1963.
Williams, W. A. *The Tragedy of American Diplomacy.* New York: Dell Delta paperback, 1962.

ADVANCED READING

Blount, J. H. *The American Occupation of the Philippines, 1898–1912.* New York, 1913. Written by a participant in the events of the period.
Conroy, Hilary and T. S. Miyakawa, eds. *East Across the Pacific: Historical and Sociological Studies of Japanese Immigration and Assimilation.* Santa Barbara, Calif., 1972.
Conroy, Robert. *The Battle of Manila Bay: The Spanish American War in the Philippines.* New York, 1968.
Dennett, T. *Americans in Eastern Asia.* New York, 1922; reprinted, 1963.
Dulles, F. R. *America in the Pacific.* Boston, 1939.
―――― *Yankees and Samurai: America's Role in the Emergence of Modern Japan, 1791–1900.* New York, 1965.
Grunder, G. A. and W. E. Livezey. *The Philippines and the United States.* Norman, Okla., 1951.
McCormick, T. J. *China Market: America's Quest for Informal Empire, 1893–1901.* Chicago, 1967.
Phelan, J. L. *The Hispanization of the Philippines.* Madison, Wis., 1959.
Pomeroy, W. J. *American Neo-Colonialism.* New York, 1970. A Marxist analysis.
Quiason, Serafin D. *English "Country Trade" with the Philippines, 1644–1765.* Quezon City, Philippines, 1966.
Rizal, J. *Noli Me Tangere.* Bloomington, Ind., 1961.
Salamanca, B. S. *The Filipino Reaction to American Rule, 1901–1913.* Hamden, Conn., 1968.
Schurz, W. L. *The Manila Galleon,* New York, 1939.
Tate, Merze. *Hawaii: Reciprocity or Annexation.* East Lansing, Mich., 1968.
―――― *The United States and the Hawaiian Kingdom.* New Haven, 1965.
Taylor, J. R. M. *The Philippine Insurrection Against the United States,* vol. I. Pasay City, Philippines, 1971. This detailed documentary history was compiled between 1902 and 1906, but left unpublished at the time. Other volumes in process.

Young, Marilyn B. *The Rhetoric of Empire: American China Policy, 1895–1901*. Cambridge, Mass., 1968.
Zaide, Gregorio F. *Jose Rizal: Asia's First Apostle of Nationalism*. Manila, 1970.
——— *Philippines Political and Cultural History*, rev. ed. Manila, 1957.

Chapter 18

Nationalism in Southwest Asia, 1914-1939

The outbreak of the First World War in 1914 ushered in vast changes in the history of the whole of Asia. In Southwest Asia the country in which these changes may be most clearly traced is Turkey. Behind these revolutionary changes which Southwest Asia underwent during this period was the force of nationalism. Nationalism, a European idea and ideal, demanded that each nationality or group of common culture, language, history, religion, and tradition must form its own independent national state. In this Asian setting it rejected the broader religious unity of Muhammadanism, and putting Islam in the background, it supplied the motive power toward clearly defined political goals. Politics were, in fact, almost exclusively devoted to the creation of independent national states. This basic force of nationalism proved to be constructive in its early stages for this area and period; it was positive, full of vitality, and in its best expressions a struggle against foreign exploitation. Evolving new forms not only in the political but also in the social and cultural order of Southwest Asia, it created a vast transformation of this area and established for it a new position in world politics. In this region between the Mediterranean and the Persian Gulf, the bridge across which passed the vital sea, land, and air communications between Europe and Asia, this new force rejected religion as the determining factor and put in its place a secular, middle-class, national consciousness united in a common resistance against the imperialism and colonial penetration of the Western powers. Political activities of the urban intelligentsia and the middle-class merchant, new types of economic activities, the new social forces released by the emancipation of women and visible in new youth movements, one and all without exception aimed to unite the members of each nationality into a political and territorial organization, the new national state.

TURKEY

Turkey in the War

At the time of the entrance of Turkey into World War I the Ottoman empire, however weak, was still intact. The Young Turks under the leadership of the military dictator Enver Pasha, and motivated by anti-Russian sentiment, took the fatal step of ranging Turkey at the side of the Central Powers in the fall of 1914. It seemed to be the great opportunity to vindicate Turkey for the many insults suffered at the hands of its great northern neighbor. Relations with Britain had also cooled, particularly when Britain requisitioned two warships at the outbreak of the war which were on the ways in England, and which had been ordered and paid for by public subscription in Turkey. The actual declaration of war by Turkey against Russia, Britain, and France was made when two German warships, after having found refuge at Constantinople and having been ostensibly transferred to Turkey, bombarded the Russian Black Sea port of Theodosia. In the war Turkey received German strategic assistance and a plan was evolved whereby Turkish forces with German aid were to seize the vital Suez Canal and to invade Transcaucasia. These great offensives came to nothing, but when it came to a defense of the homeland the Turks put up a very stout resistance. In 1915 a Dardanelles campaign inspired by Winston Churchill took shape. Success would have meant Allied seizure of the vital Straits and the reopening of communications with Russia, and it would have put Turkey out of the war. In 1915 Allied landings took place at Gallipoli, supposedly as a surprise move. The whole Gallipoli campaign was singularly ineffective. A preliminary naval bombardment proved futile and robbed the campaign of the tactical advantages of surprise, the land attacks were delayed disastrously and the supply system was in a state of complete confusion. Essential arms were loaded at the bottom of supply vessels and thus became unavailable to the landing forces. The Turks, led by the German general Liman von Sanders, resisted fiercely, and despite gallant efforts the Allies were repulsed by the 100,000 Turkish defenders. They sustained very heavy losses. Despite this Allied failure, by 1916 Turkish efforts were reduced to defensive actions and even in these the Turks suffered defeats, such as the Russian capture of Erzerum and Trebizond (Trabzon) on the Armenian front in February of that year.

While military efforts were being directed against the Ottoman empire the Allied powers had negotiated a number of agreements regarding its dismemberment. As early as March 18, 1915, Britain and France had agreed that Russia should receive its long-coveted prize, Constantinople. Further agreements became necessary with the entry of Italy into the war, and in the London Pact of April, 1915 she was promised "a just share of Mediterranean coast," which meant the Dodecanese Islands and the southeast coast of Asia Minor. The next year saw further schemes of partition. In April the other Allies promised Russia parts of northeastern Asia Minor, and in May France and England drew up the most important of these Allied plans for despoilment of the vanquished, the Sykes-Picot Agreement of May

SOUTHWEST ASIA ABOUT 1937

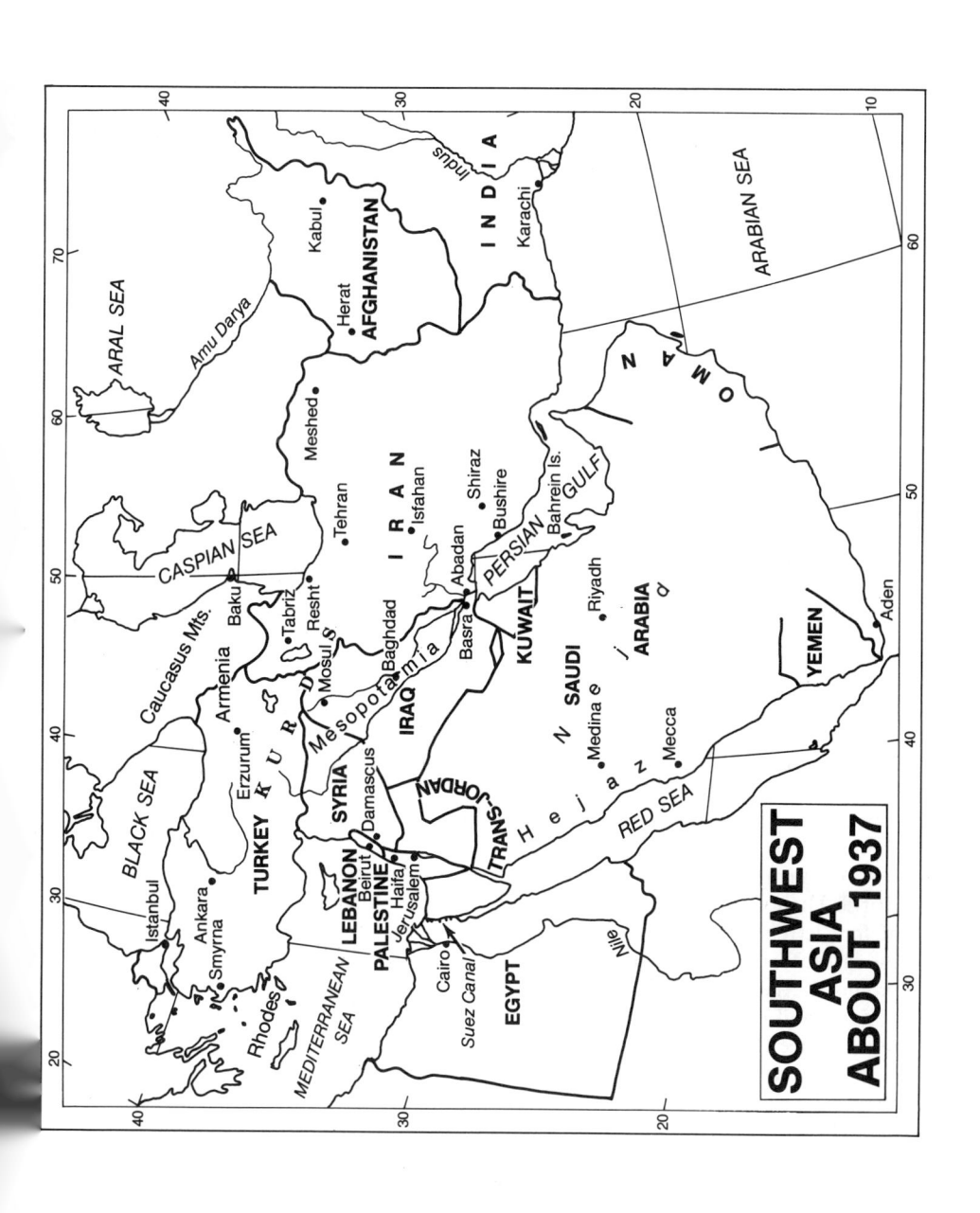

16, 1916. This agreement dealt with the Arab territories under Turkish control. It provided for French administration of Armenia, Syria, Mosul, and for the British administration in the postwar period of Palestine, Trans-Jordan, and Mesopotamia. In 1917 further promises were made to the Italians regarding western Asia Minor, and at the end of the war Greek claims to Smyrna were recognized. As seems to be frequently the case with wartime arrangements these schemes of dismemberment were premature; or at least they proved a source of great difficulty, when it came to their fulfillment. For one thing, Russia after the revolution ceased to be a partner in them, for another, Greek claims to Smyrna provided the impetus for a real Turkish rejuvenation, and finally the Sykes-Picot Agreement proved to be the source of very great troubles in the postwar period between Britain and the Arabs.

The Arab Revolt

The outbreak of the war had tremendously increased the importance of the Arabs in British policy. The Turkish sultan, in his role as caliph, had proclaimed a holy war or jihad against the infidels, and the importance of the Moslem population under British control, particularly in India but also in other parts of the world, was sufficient reason for British statesmen to devise a countermove. British policy found its logical ally in the Arabs, who were chafing under Ottoman rule. Thus British diplomacy early in the war came to the support of Husain Ibn Ali, sherif of Mecca, ruler of the Hejaz, and direct descendant of Muhammad by virtue of belonging to the house of Quraysh. Husain was basically anti-Turkish, but he had felt it wise to keep up at least an appearance of friendliness towards the sultan at the outbreak of the war. He volunteered some Arab troops in the unsuccessful Turkish attempt to break through to the Suez Canal, and he had treated the crew of a German cruiser with great courtesy, but Turkish suspicions and the drastic actions of a Turkish governor in Syria against some Arab nationalist leaders gave added reasons to Husain in his attempts to come to an agreement with the British.

Through Husain's son Abdullah negotiations were begun with the British High Commissioner at Cairo, Sir Henry McMahon, and an exchange of four letters took place between July, 1915 and January, 1916. This so-called McMahon correspondence was a masterpiece of diplomatic effort. It promised Arab independence in terms which were vague, ambiguous, and oblique, and open to wide variations of interpretation. The McMahon correspondence clashed in some important points with the British commitments to France embodied in the Sykes-Picot Agreement and these two agreements were to be the source of future trouble.

Husain was easily won over to the British cause. In his very important role of sherif of the holiest city of all Islam, he had abstained from approval of the holy war and had thus eased British fears regarding Moslem subjects of the crown. Husain then collaborated in the scheme of an Arab revolt against Turkish rule. British propaganda (which included the dropping of leaflets by airplanes on the Arabian peninsula in 1915) and occasional stoppage of grain exports from Egypt, had prepared the groundwork and in June, 1916 the Arab revolt began. A stream of corn, cash, and cartridges went to Husain whose forces under the leadership of Husain's third son, Faisal, quickly overcame the Turkish garrisons at Mecca and in the Hejaz, except for that of Medina. Here the sound strategy of not capturing that particular city, and consequently forcing the Turks to support it in a most difficult position, was successful in tying down over 65,000 Turkish troops. Their supply line, the Hejaz Railroad, was kept barely working by constant demolition attacks, never put out of commission, yet made to require constant attention.

In these attacks on the Turkish line of communication the activities of T. E. Lawrence were most spectacular and cast him soon in the role of a great British hero. A man of complex character, who after Oxford had gone into archeology in Syria and Mesopotamia where he acquired fluency in colloquial Arabic, Lawrence had the special facility of gaining Arab confidence. Leading a mixed force of about 30,000 to 40,000 Arabs and Indians with occasional support from the Royal Navy in the Red Sea, he engaged in a dramatic struggle against the Turks, the "revolt in the desert." This Arab revolt, and the defection of the Hejaz, was a serious blow to Turkey's war effort, and a severe drain on her limited resources.

The direct attack against Turkish power was started again in 1917, when General Allenby moved into Palestine from Egypt and captured Gaza and Jerusalem. It was completed with a great new offensive in September, 1918, culminating in the triumphal entry of Faisal, son of Husain, into Damascus on October 3 of that year. The success of British and Arab arms against the Turks was complete, but it did not mean that all Arabs of the peninsula had been united.

Somewhat at cross purposes with the Anglo-Egyptian plan of support to Husain, was a British policy begun during the war years of supporting yet another Arab leader, Ibn Sa'ud, the ruler of the Arab interior region of Nejd. The India office was responsible for this policy and it supplied him liberally with gold and arms so that he did not join the Turks in war. At the same time he remained neutral during the Arab revolt and used British support to build up his own strength, advancing slowly and cautiously and reaching the shore of the Persian Gulf in the north in 1915. Arabia revolted against Ottoman rule, but Arabia was not united and the dual policy of British statesmen soon caused internal repercussions.

The Dismemberment of Turkey

By 1918 Turkey had lost all her non-Turkish territories and she was forced to sign the armistice of Mudros on October 30. With this armistice the Ottoman empire dissolved and a new era began for Turkey, an era which was made possible only because of the great shock of imperial dismemberment. After the war the Allies occupied Constantinople with British, French, and Italian troops for four years. Enver Pasha and his supporters fled with the final disasters of 1918, and the Allies dealt with the weak Sultan Muhammad VI. In 1920 they forced the Treaty of Sèvres upon him.

This treaty was an example of triumphant Western imperialism and the means by which Turkey was brought to her lowest point as a power and as a nation. In this agreement not only was the end of the Ottoman state promulgated but the subjection of Turkey to the Western powers was also to become a final reality. All non-Turkish territories were lost, the Arab possessions being parcelled out: Syria to France, Palestine and Mesopotamia to Britain, and the Hejaz to the Arabs, while the Aegean Islands, Smyrna, and eastern Thrace were assigned to Greece, and Rhodes and the Dodecanese Islands were handed over to Italy. Only Constantinople, a small corner of Europe, and Anatolia were left to the Turks. Even there Western zones of influence were to be created, with southern Anatolia going to Italy and Cilicia and southern Kurdistan south of Armenia, to France. Armenia was to be independent and the Kurds were to be given autonomy. As for the vital Straits, an Allied commission was to take over their control from Turkish hands. It was no wonder that the date of signature of Sèvres was declared a day of national mourning in Turkey when all shops were closed, newspapers appeared with black borders, and prayers were being said for the welfare of the country. Sèvres would have reduced Turkey to impotence, but this treaty was soon a dead letter.

Turkish nationalism, freed from imperial responsibilities, annulled Sèvres, created a new era, and established a new Turkey. In 1919 it had seemed to the European powers that with the loss of vast territories, the end of the empire, and a prostrate and passive Turkey, which tolerated the Allied occupation of its capital, the country had definitely come under European tutelage. It appeared so even to some Turks who desired a United States mandate for Turkey. Total defeat and internal chaos raised the problem of survival of Turkey as an independent state. But the last blow against the Turks provided sudden, unexpected, and furious resistance and it led to Turkish salvation. This blow was the Greek invasion of Asia Minor.

Rise of Mustafa Kemal

Venizelos, the Greek premier, at Versailles had obtained a secret invitation from Lloyd George, Clemenceau, and Wilson to occupy Smyrna (Izmir) and the adjacent Anatolian coast. In May, 1919 Greek transports, backed by British and American naval units, debarked Greek troops in the harbor of Smyrna, and the Greek plan to "redeem Greek Anatolia" began. It was this invasion which provided the necessary challenge to awaken the Turks from the state of apathy and weariness which defeat had induced. The Greek challenge created a unified, revitalized national spirit in opposition to foreign encroachment of Anatolia, the very base of Turkish power. Local resistance to the advancing Greeks by peasant guerrillas flared up at once and was further inflamed by Greek atrocities. Turkish resistance was most fortunate in having the leadership of the founder of modern Turkey, Mustafa Kemal.

Mustafa Kemal had been born in 1881 in Salonica, the son of a petty Ottoman official and a peasant woman. In military school the boy excelled, the quality of his work in mathematics earning for him the name "Kemal" or excellence. During his education Kemal came completely under the influence of Western ideas and he rejected traditional Ottoman values. He be-

FIGURE 18.1. Ataturk.

came a radical, a "Young Turk," and an enthusiastic nationalist. His military career which began when he was posted at the age of 22 to a cavalry regiment in Damascus was uniformly outstanding. He participated in the Balkan Wars, where he gained considerable experience and he visited Germany and France. In World War I he won distinction as a military hero in the Gallipoli campaign. His personal life was hectic, full of love affairs and fits of incessant drinking. Ruthless and possessed of very great energy, he used his position as inspector-general in Anatolia, to which he had been appointed after the flight of Enver Pasha, to rally the Turks in Asia Minor against the Greeks. His personal leadership brought victory in the war against the invaders.

In 1919 two congresses were called by the Turkish nationalist leaders under the guidance of Kemal, one at Erzerum and one at Sivas, where a national assembly was formed. In October, 1919 this body drew up a document entitled the "National Pact" in which were embodied the aims of the new Turkish nationalism. It called for Turkish independence and self-determination, security for Constantinople from foreign rule, the abolition of capitulations and all restrictions imposed by foreign power, and it gave some assurance of equal treatment to the remaining minorities in Turkey. In January, 1920 this "National Pact" was also adopted by the parliament in Constantinople. In March of that year the British replied by occupying the city, arresting and deporting a number of Nationalist leaders to Malta, and making the sultan a virtual puppet. This action inflamed the spirit of the Nationalists, and when in April the National Assembly met at Ankara, which had been chosen for its good defensive position, it declared the sultan to be a prisoner of the Allies.

Kemal had little difficulty in rallying Turkish officers around him in the movement to "liberate the sultan" and to expel the Greeks. The movement soon gained rapid headway. Aid from the new Russian revolutionary leaders played some part in this. Bolshevist Russia had restored the fortress of Kars to Turkey in 1920 and it now supported the Nationalist forces by means of munitions and money in their struggle against what the Communist press denounced as "British imperialism." In 1921 the Soviet Union made a treaty with Turkey, which was of considerable importance to the government of Kemal, since it meant freedom from attack on the northern border.

In the task of expelling the Greeks, a victory was won at the village of Inönü in April, 1921 by Ismet Pasha (later called Ismet Inönü), and in the late summer of that year the decisive engagement was fought at the three weeks' battle of the Sakaria river. This terrific struggle of forces, almost equal in strength, within 200 miles of Ankara, was the turn of the tide; it had an electric effect, not only upon the two combatants, but also upon world opinion.

Despite the fact that the British still supported the Greeks (the London *Times* referred to Kemal as a "bandit"), the French in October, 1921, came to a separate agreement with the nationalist Turks. In return for various economic concessions the French agreed to withdraw from their area of influence in Cilicia. Italy soon joined the French in also agreeing to evacuate Asia Minor.

With loss of support, broken morale, and exhausted strength there was little left for the Greek forces but to retreat. This they did, burning all the villages which they passed. After a headlong flight the Greeks were driven out of Smyrna in September, 1922. Turkish forces reoccupied the port, but Smyrna was almost completely destroyed in a terrible fire which broke out soon after. The Turks, under the leadership of Mustafa Kemal, now also known as the conqueror or Ghazi, next moved to expel the Greeks from eastern Thrace in Europe, but here they were blocked by British troops; however, a tense situation was settled by an armistice between the local Turkish and British commanders.

By 1923 all the Allies were forced to recognize the changed situation created by the existence of a new and strong Turkey, and this recognition was formalized in the negotiated peace of Lausanne, which replaced the dictated peace of Sèvres. Negotiations began in the Swiss city in November, 1922, and they dragged on until July of next year. A great measure of the success of Lausanne was due to the very able handling of the talks by Ismet Pasha, the chief military collaborator of Kemal. Stubborn, shrewd, and calculating, Ismet Pasha even put his deafness to diplomatic advantage by pretending not to hear the counterproposals of the other parties.

At Lausanne Turkey again renounced her claim to non-Turkish territories, but in turn was reinstated in her Anatolian and European possessions which now also included eastern Thrace to the Maritsa river with the important city of Adrianople. Most significantly, Turkey gained complete freedom from foreign control in her internal affairs. Her military position was secured by having no restrictions on the size of her forces; in turn, Turkey agreed to the demilitarization of the Asiatic and European shore of the Bosphorus and the Dardanelles. As for the Straits, full freedom of passage was guaranteed to commercial vessels and warships of all nations both in peace and in war as long as Turkey remained neutral. The Treaty of Lausanne was a great diplomatic success for the new state. Turkey again gained recognition, respect, renewed power, and prestige. Lausanne gave to Turkey her independence and her security. Her striking success had been partially due to Allied disunity, since France in particular opposed the Greek ambitions after Venizelos had been replaced by a pro-German king; it had also been due to Russian aid against British imperialism, but most important, her success was due to her own effort and her new national spirit.

The Turkish Revolution

The defense of Turkey, led by Kemal, was but the beginning of the Turkish Revolution, and this was continued with the internal reconstruction of the Turkish state. Turkey after Lausanne was a homogeneous coherent national state with the exception of a few small minorities of Greeks, Jews, and Armenians in Constantinople. Turkish lands had been cleared of other nationalities; the Armenians had been massacred and the Greeks driven out of Asia Minor. A postwar Graeco-Turkish agreement for the compulsory exchange of population completed the process, and although the loss of Greek artisans, craftsmen, and traders was a serious economic blow to Turkey, it was a gain for the national state; Turkey was now almost exclusively Turkish. The virtues of Turkish ancestry, of steppe nomadism, and of such historic figures as Chingis Khan and Timur were extolled, and Turkish nationalism constructed a new Turkey on a solid base of Anatolian peasants.

The Nationalist government met in Ankara in 1920, a miserable, treeless town which was selected both for its military defensibility and as a symbol of the break with the past. Relations with Constantinople were bad, and by 1922 the Nationalists had captured the Ottoman capital. A few days after the Allied evacuation of Constantinople, which was stipulated under the terms of the Treaty of Lausanne, Ankara was made the new capital of Turkey, and on October 23, 1923, a republic was proclaimed. A month later the last Ottoman sultan left Turkish soil aboard a British warship. Although the sultanate was abolished in 1923, the caliphate lingered on for one more year in the person of Abdul Mejid, the nephew of Muhammad VI. In 1924 the caliphate, too, was abolished and with it the political power of Islam in Turkey was broken. Power now was held in the hands of Mustafa Kemal, as a dictator presiding over what might be described as a parliamentary despotism. The autocratic religious monarch of the Ottoman empire was replaced by the modern dictator working through the medium of a Grand National Assembly. This body chose the president, who was, of course, Kemal; in turn he chose his premier, and the premier chose his cabinet. But there never was any doubt where power resided. In 1922 a single "Popular

Republican Party" was created, and in 1927 Kemal reserved for himself the right to name all candidates for the bicameral Grand National Assembly from this party. "Selection," not election, was the method by which the parliament was chosen. In 1930 a parliamentary opposition party, which had been briefly tolerated, was finally dissolved.

Kemal was president and dictator of Turkey from 1920 to 1938, and it was he who was the driving force behind the second stage of the Turkish Revolution, the attempt to create a strong, united power by means of complete Westernization and modernization. What that meant may be illustrated by a speech which the minister of justice made in 1925: "We desire to draft our law in accordance with the methods and principles of civilized Western peoples. Medieval principles must give way to secular laws. We are creating a modern civilization, and we desire to meet contemporary needs. We have the will to live, and nobody can prevent us."

As a fundamental step the system of education was radically reformed. A ministry of education, with strongly centralized powers analogous to the French model, decreed compulsory education for all Turks. In 1928 modern numerals were introduced, in 1934 the metric system followed, and in 1935 the momentous step of using the Latin alphabet was taken. This meant a real break with the past; Arabic and Persian were no longer taught and the old Ottoman literature soon was understood by but few people. So little was the past regarded that the finance ministry of the Turkish republic sold the old Ottoman records in its possession as waste paper to Bulgaria.

Next in importance to the modernization of education and closely connected with it was the secularization of the state. When the Kurds revolted in 1925 against the abolition of the caliphate all religious orders were suppressed, and in 1928 Islam ceased to be the state religion. The number of mosques and religious teachers of the mosque schools was curtailed, to the extent that even St. Sophia was made into a museum. The Koran and all prayers were to be exclusively in the Turkish language instead of Arabic. In 1935 Sunday was introduced as rest day, along the Western model, and the clergy was required to be garbed in secular dress in public.

Of particular importance was the end of Islamic law. Turkey henceforth was governed by Swiss civil, Italian penal, and German commercial legal codes. These drastic changes in law, education, and religion were accompanied by successful attempts at social change, from which women in particular profited. Polygamy was ended, women no longer had to wear the veil, and the franchise was extended to them, with the result that the Grand National Assembly soon contained a number of women delegates. Civil marriage was made obligatory, and the right of divorce was recognized, a law which Kemal himself used to advantage. All Turks were given family names, and Kemal became "Ataturk," or father of the Turks.

Sartorially speaking, equality with the West was accomplished when the fez was eliminated, and the modern Turk wore a modern Western hat. Modernization extended, as might be expected, to the arts. European architecture, painting, and sculpture were introduced, and in 1925 appeared the first public statues to Kemal, a distinct sign of the revolution which had taken place since to orthodox Moslems the depicting of the human form was sheer idolatry. A music conservatory was established in Ankara which was headed for a time by Paul Hindemith.

Very great attention was paid to the complete modernization of Turkish military power, and the national economy. Mustafa Kemal chose state socialism as the best means to modernize Turkey. This meant that the state controlled the development of industry. The government developed and regulated all vital industries, particularly those necessary for national defense. Industry was planned by means of a series of five-year plans, protected by high tariffs, and financed by means of state banks. Opposition to foreign investments, which in the past had been equated with foreign control, was an important point in this policy, and in 1938 all railroads in Turkey were nationalized.

In agriculture the government also predominated. It distributed seed and agricultural machinery, established cooperative societies and state agricultural banks, and Kemal himself set the precedent to his countrymen by working his own model farm. Westernization and modernization were successful and they made their appeal on the basis of nationalist ideology. Some tendencies towards excesses occurred. Not only were textbooks strongly slanted along nationalist lines, but there were extremes such as the theory that all languages were derived from the Turkish language, since the language of Sumer supposedly was related to Turkish, or the doctrine that all human achievement was Turkish, since all human beings began as Turks. In order to establish their claim to Anatolia the Turks now pronounced the ancient people of the Hittites as their ancestors. Sometimes narrow-minded intolerance led to regrettable laws, such as the one of 1934 which declared that no aliens could remain in any profession or trade.

The growing strength of the new Turkey, the result of successful modernization and westernization, is shown in her improved international position, and in her foreign relations. Although Turkey had to relinquish the district of Mosul to British controlled Iraq in 1925, she was recognized as a full member of the League of Nations in 1932, she joined in a Balkan pact with Greece, Rumania, and Yugoslavia in 1934, and in the next year her growing prestige was acknowledged when an Iranian-Afghan frontier dispute was handed over to Turkish arbitration. The Treaty of Montreux of 1936 ended the demilitarization of the Straits, and consequently improved Turkey's defenses. Russia was permitted to have free passage of warships of any size in peace, while the other powers were restricted to light surface vessels. In war, if Turkey were neutral, no warships at all could pass; if Turkey herself became a belligerent, passage of warships remained at her discretion. In 1937 Turkey joined in the so-called Saadabad Pact with her Eastern neighbors Persia, Iraq, and Afghanistan. Thus, when in 1938 Mustafa Kemal died, and Ismet Inonü, his right-hand man, became Turkey's second president, Turkey was a strong and modernized state. Homogeneous, small, compact, with a population possessed of a keen patriotic sense, and strong military discipline, Turkey in some respects showed striking parallels with Japan. In both cases there had taken place the same development of a strong national state, about sixty years apart in time.

It must be realized that this revolution was one which was imposed on

Turkey from the top down. It was the leadership of men like Mustafa Kemal and his followers who, contemptuously despising the old traditional values, extracted from the majority of their countrymen a grudging acceptance of westernization. This explains to some degree the autocratic tendencies of the national government, which never hesitated to suppress any opposition to its rule from whatever side it might arise. The press soon learned its lesson. When editors of a Constantinople journal cautioned against the abolition of the caliphate they were arrested, tried, and sentenced. A watchful eye saw to it at all times that the press remained shackled, and even abstention from criticism did not mean automatic freedom from persecution, as one unfortunate editor experienced to his regret. Since he had abstained from discussing politics at all, he was prosecuted for the tacit criticism which this implied. The more dangerous and open revolt of the Kurds was ruthlessly suppressed. The pastoral Kurds had demanded some rights of autonomy, and in 1925 they revolted under the leadership of a wealthy religious-minded sheik who protested against the abolition of the caliphate. Harsh subjection was the answer, and since the Kurds lacked both unity and leadership, they were soon put down and later some of them were forcibly transplanted into European Turkey.

By 1938 the process of internal reform of the Turkish state was completely successful. Turkey in 1938 was secularized, her people were emancipated from the old traditions of Islam, and her social and economic life had been reoriented along Western models. Turkish history from 1919 to 1938 was a triumph of nationalism.

PERSIA

Nationalism had completely revolutionized the Turkish state, and the same process remolded Persia, but to a much lesser degree. Modernization and westernization were less successful and complete, and in consequence Persia was a weaker and less unified nation when it became involved in the great power politics of World War II.

World War I and Persia

In 1914 Persia was ruled by the weak and corrupt Kajar dynasty, and the country had been divided since 1907 into two spheres of influence, a northern one controlled by Russia, and a southern one in which Britain predominated (see Chapter 11). Although Persia declared her neutrality in the conflict, she at once became the battleground between Russian and Turkish forces in the northeast and northwest, while in the south the British, anxious about their oil refinery on the island of Abadan in the Persian Gulf, occupied Bahrein Island and captured Basra at the head of the Gulf. The Russians were successful in driving the Turks back into Turkish territory, but the British faced considerable German subversive activity in their sphere of influence. German propaganda stirred up some of the Persian hill tribes by declaring that the kaiser was a friend of Islam who had been a Mecca pilgrim, and some German officials succeeded in creating organized resistance against the Persian government and British interests. The former German consul at Bushire, Wassmuss, was especially effective in this. Disguised as a Persian he managed to seize the British colony at Shiraz, and the Persian gendarmerie, officered by Swedes, tended largely to support these German moves. Irregular bands of these troops would swoop down on provincial cities, capture them, rob the branches of the British-controlled Imperial Bank, and then retreat again to the hills. A number of Russian and British consuls were killed and German intrigues even extended to Afghanistan where an attempt was made to persuade the emir to attack India.

By 1916 the British retrieved the situation fully. German pressure on the Persian government to join the Central Powers was counteracted by strong remonstrances of the Russian and British ambassadors at Tehran. Pro-German hill tribes were again brought under control by the creation of Persian volunteer forces, known as the South Persian Rifles and commanded by Sir Percy Sykes, who under British and Persian officers restored order in south Persia, capturing Shiraz and Isfahan in 1916. The attempt to cause trouble for Britain in Afghanistan collapsed when the emir turned against the German emissaries, and the British set up an effective cordon system between Persia and Afghanistan, making it impossible for German agents to continue operations. Further complications in the already chaotic Persian situation came in 1917 when the Russian Revolution caused the collapse of their Trans-Caucasian front against Turkey and Turkish troops again reoccupied Azerbaijan in the northeast. Consequently British troops moved north into Tehran, and then were dispatched to support the newly independent regimes of Georgia and Armenia against the Turks. General Dunsterville was sent to Baku in 1918, but was attacked by the Turks, and had to evacuate his troops. After 1918 British power was in complete control of all of Persia.

A British-Russian agreement of 1915, which had granted Constantinople to Russia, had provided that Britain would obtain the heretofore small neutral Persian middle zone between the northern and southern spheres of influence. Further British ascendancy was established in April, 1917 when a large British loan was made to Persia, and when Britain was granted the power to supervise the Persian gendarmerie. Complete English control of Persia was attained in 1919 when a British-Persian treaty was signed between the British Minister, Sir Percy Cox, and the government of Ahmad Shah, headed by the Premier Vossugh-ud-daula. In return for a large British loan, the Persian government agreed under its terms to accept British advisors in all departments of the government, thus making Persia a vassal of the British crown. A great deal of bribery was necessary and both Persian and world opinion became disturbed as a result of this agreement. The United States protested against it, and the Persians themselves sent a delegation to the peace conference at Versailles appealing against the treaty, but they were turned down by a British declaration that Persia had not been a belligerent and consequently was not entitled to a hearing.

The outstanding effect of the British-Persian agreement of 1919 was that it aroused the Persian national spirit. As a consequence of this revived sentiment Persia came under the control of a military dictator, while it also permitted a significant change in position of Russia towards Persia. When the British-Persian treaty became known, opposition in Persia was pronounced and sharp. The press was solidly anti-British, the people protested publicly, and parliament refused to ratify the agreement. In fact, the agreement was suspended due to the resignation of the Persian premier, and British economic retrenchment, but not before it served as a vehicle for Russian propaganda, and the establishment of a strong Bolshevik influence.

Soviet Influence

As early as January 1918 the Bolshevist government had made it known that it would make a clean sweep of all the rights and privileges which Tsarist Russia had possessed in Persia. Capitulations, rights of extraterritoriality, and the outstanding Persian debts to Russia were all cancelled. In 1920 diplomatic relations between Persia and Russia were reestablished, and the first Russian envoy, Rothstein, appeared with a large staff in Tehran, determined to gain popular appeal as champion of Persia against British imperialism. Free Soviet films were distributed, a number of newspapers were started, Russian schools were opened, one and all with the object of assuring Persia of Russian support against British aims.

Violent anti-British propaganda in newspapers led to a British protest. Persia signed in February, 1921 a treaty of mutual noninterference with the Soviet Union. It allowed Persia to establish a navy on the Caspian, but a clause permitted the Soviets to send troops into Persia whenever the Soviet Union felt threatened by anti-Russian activities: "If a third party should attempt to carry out a policy of usurpation by means of armed intervention in Persia, or if such power should desire to use Persian territory as a base of operations against Russia . . . , and if the Persian government should not be able to put a stop to such menace after having been called upon to do so by Russia, Russia shall have the right to advance her troops into the Persian interior for the purpose of carrying out military operations necessary for its defense."

Bolshevik Russia posed as a friend of Persia. But this treaty with its implications, and the attempt to create a Soviet Republic on Persian territory in 1921, showed that Russian imperialism in a new garb was still a potent force. Red troops began an invasion of Persia in May 1920, when they were landed at the Caspian seaport of Enzeli near Resht in quest of some White Russian vessels of Denikin's fleet which had been interned there by the British. Inasmuch as Britain and the League of Nations both failed to oust the Russians, Persian faith in the power of British protection was further shattered, and Russia was encouraged to proceed. In June, 1920 Red troops took Resht, capital of Gilan province, and, despite frequent Persian protests from Tehran, the Russian troops stayed in occupation.

A local Socialist Soviet Republic was established in Gilan, which was sponsored by Russia and headed by an extraordinary character, Mirza Kuchik Khan. Kuchik Khan was a short, stocky, heavily bearded leader of some wild tribes, known as the "jangali" or jungle people, since they occupied the rainforests on the Caspian littoral. He rose to power by extorting ransom from large landholders, and by similar methods of near banditry. He set up in 1920 a government with a policy of land confiscation and antireligious measures. But even he was influenced by nationalist sentiment, and a rift took place between him and the Bolsheviks which led to his defection from the Russians. Since this Soviet republic seemed to be crumbling, Russia finally agreed to evacuate Persian soil in 1921. Persian troops moved into Gilan, and Kuchik was captured and executed. The suppression of this Soviet movement in Gilan made it also easier for the Persian government to suppress a revolt against it in Azerbaijan.

Reza Shah and Reforms

The most important consequence of the rise of Persian nationalism, which had been aroused by British and Russian action, was the capture of power by a military dictator, Reza Khan. Reza, physically large and strong, came from a poor branch of a landowning family in the province of Mazanderan. In his youth he had tended flocks, as did Nadir Shah, and had obtained very little formal education. Enrolled in the Persian Cossack Brigade he rapidly rose from the ranks to colonel, and he was extremely popular with his troops. Reza Khan became an ardent Persian patriot, opposed to British control, and he found as his supporter a journalist with similar ideals, Sayyid Zia-ed-din. The two combined, and making use of the prevailing Persian opposition to a government which had signed away all Persian rights to England, they successfully obtained control of the government by a coup d'état in 1921. A brief fight between Reza's cossacks and the gendarmerie was all that was needed to bring into power a government devoted to nationalism and reform. The latter in particular appealed to Zia, who was far more radical than his military collaborator, and he at once began to nationalize large landed estates, arrest recalcitrant landowners, and distribute lands held by the state. Gambling and the consumption of alcohol and opium were halted, corruption was inveighed against, but, as may be imagined, the extent and radical quality of reforms soon aroused powerful opposition. In the same year Zia was forced out of power, and he fled to Palestine, where he was given sanctuary in Haifa by the British, always willing to shelter a man who might be useful in the future. The field of Persian politics was left entirely to Reza Khan. He was commander-in-chief, and two years later became prime minister, while the shah stayed abroad in Europe. The British were faced with the alternatives of either to campaign to oust Reza Khan, or to accept him, and they chose the latter. British advisors had been decisively rejected by Persian national sentiment, but since some outside help was needed to reform the Persian economic chaos, Persia turned once again to American aid as she had before in 1911.

An American financial advisor, Dr. Arthur C. Millspaugh, was engaged from 1922-1927 by Reza Khan. Millspaugh reorganized the finances, increased revenues, and balanced the budget, despite the resistance of landlords who clamored against taxes. Income tax, import and export duties, stamp taxes, and surveys of landholdings upon which a new tax structure was based made possible the balanced budget, which is the more remarkable since at the same time a Persian army, with tanks, airplanes, and artillery, was in the making. During this period American oil companies, notably Standard Oil Company and Sinclair, gained concessions in Persia. When Millspaugh was finally dismissed by Reza, Persia was on a solid financial base.

Reza Khan had been premier since 1923, and in 1925 he established himself on the Peacock Throne as Reza Shah, the first of the new Pahlavi dynasty. There was no opposition to the dethronement of the last of the Kajars, but there was in Persia, unlike Turkey, considerable opposition to the establishment of a republic. Shi'a, dislike of the Turkish precedent, and general public sentiment all argued for a continuance of the Persian monarchy. Reza Shah understood the general mood of Persia too well to insist on the promulgation of a republic. He had little difficulty in controlling Persia effectively and the unruly tribesmen of southwest Persia, the Bakhtiari, were brought under effective administration.

Reza Shah had many things in common with Mustafa Kemal: both were successful dictators and despots, both possessed great energy and worked hard, but Reza made it a point to remain little known, and to shun the company of strangers, especially foreigners. Reza Shah also attracted far fewer loyal and capable supporters than did Mustafa Kemal, and his self-imposed tasks, to free Persia from foreign control and to achieve her modernization, were more difficult than the tasks that faced Kemal. Persia was further removed from Europe, and her reform attempts were of far more recent date. Nevertheless, Reza set in motion a reform program which, while not destroying the basic economic structure of the landholding class, attempted to make Persia a modern, strong, and military state. Reza gave his chief attention to the armed forces, and he evinced great interest in Western technical progress in this field. Swedish, Russian, and British officers were dismissed, French weapons were introduced, and a national army of about 40,000 men was created with the most modern equipment available. Reza attempted to set up the army officers as a special privileged class; they were sent to Europe, given brilliant uniforms, and sumptuous army clubs were built for their use. He also established a small navy on the Persian Gulf. The police was reorganized, and a road police enforced security of travel.

Some attempts were made to centralize the government. Secular law replaced the law of Islam, and a judicial system on the French model was created. In 1928 all capitulations and restrictions imposed upon Persia by foreign powers were revoked. Some attention was also paid to education by the government of the new shah. Free primary education was made compulsory, and many students were sent to Europe to study particularly the sciences and medicine. In 1935 the University of Tehran was opened, the metric system of weights and measures was introduced, European headgear for men was ordered, and a year later the veil for women was abolished.

If anything, it was in the economic development of Persia that the greatest progress was achieved toward the goal of creating a strong national state. Upon the sound economic structure which Millspaugh had erected a number of government industrial enterprises such as sugar, glass, and match factories, and spinning and weaving mills were established. They were financed by the state bank, which issued paper money. The determination

FIGURE 18.2. Reza Shah.

not to depend on foreign loans, which had been an entering wedge of imperialism, was well illustrated by the construction of the Trans-Iranian Railroad in 1933–1939. This great engineering project, which connected the Caspian Sea with the Persian Gulf and which in a distance of 870 miles had no fewer than 200 tunnels and 4,000 bridges made necessary while climbing and descending 9,000 feet, was managed by a Scandinavian company, but the expense was borne by the state. Government monopolies on sugar, tea, opium, and oil defrayed the entire costs. Native crafts were also encouraged by the government, and something was done for agriculture in the way of model farms, but no major irrigation project, which would have greatly aided the Persian economy, was undertaken. As a whole the reforms which accompanied Persian nationalism were weaker than those of Turkey. Some efforts at language reform were made, and Iranian motifs were introduced in art and architecture with the so-called Neo-Achaemenid style, but there was nothing comparable to the substitution of the Arabic script by a foreign alphabet as was done in Turkey. Persia also never commanded the same respect as Turkey. A claim she made in 1927 for Bahrein was ignored by Britain, and when in 1932 a dispute arose concerning the amount of royalties which the Anglo-Persian Oil Company was to pay to Persia the British at first threatened armed force against Persia and sent naval units into the Gulf. In this instance Reza Shah won out, he abrogated the British oil concession on the legal basis that it had been secured when Iran (the new name for Persia since

1935) lacked a representative government, and in 1933 he won a new agreement which provided for greater royalties, a more limited concession area, and greater employment of Persians by the Company.

In 1937 Iran joined with Turkey, Iraq, and Afghanistan in the previously mentioned pact signed at Saadabad Palace in Tehran. This pact stipulated that the signatories would guarantee their common frontiers, that they would not interfere in internal affairs, and would consult on mutual questions. But the basic problem of Persia, which made her position inferior to Turkey, lay in the fact that modernization and westernization were not as thorough as in Turkey, and were more resisted by the Iranians themselves. It also lay in the fact that Reza Shah lacked the kind of support which Mustafa Kemal had built up in his country from loyal and devoted followers. Reform in Persia was accompanied by much waste, some failures, and little insight. Everything was done quickly, at the whim of Reza, with no advance preparations. Hospitals were built, but nurses were not available, and there was no system of sanitation or preventive medicine. The streets in Tehran were paved, a number of modern buildings were constructed in the capital, but some, like the opera house, were never finished. Since the shah wanted modern transportation, he issued a decree outlawing camel caravans, but of course there was no substitute to be had for the moment. Frequently, opposition to reform took the form of riots, and some of these, like the one in Meshed, were put down with machine guns.

Furthermore, since Persia was ruled by a despot, his nature was of great importance, and Reza Shah's character had begun to change. By 1930 he had become a victim of the lust for power and for wealth, as had Nadir Shah in the eighteenth century. In this process he grew more and more suspicious and melancholy. He began to murder members of the landed aristocracy whenever he wanted some of their estates, he killed possible rivals, and in 1933 he removed in this fashion his friend and prime minister, Timurtash. The visit of the shah's personal doctor became dreaded by the Iranians; he had an unpleasant habit of injecting air bubbles in the bloodstream by way of treatment. The press was completely muzzled and the movement of all people was carefully controlled by the gendarmerie. Reza Shah's greed and ruthlessness also turned him against Islam. Religious leaders were imprisoned, and the possessions of the mosques handed over to the government. The positions of the mullas, the Moslem religious leaders, became government appointments. Terror, graft, and corruption were everywhere. Above all, criticism of the shah was not tolerated. The story is told that Reza wanted to plant some trees at a certain spot, but that his forestry expert advised him against the particular location, whereupon the "Shadow of God" declared that "they will grow any place if I order them to do so."

In line with the increasing authoritarian tendencies of Reza Shah he began to look more and more with favor toward Germany. The United States had less concern with foreign affairs during the 1930's and commerce with Iran was deterred by high tariffs. In addition, the shah himself had taken offense at the fact that his envoy to the United States had been arrested in Washington on a charge of speeding. The regimentation, greater efficiency, and totalitarianism of Germany appealed to the Iranian regime and German advisors, German investments, and German trade became more and more noticeable. By the end of this period 45 per cent of Iranian trade was with Germany, German experts in industry had built armaments plants, and there were frequent German official and tourists' visits to Persia, the land of the "pure Aryans."

Nationalism in Persia had ejected foreign control, but it had done so only ineffectively. British control had been replaced at first with Russian and later German influence, and although nationalism under the sponsorship of Reza Shah had done a great deal to reform Persia, it did not succeed in creating a really strong state. Consequently Persia entered the Second World War in a far weaker position than did Turkey.

AFGHANISTAN

Afghanistan during the years between the two World Wars showed a development similar to that of Persia. Here, too, nationalism won independence from the West, but the reform movement encountered strong internal hostility, and had to be severely curtailed. Since Afghanistan was most remote, westernization and modernization were least developed.

In 1919 Ammanullah succeeded to the throne of his father Habibullah, who had been assassinated. The new emir was strongly anti-British, and demanded that all rights be restored to an independent Afghanistan. In defiance of the British government in India, which controlled Afghan foreign relations, he sent an emissary to Moscow. Ammanullah also dispatched an army to attack India. His army was quickly defeated in May, 1919, but Afghanistan scored a great diplomatic victory with the Treaty of Kabul of 1921 in which Afghanistan was recognized as an "absolutely independent sovereign state," over which Britain had relinquished all control. A treaty was also concluded with Russia. The next step in Ammanullah's plans was to follow in the footsteps of Turkey and of Persia, that is, to modernize and westernize the country. Reforms came quickly and were somewhat hastily executed. Compulsory primary education was decreed, Afghan diplomats were sent abroad, foreign advisors were called in, and an Afghan press was created. This was followed by the establishment in 1922 of twelve colleges, of the adoption of a regular budget, and the employment of Russian technical instructors. It was all done rapidly, and it was all somewhat confusing to the Afghan tribesman.

Opposition to Ammanullah erupted in a revolt by the military in 1923-24, which was suppressed. But four years later while the emir was on a trip in Europe a new uprising occurred, and Ammanullah was forced to abdicate and to go into exile. His brother, Shah Nadir Khan, crushed the rebellion, but progress became decidedly slower. He was assassinated in 1933, and his young son, Muhammad Zadir Shah, came on the throne under the guardianship of a number of uncles.

Although a constitution was promulgated in 1931, power still remained in the hands of the ruler. Islam continued both as religion and as law, and only primary education was kept as a concession to reform. In international

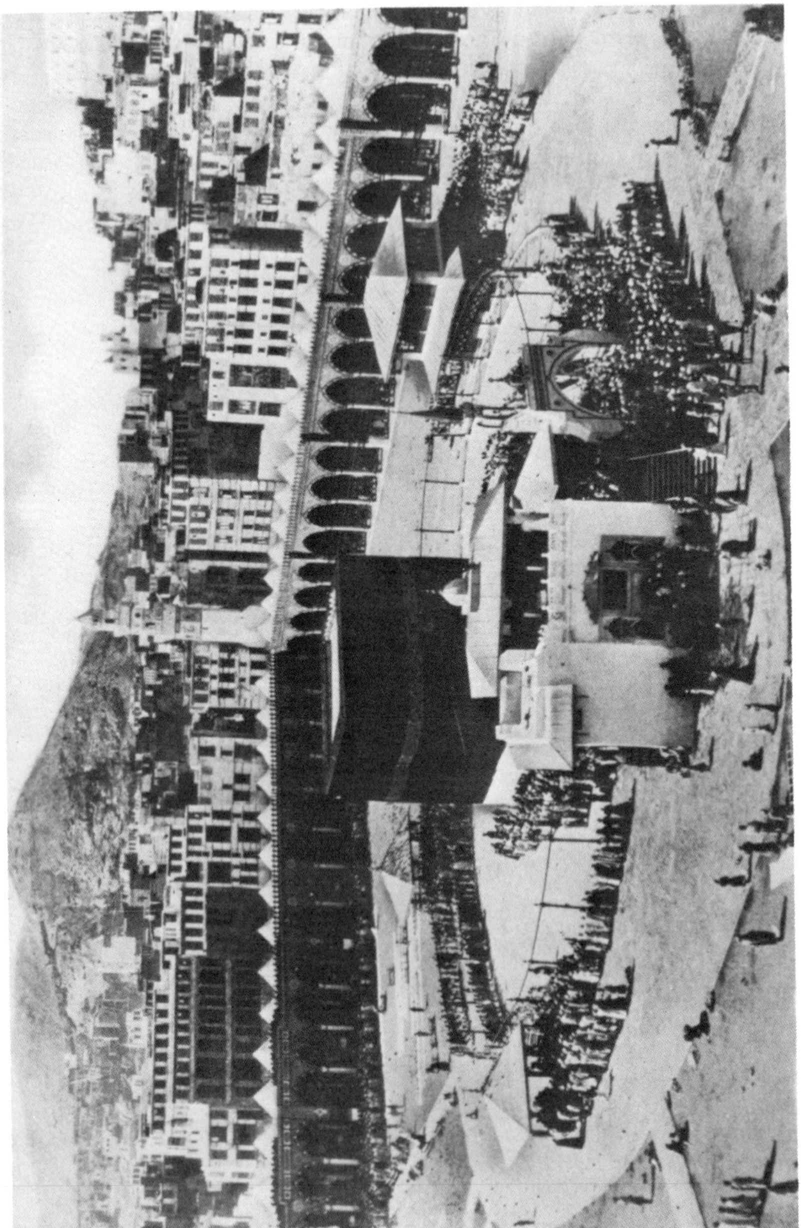

relations Afghanistan became a member of the League of Nations in 1934, and she was a signatory of the 1937 Treaty of Saadabad with Iran, Iraq, and Turkey.

THE ARAB STATES AND LEAGUE MANDATES

Ibn Sa'ud

Arab unity was originally conceived to be a product of British imperial policy. We have discussed earlier the support the Foreign Office had given to Husain, sherif of Mecca, in the successful attempt to bring the Arabs into the war on the side of the British. An even greater scheme, the Arab League, was to be the postwar fulfillment of British promises. Husain was to become the new caliph of Islam in the holy city, while his sons were to be put on the thrones of other Arab areas. As far as the Arabian peninsula was concerned, this scheme was not successful. It was not successful in large part because the India Office of the British government had supported Ibn Sa'ud, the ruler of Nejd. Ibn Sa'ud's career had been one of a steady advance from landless exile at Kuwait to successful ruler of interior Arabia with his capital at Riyadh. A treaty, which was concluded in 1915, assured him support and a £50,000 monthly allowance from the British government, for which he maintained a benevolent neutrality during the war. Ibn Sa'ud's greatest task as the leader of the fanatical Wahhabi movement and the leader of the ever restless Bedouins was to attach them to the soil and make them conscious of their unity, while relying on their religious zeal to carry out his schemes of expansion.

Ibn Sa'ud was very effective in organizing about 50,000 Bedouins into agricultural colonies, and in forming from these a disciplined standing army. This organization was known as the "Brethren" (Ikhwan), and Ibn Sa'ud was able to eliminate his chief rival in 1913 and gain access to the Syrian desert a few years later. When his power became solidified, he was ready to begin his contest against Husain of Mecca. The latter had dreamt of an Arab kingdom with himself as new caliph. Ibn Sa'ud was an obstacle, and Husain initially was the aggressor. In November, 1916 he proclaimed himself "King of the Arab countries," a move which annoyed Ibn Sa'ud who ruled the Nejd with absolute control. In 1919 the first armed clash between Husain and Ibn Sa'ud took place, both being supported by British money. British intervention put a stop to it, but the war was merely postponed, not cancelled. The issue was reopened in 1924. In that year Husain proclaimed himself in autocratic fashion as the new caliph, an impolitic move since he had little Arab support in this. Arab opinion had become hostile to him due to his indifference to the welfare of the pilgrims in the holy cities, and of his financial extortion of them. The result was a short victorious war against Husain by Ibn Sa'ud who had the better organized troops, fired with fanatic Wahhabi zeal. Within two months Husain was driven out of Mecca, forced

FIGURE 18.3. Mecca: The Kaaba.

to abdicate, and retire into exile to Cyprus where he died in 1931. His son, Ali, managed to maintain himself in the port of Jidda until December, 1924, but he too succumbed to the power of Ibn Sa'ud.

That ruler adopted a very cautious and successful policy of not permitting the desecration and destruction of the holy relics, and consequently did not arouse Sunni orthodox opinion against him as was the fate of the Wahhabi leaders when they managed to capture the holy cities once before. Caution, good organization, and careful westernization were the policies of Ibn Sa'ud, and they proved most effective. After uniting almost all of Arabia and crushing his opposition, Ibn Sa'ud determinedly restored order. The roads to Mecca were made safe for pilgrims, and drinking water and motor transportation were provided. At first the Hejaz and Nejd were ruled separately. Ibn Sa'ud became king of the Hejaz in 1926, but it was not until 1932 that the two kingdoms of Nejd and Hejaz became combined into one state which was renamed Saudi Arabia.

Gradually and slowly modern reforms were introduced by Ibn Sa'ud. Telephones, education, and some public health measures made their appearances, but it is illustrative of the sensitivity and caution with which this program was pursued by Ibn Sa'ud that when the question of the introduction of radio came up, he called an assembly of holy men, who proceeded to declare that there was nothing in the Holy Scriptures against the adoption of the wonder. The strong position which Ibn Sa'ud had created for himself was recognized by Britain in 1927 when a treaty of complete equality was concluded between Ibn Sa'ud and England. In return Ibn Sa'ud recognized the British-protected states on the Persian Gulf, such as Bahrain, Kuwait, Trucial Oman, and Muscat. Apart from these protectorates and the extreme southwest corner of Arabia, the whole peninsula was united into Saudi Arabia, and was ruled effectively by Ibn Sa'ud. His position was also strengthened by a series of treaties of friendship with his neighbors, such as the one of 1933 with Transjordan and those of 1936 with Iraq and Egypt. Southwest Arabia or Yemen, continued to be controlled by a Shi'i Imam, Yahya, who ran the country as a theocracy. He had sided with the Turks in the first war, and in 1934 he became embroiled with Ibn Sa'ud. After a brief war, successful for Ibn Sa'ud, Yahya was forced to make peace, but Ibn Sa'ud was moderate in his terms and recognized the Yemenite claims regarding its frontier. By this moderation Ibn Sa'ud won great prestige, and the fear of the Shi'ites of Yemen against the Wahhabis lessened. Yemen in the last years of the thirties became pronouncedly more anti-British, and sought in Italy, and even Japan, a force which would counterbalance British influence.

The Arab Mandates

While Arabia was united under the leadership of Ibn Sa'ud, the rest of the Arab world was partitioned by Britain and France after 1918. This division resulted in important consequences in the development of Arab nationalism. On the one hand there remained the steady demand for reunification of all Arabs, but on the other the independent development of the divided areas gave rise to disunity. This was compounded by the rivalry between Ibn

FIGURE 18.4. Ibn Sa'ud with his son, Sa'ud.

Sa'ud and the sons of Husain who gained leading positions in the areas under direct British control. It took an outside challenge, Jewish nationalism, or Zionism, in Palestine to reunify all Arabs once again and to create pan-Arab bonds of sympathy and solidarity between them. In the period between the two World Wars Great Britain maintained an unquestioned predominance in the Arab world; she ruled directly over Palestine and Aden and exercised special rights and privileges in Iraq, and even in Saudi Arabia. French rule in Syria was far less important, except that Arab resistance to France was particularly bitter and added a great deal to the rise of common resistance against Western control over the Middle East.

It will be remembered that during World War I the Allies had concluded a series of secret agreements regarding the dismemberment of the Ottoman empire. Some of these had to be modified due to the Russian Revolution and the revival of a strong nationalist Turkey. The most important agreement for the fate of Arab territories was the Sykes-Picot Agreement, concluded by Sir Mark Sykes and Georges Picot in 1916. Under its terms France was promised Syria and Mosul, while Britain was to obtain southern Mesopotamia, Baghdad, Haifa, and Acre (in Syria). The city of Alexandretta was to be made into a free port. The Sykes-Picot Agreement was later changed slightly, but it remained the base upon which the victorious powers divided the Arab territories.

In December, 1918 Lloyd George and Clemenceau agreed that Mosul and all of Palestine were to go to Britain, while France would obtain Syria. The Sykes-Picot Agreement became public when the Bolsheviks opened the Russian imperial archives, and this caused a storm of protest among the Arabs and even worried Woodrow Wilson. Under his auspices an American mission was sent, headed by Dr. A. C. King and C. H. Crane, to study the situation and to find out the wishes of the people. The report of the King-Crane mission clearly indicated that the ex-subjects of the Turks preferred to remain united, that they might acquiesce in a British mandate in Iraq, and an American one in Syria, but that they opposed the French, and that they also opposed Zionism in Palestine.

This report was ignored, and at a conference in San Remo on the Italian Riviera in 1920 the decision to put the Arab provinces under the mandate system was made a reality. All Arab provinces were made Class A Mandates under the League of Nations, which meant that after a brief period of tutelage they would arrive at eventual independence. This temporary control and training for freedom was safeguarded by annual reports which the mandatory power had to make to the League, under the theory that the mandatory power governed not for its own benefit, but for that of the mandate. In practice the mandate system resulted in considerable interference and in some evils of colonialism.

The decision to establish mandates was the result of a compromise between the promises made to France under the Sykes-Picot Agreement, and those made to the Arabs by the McMahon correspondence. The ambiguous language of the latter now could be made to serve British ends, inasmuch as Britain declared that the letters contained reservations regarding promises which might be detrimental to her French ally. Practical politics had won out over the joint British-French declaration of 1918, during World War I, that both powers would establish Arab governments in Syria and Mesopotamia. In July, 1922 the League approved the mandates, and the United States agreed to them in 1924. Syria was to be a French mandate, Iraq and Palestine to go to Britain. The disappointment of the Arabs was very great, since it had seemed to them that immediate independence was forthcoming, and bitterness and resentment against both Western Powers remained smoldering during the years which led up to World War II.

Syria

France obtained Syria because of her long-standing influence and prestige in that area which dated back to 1860 when she had come to the protection of a Christian sect and had established mission schools. France also wanted bases on the way to her East African and Far Eastern colonies. In addition France intended to be a great power and to expand her control and influence in the Mediterranean in particular and in the world of Islam in general.

At the end of the war Syria had been occupied by the victorious Arabs under Faisal and the British, with but a small French force on the coast, but an Anglo-French agreement of September, 1919 turned the entire coastline over to the French army, and the British evacuated their troops from the interior. The Arabs were very bitter when the existence of the Sykes-Picot

Agreement was made public by the Russians, and Faisal, son of Husain, protested against the presence of French troops. In March, 1920 the Syrians offered him a crown; Faisal accepted and ruled Syria from Damascus. But in the next month the San Remo Conference made Syria a mandate of France, a move promptly rejected by the Damascus government which had proclaimed Syrian independence. Faisal himself was willing to accept some French aid and advice, but he was pronounced a traitor by each side, and soon got into an impossible position. In July, 1920 came the open clash between the Syrian government and France. A French force led by General Gouraud marched toward Damascus, and on July 14 he issued an ultimatum demanding the acceptance of the mandate. Faisal accepted it, but curiously enough his reply was never received by the French general. New demands were put forward instead by the French military, and after a brief fight the French forces entered Damascus. Faisal fled, and Syrian independence ended.

The technique of French rule in Syria was simple; it was one of divide and rule. The French made it a policy to accentuate and foster communal particularism, and they made great use of the many Christian and Moslem minorities. This was not difficult since Syria contained over eighteen religious creeds, more or less mutually antagonistic. Even so, France decided to further divide the country, and she divided it into five units: Syria, the Christian Republic of Lebanon, the region of the Alaouites, that of the Jebel Druse, and the area around the port of Alexandretta. Political division and an economy designed to further French interests made it clear to the Syrians that France ruled for her own benefit, and not for that of the mandate. French advisors and a highly organized bureaucracy, French oil pipelines and railroad construction, the introduction of depreciated French paper currency, the extensive use of black Senegalese colonial troops, and the erection of a monument to the liberation of Syria by the French (when in fact this had been done by Faisal and the British) were visible indications of French policy, and they rankled among the Arab nationalists.

Nationalist resentment soon gave rise to riots, and between 1925 and 1927 a full-scale rebellion broke out against France. For this the French could partly thank General Sarrail whose anticlerical views and treachery alienated both French supporters and native chiefs. A socialist and atheist, he was sent out from Paris in 1925 to Syria, where upon arrival he refused the welcome rendered him by church officials, and he soon managed to get into a quarrel with the Catholic Church.

Sarrail also invited a party of Druse leaders, from the hill tribes of the Jebel Druse, to a parley in Damascus, and when they arrived he had them arrested and jailed. This was the spark which set off the Druse rebellion, which lasted for two years, and which for a time seriously threatened French control of the mandate. The French Army armed Christians against Moslems, and was not beyond such intimidating measures as the exposure of the corpses of rebels, a step which resulted in October, 1925 in a riot in Damascus and the three-day bombardment by French artillery of that city. About 1,200 persons were killed in the unfortified city; but the shelling turned out to be a serious psychological mistake—it aroused great hatred against the French and unified all Arab nationalists. A League of Nations investigation severely criticized French rule. Sarrail was replaced by a civilian, de Jouvenel, but the French policy of fostering separatism remained.

Lebanon was consistently favored over Syria, and it was given a constitution in 1926. Some treaties with Syria were drawn up in 1930 by the French, but all of them included military clauses which gave France the right to station troops and to use aircraft facilities. A number of constitutional schemes were also proposed, but were rejected by the Syrians. Even the treaties of 1930 were not ratified by the French parliament, and until 1939 constitutional progress remained at a stalemate. In 1939 the movement toward a constitution was suspended with the outbreak of the war. France had managed to instill in the Syrian nationalists a burning desire for the unification of the whole territory, and it also succeeded in getting a Syrian National Party together in which religious differences no longer mattered. A special problem was the future of the region of Alexandretta, which was part of the French mandate. Turkey claimed it for economic and strategic reasons, and also because a sizable Turkish minority lived in the city of Alexandretta. In 1937 it became the autonomous republic of Hatay (a Hittite term), under a joint French-Turkish Guarantee, and in 1939 France ceded Alexandretta outright to Turkey when war seemed imminent and Turkish neutrality worth having. But to Syria the loss of Alexandretta remained a fact to be resented.

Iraq

Great Britain was given the mandates over Iraq, Palestine, and Transjordan. Of these three, Iraq was the first to obtain full independence. In 1914 the British had occupied Basra at the head of the Persian Gulf, and they made good use of the anti-Turkish sentiment among the Arabs of Mesopotamia. The Indian government had looked upon the occupation of Mesopotamia as a necessary and a permanent solution to the problem of guarding India, and with the troops and the administrators there were plans to send out Indian colonists to grow cotton in the river soils. At first everything went very well, but in December, 1915 the British advance up river was decisively defeated by the Turks at the Battle of Kut-al-Amara, and the conquest of all of Mesopotamia was consequently prolonged. Baghdad was taken in March, 1917, and soon after northern Mesopotamia.

British official opinion was divided regarding the postwar future of the land; the Anglo-Egyptians and the Foreign Office supported the Arabs and favored eventual independence, while the India Office squarely opposed this and even the mandate solution which was finally adopted. Iraq (the Arab name for Mesopotamia) was given as a mandate to Britain at San Remo.

Arab nationalism, which up to this moment had been directed against Ottoman rule, now turned to opposition to Great Britain. The Arab press, the Arab intelligentsia in Baghdad, and Shi'a religious leaders all united in vociferous denunciations of the British mandate, and in 1920 a revolt broke out against the British occupying forces which had to be put down with considerable costs, and which saw particularly violent anti-British sentiments displayed in the Shi'a holy city of Kerbela. Under the sponsorship of Winston Churchill, who was then colonial secretary, and the influence of T. E. Lawrence, Britain set up a provisional Arab government at Baghdad headed by the Naqib, or hereditary marshal of that city. Sir Percy Cox was dispatched from Tehran with the aim to get Faisal on the throne of Iraq. Britain thus was able to repay her debt to Husain by promoting his son, a refugee from the French in Damascus, as king of Iraq. Faisal arrived aboard a British warship, and was installed as first king of Iraq in 1921, while his chief political rival was invited by Lady Cox to tea, arrested, and deported to Ceylon.

King Faisal

Faisal made an excellent king. He quickly gained the confidence of the Arab nationalists and of the desert tribes, and he had learned from his experience with the French not to oppose a great power too much. Faisal, who ruled until 1933, held a fine balance between the demands of the Iraqi nationalists and the wishes of Great Britain. The relations between the two countries were regulated by the Treaty of 1922, which admitted British advisors to the Iraqi government, but which also introduced two sets of officials so that Arabs had a chance to learn administrative duties. The British hold was gradually lessened, due to the high costs of occupation, and air power replaced garrison troops.

Considerable progress was made in the reforms of the country. National education and a judicial system were introduced, personnel employed in finance, education, and administration were trained by British experts, and in 1924 the first Iraqi parliament convened. On the economic side emphasis was given to agriculture, and little to industry, but the railroad from Turkey to Baghdad was completed in 1939. A motor route was established connecting Baghdad, Haifa, and Damascus, and a number of air bases were built. Iraq soon became a vital stepping stone on the air route from Europe to Asia. The discovery of new rich oil fields was of particular importance to Iraq. In 1926 Iraq obtained Mosul from Turkey, which had the strategic advantage of protecting the British buffer state on the road to India from an attack from the north while it gave great new oil fields to the government in Baghdad. Iraq also began to build up a new national army, in order to counterbalance the military effectiveness of some of the tribes which frequently had more rifles at their disposal than did the government.

Discussions between Britain and Iraq were renewed in 1928, and a new treaty was signed in 1930, effective in 1932, which terminated the mandate status. Iraq was promised independence, and in return signed this treaty which was to run for twenty-five years and which gave Britain a special position in Iraq. England was to be consulted on all external matters, Britons were to be preferred when it came to the employment of foreign officials, and the British ambassador took precedence over any other diplomatic representative. If war should break out Iraq would be England's ally, her help being limited to making available all port and railroad facilities, and the use of three air bases at which the Royal Air Force maintained planes. After the conclusion of the treaty Britain persuaded the League to end the mandate, and in 1932 Iraq became a member of the League, the first Arab state to do so. This new status did not satisfy some of the extreme nationalists, and their chance came after the death of Faisal in 1933. He died in Switzerland, worried about an uprising of the Kurds in northern Mesopotamia, who had proven as unruly under Iraqi rule as they did under Turkish.

Successors of Faisal

Faisal's successor was King Ghazi, who ruled from 1933 to 1939. Young, weak, and somewhat irresponsible, he gave headway to army influence which was strongly nationalist. In 1935 there occurred an uprising of the so-called Assyrians. These were Nestorian Christians who had fled from Turkey, been protected by the British, and given a refuge in Mesopotamia. Their rebellion was ruthlessly put down, and a number of them were massacred by the army. The army leader in command, General Bakr Sidqi, who had crushed them, emerged as a military hero, and there followed a series of plots and counterplots, far too tedious to unravel, which showed that Iraq had become more and more a victim of chauvinism and extreme nationalism. A territorial claim to Kuwait was advanced, anti-Zionism became a strong issue, and the government tended at times to lean more closely toward Germany and Italy. German trade increased rapidly, and Italian shipping predominated in the commerce of the Persian Gulf. After Ghazi was killed in 1939 in an automobile accident (he liked fast driving), his four-year-old son, Faisal II, ascended under a regency. Control passed more and more to the army and to the extreme nationalists, and Baghdad was soon overrun by anti-British, German, and Italian agents. The British consul in Mosul was murdered, and the leading opponent of the Jews in Palestine, the Grand Mufti, found ready sanctuary in Iraq.

Iraq during this period bettered her relations with Saudi Arabia by a treaty in 1936, which settled some frontier disputes, and she joined the Saadabad Pact with Iran, Turkey, and Afghanistan in 1937. Her oil resources became strategically more important with the completion in 1935 of a pipeline from the oil fields to the Mediterranean ports of Tripoli and Haifa. When World War II broke out, Iraq in consequence was a potential political danger to Great Britain, while her strategic and economic position was more important than ever.

Palestine

In Palestine Arab nationalism clashed with the nationalism of the Jews. Here the general struggle of the Middle East between Arab and Western domination became a struggle for actual possession of the land, in which opposition to British control played a lesser part, and in which the national spirit of all Arabs was united in common bonds against the force of Zionism, or Jewish nationalism. In 1897 an Austrian journalist, Theodore Herzl, an outstanding leader of Zionism, demanded Palestine, the historic land of the

Jews, as their homeland. At its first congress in Basle Zionism went on record for the creation of this political ideal, a Jewish state colonized by Jews.

Due to the exigencies of the war (1914–1918) Britain wished to gain the support of the Jewish communities in the United States. In addition she owed a debt of gratitude to the leader of the English Zionist movement, Chaim Weizmann, who greatly aided the British war effort by discovering a formula by which cordite used in munitions could be obtained from horse chestnuts. Thus the British government in 1917 made the so-called Balfour Declaration. The declaration was also designed to cause Russian Jews to support the tsarist empire and to stir up trouble for Germany and Austria-Hungary whose Jewish minorities would be attracted by the promise of a national home in Palestine. The Balfour Declaration stated:

His Majesty's government view with favor the establishment in Palestine of a national home for the Jewish people, and will use their best endeavors to facilitate the achievement of this object, it being clearly understood that nothing shall be done which may prejudice the civil and religious rights of existing non-Jewish communities in Palestine or the rights and political status enjoyed by Jews in other countries.

At the San Remo Conference in 1920 Palestine was handed over as a mandate to Britain, who desired it as a strategic region guarding the vital Suez Canal, and the Balfour Declaration was included in the mandate, its execution to be left to the British administration. This produced at once the most bitter conflict between the Arabs, the British, and the Jews. The Arabs argued that the mandate, not to speak of the Balfour Declaration, was a flagrant violation of the prior commitment of Britain to Arab nationalism obtained in the McMahon correspondence, while the British insisted that Palestine belonged to territory specifically exempted by the McMahon terms. Bitterness and resentment caused Arab refusal to participate in the government of the mandate, and it became run entirely by British officials. Arab riots took place as early as Easter, 1920 in Jerusalem, and in May the following year in Jaffa.

Under British administration Jewish immigration into Palestine rapidly increased. Working under great hardships the Jews at once set about to reclaim lands, to set up collective farms and cooperative societies, and to greatly increase agricultural production. An outstanding example was the drainage of the valley of the Esdraelon. Industry also was greatly expanded and stimulated by Jewish immigration. Large scale hydro-electric power plants provided energy for potash and mineral salts production, and for metals and textile industries. The influx of Jews and their economic activities which benefited primarily the Jewish community, although Arabs tended to benefit indirectly from them, was vigorously opposed by Arab nationalists. To the Arabs Palestine was a holy land and an integral part of Syria, not a separate province to be administered by a Western power and gradually to be taken over by the Jews. Their demands were exclusion of the Jews and immediate independence. British policy attempted to steer a middle course between the two opposing forces, and it pleased neither side.

When Weizmann made a speech in which he declared that Palestine was to be for the Jews what England was for the English, a British White Paper took exception to this statement, and pointed out that the British administration would not permit the imposition of a Jewish nationality on the inhabitants of Palestine. These official statements made in 1922 satisfied neither Arab nor Jew. The Jews interpreted the Balfour Declaration as the right to create a Jewish majority in Palestine, and the land purchased by Jews was considered to belong permanently to the Jewish national state. The Arabs resisted the Jewish attempt to reduce them to a minority in the country, at first by a policy of noncooperation with the British and after 1925 by demands for protective laws. The feeling of antagonism against the Jews and the English was demonstrated in the serious riots which broke out in Palestine and Damascus when Balfour visited the mandates in 1925. While Arab feeling became crystallized, the achievements of the Jews continued steadily. Very great efforts were made to improve agriculture, large irrigation projects were established, modern cities such as Haifa were built, and the standards of education, and of living in general, were greatly raised. This engendered renewed Arab fears of the Jewish majority in Palestine, and the British took notice of this in the Hope-Simpson Report published in 1930. This report was conciliatory towards the Arabs, and stressed the obligations of the British mandatory toward the non-Jewish inhabitants. It pointed out that Arab tenant farmers had been deprived of their land and had been reduced to poorer soils; it asked for a pause in Jewish immigration, and a more stringent control of land transfers.

Needless to say this report aroused the opposition of the Zionists. With increased Jewish immigration due to the persecutions of Hitler in Germany the Arabs developed organized resistance against the British and the Jews. Although there were many factions among the Moslems, as there were many also among the Jews, anti-British and anti-Jewish Arab nationalism was strongest in a party headed by Husain, the Grand Mufti of Jerusalem. After sizable funds had been collected resistance came out into the open by means of riots, violence, and terrorism. In 1936 a general strike was called against the British, which was accompanied by armed robbery and many acts of sabotage. The British took a strong stand, suppressed the movement, and deposed the Mufti. A royal commission was dispatched, and its report of the investigation, the Peel Report, pointed out that the underlying cause of the disturbances was "the same desire of the Arabs for national independence and their hatred and fear of the Jewish national home." The Peel Report offered a scheme of partition ("Partition seems to offer at least a chance of ultimate peace") but this was rejected by both Arabs and Jews. Again violence broke out, and some Jewish terrorist groups, notably the Stern Gang, retaliated with terroristic acts against the Arabs. In 1938 a serious Arab uprising took place, but this too was drastically suppressed by the British. British official policy was not united; the Foreign Office stood for the mandate, the Balfour Declaration, and some support to Zionist aspiration, while the Colonial Office, which was in charge of the actual administration, tended to be pro-Arab and more hostile to the Jews.

In 1939 the British government published a new White Paper which abrogated the mandate, and which in effect left it for the Jews and Arabs themselves to work out their problems. It will be noted, however, that due to the impending war, and the need to conciliate the Arabs in the conflict to come, the White Paper stipulated that all further Jewish immigration would cease unless the Arabs approved and that Jewish land purchases would be severely restricted. In 1939 the Jews were about one-third of the population of Palestine, so that they had not as yet become a majority. In consequence the Palestine problem was more acute than ever, and the rivalry between Arab nationalism and Zionism was greater than before.

Transjordan

A few words need to be added here regarding the last of the British mandates, that of Transjordan. Originally the region of Transjordan had belonged to the Damascus government of Faisal, but after his expulsion by the French it became part of Palestine. The British then appointed another son of Husain, the sherif of Mecca, as its emir. This was Abdullah, who ruled this desert border state guarding the British route to Iraq and to India. Transjordan was exempted from the Balfour Declaration, and in 1923 it was given a status of semiautonomy. The British were granted the right to station troops, and these went into action against an attack of the Wahhabis in 1924 when airplanes and armored cars decisively repulsed the invaders. In 1928 Transjordan became an independent state, but concluded a treaty with Britain whereby English advisors were accepted in its government, and Britain was responsible for the external relations of the country. In fact, the British high commissioner in Palestine still maintained effective internal control of the new state, and he was responsible for its defense, so that the government of Emir Abdullah exercised only relatively few legal and administrative rights.

In conclusion, this brief survey has attempted to point out that for the Arab world neither religion, nor ethnic boundaries were decisive. Nationalism was the greatest ideal, and this meant the creation of an independent nation for each state. Pan-Arab unity remained attractive, despite local divergence and local jealousy and the family rivalry between Ibn Sa'ud and Husain and his sons. Common opposition to the ideals of Zionism and bitter disillusionment with the British and the French were the catalysts which pointed a way towards effective Arab unity. By 1939 Arab nationalism by and large had not been satisfied and opposition to European guardianship was still a powerful force. It was clear that both the British and French Mandates were working badly; Britain herself had said that she could no longer rule Palestine under the original terms. As for Persia and Afghanistan, they had successfully obtained full external and internal independence, but they had yet to cope with the problem of modernization and westernization. Turkey alone, which had been at its lowest point in all her Ottoman history in 1918, was the one nation which emerged as a modern, strong, and united state.

BASIC DATES

1913–1918	Enver Pasha holds power in Turkey
1915–1916	Dardanelles campaign
1915	Independence of Ibn Sa'ud
1916	Arab revolt in Hejaz
1917	Balfour Declaration
1918–1921	British ascendancy in Iran
1918	Turks lose all non-Turkish territories
1918–1922	Allied occupation of Constantinople
1918–1920	Faisal rules in Damascus
1919–1922	Mustafa Kemal leads Turkish nationalist movement; war against Greece
1919–1936	French control of Syria opposed by nationalists
1919–1925	Ibn Sa'ud conquers Arabia
1919–1929	Ammanullah reigns in independent Afghanistan
1920	Treaty of Sèvres
1920–1938	Mustafa Kemal president of Turkey
1921	Reza Khan seizes power in Iran
1921–1933	Reign of Faisal in Iraq
1922	Palestine becomes League of Nations mandate
1923	Treaty of Lausanne; proclamation of Turkish republic
1923	Transjordan becomes autonomous
1923	Reform edicts in Afghanistan
1924	Abolition of caliphate
1925–1941	Reign of Reza Shah Pahlavi
1926	Lebanon becomes a republic
1929–1933	Nadir Khan in Afghanistan
1930	Iraq becomes independent
1932	Saudi Arabia created
1933	Muhammad Zahir Shah in Afghanistan; Ghazi ascends Iraqi throne
1934	Yemen becomes independent
1938	Ismet Inonü president of Turkey
1939	Trans-Iranian Railroad completed

SUPPLEMENTARY READING

Avery, P. W. *Modern Iran.* London, 1965.
Fisher, S. *The Middle East.* New York, 1959.
Haas, W. *Iran.* New York, 1946.
Hitti, P. *The Near East in History.* Princeton, N.J., 1961.
Hoskins, H. *The Middle East.* New York, 1954.
Kirk, G. *A Short History of the Middle East.* New York, 1957. Contains some unusual interpretations.
Lewis, B. *The Emergence of Modern Turkey.* London, 1961.
Royal Institute of International Affairs. *The Middle East: A Political and Economic Survey.* London, 1958.
Speiser, E. *The United States and the Near East.* Cambridge, Mass., 1950.
Thomas, L. and R. Frye. *The United States and Turkey and Iran.* Cam-

bridge, Mass. This volume and preceding entry both provide excellent introductions to the nations they deal with.
Toynbee, A. and K. Kirkwood. *Turkey.* New York, 1927. A good account of the rise of Mustafa Kemal.
Upton, J. *The History of Modern Iran: An Interpretation.* Cambridge, Mass., 1960.

ADVANCED READING

Adamec, L. *Afghanistan, 1900–1923: A Diplomatic History.* Berkeley, 1967.
Armstrong, H. *Lord of Arabia.* London, 1934. A biography of Ibn Sa'ud.
Barker, A. *The Neglected War: Mesopotamia, 1914–1918.* New York, 1967.
Coke, R. *The Heart of the Middle East.* London, 1925. Deals with Mesopotamia.
Cottam, R. *Nationalism in Iran.* Pittsburg, 1964.
De Novo, J. *American Interests and Policies in the Middle East, 1900–1939.* Minneapolis, 1963.
Gardner, B. *Allenby of Arabia.* New York, 1966.
Gökalp, Ziya. *The Principle of Turkism.* Translated from Turkish by Robert Devereux. Leiden, 1968.
Hurewitz, J. C. *The Struggle for Palestine.* New York, 1950.
Ireland, P. *Iraq: A Study in Political Development.* London, 1937.
Khadduri, M. *Independent Iraq. London,* 1951. An excellent study.
Kincross, L. *Ataturk.* New York, 1965.
Kohn, H. *Nationalism and Imperialism in the Hither East.* London, 1932.
Langsam, W. C. *The World Since 1914.* New York, 1954.
Lawrence, T. E. *Revolt in the Desert.* New York, 1928. Account of the Arab revolt in the Hejaz by the famous participant.
Lenczowski, G. *The Political Awakening in the Middle East.* Englewood Cliffs, N.J., 1970.
Millspaugh, A. C. *Americans in Persia.* Washington, 1946.
Monroe, E. *Britain's Moment in the Middle East, 1914–1956.* Baltimore, 1963.
Nathan, R. et al. *Palestine, Problem and Promise.* Washington, 1946.
Nevakiki, J. *Britain, France and the Arab Middle East, 1914–1920.* London, 1969.
Nutting, A. *Lawrence of Arabia.* New York, 1962.
Payne, R. *Lawrence of Arabia.* New York, 1962.
Sachar, H. *The Emergence of the Middle East, 1914–1924.* New York, 1969.
Searight, S. *The British in the Middle East.* New York, 1970.
Sharabi, H. *Nationalism and Revolution in the Arab World.* New York, 1966.
Sykes, P. *History of Persia.* Oxford, 1922.
Trumpener, U. *Germany and the Ottoman Empire, 1914–1918.* Princeton, N.J., 1968.
Williams, A. *Britain, France and the Arab Middle East, 1914–1967.* London, 1968.
Williams, K. *Ibn Sa'ud.* London, 1933.

Chapter 19

India, 1914-1947

MILITARY EFFORT AND DISILLUSIONMENT

In India in 1914, just before the outbreak of the First World War, the Indian National Congress, established in 1885 with British help, had begun to ask for self-rule, or *swaraj*, and liberal reforms, while the British government had responded to these demands with the passing of the Morley-Minto Act of 1909. Congress had pushed for responsible government, but the act of 1909 had fallen far short of this (see Chapter 10). Despite the fact that the legislative councils had been enlarged both at the center and in the provinces, the executive power of the viceroy and the provincial governors remained unimpaired and fully independent of the legislative bodies, whose lack of power tended to make them irresponsible. At the same time Hindu-Moslem antagonism was on the increase, and communal differences began to reassert themselves as never before. During most of the nineteenth century this antagonism had been subdued under British rule, but by 1914 the British had become the protectors of the minorities, and especially of the Moslem population in India by introducing the principle of communal representation in the legislative councils. This, and the favor bestowed by the British upon the Moslem League, did much to solidify the baneful Hindu-Moslem split.

World War I

Yet, when the great war came in 1914 India remained definitely loyal to Great Britain, and was a great source of strength to the British war effort. The overwhelming majority of Indians, to judge from the unanimous voice of the Indian press, were shocked and horrified at Germany's invasion of Belgium, and supported England wholeheartedly with contributions of soldiers, loans, and ammunition. A total of some 800,000 soldiers, all volunteers, and 500,000 noncombatants joined in India's military effort. Many of the native princes requested active duty or made significant gifts such as hospital ships or, as in the case of the nizam of Hyderabad, maintained regiments abroad out of their own pocket. Indians in active service were engaged mainly in overseas duty, since the British navy maintained complete supremacy in the Indian Ocean. Indian troops overseas served in Flanders, in East Africa, in Palestine, and in Mesopotamia. Some 44,000 Indians, or two divisions, part of the English Expeditionary Force in France, suffered losses of seventy-five per cent killed or wounded on the bloody fields of Flanders.

Some revolts did occur in 1914 and 1915 in Bengal, the Deccan, and among the Sikhs of the Punjab, but these were easily put down, and did not express much more than the attempts of German agents to foment trouble. German agents were behind the so-called Dayal movement, which operated both in the Punjab and among Hindus in California, and which advocated revolt against the British rule. Propaganda, emanating from Berlin, urged the Sikhs in the United States, in particular, to revolt upon return to India from overseas. There was trouble also among the fanatic Moslems on the northwest frontier, who launched attacks which made it necessary for the English to send several expeditions into the troublesome hills, but as long as the Afghan amir, Habibullah, kept his country neutral the border could be kept tranquil without too much effort. The 1915 Defense of India Act, which gave extraordinary powers to the British government in India to deal with disturbances such as these, was generally approved by the people of the country, a sure index of their willingness to cooperate with the British at a time of great peril.

In return for India's support and cooperation the British government made some concessions. Indians were used not only on the battlefield, but also increasingly in India's administration. Two maharajas were appointed to the Imperial War Council, and other Indians were to serve as members of the peace conference and eventually in the League of Nations, and other international conferences and organizations. At the same time, while Britain made a gesture of associating Indian personnel with herself in the great struggle against the Central Powers, the British also permitted an increase in India's tariff on cotton goods to 7.5 per cent as an economic concession to India's growing textile industry.

But the early enthusiasm of the first two years of war gradually turned into a feeling of weariness and a general malaise, as it did in all countries drawn into the horrible struggle. High wartime prices created distress among India's urban class and factory workers. Rumors that the war's end would see a reorganization of the empire in which a greater share of power was to be given to such self-governing dominions as South Africa increased India's concern with the possibility of greater discriminatory legislation, while it whetted the appetite of India's political leaders to gain for India greater power. In 1916 the Congress stated that the Morley-Minto reforms led nowhere at all, and they demanded a definite statement and free institutions. Excited by the Irish revolt of 1916, which fascinated India's nationalists, a rapprochement took place between the Hindus and the Moslems, and in

December 1916 they sponsored the so-called Lucknow Pact. This joint resolution favored home rule by which India was to be granted immediately the status of a self-governing entity within the British empire. The Lucknow Pact not only brought Hindus and Moslems together in agreement, but it also saw the return of the left-wing extremists back into the Congress, led by Tilak who was given a standing ovation.

The British government did not fulfill the expectancies of home rule, and it continued to exercise the strict emergency powers during the rest of the war which were designed to deal with manifestations of unrest and discontent. But the undercurrent of this unrest continued to increase rather than to dwindle. Inflation, for one thing, was one cause for the widespread dissatisfaction and discontent in India after 1916, and so was the terrible influenza epidemic which killed millions of Indians, more men than fell on all the battlefields of the great war. This terrible death toll and the mounting cost of living caused renewed conspiracies in India, especially among the Moslems who were also concerned with the eventual fate of the caliphate, their spiritual leadership, as the defeat of the Ottoman empire came to be steadily more of a certainty (see Chapter 18). Moslem unrest had also been partially stimulated by the heavy losses suffered by Indian troops when the Turks had won their spectacular victory against the British early in 1916 at Kut-el-Amara in Mesopotamia.

Government of India Act of 1919

The British reply to this dissatisfaction, unrest, and discontent during the latter part of the war was the famous announcement in August, 1917 by Montagu, the secretary of state for India, that the policy of the British government was to be toward "the gradual development of self-governing institutions and the progressive realization of responsible government." In November, 1917, Montagu sailed for India to consult with the viceroy, Lord Chelmsford, and in 1918 the result of their conversations was published in the form of the Montagu-Chelmsford report, which served as the basis for the Government of India Act of 1919. This act certainly was a great advance over the Morley-Minto reforms, it was liberal in approach and sympathetic to Indian aspirations, and it was welcomed as a most promising step in the right direction by all Indian leaders. Essentially, the Government of India Act of 1919 embodied a certain liberalization of the governmental structure of India by the introduction of the principle of dyarchy at the Indian provincial level. The whole country was divided into nine provinces, and in each province the beginnings of responsible government were established with the principle of dyarchy which provided for two kinds of governmental subjects, those in which the government was to be guided by Indians elected in the provincial legislature, and called *transferred* subjects, and those over which the governor and his executive council had exclusive control, and which were called *reserved* subjects. Among the transferred subjects were agriculture, sanitation, education, and some powers of local government, while the reserved subjects included the most important powers of control over finance, police, prison administration, famine and relief organization.

Under the principle of dyarchy the basic powers of finance and maintenance of law and order were still in the hands of the British, but at least the new act gave a chance to the Indian legislative bodies to gather experience in government. Responsible government had been introduced, albeit in a minor way, for the first time in Indian history, as the provincial legislative councils were at least seventy per cent elective and ministerial responsibility to their orders had become a fact.

At the center, in the viceregal government, there was no dyarchy. The viceroy had his Council of State, composed of an Indian majority but recruited from a small, restricted electorate. There was also the legislative assembly, where the majority was also elected, but without real power. In fact, the viceroy held practically unlimited powers, since he could veto any bill he disliked and could also make any bill which he desired into law by his power of certification. In short, the Government of India Act of 1919 represented a typical compromise arrangement, whereby the British government had agreed to some real though limited advances. It was a good example of the Burkean tradition of slow political evolution.

Nevertheless, despite the very real concessions embodied in the Act of 1919, the British compromise was soon nullified by the intense anti-British feeling aroused in India when the Indian government attempted to make the extraordinary British wartime powers permanent. The Rowlatt Acts of 1919 provided for a summary procedure against suspected terrorists, with secret trial and no right of counsel, jury, or appeal. The attempts to continue wartime measures designed to crush Indian terrorism and to intern suspects for long periods without trial put an end to any goodwill towards the British government among Indian nationalists, who argued that the Rowlatt Acts nullified all political advance toward responsible government in India. Thus, the passing of these acts ushered in a new era in Indian politics, that of the noncooperation movement between Indians and their British government, a movement which was the work of a most remarkable Indian leader, Mohandas Gandhi.

MOHANDAS GANDHI LEADS NATIONALISTS

The Amritsar Massacre

The decision of the British government to perpetuate its extraordinary powers by enacting the Rowlatt Acts set off at once violent protests in India. There were serious riots in Delhi and Punjab, in which Europeans were attacked and killed, trains derailed and wrecked. These disturbances came to a head in April, 1919 in the Punjab, where the Amritsar Massacre occurred. The Amritsar Massacre damaged severely the possibility of Britain's retaining India, while at the same time it propelled Gandhi into prominence in Indian political affairs.

In response to the violent anti-English riots due to the misguided attempt by the government to continue the wartime powers given to it by the Rowlatt Act, all assemblies had been forbidden. In violation of this order, a crowd, variously estimated at from 6,000 to 12,000 people, met inside a garden in Amritsar, in a small space entirely surrounded by brick houses and a high wall, with but one exit. General Dyer, arriving at this scene with some fifty infantry soldiers, without warning opened fire upon the unarmed crowd, killing 376 and wounding perhaps some 4,000 Hindus. His avowed purpose in doing so was to "strike terror in the whole of Punjab," and he coolly defended his action later by declaring that "the targets were good." The Amritsar Massacre had many consequences. General Dyer was shot to death in London in 1930 in revenge, but much more important was the profound influence the Amritsar Massacre had on Gandhi.

Gandhi's Early Life

Mohandas Mahatma ("great soul") Gandhi was born in 1869 in Kathiawar into a middle-class or Vaishya Hindu family with a strong religious background. Gandhi was thin, with plain, even ugly features, and a shaven head. As we can tell from his autobiography, he was a man of easy simplicity, considerable warmth, and humor as well as kindness. After marrying at the age of 13, he was sent by his family to London to study law. While training successfully for his profession Gandhi acquired a measure of self-discipline, detachment, and a great concern for his fellow men and their social problems. He also came strongly under the influence of Christian ethics, as preached in the gospel and expounded by such writers as Tolstoy and Ruskin. As his professional horizon widened, so did his understanding of religion and the ethical problems of man. He ceased to be confined into a narrow Hindu caste tradition, and declared that "personally I do not regard any of the great religions as false." In 1893 he returned to Bombay, but did not stay long in India. Having failed dismally as a lawyer in India, he thought better prospects might be found in South Africa working for an Indian clientele sorely beset by British and Boer discrimination. It was in South Africa that Gandhi won his first successes as the champion of the Hindu indentured laborers who were discriminated against with special poll taxes and the requirement of finger printing. It was also in South Africa that Gandhi arrived at his basic technique of soul-force or *satyagraha*, which, to put it simply, tried to win over an opponent without violence but rather by sympathy, patience, and self-suffering. Nonviolence, or *ahimsa*, and self-restraint were the basic weapons used by Gandhi who declared that "I cultivate the quiet courage of dying without killing." He was soon called upon to prove his ideas in a series of strikes and civil disobedience campaigns in which he was personally attacked and badly beaten by a mob in Durban. But Gandhi welcomed arrest, embraced prison, and glorified in his martyrdom; it was here that he gained the title of Mahatma, or great soul.

He had found his way and his technique of passive resistance. Gandhi had arrived at his own formula of success, that of fusing politics with religion. Above all, Gandhi was a religious genius, who believed that every kind of human activity derived from religious motives and that no sanctions were valid except those of religion. Gandhi's great strength was that he applied his ethical beliefs to practical humanitarian problems, such as those of the Indian indentured laborers abroad, of the untouchables in India, and finally to the political problem of Indian independence.

Gandhi, expressing himself simply, sincerely, with personal charm and as a master of prose, provided a channel for action in keeping with the traditional Hindu ideal of nonviolence.

After his initial work in South Africa on behalf of the indentured Indian laborers and after volunteering his services as an ambulance driver for the British during the Boer war, he returned to India. When World War I broke out in 1914 Gandhi was in London where he again offered his services as an ambulance driver, but ill health forced him to return once more to India. There, remaining loyal to the British cause, he went on a series of recruiting tours for the British army.

Passive Resistance and Western Nationalism

Gandhi's loyalty to the British cause soon, however, received a severe shock, first by the English government's attempt to perpetuate the hated Rowlatt Act, and then by the violent riots which began in March in Delhi and were climaxed by the Amritsar Massacre. Horrified by this free shedding of blood Gandhi protested and appealed to all Indians to begin satyagraha or a passive resistance campaign against the British, by ceasing work, closing shop, and by spending time instead in prayer. From this moment on Gandhi had ceased to be the cooperator and loyal supporter of the British regime, and he became instead the most remarkable enemy of British rule. His first move in 1920 was to make common cause with the Moslems by supporting the Moslem anti-British Khilafat movement, about which more later on in this chapter. During the same year he also successfully urged the boycott of the elections to the legislative councils, held under the new Government of India Act, and he then proceeded to launch a massive civil disobedience campaign which featured in addition to the technique of work stoppage, or hartal, refusal to pay taxes, the boycott of all foreign goods as symbols of Western materialism, the burning of foreign cloth, and the attempt to do away with the consumption of liquor, for which purpose an American prohibition leader named Pussyfoot Johnson was especially imported to India. The use of native Indian languages instead of English and the wearing of homespun cloth were other symbols of Gandhi's passive resistance movement.

The difficulty with this first Gandhian campaign of nonviolence was that it did not remain nonviolent. Soon there were new riots and renewed bloodshed. Gandhi himself called off this campaign of 1922 after some policemen were killed by a mob. Because of this violence Gandhi's prestige declined, and he was arrested, and after a dramatic trial in which he stated that it had been "a Himalayan blunder to believe that India had accepted nonviolence," he was jailed and spent the next few years in and out of prison, a rather monotonous existence punctuated by occasional fasts. It seemed, as of the year 1924, that the noncooperation program had failed, but this was merely an erroneous surface impression; in reality Gandhi succeeded in forging the chief weapon for India's nationalism, a practical tech-

FIGURE 19.1. Mohandas Gandhi.

nique of revolution which had transformed the Indian national political protest from middle-class agitation to a mass movement. As early as 1922 a shrewd eyewitness could state that:

> Gandhi has, I believe, done his work. He has made India self-conscious. He has given India a new sense of self-respect. His program had been characterized by many negative features. It has never put forward even a suggestive outline of the government it would substitute for the one it would tear down. But Gandhi has given a moral basis and a spiritual standing to India's revolution.[1]

There were many limitations to Gandhi's work. He was to contribute to Hindu-Moslem antagonism, for his stress on religion made him deeply suspect to the Moslems. He had no understanding of economics, and little love for the industrial revolution. He opposed railroads which he held were the cause for the spread of bubonic plague and caused increased famine, he considered all machinery a "great sin," and wanted to drive out most of the attributes of Western civilization in India as inherently evil, but when everything was said and done, despite the fact that his message was essentially one of the past denouncing all modern innovations, Gandhi proved to be a real genius. G. B. Shaw said of him that he was not a man, but a phenomenon.

[1] Gertrude Emerson, "Non-Violent Non-Cooperation in Asia," *Asia*, Vol. XXII (August 1922), p. 674.

Gandhi's program was simple enough. It called for the surrender by Indians of all British titles, the refusal to attend all government functions, the withdrawal of all students from schools and colleges, boycott of courts, refusal by Indians to serve in the British army, refusal to cooperate with the government in its new reforms, and refusal by Indian political leaders to stand for election. The growing effectiveness of this nonviolent resistance movement, and Gandhi's genius for popular presentation of his ideas caused Gandhi to become the unchallenged leader of Indian home rule. His personality proved to be one of magnetic attraction for all Hindus, as he combined in himself the universal and traditional veneration of a saint, who was guided in his work by an inner voice and spent one day each week in utter silence, with that of a superbly skilled politician. His trial and imprisonment by the British added to this the crown of martyrdom.

In essence, what Gandhi accomplished was to widen the appeal of the Indian National Congress to the peasant masses as well as to the middle classes, while he changed its tactics by introducing revolutionary methods. He won India's Hindus by assuming the attributes of a Hindu saint, while he kept hold of the intellectuals by talking and acting as a trained lawyer. Gandhi's services were of incalculable value because he transformed the Congress from a Western-style political body into a national cultural one embracing elements both from the East and the West, and because in the long run he thoroughly discredited the British occupation of India.

MOSLEM-HINDU DIVERGENCE

Gandhi's leadership may have given a moral basis and a spiritual standing to India's leadership, but it did not prevent a degeneration of relations between India's Hindus and Moslems. Nationalism after the First World War became an increasingly intransigent force, and it split India along religious lines.

As far as the Moslems were concerned Moslem national feeling in the immediate postwar years expressed itself in the Khilafat movement, the controversy over the fate of the caliphate. The last caliph had been, of course, the Turkish sultan who had brought his country into the war on the German side. After the Allies had defeated the Ottoman empire, occupied the city of Constantinople, and imposed the humiliating Treaty of Sèvres upon the Turks, thereby bringing them to a point lower than any since the beginnings of Ottoman power, a general cry of "Islam in danger" could be heard in all the Moslem cities of India. Sèvres, it was argued among the Islamic community, was far too severe, and it seemed to many Moslems as if Britain had joined a general conspiracy whose purpose was to abolish the caliphate and to dismember Moslem unity throughout the world. The Khilafat movement, intent on restoring to the Turkish sultan all his powers as spiritual leader of Islam, soon produced unrest and ferment. Some Moslem leaders actually preached mass exodus, away from the pollution of British rule, and in 1920 there took place a great mass migration of Indian Moslems to Afghanistan. It is estimated that some 18,000 Moslems reached Afghanistan before that country closed its borders to the stream of homeless refugees, many of whom perished en route. As mass emigration did not prove an effective release, Moslem nationalism turned increasingly against its Hindu enemies in India itself.

Communal riots and bloody clashes became increasingly more frequent in the 1920's. These began when the Moslems on the Malabar coast, the so-called Moplas in southwest India, attempted to forcibly convert local Hindus in that area. Serious bloodshed was the immediate result, and by 1927 relations between Hindus and Moslems had become exceedingly bitter, ending the temporary alliance between these two major segments of India's population which had existed since the days of World War I. In 1931, for instance, there took place a ferocious communal outbreak in the city of Kanpur in which some 300 persons were killed, many temples and mosques desecrated and destroyed, and whole quarters of the town pillaged and burnt. Hindu-Moslem antagonism was also present on the political scene, where elections to the provincial legislatures were often decided by voting on a straight Hindu versus a straight Moslem basis. The memory of the many victims of the riots and of the frequent disturbances further caused both sides to take an ever more militant stance, so that by the end of the twenties the Moslem League had been fully revived, and had begun to go its own way, standing for a dominion status for India and full autonomy in the provinces, while among the Hindus the militant Hindu society of the Mahasabha had begun to grow in numbers and in scope of action. During this period ever growing intransigence was the keyword for both Hindu and Moslem nationalism.

THE BRITISH SEEK STABILITY

In 1921 a new Indian legislature came into being, under the terms of the Government of India Act of 1919, despite the opposition and boycott by the Indian nationalists led by Gandhi. In the next elections, those of 1923, a number of Indian nationalists did decide to participate, partially because under the guidance of Pandit Motilal Nehru there had been some reaction among their ranks against the leadership of Gandhi who refused to participate in any elections whatsoever. The Indian National Congress, with no difficulty, obtained the majority of the elected seats, but, though they had participated in the elections with the announced aim to "wreck reform from within," once in power their policies were not purely obstructionist. Many members took their duties seriously in order to prove that India was ready for fuller autonomy, and their success in participating in government could be, and was, interpreted as a partial repudiation of Gandhi's leadership and the failure and disintegration of his noncooperation movement.

Simon Commission

The act of 1919 contained the provision that after ten years a parliamentary commission was to be appointed to investigate the workings of the new system and to make new recommendations for changes which might be deemed necessary. The Conservative party in Britain, then in power, announced in 1927 that such a commission was to be formed, headed by a Liberal, Sir John Simon, and composed of seven members, and it was to report whether India was to receive more extensive rights of self-government. The announcement of the Simon Commission evoked at once considerable resentment in India, since the fact that the Commission included not a single Indian was interpreted as a deliberate insult to the Indian people.

Added to the blunder of appointing an all-English commission were the policies of the British governments of South Africa and Kenya, which discriminated sharply against Indians by forcible segregation in towns and by the prohibition of landholding by Indians in the salubrious highlands; thus Indian bitterness soon reached a new pitch. At a meeting of the Indian National Congress in 1925 one delegate made a speech to the effect that "if we had some battleships today, if we had our army, a little handful of these so-called whites who were vomited forth on the shores of Africa from the slums of Europe would not have dared to do what they are doing today." These were harsh words, but they were as nothing compared to the scathing denunciations showered upon the book *Mother India*, written by an American woman and scornfully indicting the traditions of Hinduism. Many Indians felt that it was the British who stood behind this vivid attack against much that was considered traditional and good in Indian life and society.

The result of all this resentment was that both the Indian National Congress and the various provincial legislative assemblies passed resolutions affirming once more noncooperation with the British, in other words returning, among scenes of violent demonstrations, to Gandhi's leadership and policy. In the meantime, however, even prior to the release of the report of the Simon Commission, the Laborite viceroy Lord Irwin (later better

FIGURE 19.2. British district magistrate talking to villagers, near Faizabad, United Provinces, 1926.

known as Lord Halifax, a change of title presumably made in order to confuse history students) had made an important declaration in India, to the effect that the natural issue of the constitutional progress in India was to be dominion status. Lord Irwin's declaration was the result of the policies of the British Labor party which had come to power in Britain in 1929 under Ramsay MacDonald, a party far more sympathetic to Indian nationalist aspirations than had been the Conservatives. This caused a sharp flare-up of debate in Parliament where the Conservative party, led by Stanley Baldwin and others attacked the concept of dominion status for India. Baldwin made a speech, "wrapped around ponderous rhetoric, full of simple thoughts, and resounding generalities," in which he bitterly assailed Labor policy, but by this time the demand for dominion status within India had of course been greatly strengthened. By 1928 both the Moslem League and the Congress passed resolutions demanding just that, having been greatly encouraged by these events. The Calcutta Congress of December 1928 adopted a so-called Nehru report demanding Dominion status within a year. However, the British government decided to wait for the report of the Simon Commission, which was to be followed by a series of round table conferences in London which were to decide what changes should be recommended to Parliament.

In view of this British delay Gandhi issued an ultimatum to the viceroy, in the form of a letter addressed to "my dear friend," in which he insisted that unless national independence was forthcoming at once civil disobedience would be resorted to again. In March of that year Gandhi organized his famous March to the Sea in order to make his own salt in defiance of the salt tax, a shrewd move indeed as there existed a universal dislike against this measure among India's millions. He was then promptly arrested, together with some 40,000 to 60,000 followers. Gandhi and his adherents, were held in prison without trial, but he had made his point and had become again the unchallenged leader among India's nationalists.

During this turmoil the report of the Simon Commission was finally released. As a document it was rather dry and pale, reflecting accurately the ultracautious and conservative views of the British government. Specifically, the report recommended the abolition of dyarchy in the provinces, and instead the introduction of full responsible government at the provincial level, but there were to be no substantial changes in the center, and, of course, no mention was made of either home rule or of dominion status. The report also advocated the introduction of a federal system at the center, which would be composed of a central government whose representatives were to be chosen by the provincial legislatures, but the governor-general (a change in title from viceroy) would still possess the so-called "reserved" powers in the field of defense and internal peace with which he could rule by ordinance and do as he pleased. In addition, in view of the continuing hostilities between Hindus and Moslems, the Simon Commission report also asked that communal representation be continued, and it made the further point that Burma should be separated from India and governed independently.

The reception of the Simon Commission report in India, as one might have expected, was overwhelmingly negative. The Indian press rejected it, as all liberal thinkers were generally disappointed since no definite recommendation for a dominion status for India was included, and the Indian princes also made it clear that they did not approve since the report did not include the native states at all, and had made no provision for their future. In this general atmosphere of disapproval and opposition in 1931 there began in London a series of round table conferences, three of them in two years, at which representatives of the British government, of India, and of the princely states met to discuss what further progress should be made. Gandhi himself, after considerable hesitation, decided to attend the second of these conferences, dropping civil disobedience for the time being, and he appeared in London as the sole representative of the Congress. Accompanying him was Muhammad Ali Jinnah, a Moslem lawyer, born in Bombay, and trained in England in the legal profession, who represented the views of the Moslem League at the London sessions.

The second round table conference in London was to be, just as the first, a failure. Gandhi stated the demands of the Congress, and in particular opposed the idea of separate electorates for minorities in India who felt themselves threatened by communal discord, demands unacceptable to the British; on the other hand the British would not commit themselves to dominion status as the logical future goal of Indian political evolution. Gandhi returned to Bombay at the end of the conference and launched a new civil disobedience campaign upon his arrival, but the British government acted swiftly, arrested and jailed him in 1932, and proceeded also to outlaw the Congress. In return Gandhi decided that he would fast to death before he would accept communal representation. Congress now demanded that India be given complete independence, and it and the Moslem League both voted to boycott further sessions of the round table conference in London. On the other side, British public opinion hardened also, and British Conservative opposition toward the Indian nationalists was tersely expressed in Winston Churchill's comment that Gandhi was nothing but "a half-naked fakir."

The Constitution of 1935

The British government in London proceeded with the working out of a constitution based upon the recommendations of the Simon report, and it laid such a draft constitution before Parliament in 1933 in the form of a White Paper. There then ensued a period of much wrangling and bitter disputes about the constitution, so that it was not until 1935 that it became law, having the distinction, unenviable no doubt of having been a bill before Parliament which was debated longer than any other in British history.

The Constitution for India of 1935 was a compromise, since it had been opposed both by the Conservative party in England and by Indian political leaders. It created a federal union embracing both the existing provinces of British India and the territories of the princes. The federal union was to be headed by a governor-general, appointed by the British, who

FIGURE 19.3. Parliament House, New Delhi.

was to be assisted by a bicameral legislature. Dyarchy was to be introduced at the center as well, creating at least responsible government in parts, and the right of suffrage was extended from some seven million Indians to some 35 million. In addition the Constitution of 1935 included provisions for communal representation for several minority groups.

The Constitution of 1935 did represent an advance, as it provided for provincial autonomy, responsible government in parts at the center, and a better working administration by separating Burma, but it fell short of the demands of Indian nationalists: full dominion status. The governor-general, in particular, still had many powers reserved to him, as so-called emergency powers, these being, of course, the most important powers of defense and external affairs. The reception of the Constitution in India caused a split among the Indian Congress; Gandhi, who had withdrawn into private life since the collapse of his second disobedience campaign, preferred to accept what Britain offered, while the more radical and liberal elements of the Indian National Congress, now led by Jawaharlal Nehru, denounced the offer and continued to insist on full dominion status for India, as they feared the possible alliance of the British with the conservative Indian princes. Many of the great princes of India were also unhappy with the document, since they worried lest their privileges would be greatly curtailed by it, and they too rejected it.

Jawaharlal Nehru

Nevertheless, when provincial elections were held in 1937 on the new basis of the Constitution of 1935 both the Congress and the League participated.

The result of these elections was a sweeping victory for the Congress party which won some 70 per cent of the seats, and was able to install Congress ministries in seven of eleven provinces. This did not indicate, however, that there was unanimity among the leaders of the Indian National Congress. Rather, a split occurred wherein Gandhi led the moderate segment inclined to accept compromises from the British government and Jawaharlal Nehru, the son of the famous Congressman Motilal Nehru, led those sections of the Congress which were more radical in their demands and who denounced the Constitution of 1935 as "a new charter for slavery." The young Nehru had been born in 1889 in Allahabad into a wealthy Brahman family which had originally lived in Kashmir. His father had been not only a leader of the National Congress, but also a very wealthy lawyer, and the young Nehru was sent to England, to study law and to follow in the footsteps of his parent. His education there was received at Harrow and at Trinity College in Cambridge University, and Jawaharlal Nehru soon turned out to be not only an extremely able and highly intelligent young man, but also an individual sensitive to the needs of, and interested in helping the masses. As a rationalist Nehru was increasingly drawn towards the doctrines of socialism, as well as those of nationalism, so that his subsequent political views not only embodied the ideal of early independence for his country, but also support of socialist economic thought. Nehru wrote an excellent autobiography in which he described his political views and career. In early youth he had been fascinated by Garibaldi's deeds in Italy and by the victory of Japan over Russia. A forceful, eloquent, yet fastidious and scintillating young man, he, unlike Gandhi, lacked religious belief, but was nevertheless powerfully attracted by Gandhi's personality. Ever since the days of the riots produced by the Rowlatt Acts he implicitly believed in and revered Gandhi, although Nehru was at the same time much impressed by the economic achievement of the communists in the Soviet Union. As a lawyer and an active leader of the Indian National Congress he was of course highly suspect to the British authorities, who jailed him nine times during his political career. In 1936 Nehru became president of the Indian National Congress.

Congress and the League

As a whole the Indian National Congress, now led by Nehru, did cooperate more or less with the British until the advent of World War II. The Congress party, as we have seen, participated in provincial elections, and on that level it made self-government a real success. But there were still many divisions among the members of the Congress itself, and the relations between the princes of India and the Congress also left much to be desired. Nehru opposed the princely states as "sinks of reaction and incompetence," while most of the princes feared and resented the Indian National Congress. Further, there were other factions within the Congress, such as those led by Subhas Chandra Bose, who charged that Congress as a whole was far too conservative and that Gandhi was but a mystic. Bose, an uncompromising nationalist with pronounced fascist leanings, was forced to resign from the

Congress in 1939, and he was arrested by the British in July, 1940, but escaped to lead anti-British forces in Southeast Asia. These splits were serious enough, but what was really fatal to Indian national unity was the continually widening breach between Moslems and Hindus, and the steadily worsening relations between Congress and the Moslem League between 1937 and 1939. Much of this was due to increased acrimony produced by serious communal outbreaks, such as the one already mentioned in Kanpur which took the lives of some 400 people amidst scenes of terrible atrocities. That fatal gulf was now more than ever visible in the provincial governments where it was often a clear case of the Congress party voting as a solid bloc against the Moslems and vice versa.

The Moslem community in India began to benefit also from the new leadership given to it by Muhammad Ali Jinnah, who in December, 1938, feeling the upsurge of Moslem strength behind him, first began to raise the idea of a completely separate and autonomous Moslem state, "Pakistan" or the "land of the pure." In an interview given to a French journalist Jinnah argued this view as the inevitable outcome of an old tradition:

> How can you even dream of Moslem-Hindu unity? Everything pulls us apart. We have no intermarriages. We have not the same calendar. The Moslems believe in a single God, and the Hindus are idolatrous. Like the Christians, the Moslems believe in an equalitarian society, whereas the Hindus maintain the iniquitous system of castes and leave heartlessly 50 million untouchables to their tragic fate at the bottom of the social ladder. Now again, the Hindus worship animals. They consider cows sacred. We, the Moslems, think it nonsense. We want to kill the cows. We want to eat them. Another thing: no Hindu will take food from a Moslem. No orthodox Hindu will even touch Hindu food if the shadow of a Moslem or the shadow of a Hindu of a lower caste pollutes his food.[2]

MODERNIZATION

Finally, a few words must be added here about the increasing westernization and modernization which India experienced after the First World War. In the economic sphere this meant increasing industrialization, with special emphasis upon steel and textile production, but also the appearance of some new consumer industries such as sugar, matches, cigarettes, glass, cement, and chemical products. The economic pace of the twentieth century was also reflected in more efficient communications for the country, especially in the construction of new seaports, the establishment of airlines, and the nationalization of India's railroad trunk lines, while the coming of motorbuses, which soon became the most popular means of transportation, gave an unheard of increase in mobility to the rural population. Indian investments in Indian trade and industry grew and there was also a greater amount of coordination in banking affairs. Modernization of India's economy also

---

[2] Quoted in Eve Curie, *Journey Among Warriors* (New York: Doubleday, Doran, 1943), p. 462.

brought about the end of excise duties. The shaping of an Indian tariff policy protected the new Indian industries, while at the same time there also arose a trade union movement among India's industrial workers using the strike as a weapon. Gandhi himself had led a strike in Ahmadabad in 1917. Even so, despite increasing industrialization and urbanization, India's population showed no sign whatever of decreasing; rather, the population increased at a dizzying rate, some forty million in the first forty years of the twentieth century.

It is important to keep in mind that one out of every six Indians by the 1960s lived in a city, and that it is these cities of modern India which have been the focal points of political and economic change. Urbanization is of the greatest importance in terms of the important events that have taken place in India. It was in the large urban centers, such as Bombay, Madras, and Calcutta, good seaports all with important rail connections, or in Delhi, a city of political importance, that nationalism flourished, commerce and factories multiplied, and educational facilities served as centers for the diffusion of new ideas leading to the demands for independence.

In agriculture this period showed marked improvements, primarily in the introduction of new methods and in the improvement of varieties of strains of agricultural products such as wheat, cotton, and sugar cane. Qualitative and quantitative improvement was accompanied by bringing new lands under cultivation by irrigation effected by the building of great new irrigation dams such as the famous Lloyd barrage on the Indus. Among the Indian peasants great changes could be observed in their mentality, largely due to motor transport and subsequent mobility, the influence of the cooperative movements in their lives, and the fact that many Indian peasants, particularly from the Punjab, had seen the standard of living of other peasants, such as the French, during their wartime service. Among the Indian intellectuals a growing appreciation of the needs of the peasantry meant that for the first time students paid serious attention to the study of economic questions and the problem of national poverty. Great efforts were made to begin a social service on the rural level and to combat illiteracy by the spread of primary education. By 1939 perhaps one out of every twenty men and women throughout the country had become literate. Upper class Indian women were becoming the freest and best educated among women anywhere in Asia.

On the other hand, there was also growing respect and appreciation for India among countries abroad. Indian art, science, and scholarship began to equal that of Europe and such vigorous intellectual leadership as that of the great poet Rabindranath Tagore won foreign recognition and acclaim, symbolized by his award of the Nobel Prize for literature.

INDIA AND WORLD WAR II

India in the War

On September 3, 1939, the Governor-General of India, Lord Linlithgow, proclaimed by decree that India had become a belligerent in World War II,

FIGURE 19.4. Scene from the Tata steel works in Jamshedpur, India's heavy industry center.

and thus put the country into the struggle against Nazi Germany and Fascist Italy, without having consulted the Indian National Congress as to its wishes in this regard. Thereupon the Congress party met, and voiced its disapproval of this act. Indian nationalist leaders did express their condemnation of fascism and Nazism, but declared that since war had been proclaimed without seeking and obtaining consent from the Indian people, Congress could not associate itself with the war effort unless India was pronounced an "independent nation." The Moslem League supported the British declaration that India was at war but only on condition that no constitutional changes were to be made during the period of belligerency without its consent and approval, though the Moslem leaders did affirm their loyalty and offered aid to the British as did the Indian princes. Thus World War II began for India with the political problem of independence still occupying its place as the foremost problem between the British and India.

In October, 1939 the British government made an offer to Indian nationalism by reiterating that dominion status was to be the ultimate fate of the country, and that after the war the Government Act of 1935 might be reconsidered, but the idea of immediate self-government was rejected in blunt words: "the situation must be faced in terms of world politics and of political realities in this country . . . progress must be conditioned by practical considerations . . . there is nothing to be gained by phrases which contemplate a state of things which is unlikely at the present point of political development to stand the test of practical application." Since nothing short of complete independence would satisfy the Indian National Congress, a hostile Congress party resigned its ministries in the provinces and boycotted the war effort to the end of the war.

On the other hand, the Moslems, too, by this time were determined, despite all disadvantages and all risks involved, to demand a separate Moslem state. By 1940 the Moslem League and its chief leader, Muhammad Ali Jinnah, declared that the overruling demand for India's Islamic community was the creation of a future Pakistan.

Jinnah, born in Karachi in 1876 into a prominent merchant family, had become a brilliant lawyer, who practiced in Bombay, and a politician at first willing to work with Congress. But he had changed his outlook in the late twenties. A handsome and elegant man, wearing a monocle and impeccably attired in Western clothes, with a keen and sensitive mind and possessing really incisive powers of logic, Jinnah feared that Moslem interests would be jeopardized by the advances of Hindu nationalism, and after he became president of the Moslem League in 1939 he seized almost dictatorial powers as the "Great Leader" of the Moslems of India. Jinnah argued that the Moslems in India were "a nation of a hundred million, and what is more, we are a nation with our distinct culture and civilization, language, literature, arts, and architecture . . . laws, and moral codes, customs and special aptitudes and ambitions. In short, we have our own distinctive outlook on life and of life." This view naturally greatly increased the already existing friction between Hindus and Moslems making the task of creating a unified India an insurmountable one.

With the outbreak of the war Indian troops served overseas, in Aden,

FIGURE 19.5. Muhammad Ali Jinnah.

Malaya, and the Middle East. In August, 1940 Britain's position became critical with the fall of the Low Countries and of France, and as a consequence of this debacle the British government in that month made yet another offer to India, through Amery, the Secretary of State for India, which promised that the constitutional progress of India would be determined not by the British Parliament, but rather, after the war, by an Indian body. This proposal was rejected by both the Congress and the Moslem League as too narrow, and offering no solution for India's immediate demands, and Congress, after stating a blunt no, once more fell back on a nonviolent civil disobedience campaign led by Gandhi. Its result was the imprisonment of the Mahatma by the British, as well as that of thousands of his followers, and the suppression of the movement.

In July of the next year, 1941, the British government again made a gesture to appease Indian nationalism when the viceroy enlarged the Executive Council so that Indians made up a majority, or some eight out of twelve. At the same time a National Defense Council was set up for India with only one European sitting on it, and the government also released a number of prisoners from jail who had been held for civil disobedience. But these were mere gestures, as the viceroy still maintained his veto right, and thus could overrule any decision of the Executive Council, and since, furthermore, the key portfolios of finance, defense, and the home department were in British hands on the Council. Finally, not a single member among the Indians serving on the Council belonged to either the Congress party or the Moslem League.

The Cripps Mission

When in December, 1941 Japan entered the war against Britain and the Western powers, the situation became most critical for the British in India. Malaya was quickly overrun by the Japanese, the great and supposedly impregnable naval fortress of Singapore fell, Burma was invaded, and Japanese forces landed on the Nicobar and Andaman Islands. Since the days of the Afghan raids, the threat of a foreign power to India had never been so great or so real as in the spring of 1942. Added to the Japanese menace was the presence of an "Indian National army," led by the ultranationalistic Bose in Singapore, who relied upon Japanese support, only too readily given, for an attack upon the British in India and the "liberation of India." In these desperate days, Winston Churchill sent to India in March, 1942 Sir Stafford Cripps, a cabinet member, distinguished lawyer, and statesman of liberal views, to present a "draft declaration" intended to gain the support of India's nationalists. Cripps' mission was "to rally all the forces of Indian life to guard their life from the menace of the invader." Sir Stafford spent three weeks in New Delhi, and had several long talks with Gandhi in which Cripps agreed to the creation of a new Indian union that was to constitute a dominion associated with the United Kingdom and the other dominions. However, and this was the critical clause on which all negotiations were wrecked, this was not to be done at once and immediately, but only after the war when an Indian body would be set up to determine India's final constitutional progress. Furthermore, Cripps included in his offer certain provisions which also were considered unacceptable by the Indian Congress. These concerned the right of any Indian province to join or not to join the new union (a measure designed to mollify Moslem separatism), a treaty to safeguard the obligations of the British government, and finally a clause which stated that Britain would be responsible for India's defense until the new constitution actually would be working in the postwar period.

These limitations of the "draft declaration" proved unacceptable to the Congress, whose leaders particularly feared that many provinces and princely states might not join the union at all. The princes, too, fearing for their rights, were not at all agreeable to the establishment of such a future Indian union, even though their states might have nominated, rather than elected members (another provision unacceptable to the Congress).

Finally, the Moslem League also rejected the declaration, as they feared Hindu domination in the future Indian union, and as the League had come out for nothing short of a separate nation, Pakistan. Even the depressed classes looked with the greatest suspicion towards the realization of an Indian union in which they might be oppressed by the higher caste Hindus. The draft declaration also suffered unfortunate timing, as it came at a moment when British prestige was at a very low ebb indeed, and Indian nationalists felt they could well be recalcitrant and hold out for more. In view of this complex and complicated situation the negotiations between Cripps and India's leaders broke down, stalemate ensued, and Sir Stafford returned to London declaring that the "Congress wanted all or nothing."

The result of the Cripps negotiations was most unfortunate, since, instead of bridging the gulf between the British government and the Indian political parties, it only served to widen it. The manner in which the negotiations broke down strengthened the doubts and suspicions in the minds of Indian political leaders whether there really existed a genuine desire on the part of the British to part with power. In consequence Gandhi decided to resume once again his cherished civil disobedience campaign (in which he stressed the concept of nonviolence), and Congress passed a "quit India" motion advocating the immediate end of British rule and refusing to put Indians in the war on the side of the Western powers. Gandhi had implicit trust in his method. If it worked against the British and would oust them, the same policy could also be invoked against the Japanese in case they conquered the country. As he put it: "Leave India in God's hands." "Then all parties will fight one another like dogs, or will, when real responsibility faces them, come to a reasonable agreement."

There then set in a new period of acute political anxiety and frequent disturbances. All leaders of the Congress, including Gandhi and Nehru, were arrested and kept in prison, and there were widespread disorders throughout the country, in which some 750 persons were killed, telegraph lines cut, and railroad lines torn up. But all of these were suppressed by British troops, and the country fell back into a state of uneasy truce between the government and Indian nationalist aspirations.

Impact of the War

At the same time India did make an enormous contribution to the war, in terms both of manpower and of supplies. Close to two million Indians from all classes and areas served in the now separate Indian army, Indian navy, and Indian air force, commanded by Indian commissioned officers. These soldiers, sailors, and airmen were drawn not only from the traditional military groups, but from all kinds of possible backgrounds and they lived and fought together in mixed regiments. In the Indian navy, for instance, caste rules were abandoned and everyone ate the same food. Indian troops served in the east, in Hong Kong, Malaya, and Singapore, where most of them became prisoners of war of the Japanese, and also on the difficult retreat from Burma. In the west, Indian troops saw action in Iran, Iraq, Syria, and in Africa from Somaliland to Tunisia. With the fortunes of war leaning toward the Allied side, Indian forces later on participated in the reconquest of Burma in 1944 where they were active also in the building of the Ledo Road, and they were also used in the Allied conquest of Italy and the penetration of Hitler's "fortress Europe." In addition to India's contribution to manpower the country also served as a major supply base for the British empire. Indian war industries were built up, and such articles as ordnance, explosives, small arms, medical supplies, uniforms, blankets, and boots were mass produced and distributed by the Eastern Group Supply Council with headquarters at Delhi. Finally, India also made large loans to England, so that at the end of the war India had accumulated vast credits abroad, and Britain owed India a large debt in pounds sterling.

With the war years there occurred also great economic changes, the majority of which were detrimental to India's economic life. Spurting inflation, the result of huge wartime profits and insufficient imports from abroad, characterized the economic picture of the war period, and this was topped off by severe food shortages which culminated in the great Bengal famine of 1943. This stark and horrible tragedy was the result of an initial shortage of rice due to a poor crop, coupled with the cutting off of imports from Burma and belated and inefficient administrative measures. Thousands died in the streets of Calcutta alone, and a traveler arriving at one of the great Calcutta railroad stations literally had to watch where he alighted from his carriage so as not to step on the corpse of some famine victim. A total of one and a half million persons perished in this catastrophe, while by hoarding, merchants reaped huge profits, estimated at some 1,000 rupees per death. The basic cause of the famine, though, went deeper than just the fact of war; it was connected with the continuing tremendous increase of population in India, which had resulted in a 47 per cent increase between 1920 and 1947, and which once again posed the supreme problem of subsistence for the masses.

On the political scene, after the failure of the Cripps mission, there was a continued deadlock. In 1944 Gandhi and Jinnah met for some prolonged conversations, but they too were unsuccessful in view of the fact that Jinnah was determined and adamant in his demand for Pakistan. During that year, too, the British reiterated the Cripps offer with the proviso that the Indians themselves were to work out details contained in it. This took place at the Simla Conference, where the viceroy, as another concession, also made his executive council an all-Indian one, but here too failure accompanied the government's efforts. There was no agreement between British and Indian leaders, as there was no agreement between the Moslems and the Congress.

At the end of the Second World War in 1945 renewed attempts were made to find a permanent and lasting solution of India's constitutional problem, a solution which was to be favorable to Indian aspirations. In July, 1945 a new Labor government came to power in Great Britain, under Clement Attlee. Unlike Churchill, who was not willing to preside at the dissolution of the empire, Attlee's government went on record that it stood for the promotion of self-government, and that it would shortly transfer all power to India, whether to one or more governments. By the end of the war it had become obvious to the English that Britain was no longer in any position to hold India by force, and furthermore, that to most Englishmen India had become a burden rather than an asset. This was emphasized by the stopping of recruitment for the Indian Civil Service in England since 1939. By 1945 general interest in Indian affairs had dwindled so that India was no longer an issue of paramount interest to the English public. At the same time Britain's inability to hold on was also demonstrated by the general anti-Western sentiment displayed in India in 1946, when there occurred riots and attacks against Europeans, particularly in Calcutta. In January of that year a segment of the Royal Indian Air Force refused to obey orders, and in February some ships of the Royal Indian Navy also mutinied. Sailors in Bombay went on a hunger strike, seized ships and guns in the harbor, and there were riots and looting in the city itself.

The Partition of India

By 1945 India had won her promise of victory; she was to be independent. But victory was dearly bought, since the conflict between the Moslem League and the National Congress had not been healed; and since the Moslems demanded the partition of India and the creation of a separate state of Pakistan, the subcontinent now faced the prospect of disunion.

Britain no longer had either the power or the will to rule India; intransigent nationalism, exhaustion due to war, and the weariness of carrying the imperial burden had seen to that. Consequently there was no longer any question of a struggle to wrest power from the British; rather, the dispute among the nationalists in India was as to how that power should be shared by all parties concerned. The British government itself wanted to keep India united, and it proposed a cabinet plan, under which the union would be preserved, and in which the Moslems would be given wide ranging autonomy in such a way that Moslem majority provinces would be formed which would group themselves together. But these attempts to preserve unity accomplished nothing, since the Moslems were adamant in their rejection. There was a genuine fear among them that their community might not be able to maintain itself against Hindu domination, and they feared that their faith might perish, and their descendents be governed economically and socially by a "brute Hindu majority." Jinnah in particular ruled out any move in this direction, and he proclaimed time and time again that the unity of India was nothing but a myth, since in India there were two totally different and deeply rooted civilizations, and since the only possible solution was not the possibility of separate grouping, but rather total division of India.

Nehru contributed to the tenseness of the situation by making intemperate remarks in some speeches he gave, and by August, 1946 communal violence in all its horror again stalked Indian cities and the countryside. In Calcutta occurred the worst riots yet, the so-called "Great Calcutta killing," an orgy of destruction which cost some 4,700 lives and injured another 15,000, while some 150,000 refugees fled to the countryside where they spread the germ of internecine violence. This was the direct result of Jinnah's public proclamation of the end of constitutional methods and his "direct action" day. Jinnah then made the statement that civil war was inevitable unless Pakistan was granted, and when Nehru in September, 1946 formed an interim government the Moslems refused to join. Violence continued unabated in Bengal, Bihar, Assam, and the Punjab, where riots between Sikhs and Moslems took on the character of full-scale battles, and the danger of civil war had become a mounting horror.

In view of this steadily growing danger the British Labor government in February, 1947 made the bold announcement that Britain was determined to pull out of India not later than June, 1948. In March Prime Minister Attlee sent Lord Mountbatten to India as last British viceroy, with the task of handing over power to either one united or two separate dominions, as the case might be.

By June a partition plan had been worked out, under guidance of Mountbatten and some very capable aides (not an easy task, considering the problems of dividing assets, currency, the army, and drawing two boundaries), and by July, 1947 the Indian Independence bill passed Parliament. On August 15, 1947, India gained her independence, when on that day Nehru became prime minister in India and Liaquat Ali Khan became premier of Pakistan (with Jinnah as governor-general). In that month Indian independence began, but Indian unity ended.

Indian independence marked the end of an epoch of British political rule, thereby diminishing British world power and bringing to a conclusion the status of India as the world's largest colony. For 182 years, since 1765, the year when the East Indian Company had taken over the collection of revenues in Bengal, Britain had gradually built up her economic and political domination of the subcontinent. During that period England had consolidated and unified the country, had created an efficient administrative organization, and also had introduced the rule of law. When Britain ended her rule in 1947 and transferred power on a dominion basis to India and Pakistan, she left behind her, undoubtedly as her greatest contribution, the traditions of a parliamentary democracy. But she could not prevent partition which was the direct result of communalism, begun in the nineteenth century, recognized when the principle of communal representation had been included in the Morley-Minto reforms, and intensified in the succeeding years by the growth of Moslem and Hindu nationalism.

BASIC DATES

1918	Montagu-Chelmsford discussions
1919	Government of India Act
1919	Amritsar Massacre
1919–1922	Mohandas Gandhi leads anti-British movement
1923–1930	Cooperation of moderate nationalists
1927	Simon Commission
1928	Nehru Report
1930–1931	London round table conferences
1935	Constitution for India
1936	Jawaharlal Nehru president of Congress
1938	Agitation for Pakistan
1939–1945	World War II
1940	Civil Disobedience; Moslem declaration for Pakistan
1942	Japanese reach Indian border; Cripps offer; Congress leaders jailed.
1945	British Labor party victory
1946	Cabinet Mission plan; Nehru heads interim government
1947	Mountbatten proposes partition plan; Indian independence

SUPPLEMENTARY READING

Gandhi, M. *Autobiography.* Washington, D.C., 1948.
Moreland, W. H. and A. C. Chatterjee. *A Short History of India,* 3rd ed. London, 1953.
Nehru, J. *Toward Freedom: The Autobiography of Jawaharlal Nehru.* New York, 1941.
Philips, C. *The Partition of India: Policies and Perspectives.* London, 1970.

ADVANCED READING

Ahmad, A. *Islamic Modernism in India and Pakistan, 1857–1964.* London, 1967.
Aziz, K. *Britain and Muslim India.* London, 1963.
Bose, S. C. *The Indian Struggle, 1920–1942.* New York, 1964.
Broomfield, J. C. *Elite Conflict in Rural Society, Twentieth Century Bengal.* Berkeley, 1968.
Cohn, B. S. *India: Social Anthropology of a Civilization.* Englewood Cliffs, N.J., 1971.
De Bary, W. T., ed. *Sources of Indian Tradition.* New York, 1958.

Erikson, E. *Gandhi's Truth on the Origins of Militant Non-violence.* New York, 1969.
Hay, S. *Asian Ideas of East and West: Tagore and His Critics.* Cambridge, Mass., 1970.
Hutchins, F. G. *The Illusion of Permanence: British Imperialism in India.* Princeton, N.J., 1967.
Irschick, E. *Politics and Conflict in Southern India.* Chicago, 1964.
Kanshick, P. D. *The Congress: Ideology and Programme, 1920–1947.* New York, 1964.
Nanda, B. R. *Mahatma Gandhi, A Biography.* New York, 1965.
Singh, H. *The Heritage of the Sikhs.* London, 1965.
Spear, P. *India: A Modern History.* Ann Arbor, Mich., 1972.
——— *India, Pakistan and the West,* 4th ed. Oxford, 1967.
Tagore, R. *Collected Poems and Plays.* London, 1956.

Chapter 20

Southeast Asia: Colonies and New Nations, 1914-1946

COMMON CHARACTERISTICS OF MODERN SOUTHEAST ASIA

Until the First World War Southeast Asia had been part of a colonial world, a rather quiet corner of the globe with a high degree of security and political stability guaranteed by the great Western powers. This was a world in which there seemed to be discernible few new factors of far reaching significance. However, the quiet in this area was but the prelude to a period of revolution, or rather a series of revolutions. These revolutions were directed against foreign political control and against colonialism and imperialism, but they were also economic and social revolutions designed to gain freedom from poverty and economic insecurity. This period ended in the years after World War II with the rule of the Western powers over Southeast Asia mostly terminated, but with a host of political, social and economic problems still unanswered.

Southeast Asia is a vast region including Thailand, the Philippines, Indonesia, Indochina, Burma, and Malaya, and it encompasses a great diversity of peoples, customs, languages, and religions, yet in the most recent history of Southeast Asia this region did undergo the same common experiences of turbulence and of possessing to a certain degree the same common characteristics of belonging to a colonial world, politically, economically, and socially. Politically speaking, Southeast Asia was controlled by foreign, Western powers (and this is true even of Thailand to a point), who permitted various degrees of self-expression to their peoples, ranging in freedom from the Philippines to French Indochina. Economically, too, Southeast Asia as a whole shared the experience of being an area where native labor was utilized to produce export raw materials, such as oil, rubber, rice, coffee, tea, sugar, and minerals. It was an economic entity no longer self-sufficient but rather dependent on world markets. The bulk of income went to the government or to the landlords, and free economic development did not bring about a general increase in the social welfare or prosperity of the peasant cultivator. Dependence upon world market conditions also meant the sharing of prosperity before 1930, and of deep depression after that year. Southeast Asia had another facet in common. Its society was a plural one in which the white man was at the top, exercising political control and furnishing capital for investment, and the native peasant population was at the bottom of the social pyramid. Between the two extremes there had come into being an alien middle class, composed of foreigners, either Chinese or Indian, which controlled retail business, trading, and money lending, contributing thereby to social disintegration, lack of cohesion, and divisions which were accentuated and complicated by racial differences. Finally, there was yet another common factor, a new force—nationalism, the most dynamic of all of Europe's exports, which all these countries of a colonial world shared.

By definition the term nationalism describes that force which unites a people of common tradition, language, religion, history, and culture in its endeavor to overthrow foreign rule and to realize an independent state. The idea of nationalism is a product of the Western mind, particularly of the French Revolution and its aftermath, and in Southeast Asia it first made its appearance among a small group of Western-educated natives who were eager to introduce new ways of thinking and new techniques to their countries. The spirit of nationalism was revolutionary, inasmuch as it was directed towards the overthrow of foreign rule and the end of colonialism, but it also was revolutionary because it was directed just as much against the traditions and the past of each native society. The spirit of nationalism grew quickly with the rapid spread of literacy, the development of the press, and the establishment of education, but at first it only belonged to a small minority of people whose ultimate goal was unqualified national independence.

In the history of the development of nationalism in twentieth-century Southeast Asia one may discern three major milestones. In 1905 Japan's victory over Russia made a tremendous impression. Japan's signal and unexpected victory contributed greatly to the growth of national consciousness throughout Asia, since the Japanese had shown the world that an Asian people were perfectly capable of learning, and even improving upon, the techniques of the West. Next came the First World War which to many had the character of a fight for the principle of self-determination. The victory of the Allies in that colossal struggle was represented as the vindication of the rights of the small nations, and Wilson's Fourteen Points added a great stimulus to the concepts of self-rule and self-determination. By this time, too, Southeast Asia had become fully aware of the example of India's demands for *swaraj*, or self-rule. After 1918 the ideological climate, as well as the personnel of the anticolonial movements, began to change as the result of the increasing impact of foreign ideas and the growing numbers of individuals who became susceptible to them, what with the growth of education in the various Southeast Asian countries themselves, and the opportunities of education abroad which also were on the increase. The development of urbanized intellectual elites greatly facilitated the spread of radical nationalism.

Finally came World War II which changed the entire picture in Southeast Asia, and in which Asia witnessed the almost incredibly rapid and overwhelming defeat of European forces. It smashed the myth of an invulnerable West, reduced its prestige, and impaired its ability to reestablish the old order. Japan's overrunning of French Indochina, Siam, Malaya, the Netherlands East Indies, Burma, the Philippines, and most of New Guinea by 1942 was the final stimulus to Southeast Asian nationalism. Japan not only promoted nationalism in Southeast Asia by her slogan of "Asia for the Asiatics," by the promotion of native independence movements, and by her military successes against the Western powers, but she also created conditions which made national independence possible and which gave Southeast Asia the opportunity to terminate Western overlordship after the end of the war. So great was the effect of the Japanese occupation of Southeast Asia in strengthening nationalism and anticolonialism that when Japanese control came to end in 1945, everywhere the returning Europeans were opposed by revolutionary nationalism in a great variety of forms. The colonial powers had made no formal commitments to their charges during the war, as they all believed that their subjects preferred their rule to that of the Japanese, but the end of the war brought them face to face with utterly unexpected and unforeseen situations.

Actually, it had been Western rule itself which created the revolution in Southeast Asia which now faced the Western colonial powers. It had done so by introducing powerful new economic and political forces and concepts, of which the most powerful was nationalism. Nationalism frequently lacks logic and is often emotional, branding as enemies and obstructionists all those who preach caution and point to the many difficulties on the road to full independence, and some nationalist leaders did not hesitate to listen to the appeal of communism as a force which might more quickly help in realizing its cherished aims. A good example of a typical career of a nationalist in Southeast Asia who did not hesitate to make alliances with all sides, was that of the leader of Indonesia, Akmet Sukarno. What kind of political support he gained and where it came from mattered little as long as it aided him in the fulfillment of his ideas. Sukarno was a Dutch-trained engineer who early in his student days away from his native Indonesia first came under the influence of Western liberalism and Gandhian nonviolence. He then turned to Marxism in the 1920's, when he had returned to Java. An excellent orator, he was able to form in 1927 the Nationalist party of Indonesia. The Dutch interned him, first in Flores and then on Sumatra where he remained a prisoner until the arrival of the Japanese. With Indonesia in Japanese hands Sukarno next collaborated with them, which enabled him to establish an independent government at the end of World War II. In the turbulent postwar years Sukarno did not hesitate to make use of communist support, or, for that matter, turn against the communists, if he could achieve what he desired, realization of nationalist goals. Nationalism more than any force explains the history of the individual countries of Southeast Asia during the period from 1914 to the present.

THAILAND (SIAM)

Foreign Relations

This country of some sixteen million people, slightly smaller than Texas, whose economy is virtually based upon the production of rice, was the only one in the colonial world of Southeast Asia to survive as an independent nation. Siam succeeded in remaining independent largely because she was a buffer state between the British and the French, and partially, too, because of her successful "diplomacy of survival" which began in the mid-nineteenth century under Rama IV who started the country on the road to westernization. In this process Siam began to develop a degree of national awareness, and although she developed no antagonism against any external power, her embryonic nationalism began to turn inward against the economic domination of the Chinese middle-class community and the political absolutism of the Siamese monarchy.

As described in Chapter 8, Siam was fortunate in possessing a series of very able kings who continued the policies of westernization begun in the mid-nineteenth century and played a careful game of balance between her two dangerous neighbors, France and Great Britain. Although the kingdom had to suffer losses, Siam by 1896 was guaranteed her independence in a treaty by the French and the British, and she began to make some gains against imperialist encroachments. The Siamese had clearly recognized that Britain was the most powerful state, and consequently Siamese life at the end of the nineteenth century was modeled on the British pattern. Her pro-British alignment paid off dividends when Siam ranged herself on the side of the Allies in World War I and thus obtained at Versailles the abrogation of the rights of Germany and Austria to special concessions and extraterritoriality in Siam. This was followed by a series of treaties between 1920 and 1926 in which the Western powers, too, relinquished their rights to extraterritoriality. The United States under Wilson signed a treaty in 1920, rapidly followed by similar treaties concluded with Japan (1924), France, Britain, and Holland (1925). The process of terminating all unequal treaties was completed in 1927 when Siam obtained tariff autonomy.

Absolutism

All this had occurred during the regime of an absolute monarchy, which remained strong regardless of the personal nature of the occupant of the throne. Although the Siamese king was aided by an executive and a legislative council, their membership was restricted to royal princes or nominated members of the aristocracy. Royal absolutism, the rule of a parasitic clique of nobles, and considerable corruption characterized the Siamese government. Rama VI Vajiravudh, who governed from 1910 to 1925, was a rather shy person who lacked the quality of leadership and who was interested in journalism, sports, and religion. He was educated at Cambridge, and personally translated Shakespeare into Siamese, while he also wrote journalistic articles and popularized Western literature. He promoted European games, football for example, while he also led the movement for a revival of Buddhism in the country, publishing a new edition of the *Tripitaka*, the sacred Buddhist scriptures. His government, purely personal and one in which the nobles had full charge, was continued by his brother who succeeded him in 1925. This was Rama VII Prajadhipok, the 76th child of his father, who ruled until 1935.

By this time, however, there had grown in Siam among a small group of Western-educated Siamese enough spirit of opposition to royal absolutism and the rule of a clique of nobles that they came to represent a party which stood for reform and a monarchy limited by a constitution. In June, 1932 a small group of this Western-trained intelligentsia, who wanted a share in power, executed a coup d'état. In this bloodless revolution they had the support of some army and navy officers, and they were entirely successful in obtaining control of the government. This group, which called itself the "People's party," was led by Pridi Bhanomyong, a brilliant young lawyer, who was influenced by left-wing economic theories, and by a number of military men of whom the most important in terms of future development was Pibul Songgram. This group obtained from the king the grant of a constitution and the right to an assembly, but it must not be thought that this represented a great democratic victory. After all, the Siamese masses had hardly any participation in these events, and the revolution of 1932 meant merely that a different group, a different oligarchy, exercised power in the kingdom.

Pibul Songgram

Rama VII, who had rather grudgingly conceded a constitution to his subjects, in vain tried to undo the work of the People's party, and when he failed, he abdicated in 1935. A regency was then established for his nephew, the new king of Siam, Ananda Mahidol, who was still being educated in Switzerland. However, by this time, the liberal and even radical elements of the People's party, represented by Pridi, were declining in power in favor of a more conservative military group led by Pibul Songgram. In 1938 Pibul executed yet another coup d'état by which he seized the government of Siam, eliminating the liberals, and establishing a benevolent military dictatorship with definite fascist and authoritarian tendencies. In a sense the rise to power of a military dictator and the repression of liberal opinion was due to the fact that Siam closely followed in the pattern of the nation which was the strongest power in Southeast Asia, and this, by the thirties, was Japan. By 1940 Japan had become the greatest power in the Far East, and Siam decided to follow in her footsteps and to make Japan the new model. This explains why the People's party came under the control of a military clique, and it also explains many of the policies of the government of Pibul Songgram, especially its strong nationalist tendencies.

As early as 1933 it had become obvious to the Siamese that Japan had replaced France as the second power in Southeast Asia, and in consequence of this awareness the Siamese did not vote against Japan in the League of Nations when the Manchurian incident demonstrated to the world Japan's prowess and aggressive policies. In 1938 the Siamese concluded a commercial treaty with Japan, and established close economic ties with that country. Japanese textiles were substituted for the products of British mills, and Japanese businessmen were encouraged in Siam at the expense of Chinese merchants. Two years later Siam and Japan signed a treaty of friendship.

In his internal policies Pibul Songgram closely modeled himself after the Japanese authoritarian example he had chosen to follow. This did not mean that westernization and reform had been abandoned. They continued in such fields as agriculture and education (public bathing and betel nut chewing were outlawed to symbolize continuing reform), but his policies were increasingly characterized by extreme nationalism and attempts to set up a strong authoritarian nation tightly regimented and closely controlled by the dictator himself. Pibul's nationalism most strikingly could be seen in the fierce anti-Chinese legislation which now was passed, directed against the Chinese middle class in Siam, as well as in the adoption of the name of "Thailand" for the country, with its implications that all Thais, even those outside the boundaries of Siam, should be united under one rule. The Chinese were compared to the Jews in Nazi Germany, and they became the victims of a rigorous exclusion program. In education, too, Thailand adopted the pattern of Japan, with textbook control, the elimination of "dangerous thought," increasing scrutiny of teachers, and the firing of those who did not think as did Pibul Songgram himself. Censorship and thought control were only two obvious examples borrowed from the Japanese, while in economic policies, too, Thailand followed the lead of her new mentor. Rigid price and industrial controls were established, while 25 per cent of the budget was now devoted to Thailand's army. At the same time Buddhism was encouraged, Christians were persecuted, and many conversions back to Buddhism were registered.

This close following of Japan by Pibul Songgram logically led to Thailand's collaboration with that nation during World War II. In 1940, as the result of Japan's occupation of French Indochina, Thailand seized from that colony the provinces of Battambang and Siemreap along the Cambodian frontier, as well as some Laotian territory west of the Mekong river, to which concessions the French had to agree under rather humiliating circumstances in Tokyo in 1941, after Japan had offered her services as a not-so-honest broker. After Japan's attack on Pearl Harbor Pibul Songgram accepted all Japanese demands, particularly those of letting Japanese troops occupy Thailand and use that country as a base for attack against the British in Malaya. The Thai military dictator even went further when he joined Japan in a military alliance and declared war against the United States and Britain in 1942. His reward was two Shan states seized from

Burma, as well as Thai control over four Malay states in the south. Thailand had apparently become a full puppet state under the control of Japan, whose willing servant Pibul Songgram declared himself to be, but at the same time the Thai also looked toward the eventuality of an Allied victory. Pridi, the great rival of Pibul, continued to serve as a regent and a member of the Thai government, even under Japanese occupation, and he organized a Siamese resistance movement. When it had become obvious in 1944 that the Japanese were being defeated, Pridi engineered another coup which overthrew Pibul Songgram and established in Thailand a government friendly to the West. Pridi, after Pibul's fall, revived the constitution and an elective assembly, and organized a government which would be acceptable to the West. After the war Thailand was forced to surrender the territories she had seized from the British and the French, but the country managed to maintain its independence, despite rather stiff British demands upon Thailand which, if accepted, would have reduced her to the status of a British protectorate. It was United States support which saved Thailand from this fate, and it was also American influence which saw to it that Thailand was accepted as a member of the United Nations. While Pridi was in power, from 1944 to 1947, even the name Thailand was no longer used, and the country again was known as Siam.

In the whole area of Southeast Asia Thailand was perhaps least affected by Western dominance and the Japanese interregnum, thus the country emerged virtually intact in the postwar world.

THE PHILIPPINE ISLANDS

In the Philippines the idea and the demand for independence had been a reality even before World War I. This demand, which all Filipinos shared alike, received a great deal of American encouragement, particularly from the Democratic party which under Wilson's leadership had drafted a party platform opposing American imperialism. Francis B. Harrison, Wilson's appointee as governor-general in the Philippines, went on the record for pledging independence to the islands as soon as a stable government should be established. As soon as he arrived in Manila in 1913 he put Filipinos on the central government commission. In 1916 the Jones Bill was enacted in Washington, which gave the Filipinos a large measure of governmental responsibility. It ended the Philippine commission, and instead created a new legislative body for the Philippines, composed of a senate and a house of representatives. This was a firm step forward toward representative government by Filipinos, since after 1916 the Filipinos enjoyed a predominant voice both in the upper house as well as in the assembly or lower house. Not only did the Filipinos as the result of the Jones Act dominate the legislature, but an increasing proportion of appointments in the government service also went to natives of the islands. Only the governor-general, the vice-governor, and the judges of the supreme court were still appointed by the American president from Washington. In 1919 President Wilson promised complete independence for the Philippines. During these years of temporary autonomy, from 1916–1921, the Americans continued the policy of providing some training for independence (a policy which went back to the beginnings of American influence), by furnishing the country with schools, school teachers, and democratic education, as well as by raising its standards of public health by building hospitals and sewage systems. Nevertheless, the Philippine social and economic system remained very much as it had been under the Spanish regime, a system completely dominated by a small, but exceedingly wealthy class of large landholders or caciques. This class continued to receive American support as a means of avoiding violent social change.

During these years of almost complete freedom the Filipino-dominated legislature pursued what might be called a radical and perhaps even reckless policy of economic nationalism and nationalization, which resulted in a great variety of financial scandals and the outcries of American businessmen against continuing Filipinization of the government. When the Democrats were defeated by the Republicans in the 1920 elections, these complaints of American business reached the ears of the new president, Harding, who sent out a special commission, headed by General Leonard Wood and Cameron Forbes, to investigate conditions in the islands. The result of this investigation was a temporary retrogression on the road of the Philippines towards their cherished aim of independence. With the Republicans back in power American policy in the twenties was one of a greater amount of American control, and attempts were made by the new governor-general, General Leonard Wood, to retract concessions to the Filipinos and to establish tighter control. As might be expected, this policy led to solid unity among Filipino nationalist leaders, of whom Manuel Quezon and his Nacionalista party were the most prominent. The cry for independence again could be heard loudly in Manila, but it took the economic depression, beginning in 1930, to make the dream come true. The issue of political independence was closely linked with the key issue of the Philippine economy, as the latter was tied to and completely dependent upon American markets. Philippine products, notably sugar, tobacco, and coconut oil, as well as Filipino immigrants to the United States, were competing in the American economy. United States labor and American industry, especially the sugar interests, could point out in the years of bleak depression that if the Philippines were given their independence neither Filipino products nor its cheap labor would any longer compete on equal terms with American labor or American-grown sugar. Other arguments which were advanced for granting independence to the islands included the idea that the Philippines could be considered a naval liability in the American picture of national defense, and that the Philippines certainly had not come up to expectation in terms of a way station to the supposedly limitless China market.

Independence

It was as the result of these reasons, but especially the result of the depression, that the Philippines were promised their independence. In 1934 the Tydings-McDuffie Act was passed in Washington, which provided for the necessary legal machinery. Under this act the Philippines would become a commonwealth for ten years, completely autonomous except for continued control of its foreign policy by Washington, and then after this ten-year period of transition, the Philippines would become completely independent on July 4, 1944. The Commonwealth government was established in 1935, with a constitution which provided for a bicameral legislature and a governmental organization parallel to that of the United States. In the elections for the new government which were held in the same year, Manuel Quezon was elected president, with Sergio Osmena as vice-president, and almost all officials of the new government came from their party, the Nacionalista. The Nacionalista-dominated government continued to spread American ideas of self-government, and it began to wean itself gradually away from the shelter of American tariff protection towards the direction of limited free trade, but trade with the United States continued very active and the economic ties between the islands and America were far from being rapidly severed. Economic independence was to be a much more difficult process than political independence.

The new Philippine government, under Manuel Quezon, was a thoroughly oligarchic institution, despite lip service to democracy, and control remained vested in the small upper class of landlords and rich businessmen of Manila. The transition period towards full independence was rudely interrupted by the coming of World War II and the Japanese attack on America, which prevented the fulfillment of Philippine independence in 1944 as originally scheduled. Quezon fled to Washington, and a Philippine government in exile was established there, which was taken over by Osmena upon the death of Quezon. When victory came and Osmena returned once again to the Philippines he faced many problems, of which the gravest were the questions of collaboration and those of economic rehabilitation of the war-torn country. The problem of collaboration with the Japanese by many leading Filipino politicians, the majority of whom came from the upper classes, was solved when the American army by MacArthur's direction rehabilitated most of them, including José Laurel and Manuel Roxas. It has been estimated that some 75 per cent of the Philippine upper house, most of the supreme court, and 80 per cent of the officers of the Philippine army collaborated with the Japanese during their occupation. José Laurel, who had been senate president, ran for the office of president of the Japanese-sponsored puppet regime, and received a very substantial vote, but he was freed by the American military upon their return to Manila, and other politicians, notably Roxas and Quirino, were also given American support.

This problem of collaboration was to plague Osmena upon his return to the Philippines in 1945, and it cost him an election victory the year after, the first year of the Philippine republic which finally came into existence on the 4th of July, 1946. The Philippines had suffered terribly from the war, and no city, except Warsaw, had experienced what Manila had in terms of sheer wanton devastation. The great destruction which had taken place meant that Osmena and his government were very much dependent upon the economic as well as the military assistance of the American government. The Americans extended military assistance to the Philippines, but they also

FIGURE 20.1. War damage at the University of the Philippines.

retained special military rights and a number of bases. To help economically, Congress passed the Philippine Rehabilitation Act and the Philippine Islands Trade Act in 1946, the former of which gave outright financial relief to the Philippines, while the latter provided for a period of eight years of trade by the Philippines within the protection of the American tariff system to be followed by a period of graduated tariffs and eventual full application of the American tariff to Philippine goods. It also included a clause, denounced by many Filipino nationalists, which gave American citizens parity with Filipinos in industry and business ventures in the islands.

INDONESIA

Early Nationalism

In this rich, great archipelago, which extends some 3,200 miles and is inhabited by some 94 million people, mostly concentrated in Java, nationalism was a product of rather slow growth. It began among a very small group of Western-educated Indonesian idealists who were much influenced by the great example of Japan, an example which was given concrete form when after 1899 the Japanese in Indonesia were treated by the Dutch as equal in status with the European citizens, and when Japan opened its first consulate in Batavia in 1909, shortly after defeating Russia in the Far East. The first aims of incipient Indonesian nationalism were westernization and a gradual, but general, advance in the standard of living of the natives. Such aims were incorporated in the society known as the Budi Utomo, or "great endeavor," founded in 1908, but soon nationalism turned towards a more religious expression coupled with wider aims of national independence and elimination of the Chinese as an economic force. This could be discerned with the forming of the Sarekat Islam movement in 1911, a society devoted to religious revival, independence, and against the economic strength of the Chinese.

After World War I, Indonesian nationalism became much more impatient and aggressive. To the many Indonesians who were now being educated in Dutch universities the Wilsonian principles of the rights of self-determination could not but evoke a strong feeling of national injustice when they considered how Holland, one of the smallest powers on the European continent, ruled the vast East Indies along authoritarian lines. In the face of such growing sentiment the efficient Dutch government, which had managed to keep its neutrality during the difficult years 1914–1918, had no desire to make any but the slightest concessions. As a token of slow, almost snail-like political evolution, the Dutch government in Batavia did permit the creation of the Volksraad (people's council) which first met in 1918, as an advisory body of 39 members, the majority of whom were Dutch-culled from an extremely restricted franchise list. The Volksraad was given some legislative power in 1922 and the number of its Indonesian members was increased so that by 1929 only half were still Dutch, but it was in no sense an organ of representative government, its advice was often disregarded by the Dutch officials, and it exercised no control whatever over policy. Indonesian nationalism, far from being appeased by such small measures, became more strongly entrenched than ever during the twenties as the result of the great prosperity the Dutch East Indies enjoyed at that time. The great profits which flowed from Java and the other islands to the Netherlands, without doing any good to the Indonesians, were but another symbol of Dutch exploitation in the eyes of nationalist leaders who already suffered from what they considered denial of their self-determination.

Yet the nationalists themselves were not united. There was a strong internal struggle within Sarekat Islam between the moderates and the radicals and this caused a decline of Sarekat Islam and by 1923 some nationalist leaders had begun to join the newly created Indonesian Communist party. The Communists enjoyed intelligent leadership, but they were bitterly opposed by Sarekat Islam. The Communists managed to stir up labor disputes and strikes, and in 1927 they even attempted a full-scale rising against the Dutch. A few years later, in 1933, they organized a mutiny aboard the Dutch cruiser *Seven Provinces*, in protest against a pay cut, but all of these attempts were promptly and rigorously suppressed by the

FIGURE 20.2. Washing along the canals of Djakarta, Indonesia. The variety of means of transportation is indicated by the traffic on the opposite bank.

Dutch. Dutch sympathy with any kind of nationalism evaporated, and the failure of the Communists also resulted in the failure of non-Communist nationalist movements, of which one of the most important by 1927 was the National Indonesian party, or PNI, founded in that year by Sukarno. The PNI was not a strong or very large group, and it also suffered from disunity, but it was yet another expression of the political forces at work in Indonesia which the Dutch failed to recognize. The Dutch suppressed all political activities after the onset of the great depression which had a major impact on the economic life of the East Indies and after the abortive attempts by the Communists. They did this with tight political control, rigorous police work, an elaborate network of informers, and thorough press and mail censorship. By 1934 all the chief nationalist leaders, such as Sukarno and Hatta, had been interned and their activities had been drastically stopped. No thought was given by the Dutch government to conceding further measures leading towards independence. In education, too, the Dutch maintained a paternalistic outlook, natives were to be trained in trade and agriculture, but certainly not in politics.

Independence

The increasing suppression of nationalism by the Dutch in the immediate prewar years made for growing anti-Dutch feeling, and the Japanese invasion of the Dutch East Indies in 1942 gave Indonesian nationalism its opportunity. When Indonesian nationalist leaders were released from their internment by the Japanese, most of them, including Sukarno and Hatta, collaborated with their liberators. Although most Indonesians soon became very disappointed and enlightened about the nature of the Japanese military occupation (going even so far as to organize anti-Japanese resistance movements), the Japanese interlude did strengthen Indonesian nationalist leadership, its military forces, and its demand for self-government. At the moment of defeat of the Japanese in 1945, Sukarno together with Muhammad Hatta and Sjahrir (who had been active in the anti-Japanese movement) established an independent Republic of Indonesia at Batavia, the capital, which was given its old name of Djakarta. Since no Dutch troops were immediately available to effect the surrender of the Japanese, British troops arrived in Java, and the British commander recognized the de facto existence of the new independent republic, a necessity if he were to free the many Dutch who languished in internment camps. However, the Dutch government was determined to reinstate its control over the Indies, and after an uneasy interval Dutch troops landed and temporarily reestablished Dutch rule in some parts of the islands.

INDOCHINA

French Rule

French Indochina, which included one colony, Cochin China, and four protectorates, Annam, Tonkin, Laos, and Cambodia, was subject to what

FIGURE 20.3. Akmet Sukarno, first president of Indonesia.

sometimes has been referred to as the worst of all colonial administrations in Southeast Asia. Essentially, Indochina was governed by Frenchmen for Frenchmen, and the great French liberal slogans of liberty, equality, and fraternity were not considered to be export goods for overseas dominions. French imperialism in the nineteenth century had been motivated primarily by national pride, and it changed very little in the new century. The French had no intention of permitting independence to their colonial subjects in Southeast Asia; rather, they developed instead a policy of assimilation designed to make brown-skinned Frenchmen out of the Vietnamese in an ever more perfect union with France. As a consequence of this policy the French were most reluctant to train and develop native administrators, and they recoiled from the thought of eventual self-government for their subjects. If, politically speaking, the French used their overseas possessions for the greater glory of France, so in the economic field also the colonies were exploited for the sake of the mother country. The French developed rice, rubber, coal, and other resources in Indochina, but the great profits reaped from these developments went to French investors and little benefit accrued to Indochina itself, while the native cultivators remained a debt-ridden, landless class, suffering from French government monopolies on salt, alcohol, and other consumer goods.

Growth of Nationalism

The paradox of this situation was that the ideas of the French Revolution at the same time began to influence the thought of a few Western-educated Vietnamese who, after being exposed to the concepts of liberalism and nationalism, turned these ideas against their French overlords. Nationalism in Indochina was limited to a small group of educated Vietnamese most of whom had no political or administrative responsibility. But they eagerly learned from the ideas of the French Revolution, and of the Chinese Revolution of 1911. World War I further stimulated this nationalism. More than 100,000 Indochinese served as soldiers and laborers in France during World War I. Meanwhile anti-French uprisings in Tonkin and Cochin China were ruthlessly suppressed.

Dissatisfaction of the Vietnamese with colonial conditions grew rapidly in the postwar years, while the French government in the colonies viewed the growth of an ever more radical nationalism with disdain, and practically refused to make any concessions to it.

Among the Vietnamese anticolonialists Phan Boi Chau emphasized Vietnamese national traditions. In the postwar period he played an increasingly passive role. In his writing Phan was influenced by the socialism of Sun Yat-sen, but he had no comprehensive program for the Vietnamese. Some of the intellectuals turned to a "revolutionary romanticism," which was part of the nationalism of this period. Meanwhile, more active anti-French Vietnamese nationalists in Canton in the years 1921 to 1925 organized a party known as the Viet-Nam Quoc Dan Dang, the most important noncommunist party among the Vietnamese between the two World Wars.

Among Vietnamese leaders the most important one was Nguyen Ai Quoc. He later, in 1943, changed his name to Ho Chi Minh. He was in Europe from 1914 until 1923. In Paris after 1917 he came under the influence of French left-wing socialists and became a co-founder of the French Communist party in 1920. Going to Moscow in 1923, he became involved in international communism. With the Russian Borodin he traveled to China in 1925 and helped establish a Vietnamese Revolutionary Youth League at Canton.

The government of Indochina in the 1920's and 1930's was run by and for the French. They did not think in terms of developing self-government for the local peoples of Vietnam, Laos, or Cambodia but they introduced some elected members into a government council in 1927. However, admitting a few natives of Indochina on a colonial council did not win for the French the support of the organized nationalist groups.

The hopes of the Vietnamese nationalists were raised during 1925 to 1928 by the appointment of a socialist governor-general, Alexander Varenne. He paroled the anticolonialist leader, Phan Boi Chau, in December 1925. Two years later the advisory government council mentioned above was formed.

Meanwhile, the revolutionary movements continued. Liberal and progressive demonstrations took place in 1926. The Vietnamese Nationalist party was active in Tonkin and the Communist party of Indochina had its beginnings in 1929. Ho Chi Minh succeeded in unifying various groups of Vietnamese communists; the party flourished and soon outnumbered all other anti-French groups, particularly in northern Vietnam.

Communists took the lead in a peasant revolt in Nghe An in 1930. "Soviets" were established but were put down with force by the French, using airplanes, troops of the Foreign Legion, and torture in their treatment of captured dissidents. The culmination of the disturbances of 1930 was the so-called Yenbay Mutiny, during which a number of French officers and noncommissioned officers were shot down by their own men. As a result of this uprising some thirteen Nationalist party members were guillotined.

In spite of repression various Vietnamese groups sought to gain modifications of French rule. Among the official class who served under French supervision some attempted to obtain greater rights for the Vietnamese. An official named Ngo Dinh Diem was appointed Minister of the Interior by the Annamese "emperor," Bao Dai. Diem asked for a legislative assembly and when his request was rejected by the French, Diem resigned. Open revolutionary politics continued in Cochin China, the southern part of Vietnam. In that region various factions were able to elect their candidates to the Colonial Council. Ho Chi Minh meanwhile had fled to Hong Kong, where the British imprisoned him for some three years at the request of the French. In spite of repression, a communist-led hard core of Indochinese nationalism continued in Vietnam.

Among the political elements during this period were the religious sects. The Cao Dai became active in 1935. They had an organization like a political party. With their headquarters at Tayninh, they expanded to over one million adherents before World War II. The Hoa Hao sect was founded by a Buddhist preacher in 1938 and became prominent among the poor peasants of the Mekong Delta.

Indochina During World War II

With the spread of the Second World War, French active influence in Indochina came to an end. When France fell, in 1940, the Japanese moved into Vietnam to exploit its economic resources and its strategic position. Given special rights by the Vichy French administration, they succeeded in bringing the entire colony under their influence. The Japanese used Vichy sympathizers among the French officials to maintain order and to suppress nationalist and communist uprisings in 1940 with bombing, executions, and deportations. The Japanese imposed high taxes on the Vietnamese.

In December 1941, at the same time that the Japanese moved to attack Pearl Harbor and to invade the Philippines, they completed their occupation of Vietnam and forced the French to accept their intervention. The French also were compelled to relinquish territory in Laos and Cambodia which was claimed by Thailand.

During the Japanese occupation of Indochina, in 1941, Vietnamese communists in China under Ho Chi Minh formed the Dong Ming Hoi (Vietnamese national front), an umbrella organization of Vietnamese revolutionary groups, sponsored by the Chinese Kuomintang. Among these groups, the communist-dominated section, known as the Vietminh, was at first only a part of the organization.

Ho Chi Minh was imprisoned by the Kuomintang at Liu-chou in Southwest China during the years 1941 to 1943. After his release Ho became the head of the Dong Ming Hoi. Under his direction the Vietminh built up their political strength at the expense of other Dong Ming Hoi organizations. Their activity was based on a network of cells throughout Vietnam. During the war they supplied information to the Allies and received $100,000 a month from the Chinese government. Guerrillas, organized by the Vietminh leader Vo Nguyen Giap in 1942, carried out the communist program of resistance against the Japanese.

At a congress of Vietminh groups held in China at Liu-chou in 1944 Ho Chi Minh, because of his organization within Vietnam, emerged as the strongest Vietnamese leader in exile. He had financial support from the Chinese and weapons from the United States. The Vietminh army under Vo Nguyen Giap numbered some 10,000. In their struggle for power the Vietminh applied terroristic methods, not only against the Japanese but also against Vietnamese nationalist opponents who were not within their own organization. In November 1944, Ho moved into Tonkin and set up revolutionary headquarters.

The Return of the French

By the next spring the end of the war was in sight, and the Japanese, in order to leave conditions in a chaotic state within Vietnam, put an end to

French rule (March-April 1945). The shadowy authority of the French had been tolerated until it became obvious that Japan was losing the war. In order to forestall possible French underground resistance, and also to cause as much trouble as possible for the victorious Allies, the Japanese eliminated the French regime, and installed a Vietnamese authority at Hue headed by the Emperor Bao Dai. His government proclaimed the independence of the new state of Vietnam.

The Vietminh under Ho and Vo continued to organize and to oppose the Japanese. They gained control at Hanoi and in North Vietnam in August 1945, and with their organization they could count on mass support in the countryside. At the end of the war they also controlled Saigon.

When the Japanese surrendered and Bao Dai abdicated, Ho Chi Minh remained the most effective political leader in the country. As a designation for their government the Vietminh proclaimed the "Democratic Republic of Vietnam" with Ho Chi Minh as president.

At the same time, the French attempted to reestablish themselves in their former colony. Aided by British troops, who were among the first to arrive, French forces disembarked at Saigon in August 1945. In Saigon they were faced with armed resistance from all Vietnamese groups. The avowed purpose of the French was to maintain their prestige in the Far East and to preserve their extensive economic interests in Indochina. They set out to reconquer the country by military means.

French policy tended to unite the Vietnamese against them. The provisional "Democratic Republic of Vietnam" was supported by widespread nationalist feeling, especially in Tonkin and Annam. Vietnamese nationalists welcomed the leadership of Ho Chi Minh even though he was a communist. The Vietminh commenced guerrilla activity against the French as early as September 1945, and at the same time they proceeded to eliminate possible rivals among the anticolonial groups, such as the Trotskyites and the Hoa Hao. Within the Vietminh coalition the communist party of Ho Chin Minh and Vo Nguyen Giap were still only a minority.

Increasingly well established in Vietnam, the Vietminh attempted to negotiate with the French. In March 1946, the French recognized the "Democratic Republic of Vietnam" and immediately afterward proceeded to bring troops and tanks into Hanoi. In the ensuing negotiations between the French government and Ho Chi Minh the terms offered by the French to Ho did not include complete independence for all of Indochina. The government in Paris spoke of a planned union of France and her colonies, but within such a union the French were unwilling to grant autonomy to the colony of Cochin China in southern Vietnam. The results were unending disputes and eventually open war.

After an abortive conference in the summer of 1946 at Fontainebleau, at which Ho Chi Minh was present and during which the French stood adamant in refusing autonomy to Cochin China, negotiations broke down and Ho, upon his return to Hanoi, proclaimed a program of "national liberation" which in effect amounted to a declaration of war.

With the return of the French and their refusal to give way to the popular and militant nationalism of the communist-controlled Vietminh, there commenced a new phase in the history of Indochina, the start of eight years of warfare between French and Vietnamese.

BRITISH COLONIAL EMPIRE

The British empire in Southeast Asia was characterized by its wide range of power, with key bases in Burma and in Singapore in Malaya, flanked by British possessions in India on the one side, and in Hong Kong, as well as the dominions of Australia and New Zealand on the other. Independence by British colonial possessions was achieved successfully and relatively painlessly in the post-World War II period.

Burma

The largest British colony in Southeast Asia was, of course, Burma, which as late as 1937 had been a part of India, but which by 1948 had become a fully independent republic. After World War I Burma had contributed to the wealth of the British empire with its rice, petroleum, minerals, and teak, but the Burmese were given no share in their government until 1923, when as part of the Indian reforms the British extended to Burma the principle of dyarchy. Burma participated in this evolutionary development of government, just as did India, by having certain subjects of administration, the so-called transferred subjects, placed in Burmese hands, while other matters and the more important and fundamental ones such as revenue, defense, and law, were reserved subjects, in which the governor-general had the final word. This reform was welcomed by Burmese nationalists, but it did not lessen their antagonism against economic domination of Burma by the *chettyars*, the middle-class Indian moneylenders, who had come to be exceedingly unpopular in Burma due to their avariciousness and their control of the most valuable rice lands on the Irrawaddy delta near Rangoon. Nationalism in Burma was thus a two-pronged affair: it was directed against the British by demanding full self-government and independence, while at the same time it was also an anti-Indian movement, desirous of doing away with Indian influence in the Burmese economic life, and eliminating the Indian from the Burmese plural society.

Burma's constitutional development permitted rapidly increasing native participation in government during the 1930's, and a policy of cooperation with the British seemed attractive to the Burmese elite. Even so, in the last years of that decade, a more radical element, insisting on Burma's complete independence, came to the fore. These were the so-called Thakins—or "Masters"—a group of young students led by Thakin Nu, many of whom later on collaborated with the Japanese against the British raj.

When, in 1937, Burma was separated from India, the result of a recommendation by the Simon Commission on India which wanted such a reform for administrative reasons, there was intense satisfaction in Burma at this measure. Even so, occasionally, such as in 1938, the country was the scene of violent and massive anti-Indian riots in Rangoon. In 1937 a new constitution was promulgated, and Burma became practically a self-governing colony, except in the fields of finance, foreign affairs, and religion. The British went a long way in making substantial concessions in the direction of self-government, and Burma can be said to have possessed a qualified dominion status before the war broke out. It had a bicameral legislature and a full cabinet of ministers, with full franchise, while only a few, though major, rights remained the exclusive prerogative of the British governor-general. But even so, the rising nationalist spirit in Burma demanded more power and, especially, a greater share in the economic life of the country. The Burmese government, whose first Burmese prime minister was Ba Maw, was angered by the fact that although there were rich men in Burma, there were no rich Burmese. In the Burmese economy the British and Indians controlled affairs, and although the British did much to increase Burmese production of raw materials and to stimulate trade, they provided little social welfare for the Burmese themselves. Burma, in 1939, was still a backward country, with few educated Burmese, and a Burmese political life distinguished by instability and a multiplicity of political parties, united only in their demand for the ousting of the Indian and the granting of yet greater political powers from the British.

Independence for Burma. Again, it was the Japanese conquest of Southeast Asia which provided Burmese nationalism with its opportunities. The British defeat in Singapore and subsequently in Burma itself greatly reduced British prestige, and the Burmese government led by Dr. Ba Maw aided the Japanese in the occupation of the country. Other Burmese nationalists, such as the new leaders of the anti-British Thakin party, of whom Aung San who had been trained by the Japanese on Formosa soon became the most prominent, also collaborated with the Japanese. However, the first rash of enthusiasm for the Japanese liberator soon gave way to profound disillusionment at the severity, brutality, and rapacious exploitation of the Burmese economy by the Japanese, and when in 1943 the Japanese masters granted independence to the Burmese most nationalists in Burma felt that this was but an empty gesture, and that no real freedom was possible under the Japanese yoke. Opposition against the Japanese among the Burmese began to grow, and an Anti-Fascist People's Freedom League was organized designed to resist the Japanese military, in which Aung San now opposed Japan. These activities by the Burmese nationalists against their Japanese masters eased the way towards reconquest of Burma by the British at the end of World War II, but when British power returned to Rangoon once more it was with the intention of restoring prewar conditions. When the British government was faced, upon its arrival in Burma, with a Burmese national movement which had gained new leadership, experience, and a sense of assurance and power as the result of wartime developments, and which insisted upon full independence for Burma, the British government yielded, thereby preventing a course of action which in neighboring Indochina spelled disaster. In addition it was the unity, support, and military strength of the Anti-Fascist People's

Freedom League (AFPFL) which led to the victory of nationalism at a conference held in London in 1946, at which Britain promised complete independence.

Malaya

In Malaya, another British colony in Southeast Asia, the spirit of nationalism was much less strong. Malaya, an aggregation of a crown colony (the Straits Settlements), four federated, and five unfederated states, was efficiently administered by the British and for the British, but among the Malays there had been little resentment against British rule; rather, on the contrary, Malays sought protection from the British against the encroachments of foreign Asians, Chinese as well as Indian. The reason for this lack of a strong nationalist movement, and the ease with which British rule was accepted, was due partially to the great prosperity of Malaya, producing some 45 per cent of the world's supply of rubber, and 28 per cent of tin, and to the existence of a strong Chinese middle class in Singapore which seemed to threaten the economic life of the Malayan people by acting in the traditional role of middleman of the Southeast Asian plural society. It was a terrible surprise to see the great naval base of Singapore fall so easily to the Japanese, and the wartime period resulted in a rather difficult economic situation, but as a whole in Malaya the returning British troops were welcomed in 1945 as no other colonialists in any other place in Southeast Asia.

In the postwar period the British government began to draw up a series of plans for a Federation for Malaya which were to include gradual concessions toward self-government. The first of these, in September 1945, provided for a Union of the Federated and the Unfederated States under a centralized government in which the British governor was still to have wide powers, and in which Singapore was to remain as a separate colony, but this plan soon ran into trouble by being interpreted by the Malays as being too much in favor of the Chinese.

BASIC DATES

1910–1925	Rama VI in Thailand
1916	Jones Bill for Philippines passed
1918	Volksraad in Indonesia
1923	Dyarchy in Burma
1925–1935	Rama VII in Thailand
1926	Communist uprising in Indonesia
1927	End of unequal treaties in Thailand; National Indonesian Party founded; Colonial Council in Indochina
1930	Peasant and nationalist revolts in Indochina
1934	Tydings-McDuffie Act
1935	Commonwealth of Philippines under Quezon as first president
1937	New constitution instituted for Burma

1938	Pibul Songgram dictator of Thailand
1940	Japanese obtain control of Indochina
1941	Ho Chi Minh organizes Vietminh
1942	Siam joins Japan in war; Ba Maw government aids Japanese in Burma
1943	Aung San heads AFPFL in Burma
1944	Pridi assumes power in Thailand
1945	Sukarno proclaims Indonesian independence; Democratic Republic of Vietnam proclaimed by Vietminh; French troops at Saigon
1946	Philippines independent under Roxas; war between French-controlled Vietnam and Vietminh

SUPPLEMENTARY READING

Ball, W. M. *Nationalism and Communism in East Asia.* New York, 1955.
Benda, H. J. and J. A. Larkin. *The World of Southeast Asia: Selected Historical Readings.* New York, 1967.
Cady, J. *Southeast Asia: Its Historical Development.* New York, 1964.
Hall, D. G. *A History of South-East Asia.* New York, 1955.
Hammer, E. *Vietnam: Yesterday and Today.* New York, 1966.
Harrison, B. *South-East Asia,* 2nd ed. London, 1963.

ADVANCED READING

Allen, R. H. *Malaysia.* London, 1968.
Benda, H. J. *The Crescent and the Rising Sun.* New York, 1958.
Bernstein, D. *The Philippine Story.* New York, 1947.
Bro, M. *Indonesia, Land of Challenge.* New York, 1954.
Christian, J. *Burma.* Berkeley, Calif., 1942.
Dahm, B. *Sukarno and the Struggle for Indonesian Independence.* Ithaca, N.Y., 1969.
Dobby, E. *Southeast Asia.* London, 1950. A geographical account.
―――― *Malaya and the Malayans.* London, 1947.
Drachman, E. R. *United States Policy toward Vietnam, 1940–1945.* Cranbury, N.J., 1970.
Elsbree, W. *Japan's Role in Southeast Asian Nationalist Movements.* Cambridge Mass., 1953.
Friend, T. *Between Two Empires, the Ordeal of the Philippines, 1929–1946.* New Haven, 1965.
Gerbrandy, P. *Indonesia.* London, 1950.
Grunder, G. and W. H. Livezay. *The Philippines and the United States.* Norman, Okla., 1951.
Hammer, E. *The Struggle for Indochina.* Stanford, Calif., 1954.
Hartendorp, A. *The Japanese Occupation of the Philippines.* Manila, 1967.
Jacoby, E. *Agrarian Unrest in Southeast Asia.* New York, 1949.
Kahin, G. *Nationalism and Revolution in Indonesia.* Ithaca, N.Y., 1952.

Kennedy, J. *History of Malaya.* London, 1962.
Kennedy, M. *Communism in Asia.* New York, 1956.
Malcolm, G. *First Malayan Republic, the Story of the Philippines.* Boston, 1951.
Marr, D. G. *Vietnamese Anticolonialism, 1885–1925.* Berkeley, Calif., 1971.
Osborne, M. *Region of Revolt, Focus on Southeast Asia.* Rushcutter's Bay, N.S.W., 1970.
Purcell, V. *The Chinese in Southeast Asia.* London, 1951.
Roff, W. R. *The Origins of Malay Nationalism.* New Haven, 1967.
Steinberg, D. J., ed. *In Search of Southeast Asia.* New York, 1971.
────── *Philippine Collaboration in World War II.* Ann Arbor, 1967.
Trager, F. *Burma, from Kingdom to Republic.* New York, 1966.
Wehl, D. *The Birth of Indonesia.* London, 1948.
Wertheim, F. *Indonesian Society in Transition.* The Hague, 1956.
Winstedt, R. *Malaya and Its History.* London, 1951.
Wolf, C. *The Indonesian Story.* New York, 1946.

Chapter 21

Chinese "Republic" and Japan, 1914-1928

PEKING "REPUBLIC" AND THE WARLORDS

Yuan Shih-k'ai Attempts to Create a Monarchy

It was clear by 1914 that the Chinese Revolution of 1911 was a failure (see Chapter 15). Realistic military politician that he was, Yuan Shih-k'ai had betrayed the republican ideals of the Revolution just as earlier he had betrayed the reforms of 1898. Of course, it may be argued that China was entirely unprepared for representative government and needed a strong hand at the helm, an idea which Western powers seem to have endorsed in their decision to loan money to the emerging dictator in 1913, but certainly the aspiration for it was deeper than Yuan, for all his realism, estimated. This was proved in 1915-1916 when Yuan undertook to remove even the trappings of republicanism by having himself declared emperor, a move which brought him crushing defeat—the first and last of his long career.

While Yuan's plans were being laid, Ts'ai Ao, a Japanese-trained military man, declared open rebellion in Yunnan, and the flame of revolt spread again through south China. Even Yuan's hand-picked general at Nanking, Feng Kuo-chang, seemed now to be biding his time, perhaps waiting for a chance to strike for power himself. Foreign powers urged delay, and then Tuan Ch'i-jui, Yuan's war minister and Peiyang army protégé, turned against the scheme. In March, 1916 Yuan issued a contrite statement, admitting his failure to read the signs of the times and promising both a cleansing of heart and a cessation of enthronement plans. But the damage had been done. China was again split into several parts, and warlords were eyeing the future when Yuan, disappointed and dispirited, died suddenly on June 6, 1916. The shifting alliances of military governors, called *tu-chun* or warlords, were to keep China in turmoil for the next decade.

489

Shortly before his death Yuan appointed Tuan Ch'i-jui as premier, while elements of the former National Assembly met in the foreign settlement at Shanghai to revive the republic. A noteworthy attempt was made in August, 1916 to bring the various factions together when Li Yuan-hung, the almost forgotten vice-president under Yuan who it will be recalled had been with the revolutionists in 1911 and had been the embodiment of the compromise between Yuan and Sun in 1912, tried to restore parliamentary government at Peking including the Kuomintang party members who had been ousted in 1913. He invited the Assembly back to Peking, reaffirmed Tuan as premier, which kept his faction of the Peiyang army at least temporarily quiescent, and installed Feng Kuo-chang, heir to the leadership of the second largest Peiyang element, as vice-president. (Ts'ai Ao had died, so there was no need to account for him.) It was a noble attempt, but the balance was too delicate to be kept.

Warlord Politics

By the end of 1916 President Li and the parliament were being ignored as Tuan and Feng played military power politics. Ironically, Tuan caught hold of a fruitful issue early in 1917 by advocating the entry of China into World War I on the side of the Allies. He seems to have been mainly interested in the prestige and money (from foreign loans) such a step would bring to his military leadership. Most of parliament opposed the move and Li dismissed Tuan from the premiership. Tuan then threatened to take Peking with his army, which sent Li into such a panic that he called on an old Manchu military supporter, Chang Hsun, for help. Chang entered Peking with his troops, but instead of helping Li he proceeded to "restore" the Manchu boy-emperor. Tuan then announced that he would save the republic, organized a coalition of warlords, and took Peking. He ousted both Chang and Li, installed as acting president his Peiyang army colleague and potential rival, Feng, perhaps to keep him in Peking, and with most of the members of parliament in hiding or in flight joined the fight to "make the world safe for democracy" by pushing through a declaration of war against Germany on August 14. Then, while the Kuomintang members of parliament set up a rival government at Canton, Tuan consolidated his strength in the north bringing into power the so-called Anfu clique, a group of warlords which he headed and which through rather tenuous alliances with other warlords ruled most of China until 1920. During this period he sought loans from foreign powers, which materialized in the form of the lucrative but compromising Nishihara loans from Japan. Before discussing these it is necessary to review Japanese developments since 1914.

JAPAN IN WORLD WAR I

With the outbreak of World War I in August, 1914, Japan began an era of tremendous economic development and territorial expansion, which in a sense were to contradict one another. With her competitors busy in Europe and with the markets of both Asia and the West open to her as never before, she could easily have established herself as a creditor nation and raised the living standards of the Japanese people, but, unfortunately, her leadership preferred to play the power politics of territorial expansion, which in the end not only proved extremely expensive in financial terms, but laid the foundation for unhealthy domestic political developments which were to lead the nation into aggressive war in the 1930's.

Japan Enters the War

Japan entered World War I on the side of the Allies almost immediately. This was officially to fulfill her obligations under the Anglo-Japanese Alliance, wherein she and Britain were pledged to mutual aid if either were attacked by more than one other power. However, there was an interesting diplomatic sideplay connected with her entry. Sir Edward Grey, Britain's foreign secretary, promoted the idea that Japan fight, but not too hard, and he even asked Japan to delay her declaration of war until agreements about the scope of her war effort could be worked out. The Japanese foreign minister, Kato, did delay a few days, but argued that such a halfhearted approach would have "undesirable effects upon the value of the Anglo-Japanese Alliance," that Japanese public opinion was already aroused, and insisted on vengeance on Germany (though not apparently on France and Russia) for the Triple Intervention of 1895. However, Kato assured Lord Grey that Japan's war activity would in no way threaten English trade or interest. After a week of exchanging diplomatic notes in this vein Japan issued an ultimatum to Germany, at the expiration of which, on August 23, the Japanese navy attacked the German naval base at Tsingtao, Kiaochow Bay, Shantung. Britain rushed a small force to the scene to "help" the Japanese and the Germans capitulated on November 7. The Anglo-Japanese diplomatic byplay surrounding the start of World War I in the Far East is perhaps chiefly interesting to the student of history as an example of the way in which the successful diplomacy of one era can be an embarrassment in the next. The Anglo-Japanese Alliance had become an embarrassment to Britain, but there was no way out until 1922.

Having taken over the German leasehold on Shantung, the Japanese then proceeded to quarrel with the Chinese over the question of whether Japanese troops should continue to guard the German-built railway that led to the capital of Shantung province. This led to the infamous "Twenty-one Demands" on China.

Japan's Twenty-one Demands

Although the Twenty-one Demands hit China and her erstwhile advocate of territorial integrity, the United States, like a bolt from the blue, they had been in process of formulation in Japanese government circles for some two years, and as served on China represented an effort by Foreign Minister Kato to balance off conflicting interests in Japan. Kato was primarily concerned about the short duration of the Japanese leasehold in south Manchuria, 18 years as negotiated in the treaties of 1905. He wanted to increase the term for this and Japan's Manchurian railroad rights to 99 years lest, he sometimes argued, trouble arise about renegotiation and the Japanese military insist on violent measures to maintain Japan's position. He discussed the problem with Britain's Sir Edward Grey in London in January, 1913 and received Sir Edward's understanding answer that Japan had "planted blood" in south Manchuria and that Britain would not be disposed to interfere in a matter which, after all, should be decided between Japan and China.

By January, 1915 the list of demands to be presented to China had swelled to five groups, as follows: Group I, transfer of German Shantung rights to Japan and enlargement of them; Group II, extension of Manchurian leases and railway rights in Manchuria to 99 years and additional travel, business, and financial rights in Manchuria and eastern Inner Mongolia; Group III, joint control with China of Hanyehping Iron and Coal Company in the Yangtze valley; Group IV, China to grant no new leaseholds to other powers; Group V, miscellaneous, including joint Sino-Japanese control of Chinese police in areas of tension, joint Sino-Japanese control of certain arsenals, rights of ownership of land in China to be granted to Japanese institutions, right of Japanese "preaching" in China, and new railway concessions. Kato, as a seasoned diplomat, was fully aware that only a part of Group II, together with Group I in a de facto sense, had been cleared with Britain, and he was irritated that business and other interests had so inflated his original intentions with their additional demands. He therefore attached the curious designation of merely "desires" to Group V.

China at first refused the demands, but with Japanese troops in Shantung and Manchuria, and China in anything but a stable condition, only active support from other powers could stave off capitulation if Japan decided to apply real pressure. All other major powers, except the United States, were actively engaged in Europe, and no help came from them. On behalf of the United States, Secretary of State Bryan in March, after the full extent of the demands became known, sent to the Japanese government a long and stiff note listing in detail numerous Sino-American treaty clauses which were violated or impaired by the Japanese terms, but he concentrated his fire on Group V. Kato primarily wanted to gain Chinese agreement to the first four groups and after a Japanese ultimatum, China acquiesced on May 9. A new series of Sino-Japanese treaties and agreements embodying Groups I through IV of the demands was signed on May 25. Group V was left aside for "future negotiation."

However, the Japanese victory had been gained only at the cost of exciting great suspicion of Japan in the popular opinion of China, the United States and, to a considerable extent, England. Secretary Bryan sent identical notes to Tokyo and Peking formulating the later famous "nonrecognition doctrine." He stated that the United States would not recognize any agreement or undertaking impairing American treaty rights in China, the political or territorial integrity of China, or the Open Door policy. This meant that at some future international conference Japan could expect the new treaties to be challenged not only by China, but by the United States and perhaps by Britain. Unhappy at the diplomatic turmoil and damage to Japan's reputation that had occurred, the Genro, whose meddling had certainly contributed to these, now accused Kato of mishandling the whole affair and forced his resignation as foreign minister, which he submitted on August 10, 1915.

Treaties with the Allies

During the next two years the Japanese foreign office worked assiduously to gain international approval of the 1915 treaties, and to a considerable extent succeeded. First, Japan adhered to the Declaration of London by which the Allies had promised to remain united and make no separate peace with Germany. This underscored Japan's standing as a full-fledged member of the Allied team and, according to the new foreign minister, Viscount Ishii, assured Japan of the opportunity to push her claims "authoritatively" at a future peace conference. Next, treaties or agreements were negotiated with each of the Allied powers. These included a treaty with Russia in July, 1916, wherein Russia acknowledged the help in arms and supplies Japan had been sending and would continue to send her by approving Japan's enlarged position in Manchuria and Mongolia. Then secret agreements with England, France, Italy, and (again) Russia were negotiated in February and March, 1917, whereby these powers agreed to support Japan's claims for the Shantung rights and Germany's seized Pacific possessions north of the equator. Japan's part of these bargains was to provide antisubmarine protection in the Mediterranean, urge China to enter the war on the Allied side, and back British claims for German Pacific possessions south of the equator. Later in 1917 Viscount Ishii came to the United States to offer congratulations on America's entry into the war and to ease the diplomatic tension that had existed since the Twenty-one Demands. While the United States did not recognize Japan's new positions as clearly as the other powers had done, Secretary of State Lansing, after hearing arguments that China was to Japan as Mexico to the United States and reiterating jointly with Ishii the great respect both countries had for Open Door principles, acknowledged in writing that "territorial propinquity creates special interests" and that therefore the United States recognized that Japan had special interests in China, especially the "contiguous" part. This was rather vague, but it would certainly help bolster Japan's case. Lastly, Japan undertook to obtain Chinese approval of the new conditions, without benefit of ultimatum. With the Anfu clique in power at Peking the time was propitious.

The Nishihara Loans

Field Marshal Terauchi Masatake became Premier of Japan in 1916. Terauchi, like his Genro sponsors for the premiership, Yamagata and Miura Goro, was a Choshu militarist who had a large view of Japan's continental destinies. As governor-general of Korea from 1910 to 1916 he had been ruthless, but he had also acquired a measure of sophistication in the application of financial techniques to imperialism. This had been partly due to the influence of a young businessman and banker, Nishihara Kamezo, who had been very helpful to him in Seoul and who now advocated a bold adventure in international finance not only to obtain Chinese acquiescence to the still rankling Twenty-one Demands but to inaugurate a new era in Sino-Japanese relations in which China would rely on and trust Japan. In short, Tuan should be supported handsomely with money as well as advice. A graduate of Waseda University in Tokyo, Ts'ao Ju-lin, who was minister of communications and later minister of finance to Tuan, along with Nishihara, helped in arranging the financial transactions.

To funnel large, essentially political loans to Tuan, Terauchi had to bypass normal financial and foreign policy channels in Japan. Japan was a member of the International Consortium set up in 1913 to oversee loans to China, but since they could not meet Consortium regulations she could not make these loans through her Consortium representative, the Yokohama Specie Bank. Terauchi, or Nishihara, therefore utilized a Korean banking group whose leader, Shoda Kazue, was also minister of finance in the Terauchi cabinet. The Foreign Office and its minister, Motono, hardly knew what was going on and other possible opposition in Japan was sidetracked by a "war emergency" device to obtain national unity, or perhaps national acquiescence, on foreign policy. This was the Advisory Council on Foreign Relations, established by imperial ordinance on June 5, 1917, wherein political party leaders like Hara Takashi (Seiyukai) and Inukai Tsuyoshi (Kokuminto) were given titles as ministers of state and placed in the position of seeming to endorse Terauchi, whose Choshu military group, in collaboration with Satsuma navy men, really dominated the Council.

Between September, 1917 and September, 1918 Nishihara arranged the transmittal of some 150 million yen in loans to the Peking regime of Tuan Ch'i-jui, whose Anfu clique seems to have got most of the money and used it in mysterious ways. Security for the loans consisted largely of promissory notes and paper mortgages on unbuilt facilities and untapped natural resources, less than 1/30th of which were ever honored. If Terauchi intended, as he said he did, to promote the development of Chinese resources by joint Sino-Japanese cooperation, he certainly failed, and even as a purely imperialistic device to strengthen Japan's position in China this was only partially successful. It is true that, probably as a result of the loans, Tuan's government signed several new treaties with Japan in 1918, which called for a "joint" Sino-Japanese war effort, recognized the transfer to Japan of Germany's Shantung holdings, and gave the Japanese great latitude for operations not only in Shantung, but in Manchuria and Mongolia where the new Siberian question now impinged. But for Japan the loans represented a very large financial outlay that could better have been used to combat wartime inflation at home and, worse yet, they excited great bitterness against Japan and the Peking government with which she dealt among sensitive and increasingly nationalistic Chinese students and intellectuals, who became convinced that China was being sold out for money by a corrupt government. During the Versailles peace conference and thereafter their sentiments were to have political effect.

SIBERIAN INTERVENTION

Japanese expansion during World War I was made not only at the expense of Germany and China, but also of Russia, whose Bolshevik revolution opened the question of eastern Siberia.

Advocates of Intervention

Nishihara, as Premier Terauchi's personal behind-the-scenes investigator, seems to have been in touch with members of the Tairo Doshikai, the anti-Russian expansionist society which had once sought to prolong the Russo-Japanese War to "final victory," and to have brought to Terauchi's ear their advice that "the time for a Siberian expedition had come." Nishihara says he had convinced Terauchi of this before the end of December, 1917. However, Nishihara's influence should not be overestimated. The Japanese army general staff was also revising its earlier negative estimate of the feasibility of an expedition. General Tanaka Giichi, vice-chief of the general staff and a specialist on Siberia, took the lead in this, arguing that ousting the Bolsheviks from eastern Siberia and preventing any disturbances in the Russian zone of northern Manchuria would serve as an excellent joint Sino-Japanese project (under Japanese leadership) of the sort Terauchi's China policy had envisioned, and limiting its activity to the area east of Lake Baikal, it would not become involved in the long transport difficulties to European Russia of which the army had been wary. This idea won support and a Sino-Japanese military agreement of March, 1918 cleared the way.

Despite these arguments for an intervention it was recognized that to intervene in Siberia itself, as distinct from Manchuria and Mongolia, would be a dangerous move, and in critical meetings of the Advisory Council on Foreign Relations strong opposition to the idea was presented by Hara Takashi, leader of the Seiyukai party, who had "liberal" Genro Saionji's support. He cautioned especially that a move toward intervention could seriously imperil relations with the United States, and insisted that it could be undertaken only if the United States approved or cooperated. His opposition and a certain instinct for caution in Yamagata and Terauchi held up the operation until various Allied pressures had been put on President Wilson, who, on July 6, 1918, approved the idea of sending to Vladivostok a joint expedition, including both American and Japanese troops. Wilson, however, suspicious of possible Japanese enlargement of the affair, specified that the forces should concern themselves with very limited objectives. They were to take charge of Allied equipment piled up at Vladivostok because of the breakdown of rail transport to European Russia, and to assist Czechoslovak former prisoners of war who were making their way eastward along the Trans-Siberian Railway after the collapse of the Russian front, and he specified that the Japanese and American troop components should be limited to 7,000 men each.

Intervention Approved

Wilson's "invitation" to Japan to send an expedition undermined Hara's opposition and he finally approved of accepting the American proposal, though he tried to limit the number of troops to be sent. The army insisted that room must be left for expansion of the number to meet "unexpected developments," which the interventionists frankly expected and hoped for, their object being the establishment of a pro-Japanese government in eastern Siberia. Hara won a "victory in words" in the final exchange of notes with the United States, where Japan stressed its "belief" that there was no difference in view between the United States and Japan, but the fact that not 7000, but 72,000 Japanese troops were sent is instructive. Also, even though the entire intervention proved a failure, if not a fiasco, and Hara himself became premier (September, 1918–November, 1920), the fact that Japan's forces were not withdrawn from Vladivostok and northern Sakhalin until after the Washington Conference agreements of 1922 indicates the degree to which expansionist elements became entrenched in agencies of the Japanese government during World War I. The Nishihara loans and the Siberian intervention proved terribly costly to Japan, not only in money but in international goodwill, and the postwar treaty settlements saw Japan at odds with her erstwhile allies, China, Britain, and the United States.

VERSAILLES AND WASHINGTON TREATIES

Versailles Conference

Though Japan's wartime expansionist gains excited the animosity of the other Allied powers and the United States, no serious challenge to them emerged at the Versailles Conference. In general the various wartime agreements held firm. Britain, France, Italy, and ultimately the United States accepted Japanese possession of the German Shantung rights, the Caroline and Marshall Islands (as a League mandate), and refused to inquire into her relationships with China as established under the Twenty-one Demands settlements. The Chinese delegation made quite a fuss, however, despite the pro-Japan proclivities of the Tuan Ch'i-jui government and the treaties it had signed with Japan. This was because the Western-educated Chinese diplomats at Versailles, including the unrecognized Canton faction of Sun Yat-sen as well as Peking government appointees, were caught up in a spirit of nationalism, went beyond the intent of their instructions, and tried to plead China's case before the world forum. In this they were encouraged by members of the American delegation, who became their unofficial advisors.

Actually the American position was somewhat ambivalent. President Wilson, espousing international idealism, refused to recognize the secret treaties the Allies had made with Japan, and challenged the validity of her claims to Shantung, as well as, by implication, all her wartime gains in China. He read the Lansing-Ishii Agreement as merely an endorsement of Open Door principles. However, it is clear that Lansing had tried to develop a basis for a realistic bargain with Japan, an idea which the Japanese assumed to have been embodied in that agreement, and their delegates at Versailles, who represented the more liberal wing of the Japanese government, were angered and embittered at what looked to them like self-righteous deception on the part of Wilson. Therefore they tested his idealism by proposing, in effect, that since Japan was being asked to sacrifice real interests she had paid for in blood or treasure on behalf of a more enlightened international order, it should not be too much to have a clear expression of racial equality in the proposed League of Nations covenant.

The racial equality proposal stirred up a storm of protest from British empire representatives. Prime Minister Hughes of Australia, who was determined to keep orientals out of his "white Australia," was particularly vehement, but the proposal might have carried had not Wilson's own idealism cracked under the strain. Of a Southern background, which regarded segregation as a natural way of life, and elected narrowly in 1916 by the votes of a state (California) whose antioriental attitudes were notorious, Wilson could not face the domestic implications of his own international idealism, and, as chairman of the session on which the crucial racial equality vote was taken, he ruled it defeated because it was not unanimous, though the ayes were in the majority.

Defeated on racial equality, Japan was conceded Shantung and the rest. However, the repercussions were severe. The Chinese delegation refused to sign the Treaty and behind them at home thousands of students rose in vehement protest against the "betrayal" of China at Versailles. They demonstrated in Peking and other major cities, anti-Japanese boycotts were organized, and pro-Japanese ministers in Tuan's cabinet were harassed. The students could not bring down Tuan's Anfu regime themselves, but rival warlords used the "Japanese puppet" label to good effect and a coalition of them overthrew Tuan in the summer of 1920.

The ferment aroused in China was probably the most important result of the war years for the Far East in the long run, but the Western powers did not understand this at the time. Britain and the United States, and to a lesser extent France and Italy, were chiefly concerned at the vastly augmented power of Japan. American-Japanese relations were quite embittered by anti-Japanese agitation in California and a diplomatic squabble over the island of Yap, an important Pacific cable station, augmenting the larger frictions over Shantung, the Siberian intervention, and the closing door in Manchuria. A dangerous Pacific naval rivalry was in the making, and Britain was in the anomalous position of favoring the United States while being still married to Japan in the Anglo-Japanese alliance. However, there was nothing in the relationships of the three major powers which could not be settled by compromise, if the United States would accept Japan as a partner in maintaining Far Eastern balances and Japan would abandon her more extreme positions. This was accomplished at the Washington Conference, November 11, 1921–February 6, 1922.

Washington Conference

As international conferences go, the output of the Washington Conference (some seven treaties and twelve resolutions) was tremendous. And no one, seemingly, went home angry. Perhaps it was the most successful international conference of modern times. The Japanese were skeptical at first, knowing that there would be pressure on them to give up some of their recent gains, but the temptation to be a partner in momentous decisions brought them to Washington, and upon discovering that the United States was willing to bargain in what they understood to be the spirit of the Lansing-Ishii Agreement, they found the surroundings congenial. China was also represented, by some of the same men who had been at Versailles, now sadder and wiser, not expecting so much as at Versailles, but hopeful that some of the greatest wrongs done to China would be righted. Secretary of State Charles Evans Hughes demonstrated America's seriousness of purpose spectacularly in his welcoming address by offering to sink a substantial portion of the American navy and stop construction on other ships, if the other powers would cooperate in setting naval armament ratios.

The principal agreements of the Washington Conference were embodied in three major treaties: the Five Power, Four Power, and Nine Power Treaties. The Five Power Treaty, signed by the United States, Britain, Japan, France, and Italy, established naval ratios (5:5:3:1.75:1.75, respectively) on capital ships and agreements on Pacific area fortifications. Her ratio, coupled with a status quo regulation on non-Japanese fortifications east of Singapore and west of Pearl Harbor, left Japan as the policeman of western Pacific waters and the China coast. In return Japan gave up the Anglo-Japanese Alliance, which was dissolved in a face-saving Four Power (United States, Britain, France, Japan) Treaty, pledging cooperation and consultation in rather vague terms, and she accepted, for the first time in writing, the wider version of the Open Door policy, whereby the several powers would respect the sovereignty, independence, and territorial and administrative integrity of China. This was the main point of the Nine Power Treaty, which also pledged to uphold the principle of equal opportunity among nations for commercial enterprises in China (the original Open Door idea), to refrain from seeking concessions, and to provide "the fullest and most unembarrassed opportunity to China" to develop a stable government. Giving specific effect to these pledges, Japan, during the course of the Washington discussions, reached a separate agreement with China to return to her the Shantung leasehold and control of Shantung railways, on condition that certain Japanese economic rights be protected. Japan also promised to withdraw her troops from Siberia, which she did in November, 1922, although her withdrawal from northern Sakhalin Island, also Russian territory, was delayed until 1925 pending settlement of certain claims against Russia.

After the Washington Conference the world breathed easier. Balance had been restored in the Far East; the naval race was averted; the United States, Britain, and Japan had been successful, seemingly, in "freezing the Pacific." However, certain deficiencies in the arrangement should be noted. Soviet Russia was not represented at the Conference, and, although China was represented, her emerging nationalist aspirations went relatively unheeded. Nor were the voices of colonial peoples heard at all. It is ironic, but significant, that while the rich and powerful nations were settling their differences at Washington, representatives of the underprivileged were meeting in a "Congress of Toilers of the East," sponsored by Moscow, which included Chinese, Korean, Mongolian, left-wing Japanese, and even Indonesian participants. However, the challenge to the Versailles and Washington "settlements" was to come at first from nationalism rather than communism.

FAR EAST 1922

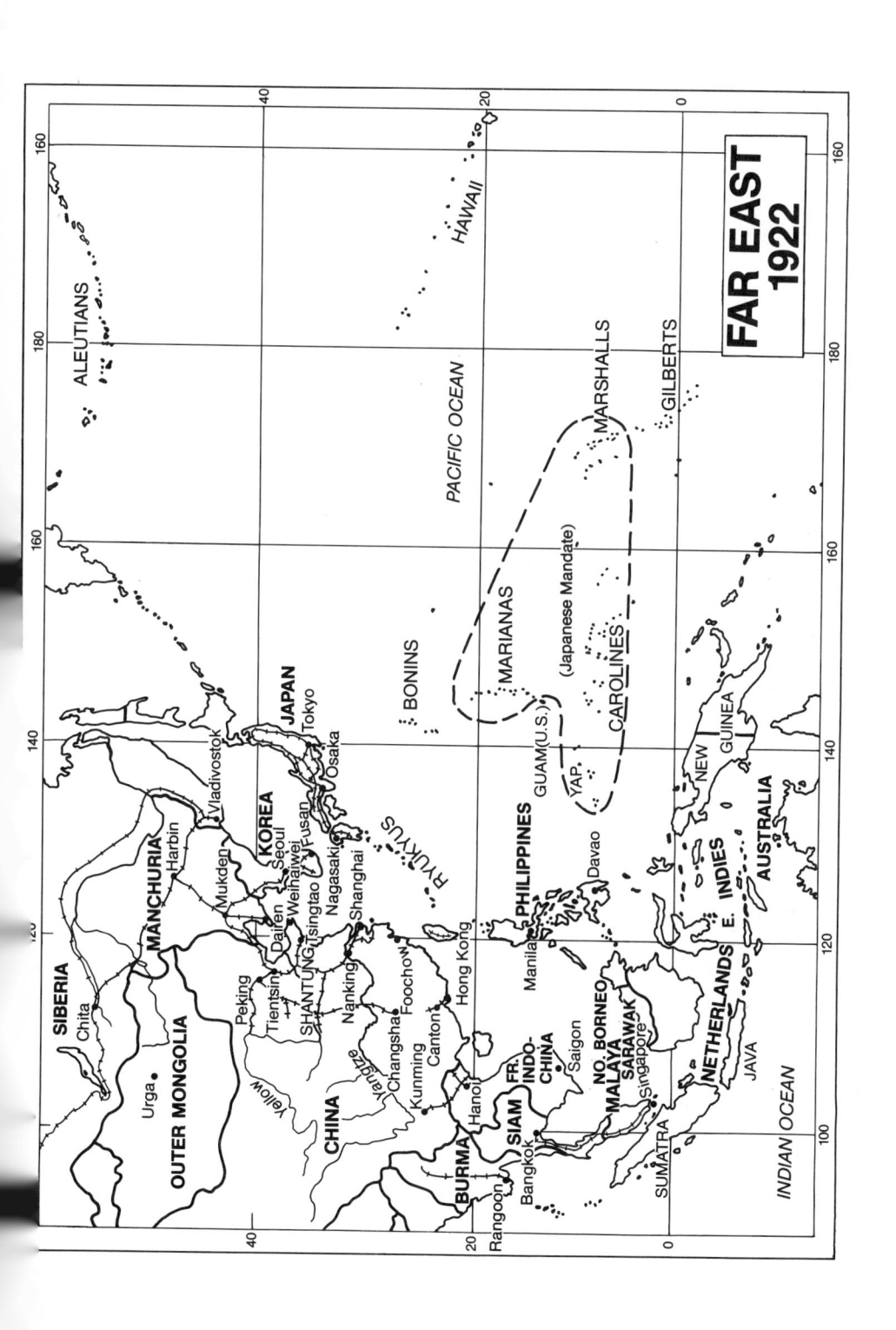

GROWTH OF THE CHINESE NATIONALIST MOVEMENT

Chinese nationalism was certainly a factor in the 1911 revolution, but in a particular anti-Manchu sense, and once the Manchus were out of the way, it did not play a significant political role for several years.

The "May 4 Movement"

Probably it can be said that Chinese nationalism in depth began with the aforementioned student demonstrations in Peking, which were climaxed by the burning of cabinet minister Ts'ao's house. This occurred on May 4, 1919, and the term "May 4 Movement" came to symbolize a vigorous new spirit which by the mid 1920's was bringing China into a new era of self-assertion. It was a compound of several elements. It was partly a "literary revolution" or "renaissance." The name "renaissance" was the name which a group of Peking University students gave to a new monthly magazine which they instituted in 1918. The heart of the renaissance was the idea, propounded most vigorously by a young Columbia University Ph.D. named Hu Shih, that the Chinese written language must be brought into conformity with the vernacular, called *pai hua*. Up to that time all serious literary work, official documents, and the like were written in classical Chinese, which as a spoken language was almost as dead as Latin or Sanskrit. Hu Shih and his friends perceived correctly that it had become a language of the elite and that it prevented wider communication with the masses of the people. Hu noted the fact that the various European nations began their rise to nationhood only with the development of a national language, one which produced a living literature. In China there were a few examples of popular novels written in the vernacular, but no scholar would use it except surreptitiously.

Hu began his campaign for pai hua while still at Columbia in 1916 with a volume of poetry called *A Book of Experiments*, followed by several articles advocating the new approach to literature published both in America and in China. On his return to China in 1917 Hu was invited to teach at Peking University, where the Dean of the College of Letters, Professor Ch'en Tu-hsiu, later the founder of the Chinese Communist party, supported his proposals. There was criticism from old scholars, but the May 4 Movement enormously popularized Hu's idea until by 1920 the Ministry of Education, despite its conservative predilections, ordered textbooks for the first two grades in the primary schools to be printed in the vernacular. In 1922 the order was extended to include all school texts.

The literary revolution spread rapidly as more and more scholars and publicists began to write in pai hua. This is not to say there were no difficulties. The principal immediate problem was that there was not one vernacular but many in China. Hu solved this by advocating that the north China or Peking Mandarin dialect be the standard one taught in all the schools.

Another problem, if mass education was to be achieved, was that offered by the sheer number of characters to be learned. A well-educated person of the old school had to spend years learning 5000 to 10,000 characters. Some effort at limitation and standardization of the number of ideographs was necessary if literacy was to cease to be the monopoly of the few who could command the leisure of years for studying them. Hence paralleling the call for patriotic scholars to write in the vernacular was a movement to limit the number of characters, to 5000, 3000, or even 1000. A former YMCA secretary, Dr. Y.C. (Jimmy) Yen, took the lead in this with his "1000 Character Mass Education Movement" and within a few years thousands of Chinese who under the old system would never have been able to read or write could read newspapers, pamphlets, and revolutionary tracts produced for popular consumption.

Although the literary revolution was probably its most spectacular aspect, there was also a more general intellectual revolution among China's young intelligentsia in these postwar years. The traditional Confucian value system was questioned, and replaced with a philosophy of science and pragmatism. Where K'ang Yu-wei had tried to find a progressive meaning in Confucianism at the turn of the century, by 1920 many returned students were ready to scoff at traditional ideas as metaphysical and unscientific. John Dewey lectured in Peking in 1919 and 1920 and his presence added to the prestige of those, like Hu Shih, who had studied with him at Columbia. With subtleties in his approach overlooked, Dewey's message emerged as "take a scientific view of life and society, the here and now, the concrete, the material." Hu Shih turned to pragmatism, while his friend, Ch'en Tu-hsiu, drew closer to philosophical Marxism, then communism. The idea of a "scientific" approach to society stirred more opposition than the idea of writing in the vernacular, because scholars like Liang Ch'i-ch'ao and others of K'ang Yu-wei's progressive Confucian school opposed it, and Ch'en Tu-hsiu's extremism brought about such a furor that he had to resign from Peking University. Perhaps no philosophical school won the broader intellectual revolution at this stage, but that may be a significant point. Even though unable to agree on philosophic fundamentals, the various camps shared a fervent desire to improve things in China. This allowed them to cooperate broadly in the cause of nationalism, and such a project as developing a popular literature that the whole nation could read was an excellent case in point.

Social Changes

The new nationalism had a social as well as an intellectual foundation. The growth of industry, often foreign-owned or financed, in the cities and of active trade along the coast gave many young rural Chinese an escape valve. And in the cities young workers, like young students, both male and female, began to reject Confucian familial relationships. Working for wages, instead of on a family farm, they developed a sense of independence from traditions and ancestors.

Competition with foreign industrial concerns also stimulated nationalism. For example, a Chinese cigarette company founded in 1905 enjoyed a tremendous expansion in the period from 1914 to about 1927, as Chinese cigarette consumption increased some twenty-five fold. The company was making excellent use of a "made by Chinese" label in the 1920's. A study of shoemaking in Tientsin reveals that out of 145 shops studied in 1931, 100 had been established since 1924. Another point of interest was that 61 per cent of the shoemakers studied could be classed as literate, with the younger apprentices providing a substantially higher percentage of literates than the older journeymen.

Of course, cigarettes and shoes were not the major industries of China. Textile mills, iron mines, and shipyards were much bigger operations. But they were even further removed from customary rural or village life, and when a young farm boy found his way into them he learned that personal ties counted for little in the job market, and that opportunity might best be enhanced through labor organizations which promoted nationalistic and revolutionary sentiments.

Nationalism on the Move

Clearly intellectuals, merchants, and city workers were feeling the quickening pulse of Chinese nationalism in the 1920's. (Parenthetically, it should be added that the peasants, as peasants, were yet to be heard from, though a young library worker at Peking University, Mao Tse-tung, was beginning to have ideas about the role they might play.) Meanwhile the urbanites showed their feelings concretely in demonstratoins, boycotts, and strikes against Japanese, against all foreigners, and against fainthearted or reactionary officials when they seemed to be dragging their feet. Perhaps the most spectacular manifestation of national feeling was in connection with the Shanghai Incident of May 30, 1925, when British-officered police fired on Chinese students who had entered the International Settlement to protest working conditions at a Japanese-owned textile mill. Nine Chinese were killed, and this "murder of Chinese by foreigners on Chinese soil" reverberated up and down the coast and along the Yangtze river as far as Chungking. The worst rioting was at Canton where foreign troops fired into a Chinese crowd.

Meanwhile the Peking "Republic," the recognized government of China, though it remained under the control of various northern warlords until its overthrow in 1928, gave at least lip service to nationalist aims, and in some ways served them.

For example, a close view of "Model Governor" Yen Hsi-shan, whose stronghold was Shansi province, shows that while his main objective was undoubtedly to stabilize his own regime so as to maintain and expand his area of control, he encouraged village assemblies as a popular check on local gentry and he instituted a four-year mass education system. These steps were soon pushing him toward more far-reaching changes than he had intended.

However, the most important contribution of the northern warlords was perhaps the negative one that while they jockeyed for power at Peking, they left the diplomacy of China in the hands of bright young patriots like Wellington Koo, C. T. Wang, and Alfred Sze, who practiced all the diplo-

FIGURE 21.1. The Bund (landing stage) at Shanghai in the 1920s.

matic tricks they could muster to regain China's long-compromised sovereignty with some success. They negotiated equal treaties with Germany, Austria, and Soviet Russia, all of whom had lost their privileged position in China as a result of World War I. Then they approached Belgium and other small powers and succeeded in negotiating several more equal treaties, which broke the solid ring of unequal treaty relationships that had been forged in the nineteenth century. Also the big powers began to give ground. The Shantung and Weihaiwei leaseholds were given up by Japan and Britain. Foreign post offices, numbering nearly 100, were closed. Tariff rates were raised and the promise of general tariff autonomy was set for January 1, 1929. Also, China's demand for an end to extraterritoriality was forcefully presented.

THE KUOMINTANG REVITALIZED AND VICTORIOUS

The above discussion of Chinese nationalism in the post-World War I era has considered the combustible material which composed it without coming to the sparks which set it afire. The latter consisted of Sun Yet-sen's Kuomintang, as revitalized by an alliance with communism.

Sun at Canton

As related earlier, Sun and his party, after being ousted from the Peking government, had entrenched themselves at Canton in 1917. There they kept up a precarious existence, with Sun, disillusioned and suspicious, trying to hold his followers with oaths of personal loyalty to him and trying to gain territory by playing warlord politics with southern militarists. Indeed, the jockeying for power in south China during the period 1917–1925 was not very different from what went on in north China except that it was even more petty, and the southern factions, including Sun's, were sometimes pawns in the games of the bigger warlords of the north.

However, Sun was actually a man of great ideas who had stooped to petty tactics only in desperation. Perhaps he learned the futility of this in 1922 when his own commander in chief, Ch'en Hsiung-ming, entered into collusion with Wu P'ei-fu's clique while Sun was temporarily cooperating with Chang Tso-lin at a time when Wu and Chang were at war. Sun completely lost control of the situation and had to flee temporarily to Shanghai.

In Shanghai in December, 1922 Sun met with Adolf Joffe, agent of the Comintern, in a meeting which was to have far-reaching consequences. Sun was not a communist and never became one. He continued to the end of his life to seek the goals of national freedom and self-respect for China, self-government for her people, and an improved standard of living. But he was rather sympathetically disposed toward Soviet Russia, whose successful revolution against an ancient tyranny (rather like the old Manchu empire) impressed him, and whose offers of aid contrasted rather sharply with the coldness he had repeatedly received from Britain, America, and Japan. He made it clear to Joffe that he would have no communist dictatorship in China, but he lent a willing ear to Joffe's offer of revolutionary know-how,

FIGURE 21.2. Chang Tso-lin.

the cooperation of a small but already well organized Chinese Communist party, and he acknowledged that at least on the goal of freeing China from imperialist controls and warlord rule his objective and the communists' were the same. Also it should be noted that, unlike Gandhi, Sun Yet-sen had no clear philosophy concerning the relationship of means and ends. He saw no contradiction in using violent means to achieve peaceful ends or temporary dictatorship to achieve democracy, and in that sense he could also agree with the communist theory of revolution.

Sun and Joffe reached agreement in January, 1923, and within a year communist advisors were re-energizing the Kuomintang. Chiang Kai-shek, Sun's choice as military commander, was sent to Moscow for a period of training with the Red Army, and Michael Borodin came out from Russia to teach Kuomintang politicians how to reorganize the party and build mass support. The party was reorganized along the lines of the Russian Communist party, with local cells, an annual party congress and a Central Executive Committee, which, once policy had been decided, could invoke party discipline. Also on the advice of Soviet General Vasilii Blücher (Galen) a military academy for officer training was established at Whampoa, near Canton. On his return from Russia Chiang, who earlier had studied in military schools in north China and in Japan, was named its president. This was highly important for Chiang's future career, for his most dependable personal support in future years was to come from officers trained at the academy.

The Three Principles of the People

One of the most important contributions made by the communists was training in the use of propaganda. Borodin set up a special institute for this and trained some 20,000 people who began to spread the gospel of revolutionary nationalism through south China. Sun Yat-sen himself provided the ideas, which, at Borodin's urging, he focused and simplified to a greater extent than ever before. Sun was widely read and had a brilliantly agile mind filled with ideas acquired from many sources, from America, Western Europe, Japan, his own China, and more recently Soviet Russia. To make them into a ringing revolutionary program was a difficult task, but Sun was equal to it. He focused his thinking in a series of lectures entitled *San Min Chu I* (The Three Principles of the People) which he expounded in 1924. He took the triplex idea from Lincoln's classic "government of the people, by the people and for the people." He called his principles Nationalism, Democracy, and People's Livelihood.

The first principle, Nationalism, reveals most clearly his differences with the communists. China must unite as a nation, self-conscious, vigorous, and recover her sovereign rights. (There was no room for communist class war or emphasis on internationalism.) The second principle, Democracy, was a three-stage goal, its implementation being preceded by military seizure of power by the revolutionary party and then a period of Kuomintang tutelage of the people. The third, Livelihood, was built on a combination of Henry George and socialist doctrines with private, but equalized, ownership of land and state development and ownership of major industries. To political scientists and economists Sun's principles seem vague and even contradictory, but to the restive people of mid-1920's China "Nationalism, Democracy, and People's Livelihood" became their chief symbol of hope.

The Northern Expedition

Sun Yat-sen died in 1925 before any clear result of the revitalization of his party could be seen, but almost with his last breath he urged the continuation of the communist alliance. Actually there was some dissatisfaction with it on both sides. Ch'en Tu-hsiu, the Chinese communist leader, had opposed it as a compromise with nationalism, and only severe pressure from the Comintern had brought him into line. Also Mao Tse-tung, who was a minor communist organizer at the time, kept advocating that more attention be paid to peasants, for the communists were being most active and successful among the urban proletariat. On the other hand, merchants and other right-wing elements in the Kuomintang feared the communist connection and disliked the growing power of the working class. However, a grand project held them all together, a Northern Expedition to unite China, which Sun had dreamed of for years.

With Chiang Kai-shek in military command and Michael Borodin as political commissar, the Northern Expedition was launched in the summer of 1926. It was remarkably successful, one prong of the revolutionary army moving northwest to Hankow and the other, which Chiang personally commanded, taking Nanking. Propaganda had been well laid, and the army was full of enthusiasm and was welcomed in cities and towns as an army of liberation. Warlord resistance collapsed throughout south China, and Hankow was proclaimed the new national capital. Madame Sun Yat-sen, Wang Ching-wei, and other Kuomintang leaders were there, as well as Borodin and other leading communists. Chiang Kai-shek was supposed to join them on the Central Executive Committee. However, Chiang had been becoming increasingly suspicious of and antagonistic to the left-wingers. He now refused to come to Hankow, and instead began negotiations with banking and merchant circles in Shanghai, who were very frightened at the revolutionary outbreaks and anxious to come to terms. A workers' revolt facilitated Chiang's capture of Shanghai, but Chiang accepted substantial "loans" from the business elements and turned his guns on the workers' "Red Guard." Ever since, communists have accused him of the vilest treachery.

The Establishment of the Nanking Government

However, Chiang triumphed. The Hankow group split, some wishing to negotiate with Chiang, and when Stalin sent rather arrogant orders, the nationalist sensitivities of most of the Chinese were injured. Borodin and the other Russian advisors were invited to leave, all communists were expelled from the Kuomintang, and the Central Executive Committee moved to Nanking where Chiang became the undisputed leader of the party and a new Nationalist government. Early in 1928 Nationalist forces moved northward against Chang Tso-lin, the entrenched warlord at Peking. Peking was taken on June 5, 1928, the "Manchurian Marshal" having fled the day before to Manchuria where he expected to resume his role as regional warlord. But Chang was assassinated by Japanese ultranationalists in a bizarre incident which presaged exceedingly ominous developments in Japan. To these we now turn.

JAPAN'S LIBERAL ERA

Although the Terauchi government (1916–1918) had been authoritarian, spendthrift, and expansionist, the immediate postwar years saw promising developments in Japanese politics. The Terauchi cabinet went down in a flood of popular indignation at its failure to raise the standard of living even in a period of unprecedented prosperity in Japan. "Rice riots" protesting inflated prices and shortages, which swept Japan in the summer of 1918, were the immediate cause of its downfall. Even the old military Genro, Yamagata, was frightened enough at the specter of popular revolt that he accepted the advice of the "liberal Genro," Saionji, that it was time for Japan to have responsible parliamentary government. Hara Takashi, leader of the Seiyukai party and a commoner who had often crossed swords with his betters, was the logical choice for premier. When he took office on September 29, 1918, the institution of "transcendental cabinet" which the Meiji oligarchs had fashioned and for so long manipulated seemed to have died a natural death.

Hara

There was a wave of popular enthusiasm, for Hara had become a symbol of the common people's many aspirations for universal suffrage, tax relief, broader opportunities for higher education, and amelioration of social inequalities, which were being voiced by politicians in the lower house of the Diet. But popular expectations were too high. Hara improved opportunities for higher education and provided some broadening of the suffrage, and he replaced military with civilian colonial government in Korea and Formosa. But he played down universal suffrage while attempting the reshuffling of election districts, and he could not give tax relief in the face of continuing military demands on the budget. (The military could point to the Siberian expedition and the impending naval race with the United States as big "defense" needs.) In addition, some of Hara's subordinates turned their good political fortune into financial fortune by corrupt means. Also the European armistice of November 11, 1918, inaugurated a period of economic retrenchment and hardship for Japan as the wartime boom subsided. Hence there was considerable disillusionment with Hara's administration which may have encouraged an unbalanced railroad employee in a successful assassination against Hara at Tokyo Station on November 13, 1921.

Hara's finance minister, Takahashi, succeeded him briefly, but then the Genro maneuvered the appointment of three successive bureaucratic cabinets while the international balances set up at the Washington Conference were put into effect.

The period from 1922 to 1924 was an era of admirals. Admiral Kato Tomosaburo was chief delegate at the Washington Conference, then took the premiership himself, and was succeeded at his death by another admiral. The admirals were able to "freeze the Pacific" and to tone down the army's adventurous northeast Asian program. These policies coincided with the aims of Saionji, the principal cabinet maker.

Kato Takaaki and Shidehara

However, the man with the greatest public backing after Hara was Kato Takaaki, the leader of the Kenseikai (later the Minseitō) party, who after burning his fingers on the Twenty-one Demands (see Chapter 22), had become a powerful exponent of popular rights in Japan and conciliatory policies abroad. He had opposed the Terauchi government on the Nishihara loans and the Siberian expedition, and he had pressed Hara for universal suffrage. He would have been premier earlier had not the Genro blocked him, but in 1924 there was no denying his political leadership, and on June 11 of that year, when he assumed the premiership, it seemed that responsible parliamentary government was at last there to stay in Japan.

True to his main promise Kato put through a bill removing all property qualifications on voting and establishing universal adult male suffrage. This increased the size of the electorate some four times to about 14 million. In addition, Kato made good on numerous secondary promises. He succeeded in cutting military budgets, over the vigorous opposition of the army, reorganized the House of Peers to give it a broader outlook, secured the appointment of a Privy Council chairman who was sympathetic to parliamentary government, and took steps to eliminate sinecure posts from the government service.

In foreign affairs Kato sought to ease outstanding tensions. In this spirit negotiations were undertaken with Soviet Russia which resulted in the establishment of regular diplomatic relations and the withdrawal of Japanese troops from northern Sakhalin, upon Russian settlement of certain claims. To China he promised sympathetic consideration and his foreign minister, Shidehara Kijuro, developed the famous "conciliatory policy" toward China. This included turning back the balance of the Boxer indemnity payments to be used for educational purposes, accepting various Chinese tariff increases and approving the tariff autonomy idea, and avoiding participation in foreign retaliation for injuries suffered by foreigners in the Nationalist capture of Nanking in 1927. He stood with the Western powers in refusing to abandon extraterritoriality until the Chinese court system had improved, but urged Western-style court procedures on the Chinese. In fact, Shidehara, who held the post of foreign minister from June, 1924 to December, 1931 except for two years (1927–1929), was perhaps more important to the era of liberalism than Kato, who died suddenly while still in office in January, 1926.

The Intellectual Scene

Responsible parliamentary government and international conciliation, which were put into practice by Kato, Shidehara, and their associates, were backed at the highest intellectual level by the teachings of Minobe Tatsukichi, Tachi Sakutaro, and Yoshino Sakuzo, Tokyo Imperial University professors who subjected Japanese political traditions to rational analysis and "proved" to the satisfaction of liberally inclined educated people that these approaches were correct. Professor Minobe, a constitutional lawyer, dealt with perhaps the thorniest problem of all, the position of the emperor in the parliamentary system. He concluded that the emperor was one of the organs of the state, along with the Diet and the cabinet, but he was not the total expression of the state, as mystically minded traditionalists tried to maintain. Minobe's views were considered very radical when first introduced about 1912, but by the late 1920's they were widely accepted and were included in school textbooks on politics. Yoshino even justified labor movements and social-democratic politics, which made his position too radical for most of his colleagues, but he was very popular with college students.

Japanese universities in the 1920's were fairly teeming with ideas. Several private institutions like Waseda and Keio and missionary-founded colleges like Doshisha and Aoyama Gakuin, competed with the imperial universities and provided the added stimulus of perspectives that were not related to national service or national goals. Some preparatory schools, like Jiyu Gakuin (the Free Academy), were so highly experimental, involving themselves even in women's rights, that they were not accredited, but they flourished anyway.

WEAKNESS OF JAPANESE LIBERALISM

Perhaps the weakness of Japanese liberalism may be epitomized by saying it was "behind the times," a nineteenth-century variety, business-dominated and imperialist, with little concern for the problems of the lower classes at home or the aspirations of colonial peoples abroad. Of course, in the 1920's even the great liberal powers with which Japan was trying to associate herself as an equal, the United States and Great Britain, were something less than paragons of progress on labor problems, the rights of minority groups, and colonial aspirations for freedom. However, in Britain and America the machinery of democratic government, wherein problems even of an unanticipated sort could be worked out, was firmly grounded. This was not true in Japan.

In Japan the idea that the cabinet should be transcendental had begun to give way only as recently as 1918, with the Hara ministry being the first to acknoweldge responsibility to the Diet. The Diet itself was still widely distrusted as an alien institution, especially at the lower levels of Japanese society, and it was extremely susceptible to manipulation by the wealthy elements. Secondly, Japan having but recently emerged from a backward state, her people were ultra-sensitive to slights and insults by foreigners, and even sophisticated Japanese were highly nationalistic beneath a suave internationalist exterior. Thirdly, Japan was economically far weaker than the powers with whom she was trying to keep up in the international arena.

National Sensitivity

Certain episodes in the 1920's reveal these conditions and point the way toward the calamities that befell Japan's parliamentary structure in the 1930's. For example, the aftermath of the tragic earthquake of September 1, 1923, shows how close to the surface nationalism and chauvinism lay. After the earthquake, fires swept the city of Tokyo and rumors spread that alien elements, Koreans, Chinese, and "socialists," were responsible. Patriotic toughs roamed the city seeking them out for punishment, and the police, instead of protecting them, joined in the persecution. Hundreds, perhaps thousands, were killed, and one noted radical leftist, Osugi Sakae, together with his wife and small nephew, were murdered in jail by a military police captain.

Another incident which helped to undermine Japanese liberalism was not Japanese but American in origin, the Oriental Exclusion Act of 1924, which refused to allow even the smallest quota of Japanese immigrants into the United States. This gave national sanction to the long-standing anti-Japanese feeling on the West Coast and the discrimination practiced there. Kaneko Kentaro, whose American ties went back some forty years to student days at Harvard Law School, resigned the presidency of the America-Japan Society in protest against the law, and hundreds of other Japanese friends of America, who were almost always friends of constitutional government also, were disillusioned or embittered.

Labor-Farmer Movement

The hostile attitudes of the major parties, the Kenseikai (which became the Minseito) and the Seiyukai, toward labor-farmer movements was another factor contributing to the weakness of Japanese liberalism. The major parties were definitively business-oriented, so much so that they were sometimes called by the names of the business combines with which they were most closely connected, Mitsubishi (Kenseikai-Minseito) and Mitsui (Seiyukai). It is interesting that when liberalism was presumably coming into full bloom with the passage of universal manhood suffrage, a Peace Preservation Law was also passed, which provided for ten years' imprisonment as punishment for participation in any organization whose object was "to change the fundamental character of the state or to deny the system of private property." Ozaki Yukio and other party members whose roots were in the "people's rights" advocacy of the Meiji era opposed the law, but the party leadership, including Kato, evidently saw no contradiction to liberalism in it. Unfortunately not only Communists, but socialists (however gentle), social democrats, labor leaders, socially conscious liberals, and eventually the major party leaders themselves were to fall under its ominous shadow as holders of something vaguely defined as "dangerous thoughts."

Nevertheless there were serious attempts in the next five years to organize labor-farmer parties. Suzuki Bunji, the "Friendly Society" labor leader, Abe Isoo, the Waseda University professor who had tried to launch a Social Democratic party as far back as 1901, and Professor Yoshino Sakuzo, who resigned from Tokyo University, took the lead. Their first attempts were branded communistic, but they persisted and were able to enter actively in the election of 1928, in which both Suzuki and Abe were elected to the Diet. However, the Home Ministry had invoked the Peace Preservation ordinances with such devastating effect that, although the new labor-farmer vote was potentially 75 per cent of the total, their parties won only 4.7 per cent, good for eight Diet seats. Two years later they won only five. This was really an ominous outcome in view of the fact that the major parties offered no program for the alleviation of farm and labor distress, and the persistent post-World War I recession in Japan found no relief before the major worldwide depression set in. Frustrated in parliamentary politics, labor-farmer distress came to support more violent types of political activity. But for the fact that its leadership was in jail, communism might have gained a mass following. As it was, in Japan, the principal beneficiary of the weakness of liberalism was the extreme right wing, which advocated ultranationalist expansionism as the cure-all for Japan's ills.

RISE OF ULTRANATIONALISM IN JAPAN

Japanese liberalism had its deficiencies, but still it might have survived and moved Japan in a liberal direction both in domestic and foreign affairs if it had not been subjected to virulent attacks from self-appointed guardians of Japan's heritage and destiny. These were individuals and groups who believed, or professed to believe, the myths of the origin of Japan and her god-emperors contained in the *Kojiki*, and who saw Japan as a special nation, destined to rule others through the peculiar benevolence of her imperial ruler. They detested the barbarian Western world and its "alien" influence in Japan and other Far Eastern countries. This earned them esteem as opponents of Western imperialism, but their egocentricity was such that they could never see Japanese expansion as anything but benevolent, righteous, and just. They talked incessantly about morality, but it was the morality of the old Confucianist-samurai world, the morality of tradition, loyalty, and emperor worship. Always vague on their ideals and goals, they were nevertheless quite specific as to methods. Disdaining parliamentary politics as a Western invention, they advocated and practiced "direct action." Assassination, violence, attack, even if suicidal, was their battle plan against the "enemies" of the emperor, but they also made adroit use of propaganda to stir up feelings of fear and hatred.

In the Meiji era they had concentrated on foreign affairs and their semi-secret Kokuryūkai (Black Dragon or Amur River Society) had played a role in molding Japanese opinion to favor war with Russia, annexation of Korea, and general continental expansion. They continued to advocate expansionism in the 1920's but in addition harnessed a good deal of support from lower-class, especially agrarian, discontent in Japan by claiming that the Western-style businessman's parliamentary government was exploiting the people.

Kita and Okawa

In 1923 Kita Ikki, who was the principal spokesman for this new social reformist element of the right wing, published an "Outline Plan for the Reorganization of Japan" which demanded the abolition of the peerage system and the various upper-class advisors surrounding the emperor, so that he could emerge as a "People's Emperor." With a "People's Emperor" reforms such as an eight-hour work day, a land reform program, and nationalization of industries and wealth could be effected. The zaibatsu-controlled Diet would never allow these things, said Kita, hence it must be overthrown. The best way would be through a coup d'état by the army, after which martial law must be proclaimed to allow the suppression of the nobility and the wealthy on the one hand and those who were importing foreign revolutionary creeds like "half-witted" democracy, "effeminate" pacifism, and "doctrinaire" socialism on the other. Japan must express "a national opinion

FIGURE 21.3. Emperor Hirohito.

in which no dissenting voice is heard" and the emperor must become again, as of old, "the commander-in-chief of an equal people." (Equal people, however, did not include women, who as "the mother of the nation and the wife of the nation" should not be involved in politics.) Having thus been "renovated" herself, Japan could then assume the leadership of China and other Asian nations and bring about a revival of Asia.

While Kita's branch of the ultranationalist movement seemed to desire an internal Japanese "renovation" first, others, led by Okawa Shumei, a research director of the South Manchurian Railroad Company, maintained that direct action on the continent would reverberate back to invigorate and purify the Japanese nation. To Okawa it would be enough to eliminate those in authority who were too blind to see this or too weak to carry it out. It is interesting that in the long run Kita's social reform ideas were dropped out of the ultranationalist movement, and Kita himself was arrested and executed in 1936 for attempting the sort of coup d'état he had long advocated, while Okawa's brand of expansion abroad without social reform at home won increasing support in government and business circles and became the basis for the "Greater East Asia Co-prosperity Sphere" idea of the later 1930's. However, the two ideas were intertwined in the 1920's and early 1930's, with the social reform element no doubt contributing much to the mass support the movement developed.

Young Officers

Of course, two ideologists like Kita and Okawa could not alone have set Japan on the path to ultranationalism and aggressive war. However, their ideas were very appealing to half-educated, ambitious young army officers, whose peasant backgrounds made them a channel for the expression of rural grievances. And the failure of the farmer-labor movement to obtain a voice in parliamentary politics left rural Japan constituting "election districts for the army," as a Japanese scholar has expressed it. Military cutbacks sharpened rural antagonism to the liberal governments, for the chief road open to advancement for rural youth had been the army. As the Black Dragon and other civilian rightist societies warned of alien dangers, reservists and active-duty young officers joined them or organized counterpart societies of their own, condemning government "appeasement" and even denouncing old-line "civilian-minded" generals like Tanaka, who were, in their view, participating in or cooperating with appeasement. It was during Tanaka's premiership, in 1928, that the rightists began to practice their "direct action" in earnest.

INTERVENTION IN CHINA

The march northward of Chiang Kai-shek and his Nationalist forces from Nanking in the spring of 1928 posed a serious problem for the Tanaka government. Japan was giving ground slowly to Chinese nationalist aspirations, but the new Chinese government, as yet unrecognized by Japan, was accelerating things. When Chiang entered Shantung province, where there were many Japanese residents and investments left from Japan's wartime holding of the German leasehold, Tanaka dispatched troops from Tientsin to "protect them." In May there were several sharp engagements between Chinese and Japanese troops, but finally the affair was settled.

Meanwhile, Tanaka was in touch with Chang Tso-lin at Peking seeking guarantees that he would honor Japanese interests in Manchuria and urging that he withdraw to Manchuria and consolidate his position there before it was too late. Marshal Chang may have been following this advice when he entrained for Mukden on June 3, accompanied by troops and guards. But on the outskirts of Mukden in the early morning hours of June 4 the train was wrecked and Chang killed in an explosion which occurred just as the train went beneath a viaduct of the Japanese-owned South Manchurian Railroad.

Since there was obvious Japanese complicity in this assassination, it was widely assumed that the Tanaka government had ordered it, and that it was part of a plan somehow associated with the "Tanaka Memorial." However, these contemporary explanations and suspicions were incorrect. Those who voiced them failed to understand the underlying forces at work in Japanese army politics, which were not revealed until after World War II. The truth was that Tanaka had not ordered the assassination; he was hoping that Chang Tso-lin would resume power in Manchuria, separate it from the rest of China, and continue to recognize Japanese interests there, whatever the Nationalists might do. But certain "Young Officers" of Japan's Kwantung (Manchurian) army, which was seething with ultranationalist sentiment, had plotted to create an incident deliberately, so as to force the hand of their own government into taking direct control of Manchuria and ceasing to "appease" Chinese nationalism and world opinion.

The plot failed in its immediate objective, because large-scale fighting between Japanese and Chinese troops did not develop, as Colonel Kawamoto, the chief perpetrator of the plot, had hoped. But Tanaka's Manchurian policy was thrown into chaos and the Army Ministry refused to carry out the sort of searching investigation that would have revealed the enormity of the plot "lest the honor of the Army be tarnished." Tanaka, himself a general, came face to face with the fact that the Kwantung army was running out of control. His Seiyukai cabinet fell on July 2, 1929, and the Minseito party, with Hamaguchi Osachi as premier and Shidehara again as foreign minister, returned to power to attempt to control the situation.

BASIC DATES

1914	Japan enters World War I, takes Shantung leasehold
1915	Twenty-one Demands
1916	Yuan Shih-k'ai fails to become emperor, dies
1917	Tuan Ch'i-jui and Anfu Clique; Nishihara loans; China enters World War I
1918	Siberian intervention; rice riots in Japan

1918–1921   Hara cabinet in Japan
1919   Japan wins demands (except racial equality) at Versailles; May 4th Incident at Peking; Chinese intellectual "renaissance"
1921–1922   Washington conference and communist conference of "Toilers of the East"
1923   Sun Yat-sen and Adolf Joffe reach agreement on Kuomintang-communist cooperation; Tokyo earthquake
1924   United States Oriental exclusion law
1925   Death of Sun Yat-sen; May 30 Incident at Shanghai; Universal Manhood Suffrage and Peace Preservation acts in Japan
1926   Northern Expedition starts from Canton
1927   Chiang K'ai-shek splits with communists; establishes Nationalist government at Nanking
1928   Nationalists take Peking; murder of Chang Tso-lin in Manchuria

SUPPLEMENTARY READING

Borton, H. *Japan's Modern Century*, rev. ed. New York, 1970.
Brown, D. M. *Nationalism in Japan*. Berkeley, Calif., 1955.
Clubb, O. E. *Twentieth Century China*. New York, 1964.
Fairbank, J. K., E. O. Reischauer, and A. Craig. *East Asia: The Modern Transformation*. Boston, 1965. Revised and abbreviated ed., 1973.
Hsü, I. C. Y. *The Rise of Modern China*. New York, 1970.
Iriye, Akira. *Across the Pacific: An Inner History of American-East Asian Relations*. New York, 1967.
Li, C. *The Political History of China, 1840–1928*. New York, 1956.
Scalapino, R. A. *Democracy and the Party Movement in Prewar Japan*. Berkeley, Calif., 1953.
Sharman, L. *Sun Yat-sen, His Life and Its Meaning*. New York, 1934.
Teng, S. Y. and J. K. Fairbank. *China's Response to the West: A Documentary Survey 1839–1923*. Cambridge, Mass., 1954.

ADVANCED READING

Arima, T. *The Failure of Freedom: A Portrait of Modern Japanese Intellectuals*. Cambridge, Mass., 1969.
Ch'en, J. *Yuan Shih-k'ai: Brutus Assumes the Purple*. Stanford, Calif., 1961.
Chow, T. *The May Fourth Movement*. Cambridge, Mass., 1960.
Duus, Peter, *Party Rivalry and Political Change in Taisho Japan*. Cambridge, Mass., 1968.
Grieder, J. B. *Hu Shih and the Chinese Renaissance: Liberalism in the Chinese Revolution, 1917–1937*. Cambridge, Mass., 1970.
Houn, F. W. *Central Government of China, 1912–1928*. Madison, Wisc., 1957.

Hu, S. *The Chinese Renaissance.* Chicago, 1933.
Iriye, Akira. *After Imperialism: The Search for a New Order in the Far East, 1921–1931.* Cambridge, Mass., 1965; New York, Atheneum, 1969.
Leng, S. and N. D. Palmer. *Sun Yat-sen and Communism.* New York, 1960.
Levenson, J. R. *Confucian China and Its Modern Fate.* Berkeley, Calif., 1958.
Marshall, B. K. *Capitalism and Nationalism in Prewar Japan: The Ideology of the Business Elite, 1868–1941.* Stanford, 1967.
Morley, J. W. *The Japanese Thrust into Siberia,* 1918. New York, 1957.
Morley, J. W., ed. *Dilemmas of Growth in Prewar Japan.* Princeton, N.J., 1971.
Roy, M. N. *Revolution and Counter-revolution in China.* Calcutta, 1946.
T'ang, L. *The Inner History of the Chinese Revolution.* London, 1928.
Wilson, G. M. *Radical Nationalist in Japan: Kita Ikki, 1883–1937.* Cambridge, Mass., 1969.
Yanaga, C. *Japan Since Perry.* New York, 1949; reprinted, 1966.

Chapter 22

Japan's Road to War: In China and the Pacific, 1928-1945

With the assassination of Chang Tso-lin the appetites of Japan's ultranationalists had only been whetted. Next they hatched an assassination plot against Premier Hamaguchi in retaliation for his "appeasement" policy at the London Naval Conference, which met in 1930 to further the reduction of naval armaments begun at the Washington Conference eight years earlier. Hamaguchi, wounded severely on November 15, 1930, was unable to resume office and Foreign Minister Shidehara became acting premier. Ultranationalists then planned a "March Incident" (1931) in which both the Minseito and Seiyukai party headquarters were to be blown up, civilian government destroyed, and Army Minister General Ugaki invited to take over the government. The March plot had to be abandoned when Ugaki refused to come forward, but the plotters, prominent among whom were Okawa Shumei and military officer members of a so-called "Cherry Society," then turned their attention to fomenting another Manchurian incident. Colonels Itagaki Seishirō and Ishiwara Kanji laid the detailed plans in Manchuria.

The Mukden Incident

This time they were successful, both in their immediate and long-range objectives. On the night of September 18, 1931, a small section of track on the Japanese South Manchurian Railway was blown up near Mukden. Claiming the Chinese had "attacked," Colonel Dohihara Kenji, a strong policy advocate, declared martial law in Mukden, and various sections of the Kwantung army fanned out to take over direct control of large sections of

Manchuria. Then, as sporadic resistance by the Chinese provided an excuse for wider and wider Japanese military activity, Japan entered a period of "dual diplomacy," wherein the Foreign Office under Shidehara sought to minimize the conflict while the military sought to expand it. This phenomenon had occurred occasionally before, and the Japanese governmental structure was peculiarly conducive to it because the premier lacked full authority over the army and navy ministries. However, never before had civilian authority been so completely ignored. Also there were wheels within wheels, wherein the military commanders in the field in Manchuria really made policy, presenting their own superiors with *faits accomplis* which were then covered by general officers and the army minister. Meanwhile the patriotic propaganda apparatus worked overtime in Japan to convince the public that only the army had an effective policy in Manchuria. With the Shidehara "conciliatory policy" shattered, the Minseito cabinet resigned on December 13, and the Seiyukai, promising to do a better job of balancing the national interests, took over under Inukai Tsuyoshi as premier.

Inukai thought he could control the situation by placating the military, and he tried to create an illusion of solidarity by appointing General Araki Sadao, who because of his frequent patriotic utterances was very popular with the Young Officers, as army minister. But Araki only encouraged them in their excesses. Dohihara had brought the ex-Manchu boy emperor of China, known in the West as Henry P'u-yi, from Tientsin to Mukden to assume office as head of the "country of the Manchus" (Manchukuo), a puppet state which the Kwantung army was busily erecting, with or without the approval of Tokyo.

Meanwhile, "direct action" was bringing Tokyo into line. Baron Dan Takuma, head of the giant Mitsui company, the principal financial backer of the Seiyukai, was assassinated by a farm boy from an ultranationalist society on March 5, and Premier Inukai himself was killed in an incredibly audacious uprising of the Blood Brotherhood League (Ketsumeidan) on May 15th. On that occasion the Seiyukai headquarters, the Bank of Japan, the Mitsubishi Bank, and other places associated with the "corrupt business government" were also attacked. The perpetrators of these crimes were arrested, but their trials became a patriotic circus as they based their defense on the claim of love for the emperor and service to the state. Army Minister Araki said that though they had broken the law, he could only admire the purity of their motive. Their sentences were remarkably light.

End of Party Government

Inukai's was the last responsible party government until after World War II. The army said definitely it would not accept another "politician" as premier, and Elder Statesman Saionji resorted to his favorite device for a time of troubles. Hoping to use military men to check the military, he recommended the appointment of an admiral to the premiership. This proved acceptable and two admirals, Saito and Okada, in succession occupied the premiership on a nonparty "transcendental" basis from 1932 to 1936. During this period the Tokyo government fell in behind the creation

FIGURE 22.1.   Saionji and Inukai.

of the new puppet state of Manchukuo, recognizing it and withdrawing from the League of Nations in 1933 after the Lytton Report, which condemned Japanese actions in Manchuria, was adopted by the League.

Politics now shifted away from the Diet, which more and more became a rubber stamp, to the military where the "Young Officer" (or "Imperial Way") faction, which embraced the radical "People's Emperor" ideas of Kita Ikki, opposed an emerging "Control Group," which rejected those ideas and showed itself not unwilling to compromise with big business and the aristocracy if they would support continental expansion. The Control Group gradually gained the upper hand, as it maneuvered out of position Army Minister Araki and the inspector-general of military education, Mazaki Jinzaburo, who were the highest ranking spokesmen for the Young Officers.

By 1936 the Young Officers saw their situation deteriorating and on February 26, 1936, they attempted the most spectacular coup of all. Former Premier Saito, Premier Okada, Prince Saionji, and numerous other government leaders and palace advisors were marked for assassination, and the Control Group's appointee as inspector-general of military education, one General Watanabe, was a special target. Okada and Saionji miraculously escaped, but most of the others, including Watanabe, were mowed down, as some 1400 insurgent troops took control of key points in Tokyo, including the prime minister's official residence and the War Ministry. However, they then waited, apparently expecting Araki or Mazaki to take command or perhaps the emperor to make a pronouncement in their favor. Instead, as martial law was declared and Control Group troops were brought into the city, they were informed that they might best show their loyalty by committing suicide, which their leader finally did. Then the others surrendered. The army leadership, now shocked to the core to see the sort of insurgency it had encouraged against civilian party governments turned against itself, meted out swift justice this time. Thirteen army officers and four civilians, including Kita Ikki, were sentenced by court martial and executed.

The disciplining of the February 26th rebels did not, unfortunately, give a new breath of life to liberalism in Japan. Army politics merely were concerned with the question of which brand of ultranationalism would be official and which faction would be at the helm. Both groups believed in rule from above by military force and neither had the slightest respect for freedom of thought, religion, or speech. Intellectuals and religious leaders who would not mouth patriotic utterances were hounded from their positions.

"Dangerous Thought"

For example, Professor Minobe, whose theory of the position of the emperor has been alluded to, came under ultranationalist attack as an advocate of "dangerous thought," and in 1935 was forced to resign from his professorship and from the House of Peers. The case provided an excuse for widespread investigations of university professors and their writings and for interference with university administration, which was accomplished most easily and directly by army pressure exerted through military training units on the campuses. Even at Doshisha, which had a long tradition of independence as a liberal Christian college, military officers on campus were able to force the resignation of the president and the rewriting of the school's constitution. Since military training was required of all male students, a college like Doshisha had to put up with the arrogance of its military unit or resign itself to becoming a women's college.

It should be emphasized, however, that although before the outbreak of full-scale war with China in July, 1937, special pressures and incidents were utilized by ultranationalist groups to bring about conformity of opinion on such matters as reverence for the emperor and patriotic support for the army and its Manchurian venture, by 1937 these were becoming generally accepted in Japan, certainly by anyone with ambitions in public life. A steady stream of patriotic propaganda in radio, public speeches, and press was reinforced in 1937 by the publication by the Ministry of Education of a book called *Kokutai no Hongi* (*Principles of the National Polity*) which was circulated to teachers with instructions that it should constitute the basis of their teaching. It was permeated with ultranationalism, and with it one can say that the propagation of ultranationalism had become official policy in Japan.

JAPANESE PRESSURE ON CHINA

If Japan had been satisfied with Manchuria, it is possible that she would in time have received at least *de facto* international recognition of her rule there. It is true that the Lytton Commission condemned the seizure by force and Secretary of State Henry L. Stimson reinvoked Bryan's nonrecognition policy and told Japan that the United States would not recognize changes made in violation of treaty commitments. However, although the League of Nations adopted the Lytton Report, its position was far from adamant. Of course, all the Western democracies were overwhelmed with their own economic problems and were viewing with alarm the activities of Mussolini and Hitler in Europe. They had no desire to become unnecessarily involved in friction with Japan.

Similarly Soviet Russia was anxious to avoid conflict on its eastern borders. The Kwantung army was intensely anti-Soviet, and made it clear that continued Russian operation of the Chinese Eastern Railroad across northern Manchuria would not be tolerated. Facing constant interference and potential large-scale conflict, Russia entered into negotiations with Japan, hoping to salvage something by selling the railroad rights. Japan insisted that the price be low and that the sale be to the "independent" state of Manchukuo. In 1935 the Soviets gave in and sold their railroad rights to Manchukuo. Even China came very close to *de facto* recognition.

FIGURE 22.2. Japanese emigrants to Manchukuo at the Meiji Shrine in Tokyo.

Domestic Strife in China

When the Japanese struck in Manchuria in 1931–1932, Chiang Kai-shek was desperately trying to keep his warlord "subordinates" in line. Though they all urged him to fight Japan, their continued jockeying for position suggested that they were perhaps hopeful he would spend his energies and his loyal troops against Japan, leaving them a new opening for a power grab. In addition, the Chinese communists, whom Chiang had ruthlessly eradicated from the cities, were holed up in a rural area in Kiangsi province in south China in open defiance of the Nanking government. It was here, in difficult hill country, that the Communists had found refuge after the 1927 split. Here too, under the leadership of Mao Tse-tung, the Chinese communists had developed the idea that if their revolution was to be successful it could no longer be based upon the support of the practically nonexistent industrial proletariat, but, of necessity, had to obtain support from the rural proletariat, the vast masses of the peasants. Chiang was especially determined to crush them. Consequently he was prepared to temporize with Japan while securing the authority of the Nanking government over all of China proper, and twice he made concessive truces with Japan. In 1933 the Tangku truce was signed, which left the Japanese in control of Manchuria and established a "no man's" line of demarcation at the Great Wall. When the Japanese were not satisfied with this because of "anti-Japanese agitation" in the Peking area, he authorized the Ho-Umezu agreement in 1935, whereby a mutually acceptable (meaning Japanese approved) administration was established in the east Hopei (Peking-Tientsin) region and also in eastern Inner Mongolia. He did not recognize Manchukuo, but trade and railway traffic was resumed on the Mukden-Peking line and postal and telegraphic services were restored.

"Long March"

However, the Japanese Kwantung army was insatiable. Feeding on the ideology of ultranationalism, and with crises on the continent interacting with crises in Japan, they would not be satisfied until China accepted the "divine leadership" of the Japanese emperor. In 1935 they found another excuse for action. This was the resettlement of the Chinese communists in northwest China in Shensi province, where they eventually made the city of Yenan their capital. Their Kiangsi stronghold having been made untenable by Chiang's attacks and by economic blockade, the communists had undertaken the later famous "Long March" westward and northward to Shensi, presumably to get closer to possible Soviet aid. The march covered some 6,000 miles and took more than a year. There was almost continuous fighting. The marchers were harassed by Nationalist forces and local armies, and only 20,000 communists completed the journey, some 70,000 being lost along the way. Nevertheless they made remarkable use of the opportunities they had to propagandize people in the villages and along the countryside as they passed through, sometimes killing officials, merchants, and landlords and distributing money, commodities, and land to the poor. Many recruits joined their band, which helped to make up for large numbers lost in the earlier stages of the journey. Their route, which seems to have been the product of necessity rather than active planning, took them westward through Szechuan as far as the borderland of Tibet before they could proceed north, and their final settling in Shensi province seems to have been dictated by the fact that it was the first place where the exhausted band could feel secure. One important effect of the march was that it solidified the leadership of Mao Tse-tung and his lieutenants, Chu Teh and Chou En-lai, in the movement, as dissident elements dropped out along the way, and it taught the remaining leaders much about guerrilla warfare and how to enlist support from the peasants.

Little Russian aid was forthcoming at Yenan, but the Communist leaders began organizing rural soviets and guerrilla armies. Also they proclaimed defiance of Japan and called for resistance to Japanese encroachment in north China. This was in line with their declaration of war against Japan, issued shortly after the Manchurian Incident of 1931, but it took on special meaning in 1935 and 1936, as will be discussed shortly.

Since the Japanese ultranationalists were vitriolically anti-Soviet and anti-communist, considering communism the most vile of all the "materialist" Western doctrines that were poisoning Asia, they insisted on the removal of this communist "threat." Former Colonel, now General, Dohihara of the Kwantung army planned to bring all of north China under Japanese control to fight the communists more effectively. This renewed pressure, however, had the reverse effect of making the Japanese all the more hated in north China, where student demonstrations and boycotts against Japan mounted. The Japanese claimed these were all communist-inspired and insisted on rooting them out. Meanwhile another army officer, Oshima, a military attaché in Berlin, was negotiating outside regular diplomatic channels with Hitler's foreign minister, Ribbentrop, on the subject of an anti-communist pact. The army pressed for its consummation in Tokyo, and the pact was signed in November, 1936 as the Anti-Comintern Pact, between Germany, Italy, and Japan, directed not against Soviet Russia, it was said, but against international communism. The pact in effect gave highest level sanction to whatever "anti-communist" activities Japanese army authorities on the continent might wish to carry out and also to further purgings of "leftist" elements in Japan itself.

Chiang's Position

Chiang Kai-shek was as anti-communist as the Japanese and he had, in fact, stationed his north China army, made up largely of Manchurian troops under the command of the "Young Marshal" Chang Hsüeh-liang (son of Chang Tso-lin), at Sian (formerly Ch'ang-an) directly south of the communist-held area in Shensi. They were under orders to fight the communists to extermination. Chiang was particularly vehement about the communists because they alone defied his authority consistently. Otherwise China was coming under his control. As a military man who thought primarily in military terms, Chiang had worked hard in the 1930's to build his power far beyond that of any potential rival in China. Using German military advisors, he remolded his revolutionary army into a professional military machine. General Hans von Seeckt, the leader of the German advisory group, helped replace revolutionary fervor with tanks, modern weapons, an elite officer corps, and absolute unity of command. He also urged Chiang to gear Chinese industry to the needs of this professional army, with the result that German precision tools were imported, and munitions factories, chemical plants, military transport, and the like received first priority in Nanking's budgetary considerations.

True, the economic foundations of the Nanking government were far from sound. Chiang's persistent attention to the military starved other sections of the economy, and such things as "People's Livelihood" had to wait. Nor was there any significant investment in long-range economic development. The financial leadership of men like T. V. Soong and H. H. Kung, Chiang's brothers-in-law, was singularly self-centered and benefited the banking circles they headed far more than the country at large. However, Chiang tried to circumvent potential grumbling and resistance to high taxes and lack of visible improvement in living standards with preachments about "moral standards," as emphasized in the "New Life Movement" launched in 1934. Also political discipline was maintained through a secret organization of "Blue Shirts" commanded by two adopted nephews of Chiang, the Ch'en brothers. (This was later called the "C. C. Clique.")

By late 1936 Chiang's position was strong. The Kuomintang party apparatus was under his control. His military position was unassailable, the last flurry of warlord opposition having died the preceding spring. However, his policy of appeasing Japan, while consolidating his strength in China, was not popular with the Chinese people. Anti-Japanese boycotts and demonstrations continued. Intellectual leaders like Hu Shih were sharply critical, and student groups, especially in the Peking-Tientsin area where they had felt the interfering hand of Japan, were smoldering with patriotic resentment against Japan, and against Chiang when he seemed to cooperate with the Japanese by banning their demonstrations. Beginning in 1935 a "National Salvation" movement developed in Nationalist China, which demanded that the government take a stronger stand against Japan.

About the same time the Chinese communists began to put out feelers for a truce with the Nanking government and a joining of forces against Japan. As noted above, the communists had already declared war against Japan, but the overtures to Chiang were also related to the decision of the Comintern made in August, 1935 to seek united fronts against fascism with "bourgeois-democratic" and "bourgeois-nationalist" forces wherever they could be obtained. The question whether Mao Tse-tung authorized these feelers merely because of the dictates of Moscow is sometimes argued with reference to the question of the degree of independence in the Chinese communist movement. But suffice it to say here that by 1936 the Chinese communist leadership wanted a united front against Japan.

Chiang Kai-shek, at first, refused to heed either the pressures within the Nationalist ranks or the feelers of the communists. However, the army of Chang Hsüeh-liang, assigned to anticommunist duty at Sian, was receptive both to the patriotism of the student movement in Peking and to the Red arguments. The fact that the Young Marshal and many of his men had been ousted from their Manchurian homeland by the Japanese and knew Japanese rule there to be harsh no doubt influenced them also. Japanese "bandit suppression" campaigns in Manchuria were notorious.

United Front

By December 1936, fighting between the communists and the Young Marshal's forces had entirely ceased; in fact it had been supplanted by considerable friendly camaraderie between the lines. On December 14 Chiang Kai-shek flew in from Nanking to check conditions, and the famous Sian "kidnapping" incident occurred. Chiang was detained by his subordinates and bombarded with arguments, and perhaps threats, to change his policy, accept a united front, and lead the nation against Japan. All the details of the affair have not been known even yet, but it seems that although at first he refused, later, after Mme. Chiang and other Kuomintang advisors came to Sian, he was won over. No documents were signed, but Chiang returned to Nanking on December 25, with Chang Hsüeh-liang "in custody." Thereafter, in the spring of 1937, various declarations from Nanking and Yenan made it clear that an understanding had been reached, and a united front against Japan now prevailed. Chiang emerged from the Sian Incident as not only a military commander, but a national hero, whose stature for the first time approached that of Sun Yat-sen.

Thus Japanese pressure tactics in north China had not only failed to split the country, or to rouse Chinese support for them in an anticommunist drive, but it had had precisely the opposite effect. Japanese army leaders were furious, and began now to claim that this unity between nationalists and communists proved the treacherous proclivities of both sides, and they declared that Japan must strike in force before the united front could be fully organized. There was some argument among them as to whether there should not also be a thrust against Soviet Siberia, but for the time being this was left aside, since on July 7, 1937, at Marco Polo Bridge (Lu-kou-ch'iao) near Peking Chinese and Japanese troops clashed in a new "incident" that touched off a full scale, though undeclared, Sino-Japanese War.

KUOMINTANG LEADERSHIP, 1928–1937

Before taking up the turbulent wartime period after 1937 a few words of summary should be said about the record of the Kuomintang during the years 1928–1937, when it had the opportunity to move Chinese politics and society in a progressive direction. Even though the Japanese were pressing in in the northeast and the communists maintained their pocket of resistance first in the south and then in the northwest, the Nanking government was freer than any government had been since the Boxer Rebellion to organize the administration of the country. It had taken control in a wave of revolutionary enthusiasm, and the Organic Act of 1928 gave the Kuomintang party complete control of the central government.

Constitution

There were certainly bright spots in the record. A provisional constitution, promulgated in 1931, emphasized the idea that constitutional government would be brought into being after five more years of Kuomintang tutelage, that citizens possessed "rights" as well as duties, that all children were entitled to a free public education, that there would be checks and balances in the central government and separation of powers between the central and local governments. Then the draft of a permanent constitution was published in 1936, which, had it been put into effect, would have granted the people the right to choose their representatives by election, to organize various types of political parties, and to carry on democratic government. One could not quarrel with the paper pronouncements, but unfortunately war intervened and the constitution was not put into effect.

Economic Conditions

The military orientation of industrialization has been mentioned, but nonmilitary industrialization was also aided by a four-year plan begun in 1933. The program concentrated on the Yangtze valley area, but the building of factories in distant provinces like Sinkiang was also encouraged. Beginning in 1938 an industrial cooperative movement for small industry was developed with considerable success, especially in textiles.

In agriculture a Land Law was promulgated in 1930 to protect tenants from arbitrary eviction and exorbitant rents, land reclamation was accomplished in some areas, and a program of government-backed agricultural credit was introduced. The development of agricultural cooperatives was encouraged, banks to aid them were set up, and the government offered attractive inducements to trained people who would work with these. Local gentry often opposed the agricultural cooperatives but the number of them grew steadily in the 1930's.

In finance, government revenues were substantially increased through tariff increases levied after tariff autonomy went into effect in 1929, and the official goals of a balanced budget and a sound currency seemed to be within reach. T. V. Soong worked hard on budgets and, although Chiang would not subject military expenditures to a fixed amount, China came closer to having a balanced budget than did many countries in the early and middle 1930's. Currency stabilization was first achieved by the adoption of a coined silver dollar as the basic unit. However, silver began to be drained from the country, especially after the United States adopted a silver purchase policy in 1934. In 1935 Frederick Leith-Ross, a British financial expert, helped the Nanking government devise a means of retrieving the situation by nationalizing silver and using it to back a nonconvertible, but for a few years relatively stable, paper currency. Of course, these sound-budget, sound-currency policies were perhaps more advantageous to business than to other segments of the economy.

Communications were much improved, with postal service, telegraph, road construction, and railroads all receiving attention. Also the New Life Movement, in which both the Generalissimo and Mme. Chiang took an active interest, sought to teach basic hygiene and cleanliness and to instil a sense of community responsibility for helping out unfortunate people and keeping up public places. However, the "New Life Movement" was ineffective. Also, as mentioned above, it had an aspect of moral preaching about it which contradicted progress, and if we turn to this ideological aspect of Kuomintang leadership and its political implications, we see that the Kuomintang at best was unimaginative and at worst became retrogressive.

Ideological Reversal

A careful analysis of the ideology of the Kuomintang under Chiang's leadership from 1928–1937 reveals a nearly complete reversal of the revolutionary ideals which had brought the party to power, and this probably played at least as large a role as Japanese aggression and communist opposition in rendering abortive the political, economic, and social reforms that were instituted. The workings of this may be seen most clearly in the new cult of Tseng Kuo-fan which was fostered in the 1930's. Officially, of course, Sun Yat-sen was the hero of the Kuomintang, and his "Nationalism, Democracy and People's Livelihood" remained its goals, to which the May 4 Movement, the Revolution of 1911, and the T'ai-p'ing Rebellion had given inspiration. Tseng Kuo-fan, who had helped the Manchus defeat the T'ai-p'ings and brought the old Confucian order back from the brink of chaos in the 1860's (see Chapter 12), was as unlikely a candidate as the empress dowager for honors in the 1920's. But by 1932 Chiang had openly adopted Tseng as his model and he referred to the T'ai-p'ing rebels as pigs and dogs. The Confucian values that Tseng had helped save were extolled and the ideas expressed in the May 4 Movement were criticized by the party leadership as radical, cheap, and dangerous. "Faithful action" and "the coordination of military and civil matters," not "science and democracy," were said to be needed for the rehabilitation of China. Of course, some Kuomintang followers of liberal inclination continued to support the course outlined by Sun Yat-sen as the course for the future, but Chiang and his most intimate associates pushed the transformation of the Kuomintang ideology from revolutionary to reactionary moorings insistently. It is rather symbolic that Chiang did not even bother to occupy the presidency of the republic, turning that over to a figurehead in 1931, while he ran the party and the government from his position as chairman of the Military Council and commander-in-chief.

By 1937 Japan and China were both on the brink of tragedy. They were about to fight each other, but beyond that internal conditions in both countries were poor. Japan had seen the liberal developments of the 1920's fall short of fruition. Through character assassination and real assassination the complexion of the government had become ultranationalist, and through dual diplomacy the Japanese military had been able to make aggressive expansionism the basic foreign policy of the country. Dissent was already difficult and shortly would become impossible.

China, beset by domestic strife, had been unable to establish a stable, popular government. The promise of the intellectual renaissance and the nationalist movement had gone unfulfilled. Now, with Japanese pressure mounting, it was too late for anything but frantic defensive measures.

Control Group and Prince Konoe

After the February 26, 1936, Tokyo Mutiny, which had seen two army factions in open contest for control of the Japanese government, there was little hope that Japan would desist from her expansionist course. However, the Control Group had won over the more adventurous Young Officers, and it might be assumed that they at least would be more careful. In two respects they were. The Young Officers had wished to overthrow what they considered to be the unholy alliance of court aristocracy and big business in order that the army and the emperor might "purify" the national structure. The Control Group was willing to have peace with these, on their terms. The Young Officers had also wished to push the Manchurian expansion northward into what they hoped would become war with Soviet Russia. The Control Group, while vigorously anti-communist, was more inclined to focus its attention southward, on "stabilizing" China by rooting out communism and anti-Japanism there and establishing a security system which would give Japan "autonomy" in her relations with east and southeast Asia.

Whatever faction ruled it, the army was restive in 1937. It had been more active in politics, both in Japan and in China, than in military campaigns for some time, since control of Manchuria had been secured. To harness its drive would require a statesman of the highest order. Some court and business circles, as well as the last surviving Genro, Saionji, felt they had such a man in Prince Konoe Fumimaro. Of Fujiwara lineage, he had been tutored in international affairs by Saionji. Yet he was also popular enough with patriotic societies and the army to be acceptable to them. There were, in fact, two strains in Konoe, one Western-oriented and liberal from Saionji, his mentor, and one anti-Western, traditionalist, and nationalistic from his father, who had been a patron of the Black Dragon Society. It was not clear which strain would predominate, but Konoe was a last hope for civilian control of the government, and on Saionji's recommendation he was offered the premiership in June, 1937. The army, which had hoped to make General Sugiyama Gen, a leader of the Control Group, premier, signified its acceptance by designating Sugiyama as army minister instead. (Since an active duty army officer had to occupy the post of army minister, refusal to designate one by the army high command could have prevented the formation of the cabinet.) Konoe was to be a very important figure between 1937 and 1941, heading three cabinets, but he was consistently to disappoint those who thought of him as a peacemaker. He had been in office barely a month when a new incident broke out in China.

JAPAN SEIZES KEY AREAS OF CHINA

The Marco Polo Bridge Incident

On July 7–8, 1937, a skirmish between Japanese and Chinese troops occurred near the junction of the Peking-Tientsin and Peking-Hankow railroads in north China, the exact location being called Marco Polo Bridge. Japanese army units were holding maneuvers there by dint of a rather extended interpretation of the old Boxer protocol, which permitted the stationing of foreign troops at Tientsin and Peking to assure the safety of the legations. The Japanese had some 5000 men in the area, well equipped with the latest weapons. It is instructive that the Chinese commander who refused to accept their version of the affair and to order Chinese troops withdrawn from the area was noted for his pro-Japanese proclivities and had been put in charge of the Hopei-Chahar political council (a Japanese-dominated local government organ) with the concurrence of the Japanese. To have roused his national feeling local Japanese had to be very arrogant indeed.

Army Minister Sugiyama demanded a call-up of reserves in the threatening situation and reinforcements were dispatched to the Peking area, despite the fact that the Japanese were winning the fight. Premier Konoe stressed that the incident was a local one and sought to institute negotiations with Nanking to settle it. Actually the whole China war, which lasted eight years, was never admitted to be more than an "incident." The Japanese terms of settlement, however, were dictated by the army; they insisted that China assume the major responsibility for the incident and that affairs in north China be arranged more to their liking. Meanwhile Japanese troops routed Chinese garrisons and took control of the whole Peking-Tientsin area.

Extension of the Fighting

Before negotiations had proceeded very far, events in Shanghai rendered them abortive. There anti-Japanese feeling was running high and an incident occurred at a Shanghai airdrome when Chinese sentries shot two Japanese marines. The Japanese, claiming the need to safeguard Japanese personnel, dispatched additional forces and warships to Shanghai. Several other incidents occurred, and, as both Chinese and Japanese troops poured into the area, full-scale fighting broke out. The Japanese navy began a blockade of the coast against Chinese shipping in late August, and Army Minister Sugiyama spoke of striking a "strong blow" to be followed by "benevolence." Chinese forces retreated from Shanghai in November, but the Chinese did not surrender or offer to negotiate.

FIGURE 22.3. Chinese troops in Shanghai, fall, 1937. Chinese resistance to the Japanese attack was surprisingly effective.

Premier Konoe, becoming alarmed at the spread of the war, sought to bring about negotiation through mediation by a third party. He preferred England, but the army would trust only Germany, so the German ambassador at Tokyo, Dirksen, was invited to initiate negotiations with Chiang Kai-shek. The Germans were pleased to do this, as Hitler and his general staff viewed the Sino-Japanese rupture as foolish, playing into the hands of Russia and communism. The German ambassador to China, Trautmann, was instructed to approach Chiang.

However, events ran ahead of diplomacy, as the Japanese north and central China armies tried to outdo each other in gaining advantages before any peace settlement could be achieved. In north China a new provisional government, manned by Japanese puppets, was installed at Peking, and in central China a determined attack was launched on Nanking, from which Chiang had already withdrawn his executive apparatus to Hankow. Nanking fell on December 13, after which Japanese troops went on a week long orgy of pillage and rape of the city. These events ended the possibility of negotiation, as the Japanese military became more arrogant and the Chinese more grimly determined to resist. The various dissident Chinese factions, including the communists, all pledged their support to the nationalist government. Chinese forces fought desperately to prevent the north and central China Japanese armies from effecting a junction, and they won a great morale

FIGURE 22.4. The Japanese army advances in Shanghai, fall, 1937. Fierce house-to-house fighting characterized the struggle.

building battle at T'aierchuang in April, 1938. When they finally had to give way, they cut the dikes on the Yellow river to impede the Japanese.

Japan's superior forces took the cities and the rail junctions, including Canton and Hankow, in September, 1938, but the nationalist government had re-established itself beyond their reach at Chungking, far up the Yangtze, and thousands of Chinese, carrying everything from seeds to machinery, had fled to the western hinterland of China. By the end of 1938 the Japanese controlled the major coastal cities and the Peking-Hankow-Canton railway axis, but their advances westward had ground to a halt.

Chinese Resistance

Chinese morale was high during the first two years of the war. Old animosities were buried and a spirit of cooperation prevailed. Yenan announced the abandonment of sovietization as its goal and reaffirmed the Three People's Principles of Sun Yat-sen. It sought and received permission from Chungking to organize a noncommunist government for the Shansi-Shahar-Hopei region in opposition to the Japanese-sponsored provisional government at Peking. This so-called "Border Government" was composed of one-third communist members and two-thirds representatives of other groups. Its tax, rent, and land policies were very favorable to the peasants, with landlords being required to accept reasonable rents or be declared "pro-Japanese," in which case their lands might be expropriated. It was here that the communists built their reputation as fair agrarian reformers.

The main communist armies were redesignated as the Eighth Route and New Fourth armies respectively, technically under the overall command of Generalissimo Chiang Kai-shek, but still led by their communist commanders. They avoided positional warfare, but organized effective guerrilla resistance to the Japanese, both in the north where the Eighth Route Army operated and in the lower Yangtze area where communist organizers had boldly penetrated under the very noses of the Japanese.

At Chungking an advisory People's Political Council was established to bring in expressions of opinion from all parts of unoccupied China and of various political groups. Its largest component consisted of Kuomintang members but seven communists sat in the body as well as representatives of smaller parties. A determined effort to rebuild industries in the hinterland was made, with considerable success at first. Strategic industries were given preference and industrial cooperatives were encouraged. Universities and other higher training institutions, whose student bodies and faculties had often fled en masse from the Japanese, were reestablished. Even the bones of the famous Peking man, the oldest human archeological specimen in China, were transported out of Japanese occupied north China, but they were lost somewhere en route. The Chinese left no doubt that they were digging in for a long struggle.

Japanese "Stabilizing" Measures

The Japanese, by their own propaganda, had convinced themselves that the Chinese people were out of sympathy with the radical elements which governed them, whether communists or nationalists. Indeed many Japanese made little distinction between the two, considering the whole Chinese revolutionary process from the 1920's on to have been one great radical aberration. They could point to the two nationalist alliances with the communists, in the 1923–1927 period and beginning again in 1937, as proof that this was so. Furthermore the Japanese ultranationalists had built an elaborate rationale in which they denounced Western influences in the Far East as alien and materialistic, contrasting them with the wonderful "spiritual" heritage of the Orient. Hence Chiang Kai-shek could be castigated as a puppet of materialistic British and American capitalism, while Mao was a puppet of materialistic Russian communism.

This ideological approach was discernible in the first stage of Japan's program for stability in China, while primary attention was being given to establishing the aforementioned provisional government at Peking. The idea was to return to pre-Nationalist days, before Sun Yat-sen and his radical Kuomintang had begun to lead China astray. The Chinese personnel who were obtained to serve in the provisional government were Confucian-minded bureaucrats of pre-Kuomintang regimes. The assumption of the Japanese was that the people of China, at least of north China, were nostalgic for the halcyon days of Confucian traditionalism and would welcome its return.

However, the Chinese response was decidedly negative, and after trying for about a year to promote Peking and Confucianism, while demoting Nanking and nationalism, the Japanese changed their tactics.

In the second stage of their effort to "stabilize China" and "solve the China problem," as they called it, the Japanese turned a sort of ideological somersault. They now admitted the strength and depth of Chinese nationalism and the importance of the role of the Kuomintang, and they sought to enter into negotiations with certain Kuomintang leaders to get them to bring about peace with Japan and to return to Nanking. Wang Ching-wei, who had been Sun Yat-sen's close associate and who was considered the number two man in the Kuomintang, next to Chiang, took up the offer. He had served in many high posts in the nationalist government, but whenever there had been an issue between the two, Chiang, with his strong military backing, had always had his way. Probably Wang saw the Japanese offer as a chance to fulfill personal ambitions for political power. It is also thought by some that Wang believed that he could genuinely serve China by restoring peace and bringing about Japanese evacuation from most areas.

Wang left Chungking on a "trip abroad" in December, 1939, and for some six months he traveled and talked with his Chinese followers and Japanese agents, in Hanoi, Hong Kong, and finally in Tokyo. He tried to drive a hard bargain with the Japanese. His was not to be a new government, but the nationalist government, reestablished at Nanking with the Kuomintang party in power, flying the nationalist flag—with characters for "peace" and "reconstruction" added. Japanese troops were to withdraw from China within two years after communism in China had been suppressed.

The Japanese expressed general agreement, and indeed not a few Japanese leaders, including some military men, like Ishiwara Kanji, who had been one of the principal planners of the Mukden incident, now saw the China war as endless, if not wrong, and genuinely wished to deescalate Japan's involvement in China. But the "pacification problem" did not permit the withdrawal of Japanese troops and Wang, declared a traitor by Chungking, was unable to attract any sizable support from his former Kuomintang following. Recognized by Japan on November 30, 1940, his government was never able to escape from Japanese "assistance" and Wang died, an unmourned "puppet," in a Japanese hospital in 1944.

JAPANESE RELATIONS WITH EUROPE

Soviet Border Strife

During the years 1937–1939 Japanese relations with Soviet Russia were very tense. It has been noted that a large section of the Japanese army, particularly the Young Officer contingent, had looked forward to war with Russia and reoccupation of Siberia as a natural outgrowth of Japan's northeast Asia expansion. The Control Group, which seized power in 1936, was more cautious about this and preferred to concentrate on the "China problem." However, border incidents occurred in Manchuria, at Changkufeng in 1938 and at Nomonhan in 1939, with the Russians more than holding their own. Japan was further embarrassed by the sudden conclusion of the German-Soviet nonaggression pact of August, 1939, and a cabinet crisis ensued in Japan, out of which a rather nondescript general, Abe Nobuyuki, emerged as premier. He promised to bring the "China problem" to a successful "solution," and a boundary settlement with the Soviets was ratified.

Japan Antagonizes Britain and France

Japan's backing down on the Soviet frontier only increased her pressure on China. While the puppet government of Wang Ching-wei was being brought into existence, the Japanese became increasingly determined to prevent foreign aid from reaching Chiang Kai-shek. On the grounds that foreign concessions in China's coastal cities were harboring Chinese "subversives" they blockaded them. At Tientsin they subjected British nationals to humiliating searches. After the outbreak of the European war in September, 1939, Japan put great pressure on Britain and France to curtail the sending of supplies into Chungking via Burma, Hong Kong, and French Indochina. Finally in the spring of 1940 the hard-pressed British promised to do so, closing the Burma Road as a gesture of appeasement (though they reopened it three months later). The French promised to send no munitions to Chiang, and they reduced their forces in China coastal cities to "skeleton size" as gestures of appeasement. However, Japan insisted that war supplies were continuing to reach Chiang from Indochina, and bombed the French-built Yunnan railway in China and then in December, 1939 and again in February, 1940 bombed the Indochina part of it.

The defeat of France in Europe left Indochina fully exposed to Japanese pressure, and Japan demanded that Japanese troops be permitted to enter Indochina to police the Chinese border. Japan would pay the expenses. In September, 1940 Japanese troops began to enter northern Indochina. Meanwhile Japan and Thailand had been conducting negotiations and Thailand entered demands for border territories in Laos and Cambodia, which were supported by the Japanese. In July, 1941 the Japanese demanded French permission to station troops and to establish air and naval bases in southern, as well as northern Indochina, in short to occupy the whole colony. The Vichy French government reluctantly gave in.

From Indochina Japan was able to gain various resources as well as to blockade China, but the ultimate economic prizes which she sought lay in the Dutch East Indies. Oil was the principal object. In September, 1940 Kobayashi Ichizō, Japan's minister of commerce and industry, journeyed to Batavia to propose a trade agreement that would guarantee Japan 3,150,000 tons of oil annually for five years. The Dutch talked, but evaded a commitment, and Kobayashi left. Actually Kobayashi was milder than others might have been. The Japanese army had proposed sending as the negotiator a general aboard a battleship empowered to bombard Batavia. After Kobayashi's departure the chairman of the board of Japan's giant Mitsui corporation carried on private negotiations with Dutch companies and obtained a one-year agreement trebling the amount of oil purchases. This was regarded only as a beginning in Tokyo, however, and a new official negotiator, Yoshizawa, soon arrived with demands not only for oil but for tin, bauxite, rubber, and other materials. The Dutch argued that such large demands must mean that Japan intended to transship some of the materials to Germany, and they asked assurances this would not happen. With the Dutch standing adamant, in June, 1941 Yoshizawa was recalled to Tokyo before an agreement was reached. The Japanese now decided to occupy southern Indochina before settling matters with the Dutch.

Tripartite Pact

Japan's ability to apply pressure against British, French, and Dutch areas in eastern Asia was, of course, related to the misfortunes those countries were experiencing in the European war. Hitler's victories impressed the Japanese military greatly, but they also worried her professional diplomats somewhat. What if Germany, having reduced the Netherlands, France, and England to subservience, should seek to take over their Asian holdings? The new Germany might even raise questions about Japanese possession of the old Germany's Pacific islands. The second Konoe cabinet, inaugurated in July, 1940 with a new civilian luminary, Matsuoka Yosuke, as foreign minister took up these matters. By that time the decision to hold peace with Russia on the northern frontier was firm; Southeast Asia was much more important than a few hundred miles of Siberia. One of the first decisions of the new cabinet was to seek to establish a new Japanese-dominated order in Southeast Asia, which by starving out Chiang Kai-shek would help to bring the China problem to solution.

It was decided that to accomplish this a firm understanding with Germany was needed, which would make it clear that Japan was Germany's ally, but that Japan alone would be the arbiter of affairs in the whole "Greater East Asian" area. There was a certain subtlety in this idea of being on the right side of the "master race" and yet containing it. Konoe was somewhat worried lest an outright alliance with the Axis might bring on war with the United States, but he was won over by Foreign Minister Matsuoka, who argued that the pact would serve as a deterrent to American interference in East and Southeast Asia.

Matsuoka knew America well. He had, in fact, spent his youth in California and Oregon, where he worked his way through high school and college. He had entered Japan's foreign service in 1904 and had served in many minor posts, including that of interpreter for the delegation at Versailles in 1919, where he had attracted Konoe's attention. He was a director of the South Manchurian Railroad in the 1920's in which capacity he mixed both with business circles and the Kwantung army. He also became a severe critic of the United States for her oriental exclusion policy. In 1932 he was appointed Japan's representative to the League of Nations, where he voiced Japan's Manchurian claims in excellent English. In February, 1933 he led the Japanese delegation out of the League, at which time he predicted that Anglo-Saxon assumption of racial superiority would someday cost Britain its East Asian colonies and America the Philippines. In 1940, as foreign minister, he began to make this prediction come true.

At any rate Matsuoka convinced Konoe that an Axis alliance would be advantageous to Japan. It would stake out her sphere in southern Asia and would deter the United States. There might, of course, be trouble, possibly even war, with Britain, France, and the Netherlands, but Germany was defeating them in Europe anyway. Russian-Japanese relations need not be worried about; they might even be "improved."

Such was the argument that led to Matsuoka's being authorized to propose an alliance to Germany. At first, Hitler was not very interested. He merely wanted Japan to say when she would enter the war. However, Matsuoka and his negotiators persisted and finally the pact was forged, much as he wanted it, with a commitment for Japan to enter the war only if one of the partners were attacked by a power not then involved in the war. "Greater East Asia" was definitely assigned to Japan as the sphere for her "new order." Germany accepted a small compensation for the former German Pacific islands. (Her envoy had suggested six bags of coffee.) Italy also adhered to the pact, which was signed in Berlin on September 27, 1940. Matsuoka thought it a great diplomatic triumph.

RELATIONS WITH THE UNITED STATES

Stiffening American Attitude

However, Matsuoka had underestimated American reaction. To them the Tripartite Pact was simply another step in Japan's allying herself with the aggressor nations of the world. Since 1939 American policy and public opinion had been becoming steadily more anti-Japanese. Though President Roosevelt had been rebuffed for his "quarantine the aggressors" speech in 1937, and that year also had seen the United States accept a Japanese apology and compensation for the bombing of the American gunboat *Panay* on the Yangtze river, the rising Japanese pressure on Southeast Asia began to bring American countermoves in abundance. Secretary of State Cordell Hull in April, 1940, as the Germans were overrunning Holland, served notice on Japan that interference in the East Indies would be regarded by the United States as prejudicial to peace and security in the Pacific. During the summer of 1940 President Roosevelt began to impose export licenses and other restrictions on trade with Japan. More attention was given to the Philippines where, since 1937, General Douglas MacArthur had been building a defense force. Meanwhile large monetary credits were extended to Chungking. The fact that the China war had remained an undeclared one, an "incident," proved very helpful to Roosevelt, for the "Neutrality Acts" might have hampered his efforts to favor China over Japan had they been admitted belligerents.

After the conclusion of the Tripartite Pact the United States began a program of returning American civilians from the Far East, curtailed, but did not end, oil and scrap iron shipments to Japan, and quadrupled the amount of assistance to Chiang Kai-shek's government. Britain reopened the Burma Road to help supply Chungking. President Roosevelt's re-election to a third term in November, 1940 made it clear that his policies would prevail, and he immediately began to press for the Lend Lease Act, which, when finally enacted in March, 1941, negated the heretofore official "neutral" stand of the United States. The United States was definitely taking sides with the Allies.

Hull-Nomura Negotiations

With American-Japanese relations deteriorating rapidly, Admiral Nomura Kichisaburo was sent to Washington to try to reverse the trend toward war. Nomura presented his credentials on February 14, 1941, and began serious negotiations with Secretary Hull on March 8. It is clear from Japanese records that Nomura represented the views of those elements of the Japanese government which were most anxious to reach an accord with the United States, including Premier Konoe, court aristocrats, and the emperor. But he did not have the confidence of the military, particularly the army, and Matsuoka's global diplomacy was beyond him. Unfortunately Nomura was so anxious to be successful that he defeated his own purpose. He represented Hull's position to Tokyo as being more flexible than it was and Tokyo's position to Hull as being more willing to compromise than was the case. By summer his diplomacy was mired in misunderstanding to the extent that Tokyo was considering the proposals which Nomura had originally presented to Hull as if they were American proposals which Hull had submitted to him. When Tokyo came back with its "answer," which included further demands, Hull was convinced of Japanese deceitfulness. And Tokyo decided Hull had changed his ground. Basically the American position was that Japan must abandon military means of handling the China and Southeast Asian situations and begin to withdraw her troops. The Japanese army would not withdraw any troops until the various China and Southeast Asia problems had been solved to their liking.

The American answer to the impasse was on July 25, 1941, to freeze Japanese assets in the United States, thus suspending all trade. The same course was followed by Britain, Burma, and India on the 26th and by the Netherlands Indies on the 28th. Thereafter Japan would have to get whatever oil she needed from the Axis.

Collapse of Matsuoka's Diplomacy

The freezing of Japanese assets, despite the ample justification for it, may have been ill-timed in the sense of extinguishing what small chance Japanese leaders like Nomura, who wished to avoid war with the United States, might have had to reverse the trend. There had been a cabinet crisis in Japan in early July which had resulted in the removal of Matsuoka as foreign minister, and with him had gone the illusion that the Axis alliance could be made to serve the cause of peace with the United States, as well as Japan's new order in "Greater East Asia."

Matsuoka fancied himself a master diplomatic and political strategist, and in a perverted sense he was. He was the only Japanese foreign minister after 1931 who was able to create the illusion that he was controlling foreign policy. It was an illusion because such military considerations as security of forces in the field set the limits of foreign policy manipulation, but Matsuoka was able to create the illusion because, in contrast to his predecessors, whose role was to urge caution on the military while rationalizing their deeds, Matsuoka was even more audacious than they. While they ploddingly advanced Japan's area of control, he expected to win "Greater East Asia" for Japan by a diplomatic blitzkrieg—without necessarily having to fight a major war.

Matsuoka had been riding high. With the Tripartite Pact he had obtained German approval of Japan's new order. With Wang Ching-wei's new regime established in China a "solution" there was presumably nearer. However, the United States was refusing to be bluffed into accepting Japanese claims to Southeast Asia, and she could make the oil question critical. Therefore in the spring of 1941 Matsuoka journeyed to Moscow and Berlin. His objectives were two: from Russia oil and a further guarantee of Russian nonaggression in Northeast Asia; and from Berlin an understanding about the Tripartite Pact so that Japan would not be drawn into war with the United States or with Russia for German reasons. His diplomacy was largely successful. He obtained the promise of oil from Russia (one million tons annually for five years, although he was not able to purchase northern Sakhalin as he had hoped to do) and a neutrality pact with border guarantees. The Germans did not oppose these arrangements. Hitler wanted Japan's promise to enter the war against Britain by attacking Singapore. Matsuoka avoided commitment on this with generalities which added up to the meaning that Japan would go to war with Britain (or the United States or Russia) only when and if it suited her. Matsuoka returned to Japan in late April to resume negotiations "from strength" with the United States, and to try to maneuver himself into the premiership.

But his strategy was ruined by two events: first, another Hitler "betrayal," the German attack on Russia on June 22, 1941. Concerning this Japan was given no real advance notice and news of it threw the Japanese cabinet into a turmoil, with much criticism being leveled at Matsuoka. After all, how could Russia supply oil to Japan if she needed it all herself? Now Matsuoka brazenly argued that perhaps Japan should also attack Russia and take what she wanted. Then Matsuoka leaped into the delicate American negotiations with even more than his customary brashness. He fired off notes to Nomura and Hull without consulting Konoe and, once, in direct contradiction to a military-cabinet decision. Nomura was so upset that he asked to resign. At this point (July, 1941) Army Minister Tojo demanded that Matsuoka be ousted from the cabinet; his diplomacy had become too audacious even for the army. Furthermore he had not solved the oil problem. Konoe, embarrassed by the diplomatic knots Matsuoka had tied,

FIGURE 22.5. Wang Ching-wei, Japan's puppet premier of occupied China, exchanges a sake toast with Japanese foreign minister, Matsuoka, the architect of a diplomacy which proved so disastrous to Japan.

agreed, tendered the resignation of the cabinet en masse, then re-formed it the next day without Matsuoka (July 17–18).

At this point Japanese policy was still susceptible to some modification away from the Tripartite Pact and toward rapprochement with the United States. But the freezing orders of July 25, 26, and 28 made oil the central issue, and General Tojo the key figure in the cabinet.

Tojo and Pearl Harbor

In contrast to Matsuoka, whose ways were complex and devious, Tojo was simple, direct, and military to the core. He was not an ideologist, but a military administrator and disciplinarian. He had risen rapidly in the Japanese army since 1936, when he had controlled seething Young Officer elements in Manchuria at the time of the Tokyo Mutiny. He regarded policy as already set: the consolidation of Japan's control of "Greater East Asia." If diplomacy could do it that was fine, but meanwhile Japan's military striking power must not be weakened. That was why the oil issue was so important.

The military compiled statistics which showed that Japan's oil reserves were being depleted at the rate of 12,000 tons per day, and in late August Tojo served notice that a time limit must be put on diplomatic negotiations. In crucial conferences held September 3–5 a mid-October deadline was adopted. If diplomacy did not show fruits by then the military would strike to take the oil fields of Southeast Asia. Konoe tried frantically to promote a last ditch meeting with President Roosevelt, but there was no response, and on October 14 he gave notice of his intention to resign. Then he consulted with the Lord Keeper of the Privy Seal, Kido, to advocate that an imperial prince, Higashikuni, should become premier. Kido vetoed the idea, urging that if the army was determined to press for war, it should also take the responsibility. On October 18 Tojo became premier.

Tojo let the diplomacy at Washington continue and sent a professional diplomat, Kurusu Saburo, to aid Nomura, but his preparations were for war. On November 10 orders were issued for a naval rendezvous in the Kurils preparatory to an attack on Pearl Harbor, which was set for December 7. On November 20 orders were issued for simultaneous military attacks on the Philippines and Malaya immediately following the Pearl Harbor strike. Many messages went back and forth between Nomura and Kurusu in Washington and Tokyo, and they were intercepted and decoded by the American cryptocomputer, but they did not reveal the Pearl Harbor scheme, for Nomura and Kurusu were kept ignorant of the actual strike plans.

Secretary Hull, realizing that a break was near, presented a summary of the American position on November 26. It demanded that Japanese forces be withdrawn from Indochina and China proper and that Japan guarantee the territorial integrity of China and Southeast Asia with a non-aggression pact. There was no demand concerning Manchuria and, if Japan accepted, the United States would rescind the freezing of assets, reopen trade, and assist the process of economic stabilization in the Far East. Tojo's cabinet was "dumbfounded" at the "harshness" of Hull's statement, and on December 1 reaffirmed the orders for attack. Neither Roosevelt nor Hull was under any illusion that Japan might accept the proposal, but they expected that if Japan attacked it would be in Southeast Asia.

THE PACIFIC WAR

The Pacific war began at 7:50 A.M. on Sunday, December 7, with the attack on Pearl Harbor. Most of the American Pacific fleet, except for its aircraft carriers, which happened to be out on maneuvers, was concentrated there. This concentration had been made partly to deter Japan with a view of American might. The strike was successful beyond the best hopes of its Japanese planners. It was a complete surprise, and so many ships were immobilized that any American counterattack had to wait for months. Meanwhile, as planned, Japan could overrun Southeast Asia, start the flow of oil and other essential materials to Japan, and seal off the western Pacific. Eventually, the Japanese strategists thought, the United States would give up the fight and negotiate a peace that would leave Japan in control of "Greater East Asia." There was really no thought of invading the con-

FIGURE 22.6. *The Japanese attack on Pearl Harbor. "Banzais" at takeoff aboard a Japanese carrier.*

tinental United States or Hawaii or of "dictating peace in the White House." The last phrase, though commonly quoted, was actually a Japanese admiral's admonition to his colleagues that, if they began the war, it might not end until they could "dictate peace in the White House." The others did not believe him.

Japan as a Totalitarian State

Unquestionably most Japanese believed that their cause was a just one. They had been conditioned by long years of their own propaganda to believe that enemies were threatening them, first radical Chinese trying to deprive them of their property in Manchuria, then the Communist menace in East Asia, then American, British, Dutch, Chinese hostility and "encirclement." Those who criticized these ideas seriously were gradually eliminated from government until in the last two years before Pearl Harbor a grand sense of a positive national mission had come to pervade Japan. The idea of an "East Asia Co-prosperity Sphere" which Japan was forging in "Greater East Asia" was heralded as the ultimate Japanese purpose. It was to be a "sacred war" led by a "sacred emperor" who had no thought other than the happiness of Asian peoples. Japan was prepared to sacrifice much to attain her goals.

There were a few grains of truth in the vast amount of propaganda. Their argument that Southeast Asian peoples had too long been exploited by Western colonial powers had validity, but the question of whether a Japa-

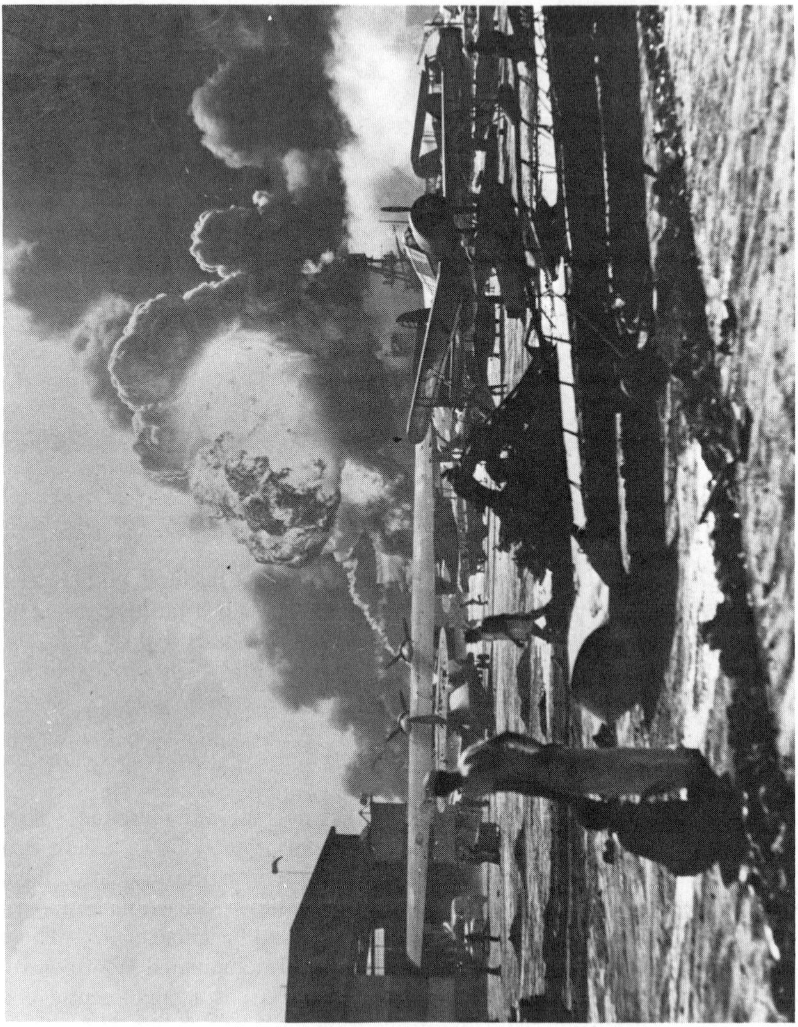

nese victory would improve their condition remained unanswered, if Japanese thinking had been critical enough to analyze the situation. Japanese leadership did not desire critical thought at this juncture. Ever since the Minobe case of 1935 the pressures for conformity in expression and in thought had operated mercilessly in the schools, the press, and in politics. Professors and teachers whose "loyalty" was suspect were ousted. Okawa Shumei's ultranationalistic book on Japanese history became a standard secondary school text. The ultranationalist tract entitled "Principles of the National Polity" published by the Ministry of Education in 1937 became the philosophic basis for teacher training.

The press was mainly sensationalist and nationalistic, but if there occurred any deviation in a liberal direction, censorship was resorted to. The horrible details of the rape of Nanking, for example, were not known in Japan until after the war. The military could always invoke "security of forces requirements" to cover up or distort whatever it wished. As for the politicians, most of them were only too anxious to make themselves popular by climbing on the ultranationalist bandwagon once it had begun to roll. But as the international situation grew more tense, after the war in Europe broke out and the Southeast Asia moves began, the call for national unity became so insistent that political parties were partly by persuasion and partly by intimidation made to disband. In 1940 Premier Konoe decreed the organizing of an "Imperial Rule Assistance Association" (IRAA) to take their place. This was a single totalitarian party whose mission was to weld the nation "into an iron-clad whole."

Through the IRAA the utmost united effort was exacted from the people. It was organized down to the village and block level, and local officials not only had to cooperate with it, but they were required to take leadership in it. Through it the Japanese military chiefs, who were its principal advisors, made known the requirements of patriotic duty for every Japanese subject.

Business and industry were for a time somewhat resistant to the organization of the totalitarian structure. Having controlled the old political parties, they were reluctant to see them go. However, by 1940 they were so much involved in military contracts and production that it would have been most uneconomic for them to persist in serious opposition. They grumbled about "controls and red tape" but they found advantages also in the system. Labor unions, which, though never strong, had been troublesome, were required to transform themselves into a "league for service to the state through industry," with the result that strikes and labor agitation became a thing of the past.

Religious groups, especially those with American or English missionary connections, resisted for a time, but the "Religious Bodies Law" passed in April, 1939 had emphasized the necessity for religious groups to conduct themselves in ways that were not inimical to the national polity and had given the Ministry of Education authority to determine if they were doing so. After 1940, when the law was implemented, the various Christian

FIGURE 22.7. The attack on Pearl Harbor.

churches were required to sever their American and English missionary connections, and their Japanese leadership was placed under strict constraint. The result was that the more nationalistic churchmen assumed leadership and found ways to please, such as organizing proselytizing missions for areas occupied by the Japanese army, ministering to the needs of servicemen and their families, and the like. YMCA's and YWCA's fitted in well with national fitness programs, which were much stressed by the military. Buddhism, which by this time was extremely nationalistic, presented no problem.

Individuals who opposed the trend could only keep silent or become expatriate, but it is interesting to note that, in contrast to the rather large numbers who left Nazi Germany, very few Japanese seized the possibility of expatriation. The conviction that the war was a righteous one was very strong, and even those who doubted took a fatalistic view that they must stand with their country.

On another important point totalitarian Japan differed from Nazi Germany or Fascist Italy. There was no single dictator of the stature of Hitler or Mussolini. Tojo was perhaps the nearest to this, but he was merely the chief of the military clique, which would have probably done much the same without him. No single person was indispensable to the Japanese course; the leadership was group leadership, and decision-making was by consensus within a general framework of ultranationalism which had grown over a decade and which no single person was either responsible for or able to control.

Military Developments

The Japanese advance into Southeast Asia was extremely rapid. Hong Kong, left completely exposed by the outbreak of war, was taken easily by late December, and then Singapore, with its large concentration of British forces, became the primary objective. From already occupied Indochina Japanese troops poured into the Malayan peninsula, and advanced southward. Singapore had extensive fortifications to defend her from seaborne attack, but little to thwart a land invasion. The causeway connecting Singapore island with the mainland was blown up, but the Japanese repaired it quickly, entered the island, and took the city on February 15, 1942. Seventy-five thousand prisoners were taken, and tremendous stores of rubber and other resources located throughout the Malay peninsula fell almost intact into the hands of the Japanese.

Simultaneously the Japanese were invading the Philippines, where a naval-air strike immediately after Pearl Harbor had destroyed most of the American planes on the ground. Actually the Philippines were not the immediate objective, for as soon as the American-Filipino defenders had been put on the defensive, the Japanese proceeded to use captured bases in the Philippines as launching points for the invasion of Indonesia, where various landings were effected and bombing raids were carried out. Batavia was taken (March 5), and the Dutch surrender was received (March 9). Then huge pressure was mounted in the Philippines, where the defenders were bottled up on Bataan peninsula and then on Corregidor rock, which finally was taken on May 6. General MacArthur, who had been ordered by President Roosevelt to leave the Philippines to take command of the whole Southwest Pacific campaign, was already in Australia planning ways to implement his famous vow, "I shall return." In their conquest of the Philippines the Japanese had again been unnecessarily brutal. They had ravaged Manila, which had been declared an open city and not defended, and their treatment of the survivors of Corregidor on a 100-mile forced march to prison camps became infamous as the Bataan Death March.

In the west the area of Japanese control was extended to include Thailand and Burma. Thailand was coerced into allowing Japanese troops to be stationed in the country and from there and from Malaya attacks on Burma were launched. Rangoon fell quickly. The United States assigned General Joseph Stilwell to try to organize a defense of upper Burma and keep open the Burma supply road into China with Chinese troops, but by May the Japanese had control of the whole country and had cut the supply route.

By May, 1942 the Japanese had their "Greater East Asia" with all its vast resources. It remained now only to consolidate and defend it. Though this was all they had intended to do, the victories had been so swift and so easy that they could not resist pushing further. They now conceived of a larger perimeter, to include the Aleutians, the Solomons, and Midway, from which Hawaii could be threatened. This proved their undoing, for though the Solomons and several of the Aleutian Islands were occupied, the strike at Midway failed. The American fleet had recovered amazingly since Pearl Harbor and, aided by excellent intelligence, it was fully concentrated for the Midway engagement and it had the advantage of land-based planes from Hawaii. In the Battle of Midway (June 3–5, 1942) Japan lost most of her aircraft carriers, and thereafter at sea she was on the defensive.

In August, 1942 an American task force attacked Guadalcanal Island in the Solomons, from which the Japanese could threaten Australia and Allied bases on the southern side of new Guinea. The battle was savagely fought for six months, but at its end the Americans had captured the first of Japan's conquered Pacific islands. Thereafter reconquest of selected islands became the pattern of counterattack. Some would be bypassed, their Japanese garrisons left isolated. In the summer of 1944 the Marianas were penetrated, and Saipan, Tinian, and Guam were taken. Saipan became the principal base for B-29 raids on Japan until Iwo Jima in the Bonins was taken in February, 1945. Meanwhile the reconquest of several islands in the Palau group of the western Carolines in September, 1944 prepared the way for the reconquest of the Philippines. American forces landed at Leyte Gulf in October, 1944. The Japanese, now fighting on their inner defense perimeter, brought up sizable naval units which, however, were so far inferior to the American that they were afraid to take advantage of certain tactical opportunities presented them by Admiral Halsey. The land fighting in the Philippines lasted six months, but after Manila, largely burned out by the Japanese, was retaken in February, the campaign was merely a matter of time.

In April, 1945 the last, and in many ways the most vicious, battle of the war was fought for the island of Okinawa in the Ryukyu (Liuch'iu) chain. Here the Japanese fought with desperate fury. With their navy and air force

JAPANESE CONQUESTS

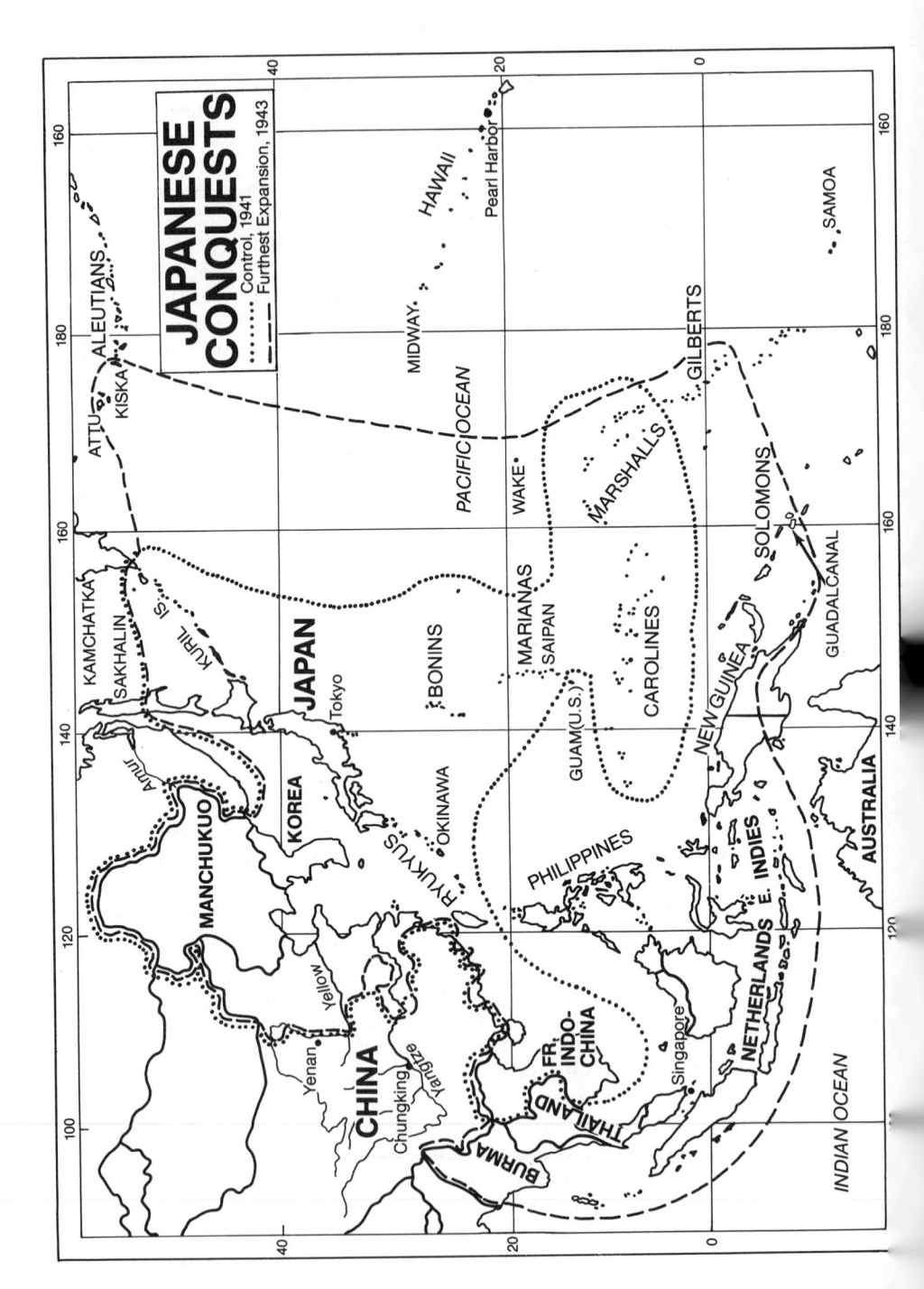

.... Control, 1941
– – – Furthest Expansion, 1943

FIGURE 22.8. American marines in the battle for Tarawa in the Gilberts.

almost gone and the home islands under constant bombardment they tried to make full use of the airplanes they had left by using them for suicide missions, whereby planes loaded with explosives would be ridden down by the pilots and deliberately crashed into American ships. While these so-called "kamikaze" attacks (named for the typhoon that defeated the Mongols in 1281) took a huge toll, Japanese defenders of the island killed thousands, including the American commander, General Bruckner, and were in turn slaughtered; at the end, many were burned to death by flamethrowers in the caves to which they had retreated.

The Surrender of Japan

With the fall of Okinawa the war was lost for Japan. The home islands were not only open to air attack from the nearby islands, but the American fleet was able to shell Tokyo. With her overseas sources of supply cut off Japan could no longer run her industrial plant. The whole economy was breaking down, and it was becoming clear that disease and starvation would soon stalk the land. Tojo had resigned in July, 1944 after the capture of Saipan had made the reversal of Japan's military fortunes clear, and since that time there had been a "peace faction" in the Japanese government.

After the Okinawa landings in early April the "peace faction" got the upper hand and a new cabinet under retired Admiral Suzuki Kantaro took over to seek ways to peace. They were hampered in their efforts by the army leadership, which now began to talk of a defense of the home islands with bamboo spears, if necessary, but they renewed the overtures to Russia with greater urgency. Meanwhile the meaning of "unconditional surrender" was being spelled out more specifically. In the Cairo Conference Roosevelt, Churchill, and Chiang had decided that in addition to stripping Japan of the empire she had conquered since 1931, Formosa and Korea would be taken from her; Formosa to be returned to China and Korea to be made independent "in due course." At Yalta in February, 1945 Russia had been promised the return of southern Sakhalin, the Kuril Islands, and her former railroad rights and naval base in Manchuria in return for entering the war against Japan "two or three months" after the defeat of Germany. At Potsdam in July, 1945 a definition of "unconditional surrender" was framed. This said that Japan would be restricted to her four main islands and that her armed forces must surrender unconditionally. But the Japanese would "not be enslaved as a race or destroyed as a nation." This was publicly proclaimed on July 26, 1945.

Premier Suzuki was noncommittal after the Potsdam Conference, using the term *mokusatsu*, literally "kill it with silence." The great problem for Suzuki was that there was no mention of the fate of the emperor in the Potsdam "terms." Without a clarification on this point Suzuki could not withstand the demands of the military establishment that he reject the Potsdam declaration. Hence his equivocating phrase, which might have been interpreted as "no comment" or even "withholding comment," seemed to the Allies an unequivocal no. Actually the Japanese cabinet was locked in indecision.

On August 6 a single American plane dropped one atomic bomb on Hiroshima. There were 80,000 casualties and most of the city was destroyed. On August 8 Soviet Russia declared war on Japan and invaded Manchuria. On August 9 another American plane dropped the second atomic bomb, on Nagasaki. The city was destroyed. In Tokyo Premier Suzuki was meeting with the Supreme War Council as Nagasaki burned in the atomic explosion. He was trying to get them to agree to accept the Potsdam declaration. The navy minister, Yonai, and the foreign minister, Togo, agreed; the army chief of staff, Umezu, the army minister, Anami, and the navy chief of staff, Toyoda, refused. The news about Nagasaki, which came during the meeting, made no difference. That afternoon Suzuki convened the cabinet. Another deadlock ensued. Suzuki and Togo then went to the palace to ask that an imperial conference be convened. This was a conference in which the emperor was usually invited merely to ratify what the cabinet had decided. Not since the fiery quarrel over the Korean question in 1873 had conflicting opinions been presented to the emperor. Now the emperor authorized Suzuki to call the conference that same evening, August 9. The military chiefs of staff, Umezu and Toyoda, and Baron Hiranuma for the privy council, as well as the full cabinet, were invited.

Dramatically Suzuki informed the emperor that the cabinet had not been able to reach a decision on the Potsdam declaration; yet a decision was necessary. He apologized in deepest reverence for troubling the imperial mind, but he would ask his Imperial Highness to hear the arguments and make a decision. The arguments were repeated, not so heatedly in the imperial presence, and at their conclusion the emperor announced his decision: Japan would "bear the unbearable" and "accept the Allied proclamation on the basis outlined by the foreign minister." The foreign minister, speaking for the peace faction, had urged acceptance of the Potsdam declaration immediately with the sole reservation that the national entity be maintained.

In the predawn hours of August 10, the cabinet made the imperial decision its own and the processes of surrender were set in motion. The Swiss government was notified that Japan accepted the Potsdam declaration "with the understanding that the said declaration does not prejudice the prerogatives of His Majesty as a sovereign ruler." The specific reference to the emperor caused a momentary problem for the Allies. They had promised that Japan would not be destroyed as a nation, but they had not made up their minds about the emperor. However, a carefully worded reply, sent by American Secretary of State James F. Byrnes with the approval of the other allied governments, avoided raising the issue. "From the moment of surrender," it said, "the authority of the emperor and the Japanese government to rule the state shall be subject to the Supreme Commander of the Allied Powers." As for the ultimate form of the government of Japan, it would "be established by the freely expressed will of the Japanese people." This reply, sent on August 11, reassured Premier Suzuki and the peace faction of the cabinet sufficiently. War Minister Anami and the chiefs of staff wished to interpose further stipulations, but they were overruled, again with a final word from the emperor. A surrender rescript was drafted, recorded in the emperor's own voice, and was scheduled for broadcasting to the nation on August 15.

Between August 12 and 15 there was real danger of a coup by fanatical army men, but an attempt to enter the palace grounds was thwarted and the surrender broadcast was performed as scheduled. War Minister Anami and a few other Japanese officers committed suicide, but most, even in remote areas where they had never tasted defeat, surrendered as instructed. General MacArthur, as Supreme Commander for the Allied Powers (SCAP), officially received the Japanese surrender aboard the battleship *Missouri* in Tokyo Bay on September 2, 1945.

CHINA AND THE PACIFIC WAR

In contrast to the victorious American counterattack which reversed the Japanese expansionist tide and defeated Japanese forces everywhere in the Pacific Ocean area in the years 1943–1945, the war in the China theater remained a stalemate. This was partly because of the low priority assigned by the top Allied command to that area, and partly due to political conditions in China which prevented a united effort against the Japanese.

Before the United States entered the war the Chinese had utilized their meager resources to resist Japan amazingly well, but the situation deteriorated rather than improved thereafter. With the closing of the supply route from Burma in April, 1942 Chungking began a period of relative isolation during which supplies dwindled, inflation developed, and general enervation prevailed. Supplies flown at great risk over the mountainous "Hump" from India appeared in black markets. Nevertheless with the aid of American bombers operating from advanced airbases at Kweilin and Liuchow in Kwangsi province, as well as from Chungking, the Chinese were able to prevent the Japanese from advancing much beyond their 1941 lines until 1944, when the Japanese broke through, and seized the advanced airbases and the city of Changsha, enabling them to forge the last link in a long interior rail line from Manchuria to Malaya. With their ocean shipping lanes under constant harassment this had become vitally important to the Japanese.

Stilwell versus Chiang

Meanwhile General Stilwell, who had been appointed chief of staff to Chiang Kai-shek as well as American commander in China, had been striving desperately to reopen the Burma Road—without success. At the Cairo Conference of November, 1943 Roosevelt and Churchill had promised a strenuous effort by Anglo-Indian and American forces to push into Burma from India. However, the priority had been lowered later since the British declined to place much confidence in the Chinese ability to hold up their end. American commando teams did penetrate Burma from the south in 1944 at great risk, but they could not link up with Stilwell.

The problem, as Stilwell saw it, was Chiang Kai-shek's unwillingness to commit enough forces to the Burma campaign. Stilwell noted that Chiang insisted on keeping large numbers of his best troops in the north, where their mission was to keep watch on his Eighth Route Army (the communists) and prevent its moving southward. This, of course, was symptomatic of the breakdown of the "united front," which still remained official policy, but since 1941 had not actually functioned. While the Chinese armies growled at and occasionally clashed with each other in the field, the People's Political Council, which had supposedly brought together in cooperation all Chinese political groups including the communists, had become a dead letter.

At Chungking the right-wing elements of the Kuomintang were in the ascendancy. The banking and commercial elements of the coast cities, which had tended to liberalize the party somewhat, lost their influence at Chungking to more conservative landlord groups. In 1943 Chiang published a treatise called *China's Destiny* which sounded extremely Confucian in its terminology. Another volume, called *China's Economic Theory*, also published under the Generalissimo's name, appeared in 1943. It denounced the theories of "alien" and Western-oriented Chinese economists, and refused to be concerned with human wants. Certainly it offered no hope of a better future to impoverished peasants and dissatisfied businessmen.

Chiang had undoubtedly intended these publications as a rejoinder to communist leader Mao Tse-tung's treatise *On New Democracy*, published in 1940, which, along with the communists' reputation for "agrarian reform" in north China, was becoming uncomfortably popular. But by castigating liberals and Western influences almost wholesale he alienated a large segment of Chinese Western-educated and -oriented intelligentsia and Americans in China as well. The fact that thought control went hand in hand with these official pronouncements made the alienation all the deeper. Chiang's adopted nephews, Ch'en Kuo-fu and Ch'en Li-fu, were very much in evidence in Chungking in the war years. They were the leaders of the so-called C.C. Clique, the ultraconservative element of the Kuomintang, and through their secret group of "Blue Shirts," they checked incessantly on loyalty and discipline. Few government officials could hold their posts without having their stamp of approval. Also they were put in charge of propaganda in the guise of "educational policy." Under them censorship and thought control were diligently attended to.

It was in this climate that General Stilwell came to detest the Generalissimo and all he stood for. Furthermore, as a military man, Stilwell could not abide the idea that Chiang should hold back his best troops from fighting the Japanese, yet kept poised for action against the communists. Stilwell wanted *both* nationalist and communist troops, the best he could get, to hold the Japanese in south China and to open the Burma Road. During the summer of 1944 the tension between Stilwell and Chiang reached the exploding point. Chiang demanded Stilwell's recall, and after sending a special envoy, Patrick Hurley, to China to see if he could patch things up, President Roosevelt recalled Stilwell in October. Washington-Chungking relations were at their lowest ebb.

After Stilwell's departure Ambassador Clarence Gauss, who was also critical of Chiang, resigned. Hurley remained as ambassador and General Albert Wedemeyer took over the China military command.

Gradually Hurley came to accept Chiang's point of view and Wedemeyer, even without the northern troops, went to work on reopening the Burma Road. Actually Stilwell had made remarkable progress, despite his difficulties, and carrying on from there Wedemeyer succeeded in opening the road, now renamed the Stilwell Road, in February, 1945. At least Chungking would not fall in the last months of the war.

The Sino-Soviet Treaty

A final round of diplomacy, not with the United States, but with Soviet Russia, filled the last weeks of the war for China. At Yalta in February, 1945 Roosevelt and Churchill had sought a guarantee of Russia's entering the war against Japan. Stalin had agreed to do so "two or three months" after the defeat of Germany providing certain conditions were met. He wanted to regain from Japan certain rights and territories taken from Tsarist Russia in the Russo-Japanese War. These included the southern half of Sakhalin Island and, more importantly for China, railroad rights in Manchuria, and the use of Port Arthur as a naval base and Dairen as an open port. Also he wanted the Kuril Islands (once claimed by Russia but conceded to Japan for Sakhalin in 1875) and a guarantee of the continuation of the status quo in Outer Mongolia (already a Soviet Republic). All of these were granted by Roosevelt and Churchill, with the stipulation that on the Manchuria-Mongolia agreements the consent of Chiang Kai-shek must be obtained. Roosevelt said he would urge Chiang to negotiate an agreement.

The death of Roosevelt in April delayed matters, but beginning in June delicate negotiations were carried on between T. V. Soong, Chiang's representative, and Russian Foreign Minister Molotov, with the United States State Department counselling Soong. Thus on the surface it would seem that Chiang was dragooned by the State Department into accepting the Yalta concessions. However, the situation was more complicated than that, for by the time the negotiations reached a climax in early August, Stalin was anxious to enter the Japanese war before it was over, and his own quid pro quo, the Chinese concession demand, was embarrassing him. The Chinese were not blind to this, and they used the opportunity to obtain certain guarantees from the Soviet. The Soviet "reaffirmed" its recognition of the nationalist government and promised to give aid to China only through that government; it recognized China's full sovereignty in the three eastern provinces (Manchuria); promised that it would discontinue interference in the affairs of Sinkiang province; and that the independence (not status quo) of Outer Mongolia would be recognized if a plebiscite showed her people wanted it. China conceded the use of Port Arthur and Dairen and agreed to establish a joint Sino-Soviet railroad company to manage the Chinese Eastern and South Manchurian railroads. The agreement, if kept, could seriously impair any underlying Soviet scheme to expand her own borders by annexing Manchuria, Mongolia, or Sinkiang or to help the Chinese communists establish a separate regime in north China. How this would work remained to be seen, but Chungking was not unhappy with the agreement, which was initialed shortly after the impatient Russians invaded Manchuria, and finally signed on August 14.

And so the Pacific war ended. As the surrender terms were implemented, new problems would arise, which will be discussed in another chapter.

BASIC DATES

1929–1931	Hamaguchi, Shidehara, Wakatsuki liberal cabinets in Japan
1930	Japan signs London Conference agreements; ultra-nationalists' opposition led by Okawa Shumei, Kita Ikki, and Cherry Society
1931	March Incident fails; Manchurian (Mukden) Incident succeeds, September 18; Fall of Wakatsuki-Shidehara cabinet
1932	Murder of Premier Inukai and end of party government in Japan
1933	Establishment of Manchukuo; Japan withdraws from League of Nations

1933–1936	Young Officers ("Imperial Way") group versus Control Group in Japanese army politics
1936	Attempted coup by Young Officers; victory of Control Group
1934–1935	Chinese communists' Long March to northwest China
1933–1936	Mounting Japanese pressure in north China
1933–1936	Chiang Kai-shek consolidates power
1936	Sian incident (kidnapping of Chiang) leads to united front
1937	Marco Polo Bridge incident begins full-scale Sino-Japanese War
December, 1937	Japanese take Nanking
1937–1941	Three Konoe cabinets in Japan
1938	Seizure of Canton and Hankow; puppet government at Peking
1938–1939	Soviet border incidents; Japanese expansion turns southward
1938–1945	Communists and border government oppose Japanese in north China
1938–1945	Nationalist government at Chungking
1939–1944	Stalemate in China war
1940	Wang Ching-wei "puppet" government established at Nanking
September, 1940	Tripartite Pact between Japan, Germany, and Italy
1940–1941	Japanese in Indochina; pressure on Dutch East Indies; mounting tension with United States
April, 1941	Japanese-Soviet neutrality pact
October, 1941	Tojo becomes premier
December 7, 1941	Pearl Harbor attacked
January–June, 1942	Japanese take Southeast Asia
1942–1943	American victories in Pacific
November, 1943	Cairo Conference
1944	Philippines retaken
1944	Stilwell-Chiang dispute in China
1944–1945	Bombing of Japan
February, 1945	Yalta Conference
July, 1945	Potsdam Conference
August, 1945	Atomic bombs dropped; Russia enters war; Japanese make surrender offer
August, 1945	Sino-Soviet Pact
September 2, 1945	Official surrender of Japan

SUPPLEMENTARY READING

Borton, H. *Japan's Modern Century,* rev. ed. New York, 1970.
Brown, D. M. *Nationalism in Japan.* Berkeley, Calif., 1955.
Clyde, P. H. and B. F. Beers. *The Far East,* rev. ed. Englewood Cliffs, N.J., 1966.
Fairbank, J. K. *The United States and China.* Cambridge, Mass., 1961.

Fairbank, J. K., E. O. Reischauer, and A. Craig. *East Asia: The Modern Transformation.* Boston, 1965. Revised and abbreviated edition, 1973.
Iriye, Akira. *Across the Pacific: An Inner History of American-East Asian Relations.* New York, 1967.
Scalapino, R. A. *Democracy and the Party Movement in Prewar Japan.* Berkeley, Calif., 1953.
Yanaga, C. *Japan Since Perry.* New York, 1949; reprinted, 1966.

ADVANCED READING

Arima, T. *The Failure of Freedom: A Portrait of Modern Japanese Intellectuals.* Cambridge, Mass., 1969.
Borg, Dorothy. *The United States and the Far Eastern Crisis of 1933–1938.* Cambridge, Mass., 1964.
Butow, R. J. C. *Japan's Decision to Surrender.* Stanford, Calif., 1954.
——— *Tojo and the Coming of the War.* Princeton, N.J., 1961.
Chiang, K. *China's Destiny.* New York, 1947.
Clubb, O. E. *Twentieth Century China.* New York, 1964.
Crowley, J. B. *Japan's Quest for Autonomy.* Princeton, N.J., 1966.
——— *Modern East Asia: Essays in Interpretation.* New York, 1970.
Feis, H. *The China Tangle.* Princeton, N.J., 1953.
——— *The Road to Pearl Harbor.* Princeton, N.J., 1960.
Grieder, J. B. *Hu Shih and the Chinese Renaissance, 1917–1937.* Cambridge, Mass., 1970.
Ike, Nobutaka, ed. and trans. *Japan's Decision for War: Records of the 1941 Policy Conferences.* Stanford, Calif., 1967.
Iklé, F. W. *German-Japanese Relations, 1936–1940.* New York, 1956.
Israel, John. *Student Nationalism in China, 1927–1937.* Stanford, Calif., 1966.
Lockwood, W. W. *The Economic Development of Japan,* rev. ed. Princeton, N.J., 1968.
Lu, D. J. *From Marco Polo Bridge to Pearl Harbor.* Washington, 1961.
Maruyama, Masao. *Thought and Behaviour in Modern Japanese Politics,* expanded ed. New York, 1969.
Maxon, Y. C. *Control of Japanese Foreign Policy, 1930–1945.* Berkeley, Calif., 1957.
Miller, F. O. *Minobe Tatsukichi: Interpreter of Constitutionalism in Japan.* Berkeley, Calif., 1965.
Morison, S. E. *History of U.S. Naval Operations in World War II.* Boston, 1956.
Morley, J. W., ed. *Dilemmas of Growth in Prewar Japan.* Princeton, N.J., 1971.
Ogata, S. *Defiance in Manchuria.* Berkeley, Calif., 1964.
Pu Yi, Ainsin Giorro (Henry). *From Emperor to Citizen.* 2 vols. Peking, 1964.
Schroeder, P. W. *The Axis Alliance and Japanese-American Relations, 1941.* Ithaca, N.Y., 1958.
Shigemitsu, Mamoru. *Japan and Her Destiny.* New York, 1958.
Storry, R. *The Double Patriots.* London, 1957.

Togo, Shigenori. *The Cause of Japan*. New York, 1956.
Toland, John. *The Rising Sun: The Decline and Fall of the Japanese Empire*. New York, 1970.
Tsou, Tang. *America's Failure in China, 1941–1950*. Chicago, 1963.
Tuchman, B. W. *Stilwell and the American Experience in China, 1911–1945*. New York, 1970.
Wilson, G. M. *Radical Nationalist in Japan: Kita Ikki, 1883–1937*. Cambridge, Mass., 1969.
Wohlstetter, R. *Pearl Harbor: Warning and Decision*. Stanford, 1962.

Chapter 23

Southwest Asia: Since World War II

Southwest Asia underwent great changes as a result of World War II. A number of significant trends have appeared in the postwar period, but it is not yet possible to discern a single development common to the whole region. While each nation developed individually, it can probably be said that there were four major underlying factors: oil, nationalism, demands for social reform, and the strategic location of the region between the two great powers of the United States and the Soviet Union.

Clearly, petroleum has played and continues to play a major role. Forty-two per cent of the world's total oil resources are to be found in Southwest Asia, and production costs there are lower than at any other point on the globe. Oil has played a vital role in filling the energy needs of both Western Europe and Japan. Increased production, the building of new refineries in such places as Saudi Arabia, Iran, and Kuwait, the construction of supertankers, and the establishment of new pipelines are all witness to this expansion, which was particularly great in the period between 1948 and 1967, when there existed a real seller's market. However, the closing of the Suez Canal, coupled with the development of natural gas resources for the European market, and the development of new petroleum fields in Algeria and Nigeria have changed this situation somewhat, to the growing anxiety of the Southwest Asian oil producing countries.

Nationalism has remained everywhere the underlying political ideology for this part of the world. It has been characterized by great suspicion toward the Western powers, the British, French, and Americans, and to a somewhat lesser degree toward the Soviet Union. Such slogans as "Down with the West," or "Down with the Foreigners," enjoy a wide appeal, with only the Turks and the Iranians an exception. In fact the only unifying factor in Southwest Asia is the constant fear and hatred of Israel, and the oustanding political problem has been and continues to be, without much hope for a future settlement, the Arab-Jewish conflict which has resulted in three major confrontations, those of 1948, 1956, and 1967. Yet xenophobia in general, and the opposition to Israel, merely mask another aspect of nationalism in Southwest Asia, namely that it is frequently also a regional or local kind of thing, making coordination and cooperation most difficult, if not impossible, between various Arab states.

Accompanying nationalism there has also been a tremendous upsurge in demands for social reform. Not only has there been a growing feeling that there should be a rise in the standard of living, and that the low-level economic status quo should be abandoned for a richer life, but there has also taken place, especially in the Arab world, a genuine social revolution whose bearers are the products of the new university education who seek to break down the walls of ancient privilege and to bring about increased material rewards for the masses. These aspirations of the young intellectuals are due to a combination of the successful achievement of national independence with the burning desire for economic improvements. Frequently impatient with the old order, and indifferent to the means employed to bring about a change, these demands often have resulted in political murder and revolution. The spearhead in this drive quite frequently is the armed forces of a country, and there has been a growing tendency toward military dictatorships in the Arab world.

Finally, Southwest Asia does occupy a strategic position between the two superpowers, America and Russia. The United States, having replaced Britain as the foremost Western power, has attempted to contain the Russians, to control oil resources, and to build up its airpower in Southwest Asia, while the Russians have attempted to counteract these moves by gaining access to oil, neutralizing American air power, and achieving access to warm water ports. In fact, especially as the result of the Arab-Israeli conflict, the Soviet Union has gained considerable successes in these aims, by not only winning the minds of many Arab nationalists who look upon the Soviet Union as a power favorable to reform, but also by gaining access to such important assets as the Iraq oil fields, or the use of Syrian and Egyptian ports for the Russian Mediterranean fleet.

In Iran all of these four major problems, feverish nationalism, oil diplomacy, Soviet influence, and demands for reform, manifest themselves to a marked degree. The two major developments in Turkey have been a most shaky progress toward a democratic state, and an increasing tendency to adopt a neutralist position between America and Russia. Iraq has undergone a number of violent revolutions, while Saudi Arabia faces primarily the oil problem and strategic questions connected with it, although the old monarchical order may also be threatened by attempts at violent overthrow. For the new nation, Israel, and its neighbors, Syria, Lebanon, and Jordan, the burning issue remains the old clash between Jewish and Arab nationalism which overshadows every other concern. For the Persian Gulf sheikdoms, as well as Aden, the major development has been British withdrawal, and in Yemen the outstanding issue has been a protracted civil war between the royalists and the republicans, which brought with it outside involvement by the Egyptians and the Saudi Arabians, and still left Yemen a hapless country, backward, and hoping to be propelled at least "into the 14th century."

IRAN

Iran, in the period from 1939 to 1954, was a most troubled country. Violent nationalism, its rich oil resources, and a position adjacent to the Soviet Union all played a part. In 1939 the country was ruled by an autocratic shah who governed a strongly centralized state by means of a large bureaucracy. The constitutional spirit glimmered faintly in the Iranian parliament, the Majlis, which represented primarily the interests of the land-owning classes and of the Shi'i religious leaders. Prior to the outbreak of the war in 1939 the Iranian ruler, Reza Shah, exhibited distinctly authoritarian traits and tended to be increasingly in sympathy with the climate of opinion which pervaded Nazi Germany. German advisors, technicians, businessmen, and teachers flooded the country, some disguised as so-called tourists, and trade with Germany and German investment increased rapidly. The German embassy, occupying the newest and most luxurious embassy building in Tehran, directed the activities of several thousand Germans at the outbreak of the conflict. Iran declared its neutrality in the struggle, but after the German invasion of Russia in June, 1941, the pro-German leanings of the shah caused the newly allied nations of Great Britain and the Soviet Union to cast a most suspicious eye upon Iran.

World War II and Iran

As a vital link between the two Allied powers, Iran and its rich oil resources could not be permitted to fall into the hands of the German army, which was advancing toward Trans-Caucasia. Russia had considered the absorption of Iran as recently as 1940. In that year Molotov was tempted by a German offer of Iranian territory from Baku to the Persian Gulf. However, Soviet policy swiftly changed towards close cooperation with the British. In August, 1941 the shah was presented with a joint Anglo-Soviet note which demanded the expulsion of all German influence. Reza Shah replied, a trifle insolently perhaps, that Iran was anxious to get rid of all foreigners. Then followed several joint notes from England and Russia asking for a supply route across Iran, but all of these were refused.

The Allies acted on August 25, 1941. British and Russian troops marched into Iran to prevent a German-instigated palace revolution. While token resistance was offered to the British in the south, none was encountered by the Russians in the north, and in a few days the whole country was brought under joint occupation. By September the Russians controlled all of north Iran, including Tehran, the capital, while the British seized south Iran, and Reza Shah, who had become increasingly unacceptable to the British, was removed and shipped into exile to South Africa where he died in 1944.

His son, Muhammad Reza Pahlavi, a serious young man with liberal ideas, succeeded him on the Peacock Throne on September 16. On January 29, 1942, he legalized the occupation of his country by a treaty between Iran, Britain, and the Soviet Union. This was a treaty of alliance, which authorized the occupation of Iran by forces of the Allies. Iran was to be defended from German aggression, her economic well-being was to be safeguarded, and Iranian sovereignty, political independence, and territorial integrity were to be respected. Under its terms the Allies were to evacuate the country six months after the end of the war. At the big Three Conference, which was held in Tehran in November, 1943, Iranian independence was once more reaffirmed, largely at the behest of the United States, which also undertook to assist the Iranian economy.

The essential task of funneling supplies to Russia and keeping the important line of communications open was also shared by the United States, whose army was brought into Iran, not by treaty but rather under British auspices, where it was organized as the Persian Gulf Service Command. Consisting of a small number of specialist troops, never exceeding 30,000, it operated the vital Trans-Iranian Railroad and ran truck lines to supplement it. Prior to the departure of United States troops from Iran material amounting to a total of five million tons, or roughly 6,000 tons a day, was being turned over to the Red army at Tehran. The United States also furnished advice for the Iranian government; Dr. Millspaugh returned once again to help with the financial system and the Iranian army and police had the benefit of American advisors.

Iran joined in the war in September, 1943, but no Iranian troops saw any fighting. Participation was motivated by the desire to join the United Nations. Despite the fact that Iran was spared the frightful ravages of modern conflict, the impact of the war on her politics and economics was very serious. As early as 1942, when there was a crop failure, the food situation had become critical. It was accompanied by hoarding, a flourishing black market, and food riots, and despite the fact that Britain, the United States, and Russia all provided food supplies, the situation remained critical for some years. Inflation increased with more and more paper money being turned out by the government.

In politics, the occupation meant that the authority of the central government was weakened and consequently the power of the local leaders was increased. Politicians were now permitted to criticize the government through the medium of a free and active press. This criticism was mainly directed against the reform and westernization attempts of the Reza Shah regime, and it demanded a return to the traditional Iranian customs and religion. Women wore veils more frequently and mosques were once more closed to tourists. However, the most important development in Iranian politics was the creation of political parties actively aided by outside powers.

The Cold War and Soviet Pressure

Iranian internal political developments began to reflect the growing estrangement and diplomatic struggle between the Soviet Union, Britain, and the

United States. Soviet influence began in Iran through the medium of the Tudeh party. A number of leftist liberals and intellectuals outside parliament founded the party in 1942. Gradually growing stronger, it enjoyed the excellent organization adopted from the model of the Soviet Communist party and soon became completely controlled by a hard core of communists. Its growth was particularly impressive in northern Iran where the Tudeh party had the active support of the Russian army. As a consequence of this activity, and since the Iranian government seemed unable to combat the spread of communism, the British in a countermove brought back to Tehran from Palestine the former journalist and reformer Zia-ed-din Tabataba'i, who had been an original partner in Reza Shah's coup of 1921. The return of Zia-ed-din, whom the British had kept on hand for a good many years, ever conscious of the wisdom of reemploying fallen statesmen, soon produced results. He was an able organizer and his opposition to communism gave him the support of some groups in the Majlis, notably the landowners, the clergy, and some tribes. Nevertheless, by 1944 Russian influence showed steady signs of an increase. Soviet propaganda libraries and a "house of Russian culture" were opened. Support was given to a great number of anti-Western newspapers and propaganda journals, and a violent press war was waged against the West.

In the fall of 1944 a large Soviet delegation, headed by Kavtaradze, the vice-commissar for foreign affairs, arrived in Tehran with the object of obtaining oil concessions in northern Iran. This direct demand by the Soviet Union resulted in the decision of the government to stop all oil concession negotiations until all Allied troops had been evacuated, and a law was passed which forbade any Iranian official from even discussing the problem of concessions under penalty of an eight-year prison sentence. The immediate result of this rebuff was mob violence against the government, led and inspired by the Tudeh party, which all along had been in favor of granting oil concessions to the Soviet Union. At the same time Soviet control of northern Iran tightened considerably. Iranian officials were no longer permitted to collect taxes in northern Iran, foreign journalists were banned, and the Soviets began to expropriate increasing amounts of grain, livestock, and the copper resources of the territory occupied by the Red Army. Iranian protests to the Soviet envoy remained unheeded, and the Tudeh party displayed even greater power.

The climax in the development of Soviet pressure on Iran was reached after the conclusion of the war when Russia attempted to detach a part of Iran and to set up a Soviet state. This was the creation of the Azerbaijan autonomous government. It was quite similar to the attempt by the Soviets to set up the Soviet republic of Gilan on the Caspian after World War I, and indeed it had as its leader an old Bolshevik, Jafar Pishevari, who had been the minister of interior in the ill-fated Soviet Gilan republic. The Russians also knew a good man when they saw one. The Azerbaijan autonomy movement had its inception in December, 1944, when a Tudeh-led rebellion occurred at Tabriz. When Iranian troops attempted to quell it, they were confined to their barracks by the Russian army, and when Iranian reinforcements from Tehran attempted to enter northern Iran they were turned back by Russian soldiers a few miles outside the capital city. By September, 1945 the autonomy movement had resulted in the establishment of an independent government at Tabriz. It was, of course, communist-dominated and conceived, and while it soon developed its own People's Army and its own secret police, it nevertheless did achieve some valuable reforms. Counting on the hostility of the people of Azerbaijan against the central government, which had drained the area of its wealth, it made an effective appeal for socialism and began to set up a program of land redistribution at the expense of landlords, of bank nationalization, and of the substitution of the disliked Persian language by the native Turkish.

Russian support was also given to yet another attempt at the creation of an autonomous region within Iran. This was the Kurdish proclamation of a noncommunist independent republic with its center at the town of Mahabad. Soviet support of the hard-to-control Kurds had particularly dangerous implications since there were also Kurds in Iraq and Turkey, and the development of a Kurdish state within Iran might well give rise to demands by all Kurds to become united. Such a state under Soviet control would be a formidable threat. By the end of 1945 the Persian government faced a very difficult situation which worsened in the spring of the next year when British and American troops left Iran under the terms of the treaty of 1942; the Soviet troops did not depart. Despite British and American protests the Soviet Union declared that her troops would have to remain in Azerbaijan and the Caspian region.

Ahmed Qavam Blocks Russian Pressure

Increasing Soviet pressure and the growth of the communist-controlled Tudeh party resulted in anti-Russian sentiment in the Iranian government, now under the leadership of Ahmed Qavam, a rich and wily landowner. Qavam appealed against Russian interference and the presence of their troops on Iranian soil to the United Nations in March, 1946, thereby precipitating a veto, a walk-out by Gromyko, and the first United Nations crisis. The Russians claimed that the problem was one to be solved directly between Iran and the Soviet Union. Since Qavam achieved little by his appeal to the U.N., he changed his tactics and now cleverly led them to believe that they would gain the coveted oil concessions in Iran if they would withdraw their troops. As a token of his pro-Soviet leanings Qavam proceeded to arrest and imprison the anticommunist Zia-ed-din and to suppress all anti-Soviet newspapers. On April 4th Qavam reached an agreement with the Soviet government; Russian troops were to be withdrawn from Iran and in return Qavam would submit the proposal for a joint Iranian-Soviet oil company to the Iranian parliament. The Soviet Union, believing Qavam and also giving heed to the pressure of world opinion, evacuated her troops from Persia in May, 1946. However, she maintained steady pressure through the Tudeh party, which, growing even more powerful, began a series of mass demonstrations in the summer of 1946 against the Anglo-Iranian Oil Company. Strikes were called and some resulted in violence in which many Iranians were wounded and a few killed. Press attacks by Russia accompanied this violence and *Pravda*, the official organ, denounced "the brazen and imperious behavior of the British oil company which is an example of the disrespect for the sovereignty of a small country." In August, 1946 Qavam began to include Tudeh party members in his cabinet, thus further demonstrating to Russia what appeared to be his sincere attempt to cooperate with the Soviet Union.

Great Britain, becoming increasingly disturbed over the trend of developments in Iran, began to take countermeasures. Since protests to Qavam seemed to have little effect, British troops were landed at Basra, and Britain began to foment revolt among the south Iranian Qashqai tribes against the Iranian government. The tribes rose, demanded autonomy for themselves, the expulsion of the Tudeh members from the government, and government reform. To give weight to their demands they seized the cities of Bushire and Shiraz. Tribal revolt was sufficient excuse for Qavam to change his policy and he now turned against the Soviet Union. Tudeh ministers were expelled from the cabinet, and in October all the leading members of the Tudeh party found themselves in jail in Tehran. Immediately after this, Iranian troops marched into Azerbaijan and after a few brief skirmishes the autonomy movement suffered an inglorious collapse. Iranian troops imposed martial law and the whole of Azerbaijan was successfully brought back under Iranian control. Next came a quick move against the Kurdish independence movement. Its leaders were arrested and executed and by the end of the year all of Iran was once more firmly united.

In the summer of 1947 Qavam, still ostensibly working for Russian interests, introduced the problem of the oil concessions in the Majlis. By now parliament was purged of Tudeh members and was firmly anti-Russian. Iran was also backed by the United States. Henry Grady, the United States ambassador, stated that Iran was free to do with her resources as she pleased, and in October the Iranian parliament rejected the Russian bid for an oil concession and passed a bill which forbade new concessions to any foreign power. In December Qavam resigned. Although denounced by the press and attacked as a traitor, Qavam seems to have negated Soviet influence by his clever and skillful handling of a most difficult problem. This defeat sustained by Russia did not lessen the activities of the Tudeh party, which organized demonstrations hostile to America and which was ably seconded by bitter Soviet radio attacks against United States influence.

In February, 1949 there was an attempt to assassinate Shah Muhammad. While he was on a visit to the campus of Tehran University, a journalist, probably working for the Tudeh, shot and slightly wounded the shah. The unsuccessful assassin was killed at once. As a result of this attempt martial law was proclaimed and the Tudeh party was outlawed by the government. Despite these setbacks, Soviet pressure on Iran did not lessen. There were still protests against the presence of United States advisors with the Iranian army and gendarmerie, and a number of border incidents took place in the northeast where the Red Army had crossed the Iranian frontier a number of times. When Tehran objected the Russians closed their consulates.

Western Aid

Russian influence worked through threats, propaganda, and attempts at subversion, while the diplomacy of Britain and the United States tried to offset Soviet pressure by economic aid, military missions, and the bolstering of the Iranian army. Britain aided Iran because she wished to guard extensive oil interests, estimated at over eighty million barrels annually. British aid took the shape of economic assistance. The United States looked upon Iran as a vital spot in the Cold War struggle between itself and Russia, and accordingly, dispatched a number of missions to reorganize the Iranian army and gendarmerie and to improve Iranian agriculture and health.

In 1949 United States aid under the Point Four Program was being extended to Iran. As stated in President Truman's inaugural address, this was an aid program to underdeveloped countries in the form of capital investment and technical assistance. In November of that year the young shah visited Washington where he obtained further promises of aid in the form of American capital. In return the broadcasts of the Voice of America were relayed through the government radio at Tehran. Yet relations between the United States and Iran cooled with the outbreak of the Korean conflict in June, 1950 and the rise to power of a new premier, General Ali Razmara, the former army chief-of-staff.

When under the first Point Four allotment 25 million dollars were granted to Iran there was a great deal of disappointment and outspoken criticism against the United States since the sum was considered insufficient. Razmara then successfully negotiated a large barter agreement with the Soviet Union and in a general way attempted to balance Persian relations between the West and Russia. A number of measures were adopted which discriminated against the West; foreigners were barred from travel near the Russian border, all military attachés were forbidden to leave Tehran, and no Persian was allowed to approach any foreign mission. In the economic field the government of Ali Razmara tried with little success to effect some land reforms which were opposed by the entrenched interest of the landlord class. The shah did distribute some of his large estates and turned part of his fortune over to a philanthropic society. A steel mill and some railroad mileage were also added to the Iranian economy. But this progress was soon undone by the great oil crisis which began in the winter of 1950 and which had far-reaching internal economic and political repercussions.

The Oil Crisis and Mossadegh

Aroused nationalism made oil the great issue. The storm which broke was directed against the Anglo-Iranian Oil Company, a vast corporation which possessed the largest oil refinery in the world on the island of Abadan in the Persian Gulf, and which had enormous investments in Iran. In the years leading up to 1950 the company had enjoyed steadily increasing profits. So did its neighbor, the Arabian-American Oil Company in Saudi Arabia which in 1950 had made a new agreement with the government of Saudi Arabia under which it shared its profits equally with that government. When the news of this fifty-fifty split reached Iran, there was an outcry for the immediate nationalization of the Anglo-Iranian Oil Company so that Iran would also benefit at an increased rate from its oil resources. However, Ali Razmara committed the blunder of underestimating the force of this demand for oil nationalization. Arguing that Iran did not have the necessary personnel to run such a vast and complex industry, he opposed its nationalization.

Ali Razmara's stand against the nationalization of the Iranian oil industry fused his opponents, consisting of landlords, religious fanatics, and violent nationalists, into a solid bloc. They were led by the ambitious and unscrupulous Ayatollah Kashani, a demagogic mulla who wanted to restore the hold of Islam over the Iranian people and who became a popular leader of the National Front party. Kashani was supported by the shrewd politician Muhammad Mossadegh, who in his vociferous opposition to Razmara had won great popular support and had also emerged as a leader of the same party. In March, 1951 Ali Razmara was assassinated in a mosque by one of the followers of Kashani. In April Iran received a new government when Mossadegh became its new premier. He had ridden to power on the wave

FIGURE 23.1. The great oil refinery at Abadan, one of the largest in the world.

of feverish nationalism, and he received an endorsement of his policy when the Majlis unanimously voted for the nationalization of the Anglo-Iranian Oil Company.

Antiforeign feeling expressed itself in strikes and mass demonstrations, and the British operating personnel of the Anglo-Iranian Oil Company were forced to leave Abadan since the Persian government turned a deaf ear to arbitration. Iran neither was able to operate the Company nor could it pay for the seized properties. On the other hand the Anglo-Iranian Oil Company retained control of the marketing organization and most of the tankers, and the British government effectively blocked the export of Iranian oil by seizing foreign-owned tankers. The oil industry suffered relatively little loss since the closing of Abadan stimulated production in other areas, notably in Iraq and Saudi Arabia, and new refineries in Basra and Bombay substituted for Abadan.

Mossadegh, the "personal symbol of Persian nationalism," tried in vain to improve his country's economic position. A seven-year plan was worked out with the aid and consultation of American engineers, but the lack of personnel and of funds hampered the plan. The premier even flew to New York and appeared somewhat dramatically before the Security Council of the United Nations but no economic aid was forthcoming. However, his political status was secure. In the Iranian elections of 1952 Mossadegh was overwhelmingly elected on the basis of his declaration that he would not compromise on the oil issue. All negotiations with the British collapsed, the Iranians refused entry to British technical personnel, and then denied the competence of the International Court of the Hague to arbitrate. Anti-British riots swept Tehran and consequently the British closed their consulates. In July, 1952 Mossadegh resigned his office since the dictatorial powers which he wished were denied him by the shah. Instead Ahmed Qavam took over, but after three days it became clear that he would not do. The Majlis refused him any support, and he was attacked by both the Tudeh and the religious fanatics of Kashani. Amid riots Mossadegh triumphantly returned to power on July 22 with full dictatorial powers. The assassin of Ali Razmara was pardoned with honors, all oil agreements were refused, and in October, 1952 Mossadegh broke diplomatic relations with Great Britain. But he did not stop here. Heady nationalism and desperation now led Mossadegh to attack the shah. He dissolved the Majlis and showed an increasing willingness to deal with Russia on her own terms. Communist influence increased steadily and the climax to Mossadegh's extreme policies came in August, 1953 when the shah fled to Baghdad while adherents of the Tudeh party pulled down the royal statues in the public squares of Tehran.

These dramatic events now produced a reaction, and opposition to Mossadegh grew rapidly from many quarters. Supporters of the monarchy and a sizable faction in the Majlis united and on August 16th the royal guard attempted a coup d'état which was suppressed. Three days later General Fazollah Zahedi led the successful counterrevolution which resulted in the tumbling of Mossadegh from power. The shah returned from Iraq amid scenes of wild rejoicing and Mossadegh was arrested, tried, and imprisoned. It has been alleged that during this episode American intelligence operatives were actively assisting the shah.

The new conservative government then attempted to reach a rapprochement with the Western powers. Diplomatic relations with Great Britain were resumed and Iran received new American loans. Negotiations were also started on the oil question and in October, 1954 a new international oil agreement was concluded which for the time being settled that vexing problem on the basis of some concessions made by the Anglo-Iranian Oil Company to Iranian national pride and a fifty-fifty split of the profits.

GOVERNMENT OF AND BY THE SHAH

Since the brief period of Mossadegh's power the most important feature of Iranian history is the fact that the monarchy continues as a living reality. Muhammad Reza Shah Pahlavi is the active symbol of traditionalism and nationalism, and at the same time he continues to be the manager of the process of modernization. "The shah is the government"; he forms the cabinet and he controls the armed forces. He has gained the reputation as the most skillful political and diplomatic brain in Tehran.

After the trouble with Mossadegh the shah consolidated his authority as ruler in fact as well as in name. During the 1950's individual freedom was curtailed and the secret police were a power in the land. Gradually the shah established his image as a paternalistic monarch with progressive intent, one who aimed to democratize the government of Iran.

For many years the shah had the backing of the large landowners and of the mullas, the teachers of Shi'a Islam, the national faith of Iran. The shah also had the loyal support of many of the educated people in his country.

Although in name the Iranian monarchy has been a constitutional one, the elected legislature had very little real authority. Administration operated through a centralized bureaucracy. The legislature, however, was respected as "a visible manifestation of constitutional government." Public opinion had a strong influence also in the actions of the administration. One of the most encouraging changes during the period after World War II was the modernization of the legal and court systems of Iran. On the other hand, defects in the government were obvious. Padding of payrolls, nepotism, land grants made to favorites of the shah's government, bribery, and corruption weakened the regime.

The shah has moved to establish his family as a ruling dynasty. In 1958 his second marriage was dissolved and in December 1959 he married Farah Diba, now the Empress Farah. A son and heir apparent was born in October 1960. The shah crowned himself and the empress at Tehran in October 1967, and in 1971, at Persepolis, an international gathering celebrated the 2,500th anniversary of the founding of the Persian monarchy by the Achaemenian Cyrus the Great.

DEVELOPMENT, LAND REFORM, AND POLITICS

Modernization and an increased population have caused many changes in Persian society. The urban population of Iran doubled between 1941 and 1968. In one ten-year period, 1956 to 1966, the population of the whole country increased by one third to a total of 25,000,000, 62 per cent of whom were in urban areas. The capital and largest city, Tehran, grew from 200,000 in about 1918 to 800,000 at the end of World War II and to 2,500,000 in 1968. The urban population included an enlarged middle class, from whom came an increasing proportion of educated technological and administrative elite and among whom were many potential revolutionists. The role of women was changing as they entered new occupations and gained the right to vote. The modernization of Iran proceeded at an accelerated pace and urbanization strained the fabric of traditional society.

Land reform was promoted by the ruler Muhammad Reza Shah Pahlavi himself. As part of a land distribution program, the shah began in 1950 to turn over large tracts of crown lands to the farmers who tilled the soil. Agricultural cooperatives were started in 1951. The shah also persuaded the legislature to arrange for the distribution of public domain lands. Such lands, formerly held by the government, were sold mainly to villagers working on the land and the proceeds were used to finance an agricultural development program.

Starting in 1954, a seven-year plan of social and economic development was begun, made possible by the increased revenue coming from oil production under nationalization. Numerous reform programs were started under this plan through a separate governmental agency known as the Plan Organization. In the field of transportation highways were improved, railroad lines extended (including lines to Tabriz and Meshed), seaports and airports developed. Automobiles were imported in quantity, to the extent that in 1960 it was said there were 100,000 automobiles in Tehran alone. In agriculture there were changes in methods of cultivation, development of irrigation, and especially a large land reclamation project in Khuzistan northwest of the Persian Gulf. Industrial production increased in many areas, including sugar, cement, electric power, and steel.

Reform activities included development of education. Schools for lower levels of education were built and new universities in Meshed, Shiraz, and Tabriz founded. Thousands of Iranian students went abroad to be educated. In 1955, for example, there were over 5,000 Iranian students studying in Western Europe and the United States.

The governmental weaknesses mentioned above were seen in the events of 1960–61. The election held in 1960 was considered unsuccessful partly because of manipulation of votes by government officials, combined with an ineptness of the two political parties who were running for office, and the boycotting of the election by the genuine opposition of the old National Front admirers of Mossadegh. As a result the shah ordered the cancellation of the 1960 election results. About this same time corruption in the army resulted in the arrest of 145 army officers including five generals. The government was faced with inflation and overspending beyond the limits of the increased revenues due to the taxing of the oil production. In spite of the need for changes, vested interests opposed any radical reforms.

New elections were called in the winter of 1960–61. When the new legislature met partisan politics seemed to be its chief concern and in May of 1961 the legislature was dissolved. Lacking a proper means of bringing about political and legislative change, some of the more vocal elements among the people were active in demonstrations against the government. Particularly noteworthy were the student demonstrations and the strike of school teachers.

By the middle of 1961 Dr. Ali Amini, an official with long experience in high office, was called upon to head the cabinet. He worked at improvement of administration and also permitted a liberalization of restrictions to the extent that speakers might denounce the government.

In November 1961 the shah announced a program of reform which included the breakup of large estates and redistribution of land among the peasants. Although the land reforms gained for the shah the approval of the peasants, nevertheless, because of his arbitrary methods and the lack of any really representative government, the shah and his officials failed to gain the support of the National Front Party.

In 1962 Dr. Amini was faced with large antigovernment meetings. He dissolved the majlis (parliament) and suppressed the public meetings for fear of real rebellious activities. Elections were postponed indefinitely.

Faced with a financial crisis and political discontent, Dr. Amini resigned (July 1962). The shah meanwhile reorganized and strengthened his security forces.

When the National Front leaders continued to attack the government of the shah their political activity was suppressed. Aided by a subservient premier, Amir Assadolah Alam, the shah had the political leaders arrested. At the same time he promoted the land reform program more vigorously than ever.

By the beginning of 1963 the reform program was already achieving results. With the promotion of rural education, the enactment of a new election law and the distribution of land, the power of the landowners had diminished, the peasants had an increased sense of unity and of confidence, and productivity increased in spite of some credit difficulties. The shah asked for and obtained popular approval through a nationwide referendum (January 1963).

Opposition to the reforms came partly from the Moslem religious leaders, who saw the traditional precepts of Islam endangered by an increased secularization of government and by the modernization process in education, land reform, and the emancipation of women.

There was also the feeling that the use of arbitrary power by the government had exceeded reasonable bounds. In February 1963 the shah seemed to be moving toward totalitarianism. Iranian students overseas (some 25,000 in Europe and America) were very vocal in their attacks. Within Iran tribal leaders in Fars rebelled and were brought under government control. Opponents of land reform promoted demonstrations against the government in Tabriz and Qum during March 1963.

The crisis came when severe rioting broke out, first at the Shi'i center of Qum during three days in June 1963 under the leadership of a religious teacher, Abdullah Khomeini (or Khumayni), who had been preaching against the shah's regime. The rioting, which also occurred in Tehran, Shiraz, and other towns, was quickly and ruthlessly suppressed by the army. Some National Front leaders, who had only joined the uprising in its second day, were arrested. Khomeini was exiled.

The shah continued with his policies of reform and modernization. Local elections were planned in municipalities and regions, in accordance with the shah's ideas of moving toward democracy in government. At a congress of "the movement of free men and women of Persia" in Tehran in August 1963, peasants, workers, women, intellectuals, and others were brought together to nominate candidates for election to the National Consultative Assembly. On the other hand, in the election which followed in September no opposition candidates were permitted to run.

In the farming country cooperatives were established to take the place of large-scale landlordism. Modern methods of farming were promoted and through the land-distribution program, by the middle of 1966, some 4,200,000 Iranians had become farmer-proprietors.

The economy, with support from the oil business, showed continued expansion. One so-called "five-year plan" followed another. Under a new premier, Amir Abbas Hoveida, the first year of a fourth five-year plan, ending in March 1969, showed a growth rate of more than 10 per cent. The central "Plan Organization" during this period gave priority to the development of water supply, electric power, and communications. With international support Iran's first steel plant was established near Ahwaz in 1969.

These were some of the elements which contributed toward an increase in per capita income and a higher standard of living. Educational reform played its part. The government established a new ministry for higher education in 1967. New administrative officers at the universities in 1968 emphasized technology and agriculture as well as history and literature and undertook to improve relations between administration and students. The government also provided new services for the average Iranian. Education and literacy had expanded by 1970. Popular interest in education was evidenced by the fact that in 1971 funds for schools and teachers were raised by public subscription.

Meanwhile in a period of worldwide student unrest the Iranian students have continued to agitate against the shah. Demonstrations about bus fares occurred in February 1970. A riot over various issues (examinations, poor teaching, etc.) broke out at Tehran University in November 1970 and the trouble spread to other universities. Ringleaders were arrested and sentenced to prison terms.

POWER AND STABILITY IN SOUTHWEST ASIA

After the fall of Mossadegh Iranian nationalist sentiment was for years directed against the communist regime of the Soviet Union. This was kept alive by continuing broadcasts of the Russians against the shah's government, and there was genuine fear of a repetition of Russian intervention in the country. At the same time, Iran during this period of the Cold War became an active part of the American system. The most noteworthy event was the signing of the Middle Eastern collective defensive agreement of October 1955, the so-called Baghdad Pact. This resulted in an alliance among the northern tier of Southwest Asian states facing on the Soviet Union. After 1958 and subsequent to the withdrawal of Iraq under the Kassem government the alliance was termed the Central Treaty Organization.

American influence continued to increase. American interest was expressed through the granting of funds up to a billion dollars between about 1951 and 1961. Private loans increased. United States government programs comprised technical assistance (including Peace Corps volunteers) and military advisors, who helped to develop effective armed services in Iran.

Iranian sentiment was largely pro-American. There was an admiration of and a friendliness toward the United States which was shown by the sending of many young men and women to study in this country. The feeling of dependence on the United States led some Iranians to stress the importance of American responsibilities and others to fear the power of the United States. Cordial relations between the two governments have continued. In spite of difficulties, American aid has helped the shah's government to maintain its authority in Iran.

Iranian relations with the Soviet Union improved during the 1960's. The shah has twice visited the Soviet Union and Russians built the steel plant arranged in 1965. Cooperative undertakings include a gas pipeline in Azerbaijan, electric power exchange, and an irrigation project. Military supplies for Iran have come from the United States, the Soviet Union, and Great Britain.

Iran's recent relations with Iraq and other Arab states have not been cordial. Border incidents, especially because of Persian influence among the Kurds, disputes over navigation rights on the Shatt al Arab, and revolutionary propaganda from Baathist Iraq in Iranian Khuzistan and in the gulf sheikhdoms have been sources of friction.

On the other hand, the Persians in the years from 1964 to 1970 sought and obtained friendly agreements with Turkey and Pakistan. At a summit conference in Karachi in December 1968 the shah met with Premier Demiral of Turkey and President Ayub Khan of Pakistan. In accordance with a tripartite partnership of "Regional Cooperation for Development," trade, communications, and banking have been promoted among the three states. A six-year construction project ending in 1971 resulted in the completion of the Turkish-Iranian railroad between the two countries.

TURKEY

The record of Turkey, which had already suffered the pains of nationalism and which did not possess vital natural resources, was quite different from that of Iran. Its chief problem has been how to maintain a semblance of democratic institutions, and how to balance its position between the two great powers, the United States and the Soviet Union.

World War II and Turkey

One year before the outbreak of the Second World War, in 1938, Mustafa Kemal, the founder of modern Turkey and its president, died after a long illness. His successor was Ismet Inonü, who became president despite the rather strained relationship which had existed between him and the sick Kemal. Ismet Inonü, the virtual dictator of a one-party republic, faced as his major task the maintenance of a precarious neutrality in World War II, thus avoiding the error of World War I. Turkey remained neutral until it was clear who would win. All major belligerent powers attempted to be on good terms with Turkey, strategically placed on the Straits. France ceded to Turkey the disputed district of Hatay in October, 1939, and signed a pact of mutual assistance. Britain bought Turkish tobacco and dried fruits in order to deny these products to Germany, while supplying Turkey with badly needed war materiel and loans. British trade with Turkey doubled in consequence of this preemptive buying and she too concluded a treaty of alliance. The Germans on the other hand, who badly needed Turkish chromite in their industrial production, made a nonaggression pact with Turkey in June, 1941.

The Battle of Stalingrad caused a marked tendency to favor the Allies. In 1944 Turkey stopped all chrome shipments to Germany, and in August of that year she broke diplomatic relations with the Reich. In February, 1945 there followed a declaration of war on Germany, timed so as to permit Turkey membership in the United Nations.

Despite the successful attempts to stay out of the conflict, the war brought its inevitable inflation, rationing, and shortages. It also brought renewed Turkish discrimination and injustice against the remaining non-Moslem minorities. In 1942 and 1943 a special discriminatory tax was levied against Greeks, Jews, and Armenians, but this policy ended again at the conclusion of the conflict.

The end of the war replaced the possibility of a German threat by the fear of the Russian menace, and the victorious Soviet Union was not slow in exerting pressure on the Turks. As early as 1945 the Soviet Union severed its treaty of friendship with Turkey and began to demand revisions in the Montreux Convention. A joint Soviet-Turkish defense of the Straits was proposed and then came a Russian demand for the Kars-Ardahan region in Armenia, while the Soviet press declared that the Turkish government did not inspire any confidence. These ominous developments were staunchly resisted by the Turks and this caused a great deal of sympathy on the part of the United States. In 1946 the *U.S.S. Missouri* was dispatched to Istanbul and in March, 1947 the Truman Doctrine was extended to Turkey.

The United States wanted primarily to promote in Turkey a stable bulwark against the U.S.S.R., and American aid was freely given and used effectively in the development of Turkish military power, natural resources, highways, and agricultural production. The great power struggle between

Russia and the United States caused further Turkish alignment with the West; in 1949 she became a member of NATO (North Atlantic Treaty Organization), in 1950 she sent troops to Korea, and in 1951 she participated in the integrated Allied Middle East Command. In a series of treaties in 1953 Turkey established amicable relations with her Balkan neighbors, Greece and Yugoslavia, and was on friendly footing with India, Pakistan, and even Israel, despite Arab League opposition.

Turkish internal development was characterized by a very shaky trend toward democracy. In 1943 Inonü was reelected president, and he met President Roosevelt and Churchill in Cairo in December. As a move toward greater democratization and to win Western support, a second party was again permitted in opposition to Inonü's own People's party. This was the Democratic party which was supported by private business interests and was led by Jelal Bayar. He was a man of humble Ottoman origin who had become a financier, a one-time supporter of statism, but who now opposed the central economic policies of the Turkish state. His party suffered defeat in the rigged elections of 1946, but in 1950 he won victory over the government after the secret ballot system had been installed. The 1950 elections were thus a great success for the democratic process. They also resulted in somewhat fewer state controls in the Turkish economy. In May 1954 new elections again brought victory to Jelal Bayar and the Democratic party under his leadership as president of Turkey.

Turkey by 1955 had seemingly become an independent, resolute, and stable state, the most Western and the most democratic of the countries of Southwest Asia. Yet the path towards a more democratic development of Turkey was to be strewn with serious difficulties. Some of these were of

FIGURE 23.2. President Ismet Inonü of Turkey.

an economic nature, such as inflation, the byproduct of too rapid industrialization. Some, and these were far more grave, were the result of arbitrary and oppressive action of the government of President Jelal Bayar and his premier, Adnan Menderes. By suppressing the freedom of the press, by arresting opposition deputies, and by similar unconstitutional and undemocratic measures, Menderes fanned political and economic discontent into open rebellion. Repeated student demonstrations against these repressive measures eventually culminated in army intervention in the spring of 1960. Menderes himself was arrested, tried, and hanged, while a military dictatorship ran the country, although the army officers promised to restore a democratic civilian government to power. New elections were held and in 1962 Ismet Inonü again became president.

Convulsions such as these indicated that democracy as a viable concept was not as yet really deeply imbedded among the Turks. Ominous signs could also be discerned in 1964 in the tense relations between Turkey and Greece as the result of the Cyprus problem.

Twenty per cent of the population of the island are Turkish, close to the Turkish shore, and violently opposed to union with Greece. The Cyprus problem contributed greatly to a cooling of relations between Ankara and Washington, and a corresponding increase in cordiality between the Turks and the Russians.

In 1962 Turkey received a new constitution, and a new National Assembly met in which the Peoples Republican Party, led by Inonü, had the largest vote, though no majority. General Gursel, the mastermind in the army coup of 1960, became president. But there was much dissatisfaction, especially among the ranks of young officers and intellectuals, who clamored for more reforms, and the role of the military became ever more important, raising the basic issue whether democracy was to be a viable proposition for the country. The following year, 1963, there was an attempted military coup, followed by the proclamation of martial law, and the formation of a new cabinet, headed by Premier Inonü until he resigned in 1965.

In that year Demirel became the new prime minister, heading a coalition government formed by the People's Republican Party and the Justice Party, and Turkey again tended to look away from its earlier friend, the United States, and to develop closer relations with the Soviet Union. Demirel experienced greater internal instability, what with increased extreme leftist activities and terrorism, and the army eventually forced him from office. Attacks against American soldiers and sailors, frequent student riots, and the proclamation of martial law have been a characteristic of the last few years, and in 1972 President Sunay, as the result of a veritable wave of anarchism, was forced to suspend the Constitution, and to give even more authority to the military.

THE ARAB LEAGUE AND ISRAEL

For the Arab world of Southwest Asia in Palestine, Syria, Lebanon, Transjordan, and Iraq the chief problem was the clash between the common trends toward unity, such as Islam, economic interests, and anti-Zionism, and the trend toward independent and divergent local nationalism. Arab unity, or Pan-Arabism, was represented by the Arab League. This organization began under British auspices early in World War II when Winston Churchill revived the World War I idea of Arab unity in order to draw the Arabs over to the British side. This turned out to be a process full of difficulties. In May, 1941 Anthony Eden announced in the House of Commons that Britain favored Arab unification and British support was given to Egyptian leadership in this program which had as its purpose the improvement of England's position in the Middle East.

Failure of Arab Unity

Nahas Pasha, the Egyptian premier since 1942, was given strong support, and after preliminary negotiations a common meeting of the Arabs was arranged at the Alexandria Conference of 1944. Despite British urgings there soon developed strong suspicions and rivalries among the assembled Arab leaders. Ibn Sa'ud in particular remained lukewarm toward the idea of Arab unity. If such a program was to be, he felt that he was the man to lead it. Furthermore, he mistrusted the ambitions of his traditional enemies, Iraq and Transjordan. Nevertheless in March of the next year the Arab League was formed in Cairo. It consisted of six states: Egypt, Iraq, Saudi Arabia, Lebanon, Transjordan, Yemen, and an Arab representation from Palestine. The Arab League was to consider matters of mutual interest and to coordinate political actions, but this attempt at unification achieved very little. Discord, rivalry, and jealousy undermined the idea of Arab unity. Ibn Sa'ud opposed the creation of a greater Syria.

In 1948 the Palestine war demonstrated the weakness of the Arab League. Each Arab state blamed the others for the failure in the war against the Jews, and this failure caused the intensification of the separate and divergent nationalism of each Arab country. All that was left of unity was hatred of the foreigner. As an editorial in the London *Times* put it, "the main, if not the only cohesive force within the League is an ingrained and traditional xenophobia, directed according to circumstances against the French, the British, or the Jews." A joint defense pact in 1950 between Egypt, Lebanon, Syria, Saudi Arabia, Yemen, Iraq, and Jordan was directed as much against the Western powers as against any other possible adversary, but in reality each nation went its own independent way. Territorial nationalism was the victor.

The ideal of Arab unity was brought much more sharply into focus as the result of the abrupt, complete, and bloodless revolution in Egypt of July, 1952 which propelled General Muhammad Naguib into power. However, Naguib was soon replaced and put under permanent house arrest two years later by his former subordinate, Colonel Gamal Abdel Nasser, who then became president of Egypt. Nasser's primary objective ever since was to become the leader of all Arab states in opposition to the Western nations. When he successfully nationalized the Suez Canal in 1956 be became the hero of the Arab world, but he also suffered a serious blow to his military prestige as the result of the speed with which the Israeli armed forces overwhelmed Egypt's army in the Sinai peninsula campaign. Nasser's interference into the affairs of other Arab states in trying to make himself the head of a Pan-Arab movement brought him into sharp conflict with some of the other Arab states. Jordan and Lebanon particularly reacted violently against such Egyptian claims, but Saudi Arabia, irked at temporary losses of oil royalties in the aftermath of the Suez affair, also remained in solid opposition to Nasser's aspirations.

The Creation of Israel

In the postwar period Palestine was the greatest problem in the Arab world. The British mandate for Palestine became an insoluble dilemma. On the one hand Britain wanted and needed the support of the Arabs, and she stood behind the Arab League; on the other hand she also wanted and needed the support of the Jews everywhere in the war against Germany. The status quo which was based on the White Paper of 1939 became rapidly untenable. Under the provisions of that document Jewish immigration was limited and Jewish land purchases were restricted, with the foreseeable result that the Jews would remain a permanent minority in an Arab state. Consequently, although there was little doubt about general Jewish support in the war against Nazi Germany, there was still a great deal of Jewish anger and irritation against the English. Jewish support was given to England at once after the first Italian air raid on the country, but there were also demonstrations and a perceptible increase in acts of terrorism.

The British moved cautiously, and did not permit the creation of a separate Jewish brigade until 1944. Jewish terrorism against the British increased gradually. Terrorist organizations, such as the one headed by the former classicist Stern and the Haganah, facilitated illegal Jewish immigration and occasionally murdered objectionable British statesmen, such as Lord Moyne, the British minister to the Middle East, who was assassinated in Cairo. When the British refused, for example, to permit the landing of a number of illegally entering Jews aboard the ship *Patria*, which was diverted from Haifa to Mauritius, the Jewish terrorists blew up the ship in 1940 in Haifa harbor at the cost of 268 lives, as a protest against the British action.

The Arabs were also troublesome to the mandatory power. Few Arab volunteers cared to join the British forces and the Mufti of Jerusalem was busily engaged in broadcasting threats from Berlin against the Anglo-Saxons and the Jews. At the same time the Zionist movement in the United States became most active. In 1942 it passed the so-called Biltmore Program which demanded that Palestine be a Jewish commonwealth, opened to unlimited Jewish immigration, and controlled by an all-Jewish army. American aid was given to the Zionist underground army, the Haganah, which became steadily more enterprising and gained access to great stores of arms by theft and robbery. By 1944 Jewish terrorism was definitely on the increase, and it had the support of American Zionist leaders. Terrorists committed sabotage against railroad lines, oil refineries, and British military installations, while a flood of illegal Jewish immigrants entered the country.

Behind these activities were American contributions. When during the victorious Allied advance into Germany in the spring of 1945 the Nazi atrocities against the Jews became widely known, President Truman appealed to the British government to admit the remaining few homeless European Jews without delay into Palestine.

Terrorism increased as a result of the conflict between Arab and Jewish nationalism, reaching its height in 1946 when the Jews blew up the King David Hotel in Jerusalem. The British government decided that a settlement was impossible, since both sides adamantly rejected any compromise solution, and declared that it would terminate its mandate for Palestine. This was announced to the United Nations in April, 1947, and a special session of the United Nations Assembly in November of that year proposed a partition of the country. When the British withdrew on May 14, 1948, terminating the mandate, the Jews declared the creation of their new independent state of Israel. On the very next day Israel had to fight for its existence, since Arab forces from Egypt, Jordan, and Iraq under the leadership of Abdullah of Transjordan began an invasion. Turkey, however, abstained from participation in the Arab-Jewish war.

In this so-called Palestine War of 1948 success went to the Jews because of their unity of purpose, organizational ability, and superior military skill. The war ended in July, 1949 by a truce and not by a treaty of peace. But there continued to be friction and constant flareups of fighting. Israel had expelled 900,000 refugees and these found refuge and scanty relief in the adjacent Arab countries. Their resettlement provided fuel for constant incidents and so did the question of boundary lines. The city of Jerusalem was to be internationalized by a decision of the United Nations, but Israel insisted on its retention as the Jewish capital under full Jewish control. Until 1967 Jerusalem remained under divided rule with the boundary line between Jordan and Israel running right through the city. A state of uneasy truce under United Nations supervision frequently punctuated by bloodshed formed the relationship between Israel and its Arab neighbors.

The first president of the new republic of Israel was Chaim Weizmann, and in the first elections David Ben-Gurion became premier. Israel was assured of considerable Zionist support from the United States, and in 1949 it obtained an American loan of 35 million dollars for agricultural development. But with the increasing tension of the Cold War between the United States and Soviet Russia, and particularly after the outbreak of the Korean conflict in 1950, Israel tended toward a neutral foreign policy. The United States position became less friendly toward the new nation since Washington felt that the support of the Arab states was necessary in the struggle with Russia. In 1954 Weizmann, the president of Israel, died after having seen the fulfillment of the Balfour Declaration and having led the Zionist movement to success.

The chief problem which Israel faced was that no final peace settlement had been achieved with the Arabs. Control of the upper Jordan river caused clashes with Syria in 1951, disputes over Jerusalem resulted in frequent incidents with Jordan in 1953, and the question of the Gaza strip led to bloody frays with Egypt in 1955. The bitter tension between Arab

THE
ARAB WORLD
AND ISRAEL
IN 1970

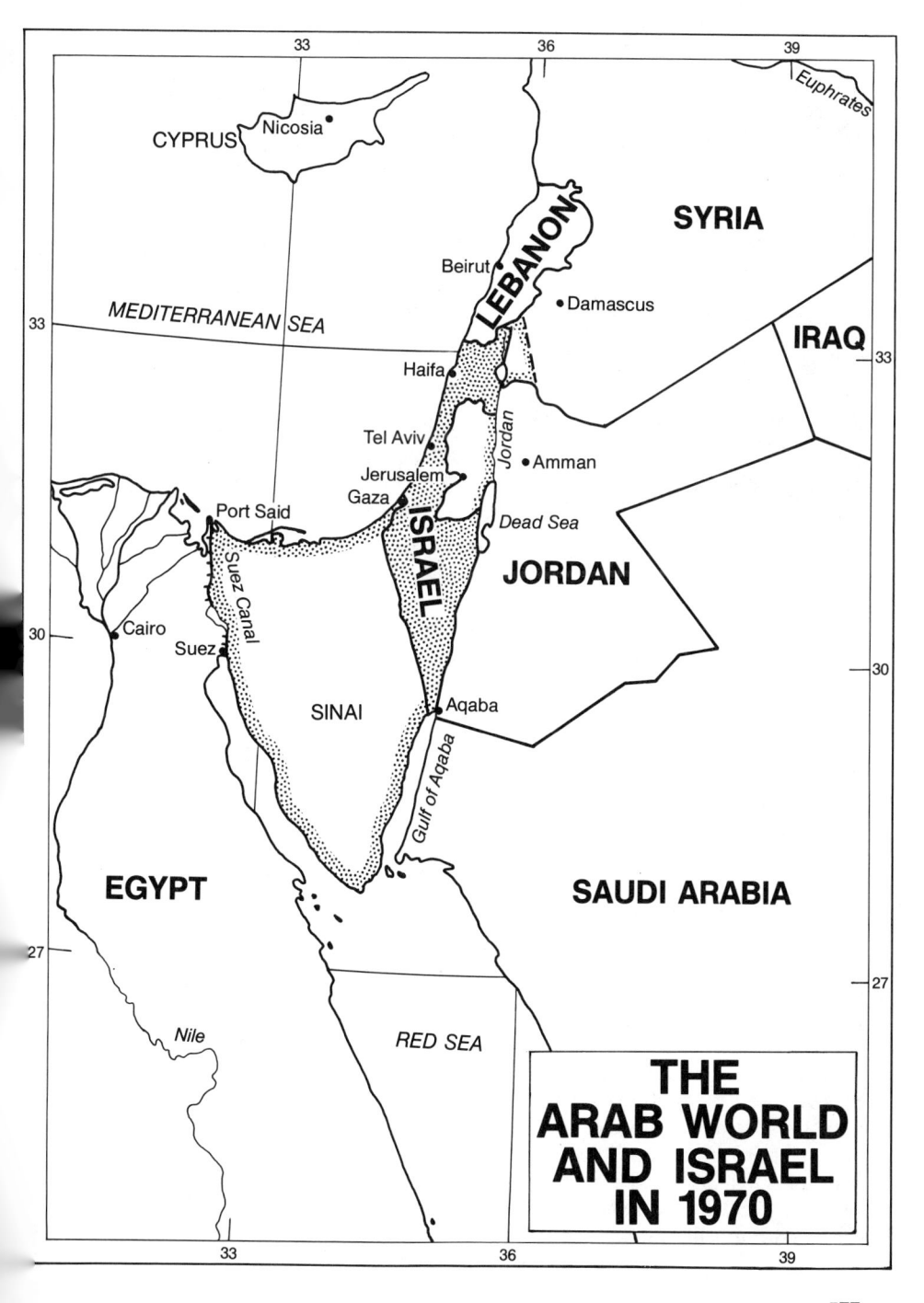

FIGURE 23.3. Golda Meir and Moshe Dayan, premier and defense minister of Israel.

and Jew continued, and the fundamental clash between the irreconcilable demands of Arab and Jewish nationalism remained a permanent factor.

Israel was also boycotted economically by the Arab states, and this threw her into the arms of the West. American aid poured into the country, while the French also supported her with arms and aircraft deliveries. In turn, the Arab states, and especially Egypt, began to look toward the Soviet bloc for military assistance. The future of the Palestinian refugees remained as the most insoluble problem of them all: Israel being unwilling to take them back for fear of a growing Arab population, the Arabs using them as a propaganda issue, and especially after 1955, as a fertile recruiting ground for guerrilla raiders, the *fedayeen*, against Israel.

A major new crisis developed in July 1956, with the coming of the so-called Sinai war, the result of Nasser's insistence to nationalize the Suez canal, when funds for the construction of the Assuan high dam were refused him by the West. War broke out in October between the Israelis and Egyptians, while the British and the French joined in November. The Israelis had no trouble conquering the Gaza strip and occupying Sharm el-Sheikh, overlooking the Gulf of Akaba, but world opinion was shocked with the attempt to invade Port Said. The United States and the Soviet Union, acting in unison, forced an end to the conflict, but not before Israel had again demonstrated her military capabilities, and had caused at least a temporary end to the fedayeen raids. Instead, United Nations forces now separated the belligerents.

While the Sinai war of 1956 had been a very successful act of deterrence against Arab hostility, the Israelis nevertheless also experienced some internal difficulties. After the resignation of Ben-Gurion in 1963 there were frequent political disputes between those who, as moderates, wanted a settled future for the country (the new Prime Minister Levi Eshkol adhering to this view), and those who argued that Israel would have to hold out for Arab recognition of Israel before such a settlement was possible (a view held for instance by Moshe Dayan, minister of defense and architect of Israeli victory). Arab-Israeli relations continued to be aggravated, and there were frequent bitter disputes over such matters as the distribution of the waters of the Jordan. Again, there was a buildup of arms, and brinkmanship on both sides resulted in yet another, the third war between Israel and her hostile neighbors. This new war in June 1967, the "Six-day war," came about when Nasser, in a fit of political impetuousness and much against the counsel of his mentors, the Soviet Union, closed the Gulf of Akaba to Israeli shipping, and ordered the UN peace-keeping force out of the Sinai area. The Israelis, challenged, and fighting to teach their enemies a lesson, attacked with great skill and vigor, defeating the Arabs everywhere in a series of rapid victories. The Arabs were defeated on all fronts, the Egyptians losing not only the Gaza strip but the whole of the Sinai peninsula with Israeli forces occupying the East bank of the Suez canal, the Syrians losing the strategic Golan heights, and the Jordanians losing Jerusalem and the entire west bank of the Jordan River. Again the Arabs had lost in battle, the result of a much lower level of education, technical competence, and leadership and lack of trust, and again the problem of the Arab refugees was compounded with thousands of Arabs fleeing from Israeli-occupied territories. The failure of the United Nations to avert the conflict also meant that the role of the great powers, the Americans and the Russians, had greatly increased. Confrontation there might easily lead to the dreaded possibility of a Third World War, and from 1967 on the "Middle East" conflict has acquired a most important, though also somewhat ironic status, in the relations between Moscow and Washington. Both sides have tried to bring about a settlement, only to be thwarted by their respective protégés, the Egyptians and the Israelis, thereby pointing out the weakness of even a superpower to settle a dispute in cases where their clients prove intractable. The Israelis have insisted on direct negotiations between themselves and the Arab states, demanding recognition before they are willing to withdraw their forces from the occupied areas, and the Arabs have insisted upon an Israeli withdrawal before negotiations could begin. While the United States and the Soviet Union have been unable to budge the issue, both have recognized that a confrontation between Russia and America over a renewed conflict must be avoided.

Hostilities between Israel and her neighbors have continued ever since. There has been frequent fighting, especially along the Suez front, with Israeli commando raids, jet strikes, and artillery bombardments. There have also been frequent clashes with the Syrians and commando raids into Southern Lebanon to root out Arab guerrillas. The Arabs have retaliated by terrorist attacks, especially against Israeli planes, or planes flying to Israel, whether German, Swiss, Austrian, or others, by bombings and sabotage within Israel, and by the shelling of agricultural cooperatives, etc. In 1969 with the death of Levi Eshkol, Golda Meir, a former schoolteacher in Milwaukee, became the New Israeli prime minister, and she has inherited this situation of almost complete deadlock. The death of Nasser and the coming to power of President Anwar Sadat in Egypt has changed little so far. Both sides hold totally opposing views. The Arabs denounce the Israelis as naked and unjustifiable aggressors, and they demand unconditional Israeli withdrawal. The Israelis have refused to withdraw until a permanent peace is signed and their right to exist has been recognized. In this deadlock each side does have a trump card: the Israelis could agree to a return of the Arab refugees, the Arabs could recognize and accept Israel, but neither card is likely ever to be played. The Arab-Israeli conflict, a product of the most intense nationalism, seems to have in it all the seeds of a long-term political conflict with no solution in sight.

Syria and Lebanon

Developments in Syria and Lebanon since the Second World War led to their full and unrestricted independence, characterized by political instability and military factionalism. In 1940, with the fall of France, Syria and Lebanon came under the regime of General Dentz, loyal to the pro-German government at Vichy. Many German spies flocked into these two countries and the region became a hotbed for anti-British subversive activities in the Near East. When the Allies decided to occupy Syria and Lebanon in June, 1941 as the result of a pro-Axis coup in Iraq, British and Free French troops occupied the countries after meeting stiff Vichy resistance. The Free French General Catroux, commander of the liberated areas, announced the end of the French mandate for Syria and Lebanon, and their independence, although France was to maintain a special position of privilege. This reflected the thinking of General de Gaulle, who for reasons of French prestige was unwilling to withdraw completely from the Levant. In 1943 the constitution was restored and in the elections the nationalist parties won. But in November, 1943, despite British and American opposition, the French arrested the Lebanese premier and his cabinet, since they felt that French interests were jeopardized. Both the United States and Soviet Russia came out in favor of full independence for both states.

A new outbreak between Syria and France took place in 1945 when the French, insisting on their special rights, reinforced their garrisons with Senegalese troops and built up their military strength. Fighting broke out between Syrian nationalists and the French, who again bombarded Damascus, the Syrian capital. Syria appealed to the Security Council of the United Nations, but a more immediately effective action came when Churchill told de Gaulle that the French would have to get out of Syria and Lebanon. In the face of this British ultimatum, a furious de Gaulle had no choice but to withdraw and French authority was finally forced out of the Near East.

Syria and Lebanon then became completely independent states and members of the United Nations after 1945. But they lacked the element of stability and were often shaken by army coups d'état. As members of the Arab League they fought in the Palestine War of 1948 against Israel without distinction. In March 1949 a revolution overthrew the first Syrian president, Shukri Quwatly, under whom the government had become corrupted and bankrupt. An army coup led by Colonel Husni el-Zaim, the chief-of-staff, inaugurated a military government. Husni el-Zaim was also very interested and instrumental in the attempt to reform Syria on the Turkish model. A civil code was promulgated, women were emancipated and the clergy curbed, and a program of public works was developed. Unfortunately the new premier exhibited dictatorial tendencies and he aroused opposition by his measures of censorship and suppression of the opposition. Husni el-Zaim became more and more arrogant (he quarrelled with Iraq and Jordan) and power-thirsty, and in a new army coup in August 1949 he was killed. For a short while Syria was governed by a council of army officers. In December of the same year Colonel Shishakli, another professional army officer, assumed dictatorial power by yet another coup, and brought Syria firmly under military rule. His control in turn was followed by a new military coup in February 1954 led by Hachem el-Abassi, who succeeded Shishakli. The latter fled and found sanctuary in Saudi Arabia. The same strong army influence was exhibited in Lebanon, Syria's sister nation, and it led to similar instability.

In February 1958 Syria became part of the United Arab Republic when she joined Egypt under Nasser, but within four years another Syrian revolution against Egyptian predominance in governmental affairs and against Nasser's social revolutionary schemes terminated this situation, and once again Syria became an independent state.

At the same time there could be felt in Syria the growing influence of the Baath party, dedicated to its own special form of Arab socialism, and much indebted to Marxist ideology. This brought with it the proclamation of a Socialist People's Republic, and much closer ties with the Soviet Union, but it did not bring about any measure of greater political stability or freedom from military coups. One of these occurred in 1963, propelling Salah al-Din al-Bitar to power as prime minister, and putting Baath ideology firmly on top, but this in turn led to a reaction by business people who went on strike, and in 1966 there was another bloody military coup, after which the Zayen government took power. Despite their militancy the Syrians fared exceedingly badly in the 1967 war against Israel, losing the important Golan heights. In 1968 al-Atasi became prime minister, but the very next year, 1969, the Syrian army again seized the reins of power. In 1971 there came into existence a new Federation of Republics, in which Syria joined the Egyptians and the Libyans, as a "bastion against Israel." But Syrian support of al-Fatah, the Arab guerrilla movement in Jordan, came to nothing, and Syrian attacks on Israel brought with them the usual reprisals. Internally, Syria, then, is a country where the Army holds the reins, permits little freedom of thought, preaches a militant form of socialism, and a militant stance toward the archenemy, the Israelis.

Compared to Syria, Lebanese politics have been far more moderate. True, due to Egyptian interference, there broke out an insurrection against

President Chamoun in 1958, after strikes, disturbances, and much terrorism. But the government appealed for and received American aid in that crisis, which was settled when American marines landed in the country. By and large, however, Lebanon has benefited from a swift economic recovery, and a more or less constitutional democratic regime. Relations with its neighbor, Syria, have been frequently hostile, especially so after 1963, when the Baath party was outlawed in Lebanon, and there were frequent incidents. Lebanon has also suffered from the terrorist activities of the Arab Palestinian commandos, headed by Yasir Arafat, who chose to occupy territory in Southern Lebanon as bases for attacks against Israel. The Israeli reprisals produced a series of clashes, and presented the government of Lebanon with yet another serious and continuing problem.

Jordan

The emirate of Transjordan, which had been under a British mandate, also achieved full independence in 1946 and Abdullah, the Hashimite emir, now assumed the title of king of Jordan. The treaty of independence concluded with Great Britain gave that power the right to maintain military bases in the country and relations continued very close between England and the new nation. Abdullah made a visit to Turkey in 1947 and established cordial relations. Jordan joined in the Palestine War against Israel in 1948 and in fact Abdullah was the recognized leader of the invading Arab armies. After the truce which terminated the war in 1949 Jordan annexed those portions of Palestine which were predominantly Arab in population, and which were not incorporated into Israel. Together with all the other Arab states Jordan maintained stout opposition against the Jewish claims for the possession of Jerusalem, and frequent border clashes and armed forays characterized the uneasy relationship with the Jewish republic. In July, 1951 King Abdullah, a skillful ruler who made cooperation with Britain the polestar of his foreign policy, was assassinated in Jerusalem, and he was succeeded by the Emir Talal who became king of Jordan in September. Since Talal proved hopelessly mentally ill he was deposed in less than a year and the crown passed to his son Husain, who after an education in England could be expected to follow Abdullah's precepts. Jordan benefited economically from both Britain and the United States. The former included Jordan in the sterling area and supported her currency, while the latter extended technical and financial aid to Jordan under the Point Four Program.

The inexperienced, but courageous, young king of Jordan, Husain, was faced with a series of plots against his regime, and even against his life, which were masterminded by Egypt and Syria, and which came to a head in 1958 when British paratroopers landed in his kingdom, in line with American intervention in Lebanon, in order to maintain the security and stability of both governments. Since that time the Jordanian government was almost constantly plagued by the intrigues characteristic of inter-Arab rivalry. The most serious challenge to Husain came from the Palestine Liberation organization, the fedayeen movement headed by Yasir Arafat, who created a state within a state. The situation became much worse as

FIGURE 23.4. Amman, the capital city of Jordan. The Husseini mosque dominates the narrow valley in the foreground, while the newer residential districts are situated higher up on the slopes.

the result of the shattering defeat the Jordanians sustained at the hands of the Israelis in 1967. The loss of Jerusalem and the entire west bank of the Jordan River was bad enough, but the new influx of Arab refugees brought about an upsurge of fedayeen activities. This was a constant embarrassment to Husain and his Bedouins, in that they faced the wrath of the guerrillas, who accused Husain of not doing enough for them. It also gave Israel excuses to attack Jordan. The meddling of Nasser contributed to growing internal violence. By 1968 there were bitter clashes between al-Fatah, the chief guerrilla organization, and the king, who was denounced as the individual who "plotted to stab the Palestine revolution and the commando activities in the back." Fighting between commandos and government forces escalated in the next years, until a bloody showdown began between the two parties in November 1970. This led to the weakening and increasing desperation of the Palestinian commandos.

Iraq

The history of Iraq in the days after the Second World War was governed primarily by the fact that it remained an area of great strategical importance between the two giants, the United States and the Soviet Union, and that its position was enormously enhanced by the possession of vast oil resources. In 1939 Iraq, the first Arab state to reach independence, was ruled by the child king, Faisal II, who was later educated at Harrow. When the war broke out anti-British factions in Iraq hoped for an Axis victory.

German and Italian influence had been very active in Iraq. Germany had permitted Iraqi students to study at Nazi universities at low fees, almost half the motion pictures shown in Baghdad were of German origin, and the Germans operated an airline from Berlin to Iraq. Although the Iraqi government of General Nuri Said broke off diplomatic relations with Germany, the Italian embassy at Baghdad remained as a center of intrigues. German subsidies supported the Mufti of Jerusalem who in the early stages of the war made Iraq his headquarters and who violently denounced British control of the Middle East. In April, 1941, when the war situation looked unfavorable for England, a pro-Axis coup took place in Iraq. It was headed by Rashid Ali who was supported by four Army colonels known as the "Golden Square." Iraqi forces attacked the British embassy in Baghdad and the great British air base at Habaniyah. Rashid Ali had hoped for and expected Vichy French and German support from neighboring Syria, and some German airplanes and a trickle of French arms and ammunitions did in fact arrive; but it was not enough. The British intervened with great promptness and with the aid of the Transjordan Arab legion the rebellion of Rashid Ali was completely crushed. The four colonels of the Golden Square fled to Iran, where Britain was able to seize them after she occupied that country, and they were tried and executed. Rashid Ali had more luck; he fled to Saudi Arabia where he was received with friendliness and was put to work. The Mufti reached Berlin where he broadcast anti-British propaganda. As a direct consequence of the abortive coup Britain decided to occupy the French Levant states and to end Vichy rule.

A new Iraqi government was installed under the leadership of Nuri Said who cooperated closely with the British. In 1943 Iraq joined the war on the Allied side, the first Arab state to do so. She also joined the Arab League, but in that organization she met rivalry from Ibn Sa'ud. As previously seen, little actual solidarity was accomplished by the League. On the other hand Iraq concluded a treaty of alliance with Turkey in 1947 and the relations between these two countries became increasingly more cordial since both stood in the path of Soviet expansion. Iraq also had become a member of the United Nations at the San Francisco Conference.

The country had to face a number of domestic problems. There was a Kurdish uprising in 1945 which was bloodily suppressed, and the regularization of Iraq's relations with Britain was punctuated by occasional riots and incidents. In 1948 the British withdrew all their land forces from Iraq but continued the maintenance of a military mission and the operation of two large Royal Air Force bases. In 1949 the riots which broke out against Britain postponed a final treaty settlement.

When the Palestine issue came to a head in 1948 Iraq joined the war against Israel. An "Arab National Liberation Army" which fought in Palestine was organized in Iraq. The Iraqis also shut off the flow of oil through the pipeline to Haifa, and engaged in harsh measures against the

Jews who had the misfortune to live in Iraq. The failure of the war badly shook Arab solidarity, since each participant accused the other of military incapacity. When a new conflict broke out between Syria and Israel over control of the upper Jordan river in 1951, Iraq again sent troops and airplanes to the aid of Syria. On the international scene Iraq pursued a rather cautious policy, abstaining from participation in the United Nations action in Korea for "technical reasons," but Iraq did join in the joint defense pact of the Arab states.

Great progress was made in the postwar period as a result of the exploitation of Iraq's vast oil resources. In 1949 a new pipeline was constructed from Kirkuk to Tripoli in Lebanon and the Nuri Said government received large British loans for railroad, oil and reconstruction projects. An agreement made the following year between Iraq and the Iraq Petroleum Company assured greater royalties to the government and a second new pipeline was constructed from the oil fields to Tripoli where a big new refinery was also built. Increased revenues from oil and loans from the International Bank were used in railroad and bridge building and in the flood control of the Tigris valley. The Iraqi Development Board set up a five-year plan for Mesopotamian land reclamation, and after it received American Point Four aid the Tigris flood control project was completed. In 1952, after three months of negotiations, a new agreement was signed between the government and the Iraq Petroleum Company and its subsidiaries whereby more Iraqis served on the board of directors and more Iraqis were employed, and under which 50 per cent of all profits accrued to the Iraqi government. This most satisfactory agreement produced revenue greater than was needed to balance the budget. Oil remained in the forefront of the economic development of Iraq, new fields were exploited, new pipelines were built, and a huge new refinery was established at Basra at the head of the Persian Gulf.

Domestic politics in Iraq showed an often baffling turnover of premiers, but underneath the facade of power Nuri Said retained firm control. Occasionally the army became quite active, as for instance in November, 1952 when pre-election disorders were followed by the military dictatorship of Nureddin Mahmud. It was succeeded in January, 1953 by the government of Premier Jamil Midfai, who had in his cabinet many supporters of Nuri Said, so that it may safely be said that up to 1955 Nuri Said retained great political power.

In July, 1958 there occurred, however, another coup d'état by the military against the government of the young king, Faisal II, and his premier, Nuri Said. This was a bloody affair in which the king, his household, as well as Nuri Said himself, were slaughtered, and which brought to power the extremely anti-Western and ultranationalist regime of Abdul Karim Kassem. The Kassem government changed Iraq from a monarchy ostensibly into a republic, though in fact it was, of course, a military dictatorship. The Kassem government tried to wipe out all Western influence in the country, Western foreign experts being released or expelled, and it embraced in foreign affairs a studied policy of neutralism. Kassem enjoyed in these actions considerable communist support, but the extent of communist penetration into this vital area of Southwest Asia is difficult to assess. In any case, the

Kassem regime was soon faced with occasional opposition not only from the always difficult-to-control Kurds, but also from the brand of Arab nationalism which emanated from Egypt. Reaction against the Kassem regime and communist infiltration led to its violent overthrow, and its replacement by a military dictatorship under Abdel Salem Arif who, at least temporarily, brought Iraq into closer alignment with Egypt. Yet, perhaps the most significant feature of modern Iraqi history is the development of its own kind of Arab nationalism, in opposition to the Pan-Arabic claims of Nasser.

Arif's type of Baath socialism led to a closer alignment with the Syrians, and it also brought with it closer ties with the Soviet Union, although Arif did not hesitate to crack down against the Iraqi communist party. By late 1963 Arif was in full control of Iraq, and he governed the country until his death, three years later, in a helicopter crash; but he, as well as his successor, his brother Abd al-Rahman Arif, who became both president and premier, were unable to solve one of the perennial Iraqi problems, that of the Kurds. Fighting between government forces and the difficult and unruly Kurds has remained a constant, though intermittent, feature of the Iraqi political scene.

The war with Israel brought defeat to the Iraqis and in 1968 Arif was overthrown in a coup which brought the military, in the figure of General Hasan al-Bakr, into power. Al-Bakr has instituted a severe regime, what with rigid press censorship, oppressive measures against Jews and other "enemies of the state," political trials, convictions, and executions in public of so-called spies. All power was to be in the hands of the "Revolutionary Command Council," headed by al-Bakr, and a series of radical reform programs were undertaken. Perhaps the most important of these was the land reform of 1969. Domestic opposition was hunted down, and much propaganda was spent in blackening the images of earlier politicians, what with Arif himself being denounced as a spy for the CIA and Israel, a somewhat dubious proposition. Al-Bakr also continued to have his hands full with the Kurds, and there have also been clashes with Iran along the Persian Gulf shore. As far as international relations are concerned Iraq has experienced a growing Soviet influence, symbolized by visits of Red Fleet units to Basra and much in the way of Russian technical and economic agreements, and the development by the Russians of Iraqi oil fields.

Saudi Arabia

For most of World War II Saudi Arabia, under the absolute rule of Ibn Sa'ud, remained neutral, but made no secret of its pro-British feelings, and in March, 1945 Saudi Arabia entered the conflict so as to assure for herself membership in the United Nations at San Francisco, where Prince Faisal, Ibn Sa'ud's son, appeared as delegate.

Oil above everything else was of chief importance in the recent history of this kingdom. In oil development the United States played the dominant role in Saudi Arabia. In 1939 the Arabian-American Oil Company (Aramco) was founded for the exploitation of the Dhahran oil fields. This led to the establishment of diplomatic relations between the United States and the Arab kingdom, and lend-lease loans were made available to the country. A huge airfield and air force base was constructed at Dhahran by the United States when they entered the war. Ibn Sa'ud sent his son, Prince Faisal, to Washington in 1943 and the cordiality between the two nations was further cemented by a meeting aboard an American destroyer in the Red Sea between President Roosevelt and Ibn Sa'ud in 1945. At the end of the war a series of new agreements were concluded, under which the United States trained and equipped the Arabian army in return for further permission to use and develop the air base at Dhahran on the southern shore of the Persian Gulf. An American financial advisor, Arthur Young, took charge of the Saudi Arabian budget. In 1951 Aramco and the Arabian government concluded a new agreement under which profits from oil were shared equally. These brought great prosperity to the kingdom. Royalties and loans from the United States Export and Import Bank made possible the construction of roads, ports and air fields, the building of a railroad to Riyadh, and of a new pipeline to Sidon in Lebanon.

As far as foreign affairs were concerned the most impressive development was the replacement of British influence in Saudi Arabia by that of the United States. Saudi Arabia was a participant in the Arab League, but opposed the greater Syrian ambitions of Ibn Sa'ud's old rival, Abdullah of Transjordan. Instead Ibn Sa'ud supported Syrian independence and, to underline this Arab policy, royal princes visited Colonel Shishakli of Syria in 1952 and 1953. The great oil riches of the kingdom gave rise to disputes with the Persian Gulf sheikhdoms of Muscat and Trucial Oman, since the frontier included a neutral zone, suspected of containing rich oil deposits. Some frontier incidents took place which the British government mediated. Border incidents also occurred with Yemen in Southwest Arabia.

In November 1953 King Ibn Sa'ud died. He had been a shrewd and able king, who by combining the nationalism and strong religious sentiment of the Arabs had created the strongest state the Arabian peninsula had known since the days of the Wahhabis, and he achieved peace and security in his kingdom. His place was taken by his son, who was enthroned as King Sa'ud. Sa'ud II, the eldest of 35 living sons, proved not to be a good choice. There was much corruption, much building of new palaces, and the acquisition of vast fleets of luxury automobiles, and little in the way of reform.

While the foreign relations of Saudi Arabia in the late 1950's were primarily concerned with stopping the ambitious claims of Nasser to become the leader of all the Arabs, domestic problems were perhaps more urgent. The huge income from oil royalties did not result in a social revolution improving the standard of living of the population as a whole, and this soon became a critical issue within the government. In March, 1958 the crown prince, Faisal, who believed in moderate social reform, took control of the government. This resulted in greater financial stability and a certain amount of modernization of the government machinery.

Sa'ud II went into exile, and in 1964 Faisal officially became the king of Saudi Arabia. In 1967 the country was involved in the protracted and bitter civil war fought in Yemen, where Faisal supported the royalists against the Egyptian-supported republicans. The chief question for the future of Saudi Arabia probably still concerns the viability of a monarchical, if not a

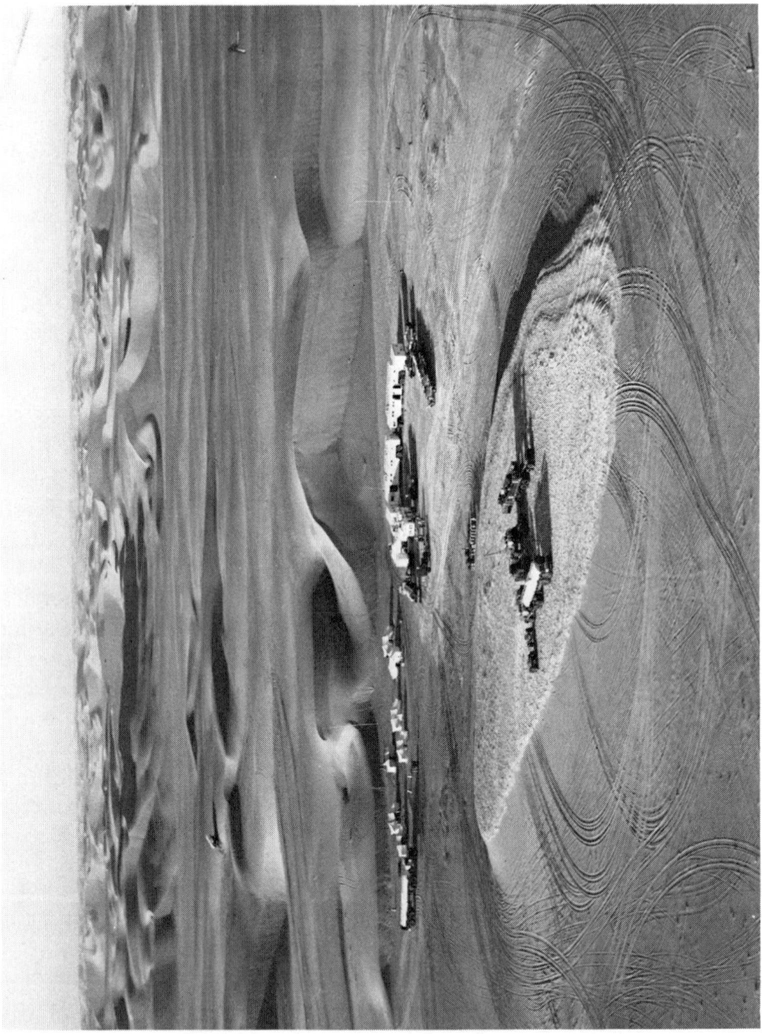

somewhat feudal system, against the upsurge of social revolutionary demands within the Arab world.

Persian Gulf Sheikhdoms

The various Arab sheikhdoms which border on the Persian Gulf, notably Kuwait and the island of Bahrain, also achieved a significant status as major oil-producing areas of the world. In contrast to Saudi Arabia, where American influence predominated, Kuwait and Bahrain were British oil concessions. In their possession was an estimated one-seventh of the total world oil resources, and their wealth was fabulous. The ruler of Kuwait received an estimated ten million dollars a month from royalties, and there was a problem as to what to do with it. This illustrates a problem common for the area: the tendency for rulers to regard the oil resources as their private possession.

Iran and the Arab states were concerned with the changes which would occur when the British in 1971 withdrew their protection over the Persian Gulf sheikhdoms, including those of Trucial Oman. In all of this area the matter of oil exploitation was an important issue.

In the politics of the Persian Gulf, Iran, Saudi Arabia, and Kuwait were brought together by a common interest in preventing Iraq from having influence in the sheikhdoms to the south. On the other hand, the historic suspicion of powerful Shi'i Iran among the small Sunni sheikhdoms was somewhat alleviated when in 1970 the shah abandoned the Persian claim to Bahrain.

In the Gulf area Bahrain became an independent emirate in August 1971, when the British ended 151 years of protection and military occupation. Meanwhile the Persians in 1970 laid claim to two small islands near the Straits of Hormuz, Abu Musa and the larger of two Tunb islands. The Iranians landed troops on these islands in November 1971 and at the same time promised economic aid to Sharjah, the emirate claiming Abu Musa. Thus British withdrawal led to an expansion of Iran's military power.

Meanwhile in the autocratic semifeudal sheikhdoms of Trucial Oman an effort was made to bring them together. Concern over influences from Iraq, Iran, and Russia resulted in six out of seven coastal sheikhdoms joining to form the "Union of Arab Emirates" (December 2, 1971). British withdrawal from the Gulf was not complete, in that the defense forces of the U.A.E. and of Oman were still British-officered. Bahrain and the Arab Emirates became independent members of the United Nations.

Yemen

The last of the Arab countries in the peninsula, Yemen in the extreme southwest corner, remained also the most backward area. In the war it stayed neutral, though because of strong Italian influence, it leaned towards the Axis in its sympathies. A member of the Arab League, its chief foreign

FIGURE 23.5. Exploring for oil in the Arabian desert.

policy was to maintain its independence against its mighty neighbor, Saudi Arabia. In 1946 Yemen opened diplomatic relations with the United States.

Yemen was ruled by an autocratic religious head, the imam. Imam Yahya, old and reactionary, was assassinated together with two of his sons in a revolt which broke out against him in 1948. It was headed by the reformer Sayyid Abdullah, but the crown prince Ahmad escaped and in a short civil war, during which the imam's son enjoyed aid from Ibn Sa'ud, the revolution was suppressed. Ahmad became the new imam and returned to the previous conservative status quo, ruling a backward theocracy.

Yemen followed Nasser's foreign policy rather closely, and came to be federated with Egypt and Syria into what was called the United Arab States, but the breakup of the United Arab Republic in 1962 shook this alignment, and Egypt's influence lessened somewhat until a revolution against the imamate in 1962, when Ahmad was killed. A Yemen Arab Republic was proclaimed by the leader of this revolt, Sallal, who promptly obtained military support from Egypt in his struggle against the royalist forces who in turn were supported by Saudi Arabia. Revolutionary Yemen served as a base for communist entry into the Red Sea area, and also engaged in border warfare with the British at Aden.

The unfortunate Yemeni civil war which lasted, intermittently, and with much outside meddling, until 1967, was a bloody and somewhat inconclusive affair. It gave the communist bloc a chance to seize a foothold in Yemen, and both the Soviet Union and Peking made available much technical and economic aid for highways, loans, technical schools, and student exchanges. By 1968 Ami, the republican leader, became prime minister. He and his regime faced the formidable task of bringing Yemen, the most backward country of them all, into the modern world.

The story of the former British colony of Aden has some analogies with Yemen. The rapid rise of nationalism led to a virulent and militant movement, which, after much terrorist activity, forced the British to leave Aden in 1967. There then came into being the People's Republic of Aden, a radical leftist regime, battling with the royalists in Yemen, and with the more conservative neighboring Arab sheikhdoms. Internally, this also meant much repression, and externally, a clear alignment with the communist world, symbolized by such things as visits to Aden of units of the Soviet fleet, the presence of Chinese aid personnel such as doctors or engineers, and the signing of various loan and trade agreements.

AFGHANISTAN

Finally, to end this survey of Southwest Asia, a few words should be said about developments in Afghanistan. As in all other states of the region, World War II brought economic hardship and inflation. Reforms were gradual and slow. In 1946 the University of Kabul was established and girls' schools were built. In 1951 under an agreement with the United States Point Four economic aid was given to Afghanistan.

In foreign policy Afghanistan remained a highly strategic region, situated between the Soviet Union and India. Relations with the Soviet Union were very friendly, since the Soviets in a treaty of 1946 returned some disputed islands in the middle of the boundary stream, the Amu Darya, to Afghanistan. Russia also promoted a trade agreement and Russian engineers were employed in Afghanistan to build public works. Relations with India remained correct, and even friendly, but the situation was different in regard to Pakistan. The Afghan government supported the Pushtunistan movement within the Pakistan boundary. This was a movement of Pushtu-speaking peoples to achieve autonomy, and at times the relations between Kabul and Karachi became so strained over this issue that the roads were closed and troops were mobilized.

The Afghan-Pakistani conflict came to a head in 1961 when the Karachi government blocked the transit of goods destined for Afghanistan. This produced much closer relations between Afghanistan and the Soviet Union, since the Russian government, with a border of some 1,250 miles with Afghanistan, did not wait long in offering to the Afghans easy trade terms and importation of goods from the Soviet Union. Despite the official Afghan policy of neutralism in its foreign relations, which permits Afghanistan to accept both American as well as Soviet assistance, these difficulties with Pakistan have tended to bring the country closer into the Russian orbit. Nevertheless, the ruler of Afghanistan, Mohammed Zahir, has attempted to maintain his country's policy of nonalignment rather successfully. Visits to Kabul of such dignitaries as Brezhnev of the Soviet Union (1963) and the signing of a Sino-Afghan treaty, have alternated with renewed agreements between Afghanistan and the United States providing for economic aid and cultural exchanges.

BASIC DATES

1938	One-party republic in Turkey under President Inonü
1939	Iran declares neutrality in World War II; Faisal II ascends Iraqi throne; Ibn Sa'ud rules Arabia
1940	Vichy control over Syria and Lebanon
1941	British and Soviet occupation of Iran, Reza Shah Pahlavi deported; pro-Axis coup in Iraq led by Rashid Ali; Nuri Said cooperates with British; Free French control Syria and Lebanon
1943	Iran declares war on Axis
1945	Turkey declares war on Germany; Russia exerts pressure on Iran; Arab League formed
1946	Soviet demands presented to Turkey; U.N. intervention in Iran; French withdrawal from Syria and Lebanon
1947	Truman Doctrine; U.N. plans for Palestine
1948	Jordan gains independence under King Abdullah; Republic of Israel proclaimed; Palestine War
1949	Turkey joins NATO; Tudeh party dissolved in Iran
1950	Jelal Bayar elected president of Turkey; Arab League pact
1951	Mossadegh nationalizes Iranian oil; King Talal ascends Jordanian throne

1953	Fall of Mossadegh; death of Ibn Sa'ud; King Husain ascends Jordanian throne
1954	Nasser comes to power in Egypt; founding of "Plan Organization" for oil income in Iran
1956	Suez Canal affair
1958	Fall of Nuri Said and Faisal in Iraq, Kassem obtains power; Syria becomes part of United Arab Republic; United States intervention in Lebanon; Crown Prince Faisal gains control of Saudi Arabia
1960	Revolt in Turkey by students and army; birth of Iranian Crown Prince Reza
1961	Shah of Iran announces reform program
1963	Riots in Iran; Kassem assassinated and Arif in power in Iraq; elections to National Consultative Assembly in Iran; Levi Eshkol, Israeli prime minister
1964	Start of Tripartite cooperation between Iran, Turkey, and Pakistan; Faisal king in Saudi Arabia
1965	Inonü resigns in Turkey; Demirel prime minister
1966	Arif killed in Iraq; military coup in Syria
1967	"Six-Day War" of Israel against the Arabs; British withdraw from Aden
1968	al-Bakr assumes power in Iraq; Atasi government in Syria
1969	Golda Meir prime minister of Israel
1970–1971	Student agitation in Iran
1971	British withdraw protection from Persian Gulf sheikhdoms
1971	Bahrain, Qatar, Union of Arab Emirates, and Oman independent; enter United Nations
1971	Celebration of 2,500th anniversay of Persian monarchy
1971	Iran occupies islands near Straits of Hormuz

SUPPLEMENTARY READING

Anderson, J. N. *Islamic Law in the Modern World.* New York, 1950.
Avery, P. *Modern Iran.* New York, 1965.
Fisher, S. *The Middle East.* New York, 1959.
Hitti, P. *The Near East.* Princeton, N.J., 1961.
Kirk, G. *A Short History of the Middle East.* New York, 1957.
Lenczowski, G., ed. *The Political Awakening in the Middle East.* Englewood Cliffs, N.J., 1970.
Lewis, B. *The Emergence of Modern Turkey.* London, 1961.
Royal Institute of International Affairs. *The Middle East: A Political and Economic Survey.* London, 1958.
Upton, J. *The History of Modern Iran: An Interpretation.* Cambridge, Mass., 1960.
Yale, W. *The Near East.* Ann Arbor, Mich., 1958.

ADVANCED READING

Bauer, Y. *From Diplomacy to Resistance: A History of Jewish Palestine, 1939–1945.* Philadelphia, 1970.

Bayne, E. A. *Persian Kingship in Transition: Conversations with a Monarch Whose Office Is Traditional and Whose Goal Is Modernization.* New York, 1968.
Berger, E. *The Covenant and the Sword: Arab-Israeli Relations, 1945–1956.* Toronto, 1965.
Cottam, R. W. *Nationalism in Iran.* Pittsburgh, 1964.
Esen, N. *Turkey Today and Tomorrow, An Experiment in Westernization.* New York, 1963.
Fatemi, N. *Oil Diplomacy.* New York, 1954.
Feis, H. *The Birth of Israel.* New York, 1969.
Frye, R. *Iran.* New York, 1953.
Haim, S. G., ed. *Arab Nationalism: An Anthology.* Berkeley, Calif., 1961.
Harris, G. *Iraq.* New Haven, 1958.
Hitti, P. *Lebanon in History.* New York, 1957.
——— *Syria: A Short History.* London, 1959.
Hourani, A. H. *Minorities in the Arab World.* London, 1947.
Hudson, M. *The Precarious Republic: Modernization in Lebanon.* New York, 1968.
Ingrams, H. *The Yemen.* New York, 1964.
Khadduri, M. *Republican Iraq.* New York, 1969.
Lambton, A. K. S. *The Persian Land Reform, 1962–1966.* Oxford, 1969.
Laqueur, W. Z. *Communism and Nationalism in the Middle East.* New York, 1956.
Lenczowski, G. *Russia and the West in Iran, 1918–1948.* Ithaca, N.Y., 1950.
Longrigg, S. *Oil in the Middle East.* London, 1954.
——— *Iraq, 1900–1950: A Political, Social and Economic History.* New York, 1953.
McDonald, R. *The League of Arab States.* Princeton, N.J., 1965.
Peretz, D. *Israel and the Palestine Arabs.* Washington, 1958.
Qubain, F. *The Reconstruction of Iraq.* New York, 1958.
Safran, N. *The United States and Israel.* Cambridge, Mass., 1963.
Tibawi, A. L. *A Modern History of Syria, including Lebanon and Palestine.* New York, 1970.
Toukan, B. *A Short History of Trans-Jordan, 1950–1957.* New York, 1958.
Twitchell, K. S. *Saudi Arabia.* Princeton, N.J., 1947.
Wilber, D. *Afghanistan.* New Haven, 1962.
Williams, A. *Britain and France in the Middle East and North Africa.* New York, 1968.
Ziadeh, N. *Syria and Lebanon.* New York, 1957.

Chapter 24

India and Pakistan, Since 1947

INDEPENDENCE AND ITS PROBLEMS

The achievement of independence for India and Pakistan in August 1947 plunged the subcontinent at once into vicious communal strife, violence, and chaos, with partition looming as the foremost and most fundamental problem. It produced two mutually antipathetic and suspicious nations which, due to the corrosive inheritance of the past, clashed discordantly on a number of basic issues. Partition had disrupted their economy, their communications, their administration, and it brought acute suffering to untold millions. Some ten million people were on the march, exchanging one country for the other, and no one will ever know exactly how many tens of thousands of these victims of disunity perished, but best estimates run to half to three-quarters of a million. Partition furthermore seriously weakened the defense of the subcontinent, and it is not overly difficult to agree with the ironic comment of an Indian official to the effect that "the British are a just people. They have left India in exactly the same state of chaos as they found it."

Pakistan

As the result of partition two new dominions, India and Pakistan, were brought forth in August 1947, with assets divided in such a way that India was to obtain 82.5 per cent and Pakistan 17.5 per cent. Pakistan, the new nation, consisted of two areas, East and West Pakistan, both governed from the new capital of Karachi (near the mouth of the Indus) and separated by almost 1,000 miles. The undisputed leader of Pakistan was, of course, Muhammad Ali Jinnah, who was governor-general until his death in September 1948. The government of Pakistan was based on the Act of 1935 in such a way that its Constituent Assembly became its legislative assembly.

Pakistan was to be an "independent Islamic democracy," with guarantees extended to non-Moslem minorities and with promises of equal civil status, religious freedom, and cultural autonomy to all of its subjects.

The chief immediate difficulty of Pakistan after partition resulted from the fact that the new state was composed of two widely separated areas, and from its economic structure. Although Pakistan had a surplus of food, it had practically no industry, and these problems were compounded by the presence on its soil of large Hindu minorities. When Jinnah died after only one year of independence, and was succeeded by Nazimuddin as the new governor-general, with Liaquat Ali Khan serving as premier until his assassination in 1951, the basic problems of the new dominion still remained unsolved.

Indian Economic and Social Problems

India, a British-type parliamentary democracy with able men to lead her, such as Gandhi, Nehru, and Patel, also faced immediate grave issues as the result of partition, of which the most important were the economic problems, and the problem of fragmentation resulting from the presence of many princely states.

The problem of economic reform was, of course, not new but a heritage from the pre-British past and the results of British colonial rule which had produced economic imbalance. Essentially, the economic problem of India was and is one common to many parts of the world, that of underdevelopment. Its chief issue is how to raise the standard of living in a nation subject to tremendous population pressure. A large proportion of India's population is undernourished, inadequately clad, and miserably housed. If, by industrialization and other measures, the standard of living is raised, are these gains to be immediately swallowed up by resultant increase in births?

After independence India's leaders developed the so-called Bombay Plan, the first step toward a planned economy, which provided for three successive five-year plans on the model of the U.S.S.R. designed to increase India's industrialization. The plan was coupled with an increase in the scope of compulsory education and in emphasis on birth control information. To many economists the Bombay Plan was not realistic but based upon wishful thinking, and they characterized India as the economic "never-never land," and indeed, industrialization so far has not been able to take care of India's additional population. The economic problem is made much more difficult by the importance of tradition in India's life. A good symbol of this is the problem of the holy cow. The fact that cow protection is one of the main tenets of Hinduism, characterized in these words by Gandhi: "Man through the cow is enjoined to realize his identity with all that lives. She is the mother to millions of Indian mankind. The cow is a poem of pity," saddles India with a burden of some 215 million undernourished, unproductive beasts which cannot be killed due to the concept of sanctity of animal life, and which add nothing to India's economy. Other Indian traditions, such as the habit of hoarding wealth rather than investing it, or the existence of a large unproductive class of some three million holy men and beggars, are added complications from an economic point of view.

FIGURE 24.1. An Indian woman tends her baby and spinning machine in a cotton mill.

The problem of caste also has not vanished. It is true that since partition one could observe the accelerating secularization of India's life; fewer pilgrims were on the road, and fewer temples and shrines were visited. Nehru implicitly repudiated the doctrine of position by birth, and the physical contact between members of different castes is now a commonplace occurrence, so that today members of different castes will sit side by side on trains and buses, will be comrades in labor unions, and will marry across caste lines. However, caste lines are not vanishing; rather, they are merely modified in their superficial features. Gandhi, for instance, had believed in caste; his only interest had been to "humanize" the institution. And as long as the caste problem survives it will also constitute an economic burden.

But the most important factor in Indian life is pressure on the land. Agriculture remains the basic occupation of India's millions, as only one-half of one per cent of the population work as industrial laborers, and only 6 per cent live in cities. Land provides merely for the barest of subsistence, and sometimes not even that. Land holdings are small, and they are divided upon the death of the landholder. Fragmentation of the land may result in some fields, in the Punjab for example, being a yard wide and over one mile long, a condition which obviously does not lend itself to modern, mechanized farming. Despite the new irrigation developments, which are themselves limited primarily to the Punjab region, there is in India only a limited possibility of increasing acreage, and due to considerable soil deterioration the crop yield per acre of Indian agriculture is low. Added to this is the problem of peasant indebtedness, which is so great that it is estimated

FIGURE 24.2. Paddy cultivation in Oyla Village District, Satna, India: seedlings being transplanted (improved method).

that about 75 per cent of all peasants are in debt to the extent of three times their annual net income, paying interest rates which sometimes climb to 300 per cent. This produced a grim situation, in which the average income of the Indian peasant was estimated by the U.N. in 1950 to be $57. At the same time the population continued to increase, and some 48 million mouths were added to India in the decade 1941–1951. It was estimated that, at the current rate of population increase, India by the year 2005 will contain 840 million people, or a third of the total world population, without compensatory and corresponding increase either in food production or industrial development. In 1960 the average individual was more poorly fed than he was in 1901, and individual poverty was worse than at any time before this century. Farming was poorer, and so was housing; sanitation and health services were hopelessly inadequate. It has been said that the life of the poor Indian is one of semistarvation, high mortality, and low life expectancy, and that there have never been so many people who lived in such misery. The wretchedness of living conditions is sometimes unbelievable to the Westerner, and it is accentuated by the enormous gap in wealth between the poor and the rich, since 5 per cent of the population possessed 33 per cent of all wealth. In addition, the progress of public health was also far behind other countries, and malaria was not merely endemic in India, but actually was on the increase. There was one doctor for 6,300 patients, and one nurse for some 43,000 people. There was widespread undernourishment, few water supplies were protected, and the cities which possessed sanitary sewage systems could be counted on the fingers of one hand. Modern Western medicine is paralleled by the traditional Hindu Ayurvedic system, which is taught in so-called medical universities and which in turn contributes to the formidable mortality. This is tolerated by the government (under the assumption that any system is better than none).

In education India has decreed free and compulsory training through the age of 14, in order both to help the country attain rapid economic development, as well as to ensure a government based upon democratic principles, but the ideal is a far cry from reality. This task has simply proven impossible, and much of India's elementary education is of poor quality, due to lack of funds, notoriously ill-paid teachers, and absence of textbooks. On the level of university education, India also faces a most serious problem: the production of large numbers of unemployed college graduates, many of them in the liberal arts, with no prospect of finding useful lives, and furnishing cadres for extreme political movements, whether among the Maoist Naxalites in Bengal or in the South, or among the extreme rightist movements of North India.

In view of the fact that India simply does not possess sufficient natural resources herself (oil, for instance, is a good example), how can the economic problems be solved? Industrialization so far has not alone provided the answer. India's industrialization has been weak and somewhat lopsided, with development concentrated in traditional cotton textile and jute factories and in the enlargement of existing heavy industry, but there still remain many gaps in the industrial structure, and industry as a whole is far below India's needs and potentiality. Industrial owners are interested in excessive profits, anything below 10 per cent being scorned. Industrial labor is ill-fed, inefficient, and is distinguished by high turnover and low productivity. It leads a life of really wretched substandard conditions. Trade unions are poorly financed and, so far, have organized few effective strikes. Without some such revolutionary transformation as occurred in China it seems the answer to India's gigantic economic problems must come from outside. A beginning of such aid can be seen in such schemes as the U.S. Point Four program, or the Colombo Plan, but these and other plans would have to be continued far into the future, and India's birthrate would have to be curbed, if there is to be any amelioration of the formidable economic problems of India.

The most immediate internal economic problem for India is to secure sufficient food to feed her vast population. The age-old specter of famine still continues to stalk the country, as demonstrated by the hunger marches, demonstrations, and riots in all the major cities during the summer of 1964. Land reforms have frequently remained a matter of form rather than fact, and the problems of landholdings of uneconomic size, of fragmentation, and of disguised unemployment in the countryside clearly are still unsolved. The second major problem is that of increasing unemployment despite protracted economic efforts. Rural India today has had underemployment estimated at 100 million, and the unemployed intellectuals in the cities also constitute a great problem for India's economic and political welfare, facts which probably loom larger than the creation of India's first atomic energy

FIGURE 24.3. Power for India's industrialization; part of the Damodar valley development project.

plants, or progress made in steel production, or the development of India's textile industry. Even the series of five-year plans, initiated since 1951, have been less successful since 1962, as the result of India's need to spend more on defense costs.

The late 1960s saw some mitigation of India's appalling economic situation as a "green revolution" in agriculture increased crop yields remarkably. This was accomplished through the use of fertilizers, new types of grain, and better irrigation. Also, birth control showed signs of taking hold in the early 1970s. However, India remains today one of the most disease-ridden and poverty-stricken areas of Asia, with an average life expectancy of 26 years and an annual per capita income well below $100. India faces large-scale economic problems, which can be solved only by large-scale economic efforts. The chief questions remain whether India can indeed succeed in raising the standard of living of her masses fast enough to avert widespread and violent popular discontent, whether she can attain self-sufficiency in food production, whether her population growth can be effectively curbed, and whether new resources can be found for her industrial growth. No clear answers are possible; what is clear is that since India's economy is based upon agriculture, progress in that area is crucial. The economic problem is, of course, also interrelated to political stability, and whether the Congress party will maintain its position of dominance, shaken in 1967, but restored as the result of the 1971 war with Pakistan, is another matter, given the many centrifugal tendencies of Indian political life, and the rise of political extremism. India thus faces not only an uncertain economic future, but an uncertain political future as well.

Political Problems

A problem initially no less crucial than the economic one, is the political problem of loss of unity and the relations between India and Pakistan. As already indicated the partition of the subcontinent in 1947 brought in its train an immediate and violent crisis between the two new dominions. Due to religious fanaticism and mob action the violence which shook both Pakistan and India was on a truly colossal scale, and its savagery appalling. Moslems murdered Sikhs and Hindus, Sikhs and Hindus murdered Moslems, particularly in the Punjab and the Sikh states in the northwest, and in parts of the United Provinces. In these scenes of horror peaceful villages suddenly turned into desolate camps, and terrorism stalked the streets of great cities such as Lahore and Delhi, where houses burned, looted goods spilled into the gutter, and corpses were found at every intersection, symbols of the anarchism which had overtaken both countries. These dreadful riots which killed at least 500,000 persons led to one of the greatest exchanges of population the world has ever seen. Some twelve million fled to find refuge among their coreligionists whether that meant Pakistan for Moslems or India for Hindus. But even the refugees were not safe, as trains were derailed and people were slaughtered on the highways. These scenes of civil war boded no good to the critical relations between these two countries, and these were further embittered by the rivalry over control of two princely states, Hyderabad and Kashmir.

Hyderabad. Hyderabad was the largest princely state in India. It was ruled by the nizam, a Moslem who had some 16 million subjects, of whom some 87 per cent were not Moslems but Hindus. Economically and geographically, Hyderabad was linked directly to India, being a landlocked state entirely surrounded by Indian territory. His Exalted Highness, the nizam, a miser of heroic proportions possessing incredible wealth but frequently addressing his guests clad in semi-rags and old, worn slippers fit only for the second-hand bazaar, had no desire whatsoever to come under the control of India. He wanted to become the independent ruler of an independent country. His state was a conservative one, in which the Moslems formed the ruling class. For a short time he managed to remain independent, severing relations and imposing duties and restrictions on traffic between Hyderabad and India. Eventually, though, pressure for accession of his territory to India forced him into some limited concessions, and in September, 1948 Indian troops finally marched into Hyderabad in the so-called "100-hour War" and took over the state by force, thereby ending its independence and further irritating all Moslems in Pakistan.

Kashmir. More serious, however, than the Hyderabad issue, for which India could argue plausible excuses, was the Kashmir problem, a problem which was one of the most critical issues dividing India and Pakistan. The situation in Kashmir was the exact opposite of that which existed in Hyderabad. Kashmir, an area economically and geographically related to Pakistan, was ruled by a Hindu ruler whose subjects were very largely Moslems. In October, 1947 trouble broke out when a revolt occurred among his Moslem subjects against the maharajah. This revolt, in which Hindus and some Europeans were massacred, was aided by Pakistan which came to its help by sending Moslem tribesmen across the frontier. It almost succeeded, since Moslem forces came within 18 miles of Srinagar, the capital of Kashmir, but at the last moment, the maharajah of Kashmir, Hari Singh (a ruler heretofore primarily interested in race horses rather than in politics), was saved when his frantic appeals for help from India were rewarded by the most timely arrival of Indian troops by air at Srinagar. These managed to defeat the Moslem forces, but the situation was one of extreme tension as war loomed between India and Pakistan. For Pakistan the Kashmir issue was one in which her economic, political, and strategic stakes were definitely involved, while for India, Kashmir overnight had become a symbol of her international prestige and of justice. War was only narrowly averted when both sides appealed to the United Nations. India appealed to the Security Council, charging Pakistan with aggression. Pakistan levied countercharges which insisted that a plebiscite should be held in Kashmir, but Nehru refused these conditions. The United Nations was able to obtain a truce, but nothing more. No real settlement was accomplished, no plebiscite was ever held, and an armed stalemate and a negotiated deadlock continued despite repeated efforts at mediation. Kashmir remained a problem, despite the fact that it was a serious drain upon the slender economic resources of both dominions, neither of which could afford budgets which provided for some 50 per cent of total income to be spent on military expenditures. The Kashmir issue in particular originally contributed greatly to the bitter relations between India and Pakistan and brought about war in 1965 but there were also others, such as the question of control of irrigation water in the Punjab, the problem of cow protection, and the economic warfare which was waged until 1951 between the two new states. To these many difficulties later on was added the problem of the autonomy or independence of East Pakistan, which again brought about full-scale warfare between India and Pakistan in 1971, Indian intervention in East Bengal, and the setting up of a new, and independent, nation, that of Bangladesh.

Death of Gandhi

The death of Gandhi can be attributed directly to Hindu-Moslem tension and communal warfare. Gandhi had done his very best to minimize fraternal strife, and in the holocaust of riots and wholesale bloodshed that convulsed Bengal in January 1947 it had been his influence that had moderated the worst excesses. In particular, by his appeal for forbearance he had prevented an outbreak in Calcutta, but his tolerance had merely enraged Hindu extremists. It was one of these, a member of the Hindu Mahasabha, the violently ultranationalist anti-Moslem organization devoted to a passionate defense of caste and cow protection, who fired three rounds of revolver shot into Gandhi on January 30, 1948, as Gandhi was going to a prayer meeting. The assassination of Gandhi was a tremendous shock to India. The ashes of the Indian patriot and prophet were minutely divided and scattered in India's rivers and lakes, and Nehru broadcast to a bereaved nation that the "light has gone out of our lives and there is darkness everywhere." Gandhi's influence had been profound, and in the opinion of some he had been the most influential Indian since Buddha or Asoka. It was above all his prodigious influence among the masses where he had caught their imagination that made Gandhi such an important personality in Indian history. Beyond his concrete ideas of social and moral reform, such as village welfare, universal education, prohibition of liquor, franchise for all adults, and his influence in the Congress party, Gandhi remained as the man who had shown India that religion is politics and politics religion.

New Constitution

With Gandhi gone, the dominant Congress party was led by Nehru and by Vallabhbhai Patel, the "iron man" of the party who had been active and successful in integrating the princely states into India and ending their autocratic rule. Under the leadership of the Congress party a written constitution for India was drawn up in 1949. India's constitution provides for a sovereign democratic republic, a federation of 28 states, in which power is divided between the states and the union. India is a republic, fully independent, with no legal ties with the British Commonwealth except for the fact that she recognizes the queen as a symbol of the free association of the independent member nations. India is a secular state, enshrining the inviolability of law, and separating state and religion. The constitution provides for a bicameral parliament, comprising an upper house, the "council of states," and a lower house, the "house of the people," and for an independent judiciary. In the constitution of India many ideas of Gandhi's social and moral reforms are embodied, such as the abolition of untouchability, prohibition of child marriage, rejection of communal representation, institution of compulsory education within ten years (impossible to accomplish), and a statement of the fundamental rights of Indian citizens all of whom are declared to be equal. In 1948 two untouchables were high officials of state of whom one, the minister of justice, was married to a Brahman. The constitution says that Hindi is to be India's national language, but on this point serious difficulties arose at once, since English was the only universally understood and spoken language, and some claimed Urdu and some Dravidian dialects to have equality with Hindi.

In the winter of 1951–1952 elections, based upon this constitution, were held in an orderly and democratic manner (the effect of British tradition), and 74 per cent of the total seats of parliament were won by the Congress party which demonstrated in this way its overwhelming strength. Ever since that great victory the Congress party has been the dominant force in Indian political life, despite criticism of corruption, and some fissures and cracks within its structure. A party stalwart, Dr. Prasad, became the first president of India, while Nehru became prime minister. The Congress

FIGURE 24.4. Prime Minister Jawaharlal Nehru in 1961.

party stands for a secular, socialist state, and for economic progress as the first priority among India's needs. It has encountered opposition from the extreme right, the Mahasabha, actively hostile to Pakistan and attacking Moslems in India, and from the left from the Communist party of India. The government of Nehru had repressed the communists in India, especially during the railway strike of 1949, but the Communist party conceivably represents the greatest rival for the Congress party in India's future, depending on the world situation.

The death of Nehru in 1964 deprived India of his able leadership, and, without question, ushered in a period of less political certainty for the Congress party.

Nehru was succeeded in 1964 by Lal Bahadur Shastri as prime minister. Shastri, a thin, frail, short individual, had been former home minister, and as such had gained a reputation as a born compromiser, though there were many who criticized him for lack of leadership. His major test came in the 1965 war between India and Pakistan, again triggered by each side's claims to Kashmir. The fighting, though it lasted but three weeks, was sharp and intense, especially in the arid Rann of Kutch area, and it was terminated with the Tashkent agreement, when the Soviet Union mediated between the two

FIGURE 24.5. Indira Gandhi, prime minister of India.

parties by providing for mutual withdrawal. By this time Shastri had become a most popular figure, and when he suddenly died in Tashkent in January 1966 as the result of a heart attack, he was deeply and genuinely mourned throughout India.

Shastri's successor was Indira Gandhi, Nehru's only daughter. A person of immense energy, great willpower, and much charm, she has managed to gain control over Indian politics. Her rule and that of her party were severely challenged in the 1966 elections when the Congress party suffered a major setback, but the clash with Pakistan in 1971, and India's great success in creating an independent Bangladesh in East Bengal, formerly East Pakistan, have given her and the Congress party a new and solid lease on life. She still faces formidable problems, Kashmir for one, and dangerous opposition, especially from among the militant Maoist Naxalites in Bengal and Calcutta; but her government, and her party, so far have found favor among most Indians.

WORLD RELATIONS

India

Until independence India had been, of course, under British protection on the international scene. After independence both India and Pakistan retained membership in the British Commonwealth, but with no legal ties, and both dominions soon had to face the great postwar struggle between the United States and the Soviet Union. In the Cold War which characterized this struggle India adopted a neutral position, defined by Nehru as "constructive nonalignment with other power blocs." He felt that the great social and economic revolution in which India was engaged was more important than the struggle between America and Russia, and he also made it clear that India did not fear the influence of communistic economic and social ideas which might be helpful to the progress of India as long as there was no aggressive political expansion. Pakistan, on the other hand, identified its interests by and large with those of the Moslem world. Both new nations were members of the United Nations, and firm supporters of that organization, and both were extremely sensitive to any infringement upon the independence of any other Asian nation. They opposed all forms of colonialism and any kind of interference from Western nations, while they stood for the principle of Asian autonomy and the support of Asian nationalist revolutions. As a case in point, India fully supported the Indonesians against the Dutch whom Nehru denounced in 1948 as "naked and unabashed aggressors." In Nehru's words Asia had been "too long submissive and dependent and a plaything of other countries . . . and she will no longer brook any interference with her freedom." India's relations with Britain were, as a whole, excellent, but there was a great deal of bitterness between India and South Africa over race discrimination and exclusion policies. As far as the minor European colonies in India were concerned, the French had sense enough to evacuate their small possessions and hand these over to India, but the Portuguese in Goa did not, and clung to what Nehru called a "pimple of imperialism," which contributed to occasional violence and dissatisfaction between both powers until the forceful seizure of Goa by India in 1961.

Far more important were India's relations with China. Until 1950 Nehru maintained that all revolutionary movements in Asia, including the Chinese one, were basically nationalistic, and that they used communist techniques only because they had no other alternatives to obtain their aims. Once the revolution had been successful and had become consolidated, Nehru believed, China too would stand on her own as an independent Asian national entity. The People's Republic had been motivated by understandable and sincere suspicions and fear of the United States, which supported Chiang Kai-shek in Formosa, protected that island with American naval and military power, and blocked Chinese seating at the United Nations. Thus Nehru, who also showed an interest in Red China's solution to her agrarian problems, supported that country during the period of the Korean War. India felt that the crossing of the 38th parallel in Korea by United Nations forces had been a serious mistake, by threatening Manchuria, and Nehru in consequence, although he agreed with the resolutions of the United Nations, sent no contingents to the United Nations force, but rather attempted a constant policy of mediation, despite the fact that his government cracked down hard upon the domestic Indian Communist party after 1949 when a general strike was narrowly averted. In the Korean conflict

Nehru unceasingly was the champion of mediation and cautiousness. He tried to bring about a cease-fire, which, while it was rejected by Peking, irritated and angered the Americans. India served as the referee in the Korean truce arrangements, while later on she also participated in the Vietnam International Control Commission. India further supported the United Nations as a participant in the U.N. force in the Congo. At the Bandung Conference of 1955 Nehru argued for the admittance of communist China to the United Nations, and for conciliation between America and China, but by this time the relations between Peking and Delhi had already begun to change for the worse.

After Chinese forces had invaded Tibet in October, 1950, and Peking rejected the protest of India, a growing sense of dissatisfaction with Nehru's foreign policy could be detected in India. The cooling relations between India and China produced defense treaties between India and Sikkim and Nepal. Relations between Peking and India suddenly became most tense when the Chinese suppressed the Tibetan revolt, resulting in the flight of the Dalai Lama to India, and when they then in 1959 occupied important areas in Ladakh and the northeast frontier zone, disputing possession over these areas with India, and resorting to open violence by attacking, killing, and capturing some Indian soldiers and policemen. These events produced a violent reaction in India and a determination not to yield

FIGURE 24.6. Prime Minister Nehru and United Nations Secretary-General Dag Hammarskjöld in New Delhi, 1959, to discuss China's attack.

to Chinese "aggression," and they ushered in a new stage in Indian foreign policy in which neutralism, although perhaps still not completely abandoned, has nevertheless definitely receded.

The war between India and China which broke out in 1962 was a result of the failure of Indian foreign policy, as well as an example of Nehru's intransigeance. After 1959 the Chinese not only established themselves in the Aksai Chin region of Ladakh in the Western Himalayas, but they also built a road traversing the territory and connecting Lhasa in Tibet with Chinese Turkistan. In addition there were growing problems, and incidents, on the northeast frontier. An attempt was made to solve these issues between China and India at talks in Delhi between Nehru and Chou En-lai, but in vain, and by 1962 Nehru insisted that "all our territories must be taken back from the Chinese aggressor." Talk was one thing, but the sending of Indian army units into Ladakh was quite another, and India soon discovered that her forces were no match for the Chinese. The better armed and better trained Chinese units outfought the Indians, and during October and November of 1962 there were a series of massive Chinese attacks on both ends of the Himalayan frontier which simply overwhelmed their opponents. The Chinese, who had some legitimate claims to Ladakh, then unilaterally announced a cease-fire in November, and withdrew some of their units. By this time, however, Nehru's cherished policy of nonalignment had been shattered as India had received American and British military supplies, aircraft, etc. From 1962 on India has always been the recipient of great-power support, first from the West in her confrontation with the Chinese, and in later years from the Soviet Union. In the new crisis over East Bengal, India gained invaluable political and military support from the Russians, in contrast (ironically enough) with Pakistan, which relied upon American and Chinese support.

Pakistan

Pakistan's position in world affairs has been determined largely by the fact that it is, of course, a Moslem state, and consequently tends to lean toward the Moslem world in Asia and Africa. Both her political and her economic stability deteriorated after the death of Jinnah and the murder of Liaquat Ali Khan and with the fall of the price of jute and cotton after 1951. Pakistan is a republic but after 1951 her increasingly inefficient government, characterized by ineptitude and intrigue and many constitutional wrangles, led to the coming to the fore of the army in politics. The army, having been built up energetically in the postwar years, finally took over the country and a military dictatorship under Ayub Khan was established. One early result of this development was that Pakistan's quarrel with India came into a new perspective, and questions of defense rather than religion seemed to point out the overwhelming necessity of getting along with the other dominion. Yet, the basic clash with India over Kashmir at first, and later on over East Bengal, was given priority in Pakistan's foreign policy. This resulted, during the first few years of Ayub Khan's regime, in Pakistan being aligned with the United States, and receiving American military aid. Pakistan also became a member of CENTO, the alliance between Turkey, Iran, and herself designed to contain communist expansion and sponsored by the West. The fact that the United States also gave military supplies and aid to India gradually set in motion a cooling of relations between the two countries, and resulted in a Pakistan approach to Peking. After 1963 especially, the relations between Peking and Pakistan rapidly improved. In that year a border agreement, as well as an air transport agreement, was signed between the two countries. By 1966 Pakistan began to acquire Chinese military hardware, including jets and tanks, and the caravan route between Gilgit and Sinkiang was opened once again. Liu Shao-chi, as well as Chou En-lai, made official visits, and the Chinese also provided economic and technical assistance. American support, in the form of military aid, loans, and grain shipments, did not cease, but clearly Washington became less pleased with Ayub Khan's policies, which at the same time became also more repressive in internal affairs, what with press censorship and the squashing of a burgeoning "autonomy" movement in East Pakistan. Growing internal opposition to Ayub led to his overthrow and replacement by another military man, Yahya Khan. He, however, exacerbated the already strained relations between West and East Pakistan, producing a major conflict with India, and the loss of the East.

East Pakistan, the geographical area of East Bengal, had many reasons to resent West Pakistan. To begin with, the Bengalis felt that they were at the mercy of government officials from the West, imposed upon them from the Punjab, with little knowledge or concern for the affairs of East

FIGURE 24.7. India's prime minister, Shrimati Indira Gandhi, with Sheikh Mujibur Rahman, president of the People's Republic of Bangladesh, when she called on him at Rashtrapati Bhavan in New Delhi on January 10, 1972.

Pakistan. The money earned, primarily in the export of jute, by the East also was used to bring about an uneven economic development of West Pakistan at the expense of the East. Religion, the only common bond, soon was no longer sufficient to overcome the basic incompatibility in character and outlook of the two widely separated sections of Pakistan, and in the December 1970 elections many voted against the arbitrary dictatorship of Yahya Khan, demanding a measure of autonomy. Yahya Khan, in a singularly inept and callous fashion, declared these elections null and void, proceeded to arrest the East Bengali leader, Sheik Mujibur Rahman, and sent an army of Punjabi soldiers to the East. There then began a systematic process of terrorism and oppression, with attempts made to remove, by execution, the whole of the East Pakistani leadership. Many individuals were shot, tortured, or fled in utter fear to neighboring India, and East Pakistan erupted into wholesale insurrection. The local guerrilla movement, fighting the Pakistani soldiers, was given increasing support from India, at first covertly, but by 1971 a new, dangerous, and full-fledged war broke out again between Pakistan and India. Russia gave full backing to Mrs. Gandhi, providing India with new jet aircraft, tanks, and welcome diplomatic support, while the Pakistanis counted upon Chinese and American assistance. The war itself resulted in a smashing defeat for the Pakistanis both in the East and the West. In fact, one half of Pakistan ceased to exist with the proclamation of East Pakistan as a new nation, Bangladesh, created with Indian support. The situation of Pakistan became so grim that Yahya Khan was overthrown, and Zulfikar Ali Bhutto, the former foreign minister of Ayub Khan, and a more moderate leader, seized power.

FIGURE 24.8. President Zulfikar Ali Bhutto of Pakistan.

All that is left of Pakistan today is the West, truncated, militarily weak, and propped up by outside forces. In contrast, India's strategic position has greatly improved. As for the new nation, Bangladesh, the child of conflict, its problems also seem overwhelming. With 75 million people it is the second-largest Moslem nation (after Indonesia) in the world. But it is also desperately overcrowded, incredibly poor, subject to endemic floods and tidal waves, and can exist only with outside economic support.

Ceylon (Sri Lanka)

A word might be said here concerning the island of Ceylon. After the British Parliament in 1947 passed the Ceylon independence bill, this island, inhabited by seven million Buddhists, in February 1948 also achieved full dominion status as a self-governing member of the British Commonwealth. Ceylon's constitution was based on the British model of a bicameral parliament. The premier of the government is fully responsible to parliament. An agreement was concluded between Britain and the island concerning its defense, by which the British were given the right to maintain air and naval bases, but these facilities have been sharply curtailed as the result of nationalist agitation. At first, Ceylon, with its wealth of coconuts, tea, and rubber, enjoyed a quiet but prosperous economic development after independence, with close economic ties with Britain fully maintained. Economic improvements were such that Ceylon possessed the highest standard of living of any country in Southeast Asia. Yet rubber and coconut (Ceylon's two chief crops) price fluctuations were so great that the island could not control its economy. This led to trade agreements with the Sino-Soviet bloc, an increasingly neutralist foreign policy, and efforts to diversify its economy.

Unlike India, it remained more closely linked with Britain, for reason of the fear of the large Indian (Tamil) minority inhabiting the island. Ceylon in recent years has moved rather rapidly toward socialism of the British type, with state ownership of railways, telephone and telegraph, radio, and some factories. Ceylon's political life has seen the presence of a great variety of parties, ranging from communist and all kinds of communist splinter parties, such as the Trotskyists on the left, to some Buddhist parties on the right. Political development at first seemed quite balanced, following the British pattern of political democracy, but economic difficulties, the conflict between Tamils and Sinhalese, and political irresponsibility led to communal rioting (1958) and the assassination of Bandaranaike, the premier of Ceylon (1959). After a brief interval he was succeeded by his widow, Mme. Bandaranaike. Despite her reputation as an able politician she soon was beset with many problems, among which were fear of the large Indian minority on the island, inflation, strikes, and rapidly growing unemployment. Her attempts at socialist policies and nationalization led to her defeat in 1965. She then was succeeded by Dudley Senanayake as premier, who also inherited the problems of strong challenge from the left, and of what to do to improve and change the economy of the island away from a traditional plantation economy to one that would take care of the rapid population growth. Internal unrest and leftist militancy led to the fall of his government, the return to power of Mme. Bandaranaike and her United Party (1971), and the changing of Ceylon's name to Sri Lanka (1972).

A Merging of Cultures

Three influences from the past have shaped the history of India, two by invasion from the northwest, and the third from overseas. The Aryan descent into India gave the country its oldest and most powerful culture, with Brahmanism, Buddhism, caste, and its art and philosophy. The second, Islam, with its doctrine of the universal brotherhood of men in religion and with its own civilization and art, greatly modified Indian culture, but it also introduced the problem of communal strife. The third force was Western influence, borne by the British, who introduced India to political stability, Western political ideals, and the concept of political democracy. Out of this past arises the chief problem of India and Pakistan, how to adjust to the modern world?

Western influence is more than just a thin veneer and the matter of adopting modern conveniences and instruments of power. This is well illustrated by the fact that India still uses English as an "associate language," and that this still seems a good compromise in multilingual India. It has penetrated Indian soil, it has changed the Indian outlook, and it has produced ferment in the Indian mind. The question is, how deep has it penetrated, how radically does it change the outlook and what will the final result be like? In the modern world, both in India and in Pakistan, two sets of values live side by side, the values of the past and those of the West. Can these two sets of values live side by side indefinitely, or will one dominate the other? Can there be borrowing without radical transformation, or will there develop a synthesis of the two? On the one hand there is the belief, perhaps best expressed by Ram Mohun Roy, that both Hinduism and Islam have, by a logical process, built up a system of life and thought which endeavors to absorb Western ideals without abandoning their own; on the other side the idea is expressed that India's need is a happy balance between the past and the new, as stated by the great poet Tagore: "There should be a collaboration of East and West, each giving its best and taking the best the other can offer." Whatever the future may hold, to the historian it will be one of great fascination as this riddle of the old and the new, of the East and the West, will continue to be unravelled.

BASIC DATES

1947	India and Pakistan independent; Kashmir crisis
1948	Gandhi assassinated; Ceylon independent
1949	Written constitution promulgated in India
1959	Tibetan revolt; border dispute with Red China begins; Bandaranaike assassinated
1960	Mme. Bandaranaike premier in Ceylon

1961 India seizes Goa
1962 Northern borders invaded by Chinese
1964 Death of Nehru
1965 L. B. Shastri premier in India; war with Pakistan; D. Senanayake prime minister in Ceylon
1966 Tashkent agreement; death of Shastri; Indira Gandhi becomes prime minister of India
1968 Fall of Ayub Khan in Pakistan
1971 East Pakistan crisis; India-Pakistan war; establishment of independent Bangladesh

SUPPLEMENTARY READING

Brown, W. N. *The United States and India and Pakistan,* rev. ed. Cambridge, Mass., 1965.
Lamb, B. P. *India, a World in Transition,* 3rd ed. New York, 1968. Fine study.
Ludowyk, E. F. *The Modern History of Ceylon.* London, 1966.
Spear, P. *India, Pakistan and the West,* 4th ed. Oxford, 1967.
———— *India: A Modern History.* Ann Arbor, Mich., 1972.
Stephens, I. *Pakistan.* New York, 1967.

ADVANCED READING

Abbott, F. *Islam and Pakistan.* Ithaca, N.Y., 1968.
Ashe, G. *Gandhi.* New York, 1968.
Aziz, K. K. *The Making of Pakistan: A Study in Nationalism.* London, 1967.
Bailey, S. D. *Ceylon.* New York, 1952.
Brecher, M. *Nehru: A Political Biography.* London, 1959.
Brines, R. *The Indo-Pakistan Conflict.* London, 1968.
Choudhury, G. W. *Pakistan's Relations with India, 1947–1966.* New York, 1968.
Masani, M. *The Communist Party of India.* London, 1954.
Menon, V. P. *The Transfer of Power in India.* Princeton, N.J., 1957.
Moraes, F. *J. C. Nehru: A Biography.* New York, 1956.
Nair, K. *Blossoms in the Dust.* New York, 1962. A superior study of rural India.
Palmer, N. D. *The Indian Political System.* Boston, 1961.
———— *South Asia and United States Policy.* Boston, 1966.
Smith, D. E. *India As a Secular State.* Princeton, N.J., 1963.
Weekes, R. V. *Pakistan, Birth and Growth of a Muslim Nation.* Princeton, N.J., 1967.

Chapter 25

New Nations of Southeast Asia, Since 1946

GENERAL

As a whole, conditions in Southeast Asia have been poor since 1946, the whole vast region being characterized by growing instability, violence, and insecurity. Examples are easy to furnish, whether they be Burma, plagued by insurgency since independence and being controlled by an authoritarian military dictatorship; Indonesia, which suffered chaos and mismanagement under the late Sukarno; or Vietnam, where there has been no peace since the Second World War. The most powerful force remains nationalism, but the involvements of the great powers have made a revolutionary situation even more perilous. The revolutions which take place are actually of two kinds, a nationalist revolution directed against Western rule or Western influence, and social revolution against the old native elites with its search for new standards, and the coming to power of a new revolutionary intelligentsia. The latter, frequently accompanied by communist influence and guerrilla activity, have taken place in Burma, Indonesia, Vietnam, Malaya, and even in the Philippines.

While each of these countries has evolved its own political system in the postwar years, there has also taken place growing interaction so that what happens in one area is now important for the rest, a situation different from the colonial past. A number of common problems have emerged. One of these clearly is the problem of modernization and industrialization, a second the need for increased food production, the latter especially for the Philippines, Indonesia, and Malaysia. Another shared problem concerns the demarcation of arbitrary boundaries going back to colonial days, where controversies have taken place between Malaysia and Indonesia and the Philippines. Yet a fourth common problem has to do with ethnic minorities, such as the presence of Malays and Lao tribes in Thailand, or Shan tribes in Burma with their close connections to Thailand.

The industrial revolution, the Cold War, and the meddling of the great powers, as well as the growing economic interdependence for all of Southeast Asia, have made isolation impossible, but at the same time they have done nothing to lessen unpredictability of events. Ne Win's coup in Burma in 1962 and the establishment of a military dictatorship, or the hunting down of Communist party members and sympathizers in Indonesia in 1965 were all events no one really expected, emphasizing the political instability of the area. In general, there has been a movement away from democratic political forms, as seen in Burma, Indonesia, Cambodia, North and South Vietnam, Thailand, and recently the Philippines. Malaysia and Singapore remained democracies. At the same time external factors tended to become increasingly decisive, whether the actions of the United States, the Soviet Union, or China.

THAILAND

The government which had been put in power by Pridi had seen the successful transition of Thailand from an ally of the Japanese and an enemy of the West to an accepted member of the United Nations and a friend to the United States, thereby again illustrating the adaptability of Thai politics. However, Pridi's control of Siam was not destined to last long. A difficult economic situation, the result of wartime conditions, as well as scandals which seemed to implicate Pridi in the mysterious death of the new young king, Ananda Mahidol, who was found shot dead in the palace in Bangkok amidst circumstances which remain mysterious, led to a new, one-day, bloodless coup in 1947. In this coup, Pibul, who had managed to escape trial as a collaborator with the Japanese, made a successful comeback. The army supported him, and Pridi was forced to flee the country when he was accused in the death of the king. He fled to China, where he was active in organizing an "autonomous" Thai movement, which presumably could be used in the future to restore him to power.

Meanwhile in Bangkok Pibul Songgram and a new king, Phumiphon Adundet, re-established a government in which the military was once again in full power. In this they had the support of the United States, who looked to Pibul as a man willing to help fight America's battle against communist danger. Heavy American financial and military support was extended to Thailand (again the name of the country after Pridi's expulsion in 1947). American support also gave Thailand a seat in the United Nations in 1947, while it made her an important member of SEATO, the treaty organization designed to stop communist expansion in Southeast Asia. In fact, Thailand had become virtually an American protectorate, due to its willingness to follow the model of what seemed the strongest power in world politics at that particular moment. The somewhat reactionary military rule of Pibul was challenged in 1950 by an abortive putsch, backed by the Thai navy which traditionally was envious of the army, but the result was only a strengthen-

FIGURE 25.1. Field Marshal Sarit of Thailand.

ing of the dictatorial policies of Pibul. He suppressed all opposition activity, but corruption in his government, scandals arising over opium, and discontent over manipulations of elections weakened his power so that in September, 1957, a number of young intellectuals and navy officers were able to bring off yet another (and typically bloodless) revolution. Pibul went into exile, and went to India where he became a Buddhist monk, while government in Thailand was seized by Marshal Thanarat Sarit. Sarit ran the country as a military dictator, paying attention to economic and social development, but having no interest in modernizing political processes. As an individual he was given to hard drinking and high living, but he also gave Thailand a purposeful leadership. This resulted in greater efficiency in government, economic prosperity which in turn attracted foreign investment, and various plans of development which even saw the establishment of the first University outside Bangkok, in Chiengmai. Sarit died in 1963, as the result of prolonged dissipation, and was succeeded by his deputy, General Thanom Kittikachorn. Thanom has continued the same policies, again paying much attention to Thailand's economic future, but also permitting a somewhat greater influence of the civilian element in politics.

Thailand during all of these years has been most apprehensive and fearful of the communist threat from the outside, and the terrible turmoil in neighboring Indochina, and as a result of this has looked for ever closer ties with the United States. Thailand, with the exception of the Philippines, is the only country of Southeast Asia to have become a member of SEATO, and American influence has been most pervasive and widespread. In fact, Thailand, by permitting the Americans the construction of military facilities and the buildup of airpower on her soil, really became a kind of staging area for the American military effort in Indochina, a situation somewhat reminiscent of the times when the Japanese were given similar facilities during World War II. In such involvement there is, of course, a danger, and Thailand has had to cope with a certain amount of communist subversion, especially in the economically backward northeast part of the country where there exists a minority problem of the Lao communities on Thai territory. Infiltration from Laos, terrorism, and the assassination of Thai officials has been increasing, despite American technical support and advice in how to combat insurgency. But Thailand is an economically stable and prosperous country with a contented peasantry, and the dangers of internal revolt seem minimal, despite rumors of plots. Should there occur a general withdrawal of American power from Southeast Asia, in the event of a settlement in Indochina, Thailand would have to come to terms with the People's Republic of China, the new great power in that part of the world. Given the ability of the Thais to accommodate themselves in the past, a safe prediction would be that the Thai political leadership of the future will succeed in doing so. In 1968 a new constitution was promulgated, and in the 1969 elections Thanom's party, the United Thai People's Party, won a commanding position.

PHILIPPINES

The aid which America gave to the new, but shattered, Philippine republic did little to come to grips with the old and basic problem of the great inequality of income which existed in the Philippine social structure, a structure in which some 3 per cent of the population owned 98 per cent of the land. The problem of economic reform became acute in the immediate postwar years when communism made use of economic distress to challenge the established order and to produce an armed revolutionary force, the Hukbalahaps, or Huks. This movement began as the outgrowth of an anti-Japanese guerrilla force, operating mostly in central Luzon, which refused to surrender its arms after the war had ended. Instead, under such leaders as Luis Taruc, it came to be communist-led, and began to demand the blood of collaborationists as well as ouster of the landlords. The Huks were outlawed by the Osmena government, but not suppressed, and violence and bloodshed became a feature of the Luzon countryside.

Amidst these difficult circumstances a new election was held in 1946, in which Osmena lost to Manual Roxas and his new Liberal party. After winning the presidency, Roxas began a strong policy designed to suppress all opposition, including that of the Huks, but he was assassinated and was succeeded by Quirino in 1948. Quirino was re-elected (with considerable fraud) in 1949, but not by a very large vote. (Laurel, the ex-collaborationist, was his opponent, and he made a strong showing.) The period of Quirino's tenure only brought the problems of economic reform to the forefront, since his regime was the most inefficient and corrupt that the Philippines had yet suffered. In 1950 the American government sent the Bell mission to the Philippines, which severely censured the government and exposed a great variety of administrative abuses, and these concerns with economic reform and the communist guerrilla movement were also shared by the minister of defense in the Philippine government, Ramon Magsaysay. Magsaysay denounced government corruption and fought the Huk movement most successfully by taking away the basic cause of discontent of the Philippine small farmer. He provided land and homes, mostly in Mindanao, to those of the Huks who surrendered, and in this way broke the back of the communist insurrection. His great success and his patent honesty made him a most popular leader with great mass appeal, and in 1953 Magsaysay defeated Quirino and became president. Magsaysay, a former guerrilla fighter and auto mechanic, who had been educated at the University of the Philippines, earned his popularity by his constant concern with the affairs of the little people, his honesty, and his attempts at economic reform. In foreign affairs Magsaysay continued strong ties with the United States, and he caused the Philippines to play an active role in international affairs, particularly after the country became a member of SEATO. Unfortunately, Magsaysay was killed in an airplane crash in 1957. He was succeeded by his vice-president, Carlos Garcia, who was then elected president in the 1957 elections. The regime of Garcia, however, seemed to be very much controlled again by the caciques, and the program of economic reform now receded into the background. In 1960, corruption, nepotism, and inefficiency once again were the hallmark of Filipino politics. At the same time, Philippine nationalism continued to agitate from time to time against American influence and American bases in the islands, but to most Filipinos this was not much more than a rhetorical exercise, since the need for American support and friendship was only too obvious. In 1962 the Garcia regime was defeated, and Macapagal was elected as the new president of the Philippines.

The victory of Macapagal, with his Liberal party, again illustrated that the two-party system, and a measure of political democracy, was working in the Philippines, although it must be remembered that it is still a very small elite in Philippine society which commands weight and power, and that Philippine politics might best be characterized as a combination of democracy with oligarchy. The Macapagal government attempted once again to stem corruption by ending foreign exchange controls and reducing graft, and it also engaged in various nationalist gestures against the Chinese community in the islands. In foreign affairs Macapagal claimed control over Sabah, or North Borneo, to the discomfiture of Malaysia, although these claims have subsequently been underplayed.

In 1965 the Nacionalistas won again in the presidential elections, with Ferdinando Marcos being elected the sixth president of the republic. His problems have been both economic and political. Despite the fact that the Philippines are a rich agricultural land, the country does not grow sufficient rice and continues to depend on rice imports. Also, its economic growth has been moderate at best, much of it being negated by a continuously high population increase, with about one million Filipinos added each year, with resulting underemployment and unemployment. The wide gap between the rich and the poor remains a basic problem as does ingrained corruption. On the political scene there has been trouble with the Moslems of Mindanao and the Sulu archipelago.

The relations between Manila and Washington continued close, and the Philippines, with U.S. financing, even contributed some token military support to the American effort in Vietnam. A 1965 adjustment on military base jurisdiction eased tension on that long-festering issue and permitted the United States to use Philippine bases very actively during the Vietnam war. However, President Marcos, for a variety of reasons primarily associated with his effort to perpetuate the rule of a *nouveau riche* group with himself at the center, declared martial law on September 23, 1972. While suspending civil liberties, silencing the press, and imprisoning political opponents in the Philippines, he assured American business and government leaders that these were necessary anticommunist moves. All this seemed singularly inappropriate at a time when Washington and Peking were resuming relations.

INDONESIA

Independence

Since the government of the Hague was unwilling to recognize Indonesian independence, the Dutch by 1946 found themselves embroiled in intermittent fighting with the Indonesian Republic. The Dutch tried to cut off exports from territory under control by the Indonesians, thereby causing economic disorganization and hardship. Yet resistance and opposition by the Indonesian Republic was unexpectedly stiff, and the Dutch were forced into negotiations that led to a truce and two agreements. The first of these was the Linggadjati Agreement in 1947 in which the Dutch recognized the de facto existence of the republic and agreed to a union of Indonesia and Holland; the second was the Renville Agreement in January 1948, which was never ratified. In these negotiations the Indonesians had American support for their independence, but neither of these agreements was successful, as the Dutch had no intention of honoring them. Rather, the Dutch government in Holland planned to crush the Republic by force, and in December 1948 they began a "police action" and captured President Sukarno and his government. Dutch aggressiveness led to an appeal to the Security Council of the United Nations in that month, and the United Nations intervened, proclaiming an immediate "cease-fire." Indignation at Dutch military action and strong United States pressure led to new negotiations at the Hague Round Table Conferences of 1949 in which a sovereign United States of Indonesia was accepted by the Dutch, largely because of American support for the Indonesian cause. This was to be a sovereign federal republic, an equal partner with Holland under the Dutch crown, and it was to consist of 16 republics, of which Java was the most powerful. The victory of the Indonesians at the Hague was also due, in part, to the success of the new government in crushing a communist uprising in 1948 at Madiun in central Java. The chief communist leader, Muso, was shot, while many of his followers were exiled, and this action made it clear that the new state was strong enough to fight communist subversion, thus earning American support.

The arrangements for a federal republic did not last long, however, as by 1950 a united and unitary Republic of Indonesia replaced the United States, despite the protests of the outer islands. In 1954 Indonesia severed all political links with Holland, the Dutch-Indonesian union being dissolved at the insistence of the Indonesian Republic. From 1957 on, Dutch-Indonesian relations steadily deteriorated due to the Indonesian claim to Western New Guinea which the Dutch controlled and the reluctance of the Dutch government to yield on that issue. In that year the Indonesian government seized Dutch property in Indonesia, and many Dutch left the Indies in consequence. In 1960 diplomatic relations between the two countries were severed, bringing to a formal end the period of Dutch influence, which had begun when Van Houtman dropped anchor off the port of Bantam late in the sixteenth century, and which ended amidst rampant nationalism and mutual bitterness.

Recent Problems

Independence had been accomplished, but independence brought no end to Indonesian problems. Rather, it brought many new ones. Perhaps the most immediate of these was the question of internal political stability. The new Indonesia was a country in which illiteracy ran to some 50 per cent, in which there was no experience with democracy thanks to the Dutch reluctance to institute responsible government, and in which authoritarian traditions were firmly entrenched. There were almost constant crises, rebellion, corruption, scandals, constitutional problems, and instability. Sukarno decided to "bury all political parties," and to replace them with his concept of a "guided democracy," in effect an authoritarian state under the direct guidance of Sukarno as president whose more or less obedient premiers, such as Muhammad Hatta, Ali Sastroamidjojo, and Djuanda, were selected from a narrow clique of politicians. But Sukarno's decision for a "guided democracy" did not end internal weakness and civil war. The most important political forces in Indonesia were, in addition to the PNI and the communists, the Moslem Masjumi party which was strongly anticommunist, and the violently anticommunist politico-military organization known as the Darul Islam. These were responsible for a major rebellion in Sumatra in 1957 against the government at Djakarta, when they accused the government of toleration of communists. The lack of an effective public administration and trained civil servants, as well as the spirit of separatism of some of the outer islands, Celebes, for instance, also contributed to almost continuous uprisings and extreme political insecurity in Indonesia. A strongly anticommunist army, strong communist penetration, and a president who flirted with communism on and off while maintaining a neutralist position in international affairs were other elements which contributed to a situation which became ever more explosive, culminating in a series of dramatic events in 1965. In that year Sukarno's game of counterbalancing the power of the

FIGURE 25.2. Djalan Thamrin, busy boulevard in Djakarta.

military against the growing internal power of the PKI, the Communist party of Indonesia, came to a sudden and violent end in a setting of mounting restiveness occasioned by both continuous economic downward trends, and the arbitrary excesses of the "guided democracy," with its rigid censorship, strident indoctrination, burning of "ideologically subversive" books, and excessive propaganda. During a speech he was giving in the fall of 1965 Sukarno collapsed, probably as the result of growing kidney troubles, and thereby furnished the trigger for a communist-inspired revolt, led by an obscure commander of Sukarno's bodyguard, against the military. A number of junior officers, as well as segments of the Indonesian air force, attempted to do away with the army's general staff by brutally murdering six senior officers. Two others, Generals Nasution and Suharto, managed to escape, and by quick action and cool thinking caused the army to regain complete control. There then ensued the systematic destruction of the Indonesian Communist party, with practically all party members and communist sympathizers and many noncommunist Chinese being hunted down and killed. The bloodbath was widespread and thorough, with the Moslems taking a leading part in it, and it is estimated that close to half a million Indonesians perished. Whether Sukarno himself was implicated in the communist plot remains doubtful, but his reputation was thoroughly undermined, and despite his tenacious political skill his powers were increasingly reduced. By 1967 Sukarno was deposed as leader, and put under house arrest. He died

FIGURE 25.3. President Suharto of Indonesia.

soon thereafter and General Suharto became president. A quiet and skillful professional soldier of considerable reputation, Suharto has given Indonesia a much more calm political life. While many more military men today occupy high governmental positions than before, there is nevertheless more freedom in political life, and greater economic and fiscal stability. Foreign capital investment has again been flowing into Indonesia, and by 1970 Djakarta had all the appearances of a modern boom town. In foreign affairs Suharto put an end to confrontation with Malaysia and returned the country into the ranks of U.N. members.

BURMA

The British government having promised independence for Burma, a new constitution was drafted, and elections were held in 1947 prior to independence which developed into a contest between Aung San, the master of the AFPFL, and his political rival, U Saw. The latter resorted to wholesale murder in order to rid himself of opposition, and he hired some gunmen who, in the best Chicago style, mowed down with machine-guns the Burmese cabinet, including Aung San, at one of its meetings, but U Saw did not live to profit by this deed. He was hanged, and the result of the assassination of Aung San was that another leader of the Thakin party, U Nu, became premier of the new Burmese government, which proclaimed on January 4, 1948 (a date most carefully selected by astrologers) the independence of the country.

Postindependence Problems

Political independence did not, however, solve the many problems that Burma faced; quite the contrary. For one thing, as the result of wartime destruction, the country was economically ruined. Eventually, the government adopted a policy of limited socialism, and it willingly accepted outside aid, from both the British and nations of the communist bloc. Another, and even more serious problem, was ethnic nationalism. With independence armed conflict broke out between several separatist groups and the government, the former all wanting full autonomy. The most important among these were the Karen hill tribes and the Mons of the Arakan coast. The local Burmese communists contributed to this civil war and to economic chaos by armed raids against the government and the levying of tolls on teak logs floating down the Chindwin river. Communist participation in civil war soon assumed international implications when the Chinese began to claim certain frontier areas from Burma and when Chinese communist irregulars not only violated the northeast border of Burma but even attempted to set up a People's Republic among the discontented Kachin tribes.

U Nu managed to come to an agreement with the local dissidents, and also to arrive at a settlement with Peking. After recognizing the Peking government as the government of China, the first non-communist state to do so, he was able to sign a frontier agreement and to eliminate the threat of communist subversion within the borders of his own country. But instability continued to characterize developments in Burma until the 1956 elections, when the military took over and U Nu retired for a period of some ten months into the quiet of a Buddhist monastery for a period of contemplation and ascetic practices, after which, purified, he emerged to take over once more briefly the helm of government before being ousted by yet another military coup. In the field of international relations Burma carefully followed a policy of neutralism, belonging to the neutralist bloc in the United Nations. A Burmese, U Thant, became Acting Secretary General of the U.N. in 1961.

U Nu's increasingly parliamentary regime, which was also favorable to the Buddhists, was overthrown in a second military coup in 1962, a coup again led by General Ne Win. Disdainful and impatient with democracy, General Ne Win, of Chinese-Burmese parentage and trained in guerrilla warfare by the Japanese, set up a military junta with the aim of making Burma a unitary, socialist, and secular state. This meant fewer concessions to the Buddhists, and to the Burmese minorities, such as the Karens, Shans, and Kachins, and the adoption of a program of "Burmese socialism." All power is vested in an autocratic military "Revolutionary Council," and by 1964 Burma had become a near-totalitarian state. All parties had been outlawed, all businesses, mines, mills, banks, even small shops, had been nationalized, missionaries had been expelled, and private schools taken over. Burma's nonalignment in foreign affairs has become much more marked, and in fact the country exhibits xenophobia to the extent that foreigners are not welcomed, even for a short visit. Fear of China has also led to some anti-Chinese riots, such as those that took place in 1967. But a policy of voluntary isolation and centralized military control has not removed all of Burma's present problems. Internal insurrection, whether by ethnic minorities or communist factions, is one of these; another one is the expansion of rice production, and a third is the difficulty of industrialization without outside capital.

MALAYSIA

The British government had drawn up a plan for a Federation of Malaya in 1945 which was considered by the Malays as being too much in favor of the Chinese. Malay resentment at this plan led to a new plan in 1948, a plan for federation which this time, however, was considered to be anti-Chinese. The Chinese opposed this plan for federation, and after 1948 Chinese communist guerrillas began a series of attacks in the jungles of Malaya, designed to undermine the sources of British prosperity and dollar income by striking at the rubber plantations. In the next three years a vicious jungle war was fought in which hundreds of British planters were killed by terrorists, and to which the British committed large military forces. British persistence and determination finally produced results, and the communist guerrillas were, for all practical purposes, eliminated. This jungle war had obstructed political evolution, and delayed British grants of political power in answer to demands for self-rule, but in 1952 the British government was able to reaffirm its position that Malaya would in due course become a self-governing nation. In 1955 elections were held, and in 1957 Malaya became a fully self-governing dominion, with Tunku (Prince) Abdul Rahman as its first premier. The transfer of power from Britain to Malaya was a friendly one. Singapore, separately governed, had a large Chinese population, subject to chronic labor troubles, mob riots, and the ever present danger of communist interference. In early 1961 Tunku Abdul Rahman, the prime minister of the Federation of Malaya, suggested a new entity, the Malaysian Federation, which was to include the British colonies of Sarawak and North Borneo and the British protectorate of Brunei. By late 1961 both the British and the Malayan governments gave their agreement to this plan. The new nation of Malaysia, not including Brunei, which opted out, came into existence in 1963. But the new Federation, which then included Malaya, Singapore, Sabah (formerly North Borneo), and Sarawak, soon began to encounter difficulties. There was trouble with Indonesia when Sukarno demanded territories on Borneo, and the relations between Singapore and Malaya also deteriorated.

In 1965 Singapore, under its prime minister Lee Kuan-yew, a primarily Chinese city, seceded (or was expelled)—depending on one's viewpoint—from the Federation to become a republic. Singapore has remained a most successful combination of welfare socialism with commercial capitalism, and is today one of the most active ports in the world, enjoying the highest

FIGURE 25.4. Tunku Abdul Rahman, prime minister of Malaysia.

standard of living in Asia outside Japan, and being firmly ruled by Mr. Lee's Action Party.

Malaya remains in the hands of Tunku Abdul Rahman's Alliance Party, pledged to an anticommunist stance and further economic development. Sabah, a prosperous unit of the Federation, based on a rubber and lumber economy, strongly supports the Federation, and has rejected threats from both the Philippines and Indonesia. In Sarawak there is a strong pro-communist element present, but it too adheres to Malaysia, while Brunei remains a British protectorate enclave within Sarawak, and is not a member of the Federation. There are of course some problems, the most important of which seems racial extremism, pitting Chinese versus Malays, which has resulted in some unpleasant riots, especially in Kuala Lumpur. Economically, of course, Malaysia depends primarily upon rubber and tin exports, and as their prices fluctuate on the world market, so does Malaysia's political stability.

INDOCHINA

French vs. Vietminh

During the first years after the end of World War II the French attempted to regain complete control in Indochina. After eight years of warfare they were forced to acknowledge their failure and withdraw.

The "Democratic Republic of Vietnam" had been proclaimed in northern Vietnam in September 1945. The French recognized this provisional government organized at Hanoi with the communist Ho Chi Minh as president, but they were unwilling to grant Vietnam its autonomy; and the negotiations of 1946 had no result. Friction continued over who was to control in the larger towns of Vietnam; war commenced in December 1946.

In the war between the French and the Vietminh the French managed to gain cities and towns, highways, and the borders with China. The Vietminh, on the other hand, developed guerrilla warfare and controlled most of the countryside. Soon, during the years 1947–1948, the French found themselves on the defensive.

On the political side, the French attempted to set up another regime, under the Vietnamese prince Bao Dai (then in France), as an alternative to the government of Ho Chi Minh. Although Bao Dai did not have popular support he did have adherents among anticommunist nationalists and some leaders of the religious sects, the Cao Dai and the Hoa Hao.

In 1948 the French recognized the "independence" of the "Associated State of Vietnam" as part of the French union while they continued to bring in more troops of their own.

In the next year they granted Bao Dai the title of "Chief of State," under their protection but without real autonomy. They were very slow in ratifying their agreement. The regime was to be a "republic," but it had no administration, no army, and no funds. Bao Dai stayed in France to bargain with the French and finally returned to Vietnam with as much as he could get, in April 1949.

Meanwhile the Chinese communists were gaining control of the whole of China, and in January 1950 they formally recognized Ho Chi Minh as president of Vietnam and sent him aid in his fight against the French. The United States government, on the other hand, on the assumption that the Bao Dai regime had the support of the Vietnamese people, began to send regular aid to the French and the Republic of Vietnam.

The Vietminh during the period 1948–1950 were taken over by hard line communists and were encouraged in their political faith by the government of Mao Tse-tung. With aid from the Chinese the organized forces of the Vietminh were able to gain victories over the French in northeastern Tonkin in the fall of 1950.

As a result of these defeats the French sent out a dynamic general as high commissioner in command of their forces in Vietnam. General Jean de Lattre de Tassigny was a crusader against communism, but nothing was done to promote the formation of a real Vietnamese national army. Most of the fighting men supporting the Bao Dai regime were French.

To carry on their struggle against the French the Vietminh formed a workers' party, Lao Dong, which was organized by Truong Chinh, a pro-Peking communist, and this party in turn was made the central feature of a "National Union Front" which took within it peasants, workers, youths, and other groups.

End of an Era

The climax of the war came when the French were forced to surrender to the Vietminh at Dien Bien Phu on May 7, 1954, after a siege of 55 days.

A new French commander, General Navarre, had attempted to risk all by supporting a forward base in the green wilderness of Dien Bien Phu against a full-scale Vietminh offensive.

Meanwhile at Geneva an attempt was made to find a solution to the Vietnamese problem. An international conference, under the chairmanship of the Soviet Union and the United Kingdom, met from April to July 1954. Communist China participated and the United States also had a delegation at the conference.

The actual agreement reached at Geneva was only between the Vietminh and the French. By its terms the French granted full independence to the Democratic Republic of Vietnam. The country was divided at a provisional "military demarcation line" along the seventeenth degree of latitude, and reunification was to be undertaken on the basis of elections two years later (these elections never took place). Neither the South Vietnamese government of Bao Dai at Saigon nor the United States were parties to this agreement. Arrangements within Vietnam were to be supervised by an international control commission. Cambodia and Laos became independent, and the French began a withdrawal of all their forces from Vietnam.

With the defeat and withdrawal of the French the American government took on the protection of South Vietnam and of Laos. While continuing and increasing American aid to South Vietnam the United States reinforced its position by the formation of a Southeast Asia Treaty Organization proclaimed as an international group designed to promote common action against the spread of communism.

Diem and the Civil War

With the partition of Vietnam in 1954 and the withdrawal of the French, the communist republic of Ho Chi Minh in the north was confronted with an American-supported anticommunist regime extending from Quangtri and Hue in central Vietnam down to and including Cochin China in the south. As the result of a referendum in southern Vietnam in 1955 the independent "National Republic of Vietnam" succeeded the French-sponsored regime of Bao Dai. Bao Dai was deposed and replaced by Ngo Dinh Diem as chief of state. Diem was a devoted anticommunist and Catholic politician who enjoyed American support and who had for a time achieved considerable popularity as the result of a land reform program carried through in 1952. In 1955 Diem became president of the republic, but he speedily lost his popularity by severely suppressing opposition to his authority. The private armies of the Cao Dai and Hoa Hao religious sects were defeated. He also faced the problem of resettling large numbers of refugees from the north, in which he received American assistance.

Communist guerrillas (known as Vietcong) continued some activity in South Vietnam even after the settlement at Geneva. But the country was relatively quiet and the adherents of Ho Chi Minh in the south devoted themselves mainly to "political struggle" in anticipation of the elections to be held in 1956. After the Diem government failed to arrange for such elections the dissident cadres in South Vietnam began a serious insurgency, especially noticeable in 1958 and after.

In the north the Hanoi government during this same period was faced with a peasant revolt because of the enforcement of a harsh land-reform program in 1956. But by the end of 1958 the decision was made at Hanoi to endorse the "armed struggle" in the south. Small-scale infiltration for guerrilla operations was begun in 1959.

In South Vietnam in 1960 the Vietcong organized a "National Liberation Front" which maintained a network of supporters in the villages. Later, in 1962, a "People's Revolutionary Party" was founded. Within this party the central leadership, representing the communist Lao Dong Party of North Vietnam, had direct control in all the Front villages.

To help meet this insurgency advisors both civilian and military were sent from the United States to South Vietnam. Americans trained special counterinsurgency forces and brought in helicopters. The military advisor system, however, failed in persuading the Vietnamese to engage in counterguerrilla tactics. Observers in 1960–1961 noted a lack of leadership or motivation among the South Vietnamese. On the other hand, the Americans were often ineffective because of impatience and because they were usually in Vietnam for only one year.

By 1961 both the North Vietnamese and the Americans were actively engaged in direct intervention in South Vietnam. Hanoi was sending supplies and weapons to the insurgents through Laos. Washington increased American intervention in Vietnam to include combat forces as well as advisors. The escalation of armed confrontation had begun.

Meanwhile the arbitrary government of Ngo Dinh Diem and members of his family lost favor with his own people as well as among the Americans. After severe repression of Buddhists and students in 1963 Diem and his brother, Ngo Dinh Nhu, were killed in a military uprising. This was followed by a period of political confusion.

Government of the Generals

There were four separate governments at Saigon between the end of 1963 and the middle of 1965. In June 1965, the leaders in control were Generals Nguyen Van Thieu and Nguyen Cao Ky. Ky was head of the government from 1965 to 1967; Thieu has been president since 1967. Military men have controlled the politics of South Vietnam ever since the end of Diem's regime. Other elements to be reckoned with were Buddhists, who used the peace issue as a political weapon, and Catholics. Behind the political changes which took place was the influence of the United States; this became even more important with the greater military involvement in the following period.

The communists in South Vietnam meanwhile gained control of almost two-thirds of the countryside. They increased in strength from 25,000 in 1963 to 279,000 (including 50,000 North Vietnamese) in 1966.

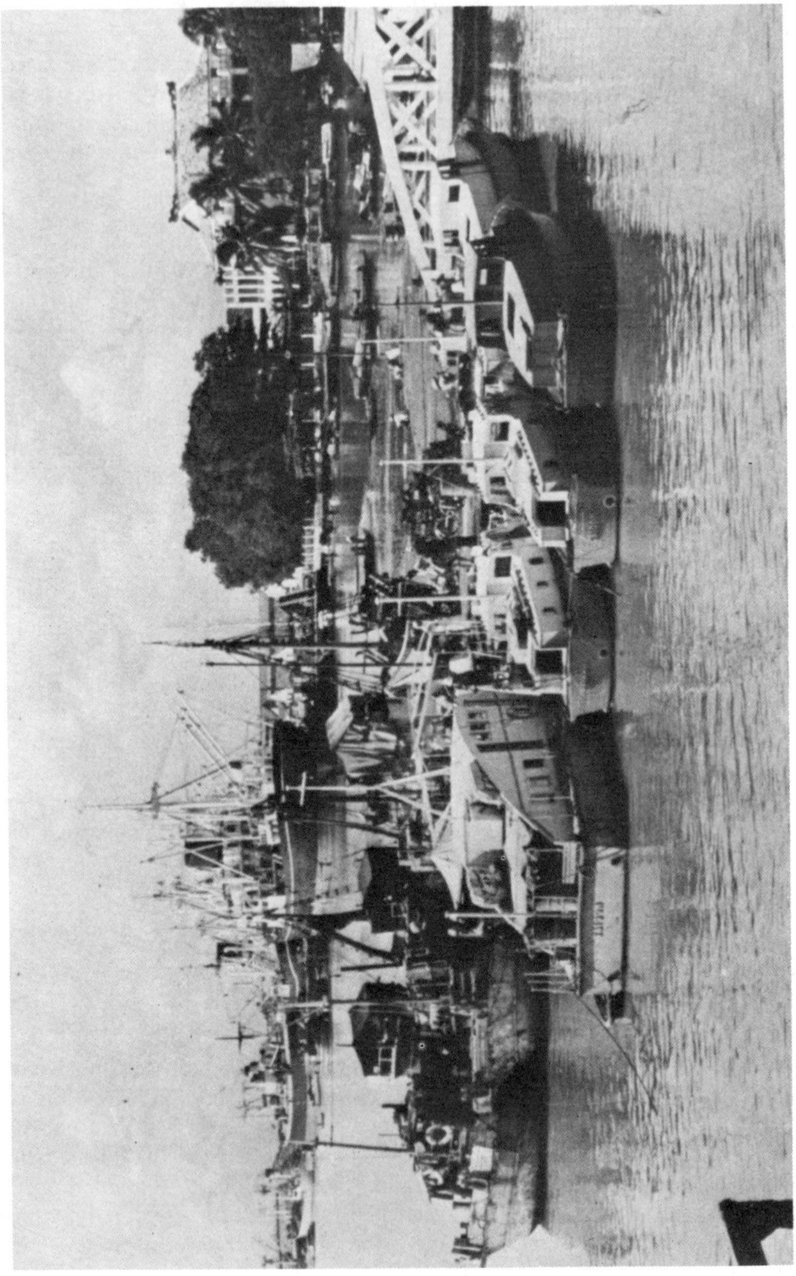

Vietnamese Politics, 1965–1972

After the confusion of the years immediately following the fall of Diem there was a thread of continuity in Vietnamese politics, in that Nguyen Van Thieu and his colleagues of the "Directory" have been the ruling group in South Vietnam since 1965. This Directory which ran the government in Saigon under Thieu and Nguyen Cao Ky consisted of ten generals and ten civilians. The military men, headed by the four Army Corps commanders, were the dominating group.

Buddhists and others clamored for civilian control and demonstrated against the government at Danang, Hue, and Saigon. The dissension of 1966 was calmed somewhat by the promise of an election.

Steps were taken in the direction of establishing a constitutional government, at the insistence of the Americans. Election of a Constituent Assembly in 1966 led to the adoption of a constitution in 1967. Thieu was elected president and Ky vice-president; the military remained in power. But executive authority was split up into about ten different parts, with an accompanying lack of unity or purpose. Divisiveness prevailed in the Army, among politicians, and in religious groups.

In order to establish their authority in the countryside the Saigon government, with American support, undertook pacification programs and the organizing of "Popular Forces" in the villages with some success.

This was the situation in 1968 when the communists struck a decisive blow at the whole fabric of the Thieu regime. The Tet Offensive of February 1968 is described further on. Through the military attack on towns and government centers throughout South Vietnam, the communists attempted to establish a new revolutionary political organization. They failed to gain the support of the people in the various communities, but on the other hand Thieu showed no signs of leadership in the crisis.

In May 1968, President Thieu appointed Tran Van Huong as prime minister. This meant civilian leadership, but the prime minister was subject to orders from Thieu. The rivalries of politics were reflected in such details as that Thieu headed a new six-party coalition in May 1969, and that in an election for the national senate in 1970 a group of Buddhists received the largest vote. On the other hand, the communists of the National Liberation Front were excluded by Thieu from any coalition government.

While the government at Saigon was gradually gaining greater control in South Vietnam, there was serious inflation.

At Hanoi during the period from 1965 to 1969 the government continued to be that of Ho Chi Minh and the communists, organized principally in the Lao Dong, or Workers' Party. That party and the North Vietnam Politburo completely controlled the so-called "People's Revolutionary Party" and the "National Liberation Front" which, as we have seen, operated in South Vietnam. The North Vietnamese, in their struggle against Thieu and his allies, were receiving increased military aid from the Soviet Union.

President Ho Chi Minh died at Hanoi on September 4, 1969. After

FIGURE 25.5. Saigon.

FIGURE 25.6. Ho Chi Minh.

Ho's death the most important person in the power structure in North Vietnam was the Communist Party secretary, Le Duan, who managed the government of President Ton Duc Thang and Premier Phan Van Dong. Agreements with Communist China as well as the Soviet Union guaranteed the receipt of further supplies, both economic and military.

Laos and Cambodia

Laos and Cambodia were independent constitutional monarchies and members of the United Nations, but both were unstable politically and had difficulty in coping with outside pressures, particularly from communist North Vietnam. They were both recipients of American technical and military aid.

Laos, governed in part by the neutralist Prince Souvanna Phouma and faced with the communist Pathet Lao insurgency in the north, was the subject of international deliberations at Geneva in 1962. The Prince's "right-wing neutrality" was supported since 1964 by American arms and Thai volunteers in an inconclusive war against Pathet Lao and North Vietnamese forces. Southern Laos was used as an infiltration route for North Vietnamese reinforcements entering South Vietnam.

In Cambodia Prince Norodom Sihanouk was the ruler from 1941 to 1955 and from 1960 until he was deposed in 1970. In spite of his "neutralism" he permitted the North Vietnamese to use Cambodian border territory for bases in operations against South Vietnam. He was deposed after an army coup and his successor, Premier Lon Nol, in April 1970, requested military assistance from the United States. American troops, together with South Vietnamese, operated against the communists in Cambodia during May and June 1970. In spite of this aid, the Cambodians in the subsequent warfare lost to the communists by the end of 1971 about one-half of their national territory.

American Involvement

American forces were increasingly involved in military activity in Indochina from 1964 to 1969, although de-escalation officially commenced in 1968. This period began with the controversial Tonkin Gulf incident of August 1964, when American destroyers were allegedly attacked by North Vietnamese PT boats off the coast of North Vietnam and when the American Congress, at the request of President Johnson, passed the "Gulf of Tonkin Resolution." Plans were made for the extensive use of United States combat forces in Vietnam, and after American troops were attacked at Pleiku in February 1965 the escalation began. American planes and land forces were used against the Vietcong in the South and bombing raids commenced against North Vietnam. From a total of 3,500 Marines at Danang in 1965 American forces increased up to 510,000 troops in 1968.

The most intensive military phase of this Vietnam War, from 1966 to 1968, saw American troops participating in combat against the communists in many parts of South Vietnam: the northern part near the "Demilitarized Zone," on the Cambodian border, in the Central Highlands, the Mekong Delta of Cochin China, and in coastal areas of South Vietnam. Meanwhile the war continued in Laos. There, government forces, who received aid from the United States, fought an inconclusive war against the Pathet Lao.

Bombing raids by United States planes carried the war in 1966 beyond South Vietnam and Laos and into the heart of North Vietnam, to the vicinity of Hanoi and Haiphong, where the objectives included oil supplies of the North Vietnamese.

Although there were many in the United States who challenged the legality or the wisdom of American involvement in Vietnam, there were also in this period those in other countries who expressed their approval of American policy. These included the British government (except in the case of raids on the oil depots), the Philippine government, which announced that they would be sending 2,000 troops to South Vietnam, and the Thai, which joined in the fighting in South Vietnam and provided bases for the use of American bombers. South Korea, Australia, and New Zealand also sent forces to share in the fighting against the communists. The sending of Korean, Thai, and Philippine troops to aid the South Vietnamese was undertaken with financial support from the United States.

The most important military event of 1968 was the famous Tet Offensive. During the Lunar New Year holiday season the communists in South Vietnam made surpise attacks on a total of 102 towns and cities, including Saigon, Hue, and thirty other provincial capitals. In most places the hoped-for popular uprisings did not occur. Assassinations and maiming were inflicted on their enemies by the communists; in Hue alone nearly 2,900 South Vietnamese were "eliminated."

Heavy fighting continued throughout the country during a large part of 1968. In the next two years the South Vietnamese army was strengthened and its control reestablished.

In 1968 the United States called a halt to the bombing and shelling of North Vietnam, "peace talks" between the chief opponents in the Vietnam War commenced in Paris, and the withdrawal of American land forces from Vietnam was begun. The war continued on a somewhat different scale during the next four years.

The Paris peace talks were enlarged in 1969 to include all four major opponents: the Vietcong with the North Vietnamese, and the Saigon government of South Vietnam with the Americans. Three years later the participants still had failed to arrive at any agreement.

Simultaneously with the gradual withdrawal of American land forces President Nixon proclaimed a policy of "Vietnamizing" the war against the communists. Land fighting continued, especially in the northern parts of South Vietnam and against guerrillas in many regions. A carefully planned campaign was undertaken by South Vietnamese troops in March 1971 to cut communist communications along the so-called Ho Chi Minh Trail through southern Laos. In spite of American bombing support the South

FIGURE 25.7. General Vo Nguyen Giap, defense minister and commander in chief of the North Vietnam armed forces at Hanoi.

Vietnamese suffered heavy losses. The campaign was unsuccessful and resulted in a decline of morale. Heavy bombing by American planes was resumed and by the end of 1971 was extended into Tonkin, to the region near Hanoi. American aircraft were also used against the communists in Laos and Cambodia.

In the spring of 1972 the North Vietnamese commenced a series of strong offensives into various parts of South Vietnam. The United States retaliated with further bombing of North Vietnamese communications and with a blockade through mining of North Vietnamese ports. Bombing by American planes during 1972 was the most intensive and destructive of the whole war.

American ground forces continued to be withdrawn. Meanwhile South Vietnamese forces successfully resisted attacking communist tanks and artillery on three fronts. Particularly bitter fighting took place at the provincial capital of Quangtri, where the North Vietnamese held the city for five months before being forced to retire.

By 1971 the South Vietnam economy had shown some improvements and the Thieu government was well established, but the withdrawal of American troops and the reverses suffered in 1971 resulted in a weakening of the regime. Defects in the "pacification" program and in the operation of the "people's self-defense forces," the development of urban ghettoes (comprising half the population of Vietnam), corruption in the army and in the public services were some of the elements which led to unrest and dissatisfaction. In the United States those who opposed the war were increasingly frustrated and organized demonstrations against its continuance.

Politically, Thieu's regime made a show of conforming to the written constitution of 1967. Within an elected legislature various blocs reflecting the political and religious diversity of Vietnam were free to struggle for legislative autonomy against the executive. But there was no effective party system. While an uncontested presidential election in October 1971 was conducted without regard for the provisions of the constitution, the various politicized groups avoided any decisive action.

Thieu and his military directory continued in power. In May 1972 he proclaimed martial law and rule by decree. In September Thieu put an end to the election of hamlet officials.

During the war, the North Vietnamese had the moral backing of the Chinese and, until the blockade of 1972, a steady supply of munitions of war from the Soviet Union. Laos was torn apart. South Vietnam and the southern part of Cambodia, under the protection and with the military support of the United States, continued the war against the communists into 1973.

Meanwhile throughout 1972 the American government was involved in protracted negotiations with the North Vietnamese. The result was a series of compromise cease-fire agreements signed at Paris on January 27, 1973. Negotiations in Laos led to a cease-fire agreement for that country signed February 21, 1973. Hostilities did not end immediately; fighting continued at Tayninh and elsewhere in South Vietnam.

BASIC DATES

1946	Philippines independent; Democratic Republic of Vietnam proclaimed by Vietminh with Ho Chi Minh as president
1946–1954	Vietminh war against French
1947	Pibul returns to power in Thailand
1948	Quirino president of Philippines; Dutch "police action" in Indonesia; Burma independent; French set up "Associated States of Vietnam, Laos, and Cambodia"
1949	United States of Indonesia established; Bao Dai in South Vietnam
1950	Republic of Indonesia established; U.S. commences aid to Vietnam
1951	Lao Dong (Workers' Party) organized by Vietminh
1953	Magsaysay elected president of Philippines
1954	Fall of Dien Bien Phu and Geneva conference; Cambodia and Laos independent; Ngo Dinh Diem becomes premier in South Vietnam; SEATO established
1955–1963	Diem president of South Vietnam
1956	Vietcong insurgency commences
1957	Sarit seizes power in Thailand; Malaya becomes a Dominion
1960	"National Liberation Front" established in South Vietnam
1960–1970	Prince Norodom Sihanouk head of state in Cambodia
1962	Laos "neutralized" at Geneva conference; Ne Win seizes power in Burma
1963	Indonesia annexes West New Guinea; formation of Malaysia; Diem assassinated; start of military governments in Saigon
1964	Gulf of Tonkin incident and resolution
1965	Attempt at communist coup in Indonesia fails; Singapore an independent republic; President Marcos in Philippines; rule of Nguyen Van Thieu and "Directory" in South Vietnam; American use of land forces and bombers against Vietnamese communists
1967	Death of Sarit; Thanom in power in Thailand
1968	Tet offensive; U.S. bombing reduced and halted; start of Paris peace talks
1968–1969	Largest number of U.S. troops in South Vietnam
1969	Death of Ho Chi Minh
1970	U.S. bombing resumed; Sihanouk replaced by Lon Nol; U.S. and South Vietnam forces in Cambodia; communists control large section of Cambodia
1972	North Vietnamese major attacks in South Vietnam; Thieu at Saigon and Lon Nol at Pnom Penh assume dictatorial powers under American protection
1973	Cease-fire agreements for Vietnam and Laos

SUPPLEMENTARY READING

Bastin, J. and H. J. Benda. *A History of Modern Southeast Asia.* Englewood Cliffs, N.J., 1968.

Benda, H. J. and J. A. Larkin. *The World of Southeast Asia: Selected Historical Readings.* New York, 1967.
Cady, J. *Southeast Asia: Its Historical Development.* New York, 1964.
Hall, D. G. *A History of South-East Asia.* New York, 1955.
Hammer, E. *Vietnam Yesterday and Today.* New York, 1966.
Harrison, B. *South-East Asia,* 2nd ed. London, 1963.
Shaplen, R. *The Lost Revolution: The U.S. in Vietnam, 1946–1966,* rev. ed. New York, 1966.
Vandenbosch, A. and R. Butwell. *The Changing Face of Southeast Asia.* Lexington, Ky., 1967.
Young, K. T. and others. *Vietnam: Evolution of the Crisis in Asia, No. 4.* New York, Winter 1966.

ADVANCED READING

Allen, R. H. *Malaysia.* London, 1968.
Bone, R. C. *Contemporary Southeast Asia.* New York, 1962.
Bro, M. *Indonesia, Land of Challenge.* New York, 1954.
Clutterbuck, R. *The Long, Long War: The Emergency in Malaya, 1948–1960.* London, 1967.
Crozier, B. *South-East Asia in Turmoil.* Baltimore, 1965.
Dahm, B. *Sukarno and the Struggle for Indonesian Independence.* Ithaca, N.Y., 1969.
Fall, B. B. *Hell in a Very Small Place: The Siege of Dien Bien Phu.* London, 1967.
———— *The Two Viet-Nams: A Political and Military Analysis.* New York, 1963.
———— *Viet-Nam Witness, 1953–1966.* New York, 1966.
Fifield, R. H. *Southeast Asia in United States Policy.* New York, 1963.
Gray, M. M. *Island Hero: The Story of Ramon Magsaysay.* New York, 1965.
Grunder, G. and W. Livezay. *The Philippines and the United States.* Norman, Okla., 1951.
Hammer, E. *The Struggle for Indochina, 1940–1955.* Stanford, Calif., 1966.
Hindley, D. *The Communist Party of Indonesia, 1951–1963.* Berkeley, Calif., 1964.
Hoang-Van-Chi. *From Colonialism to Communism: A Case History of North Vietnam.* New York, 1964.
Hunter, G. *South East Asia—Race, Culture and Nation.* London, 1966.
Kahin, G. *Nationalism and Revolution in Indonesia.* Ithaca, N.Y., 1952.
Kahin, G. and J. W. Lewis. *The United States and Vietnam.* Ithaca, N.Y., 1970.
Kennedy, M. *Communism in Asia.* New York, 1956.
Kim, S. Y. *United States-Philippines Relations, 1946–1956.* Washington, 1961.
Kunstadter, P., ed. *South East Asian Tribes, Minorities and Nations.* Princeton, N.J., 1967.
Lacouture, J. *Ho Chi Minh: A Political Biography.* New York, 1968.
———— *Vietnam: Between Two Truces.* New York, 1966. From 1954 to 1965.

Lancaster, D. *The Emancipation of French Indochina.* London, 1961.
Malcolm, G. *First Malayan Republic, the Story of the Philippines.* Boston, 1951.
McVey, R. *The Rise of Indonesian Communism.* Ithaca, N.Y., 1965.
Meyer, M. *A Diplomatic History of the Philippine Republic.* Honolulu, 1965.
Purcell, V. *The Chinese in Southeast Asia.* London, 1951.
Pye, L. *Guerrilla Communism in Malaya.* Princeton, N.J., 1956.
Roff, W. R. *The Origins of Malay Nationalism.* New Haven, 1967.
Schell, J. *The Village of Ben Suc.* New York, 1966.
Shaplen, R. *The Road from War: Vietnam, 1965–1970.* New York, 1970.
Sheehan, N. and others. *The Pentagon Papers as Published by the New York Times.* New York, 1971.
Smith, R. *Philippine Freedom, 1946–1958.* New York, 1958.
Trager, F. *Burma from Kingdom to Republic: An Historical and Political Analysis.* New York, 1966.
Tregonning, K. G. *A History of Modern Malaya.* New York, 1967.
Wertheim, F. *Indonesian Society in Transition.* The Hague, 1956.

Chapter 26

Divergence and Division in East Asia: Japan, China, and Korea, 1945-1960

By 1945 Japan and China had been intimately, though not very happily, involved with each other for half a century. Now suddenly they were to go very separate ways, Japan toward democracy, China toward communism. Even in the years immediately after the Pacific war, when the lines of division between the communist and noncommunist worlds had not yet solidified, there was little contact between China and Japan or between Chinese and Japanese. For as Japanese were being repatriated to their home islands and life under American occupation, China was becoming a battleground of civil war to the extent that even the nationalist government, which had been expected to play a considerable role in shaping the postwar Far East, had neither time nor energy to devote to matters Japanese. The idea that Japanese factories and reparations should contribute to the rehabilitation of China was put aside amidst developing Cold War tensions, and except for Chinese involvement in a few Japanese war crimes trials, the two greatest civilizations of eastern Asia had practically no contact with each other for over six years. Finally in 1952 the Chinese nationalist government on Formosa and the Japanese government resumed relations, but the mainland areas of China proper, Manchuria, and Korea, which the Japanese had regarded as the "inner core" of their "co-prosperity sphere" remained entirely out of contact with Japan. Perhaps another day for East Asia "co-prosperity" would come, on a happier basis than Japan had provided, but the Cold War had cut the region in half by 1952.

THE OCCUPATION OF JAPAN

An analytical description of the occupation of Japan might divide it into two main phases: (1) the phase of democratization, from 1945 to 1948;

(2) the phase of recovery, from 1948 to 1952. The primary emphasis of the first phase was political, and to a lesser extent social; the primary emphasis of the second phase was economic. The first phase dealt with such matters as demobilization and demilitarization, including war crimes trials, the release of political prisoners, the purging from office of leaders of the ultranationalist movement, the making of a new constitution, which shifted sovereignty from the emperor to the people, the establishment of civil rights safeguards for all Japanese citizens, and the curtailment of economic and social aristocracy. The second phase turned to such matters as the rehabilitation of business and trade and a reconcentration of political and economic control in conservative hands.

The Setting

This analysis will be developed directly, but before doing so, since the occupation of Japan was one of the most remarkable encounters in modern history, one should first try to recapture something of its drama. As the occupation forces landed neither Japanese nor Americans knew what to expect. The Pacific war had been a ferocious struggle, wherein hatred and bitterness, built upon several decades of increasing suspicion and misunderstanding, had reached unprecedented heights. The last battles, on Okinawa, had been the fiercest of all. No quarter was given or expected, and the Japanese defenders preferred suicide to surrender. In the homeland Japan's main cities were a shambles from the months of B-29 saturation bombing raids that had preceded the atomic blasts, and Japanese families who could find the means to do so evacuated wives and children to country areas to protect them from anticipated ravagings of occupation troops. The American occupiers erected various safeguards against sabotage, putting most of their best-trained language officers and crews to checking postal and telecommunications centers for plots.

The Tokyo-Yokohama area, formerly the heart of Japan's vast empire, had the look of a dead city to the occupying forces entering in September and October 1945. The ride to Tokyo from Atsugi airdrome where many Americans landed was an eerie experience. Where a vast industrial complex had been, only smokestacks and steel safes remained as identifiable objects amidst the debris that represented flattened factories. Somehow the bombing had failed to fell the smokestacks, and the steel safes stood in mute testimony to their strength of construction, though no one now seemed to care what they contained.

In Tokyo, whose population had been reduced by evacuation from some seven million to around three million, life moved at a snail's pace. A few charcoal-burning ten-year-old automobiles were to be seen; some trolleys were running, with the occupants having to alight every few blocks to help push them up an incline. Some shops were open, but their shelves contained few goods. The railroad stations were crowded with people, either trying to go to the country or returning from it. Those going carried empty sacks which they hoped to fill with rice; those returning, if they had been lucky, had full or half full sacks which they guarded with their lives. All buildings were without heat, though corner lots were sometimes piled with radiators removed from office buildings in the final desperate drives for scrap iron. Government offices were open, with their personnel loyally reporting for duty each day and going through the motions of their jobs while awaiting orders. Japanese police, in worn uniforms, tried to maintain a show of decorum standing behind American military police at all the major traffic intersections. Furtive figures lurked in every alleyway trying to make black market exchanges. American cigarettes and other Post Exchange supplies speedily became almost a medium of exchange in the early months of the occupation.

Though Japanese were fearful and silent and Americans were suspicious during the first two or three months of occupation, as practically no untoward incidents occurred, tension eased and an amazing degree of mutual confidence and even cordiality speedily developed. Having been ordered by their emperor to cooperate with the conquerors, the Japanese could do so in good countenance and, according to their own traditional mores, the appearance of a new military ruler (a shogun), giving orders with the sanction of the emperor, was something that had happened before and could be accepted again. Also they were desperately tired of war and disillusioned by it, so that peace at almost any price might have had a grudging acceptance. However, these are only negative reasons for the successful start of the occupation. In addition, the Japanese were amazed to find that Americans were not the villains their wartime posters had portrayed them to be, and the Americans found much they could admire and like in the Japanese—their industry, their patience, their courage in the face of hard times.

FIGURE 26.1. General Douglas MacArthur, supreme commander of Allied Forces in Japan, leaves his Tokyo headquarters on his seventy-first birthday, in 1951.

The character and personality of General MacArthur, who, as supreme commander for the Allied Powers (SCAP), wielded final authority over the Japanese emperor and government, were well suited to his task. Though he was criticized by many Americans for his pompous ways and dramatic effects, and his political conservatism was behind the times in America, he gave a posture of benevolent dignity to the occupation and provided the Japanese with a sense of security. The changes to be demanded were so extensive that it was well, perhaps, to have a man of basically conservative temperament implementing them, so that an aura of stability might be preserved amidst rapid change. This is not to say that General MacArthur's leadership was indispensable, or that it remained as effective in the later stage as it was in the beginning, but his stern countenance and commanding ways probably helped to prevent liberty from being confused with license in the newly emerging Japan.

Lastly, the importance of the promise of freedom to a people who had never been free should not be underestimated as a factor in making the occupation so congenial an operation. Many writers, expressing amazement that a people so steeped in authoritarian political and social traditions could become so enthusiastic about democratizing their country, do not consider the question whether the Japanese really loved those old traditions. There is much evidence in Japanese history to show that the lower classes, the politically dispossessed, the intellectually curious again and again had sought ways to liberalize their society and their country. The bourgeois culture of the Tokugawa era, the people's rights movement of the early Meiji years, and the liberal currents of the 1920's had some popular enthusiasm behind them. But in each case the classes had thwarted the masses. Now the occupation provided a new opportunity, a better opportunity than the people of this heretofore tight-knit, never invaded semi-isolated "island country" had ever had, to make some changes. To many Japanese freedom and democracy were not merely the creed of the conqueror, but something they had wanted for a long time, and the chance was at hand to obtain them.

ORGANIZATIONAL STRUCTURE AND POLICY OBJECTIVES

Neither the policy objectives nor the organizational structure for the occupation of Japan had been fully settled at the time of surrender. In the spring of 1945 an attempt to coordinate policy was made by the creation of the State-War-Navy Coordinating Committee (SWNCC). As the end of the war approached, this committee worked rapidly and even frantically to draw up both a postsurrender policy and to make recommendations on a postsurrender organizational structure. One thing that complicated its labors was uncertainty about the future relationships of the Allied powers in any occupation of Japan. This became particularly crucial after it became clear that Russia would enter the war.

Regarding organizational structure, the basic principle that SWNCC decided on was that the United States should be the occupying power for all Japan, with perhaps token occupation forces from other countries but no division of the islands into occupation zones. It was hoped that the other Allied powers, including Soviet Russia, would give congenial assistance to the United States.

Accordingly, to give effect to this, the United States proposed that a Far Eastern Advisory Commission (FEAC) be created to include representatives of all powers that had participated in the Pacific war. This arrangement was not accepted by the Russians. They refused to participate in a commission with only advisory functions and the matter remained unsettled through the fall of 1945 as the occupation settled in and American policies took effect. A compromise was reached at the Moscow Conference in December 1945, when Soviet Foreign Minister Molotov agreed that Russia would join a Far Eastern Commission (FEC) which would possess authority "to formulate the policies, principles, and standards in conformity with which the fulfillment by Japan of its obligations under the terms of surrender may be accomplished," and in which all of the four major powers, the United States, Britain, Soviet Russia, and China, had to agree on these for action to be taken. France, the Netherlands, Canada, Australia, New Zealand, India, and the Philippines were also members of the Commission. The Commission's headquarters was in Washington. Its arm in Tokyo was called the Allied Council for Japan, which had the duty of "consulting with and advising the Supreme Commander in regard to the implementation of the terms of surrender, the occupation and control of Japan, and of directives supplementary thereto."

With the Cold War developing, however, the Far Eastern Commission was soon deadlocked on many matters, whereupon American policy prevailed through "interim" directives. General MacArthur regarded the Allied Council for Japan as of nuisance value only, and he treated it with such contempt as to irritate not only the Russian member, whom he intended to irritate, but even the representative of the United Kingdom, an Australian, W. Macmahon Ball, who was so incensed that he wrote a book about General MacArthur's high-handed methods. Thus, the organizational structure of the Far Eastern Commission and the Allied Council, taken together with American determination not to let them interfere seriously with the management of the occupation, meant that the occupation, though officially international under a supreme commander for the Allied Powers, was nevertheless an American show.

Under General MacArthur, as supreme commander, the occupation organization was divided into twelve sections, the most important of these being the government section, the economic and scientific section, civil information and education section, natural resources section, and international prosecution section. The activities of these branches will be discussed subsequently.

Overall policy objectives were provided by the wartime pronouncements at Cairo and at Potsdam, but the first specific policy directive issued to General MacArthur was drawn up by SWNCC, approved by President Truman, and issued as the United States' "Initial Postsurrender Policy for Japan" dated September 6, 1945. Considering the haste with which the document had to be drawn up and the differences of opinion involved, it is a remarkably clear and thorough set of instructions for the supreme commander, most of which step by step he carried out. Although subsequently it often appeared that MacArthur was making policy, one need only refer back to the document to see that through the "stage of democratization" at least, until 1948, he was following these orders. At any rate the general directive under which General MacArthur began the occupation included the following main points. The occupation was to insure that Japan would "not again become a menace to the United States or to the peace and security of the world." It was to bring about

> the eventual establishment of a peaceful and responsible government which will respect the rights of other states and will support the objectives of the United States as reflected in the ideals and principles of the charter of the United Nations. The United States desires that this government should conform as closely as may be to principles of democratic self-government but it is not the responsibility of the Allied Powers to impose upon Japan any form of government not supported by the freely expressed will of the people.

These were called the "ultimate" objectives. The following "means" were to be utilized to attain them: (a) Japan would be limited territorially to the four main islands, (b) Japan would be completely disarmed and demilitarized and the authority and influence of militarists and militarism would be totally eliminated from her political, economic, and social life, (c) the Japanese people would be encouraged to develop a desire for individual liberties and respect for fundamental human rights and they should also be encouraged to form democratic and representative organizations, (d) the Japanese people would be afforded an opportunity to develop themselves an economy which would permit the peacetime requirements of the population to be met.

The initial postsurrender policy document also spelled out in some detail certain areas in which the supreme commander would implement the above general policies. These included immediate disarmament and demilitarization, the meting out of stern justice to war criminals, the swift release of unjustly imprisoned persons, the reform of judicial, legal, and police systems to conform to the protection of individual liberties and civil rights. Furthermore the economic basis of Japanese military strength was to be "destroyed and not permitted to revive," and this would involve both reparations for damages done overseas and the limitation of the future size and character of Japan's industry. There was also to be encouragement of democratic organizations in labor, in industry, and in agriculture.

The supreme commander was "to exercise his authority through Japanese governmental machinery and agencies, including the emperor" to the extent that he could do so and still satisfactorily pursue occupation objectives. The Japanese government was to be permitted under SCAP's instructions to exercise "the normal powers of government" in "matters of domestic administration," though it would be "the right and duty of the Supreme Commander to require changes in governmental machinery or personnel or to act directly" if the actions of these did not meet his requirements.

These directives, which were put in final form in instructions sent to

General MacArthur in November, 1945, were not approved by the Far Eastern Commission until nearly two years later. However, it was under them that the occupation undertook its task of remaking Japan.

THE STAGE OF DEMOCRATIZATION, 1945–1948

With the exception of the Japanese Foreign Office, which was abolished, and the war and navy ministries which were reconstituted as demobilization agencies, SCAP left the Japanese government temporarily intact, and the various sectional subdivisions of the occupation authority were instructed to work with their counterparts in the Japanese government to effect the changes implied by the initial postsurrender policy document.

Demilitarization

Demobilization of the Japanese military was given a high priority and swiftly accomplished. Some four million Japanese under arms were mustered out within a few months and even those who were scattered through Pacific islands and Southeast Asia were soon repatriated to Japan. An exception was those Japanese who were taken prisoner by the Russians in Manchuria. These were held much longer, some of them not being repatriated until after the end of the occupation.

Related to the military demobilization was the purging of militaristic elements from government. SCAP's International Prosecution Section undertook the task of singling out those Japanese who had been guilty of "plotting aggression" before the war and of "crimes against humanity" during the conduct of the war and of bringing them to trial. Such leading militarists as ex-premier Tojo, General Dohihara, who had played such an important role in the conquest of Manchuria and north China, General Matsui, who had ordered or allowed the rape of Nanking, ex-foreign minister Matsuoka, and the ideologist of expansion, Okawa Shumei, were among those arrested. After indictments were prepared 28 major defendants were brought to trial and 25 were convicted; two, including Matsuoka, died during the course of the trial and only one, Okawa, was freed (Okawa was ruled mentally incompetent at the trial). Seven, including Tojo, were executed. The purging of militarists from government, however, went much deeper than these spectacular trials which, lasting nearly two years, tended by their very length to lose the sense of purpose for which they had been intended, although the mass of material presented at them is of inestimable value to historians and researchers into the course of modern Japanese expansion. But in addition to the purging by imprisonment or execution of those leaders convicted at the trials, thousands of Japanese who had belonged to organizations designated as militaristic or ultranationalistic were by virtue of their membership in those organizations deprived of the right to hold public office. Since a large number of key persons in the Japanese government had belonged to such organizations, this meant a very considerable turnover of government personnel. This turnover went on simultaneously

FIGURE 26.2. Tojo Hideki, former general, premier, and war minister of Japan, testifies in his own behalf during the trials of the International Military Tribunal for the Far East in Tokyo (1947).

with the application of pressure from SCAP Government Section toward the democratization of the political processes.

The Constitution

A key issue here was the matter of the constitution of Japan. By the old Meiji constitution of 1889 sovereignty rested entirely with the emperor. His ministers were above the representatives of the people in the Diet, the concept of transcendentalism never having been fully breached. Now, however, SCAP insisted that the Japanese draw up a new constitution which would place sovereignty squarely in the hands of the people. The SCAP-approved interim Japanese government, which was headed by the now elderly former foreign minister Shidehara, who had unsuccessfully opposed the militarists in 1931, was reluctant to assume this task. However, former premier Prince Konoe, who had changed colors so often, made known his availability to head a committee for revision of the constitution. SCAP vetoed this by listing Konoe as a war criminal suspect, and Konoe committed suicide in November 1945.

Then a committee headed by Dr. Matsumoto Joji undertook the task, but it could not bring itself to be so disrespectful to the throne as to change the location of sovereignty. General MacArthur became impatient and finally ordered SCAP Government Section to draw up a constitution which would be given to the Japanese as a satisfactory prototype for their adoption. Relieved at not being forced to go through with the onerous duty of demoting their emperor, the Japanese adopted the American draft as their own without changing a word, with peculiarly American expressions like "life, liberty, and the pursuit of happiness" being rendered dutifully into Japanese. Though there were many dire predictions about the future of a Japanese constitution that had been "first written in English," it is perhaps a significant testimony to its excellence that after the end of the occupation it remained the constitution of Japan, with Japanese public opinion becoming extremely averse to suggestions for changing it. Perhaps the Japanese people at large were more willing and anxious to have a truly democratic constitution than their government officials, even those moderate ones who were acceptable to occupation authorities, were willing to concede.

At any rate the new Japanese constitution, which was adopted in 1946 and promulgated in May 1947, is a truly remarkable document. It is probably a better expression of democracy than the American constitution.

The new constitution makes the emperor the "symbol" of the state, rather than its sovereign, a change which the emperor himself manifestly assisted by his public renunciation of his "divinity" in a New Year's message in January 1946, and by his timid yet increasingly effective efforts to show himself and members of his family to Japanese "citizens" (no longer subjects) in a "democratic" light.

The Diet, entirely elective, became the "highest organ of state power." The titled aristocracy was abolished except for immediate members of the royal family, and the House of Peers was reconstituted as an elected House of Councillors, inferior in legislative authority to the "lower" House of Representatives (it might delay, but could not block legislation enacted by the House of Representatives). The prime minister, selected by the Diet, was made clearly responsible to it, and must resign on a vote of no confidence. Freedom of religion, speech, and association, including the right of labor to organize, were guaranteed, and every adult Japanese, male and female, was given the right to vote, to change his residence or his occupation, to receive an equal education according to his ability, to choose his spouse, and to "life, liberty, and the pursuit of happiness." An independent judiciary was established and access to the courts guaranteed to all citizens. Local government was protected from the encroachment of national authority.

In addition, a unique clause, Article 9, provided a presumably final safeguard against a resurgence of militarism. This, the "no war" clause, renounced the right of the belligerency of the state and pledged that Japan in the future would not maintain military forces.

Other Reforms

While the new constitution was being drafted and put into effect to safeguard democracy for the future, numerous institutions of the old order were being reformed. The Civil Information and Education Section of SCAP was concerned with the educational structure and curriculum. As a result of its endeavors the power of the old Japanese Ministry of Education was sharply curtailed, local school boards were given authority over lower education, textbooks were revised, with their nationalistic teachings being expurgated. Some of the educational reforms, such as the institution of the American-style junior high school system, were more mechanical than meaningful, but Japanese educators, released from the bondage of thought control, speedily injected a new spirit into education. The Natural Resources Section looked to agrarian problems particularly, and remarkable progress was made in bringing about a deconcentration of agricultural landholdings, without outright confiscation. Tenants were encouraged to buy the lands they tilled at controlled prices, and thousands did. One area, however, was largely overlooked. Forest lands remained in the hands of a few, which later had serious consequences for home rebuilding programs, as the price of lumber soared.

Edwin Pauley, who headed a commission to investigate Japan's capacity for reparations payments in 1946, recommended the breakup of Japan's financial and industrial combines, the zaibatsu which, his report said, were as responsible for war as the militarists. SCAP's Economic and Scientific Section drew up an ambitious program of trustbusting. Many business leaders were "purged" (i.e. ousted from management positions), though it was often said that this merely saved them a trip to the office, for they continued to manage their financial empires from behind the scenes. However, corporation stock was required to be sold widely, and a large number of corporations were broken up with their component parts being set into competition with each other. Japanese businessmen resisted these measures, not overtly, but by simply biding their time on undertaking plant renewal and raising production levels. Unsure of whether a rebuilt Japanese industrial plant would be dismantled and shipped abroad for war reparations, they simply waited for the occupation to lose its vigor on this matter, which it eventually did.

More successful was the stimulation of labor organization, also under the auspices of the Economic and Scientific Section. Actually only an initial stimulus was needed, for Japanese labor organized with alacrity, and despite the cautious urgings of its American advisors had soon gone into politics and aligned itself with the political left. In 1947 a general strike was proclaimed, which General MacArthur banned as politically inspired and potentially injurious to the national welfare. However, labor had found its voice, which business in the future would have to take into account.

Japanese Politics

With the release of political prisoners and the encouragement of the formation of new political parties, very active Social Democratic, Socialist, and Communist parties emerged to challenge the old Seiyukai and Minseito which were speedily reformed as "Liberal" and "Progressive" parties. The latter, as they had been in the 1920's, were backed by business and financial interests and were very conservative in domestic affairs, though internationalist in their world outlook.

Although the strength of the new leftist-oriented parties, backed by the emerging labor movement and by many intellectuals, grew rapidly, the government remained in conservative hands. Shidehara continued as premier until SCAP ordered elections in April, 1946. In these the conservative parties with their superior organization and financial backing won over two-thirds of the Diet seats, and Yoshida Shigeru became the first elected postwar premier at the head of a "Liberal-Progressive" (conservative) coalition. Yoshida, who was a member of the "Liberal" party, had been known as a peace advocate during the war and had avoided membership in ultranationalist organizations. He assumed the premiership after the party chief, Hatoyama Ichiro, was declared by SCAP to be ineligible for public office because of past ultranationalist associations.

Yoshida reluctantly put through the vast array of reforms the occupation authorities demanded, but was forced out of office in May 1947 by a potent coalition of Social Democrats, Socialists, and dissident conservatives, and for ten months Katayama Tetsu, a right-wing Socialist (or Social Democrat) headed a coalition cabinet which promised sweeping economic reforms. However, Yoshida would return. Katayama's coalition quarrelled among themselves, business sat on its hands, and the economy careened into a worse condition than before. Katayama could take no really radical mea-

FIGURE 26.3. Yoshida Shigeru, postwar prime minister and architect of Japan's recovery in 1959.

sures to force cooperation of business; his government floundered and he resigned in March 1948.

THE STAGE OF RECOVERY, 1948–1952

By January 1948 SCAP believed that democratization had proceeded far enough, or perhaps too far, in Japan, and that economic recovery was the most pressing problem. Occupation authorities had become more worried about communists than about ultranationalists. They had had enough of labor demonstrations and strikes. They were acutely aware of the fact that despite the original disavowal of American responsibility for supporting the Japanese economy, American aid had had to be given to prevent economic chaos. In the face of Cold War developments they now wanted a strong, not a weak, Japan. Pauley's recommendation that Japanese industrial equipment be shipped abroad as reparations and that the zaibatsu be destroyed were therefore reconsidered and reversed. Though the decision was probably made earlier, the report of an investigatory commission headed by William H. Draper and Percy Johnstone and loaded with American businessmen, which visited Japan in the spring of 1948, verified the need for this. Significantly the number of Japanese companies marked for dissolution was suddenly reduced from 325 to 100. Japanese businessmen were quick to read the signs.

In October 1948, when Yoshida Shigeru was returned to the premiership with solid conservative backing, he had a much more congenial atmosphere than formerly in which to promote business revival and expansion. From this time until Yoshida left office in 1954 after five consecutive premierships, business was in control, and economic recovery proceeded. Austerity continued for several years, but Japanese industry began to produce, largely for export, and as Japan's international payments were brought more nearly into balance, the yen currency was stabilized and inflation gradually halted. Then the Korean War, which broke out in 1950, actually helped this process since many supplies for the U.N. armies in Korea were purchased in Japan, but the principal aid was the maintenance of liberal tariff policies vis-à-vis Japan by the United States. Thus a larger and larger volume of Japanese manufactures, as they were produced, could be sold in the United States.

End of the Occupation

With economic recovery on the way, and the presence of the American occupation authorities in Japan becoming a source of embarrassment to the Yoshida regime, negotiations for a peace treaty to end the occupation were undertaken by the United States. This was complicated by the fact that the other Allied powers who had been at war with Japan had not yet officially ended the state of hostilities, nor were some of them inclined to do so until suitable reparations had been received. Neither Communist nor Nationalist China, nor the Soviet Union, nor India, nor a number of smaller countries would agree to the treaty which John Foster Dulles negotiated with the Japanese, but the United States and a majority of the Pacific war adversaries of Japan signed at San Francisco on September 8, 1951. Japan accepted the territorial settlements as they had earlier been arranged, and agreed to negotiate reparations agreements with countries still demanding them, it being stated that she would pay through services rather than with her industrial equipment. On the same day a security treaty was signed with the United States which gave the United States the right to maintain land, sea, and air forces in Japan as a protection against possible communist aggression, and envisioned, despite Article 9 of the Constitution, that Japan would eventually contribute military forces to her own defense. The Occupation officially ended when these agreements went into effect on April 28, 1952.

RENEWAL OF CHINESE CIVIL WAR

The end of the Pacific war in September 1945 found Nationalist China in a state of exhaustion, corruption, and inefficiency. Serious inflation had set in, the Kuomintang party machinery was in the hands of its most reactionary element, and the government had lost the confidence of most Chinese intellectuals and liberals. The nationalist armies, though numerous, were poorly organized, in a state of low morale and, most important of all, could no longer elicit the support of the populace as they had been able to do in the early days of the revolution and again during the days of Japanese invasion.

Nevertheless, the official international position of the nationalist government was strong. President Roosevelt had made every effort to include China in the ranks of the great powers and to emphasize that China would be one of the Big Four in the Far East after the war. He had hoped that there would be a truly unified China by the end of the war but, with the removal of General Stilwell, he showed he had decided not to press the issue with Chiang while the Pacific war continued. The Truman administration continued this same hope for Chinese unity but likewise regarded Chiang and his nationalist government organization as the main pillar of postwar China. In addition, Chiang had obtained clear-cut Soviet recognition of his government in the Sino-Soviet Treaty of 1945, and, since the Manchurian-Mongolian concessions to Russia granted in that treaty would presumably depend on the cooperation of the nationalist government for fulfillment, he could have confidence that the Soviet recognition would continue, at least if he could assert nationalist hegemony. Finally, China was a member of the Security Council, the inner circle of the United Nations.

Perhaps these invitations to great power status helped to encourage Chiang to extend himself beyond logical limits. Though his forces were not even in a position to receive the Japanese surrender in many areas of China proper, American planes being required to airlift nationalist units to the main coastal cities, including Nanking, so that they could reoccupy them before communist or independent local guerrillas could take over,

Chiang's immediate objective was to reestablish exclusive nationalist hegemony over as wide an area as possible, including Manchuria. He refused to allow the Chinese communists to act as his agents in receiving the Japanese surrender in those parts of China which they controlled. This they bitterly resented, and soon there was a race in progress between communists and nationalists for control of former Japanese-occupied areas. During the fall of 1945 it became increasingly clear that unless some mediation were attempted China would soon be engulfed in civil war.

The Marshall Mission

In December 1945 President Truman designated General George C. Marshall, formerly United States Army chief of staff, to go to China as his personal representative to talk frankly with leaders of both the nationalist government and the Chinese communists and to try to obtain their agreement to bring about the unification of China by peaceful democratic methods as soon as possible. In a public statement made by President Truman just after Marshall's appointment, it was implied that an end of the civil strife in China might be a necessary precondition for the giving of the American aid that was so much needed for the reconstruction and rehabilitation of the country. It should be noted, however, that American aid through the United Nations Relief and Rehabilitation Administration (UNRRA) was already being poured into China and that the nationalist government had substantial American dollar credits on which to draw for various purposes, including military.

General Marshall began his negotiations in Chungking in early January, 1946, with General Chang Chun appointed by Chiang to represent the nationalist government and Chou En-lai speaking for the communists. Marshall's invitations to the conferences had been quickly accepted by both sides, and the negotiations started off well. The principal problems were taken up under three headings: first, cessation of hostilities (a truce); secondly, political matters; and thirdly, military reorganization. A cease-fire agreement was speedily concluded on January 9th and put into effect on January 13th. By this the various nationalist and communist armies were to hold their respective positions, with the exception that the nationalists were to be allowed to continue to bring units into Manchuria and to consolidate certain other positions in former Japanese-occupied areas in north and central China.

As to Manchuria it should be noted that after the Japanese surrender Russian forces had occupied that area and at this time were still in possession of the main cities and communication lines. The Russians had been rapidly dismantling the industries of Manchuria to take back to Russia as war "reparations" (or booty), and they were scheduled to leave in March, six months after the surrender, at which time the nationalists would presumably take over full control. The Russians were not at this stage trying to block the resumption of nationalist sovereignty in Manchuria, for Stalin, who had never thought highly of Mao and his band, apparently still did not take seriously the Chinese communists' chances for greatly enlarging their sphere of control.

To supervise the truce an executive headquarters consisting of three commissioners, one American, one nationalist, and one communist, was established at Peking to supervise a network of truce teams who went into the field. The news of the truce was widely circulated throughout north China by leaflets dropped from airplanes as well as by regular communications.

Political problems were taken up at a meeting of the long defunct Political Consultative Conference which convened the day after the cease-fire was agreed to, on January 10. Generalissimo Chiang took the initiative, as a result of agreements worked out in Marshall's mediation discussions, in calling this conference and to it he made a remarkably conciliatory speech, emphasizing that the time had come for the establishment of basic freedoms for the people, legalization of all political parties, the preparation for popular elections, and the release of political prisoners. The communist delegates, as well as delegates from middle-of-the-road parties, similarly gave evidence of conciliatory feelings, and the conference voted that a new constitution should be drawn up to be presented to a multiparty National Assembly, meeting in May 1946. Meanwhile a political liberalization program based on the draft constitution of 1936 would be put into effect. The Political Consultative Conference adjourned on January 31st.

After this negotiations were held between communist and nationalist representatives, with the assistance of General Marshall, to work out a "military reorganization agreement." Such an agreement was signed on February 25, 1946, and it called for the gradual integration of communist and nationalist armies into a nonpolitical military force, considerably reduced in size, as a standing army for the protection of the country. Some detailed plans were outlined for the process and ratios by which this integration was to be made. Hence on all three problems great progress had seemingly been made by March 1, 1946.

Despite or perhaps because of these agreements there was great tension in many quarters. Right-wing elements of the Kuomintang were most unhappy and accused the negotiators of giving in far too much to the communists. From communist quarters also came accusations, particularly that the United States was continuing aid to the nationalists, thus implying that Marshall's mediation was not neutral. However, General Marshall felt that sufficient progress had been made to permit his return to Washington to report partial success and to confer on the matter of financial aid to China. He was absent from China from March 25 until April 18, during which time there was a rapid deterioration of the situation in China. Chiang laid plans to return the government to Nanking in May but decided that the meeting of the National Assembly must be postponed until the fall, and a crisis developed in Manchuria, as the Russian forces withdrew. The Chinese communists, accusing Chiang of deceit and delay on the political agreements, refused to allow the nationalists to take over the city of Ch'angch'un in central Manchuria, and the truce agreements began to break down at several other points as well.

By the time Marshall returned so much damage had been done that he was never able to make the truce effective again, and with the truce ineffective the longer-range political and military agreements were not invoked. Though the nationalists took Ch'angch'un and Kalgan, which had also become a bone of contention, by military force, the effect of these victories was to harden the communist resistance to further proposals to negotiate, and by the late fall of 1946 civil war was again raging. On November 15 Chiang convened the National Assembly without the communists and in a setting dominated by the Kuomintang. Though the constitutional document the Assembly drew up was fairly liberal in tone, and promised the end of the period of Kuomintang party tutelage, it gave wide "emergency powers" to the president, that is to Chiang. The communists could come and participate in the new government if they wished, but it was clear that the Kuomintang, now increasingly self-confident, would dominate it. The communists not only refused to participate but said that the National Assembly as then constituted would have to be dissolved and the nationalist forces would have to be pulled back to their positions of the preceding January before they would negotiate further.

Seeing no hope for further mediation, General Marshall requested his own recall, and he returned to Washington to report to President Truman and the American people in January 1947 that "extremist elements on both sides" had frustrated his efforts at peaceful settlement.

The Communist Victory

For a time the fortunes of war seemed to favor the nationalists. Their forces even captured Yenan. However, the communists were well organized, especially for countryside fighting, and the loss of any city or town did not seem to bother them. Their arsenal of weapons had been increased considerably by the acquisition of Japanese arms, both taken by themselves and turned over to them by the Russians as the latter evacuated Manchuria. In addition they began to receive some direct aid from Russia, and nationalist supplies began to fall into their hands.

The last process was symbolic of a breakdown in the whole fabric of nationalist China. The government, with some of its officials living well in Nanking and Shanghai, could produce no program of reform to capture the imagination and the hopes of the Chinese people. UNRRA goods went into black market channels, as did direct United States aid, which was given in increasing amounts despite the failure of Marshall's mediation. Inflation became rampant during 1947 when the CNC (Chinese National Currency) depreciated to near worthlessness. Government officials and leading businessmen with huge fortunes in foreign currencies kept them secure in foreign banks.

In the summer of 1947 General Albert Wedemeyer, an earnest supporter of the nationalists, who had warned Chiang for his own good not to divide his troops by occupying Manchuria, went to China on a fact-finding mission. The report he made was very gloomy and, since it contained a recommendation presumed to be obnoxious to Chiang, namely, that Manchuria might best be placed under a U.N. trusteeship, it was not made public.

By 1948 the military tide had turned in favor of the communists.

DIVERGENCE AND DIVISION IN EAST ASIA

FIGURE 26.4. Chinese communist leaders at Yenan during the Chinese Civil War. From left to right, Chou En-lai, in charge of foreign affairs, Chu Teh, creator of the Red army, and Mao Tse-tung, the master of the Chinese revolution.

Whole units of the nationalist army in north China and Manchuria began to surrender to or make deals with them. Peiping was taken in January 1949, with the populace at large generally accepting the communist propaganda that this was a "liberation," not a conquest. After that the communist conquest of the rest of China was so rapid as to suggest that the people of China had concluded, as in the declining days of dynasties of old, that the "Mandate of Heaven" had been lost by the nationalists and the time had come to cast one's lot with the new order. Shanghai and Nanking were taken in the spring of 1949, and the nationalist government fled to Formosa. In September the communists proclaimed a new "People's Republic of China" at Peiping, renamed Peking to symbolize its being the capital of China again.

THE PEOPLE'S REPUBLIC ESTABLISHED

Though the Chinese communist leaders had repeatedly voiced their dedication to Marxist-Leninist principles and the ultimate creation of a communist society in China, their road to power had been eminently practical and pragmatic. The "border government" which they had erected in north

China during the war with Japan had been much more concerned with practical agrarian problems than with communist theory, which accounts in large measure for its success and for the popularity it won for the communist cause.

In establishing the new government in Peking Mao Tse-tung and his comrades again moved carefully and pragmatically. They established a new "People's Consultative Conference," to which noncommunists, excluding "reactionary" elements, were invited. The official line which the Conference took was that the new China, though led by the communist party, was to be a joint effort, not only of workers and peasants, but also of small businessmen and even "capitalists," if they proved patriotic. An organic law and a so-called Common Program for the new government were drawn up by the PCC. According to the organic law a National People's Congress would become "the supreme organ of the state power." However, this would not be elected until 1954 and in the meanwhile a Central People's Government Council of fifty-six members, chaired by Mao Tse-tung, would run the government, subject to the approval of the People's Consultative Conference. The location of key chairmanships, army control, and other important functions in the hands of communist party members, especially of Mao's original Kiangsi group, indicated that the communists would actually run the government under a probably temporary show of coalition.

Programs of economic recovery and social reform were immediately announced and put into effect. These proceeded effectively and not too ruthlessly at first. Remarkable progress was made in the control of inflation, through the establishment of a national budget, in the centralization of the taxation system, and in price control policies. In agriculture, an agrarian reform act continued the general policies used with success in the border regime earlier. However, beginning in 1951 pressures were applied with increasing harshness. A system of public trials was instituted whereby those persons who were deemed "reactionary" were hounded into public confessions and sentenced to execution, prison, or forced labor. This technique was particularly applied to former landlords among whose tenants many could be brought forth to level accusations. Also a so-called "Five Anti-Movement" was launched against businessmen who were accused of being "traitors" to the people for overcharging, cheating, and tax evasion. Again sufficient numbers were executed or imprisoned to produce a wave of fear in the business community and bring compliance with the new regulations of the new regime, which taxed business very heavily. Another campaign called the "Three Anti-Movement" sought out "traitors" and "corruptionists" in public office and eliminated a great many officials who had temporarily been used as carryovers from the old regime.

While these campaigns of fear were designed to enforce compliance with official edicts, a propaganda campaign was undertaken to promote positively the goals of the regime. The keynote here was re-education and re-thinking, or "brainwashing," as it came to be called in the Western world. Communist indoctrination teams taught the techniques of correcting "erroneous attitudes" to every kind of group from sophisticated intellectuals and professional people to farmers and factory workers. These rethinking sessions often took the form of public confessionals where individuals would frankly admit their past "antisocial attitudes" and promise to go forth with the interests of "the people" at heart. The process of re-education was no doubt assisted by the fact that the Korean War was raging at this time, and the Chinese communist regime used the "threat of American aggression" as a major argument for reconsidering past reliance on "imperialists" and their "running dogs" among the "gentry" and "capitalists" of China. No one wanted to appear in these unsavory classifications and the stampede to communist ideology was very rapid.

By 1952 communist control was secure. Opponents of the regime had been killed or silenced; many converts had been won, who could now be counted on to fill administrative positions with zeal; and the mass of the Chinese people waited, half in hope and half in fear, to see what the new era would bring. An official blueprint, the "First Five-Year Plan," was announced in December 1952.

NATIONALISTS ON FORMOSA

Prior to the escape of the Chinese nationalist government to Formosa in 1949, the nationalists had been involved in Formosan affairs for four years. According to the wartime Cairo Conference decisions Japan was to be required to return the island of Formosa to China, and Chiang Kai-shek had assigned Chinese nationalist administrators to it in 1945. When Chinese nationalist troops arrived to receive the surrender of the Japanese and the administrators installed themselves in the government at Taipei, the Formosans at first greeted them as liberators. However, there were many temptations for the mainlanders on Formosa. Its economy was actually considerably richer than that of the mainland, and despite the fact that the Japanese had exploited the island, the standard of living of the native Formosan was considerably higher than that of the Chinese mainlander.

The Chinese administrators, under a former warlord named Chen Yi, were soon acting like a gang of carpetbaggers who found Formosa to be a marvelously rich plum for exploitation. They treated the Formosans as a conquered people and their leaders as Japanese collaborators, and they used the excuse of the islanders' "Japanese-ness" to justify the seizure of all valuable properties on the island and to organize lucrative government monopolies of key products. At the same time they neglected essential services as too expensive to keep up. For example, public health was neglected while the officials in charge profiteered in drugs and medical equipment, with the result that cholera, bubonic plague, and smallpox, long since wiped out by the Japanese, reappeared. UNRRA medical teams intervened and prevented public health chaos, though smallpox was not brought under control until 1950.

The Formosans, having tried in vain to receive redress or even hearings for their grievances, finally resorted to demonstrations in February and March of 1947. When these were put down brutally by the nationalist forces present, a full-scale revolt broke out. Troops hastily summoned from the mainland suppressed it with great severity, but the situation had become so scandalous that Chiang Kai-shek removed Chen Yi as governor and promised an improvement in the administration.

The situation was but little improved and tensions between mainlanders and native Formosans were still running high when in 1949 the nationalist government, after the defeat on the mainland, was moved to Formosa. With it came thousands more mainlanders, both military and civilian, seeking refuge from the communists. About one-third of the membership of the National Assembly, representing the various provinces of China, came, as well as most of the leading members of the Kuomintang. The government in Formosa now became two governments, a national government of which Chiang Kai-shek was the president and in which all of the provinces of China were represented by mainlanders except the province of Formosa, and the Formosan provincial administration which had been established previously and which was also dominated by mainlanders. Formosa's seven million native inhabitants, with practically no part in the government, were extremely restive, and, as of the beginning of 1950, it was a moot point whether the nationalist government would survive at all.

Nevertheless, the administration improved somewhat. Chiang and his Kuomintang colleagues had suffered a terrible defeat and they now were determined to rebuild for eventual reconquest of the mainland. Chiang did not want Formosa to become a hotbed of communist intrigue and, while maintaining the strictest security regulations and government controls, he did institute a program of economic and political reform designed to obtain at least a modicum of support from the Formosans. K. C. Wu, the American-educated former mayor of Shanghai, was appointed governor of Formosa in December 1949, and he introduced measures that promised both economic improvement and greater Formosan political participation at the provincial level.

During the crucial winter of 1949–1950, while in the United States people were arguing China policy fiercely, with no clearcut decision yet reached, American goods were rushed to Formosa in sufficient quantity to stave off drastic inflation and general chaos. No commitment to further military aid was given, however, and it was only the outbreak of the Korean War in June 1950 which brought American commitments to Formosa's defense. On June 27, two days after the North Korean attack on South Korea, President Truman announced that he had ordered the United States Seventh Fleet to prevent any Chinese communist attack on Formosa. By 1952 United States economic and military aid to Formosa was flowing rapidly, and there were signs of excellent economic progress. This was particularly true in agriculture, where a Sino-American Joint Commission on Rural Reconstruction brought about irrigation, seed and fertilizer improvements, and a rent ceiling of 37.5 per cent of the crop yield. Also farmers were encouraged to purchase public land, on which 37.5 per cent of the yield became the maximum payment figure per year, including taxes. Rice production reached a record level in 1951. Electric power, road building, and other developmental programs also proceeded. But politics remained tightly controlled by Chiang.

THE QUESTION OF RECOGNITION

With the establishment of their People's Republic at Peking in September, 1949, the Chinese communists for the first time laid claim to being the government of China. Previous to this they had officially sought only participation in the nationalist government, but now they claimed they had replaced it entirely. In fact in their Common Program they stated that they would establish diplomatic relations only with those governments who would "sever relations with the Kuomintang reactionaries." The nationalists, on the other hand, though their area of control was limited to Formosa, the Pescadores, and a few offshore islands, still claimed to be the legitimate government of all China. Foreign governments therefore could recognize one or the other, but presumably not both. The question was complicated by the fact that China held a permanent seat on the Security Council of the United Nations, and the question whether a nationalist or communist delegate would occupy it was also at issue.

Soviet Russia recognized the new Peking government immediately, followed by Czechoslovakia, Poland, Hungary, and other communist states, and in the fall of 1949 the Soviets began an active campaign in the United Nations to turn over to Peking the China seat on the Security Council. Among noncommunist nations India, Burma, and Pakistan speedily recognized Peking and on January 5, 1950, in a dramatic move, Great Britain recognized the People's Republic. British emphasis on the de facto situation in China, together with considerations of the sensibilities of Asian Commonwealth members, worry about the status of Hong Kong, and hope for normal trade with the new China help to explain the British action. By June 1950 six other Western European nations, Sweden, Norway, Finland, Switzerland, the Netherlands, and Denmark, had recognized the Peking government.

However, the United States adopted a waiting policy, and as the months went by moved further away from any consideration of recognition. In October 1949 Angus Ward, American consul at Mukden, and four associates were arrested by the communists on charges of "beating a Chinese manservant," convicted by a "people's court," and ordered deported from China. This and other arrests and detentions involving American missionaries and other civilians, as well as seizures of American property and denunciations of the United States, prompted the withdrawal of all American diplomatic and consular officials from the mainland in January 1950. Meanwhile at the U.N. the United States countered Russia's moves to have Peking's representatives seated there, and after the United States had mustered enough votes to defer action (which procedure was to be repeated year after year), the Soviet delegate in late January 1950 began to boycott meetings of the Security Council in protest against the continued presence of the Chinese Nationalist representative there.

On February 14, 1950 Peking and Moscow signed a new Sino-Soviet Treaty, which replaced the one of August 1945. It promised friendship, alliance (against "any resumption of aggression by Japan or any state allied with her"), and mutual assistance (i.e., Russian technical and economic aid). Russia promised to turn back management of the Manchurian railroads and Port Arthur to the Chinese by 1952. The railroads were returned on schedule, but the naval base remained in Russian hands until after the Korean War.

The Korean War impinged on many matters. It ended the rash of recognitions of the Chinese People's Republic by noncommunist nations, fixed the separation of Formosa from the China mainland, put off far into the future any settlement that might allow easy contact among East Asians without reference to Cold War issues, and it dramatically sharpened issues in the Far East. However, before taking up that episode a final word on the recognition question as it related to Japan and her relations with China remains to be said.

In 1951, when the treaty to end the Japanese occupation was being negotiated, the question of the status of Formosa was involved. In the Cairo declaration Britain and the United States had promised to return Formosa to the "Republic of China," but now Britain recognized the Peking government, while the United States continued to recognize the nationalist government. Difficulty was avoided by having Japan in the Treaty of San Francisco merely relinquish her past sovereignty over Formosa and the Pescadores, without saying who should have it. Neither nationalist nor communist China signed the treaty. However, in January 1952, Premier Yoshida announced publicly that the Japanese government favored the nationalist regime, and on April 28, the day the San Francisco Treaty went into effect and Japan regained her independence, her representatives signed a bilateral treaty with nationalist China, by which the "state of hostilities" was ended, and diplomatic and trade relations were established.

The period from 1945 to 1952 brought many surprises. The occupation of Japan proved to be surprisingly easy and congenial, both from the American and the Japanese points of view. Former enemies became fast friends and began to wonder how they could have thought so ill of each other. Japanese who had been a part of the war machine of the 1930's became active practitioners of democracy. The "divine" emperor became a constitutional monarch. And after a slow start, Japan's economy recovered to a remarkable degree.

On the other hand, China, whose worst problem had presumably been eliminated with the defeat of Japan, became a tangle of conflicts and problems. The nationalist government proved its ineptness on a scale so vast that even its best friends were appalled, while the Chinese communists succeeded in giving their bid for power the aura of a "liberation" movement. Once in power they began, slowly at first, to change the whole political, social, and economic fabric of "unchangeable" China, as well as its international orientation.

During these years Japan and China went separate ways, at first because of China's preoccupation with civil war and later because of rising hostility between the United States, as guardian of occupied Japan, and Soviet Russia, as sponsor of the Chinese People's Republic. The Korean War brought this hostility to a climax and hardened the lines of division.

THE DIVISION OF KOREA

When Russian and American troops entered Korea in September 1945 to liberate that country from Japanese rule, there were two basic agreements on Korea. First, from the Cairo Conference had come the promise that Korea would "in due course be free and independent," a promise which had been subscribed to by the Russians at Potsdam. Secondly, at Yalta the decision had been made to divide the responsibility for ousting the Japanese between the United States and Russia, and at Potsdam the 38th parallel had been set as the line south of which American troops would enter to disarm the Japanese and north of which the Russians would do so. What kind of government would be established in Korea was not decided. However, in the background rival regimes were already forming.

To understand the formulation of these we must observe certain events that involved Korea at the end of World War I. One of the side effects of the Siberian intervention in 1918 was the enlistment of numerous Koreans in the Soviet cause. These were Koreans who had fled across the border of their country into Manchuria or Siberia to escape the oppression of Japanese colonial rule, and, when the Japanese intervention forces arrived in Siberia and northern Manchuria, they were, needless to say, anti-Japanese. Opposed to any extension of Japanese rule, which they bitterly detested in their homeland, they worked as anti-Japanese agents and in so doing became intimately associated with Russian communist groups also opposing the Japanese. This association ripened into a hard-core Korean communist element.

Korean Politics

Also in 1918 and 1919 Korean nationalists, inspired by Wilson's famous Fourteen Points and the principle of national self-determination he voiced at the Paris Peace Conference, began an active campaign to bring an end to Japanese rule of their country. Korean political exiles living in the United States and other Western countries sought a hearing at Paris, and, though they failed, great excitement and anticipation swept through Korea. In February 1919, rather opportunely, the old abdicated king, Kojong, died and thousands of Koreans assembled in Seoul in early March to celebrate his funeral. To the assembled throng a group of distinguished Koreans issued a proclamation of Korean independence. Mass demonstrations, peaceful but insistent, followed. Thoroughly alarmed, the Japanese cracked down ruthlessly. Thousands were imprisoned and hundreds were killed.

Nevertheless Korean exiles everywhere were exhilarated by the show of courage in their homeland, and during the summer of 1919, in the French concession at Shanghai, representatives of various Korean groups came together, both communist and noncommunist, to form a Korean provisional government, with a communist, Yi Tong-hwi, named premier. Thereafter numerous arguments and splits occurred, with the result that by 1924 the communist element was entirely eliminated and had returned to Siberia.

There the communists split into two groups, one with its headquarters at Irkutsk and the other at Chita. Little is known of these groups during the intervening years to 1945, but it is clear that by that time they had been welded into a Soviet-sponsored Korean communist party which had established some underground contacts inside Korea. A Korean communist named Kim Il-sung, who worked against the Japanese in Manchuria during the 1930's, had become the most important figure in the movement by 1945.

Meanwhile the Shanghai provisional government proceeded without the communists. It, too, was ridden by factionalism, with Syngman Rhee, American-educated and with his headquarters in Hawaii or Washington, leading one, the "American" faction, and Kim Koo, who went to Chungking with the Chinese nationalists in the late 1930's, leading a "China" faction. The two groups maintained a show of unity during the Pacific war, with Rhee as the most prominent figure in American eyes, although Kim Koo claimed to be the president.

Korea at the Time of Japan's Surrender

When the Russians entered North Korea they brought with them Kim Il-sung and a large group of other well-trained Korean communists who speedily became the nucleus of a Soviet-sponsored regime in North Korea. Syngman Rhee was brought to South Korea by plane from Washington. Other members of the Korean provisional government came in as rapidly as they could arrange transportation from China. Rhee, even though he was not the president of the Korean provisional government, because of his Washington connections and his fluent English was soon the leader of the group and its spokesman in discussions with the American occupying forces which, while not at first giving outright support to Rhee's group, tended more and more to favor it.

Another possibility was the formation of a government by resident Koreans and, in fact, a former political prisoner of the Japanese, Lyuh Woon-Hyung, succeeded in doing so, at Seoul, before American forces under Lt. General John R. Hodge arrived on September 8. Though Lyuh's government was functioning in both north and south Korea, Hodge refused to deal with it except as a political party and after the arrival of Rhee from Washington a month later, Lyuh's group gradually lost ground in the competition for leadership in South Korea. Rhee became the head of an interim government for South Korea in December 1946. Lyuh was assassinated in Seoul in July 1947.

Meanwhile, before the final polarization of Korea into two zones, various efforts were made to unify the country. At the Moscow Conference in December 1945 Secretary of State Byrnes and Foreign Minister Molotov agreed that Korea should be unified under a United Nations trusteeship. However, Rhee's party in South Korea took a very strong antitrusteeship stand and denounced any idea of rapprochement with the north. The Russians then insisted that only those groups in Korea which would accept the idea of trusteeship should be allowed to participate in the government. This was rejected by the United States, which, though embarrassed by

Rhee's opposition to the trusteeship idea, wanted some right-wing pressure to counteract the communists. Rhee won a great deal of popularity by his vehement antitrusteeship stand, which was misunderstood by many Koreans to mean a continuation of something like Japanese colonial rule.

The Division of Korea

In September 1947, all efforts at compromise having failed, the Russians, who had built up a strong North Korean army, proposed that all foreign troops leave Korea and announced that Russian troops would withdraw. The United States, dissatisfied with the military preparedness of South Korea, refused to accept this and proposed instead turning over the whole question to the United Nations. A commission of nine U.N. members was appointed to supervise Korean elections but this included only one Soviet-bloc member and the Russians announced their intention of boycotting the commission. In November 1947 the United Nations, over Russian opposition, voted to dispatch members of the commission to Seoul to arrange elections throughout Korea. When the commission arrived in Korea in January 1948, it found that the Russians would not allow them to enter the north. Nevertheless, they went about organizing elections which were held in May, but only in South Korea. Syngman Rhee was overwhelmingly elected to a term of four years as president. Since Rhee had already been in office at the head of the interim government his election was not unexpected. The new government was called the Republic of Korea and seats in the assembly were kept open for those North Koreans who might one day participate. Meanwhile in North Korea the communists also organized a permanent government. This was proclaimed in September as the Democratic People's Republic of Korea and it too considered itself officially the government of the entire peninsula. South Koreans were invited to come to Pyongyang, the North Korean capital, to participate. Russian troops left North Korea in December 1948 and American forces, after hurriedly organizing South Korean defense forces, left in June the following year.

Between 1948 and 1950 the rival Korean regimes eyed each other across the 38th parallel. There were many border incidents and persons suspected of being leftists in South Korea were jailed, while those suspected of being rightists in the north were no longer heard of. Suddenly, on June 25, 1950, North Korean forces launched a general attack on South Korea. The Russians, who had trained the North Korean army and supplied it with guns, tanks, and munitions of all sorts, apparently also gave the order for the North Korean attack on June 25th, though curiously they played their own role badly. For, when the United Nations Security Council met in session later that day to consider the new threat to the peace of the world, the Soviet representative was absent. This was because the Soviet Union had been boycotting the Security Council since January to protest the fact that the Peking communist government had not yet been awarded the Security Council seat being held by the nationalists. The absence of the Soviet delegate gave the Council an opportunity to take action, which a Soviet veto would have blocked. In response to an American proposal, the Security Council designated the "armed invasion of the Republic of Korea" as a breach of the peace and called upon the North Koreans to cease hostilities and withdraw their armed forces to the 38th parallel. Member nations were urged to give "every assistance" to the United Nations in bringing about this result. Three days later, as it became apparent that the North Koreans were going to conquer South Korea, President Truman ordered American forces into action and urged other U.N. members to provide forces for an international army. General MacArthur, as the supreme commander for the Allied Powers in Japan, was the logical choice as commander of this U.N. army in Korea. Although during the next three years of war the United States provided the vast majority of the troops and almost all of the equipment involved, the fact that fifteen other U.N. member nations sent token forces and participated in various ways was very important, for it made this Korean War something more than merely a great power struggle between Soviet Russia and the United States. It emphasized that the principle of collective security was being applied against aggressive military action, and U.N. involvement in the truce negotiations helped break deadlocks, factors unfortunately absent in the Indochina conflict.

WAR AND TRUCE IN KOREA

Course of the War

During the summer months of 1950 victory after victory went to the communists, and the South Koreans and the U.N. forces supporting them were almost ousted from the peninsula, holding at one point only a small perimeter around Pusan. However, on September 15, 1950, a masterful landing behind the communist lines at Inchon was effected by American amphibious units and with the communists now under attack on the rear, the U.N. forces broke through the Pusan perimeter. Not only did the communist offensive collapse entirely, but their forces were soon in pell-mell retreat, being forced back across the 38th parallel in early October. General MacArthur demanded the unconditional surrender of the North Korean communist regime. At the United Nations the Security Council was now deadlocked because Russia had returned with her veto, but a decision was needed on whether, by reaching the 38th parallel, the U.N. forces had carried out the original resolution. The General Assembly debated this question and on October 7, 1950, adopted a resolution setting the goals of the United Nations's action as "stability throughout Korea" and the "establishment of a unified, independent, and democratic government in the sovereign state of Korea."

While this did not specifically authorize the crossing of the 38th parallel, it certainly implied it and General MacArthur, determined to pursue the war to a successful conclusion, sent advanced units far north into the region of the Yalu river in late October and early November. However, at this point, Chinese "volunteers" began to appear among the North Korean forces still resisting south of the Yalu river. Also Russian warplanes were increasingly in evidence. By December the tide of the war was again turning and, as thousands of Chinese troops entered the fray, United Nations forces were pushed back beyond the 38th parallel and Seoul was taken by the communists for a second time in January 1951. However, the United Nations forces held the line at about the 37th parallel and a stalemate ensued.

Now among United Nations members there were recriminations from all sides. General MacArthur, saying that the presence of the Chinese "volunteers" made this a "new war," demanded that he be authorized to attack communist air bases in Manchuria, feeling that no Manchurian "sanctuary" of communist power could be permitted. More cautious voices pointed to the danger of broadening the Korean War into a world conflagration, and pointed out that if the communists enjoyed a "sanctuary" in Manchuria, so did the United Nations forces enjoy one in Japan where Soviet planes had so far not attacked American air bases. India was especially critical of MacArthur's desire to push the war further and sought to bring about a compromise. However, the United States pushed a proposal in the Assembly of the United Nations to label Communist China an aggressor nation. This proposal was passed, but it was significant that most of the Arab-Asian nations, led by India, abstained. Meanwhile, in bitter fighting the United Nations forces gradually pushed back to the 38th parallel at some points and once again the question of whether to cross it came up. President Truman now instructed MacArthur that he might cross the 38th parallel for purposes of "security of his forces" but that any large movement into North Korea involved political considerations which would have to be decided in Washington and at the U.N.

Soon thereafter it became apparent that MacArthur and his superiors in Washington were at odds. MacArthur tried to take his case to the American public through an open letter to House Speaker Joseph Martin in which he advocated the employment of nationalist Chinese forces from Formosa to invade the Chinese mainland and a general broadening of the scope of the war. At this, President Truman on April 11th relieved MacArthur of all his commands and ordered him to return to the United States. He was replaced by General Matthew Ridgway, who now also became commander-in-chief of the occupation in Japan for its last phase. Meanwhile the British and Indian representatives at Peking were taking soundings on the possibility of truce talks and behind the scenes at the U.N. there were discussions between the Russians and some members of the Arab-Asian bloc.

Korean Truce

Late in June, Jacob Malik, the Russian delegate to the United Nations, said that he thought a truce could be arranged. The U.N. command immediately followed this up by offering to negotiate on the field in Korea. Truce talks began on July 10, 1951, but they had a thorny path. Begun at Kaesong on the 38th parallel, they were soon deadlocked and suspended. Late in October they were resumed after the site had been moved a few miles to Panmunjom. There, despite violent recriminations, threats, and

FIGURE 26.5. American marines in Korea, 1951.

walkouts, they continued for 21 months more. Meanwhile, the war went on, with no major changes in the battle line but with heavy casualties on both sides. The first major issue concerned the location of the future truce line. The communists demanded that it be the 38th parallel but the U.N., whose forces were in most sectors now north of the parallel already, held that it was not defensible and the "line of [military] contact" should mark the division. Finally the communists accepted this, but drawing the "line of contact" was a very bitterly contested task. The biggest problem of all concerned the exchange of prisoners. The U.N. held far more prisoners from the communist side than the communists had from the U.N. side, and the U.N. command had learned by interviews that many of the prisoners it held did not wish to be repatriated to life under communism. It therefore insisted on the principle of voluntary repatriation. At first the communists refused absolutely to consider this, but finally, after a preliminary exchange of sick and wounded prisoners had been made, a compromise Indian proposal was accepted whereby a neutral nations repatriation commission would interview all prisoners who did not immediately exercise their right to be repatriated and discover whether or not such repatriation was desired. Arguments could be presented by communist or U.N. representatives in the presence of the commission. After that the prisoners could choose whether to accept repatriation, remain with their captors, or go to a neutral country.

President Rhee, who wanted no armistice at all, but hoped that the war would continue until control of North Korea had been secured, at first refused to accept this arrangement, and at a crucial point in the negotiations opened prisoner stockades in South Korea to allow some 25,000 prisoners to escape. The U.N. command assured the communists that this had been done without their authority and that they would henceforth undertake to hold Rhee to the armistice terms; at the same time the United States gave Rhee assurances of military and economic support for post-armistice protection and rebuilding of South Korea. Grudgingly Rhee gave in, and finally on July 27, 1953, after more than two years of negotiation, the armistice was signed at Panmunjom. Korea remained divided, not at the 38th parallel, but along a zigzag line near there, the finally determined "contact of forces" line.

After the armistice a "Big Switch" of prisoners who wished to be repatriated was swiftly accomplished, with some 48,000 being returned by the U.N. command to the communists and 11,000 by the communists to the U.N. Then followed 120 days of tense interviewing of prisoners who had refused repatriation. Nearly 23,000 men of the communist army had signified their desire not to be repatriated, and despite ardent communist persuadings nearly all of them remained adamant, most of the Koreans choosing to remain in South Korea and the Chinese to go to Nationalist China. A few went to neutral countries. This was a tremendous blow to communist prestige, but the communists accomplished some face-saving when about 350 U.N. troops, including 20 Americans, chose to remain with them.

The world breathed a little easier after the Korean truce. Although no one was satisfied with the result, at least full-scale atomic war had been avoided. No political settlements had been accomplished at the truce talks. The Korean question was put on the agenda of the Geneva Conference which opened in April 1954. However, by that time the Indochina problem had surpassed the Korean one in urgency and the Korean political issues were left unsolved while the conference worked out the Indochina truce (see Chapter 25).

EAST ASIA IN THE LATER 1950's

Although during the Korean War Soviet pilots in Soviet planes had fought aerial battles with American pilots in American planes and it had seemed that Soviet Russia and the United States were on the brink of war, after the Panmunjom armistice, tensions in East Asia relaxed considerably and the accent returned to internal development in the two Koreas, Japan, and China, both the People's Republic and Taiwan.

North Korea

North Korea inherited a sizable industrial plant from the era of Japanese control, larger than that of South Korea, which remained almost exclusively agricultural. Though much of this plant was destroyed during the Korean War, it was largely rehabilitated with Russian assistance. Hydroelectric power and mining (especially coal) are the basis of it. Although this industrial production has permitted the maintenance of a large mechanized military establishment, the construction of buildings, the repair of cities, and the rehabilitation of the transportation system, it has probably produced only minimum supplies of consumers' goods. In 1950 there were only 15,000 cotton and rayon spindles in North Korea, as compared with 250,000 in South Korea, and with the stress on heavy industry shortages of clothing and other consumers' goods were only slowly overcome.

Also agricultural production presented a great problem. The amount of arable land is insufficient for population needs. When the Soviet forces took over in 1945 they redistributed the holdings of "landlords" and Japanese "collaborators" to small farmers, but since 1953 the accent has been on collectivization. Improved use of fertilizers and larger-scale collectivized farming methods have increased production, though not enough for comfortable living. Fishing was stressed, but at the same time several thousand Korean fishermen went into Soviet fishing enterprises in Sakhalin and Kamchatka, which meant minimum supplies of sea products available to Koreans. Hence living standards remained low. However, farms and factories were soon operating at full capacity. There developed a labor shortage in North Korea, as evidenced by the fact that in 1958–1959 the regime went all out in offering inducements to Koreans living in Japan, who were to be repatriated, to come to the north instead of to the south. It was disquieting to South Korea and its friends that the great majority of the repatriates, some 70,000, chose the north.

The government is characterized by the vesting of theoretical power in an "elected" Supreme People's Assembly, but of actual power in its executive apparatus. Similarly there is a "Democratic Front" comprising a number of political parties, from which the so-called North Korean Workers' party (which is the name given to the communist party in North Korea) provided the personnel for important government positions. It is, of course, run from the top. This party was built up rapidly to a membership of some 700,000 before the outbreak of war in 1950. After that, with various membership screenings and purges to guarantee ideological solidarity, its membership was built up more slowly, reaching about 1,300,000 in 1961.

Kim Il-sung, the premier, remained the leading figure. A serious challenge to his leadership developed after the death of Stalin in 1953 and came to a head in 1956. At that time a group of Yenan, China-trained Korean communists, headed by one Kim Tu-bong, tried to discredit him on various charges, including insufficient attention to the people's needs and indulgence in "the cult of personality." However, Kim Il-sung, who had journeyed to Moscow and successfully identified himself with Khrushchev's leadership, returned to oust them and emerge stronger than ever.

For a time after that there was little or no Chinese influence in the government. Kim's links led directly to Moscow and it was significant that a Soviet citizen Nam Il, the truce negotiator, remained as foreign minister. However, Kim did not defer completely to Moscow, and by 1960 he was emphasizing that while it was necessary to follow Moscow's leadership as head of a "family" of communist states, some differences and rivalries were natural. Korea had problems of its own, he indicated, and avoiding both "revisionism and dogmatism" it should solve them. This prepared the way for a more studied "neutralism" as ideological disputes began to impair relations between Moscow and Peking.

Meanwhile after three years' preparation, the first Korean Five-Year Plan was launched in 1957. Industrial output was to be increased 3.5 times. It was subsequently claimed that this goal was reached ahead of time in 1960. Compulsory education through the sixth grade was first decreed, then raised to the tenth. Also technical and higher education was stressed, and colleges were established on factory premises to permit workers to attend in off-work hours. By 1960 North Korea had become a tightly knit, hardworking communist state, not likely to collapse.

South Korea

In contrast to the communist-style development in North Korea, South Korea became a political maelstrom. Nominally a democracy, it fell far short of that form, but neither was it a rigid dictatorship. Between 1953 and 1960, when it was toppled by student riots, the Rhee regime became more and more an embarrassment to Americans who tried to help it. The United States, unlike Soviet Russia in the north, respected the sovereignty of the republic it supported, but with the result that all sorts of follies were committed. Emerging from the Korean War as a hero to his people, President Rhee increasingly lost touch with reality as he passed his eightieth birthday. His administration, despite some two billion dollars in American economic aid, was not able to develop a viable economy. In 1960 the export-import ratio still stood at an adverse 10 to 1. Part of the problem was imbalance of agriculture and industry created by the unhappy division of the country. With few power resources and no heavy industry in the south the area was almost wholly dependent on an overburdened agriculture, but the administration did not even take the steps for improvement open to it. Reforestation and agricultural reform programs broke down in scandal, unemployed squatters ringed the cities, especially Seoul, and black markets flourished as the administration desperately clung to power by operating an inefficient authoritarian rule, largely through bribery and corruption.

However, lessons were learned during the last Rhee years and plans were laid. While no open criticism of the regime was permitted, the universities and the army were seething with discontent, and students, professors, and army officers were thinking of numerous improvements that might be made once "the King" (Rhee) and his "dynasty" were ousted. The best hope seemed to rest in a weak and harassed opposition party headed by John M. Chang, who was elected vice-president in 1956 in a striking demonstration of the growing antagonism to the regime. By rigging the elections of March 1960 Rhee made certain that such a thing would not happen again, but the audacity of police intervention at that time triggered a reaction in the form of student-led mass demonstrations in

Seoul and other cities, which the army refused to quell and which brought down the regime in April. Rhee was allowed to retire into exile to Hawaii, and John Chang became premier under a reorganized government that greatly reduced the powers of the presidential office. Free elections endorsed the changes enthusiastically. But with general conditions so poor the prospects for the successful operation of democracy were minimal, and the army was waiting in the wings.

Japan

By the end of the occupation in 1952, both democracy and economic recovery had made a good start in Japan. Subsequently, into the 1960's, the government remained in conservative hands. Yet there was also strong opposition from the Socialist party or parties, depending on the degree to which the Socialists could achieve unity, and strong criticism from intellectuals and the press. This combination of conservative leadership amidst vehement criticism on various issues produced generally happy results.

Under the guidance of the business interests the economy grew steadily, showing a phenomenal nine per cent average annual growth during the 1950's. Not only did the level of exports rise to the point that necessary imports could be paid for and the yen currency stabilized, but by the end of the decade there were ample supplies of consumers' goods in Japan and the Japanese standard of living had risen to between 30 and 40 per cent above the best prewar levels.

A combination of factors made this possible. First, in the export category new products, such as processed steel, plastics, radios, and cameras were added to the more traditional items, textiles, toys, and shipping services. Ingenious new production devices, an accent on precision and quality, patent sharing agreements with American companies, and, in the case of steel, the availability of American scrap iron, assisted greatly. With no large drain for military expenditures, this huge item in prewar budgets was eliminated. Also American tariff policies remained favorable, and the new nations of Southeast Asia found that they could deal profitably with Japan. Japan could supply the simple tools they needed at minimum cost, and items such as Japanese thong rubber sandals, which wear like iron, were sold by the millions through southern Asia, from Hong Kong to Arabia.

A home austerity program was maintained through the Yoshida years, which ended with Yoshida's resignation after his sixth term as prime minister in December 1954, but gradually, as conditions continued to improve and Japanese production was capable of supplying most of the needs of the Japanese people, even motor bikes and automobiles, this was relaxed. By 1958 the Japanese people for the first time in their history began to enjoy something like a feeling of prosperity. This had a profound political effect, for people who could feel their economic condition improving were not so likely to be disposed to revolutionary action, whatever the ideological issues.

Yoshida was succeeded by Hatoyama, who served as premier from December 1954 to December 1956. Hatoyama's chief contribution was the regularization of relations with Soviet Russia, which, together with the end of the Korean War, removed the threat of Russian anti-Japanese actions on the pretext that World War II issues had not been settled. Also it pleased the Japanese socialists, who had been arguing that Japan was too much tied to American coattails and should pursue a neutralist course. Actually the negotiations did not result in any enhancement of Soviet prestige and influence in Japan, for the negotiations were hard and the results embittering to the Japanese.

In return for the "restoration of peace," the repatriation of those Japanese still being held in Russia, and what the Japanese consider inadequate fishing rights in the Russian-dominated seas north of Hokkaido, the Russians demanded that Japan abandon any and all claims to southern Sakhalin and the entire Kuril Island group. The Japanese expected to lose Sakhalin and the northern Kurils but had hoped to retain the southern Kurils and they refused to abandon all claims to them, whereupon the Russians added Shikotan and the Habomai Islands, traditionally a part of Hokkaido, to their definition of Kurils. The issue of these islands had to be put aside, but agreement was reached on the other matters and regular diplomatic relations between Russia and Japan were resumed by a joint declaration signed in October 1956. Russia now dropped her opposition to Japan's entry to the United Nations, and the latter became a member in December 1960.

The principal differences between the new independent Japan and the United States revolved around the related issues of American military bases in Japan, hydrogen bomb testing, and the continued American occupation of Okinawa. These, taken together with the long standing presence of American troops in Japan—which contrasted with the fact that Russian soldiers were never seen—created an impression, particularly strong among students and intellectuals, that America was to be identified with militarism. The reaction against militarism had been very strong, not only among these groups, who voiced it, but generally throughout the Japanese population. A vision of Japan as a "Switzerland in the Pacific," the only nation with a "no war" constitution and the peacemaker of the future, took strong root among the only people in the world who had suffered the horror of atomic bombings. Consequently there was great popular resistance to being drawn into the Cold War.

The government, run by conservatives who were well aware of the great economic dependence of Japan on the United States, wished to follow the American lead on Cold War issues, but still it could not ignore the extent of "neutralist" sentiment in the country. The efforts of the conservative premier, Hatoyama, to reach agreement with the Soviets are partly to be explained as his attempt to mollify this sentiment or capitalize on it. The American hydrogen bomb test in the Pacific in March 1954, which had accidentally cost the life of a Japanese fisherman, was a factor in the decline of Premier Yoshida's popularity, he being regarded as too pliant to American policies. The testing moratorium which prevailed in the later 1950's eased tension on the bomb issue. However, a large segment of vocal Japanese opinion insistently demanded progress on the curtailment of American bases. Every time a base issue came up, whether it involved a fracas between an American soldier and a Japanese civilian or the extension of an airplane runway, there were demonstrations and recriminations. The seemingly permanent American installations on Okinawa became an object of denunciation, and the question whether the treaty-stipulated "residual sovereignty" of Japan over this island should be actively asserted became an issue.

The policies of Premier Kishi Nobusuke, who held office from 1957 to 1960, intensified these issues. Kishi made it plain that he regarded these antiwar sentiments as communist inspired and he determinedly followed the American lead on Cold War issues. He pushed the building up of a Japanese "Self-Defense" force, which had been begun quietly under Yoshida and continued apace, despite vehement opposition from the Socialists. The fact that Kishi had been a member of Tojo's wartime cabinet made him especially vulnerable to charges of "militarist." A climax came in the spring of 1960 when Kishi, having signed an extension of American mutual security and military base agreements in Washington, committed the tactical blunder of arranging to celebrate the ratification of the new treaty with a visit by President Eisenhower. After a stormy session of the Diet in which socialists tried to prevent ratification first by filibuster and then by physically blocking the Speaker from ascending the rostrum to extend the session, police were called into the Diet Chamber, the session extended, and the treaty ratified with the socialists boycotting what they called the "illegal" extension of the session. The treaty would automatically go into effect one month later in June, at which point President Eisenhower was scheduled to arrive.

As the date of President Eisenhower's visit approached, criticism of the premier's "strong arm" tactics mounted. Demonstrations on the Diet premises in Tokyo, and also in other cities, attracted larger and larger numbers. Although these were initiated by the communist-oriented student federation, Zengakuren, whose members mobbed presidential press secretary Hagerty when he arrived at Tokyo's Haneda Airport to make preliminary arrangements for Eisenhower's visit, they were joined in by the general student population, by organized labor, and by large sections of the general public. Newspapers were vehemently anti-Kishi, although stress was also laid on the idea that Kishi was to be blamed, not "Ike." Eisenhower's visit was postponed by mutual agreement, and on June 20, as the treaty went into effect, Kishi announced that he would resign.

Tension gradually subsided as Kishi stepped aside and turned over the reins to a less controversial conservative leader, Ikeda Hayato, whose specialty was finance. Taking office in July 1960, Premier Ikeda stressed continued economic development, avoided further rousing of the militarism issue, and conservative leadership again became secure.

Nationalist China (Taiwan)

Formosa, the Pescadores, and certain small islands off the China mainland shoreline, such as Quemoy and Matsu, remained under the control of the nationalist government, which considered itself the rightful government of the entire China mainland. The United States officially continued to support this view, although it harbored no expectation that the nationalists would recover the mainland and enjoined them from military attempts to

FIGURE 26.6. Generalissimo Chiang Kai-shek on Taiwan.

do so. Despite official pretenses, which were maintained largely to prevent the loss of the Chinese seat on the Security Council of the United Nations to the Chinese communists, the term Taipei or Taiwan (Formosa) government was increasingly used by all save irredentists.

Another result of the pretense that Taipei was the "national" government of China was the maintenance of control of it by mainlanders "representing" the various provinces of China. Native Formosans were largely excluded, though gradually they were admitted to local government and accommodated themselves to the situation. This was no doubt largely because, despite the continuation of political rule by a very few, remarkable economic progress was made.

National income doubled, as did the volume of industrial production. The rural reconstruction program developed handsomely, with some eighty per cent of the farmers owning their own land and making a reasonably good living off it by 1960. With the population adequately fed surplus food became available for export. A network of roads and electrification was built. Education was much improved. The biggest problem was the huge military budget, but most of the cost of this was borne by the United States. Likewise American economic aid was very large, but the investment paid off in producing a nearly viable economy. In short, Formosa, though not a showcase for democracy, became something of an example of economic recovery.

Communist China

During the first Five-Year Plan, which was begun in 1953, the People's Republic sought to double industrial production. To do this living standards were kept at a minimum level while surpluses from the agriculture and business sectors of the economy were channeled into industrial development. To obtain surpluses agricultural production had to be increased, and the government now reversed the trend of distributing land in small parcels to peasants, and brought pressure to bear on the farming population to farm more efficiently by cooperative means. This applied to both production and marketing. During this period the peasants were persuaded rather than forced, for they had vastly enjoyed receiving title to the lands of former landlords, and the government wished to avoid antagonizing them immediately by making them give up this sense of ownership. Hence the emphasis on "cooperatives" rather than collectives. Collectives, wherein the farmer was required to give up his title to the land and become a wage earner for the state, were minimized in this period. Profits from business, however, were drained off mercilessly, through high taxes and state control of certain products.

Relieved of Korean War costs and enjoying the general cooperation of the populace, the first Five-Year Plan succeeded in accomplishing its objectives to a remarkable extent. So great was the government's confidence that in 1957 it announced two bold programs: (1) the so-called "One Hundred Flowers" campaign and (2) a "Great Leap Forward" vastly augmenting industrial production for the next five-year period. Both of these backfired.

The "One Hundred Flowers" campaign was an invitation to free speech and criticism offered by Chairman Mao in a moment, perhaps, of excessive optimism. In a speech delivered on February 27, 1957, he admitted that there were differences of opinion in China and acknowledged the criticism of Western countries that China lacked a two-party system. However, he said that "democratic centralism" was better than "bourgeois democracy" even in the area of freedom of expression, for Marx had seen that the employment of "contradiction" could bring forth the best ideas and promote the welfare of the people. Hence criticism was welcome. "Can Marxism be criticized? Certainly it can." "Questions of right and wrong in the arts and sciences should be settled through free discussion in artistic and scientific circles." "Let one hundred flowers bloom; let one hundred schools of thought contend."

Scholars, writers, and leaders in various fields took up the invitation with alacrity, and for several months amazingly outspoken criticisms of the regime were voiced, much more, apparently, than had been expected. Soon the government was backtracking, and noting that there was a difference between constructive and destructive criticism. Then critics began to be arrested, and abruptly the "hundred schools" ceased to contend. A stony silence settled over the intellectual world of mainland China.

In announcing the beginning of the second Five-Year Plan Mao claimed that the objectives of the first had been exceeded and that it was time for a "great leap forward." Astonishing new production goals were announced and almost the entire population was to participate. Steel production was to be practically doubled every year through the building of backyard steel furnaces in the domiciles of the nation. At the same time a grand new scheme was announced for agriculture: the commune system. By this cooperatives and collective farms were to be merged into huge communes, in which the farmers and their families would live and work together, with production and marketing to be organized by the state. Also millions of peasants were conscripted for irrigation and road building projects.

However, the new plans were soon bogged down. One important factor that had been neglected was the importance of Soviet technicians, who during the early 1950's had made a large contribution to the industrial and technological advances that had been accomplished. By 1958 most of these had gone home. Also Soviet loans and direct aid had been curtailed. Now the "backyard furnace" steel, which took tremendous effort to produce, proved to be of inferior, almost unusable quality. And the commune system produced less instead of more agricultural product. By 1960 the "Great Leap Forward" was in such serious trouble that famine stalked the land. Despite this the communists pressed on, refusing to plead for aid from the outside world. The People's Republic was obviously badly shaken, but it survived and projected a future without Soviet aid.

In foreign affairs the People's Republic was obviously relieved to see the end of the Korean War, but having been branded an aggressor by the U.N. and having no immediate prospect of gaining membership there, she began to woo the Arab-Asian bloc of "neutrals." Having pledged noninterference and peaceful coexistence in the Panch Shila agreements with India and Burma in 1954, Chou En-lai made a bid to assume leadership of a budding Third World organization at the Bandung Conference in 1955. However, much of the popularity China gained from these moves was

FIGURE 26.7. Chou En-lai addressing the Twenty-first Congress of the Soviet Communist party in Moscow, January, 1959, at the beginning of the rift in the Sino-Soviet bloc.

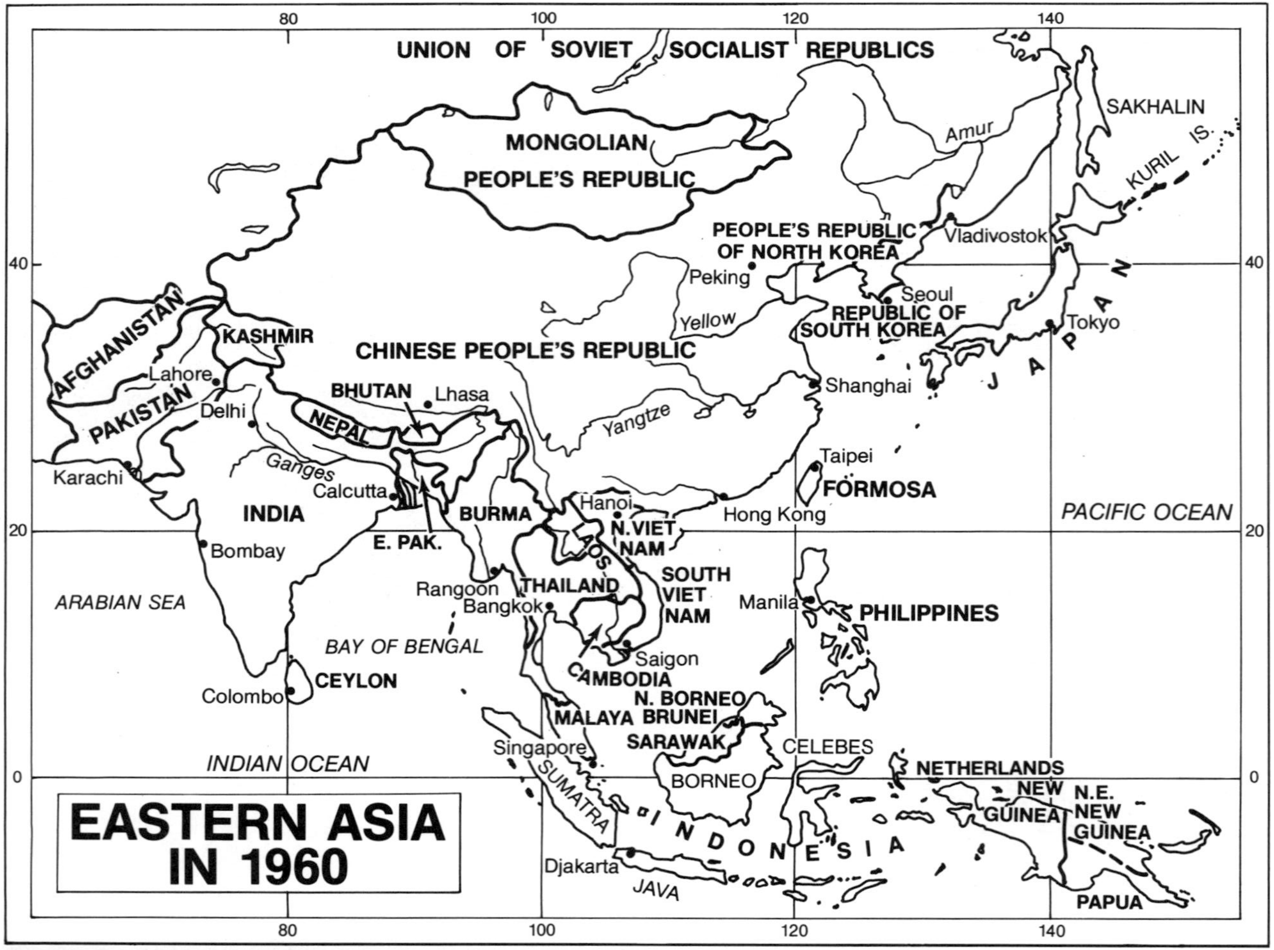
EASTERN ASIA
IN 1960
UNION OF SOVIET SOCIALIST REPUBLICS
MONGOLIAN PEOPLE'S REPUBLIC
CHINESE PEOPLE'S REPUBLIC
PEOPLE'S REPUBLIC OF NORTH KOREA
REPUBLIC OF SOUTH KOREA
JAPAN
SAKHALIN
KURIL IS.
Amur
Vladivostok
Peking
Yellow
Seoul
Tokyo
Shanghai
Yangtze
Taipei
FORMOSA
Hong Kong
PACIFIC OCEAN
AFGHANISTAN
PAKISTAN
KASHMIR
Lahore
Delhi
BHUTAN
Lhasa
NEPAL
Karachi
Ganges
Calcutta
INDIA
E. PAK.
Bombay
BURMA
Hanoi
N. VIET NAM
LAOS
THAILAND
SOUTH VIET NAM
Rangoon
Bangkok
Saigon
CAMBODIA
PHILIPPINES
Manila
ARABIAN SEA
BAY OF BENGAL
CEYLON
Colombo
INDIAN OCEAN
MALAYA
N. BORNEO
BRUNEI
SARAWAK
Singapore
SUMATRA
BORNEO
CELEBES
NETHERLANDS NEW GUINEA
N.E. NEW GUINEA
PAPUA
INDONESIA
Djakarta
JAVA
80
100
120
140
40
20
0

dissipated in the later 1950's as she sent Chinese forces into Tibet and staked out claims to the farthest extent of Tibetan borders. This especially antagonized India, to which Tibet's Dalai Lama fled for refuge in 1959. At the end of the decade Peking and New Delhi were locked in argument over the Tibeto-Indian border question.

Meanwhile a rift was developing between the People's Republic and her erstwhile sponsor, the Soviet Union. After several years of very cordial relations during which the Soviets relinquished control of the Chinese Eastern Railroad and the naval installations at Port Arthur and gave a great deal of technical and financial assistance to the new China, Peking and Moscow began to argue. Moscow regarded Peking's Bandung efforts as "racist" and her Chinese border concerns as "nationalist" and Peking did not respond favorably to Khrushchev's de-Stalinization campaign. By 1960 Peking was openly contesting Soviet leadership in communist party conferences.

The complete divergence of Japan and China, which began in 1945 and solidified amidst American-Soviet Cold (and Korean) War rivalries, remained the central fact of East Asian history in 1960, but a new stage had been reached. The New Japan and the People's Republic of China were on the threshold of rapid independent development, far beyond their respective American and Soviet sponsors' original expectations. In fact Japan, in terms of economic growth, was soon to be the leading capitalist nation of the world, and China, in terms of socialist inventiveness, the leading communist nation. The future impact of these two great Asian nations was only dimly to be seen.

BASIC DATES

1945, September	Japanese surrender
1945–1952	Occupation of Japan
1945–1949	Chinese Civil War
1945, December	Moscow Conference
1945–1947	Marshall Mission to China
1948	Two regimes in Korea
1949, September	People's Republic of China established at Peking
1949	Nationalist government to Formosa
1950–1953	Korean War
1951	San Francisco Treaty with Japan
1952	End of occupation of Japan; Japan-Nationalist China Treaty signed
1952	Chinese communists announce first Five-Year Plan
1954	End of Yoshida premiership in Japan
1955	Bandung Conference
1956	Japan-Soviet settlement; Japan admitted to the U.N.
1957	"One Hundred Flowers" campaign in China
1958	"Great Leap Forward"; Sino-Soviet rift
1960	Anti-American demonstrations in Tokyo; fall of Rhee government in South Korea

SUPPLEMENTARY READING

Berger, Carl. *The Korea Knot,* rev. ed. Philadelphia, 1964.
Borton, Hugh. *Japan's Modern Century,* rev. ed. New York, 1970.
Clyde, P. H. and B. F. Beers. *The Far East,* rev. ed. Englewood Cliffs, N.J., 1966.
Clubb, O. E. *Twentieth Century China.* New York, 1964.
Fairbank, J. K. *The United States and China,* 3rd rev. ed. Cambridge, Mass., 1971.
Fairbank, J. K., E. O. Reischauer, and A. Craig. *East Asia: The Modern Transformation.* Boston, 1965. Revised and abbreviated ed., 1973.
Hsü, I. C. Y. *The Rise of Modern China.* New York, 1970.
Iriye, Akira. *Across the Pacific: An Inner History of American-East Asian Relations.* New York, 1967.
Ishida, Takeshi. *Japanese Society.* New York, 1971.
Pye, Lucian W. *China: An Introduction.* Boston, 1972.
Reischauer, E. O. *Japan: The Story of a Nation.* New York, 1970.
―――― *The United States and Japan,* 3rd. ed. Cambridge, Mass., 1965.

ADVANCED READING

Abegglen, J. C. *The Japanese Factory.* New York, 1959.
Ayusawa, Iwao. *A History of Labor in Modern Japan.* Honolulu, 1963.
Ball, W. M. *Japan: Enemy or Ally?* New York, 1948.
Barnett, A. D. *Communist China: The Early Years.* New York, 1964.
Bodde, D. *Peking Diary.* New York, 1950. The author was in Peking when the communists entered.
Burks, Ardath W. *The Government of Japan,* rev. ed. New York, 1964.
Ch'en, Jerome. *Mao and the Chinese Revolution.* New York, 1967.
Cho, S. S. *Korea in World Politics, 1940–1950: An Evaluation of American Responsibility.* Berkeley, Calif., 1967.
Chung, K. C. *New Korea.* New York, 1962.
Cohen, J. *Japan's Economy in War and Reconstruction.* Minneapolis, 1949.
Crowley, J. B., ed. *Modern East Asia: Essays in Interpretation.* New York, 1970.
Dore, R. P. *City Life in Japan: A Study of a Tokyo Ward.* London, 1958.
Dunn, F. C. *Peacemaking and the Settlement with Japan.* Princeton, N.J., 1964.
Fearey, R. *The Occupation of Japan: Second Phase, 1948–1950.* New York, 1950.
Feis, H. *The China Tangle.* Princeton, N.J., 1953.
―――― *Japan Subdued.* Princeton, N.J., 1961.
―――― *Contest Over Japan.* New York, 1967.
Henderson, D. F., ed. *The Constitution of Japan: Its First Twenty Years, 1947–1967.* Seattle, 1968.
Hinton, W. *Fanshen.* New York, 1966.
Ho, Ping-Ti and T. Tsou, eds. *China in Crisis,* 2 vols. Chicago, 1968.
Kawai, K. *Japan's American Interlude.* Chicago, 1960. The author is an American-educated Japanese professor who was in Japan during the war and the occupation.

Keene, D. *Living Japan.* New York, 1959.
Koo, A. Y. C. *The Role of Land Reform in Economic Development: Taiwan.* New York, 1968.
Langdon, F. C. *Politics in Japan.* Boston, 1967.
Langer, P. F. *Japan, Yesterday and Today.* New York, 1966.
Lee, C. S. *The Politics of Korean Nationalism.* Berkeley, 1963.
Lockwood, W. W., ed. *The State and Economic Enterprise in Japan.* Princeton, N.J., 1965.
Mancall, Mark, ed. *Formosa Today.* New York, 1964.
Mao, T. *Quotations from Chairman Mao Tse-tung.* Peking, 1968. Mao's *Selected Works* in four volumes is also available.
Martin, E. M. *The Allied Occupation of Japan.* Stanford, Calif., 1948. A careful analysis of the first phase of the occupation.
Mendel, D. *The Politics of Formosan Nationalism.* Berkeley, Calif., 1970.
Minear, R. H. *Victors' Justice.* Princeton, 1971.
Morley, J. W. *Japan and Korea: America's Allies in East Asia.* New York, 1965.
Olson, L. A. *Dimensions of Japan.* New York, 1963.
Packard, G. B. III. *Protest in Tokyo: The Security Treaty Crisis of 1960.* Princeton, N.J., 1966.
Paige, Glenn D. *The Korean Decision.* New York, 1968.
Scalapino, R. A. and C. S. Lee. *Communism in Korea.* 2 vols. Berkeley, Calif., 1972.
Scalapino, R. A. and J. Masumi. *Parties and Politics in Contemporary Japan.* Berkeley, Calif., 1964.
Schram, Stuart. *Mao Tse-tung.* New York, 1966.
Schurmann, H. F. *Ideology and Organization in Communist China.* Berkeley, Calif., 1971.
Schurmann, H. F. and O. Schell. *The China Reader.* Volume III: *Communist China.* New York, 1967.
Sheldon, W. L. *The Honorable Conquerors: The Occupation of Japan.* New York, 1965.
Snow, Edgar. *The Other Side of the River: Red China Today.* New York, 1962.
Suh, D. S. *The Korean Communist Movement, 1918–1948.* Princeton, N.J., 1967.
Tsou, Tang. *America's Failure in China, 1941–1950.* Chicago, 1963.
Van Slyke, L. P. *Enemies and Friends: The United Front in Chinese Communist History.* Stanford, Calif., 1967.
Ward, Robert E., ed., *Political Development in Modern Japan.* Princeton, N.J., 1968.
Yoshida, Shigeru. *Memoirs.* Boston, 1962.
Zagoria, D. *The Sino-Soviet Conflict, 1956–1961.* Princeton, N.J., 1962.

Chapter 27

New Giants of Asia: Japan's Capitalist Democracy and China's People's Republic, Since 1960

The Tokyo demonstrations against the American Security Treaty of 1960 and Chinese accusations against Khrushchev as a "revisionist" in the same year foreshadowed the growing independence of the New Japan and the People's Republic from their former sponsors, the United States and the Soviet Union respectively. During the decade that followed, Japan and China were to continue in the divergent patterns established previously, Japan as a capitalist-democracy and China as a socialist-people's republic, with little contact between them, but both were to emerge by 1970 as Asian and even world powers in their own right, far beyond the client roles which the Cold War had earlier assigned them. Indeed, Japan, as the fastest growing economy in the world, became a leading economic rival of the United States, and China surpassed the Soviet Union in developing new communist techniques and goals.

While neither nation could, or attempted to, match its former sponsor in military power, each found diplomatic means to enhance its position in East Asia, Japan by successfully asserting its "residual rights" to sovereignty over Okinawa and by forging active economic relationships with Southeast Asia and South Korea, and China by neutralizing Soviet influence in North Korea, by vigorously asserting boundary claims along its frontiers, including those with the Soviet Union, and by becoming the favorite host for communist leaders of the Third World and even dissident European communists, like the Albanians.

It should be emphasized, of course, that neither the new Japan nor the

People's Republic of China was in any sense merely the product of its postwar sponsor's design. Both countries have histories far too long and cultural traditions far too deeply imbedded to permit foreign implants to escape serious alteration, even when they are undertaken in the face of political or economic necessity.

While it is true that in the nineteenth century both Japan and China were far behind the West in scientific and technological know-how and the skills commonly associated with the organization and management of modern nations, they by no means lost their cultural identities even in the subsequent mood of desperate catching up. There was a vogue of westernization in early Meiji Japan, with Western advisors of all sorts being allowed to introduce new methods and techniques in many fields, but by the time Japan's "modern" state was in full operation, by about 1900, it was noteworthy that such traditional Japanese phenomena as Shinto, family-feudal business structures, Genro-consensus political decision making, and the Japanese ideographic-kana script were far from displaced by such Western counterparts as Christianity, corporations, presidents, and roman letters. Indeed, the "new" Japan that emerged in Meiji times turned out to be modern, but by no means Western.

China, too, while seeking Western technology, not only clung to Confucian traditions, perhaps too long, but as with K'ang Yu-wei attempted to construct a Confucian rationale for modernization. Even after "the day Confucius died" (May 4, 1919), when the castigation of traditions associated with his name reached a peak of intensity, Confucianism was not really dead, as witnessed by the cult of Confucian modernizer Tseng Kuo-fan in the 1930's.

Another point to be made is that regardless of the risings and fallings in the fortunes of Confucianism as the creed of the traditional leadership of China, customs and traits derived from the earthy and pragmatic existence of China's vast peasant population endured like "the good earth" through all manner of upheavals, as did a general faith in China's revival from a time of troubles. And Mao Tse-tung, the Marxist-Leninist, had a full awareness of these.

Thus, although Japan was "Americanized" and China "communized" in the decade and a half following the Pacific war, by 1960 the native genius of both countries was about to burst forth, and the following decade was to show that both of these Asian nations were quite capable of operating in the modern world, regardless of what Western nations, whether capitalist or communist, thought, said, or did about them.

JAPAN

Considering Japan first, it might be said that an early indicator of the Japanese potential for thriving in the capitalist world was the appearance of a camera called *Canon*. Canon cameras were much sought after by knowledgeable tourists of the world in the 1950's as *the* quality camera at a reasonable price, and Canon's producer, a former physician named Takeshi Mitarai, knew exactly what he was about; quality, convenience of operation, and reasonable price were built into every camera he produced. It is symbolic that the name Canon came not from the Western "cannon" but from the Buddhist "Kannon," and the entire production operation was an example of Japanese skill focused on a modern product.

Meanwhile the narrow streets of Tokyo were the testing ground for a new variety of small vehicles, including the three-wheeled delivery truck, the two-seated motor scooter, and then in rapid succession Honda, Toyota, and Datsun. Who would have believed in 1960 that by the early 1970's Honda would have surpassed Harley-Davidson in the cycle field and Toyota and Datsun would have Ford and General Motors scurrying to produce competitive small cars?

Again in shipbuilding, Japan caught the needs and realities of the modern world in the 1960's. Previously oil tankers had been built small, with the Suez canal in mind, but pragmatically assuming that political instability in the Middle East would render the canal's use at best uncertain, the Japanese opted for huge tankers whose volume more than offset the increased distance cost of nonuse of narrow waterways. In electronics, the transistor was the revolutionary element, which the Japanese perfected with amazing speed, first in the pocket radio, then in television and recording devices. While older and bigger American and European companies were still regarding the small set market as marginal or secondary, Sony, Hitachi, and other Japanese companies, which by 1970 were household words around the world, gave it their primary attention. Big in tankers, small in cars and electronics, Japanese pragmatism caught the real demand in all three areas of the market.

Japanese political leadership remained in the conservative hands of the Liberal Democratic party, and, indeed, became even more business oriented than in the 1950's. Ikeda, Kishi's immediate successor as premier when the latter resigned in the aftermath of the United States Security Treaty crisis of June 1960, assumed a very low posture on both foreign and political affairs, and concentrated on improving the economy. When he called elections to confirm his leadership in November 1960, he received a resounding endorsement, with the opposing Socialists losing more than twenty Diet seats.

Ikeda's economic promises were more than fulfilled, and when he had to resign because of ill health in 1964 his choice as successor, Sato Eisaku (Kishi's younger brother who had served as finance minister in the Kishi cabinet), was broadly supported by business interests, and the continuing prosperity of the country confounded his critics. Sato had to reshuffle his cabinet occasionally to take account of the waxing or waning of the various leader-follower (oyabun-kobun) factions which provided the intramural politics of the LDP, but he continued into the 1970's at the helm of his party and the country as the growth rate of Japan's gross national product averaged well over ten per cent per year.

While labor complained that they were not getting enough of the increasing wealth, the Socialist party was not able to mount a serious challenge to the LDP. This was partly because of ideological quarrels among the socialist factions, but also because a new phenomenon arose on the political horizon, which captured the imagination and support of heretofore unorganized elements of the working class, especially those who felt themselves lacking in education. This was the Soka Gakkai (Value Creating Society), an offshoot of the Nichiren sect of Buddhism, which built a mass following in the late 1950's and early 1960's and then, after a few preliminary political forays (all victories), launched a new political party, the Komeito (Clean Government Party) in 1964. By 1970 the Society had an amazingly large membership of over 15 million (far larger than the membership base of either the LDP or the Socialist party) and its Komeito candidates were polling over ten per cent of the votes cast.

Explanations of the phenomenal growth of Soka Gakkai are varied. In part it provided a kind of materialist religion: you will get a better job and more material possessions if you believe in the Lotus Sutra (basis of Nichiren's teaching) and have a happy, positive outlook. In part it provided a "higher" educational experience for millions who aspired to go to college, but who failed to get in because of high entrance requirements and/or lack of funds. In part it provided low cost social life on a mass basis, meetings, discussion groups, picnics, and festivals.

While the Soka Gakkai creed is antirational and its organization undemocratic, the movement has not developed the fascistic tendencies some of its critics predicted. Its stance on militarism has been to condemn it, both in terms of enlargement of the military establishment in Japan and following the United States in Cold War policies and also in terms of the violent confrontation tactics of Japanese leftists. Meanwhile its demands for ethics in government and a greater share of the prosperity pie for Japanese consumers have kept pressure on the business leadership to develop some humanistic concerns.

The student movement is another fact of Japanese political life, though taking place more in the streets than at the polls. The leadership of the student federation, Zengakuren, which was organized throughout the country in the postwar years, was early captured by communists and their sympathizers, but the Japan Communist party, from 1955, stressed legality, lovability, and only peaceful opposition to rearmament and involvement with the United States in the Cold War. The demonstrations of 1960, which developed broad popular support, were actually conceived in this vein. However, when the Security Treaty became effective despite this, many student leaders lost patience, and the phenomenon of ultraleftism began to develop. In the 1960's the communist faction became the conservative wing of the Japan student movement, with the new radicals becoming interested in a far wider range of problems. Their attention turned particularly to their own universities, which, despite postwar reforms, remained quite paternalistically organized, and during the later 1960's practically every major Japanese university was shut down by student strikers at one time or another, often for months at a time.

Sometimes the issue involved "United States militarism," as at Kyushu University in the spring of 1968, when an American Phantom jet on a training flight crashed into a (fortunately) unfinished and unoccupied university building after the pilot bailed out. Students surrounded the building and demanded that the wreckage be left there as a symbol. At other times the issues were entirely Japanese, as the organization of the Tokyo University medical school, tuition costs, or merely quarrels among the factions of Zengakuren. Marathon "collective discussions" (*dankai*), in which students by their numbers and energy literally wore out university administrators and faculty members, were necessary for reopening agreements. When police were called in, intense confrontations developed, with both sides wearing crash helmets and engaging in physical violence. Fortunately, certain rituals developed, whereby most of the fighting would be done with old fashioned samurai type staves, and though many a helmet was dented and some bones broken, few were killed.

By 1970 the student movement was arrayed against all the ills of society, from war in the world to pollution (*kogai*, public damage) at home. Its excesses were deplored by older (voting) Japanese and the public at large was far less sympathetic to *demo* (demonstrations) in the streets than it had been in 1960, but student politics in some form had something to say on almost every issue.

In a curious way all of the above mentioned political factors contributed to the continued economic growth of Japan and to keeping the conservatives in power. Japanese business was incredibly successful, both abroad and at home, and its critics, whether socialists, Soka Gakkai, or student movement, may have unwittingly contributed something to that, by keeping up the pressure against military expenditures, which would waste Japanese resources, and by voicing consumer demands and complaints. Thus business in the new Japan had a volatile Japanese population to satisfy, not as in the 1920's merely international trade balances to meet, or in the 1930's merely a military machine to feed, while the general populace did without. Conversely, the general population supported the conservatives in power, knowing instinctively, perhaps, that their critics served them better in voicing complaints than in managing the economy.

Of course, it can be argued that the Japanese economy (and society) has not yet met the real tests. Under American military protection, it has escaped the staggering costs of "defense" in the modern world. However, Japan's relations with potential "enemies" have improved. Since her 1956 reopening of relations with the Soviet Union, she has developed mutually beneficial trade arrangements. The only thorny issue is that of conflicting claims to Habomai and Shikotan islands north of Hokkaido, which the Russians continue to occupy. Japan has avoided raising this issue. In January 1966 the Soviet Union placed an order for 100 Japanese-built merchant ships, to be delivered in the next five years, and shortly thereafter a trade agreement, a civil aviation treaty, and a cultural cooperation agreement were signed by Japan and the U.S.S.R.

The People's Republic of China could be a threat. It exploded a "nuclear device" in October 1964, another in May 1965. In February 1966 it accused the Soviet Union of attempting to build an "encirclement" of China, from India to Japan. In May 1966 the People's Republic exploded a "thermonuclear device," and in June 1967 its first "hydrogen bomb." Of course, Peking has often accused Japan of being in the camp of the "American imperialists." Despite these happenings, the Japanese have not felt it necessary to undertake any special "defense" procedures against China. Instead, Japan has sought to avoid enmity and develop trade, with modest success. This began in the mid-1950's, was interrupted by a quarrel over flags at a trade fair in 1958, but resumed in the 1960's and a long-term trade agreement "in principle" was signed in May 1966. Probably more Japanese have visited China than any other noncommunist nationals. As former Premier Yoshida had said, Sino-Japanese differences were "merely political." The key problem of recognition was a thorny one, because Japan continued to honor her treaty of 1952 with the nationalists. This ended the war with "China" and established trade relations with Taiwan, which have since flourished. Of course, Peking demanded termination of this treaty in return for any official "normalization" of Tokyo-Peking relations. But in 1972, after her new premier, Tanaka, visited Peking, Japan found a way to accomplish this and to continue relations with Taiwan on a "trade mission" basis.

South Korea might be considered a potential enemy. It has a strong army and a deep tradition of bitterness for Japan, which was a prominent feature of the Rhee era of the 1950's. But the new leadership which emerged after Rhee's overthrow in 1960, specifically the military government of General Park Chung-hee, which seized power in May 1961, saw advantages in normalization of relations with Japan. (Park had graduated from military school in Tokyo and had been an officer in Japan's Kwantung army.) After he was elected president in 1963, Park let it be known he was willing to negotiate, and the Japanese, with an eye on Korean trade, responded eagerly. There were some thorny problems, and many Koreans were opposed, but finally a treaty was signed and diplomatic relations between South Korea and Japan were instituted formally on December 21, 1965. Despite earlier demonstrations against the treaty, Korean opposition to it melted away rapidly after the event, and Japanese-Korean trade and exchanges became a large factor in Korean economic and cultural life subsequently.

Somehow, through all this, the Japanese also managed to maintain some relationships with North Korea, built out of a repatriation program for Koreans in Japan who wished to return there in the 1950's.

In short, by the end of the 1960's Japan, which had been hated by all her neighbors in the 1930's, really had no enemies. Having desisted from arrogant behavior, her defense needs were minimal.

It can also be argued that Japan has not met the "real" test of economic life, because of an unusually favorable trade relationship with the United States. Thus Japan has been allowed to maintain protective tariff barriers against American manufactures, such as automobiles and television sets, while selling her own manufactures very freely in the United States. The trade balance has only gradually made this apparent, because Japan has been importing large quantities of food and raw materials, especially soy beans, wheat, cotton, and scrap iron. However, a crisis developed in 1970 as the dollar, weakened by worldwide American trade deficits and inflationary spending related to the Vietnam War, became clearly overvalued in relation

FIGURE 27.1. Eisaku Sato, Prime Minister of Japan, 1964-1972.

to the Japanese yen, at 360 to 1, a ratio that had been held firm since the early 1950's. With the dollar overvalued, of course, Americans could buy Japanese imports more cheaply than competitive American products.

In 1971 President Nixon, in effect, devalued the dollar, not a specific amount, but by cutting it free of gold to find its own level in international monetary markets. In relation to Japanese yen this resulted in a devaluation of about 15 per cent, and meant higher prices on Japanese imports to the United States, and lower prices on American exports to Japan. In addition President Nixon threatened tariff barriers unless the Japanese extended an already established voluntary quota system for Japanese exports to the United States.

This, coupled with the surprise announcement of the forthcoming Nixon visit to Peking, became known in Japan as the "Nixon shocks" of 1971. Was Japan's great postwar sponsor forsaking her? Hasty conferences smoothed things over. Premier Sato visited President Nixon at San Clemente, California, after Nixon's return from Peking in 1972, and trade conferences ironed out problems created by the dollar revaluation. But it was clear in the aftermath that Japan could no longer count on the very special economic advantage she had held in trade with the United States.

However, Japan, with full employment and a thriving economy, was well able to stand the shock of the economic readjustment. Her trade is global, and though there may be some curtailment of the American sector, increases in other areas, such as southern Asia, Africa, the Soviet Union, and eventually perhaps China, will no doubt offset this and render Japan's position the more independent overall. Also, the diplomatic "slight" of President Nixon's going to Peking without prior consultation with Japan was offset by the reversion of Okinawa to Japanese sovereignty in 1972. This had become a major demand of all political sectors in Japan, and while the concomitant agreement allowing American military forces to remain there was denounced by Japanese antiwar groups, the compromise result was enough to defuse Okinawa as a political issue against Prime Minister Sato. Similarly, his finessing of the problem of renewal of the United States Security Treaty, by simply allowing it to renew itself automatically in 1970, must be counted a victory for Sato.

In June 1972, after the longest single-term premiership in modern Japanese history, Sato announced his intention to retire voluntarily and invited the Liberal Democratic Party to elect a new party president, who would automatically thereby become prime minister, since the LDP had an absolute majority in the Diet. Sato seemed to favor Foreign Minister Fukuda Takeo as his successor, but he did not intervene actively to support Fukuda's candidacy, and when the results of a four-way race were announced on July 6, it was not Fukuda, but the minister of international trade and industry, Tanaka Kokuei, who had won the party presidency and the premiership. This was considered something of a victory for younger, more liberal elements of the LDP, for Tanaka, only 54, stood out from his rivals as a "commoner" type, with neither a university degree nor previous experience as a bureaucrat. However, there was little doubt that Japan's business orientation would continue.

Thus Japan's capitalist-democracy continued under conservative leadership into the 1970's, and a successful blend of old and new prevailed. Businesses retained enough of the old "family" style internal loyalty to give them both stability and devoted service, while early retirement made room at the top. Politics was "faction ridden" as of old, but curiously, it produced viable compromises. Mr. Average Japanese suffered much from crowds, traffic, and air pollution in getting to his place of work, but his samurai stoicism saw him through and his leisure hours could be spent in the quietude of traditional Japanese gardens and hot springs on the "other side of the tunnel" (see the Kawabata novel *Snow Country*) if he so desired. The architecture of new buildings was modern and functional, but some corner was always preserved for the traditional art of contemplation.

In literature and the visual arts old values and sensitivities were given new modes of expression, and the wider world began to appreciate them as never before. Movies like *Rashomon*, *Gate of Hell*, *Woman in the Dunes*, and, above all, *Ikiru* (Living) spoke in a Japanese idiom to eternal human problems and captivated audiences fortunate enough to see them. Kawabata Yasunari wrote in a manner as Japanese as Chikamatsu, and won a Nobel prize for it (in 1968).

The new Japan was perhaps not the "emerging superstate" an American writer called it, but it was a self-confident, able, and functioning capitalist-democracy. And its low posture in world affairs showed that it had learned a lot since its days of arrogant militarism. If there was a malaise present, it was no more than a general uneasiness that in attaining maximum productivity and efficiency, human values and human happiness may be lost sight of. But Japan has perhaps stronger traditional safeguards than most nations, at least in the realm of philosophies of retreat, like Zen. And if newer, better answers are to be found, her increasingly uninhibited and volatile young people ought to be able to find them.

CHINA

While Japan was charting her course of industrial and commercial expansion for the 1960's, across the Yellow Sea the Chinese People's Republic was faced with the problem of furthering Chinese development without Soviet aid.

The failure of the Great Leap Forward (1959) was a great blow to China's leadership, especially to Chairman Mao, who resigned from his position as head (chairman, later called "president") of the government and was replaced by Liu Shao-ch'i, though Mao remained as chairman of the Communist party. Liu, like Mao a Hunanese, had been in the background for a long time, a practical organizer even in Yenan and pre-Yenan days. While Mao had planned the major strategies and articulated them in his writings, Liu had been Mr. Organization. There is no doubt that this was a demotion for Mao.

In the countryside the huge "10,000 family" commune system which during the Great Leap had been designated as the "basic accounting unit" was now decentralized, and by 1960 the "production team" which approximated the size and organization of the traditional village structure undertook this key economic role, with the commune temporarily, at least, relegated to paper-plan status. Along with this came the reintroduction of capitalistic practices such as material incentives (more pay for more work), rural farm markets where peasants could buy and sell goods at prices set by natural market forces of supply and demand, and private plots in which a percentage (no more than twenty per cent) of the income could be used to supplement yearly income. In local leadership, there was a return to the old cadres who had been eased out during an "antirightist" movement following the Hundred Flowers and during the Great Leap.

These measures represented a more pragmatic and rational approach to the problem of China's development and bore the stamp of Liu Shao-ch'i, who began to assume control of the party apparatus also. Mao seemed to be slipping into the role of a deity to be revered but not to be involved in decision making.

The sharp contrasts which manifested themselves in the Great Leap and the post-Leap period (and culminated in the Cultural Revolution) can perhaps be explained by noting that by 1960 there had developed in the

Chinese leadership two "visions" or models for China's development. These may be labeled as the Maoist model and, for convenience, the non-Maoist model. The former was, of course, propagated by Mao. The latter came to be identified with President Liu.

There were two main elements in Maoism, voluntarism and egalitarianism. By voluntarism, is meant that by relying on one's own resources, China could overcome almost insuperable odds. This theory was derived from Mao's great faith in the peasants, a faith built out of his reliance upon them as they formed the Red Army which defeated the Kuomintang in 1949. Implicit is a distrust of bureaucracy and elite institutions.

The second, and related, element in Maoism was the vision of a completely egalitarian society, a society which would treat as equals both men and women, educated and uneducated, old and young, rich and poor. It contained a desire to negate the very basis of capitalist society. Thus, the Maoist man must be liberated from such bourgeois values as the desire for material incentives and competition, that is working longer and/or harder for the prospect of material gain and the desire to retain private plots.

The Maoist man would be motivated by the general good and be willing to exert himself for the betterment of society for no immediate individual reward. This idea seems to have had roots in the traditional Chinese ideal of the gentleman, or *chün-tze*, who, theoretically, sought only the cultivation of a better society. Mao wanted to apply this to all.

The second, the non-Maoist model, made pragmatism the watchword. In this concept development should proceed along rational lines with due weight given to the "natural" law of human competition, profit and loss accounting, and the need for material incentives. In other words, this model assumed that basic human nature could not be changed. Thus the period which followed the Great Leap (a product of the Maoist vision) emphasized concepts of President Liu and it was a period in which policies were more "expert" than "red," more realistic than idealistic, and more accommodating than dislocating. Liu seemed to be following the Russian model in the development of China's economy.

During this period, the traditional bourgeois values which Mao had been trying to eradicate were allowed to reappear, especially among the party cadres. This aspect was especially disturbing to Mao, since the cadres occupied the important position of liaison between the party and the masses. Theirs was the function of transmitting modernizing values from the leadership to the masses and if they lost Mao's vision, there was little hope of transforming the vast society along Maoist lines. During the early 1960's the cadres unashamedly developed a careerist outlook.

Chairman Mao was not completely powerless in this period, wielding considerable influence behind the scenes and especially in the army, which he built into a bastion of support by the mid 1960's. This had its inception in events which had occurred during the Great Leap.

That there were serious dissenters to the Great Leap became evident when Marshal P'eng Teh-huai was revealed to have criticized the commune effort in a letter to Soviet Premier Khrushchev in 1959. In his criticism he also alluded to the party policy of using the People's Liberation army (PLA) as an element of mobilization and revealed army opposition to the lack of professionalization of the armed forces. P'eng's subsequent dismissal from the army not only quelled army opposition, but also boosted Lin Piao, a fervent supporter of Mao, into the position of head of the army.

The rise of Maoist influence in the army developed rapidly during the years 1962–1966, dubbed the Socialist Education Movement period, when the people were urged to "learn from the PLA." Under the leadership of Lin Piao, the army rapidly became the most powerful force in support of Maoist thinking. On the other hand, the communist party began responding to the incentive ideas of Liu Shao-ch'i.

In this period in the area of foreign affairs, two major problems loomed. One was the expanding war south of the border being waged by an America which claimed that by fighting communism in Vietnam it was actually halting Chinese expansion. The second was the deteriorating relationship with the Soviet Union, which Mao, in his quarrels with Khrushchev, had done much to exacerbate.

As United States bombing intensified and crept northward and as American troop levels in Vietnam increased, the role of China became important in the eyes not only of American policy-makers, but also in Vietnam and other Third World countries.

As ominous-sounding threats emanated from Washington because of China's policy of supplying weapons and acting as a rear base sanctuary for the North Vietnamese war effort, Lin Piao made a famous policy speech in 1965 entitled "Long Live the Victory of the People's War." This document spelled out China's policy vis-à-vis those countries engaged in wars of national liberation. Lin said that while China encouraged such people's wars and would help with advice and perhaps arms, the nation in question must rely upon its own resources, just as China did in its own revolution. While putting forth the Chinese experience as an example to emulate, Lin stressed that each country must find its own way to achieve victory and cannot count on active support from China.

This important pronouncement was intended not only to allay possible fears in the United States of massive intervention as in Korea in 1950, but also to calm the worries of North Vietnam's leadership, who feared a possible attempt to take over the war with the massive introduction of PLA troops.

In order to strengthen her independent line, China further cultivated ties with little Albania and scored an international coup in 1964 by establishing diplomatic relations with France.

In 1965 a further effort to avoid war with the United States appeared. This was also involved in a new aspect of the Sino-Soviet split. In an intraparty dispute over foreign policy, two important party members, Lo Jui-ching and P'eng Chen, were purged for advocating a united front with the Soviet Union against American imperialism. Their position was that, of the two evils, American "imperialism" and Russian "revisionism" (or "social imperialism"), the former was the more serious problem and that China and the Soviet Union should bury their differences and prepare for war against the United States by pooling their nuclear arms and preparing the Chinese army as a professional army. This view was quashed by the dominant faction of the inner elite who branded Russian "revisionism" as the more serious problem and discounted any threat of a United States attack. Thus, from the hindsight of the Nixon visit to China (1972) it is evident that, by 1966, certain elements in China saw the Soviet Union, not the United States, as her main enemy. Indeed, by the end of the decade relations with America were to improve greatly, while relations with the Soviet Union were to deteriorate into actual armed clashes.

But beginning in 1966, for three tumultuous years, foreign affairs were all but neglected as China entered perhaps the most turbulent period of her modern history since the civil war of 1946–1949. This was the period of the Great Proletarian Cultural Revolution which engulfed China from 1966–1969 and which captured the attention not only of the entire Chinese nation but also the world.

Foreigners were ushered out of China while a most massive struggle began. It was touched off by Mao, himself, who in mid-1965 went to Shanghai to set it in motion. For this he used a literary format, an attack on a play by one Wu Han, one of Liu's literary supporters. He had forgotten the revolution, said Mao, and the nation was being led down the road of "revisionism" for which he had upbraided the Soviet Union. The men who had implemented or allowed the revisionist tendencies would have to be removed from power. Revolution was a continuing process and China's youth should have a revolutionary experience similar to that which he and his compatriots had undergone: rigors such as the Long March and the successive wars of resistance against the Japanese and the nationalists.

Mao called for a closing of the schools and the going forth of students as Red Guards—students-turned-soldiers—to purge the bureaucratized Communist party. With the sympathy of the army, the students sallied forth, calling for self-criticism by the party bureaucracy. In the end fully 80 to 90 per cent of the party bureaucracy were criticized or dismissed for their bourgeois tendencies. This campaign to oust "rightist bourgeois influences" from the party led to a struggle for power at the highest echelons of party leadership. The Red Guards with "large-character posters" were soon lambasting "China's Khrushchev," and shortly after this person was revealed to be Liu Shao-ch'i, the president of China. Lin Piao's troops took control of the mass media of Peking, "declared war against the literary world," and subsequently placed Liu under house arrest. Lin was formally named Mao's heir apparent in 1969.

Meanwhile, the Red Guards were busy removing cadres who "put work points in command," "took the capitalist road," and "acted as overlords over the masses." The purged cadres were replaced by the young Red Guards, who had no experience in running a bureaucracy. Oftentimes, cadres fearing Red Guard onslaughts would organize their own group of Red Guards from the area who would mouth slogans of Mao and would protect their cadres from the Maoist Red Guards. Thus various factions of Red Guards frequently clashed and the few foreign observers often had difficulty distinguishing between Maoist and anti-Maoist groups.

Other Red Guards, especially the younger ones, were organized and

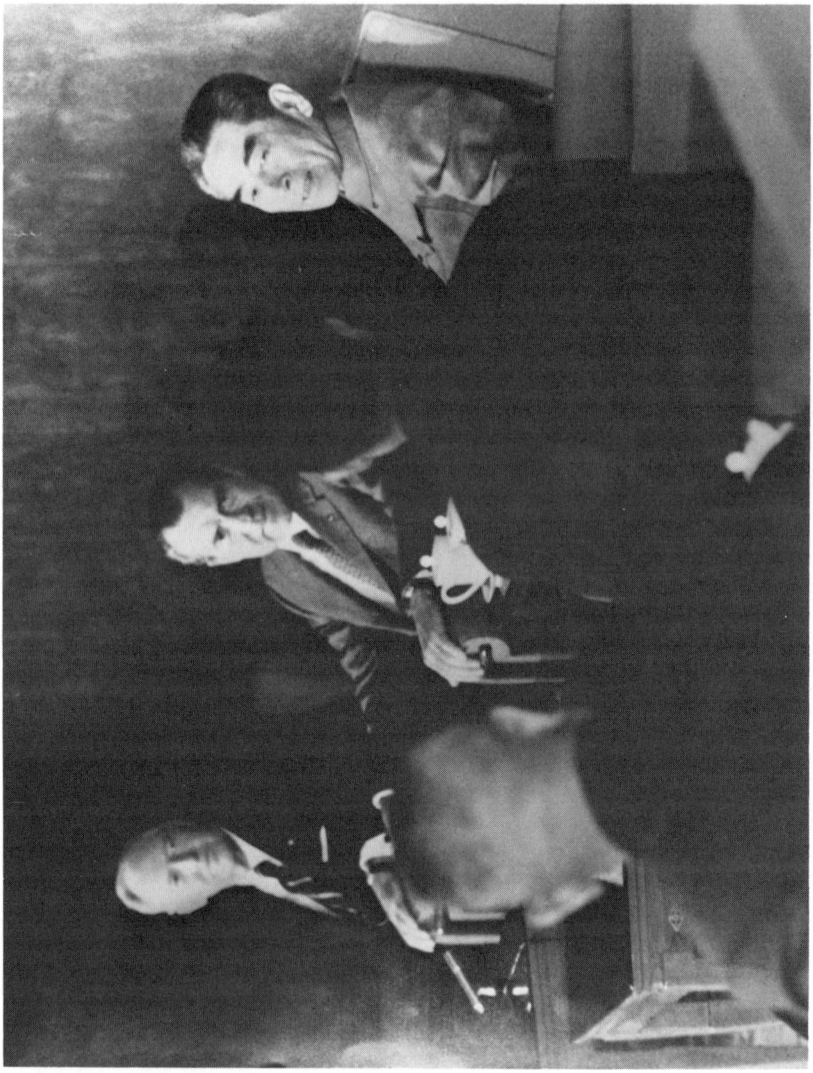

sent out to the country, often on foot, to simulate the Long March experience of their elders. These youngsters would go on marches of several months' duration chanting Maoist slogans and praising the Cultural Revolution.

In foreign affairs, all Chinese ambassadors were recalled for criticism with the exception of the ambassador in Cairo (who was later appointed ambassador to Canada and in 1971 to the United Nations), leaving China virtually isolated from international contact. One Red Guard unit, in their zeal, burned down the British minister's residence. A diplomatic incident was avoided when Chou En-lai announced that the youths would be punished and the building rebuilt at China's expense.

China, as it seemed from the West, had turned into the chaos of anarchy. Farmers, caught up in the campaign, could not produce; students could not learn because the schools were closed; managers were afraid to continue on in their ways for fear of criticism. The party apparatus was shattered with the purge of the great majority of the party cadres and a power vacuum was created. Warring factions of Red Guards clashed all over the countryside. Even the army was engaged in factional struggles over which group of Red Guards to support.

After some 18 months of this, Mao, whom critics assumed to have gone mad, saw that things were getting out of hand. Coupled with this was the fear of facing the Soviet Union with a divided nation. Suddenly he relaxed his line and began criticizing left-wing "adventurism" and Red Guard excesses. Soon afterward, he announced that 95 per cent of the cadres were good or comparatively good, and ordered the army, which as noted above had been a bastion of support for Mao since 1960, to restore order to the country. The PLA was given the task of taking over from the Red Guards and administering the provinces and municipalities. In this new order a new organization was created, so-called revolutionary committees which came to be dominated by army men and served as provisional organs of power until the party bureaucracy could once again be built up. By early 1969 revolutionary committees had been established throughout China. Their main tasks were to fill the vacuum left by the purged cadres or the Red Guards and to persuade the cadres who had been wrongly purged to return to their old positions.

The Cultural Revolution ended with the military firmly in command and wielding great power in the different regions of China. Their power may have become so great that regionalism began to reappear. This may have been the impetus for Mao to authorize an attack on the Russian-held (but Chinese-owned) islands in the Ussuri River, a tributary of the Amur River, in 1969. By creating a threat of war, the army would become united in the desire to remain vigilant in the face of an external enemy and thus to resolve their factional and regional squabbling. Whatever the cause of the incident, it seemed for a time that war was a distinct

FIGURE 27.2. Secretary of State Rogers, President Nixon, and Premier Chou En-lai at Peking, Feb. 21, 1972.

possibility between the two nations. However, tensions eased somewhat and border talks resumed the following year.

As students returned to their schools and the newly formed revolutionary committees began to function, the country seemed to be back to normal domestically. In foreign affairs, a similar easing of tensions could be observed. Border negotiations with the Russians began. In another initiative the Chinese began a diplomatic offensive which sought maximum recognition for their regime and a seat in the United Nations. That China was a power to be reckoned with was amply demonstrated by the orbiting of a satellite in 1970 which demonstrated that it had ICBM capability, although China proclaimed that it would never act like a "big power." Peking's pronouncements became moderate and compromising. In 1970 China exchanged ambassadors with several countries, but the big push came in 1971. In the spring of that year the United States's table tennis team, on tour in Asia, was invited with reporters to visit China. The offer was accepted. In July Henry Kissinger, President Nixon's top foreign policy advisor, secretly conferred with Chou En-lai in Peking. Later that month, President Nixon announced that he would visit China in early 1972. This turn of events was certainly a diplomatic victory for the PRC and a blow to the prestige of the nationalist regime on Taiwan. Next, the Peking government was accorded the China seat in the United Nations, replacing the nationalists, who were expelled, although the United States attempted to have Taiwan remain in the U.N., in an abortive attempt at a two-China policy. Then, at the conclusion of President Nixon's visit in February 1972, a joint communiqué was issued stating that the United States would eventually withdraw all of its troops from Taiwan. It seemed that the ultimate objective was the diplomatic recognition of Peking by the United States and the exchange of ambassadors.

Meanwhile Chou En-lai, who as premier, had been the third ranking man in the Chinese hierarchy, behind Mao and Liu, gradually assumed Liu's former role as head of the government. The office of "president" was left vacant. A close associate of Mao since the days of the Long March, he had specialized in foreign affairs, had been China's spokesman at the Bandung conference, had articulated the various shifts in Peking's foreign policy with soft-spoken suavity over the years, and had stood somewhat aside, while leaning to Mao, in the Cultural Revolution. It may be significant that Mao launched that affair from Shanghai, Chou's special bailiwick. At any rate, Chou's mediatory talents were much in evidence in settling things down in the aftermath of the Cultural Revolution and in bringing the reconstituted party cadres back into operation.

Lin Piao, the army chief, and several other army leaders now became a problem. They seemed reluctant to let go of the increased political influence of the PLA. It was rumored that Lin had forced Mao to name him heir apparent before throwing the support of the army to the Cultural Revolution. Suddenly, in 1971, Lin disappeared, rumored to have died in an airplane crash in Mongolia, and Chou En-lai was clearly the active head of state when visitation to China opened up in 1972.

What visitors have seen depends on whose eyes one believes. From widely televised scenes of snow shoveling in Peking some saw China as an army of hard working ants. Others saw it as a miracle of communal cooperation for the common good. Several observations based on historical analysis may put us somewhere in between:

(1) The People's Republic won a revolution and, although the vicissitudes of its first twenty years were many, dramatic, and even, during the Great Leap and the Cultural Revolution, traumatic, it not only survived but by the early 1970's had achieved self-sufficiency at a level of modest livelihood for 800 million Chinese. This was an incredible feat, considering the appalling poverty of the Chinese masses during the first half of the twentieth century, and the cutoff of foreign (Soviet) aid in the late 1950's.

(2) The People's Republic had asserted its control over most of the territory formerly associated with the "Middle Kingdom's" historical boundaries. Indeed, the term *Chung Kuo* (literally Middle Kingdom) was the term it officially used for "China."

(3) Not content with these achievements, the People's Republic had, for better or worse, attempted to reassume the "civilizing" role of the "Middle Kingdom" in teaching by example a "proper" way of life for East Asian peoples and by implication, at least, the world. This is the concept of continuing revolution, held by Mao to be so important that he risked wrecking the whole structure of the communist state he and his fellow revolutionaries had erected. Its dynamic is SUS (struggle-unity-struggle), whereby in every generation presumably the Chinese will take themselves and their institutions apart and put them back together in an effort to avoid elitism and bureaucratic stagnation. The message of the Cultural Revolution was that production, and even livelihood, are subordinate to this.

(4) Although the message was new, the way of teaching had strong Confucian overtones. Mao had become a latter-day Confucius, teaching a kind of communist humanism by proverbs and example. His "Analects" were contained in the little red book of *Quotations from Chairman Mao Tse-tung*. The emphasis on morality and ethics in government and society and the use of slogans and shame as a pressure device in the educative process are also in the Confucian tradition, as is the acceptance of authority established in those terms.

(5) In foreign relations, despite much revolutionary rhetoric, a generally pragmatic approach has prevailed. This too is in line with Chinese traditions. Alhough its assumption of the "Middle Kingdom" role gave China pretensions to suzerainty over the whole Far East, when others like Japanese, Mongols, or Vietnamese chose to reject these pretensions and remain outside, the Chinese found ways to accommodate to the situation.

***

Out of the postwar wreckage of East Asia, by the 1970's two new-old giants had emerged. Japan and China had reentered the world stage in different garb from different wings. How they would play out the century remained to be seen, but it had become clear that their major decisions would be made in Tokyo and Peking.

BASIC DATES

1959–1960	China retrenches from failure of Great Leap Forward; Liu Shao-ch'i replaces Mao as head of government
1960	Anti-Security Treaty demonstrations in Japan; Prime Minister Kishi resigns, replaced by Ikeda; demonstrations in Seoul lead to ouster of President Syngman Rhee; brief attempt at democracy
1961	General Park Chung-hee takes control in South Korea
1962	Chinese fight India; seize disputed border area
1963	Park elected president of South Korea
1964	China explodes "nuclear device"; Sato replaces Ikeda as Japanese prime minister; Soka Gakkai launches Komeito political party
1965	Japan and South Korea establish diplomatic relations
1966	Mao challenges Liu Shao-ch'i; beginning of Great Proletarian Cultural Revolution in China
1967	Lin Piao and People's Liberation Army enter Cultural Revolution, replace party cadres
1968	Kawabata Yasunari awarded Nobel prize in Literature
1969	Cultural Revolution ends with purge of "ultraleftists"; U.S. agrees to restore Okinawa to Japan
1970	U.S.-Japan Security Treaty extended automatically
1971	President Nixon "shocks" Japan with announcement of dollar revaluation and forthcoming Peking visit; People's Republic awarded China's seat at United Nations
1972	President Nixon visits Peking; Okinawa reverts to Japanese sovereignty; Japan establishes relations with Peking

SUPPLEMENTARY READING

Borton, Hugh. *Japan's Modern Century,* rev. ed. New York, 1970.
Hsü, I. C. Y. *The Rise of Modern China.* New York, 1970.
Ishida, Takeshi. *Japanese Society.* New York, 1971.
Pye, Lucian W. *China: An Introduction.* Boston, 1972.
Reischauer, E. O. *Japan: The Story of a Nation.* New York, 1970.

ADVANCED READING

Anderson, J. L. and D. Richie. *The Japanese Film.* New York, 1960.
Barnett, A. D., ed. *Chinese Communist Politics in Action.* Seattle, 1969.
Cole, R. S. *Japanese Blue Collar.* Berkeley, 1971.
Committee of Concerned Asian Scholars. *China: Inside the People's Republic.* New York, 1972.
Fairbank, J. K. *The United States and China.* 3rd rev. ed. Cambridge, Mass., 1971.
Jan, G. P., ed. *Government of Communist China.* San Francisco, 1966.
Kawabata, Yasunari. *Snow Country.* New York, 1956.

——— *Sound of the Mountain.* New York, 1970.
Kawasaki, Ichiro. *Japan Unmasked.* Tokyo, 1969.
Lifton, R. J. *Revolutionary Immortality: Mao Tse-tung and the Chinese Cultural Revolution.* New York, 1968.
Ojha, I. C. *Chinese Foreign Policy in an Age of Transition.* Boston, 1971.
Olson, Lawrence. *Japan in Postwar Asia.* New York, 1970.
Packard, G. R. III. *Protest in Tokyo.* Princeton, N.J., 1966.
Plath, D. W. *The After Hours: Modern Japan and the Search for Enjoyment.* Berkeley, Calif., 1964.
Vogel, Ezra. *Canton Under Communism.* Cambridge, Mass., 1969.
——— *Japan's New Middle Class.* Berkeley, 1965.
Yanaga, Chitoshi. *Big Business and Japanese Politics.* New Haven, Conn., 1968.

Chapter 28

The United States and Asia

Despite large reservoirs of friendship of Americans and Asians at individual and private institutional levels going back more than a hundred years, considerable largesse given by the United States government to Asian nations in need or in peril, and a generally mild and friendly occupation of Japan, the United States's relations with Asia since World War II have been badly hurt by two complexes of factors, the one highly visible and the second subliminal.

These are (1) ideological and power rivalry with the Soviet Union, and (2) attitudes of superiority deeply imbedded in the American psyche.

To begin with the visible, let us review briefly American-Russian relations in Asia.

RUSSIA AND THE FAR EAST TO 1945, AND RUSSIAN-AMERICAN RELATIONS

During the nineteenth century Russian-American relations were very cordial. There was little contact, but such things as expressions of Russian sympathy for the Union cause in the American Civil War, in contrast to England's favoring the Confederacy, the sale of Alaska, and general Russian withdrawal from Pacific area competition created a tradition of friendship. However, a few power-conscious Americans, such as Commodore Perry, predicted that one day the United States and Russia would be rivals on a global scale.

Open Door

In 1899 and 1900 came the first sign that this rivalry might develop. Already active in Manchuria and Korea in various economic and political ventures, Russia used the Boxer movement in China as an excuse to send troops into Manchuria and place the area effectively under Russian occupation. The American enunciation of the Open Door policy was to a large degree an answer to this Russian thrust. While the Open Door policy aimed to dissuade *all* the imperialist powers from dismembering China, as well as to prevent the closing of any part of China to American commercial interests, the Anglophile sympathies of John Hay plus the fact that Russia was at the time the most aggressively expansionist of the powers active in the Far East focused the Open Door notes to a peculiar degree on Russia.

Russo-Japanese War

During the Russo-Japanese War American policy and opinion was generally pro-Japanese, though at the very end President Theodore Roosevelt began to feel that American interests would be better served by a compromise peace than by a complete Japanese victory. This he worked for and achieved at Portsmouth. With Russian expansion in abeyance after the war, American Far Eastern policy became more concerned with Japan than with Russia, although the Russo-Japanese agreements of 1907 and 1910, which divided Manchuria into spheres of interest, irritated Washington profoundly and prevented the incipient Far Eastern rivalry with Russia from lapsing entirely.

Early Soviet Policies

American-Russian rivalry resumed in 1917, after the establishment of the Soviet regime, in the form of the Siberian intervention. This time the issues were complex, involving wartime strategy, internal Russian affairs, and Far Eastern international relations. Uncomfortable from the outset in the interventionist role, the United States tried to limit the scope of the intervention and soon became so disgusted with the conduct of her erstwhile allies, especially the Japanese, that she withdrew from it as soon as possible, despite the fact that the United States government was very displeased with the radical turn of events in Russia and the radical nature of the Soviet regime. During the whole period of the 1920's the United States did not recognize Soviet Russia and in the great conferences of that decade involving the Far East, the Washington and London Conferences, Soviet participation was not invited.

The new Soviet government was officially not interested in territorial aggrandizement, even for the sake of obtaining warm water outlets. In pamphlets spread through northern China it denounced the imperialism of the tsars, offered to abandon the complex of extraterritorial rights and Russian special privilege in China, including, according to one version, the Chinese Eastern Railroad across Manchuria. Its interim object, it said, prior to socialist revolution, was the liberation of Asian peoples from imperialism, and Asian communists were instructed to support national liberation movements.

However, the Soviet leaders discovered to their sorrow that national anti-imperialist movements did not necessarily bring them closer to communist goals; in fact sometimes it was the reverse, as in Turkey, Iran, and China. In each of those countries the Soviets supported the nationalist movements of Mustafa Kemal, Reza Shah Pahlavi, and Sun Yat-sen, respectively, but in each case the success of the movement resulted in the ousting of communist influence. In China this was an especially bitter experience for the Soviets, for their agents, such as Borodin, had been primarily responsible for the revitalization of the revolutionary movement. In fact, in only one non-Russian area, Outer Mongolia, was communist revolution successful, and there only because of the intervention of Soviet arms and the prior influence of tsarist Russia.

Mongolia

The Mongolian case is interesting and should be discussed briefly here. Imperial Russia had exacted a treaty from China in 1913, which permitted Mongol "autonomy" and considerable Russian influence, although Chinese "sovereignty" over the area was upheld. Then after the Russian Revolution Outer Mongolia became a hotbed of intrigue. In 1919 Chinese forces moved into the Mongolian capital, Urga, to assert Chinese sovereignty, but they were ousted in 1921 by White Russian contingents under Baron Ungern-Sternberg. In July 1921 units of the Soviet Red army appeared. They soon set up a Soviet-style puppet government and changed the name of the capital to Ulan Bator (Red Hero). China protested, but could do nothing.

However, there were other issues to be settled. The Soviets wanted Chinese recognition and, by now, had decided that the Chinese Eastern Railway, so dear to the tsars, was also necessary to them. In 1924 a Sino-Soviet treaty was concluded, by which the Soviets surrendered all tsarist privileges in China proper, as promised, but by which they retained the Chinese Eastern Railroad under Russian management. By this treaty Outer Mongolia was made an autonomous "People's Republic" from which both Soviet and Chinese troops were barred. Russian influences continued to predominate there through economic and cultural ties and in 1936 a special Mongol-Soviet treaty further tightened the Russian hold. Thus in territorial terms the Soviet position vis-à-vis China and Monoglia was very like the former tsarist position.

Soviet Policies Toward Japan

With Japan the Soviet leaders did the best they could to regain the position of the tsars. Aided indirectly by Anglo-American pressure exerted on Japan at the Washington Conference they were able to obtain an end to the Siberian intervention, and in 1925 they secured an agreement with Japan whereby, in exchange for fishing rights in Siberian waters and certain oil and mineral rights in northern Sakhalin, Japanese troops entirely evacuated Russian soil, the last being withdrawn from northern Sakhalin in that year. However, in the next decade the Russians lost ground as Japanese pressure mounted in Manchuria (see Chapter 22). By 1933 they were able to run the Chinese Eastern Railroad only with the sufferance of the Japanese and in 1935 rather than contest the situation they sold their

Manchurian railroad rights to Japan's puppet state, Manchukuo. At the Siberian and Mongolian border they held firm against Japanese pressure, but while the Japanese expanded, the Soviet government had no opportunity to reassert the pre-1905 claims of tsarist Russia to places like southern Sakhalin, south Manchuria, and north Korea.

Thus during the 1920's and 1930's, despite the not inconsiderable attractions of communist ideology to Asian peoples, the Soviet Union was not able to extend its influence in Asia much beyond its own borders, not as far, indeed, as tsarist Russia had done. This does not mean that Russian power in Asia was not growing, but its growth was largely in terms of internal developments in Siberia. There railroads, industrial centers, and great cities were built, and irrigation projects improved agricultural production. Also the Soviet government found techniques of tying Russian-controlled areas of Central Asia, like Kazakhstan and Turkistan, more closely to Russia than the tsarist regime had been able to do. These were organized into "federated" Socialist Soviet republics and governed through the Communist party organization.

However, these were internal matters, and since at its Far Eastern rim Soviet Russia was not involved in challenges to the Open Door policy, as the tsars had been, American suspicions were not aroused.

World War II

Indeed, with the development of the common cause against fascism in Europe and Japanese imperialism in Asia, Soviet-American relations improved rapidly. The recognition of Soviet Russia by the Roosevelt administration in 1933 paved the way for this, and the Comintern's United Front politics after 1935 helped it along. During World War II Soviet-American friendship and cooperation reached a height that can hardly be believed by those who have grown up during the Cold War era. Under the Lend-Lease program American supplies were funneled into the Soviet Union, especially through the Persian Gulf and over the Trans-Iranian Railroad. And the resistance the Soviets had put up against the Nazi invasion was much admired and appreciated in the United States. Most Americans, including President Roosevelt, felt that there were no insuperable odds to continued Soviet-American cooperation after World War II, although Roosevelt hoped and expected that the nature of the Soviet regime would be changed in a more liberal direction.

However, great power, as distinguished from ideological, rivalry began to emerge toward the end of World War II. At the Yalta Conference in February 1945, Stalin could have been mistaken for a tsar of all the Russias in the demands he made for the Kuril Islands, southern Sakhalin, railroad rights in Manchuria and the naval base at Port Arthur, as his *quid pro quo* for entering the Japanese war. These were granted. The Soviets also wanted to occupy the Japanese northern island of Hokkaido, and being denied this, they insisted on receiving the Japanese surrender in Manchuria and part of Korea. Since their forces were in a position to carry out the occupation of these areas with or without American approval, the agreement to divide the line of Japanese surrender at the 38th parallel in Korea, which left the capital, Seoul, in American hands, seemed at the time to be a good arrangement from the American point of view. However, this line at the 38th parallel in the months that followed the Japanese surrender became the first Iron Curtain and the point of sorest tension between the communist and noncommunist worlds.

COLD WAR

It should be remembered, as one discusses the build-up of tension in Korea leading to the Korean War, that Soviet-American rivalry was very tense at several other points in Asia, as well as in Europe. In 1946 and 1947 the Soviet Union was putting direct pressure on Turkey and Iran (see Chapter 23). This was resisted by the United States program known as the Truman Doctrine, developed in 1947, which provided economic and military aid to countries beset by Soviet pressure. In addition, whether the Soviet Union was directly involved or not, there were now active communist elements in Southeast Asian countries, like the Hukbalahaps in the Philippines, the Vietminh in Indochina, and communist groups in Burma, Malaya, and Indonesia; also there was communist activity in Japan and in India; and, of course, the communist-nationalist civil war in China was being renewed.

Actually the war that began with the Soviet-sponsored North Korean invasion of South Korea on June 25, 1950, was the second Korean war of our century. The first was the Russo-Japanese War of 1904-1905 (see Chapter 16). In the years immediately prior to that earlier Korean war imperial Russia had been trying to bring Korea into its sphere and turn the Yellow Sea into a Russian warm water outlet. And this was merely one aspect of a general Russian pressure all across Asia, from the Dardanelles to the Pacific, a pressure matched by that of Britain extending northward from southern Asia. It was a "cold war" of the late nineteenth century, an intense imperial rivalry between Great Britain and Tsarist Russia. With the formation of the Anglo-Japanese Alliance in 1902 the means for "containing" Russia was found. Japan, whose proximity to Korea made her peculiarly interested in blocking Russian expansion there, after offering to halve the peninsula at the 39th parallel and being refused, challenged Russia and, with Britain providing financial and moral support from a position of benevolent neutrality, defeated her. Russian expansion was blocked and both Korea and southern Manchuria fell into the Japanese sphere, which then served as a buffer between British and Russian interests in the Far East. With British fear of Russia now diminished and the Russian expansionist sails somewhat trimmed the way was opened for a general Anglo-Russian settlement of their "cold war" in Asia. This was accomplished in 1907 with the aforementioned agreement on Persia (see Chapter 11).

In this Korean war of 1904-1905 there were no clear-cut ideological issues. It mattered little to Koreans which sphere they were in. For Korea a Russian victory at that point would probably have been no worse than the

Japanese one which occurred. And the fact that England's government was parliamentary and Russia's was autocratic did not elevate the issues between them above the realm of power politics. In geopolitical terms it might simply be said that the greatest land power of the age (Russia) was vying with the greatest sea power (Britain), and lesser states were pawns in the game.

Now the Korean War of 1950–1953 can be interpreted in similar terms, with Soviet Russia having assumed the role of Tsarist Russia and the United States the role of Britain. This would, of course, be a cynical interpretation, equally disquieting to those who saw the Korean War as freedom's fight against communist tyranny or, conversely, if viewed from the communist side, as a "people's war" against reactionaries. It is certainly not a sufficient explanation, for the issues between democracy and communism were real ones, even in Asia where poverty intervened to cloud them. However, there was enough old-fashioned great power rivalry present in the post-World War II situation to cause the historian to be cautious in accepting exclusively ideological explanations of the 1950 Korean imbroglio, and it is possible that an unadmitted but nevertheless actual realization of this among the government leaders involved permitted a truce to be made, even though the ideological issues were as far from resolution as at the start of the war.

However, the power politics explanation of the struggle was not acceptable to the general American public, whose sensitivities were outraged by what it believed to be "Moscow-inspired communist aggression," and an articulated belief that communism posed a global threat to the "American way of life" became a prerequisite for anyone aspiring to public office in the United States.

Containment

Although McCarthyism demanded the rooting out of communism everywhere, "containment" became the established United States policy toward it. The containment policy was first proposed in 1947 by Ambassador George F. Kennan in his later famous "Mr. X" article in *Foreign Affairs* on "The Sources of Soviet Conduct." Warning that Soviet expansion was on the move, Mr. Kennan advocated an American stance that assumed long-term hostility and rivalry and would confront the Russians with counterforce wherever and whenever they might attempt to enlarge the area of communist control.

Actually containment was already in operation as Kennan wrote, for President Truman, after applauding Winston Churchill's proclamation of Cold War in his Fulton, Missouri, "Iron Curtain" speech of March 1946, had been proceeding in that vein, it being noteworthy that he dismissed the only serious advocate of continuing to seek rapprochement with Russia, Secretary of Commerce Henry A. Wallace, in September 1946. Thereafter the aforementioned Truman Doctrine was developed and put into operation. What Kennan did was to rationalize and project these moves into the long-range future as the American containment policy. Many years later, after the Vietnam War had become a tragedy, Kennan told an American Historical Association meeting on the origins of the Cold War in Asia (Toronto, 1967) that he had not intended that the containment policy be applied in Asia, but only in Europe.

However, John Foster Dulles and Dean Rusk, who were the most influential men in formulating American policy toward Asia from about 1951 to 1968, decided otherwise. The question became how to stop the spread of communism in Asia, not whether Asian factors such as poverty and anticolonialism made the problem different from that faced in Europe. Dulles avoided the commitment of American ground forces to the task, by relying on the threat of "massive retaliation," presumably atomic, for any upsetting of the communist-Free World balance in Asia after the Korean truce of 1953. He also constructed a Southeast Asia Treaty Organization (SEATO) in 1954, which lacked the military muscle of NATO, but which presumably would provide diplomatic assistance. Nevertheless, by the end of the 1950's it was becoming clear that the threat of "massive retaliation" with or without SEATO diplomacy was not an effective way to contain the sort of guerrilla insurgency that was developing in Indochina, and the State Department, after Rusk became secretary of state in January 1961, came gradually around to the view that American ground forces should be used in Indochina. The governing assumption continued to be that communism was felling nations like dominoes in a row. Emanating from Moscow, it had expanded through China and was now seeking to engulf Southeast Asia. (The "falling domino" terminology was first used by President Eisenhower in a news conference in 1954.)

The stages and extent of American involvement in Indochina have been described in Chapter 25. A key incident in this involvement was the passage of the so-called Gulf of Tonkin resolution by the United States Congress in August 1964. This was passed at President Johnson's request after North Vietnamese torpedo boats allegedly fired on two American destroyers in the Gulf of Tonkin, about fifty miles from the shore of North Vietnam. Calling this "open aggression on the high seas," the president asked for and received congressional authorization "to take all necessary measures to repel any armed attacks against the forces of the United States and to prevent further aggression." Though repealed six years later, amidst criticism that it had permitted presidential misuse of Congress' warmaking power, it was utilized in the interim to send over 500,000 American troops into a war against communism in Vietnam, Laos and, ultimately, Cambodia.

Meanwhile the question whether communism could or should be contained in Asia was lost sight of as the tactics for containing it came to be debated not only in government but in research institutes around the country. But gradually a few voices were raised to challenge the containment assumption.

Dissent

So-called "New Left" scholars began to argue that Soviet policy in the immediate post-World War II era had been essentially defensive, not expansionist, and that American "open door diplomacy," which provided an entering wedge for American business to assume control of poor countries on a worldwide scale, was the real expansionist force. Only by "escaping" from the Free World could an underdeveloped country avoid American capitalist entanglement. This argument had no effect in policy-making circles, which looked upon a succession of United States aid programs as genuinely improving the lives and livelihoods of Asian peoples, as well as assisting them in "nation building" and in defense against communism.

However, the escalation of the Vietnam war brought much soul searching among scholars and students, and through teach-ins and demonstrations their questioning of the basic assumptions of the Cold War against communism, or more specifically of the hot war that had developed in Vietnam, began to be voiced. In 1966, amid demands that scholars of Asia take a stand against the war, a "Committee of Concerned Asian Scholars" was formed, which challenged official United States interpretations of the Vietnam situation and the justifications for American involvement. By 1968 this had become a leading political issue, with several Democratic senators, including Senator Fulbright, Chairman of the Senate Committee on Foreign Relations, becoming critical of the Johnson administration's conduct of the war. In November 1968 Republican Richard Nixon, though formerly a supporter of the Vietnam intervention, was elected president on a platform of "winding down the war" and withdrawing American troops. In 1970 the Tonkin Gulf resolution came under fire by the now many critics of the war in Congress, the Senate twice voted overwhelmingly to repeal it, and the House finally concurred in a compromise whereby its repeal was inserted into a Foreign Military Sales Act. President Nixon signed the measure on January 14, 1971. The "authorization" for the Vietnam war had ended, but not yet the war itself.

Not only did the Cold War produce two hot wars, Korea and Vietnam, but it also produced outright or clandestine intervention for political purposes by both the Soviet Union and the United States in most of the countries of Asia, which as developing countries could ill afford the dubious luxury of internecine plotting and quarreling beyond what could be considered normal for the region. Such would include: the landing of American marines in Lebanon in 1958 to offset pro-Egyptian intrigues; Soviet meddling in Iraq, where Russian technicians have been developing Iraqi oil fields; American complicity in the overthrow of Mossadegh and the refurbishment of the shah in Iran, to the advantage of American oil interests; both American and Russian intrigue in Afghanistan, where geography has tended to favor the Russians; in Indonesia, where the United States seems to have come out ahead; and strange support patterns in India and Pakistan, where for Cold War reasons the United States leaned toward authoritarian Pakistan while the USSR supported democratic India in their brief war over Bangladesh in 1971. This is to say nothing of Laos and Cambodia, where the extent of intrigue staggers the imagination.

Of course, it can be argued that these Asian states would be divided or unstable even without the intrigues that have accompanied the Cold War, for the factions within are well nigh irreconcilable, and none of these states, with the exception of India, has a parliamentary means of dealing peacefully with their conflicts. It can also be said that considerable real economic and technical assistance has been given these Asian states by the superpowers.

Aid

Concerning this a brief discussion may be appropriate here. United States "economic" (as distinguished from military) assistance programs for Asian countries were generally based on Marshall Plan concepts, which had greatly assisted the postwar recovery of Western Europe. They began with Point Four (of President Truman's Inaugural Address, 1949) and proceeded through MSA (Mutual Security Act, 1951), which coalesced economic, military, and technical assistance programs and made it difficult to distinguish nonmilitary items, and continued on through the 1950's and 1960's under various names, such as Mutual Aid, Mutual Security, Foreign Aid, Foreign Assistance, Food For Freedom (also Public Law 480), and AID (Agency for International Development). An Export-Import Bank and an Asian Development Bank, willing to make "soft loans" to needy countries, agricultural assistance programs which produced a "green revolution" of immensely improved food production in southern Asia and a booming economy in Taiwan, educational aid programs in those areas, and Mekong River basin development were impressive subprograms of American aid, which over two decades (1946–1966) totalled some 33 billion dollars of nonmilitary aid. This was for all of Asia, including the Middle East. India and Pakistan, with over nine billion, and South Korea and Taiwan, with six and a half billion, were the largest recipients in the years before the Vietnam War (to 1966). The Soviet Union also gave considerable economic aid, though much less than the American total. For the twelve years, 1955–1966 inclusive, for which good estimates are available, the Soviet total (to Asia and the Middle East), was approximately five billion dollars. This does not include aid to China or other communist nations. India, with one and a half billion, and the United Arab Republic, with approximately one billion, received the largest amounts, with Afghanistan and Indonesia following.

The extent to which this nonmilitary aid was for Cold War political purposes is the subject of a growing literature, but regardless of that much of the good and goods it produced were compromised by the immense impact of military aid programs. United States military expenditures on Vietnam were to reach 30 billion dollars per year, and over the period since World War II the weaponry given, loaned, or sold to Asian states and/or factions within them for Cold War purposes has killed, maimed, and disrupted the lives of millions of Asians to such an extent that a retired American general has referred to the Cold War era as "twenty-six disastrous years."[1]

AMERICAN ATTITUDES AND POLICIES TOWARD ASIANS

The second unhappy strain in United States relations with Asia has been the superiority complex, sometimes racist, sometimes merely cultural, with which Americans have viewed Asians.

[1] *Congressional Record*, Nov. 9, 1971, E12032-33.

The origins of this were by no means peculiarly American. They lay in European colonialism in Asia, beginning with the Portuguese intrusion there in 1498 and coming to a climax in the later nineteenth century when European colonial rule reached its apogee. In this setting occidentals with few exceptions came to regard themselves as "naturally" superior to the backward peoples they were ruling or teaching, and Asians, aware of their backwardness, at least in technological and administrative know-how, generally acquiesced in the judgment. It should also be said, however, that previous to the European colonial era the Chinese had considered themselves the superior people of the world and outsiders "barbarians," the Japanese had entertained lofty "race of the gods" concepts of themselves, the Muslims thought themselves the elect of Allah, and but for the Muslim conquest of India, the Hindus might have had similar delusions of grandeur.

Americans came into Asia late, with somewhat conflicting basic attitudes. They were opposed to imperialism and colonialism as practiced by Europeans, and their foundation documents, the Declaration of Independence and the Constitution, proclaimed lofty ideals of equality and human rights. However, these basic documents were interpreted not to apply to Indians and to apply only partially to blacks in America. In their dealings with Asians in Asia, Americans were generally more friendly and equalitarian than their European counterparts, as evidenced by very cordial and equal relationships between American merchants like Girard of Philadephia and Chinese cohong members. American treaties, such as the Burlingame Treaty with China of 1868, contained more emphasis on equality and reciprocity, although it should be remembered that "most-favored-nation" clauses allowed the United States to claim advantages from European treaties when it chose.

Exclusion Laws

While there was thus a good deal of emphasis on friendship and equality in nineteenth century American dealings in Asia, relations with Asian immigrants to the United States were very bad, even before the turn of the century. Chinese, brought in as "coolie" labor for railroad building, were no longer needed or wanted after the railroads had been built, and the 1882 Exclusion Law indicated as much. Those who stayed retreated into Chinatowns, where they were afraid to exercise whatever legal rights they had as unwelcome aliens. They were often victimized by toughs and mobs. The Chinatowns became ghettos of a special kind, where women were too few in number to provide a healthy balance of wives and families, and they became stereotyped as rife with gambling and prostitution. Despite this some Chinese became naturalized citizens, raised families of native-born Chinese Americans, and made modest livelihoods in various lines of business. But even these were victims of social, if not legal, discrimination by the dominant white population.

Japanese were treated similarly, although because of Japan's rising power as a nation, with somewhat more circumspection. Rather than outright exclusion, the "Gentlemen's Agreement" system finalized in 1907 was used to hold down their numbers. By this an economic test was applied, with only unskilled laborers absolutely excluded. Meanwhile, in the 1910's and early 1920's, the courts began to block Oriental applications for citizenship on the grounds that persons of the "Mongolian race" were unassimilable, and after the Supreme Court in the Ozawa case (1922) upheld the ineligibility of Japanese to citizenship on the grounds that they were not "free white persons" as defined in the Naturalization Eligibility Law of 1790, the way was opened to total exclusion of all Asians deemed "colored." In 1924 Congress seized upon the opportunity and passed a law excluding all "aliens ineligible to citizenship."

While the immigration door was thus closed, Asian aliens resident in the United States were subjected to various forms of legal discrimination, such as the Alien Land Laws of California which prevented them from owning land. However, their American-born children were citizens by birth, and they were able to "circumvent" these laws to some extent by putting property in their children's names, and for a time in the 1930's, as this American-born generation was growing up and often distinguishing itself in educational pursuits, it seemed that the most overt forms of discrimination against persons of Asian ancestry were being dissipated.

Japanese Relocation

Then, in 1942, amid wartime hysteria, a new form of discrimination was applied to "persons of Japanese ancestry"—alien and citizen alike—in the form of "relocation" from West Coast states. Clearly unconstitutional in any ordinary reading of that document, this was done and upheld under the guise of military necessity, and over 100,000 people were incarcerated in relocation camps in various mountain states and Arkansas. Fortunately, the administration of the camps was placed in the hands of a wise and humane director, Dillon Myer, whose staff worked to mitigate the sufferings of the evacuees as much as possible and to pursue the "relocation" idea by promoting their release from the camps to educational or job opportunities in the Middle Western and Eastern states.

While the Japanese suffered the additional indignity of relocation during the war, with China as our Pacific ally the Chinese exclusion laws were at last repealed by Congress in the fall of 1943, with President Roosevelt signing the repeal measure on December 17 of that year. It should also be observed that much of what has been described above did not apply to Hawaii, where the population was about equally divided among Chinese, Japanese, Caucasians, Hawaiians, and Filipinos, and there was a tacit assumption that they would all live together as harmoniously as possible. Significantly, there was no attempt at mass evacuation or incarceration of Japanese elements of the population, despite Pearl Harbor, and Hawaii's Japanese American young men formed the nucleus of the famous 442nd Division of the U.S. Army in Europe.

It was against this historical background that American military forces and civilians drawn from all the forty-eight states, with a few from Hawaii, moved into postwar East Asia to occupy Japan, "liberate" Korea, "restore" China, and block the spread of communism. Most had never known an

Asian, some were definitely racist (toward all "colored" people), some were "colored" themselves (blacks), many were indifferent. The Asia they saw was war-torn and poverty-stricken. Most, including those who could be called racist, quickly developed feelings of sympathy and pity for the Asians they saw, gave them chocolate bars and cigarettes, and came to like Asians, especially Asian women. There was a large degree of condescension in this friendly sympathy, but as shown in the case of Japan, with time and nonanimosity it might have become something better. In fact, it did in Japan. As the Japanese began to rebuild their country sympathy turned into admiration, first for their pluckiness, then for their achievements, until by the late 1960's there were probably minimal feelings of superiority on the part of Americans toward Japanese.

Vietnam

In certain other areas, however, particularly in Korea and Vietnam, where there was tension, danger, and war, the basic American assumptions of superiority were intensified by nervousness about the capability, dependability, and even trustworthiness of their Asian allies. Fortunately, the Korean war ended before many untoward incidents could happen, and the South Korean populace seemed genuinely to have opposed the North Korean regime. But the Vietnam war, with the South Vietnamese countryside often and obviously giving aid and comfort to the Vietcong and infiltrators from the north, rendering abortive time after time the efforts of over 500,000 Americans (at the peak involvement point in 1968) to estab-

FIGURE 28.1. Refugee from Quang Tri Province holds her ears at the sound of artillery on Highway One, Vietnam, July 1972.

lish order there, brought out the worst in the American superiority complex. Forced evacuation and destruction of villages such as Ben Suc (1967) and My Lai (1968) produced situations in which civilians were the principal victims, nor was bombing from the air particularly selective in its victims. In the "body count" a dead Vietnamese was always presumed to be a Vietcong. The term "ARVN" (for Army of the Republic of [South] Vietnam) also took on a derogatory meaning, as American military and newspaper men on the scene reported evidence of their unwillingness or lack of ability to fight.

By 1968 Americans had largely taken over the war in Vietnam. American casualty rates were increasingly high, and the American public became disenchanted with the war. Then President Nixon came into office with a new approach to the war: "Vietnamization," the doctrine announced at Guam in July 1969. According to this, American ground forces were to be withdrawn gradually, and the South Vietnamese would then have to take over the ground fighting. During the next four years this program was followed, while peace talks in Paris, initiated under President Johnson, got nowhere. By 1972 American troop levels were reduced to well below 100,000, and American casualty rates to an average of less than a dozen per week.

This was widely accepted as "winding down the war" by the American people, and Vietnam (except for sporadic flareups) no longer took the headlines. However, it was observed by many critics of the war that this Vietnamization policy simply "changed the color of the bodies." And the revised American role of concentrating on air support put Americans in the position of fighting the war "from 40,000 feet up," with the bombs raining down in so-called "free fire zones" on whomever might get in the way. Vietnamization seemed clearly to be a policy of saving American lives at the expense of Vietnamese ones, and antiwar literature began to emphasize the racism implicit in this and its relationship to racism in the United States.

One particularly ironic feature of the Vietnam war was its relation to the drug (opium-heroin) problem in the United States. This increased by leaps and bounds as the war continued, until many Americans returning from Vietnam had to be given special antidrug therapy as part of their demobilization procedure.

Progress

During 1971–1972 American ground forces were steadily withdrawn from Vietnam in line with President Nixon's Vietnamization policy. However, in other aspects the war seemed to be reescalating, with renewed bombing of North Vietnam, mining of Haiphong harbor, and increasing military activity in Laos and Cambodia. President Nixon explained this as necessary to his quest for "peace with honor," which precluded a unilateral withdrawal of the United States which would leave South Vietnam open to conquest by the North. Dissent in the United States showed signs of reescalating also. The publication in mid-1971 by the *New York Times* of

ASIA IN 1971

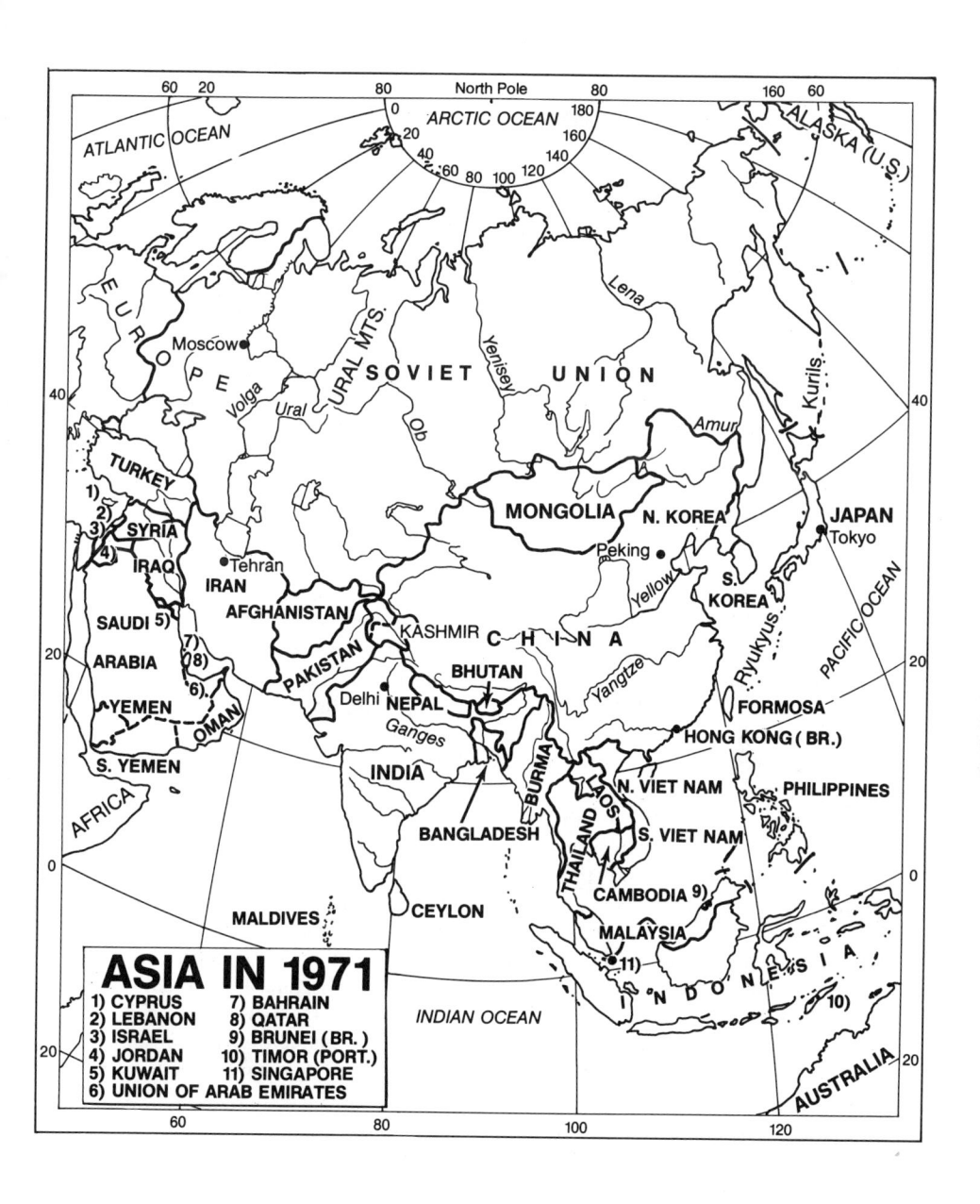

1) CYPRUS
2) LEBANON
3) ISRAEL
4) JORDAN
5) KUWAIT
6) UNION OF ARAB EMIRATES
7) BAHRAIN
8) QATAR
9) BRUNEI (BR.)
10) TIMOR (PORT.)
11) SINGAPORE

the *Pentagon Papers*, a classified history of the Vietnam war done by government researchers of the RAND Corporation, had revealed to the public the deceptions in facts and figures about the war practiced by the Johnson administration and its euphemistic terminology (such as "Rolling Thunder campaign" for bombing), and helped to make the war so unpopular that the only practical political course was to end it. The question was *how?*

While antiwar activists made headlines with renewed demonstrations in Washington, at Harrisburg, Pa., where a "conspiracy" trial of some of them was being held, and with attempted "canoe blockades" of munitions ships leaving for Vietnam, the major political parties developed their 1972 campaign approaches to the Vietnam issue. Democratic candidate George McGovern was for "immediate withdrawal." President Nixon reiterated his "peace with honor" theme and succeeded in giving it greater credibility with the revelation in the fall of 1972 that presidential advisor Henry Kissinger had been engaged in secret talks with the North Vietnamese. In October Kissinger made the spectacular announcement that an agreement had been reached and that "peace is at hand." Clearly, the president won at least half the "peace votes" in his resounding reelection victory in November.

The peace process suffered a temporary setback in December, when the Kissinger-Le Duc Tho (Hanoi representative) talks were suspended over disagreements on "terminology" and President Nixon reopened bombing of North Vietnam, December 18–28. But whether because of, or in spite of, this (the question may long be argued), the talks were resumed in January 1973 and cease-fire agreements signed on January 27 at Paris. The agreements, as emphasized by Dr. Kissinger, whose doctoral dissertation was on the diplomacy of Metternich and Castlereagh, simply represented the totality of the negotiating situation, including the surrounding pressures and history. They were quite vague and ambiguous. Except for one crucial point of exchange, whereby Hanoi would release all American prisoners of war within sixty days and all remaining American troops would be withdrawn from Vietnam during that same period, the signatory "parties" (who were not very clearly defined, but were understood to be Hanoi, Saigon, the Vietcong, and the United States) simply agreed to cease fighting and let history take its course in Vietnam, and hopefully in Laos and Cambodia also. There was to be an international truce watching team, and eventually a political conference and hopefully a settlement. All this was reminiscent of Korea and Geneva twenty years before, but so many parties had been seared by fire since then that it seemed Dr. Kissinger might be right in his prediction that the agreements could be made to work. Even though serious fighting continued in many parts of Indochina and the United States retained strong air forces in neighboring Thailand, Americans generally had no desire to continue participating in the war.

Red carpet welcomes marked the return of American prisoners (POWs) during February and March 1973. These provided at least a pleasant illusion that the Vietnam struggle had been concluded "with honor" and that the principal problems remaining therefrom were domestic ones. These included control of inflation, rehabilitation of returnees—

not only POWs, but ordinary demobilized soldiers, for whom there was no hero's welcome, and ultimately the "exiles," those who had fled to Canada or abroad to avoid being conscripted for Vietnam, drug abusers, alienated youth, and a sorry heritage of political trials. American casualties from the war were 45,933 killed, 1,344 missing, 303,616 wounded, 587 prisoners of war, about 70,000 exiles. The Vietnamese killed numbered from one to two million.

While the Cold War and the Vietnam conflict brought out the bad side of American relations with Asia, it should not be assumed that there was no progress at all in the 1950s and 1960s. In the United States Asians became much more welcome than formerly. The Immigration and Nationality Act of 1952 (McCarran Act) placed all Asians under the national origins quota system, along with Europeans and others, thus dispelling the onus of inequality, though their percentage of population-based quotas was very small. Then, in 1965, a new law abolished the national origins system and moved (within three years) to a system of processing immigration applications in order of their receipt, without regard to nationality—up to an overall quota of 170,000, with no one country to be allowed over 20,000. This had a very healthy effect on the Asian immigrant population in allowing it to reach a balance of male and female. Indeed, it may be a sign of the times that Asian elements of the American population are playing an increasingly important role in mediating tensions between blacks and whites. Examples of this are the presidency of a Nisei, S.I. Hayakawa, at San Francisco State College and the election of three Chinese Americans to mayoralty posts in Mississippi.

Relations with Israel remained quite cordial, and considering the tensions of the Arab-Israeli conflict, have been fairly cordial with the Arab nations, Iran and Pakistan. Relations with India were damaged by the decision, dictated by Cold War considerations, not to support her in her handling of the Bangladesh problem in 1971, but a considerable reservoir of good will remains in India despite this. During the early 1970s some tension crept into the economics of Japanese American relations. American overspending abroad, largely the result of Vietnam War costs, weakened the dollar while Japanese dollar earnings zoomed. Some thorny trade negotiations were emerging, but the reservoir of twenty-five years of intimate association and general good will made the outlook positive.

Most hopeful of all were the 1972 summit meetings between President Nixon and the leaders of the People's Republic of China and the Soviet Union. These and subsequent meetings between Chinese and American officials and Soviet and American officials respectively seemed to indicate that the Cold War was at last winding down. Small courtesies were supplemented by arrangements for selling wheat to Russia and the establishment of official relations with China. Certainly these lessenings of tension with the large communist powers were factors of importance in making the Vietnam truce possible. Now, if overall Southeast Asian and perhaps Korean settlements could occur as part of winding down the Cold War, the later 1970s could see United States relations with Asia take on a more relaxed character than had been the case since the fateful Manchurian Incident of September 1931.

BASIC DATES

1790	U.S. naturalization law ("free white persons")
1844	Treaty of Wanghsia
1854	U.S. opening of Japan
1868	Burlingame Treaty with China
1882	Chinese exclusion law
1899	Open Door notes
1907	Gentlemen's agreement with Japan
1917	Siberian intervention
1924	U.S. immigration law (Japanese exclusion)
1941–1945	Pacific War
1943	Repeal of Chinese exclusion laws
1945	Yalta conference
1947	Truman doctrine
1950–1953	Korean War
1951	Treaty with Japan
1952	McCarran Immigration Act
1954	Southeast Asia Treaty Organization established
1964	Tonkin Gulf resolution
1965	Start of American use of land forces and bombers in Vietnam
1968	Start of Paris peace talks; Nixon elected president
1969	U.S. Vietnamization policy announced; U.S. troop withdrawal begins
1971	Repeal of Tonkin Gulf resolution
1972	Nixon to Peking and Moscow; U.S. relinquishes control of Ryukyu Islands
1973	Vietnam, Laos cease-fire agreements; Washington-Peking relations begin

SUPPLEMENTARY READING

Brewster, Kingman. "Reflections on Our National Purpose," *Foreign Affairs,* April, 1972.

Kennan, George F. "The Sources of Soviet Conduct," *Foreign Affairs,* July, 1947.

New York Times. The Pentagon Papers. New York (Bantam paperback), 1971.

Note: The Kennan and Brewster articles will give the student a capsule view of the evolution of sophisticated American thinking on world problems between 1947 and 1972; intervening, of course, was the searing experience of the Vietnam war, concerning which the *Pentagon Papers* show the process of escalating involvement.

ADVANCED READING

Bernstein, B. J. and A. J. Matusow, eds. *Twentieth Century America: Recent Interpretations.* New York, 1969.

Clergy and Laymen Concerned About Vietnam. *In the Name of America.* Annandale, Va., 1968. Shows contradiction between terminology and reality of the Vietnam war.

Daniels, Roger. *America's Concentration Camps.* New York, 1972. A critical analysis of the Japanese relocation during World War II.

Ekirch, A. A., Jr. *Ideas, Ideals, and American Diplomacy.* New York, 1966. Good long-range analysis.

Fitzgerald, Frances. *Fire in the Lake: The Vietnamese and the Americans in Vietnam.* Boston, 1972. Pulitzer prize-winning study.

Fleming, D. F. *The Cold War and Its Origins, 1917–1960,* 2 vols. New York, 1961.

Fulbright, J. W. *The Arrogance of Power.* New York, 1966. By the chairman of the Senate Committee on Foreign Relations.

Graebner, N. A. *Cold War Diplomacy: American Foreign Policy, 1945–1960.* Princeton, N.J., 1962.

Hachey, Thomas, ed. *The Problem of Partition: Peril to World Peace.* Chicago, 1972.

Halle, L. J. *The Cold War as History.* New York, 1967.

Holbik, Karel. *The United States, The Soviet Union and the Third World.* Hamburg, 1968.

Johnson, L. B. *The Vantage Point.* New York, 1971. Contains the president's view of the Vietnam conflict.

Kissinger, H. A. *American Foreign Policy: Three Essays.* New York, 1969. By President Nixon's chief foreign policy advisor.

—— *Nuclear Weapons and Foreign Policy.* New York, 1957.

Kolko, Gabriel. *The Roots of American Foreign Policy.* Boston, 1969. Challenging revisionist study.

Kolko, Gabriel and Joyce. *The Limits of Power: The World and United States Foreign Policy, 1945–1954.* New York, 1972.

Lafeber, Walter. *America, Russia and the Cold War, 1945–1966.* New York, 1967.

Lukacs, J. A. *A New History of the Cold War.* Garden City, N.Y., 1966.

Myer, Dillon. *Uprooted Americans.* Tucson, Ariz., 1971. The director's story of the Japanese relocation.

Neumann, W. L. *After Victory.* New York, 1967.

Schell, Jonathan. *The Village of Ben Suc.* New York, 1967. Brings Vietnam War up close.

Sung, B. L. *The Story of the Chinese in America.* New York, 1967.

Williams, W. A. *The Tragedy of American Diplomacy.* New York, 1959; rev. ed. (Delta paperback), 1962. This early critique of Cold War assumptions stimulated much of the subsequent "New Left" scholarship.

Index

Abadan, 420, 563, 565
Abahai, 85–86
Abassi, Hachem el, 581
Abbas I, Shah, 25–28, 29, 31, 52
Abd-al-Wahhab, Muhammad, 9
Abdul Aziz (Ottoman), 264, 265, 267
Abdul Hamid II (Ottoman), 266, 267–268, 270, 271, 273
Abdul Mejid (Ottoman caliph), 417
Abdul Mejid (Ottoman sultan), 19 (See also Murad V)
Abdul Rahman, Tunku, 623, 624
Abdullah (Jordan), 412, 439, 576, 582, 587
Abdurraman, 235
Abe Isoo, 370, 511
Abe Masahiro, 154
Abe Nobuyuki, 534
Aboukir, Battle of, 15
Abu Musa, 589
Abul Fazl, 61
Achin, sultanate of, 185
Acre, 44, 431
Adams, Will, 137
Adat (law), 177, 186
Aden, 10, 19, 67, 431, 557, 590
Adi Granth, 64
Adrianople, 4, 17, 44, 269, 417
Adrianople, Treaty of (1829), 17
Afghanistan: conquest of Persia, 32–33; conquest by Nadir Shah, 34; Durani dynasty, 37, 44, 46, 64; Barakzai dynasty, 41, 42, 46–47, 63, 64; wars with Britain, 65, 75, 76, 225, 234–235; British in, 78, 254, 255, 257; Russian pressure on, 225; Anglo-Russian rivalry in, 234–235; education in, 427, 590; foreign relations, 427, 429, 443, 449, 590, 591; internal politics, 427
Aga Khan, 241
Aga Muhammad Khan, 37-38, 39
Age of Consent Bill, 245
Agha Riza, 29
Agra, 50, 54
Aguinaldo, Emilio, 397–398, 403–404
Ahimsa (nonviolence), 446
Ah-Lum, 281
Ahmad, Imam (Yemen), 590
Ahmadabad, 457
Ahmadnagar, 50, 53
Ahmad Shah (Afghani), 44, 46, 63
Ahmad Shah (Persia), 262, 421
Ahmed I (Ottoman), 7
Aigun, Treaty of, 221
Akbar, 50, 58, 60, 61, 64
Aksai Chin, 607
al-Afghani, Jamal-ud-din, 259
Alam, Amir Assadolah, 568
Alaouites, 433

Alaska, Russians in, 212, 213, 215, 216, 219, 220, 221
Alaungpaya, 187
Albazin, 94, 216, 217, 218, 219
Albuquerque, 66
Alcock, Rutherford B., 290
Aleutians, 212, 215, 545
Alexander, Tsar, 15, 39
Alexander, William, 402
Alexandretta, 431, 433, 434, 571
Alexandria Conference, 574
Alexis, Tsar, 217
Ali (son of Husain Ibn Ali), 430
Aligarh, University of, 241
Allahabad, 72, 78
Allen, Dr. H. N., 331
Allenby, General, 413
Ambans, 96
Amboina, 164, 165, 166, 167, 172
Amboina Massacre, 114, 166, 167
Amery, Leopold, 460
Amherst, Lord, 122
Ami (Yemeni), 590
Amini, Dr. Ali, 568
Ammanullah, 427
Amoy, 87, 113, 114, 119, 128, 373
Amritsar, 64, 65, 446
Amritsar Massacre, 445–446
Amu Darya River, 35, 224, 226, 591
Amur basin, 94, 220, 221
Amur River Society (See Kokuryūkai)
Amursana, 95
Anami, 548, 549
Ananda Mahidol, 471, 614
Anatolia, 15, 414
Andaman Islands, 460
Andō Shōeki, 150
Anfu clique, 490, 493, 494, 497
Anglo-Iranian (Persian) Oil Company, 425–426, 561, 563–564, 565
Anglo-Japanese Alliance, 366, 374, 375–376, 377, 378, 383, 491, 497, 498, 700
An Hyang, 319
Ankara, 270, 416, 417, 419
Annam, 89, 192, 194, 195, 294, 479, 483
Ansei, Great Persecution of, 154, 158
Anson, John, 115
Anti-Comintern Pact, 523
Anti-Fascist People's Freedom League (AFPFL), 485, 486
Arabia, under the Ottomans, 9–10, 247, 412 (see also Saudi Arabia)
Arabian-American Oil Company (Aramco), 563, 586, 587
Arab League, 572, 574, 575, 581, 584, 587, 589
Arafat, Yasir, 582
Arai Hakuseki, 141
Arakan coast, 55, 188
Araki Sadao, 518, 519, 520

714

Arcot, nawab of, 70, 71, 74
Ardebil, sack of, 40
Arif, Abd al-Rahman, 586
Arif, Abdel Salem, 586
Arima Incident, 137
Arjuna, guru, 64
Armenia, 22, 25, 269, 271, 273, 412, 414, 421, 571
Armenians, 27, 417
Arrow Incident, 280
Arya Samaj, 242, 248
Ashikaga, 83, 107, 136
Ashraf (Afghani), 33
Assam, 55, 188, 464
Assaye, Battle of, 64, 75
Assyrian uprising, 436
Astrabad, 41
Astrakhan, 205
al-Atasi, 581
Ataturk (See Kemal, Mustafa)
Atbak-i-azam, 261–262
Atlasov, 212
Attlee, Clement, 463, 464
Aulick, James, 401
Aung San, 485, 621
Aurangzeb, 54, 55–58, 61, 62, 63, 64, 91
Austria, and the Ottoman Empire, 10, 11, 12, 19
Ava, 187, 188
Ayn-ud-dola, 260
Ayub Khan, 570, 607, 608
Ayuthia, 187, 188, 196, 197
Azerbaijan, 25, 27, 32, 34, 421, 423; autonomous republic in, 560–561, 562, 570

Babism, 42–44
Babur, 50, 61
Bactria, 34
Baghavand, Battle of, 11, 34
Baghdad, 10, 25, 27, 32, 270, 273, 274, 431, 434, 584
Baghdad Pact, 570
Bagyidaw, King (Burma), 188
Baha Allah, 44
Bahadur Shah, 58
Bahai, 44
Bahrain, 35, 269, 420, 425, 430, 589
Baikov, 217
Bakhtiari tribe, 424
al-Bakr, Hasan, 586
Baku, 32, 34, 38, 40, 421
Baldwin, Stanley, 452
Balfour Declaration, 437, 438, 439
Bali, 185
Balkh, 54
Ball, W. Macmahon, 641
Baluchistan, 44, 50, 234
Ba Maw, 485
Banda Islands, 164, 165, 166, 168, 172
Bandaranaike, Madame, 610
Bander Abbas, 27
Bandung Conference, 606, 673, 692
Bangka, 184
Bangkok, 197, 200
Bangladesh, 601, 604, 609, 610, 703, 711
Banners, Manchu, 85, 89, 97, 349

Bantam, sultanate of, 67, 164, 165, 166, 172, 174
Bao Dai, 481, 483, 625, 626
Barakzai dynasty (see Afghanistan)
Barangay, 387, 390
Baranov, 215
Baroda, 63
Basra, 35, 37, 273, 274, 420, 434, 562, 565, 585
Bataan, 544, 545
Batavia (Djakarta), 167, 170, 171, 175, 177, 477, 479, 544
Battambang, 194, 472
Bayar, Jelal, 572, 573
Bazaar (merchant community), 259
Bedouins, 429
Behaine, Pigneau de, 193
Beirut, 269
Belgrade, 12
Bell Mission, 616
Bencoolen, 190
Bengal, 53, 68, 71, 72, 73, 75, 77, 78, 79, 237, 238, 246, 248, 250, 443, 464, 601
Ben-Gurion, David, 576, 579
Ben Suc, 708
Bentinck, 76, 79
Benyovsky (Hangenboro), 151, 152
Beresford, Lord Charles, 344
Bering, Vitus, 212–213
Better Government of India of 1858, Act for the, 229, 232
Bezobrazov, 374
Bhakti movement, 62, 64
Bhutan, 233–234, 294
Bhutto, Zulfikar Ali, 609
Biddle, James, 400
Biddle Mission, 152
Bihar, 72, 464
Bijapur, 50, 53, 56, 57, 62, 63
Billiton, 184
Biltmore Program, 575
Bingham, John A., 403
al-Bitar, Salah al-Din, 581
Black Dragon Society, 355, 513
Black Flags, 194
Black Ocean Society (see Genyosha)
Blood Brotherhood League (Ketsumeidan), 518
Blücher, Vasilii (Galen), 505
Bogle, 236
Bohol, 391
Bombay, 68, 69, 73, 231, 237, 240, 244, 457, 463, 565
Bombay Plan, 594
Bonifacio, Andrés, 396
Bonins, 545
Borneo, 164, 180, 184, 185, 191–192
Borodin, Michael, 486, 505, 506, 698
Bose, Subhas Chardra, 455–456, 460
Bosphorus, 12, 22, 417
Boxer Rebellion (I Ho Ch'üan), 345–349, 373–374, 696
Brahmans, 63, 64, 242
Brahmo Samaj, 80, 241–242
Brezhnev, 591
British East India Company, 229; in Burma, 187, 188; in China, 114,

715

118–120, 123, 124; in India, 51, 52, 67, 68–76; in the Philippines, 393
British North Borneo Company, 192
Brooke, James, 192
Bruce, James (Lord Elgin), 281, 282
Bruckner, General, 547
Brunei, 192, 623, 624
Bucharest, Treaty of, 15
Bryan, William Jennings, 492, 521
Buddhism: in Burma, 187, 622; in Ceylon, 610; in Japan, 137, 149, 303, 304, 544, 681; in Korea, 318; in Siam, 471; in Vietnam, 193, 481, 627, 629
Budi Utomo, 186, 477
Bugis, 190
Buke Sho-Hatto, 135
Bukhara, 25, 26, 32, 35, 44, 224, 226
Bulgaria, 266
Bunraku, 143, 145
Buriats, 204, 216
Burlingame, Anson, 290, 292, 399
Burlingame Treaty, 292, 402
Burma: native kingdoms of, 187; Chinese suzereignty in, 89, 96, 187–188, 197; British conquest of, 75, 188–189, 294; British rule in, 189–190, 231, 234, 452, 454, 484, 485; World War II in, 460, 473, 485, 545; since independence, 621–623; government in, 484, 485, 486; nationalism in, 484, 485, 486; plural society in, 484, 485
Burma Road, 534, 537, 550, 551
Bushire, 37, 42, 562
Byrnes, James F., 549, 660

Caciques (landholders), 474, 617
Cairo, 572, 574
Cairo Conference, 548, 641, 655, 658, 659
Calcutta, 68, 69, 72, 73, 77, 237, 240, 250, 457, 462, 463, 464, 601
Calcutta Congress, 452
California, Russia in, 212, 216
Cambodia: Vietnamese rule of, 192, 193; French rule of, 194, 195, 479, 481, 482; Siamese rule of, 197; since independence, 626, 630–631, 633
Canning, Charles John, 78, 229
Canning, George, 17
Canning, Stratford, 19, 20, 21
Cantlie, Dr. James, 354, 355
Canton, 87, 107, 108, 112, 113, 114, 116, 117, 118, 119, 123, 127, 128, 279, 280, 281, 357, 502, 531
Canton system, 114, 116–118, 119, 120
Cao Dai sect, 481, 625, 626
Capitulations: in the Ottoman Empire, 6–7, 415; in Persia, 422, 424
Capron, Horace, 402
Carnatic, 62, 70, 71
Caroline Islands, 496, 545
Caspian Sea, 40, 223
Cathcart, Lt. Col., 120

Catherine the Great, 12, 38, 39, 213, 219
Catroux, General, 580
Cavagnari, 235
Cavendish, 113
Cavite, 395
C. C. clique, 524, 550
Cebu, 387
Celebes, 164, 190, 619
Central Treaty Organization (CENTO), 570, 608
Ceylon (Sri Lanka), 169, 172, 610–611
Chakkri dynasty (Siam), 197
Cham, 192
Chamoun, President, 582
Ch'an sect, 193
Chandernagore, 69, 72
Chang, John M., 667, 668
Chang Chih-tung, 289, 338, 349, 350, 351, 352
Chang Chun, 650
Ch'angch'un, 651
Chang Hsueh-liang, 523, 525
Chang Hsun, 490
Changkufeng, 533
Changsha, 550
Chang Tso-lin, 504, 507, 514, 517
Chapdelaine, August, 280–281
Chao-hui, 95
Chao Phraya, 196
Charles V, Emperor, 2, 162
Charles II (England), 31, 68
Charter Act of 1833, 80
Chefoo Convention of 1876, 292
Chelmsford, Lord, 444
Ch'en Hsiung-ming, 504
Ch'en Kuo-fu, 551
Ch'en Li-fu, 551
Ch'en Tu-hsiu, 500, 501, 506
Chen Yi, 655, 656
Cheng Ch'eng-kung (See Koxinga)
Cheribon, 174
Cherkassky, Prince Bekovich, 223–224
Chernaiev, General, 224
Chesme, Battle of, 12
Chettyars, 189, 484
Chia-ch'ing, Emperor, 98–99, 122
Chiang, Madame, 525, 527
Chiang Kai-shek, 505, 506, 513, 514, 522, 523–524, 525, 527, 530, 532, 533, 534, 548, 550–551, 552, 649, 651, 652, 655, 656
Ch'ien-lung, Emperor, 91, 94, 95–97, 98, 100, 121, 188
Chihli province, 347, 398, 399
Chikamatsu Monzaemon, 145, 146
Child, Sir Josiah, 69
Chin empire (Mongol), 84
China, Imperial: early trade with India, 68, 76; influence on Europe, 102; Jesuits in, 108–111; and France in Vietnam, 194; wars with Great Britain, 127, 128, 220, 221; and Korea, 317; revolution of 1911 in, 356–358, 489, 500; Confucian political system in, 88–89; culture in, 94,

96–97, 99–102; education in, 349, 350–351; eunuchs in, 84; military in, 349, 351; population pressure in, 97–98, 294–295 (see also Manchu dynasty; Ming dynasty)
China, Republic of: formation of, 358; at the Versailles Peace Conference, 497; Twenty-One Demands, 490–493; detente with the communists, 504–506; the Northern Expedition, 506; Nanking government established, 506–507; united front in, 524–528, 550; war with Japan (1937–1945), 529–533, 534, 537, 549–551; civil war in, 649–653; on Formosa, 670–671; economy in, 501–502, 526–527; education in, 500–501; government in, 526; nationalism in, 500–503; relations with Japan, 508, 522, 524; relations with the Soviet Union, 551–552; U.S. aid to, 534, 537, 650, 652, 656
China, People's Republic of: establishment of, 653–655, 686–693; Cultural Revolution, 689–691, 693; incursions into Burma, 622; wars with India, 605–607; troops in the Korean War, 663; aid to Vietnam, 625; aid to Yemen, 590; economy in, 654, 671–673; foreign relations, 673, 675, 688–689, 691, 692; problem of diplomatic recognition, 657–658, 661, 683
Chinese, overseas: in Burma, 190, 623; in Dutch East Indies, 175, 186; in Indonesia, 477, 620; in Malaya, 191, 624; in Vietnam, 192
Chinese Eastern Railroad, 339, 372, 521
Ch'ing dynasty (see Manchu dynasty)
Ching-te-chen, 99
Chinkiang, 128
Chios massacre, 17
Ch'i-shan, 127
Chitral, 235
Ch'i-ying, 128, 129, 279, 280, 281, 284
Ch'oe (Choi), 332
Chong Ta-san, 322, 323
Chōshū, 154, 155, 156, 157, 300, 366
Chota Nagpur, 237
Chou En-lai, 523, 607, 608, 650, 673, 691, 692
Christianity: in China, 109, 111, 129, 280, 285, 290, 292, 346–347; in Iran, 27; in Iraq, 436; in Japan, 137–138, 304, 543–544; in Korea, 322, 323, 325, 332; in the Ottoman Empire, 12, 13, 20–21, 22, 264, 266, 269; in the Philippines, 387, 388–389, 390–391, 392, 393, 405; in Siam, 472; in Syria, 433

Christian missionaries: in China, 106, 280, 282, 285, 290, 657; in the Dutch East Indies, 175; in India, 77, 79, 248; in Korea, 323, 328; in the Ottoman Empire, 22; in the Philippines, 388, 389; in Siam, 197; in Siberia, 210; in Vietnam, 192, 193
Chuang, Prince, 347, 348
Chu Hsi, 139, 149, 318, 322
Ch'un, Prince, 352
Chun Chi Ch'u (Grand Council), 89
Ch'ung-cheng emperor, 86
Ch'ung Hou, 293
Chungking, 339, 531, 550
Churchill, Winston, 410, 435, 453, 460, 463, 548, 550, 551, 552, 572, 574, 580, 701
Chusan Islands, 119, 120
Chu Teh, 523
Cilicia, 414, 416
Clemenceau, 414, 431
Clive, Robert, 71–73
Cochin China, 193, 194, 195, 479, 480, 483, 626
Coen, Jan Pieterszon, 112, 167–169, 170
Cohong, 116–117, 118, 119, 125, 126, 128
Colbert, 69
Colombo Plan, 598
Communism, 498, 700, 701, 702; in Burma, 622; in Cambodia, 631, 633; in Ceylon, 610; in China, 504, 522–523, 524–525, 530, 531–532, 550, 551, 649–650, 651, 652, 653, 654; in India, 603, 605; in Indonesia, 477–478, 618–619, 620; in Iran, 560, 561, 565; in Iraq, 586; in Japan, 681; in Korea, 659–660; in Laos, 630, 633; in Malaysia, 623; in the Philippines, 616, 617; in Thailand, 616; in Vietnam, 481, 482, 483, 624, 625, 626, 627, 629, 630, 631
Compagnie des Indes Orientales, 69
Compradore, 118
Confucianism: in China, 339–341, 679, 693; in Korea, 317–318, 318, 325; in Meiji education, 305–306
Congress of Berlin, 269
Congress of Toilers of the East, 498
Constantin, Catherine's son, 112
Constantinople, 4, 13, 15, 16, 410, 413, 414, 415, 417, 421, 449 (see also Istanbul)
Constantinople Conference, 267
Convention of Chuenpi, 127
Cornwallis, Lord, 74
Corregidor, 544, 545
Cossacks, 207, 212, 214
Courteen Association, 114
Cox, Sir Percy, 421, 435
Crane, C. H., 432
Crimea, 12
Crimean Tartars, 207

717

Crimean War, 20, 21–22, 264
Cripps, Sir Stafford, 460, 461
Cripps mission, 460–461, 462–463
Curzon, Lord, 236, 238, 245–246, 249
Cushing, Caleb, 129, 399, 400
Cyprus, 269, 573

Daendels, Hermann, 176–177, 178, 179
Daghestan, 35
Daimyo, 132, 133, 140, 141, 301–302; fudai, 132, 154, 155; tozama, 132
Dairen, 551, 552
Dajokan (Council of State), 303
Dalai Lama, 93, 94, 95–96, 236, 606, 675
Dalhousie (governor-general of India), 66, 76–77
Damascus, 413, 433, 438, 580
Dan Takuma, 518
Danang, 193, 629, 631
Dara Shukoh, 54, 55
Daraiya, 10
Dardanelles, 22, 410, 417
Darul Islam, 619
Date Masamune, 137–138
Dato (local chief), 387
Dauri tribes, 217
Davidov, 152, 213
Davis, 67
Dayal movement, 443
Dayan, Moshe, 579
Dayanand, Swami, 242, 248
de Andrade, Simon, 107, 112
de Bussy, Charles, 71
Deccan, 50, 52, 53, 54, 58, 62, 443
Declaration of London, 493
de Gaulle, General, 580
de Goyer, Peter, 112
de Jouvenel, 434
de Keyzer, Jacob, 112
Dekker, Douwes (Multatuli), 180
de la Cruz, Apolinario, 391
de la Torre, Carlos, 395
Delhi, 35, 44, 46, 55, 58, 77, 78, 445, 447, 457, 462
Demiral, Premier (Turkey), 570
Denikin, 422
de Nobili, 79
Dentz, General, 580
Derbent, 32, 34, 38, 40
Derebeys (Lords of the Valley), 9, 13, 15
de Reuter, Julius, 256
Deshima, 138, 141
de Tott, Baron, 13
de Tournon, 111
Dewey, Admiral, 403
Dewey, John, 501
Dhahran, 586, 587
Diebitch, General, 17
Diem (see Ngo Dinh Diem)
Dien Bien Phu, 625, 626
Dipo Negara of Jogjakarta, 179
Dirksen (German ambassador), 530
Disraeli, Benjamin, 233, 234, 266

Diwan (Ottoman), 15
Diwan (revenue administrator), 72
Djakarta, 167, 479 (see also Batavia)
Djuanda, 619
Dodecanese Islands, 410, 414
Doihara Kenji, 517, 523, 643
Dollar Diplomacy, 383–384
Dong Ming Hoi (Vietnamese National Front), 482
Dorjeff, 236
Dost Muhammad, 46–47, 234
Doumer, Paul, 195
Drake, Sir Francis, 67, 165
Draper, William H., 648
Druse Rebellion, 433
Dufferin, Lord, 235
Dulles, John Foster, 649, 702
Dun, Edwin, 403
Dunsterville, General, 421
Dupleix, Joseph, 70–71
Durani dynasty (Afghani), 37, 44, 46
Dutch: in China, 111–113, 114, 123; in Europe, 161–163; in Formosa, 87, 113, 169; in India, 72; in Japan, 137, 138, 141, 150–151, 152, 170, 172; in Siam, 196, 470; in Vietnam, 193
Dutch East India Company, 66, 68, 112–113, 165–166, 168–169, 170, 172, 175–176
Dutch East Indies: expansion of trade empire in, 165–172, 390, 391, 393; plantation system in, 174–175; British in the, 176–179; culture system in, 179–180, 183; government rule of, 182–186; agrarian law of 1870, 183–184; rise of Indonesian nationalism in, 477–478, 479; Indonesian independence, 618, 619
Dyer, General, 446

Eden, Anthony, 574
Edo, 138, 139, 140, 141, 142, 143, 146, 152, 303, 321 (see also Tokyo)
Egypt: and Arab unity, 574–575, 581, 586, 590; under the Ottomans, 10, 14, 16, 17, 18, 19, 38; wars with Israel, 576, 578, 579, 580
Eisenhower, Dwight, 670, 702
Eleuths (see Mongols)
Elgin, Lord (see Bruce, James)
Elizabeth I, 113
Elliot, Captain, 126, 127
Encomienda system, 389–390
Enlightenment: Chinese influence on the, 102; Persian influence on the, 31
Enver, Bey (Pasha), 271, 274, 410, 413, 415
Enzeli, 422
Erivan, 11, 27, 34, 40
Erzerum, 410, 415
Erzerum, Peace of, 41
Eshkol, Levi, 579, 580
Eta, 302
Eto Shimpei, 301, 308

Extraterritoriality, 278, 292; in China, 129, 508; in Japan, 371; in Korea, 328; in Persia, 41, 422; in Siam, 197, 198, 470

Faisal, King (Iraq), 413, 432, 433, 435, 436, 439
Faisal II, King (Iraq), 436, 584, 585
Faisal, King (Saudi Arabia), 586, 587
Farah Diba, 566
Far Eastern Advisory Commission (FEAC), 641, 643
Fars, 568
al-Fatah, 581, 583
Fath Ali Shah, 38–41, 46
Fathpur Sikri, 60
Fedayeen, 578, 583
Federated Malay States, 191
Federation of Republics (Arab), 581
Feng Kuei-fen, 289
Feng Kuo-chang, 489, 490
Fenollosa, Ernest, 402
Feron, 324
Ferry, Jules, 188, 194
Fidalgo, 108
Fillmore, President, 152
Finkenstein, Treaty of, 39
First Treaty of Settlement, 220
Floating World (see Ukiyo)
Fontainebleau Conference, 483
Foochow, 114, 128, 194
Forbes, Cameron, 474
Formosa: under the Manchu dynasty, 93, 97, 99; under the Dutch, 87, 112, 113, 123, 138, 169, 172, 393; Japanese acquisition of, 313–314, 334, 335, 403; Nationalist Chinese takeover of, 653, 655–656, 670
Fort Ross, 216
Fort St. George, 68
Fort Zeelandia, 112, 169
Foulk, Ensign George, 331
France: and Burma, 188; and China, 115, 281, 282, 291, 294, 339, 373; and India, 69–71, 74, 75; and Indochina, 192, 193–194, 480, 624–626; and Israel, 578; and Japan, 335, 534; and Korea, 323, 325, 328; and the Ottoman Empire, 14–15, 18, 19, 20, 21, 22; and Persia, 39; and Siam, 196, 198, 199, 200, 470; and Syria, 431, 432–434, 580; and Turkey, 416
French East India Company, 70
Frobisher, Martin, 113, 165
Fudai (see Daimyo)
Fujiwara Seika, 139
Fukien, 87, 99, 175
Fukuda Takeo, 685
Fukuoka Kotei, 301
Fukuzawa Yukichi, 305, 328
Fulbright, Sen. William, 703

Galdan, 93
Gallipoli, 410
Gama, Vasco da, 108

Gandamak, Treaty of, 235
Gandhi, Indira, 604, 609
Gandhi, Mohandas, 445, 446–449, 450, 451, 452, 453, 454, 455, 457, 460, 461, 462, 595, 596, 601–602
Ganges provinces, 231
Garcia, Carlos, 617
Gardanne, General, 39, 40
Garnier, Francis, 194
Gauss, Clarence, 551
Gaza, 413, 576, 578, 579
Geneva Conference (1954), 626, 665
Geneva Conference (1962), 630
Genrō (elder statesmen), 365, 366, 367
Genroku era, 143
Gentlemen's Agreement, 382, 705
Genyosha (Black Ocean Society), 308, 311, 355
Geok Tepe, 225
George III, 40, 120
George V (England), 248
George, Lloyd, 414, 431
Georgia, 25, 39, 40, 421
Georgians, 27, 35
Gerbillon, Father, 109
Germany: and Afghanistan during World War I, 421; and China, 339, 351, 372-373; and Iraq, 436, 584; and Japan, 335, 375, 535, 536, 538; and the Ottoman Empire, 270, 275, 410; and Persia, 420–421, 426–427, 558; and Siam, 470; and Turkey, 571
Ghazi, King (Iraq), 436
Ghazni, 47
Gia Long, 193
Gilan, province of, 422, 423; Soviet Republic of, 560
Giliaks, 204
Gladstone, William, 234, 266
Goa, 165, 169, 605
Godunov, Boris, 209, 210
Gokcha district, 40
Gokhale, Gopal Krishna, 244
Golan Heights, 579, 581
Golconda, 50, 53, 56, 63
Golden Horde, 205 (see also Mongols; Kipchak Tatars)
Golovnin, 152
Gordon, George "Chinese," 286
Gortchakoff, Prince, 254
Goto Shojiro, 301, 311
Gouraud, General, 433
Government of India Act (1919), 444–445, 450
Grady, Henry, 562
Grand Canal, 128, 345
Grand Dragoman, 13
Grand Mufti of Constantinople, 6, 15, 16
Grand Vizir, 4, 5, 7, 15n
Great Britain: and Aden, 10, 19, 67, 431, 557, 590; in Afghanistan, 46–47, 225, 427; and the Arab states, 412–413, 429, 589; and Burma, 187, 188–190; and Bor-

719

neo, 191; rivalry with Russia in Central Asia, 234–235; and China (Imperial), early trade with, 113–116, 118, 119, 129; Macartney's Mission to, 120–122; Amherst Embassy to, 122; diplomatic recognition from, 124–125; concessions gained from, 278, 279, 280, 281, 282, 287, 291, 293–294; and China (People's Republic of), recognition of, 657; in the East Indies, 166–167, 177–179; and India, arrival in, 51; aid to the Peshwas in, 63–64; conquest of the Punjab in, 65–78; imperial rule in, 229, 231–232, 236–239, 240, 242, 244, 245–250, 442; and Indonesia, 479; and Iraq, 431, 434–436, 584, 585; and Japan, relations with Tokugawa, 137, 138, 152; Anglo-Japanese Alliance with, 375–376; entry into World War I by, 491, 492; relations before World War II with, 534; and Jordan, 582; and Korea, seizure of Port Hamilton in, 331; and Malaya, 486; and Palestine, 436, 575, 576; and Persia, early relations with, 25, 27, 39–40, 41, 42; rivalry with Russia in, 254–257, 259–263, 423, 560, 561; World War I intrigues in, 420, 421, 422; World War II intrigues in, 558, 559; Anglo-Iranian Oil Company in, 562, 563, 565, 566; and the Ottoman Empire, 266–267, 268–269, 410, 414; and Saudi Arabia, 430, 431; and Siam, commercial treaties with, 197, 198; rivalry with France in, 199–200; relations after World War I with, 470, 472, 473; and Tibet, rivalry with Russia in, 235–236; and Transjordan, 439, 582; and Turkey, 415–416

Greater East Asia Co-prosperity Sphere, 513, 541

Greece: independence of, 17; Ottoman rule in, 13, 14; revolts against Ottomans, 12, 17; war with Turkey, 412, 414, 416

Grey, Sir Edward, 257, 491, 492
Griffis, William E., 402
Gromyko, Andrei, 561
Gros, Baron Jean Louis, 281, 282
Guadalcanal Island, 545
Guam, 403, 545
Gubernia (province), 215
Gujarat, Battle of, 66
Gulistan, Peace of, 40
Gulnabad, Battle of, 32
Gurkhas, 75, 96
Gursel, General, 573
Guru (teacher), 64
Guru Nanak, 64
Gvosdev, 213

Gwalior, 63

Habaniyah, 584
Habibullah, 427, 443
Habomai Island, 669, 682
Haganah, 575
Hagerty, James, 670
Hague International Peace Conference, 380–381
Hague Round Table Conferences (1949), 618
Haidar Ali, 74
Haifa, 431, 436, 438, 575
Hainan, 99
Haiphong, 631, 708
Hakodate, 151, 152, 213, 402
Halifax, Lord (see Irwin, Lord)
Halsey, Admiral, 545
Hamadan, 34
Hamaguchi Osachi, 514, 517
Hami, 93
Hangenboro, 151
Han-gul, 318
Hankow, 357, 506, 531
Hanlin Academy, 89, 109
Hanoi, 192, 193, 194, 195, 294, 483, 631
Hara, 138
Hara Takashi, 494, 495, 496, 507, 508, 509
Harappa, 246
Harding, President, 474
Hardinge, Lord, 250
Hari Singh, 601
Harriman, E. H., 381, 383
Harris, Townsend, 154, 402
Harrison, Francis B., 473
Hart, Robert, 291–292
Hartal (work stoppage), 447
Harunobu, 147
Hastings, Warren, 63, 73–74, 79, 236
Hatay Republic, 434 (see also Alexandretta)
Hatoyama Ichiro, 647, 668, 669
Hatta, Muhammad, 478, 479, 619
Hatti-i-Humayun, 22
Hatt-i-sherif of Gulhané, 20
Hawaii, and Japan, 314, 382
Hawkins, William, 51–52, 67
Hay, John, 344–345, 381, 697
Hayakawa, S. I., 711
Hayashi Razan, 139
Hayashi Tadasu, 375, 376
Haydar Pasha, 270
Heimen, 302
Hejaz, 412, 413, 414, 430
Hejaz Railroad, 413
Herat, 25, 34, 41, 42, 44, 47, 254
Herzl, Theodore, 436
Heusken, 157
Hidetada, 393
Hideyori, 133
Hideyoshi, 84, 135, 136, 318, 320
Higashikuni, Prince, 540
Hindu Kush, 235
Hippisley, Alfred E., 344
Hirado, 170
Hiranuma, Baron, 548

720

Hiroshige, 147
Hiroshima, bombing of, 548
Hitler, Adolf, 523, 530, 535, 536
Hizen, 157, 300, 303, 307, 309
Hoa Hao sect, 481, 483, 625, 626
Ho Chi Minh, 196, 481, 625, 626, 629
Hodge, John R., 660
Hokkaido, 151, 152, 156, 213, 309, 310, 371, 402, 699
Hokusai, 147
Honan, 86, 97
Hong (see Cohong)
Hong Kong, 126, 127, 128, 278, 280, 281, 544
Honshu, 137, 155
Hooghly, 53
Hope-Simpson Report, 438
Hopei, 522
Hoppo, 116, 118
Hormuz, 27, 67
Ho-shen, 97, 99, 283
Hotta Masayoshi, 154
Ho-Umezu Agreement, 522
Hoveida, Amir Abbas, 569
Hsien-feng, 284, 287
Hsing-Chung-hui (Revive China Society), 354
Husan-t'ung (see P'u-yi, Henry)
Huang Hsing, 359
Hubbard, Richard B., 403
Hue, 192, 195, 629, 631, 632
Hughes, Charles Evans, 497, 498
Hu Hanmin, 356
Huk movement (Hukbalahaps), 616, 617
Hull, Cordell, 536, 537, 538, 540
Hull-Nomura Negotiations, 537
Hume, Allen O., 244
Hung Hsiu-ch'üan, 284–285, 286
Hunza, 235
Hupei province, 99
Hurley, Patrick, 551
Husain, Grand Mufti of Jerusalem, 438, 575, 584
Husain, King (Jordan), 582, 583
Husain Ibn Ali, sherif of Mecca, 274, 412, 413, 429–430, 435, 439
Husein, Shah, 32
Hu Shih, 500, 524
Hyderabad, independent state of, 58; French intervention in, 70, 71; Indian takeover of (1948), 600; protected state under the British, 231, 233; war against Britain, 74, 75
Hyderabad, nizam of, 70–71, 443

Iasak, 210, 212
Ibn Sa'ud, 274, 413, 429–430, 431, 439, 574, 584, 586, 587, 590
Ibn Sa'ud, emir of the Nejd, 9
Ibrahim Pasha, 17, 18
Iemitsu, Tokugawa, 133, 136, 140
Iemochi, Tokugawa, 154
Ieyasu, Tokugawa, 132, 133, 136, 137, 138, 139, 140, 393
Ignatiev, General, 221, 282

Ihara Saikaku, 145
Ii Naosuke, 153, 154, 158
Ikeda Hayato, 670, 680
Ikhwan (Brethren), 429
Ilbert Bill of 1883, 245
Imam, 42, 43
Imperial Rule Assistance Association (IRAA), 543
Inchon, 327, 662
India: Nadir Shah's invasion of, 35; Mogul Empire in, 50–58, 59–62, 63, 64, 67, 68, 75; Hindu resurgence in, 57, 62–66; Anglo-French rivalry in, 69–71; rule of the British East India Company in, 67–78; source of Chinese opium in, 120, 123; British administration of, 74, 76, 78, 229, 231–232, 249; public health reform under the British, 238–239; economy under the British, 237–238, 443, 456–457, 462; rise of the middle class, 239–240; Hindu renascence, 241–243; Anglo-Indian racial tension, 245–248; rise of nationalism, 240–241, 242, 243–245, 248, 249–250; Hindu-Moslem tension in, 240–241, 242, 243, 245, 248, 448–450, 456, 463; in World War I, 442–443; dyarchy in, 444–445, 452, 454; home rule issue in, 444, 449, 458-459, 461, 463; anti-British sentiment in, 445, 456; in World War II, 457–463; partition of, 463–464, 594; communal violence in, 600, 601; economy of, 595–600; education in, 61, 76, 77, 79–80, 240, 241, 246, 457, 598, 602; famines in, 238–239, 462, 598; foreign relations of, 605: with the People's Republic of China, 605–607, with Pakistan, 600–601, 603, 604, 609; government of, 445, 450, 452, 453–454, 460, 602; population of, 238, 239, 457, 462, 597
India Act, 73
Indian Civil Service, 231, 240, 242, 244, 463
Indian Mutiny (1857), 58, 77–78, 229
Indian National Congress, 241, 243–245, 246, 250, 442, 443, 444, 449, 450, 451, 453, 454, 456, 458, 459, 460, 461, 463
Indochina: French takeover of, 294; French rule of, 195–196, 479–480, 481; in World War I, 480; rise of nationalism in, 480–482; in World War II, 482–483 (see also Cambodia; Laos; Vietnam)
Indonesia: before the Dutch, 163–164; rise of nationalism in, 186, 469, 476–479; in World War II, 478–479, 544; Republic estab-

721

lished, 479; Republic of, independence for the, 618–619; since independence, 619–621 (see also Dutch East Indies)
Indore, 63
Inner Mongolia, 92, 93, 522
İnönü, 416
Inoue Kaoru, 301, 327, 335
Inoue Kowashi, 311
International Consortium, 494
International Court of the Hague, 565
Inukai Tsuyoshi, 494, 518
Iran: name of Persia changed to (1935), 425; during World War II, 558–559; Soviet pressure on, 559–562; nationalization of oil interests in, 563–564, 565; under Muhammad Shah, 566–569; foreign relations of, 562, 570, 589 (see also Persia)
Iraq: Ottoman rule in, 273–274; British mandate in, 431, 434–436; during World War II, 580, 584; wars with Israel, 576, 584–585, 586; since World War II, 419, 426, 574, 585–586, 589
Irkutsk, 215
Irwin, Lord, 451–452
Irwin, Robert W., 402–403
Ise Shrine, 306
Isfahan, 28–29, 30, 32, 421
Ishii, Viscount, 493
Ishii-Lansing Agreement, 496, 497
Ishiwara Kanji, 517, 533
Islam: Shi'a sect, 25, 27, 32, 34, 42–43, 273, 424, 430, 434, 569; Sunni sect, 32, 33, 34, 273, 430; Wahhabi movement, 9–10; in Afghanistan, 427; on the Indian subcontinent, 241, 248, 444, 447, 449–450, 459, 464, 611; in Indonesia, 163–164, 179, 477; in the Ottoman Empire, 4, 6, 13, 20, 268, 273, 412; in Persia, 27, 32, 33, 34, 424, 426, 564, 568; in the Philippines, 386, 388, 618; in Turkey, 417, 418, 420
Ismailov, 219
Ismet Pasha (İnönü), 416, 419, 571, 572, 573
Israel, 557, 576–579, 581, 582, 583, 585, 586
Istanbul, 571 (see also Constantinople)
Isvolsky, Alexander, 257
Itagaki Seishiro, 517
Itagaki Taisuke, 301, 309, 311, 364, 365
Italy, 410, 412, 416; and Iraq, 436, 584
Itelmen, tribe, 212
Ito Hirobumi, 299, 300, 301, 305, 310, 311, 312, 313, 330, 334, 363, 364, 365–366, 367, 373, 375, 376, 380, 381
Ito Jinsai, 149
Ivan III, the Great, 205
Ivan IV, the Terrible, 205, 209, 210
Ivan Kalita, 205

Iwakura Tomomi, 155, 156, 301, 303, 308, 310, 314
Iwasaki, 368
Iwo Jima, 545

Jahangir, 50, 52, 60, 61, 64, 67
James I (England), 52
Jamshedpur, 237
Jangali, 422
Janissaries, 5, 9, 10, 13, 14, 15, 16
Japan: establishment of the Tokugawa Shogunate, 132; Tokugawa system, 133, 135, 136; Dutch learning, 150–151; internal disintegration of the Shogunate, 153–156; overthrow of the Tokugawa Shogunate, 301; Meiji Restoration in, 156, 157; Charter Oath, 298–299; abolition of feudalism, 301–302; industrialization of, 367–370; constitution promulgated in, 310, 311–312; development of the party system in, 309–311, 313; Genro Era in, 365–366; Sino-Japanese War, 331–334; Treaty of Shimonoseki and the Triple Intervention, 334–335; rivalry with Russia in Korea, 371–378; Anglo-Japanese Alliance, 375–376; Russo-Japanese War, 377–378, 380; Twenty-One Demands on China, 490–493; entry into World War I, 490–496; rise of party government in, 507–511, 517–518; ultranationalism in, 511–513, 514, 517–521, 544; young officers movement in, 513, 514, 518, 519–520, 528, 533, 539; war with China, 529–533, 534; the Pacific War, 478–479, 482, 483, 485, 534, 540–541, 544–547; during the war, 541, 543–544; surrender of, 547–549; U.S. occupation of, 637–649; and the Korean War, 648; peace treaty concluded, 648–649; since occupation, 668–670, 680–686; culture, Tokugawa, 143–151; economy: Tokugawa, 140–143, Meiji, 306–307, 367–368, 369, 371, post-Meiji, 646, 647, 648, 668, 679–680, 682, 683–685; education: Meiji, 299, 304–306, post-Meiji, 509, 520, 543, 646; foreign relations: Tokugawa, 136–139, Meiji, 300, 313–315, 335, 375, 381, 404, 477, post-Meiji, 472, 658, 682; government: Meiji, 303, 307, post-Meiji, 644–645; population, Meiji, 368–369; relations with China, 508, 513–514, 522, 523, 524; relations with Germany, 335, 375, 535, 536, 538; relations with Korea, 308, 314, 320, 321, 324, 325, 327, 328, 329–330, 331, 333–334, 336, 366, 380–381; religion: Tokugawa, 303, 304, Meiji, 303–304; and

Russian relations, Tokugawa, 213–214, 223, Meiji, 223, 375, 376, 377–378, 380; relations with the Soviet Union, 508, 521, 533–534; relations with the United States: Tokugawa, 399, 400, 401–402, Meiji, 377–378, 382–384, 402, 403, post-Meiji, 535, 536, 537, 669–670, 681–682, 683–684, 685
Jardine, 128
Jassy, Peace of, 12
Jaubert, 39
Java, 108, 163, 164, 165, 167, 172, 174, 175, 177, 178, 179, 180, 184, 186, 190, 476, 477, 618
Jebel Druse, 433
Jehol, 97
Jenkins, 324
Jerusalem, 413, 437, 576, 579, 582, 583
Jesuits, 322, 388, 391; in China, 108–111, 218; in India, 50, 60, 67, 79; in Vietnam, 193
Jews, in Palestine, 437, 438, 439, 575, 576
Jidda, 430
Jihad (holy war), 9, 412
Jinnah, Muhammad Ali, 453, 456, 459, 462, 464, 594, 595
Jippenshu Ikku, 145–146
Joffe, Adolf, 504, 505
Johnson, Lyndon B., 631, 702, 703, 708, 710
Johnstone, Percy, 648
Johore, sultanate of, 190, 191
Jōi, 301
Jones, Sir Hartford, 39
Jones, Sir William, 79
Jones Act, 473
Jordan, 574, 575, 576, 579, 581, 582–583 (see also Transjordan)
Joseph II (Austria), 12
Jung-lu, 342, 343
Jurchen, 84, 318

Kabir, 64
Kabuki, 143, 145
Kabul, 34, 47
Kabul, Treaty of, 427
Kachins, 622
Kadi, 6
Kaesong, 663
Kaga, 132
Kagoshima, 157
Kajar dynasty, 258, 262, 420, 424
Kalgan, 652
Kamchatka, 151, 212, 219
Kâmil Pasha, 271
Kanagawa, 152
Kanagawa, Treaty of, 153, 154, 402
Kandahar, 32, 34, 44, 47, 52
Kaneko Kentaro, 510
K'ang-hsi, 91–94, 100, 109, 111, 114, 218, 219
Kanghwa Island, 323
Kang I, 347, 348

K'ang Yu-wei, 196, 339, 341, 342, 343, 344, 350, 353, 501
Kanpur, 450, 456
Kansai, 306
Kanto, 306
Kara Mustafa, 11
Karachi, 594
Karens, 622
Karim Khan of Zand, 37
Karnal, 35
Kars, 12, 36, 416, 571
Kashani, Ayatolalh, 564, 565
Kashgar, 93, 95
Kashmir, 44, 50, 65, 66, 231, 233; Indo-Pakistani dispute over, 600–601, 603
Kassem, Abdul Karim, 585–586
Katayama Sen, 370
Katayama Tetsu, 647
Katipunan, 396–398
Kato Takaaki, 375, 491, 492, 493, 508, 509, 510
Kato, Admiral Tomosaburo, 508
Katsura Taro, 365, 366, 367, 376, 378, 381
Kauffman, General, 224–225, 226
Kavtaradze, 560
Kawabata Yasunari, 685
Kawamoto, Colonel, 514
Kazakhstan, 224, 699
Kazan, khanate of, 205, 206
Kazoku, 302
Kedah, sultanate of, 190, 191
Keiki, 154, 155, 156
Keio University, 305
Kelantan, 191
Kemal, Mustafa (Ghazi), 271, 414–416, 417, 418, 419, 420, 424, 426, 571, 698
Kendrick, John, 399
Kennan, George F., 701–702
Kerbala, 435
Kermanshah, 34
Ketsu eki, 307
Ketsumeidan (Blood Brotherhood League), 518
Khabarov, 216–217
Khabarovsk, 216, 217
Khalifat movement, 447, 449
Kharg, 41, 42
Khitan, 318
Khiva, 35, 40
Khiva, khanate of, 224, 226, 256
Khomeini (khumayni) Abdullah, 569
Khorasan, 25, 37, 38, 40, 44
Khotan, 95
Khrushchev, Nikita, 666, 675, 678, 687, 688
Khurram (see Shah Jahan)
Khusrau, 64
Khuzistan, 567, 570
Khvostov, 152, 213
Khyber Pass, 235
Kiakhta, 219
Kiakhta, Treaty of, 219
Kiangsi province, 99, 522
Kiaochow, 373
Kido, 540

723

Kido Koin, 301, 303
Kim Il-sung, 660, 666
Kim Koo, 660
Kim Ok-kiun, 328, 329, 330, 332, 333
Kim Tu-bong, 666
King, Dr. A. C., 432
King, Charles W., 399–400
King-Crane Mission, 432
King David Hotel, 576
Kipchak Tatars, 207
Kirghiz, 204, 212
Kirkuk, 585
Kirkuk, Battle of, 11
Kishi Nobusuke, 670, 680
Kissinger, Henry, 692, 710
Kita Ikki, 512–513, 519, 520
Kitchener, Lord, 246
Kiyonaga, 147
Knox, Philander, 383, 384
Kobayashi Ichizō, 534
Kobe, 306
Koguryo, 317
Kojiki, 150
Kojong, King (Korea), 659
Kokand, 224, 226
Kokonor, 97
Kokuryūkai (Amur River Society), 511
Kolp'um, 318
Komei, Emperor (Japan), 155
Komura, Jutaro, 378
Konoe Fumimaro, 528, 529, 530, 535, 536, 537, 538, 540, 543, 644
Koo, Wellington, 502
Koprulu, Ahmed, 11
Koprulu, Muhammad, 10–11
Koprulu, Mustafa, 11
Korea: early history, 84, 86, 89, 106, 136, 143, 317–318; in the Confucian system, 317; Yi dynasty, 318–321, 323; under the Taewongun, 322–336; opening of, 324–325, 327; treaties with the European powers, 328; progressive movement in, 328–330; Sino-Japanese War in, 330-334; Japanese reforms in, 335–336; Russo-Japanese rivalry in, 372, 374, 375–376; foreign relations before annexation, 314, 317–318, 319–321, 323, 324–325, 327–331, 333, 334–336, 366; Japanese annexation of, 380–381; independence movement in, 659–660; Soviet-American liberation of, 660–661; division of, 661; Republic of, 661, 667–668, 683; Democratic People's Republic of, 661, 665–667, 683 (see also Korean War)
Korean War, 605–606, 648, 656, 658, 661–663, 701
Koriak tribe, 212
Koryo, 318
Kotoku Shusui, 366, 370
Kowloon, 282, 339
Kowtow, 113, 122, 217, 219
Koxinga, 87, 113, 172, 393
Kuala Lumpur, 191, 624
Kuang-hsü, 339, 341, 352, 353'

Kuchuk Kainarji, Treaty of, 12, 15
Kuchum, 205, 206, 208
Kuei Wang, 87
Kumazawa Banzan, 149
Kung, H. H., 524
Kung, Prince, 221, 282, 287, 288, 290
Kurdistan, 27, 414
Kurds, 273, 414, 418, 420, 436, 561, 562, 570, 584, 586
Kuril Islands, 152, 212, 213, 215, 223, 314, 548, 551, 669, 699
Kuroda, 325, 327
Kurusu Saburo, 540
Kut-al-Amara, Battle of, 434, 444
Kutb Minar, 77
Kuwait, 269, 430, 436, 589
Ku Yen-wu, 101
Kwantung Army, 514, 517, 518, 521, 522, 523
Kwangtung province, 116, 122
Kweilin, 550
Kyoto, 135, 137, 146, 149, 155, 156, 303, 306
Kyushu, 137, 138

Labuan, 191, 192
Ladakh, 606, 607
Lahore, 63
La Liga Filipina, 396
Lally, 71
Langson, 194
Lansing, Robert, 493, 496
Lao Dong, 625, 627, 629
Laos: French conquest of, 194–195; French rule in, 479, 481, 482; independence of, 626, 630, 631, 633; member of the Chinese tributary system, 89
Laurel, José, 475, 616
Lausanne, Peace of, 416, 417
Lawrence, Sir Henry, 66
Lawrence, John, 66, 254
Lawrence, T. E., 413, 435
Laxman, Adam, 151, 213
Laxman, Eric, 151
Lay, H. N., 281
League of Nations, 419, 429, 432, 434, 436, 443, 472, 496, 519, 521
Lebanon, Christian Republic of, 433, 434, 574, 575, 579, 580, 581–582, 703
Ledo Road, 462
Le Duan, 630
Le Duc Tho, 710
Le dynasty, 192
Lee Kuan-yew, 623, 624
Legalism, 149
LeGendre, Charles, 403
Leith-Ross, Frederick, 526
Lend Lease Act, 537, 699
Lepanto, Battle of, 10
Lesghians, 35
Leyte, 387
Lhasa, 93, 94, 236
Li, 106
Liakhoff, Colonel, 256
Liang Ch'i-ch'ao, 196, 341, 343, 353, 356, 501

Liaotung peninsula, 85, 334, 335, 372
Liaquat Ali Khan, 464, 595, 607
Lifeguards, 219
Li-Fournier Convention, 294
Light, Francis, 190
Li Hung-chang, 194, 286, 287, 290, 294, 325, 327–328, 330, 331, 334, 338, 342, 348, 349, 372
Li-Ito Convention, 330
Lin, Commissioner, 278, 279, 284
Lindsay, Henry, 40
Linggadjati Agreement, 618
Linlithgow, Lord, 457
Lin Piao, 688, 689, 692
Linschoten, Jan, 163
Lintin Island, 126
Lin Tse-hsu, 126–127
Li Tzu-ch'eng, 86, 87
Liu-ch'iu Islands, 89, 294, 313–314, 327
Liu-chou, 482
Liuchow, 550
Liu K'un-i, 349, 350
Liu Shao-chi, 608, 686, 687, 688, 689, 692
Li Yuan-hung, 357, 360, 490
Lobanov-Yamagata Agreement, 372
Lo Jui-ching, 688
Lombok, 185
London Pact, 410
London Naval Conference, 517, 697
Long March, 522–523
Lon Nol, 630–631
Lopez, Miguel de Legaspi, 387, 388
Lorcha, 280
Louis XIV, 197
Louis Napoleon, 21
Louis Philippe, 19
Low, Frederick P., 323
Lucknow Pact, 444
Luzon, 387, 388, 391, 392, 616
Lytton, Lord, 234
Lytton Report, 59, 521
Lyuh Woon-Hyung, 660

Macapagal, 617
Macao, 107, 108, 112, 114, 117, 122, 169, 280
MacArthur, General Arthur, 403
MacArthur, General Douglas, 475, 536, 544, 549, 640, 641, 642, 643, 645, 646, 662, 663
Macartney, Earl of, 120–122
Macaulay, 76, 79, 80
MacDonald, Ramsay, 252
McGovern, George, 710
McKinley, President, 345, 404
McMahon, Sir Henry, 412
McMahon correspondence, 412, 432, 437
Mactan, 387
Madiun, 618
Madjapahit, 163
Madras, 68, 69, 70, 73, 231, 240, 457
Madura, 174, 186
Maeda, 132, 143
Magellan, Ferdinand, 386, 387
Magsaysay, 617

Mahabad, 561
Mahan, Alfred, 403
Mahasabha, 601, 603
Mahatma Ghandi (see Ghandi, Mohandas)
Mahmud II (Ottoman), 10, 15–19
Mahmud Shah (Afghan), 46
Majlis, 256, 260, 262, 263, 558, 560
Malabar coast, 169
Malacca, 107, 163, 164, 166, 169, 190, 191
Malaya: Dutch in, 169; independence of, 486; plural society in, 191, 486; in World War II, 460, 472, 473
Malaysia, 623–624
Malcolm, John, 39
Malik, Jacob, 663
Mamluks, 18
Manchu dynasty: conquest of China, 86–88; K'ang-hsi period, 91–94; beginning of the decline of, 97–99; early trade relations with the West: Portugal, 106–108, Dutch, 111–113, Great Britain, 113–116, United States, 120; Canton system of trade in, 116–123; British wars with the, 123–129; response to Western pressure, 278–283; bureaucratic breakdown in, 283–284; border pressures, 293–294; population pressure, 294–295; foreign concessions of the, 339, 341; 100 days reform, 341–343; Boxer Rebellion, 345–349; last reforms of the, 349–352; abdication of the last emperor of the, 358; culture, 94, 96–97, 99–102; government, 88–89; foreign relations: Burma, 187–188, France, 339, 373, Germany, 339, 351, 372–373, Korea, 318, 320–321, 330–331, Russia, 94, 217–219, 221, 225, 328, 339, 372, 373, United States, 344–345, 403
Manchukuo, 518, 519, 521, 522, 699
Manchuria, homeland of the Manchus, 84, 85, 89, 221, 334; Japanese preponderance in, 378, 380, 381, 382, 492, 493, 494, 698, 699; Japanese takeover of, 517–518, 519, 528; Russian occupation of, 548, 650, 651, 652 (see also Manchukuo)
Manchurian Incident, 472, 523
Manchus, 84–85
Mandalay, 189
Mandarinate (Vietnam), 195
Mandate system, 432
Manilla, 111, 387, 388, 390, 391, 392, 394, 395, 403, 475, 545
Manilla Galleon, 392–394
Man Kan Kokan, 376
Mao Tse-tung, 502, 506, 522, 523, 524, 532, 550, 654, 679, 686, 687, 688, 689, 691, 692, 693
Marathas, 46, 57, 58–59, 62–64, 66, 69, 73, 74, 75, 77

Marco Polo Bridge (Lu-kou-ch'iao), 525, 529
Marcos, Ferdinando, 617, 618
Margary, 292
Marianas, 545
Maritime Province, 221, 223, 282, 293
Marshall, George C., 650, 651, 652
Marshall, John, 246
Marshall Islands, 496
Marshall Mission, 650–651
Marshall Plan, 704
Martin, Joseph, 663
Masjid-i Shah, 29
Mataram, 164, 169, 172, 174
Matsu, 670
Matsui, General, 643
Matsukata, 312, 363, 366
Matsumae City, 151, 152
Matsumoto Joji, 644
Matsuoka Yosuke, 535–536, 537, 538, 539, 643
Matsuycker, Jan, 169–170
May 4 Movement, 500
Mazaki Jinzaburo, 519, 520
Mecca, 413, 429, 430
Medina, 413
Meerut, 78
Mehemet Ali, 10, 17–18, 19
Meiji Emperor, 155, 298
Meiji Era (see Japan)
Meiji Constitution, 300, 311–312
Meir, Golda, 580
Menam, 196
Menchikov, Prince, 21
Menderes, Adnan, 573
Mergui, 197
Merritt, General Wesley E., 403
Merv, 37, 225, 254, 256
Meshed, 25, 27, 43, 426, 567
Mesopotamia, 19, 265, 273, 412, 414, 431, 434
Mezzabarba, 111
Miao, 97, 99, 287
Middendorf, 220
Midfai, Jamil, 585
Midhat Pasha, 264, 265, 266, 267, 271
Midway, Battle of, 545
Midway Island, 545
Migeon, 30
Mill, Colonel James, 71
Millet, 6–7
Millspaugh, Arthur C., 423, 424, 559
Min clan (Korea), 323, 327, 328, 329, 331, 335
Mindanao, 386, 388, 391, 618
Ming dynasty, 83–84, 85, 86, 87, 106, 107, 319–320
Minobe Tatsukichi, 509, 520, 543
Minto, Lord, 177, 249
Min Yong-ik, 329
Mir Jafar, 72
Mir Mahmud, 32–33
Mir Vais, 32
Mirza Kuchik Khan, 422–423
Mirza Taki Khan, 42
Mito, 150, 153, 154, 155, 156, 157
Mitsubishi, 311, 368, 510

Mitsui, 158, 302, 311, 368, 510, 518, 534
Mitsukuni, 150
Miura Goro, 335, 493
Mogul Empire (see India, Mogul Empire in)
Moguls, 32, 35, 44
Mohenjo-Daro, 246
Moldavia, 17, 21
Möllendorff, 331
Molotov, Vyacheslav, 558, 641, 660
Moluccas, 163, 164, 165, 166, 169, 172 (see also Spice Islands)
Mongolia, 85, 89, 93, 358, 493, 494
Mongols, 83, 85, 93, 204, 205, 207; Chahar, 92, 93; in Burma, 187; Eleuths, 93, 95, 218; Kalmuks, 93, 95; Khalkas, 93, 95; Korean invasion by the, 318
Mons, 622
Montagu, 444
Montagu-Chelmsford Report, 444
Montreux, Treaty of, 419
Montreux Convention, 571
Moplas, 450
Mori Arinori, 305, 325
Morley, John, 249
Morley-Minto Reform, 249, 250, 443
Moros, 388, 391–392
Moscow, 205, 206
Moscow, Grand Dukes of, 205
Moscow Conference, 641, 660
Moslem League, 241, 450, 452, 453, 454, 456, 458, 459, 460, 461, 463
Moslems (see Islam)
Mossadegh, Muhammad, 564, 565, 566
Most-favored nation, 129
Mosul, 35, 273, 412, 419, 431, 435
Motoda Eifu, 305, 306
Motono, 494
Motoori Norinaga, 150
Mountbatten, Lord, 464
Moyne, Lord, 575
Mu-chang-a, 279
Mudros, armistice of, 413
Mufti, 6
Muhammad II (Ottoman), 4
Muhammad III (Ottoman), 7
Muhammad VI (Ottoman), 413, 416, 417
Muhammad Ali, 260–261, 262, 263
Muhammad Shah (Mogul), 35
Muhammad Shah (Persia), 41
Muhammad Zadir Shah (Afghan), 427
Mukden, 85, 89, 374, 517
Multan, 65
Multatuli (pseud. Douwes Dekker), 180
Mumtaz Mahal, 52
Murad IV (Ottoman), 10, 32
Murad V (Ottoman), 265–266
Muraviev, Count Nicholas, 220, 221, 223, 372
Murray, David, 305
Muscat, 430, 587
Muso, 618–19
Mutsuhito, 155
Mutual Security Act, 704

726

Muzaffar-ud-din, Shah, 256, 258, 259
Myer, Dillon, 706
My Lai, 708
Mysore, 58, 73, 74, 75, 77, 231, 233

Nabobs, 72
Nadir Khan, Shah, 427
Nadir Shah (Persia), 11, 33–37, 44, 58
Nagar, 235
Nagasaki, 136, 137, 138, 151, 170, 213, 399, 548
Naguib, Muhammad, 574
Nahas Pasha, 574
Nakhichevan, 40
Nam Il, 666
Nanking, 87, 112, 284, 286, 357, 506, 508, 530, 649, 653
Nanking, Treaty of, 18, 128, 279
Nan-yang, 83
Napier, Lord, 124–125
Napoleon, 14, 15, 37, 38, 39, 122, 177
Napoleon III, 193
Naqib of Baghdad, 435
Nasir-ud-din, Shah, 42, 256, 258, 259
Nasser, Gamal Abdel, 574–575, 578, 579, 580, 581, 583, 586, 587, 590
Nasution, 620
National Liberation Front, 627, 629
Nationalism: 409, 556–557; in Afghanistan, 427; Arab, 430, 433, 434, 435, 436, 437, 438, 439, 574–575, 578, 586, 590; in Burma, 484, 485; in China, 500–503; in India, 240–241, 242, 243–245, 248, 249–250, 443–444, 447–448, 449–450, 452, 455–456, 460, 461; in Indonesia, 186; in Iraq, 274; Jewish, 431, 436; in the Ottoman Empire, 16–17; in Persia, 421, 423, 425, 427, 563; in Southeast Asia, 468–469; in Turkey, 271, 273, 414, 415, 419; in Vietnam, 196, 480–482, 483–484
National Pact (Turkey), 415
Navarino, Battle of, 17
Navarre, General, 626
Naxalites, 598, 604
Nazimuddin, 595
Negri Sembilan, 191
Nehru, Jawaharlal, 454, 455, 461, 464, 596, 601, 602, 603, 605, 607
Nehru, Pandit Motilal, 450, 455
Nejd, 413, 429, 430
Nemuro, 151
Neo-Confucianism, 102; in Japan, 139, 140, 149–150; in Korea, 318–319, 322
Nepal, 75, 78, 89, 96, 187, 229, 232, 233, 606
Nerchinsk, 217, 218, 219
Nerchinsk, Treaty of, 94, 109, 218, 219
Nesib, Battle of, 19
Nesselrode, 221
Nestorians, in Iraq, 436
Netherlands Trading Company, 179, 180
Nevelskoi, 220–221
New Guinea, 180, 185, 619
Ne Win, 622
Nghe An revolt, 481
Ngo Dinh Diem, 626, 627, 481
Ngo Dinh Nhu, 627
Nguyen, family, 192–193; dynasty, 193, 195
Nguyen Ai Quoc (see Ho Chi Minh)
Nguyen Anh (see Gia Long)
Nguyen Cao Ky, 627, 629
Nguyen Van Thieu, 627, 629, 633
Nicholas I, 17, 18, 20, 21, 22, 221
Nicholas II, 251
Nicobar Islands, 460
Nien-fei, 286–287
Nikko, 140
Ningpo, 114, 120, 128
Nishihara Kamezo, 493, 494, 495
Nishi-Rosen Convention, 372, 373
Nixon, Richard M., 632, 684, 689, 692, 703, 708, 710, 711
Nobunaga, 137
Nomonhan, 534
Nomura Kichisaburo, 537, 538, 540
North Atlantic Treaty Organization (NATO), 572
North Borneo, 192, 617, 623
Northern Expedition, 506
Northwest Frontier Province, 236
Northwest Passage, 67, 165
Novgorod, 205, 206
Nureddin Mahmud, 585
Nurhachi, 85
Nur Jahan, 52

Oi Kentaro, 311, 369
Oil interests, 556, 557; in Iraq, 435, 436, 557, 565, 584, 585, 586; in Japan, 534–535, 537, 538, 539–540; in Kuwait, 556, 589; in Persia (Iran), 420, 424, 425–426, 556, 558, 560, 561, 562, 563, 564, 565, 567, 568, 570; in Saudi Arabia, 556, 557, 563–564, 565, 586, 587; in Syria, 430
Okada, Admiral, 518, 519
Okawa Shumei, 513, 517, 543, 643
Okhotsk, 211, 216
Okinawa, 545, 547, 638, 669, 670, 678, 685
Okubo Toshimichi, 156, 158, 299, 300, 301, 303, 308, 310, 313
Okubo Conspiracy, 137
Okuma Shigenobu, 301, 309, 310, 311, 314, 353, 364, 365
Oman, Trucial, 269, 430, 587, 589
Omsk, 224
Open Door Policy, 344–345, 378, 381, 383, 404, 492, 493, 496, 498, 697
Opium, 278, 279, 282, 352; trade in, 120, 123–124, 126–127
Oppert, 324
Oriental Exclusion Act of 1924, 510
Orissa, 238
Osaka, 133, 138, 142, 143, 145, 306
Oshima, 523

Osmena, Sergio, 475, 616
Ostrogs, 210, 212, 214, 224
Ostiaks, 204, 212
Osugi Sakae, 510
Ottoman Empire: decline of, 7–23; reforms in the, 10–11, 12, 13, 14, 15, 16, 19–20, 22; bulwark against Russia, 16, 18, 19, 20, 22; under Midhat Pasha, 264–267; European intervention, 268–270; rise of the Young Turks in, 270–271; in World War I, 410–413; dismemberment of, 413–414; education in the, 4, 13, 22; government in the, 1, 2, 3–7; military, 5; wars with Arabia, 9–10; wars with Christian Europe, 10, 11, 12, 15, 17; wars with Persia, 10–11, 12, 32, 41, 42; wars with Russia, 11, 12, 15, 17, 21–22; Western influence on, 14, 16–17, 18, 22–23; Westernization of, 19–20 (see also Turkey)
Oudh, 50, 72, 75, 77
Outer Mongolia, 219, 552, 698
Ōyōmei, 149
Ozaki Yukio, 365, 366, 510
Ozawa, Case, 706

Paekche, 317
Pahang, sultanate of, 191
Pahlavi, Muhammad Riza, 559, 562, 563, 565, 566, 567–569, 570
Pahlavi dynasty, 424
Pai hua, 500
Pakistan: pressure for the creation of, 456, 459, 461, 462, 463, 464; independence of, 464, 594–595; communal violence in, 600, 601; rise of East Pakistani nationalism in, 608–609; Bangladesh, independence from, 609; foreign relations, 591, 605–608, with India, 600–601, 603, 604, 609
Pak Young-hyo, 328, 329, 330, 332, 335
Palau, 545
Palestine, under the British mandate, 412, 413, 414, 431, 432, 436–439, 575, 576; Jews in, 431, 436, 437, 438, 439, 575, 576; war in, 574, 575–576
Palestine Liberation Organization, 582
Palestine War (1948), 574, 576, 581, 582, 584
Palmerston, Lord, 19, 21, 47, 124, 127
Pan-Arab movement, 574–575, 586
Panay Incident, 536
Panchen Lama, 96
Panch Shila agreements, 673
Panipat, Battle of, 46, 63
Panjdeh Incident, 225, 235
Panmunjom, 663, 665
Paramountcy, 77, 233
Paris, Treaty of (1856), 22, 263, 264
Paris, Treaty of (1857), 42, 47
Paris, Treaty of (1898), 403
Paris Peace Talks (1969–1973), 632, 708, 710

Park Chung-hee, 683
Parkes, Sir Harry, 280, 281
Parsees, 237
Paskievich, General, 40
Patel, Vallabhbhai, 602
Pathan tribes, 236
Pathet Lao, 630, 631
Patna, 72
Paul V (Pope), 27
Paul, Tsar, 39
Pauley, Edwin, 646, 648
Peace Corps, in Iran, 570
Peacock Throne, 35, 54, 58
Pearl Harbor, 540
Peel Report, 438
Pegu, 188
Pei-yang (Northern Army), 351, 358, 359, 490
Peking, 86, 87, 89, 91, 105, 107, 112, 120, 122, 219, 221, 347, 348, 490, 507, 653
Peking, Treaty of (1860), 221
Peking, Treaty of (1905), 381
Peking Convention of 1860, 282, 286, 287
Penang, 190, 191
P'eng Chen, 688
P'eng Teh-huai, 687–688
Perak, sultanate of, 191
Perlis, 191
Permanent Settlement of Bengal, 74
Perry, Matthew Calbraith, 152, 154, 157, 401–402, 696
Persia: Safavid dynasty, 25–32, 33, 34; Afghan conquest of, 32–33; reign of Nadir Shah in, 33–36; Zand dynasty, 37, 38; Kajar dynasty in, 37–44; European pressure in, 38–42; Anglo-Russian rivalry in, 254, 257, 259–263; national consciousness in, 258–259; constitutional movement in, 259–263; during World War I, 420–422; under Reza Shah, 423–427; education in, 424, 567, 568, 569; foreign relations, 225, 419, 426; with the Afghans, 34, 41, 42, with Great Britain, 42, with Mogul India, 35, with the Ottoman Empire, 10–11, 12, 27, 33–34, 36, 41, with Russia, 34, 39, 40 (see also Iran)
Persian Gulf Service Command, 559
Pescadores Islands, 112, 169, 334, 657, 658, 670
Peshawar, 65
Peshwas, 63–64, 75, 77
Petchora, 205
Peter the Great, 31, 32, 34, 91, 212, 215, 218, 223
Phan Boi Chau, 196, 480, 481
Phan Van Dong, 630
Phaulkon, Constantine, 196–197
Philip II, 112, 162
Philippines: early history, 111, 113, 386–387; under Spain, 387–398, 403; wars with the Dutch, 390, 391, 393; trade with Mexico, 388, 392, 394; Chinese emigration to,

393; Propaganda Movement in, 395–396; under the United States, 403–406, 473–474; Commonwealth, 474–475; in World War II, 475, 544–545; Republic of, 475–476; economy of, 474, 475, 476, 616, 617; education in, 474; government, 473–474, 475
Phnom-Penh, 194
Phra Narai, 196, 197
Phumiphon Adundet, 614
Pibul Songgram, 471, 472–473, 614–615
Picot, Georges, 431
Pires, Thomas, 107
Pishevari, Jafar, 560
Pitt, William (the younger), 16, 73
Plassey, 72
Pleiku, 631
PNI (National Indonesian party), 478
Poiarkov, Vasily, 216
Point Four Program, 598, 704; in Afghanistan, 590; in Iran, 563; in Iraq, 585; in Jordan, 582
Pondicherry, 69, 71
Poona, 62, 63, 245
Port Arthur, 372, 373, 376, 377, 551, 552, 658, 675, 699
Port Hamilton, 331
Port Said, 578
Portsmouth, Treaty of, 377–378, 380, 697
Portugal: and China, 106–107, 112, 114, 115, 169, 280; and the East Indies, 161, 164–165, 166, 169; and India, 51, 53, 66, 67, 68; and Japan, 136, 138; in Vietnam, 193
Potsdam Conference, 548, 549, 641, 659
Pottinger, Sir Henry, 127
Prasad, 602
Preanger, 174
Press: in Afghanistan, 427; in the Dutch East Indies, 478; in India, 453; in Iraq, 586; in Japan, 366, 370, 543; in Pakistan, 608; in Persia, 422, 426, 559, 561; in the Philippines, 618; in Turkey, 420, 573
Press Act of 1908, 250
Pridi Bhanomyong, 471, 473, 614
Prikaz, 214
Primorsk (see Maritime Province)
Promyshlenniks, 209–210, 211, 212
Protect the Emperor Society, 356
Province Wellesley, 190
Punjab, 44, 46, 56, 57, 61, 63, 65, 66, 75, 76, 229, 231, 232, 238, 250, 443, 445, 457, 464, 596, 601
Pusan, 136, 321, 324, 327, 372, 662
Pushtunistan, 591
Putiatin, Count, 281
P'u-to Shan, 113
P'u-yi, Henry, 352, 518
Pyongyang, 661

Qashqai, 562
Qavam, Ahmed, 561–562, 565
Qizilbash tribe, 26, 27
Quangtri, 633
Quemoy, 670
Quetta, 234
Quezon, Manuel, 406, 474, 475
Quinhon, 192, 193
Quirino, 616, 617
Qum, 568, 569
Quwatly, Shukri, 581

Raffles, Thomas Stamford, 177–179, 190, 191
Raghib Pasha, 12
Rahman, Sheik Mujibur, 609
Rajputs, 50, 56, 58
Rama I, 197
Rama IV Mongkut, 198–199, 200
Rama V Chulalonkorn, 200
Rama VI Vanjiravudh, 471
Rama VII Prajadhipok, 471
Ramakrishna, 242
Rangoon, 188, 485, 545
Ranjit Singh, 64–65, 66
Rann of Kutch, 603
Rashid Ali, 584
Rawlinson, Sir Henry, 255, 256
Razmara, General Ali, 563, 564, 565
Red Guard, 506, 689, 691
Reed, William D., 281
Reform Act of 1832, 76
Regional Cooperation for Development, 570
Regulating Act of 1773, 73
Renville Agreement, 618
Resht, 422
Reza Khan, 423–424, 425, 426, 427, 558, 559, 560, 698
Rezanov, Nicholai, 151–152, 213, 214, 215–216
Rezhid Pasha, 20
Rhee, Syngman, 660, 661, 664–665, 667, 668
Rhodes, 414
Ribbentrop, 523
Ricci, Matteo, 108–109, 111
Richardson affair, 157
Ridgway, Matthew, 663
Rites Controversy, 111
Riyadh, 429, 587
Riza, Mirza Muhammad, 259
Rizal, José, 396, 397
Robert, Charles, 22
Rockhill, William W., 344
Roe, Sir Thomas, 52, 67
Romanov, Michael, 210
Rōnin, 154
Roosevelt, Franklin D., 536, 537, 540, 545, 548, 550, 551, 552, 572, 587, 649, 699, 706
Roosevelt, Theodore, 377, 378, 382–383, 384, 403, 697
Root-Takahira Agreement, 382
Rothstein, 422
Round Table Conferences, 453
Rowlatt Act, 445, 447, 455
Roxas, Manuel, 475, 616
Roy, Ram Mohun, 80, 611

729

Royal Company of the Philippines, 394
Royal Dutch Oil Company, 184
Rudolph II, Emperor, 27
Rusk, Dean, 702
Russia: Asian boundary geography, 203–204; expansion into Siberia, 206–212, 214–215, 220–221; in Afghanistan, 46–47, 225; rivalry with the British in Central Asia, 234–235; and China, 217–219, 221, 225, 282, 293, 339, 372, 373; relations with Japan, 151–152, 213–214, 223, 314, 375, 376, 377–378, 380; and Korea, 331; expansion into Manchuria, 372, 373–374; and the Ottoman Empire, 11, 12, 15, 16, 17, 18, 19, 20, 21–22, 269; and Persia, 25, 32–34, 39, 40–41, 225, 254–257, 259–263, 420, 421; rivalry with the British in Tibet, 235–236; war with Turkey, 234 (see also Soviet Union)
Russian-American (Fur) Company of Alaska, 151
Russian Revolution, 421
Russo-American Company, 215, 216, 220
Russo-Japanese War, 369, 376, 377–378; impact of the, 245, 249, 257, 697, 700
Ryerszon, Admiral Cornelius, 112

Saadabad Pact, 419, 426, 436
Sabah (North Borneo), 617, 623, 624
Sadae, 321
Sadat, Anwar, 580
Safavid dynasty (see Persia)
Safi, Shah, 31
Said, Nuri, 584, 585
Saigo Takamori, 156, 158, 301, 303, 306, 308, 324
Saigon, 192, 193, 483, 629, 631
Saigon, Treaty of, 193
St. Francis Xavier, 108
St. Gotthard, Battle of, 11
St. John's Island, 107
Saionji Kimmochi, 365, 366, 367, 495, 507, 508, 518, 519, 528
Saipan, 545, 547
Saito, Admiral, 518, 519
Sakaria River, Battle of, 416
Sakhalin, 152, 212, 213, 220, 221, 223, 314, 378, 380, 496, 498, 508, 538, 548, 551, 669, 698, 699
Sallal, 590
Salonica, 271
Samar, 387, 391
Samarkand, 224, 254
Sambhaji, 63
Samoyed, 212
Samurai, 135, 140, 141, 158, 301, 302, 307, 308, 314, 324
Sanchi monument, 246
Sanders, General Liman von, 410

San Fan Rebellion, 92, 175
San Francisco Conference, 584, 586
San Francisco, Treaty of, 658
Sangleys, 393
Sanjo Sanetomi, 155
Sankin kōtai, 133
San Min Chu I (Three Principles of the People), 505–506
San Remo Conference, 432, 433, 434, 437
San Stefano, Treaty of, 269
Sarawak, 191, 192, 623, 624
Sarekat Islam, 186, 477
Sarit, Field Marshal, 615
Sarrail, General, 433, 434
Sastroamidjojo, Ali, 619
Sat-Cho Do-Hi, 300, 302, 306
Sato, Eisaku, 680, 684, 685
Satsuma clan, 132, 153, 154, 155, 156, 157, 300, 307, 366
Satyagraha, 446, 447
Sa'ud II, King, 587
Saudi Arabia, 274, 430, 556, 557, 574, 586–589, 590
Sayid Ali Muhammad, 42
Sayyid Abdullah, 590
Sayyid Ahmed Khan, 241
SCAP (Supreme Commander of the Allied Powers), 640, 641, 642, 644, 645, 646, 647, 648
Schall, Adam, 109
SEATO, 614, 615, 617, 626, 702
Sebastiani, 15
Sebastopol, 22
Seeckt, Hans von, 524
Sejong, King (Korea), 318
Sekigahara, 132
Selangor, 191
Selborne, Lord, 375
Selim the Sot, 7
Selim III (Ottoman), 14–15
Semarang, 174
Semipalatinsk, 224
Senanayake, Dudley, 610
Sendai, 137
Seoul, 86, 318, 322, 327, 328, 329, 332, 334, 372, 659, 663, 667, 668, 699
Sepoy Mutiny (see Indian Mutiny)
Sepoys, 70, 71, 78
Serbia, revolts against the Ottomans, 15, 17
Seringapatam, 75
Sèvres, Treaty of, 413, 414, 416, 449
Seymour, Admiral, 347
Seymour, Hamilton, 20
Shah Durani (see Ahmad Shah)
Shah Jahan, 52–54, 55, 59, 61, 64, 68
Shah Savan tribe, 27
Shahji, 62
Shameen district, 118
Shan, migrations into Burma, 187; resistance to British, 189
Shanghai, 128, 281, 286, 291, 506, 529, 653
Shanghai Incident, 502
Shansi province, 99
Shantung, 286, 334, 339, 347, 491,

492, 493, 494, 495, 497, 498, 514
Sharjah, 589
Sharm el-Sheikh, 578
Shastri, Lal Bahadur, 603–604
Shatt al Arab, 570
Shaw, Samuel, 398
Shensi province, 86, 522, 523
Sher Ali, 234, 235
Sherifs, 9
Sherley, Anthony, 26, 27, 28, 256
Sherley, Robert, 26, 28, 256
Shi'a (see Islam, Shi'a sect)
Shidehara Kijuro, 508, 509, 514, 517, 518, 644, 647
Shikoku Island, 155
Shikotan Island, 669, 682
Shimazu, 132
Shimbara Revolt, 138
Shimoda, 152, 213, 402
Shimonoseki, 157, 334
Shimonoseki, Treaty of (1895), 334–335
Shimpan, 132
Shingaku, 143
Shinto, 149–150, 303–304
Shiraz, 37, 421, 562, 567, 569
Shishakli, 581, 587
Shivaji, 57, 62–63, 69, 245
Shizoku, 302
Shoda Kazue, 494
Shu ching, 102
Shufeldt, Commodore, 327–328
Shuja Shah, 46, 47
Shu-kuo (dependent country), 319, 320
Shun-chih (China-Manchu), 88, 109
Shushi Learning (see Neo-Confucianism, in Japan)
Shuster, W. Morgan, 262–263
Siam: Chinese tributary, 89; war with Burma, 187, 188, 197; and the French, 194, 195, 196–197, 200; under the monarchy, 470–471; constitution in, 471, 473; military dictatorship in, 471–472; in World War II, 472–473; foreign relations, 470, 472; government in, 470–471 (see also Thailand)
Sian, 525
Sian Incident, 525
Siberia: early history, 204–206; Russian expansion into, 94, 151, 206–210, 211–212, 220–221; growth of, 219–220, 223; Russian administration in, 210, 214–215, 699
Siberian Intervention, 494–496, 498, 507, 508, 697, 698
Sibir, khanate of, 205, 206, 208
Sidon, 587
Siemreap, 194, 472
Sidqi, General Bakr, 436
Sihanouk, Prince Norodom, 630
Sikhs, 46, 62, 64–66, 75, 76, 78, 443, 464
Sikkim, 294, 606
Silla, 317, 318

Simla Conference, 463
Simon, Sir John, 451
Simon Commission, 450–451, 452, 453, 484
Simonich (Russian envoy), 41
Sinai, 579
Sinai peninsula campaign, 575
Sinai War (1956), 578–579
Sinclair, 424
Sind, 46, 76, 238
Singapore, 190, 191, 460, 484, 485, 486, 544, 623–624
Sinhalese, 610
Sinkiang, 89, 95, 99, 235, 293, 552
Sino-Japanese War (1894–1895), 294, 298, 313, 334, 363
Sino-Japanese War (1937–1944), 525, 529–533, 534, 549–551
Sinope, 21
Sino-Soviet Treaty (1945), 552, 649
Sino-Soviet Treaty (1950), 657–658
Siraj-ud-daula, 71–72
Sirhak, 322
Sivas, 415
Six-day war (1967), 579, 581, 583, 586
Sjahrir, 479
Smyrna (Izmir), 412, 414, 416
Soka Gakkai, 681
Solomon Islands, 545
Sonnō, 301
Sonnō-Jōi, 155, 156–157
Soong, T. V., 524, 526, 552
Souvanna Phouma, Prince, 630
Soviet Union: and Afghanistan, 427, 591; and the Arab nations, 557, 578, 579, 580, 586, 590; and China, 551–552, 657; and India, 603–604, 609; mediation of 1965 Indo-Pakistani Kashmir dispute, 603–604; and Japan, 508, 521, 533–534, 548, 640, 641, 668, 669, 682; and Korea, 659, 660, 661, 662; invasion of Manchuria, 650, 651, 652; and Persia, 422–423, 558, 559–562, 563, 570; and Turkey, 416, 419, 571, 573
Spafarii, 217
Spain: and the East Indies, 161, 164, 169; in the Far East, 111, 112; and Japan, 136, 137, 138, 393; and the Philippines, 387
Spanberg, Martin, 151, 213
Spanish-American War, 403
Speransky, Count Michael, 215
Spice Islands, 66, 67, 108 (see also Moluccas)
Squeeze, 117, 118, 124, 283–284, 289, 291
Sri Lanka (see Ceylon)
Srinagar, 601
Stalin, Joseph, 506, 551, 552, 650, 666, 699
State-War-Navy Coordinating Committee (SWNCC), 640
Stepanov, 217
Stern, 575
Stern Gang, 438

Stilwell, General Joseph, 545, 550, 551, 649
Stimson, Henry L., 521
Stokes, Major C. B., 262, 263
Stolietov, General, 234
Straight, Willard, 381–382, 383
Straits Settlements, 191, 486
Streltsy, 214
Stroganovs, 206, 208
Suez Canal, 232, 237, 410, 412, 437, 556, 574, 578, 579
Sugita Gempaku, 151
Sugiyama Gen, 528, 529
Suharto, 620, 621
Sukarno, Akmet, 469, 478, 479, 613, 618, 619, 620, 621
Suleiman, the Magnificent, 1, 9
Suleiman (of Manilla), 387
Sultan, 4, 7, 13
Sulu, sultanate of, 391
Sumatra, 166, 169, 180, 184, 185, 190, 619
Sumitomo, 368
Sunay, President, 573
Sung Chiao-jen, 359
Sunni (see Islam)
Sun Yat-sen, 353–356, 357, 358, 359, 360, 373, 490, 503–505, 506, 698
Sun Yat-sen, Madame, 506
Supreme Commander for the Allied Powers (see SCAP)
Surabaya, 174, 177
Surat, 51, 62, 67, 68, 69
Susuhunan, 174
Sutomo, Radin, 186
Suttee, 76
Suzuki Bunji, 370, 511
Suzuki Kantaro, 548, 549
Swaraj, 245, 468
Sykes, Sir Mark, 431
Sykes, Sir Percy, 421
Sykes-Picot Agreement, 410, 412, 431–432, 433
Syr-darya River, 226
Syria: under the Ottomans, 18, 19, 412; under France, 412, 414, 431, 432–434, 580; during World War II, 580; independence of, 580–581, 582, 587, 590; war with Israel, 579; foreign relations, 574, 576
Sze, Alfred, 502
Szechuan, 86, 87, 91, 96, 97, 99

Tabriz, 27, 32, 34, 40, 262, 263, 560, 567, 568
Tachi Sakutaro, 509
Ta Ch'ing, 85
Taewongun, 322–323, 324, 325, 327, 328, 330–331, 332, 333, 335
Taft, William Howard, 378, 383, 404–405
Tagalog, 387
Tagore, Radindranath, 248, 457, 611
Tahmasp II, Shah, 33, 34
T'aierchuang, Battle of, 531
Taika Reform, 298
Taipei, 655

T'ai-ping Rebellion, 284–286, 288, 291
Tairo Doshikai, 495
Taj Mahal, 52, 54, 59, 246
Takahashi, 507
Takeshi Mitarai, 679
Takezoe, 329–330
Takizawa Bakin, 145
Taku, 349
Talal, Emir, 582
Talbot, Major G. F., 259
Tamils, in Ceylon, 610
Tanaka Giichi, 495, 513, 514
Tanaka, Kokuei, 683, 685
Tangku Truce, 522
T'ang Shao-i, 359
T'an Ssu-t'ung, 341, 343
Tao-kuang, 99, 279, 284
Tarim basin, 89, 95
Taruc, Luis, 616
Tashkent, 224
Tashkent Agreement, 603
Tasman, Abel, 172
Tassigny, Jean de Lattre de, 625
Tatars, 205, 212
Tatnall, Commodore, 282, 399
Taxila monument, 246
Tayninh, 481, 633
Tayson Rebellion, 193
Tehran, 38, 256, 259, 262, 421, 426, 558, 559, 565, 566, 567, 569
Tenasserim, 188
Terauchi, Masatake, 381, 493, 494, 495, 507, 508
Ternate, sultanate of, 164, 165, 166, 172
Tet Offensive (1968), 629, 631
Thailand: name adopted, 472; Japanese occupation of, 545; after World War II, 614–616
Thakin Nu, 484
Thakins, 484, 485
Thanom Kittikachorin, 615, 616
The Thien (Buddhist sect), 193
Theodosia, 410
Thibaw, 188, 189
Thrace, 416
Three Kingdoms, 317
Thuggee, 76
Tibet, 89, 93–94, 95–96; under Manchu, 187; Anglo-Russian rivalry in, 235–236; in Anglo-Russian Convention, 251; and Chinese Republic, 358; Chinese invasion of, 606, 607
Tidore, sultanate of, 164, 165, 166
Tientsin, 120, 282, 502
Tientsin, Treaties of (1858), 281, 282, 283
Tientsin, Treaty of (1871), 294
Tientsin, Treaty of (1885), 194, 294
Tientsin Convention (see Li-Ito Convention)
Tientsin Massacre, 290
Tiflis, 11, 32, 34, 38
Tilak, Bal Gangadhar, 245, 249, 250, 444
Tilsit, meeting at, 39

Timur, 37
Timur (son of Ahmad Shah), 46
Timurtash, 426
Tinian, 545
Tipu, 74, 75
Tobolsk, 209, 211, 215
Togo, Admiral, 377
Togo Shigenori, 548, 549
Tojo, 538, 539–540, 544, 547, 643
Tōkaido, 146
Tokugawa Shogunate (see Japan)
Tokyo, 156, 303, 547, 638
Tokyo Mutiny, 519–520, 528, 539
Ton Duc Thang, 630
Tonghak Society, 332–333
Tonkin, 192, 194, 195, 479, 480, 481, 482, 483, 625
Tonkin Gulf Resolution, 631, 702, 703
Torguts, 218
Tosa, 155, 156, 157, 300, 303, 309
Toungoo dynasty, 187
Tovarishch, 214
Toyoda, 548
Tozama (see Daimyo)
Transbaikalia, 216
Transbaikalia, Irkutsk, 216
Transcaucasia, 40, 410
Trans-Iranian Railway, 425, 559
Transjordan, 412, 439, 576, 582
Trans-Siberian Railway, 223, 334, 339, 372
Trautmann, 530
Tran Van Huong, 629
Trebizond (Trabzon), 410
Trengganu, 191
Triad Rebellion, 286, 291
Trinh (family), 192, 193
Tripartite Pact, 535–536, 538
Tripitaka, 471
Triple Entente, 254
Triple Intervention, 335, 372
Tripoli, 436, 585
Tromp, Admiral, 169
Truman, Harry S., 563, 576, 641, 649, 650, 652, 656, 662, 663, 701, 704
Truman Doctrine, extended to Turkey, 571, 700, 701
Truong Chinh, 625
Ts'ai Ao, 489, 490
Tsao Hsüeh-ch'in, 100
Ts'ao Ju-lin, 494, 500
Tseng Kuo-fan, 286, 287, 289, 290, 338, 527, 679
Tsewang Rabdan, 93–94
Tsingtao, 491
Tso-Tsung-T'ang, 225, 286, 287, 293, 338
Tsunayoshi, Tokugawa, 140
Tsungli Yamen, 288, 290
Tsushima Island, 136, 320, 321
Tsushima Straits, Battle of, 377
Tuan, Prince, 347, 348
Tuan Ch'i-jui, 359, 489, 490, 493, 494, 496, 497
Tu-chun (military governors), 489
Tudeh, 560, 561, 562, 565

Tu-Duc, 193
Tulsi Das, 61
Tunb Islands, 589
T'ung-chih Restoration, 287–290
T'ung-meng-hui (Together Sworn Society), 355, 357, 359
Tungus, 204
Turfan, 93
Turkey: in World War I, 410–413; revolution in, 416–417; Westernization of, 418–419; during World War II, 571; economy, 419; education in, 418; foreign relations, 418, 419–421, 571–572, 573
Turkistan, 93, 204, 223, 226; conquest of, 224, 225; Chinese (Zungaria), 224–225; Russian, 234, 254, 699
Turkmen tribes, 225
Turkomans, 256
Turkomanchai, Treaty of, 40–41, 225
Turner, Samuel, 236
Twenty-One Demands, 491–493
Tydings-McDuffie Act, 474–475
Tz'u-hsi, Empress Dowager, 287–288, 290, 339, 342, 343, 348, 349, 350, 352

Uchida Ryōhei, 355
Uchimura Kanzo, 370
Ugaki, General, 517
Ukiyo, 143–149
Ulama, 6, 13
Ulan Bator, 198
Umezu, 548
Unfederated Malay States, 191
Ungern-Sternberg, Baron, 698
Union of Arab Emirates, 589
United Arab Republic, 581
United Dutch East India Company (see Dutch East India Company)
United Nations, 473, 559, 561, 565, 571, 576, 578, 579, 580, 584, 585, 586, 589, 605, 606, 614, 618, 621, 622, 630, 649; and the problem of Chinese recognition, 657, 671, 692; and the Korean War, 660–661, 662–665, 669; and Kashmir dispute, 601
United Nations Relief and Rehabilitation Administration (UNRRA), 650, 652, 655
United States: and Afghanistan, 591; and China trade, 120, 129, 398–399; and China, 281, 282, 292, 344–345, 403; and the China recognition problem, 657, 670–671; aid to Nationalist China, 650, 652, 656, 671; and India, 598, 606, 608; and Indonesia, 618, 619; and Iran, 421, 423, 426, 559, 561, 562, 563, 566, 570; and Israel, 576, 578, 579; and Japan, 152, 377, 382–384, 399–403, 493, 497, 521, 536–537; response to Japan's Twenty-

733

One Demands to China, 492–493; oriental exclusion policy of, 382–383, 510, 705–706; internment of Japanese-Americans during World War II, 706–707; occupation of Japan, 640–649; Security Treaty with Japan, 670, 678, 681, 685; and Jordan, 582; and Korea, 323–324, 327–328, 331, post-war, 659, 660, 661, 662, 665, 667; and Laos, 631; and Lebanon, 580, 582; and the Pacific War, 540–541, 544–547; and Pakistan, 607, 608, 609; and the Philippines, 403–406, 473–475, 476, 616–617, 618; and Saudi Arabia, 586–587; and Siam, 197, 198, 470, 473; and Syria, 580; and Thailand, 614, 615–616; and Turkey, 414, 571–572, 573; in Vietnam, 482, 625, 626, 627, 629, 631, 702, 703, 704, 707–708, 710, 711
Universities Act, 246
Unkiar Skelessi, Treaty of, 18
U Nu, 621, 622
Unyo, 325
Urdu, 241
Urga, 698
Urmia, Lake, 27
U Saw, 621
Usted Isa, 59
Utamaro, 147
U Thant, 622
Uzbeks, 25, 32, 44

Vandenbosch, Johannes, 179
Van Deventer, C. Th[eodore], 184
Van Diemen, Anthony, 169
Van Hoorn, Schouten, 166
Van Houtman, 165
Varenne, Alexander, 481
Venizelos, 414, 417
Verbiest, Ferdinand, 109
Vernacular Press Act, 1882, 244
Versailles Peace Conference, 414, 421, 470, 496–497
Victoria, Queen of England, 78, 127, 233, 256
Vietcong, 626, 627, 631, 632, 707
Vietminh, 482, 483, 625, 626
Vietnam: Chinese tributary, 84, 96, 192–193, 194; French takeover of, 294; nationalism in, 480–482, 483–484; under Bao Dai, 483; National Republic of, 626–627, 629, 631–633; Democratic Republic of, 483, 624, 626, 627, 629–630; U.S. bombing of, 631, 632, 633
Vietnam International Control Commission, 606
Viet-Nam Quoc Dan Dang, 480
Vietnam War, French phase, 625–626; United States intervention, 627, 629, 631–633, 702, 703, 704, 707–708, 710, 711

Vietnamese Revolutionary Youth League, 481
Vikovich, Captain, 46
Village Act of 1906, 186
Villalobos, 387
Vivekenanda, Swami, 242
Vladivostok, 221, 339, 495, 496
Voevodas, 210, 214, 215
Vogul, 212
Volksraad, 477
Vo Nguyen Giap, 482
Vossugh-ud-daula, 421

Wahhabi, 9–10, 18, 274, 429, 430, 439
Wake Island, 403
Wako, 107
Waldersee, General, 373
Wallace, Henry A., 701
Wallachia, 17, 31
Wang, C. T., 502
Wang Ching-wei, 356, 506, 533, 534
Wanghsia, Treaty of (1844), 129, 399
Wang Yang-ming school, 149
Wan-li, 84
Ward, Angus, 657
Ward, Frederick Townsend, 286
Washington Conference, 497–498, 517, 697, 698
Wassmuss (German consul), 421
Watanabe, General, 519, 520
Weber-Komura Agreement, 372
Weddell, John, 114
Wedemeyer, Albert, 551, 652
Wei Chung-hsien, 84
Weihaiwei, 334, 339, 373
Weizmann, Chaim, 437, 438, 576
Wellesley, Col. Arthur, 75
Wellesley, Marquess, 63, 74–75
Weng T'ung-ho, 344
Whampoa military academy, 505
Whampoa, Treaty of, 129
White Lotus Society, 97, 99
Wilhelm II, Kaiser, 257, 270
William II (Holland), 152
Willoughby, Sir Hugh, 113
Wilson, Woodrow, 383, 414, 432, 470, 473, 495, 496, 497
Witte, Count, 223, 374, 376, 378
Wonsan, 327, 372
Wood, Benjamin, 113-114
Wood, Leonard, 474
Wu, K. C., 656
Wuchang, 357
Wu Ch'ung-yueh (Howqua), 278
Wu Han, 689
Wuhan, 352, 357
Wu P'ei-fu, 504
Wu San-kuei, 86–87, 91–92, 93

Yahya, Iman, 430, 590
Yahya Khan, 608, 609
Yakub Beg, 293
Yakub Khan, 235
Yakutsk, 211, 216
Yalta Conference, 548, 551, 699
Yamagata Aritomo, 301, 307, 312,

363, 364, 365, 366, 367, 372, 493, 495, 507
Yamamoto Gombei, 367
Yangban, 319, 332
Yang Ch'u-yün, 355
Yangtze River, 128
Yap, 498
Yarkand, 95
Yasuda, 368
Yawata Iron Works, 367
Yeh Ming-ch'en, 280, 281
Yemen, 430, 557–558, 574, 587, 589–590
Yen, Y. C. (Jimmy), 501
Yenan, 522, 652
Yenbay Mutiny, 481
Yen Hsi-shan, 502
Yenisseisk, 211
Yermak Timofeyevitch, 206, 207–208, 209
Yi dynasty (Korea), 318
Yi T'aejo, 318, 319
Yi Tong-hwi, 659
Yodoya, 143
Yonai, 548
Yoshida Shigeru, 647, 648, 658, 668, 669, 670, 683
Yoshida Shōin, 154, 157

Yoshimune, 151
Yoshino Sakuzo, 509, 511
Yoshizawa, 535
Young, Arthur, 587
Younghusband, Colonel, 236
Young Turks, 270–271, 274, 275
Yuaikai (Friendly Labor Society), 370
Yuan Shih-k'ai, 330, 331, 333, 342, 343, 347, 348, 349, 350, 351, 352, 357–358, 359–360, 489, 490
Yugria, 205
Yung-cheng, 94, 95
Yunnan, 87, 91, 188, 194, 287

Zahedi, General Fazollah, 565
Zahir, Mohammed, 591
Zaibatsu, 306–307, 368, 646, 648
El-Zaim, Husni, 581
Zaman Shah, 46
Zamindar, 74, 240
Zand dynasty (see Persia)
Zayen, 581
Zen Buddhism, 139
Zengakuren, 670, 681, 682
Zia-ed-din, Sayyid, 423, 560, 561
Zionism, 431, 432, 436, 437, 438, 439, 575, 576
Zungaria, 93